# Handbook of the Canadian Rockies

*Photo of raven by Barry Giles. Retouched by Toby Gadd.*

# Handbook

*of the*

# Canadian Rockies

*Second edition*

# Ben Gadd

*Wildlife drawings by Matthew Wheeler*

*Corax Press*

**Canadian Cataloguing in Publication Data**

Gadd, Ben, 1946-
Handbook of the Canadian Rockies

Includes bibliographical references and index.
ISBN 0-9692631-1-2

1. Natural history--Rocky Mountains, Canadian, (B.C. and
Alta.)--Guidebooks. 2. Rocky Mountains, Canadian (B.C.
and Alta.)--Guidebooks. I. Title.
FC219.G33 1995        508.711        C95-910236-1
F1090.G33 1995

No financial assistance was received from any government agency in the writing or production
of this book. Not that we didn't try.

**Corax Press**
Box 1557, Jasper, Alberta, Canada  T0E 1E0 • 780-852-4012
corax@bengadd.com
www.bengadd.com

Design, layout and electronic prepress by Toby Gadd
Copy editing by Cia Gadd
Proof-reading by Jill Seaton
Printed and bound in Canada by Friesens, Altona, Manitoba

Some illustrations based on photographs copyright Dennis and Esther Schmidt, 1991, and
published in *Photographing Wildlife in the Canadian Rockies* (Lone Pine Publishing:
Edmonton, 1991). Used by permission.

*Front cover:* Cottonwood Slough and Pyramid Mountain, near Jasper. For views of this scene
in other seasons, see the chapter on seasonal ecology, page 671.
*Spine:* American kestrel (see page 535) by Matthew Wheeler
Back cover photo by Toby Gadd

*Approaching the summit of Mt. Henry, Jasper National Park*

# *Preface*
## *Someone* had to write this book

Pity the poor naturalist, lugging all those books around. Bird books, flower books, tree books, fish books, snake books, bug books, geology books—filling up the pack, poking with their sharp corners.

Well, for naturalists in this part of the world, the first edition of *Handbook of the Canadian Rockies* seems to have eased the load somewhat. Published in 1986, it gathered a great deal of relevant information into a single volume that went into a pack pocket—a *large* pack pocket, admittedly—and it sold 23,000 copies. The second edition follows those same principles, updated with changes in the information and adjusted to reflect the comments of users. The main thing they wanted was COLOR, and here it is.

As before, the information in the *Handbook* is specific to the Canadian Rockies. Excluded is everything that doesn't live here or doesn't outcrop here or didn't happen here. Not to belittle the creeping vole of western Washington or the woodland jumping mouse of Ontario, but it's better not to have to flip through items about them when trying to identify the little gray thing that is licking up the spilled soup in the corner of the cabin. It will be gone in about 15 seconds.

This book is more than a field guide, however. In leisurely circumstances you may wish to read entire sections. For example, what about the pika? Does it really eat its own droppings? See page 619 for the answer. What is it like to climb Mt. Robson? Who discovered Banff Hot Springs? Forget about the leak in the tent for a while and read about how British Columbia collided with the rest of Canada back in the Mesozoic.

*Handbook* also has advice to offer. I have been exploring these mountains for 27 years, discovering places to go and things to do. A recreational chapter passes along some of what I have learned about hiking, climbing, skiing and bicycling here. New in this edition: a section on boating.

I had one other idea in mind when I began this project. People who know the value of something are inclined to cherish and protect it. The Canadian Rockies—beautiful, savage, delicate, unique—are worthy indeed. See the afterword, page 783, for some current concerns about the status of the region, particularly the northern half.

Has the *Handbook* been good for the Rockies? I hope so.

*Ben Gadd*
*Jasper, Alberta*
*May 17, 1995*

# Acknowledgements
## Many thanks to everyone who helped to produce this book

Many academic, government and private-sector specialists supplied information and checked drafts of the first and second editions of *Handbook of the Canadian Rockies,* giving freely of their time in correcting my errors and omissions. The remaining mistakes are strictly my own.

### Geology
Jim Aitken, Wayne Bamber, John Clague, Helmut Geldsetzer, Dale Leckie, Margo McMechan, Jim Monger, Brian Norford, Ray Price, Barry Richards, Don Stott and Chris Yorath, all with the Geological Survey of Canada; Norm Catto, Vic Levson, Nat Rutter and Mel Reasoner, University of Alberta; Jerry Osborn, University of Calgary; Brian Luckman and Chris Smart, University of Western Ontario; Eric Mountjoy, McGill University; Brian Pratt, University of Saskatchewan; Eric Erslev and Chris Hedlund, Colorado State University; Joe Meert, Indiana State University; Martin Teitz, Dome Petroleum, Calgary; Robert van Everdingen, Calgary.

### Weather and climate
Ben Janz and Nick Nimchuk, Alberta Land and Forest Services; Bob Charlton, University of Alberta.

### Botany
Elisabeth Beaubien, Patsy Cotterill and Dale Vitt, University of Alberta; Julie Hrapko, Alberta Provincial Museum; Derek Johnson, Canadian Forestry Service; Job Kuijt, University of British Columbia; George Scotter, Canadian Wildlife Service; Leni Shalkwyk, Edmonton; Barbara Zimmer, Tête Jaune Cache. Many thanks to Job Kuijt for permission to reprint his botanical drawings, and to Dale Vitt for allowing me to publish his photos of lichens and mosses. Elisabeth Beaubien researched the French botanical common names. Cia Gadd gathered the color data for the wildflower illustrations, assisted by Jill Seaton and Barbara Zimmer. Toby Gadd spent hundreds of hours on the computer applying these colors to the original black-and-white drawings. Special thanks to Barbara Zimmer, who checked the flower colors, edited the botany section of the manuscript twice and did other indispensable botanical jobs.

### Insects
Syd Cannings, Chris Guppy and Jens Roland, University of British Columbia; Charles Dondale, Agriculture Canada; Norbert Kondla, British Columbia Forest Service; H.R. Wong, Canadian Forestry Service.

### Fishes
Brenda Dixon, British Columbia Fish and Wildlife; Joe Nelson and Wayne Roberts, University of Alberta; Michael Sullivan, Alberta Environmental Protection.

### Reptiles and amphibians
Wayne Roberts, University of Alberta.

### Birds
Geoff Holroyd and Bruce Turner, Canadian Wildlife Service; Andy Miller, University of Alberta; Roy Richards and Volker Schelhas, Jasper; Kevin Van Tighem, Parks Canada.

### Mammals
Robert Barclay and Val Geist, University of Calgary; Allan Brooks, Parks Canada; Lu Carbyn, Canadian Wildlife Service; Eldon Bruns, John Gunson, Orval Pall, Margo Pybus and Arlen Todd, Alberta Fish and Wildlife; Brian Horejsi, Western Wildlife Consultants, Calgary; Cliff Martinka, Glacier National Park. Jan Murie and Wayne Roberts, University of Alberta; Alan Ross, ARC, Calgary; Gilbert Proulx, Alpha Wildlife Research & Management, Sherwood Park; Hugh Smith, Alberta Provincial Museum; Jim Vashro, Montana Fish, Wildlife and Parks.

## History
Don Beers, Calgary; Hugh Dempsey, Glenbow Museum; Jim MacGregor, Edmonton; Peter Francis, Parks Canada; Cyndi Smith and Glenda Cornforth, Jasper; Cam Finlay, Edmonton.

## Recreation
Stuart Smith, Alberta Whitewater Association; Catherine Wilde, Canadian Hostelling International.

## Safety and first aid
Tim Auger, Warden Service (mountain rescue), Banff National Park; Scott Lamont, R.N., Banff; Martin Lesperance, EMT-P and First Aid Instructor, Cochrane; Peter Callegari, M.D., Jasper.

## *Picture credits and key to initials next to illustrations*

Artist Matthew Wheeler, of McBride, B.C., spent many, many hours preparing the hundreds of wildlife drawings for this book. They are outstanding; I hope you enjoy seeing them as much as I have enjoyed working with Matthew. Key: *MW*

Job Kuijt, University of British Columbia, gave permission to reprint some 500 of his drawings from *A Flora of Waterton Lakes National Park*, published by the University of Alberta Press but sadly now out of print. These drawings were originally in black-and-white, but we have colored them in this edition to make identification easier. The colors have come from field-matching with a standard Pantone color-swatch book, from photos and from published sources. Key: *JK*

A number of other illustrations in this book have come from other publications, reprinted with permission. Where many drawings came from the same source, the author, publisher and illustrator, if known, have been credited by placing a set of initials next to each borrowed picture. See the block credits below for matching initials with sources. Where only one or two items were used, they have been credited individually. Uncredited illustrations are by the author.

**The author and publisher gratefully acknowledge permission to reprint as follows:**
- Archives of the Canadian Rockies (Whyte Museum, Banff): permission to reproduce historical photos from the Mary Schäffer collection.
- The British Columbia Provincial Museum and T.C. Brayshaw: permission to reprint some of Dr. Brayshaw's drawings of willows from *Catkin Bearing Plants of British Columbia.* Key: *BCPM*
- Canadian Wildlife Service: permission to reprint drawings of aquatic invertebrates in *Limnological Studies in Jasper National Park*, by R.S. Anderson and D.B. Donald. Key: *CWS*
- W.H. Easton, University of Southern California, Los Angeles: permission to reprint fossil drawings from his *Invertebrate Paleontology*, published by Harper and Row in 1960. Key: *WE*
- Fitzhenry & Whiteside, Toronto: permission to reprint tree profiles from *Native Trees of Canada*, eighth edition, copyright Minister of Supply and Services Canada. Key: *FW*
- Geological Society of America and University Press of Kansas: permission to reprint fossil drawings from *Treatise on Invertebrate Paleontology*, courtesy of the Geological Society of America and University of Kansas. Key: *GSA*
- Geological Survey of Canada, Ottawa: permission to reprint illustrations from several of their publications, credited individually. Special thanks to S. Conway Morris of the University of Cambridge, UK, coauthor of *Fossils of the Burgess Shale*, GSC Miscellaneous Report 43, 1985, and to Minister of Supply and Services, Canada. Key: *GSC*
- Government of Canada: illustrations from *Freshwater Fishes of Canada*, reproduced by permission of the Minister of Supply and Services Canada. Key: *CAN*
- Illustrations from *A Field Guide to Western Reptiles and Amphibians*, copyright 1966 by Robert C. Stebbins, reprinted by permission of Houghton Mifflin Co. All rights reserved. Key: *HM*

• National Museum of Natural Sciences, National Museums of Canada: drawings of mammal skulls from *The Mammals of Canada*, by A.W.F. Banfield. Key: *NMC*
• Natural Resources Canada: the satellite image on page 15, and the maps in the atlas section that begins on page 785.
• Oxford University Press Canada: drawings from *Mammals of Eastern Canada* (1966) by Randolph Peterson. Key: *OUP*
• Provincial Museum of Alberta, drawings of skulls from Hugh Smith's *Alberta Mammals,*1993. Artist was Diane Hollingdale. Key: *DH*
• University of Washington Press, Seattle: drawings from *Flora of the Pacific Northwest* (1973) by C.L. Hitchcock and Arthur Cronquist. Key: *UWP*

## Artist's acknowledgements

Matthew Wheeler expresses his gratitude for the valuable assistance he received in illustrating the butterflies, moths, caterpillars, birds and mammals for this book.

For permission to work from their photography, he thanks Esther and Dennis Schmidt; W.S. Metcalf/Bear's Lair Studio/Gallery and the South Croydon Wildlife Holding Facility; Mark Kolasinski, Jasper National Park photo curator; Glen Frear; David Greer; Ron Hammerstedt; Debra Harder; Marilyn Wheeler; Paul Wildeman; John Winnie; Julie & Rick Zammuto; Barbara and Joe Zimmer.

The following publishers were kind enough to provide permission to use their material for reference: Paul Johnsgard and Indiana University Press, Lone Pine Publishing, Altitude Publishing, Doubleday and Massachusetts Fisheries and Wildlife. Thanks also to Hugh Smith and the Provincial Museum of Alberta, for extending the same courtesy for drawing from photos in their excellent *Mammals of Alberta.*

Special thanks to Norbert Kondla, for loan of his butterfly specimens and expertise; to Chuck McNaughton, who lent mammal specimens; to Ann Cousineau, Elaine Gillette and the Robson Valley Birdwatchers for bird specimens; to Wayne Roberts, University of Alberta, for bat and rodent specimens, and to Isabel and Maurice Bonneville for access to Oscar's Wildlife Museum, McBride.

Thanks also to Dave Kraby, Elke and Mike Popp, Mark Hoddinott, Sara Davidson, Sarah Flynn, the Fraser - Fort George Regional Museum—and to all the birds and mammals that posed outside the artist's studio window at such convenient times.

## Others who helped

Staff of the national parks of Canada and the United States, including the interpretive services of Banff National Park, Kootenay National Park, Yoho National Park, Waterton Lakes National Park and Glacier National Park, Montana, provided information and access to documents, as well as some of the photos. Thanks particularly to Jeff Anderson, Mark Kolasinski and Jim Todgham of Jasper National Park, who let me use their library and special equipment.

Other provincial and federal agencies: the British Columbia Ministry of Environment, Lands and Parks, and Alberta Environmental Protection, Parks provided information on natural features and wildlife in provincial parks in the Rockies. Provincial and state agencies provided population data for the table on page 708. Entomologists Norbert Kondla (British Columbia Forest Service), Patrick Schofield (Alberta Environment, Calgary) and Diane Szlabey (Canadian Forestry Service, Edmonton), helped with a couple of insect identifications and provided some illustrations. Bruce Turner, Canadian Wildlife Service, St. John's provided information about gosling-stealing among Canada geese. David McIntyre, well-known naturalist in the Crowsnest Pass area, came through with several photos required at the last moment. He also contributed many useful updates and corrections to the second printing of this edition, as did George Scotter, Canadian Wildlife Service.

The difficult geology chapter could not have been written without the help of the Geological Survey of Canada. Besides the GSC reviewers listed previously, my thanks to Lionel Jackson, Rudy Klassen, Neil Ollerenshaw, Willy Norris, Alan Pedder, Dave Proudfoot, Archie Stalker, Art Sweet and Gordon Taylor.

Peter Sherrington, the naturalist from Cochrane who discovered the great Canadian Rockies eagle-migration route, provided the information about it that appears on page 541.

After years of wondering what the "boulderfield spider" was, I found out courtesy of Robin Leech, Northern Alberta Institute of Technology, who knew exactly what I was talking about. See page 461.

David Scollard copy-edited the first-edition text, solving editorial problems and tossing out the worst of my patronizing remarks. Jose Botelho checked all the Latin genus and species names, so that they would go into my word-processor correctly, never to emerge misspelled (maybe). Jill Seaton did the proof-reading of each chapter. Rowsby Woof, the Corax Press dog, thanks Basil Seaton for taking him on walks when everyone else was too busy.

Cia Gadd, my wife, was essential to the successful completion of both editions, doing fieldwork, editing the text, offering advice, feeding the crew, showing forbearance and keeping things together no matter what. My son Toby, who kept his dad's old Radio Shack computer going long enough to finish the first edition in 1985, found himself on the "bleeding edge" of color desktop publishing ten years later in doing the electronic prepress work for this edition. He did an outstanding job. His partner Alix Craig held the fort in Colorado and kept the computer hardware flowing north. More recently she contributed a number of updates and corrections to the second printing of this edition.

*To all these people, my sincere thanks.*

## How to use this book

There are at least three ways:

1. Read it from the beginning. *Handbook* is a multidisciplinary work with some depth, and it proceeds from one topic to the next in a manner that I hope is logical. Technical concepts and terms are explained along the way. Some colleges and universities use the book as a text.

2. Use it to look things up, which is what most readers do. For that, there is a detailed index at the back. If you come across an unfamiliar term or idea, check the index. Go to the first page number listed for that item; there you will find either the definition or a cross-reference to the appropriate page number. Most places mentioned in the text are found in the atlas, which begins on page 785. There is a special map index on pages 786 and 787.

3. Or just go browsing. The cross-references will help those who like to skip around in the various sections. Surf the index.

## Errors? Please let me know

This is the second edition, and mistakes found in the first edition have been corrected. Of course, some errors may remain, and no doubt others have been introduced. These can be corrected in the next edition, with the help of readers. *If you see something that is incorrect, I would like to hear about it.* Please contact me, Ben Gadd, at Corax Press, Box 1557, Jasper, Alberta  T0E 1E0.

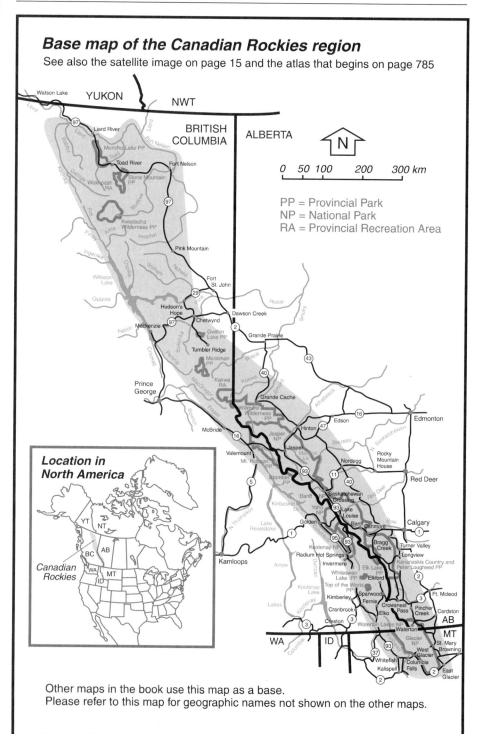

# Base map of the Canadian Rockies region

See also the satellite image on page 15 and the atlas that begins on page 785

PP = Provincial Park
NP = National Park
RA = Provincial Recreation Area

**Location in North America**

Canadian Rockies

Other maps in the book use this map as a base.
Please refer to this map for geographic names not shown on the other maps.

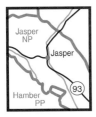

# Introduction
## The shining mountains

The mountain range we now call the Canadian Rockies was known to aboriginal peoples as the "Shining Mountains," referring perhaps to the glint of snowy peaks. "Rocky Mountains" comes from the Spanish "sierra," which means "a rocky mountain range." The term was applied descriptively to the southern end of the Rockies in the 1500s by the Spaniards Cabeza de Vaca and Coronado. In the 1752 journal of Jacques Legardeue de Saint Pierre, the name in its French form "Montagnes de Roche"is applied to the entire range, including the Canadian portion.

The Canadian Rocky Mountains, as shown on the federal government's official *Physiographic Regions of the Canadian Cordillera* (Geological Survey of Canada, 1986) and *Physiographic Regions of Canada* (Geological Survey of Canada, 1970) comprise a mountainous part of western Canada extending from the Interior Plains on the east to the Rocky Mountain Trench on the west, and from the Liard River in northern British Columbia to the international boundary on the south. Here are the basic stats on the Canadian Rockies:

- Length 1450 km, width 150 km
- Area 180,000 km²
- Highest point: Mt. Robson, 3954 m above sea level
- Lowest point: confluence of the Liard and Toad rivers, 305 m

For the purposes of this book the region is considered to extend south from Canada 100 km into Montana, to the southern boundary of Glacier National Park, because the mountains of Glacier are geologically and biologically part of the Canadian Rockies.

Within the Canadian Rockies there are four east-west physiographic divisions: the foothills, front ranges, main ranges and western ranges. There are three north-south divisions: the northern, central and southern regions. These names are not officially gazetted, so they are not capitalized.

Note that the Rockies do not include all the mountains lying between the plains and the Pacific. The Rocky Mountains are only one range of several within Canada's western cordillera. But you can cross the Rockies anywhere and recognize them immediately. That such a long, narrow region could have this degree of integrity is remarkable.

What is the nature of that integrity? It can be summarized in four points:

**1. Geology.** Sedimentary rock up to 1.5 billion years old, deposited mostly below sea level, has been bent, broken and piled up. Mountain-building in the Rockies area began about 140 million years ago and tapered off about 45 million years ago.

**2. Topography**. Ridges trending northwest/southeast are separated by parallel U-shaped valleys. A few large, deep valleys carry major rivers southwest to northeast, across the grain of the land. Glacial erosion has been heavy, and glaciers up to 300 km² in size still exist along the crest of the range.

**3. Climate**. The average mean annual temperature for all public weather stations on valley floors is a cool 2.6°C, with average mean annual precipitation of 571 mm. The weather pattern is influenced strongly by the barrier-like nature of the Canadian Rockies. The eastern slope is noticeably cooler and drier than the western slope, and strong chinook winds warm the eastern slope suddenly in winter.

**4. Ecology**. Plant and animal communities in the Rockies are stratified by elevation. There are two widespread, easily recognizable life zones—subalpine and alpine—plus a lot of ecological variety at low elevations. Limestone-rich areas and quartzite-rich areas have distinctive biological features. Much of the Rockies is still unsettled, with few roads, so a great deal of wilderness remains and nearly all the native animal species are still present. But the situation is deteriorating rapidly.

## Old rock, middle-aged mountains, young landscape

In the satellite photo on the opposite page, the long ridges of the Canadian Rockies look rather like wrinkles at the edge of a rug. This analogy is appropriate. Think of a thin layer of sedimentary rock (the rug) lying on top of the granite and gneiss that make up most of our continent (the floor of the room). Now think of someone shoving the edge of the rug toward the middle of the room. The rug wrinkles up. This is much the same mechanism that built the Rockies. The shove came from a collision between crustal plates.

Prior to the collision, the Rockies region was part of a wide continental shelf covered by the sea. Sedimentary rock had been collecting there for 1.5 billion years. That's a long time, even by geological standards, and there were few interruptions; continued slow subsidence allowed the pile to reach a thickness of 20 km in some places.

The strata now provide geologists with one of the better, more complete sedimentary records to be found anywhere in the world. The lower layers are Precambrian, showing signs of simple forms of life—algae, jellyfish, worms—that evolved into the Cambrian trilobites so beautifully preserved in Yoho National Park's world-famous Burgess Shale. Higher in the sequence one finds corals, brachiopods, snails and cephalopods in the Devonian and Carboniferous layers of the front ranges. The soft sandstone and shale beds of the foothills hold clams, oysters and plant fossils of the yet-younger Mesozoic and Cenozoic eras.

There are riches in these rocks: oil and natural gas from Devonian reefs; coal from the Cretaceous forests of 100 million years ago. But don't look for gold and silver in the Canadian Rockies. There's very little—although a lead/zinc deposit was mined in Yoho National Park, there was a little copper mining in Glacier National Park, and finely disseminated gold is found in volcanic rocks near Crowsnest Pass.

During a 100-million-year period that began about 140 million years ago, the sediments of the west-coast continental shelf were pushed inland to the northeast, coming loose from the underlying granite and sliding along. Accordioned up to 300 km, the originally flat layers bent into folds and broke into moving sheets of rock—thrust sheets, page 140—that slid up and over one another, stacking skyward. Fossils of corals that once formed tropical reefs now decorate the walls of peaks standing 3000 m above the tides.

Relatively recently, over the last two million years, glaciation has intensified in the region, carving deep, wide valleys between steep-walled ridges and sharp summits. This is a young landscape, freshly cut by ice. Along the continental divide hundreds of glaciers are still rasping away at the range, dumping fragments of it into milky-looking rivers that feed their rock flour into lakes of gem-like blues and greens. A detailed look at the geology of the region begins on page 45.

## Interesting weather

This is a cool place, literally, with average annual temperatures on the valley floors ranging from -1.1°C at Fort Nelson to 5.7°C at Canal Flats. Compare with 9.9°C at Vancouver, or 10.1°C at Denver, Colorado, in the southern part of the Rocky Mountains. At Jasper, close to the divide and midway between the north and south ends of the Canadian Rockies, the temperature touches -35°C in January. Hot spells in mid-July can reach +35°C. Neither of these extremes is as uncomfortable as it might seem, because the air is dry.

The crest of the Rockies is a climatic divide. It is generally wetter and warmer on the western slope, especially in winter; drier and cooler on the eastern side. When Pacific storms roll in across the coast of British Columbia, they unload most of their rain and snow on the Coast Mountains and Columbia Mountains, leaving much less moisture to fall over the Rockies to the east. Typical annual precipitation figures are 400–700 mm, compared with 950 mm at Revelstoke in the next range to the west, or 2552 mm in the Coast Mountains at Prince Rupert.

But although it may rain less here, there is still enough summer storminess to ruin many a vacation, and enough winter snow to please the skiers. As in other mountainous regions, the daily weather is difficult to predict. The chapter on weather and climate starts on page 205.

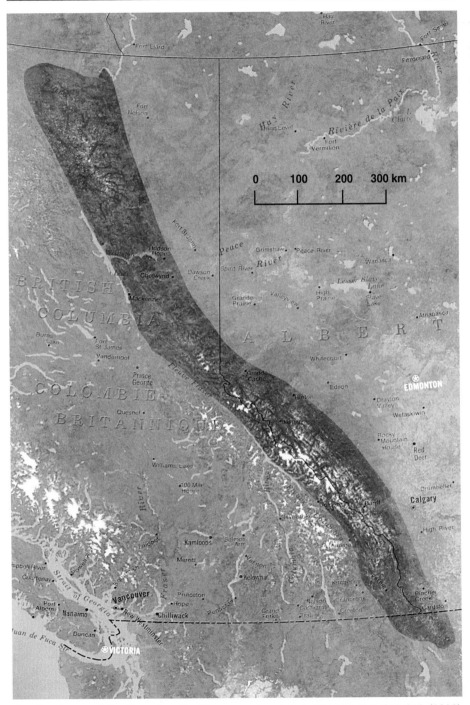

*Satellite image of the Canadian Rockies, reproduced from* Canada 1: 5 000 000 (1992), *courtesy Natural Resources Canada, Ottawa*

# *There is still wilderness, but it's going fast*

The Canadian Rockies are well-wooded with pine, spruce, fir, aspen and poplar, with hemlock and red-cedar on the western slope. Travellers along the TransCanada Highway see mostly forest, perhaps coming to the conclusion that the Rockies are about nine-tenths trees. But that's a false impression. Anyone venturing up high, or getting a view from an airplane window, can see that much of the region is above treeline—about 40 percent of Jasper National Park, for example.

These mountains are famous for wildflowers. Pink moss-campion cushions and brilliantly orange arctic poppies adorn the heights. Down in the valleys, sky-blue harebells stand out above green carpets of kinnikinnik. In late July every meadow at every elevation is full of color. In late August the breeze carries the fragrance of blueberries.

Canadian Rockies botany is surprisingly similar from one end of the range to the other. If you learn to identify a dozen common plants around Banff, you will see most of them again 275 km south at Waterton or 800 km north along the Alaska Highway. The Waterton/Glacier area has the greatest diversity: about 1500 species. This book describes and illustrates some 700 species of trees, shrubs, wildflowers, grasses, sedges, rushes, ferns, horsetails, mosses, lichens and fungi. The listings begin on page 249.

Despite the regional consistency, there are differences between eastern-slope and western-slope floral checklists, and at low elevations there is striking ecological variety. See page 221 for a discussion, and page 231 for pictures of 31 common ecological communities.

The Canadian Rockies are home to the sort of creatures one expects to find in a northern mountain wilderness: grizzly bears to keep you on your guard; wolves that watch you quietly from the forest edge; coyotes that wait patiently a few metres away from your picnic; cougars, lynx and wolverines to spot once or twice in a lifetime. There are beavers in the brooks and weasels in the willows.

*An elk, which we should really call a wapiti, in Jasper National Park. Parks Canada photo by Larry Halverson.*

*Wild gaillardia growing on purple argillite, Glacier National Park, Montana*

Moose eat those willows. Caribou wander the tundra from one tasty lichen patch to the next. Mountain goats lick the salty shale at Disaster Point east of Jasper, their babies frisking about before the smiling, lucky onlookers.

Elk and deer nibble the shrubbery and the lawns in Banff; bighorn sheep lie in the dust beside Highway 16 east of Jasper. Dall's sheep do the same near Summit Lake along the Alaska Highway. For more on the 69 species of mammals, turn to page 593.

There are at least 211 species of birds in the air and on the lakes, 44 species of fish in the water—but only one species of turtle, two kinds of toads and four kinds of snakes. Still, there are six species of frogs in the Canadian Rockies, including one that survives above treeline and freezes solid every winter. See page 501 to find out more.

A hundred kinds of butterflies grace the flowery mountain meadows, some species appearing among the early-April snows. There are crane flies that walk the drifts in mid-winter, worms that eat the algae that grow on summer snowbanks, and primitive ice insects that live under rocks on glaciers. The mosquitoes and flies here are just as fond of humans as they are anywhere; the ticks perhaps more so. The chapter on insects begins on page 435.

Despite near-extirpation of elk before the turn of the century, the only mammal driven to extinction here—so far, anyway—is the bison, a few of which are currently kept captive at Waterton and Banff. Yet bison are making a comeback in the northern Rockies, where a feral herd has established itself in the wilderness near Pink Mountain. At time of writing a single animal that escaped from a foothills ranch wanders the Rocky River area in eastern Jasper National Park. See page 653.

We have no black widows, no rattlesnakes, no scorpions. And very little poison ivy.

The wildlands of the Canadian Rockies are in decline proportionate to the worldwide human population explosion. Clear-cut logging, mining, oil and gas extraction, dam-building, road-building, ranching, resort-building and settlement are all assaulting these mountains as never before. Fortunately some of the land is protected in spacious national and provincial parks.

## *We love to visit, but most of us can't stay*

People have been present in the Canadian Rockies for a very long time. Archeological test pits dug ahead of highway construction near Banff in the 1980s revealed an 11,000-year-old campsite. See page 687.

Few of those early campers seem to have lived year-round in the mountains proper, nor do very many people now. There are only nine towns between the mountain front and the Rocky Mountain Trench with over 1000 residents. The total permanent population of the whole region, including the larger centres in the foothills and on the floor of the trench, is about 167,000. That works out to about one person per square kilometre, a blessedly low population density.

A lot of people come here seasonally, though, for mountain holidays. Jasper National Park, resident population 4200, swells to 20,000 on long weekends in July and August.

What do they do, all these visitors?

Parks Canada figures show that, by and large, they drive to the mountains, eat, sleep, excrete and go home. On page 716 you'll find the tourist's must-see list for the region.

Of the ten percent of visitors who do more than stroll down Banff Avenue, the majority go for walks of a couple of hours. Day-hikers get good value for their small investment in time and energy. A walk past Lake Louise to the Plain of Six Glaciers fills the senses with mountain sights and sounds. There you are, among the great peaks of the continental divide. A blue-white glacier lies in its brown, bouldery bed. Ice breaks from Mt. Lefroy, booming down the cliffs. The clean fragrance of subalpine fir goes deep into the lungs when the trail gets steep. Turn to page 723 for a list of recommended day-hikes.

Smaller yet are the number of people who hike for two days or more in the back country, getting the full course: sun and storms, bug-bites and fields of flowers, bears snuffing about in the night and eagles cruising the ridgelines by day. In Jasper park, especially, there are long trails that take only a few hundred people each year into a landscape that still looks much as it did a thousand years ago. Advice for back-packers is given on page 725.

*Castleguard Meadows, in northern Banff National Park*

More people every summer are seeing the Canadian Rockies by bicycle. I have spoken with cyclists from all over the world, and they tell me that the Banff-Jasper ride is the best short tour on earth, offering good pavement, cheap hostel accommodation, camaraderie around the evening fire, splendid scenery and spicy weather. For information on how to do it, see page 746.

A new breed of machine has taken bicycling in another direction: off the highway and onto the trails. While mountain-biking is healthy, self-propelled and sporting, the generally negative reaction of hikers is understandable. Their paths are already muddied and polluted by horses; who needs tire tracks in the wilderness? I have mixed feelings about trail bicycling, too, and so does Parks Canada, but I enjoy my mountain bike and appreciate its advantages. See page 748 for some fat-tire advice.

You can't bicycle up Mt. Assiniboine (yet), or ride a horse up. Mountaineering is still the most personally demanding, most rewarding way to experience the heights. No doubt every summit in the Canadian Rockies has been reached, but unclimbed faces and untraversed ridges remain. Rock-climbers will find the moves here as challenging as they are anywhere else in the world, with the added beauty of wilderness surroundings. See page 731 for mountaineering highlights.

We have fine skiing, of both the uphill and downhill varieties. There are several ski areas here, with the usual offerings, but for the cross-country skier there is much more. You can choose a gentle trail in the foothills or a crossing of the Columbia Icefield. The skiing section begins on page 737.

The icy glacial waters of the Rockies offer much to canoeists and kayakers. For paddling information, turn to page 749.

A few outdoorspeople are killed each year in these mountains, for the Canadian Rockies are unforgiving of errors in judgement. A section on safety, emergencies and first aid begins on page 761.

If you are not interested in careening through the rapids or hanging from your fingers over an abyss, there are gentler avenues to explore. In Jasper park, for example, you might take the kids picnicking at Lake Annette. The water is wonderfully clear, warm enough for swimming on a hot afternoon in July or August. After supper go for a walk up nearby Old Fort Point and listen for Swainson's thrush singing flute-like in the aspen. As night falls, head over to Whistlers Campground for an interpretive program by a park naturalist.

This emphasis on recreation, and nondestructive forms of it, is in line with the history of the region, outlined beginning on page 687. A strong conservationist element in Canadian society has held the nation's favorite mountains dear for a hundred and ten years; thus do we have the large national and provincial parks of Alberta and British Columbia. Explorers and settlers reached the Canadian Rockies so recently that government control preceded them. This lucky occurrence, and a paucity of easily exploitable natural resources, have helped the Canadian segment of the Rocky Mountains, and Glacier National Park, Montana, to avoid much of the environmental damage seen in the mountains of Colorado and New Mexico.

But human pressure is increasing. Outside the national parks the perennial tamers of wildlands—industry, agriculture, human occupation and auto access—keep gnawing away at the 87 percent of the area that lacks federal protection. Within the national parks, the rapid rate of tourist-industry development is disturbing. The afterword, page 783, deals with some pressing concerns and proposes a new national park in the northern Rockies.

Anyone seeing the Canadian Rockies for the first time is likely to feel an awestruck admiration for the place. It's a feeling that stays and grows. I hope you will join me in giving this incredible land the sensitive treatment it deserves—and in urging our governments to do the same.

*What the ground squirrels see at the Peyto Lake Viewpoint*

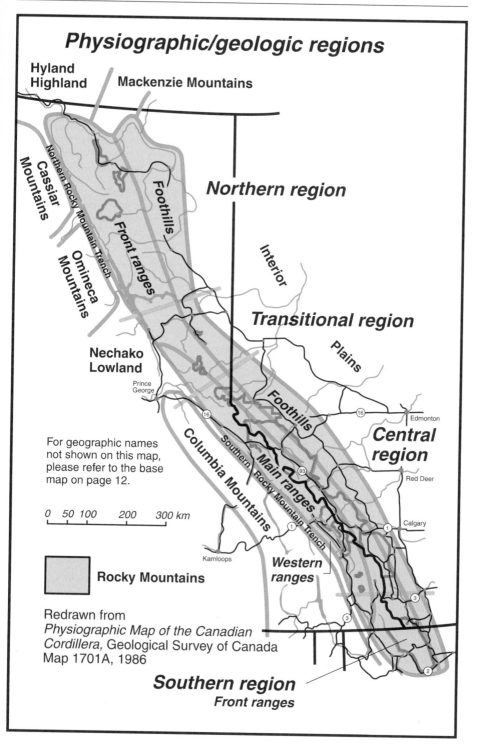

# Physiographic/geologic regions

Hyland
Highland    Mackenzie Mountains

Northern Rocky Mountain Trench

Cassiar
Mountains

Foothills

Northern region

Front ranges

Omineca
Mountains

Interior

Transitional region

Nechako
Lowland

Plains

Prince
George

Foothills

For geographic names
not shown on this map,
please refer to the base
map on page 12.

Columbia Mountains

Southern Rocky Mountain Trench

Main ranges

Central
region

Red Deer

0   50  100    200    300 km

Calgary

Kamloops

Western
ranges

Rocky Mountains

Redrawn from
*Physiographic Map of the Canadian
Cordillera,* Geological Survey of Canada
Map 1701A, 1986

Southern region
Front ranges

Edmonton

# *Lines*
## Boundaries and divisions

Where are the Canadian Rockies, what are the physical boundaries of the region and how is it divided up?

The Rockies are the easternmost part of the **Canadian Cordillera,** the physiographic name for all the mountains of western Canada. When combined with the mountains of the western United States and those of Alaska, the whole region is called by Canadian physiographers the **Western Cordillera of North America.**

A note on pronunciation. "Cordillera" is Spanish for "mountain range." It should be pronounced "core-dee-YAIR-uh," a lovely sounding word that Anglophones often pronounce as, ugh, "core-DILL-er-uh."

### Eastern boundary: the Interior Plains

In Canada, the Interior Plains (a gazetted name and thus capitalized) are the vast expanse of level land that lies between the Canadian Shield and the Rocky Mountains. In the United States the equivalent region is called the Great Plains.

Travellers approaching from the plains see the Rockies first as a blue line on the horizon. Later, face to face with the front ranges, they can see why the term "wall-like" is applied so frequently to the eastern aspect of these mountains.

The geological contrast is just as impressive as the topographic one. The layers lie flat under the plains, but in the mountains it seems that everything is at an angle to everything else. At the plains/foothills boundary west of Calgary or Edmonton, the riverbanks and road-cuts display folds and faults. Even though the topography is still plains-like, the geology shows that you're in the Rockies. North of the Peace River the plains/foothills boundary is more obvious: the plains end abruptly at an impressive escarpment that faces the mountains.

*Looking northwestward along the Rocky Mountain Trench between Valemount and McBride*

## Western boundary: the Rocky Mountain Trench

The Rocky Mountain Trench is one of the great lines on the globe, a long valley that runs from the international boundary to the Liard River, then resumes as the Tintina ("tin-TEEN-uh") Trench, which continues to Alaska. The Rocky Mountain Trench has existed for at least 45 million years, and it is visible in photos taken from the moon; it *has* to be some kind of major break in the earth's crust.

Indeed, it is. From Prince George north, the trench is a magnificent fault along which the rest of British Columbia has ground its way northwest for about 500 km relative to the Rockies. South of Prince George the nature of the faulting is different. The ditch-like character of the trench betrays an underlying down-dropped block of crust. See page 142 for a more detailed discussion.

Near the international boundary the trench splits into two diverging valleys. The western valley is that of the Kootenay River, now flooded by Lake Koocanusa, a long reservoir that extends south to the Libby Dam in the United States. The eastern valley is that of the Stillwater and Tobacco rivers, the route of Highway 93. East of that, along the western boundary of Glacier National Park, Montana, the Flathead River follows a third big valley, which would be a convenient place to put the western physiographic boundary of the Rockies except that the Flathead Valley doesn't connect either geologically or topographically with the Rocky Mountain Trench in Canada. It's east of the trench, and therefore part of the Rockies.

The Whitefish Range, found west of Glacier park and east of the Stillwater Valley, is the American name for the southern ends of two mountain groups that lie mostly in Canada: the Galton Range and the MacDonald Range. The Galton and MacDonald ranges are located east of the Rocky Mountain Trench and thus are unequivocally part of the Canadian Rockies. So it makes sense to include the Whitefish Range in the Rockies as well.

The mountains west of the Stillwater are not part of the Canadian Rockies; they are southern extensions of Canada's Columbia Mountains, one of the ranges lying west of the Rockies. Thus, the Stillwater Valley makes a good southwestern boundary.

West of the Rocky Mountain Trench lie the Columbia Mountains, the Omineca ("Oh-min-EEK-uh") Mountains and the Cassiar ("CASS-ee-yar") Mountains, known collectively to geologists as the **Omineca belt.** Although the Omineca belt began to rise 35 million years before the Rockies, and even though the Omineca area includes granite and high-grade metamorphic rock not found in the Rockies, the Omineca belt and the Rockies were essentially one mountain range until the Rocky Mountain Trench divided the region about 40 million years ago.

Topographically, the ranges west of the trench are not quite as high as the Rockies, although the valleys are deeper. Climatically, the Columbias, Ominecas and Cassiars are wetter and warmer than the Rockies, which gives them a different biological character.

## Northern boundary: the Liard River

The Liard ("Lee-YARD") River, in its deep canyon, separates the Rockies from the Liard Lowland and the Hyland Highland (yes, it's "Hyland Highland") to the north. These areas are not mountainous on the scale of the Rockies. Geologically, too, there is a change at the Liard River: the rock is younger on the north side. The grain of the land, which is southeast to northwest in the Rockies, bends 30° as the underlying folds and faults run northeasterly into the Mackenzie Mountains and Franklin Mountains of the Yukon and Northwest Territories. These ranges have much in common geologically with the Canadian Rockies, as do the Selwyn Mountains, Ogilvie Mountains, Arctic Mountains and Brooks Range even farther north, but they are considered to be major mountain ranges on their own, separate from the Rockies.

## Southern boundary: Marias Pass

Surprise: the Canadian Rockies include Glacier National Park, Montana. Nature does not respect political boundaries, especially those drawn arbitrarily along lines of latitude. The Canadian-*style* Rockies continue into the United States.

How far? The Lewis Thrust, page 36, the fault along which the rock of the Waterton/Glacier region was shoved into the area, runs south into Montana for 125 km, so one could make a case for carrying the name "Canadian-style Rockies" that far south. But consider Marias Pass, 40 km south of the international boundary along the southern edge of Glacier park. Marias Pass is low (1609 m), a major gap in the range, and the peaks south of it are smaller, not as heavily glaciated, not as rugged as peaks to the north. Further, the rock immediately south of Marias Pass is younger than the rock north of it. This is as good a place as any to draw the line. Highway 2 follows that line.

# *Comparison with the American Rockies*
## It used to be apples and oranges, but no longer

What do the Canadian Rockies and the American Rockies have in common geologically? At first glance, not much. The Canadian Rockies are made of layered sedimentary rock such as limestone and shale; the American Rockies as seen in Colorado are made mostly of metamorphic and igneous rock such as gneiss and granite. For many years it has been known that the sedimentary rock of the Canadian Rockies was shoved northeastward, sliding along the ancient underlying granite and gneiss of the North American continental plate. The plate was not broken, uplifted or folded, except at a few places. Think of a bulldozer scraping a thin layer off the undisturbed ground beneath and pushing it ahead; that's a rough analogy for the origin of the Canadian Rockies.

In contrast, the American Rockies look as if they have been built by straight uplift, from below, because the granite and gneiss seen in them is the stuff of the continental plate itself— the **basement,** to use a popular geologic term for it. No bulldozer is required for this scenario; the ground itself would have risen.

Until recently geologists were hard-pressed to explain how a single, continuous mountain chain—the Rockies of the U.S. and Canada—could have such disparate sections. There just had to be some sort of unifier. In the last ten years that unifier has been discovered. It turns out that the Canadian and American parts of the Rockies have formed essentially the same way, despite the difference in appearance, as follows.

The entire Rockies area was once the edge of the North American continent. Because today's continental edge lies so far west of the Rockies, the old continental edge was not recognized until geologists realized that most of the land between the Rockies and the west coast had been added to the continent through the mechanism of plate tectonics, page 135. North America has moved northwestward, overriding the northeastward-moving crust of the ocean floor and bumping into smaller landmasses sitting on that oceanic crust. As the smaller landmasses were scraped off the oceanic crust and added to North America, they pushed against the sedimentary rock that lay along the old continental edge, acting as the bulldozer described earlier.

Some 80 million years ago, the American Rockies and the Canadian Rockies probably looked much the same: mountains of folded and faulted sedimentary rock. The differences developed later, and they involved the amount of plate-overriding. Under western Canada, the overridden oceanic plate tilted steeply down into the hot rock of the earth's mantle, where the lower edge is now melting away at great depths west of the Rockies. But under the United States the overridden oceanic plate behaved differently. It slid along under the continent, reaching at least as far east as the Rockies of Wyoming and Colorado. In forcing its way eastward, the oceanic plate has broken up the basement rock along faults that probably reach all the way from the base of the continent, 40–50 km down, to the surface. Large areas of the crust have been shoved over one another along these faults, raising the basement rock high.

This is the big difference between the American Rockies and the Canadian Rockies. In the American Rockies the basement was broken and thrust up. We see it now at the surface. In the Canadian Rockies the basement wasn't disturbed much. We see the broken and piled-up sedimentary rock at the surface, not the smooth top of the intact basement 8–10 km down.

What about the 3–4 km of sedimentary rock of the American Rockies, the rock that was overlying the basement? What happened to it? A lot of it has been stripped off the basement by erosion, especially where the basement was uplifted highest.

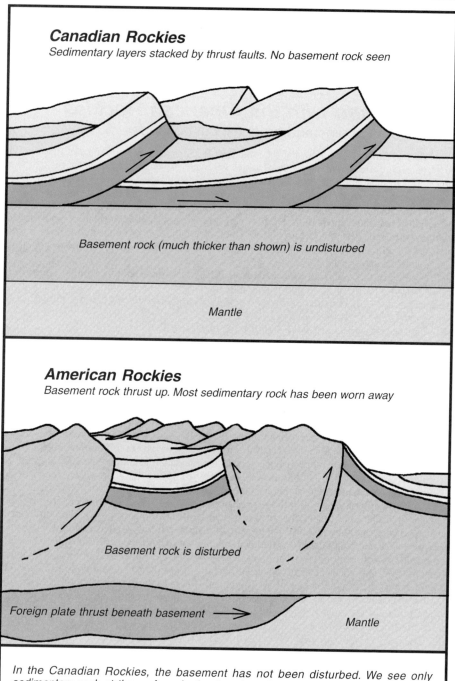

## Canadian Rockies
Sedimentary layers stacked by thrust faults. No basement rock seen

Basement rock (much thicker than shown) is undisturbed

Mantle

## American Rockies
Basement rock thrust up. Most sedimentary rock has been worn away

Basement rock is disturbed

Foreign plate thrust beneath basement ⟶

Mantle

In the Canadian Rockies, the basement has not been disturbed. We see only sedimentary rock at the surface. In the American Rockies, the basement has been broken by motion of a plate moving underneath. We see basement rock at the surface.

Another geological difference is that the American Rockies have received additional uplift from rising masses of magma, some possibly associated with actions of the underlying oceanic plate and others from a hot spot in the mantle. Molten rock has reached the surface at many points in the American Rockies, such as the Yellowstone region and the San Juan Mountains of Colorado, producing volcanoes and lava flows, which are rare in the Canadian Rockies.

The American Rockies region is, on average, higher in elevation than the Canadian Rockies region, with many summits standing over 4000 m above sea level. In the Canadian Rockies there are only 17 peaks 3500 m or higher, and none over 4000 m (see table on page 736). But the topographic relief, meaning the elevation gain from the base of any particular mountain to its top, is typically *less* in the American Rockies than in the Canadian Rockies.

For example, the greatest topographic relief in the American Rockies is found at Pikes Peak, elevation 4301 m, whose summit stands 2351 m above its base at Manitou Springs, Colorado, elevation 1950 m. At Mt. Robson, elevation 3954 m, the highest peak in the Canadian Rockies and also the point of greatest topographic relief anywhere in the Rockies, Canadian or American, the base is at 985 m, for a total relief of 2969 m, 618 m more than at Pikes Peak. Other peaks in the Canadian Rockies have less relief than Mt. Robson does, but then other peaks in the American Rockies have less relief than Pikes Peak does. On average, American Rockies peaks are shorter from base to top, even though they reach higher elevations.

The difference comes from valley depth. Valleys of the Canadian Rockies have been eroded deeper, relative to the peaks, than those in the American Rockies. The Great Plains spread out below the Colorado Rockies at elevations of 1500–2000 m. In Alberta the plains lie at 1000 m. Given the 3500-m elevation of a typical high peak in the Alberta Rockies, this allows a maximum topographic relief of 2500 m, on par with that in Colorado. But on the western slope of the Canadian Rockies the major valley floors lie at elevations of only 600–800 m above sea level, allowing for additional relief.

Further, the higher Canadian Rockies peaks lie close to those low points, meaning that they rise more steeply from base to top than do American Rockies peaks. For example, the summit of Pikes Peak lies 11 km away from its base at Manitou Springs. The summit of Mt. Robson lies only 4 km from its base at Kinney Lake.

An important factor in the steepness of the Canadian Rockies, and another difference between the American and Canadian Rockies, is that the Canadian Rockies have been more heavily glaciated. Glaciers tend to cut sideward more than they cut downward, producing wide, straight, U-shaped valleys with steep walls. Practically every valley in the Canadian Rockies has been modified this way. In contrast, glaciation in the Colorado Rockies has been restricted to higher elevations. You travel a long way up a narrow, winding, stream-cut valley before reaching the straight, U-shaped glaciated section near the head of the watershed.

This brings up a final, fundamental physical difference: latitude. Pikes Peak is located 39° north of the equator. Mt. Robson lies 53° north of the equator. At 60 nautical miles per degree, that puts Mt. Robson 840 nautical miles, or 1550 km, closer to the north pole. This far north the climate is significantly cooler than that of Colorado. (See page 205 for a discussion of latitude and angle of sunlight.) The amount of precipitation is roughly equal in both areas, but Colorado's warmth ensures that more evaporation and snowmelt occur there. Overall, this makes Colorado drier. The coolness of the Canadian Rockies reduces the amount of evaporation and dryness, giving the Canadian Rockies moister soil, bigger rivers and more glacial ice. The growing season is shorter and the soil is colder, explaining why treeline, page 227, is much lower in the Alberta Rockies (2000–2300 m) than it is in Colorado (3300–3600 m).

A word about names. Americans call the mountains of Glacier National Park the "Northern Rockies," extending that term to include several ranges to the west—well west of the region Canadian physiographers think of as the Rocky Mountains. By all means, call the American section of the range whatever you like. But to be consistent throughout this book, "northern Rockies" refers to the northern part of the *Canadian* Rockies, not to mountains south of the international boundary.

# A physiographic tour
## Well, *three* physiographic tours

The Canadian Rockies chain is long and narrow. But within the range are even-narrower strips:
- The **foothills,** between the prairies and the mountains.
- The **front ranges,** which mark the eastern mountain front.
- The **main ranges,** backbone of the Rockies between Crowsnest Pass and the Peace River. These are subdivided into **eastern main ranges** and **western main ranges,** which have differing rock types—the western main ranges are shalier—and thus a different topographic style.
- The **western ranges,** a minor part of the Rockies bordering the Rocky Mountain Trench between Radium Hot Springs and Golden. In this area the strata are bent backward.*

In addition to the lengthwise divisions, the Canadian Rockies can be divided into three main crosswise strips, creatively designated the **southern** Canadian Rockies (south of Crowsnest Pass), the **central** Canadian Rockies (Crowsnest Pass to the Peace River) and the **northern** Canadian Rockies (north of the Peace). The geological transition between the southern and central Rockies at Crowsnest Pass is fairly sharp, but the transition between the central and northern Rockies is more gradual. The geology changes between Grande Cache and the Peace River.

These divisions are shown on the map on page 20. Note that not all the east/west divisions (foothills, front ranges, main ranges, western ranges) exist in all the north/south divisions (southern, central, northern).

Now for our three tours: #1 across the central region, #2 across the southern region and #3 across the northern region. To avoid duplication, I have emphasized the differences among these transects rather than the similarities. The central-region tour is described first, for the central Rockies are the standard with which the other regions are compared.

## The central Rockies: Calgary to Golden

We'll start with the classic transect of the central Canadian Rockies, describing the lengthwise divisions as they appear on a trip from Calgary to Golden along the TransCanada Highway.

In Calgary, sandstone outcrops along the shores of Glenmore Reservoir tell us that we are on the Interior Plains, because the layers are nearly flat-lying (see the Paskapoo Formation, page 133). Some 25 km west of the city we come to the first of the foothills: a low ridge that the highway goes straight over. The next ridge includes a road-cut that displays tilted bedding. The layers show curvature, and the rock has been disturbed by mountain-building. Believe it or not, we are in the Rockies.

### Foothills

The ridges become taller and steeper to the west. At the crest of many there is an upturned edge of sandstone that is tougher to erode than the shaly rock on either side of it. On some of the hills the sandstone pokes through the soil, looking like the backbone of a skinny hog, and there you have the geologist's name for such ridges: **hogbacks.** They run from southeast to northwest, as does the grain of the Canadian Rockies generally.

Under the parallel rows of foothills the geologic structure is complicated. There is one fault after another. These are **thrust faults,** important elements in Canadian Rockies geology.

---

*These informal physiographic names are frequently capitalized in the literature (e.g. "Main Ranges"), but they really shouldn't be. The regions to which they refer have not been strictly defined, the names are plural, and with the exception of the foothills they do not appear on the official physiographic map of Canada. The foothills are shown separately from the Rockies on that map, where they are labeled "Rocky Mountain Foothills." In this book I have left the divisions of the Rockies uncapitalized, choosing to capitalize such gazetted (officially recognized) terms as "Interior Plains" and "Rocky Mountain Trench."

Along these faults, slabs of sedimentary rock have moved up and over one another, stacking like shingles on a roof. See page 140 for more on thrust faults.

Coming over the last foothills ridge on the TransCanada Highway, we go down a long grade and out onto the grassy plain that lies along the Bow River. This is Morley Flats, home reserve of the Stoney aboriginal band. Morley Flats is gravelly, windy, and often a cheerless place, but it has proved valuable to the Stoneys, for under it lies a natural-gas field.

*Hogback ridge along the TransCanada Highway west of Calgary*

## Mountain front

At the west end of Morley Flats, just before the TransCanada Highway enters the mountains, it crosses Highway 1X at an overpass. At this point look north toward Yamnuska, a mountain with a long, flat, vertical face of gray-and-buff limestone. The McConnell Thrust, a major fault, runs along the base of Yamnuska's cliff.

*Yamnuska, elevation 2235 m, also called Mt. Laurie. The McConnell Thrust runs along the base of the cliff, which is 350 m high.*

The McConnell Thrust separates the foothills from the front ranges. It lies along the foot of the mountain front from just south of the Bow River nearly to the Athabasca River. Above this fault, a huge slab of tough Paleozoic limestone has been pushed from the southwest to the northeast, up and over much-younger, much-softer Cretaceous sandstone and shale.

You could think of the mountain front as the leading edge of that great thrusted slab, stopped at its point of maximum northeasterly advance, but that wouldn't take into account the 85 million years of erosion that have occurred since thrusting began. The edge of the slab, along with a great deal of rock in the upper part of the slab, has been eroded back several kilometres. Further, the tough limestone at the mountain front has weathered more slowly than the soft shale and sandstone of the adjoining foothills, so the mountain front now stands high above the foothills, a product of **differential erosion.**

Peaks along the mountain front west of Calgary average around 2500 m in elevation. The highest is Mt. Oliver, 3009 m. (The highest peak anywhere in the front ranges of the Canadian Rockies is Mt. Brazeau, 3470 m, near the south end of Maligne Lake in Jasper National Park.) Valley-floor elevations along the TransCanada Highway are around 1300 m, and the topographic relief—the difference between high and low points—is about 1200 m at the mountain front. At Banff, in the heart of the front ranges, the relief is greater, typically 1600 m.

## Dip slopes and alternation of limestone ridges and shale valleys

Mt. Rundle is a well-known peak overlooking Banff. Viewed from the Vermilion Lakes overlook west of Banff, the mountain illustrates another front-range characteristic: the layers **dip** (geologese for "tilt downward") toward the southwest.

Mt. Rundle is a classic example of how the southwesterly dip of the bedrock in most front-range mountains has given them a characteristic writing-desk shape. Glaciers whittled away at the southwestern side of Mt. Rundle, cutting across the down-dip edges of the layers. This allowed entire beds to break loose from that side of the peak and slide into the valley. These slides reduced the slope-angle of the southwestern side of the mountain to the same angle as the dip of the bedrock—a **dip slope.** (See page 157 for more.) On the northeastern side of Mt. Rundle, where the up-dip edges of the beds are exposed, such slides could not occur, because the rock would have had to slide up the dip; that is, uphill. Erosion was slower, so the northeast-facing cliffs stand tall. This is the typical shape of front-range peaks: moderately sloping on the southwestern, dip-slope side, steep on the northeastern, up-dip side.

Thrust faults in the front ranges cause the same rock units to repeat several times from east to west. Between the mountain front and the town of Banff, the unit of rock that makes up Mt. Rundle is crossed four times along the TransCanada Highway. And you cross it twice more before reaching the Sunshine turnoff only 10 km farther.

This explains another important feature of front-range physiography: the alternation of limestone ridges and shale valleys. In the geological sequence of bedding, which is much the same throughout the central-Rockies front ranges, a soft layer of siltstone and shale about 1300 m thick overlies an equally thick, tough layer of limestone. When the two units are tilted together to the southwest, the layers look like parallel ribbons on the land surface. The soft ribbon of shale is readily attacked by rivers and glaciers. It becomes a valley. The hard ribbon of limestone erodes more slowly and eventually stands high as a ridge.

*Mt. Rundle from Vermilion Lakes Drive near Banff, showing the prominent dip slope on the southwestern side of the mountain*

Both these units—the soft shale and the tough limestone—repeat from east to west through thrust-faulting, so their topographic expression—the peak and the valley—repeat as well. That is what produces the parallel ridges of the front ranges. The ridges of the foothills are similar, but on a smaller scale.

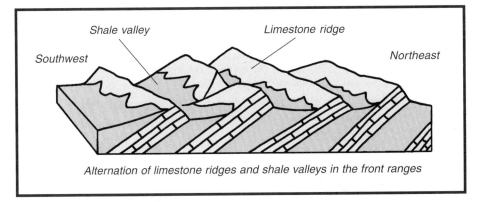

*Alternation of limestone ridges and shale valleys in the front ranges*

## Coal-mining

One of the repeating units in the front ranges is the Kootenay Group, page 127, which is rich in coal. Between 1898 and 1979, miners took three million tonnes of coal from the seams below the thrust fault that runs along the lower slopes of Mt. Rundle and Cascade Mountain. Parks Canada has prepared an exhibit on the subject at the abandoned mining town of Bankhead. Take the road to Lake Minnewanka from the Banff interchange; it passes right by Bankhead.

The geology of the Bankhead coal deposits and the method of extraction became a model for underground coal-mining elsewhere in the Canadian Rockies during its heyday, from the 1900s to the early 1920s. In the mid-1990s coal is still being mined by the open-pit method at several locations in the foothills. For more on coal-mining, see page 697 in the human-history section. You might want to read *Bankhead, the Twenty Year Town*, my short book on the subject. (See the bibliography for the history chapter, page 709.)

## Trellis drainage and flash floods

Front-range streams and rivers reflect front-range geology. Consider the Bow River. It follows a shale valley for a while, then cuts across a limestone ridge and bends into another shale valley, working its way out of the mountains in a series of right angles. The smaller streams flow in the shale valleys only, while many little creeks drain the limestone valley walls. The resulting pattern on a map is regular and angular, known as **trellis drainage.** Trellis drainage is a hallmark of the front ranges.

If you walk up almost any front-range valley in mid-summer you will discover that many of the smaller streamcourses coming in from the sides are dry. Yet the dry channel is often 10 m wide and over a metre deep. The vertical or overhung banks show that water has cut deeply into coarse gravel and angular rock fragments. In other places, trees are partly buried in these deposits.

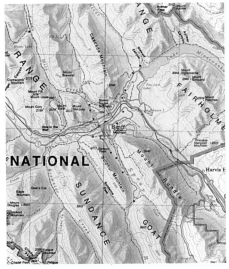

*Trellis drainage. Map: Nat. Resources Can.*

Conclusion: this is flash-flood country. I have witnessed a couple of these events. They sometimes happen in May or June from rapid melting of snow, but more often they occur in July or August from thunderstorms.

Such storms can drop a couple of centimetres of rain in less than an hour. The runoff quickly swells the creek. The velocity of the water increases to the point at which it can move head-size boulders with ease, and the little brook, now a muddy torrent, carries the top layer of its bed downstream. When the flow subsides, the channel configuration will have changed noticeably. Thus are the front ranges washed to the sea.

And thus do we finish with the front ranges. A few kilometres before reaching the junction with Highway 93, which is the turnoff for Radium, the TransCanada Highway crosses the Simpson Pass Thrust and enters the main ranges.

*The dry bed of Exshaw Creek, a typical flash-flood-prone streamcourse in the front ranges southeast of Canmore*

## Eastern main ranges

"Main" is appropriate, for this strip of mountains is the backbone of the central Rockies. The peaks of the eastern main ranges are about 500 m taller than those of the front ranges, but the valley floors are correspondingly higher, too, so the topographic relief–typically 1500 m from the Bow River to the tops of the peaks–is actually less than it is at Banff. Owing to their higher elevation, though, the main ranges receive more rain and snow than the front ranges. The climate is wetter and glaciers are more common. At Lake Louise you can see several glaciers from the highway.

Castle Mountain, easily recognized northeast of the junction of Highway 93 and the TransCanada Highway, is a classic example of an eastern-main-range peak. It is castle-like, all right, with steep walls and a tower at the south end.

The layered rock of the eastern main ranges is nearly flat-lying. Folds are broad and gentle. This produces topography strikingly different from that of the steeply dipping and more tightly folded front ranges next door. Main-range peaks are often castle-like, and dip slopes are not as common here as in the front ranges. The drainage lacks the neat trellis configuration typical of dip-slope mountains; rather, it tends to spread irregularly from the higher peaks.

Glaciers and other agents of erosion cannot cut away flat-lying rock as quickly as they erode tilted beds, which explains why the main ranges are higher than the front ranges. See the boxed item on page 157 for more on this.

The rock in which the main ranges are carved can be thought of as a single thrust sheet several kilometres thick. It was pushed in some 40 km from the southwest over 100 million years ago along the Simpson Pass Thrust, a major fault like the McConnell.

The main-range thrust sheet moved far, yet it held together well. It slid along almost horizontally, which explains the low angle of dip in this part of the Rockies. Regionally, the main ranges dip gently to the southwest.

Main-range rock is old; the oldest we have encountered so far on our east-to-west tour. The lowest layers in the thrust sheet are Precambrian, up to 800 million years old, made of the purplish slate and brown-weathering gritstone of the Miette Group, page 62. Higher in the sequence comes the pinkish, cliff-forming Gog quartzite, page 71, then the dark limestone and pale dolomite of the Middle Cambrian units, topped by buff-colored Late Cambrian units. So eastern-main-range rock is more colorful than the subdued grays and tans of the front ranges.

*Castle Mountain, 2728 m, lies midway between Banff and Lake Louise along the TransCanada Highway. The upper and lower cliffs are made of erosion-resistant limestone and dolomite, divided by a layer of easily eroded shale that forms the prominent ledge halfway up.*

### Continental divide

West of Lake Louise the highway climbs moderately up to Kicking Horse Pass on the continental divide. A raindrop falling exactly on the divide at this location theoretically could send its moisture to both the Atlantic and Pacific oceans: to the Atlantic by way of Hudson Bay, and to the Pacific by way of the Columbia River. On the Columbia Icefield, farther north in the Rockies, the continent divides three ways: Atlantic, Pacific, and Arctic.

Wapta Lake sits beside the highway near the summit of the pass. Major passes in the Rockies often have lakes and marshes at their crests. During some of the Pleistocene glacial advances, ice overtopped the divide from the west and flowed eastward through passes such as Kicking Horse, cutting deep gaps in the main ranges. Ice also moved down to these passes from neighboring peaks, complicating the flow and causing the glacial floors to erode unevenly. Masses of stagnant (non-moving) ice melted in the passes under coverings of silt, sand and gravel, leaving hollows that became ponds and lakes. Wapta Lake is one such hollow.

Shortly after passing Wapta Lake, the road starts to drop down the western side of the pass. The hill is long and the grade is steep, quite different from the eastern approach to the pass, which is gentle. Indeed, western-slope valleys are noticeably deeper than eastern-slope valleys. The highway at Lake Louise is at an elevation of 1539 m. The pass is at 1643 m, for a climb of 104 m. But the elevation of the town of Field, at the foot of Kicking Horse Pass on the

Climbers following the crest of the continent north of Kicking Horse Pass. View is to the southeast from Mt. Balfour, 3272 m, highest peak on the Wapta Icefield. Alberta is on the left, B.C. to the right. Photo was taken in March.

western side, is 1250 m, so the descent on that side is 393 m. The valley floor on the western side of the pass is nearly 300 m deeper than the valley floor on the eastern side.

Why this difference in valley depth? There are several factors that may be involved:

- Western-slope rivers have a shorter distance to go to the sea than eastern-slope rivers do. This produces a steeper streamcourse, faster water flow and hence more erosive power with which to deepen the valleys of the western slope.
- The Rocky Mountain Trench, into which all central-Rockies western-slope rivers flow, is a valley deepened by downward movement of the earth's crust. This has made it extraordinarily deep, and its closeness to the continental divide has steepened western-slope rivers considerably, increasing their erosive power.
- There were thicker ice buildups on the western slope during glacial advances. This resulted in heavier glaciation and thus deeper valleys.

Road-cuts along the descent to Field show that although we're on the western slope, we're still in eastern-main-range rock. At the top of the hill, the Cathedral and Eldon limestones sandwich a band of greenish Stephen shale. Past the bridge there are exposures of the underlying Gog quartzite. See the individual descriptions of these rock layers for more detail; the names are in the index.

Field sits on a large **alluvial fan**: a fan-shaped deposit of river-carried sand and gravel. The steep Yoho River carries this sediment down to Field, where the valley floor is flatter and the water speed slows. The coarser alluvium drops out, adding to the fan year by year. Most of these deposits are glacial outwash dating to the Little Ice Age, page 152, but upstream, in the Yoho Valley, the Wapta and Waputik icefields still supply substantial quantities of gravel.

*View southwest along the gravelly streamcourse of the glacially fed Kicking Horse River near Field. In the background are shaly peaks of the Van Horne Range, typical of the western main ranges.*

### Western main ranges

Field is the site of a dramatic change in the bedrock. East of Field the peaks are made of tough quartzite, limestone and dolomite. West of Field the mountains are mostly of easily eroded shale. Thus, geologists divide the main ranges into eastern and western parts. Handily, the dividing line is generally just west of the continental divide. The eastern main ranges are tougher and hence higher than the shaly western main ranges, which are more rounded and less impressive.

From Field to Golden the bedrock is generally soft and crumbly. There is one exceptional unit, though: the Ottertail Formation, page 84. The Ottertail is a thick, tough limestone that supports the ramparts of Mt. Hurd and Mt. Vaux about 10 km west of Field on the south side of the highway. Even though "Vaux" is a French name, it is pronounced "Vox" (rhymes with "fox") in this case, not "Voe." The mountain is named for W.S.W. Vaux, an Englishman.

While the strong rock of the eastern main ranges lies in gentle folds, the weak, shaly rock of the western main ranges is quite deformed. Road cuts show wildly contorted beds, with tiny folds only a few centimetres across.

Most shale is dark-colored, but road-cuts through the western main ranges display rock that is often greenish-silver. The reason: heat and pressure during mountain-building have altered the minerals in the shale slightly, creating silvery mica and greenish chlorite from what were originally clays. So this rock is mildly metamorphic. The proper term for it is **phyllite** ("FILL-ite"). Many geologists just call it **slate,** which is shale in the first stage of metamorphosis, before it goes to phyllite. The rock here breaks as slate does: according to the direction of stress, not according to the original layering. See the diagram on page 64.

### Western ranges

Coming up: the head of Kicking Horse Canyon, which means we are crossing into the western ranges. Not western *main* ranges, but western ranges, which are subtly different.

Both mountain groups are made of weak, slaty rock that has been intensely folded and faulted. The topography is similar. However, the faults in the western main ranges dip mainly to the southwest, while they dip to the northeast in the western ranges. The rock here has been **overturned**—bent upward and backward, beyond the vertical. Followed downward, the overturned rock curves back to the southwest as Rockies thrust sheets normally do.

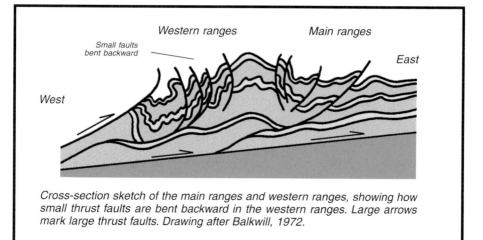

*Cross-section sketch of the main ranges and western ranges, showing how small thrust faults are bent backward in the western ranges. Large arrows mark large thrust faults. Drawing after Balkwill, 1972.*

This overturned zone is narrow and not very long, found only between Radium Hot Springs and Golden, so it is not characteristic of the central Rockies generally. But the western ranges are significant to geologists because they show where a major thrust sheet from the neighboring Purcell Mountains became jammed in the rock of the western Rockies. Rather than riding smoothly up and over the underlying layers as most thrust sheets do, the Purcell sheet plowed into the malleable shale/slate/phyllite, forcing it into the amazing, upward-spreading shape shown in the diagram.

The road descends steeply through Kicking Horse Canyon, which resembles the stream-cut John Stevens Canyon west of Marias Pass at the southern end of Glacier National Park, Montana. Other narrow, twisting valleys descend steeply into the southern section of the Rocky

Mountain Trench, among them Sinclair Canyon, which winds down to Radium Hot Springs. Such valleys look more like they belong in unglaciated parts of the American Rockies than they do in the heavily glaciated Canadian Rockies.

Speaking of the Rocky Mountain Trench, it is coming into view as we approach Golden. The trench is a deep, straight valley that marks the western edge of the Rockies, as discussed on page 141.

## Summary of central-Rockies features

- **Boundaries:** Crowsnest Pass on the south, transitional between Grande Cache and Peace River on the north, Rocky Mountain Trench on the west; indistinct boundary on the east, marked by the most-easterly foothills folds.
- **Highest point:** Mt. Robson, 3954 m, northwest of Jasper in Mount Robson Provincial Park. Treeline drops from about 2300 m at Banff to 2100 m at Jasper.
- **Foothills:** 40–50 km wide, underlain mostly by Cretaceous sandstone and shale that was folded and repetitively thrust-faulted 50–60 million years ago. The rock dips mainly to the southwest; harder beds form parallel hogback ridges aligned southeast-northwest.
- **Front ranges:** 40–50 km wide, underlain mostly by Late Paleozoic limestone (forming ridges) and Mesozoic shale (forming valleys), with spectacular folds and repetitive thrust faults formed about 50–85 million years ago. The rock dips mainly to the southwest; ridges align southeast/northwest, with steep sides to the northeast and dip slopes to the southwest. Trellis drainage.
- **Main ranges:** 40–50 km wide (20–30 km wide in the small area where the western ranges lie to the west), underlain by Precambrian and Early Paleozoic rock. Mostly quartzite and limestone east of the continental divide, in the eastern main ranges, and shale or its metamorphic equivalents west of the divide, in the western main ranges. The eastern main ranges have been carved from a single, tough thrust sheet that began to move about 120 million years ago. The mountains are castle-like, with steep sides all around. In contrast, the western main ranges are cut in tortuously folded and intricately faulted shale; they are irregular and more rounded. Irregular drainage.
- **Western ranges:** an arc-shaped region about 100 km long and 20 km across at its widest point. Topographically similar to the western main ranges, with Cambrian and Ordovician rock that has been rammed by the Purcell Thrust Sheet and forced into a fan-shaped structure in which the rock dips to the northeast. The western ranges form the eastern wall of the Rocky Mountain Trench between Radium and Golden. They began forming at about the same time as the western main ranges some 140 million years ago.

## *The southern Rockies: Waterton/Glacier area*

On this tour we'll cross the southern Canadian Rockies through Glacier National Park, Montana, on the spectacular Going-to-the-Sun Highway over Logan Pass, comparing what we see here with what we saw in the central Canadian Rockies west of Calgary. A major difference is immediately evident: the peaks of Glacier are colorful and castle-like, cut into ancient red and green argillite of the Purcell Supergroup. The gray limestone of the central Rockies seems dull in comparison. A detailed description of the Purcell Supergroup begins on page 52.

In cooperation with the United States Geological Survey, Glacier National Park has established a fine geology tour along the highway. The stops are marked with numbered signs that match a non-technical but meaty guidebook called *Geology along Going-to-the-Sun Road,* by Omer Raup and others, that you can pick up locally or order from the USGS in Denver. (See the bibliography on page 202.)

### Foothills

Saint Mary, Montana, is the eastern gate to Glacier National Park. This little community sits in the foothills, which are geologically very much like those west of Calgary. Glacial outflow from the mountains has carved wide valleys right across the foothills belt here. There are thick glacial deposits of mud, stones and gravel as well. This combination has both eroded and masked the parallel southeast–northwest ridges typical of the foothills elsewhere in the Canadian Rockies. Drilling for oil and gas in the Waterton area has shown that the faults and folds align southeast/northwest, and thus the underlying geological structure of the southern foothills is like that of the foothills farther north, in the central Canadian Rockies.

## Mountain front and Lewis Thrust

Peak elevations in eastern Glacier park reach 2600 m. Saint Mary Lake lies at 1363 m, so the topographic relief along the mountain front in the region is roughly 1300 m—some 100 m greater than that seen west of Calgary.

At Rising Sun Campground along the shore of Saint Mary Lake we cross the Lewis Thrust, the huge horizontal fault that underlies the mountains of Glacier and Waterton parks. Colorful Purcell rock has been pushed northeastward into this area as a sheet nearly 9 km thick, gliding along over slippery Cretaceous shale for a distance of 60–70 km. There is little folding in the Lewis thrust sheet; the beds lie nearly flat.

Deep erosion along the mountain front has exposed the Lewis Thrust near the bases of most peaks. The plane of the thrust is practically horizontal here, dipping slightly eastward over slippery Cretaceous shales. This situation has proved to be geologically unstable: rock faces above the fault creep slowly forward, opening cracks behind and causing slides. These slides are plainly visible at many points along the mountain front.

## Front ranges—and no main ranges

Followed north of Crowsnest Pass into the central Rockies, the Lewis Thrust intermingles with the folds and faults of the front ranges, indicating that the Lewis Thrust began to move at the same time as those faults, about 85 million years ago. There are no major faults within the Lewis thrust sheet, nothing to divide the mountains of Waterton/Glacier into front ranges and main ranges, as found in the central and northern Rockies. The mountains of Waterton/Glacier are all in the front ranges.

Even though the Lewis Thrust Sheet is part of the front ranges of the Rockies, it differs from the front ranges we saw around Banff on the central-Rockies transect. In addition to the difference in bedrock type, as outlined above, the mountains of Glacier are not arranged in long northwest/southeast ridges like those of the central Rockies, nor do the mountains of Glacier have the writing-desk shape seen in Mt. Rundle and many other front-range peaks of the central Rockies. Instead, they look more like the peaks of the central main ranges. The difference is two-fold:

- The rock of the central front ranges dips to the southwest, while the rock of the southern front ranges is essentially flat-lying (it sags a little in the middle).
- The central front ranges are divided into strips by parallel thrust faults, which cause repetitions in the rock sequence that register in the landscape as parallel ridges, while the southern front ranges lack such faults and ridges.

A few kilometres before the Going-to-the-Sun Highway reaches Logan Pass, it takes a hairpin curve at Siyeh Creek and then climbs through the only major limestone layer in the Purcell Supergroup, the pale-colored Siyeh Formation, page 57, named for the creek. In contrast, the central Rockies have much more limestone.

## Continental divide

In line with the rule that flat-lying layers resist erosion better than more steeply tilted layers, page 157, the mountains of Glacier are respectably high despite the crumbly nature of the shaly rock. Summits of peaks along the continental divide stand typically 2500–3000 m. This is storm-spawning topography, which helps to explain the intense glaciation that has occurred in the Waterton/Glacier area. The result is a deeply dissected landscape of Matterhorn-like peaks standing 1300 m above classic U-shaped glacial valleys holding long lakes. At higher elevations there is very little flat land in the southern Rockies; on the trails it seems that one is either climbing steeply up or dropping steeply down.

*Reynolds Mountain (2788 m), a classic glacial horn peak seen near Logan Pass.
Photo by John Winnie.*

As we cross Logan Pass, we note that the change from limestone to shale seen along the continental divide in the central Rockies doesn't occur here; all of Glacier is in Purcell rock, shaly throughout. But as usual in the Canadian Rockies, the western-slope valleys are deeper—400 m deeper—than the eastern-slope valleys, and for the same reasons given on page 33: down-dropped valley floors, more active river erosion and/or heavier glaciation.

### Flathead Fault and Flathead Valley

The Going-to-the-Sun Highway crosses the Flathead Fault at the east end of Lake McDonald. Lake McDonald and West Glacier sit on the down-dropped fault block that forms the Flathead Valley. Here is a similarity between the central Rockies and the southern Rockies: the Flathead Valley and the southern Rocky Mountain Trench were formed in the same way, from stretching of the crust. But they are two separate valleys, and the Flathead Valley is not the western boundary of the Rockies. The boundary is farther west, beyond the Whitefish Range.

The Flathead Fault dips steeply to the west and forms the western wall of Glacier park. It began to lower the floor of the Flathead Valley about 40 million years ago, but it may have existed as a thrust fault—moving the opposite way—long before that, during the upward-building phase of the Rockies. Total downward movement along the Flathead Fault has been 6100 m, enough to drop the whole Purcell sequence here below sea level and produce a depression deep enough to hold 2500 m of coarse material eroded from the surrounding heights. This sediment is the Kishenehn Formation, page 143.

### Summary of southern Canadian Rockies features

- **Boundaries:** Marias Pass on the south, Crowsnest Pass on the north; the most-easterly foothills folds and faults on the east—typical locations Pincher Creek, Cardston, Browning—and the Tobacco/Stillwater valley (Highway 93) on the west.
- **Highest point:** Mt. Cleveland, 3190 m, in Glacier National Park near the international boundary. Treeline is around 2400 m.
- **Foothills:** 25–40 km wide, geologically similar to those of the central Rockies, but due to glacial erosion and deposition the northwest/southeast alignment of folds and faults is not as obvious at the surface.
- **Front ranges:** 20–40 km wide and different both geologically and physiographically from the front ranges of the central Rockies. The Waterton/Glacier front ranges resemble the central-Rockies main ranges: castle-like, cut into a single thrust sheet in an irregular drainage pattern. But there are no distinct main ranges in the Waterton/Glacier area.
- **Flathead Valley:** a down-dropped block of crust rather like the southern Rocky Mountain Trench. The two valleys formed similarly, from stretching of the crust, but they do not connect.

## The northern Rockies: Fort St. John to Liard Hot Springs

This is the far northern end of the entire Rocky Mountains chain. (The southern end is in New Mexico, north of Sante Fe.) The central Canadian Rockies west of Calgary are far away from the northern-Rockies peaks west of Fort Nelson, so one must expect some differences between the two areas. To see what they are, let us begin at Fort St. John on the Peace River, driving north along the Interior Plains margin to Fort Nelson, then west over the Rockies.

### Plains margin

The western edge of the Interior Plains is different here than it is in the central or southern Rockies. The edges of the rock layers tilt up to the west rather than down to the west (see the geological cross-section on page 194). Hard sandstone and conglomerate layers of the Dunvegan Formation, page 132, are exposed at the plains margin; resistant to erosion, they form a west-facing escarpment 200 m high. This escarpment overlooks a long valley, 10–20 km wide, that parallels the Rockies, separating the plains escarpment from the foothills. This unnamed valley has no counterpart south of the Peace River; it runs from just north of the Peace to the Liard and beyond, worn into soft Cretaceous shale. The Prophet and Muskwa rivers flow through the shale valley today; perhaps they cut it originally.

See this from the Trutch Viewpoint, just past Milepost 200. The Alaska Highway follows the shale valley at this point, but a side road leads up the escarpment to the abandoned site of the Trutch service centre. From there you can look west to the foothills and mountain front. South of the Peace River the plains/foothills boundary is difficult to detect from the topography, but here it is obvious.

West of Fort Nelson, you climb up the plains escarpment on its gentle northeastern side. Of interest here are **cuestas,** which are like hogback ridges, page 26, but with the hard layer lying at a gentle angle. Occasional patches of till, page 145, show that glacial ice has existed in this area, but either a long time ago and/or not in great depth, for beds of sandstone and conglomerate capping the cuestas overhang shaly slopes beneath, and the land is much-dissected with small streamcourses. These are relatively fragile landforms that are destroyed by glacial erosion. They are more typical of the plains margin around unglaciated Denver than they are of the Canadian Rockies.

*Typical topography in the northern Rockies. This is the valley of MacDonald Creek, as seen along the Alaska Highway near Summit Lake.*

*A cuesta along the plains margin west of Fort Nelson, seen from the Alaska Highway*

## Foothills

The Alaska Highway enters the foothills along the Tetsa River. These are large hills, bringing to mind the Appalachians of eastern North America. In the central and southern Rockies the foothills belt is marked by west-dipping thrust faults and tight folds, but here the rock is gently folded and there are no thrust faults at the surface, although geologists infer that they exist farther down. The rock itself is rather like that found elsewhere in the foothills of the Canadian Rockies—Mesozoic shale and sandstone—but it lacks the coal content of the foothills south of the Peace River.

The northern-Rockies foothills rise about 600 m above the river; summit elevations are typically 1350–1650 m. The hills are steep-sided and convex, following the underlying bedrock folds. This suggests a landscape that is more water-worn than glacier-worn. Could the northern foothills have escaped the most recent major ice advance, the late-Wisconsinan? Possibly, but no detailed glacial-history study has been done here.

*The northern foothills as seen from the Alaska Highway along the Tetsa River. Note the flat, gravel-covered valley floor of glacial outwash.*

## Mountain front

Cross-cutting valleys like that of the Tetsa River are narrow. A deep gravelly fill gives these valleys flat floors. At the mountain front, where one enters Stone Mountain Provincial Park, the source of that gravel is revealed: glaciation. The valley broadens and becomes U-shaped; the peaks exhibit glacial cirques, page 147. This is the familiar physiographic style of the central and southern Canadian Rockies. The rock at the mountain front is gray limestone that dips to the southwest, producing steep eastern faces and gentler western ones—the rock type and dip slopes so typical of the front ranges of the central Rockies. The landscape of Stone Mountain Provincial Park bears a striking resemblance to that seen in Crowsnest Pass, over 1200 km away. This demonstrates the remarkable physiographic integrity of the Canadian Rockies.

Although familiar-looking, the mountains along the Alaska Highway are smaller. From base to summit the topographic relief is typically 750 m, 400–500 m less than that seen in Crowsnest Pass, or at the mountain front west of Calgary or in Glacier National Park. The limestone of the northern Rockies is somewhat different, too. Summit Pass is a good place to see Late Silurian and Early Devonian rock not present in the central Rockies.

## Main/front ranges

Geologists do not divide the northern Rockies into front ranges and main ranges. The country west of Summit Lake *looks* like the main ranges: old rock, faulted here and there, gently dipping west until it runs into a shale belt like that of the western main ranges, where it becomes intensely deformed. This would make the main-range belt very thick here, over 100 km across, and the front ranges very thin, only about 5 km across.

However, the big main-range faults of the central Rockies angle west into the Rocky Mountain Trench as they are traced north. Thus, the main ranges gradually taper out between Jasper and the Peace River, and in the northern Rockies there are only foothills and front ranges, rather like the situation in the Waterton/Glacier area 1400 km south, at the other end of the Canadian Rockies.

## Summit Lake and the non-continental divide

Back to our tour. "Summit Lake" is just that: a lake lying close to the highest point along the Alaska Highway, 1340 m. Summit Lake is yet another of the ponds so common in major Rockies passes. But the divide here—Summit Pass, a kilometre west of the lake—is not the continental divide. North of the Peace River the continental divide swings west of the Rockies, so water flowing west from Summit Pass eventually hits the eastward-flowing Liard River and cuts back across the Rockies. Nothing winds up in the Pacific; it all goes to the Arctic Ocean via the Mackenzie River. This means that the eastern slope of the northern Rockies is lower in elevation than the western slope, the opposite of the situation in the central and southern Rockies, where the eastern slope is higher. The downhill ride west from Summit Lake is steep, typical of the abrupt western-slope descents one finds throughout the Canadian Rockies, but the valley floor is not lower on the western side, as it is in the central and southern regions. It's higher.

Moraines in the pass and east of it look old, as do east-facing cirques (photo on page 146). They have been rounded by weathering and incised by running water. Coupled with the lightly glaciated look of the foothills and plains margin, this suggests that eastern-slope glacial features in the northern Rockies, at least as displayed along the Alaska Highway, are older than late-Wisconsinan. I hope a detailed glacial study will soon be made here.

## Purcell-like rock

From just west of Summit Pass, the view south along MacDonald Creek displays mountains with colorful rock that looks very much like the Purcell Supergroup, page 52, found in the Waterton/Glacier region at the other end of the Canadian Rockies. The Purcell-like rock of the northern Rockies is roughly the same age as the Purcell strata, too, but geologists have found that it does not match the Purcell Supergroup closely enough to be given the same name. Instead, it is called informally the Muskwa assemblage.

This ancient rock is not characteristic of most of the northern Canadian Rockies. The Muskwa assemblage is found only from the Prophet River north, in patches, the largest of which lies between the Alaska Highway and Tuchodi Lakes. The age of most rock in the northern Rockies is about the same as it is farther south. Whether Purcell-type rock ever extended from one end of the Canadian Rockies area to the other is unknown; the resemblance shows mainly that environmental conditions were much the same at two distant locations on the coast of North America 1.5 billion years ago.

## Western slope

In the valley of MacDonald Creek, the freshness of glaciation strikes the eye. Cirques and valleys have the rough look of late-Wisconsinan ice attack. Farther west the road crosses the Purcell-like rock. Cutting across these ancient sedimentary layers are igneous dykes of diabase, page 60. Look for one of these dykes at the first bridge over the Toad River. At Muncho Lake the road runs beside cliffs of coarse conglomerate of the Atan Group, page 75.

Following the Trout River down to the Liard River, the Alaska Highway leaves the Canadian Rockies without crossing the Terminal Range, which is the most westerly range in the Rockies here. So the northern Rocky Mountain Trench is not seen from the highway. It looks much like the rest of the trench, although the nature of the faulting here is different from that of the southern segment of the trench. There the trench is a down-dropped block of crust. Here it follows a major transcurrent fault, page 141.

The Trout River has terraced sand-and-gravel deposits beside it, and the river cuts deeper and deeper into these terraces as it approaches the Liard. The terraces are probably all that remain of valley fill deposited here when the Liard River Valley nearby was full of glacial ice, damming up the Trout River.

The Liard River seems to have maintained its course across the mountains during their creation. A rough road leads east to the Grand Canyon of the Liard, where this river, the biggest in or near the Rockies, is still busily cutting itself into the earth.

Liard Hot Springs marks the end of our journey. We ease into the clear, steamy, sulphurous water. Aaaah …

*Liard Hot Springs*

## Summary of northern-Rockies features

- **Boundaries:** the Liard River (north), transitional between Grande Cache and Peace River (south), the Interior Plains escarpment (east) and the northern Rocky Mountain Trench (west).
- **Highest point:** there are few verified summit elevations in the northern Rockies and several candidates in the range of 2970–2990 m. Mt. Smythe, 2990 m in Kwadacha Lakes park, is probably the highest, although Mt. Ulysses, a peak at the headwaters of the Besa River, is given the same elevation. Treeline is around 1700 m in the mountains beside the Peace River and 1500 m at the Liard River.
- **Foothills:** 25–50 km wide, in large, rounded folds rather than tightly thrust-faulted and folded like the rest of the Canadian Rockies foothills. Made of Mesozoic shale and sandstone like the central and southern foothills, but lacking the coal. Aligned in parallel rows and rather high, so there is trellis drainage. Little obvious glacial character except for outwash along through-going streams. The eastern boundary of the foothills is well defined by a shale-floored valley and the erosional edge of the Interior Plains.
- **Front ranges:** up to 110 km across in total. No main ranges. The rock is not as extensively folded and thrust-faulted as in the central Rockies, and shalier, but with the same gentle westerly dip to the beds. Old Purcell-like rock along the divide in the north end—the Muskwa assemblage—produces Waterton-like color in the peaks, although most of the area is shaly and drab, with lower summits and less-rugged topography.
- **Rocky Mountain Trench:** follows a major transcurrent fault.

## *Further introductory reading on the Canadian Rockies*

Bezener, A. and L. Kershaw (1999) *Rocky Mountain Nature Guide*. Lone Pine Publishing, Edmonton. Handy guide that provides natural-history basics (very little geology) for the whole Rockies region, from British Columbia to New Mexico. Good color species drawings, maps, reading list, index; 192 pages.

Cameron, K., and L. Chevalier (1997) *Yoho National Park*. Kicking Horse Publications, Field, BC. Short, inexpensive guide to natural and cultural history. Illustrated, 27 pages.

Cameron, W. (1996) *Kananaskis*. Altitude, Canmore. Good all-in-one guide to Kananaskis Country, with much historical information. Many color photos, maps, reading list, index; 160 pages.

Elias, P. (1999) *From Grassland to Rockland: an Explorer's Guide to the Ecosystems of Southernmost Alberta*. Rocky Mountain Books, Calgary. Describes 37 trips, with useful info on the natural history of the southern foothills and front ranges. Illustrated, 288 pages.

Kavanagh, J. (1991) *Nature Alberta*. Natural-history guide to the whole province, including the mountains, with 351 common species described. Illustrated, indexed, 180 pages.

Patton, B. (1995) *Parkways of the Canadian Rockies: an Interpretive Guide to Roads in the Mountain Parks*. Summerthought, Banff. Descriptions of roadside features in Banff, Jasper, Yoho and Kootenay parks. Illustrated, indexed, 160 pages.

Pole, G. (1997) *Canadian Rockies*. Altitude Publishing, Canmore. Covers interesting features of the mountain national parks. Well-written and beautifully illustrated, indexed, 288 pages.

Pringle, H. (1986) *Waterton Lakes National Park*. Douglas & McIntyre, Vancouver. Handy guide, with better-than-average historical section. Illustrated, indexed, short reading list; 128 pages.

Root, J. et al. (1981) *Rocky Mountain Landmarks*. Hosford, Edmonton. Two-page descriptions of selected natural features and topics in the mountain-park block. Illustrated, 128 pages.

Sandford, R. (1994) *The Book of Banff: an Insider's Guide to Being a Local in Banff*. Friends of Banff National Park. True to its title, this well-written and entertaining book has a bit of everything. Illustrated, 242 pages.

Spalding, A., Ed. (1980) *A Nature Guide to Alberta*. McClelland and Stewart, Toronto. Mapsheet-by-mapsheet guide to the province, with good introductory material and mountain coverage. Illustrated, indexed; 368 pages.

*Devonian corals seen high in the Rockies near the Columbia Icefield—meaning in Jasper National Park, where collecting fossils is not allowed.*

# Geology
## *Up through the layers, one by one*

Welcome to the geological details. Readers with no earth-science background may find this chapter heavy going, but I have tried to keep the jargon to a minimum and to define terms the first time they are used, or to give the page number of the complete definition. Important concepts are explained in boxed items. When in doubt, use the index at the back of the book to get to the explanation you need.

## *The short course*
### A lot of sedimentary rock piled up on the continent

If you could stack all the sedimentary layers that make up the Canadian Rockies, the collection would be about 30,000 m thick. Thirty kilometres of sandstone, limestone, shale, dolomite, gritstone, slate, conglomerate, argillite, etc. have been examined centimetre-by-centimetre and described in technical publications totalling tens of thousands of pages. How can all this detail be condensed and put into a non-technical guide like this one?

Thanks to the large-scale integrity of the Canadian Rockies, it can be done. I think of the sedimentary rock of the Rockies as four great layers, lying on that huge raft we call the North American continent. Topping the pile is a skiff of soft, geologically recent glacial and post-glacial sediments, really too thin to be thought of as a fifth great layer. This four-layer scheme is highly simplified, but it fits the basic geological history of the region. Further, each of the four great layers has a characteristic geographic distribution.

No formal names are available for the four great layers, so for the purposes of this book I have given them informal names. Here they are, from the oldest layer at the bottom to the youngest layer at the top, along with a brief outline of the geological history each great layer records.

### The basement

If you were to drill down through all the sedimentary rock of the Rockies, you would eventually hit granite and **gneiss** (banded metamorphic rock). This is the essential stuff of the North American continent, 40–50 km thick and 1.8–2.9 billion years old under the Canadian Rockies. Geologists call it "the basement." Below that is rock congealed from the earth's hot, nearly molten **mantle,** upon which North America drifts slowly about.

In most of the Canadian Rockies the basement is deeply buried, but in three localities it can be seen at the surface. See page 50 for more.

### Rodinia rock

Rodinia, described in more detail on page 51, was a huge supercontinent that formed 1.7–1.9 billion years ago and broke up 550–800 million years ago. Prior to the breakup, the Canadian Rockies area was part of Rodinia, as was much of North America, and some of the sedimentary rock deposited at the time can be seen in the Rockies today. This rock is very old (Mesoproterozoic, about 1.5 billion years), yet it contains clear evidence of life. The Rodinia rock was deposited in a shallow inland sea, something like the modern Caspian Sea or Black Sea of eastern Europe. Much of the Rodinia rock is colorful, in shades of red and green. ("Rodinia" comes from the Russian "rodit," meaning "to beget.")

There are two areas in the Rockies where Rodinia rock is found at the surface: in the southern part of the region, mostly south of Crowsnest Pass in the Waterton/Glacier area, where it is known as the Purcell Supergroup or the Belt Group, and near the north end of the Rockies, where it is called the Muskwa assemblage. The Rodinia rock is 9 km thick in Waterton/Glacier and 8 km thick in the northern Rockies.

## Old clastic unit

The next great layer is 8–9 km of gritstone (coarse sandstone), slate, quartzite, conglomerate and hardened glacial till, with very little limestone. This is **clastic** rock, meaning rock made of *eroded particles* weathered from land and deposited in seawater. Thus the name "old clastic unit." (There is a young clastic unit, too.)

The old clastic unit is characteristic of the main ranges of the Canadian Rockies, found continuously from Banff National Park north. Within this great layer, the formally named units include the Windermere Supergroup and the Gog and Atan groups. They span the period 525–780 million years ago.

The old clastic unit represents mostly rapid deposition of coarse sediments along a new continental edge formed by the breakup of Rodinia. Think of rivers carrying sand and gravel into the sea from mountains along the shore—something like the situation today along the coast of British Columbia. Glaciers flowed into the sea then, just as they do now, as shown by layers of glacial deposits hardened to rock in the Windermere Supergroup.

## Middle carbonate unit

Above the old clastics lies a very different great layer some 6.5 km thick. Much of it is limestone, or its close relative, dolomite, which has formed *in place,* in the sea, from crystals of lime generated by living things. For the details of this process, see page 55. Limestone and dolomite are called the **carbonate** rocks, for they contain mainly calcium carbonate ($CaCO_3$, the mineral **calcite**) and/or magnesium carbonate ($CaMg(CO_3)_2$, the mineral **dolomite**).

About 525 million years ago, when the ancient mountains that had supplied the sediments of the old clastic unit had been worn flat by erosion, the sea crept inland. At this time the continent was moving northeastward, relative to today's orientation, and western Canada lay along its trailing edge. The trailing edges of continents—their **passive margins** in geological parlance—are low-lying areas that often form wide continental shelves, like the modern Grand Banks of Newfoundland. The middle carbonates were laid down on such a shelf, in shallow water that was full of life. The climate of western Canada was warm, for it lay near the equator. This is the time in which most of the oil and gas in western Canada accumulated. By 245 million years ago at the end of the Paleozoic Era, North America and most of the world's other landmasses had drifted together to form a second supercontinent, this one called **Pangea.**

The middle carbonate unit is found in the front ranges and eastern main ranges of the Canadian Rockies from Crowsnest Pass north. In the western main ranges and western ranges the middle carbonates are mostly limy shales. These shaly areas were laid down in deeper water at the edge of the continental shelf. North of the Peace River this unit is shalier throughout than it is in the central Rockies, but it occupies the same time slot, from 245—525 million years ago, Middle Cambrian to Permian, and it outcrops in the same place: from the mountain front west, seldom in the foothills.

## Young clastic unit

Above the middle carbonates is the other great layer in our area: 5 km of rather soft sandstone and shale. These are clastic rock types, made of eroded particles. The young clastics are well-exposed in the foothills, and to a lesser extent in the front ranges. They are Mesozoic and Cenozoic, ranging in age from early Triassic, 245 million years ago, to the beginning of Pleistocene glaciation 1.9 million years ago. Much of this rock is nonmarine; that is, deposited in fresh water or on land.

The young clastics record a major change in the geological history of North America at about 210 million years ago in the late Triassic. Prior to that, sediments had been accumulating on the passive margin, the trailing edge of the continent. But in the Triassic, Pangea began to break up, just as Rodinia had broken up 600 million years earlier. North America changed its

## Great layers of the Canadian Rockies

**Surficial deposits**
*Glacial, river, lake and windblown deposits, slides and talus, soil*
*Quaternary (1.9 million) to the present, up to 300 m thick*
*Found in all areas*

**Young clastic unit**
*Sandstone, shale, conglomerate, coal*
*Mesozoic and Cenozoic (5–245 million), 5 km thick*
*Foothills and front ranges, Rocky Mountain Trench, Flathead Valley*

**Middle carbonate unit**
*Mostly limestone, dolomite and shale*
*Middle Cambrian to Permian (245–525 million), 6.5 km thick*
*Front ranges and main ranges*

**Old clastic unit**
*Gritstone, slate, hardened till, quartzite, limestone*
*Neoproterozoic to Early Cambrian (525–780 million), 8–9 km thick*
*Main ranges and front ranges in central and northern regions*

**Rodinia rock**
*Mudstone, argillite, siltstone, limestone*
*Mesoproterozoic to Neoproterozoic (900–1500 million), 8–9 km thick*
*Southern and northern regions*

**Basement**
*Gneiss and granite*
*Archean and Paleoproterozoic (1.8–2.9 billion), 40–50 km thick*
*Covered by younger rock, except at three places*

direction of movement toward the northwest, putting western Canada on the leading edge—the **active margin**—of the continent. "Active" is too mild a word; North America plowed westward into chains of large islands lying offshore on oceanic crust, scraping these landmasses from the crust and adding them onto western Canada. In this way most of British Columbia was created. The plate collision wrinkled B.C. into mountain ranges. There were enormous volcanic eruptions, and earthquakes were frequent.

The sediment worn from these rising mountains and spread along their eastern and western slopes is the young clastic unit. In the young clastic unit we find a record of the progress of mountain-building from west to east. The Rockies were the last, easternmost range to form. As the Rockies rose, the young clastics themselves were caught in the folding and faulting.

### Surficial deposits

Geologically recent layers of glacial till, stream gravel, lake silt, volcanic ash, wind-blown silt, sand dunes and soils form a thin layer—up to 300 m, which is thin compared to the other great layers—on the bedrock.

# Geology 101
## Answers to some questions you may be asking

### How geologists study sedimentary layers

This is the branch of geology known as **stratigraphy.** Stratigraphers think of a large area of sedimentary rock as something like a floor covered with pancakes. Some of the pancakes are thin and some are thick; some are large and some are small.

The various pancakes overlie and overlap one another. Most are intergrown at the edges. For example, one pancake may be made of sand carried by a river into the sea at one point along an ancient coastline, while a hundred kilometres away along the same coastline another river was carrying in mud. Each deposit spread out just offshore, thickened and eventually hardened to rock as a separate layer, one of sandstone, the other of mudstone. They are the same age, and the edges of the layers feather into each other, but the rock type is different.

Suppose that, as time went by, a third river appeared along the coast, halfway between the other two. This one was carrying coarse gravel, which accumulated as a conglomerate layer that overlay the sandstone and mudstone layers.

Deposition from all three rivers continued, so the conglomerate intergrew at the edges with the other units. The diagram shows the stratigraphy resulting from this geological history. The geologic columns in the diagram show what the stratigrapher would see of the stack at different locations.

By drawing geologic columns of the stratigraphy at several places in the region and linking the tops and bottoms of the various layers with lines, it is possible to figure

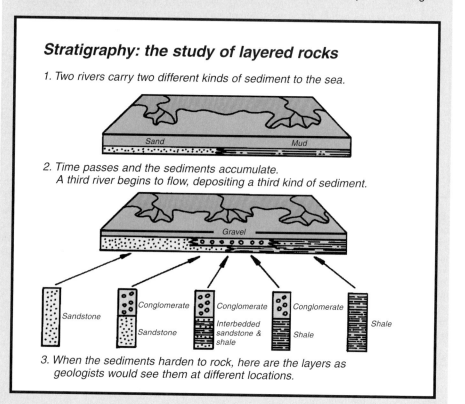

**Stratigraphy: the study of layered rocks**

*1. Two rivers carry two different kinds of sediment to the sea.*

Sand    Mud

*2. Time passes and the sediments accumulate.*
*A third river begins to flow, depositing a third kind of sediment.*

Gravel

Sandstone

Conglomerate

Sandstone

Conglomerate

Interbedded sandstone & shale

Conglomerate

Shale

Shale

*3. When the sediments harden to rock, here are the layers as geologists would see them at different locations.*

out how the layers overlie and overlap. Figuring out such natural three-dimensional puzzles can become quite complicated—especially when the layering has been bent by folding and broken by faulting, as is the case in the Canadian Rockies.

### How geologists determine the age of rock

Igneous rock, meaning rock that was once molten, can be dated directly by measuring the products of radioactive decay in it, because the decay starts when the rock crystallizes from its magma. One radioactive element or isotope changes to another at a known rate, and by comparing the proportions of the two it is possible to compute the time that has elapsed.

Sedimentary layers must be dated differently. Sediments are mostly mineral grains worn from much-older igneous rock; the atomic clocks in those grains began running long before the grains collected into the layer.

However, carbonate (limy) sediments *do* crystallize, and the minute amounts of uranium and thorium present in some kinds of limestone have been used for dating. Unfortunately the isotopes decay so quickly that if a limestone is older than about 350,000 years it is not possible to get good results with current techniques.

Lacking much directly datable rock, stratigraphers in the Canadian Rockies have had to rely mainly on **index fossils** in finding the ages of the formations.

A good index-fossil is any readily identifiable fossil species that appears and disappears in the geologic record within a rather short time, geologically speaking—meaning a few million years in the case of the older formations. If several locations can be found anywhere in the world in which igneous rock lies above or below sediments holding a particular index fossil, *and* if that igneous rock gives reliable dates, then it is possible to bracket the age of the fossil fairly accurately. In lucky cases, the fossil occurs in directly datable volcanic rock, such as a layer of volcanic ash that fell into the sea, covering the animals on the seabed.

It follows that any layer containing the same index fossil has to be more or less the same age, regardless of where it is found, provided that the organism was preserved in place. Thus the Sullivan Formation, with its Late Cambrian trilobites, is a Late Cambrian formation.

Of the thousands of different fossils appearing in Canadian Rockies strata, 87 are particularly characteristic and common. They are illustrated on pages 191–201. If you wish to collect, do so outside the national and provincial parks. Collecting in these parks is illegal.

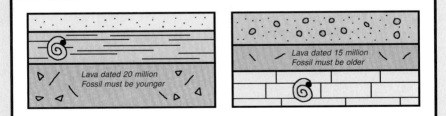

*Older layers underlie younger layers, a basic geological principle. So the age of this fossil can be bracketed by the isotopically dated igneous layers found above it at one location and below it at another. Age: 15 to 20 million years.*

For Geology 201 and higher, see the geology picture pages, which begin on page 183. See also "What every geologist should know" on page 203.

### On to the details

The rest of this long chapter examines the four great layers in greater detail, formation by formation, from the bottom up. I have included the major rock-unit names currently in use in the geological literature on our area. Sometimes one heading covers several related formations, which are named in the text under that heading. The next line under that heading gives the geological period in which the unit was deposited, its approximate age and its thickness. To save space, absolute ages are given in millions of years, abbreviated **Ma,** which stands for the metric "Mega-annums." Two dates usually appear. These bracket the age of the unit. In a few cases just one date is given; these are for igneous units, which can be dated more accurately. The last item on the age line is the thickness of the unit, in metres. See also the correlation charts on pages 192–194.

The absolute ages assigned to the geologic periods keep changing as the accuracy of the time scale improves. The dates for rock units listed used in this book are those provided to me by the expert geologists who reviewed this chapter.

# *The basement*
## Oldest rock in the Rockies

Underlying all the sedimentary rock of the Rockies is the **basement:** the ancient gneiss and granite of the North American continental plate, which is 40–50 km thick in this part of western Canada. What's under the basement? Rock of the upper mantle, which is iron-rich and thus denser than continental rock. Thus, the continents float on the mantle.

Going back over three billion years, the geological history of North America's basement rock includes many cycles of mountain-building and erosion, with several periods of continental breakup and reassembly—a complex story that will require decades of difficult investigation to understand. The basement was already old before it began to collect the sediments of the Rockies' first great layer.

The basement is buried 6–10 km down under most of the Canadian Rockies region, but deep drilling for natural gas in the foothills has shown that the rock belongs to four different **geological provinces,** or areas of the North American plate. From Glacier National Park to the south end of Kananaskis Country (Highway 932), the basement is part of the Wyoming province, 2900 Ma and the oldest rock in the Rocky Mountains, Canadian or American. Through Kananaskis Country to Canmore the basement is part of the Hearne province, 2700 Ma. From Canmore to Tumbler Ridge (between Grande Cache and the Peace River) the basement is part of the Rae province, 2800 Ma. And from Tumbler Ridge to the northern end of the Rockies the basement is part of the Slave province, varying from 1800–2400 Ma.

Despite its deep burial in most of the region, basement rock can be seen at the surface in three locations, all of them along the eastern side of the Rocky Mountain Trench. Two of the these patches border Kinbasket Lake south of Valemount, where thrust faults have carried Hearne-province gneiss to the

*The Malton Gneiss, as seen southwest of Valemount along Highway 5 near Albreda Pass*

surface from Bulldog Creek to Yellowjacket Creek, and from Hugh Allan Creek to Mt. Blackman. Access to these outcrops is not easy, but the same sort of banded, black-and-white high-grade metamorphic rock can be inspected conveniently on the other side of the trench, just west of the Rockies, where Highway 5 passes through the Malton Gneiss near Albreda Pass. The Malton Gneiss is probably the same Hearne-province rock as the Bulldog-Yellowjacket and Hugh Allan - Blackman gneisses.

The third outcrop of basement rock in the Canadian Rockies is the Deserters Gneiss, a patch of metamorphosed Slave-province granite found on the eastern wall of the Rocky Mountain Trench well to the north, at Bevel Mountain in the Deserters Range, where Williston Lake cuts across the Rockies.

Travellers along the TransCanada Highway can view basement rock in Mt. Revelstoke National Park, where gneiss of the Shuswap Complex shows the typical banded character of the other upthrust basement rock mentioned.

# Rodinia rock
## Purcell/Belt Supergroup and Muskwa assemblage

By about 1900 Ma, most of the world's continental landmasses had drifted together to form a supercontinent called Rodinia. Rodinia had a sag in it, filled with an inland sea rather like today's Black Sea or Caspian Sea. The region that would one day become the Rockies lay under this sea, into which rivers carried mud, sand and gravel. Hardened to rock, the Rodinia sediments became the lowest, oldest of the four great layers in the Rockies stack, laid down about 1.5 billion years ago in the Proterozoic Era. Life consisted mainly of bacterial colonies that took calcium out of the seawater to form layers of limestone, the oldest in the Canadian Rockies.

There are two patches of Rodinia rock in the Canadian Rockies, and they are found in two widely separated places: the Waterton/Glacier area at the southern end of the range, and the Muskwa/Tuchodi area at the northern end. The Waterton/Glacier rock is known as the Purcell Supergroup, called the Belt Group in the United States. It's about 9 km thick. The Muskwa/Tuchodi-area rock is known as the Muskwa assemblage. It's about 8 km thick. The two parts are surprisingly similar overall, considering that they are found 1000 km away from each other.

The Rodinia rock is among the older sedimentary sequences in North America. In the Rockies it has escaped the **metamorphism** (alteration through heat and pressure) that masks the features of most other Proterozoic formations, so the Rodinia rock is important in recording geological events of that long-ago age. It shows a lot of variety—mudstone, limestone, sandstone, turbidites (undersea mudflow deposits; see page 61), even volcanic layers—and that's not surprising, since the first great layer covers 600 million years of geological time.

---

## Geologic formations, groups and supergroups

Geologists give names to rock layers, much as botanists give names to plants. A particular rock layer is called a **formation,** and it is named for the place at which it was first studied. The Banff Formation, for example, is a layer of shaly limestone first studied near Banff.

Any sequence of sedimentary layers that are essentially similar can be called a formation, regardless of thickness. Most formations in the Rockies are hundreds of metres thick.

A stack of formations can be called a **group,** and related groups can be called **supergroups.** Conversely, formations can be split into **members,** and the members can be split into **lentils**—"lentil" is Latin for "lens"—of a type never found, we hope, in your soup.

*In this book, the ages of formations are given with the minimum date first and the maximum date second,* e.g. "515–525 Ma," rather than the other way around, as found in most geological writing. This emphasizes an important truth about sedimentary layers: a given rock unit formed sometime within a geological time division, not necessarily during all of it.

## Rodinia rock, southern area: the Purcell/Belt Supergroup

"Purcell Supergroup" is a Canadian identifier derived from the Purcell Mountains west of the Rockies and pronounced "Pur-CELL," even though the name is that of Irish physician Goodwin Purcell ("PER-sull"), who was on the selection committee for members of the Palliser Expedition (page 694). Americans use the older term "Belt Supergroup" for Purcell rock, naming it for the Belt Mountains of Montana. They divide the Belt Supergroup into the Ravalli Group (lower) and the Missoula Group (upper). Saying "Purcell/Belt" all the time is awkward, so I will just use "Purcell" from this point on.

The Purcell Supergroup is Mesoproterozoic in age, 1400–1470 Ma, and up to 8800 m thick in the Rockies. It is exposed most prominently south of Crowsnest Pass in the Clark, MacDonald, Galton, Lewis and Livingstone ranges of the Waterton/Glacier area, and north of Highway 3 in the Lizard and Hughes ranges, which form the eastern wall of the Rocky Mountain Trench south of Canal Flats. Purcell beds also form the rolling Flathead and Whitefish ranges west of Glacier park. North of the Canada/U.S. border, where the Rocky Mountain Trench becomes well-defined, Purcell strata are exposed along the eastern wall of the trench to a point about 10 km north of Skookumchuck in the Hughes Range. Purcell rock floors the trench itself from Radium South, but you don't see it under the gravelly valley fill.

West of the trench the Purcell is at the surface again, propping up the Purcell Range of the Columbia Mountains. The Purcell extends south and southwest into southern Montana and central Idaho, where it disappears under lava flows or merges with igneous intrusions.

A couple of outcrops showing Purcell beds lying on the granitic continental basement rock have been found in Montana, but in the Canadian Rockies (meaning from Glacier park north), the base of the Purcell is not seen. The whole unit has broken loose somewhere above the base and been shoved eastward along the Lewis Thrust, which underlies all the Purcell rock south of Crowsnest Pass.

The Purcell thickens southwestward and the sediments grow coarser northeastward, indicating that the shoreline ran from southeast to northwest at the time the Purcell was being laid down. To the northeast lay a pinkish landscape of low granite hills and sandy washes— bare basement rock, without vegetation, because at this time there was no life on land. Every day the tide would come sweeping in from the southwestern horizon, gurgling across endless mudflats and feeding the primitive organisms growing there: primarily slimy mats of **cyanobacteria,** the proper name for "bluegreen algae," which are not algae at all. Vary that scenario with occasional storms tearing up the bacterial colonies, and occasional earthquakes jarring them, and you have a pretty good picture of life in the area 1.5 billion years ago.

Sometimes the seabed sank a little quicker than the streams could supply sediments, so the shore moved inland and the water grew deeper. Sometimes a ripple of uplift brought the mudflats above sea level and erosion removed a few layers. Uplift plus tilting came at about 1250 Ma, bringing part of the region above sea level and allowing erosion to bevel off the beds at a gentle angle.

Half a billion years later, in the late Proterozoic, a good-sized chunk of Rodinia separated from the supercontinent—**rifted** is the proper term—and drifted away. Much of the Purcell Supergroup may have gone with it. Where did it go? Brace yourself: the rifted-off landmass is now most of Australia!

Purcell rock that did not rift away can be seen in the Waterton/Glacier area. The upper layers were raised above sea level at various times until the middle of the Cambrian Period, when the sea moved back into the southern and central Rockies and the next round of sedimentation began. So the top of the Purcell is overlain in the Rockies by much-younger Middle Cambrian rock, a major unconformity (see page 99 for more on unconformities).

Canadian experts on the Purcell Supergroup recognize four main divisions in this varied collection of ancient rock:

- The thick *basal division* has two east-west subdivisions: turbidites (page 61) found mostly west of the Rockies, where the sea was deep, and some shallow-water formations found mostly in Glacier and Waterton parks.

- The *lower division* holds the beautiful red-and-green argillite beds for which these parks are famous.
- The *middle division* is mostly limestone laid down in shallow, clear seawater.
- The *upper division* is a tidal-flat and river-floodplain deposit, quite varied from layer to layer and all deposited in very shallow water.

We'll deal with the western half of the basal division first: the Fort Steele and Aldridge formations. These units are all clastic, particulate rock, not limestone or dolomite, and they are found entirely in British Columbia. To the east, they grade into limy/dolomitic units of the same age.

In the discussion that follows, you may notice that the formation names in the Lizard Range and Hughes Range follow those of the Purcell Mountains on the other side of the Rocky Mountain Trench. That's because the rock in the Lizard and Hughes ranges resembles Purcell Mountains rock more than it resembles Rockies rock.

### Fort Steele Formation (lower part of the Purcell's *basal* division, western part)
*Mesoproterozoic (about 1500 Ma), more than 2000m*

The oldest exposed unit in the Purcell Supergroup and thus the oldest known sedimentary rock in the Canadian Rockies, the Fort Steele is seen only in the Hughes Range, which forms the eastern wall of the Rocky Mountain Trench between the Bull River and the Lussier River, south of Canal Flats. Fort Steele is a historical park located along Highway 93/95 at the junction of the St. Mary and Kootenay rivers.

The Fort Steele Formation is a unit of quartzite (hardened sandstone), siltite (hardened silt, which is very fine sand), and argillite with mud cracks, showing that it was laid down in very shallow water. Thus, the shoreline was nearby; in fact, the Fort Steele may be partly a river-bed deposit. Its base has not been found, so its maximum thickness is unknown.

### Aldridge/Pritchard Formation (upper unit of the Purcell's *basal* division, western part)
*Mesoproterozoic (about 1500 Ma), about 3000 m*

Mostly argillite, siltite and sandstone. In the Hughes Range there is a limy/dolomitic bed in the lower part . Some thin gray carbon-rich siltite layers in the middle section can be traced, lamination-by-lamination, for distances of up to 300 km south and west—an amazing distance considering the thinness of the beds. Aldridge beds are mostly turbidites, meaning underwater mud-flow material that moved downhill from just offshore into deeper water to the west (see page 61). The laminar beds give an idea of the distances fine-grained turbidites can travel.

The Aldridge is prominent in the Purcell Mountains west of the Rockies, but within the Rockies it is seen only in the Hughes and Lizard ranges, along the eastern wall of the Rocky Mountain Trench from about Skookumchuck south. In western Glacier park, Montana, rock equivalent to the upper part of the Aldridge is known as the Pritchard Formation. A good place to view Aldridge beds is in the Lizard Range northeast of Galloway, a tiny community along Highway 3/93.

Together, the Fort Steele and the Aldridge make up the western part of the Purcell Supergroup's basal division. Discussed next are the eastern representatives of the basal division, equivalent in age to Fort Steele and Aldridge rock.

### Subsurface units (lowest in the Purcell's *basal* division, eastern part)
*Mesoproterozoic (about 1500 Ma), more than 810 m*

Drilling for oil along Sage Creek, northwest of Waterton park in British Columbia, has brought up samples of four previously unknown rock units. They don't seem to outcrop anywhere at the surface, and they remain unnamed. From bottom to top, these subsurface units include 170 m of dark-gray muddy dolomite (base undetermined; the drill didn't go deep enough); 219 m of varicolored gray, green, red and white dolomite and limestone; 314 m of gray, red and green muddy dolomite and black argillite; and 107 m of dark-to-black argillite, some of which is limy. Above these four, the formations are named and thus discussed individually below.

## Haig Brook Formation (middle *basal* Purcell, eastern part)
*Mesoproterozoic (about 1500 Ma), more than 150 m*

On the eastern side of the Flathead Valley, in the Clark Range, this newly recognized formation is primarily gray limestone and dolomite, with some muddy red and green limestone/dolomite layers. It's named for Haig Brook, a tributary of the Flathead River about 25 km northwest of Waterton park.

## Tombstone Formation (middle *basal* Purcell, eastern part)
*Mesoproterozoic (about 1500 Ma), more than 175 m*

Above the Haig Brook beds, the rock is still limy/dolomitic, but muddier and dark gray. Tombstone Mountain is found a few kilometres west of the continental divide, near the headwaters of Haig Brook.

## Waterton Formation (upper *basal* Purcell, eastern part)
*Mesoproterozoic (about 1500 Ma), 170–248 m*

Pale gray or brownish limestone and dolomite. Cliff-maker. Once thought to be the lowest exposed unit in the Purcell Supergroup, cut off at the base by faults associated with the Lewis Thrust, but now known to overlie the newly identified formations on the western slope (see previous items). Rarely exposed, but well-displayed at Cameron Falls in Waterton Park townsite and along the opening stretch of the Cameron Lake Road. Not seen in Glacier park. Interesting for its primitive fossils: stromatolites, page 58, and wavy structures formed by cyanobacteria that grew in warm, shallow seawater. Imagine a warm mudflat covered by sticky colonies of cyanobacteria, alternately covered by the tide and exposed to the air. This is the oldest carbonate (limy) rock unit that is easy to inspect in the Rockies.

## Altyn Formation (upper *basal* Purcell, eastern part)
*Mesoproterozoic (about 1500 Ma), 145–375 m*

Pale-gray sandy limestone at the base, then black argillite, followed by gray limestone and dolomite with greenish/brownish argillite at the top. The lower part tends to erode easily, forming talus slopes and wooded areas, while the middle dolomite forms cliffs. Lies at the base of peaks forming the mountain front from Lower Waterton Lake south. Lower contact is usually the Lewis Thrust, except where underlain by the Waterton Formation and older units. The Bear's Hump above Waterton Park townsite is made of the dolomite unit of the Altyn Formation. Another good Altyn outcrop is at Geology Stop 2 along the Going-to-the-Sun Highway in eastern Glacier park. The rock is shallow-water marine, with ripple marks, cross-bedded sandy layers and cyanobacterial structures. Altyn Peak sits above Many Glacier in Glacier park.

In 1902 Canada's first oil well was drilled in the Altyn Formation in Waterton Lakes National Park, at an oil seep along Cameron Creek. Penetrating to 312 m, the well produced about 475 m³ (300 barrels) per day at first, and a town to be called "Oil City" was surveyed for the site. But the flow soon dropped to nothing, and the plans were abandoned. Finding oil in Precambrian rock is quite unusual; in this case it had worked its way up from oil-bearing Cretaceous rock beneath the Lewis Thrust, page 36.

## Appekunny/Greyson Formation and Creston Formation
(Lower part of *lower* division of Purcell, and lower part of the Ravalli Group)
*Mesoproterozoic (about 1500 Ma), 820 m*

Dark gray-green and purple argillite and siltite, outcropping mostly in the lower slopes of peaks in the Waterton/Glacier area. Ledgy and loose. Two prominent bands of pale quartzite make good identifiers, as does the sharp contact between the sombre Appekunny and the brilliantly red Grinnell/Spokane Formation above.

Named for Appekunny Creek in Glacier park, Montana, this unit has been correlated with the more-widespread Greyson shale of Montana. Some American geologists have thus begun calling it "Greyson" because "Greyson" is the older name. In the Lizard Range and Hughes

## Making limestone

Limestone is a very common rock type, making up 10 percent of all sedimentary rock, but geologists didn't really know how it formed until the 1970s. The connection between limestone and life was well established—limestone is often richly fossiliferous—so it seemed likely that somehow sea life produced limestone by chemically removing dissolved lime ($CaCO_3$, calcium carbonate to a chemist; calcite to a geologist) from the water and using it to form shells and colonies. But the fossil content is a minor part of most limestone. Much of it is simply tiny crystalline bits of calcite. Where did the crystals come from? Not from land, for calcium enters the sea dissolved in water, seldom as particles. So limestone has to be made in place, in the sea.

As it turned out, the source was obvious but overlooked. In the 1950s, geologists began to look closely at spots where lime mud, the forerunner of lime-*stone,* was accumulating on the seabed. In the science of geology, the present is often the key to the past, and so it was here: studies of lime deposition in the shallows of the Caribbean have shown that the vast proportion of lime mud begins as microscopically small, needle-like crystals of **aragonite** (a variety of calcite, meaning lime) produced inside the tissues of floating and suspended **cyanobacteria**, which used to be called "bluegreen algae." But cyanobacteria are not algae; they lack cell nuclei, which algae possess. Cyanobacteria are bacteria with chlorophyll in them, and they have been present on earth for at least 3.2 billion years, while algal cells came along much later. Like green plants, algae incorporate cyanobacteria inside their cells to do the work of photosynthesis.

The individual aragonite crystals produced inside cyanobacteria are so tiny that an electron microscope is needed to see them. When the cyanobacteria die and decompose, the aragonite needles drift to the bottom, building up deposits on the seabed.

Aragonite spontaneously recrystallizes to calcite, which has the same formula but a different arrangement of the calcium, carbon and oxygen ions in the crystal (calcite is trigonal, aragonite is orthorhombic). Most of the world's limestone is old enough for the aragonite to have converted itself to calcite; only rock formed relatively recently contains much aragonite.

It is reasonable to assume that the biochemical processes at work today off the Bahamas are much the same as those that produced the organic calcite of the Purcell Supergroup 1.5 billion years ago. The same kinds of cyanobacteria existed then and now, and when allowance for aging is made, the rock is chemically identical. So it seems plausible that cyanobacteria have been the prime producers of limestone for as long as there has been limestone; that is, for some 2.7 billion years.

Can limestone be produced inorganically? Yes. In warm, shallow tropical seas the water is saturated with dissolved calcium carbonate. Further warming of the water can cause a significant amount of calcite to precipitate (crystallize out). To a much lesser extent, evaporation of seawater can also produce carbonate rock.

Range, equivalent rock belongs to the Creston Formation, found to the west in the Purcell Mountains. Creston is a town in southeastern British Columbia.

The cliffs on Singleshot Mountain along the north side of the Going-to-the-Sun Highway in eastern Glacier park are made of Appekunny argillite and provide a good distant view of the unit. See the formation up close at Geology Stop 4 beside Saint Mary Lake.

During Appekunny time, fine sediment rapidly accumulated in fairly shallow water, suffocating the cyanobacterial colonies of the underlying Altyn Formation. Much of the bedding in the Appekunny is thin and straight, but some layers are wrinkly and distorted. This occurs when a thick, heavy layer of sediment presses down irregularly into a soft layer underneath.

The greenish tint in the Appekunny is from iron deposited in oxygen-poor (reducing) conditions. Mild heat and pressure from overlying rock have concentrated the iron in tiny green flakes of the mineral chlorite.

Together, the rock of the Appekunny/Greyson Formation and overlying Grinnell/Spokane Formation, next item, is known as the Ravalli Group in the United States. No equivalent name exists in Canada.

### Grinnell/Spokane Formation
(Upper part of *lower* division of Purcell, and upper part of Ravalli Group)
*Mesoproterozoic (about 1500 Ma), 100–335 m*

Brick-red thin-bedded argillite in Montana, silty in Canada. Iron-rich and laid down near the shore, like the underlying Appekunny/Greyson, but red rather than green because there was plenty of oxygen to rust the iron. Weathers into slopes rather than steep cliffs. These beds have been matched with a more-widespread American formation that has the older name "Spokane Formation."

The Grinnell/Spokane is the easiest formation to pick out in the Waterton/Glacier region because of its bright red color, prominent in many peaks and beautifully exposed in Red Rock Canyon in Waterton park. Geology Stop 5 on the Going-to-the-Sun Highway in Glacier park is another good place to examine it. Grinnell Peak is in the Many Glacier area.

This is a shallow-water unit, displaying the ripple marks and sun-dried cracks of a typical warm-water tidal mudflat or of a wide, shallow riverbed near the coast. Storms ripped up the surface from time to time, leaving soft chips of red mud embedded in layers of coarse white sand. A few greenish layers indicate periods of lower oxygen concentration, owing either to deeper water or a change in water chemistry. Despite the shallow water and warm climate, there was not enough cyanobacterial growth in the area at this time to leave fossil evidence, possibly because the water was too muddy or because it was fresh (in the case of a river deposit) and thus would not support marine cyanobacteria.

### *Argillite*

The word "argillite" is used often in describing Purcell units. This is a technical term applied to shale that has been weakly metamorphosed. The rock is harder than shale, but it shows too little heat-and-pressure-induced cleavage to be called slate, page 64. The Waterton/Glacier area is famous for brilliantly red and green argillite. The red color is from oxidized (i.e. rusted) iron, in which oxygen has been added, and the green color is from reduced iron, in which oxygen has been removed.

*Argillite of the Grinnell Formation seen at Red Rock Canyon in Waterton Lakes National Park. Parks Canada photo.*

## Siyeh/Kitchener Formation, Helena and Empire/lower Snowslip formations
(The *middle* division of the Purcell Supergroup, and base of the *upper* division)
*Mesoproterozoic (1450 Ma), 800–1000 m*

A thick, cliff-forming argillaceous limestone/dolomite unit, with some sandy and silty layers. In Canada, geologists still refer to this unit as the Siyeh ("SIGH-yuh") Formation, named for Mt. Siyeh in central Glacier park. But in 1967 American geologists began discarding the name in favor of individual names for the various parts.

The lower 250 m of the Siyeh is known in the United States as the Empire Formation, which is siltier and sandier than the overlying Helena, with greenish argillite beds. The Empire is transitional between the muddy-water Grinnell and the clear-water Helena.

Americans call the middle part of the Siyeh the Helena Formation, for Helena, Montana. It is mostly black limestone and dolomite, frequently weathering tan or gray on exposed surfaces. Igneous rock is present in the Helena Formation, in the form of a lava flow dated older than 1350 Ma (see next item) and a sill (see page 59) injected between Helena layers at about 800 Ma. Technically speaking, the sill is not part of the formation, because it came later in time.

The Empire and Helena often form one cliff together, so Canadians have been content to keep them together and call them the Siyeh Formation. The Helena/middle-Siyeh resists erosion strongly; it is the most prominent cliff-former in the Waterton/Glacier region, buttressing the peaks along the continental divide. The best exposures occur along the Going-to-the-Sun Highway in Glacier park, where geology stops 7 and 8 provide a close look. In the Lizard Range and Hughes Range bordering the Rocky Mountain Trench, Siyeh-like rock takes the name Kitchener Formation, from the Purcell Mountains to the west.

Like the older Waterton and Altyn formations, the Siyeh Formation was deposited in clear, very shallow seawater. Abundant colonies of cyanobacteria produced the rock. As it started to harden, it was enriched with magnesium ions from seawater, changing much of it to dolomite (dolomite discussion: page 78). The rock is wavy-bedded and loaded with stromatolites, discussed in the boxed item on the next page.

The upper Siyeh, equivalent in U.S. geological usage to the lower part of the Snowslip Formation, is brightly-colored, current-rippled argillite and siltstone. It shows that the water remained shallow, but it became muddy.

## Purcell Lava
*Mesoproterozoic (1443 Ma), 60–150 m*

The Purcell Lava is a basalt flow, a common type of volcanic rock that comes from melted oceanic crust, showing that the continental plate was thin and weak in this area in Purcell time. If the plate had been thick and strong, then the basalt coming up would have mixed with melted continental-crust granite to produce other kinds of magmas. The lava shows pillow-shaped structures characteristic of magma that oozed out under seawater. The rock is full of small cavities filled with white calcite. Look for dark, purplish boulders of this **amygdaloidal basalt** in any Waterton/Glacier stream; the white calcite speckles make it easy to spot.

The Purcell Lava caps the Siyeh Formation (Canadian terminology). It divides the lower part of the Snowslip Formation, which is the same as the upper Siyeh, from the upper part of the Snowslip Formation, which is equivalent to the lower part of the Sheppard Formation, which overlies the Siyeh. (Got that?) In the Lizard Range and Hughes Range, the Purcell Lava grades into mixed sedimentary and volcanic rock known as the Nicol Formation, up to 750 m thick.

There is a good exposure of Purcell Lava pillow basalt at the gas plant on Drywood Creek, north of Waterton park. In Glacier park there is no road access to the unit; the approach is via trail to Granite Park. There is no granite in Granite Park; the lava has been taken for granite, so to speak.

## Missoula Group (*upper* division of the Purcell Supergroup)
*Mesoproterozoic (younger than 1400 Ma), about 2500 m*

Thinly bedded pale red, green, yellowish and purplish argillite and sandstone, with a few stromatolite beds, and quartzite near the top. Found mostly west of the Flathead River, but also in the northern part of Glacier park and in the western part of Waterton park. Easily eroded and

## Stromatolites

A stromatolite is a succession of thickened, domed-up layers. They are caused by colonies of cyanobacteria, previously called "bluegreen algae." Stromatolites are found in many formations of the Canadian Rockies, and they exist in tropical regions today. Living stromatolites in Shark Bay, Australia are identical to those found in the Siyeh Formation, 1.3 billion years old.

Consider a single bacterial colony, a mat of cyanobacterial filaments covering an area perhaps 10–20 cm across; one of many that are growing on tidal flats. When the tide is in, the mat is covered with perhaps a metre of water. The water is very clear, or the cyanobacteria will not grow. The cyanobacteria produce a residue of calcite (lime), and the tiny calcite crystals catch among the sticky filaments. If the mudflat is gradually sinking, this trapped material allows the stromatolite to grow upward, keeping pace with the rate of subsidence. A trench dug into the mudflat shows cross-sections of domed stromatolite columns that have developed over thousands of years.

*Conophyton* stromatolites *seen at Stop 16 along the Going-to-the-Sun Highway in Glacier National Park. Photo by Christian Gronau.*

The centres of many stromatolites in the Siyeh Formation are concave downward rather than domed upward, as if they have collapsed. This may, indeed, have happened. The region lay close to the edge of the continent, where frequent earthquakes would have shaken the stromatolites, perhaps damaging them in this way.

thus often tree-covered at lower elevations; best viewed around Logan Pass, where it forms the upper part of the peaks.

"Missoula Group" is a name applied by American geologists in the late 1970s to unify several formations. From bottom to top, the Americans place the Snowslip, Shepard (note American spelling of this formation name has one "p"), Mount Shields, Bonner and McNamara formations within the group. Canadians use the older names upper Siyeh, Sheppard (two "p"s), Gateway, Phillips and Roosville for units that roughly match the American formations. A basal unit 200–420 m thick, the Van Creek Formation, has been identified in the Lizard Range and Hughes Range, and to the west in the Purcell Mountains. It overlies the Kitchener Formation and is equivalent to the upper Siyeh.

The lowest formation in the Missoula Group, the Snowslip, is fairly typical of the whole group: shallow-water sediments deposited on seashore mudflats, or perhaps in a brackish lake. At times, cyanobacterial colonies formed stromatolites in spots on the delta where the water wasn't too muddy. These stromatolites are uniquely colorful; they incorporate the reddish argillite that was choking them as mud at that time. See them at Geology Stop 13 along the Going-to-the-Sun Highway in Glacier park.

Coarse, sandy layers higher in the group (Phillips/Bonner Formation) show that river water was reaching this part of the seabed. The shoreline was creeping seaward because the land surface was starting to rise. Eventually the shoreline passed through the area, exposing the upper Purcell layers to erosion that continued until the Middle Cambrian—a period of 800 million years—when the erosion surface was buried beneath new sediments. How much rock was lost in the interim? Possibly thousands of metres.

## Purcell Sill and dykes
*Neoproterozoic (about 800 Ma), 1–30 m*

Found in the eastern parts of Waterton and Glacier parks as a diabase sill (magma injected horizontally between rock layers) near the top of the Siyeh Formation. **Diabase** is the coarse-grained equivalent of basalt, a black volcanic rock. The essential difference is that diabase cools slowly, deep underground, which gives the mineral crystals time to grow large, while basalt cools quickly as it spreads out on the surface, so the crystals are small. The main minerals in either rock are grayish plagioclase feldspar, chemical formula $(Ca,Na)(Al,Si)AlSi_2O_8$), which often forms star-shaped clusters, and greenish-black augite, $Ca(Mg,Fe,Al)(Al,Si)_2O_6$.

**Dykes** (magma injected across layers) branch off from the Purcell Sill. Igneous rock is rare in the Canadian Rockies, and this batch is the most widespread. For information on the others, turn to page 68.

The Purcell Sill is easily approached on the Going-to-the-Sun Highway, which crosses the sill at Geology Stop 9. It is also prominent along the road to Red Rock Canyon in Waterton park, seen high in the cliffs of Mount Blakiston. Look for a horizontal greenish-black band against the tan or gray cliffs.

The sill follows one layer for some distance, then cuts up or down to a different layer. Forced between layers under tremendous heat and pressure, the magma baked the limestone above and below it, removing dark organic material and bleaching the limestone white. In some places the bordering limestone has recrystallized as a thin zone of white marble.

Turn-of-the-century prospectors found small bodies of copper ore associated with the Purcell Sill in Siyeh limestone. Mines were opened in what would soon become Glacier National Park. Locations: Grinnell Point and Mt. Siyeh, in the Many Glacier area. The mines soon failed, but not before the boom camp of Altyn, long since abandoned, was built on Cracker Flats, an alluvial fan about 2 km downstream from the modern location of the Many Glacier Hotel.

Other metallic and non-fuel mines in the Rockies include the lead-zinc mines in Yoho park, page 697; the silver prospects at Silver City, same page, and a talc mine near Redearth Pass, page 705.)

*The Purcell Sill forms a prominent dark line in Mt. Gould, upper left, and in the Garden Wall, at centre, Glacier National Park. Grinnell Lake at lower left. Photo by David McIntyre.*

## Rodinia rock at the northern end of the Rockies

Six thousand metres of ancient sediments that are thought to be about the same age as the Purcell Supergroup, and look similar, form the crest of the northern Canadian Rockies between the Toad River and the Tuchodi Lakes area. So the older layered rock in the Canadian Rockies occurs at opposite ends of the area.

The northern Mesoproterozoic sequence is called informally the Muskwa assemblage, because it was first studied along the Muskwa River. The unit is well-exposed in the peaks just southwest of Summit Lake along the Alaska Highway. Walk 3 km up the gravel flats of MacDonald Creek to reach the formations. The oldest is the Chischa Formation (>940 m), a light-colored dolomite with stromatolites and some quartzite; it resembles the Waterton and Altyn formations of the faraway Purcell. Next younger is the Tetsa Formation (320 m), a dark, apparently deep-water argillite that overlies the Chischa above an erosion surface. Above that, the George Formation (360–530 m) is a tan carbonate (limestone/dolomite) rather similar to the Empire/Helena/Siyeh, containing the same sort of collapsed-centre stromatolites. Above that, the Henry Creek Formation (460 m) is a limy argillite resembling the Snowslip Formation (lowest Missoula Group member).

Higher still, the formations are thick and varied in rock type, with less limestone/dolomite and many shaly beds. The Tuchodi Formation (1500 m) includes quartzite, dolomite, siltstone and red shale like that of the Missoula Group. But above the Tuchodi the similarities with the Purcell, or with any other rock in the Rockies, end. The Aida Formation (1200–1800 m) is mostly deep-water argillite, deposited as turbidites from undersea landslides (see page 61), while the overlying Gataga Formation (over 1200 m) holds turbidites of argillite, siltstone and sandstone, much of the rock quite slaty. Thus, the Muskwa assemblage of the northern Rockies records deeper-water conditions in its upper layers, while the Purcell Supergroup of the southern Rockies records shallowing conditions.

Like the Purcell, the Muskwa assemblage was uplifted late in the Mesoproterozoic and has lost an undetermined thickness of rock to erosion. Neoproterozoic rock of the Misinchinka Group, page 68, has been found lying atop the Muskwa assemblage. The contact between these two can be seen only in Mt. Lloyd George, in Kwadacha Wilderness Provincial Park, where a thin layer of Misinchinka rock overlies the Muskwa assemblage. Elsewhere early Cambrian rock overlies the Muskwa.

Like the Purcell Supergroup, the Muskwa assemblage has been intruded by igneous dykes of diabase that crystallized from ocean-crust magma, rather like the magma that provided the Purcell Sill, Purcell Lava and dykes in the Waterton/Glacier area. No radiometric dates have been obtained from these northerly dykes, and the age of the Muskwa assemblage has not been firmly established.

That takes care of the Rodinia rock, the oldest great layer of the Canadian Rockies. On to the next layer up: the old clastic unit.

## The end of Rodinia

In the late Precambrian, the old supercontinent of Rodinia rifted; that is, it broke up. It wasn't until the 1980s, after a worldwide hunt, that much of Australia was identified as a sizable chunk of the ancient supercontinent. The basement rock of Australia is the same age and type as that found in western North America, complete with Rodinia-type rock lying on it.

Given that Rodinia rock in this country occurs at the northern and southern ends of the Canadian Rockies, with a big gap between, it's natural to wonder whether the segment between Waterton/Glacier and Kwadacha park was deposited farther west, on the part of Rodinia that split off some 800 million years ago for the long ride to Australia. This is quite likely.

# Undersea landslides and Precambrian glaciation
## The Windermere Supergroup, lower part of the old clastic unit

As Rodinia rifted apart, blocks of continental crust were pulled away from the edge, tilting sideways as they slipped slowly downward along curving faults toward the deep ocean floor. Block-diagram 2 on page 186 illustrates this process, which had the paradoxical effect of creating mountain ranges as one edge of each block tilted upward. Mountain ranges of this sort can be seen today in the Basin and Range geological province of the western United States.

As rifting continued, the ranges were pulled away from the continent, sticking out of the sea as mountainous islands for some millions of years before erosion wore them back down to sea level.

Mountains of this type also lay along the shore. The continental shelf was narrow, so sediments eroded from the mountains didn't have far to travel before they reached the sea. They piled up quickly on a fairly steep continental slope cut by submarine canyons. One such

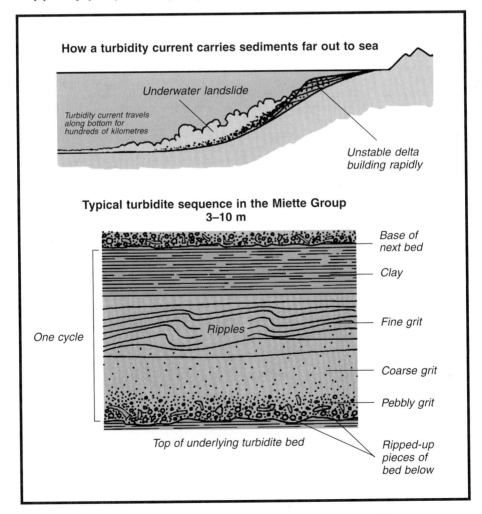

**How a turbidity current carries sediments far out to sea**

*Underwater landslide*

Turbidity current travels
along bottom for
hundreds of kilometres

*Unstable delta
building rapidly*

**Typical turbidite sequence in the Miette Group**
**3–10 m**

*Base of
next bed*

*Clay*

*Ripples*

*Fine grit*

*One cycle*

*Coarse grit*

*Pebbly grit*

*Top of underlying turbidite bed*

*Ripped-up
pieces of
bed below*

gully, 150 m deep and filled with coarse debris, has been discovered in rock of this age near Lake Louise. The scene it evokes is one of mountain streams carrying mud, sand and gravel into the sea, where a growing fringe of deltas was building up along the edge of the continent.

Imagine also the earthquakes generated as Rodinia tore apart. Those quickly growing deltas, hundreds of metres thick, were perched precariously on the steep continental slope. The result? Underwater landslides occurred every now and again for more than a hundred million years as the deltaic sediments were jarred loose and flowed downhill into deeper water. Such slides are termed turbidity currents. The rock of the Windermere Supergroup, 10 km thick in total, is largely the detritus from all those underwater slides. Sediments of this sort are termed turbidites. During the building of the Rockies the pile of turbidites was pushed back up on the continent, where we see it today. For more on turbidites, see next page.

The Windermere Supergroup lies in a belt from the south end of Banff park to the Liard River, and beyond, north through the Mackenzie Mountains across the Yukon and into Alaska. This is the lower part of the old clastic unit introduced on page 46. Windermere rock includes the Miette Group and the Misinchinka Group. The Miette Group is southern and central; the Misinchinka is northern. "Windermere" is from a creek running into Windermere Lake, which lies between Fairmont and Radium Hot Springs.

## Miette Group

The Miette Group is Neoproterozoic (570–780 Ma) and 4500–5000 m thick in the Rockies. It is easily identified by its middle part: alternating layers of buff-colored **gritstone** (very coarse sandstone, with a fair proportion of minerals other than quartz), conglomerate, and gray, green or brown shale that has been metamorphosed to slate and phyllite. The slate weathers a deep, rusty brown color. Stronger metamorphism has turned the Miette slate to schist in the Selwyn Mountains southwest of Jasper.

The Miette Group underlies much of the Canadian Rockies. It is exposed at the surface mostly in the main ranges near the continental divide and west of it, sometimes east of the divide as at Jasper and Lake Louise. The group is named for the Miette River west of Jasper, where it was first described. From a thin edge in northern Montana and southern B.C., where the Miette fringed an offshore landmass called Montania, the group thickens to 15 km in the adjacent Purcell Mountains, where it is somewhat finer-grained. Within the Rockies the Miette is thickest in the Selwyn Range southwest of Jasper, where it may reach 9 km, making it the thickest of all measured Rockies units.

Miette rock overlies the older Purcell Supergroup, page 52, at several locations west of the Rocky Mountain Trench, and in central Montana, but in the Canadian Rockies proper the bottom of the Miette Group is known only from Hugh Allan Creek near Valemount, where Miette rock was deposited directly on gneiss of the continental crust, then faulted along this basement rock later on. There the Purcell Supergroup is missing. Either it was never deposited or it was eroded away before the Miette Group was laid down.

Mild uplift and a drop in sea level near the end of the Neoproterozoic exposed the Miette group to erosion. At least a few hundred metres of the upper part were removed before the sea moved back in and began a new round of deposition. Slight tilting accompanied the uplift, and thus the overlying Gog Group lies at a very low angle to the top of the Miette.

*Miette Group schist seen at the junction of Highway 16 and Highway 5 near Tête Jaune Cache*

The best place to see this is from the Icefields Parkway at Bow Peak, 26 km north of Lake Louise. If you sweep your eye back and forth along the cliffs of Bow Peak, you can see that the rusty layers of the upper half (Gog) meet the dark-brown layers of the lower half (Miette) at a very slight angle that opens to the north. The angular unconformity at this site is plainly discernible; at most other localities the contact appears flat. (See page 98 for more on unconformities.)

Mountains carved in Miette and Misinchinka strata tend to be rounded and lumpy rather than pointed and cliffy, because overall the Windermere Supergroup is rather easy to erode. The hard gritstone layers are not very thick (about 100 m at most), and they are interbedded with crumbly slate.

From Castle Junction north, there are many good places to view Miette rock. Along the TransCanada Highway at the point where the Icefields Parkway splits off just north of Lake Louise, look for curving slaty slabs of Miette rock beside the road. A couple of kilometres north, on the road to Jasper, the low cliffs on the west side of the highway look like granite, but they are not; they are very coarse, mica-rich Miette gritstone, crisscrossed with veins of white quartz. Road-cuts west of Jasper along Highway 16 display the group exceptionally well.

The Miette Group has been studied most in the Jasper area and west to the Rocky Mountain Trench. Here are the formations identified so far.

### Lower Miette/Cushing Creek Formation
*Neoproterozoic (570–730 Ma), about 500 m*

Recent field work in the Selwyn Mountains southwest of Jasper has found the bottom part of the Miette Group, resting on the Hugh Allan - Blackman Gneiss, page 51. A formal name for the new material has not been established yet. For now the name is just "lower Miette," although the Cushing Creek Formation, studied in the 1970s along Cushing Creek north of McBride, may incorporate the top of this unit and thus provide it with a proper name. The lower Miette was originally dark-gray shale laminated with silt beds and a few thin sandstones, but most of this has been metamorphosed to schist.

### Middle Miette grits, including the McKale, Corral Creek and Hector formations
*Neoproterozoic (570–730 Ma), maximum thickness 3000 m*

Massive gray-green, tan-weathering gritstone beds typically 5–10 m thick, but can be much thicker, alternating with cleaved dark gray shale, slate or phyllite (mica-rich slate) beds, rusty-weathering from the presence of iron and about the same thickness. Fresh exposures of the gritstone beds are tinted gray-green by tiny flakes of chlorite, a low-grade metamorphic mineral. Sometimes the chlorite appears in quartz veins.

**Gritstone** is an old British term for coarse sandstone. Around the turn of the century, geologists began to look at gritstone in detail. They found that it is made mainly of bits of quartz, feldspar and mica. These are the major components of granite. Further study showed that gritstone does indeed come from eroding granite, carried away in fragments by rivers and dumped into a nearby ocean. Here was a step forward in understanding.

But what could explain the alternation of coarse gritstone and fine-grained shale in such deposits? In the 1930s it became clear that sediments like this are **turbidites** ("TUR-bid-ights"): deposits that have resulted from underwater landslides down the long continental slopes and out into the ocean basins. These are common today, especially where the continental shelf is narrow and mountains are eroding into the sea, as is the case along the coast of British Columbia or California. See the diagram on page 61.

With the rapid accumulation of sediments, the edge of the shelf collapses from time to time—perhaps during earthquakes—and the underwater slides occur. These slides set up strong currents that carry muddy slurries of rock fragments far out to sea. Such currents are termed **turbidity currents,** from "turbid," meaning muddy. Turbidity currents are loaded with rock particles. The debris carried in the current makes it denser than the surrounding water, so a turbidity current flows along the bottom, whether it is a lakebed or a seabed.

As a turbidity current slows down, the heavy, coarse particles drop to the bottom first, followed by the finer particles. So the resulting sedimentary layer is **graded:** it gets finer upward and outward, from conglomerate to very coarse sandstone to medium sandstone and fine sandstone, then to silt and finally to shale. The Miette grits along Highway 16 just west of Jasper display grading.

Science now knows rather a lot about the Miette grits: what they are made of, where they came from, where they ended up and how they got there. As usual in sedimentary geology, knowledge was gained by finding modern examples of events that happened long ago.

Well, *how* long ago? The Miette grits do not contain fossils to use in correlating them with other formations of known age. Also, there is no point in trying radiometric-dating techniques. Applied to the grits, this would tell us when the individual grains crystallized in the igneous granite, but that happened long before those grains were eroded from the Canadian Shield and spread over the seabed.

However, the imprints of jellyfish found in the *upper* Miette (see next item) occur only in Neoproterozoic rock. We note also that the Malton Gneiss, which underlies the Miette Group southwest of Jasper, has been dated to about 800 Ma. This narrows the age range of the Miette to 800–545 Ma, which is pretty good accuracy for a Precambrian sedimentary unit.

Recently named the McKale Formation, for the McKale River, north of McBride, the middle Miette grits are known by two formation names around Lake Louise. Here the grit-bed/slate-bed sequence is interrupted by a layer of purplish/greenish slate and a limestone-rich conglomerate thought to be an underwater debris flow similar to the Old Fort Point Formation of the Jasper area, next item. This unit forms the base of the Hector formation, named for

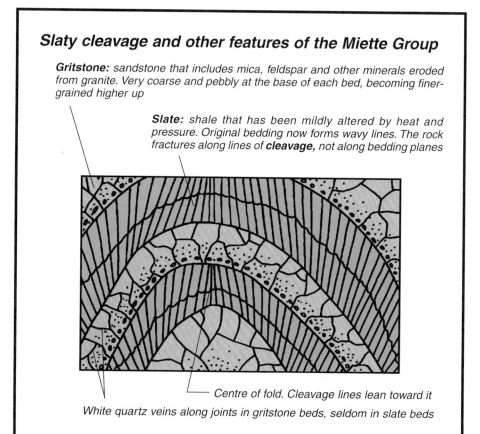

## *Slaty cleavage and other features of the Miette Group*

**Gritstone:** *sandstone that includes mica, feldspar and other minerals eroded from granite. Very coarse and pebbly at the base of each bed, becoming finer-grained higher up*

**Slate:** *shale that has been mildly altered by heat and pressure. Original bedding now forms wavy lines. The rock fractures along lines of* **cleavage,** *not along bedding planes*

*Centre of fold. Cleavage lines lean toward it*

*White quartz veins along joints in gritstone beds, seldom in slate beds*

Mt. Hector nearby. The Hector Formation includes all Miette strata from the debris flow to the top of the group. Everything below the debris flow is known as the Corral Creek Formation, base not exposed. Together, the two units total 850 m.

In the Athabasca valley around Jasper the McKale gritstone layers have been bent into folds, with steeply inclined bedding. They have been ground down by heavy glaciation to form low ridges, while the shale beds have been eroded slightly deeper to form the intervening small valleys. The trail to Valley of the Five Lakes beautifully illustrates this interesting hard-and-soft alternation, a classic example of **structural control,** in which the geology controls the topography.

Creamy white quartz veins cut across the gritstone layers. Very hot water, under so much pressure from overlying rock that it would not boil even at temperatures high enough to carry quartz in solution, has dissolved quartz from grains in the rock and redeposited the mineral in cracks and joints. The slate layers are seldom

*Slabs of rusty-weathering middle-Miette slate at the junction of the TransCanada Highway and Highway 93 near Lake Louise*

cut by quartz veins; this is because shale, forerunner of slate, compacts under pressure, closing any fissures that might otherwise carry mineral-laden water. Rusty streaks of iron oxide stain the rock surfaces below blobs of bacterially produced pyrite (see page 111). Chlorite occurs as dark-green flecks and patches in the veins. Placing geologist's hydrochloric acid on the chlorite dissolves some of it, staining the surrounding quartz yellow.

*Gritstone bed with slate beds above and below, seen beside Highway 16 west of Jasper*

## Old Fort Point Formation/middle member, McKale Formation
*Neoproterozoic (545–800 Ma), 360 m*

Within the gritstone-and-slate sequence of the middle Miette lies the peculiar Old Fort Point Formation: pinkish/purplish limestone and gray-green shale and siltstone. Where the name McKale Formation is applied to the middle Miette grits, the Old Fort Point Formation divides the McKale into lower and upper members, not individually named.

Old Fort Point limestone is a carbonate bank built up by simple marine organisms, cyanobacteria, probably, during a time when sea level rose somewhat and stayed high for a long time. Found as far away as the Selkirk Mountains, the Old Fort Point is a good marker bed in the Windermere Supergroup. The formation is thickest around Jasper at about 360 m. In the Selwyn Mountains to the west, it is 45 m of thin-bedded green and maroon shale, then 14 m of brown carbonate, then 5 m of black shale. Rock resembling the maroon unit can be seen beside the Icefields Parkway about 10 km north of Lake Louise.

The formation looks rather like parts of the Purcell Group (page 52) found 450 km to the south, in the Waterton/Glacier area. Along Highway 16, 14 km west of Jasper, most of the unit is smoothly laminated, looking very Purcell-like. But on Old Fort Point itself, a hill across the Athabasca River from Jasper townsite (a road leads right to it), the bedding is quite strange. In some layers, angular, thumb-size to platter-size pieces of limestone are embedded at crazy angles in a fine, silty matrix. This type of rock is called **breccia** ("BRETCH-yuh"). In the Old Fort Point breccia, the angular pieces weather more quickly than the surrounding matrix, forming indentations in exposed surfaces.

*Breccia seen at Old Fort Point, near Jasper*

How did this odd-looking rock form? The angular pieces have broken loose from laminar beds, have swirled around in mud, then become locked in the surrounding sediment at random angles. This happened while the rock was still soft, for the pieces are often bent and curved. Study has shown that portions of the formation slid in masses down into deeper water, breaking up the bedding. Thus, after the Old Fort Point was laid down, the continental edge in our area once again became the scene of undersea landslides and the rest of the middle Miette grits were deposited that way.

## East Twin Formation
*Neoproterozoic (545–800 Ma), up to 1500 m*

Greenish-gray or brown slate, phyllite and shale that weather rusty and purplish. The rock is variously soft, brittle and splitty, so it weathers back into slopes covered with vegetation. In the Jasper area a couple of thin quartzite beds are good markers about 1000 m above the base of this rather monotonous stack of slate. In the Selwyn Mountains west of Jasper, a boulder conglomerate bed lies near the base of the East Twin Formation, and there are many quartzite beds in the upper part. One such is prominent just east of Jasper along Highway 16, at the junction with the Maligne Road, where it abuts the Pyramid Thrust, a major fault separating the main ranges and the front ranges here.

Along Highway 16 there are good exposures of East Twin slate 20–30 km west of Jasper. In some road-cuts the cleaved rock spalls off in thin, rusty-looking sheets that stack like pieces of paper at the base of the cliff.

The earliest known animal fossils in the Rockies have been found in East Twin shale. Impressions of the Neoproterozoic jellyfish *Cyclomedusa* and *Irridinitus* have been found recently in greenish siltstone beds about 330 m below the top of the East Twin Formation on Mt. Fitzwilliam, near Yellowhead Pass. Tracks and trails identified as *Planolites*, which may have been made by marine worms, have been found in the upper Miette near Mt. Robson.

To the south, around Lake Louise, micro-fossils have been identified as that of the cyanobacterium *Spaerocongregus variabilis*. They come from fine-grained East Twin shale that is probably slightly older than the exposures in the Mt. Robson area, which would make these tiny clusters of cells the oldest preserved organisms known in the Rocky Mountains. (The stromatolites of the Purcell Group, although older, do not preserve the actual shapes of their cyanobacterial builders. See page 58.)

## Byng Formation, and other dolomite units in the upper Miette Group
*Neoproterozoic (545–800 Ma), 0–180 m*

Orange-weathering gray or bluish dolomite, with wavy bedding, stromatolites (cyanobacterial mounds, page 58) **pisoliths** (concentrically layered, pea-sized cyanobacterial balls) and zones of fragmented rock caused by underwater landslides.

The Byng Formation is not named for Mt. Byng, west of Banff near Mt. Assiniboine—the formation is not found that far south—but for Byng Pass, at the head of the Snake Indian River in northern Jasper park. The unit outcrops sporadically at the top of Miette Group exposures in the main ranges from Monte Cristo Mountain in northwestern Jasper park to The Colonel, a peak northwest of Yellowhead Pass.

Another dolomite at about the same level in the upper Miette as the Byng Formation, but unnamed, is found south of Yellowhead Pass in the Ramparts area. Mt. Fitzwilliam, the south buttress of Yellowhead Pass, has a thick, highly visible band of this dolomite, easily seen from the Fitzwilliam Viewpoint along Highway 16 (photo). To see the unit up close, go to Jasper and follow Trail 7 for about 5 km from Old Fort Point to a large outcrop of steeply tilted, pale-orange dolomite in the hillside south of the trail. Farther north, in the Miette-equivalent Misinchinka Group of the northern Rockies, next item, a dolomite unit named the Framstead Formation is found in the upper part of the group. It is older than the Byng.

Within the upper-Miette dolomite around Yellowhead Pass, a steep slope is preserved in the rock. This is the edge of the oldest known reef-type deposit in the Canadian Rockies. Alternatively, it might have been a landslide scarp. This was the edge of the Yellowhead Platform, an area of shallow water in the Neoproterozoic sea. The platform was built by cyanobacterial colonies long before corals, the usual reef-builders these days, had evolved.

*The lower half of Mt. Fitzwilliam, at Yellowhead Pass, is dolomite. The upper half is Gog quartzite, covered with lichens that look uniformly gray from a distance.*

From time to time, boulder-size pieces of the platform edge would crumble, perhaps under the onslaught of heavy storms or jarred by earthquakes, and spill down the underwater slope. Perhaps larger sections of the edge would break away in landslides, as happened in the Middle Cambrian, page 83. There they would be buried under the steady rain of cyanobacterially generated lime mud and thus be reincorporated into the platform. The outcrop at Jasper doesn't seem to show these embedded chunks, but it does show the wavy bedding characteristic of limestone layers formed in and around cyanobacterial colonies. Like other occurrences of dolomite, this one began as limestone and changed to dolomite through chemical interchange with magnesium-rich seawater. See page 78 for more on dolomite.

The dolomite in the upper part of the Miette Group is patchy in the Rockies, occurring at slightly different stratigraphic levels separated by interfingering shale and quartzite. The current interpretation is that it represents reef-building on a shallow, muddy seabed in different places and at slightly different times. The unit may have been much more extensive before the Miette Group was raised above sea level at the end of the Neoproterozoic Era and lost layers to erosion.

## Misinchinka Group

The Misinchinka Group is mainly a northern Rockies unit. About 3000 m thick, it's named for the Misinchinka River, along which Highway 97 approaches Pine Pass. To the south, the Misinchinka Group grades into the Miette Group at the latitude of Grande Cache; it runs north through the northern Rockies and into the Mackenzie Mountains. Younger than 728 Ma and older than 525 Ma, the Misinchinka is similar to the Miette Group in age and rock type, and thus part of the Windermere Supergroup, page 61, but it is even shalier. In the upper part there is a limestone unit that looks a great deal like the Miette's upper carbonate units but is probably older. The discovery of archaeocyathid fossils, page 74, in the upper Misinchinka shows that it is Early Cambrian near the top in some places.

The Misinchinka holds a great deal of **diamictite:** hardened glacial till. In this case it was till deposited by glaciers flowing into the sea, much as they do today in northern British Columbia or Alaska. Up to 2000 m of diamictite is present in northerly exposures of the group, and **dropstones** (rocks that melted out of icebergs) are present. Neoproterozoic glaciation is known also from Africa and Australia. It seems to have happened here as well—although "here" was elsewhere back then, for the world's plates have moved a good deal since the Neoproterozoic. Still, when the geography of the time is reconstructed, it is obvious that the world went through an ice age during the late Precambrian. The amount of diamictite is used to differentiate the Miette Group from the Misinchinka Group: lots in the Misinchinka, little in the Miette.

Highway 97 runs through topography cut in Misinchinka rock for many kilometres between the turn-off for the town of Mackenzie and the summit of Pine Pass. The Alaska Highway crosses Misinchinka beds from west of Coal River to west of Fireside. At the northern end of the Rockies, the Misinchinka Group lies in at least one locality on Rodinia rock of the Muskwa assemblage (see page 60). East of Williston Lake, at Bevel Mountain in the Deserters Range, the Misinchinka was deposited on granite gneiss of the basement that was metamorphosed at 728 Ma, so the base of the Misinchinka is younger than 728 Ma. A quartzite basal unit there, 200 m thick, is overlain by 1100 m of schist, quartzite and marble, showing that temperatures and pressures were high during later mountain-building. Diamictite beds lie above, then a prominent cliff-forming bed of marble and other carbonates 150 m thick. The upper 400 m are sandier/shalier and less metamorphosed, with more diamictite.

Farther south, around Monkman Pass, two vertical kilometres of diamictite are found in the Vreeland Formation, named for Mt. Vreeland. Above the Vreeland diamictite lies the Framstead Formation, which is a limestone, dolomite and shale unit about 400 m thick, and the Chowika Formation (Chowika Creek is near the north end of Williston Lake), 275 m of quartzite with a middle shale bed. Above that, the Cut Thumb Formation (named for Cut Thumb Creek, north of Pine Pass) is a shale unit like the East Twin Formation, but less than 100 m thick; it marks the top of the Misinchinka Group.

Differences between the Miette and the Misinchinka may relate to the presence of a recently discovered, as yet unnamed westerly bulge in the Precambrian shoreline between Grande Cache and the Peace River. This would have tended to separate the sediments into a northern lobe (Misinchinka) and a southern lobe (Miette).

## Crowfoot Dyke and other minor intrusives in the Rockies

West of the Rockies, in the Columbia, Omineca and Cassiar mountains, igneous (once-molten) rock is common. It includes many **dykes:** igneous veins that have cut across other rock. But in the Rockies themselves, any kind of igneous rock is rare. Such is the Crowfoot Dyke, a sheet of greenish-brown diabase about 50 m thick crossed by the Icefields Parkway just south of Bow Lake, 1 km south of the Crowfoot Glacier viewpoint. **Diabase** is essentially basalt, a common type of lava, that cooled slowly underground and thus became more coarsely crystalline.

*One of several orange-weathering dykes exposed after recent glacial melt-back on the southwestern slopes of Castleguard Mountain in northern Banff National Park. The unweathered rock is greenish.*

The Crowfoot Dyke has been traced from the Bow River northeast across the highway, through a ridge and into the next valley, where it ends just short of Helen Creek (total length 2.8 km). The dyke is Neoproterozoic; it cuts through upper Miette beds but does not cut into the overlying Gog quartzite, indicating (a) that it is younger than the Miette, (b) that it is older than the Gog and (c) that a good deal of Miette rock has been removed by erosion, because the rock exposed in the dyke must have cooled at least a few hundred metres below the surface.

Other minor intrusives in the Rockies include diabase dykes along Icefall Brook (north tributary of Valenciennes Creek, west of the Lyell Icefield), in the Freshfield Icefield area, and a diabase sill in the Mt. Assiniboine area. A highly deformed diabase dyke cuts through the Old Fort Point Formation west of Jasper (location: 1 km northwest of Geikie siding along the old road to Decoigne).

There are orange-weathering greenish dykes of unknown igneous composition—perhaps diabase—just off the Columbia Icefield near Castleguard Mountain. Nearby I have seen boulders of **pegmatite,** which is any igneous rock with very coarse grains, lying on the west side of Castleguard Meadows, near the north end. Thumb-size crystals of white mica make these blocks very distinctive; their source is unknown.

**Diatremes,** which are small volcanic pipes containing pieces of the surrounding rock and sometimes diamonds, have been discovered at several locations in the western Rockies. Some 40 pipes are located between Mt. Joffre and Cranbrook, and a few lie farther north in the Columbia Icefield area. Near the place where the Peace River flows out of Williston Lake, another diatreme is associated with a body of **carbonatite:** igneous rock with the same constituents as limestone or dolomite. Some of these diatremes have been dated to 427–445 Ma, in the Late Ordovician and Early Silurian periods; others are Carboniferous and Permian.

Elsewhere in this book there are descriptions of the Purcell Sill and dykes, page 59, and similar dykes in the Muskwa assemblage of the northern Rockies, page 60. See also the Ice River Alkaline Complex, page 119, the Crowsnest volcanics, page 131, and dykes in the Kechika Group, page 96.

# The hardest rock in the Rockies
## Quartzite of the Gog and Atan groups

The Gog and Atan groups form the upper part of the old clastic unit of the Canadian Rockies, lying atop the Windermere Supergroup, the lower part. Up to 9 km thick, the old clastic unit accounts for about a third of the sedimentary stack in the region.

To build up a lot of sedimentary rock requires a hole in which to dump it. In the case of both the Windermere and the Gog/Atan the hole was the ocean, gradually widening as the supercontinent of Rodinia broke up. In Windermere time the edge of the continent sloped steeply into the deep ocean basin; by Gog/Atan time, the continental shelf seems to have been wider and shallower, with a line of troughs along it parallelling the edge.

One of these troughs was the Robson Basin, a major sag in the crust that coincided with the position of what would eventually become the Rockies from about Pine Pass southward to Crowsnest Pass. The Robson Basin collected sediment throughout the Cambrian Period and into the Early Ordovician. The name comes from the Mt. Robson area, where the accumulation of sedimentary rock was thickest.

North of the Robson Basin, a nose of low-lying land jutted westward out to sea in the area of the present Peace River. That nose is known as the Peace River Arch, and it divided the Robson Basin to the south from the Kechika Basin to the north, which was a crustal depression similar to the Robson Basin. The Kechika Basin, named for the Kechika River of the northern Rockies, extended north to about where the northern end of the Rockies is now, at the Liard River. It acted as a sediment trap even longer than the Robson Basin did, staying below sea-level through the Ordovician and Silurian periods. The Gog Group was deposited in the Robson Basin; similar rock of the Atan Group was deposited in the Kechika Basin.

The top of the Gog/Atan is a conspicuous geological boundary in the central and northern Canadian Rockies: it marks the top of the old clastic unit (page 46), a thick succession of rock made of particles carried into the sea. From that time on, many thick carbonate layers—limestones and dolomites formed in place by biological action—were deposited until the end of the Paleozoic Era.

## Gog Group

The Gog Group is mostly **quartzite:** extremely hard sandstone, in which the quartz sand grains are themselves cemented together with quartz. This is the hardest rock in the Rockies, for much of it is nearly pure quartz, the hardest common mineral in the world, 7 on Moh's scale, harder than steel. But with that hardness comes brittleness, and while the Gog stands up in great gray or reddish cliffs, climbers on those cliffs discover that the handholds tend to be portable. Every layer is cracked and broken—except a few, such as the one at the Back of the Lake climbing area at Lake Louise, where the rock is excellent. (See page 732.) You don't have to be a climber to discover that Gog quartzite is very slippery when it's wet. Just try crossing a boulderfield of Gog rock in the rain.

The base of the Gog Group is perhaps Neoproterozoic in its western exposures, and early Cambrian to the east, spanning the period from about 600 Ma to 525 Ma. It ranges in thickness from 75–4000 m. Gog rock is mostly fine-grained white, buff, pink or purple quartzite beds, typically 1–10 m thick, separated by thin layers of brown, reddish or purplish siltstone and the odd sandstone bed. There are layers of pebble conglomerate near the base. Bedding planes and fractures are often stained red or orange with iron oxide from the weathering of the small iron pyrite crystals that are common in the Gog. Some iron-oxide-rich zones weather into brilliantly reddish-orange patches on mountainsides. Lichens (mostly greenish *Rhizocarpon geographicum,* black *Umbilicaria* species and many gray encrusting types) grow thickly on talus slopes and boulderfields of Gog rock, giving them an overall gray look from a distance.

Gog quartzite is easy to identify and interesting; it should be on any naturalist's short-list of formations to know. The name is from Gog Lake, near Mt. Assiniboine.

*Mt. Edith Cavell, 3363 m, has been carved from a block of Gog quartzite*

From central Jasper park north a layer of gray/pinkish limestone/dolomite occurs in the upper half of the Gog: the Mural Formation, up to 380 m thick. Between Lake Louise and Mt. Chown (northwestern tip of Jasper park), the Peyto Formation occurs at the top of the group. These are discussed in more detail below.

Gog rock is present continuously from Mt. Assiniboine to the Peace River. North of there the Gog contains more conglomerate, including embedded boulders up to 3 m across; the name changes to Atan Group. South of Mt. Assiniboine the Gog is patchy. Gog-type rock in the Hughes Range, bordering the Rocky Mountain Trench south of Canal Flats, is known as the Cranbrook Formation. There are also a few patches of Gog-like rock south of Crowsnest Pass, lying on the Purcell Supergroup. But these patches may be younger (Middle Cambrian) and they are much thinner, hence given a different name: Flathead Formation.

The Gog Group is exposed mostly in the main ranges, sometimes in the western part of the front ranges, but seldom at the eastern mountain front. Gog quartzite is very resistant to erosion and thick enough to form enormous cliffs. The thickness varies a lot geographically, suggesting that faults along the western edge of the continent were moving during Gog time, causing the seabed to sink irregularly and thus to collect thicker amounts of sand in some places than others.

If you want to see the Gog at its best, go to Jasper, where Pyramid Mountain and the other peaks of the Victoria Cross Range are made of it. So is Mt. Edith Cavell. The road-accessible north face of the peak is the best place to appreciate this important Rockies building block.

There are many other good Gog outcrops along the Icefields Parkway. Gog rock makes up all the reddish peaks along the west side of the Icefields Parkway between Jasper and Poboktan ("Po-BOCK-tun") Creek. Endless Chain Ridge, on the east side of the road from Sunwapta Falls south to Poboktan, is a classic dip-slope ridge (page 28) made of tilted Gog quartzite.

Farther south the Gog makes up the reddish lower cliffs of peaks around Lake Louise. There are good Gog outcrops beside the trail at the west end of the lake. The Ten Peaks above Moraine Lake are Gog quartzite from base to middle, and the big slide damming the lake provides a terrific collection of Gog boulders that visitors enjoy exploring. Forestry roads into the Rockies between Tête Jaune Cache and Prince George pass through the thick Gog sequence there.

North of Prince George the Gog is less spectacular, but 10 km east of Pine Pass, Highway 97 crosses an area of Gog rock between Mt. Murray and Mt. Garbitt.

Much of the Gog was laid down as sand in shallow water on a sea bed that was gradually sinking. So the sand layer became very thick—so thick, and so pure, that geologists think the Gog sand was probably redeposited, that is, washed in from some preexisting eroding sandstone. Much-older sandstone remnants, some of them Paleoproterozoic (over 1600 Ma) are found to the northeast on the Canadian Shield. This area was above sea level and thus eroding throughout Gog time; the hard quartz grains would have withstood the long river journey to the sea, where they may have been redeposited as the Gog. More evidence: the Gog thins and coarsens to the northeast, and the alignment of cross-beds also indicates a northeasterly source area. Alternatively, the Gog sand may simply represent quartz grains eroded from the quartz-rich granite and gneiss of the Canadian Shield itself.

You can see worm burrows over half a billion years old in the Gog. Look for vertical rods 1–20 cm long and up to 2 cm across at the tops of thick buff-colored layers. On the surface of a burrowed layer the rods show up as clusters of various-sized circles. For

*Planolites: the trails of seabed worms over half a billion years old*

convenience paleontologists have named these burrows *Skolithos*, as if they were fossils of the animals themselves, which they are not. Sinuous trails *(Planolites)*, decorate some bedding planes. Small raised spots that look like impressions of coffee beans can be seen on the undersides of rare sandstone layers. These are called *Rusophycus*; they are thought to indicate places where small trilobites dug themselves into the mud. In other places the tracks of an unknown animal *(Cruziana)* can be seen. See the illustrations of fossils, page 199.

There is a lot of iron pyrite ("fool's gold") in the Gog. Most buff-colored layers are speckled with black, brown or reddish dots of pyrite; bedding-plane surfaces are often coated with paint-thin deposits that have an iridescent sheen. Pyrite weathers to iron-oxide minerals that color the rock pink or orange.

*Worm burrows called* Skolithos

## *Origin of sandstone and other common clastic rock*

The Gog quartzite accumulated as grains of sand. Sand is mostly quartz crystals eroded from granite or other quartz-bearing rock. River transport quickly grinds up to powder or dissolves most other minerals, but quartz is hard stuff, and practically insoluble at normal temperatures, so it arrives at the ocean in fragments up to the size of pebbles. There, the waves sort the sediments out by size. Under ideal conditions the pebbles pile up where the surf is heavy. The sand-size grains collect in a belt from the shoreline out a few hundred metres into deeper water. The silt (grains somewhat smaller than sand) comes to rest a little farther out, in places with gentle currents, and the clay-size particles settle out farthest offshore. Hardened to rock, the pebbles become **conglomerate**, the sand becomes **sandstone**, the silt becomes **siltstone** and the clay becomes **shale**.

*Gog quartzite shows the cross-bedding (angled, intersecting beds) common in sandstone*

This is a common geological process, accounting for most of the world's **clastic** (particulate) sedimentary rock. The Gog Group is a classic example of clastic rock. That it has been hardened further to quartzite shouldn't obscure that fact.

**Cross-bedding** is often found in sandstone, and it is prominent in the Gog. Look for lines that are at an angle to the bedding surfaces above and below a layer. Cross-beds show that the sand grains were carried by currents to the growing edge of a layer, then dumped over. In this way the edge grew forward, just as a delta grows out into a lake. Another kind of Gog cross-bed occurred when a current cut a channel through a layer and then filled the channel with sand.

## McNaughton, Fort Mountain, Lake Louise and St. Piran formations
*Early Cambrian (525–545 Ma), up to 1750 m*

The McNaughton Formation is typical of the Gog Group, with massive quartzite beds up to 200 m thick divided by thinner beds of hardened siltstone and shale. There are a few unhardened sandstone beds. Mt. McNaughton is in Mount Robson Provincial Park. This name is applied to the lower half of the Gog Group from the Peace River south to the Brazeau River. Farther south, where the overlying Mural Formation, next item, is absent, different formation names are used for the Gog Group: bottom to top, the Fort Mountain Formation (cross-bedded quartzite), Lake Louise Formation (shale and siltstone) and St. Piran Formation (thick, varied unit of quartzite, sandstone, siltstone and shale).

## Mural Formation
*Early Cambrian (525–545 Ma), up to 380 m*

The Mural Formation, found in the upper half of the Gog Group, divides the underlying McNaughton Formation from the overlying Mahto Formation. It is mostly gray-weathering limestone, with a middle siltstone unit, although some beds have been altered to pinkish dolomite. In Mural time sand was not being laid down, so organisms dependent on clear water could survive. It's also likely that the climate warmed somewhat, favoring the growth of the cyanobacteria, sponges and other lime-depositing organisms that produced the rock.

The Mural contains the trilobite *Olenellus,* which has been used to date the Gog Group as Early Cambrian. **Archaeocyaths** are also common, usually as reef-formers. They look rather like horn corals, but they were actually sponges. Archaeocyaths became extinct after the Early Cambrian.

Mural limestone is found in the main ranges and western front ranges from Fortress Lake, near the southwestern corner of Jasper National Park, to the Peace River. It reaches thicknesses of up to 380 m in the area north of Jasper, but thins quickly to the south. You won't see it in road-cuts along major highways, but from the Icefields Parkway at Athabasca Falls the Mural is fairly obvious as a gray line running through Mt. Kerkeslin near treeline. The rough road up the Small River, branching off Highway 16 about 20 km northwest of Tête Jaune Cache, crosses the formation at kilometre 18. Above and to the west, close to the glacier, there are wonderful glacially polished exposures. The Mural is becoming known as a cave-forming unit (see page 168).

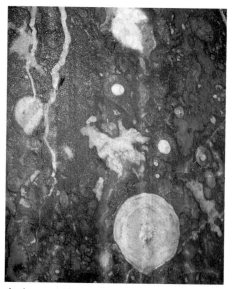

*Archaeocyaths (circles) seen in cross-section in the Mural Formation*

Limestone deposition ended after Mural time when the choking sand returned, covering the Mural with more Gog-type deposits.

## Mahto Formation
*Early Cambrian (525–545 Ma), up to 390 m*

Quartzite much like the McNaughton Formation, top of page. The name "Mahto" is applied where the underlying Mural and McNaughton formations are present, meaning from the Brazeau River to the Peace River. South of the Brazeau, equivalent rock is the St. Piran Formation. The trilobite *Olenellus* is locally common in red pyritic beds at the base of the Mahto.

### Peyto and Hota formations
*Early Cambrian (525–545 Ma), up to 128 m*

At the top of the Gog there is a peculiar limestone unit called the Peyto Formation, found capping the Gog Group in the main ranges and western front ranges from Lake Louise to Mt. Chown. A road-cut exposes it at Whirlpool Point on the David Thompson Highway, 21 km east of Saskatchewan Crossing near the Banff park boundary. Thickest around Mt. Robson (128 m), where it is called the Hota Formation, the Peyto Formation thins southward to only 6 m at Lake Louise. Trilobites such as *Bonnia* and *Olenellus* fix the Peyto as late Early Cambrian in age.

An interesting highway view of this rock is in Mt. Kerkeslin south of Jasper. Look for a couple of thin but prominent red bands in the cliffs about halfway up the mountain. The layer is loaded with red **ooids** ("OH-ids," also called "oolites"): round bits of limestone up to the size of small peas that formed when concentric rinds of calcite, the main mineral in limestone, grew around a nucleus of some kind, often a speck of sand. In the Bahamas, ooids are forming today; they roll about in shallow water that is rich in dissolved minerals and agitated by currents. Such conditions favor sand deposition, too, and thus the Peyto is sandy. Farther east the unit thins and becomes a sandstone layer.

Not long after the unit was deposited, there was a worldwide drop in sea level. The seabed was exposed to erosion, which cut into the Peyto/Hota. So there is an unconformity on top of the Gog Group.

## Atan Group

A northern Rockies unit, pronounced "At-TAN" and named for Atan Lake, in the Cassiar area of northern B.C. This is a very coarse gray conglomerate up to 1500 m thick, found near Cambrian faults. It grades into reddish quartzite and siltstone a few kilometres away from the faults, then to marine limestone still farther away. The age is Early Cambrian and perhaps Middle Cambrian (515–545 Ma).

Found from the Peace River to the Liard and beyond, the Atan Group is a classic example of what happens when the edge of a continental plate is breaking up. This was happening throughout the Canadian Rockies region during Miette time, but rifting in the northern Rockies continued into the Cambrian, after it had stopped to the south. The faulting reached farther eastward, deeper into the plate.

In the process some of the seabed was tilted above sea level, much like the tilted blocks in Miette time (see page 61). The effect was to create islands, which shed very coarse material— the Atan Group—into the surrounding sea. This sea lay in the Kechika Basin, a fault-bounded depression in the continental shelf rather like the Robson Basin south of it. The ancient faults have been located in the Tuchodi Lakes area, and next to them the conglomerate contains boulders up to 3 m in diameter. Along the Alaska Highway in the last few kilometres south of Muncho Lake, you can see some of this coarse material. Farther away from the faults, the Atan is red quartzite with siltstone beds, roughly resembling the Gog Group.

West of the fault lines the water was clearer. There, the Atan Group is limestone. The limestone ends along what must have been a slope into even deeper water farther west. And here some unusual geology occurred: pieces of the limestone layer up to the size of a city block broke off the edge and slid, intact, partway down the slope. There they were buried in mud that became shale. At first these big limestone blocks were thought to be reefs, but the water was too deep here for reef growth and the inclined beds show how the blocks tilted as they moved. To see them, hike 15 km up the West Toad River, where the white limestone blocks contrast with dark shale in the peaks. And see page 83 for more on sliding masses of limestone.

The Atan Group was uplifted late in the Cambrian and gently folded. It lies at various angles below Ordovician rock (see the drawing of an angular unconformity, page 99).

---

***New info on Cambrian dates:*** recent research has updated the beginning of the Cambrian to about 545 Ma and the beginning of the Middle Cambrian to about 525 Ma.

# *Life on the edge of the continent*
## The early Paleozoic of the central Rockies

We are now into the third great layer of the Rockies: the middle carbonates, ranging in age from Middle Cambrian to Permian (525–258 Ma). This rock is mostly limestone, dolomite and shale. Within the middle carbonates, the Cambrian, Ordovician and Silurian layers have a theme in common, which is the topic of this section: the rise and fall of sea level on the outer edge of an ancient continental shelf that was gradually breaking away.

## *The Middle Cambrian sandwich*

There are two geologic sandwiches in the central Rockies, this one and the late Paleozoic sandwich, which is described on page 112. Each consists of two thick layers of limestone or dolomite with a layer of shale between.

A classic view of the Middle Cambrian sandwich may be had at Castle Mountain, between Banff and Lake Louise at the junction of the TransCanada Highway and the road to Radium. The peak has two cliffs: an upper one and a lower one, divided by a ledge. The lower cliff is Cathedral dolomite, the ledge is Stephen shale, and the upper cliff is Eldon limestone. A sandwich.

Another fine view is along the west side of the Icefields Parkway between Bow Summit and Saskatchewan Crossing, in the Kaufmann Peaks and Mt. Sarbach. Again, the Cathedral-Stephen-Eldon sandwich is well displayed. The cliffs below the glaciers are Cathedral limestone, divided horizontally by two shale layers. The glaciers sit on a bench carved from Stephen shale, and the cliffs above the glaciers are Eldon limestone.

Between the Bow River and the Brazeau River the unit makes up the cliffs at the mountain front—but the formations are much thinner there than in the main ranges, for the sandwich thickens quickly to the west. The maximum is reached in the peaks west of Saskatchewan Crossing, where the middle Cambrian sandwich is about 1000 m thick; at the mountain front the total thickness is only 250 m.

*The Middle Cambrian sandwich at Castle Mountain, between Banff and Lake Louise. Lower cliff is Cathedral dolomite, middle ledge is Stephen shale, and upper cliff is Eldon limestone.*

These thickness figures include the Mt. Whyte Formation, next item, a thin but interesting shale-and-limestone unit found just below the Cathedral.

North of the Columbia Icefield the sandwich analogy breaks down, for the Cathedral Formation is replaced by the Snake Indian Formation, a shaly unit that doesn't weather into cliffs. The same thing happens west of Field in the main ranges, where all the Middle Cambrian limestones change abruptly to shale over a short distance. (See page 93 for the reason.) North of the Peace River there was mild uplift in the Middle Cambrian, which prevented deposition in the eastern part of the northern Rockies area until the Early Ordovician. However, deposition continued in what would become the western part of the northern Rockies. South of Mt. Assiniboine the Middle Cambrian sandwich is covered by younger rock. But Middle Cambrian rock reappears farther south, just east of the continental divide and just north of Waterton park, where the Windsor Mountain Formation lies on ancient Purcell Supergroup sediments.

South of Elko, the southern sequence includes four formations that total about 900 m in thickness. These include the Gog-like Flathead sandstone, Mt.-Whyte-equivalent Gordon Formation, Cathedral-equivalent Elko Formation, Eldon-equivalent Windsor Mountain Formation and a younger, poorly understood dolomite called the Jubilee Formation that seems to take the place of the Stephen, Eldon and possibly even younger formations. South of there, all Middle Cambrian rock in our area has been eroded away.

## Mount Whyte and Naiset formations
*Middle Cambrian (515–525 Ma), up to 200 m*

The Mt. Whyte overlies the Gog Group. Not very thick, the Mt. Whyte is nonetheless quite varied: green shale, thin-bedded limestone with ooids and oncoids (ooids discussed on page 75; oncoids in this item), limy siltstone and the odd thin sandstone layer. There are stromatolites in the Mt. Whyte, their first appearance in our area since the Neoproterozoic. Why were they back? After 75 million years of cold, deep, muddy conditions in the sea, the water in the region became clear enough, shallow enough and warm enough for their builders to survive. The climate warmed worldwide in the Middle Cambrian.

"Mt. Whyte" is one of the peaks above Lake Louise. The formation is thickest around Sunwapta Pass (140 m). At Kicking Horse Pass the Mt. Whyte is only 43 m thick; south of Mt. Assiniboine it is not exposed, except in the Middle Cambrian patches mentioned in the previous item; there, it is called the Gordon Formation. The unit goes shaly north of the Columbia Icefield, where it is equivalent to the lower part of the Snake Indian Formation, next item. Under the foothills and prairies the rock is mostly red-and-green shale, siltstone and sandstone.

After the Gog Group lost some layers to erosion, the sea moved back in and deposited the Mt. Whyte. The water was shallow, and the shore was not far away to the northeast. Flattened balls of limestone the size of marbles were produced by calcareous algae or cyanobacteria in hollows where wave motion above could wash these **oncoids** gently back and forth.

There are trilobite fossils in the Mt. Whyte Formation. Many species have been found, but the more common ones are *Plagiura*—which fixes the age of the unit as earliest Middle Cambrian in western exposures—*Amecephalus, Onchocephalus, Wenkchemnia* and *Albertella*. This last one is found only in easterly outcrops, and it shows that the formation is millions of years younger there. Thus, the shoreline moved steadily inland over a long period, leaving a trail of Mt. Whyte deposits to mark its progress. Sea level was on the rise.

The Naiset Formation, up to about 200 m thick and named for a peak in the Assiniboine area, is a minor unit lying in a narrow band that runs from the south end of Banff park through the Kicking Horse Pass area. Equivalent in age to the Mt. Whyte, the Naiset is the thin-bedded siltstone and mudstone that accumulated in somewhat deeper water west of the shallow-water, limy Mt. Whyte. It seems to merge to the west with the deep-water limy shales of the Chancellor Group (page 94).

## Cathedral, Snake Indian, Chetang-Tatei and Elko formations
*Middle Cambrian (515–525 Ma), up to 350 m*

The Cathedral is composed of massive, cliff-forming buff-to-pink dolomite rock from Lake Louise south, and dolomitic limestone to the north. Individual beds can be up to 10 m thick. Usually there are two shale layers 10–20 m thick that break up what would otherwise be a single cliff. The name comes from Cathedral Mountain, a craggy peak along the TransCanada Highway just west of Kicking Horse Pass.

This is the lower slice of bread in the Middle Cambrian sandwich (page 76). The Cathedral Formation is found between Mt. Assiniboine in the south end of Banff park and the Columbia Icefield area. Most prominent in the eastern main ranges, where it forms big cliffs, the Cathedral is thick along the continental divide west of Saskatchewan Crossing in the Mt. Forbes area, and perhaps thickest in Mt. Stephen, near Kicking Horse Pass.

North of the Columbia Icefield the Cathedral becomes shaly. Rather than differentiating it from the overlying Stephen Formation and the underlying Mt. Whyte Formation, which are also shaly, the three are known from Tangle Ridge north as the Snake Indian Formation, named for Jasper park's Snake Indian River. The Snake Indian Formation carries on nearly to the Peace River.

## Dolomite

Dolomite is a mineral as well as a rock type. (Properly speaking, dolomite rock should be called **dolostone,** but few geologists use the term.) In pure form the mineral is magnesium carbonate, chemical formula $CaMg(CO_3)_2$. It forms mainly through recrystallization of calcite, the main mineral in limestone, which is calcium carbonate, chemical formula $CaCO_3$. In practice, rock termed "dolomite" can still have a lot of calcite in it.

Most dolomite is probably produced by bacteria in shallow seawater that is very low in oxygen. The bacteria take in some magnesium from the seawater as a nutrient. The magnesium tends to be excreted as dolomite.

Dolomite can occur nearly anywhere in rock that was once limestone, from tiny crystals or small infillings of joints and cracks to entire formations that are solidly dolomite. Sometimes the mineral is in thin, wavy sheets that follow bedding planes.

*Eldon Formation dolomite in a road-cut near Saskatchewan Crossing*

Sometimes it follows the burrows of marine worms, preserving them as a network called **dolomite mottling,** which is very common in the Palliser and Eldon formations. Sometimes there will be alternating layers of limestone and dolomite, such as those in the Lynx Group. Sometimes dolomite occurs in blobby masses that cut randomly across the bedding. These blobs may be fist-sized to mountain-sized; the Cathedral and Eldon formations are well known for them.

In the Canadian Rockies it is usually easy to tell dolomite from limestone because dolomite typically weathers buff or pink, often apricot-colored, while limestone weathers gray. The next time you see a gray cliff with a big pinkish or buff spot on it, you may be looking at a dolomite patch. Limestone protected under overhangs also weathers light buff and looks rather like dolomite.

To differentiate limestone from dolomite confidently, you need hydrochloric acid, diluted to 7–10 percent in water. A drop of this acid bubbles and fizzes actively on limestone as it releases carbon dioxide from the rock, but it reacts only a little on dolomite—until you scratch the acid-bathed surface, at which point the scraped-off bits will fizz noticeably.

In the Mt. Robson area the Snake Indian is thicker and limier; it has been known for many years there as the Chetang-Tatei ("tat-EH-ee") Formation, which also may include the Stephen Formation. "Chetang" and "Tatei" are peaks near Mt. Robson. In the patch of Middle Cambrian rock north of Waterton and Glacier parks the Cathedral equivalent is the Elko Formation, named for the little settlement of Elko along Highway 3 west of Crowsnest Pass.

West of the continental divide, in the western main ranges, the whole Middle Cambrian sandwich (Cathedral, Stephen and Eldon formations) abruptly changes to shale, as detailed beginning on page 93.

East of the Rockies the Cathedral exists under the prairies. From Prince George south the ocean moved inland in a great bay that reached nearly to central Saskatchewan; the area it invaded is delineated by Middle Cambrian units such as the Cathedral. This invasion left the Rockies region well out to sea, although the ocean was shallow and the Cathedral was laid down in water less than 100 m deep, sometimes only a metre or two deep. The water was clear, favoring an increase in cyanobacterial growth and other organic activity. Slow subsidence resulted in a thick accumulation of lime mud, which hardened to limestone. Much of the rock changed later to dolomite (see boxed item on dolomite, facing page). In the Columbia Icefield area the formation is beautifully banded and blotched with dolomite, apricot-on-gray; the locals call it "tiger rock." Collecting it is illegal, as is all rock collecting in the national parks.

Although limy parts of the Cathedral and its equivalents are mottled with intersecting worm burrows, true fossils are found only in the two shale beds. Look for *Albertella* in the Ross Lake Member (lower of the two shales, named for Ross Lake near Lake Louise) and *Glossopleura* and *Zacanthoides* in the upper shale. The Snake Indian Formation is shalier throughout and trilobites are common in it, except in the Mt. Robson area. When looking for trilobites keep in mind that they are seldom found whole. One usually finds a hash of spines, heads, tails and other parts.

## Stephen Formation and the Burgess Shale
*Middle Cambrian (515–525 Ma), 20–150 m*

Mostly green shale, often appearing olive-drab or leathery brown at a distance. It is limy, with minor thin limestone/dolomite beds that contain ooids or oncoids (page 77) and limestone-pebble conglomerate.

Like the other Middle Cambrian formations, the Stephen shale runs east under the prairies as a thin tongue; to the west it merges with the limy shales of the middle Chancellor Group. Because it is shale, the Stephen provides evidence of deepening water caused by shifting of the ocean shoreline eastward. Wave action caused erosion as the shore advanced, and the finer eroded particles were carried out to sea by currents, accumulating as the shale layer.

The Stephen dips out of sight south of Mt. Assiniboine. North of the Brazeau River the formation loses its identity and is included in the Snake Indian Formation, page 77, which can be traced to the Peace River.

The Stephen shale is **recessive,** meaning that it weathers back into ledges. It is the filling in the Middle Cambrian sandwich (Cathedral-Stephen-Eldon), often covered with debris from the Eldon cliffs above. For this reason the Stephen is seldom well-displayed except at high elevations in the faces of peaks in the main ranges, where it is adorned with brilliant green and yellow lichens. A road-cut exposes the Stephen Formation, with some of the underlying Cathedral and overlying Eldon formations, along the TransCanada Highway between Lake Louise and Field. Watch for olive-drab Stephen shale at the first highway bridge west of Wapta Lake in Kicking Horse Pass.

The Stephen Formation is named for Mt. Stephen, which hulks over the little community of Field in Yoho park. "Stephen Formation" may not ring a bell with many park visitors, but a particular part of the Stephen Formation does: the Burgess Shale. See the next page.

## Eldon Formation
*Middle Cambrian (515–525 Ma), 300–500 m*

Massive dark-gray limestone mottled with burrows, or white/bluish dolomite. Fresh surfaces look very much like the Cathedral Formation (page 77), although in weathered surfaces the

# Creatures of the Burgess Shale

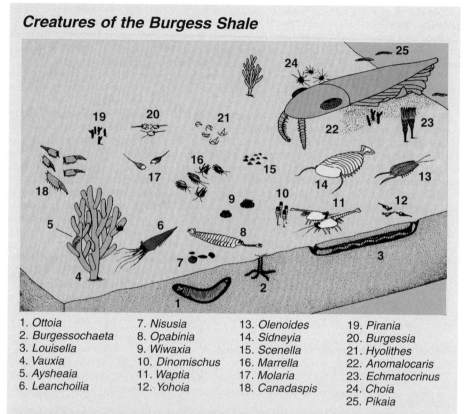

| | | | |
|---|---|---|---|
| 1. *Ottoia* | 7. *Nisusia* | 13. *Olenoides* | 19. *Pirania* |
| 2. *Burgessochaeta* | 8. *Opabinia* | 14. *Sidneyia* | 20. *Burgessia* |
| 3. *Louisella* | 9. *Wiwaxia* | 15. *Scenella* | 21. *Hyolithes* |
| 4. *Vauxia* | 10. *Dinomischus* | 16. *Marrella* | 22. *Anomalocaris* |
| 5. *Aysheaia* | 11. *Waptia* | 17. *Molaria* | 23. *Echmatocrinus* |
| 6. *Leanchoilia* | 12. *Yohoia* | 18. *Canadaspis* | 24. *Choia* |
| | | | 25. *Pikaia* |

In 1886 a railway surveyor/engineer named Otto Klotz discovered some excellent trilobite fossils on Mt. Stephen. Charles Walcott, a paleontologist with the Smithsonian Institution of Washington, D.C. (and later its director), learned of Klotz's find and arrived at the locality in 1909, as part of a general study of Cambrian rock Walcott was engaged in. While collecting in the area, he discovered fossils of many creatures new to science high on a ridge connecting Mt. Burgess and Wapta Peak. This was a sensational find, and Walcott returned to his Burgess Shale fossil quarry each summer for many years. The Burgess Shale now ranks as one of the more important fossil localities in the world. In 1980 it was declared a World Heritage Site.

The fossil beds are in Yoho National Park, and collecting by the public is not allowed. However, you can visit Walcott's quarry in the company of a park-licenced guide. For more information about these tours, for which a fee is charged, call Yoho park at 250-343-6324. Some of the fossils are on display at the park information centre beside the TransCanada Highway at the turnoff for the town of Field.

The Geological Survey of Canada has produced a beautifully illustrated, inexpensive non-technical publication called *Fossils of the Burgess Shale: a National Treasure in Yoho National Park, British Columbia,* by S. Conway Morris and H. Whittington, two scientists who have worked for many years on the fossils. The renowned Harvard paleontologist and evolutionary theorist Stephen Jay Gould has made the Burgess Shale the centrepiece of a brilliant, very readable book about the nature of scientific enquiry entitled *Wonderful Life.* See "Further reading," page 202.

The illustration above (colors for effect only) was adapted from *Fossils of the Burgess Shale,* Geological Survey of Canada, 1985.

Cathedral shows wavy orange banding, while the Eldon tends to weather uniformly very light gray. Eldon is a rail siding near Banff.

Like the Cathedral, the Eldon Formation is common throughout the eastern main ranges from Mt. Assiniboine north. But while the Cathedral goes to shale in the Columbia Icefield area, the Eldon remains a carbonate rock (limestone/dolomite) all the way north to the Jackpine River in Willmore Wilderness Park.

In the western main ranges the Eldon is replaced by its shale counterpart, the middle part of the Chancellor Group, page 94. South of Mt. Assiniboine it goes under cover of younger layers; it may pop up again as the Windsor Mountain Formation north of Waterton park.

Thickest around Lake Louise, Eldon rock tends to form the upper parts of high peaks such as Mt. Victoria. East of there, it is thick even at the mountain front (240 m), and that is perhaps the best place to look at it. The TransCanada Highway punches through a glacially smoothed Eldon outcrop exactly at the mountain front west of Calgary. The west-facing slabs are so white that from a distance they look snowy in midsummer. Great cliffs of Eldon limestone rear up on either side of the Bow River here; the impressive one facing the highway to the north is Yamnuska Mountain (see photo on page 196), a favorite among rock-climbers.

The same situation occurs at Windy Point on Highway 11 west of Nordegg, where the Eldon marks the mountain front and is quite pale. But if an Eldon road-cut is fresh, or if chunks have fallen off recently, note how dark the unweathered rock is: practically black from embedded organic material. It closely resembles the Palliser Formation, page 113, in both weathered and fresh exposures, as I learned the hard way by confusing the two on a university field project. But the Palliser has fossils in it, while the Eldon has very few (trilobites have been reported from a particularly dark-colored unit in it).

In some main-range locations the unit is pale from patchy dolomitization. A quarried outcrop beside the road near the entrance to Waterfowl Lakes Campground along the Icefields Parkway is in gray-weathering massive black limestone; a kilometre north the same unit is dolomitic and cliffs above the highway have weathered brownish and loose. Frequently just the intersecting worm burrows of this formation will be dolomitized. They erode more slowly than the limestone around them and stand out beautifully on weathered surfaces.

Eldon limestone often forms the summits of the bigger peaks along the continental divide in Banff National Park. Here it often appears quite dark. Although it stands in great cliffs, the rock is surprisingly rotten. The dolomite patches look solid but aren't, and pieces are likely to fall off—as I discovered to my horror halfway up Hungabee Mountain above Lake O'Hara. A block of dolomite came loose while I was hanging onto it, unroped, just above a steep ice slope that would have led, after an unstoppable slide of 200 m, over a cliff about twice that high. Thanks to a lucky jump sideways onto firmer ground, I lived to learn my lesson: stay roped-up on dolomite. In the front ranges the Eldon is limestone, much more solid.

## The carbonate platform and its sedimentary cycles

In the stack of formations that span the Middle Cambrian to Late Ordovician periods in the central Canadian Rockies, the rock types keep repeating. This is not a case of thrust-faulting, as described on page 28. In the stack I'm talking about, a shale formation is overlain by a limestone/dolomite formation, then by more shale, then by limestone/dolomite again, shale again and so on, for a total of seven sedimentary cycles. The layers are not only repetitive, they were all laid down in water less than 50 m deep. And the limestone beds are complicated, full of strange textures that are difficult to explain. How has this rock been formed?

The answer lies in the shallowness of the seabed during that 80-million-year interval, and in events along the edge of the continental shelf, where the rock of the Canadian Rockies was formed.

The western continental shelf of North America was wide, reaching as far inland as what is now eastern Saskatchewan, and the sea that covered it was shallow. There, living things deposited limestone that built up practically to sea level. This **carbonate platform** reached at least as far south as Nevada, where there is a region of similar sediments in the Basin and

Range geological province, and north through the Arctic. At this time North America was oriented sideways, with the Pacific coast facing north, so the continental edge ran east-west, with the sea to the north. For simplicity, though, let's think of it in its present, north/south orientation.

On the platform, the water was only a few metres deep in many places, even though the shore was hundreds of kilometres away. Such regions are very sensitive to changes in water depth, tidal effects and currents. These conditions exist in and around modern-day reefs, producing fascinating rock. And that is how the limestone-shale-limestone cycles in the Cambrian and Ordovician strata of the Canadian Rockies developed. When the water depth was stable, abundant sea life would produce a layer of limestone. It would thicken quickly, reaching nearly to the surface and spreading over vast areas of the continental shelf. The water was so shallow that the larger waves would be damped and thus kept from reaching the coast.

Then a slight but rapid increase in water depth—meaning an increase that limestone deposition could not keep up with—would disrupt things. Given deeper water, large waves would roll eastward over the edge of the platform and on across the limy flats beyond. They would reach the coast, battering the shoreline and causing rapid erosion along it. The rise in sea level would have sent the shoreline advancing inland, further aiding erosion.

Return currents moving along the bottom, especially strong during storms, would carry eroded material (mostly fine mud) over the limestone flats and the reef, smothering the sensitive organisms living there. Limestone deposition would slow considerably, and a layer of shale—the fine material—would be laid down.

Later, when sea level stopped rising, erosion along the shore would taper off, clear-water conditions would return, and the lime-producing organisms would establish themselves again, completing the cycle.

What caused the jumps in sea level? This is still unknown, but it may relate to the motions of the world's crustal plates. At that time the Rockies area was on the trailing edge of a continent moving eastward, relative to today's directions—on a **passive margin,** to use the technical term. In such situations bits and pieces of the passive margin break off and are left behind. The passive margin heats up in the breaking-off process, rising somewhat, and cools down later, becoming denser and subsiding farther into the mantle.

The swelling and shrinking of the mid-oceanic ridges as they discharged new material from the mantle could also have affected the level of the sea in the Cambrian. Cyclic worldwide cooling and warming could have lowered and raised sea level as the earth's ice caps built up or melted, just as has occurred more recently in the Pleistocene Epoch. Maybe a combination of these processes was at work.

The name "Kicking Horse Rim" has been applied to the edge of the platform in the main ranges of the Canadian Rockies. Until the early 1990s, geologists had thought that the Kicking Horse Rim was fixed, and that it had stood as a steep-sided reef overlooking deeper water to the west for many millions of years. But new evidence shows that the Kicking Horse Rim was not as stable as had been believed. The steep edge of the carbonate platform was not an organically-built reef so much as an underwater landslide scarp along which the edge broke away. It broke away repeatedly, just as happens commonly at the edges of modern reefs in places such as the west coast of Florida. Large pieces at the edge of the carbonate platform would go sliding down a gentle but very slippery incline toward the ocean floor. Such slides may have been creeping, snail's-pace affairs, or they might have been catastrophic, all-at-once landslides. The sliding chunks could have been measured in square kilometres, although most seem to have been smaller.

Between slides, reef-building organisms would have been hard at work producing limestone and extending the edge outward into deeper water, creating a true reef-front. Some of these reef-fronts can be seen in places where the edge had not broken off for a long time. But in most places, eventually another slide would carry the reef-builders and their hard-earned limestone away into the depths.

This had been going on farther north in the Canadian Rockies somewhat earlier in the Cambrian, and perhaps even in the late Proterozoic. See the items on the Atan Group, page 75, and the Byng Formation, page 67. The underlying cause of the Atan slides seems to have been the same as the cause for the Kicking Horse Rim slides: rifting of the passive margin of the continent. The rock of the Rockies records that process, and it shows how far east rifting spread until it stopped. In addition to the Middle Cambrian formations discussed so far, all the rock units described from here to page 98 were involved in the story.

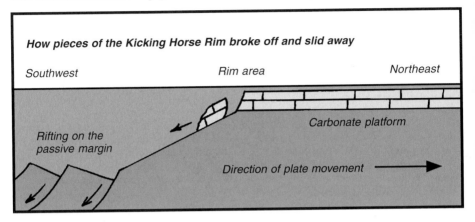

**How pieces of the Kicking Horse Rim broke off and slid away**

*Southwest*     *Rim area*     *Northeast*

*Rifting on the passive margin*

*Carbonate platform*

*Direction of plate movement* ⟶

## Pika Formation
*Middle Cambrian (515–525 Ma), 90–275 m*

Dark-weathering brown limestone and dolomite, mostly thinner-bedded than the underlying Eldon Formation and shalier, with worm burrows and fossils (the Eldon is mostly barren). The rock is moderately resistant to erosion but is not the outstanding cliff-former the Eldon is. There is a recessive zone at the base, which helps to separate Pika beds from the underlying massive Eldon. Named for Pika ("PIE-kuh") Peak, east of Lake Louise.

The Pika thickens southwestward. It is thinnest at the mountain front and thickest around Kicking Horse Pass. West of there the formation loses its identity as it merges with rock of the middle Chancellor Group, page 94. South of Mt. Assiniboine it is covered by younger rock. North of Jasper the Pika becomes shaly, resembling the overlying Arctomys Formation, described next; the two can be traced as a single unit as far as the Jackpine River in central Willmore park.

A good place to see the Pika up close is in outcrops of glacially smoothed rock 100 m west of the parking lots at the Columbia Icefield visitor centre along the Icefields Parkway. Here the white-veined Pika lies beside red and green bands of Arctomys shale. There is a road-cut through the Pika just west of extensive Eldon outcrops at the mountain front along the TransCanada Highway, and another in a similar geological setting at Windy Point on Highway 11, 55 km east of Saskatchewan Crossing. Fossils: the trilobites *Modocia, Marjumia* and *Glyphaspis*.

## Arctomys Formation
*Middle Cambrian (515–525 Ma), 30–340 m*

Red and green shales, interbedded with orange or buff dolomitic siltstone. The Arctomys, properly pronounced "ARK-toe-miss," is a formation to know in the Rockies; it is found throughout the front ranges and eastern main ranges between the Bow River and the Peace River, readily identifiable as a colorful unit between the sombre gray and brown formations above and below. Even though Arctomys shale is soft and thus recessive, you can still see the formation above treeline as a deep-red, orange or yellowish stripe in the mountainside.

Named for Arctomys Peak, west of Saskatchewan Crossing, the unit is thinnest at the mountain front and thickest west of Jasper in the Mt. Robson area. It shows very well as a buff layer in the face of Mt. Robson, as seen from Highway 16 (photo on page 198). In the western main ranges the Arctomys merges with shales of the upper Chancellor Group, page 94, but in the eastern main ranges and front ranges it can be followed to at least the Jackpine River.

Not only is the Arctomys colorful; it is interesting for its salt-crystal casts. These casts are up to 3 cm across, although usually less than a centimetre wide, and often hopper-like, weathering as boxes-within-boxes. This shows that the water here was not only very shallow, as verified by ripple marks and mud cracks; it was drying up. Don't expect to find fossils in the Arctomys; they are extremely rare (just a few lingulid brachiopods).

*Casts of large salt crystals in Arctomys shale*

## Waterfowl Formation
*Middle Cambrian (515–525 Ma), 12–200 m*

Mostly buff-weathering dolomite at the mountain front, where the formation is thinnest. Thickens westward in the main ranges, where it is usually gray limestone, often with wavy or mottled bedding between thin yellow or white dolomite bands.

There are thick Waterfowl sections around Glacier Lake west of Saskatchewan Crossing and above Kicking Horse Pass. West of the continental divide, the shaly time-equivalent is part of the upper Chancellor Group. The Waterfowl runs south to Mt. Assiniboine; north of Jasper it merges with the Lynx Group, page 87.

The Waterfowl Lakes themselves lie along the Icefields Parkway south of Saskatchewan Crossing. The formation can be seen high on the eastern valley slope there, but handier exposures are available farther south, only a few minutes' walk above the Bow Valley Parkway 2 km west of its junction with the TransCanada Highway west of Banff. The section here runs from the Eldon Formation on the east to the Survey Peak Formation on the west, before hitting the sub-Devonian unconformity, page 98, and Cairn Formation beds above—an excellent stop for geological field trips.

The Waterfowl is a limestone-student's formation, full of varied strata: massive ones, in which the bedding was destroyed by burrowing organisms when the sediment was still soft; crinkly layers and stromatolites from cyanobacterial growth (see page 58), ooids (page 75) and dolomite mottling in the form of buff squiggles against featureless massive limestone—all quite interesting to examine layer by layer. North of the Athabasca River there are also sandstone beds with limestone pebbles in them. Missing in the Waterfowl: fossils. None has been found.

## Sullivan Formation
*Late Cambrian (505–515 Ma), 12–200 m*

Mostly soft olive-drab shale with occasional thin limestone and siltstone beds. The Sullivan is thin at the mountain front and nearly always covered by soil or talus, but thicker to the west, especially between Saskatchewan Crossing and Sunwapta Pass, where it is well exposed at higher elevations. Named for Sullivan Peak, west of Saskatchewan Crossing. Distribution: from near Mt. Assiniboine to southern Jasper park, north of which it becomes limy and loses its identity in the Lynx Group. It is present (but thin) at Maligne Lake.

Sullivan shale occurs in a road-cut 1 km west of Windy Point along Highway 11 near the mountain front. In the main ranges you can see the upper part in the slope behind the Columbia Icefield visitor centre. The formation outcrops along the Icefields Parkway some 15 km farther north, in low hills beside the highway.

Among the shale beds of the Sullivan are layers of gray limestone containing bits and pieces of trilobites, including *Cedaria*, a marker fossil that places the Sullivan Formation at the beginning of the Late Cambrian. Other common trilobites are *Coosella, Cedarina,* and a small, eyeless trilobite called *Kormagnostus*. It looks the same at both ends.

## Lyell/Ottertail Formation
*Late Cambrian (505–515 Ma), 100–600 m*

Banded limestone and dolomite, commonly gray at a distance, with dull yellow or buff stripes. Up close many of the gray beds are seen to be silty or sandy limestone, with shallow-water features such as cyanobacterial structures. The buff beds are dolomitic. "Lyell" is from Mt. Lyell (properly "LIE-ull," but mispronounced "Lie-ELL" in Canada), near Glacier Lake in the north end of Banff park. Under that name it is found in the eastern main ranges and front ranges from White Man Mountain in the south end of Banff park to Tangle Ridge in the Columbia Icefield area. To the north it becomes an anonymous part of the Lynx Group, page 87, but westward it continues as the Ottertail Formation in the western main ranges and runs south through Yoho and Kootenay parks.

The Lyell and Ottertail are the odd layers out in the Middle Cambrian to Ordovician carbonate sequence hereabouts. All the others are limestone/dolomite east of the continental divide and shale to the west except these, which are carbonate throughout. The Ottertail lies between the Chancellor and McKay shales, page 95, keeping its identity all the way to the Rocky Mountain Trench.

The Lyell is banded buff and gray from dolomitization of alternating layers. In the lower part the beds contain ooids, page 75. In the middle part the bedding is much thinner

*"Zebra rock": interbedded gray limestone and pale dolomite of the Lyell Formation*

*The Rockwall at Floe Lake, in Kootenay National Park, a 600-m cliff of Ottertail limestone*

and so is the banding. This is the weak part of an otherwise erosion-resistant formation; in the main ranges the Lyell produces two very steep cliffs—often vertical or overhanging—with a slope in between that marks the weaker middle section. In the slopes of Wilcox Peak across from the Athabasca Glacier, these middle-section beds are buff dolomite and gray limestone only a few centimetres thick. The pieces lying about look as if a zebra had shattered. This is one of the better places to look at the Lyell Formation; just wander up the slope between the Icefield Centre and Icefield Campground. But don't collect; it is illegal in the parks. Lyell rock is found right beside the Icefields Parkway about 2 km north of the Columbia Icefield visitor centre, at the north end of the gravel flats where the road climbs up a hill.

"Ottertail" is from the Ottertail River in Yoho park. The Ottertail limestone is similar to the Lyell in both age and rock type, but separated geographically from the Lyell and up to 600 m thick, compared to a maximum of 345 m for the Lyell. The two units were studied independently and at time of writing still maintain separate names, even though they are really the same formation.

Ottertail rock appears just north of the Blaeberry River, north of Golden, and it runs south into western Yoho park, through the twin peaks of Mt. Goodsir—although the enormous faces of the Goodsirs are made of McKay shale, not Ottertail limestone—and then into Kootenay park, where the unit forms the spectacular Rockwall. South of the Vermilion River the Ottertail dips out of sight, having formed a seldom-broken 53-km cliff that is the epitome of what geologists call structural control: a landscape dominated by the underlying geology.

The Lyell/Ottertail represents a time when the seabed west of the Kicking Horse Rim, normally deeper than the rim, had collected so much shale that the water was shallow. This encouraged rim-dwelling organisms to advance westward, laying down telltale limestone as they went.

Few fossils appear in Lyell/Ottertail rock, although the trilobite *Crepicephalus* appears at the base of the Lyell and *Elvinia* can be found at the top, placing the Lyell/Ottertail in the middle of the Late Cambrian.

## Bison Creek Formation

*Late Cambrian (505–515 Ma), 10–210 m*

Interbedded limestone and shale, reminiscent of the Sullivan Formation, page 106, but less easily eroded. Bison Creek is a small stream on the south side of Mt. Murchison, which is the big peak beside (east of) the Icefields Parkway just south of Saskatchewan Crossing. But the best place to see this unit at a distance is in Mt. Wilson, the mountain just north of the crossing. The Bison Creek and all the other Late Cambrian and Ordovician formations are beautifully exposed there, right up to the sub-Devonian unconformity, page 98, when viewed from the Icefields Parkway near the Mistaya Canyon. See the photo on page 197.

Like the underlying Lyell Formation, the Bison Creek falls mostly within Banff and Yoho parks. Followed west, it goes to shale in the western main ranges, where rock of that age is part of the McKay Group, page 95. To the north and to the east it blends into the limestone/dolomite Lynx Group, next page.

Bison Creek rock is recessive and seldom well exposed right beside a highway, but you can see it beside the Icefields Parkway a few kilometres north of the Columbia Icefield visitor centre, from Tangle Falls north to the bottom of the long highway grade.

*Nodular limestone of the Bison Creek Formation*

The more resistant beds are full of **thrombolites:** gray, rough-weathering blobs averaging a metre tall and perhaps half as wide. "Thrombo-," meaning "clot," is a perfect description. Like stromatolites, page 58, thrombolites are cyanobacterial mounds; they simply lack the curved laminations found in stromatolites.

Limestone Bison Creek strata are rich in fossils, mostly broken-up trilobites of the genera *Elvinia* and *Ptychaspis.* **Cystoids,** which were members of the crinoid (sea-lily) branch of the echinoderm phylum, had appeared on the scene by then, and some Bison Creek beds are loaded with snowflake-shaped pieces from the platy columns and cup-shaped body cavities of these animals. The Banff Formation, page 115, and Rundle Group, page 116, are the only other crinoid-rich units in our area, and they are much younger (Early Carboniferous).

## Mistaya Formation
*Late Cambrian (505–515 Ma), 45–160 m*

Massive limestone beds, often a metre thick or more and weathering pale gray. Mistaya rock looks obviously different from the underlying thinner-bedded Lyell and Bison Creek formations (see previous items). Named for the Mistaya River, which parallels the Icefields Parkway from Mistaya Lake to Saskatchewan Crossing.

This resistant limestone stands out between the shaly formations above and below. Often it forms a cliff. The formation is entirely a shallow-water deposit, and it contains the biggest Cambrian stromatolites in our area: they are frequently 1.5 m tall, found side-by-side in the massive limestone layers. Above the Mistaya, stromatolites are less common. (For more on stromatolites, turn to page 58.)

The Mistaya Formation follows the same geographic distribution as the underlying Bison Creek beds, previous item. It is well-exposed in a gully cutting through the cliffs of Mt. Murchison, south of Saskatchewan Crossing. This is where it was originally studied. Tangle Falls, found along the Icefields Parkway north of the Columbia Icefield visitor centre, flows over the Mistaya Formation, and the double-sided road-cut just uphill passes through the unit.

Fossils: the trilobites *Saukia, Dikelocephalus* and *Briscoia,* dating the formation as latest Late Cambrian.

## Lynx Group
*Late Cambrian (505–515 Ma), up to 1060 m*

Interbedded gray limestone and dolomite, often silty or sandy, with wavy cyanobacterial laminations. Weathers in gray and buff bands. Resistant, forming ledgy cliffs.

*Gray limestone and buff dolomite of the Lynx Group, seen near Mt. Oliver in Jasper National Park. Note how the limestone beds, which are more soluble in water than the dolomite beds, are more deeply weathered. Parks Canada photo.*

The Lynx Group is simply the Waterfowl, Sullivan, Lyell, Bison Creek and Mistaya formations all lumped into one unit. Reason: traced east from the main ranges, the Sullivan and Bison Creek shales change to limestone/dolomite. This makes it impractical to separate them from the other formations, which are themselves limestones and dolomites. So where this happens the whole works is called Lynx Group. The formations the Lynx Group replaces lie mostly in Banff and Yoho national parks; the Lynx Group surrounds this area, except on the west side, where rock of that age is shaly (except for the Lyell/Ottertail, page 84). "Lynx" is from Lynx Mountain, a peak near Mt. Robson.

The Lynx Group has turned up in other places in the Canadian Rockies. To the north it can be traced to Pine Pass. To the south it has been found as far as the Ghost River east of Banff. There are no Lynx exposures along the TransCanada Highway or the Icefields Parkway; the handiest outcrop is at Cold Sulphur Spring, 20 km east of Jasper along Highway 16. The first break in the cliff east of the spring occurs in Lynx rock. See page 99 for a description of the sub-Devonian unconformity at this site.

Fossils have not been found in the Lynx, although the formation has many irregular beds attributed to cyanobacteria.

## Survey Peak Formation

*Late Cambrian and Early Ordovician (490–506 Ma), 345–400 m*

Mostly gray-green shale, but in three distinct parts: silty at the base, shaly higher, then limy in the top third. There are limestone flat-pebble conglomerates and thrombolites throughout. Not resistant to erosion except at the top, but thick and thus well-exposed at higher elevations. Named for Survey Peak, west of Saskatchewan Crossing near Glacier Lake.

The Survey Peak Formation is easy to recognize at a distance by the putty-like color of the shale in it. Geologists refer to the "putty shales" of the Survey Peak. Survey Peak itself, the rounded mountain west of the Icefields Parkway just north of Saskatchewan Crossing, gives a good distant impression of the color. Access to exposed Survey Peak beds usually requires a trip well above treeline; perhaps the shortest approach (one-half hour) is via the Wilcox Pass Trail, which begins at the turnoff for Wilcox Campground, near the Columbia Icefield visitor centre.

This unit has by far the widest distribution of any Ordovician or Silurian formation in the Rockies; Survey Peak rock can be found under one name or another from just north of Fernie to the north end of the Rockies, and from the front ranges to the Rocky Mountain Trench.

North of Sunwapta Falls the Survey Peak is sometimes identified by an older name: Chushina Formation, which also includes the northern equivalent of the Outram Formation, next item. Between Pine Pass and the Alaska Highway the rock becomes limy again and is placed in the Kechika Group, page 96. On the western slope the unit makes up part of the McKay Group shales, page 95.

The Survey Peak contains lots of trilobite parts, including species that peg its age as Early Ordovician in its middle and upper layers.

## Outram Formation

*Early Ordovician (472–490 Ma), 170–440 m*

Peculiar nodular, cherty limestone beds and brown shale with limestone nodules that have chert blobs in their centres. (See page 119 for more on chert.) Good exposures are banded sombre brown and dark gray. "Outram" is from Mt. Outram, a prominent peak west of Saskatchewan Crossing that many people mistake for Mt. Forbes; Forbes is higher but is mostly hidden behind Outram. Sir James Outram was a Scottish climber who made the first ascent of Mt. Assiniboine; he pronounced his name "OOT-rum," and so should we.

The Outram limestone tends to form the upper part of a rotten cliff, the lower part of which is the limestone of the upper Survey Peak Formation. Not widespread, the formation is most prominent in the eastern main ranges from Copper Mountain northwest of Banff to Tangle Ridge along the Icefields Parkway just north of the Columbia Icefield area. North of there Outram-type rock is included in the Survey Peak Formation, previous item; to the west it merges with the McKay Group and the Glenogle Shales. To the east, the Outram interfingers with the Skoki and Owen Creek formations. It was also being laid down at the same time as the Tipperary Quartzite farther south. So the relationship of the Outram to neighboring rock units is complex.

Outram rock also includes lacy black silica (microcrystalline quartz) in the limestone beds. The silica weathers away more slowly than the limestone and so stands out in bold relief. Trilobites and other fossils are present, but they tend to be in very small pieces.

The Outram Formation is visible in the cliffs of Mt. Wilson above Saskatchewan Crossing. The formation outcrops in gullies on the southeastern slope of the mountain, about two hours' walk from the road. Perhaps the best exposure near a highway is in Wilcox Pass, in the southern end of Jasper National Park.

## Monkman Quartzite and Tipperary Quartzite
*Early Ordovician (469–472 Ma), 0–300 m*

The Monkman and Tipperary quartzites resemble the other quartzite units in our area: the Gog Group, Flathead Formation and Mt. Wilson Quartzite. They are all hardened, cross-bedded sandstone in shades of white, gray or buff, sometimes yellowish or pink. They weather buff, orange or pink.

"Monkman" is from the Monkman Pass area northeast of Prince George; "Tipperary" is from Tipperary Lake, near the head of the Palliser River just west of Kananaskis Lakes. Both formations grade into shale to the west and thin out to the east against the sub-Devonian unconformity, page 98.

Monkman rock is found in the eastern main ranges from Kakwa Lake, just northwest of Willmore Wilderness Provincial Park, to the Peace River. The most accessible outcrops are right in Pine Pass, in cliffs below the highway. Tipperary rock is harder to get to. Outcrops at the western end of Spray Lake, west of Canmore, can be approached via the rough Calgary Power road on the northwest shore of the lake.

One might think that these two patches of Early Ordovician quartzite (Monkman and Tipperary), so similar in rock type and age, had been deposited as part of a larger sheet of sand. But such is not the case; each thins out toward the other, and the intervening space is occupied by the Skoki Formation, next item, so the Monkman and Tipperary units were never connected. They look so much alike that they may have had the same source: possibly ancient Mesoproterozoic sandstone uplifted on the Canadian shield to the northeast and eroding into the sea at both places. Alternatively, could uplifted Gog Group sandstone have been the source? This is unlikely: Gog-derived sand would have had to come from the west or south, where the sea lay.

No fossils have been found in Tipperary or Monkman rock, which is typical of quartzite, but the underlying and overlying beds contain fossils that date both units as Early Ordovician.

## Skoki Formation
*Early and Middle Ordovician (462–472 Ma), up to 230 m*

Light-gray dolomite, medium-bedded to massive, weathering buff to yellowish or pale orange, with one excellent identifier: a single bed filled with large fossil snails (*Palliseria* and *Maclurites*) near the top of the formation. Oncoids, page 77, are also common in the upper layers.

"Skoki" (pronounced "SKO-key," like the name of the Chicago suburb) is from Skoki Mountain, in the front ranges east of Lake Louise. Skoki dolomite is found in the eastern main ranges and western front ranges from the northern Rockies south to about Mt. Peck along the Elk River north of Fernie. The formation is thickest around Mt. Sir Douglas in the Kananaskis area, and is also thick near the Peace River.

This formation relates to its neighbors in complex ways. Skoki beds interfinger here and there with Outram limestone, and to the west the Skoki merges with the Glenogle Shales. The Skoki Formation appears to overlie an eroded surface (a disconformity, page 98) on the Tipperary Quartzite in some places and to grade into the Tipperary in others. Skoki rock feathers into the Monkman Quartzite to the north. The eastern edge of the Skoki is the sub-Devonian unconformity, page 98. Is that all clear, students? It will be on the final exam …

Getting your hands on good Skoki outcrops isn't easy, despite the wide distribution. The best exposures are probably at Skoki Mountain and nearby Fossil Mountain, a hike of 20 km from Lake Louise. Skoki dolomite runs through Mt. Wilson, quite high up on the huge west face above the Icefields Parkway at Saskatchewan Crossing, but it gets closer to the highway as you drive north. Just south of Cirrus Mountain Campground, which is found a few kilometres south of the viewpoint at the Weeping Wall, the formation crosses the road and outcrops are fairly close by on the east side. Walking up from Wilcox Campground to Wilcox Pass will take you to Skoki outcrops there; the cairn at the summit of the pass is right on the formation. A slab covered with its characteristic snails lies nearby. Like other fossils in the national parks, these are protected from collectors.

Soon after the Skoki was deposited, some parts of it were raised above sea level and caves formed in it. The passages were later filled with sand, which has hardened to veins of white quartzite. West of Saskatchewan Crossing near the Lyell and Mons glaciers, the filled passages are up to 10 m wide, although most passages are much smaller. Smaller cave remnants can also be seen in Wilcox Pass.

## Owen Creek Formation
*Middle Ordovician (458–462 Ma), 45–190 m*

Mostly gray- or buff-weathering dolomite, darker than the underlying Skoki, with reddish or greenish shale in the lower part and sandstone in the upper part. Most easily identified by its position under the distinctive pale cliffs of the Mt. Wilson Quartzite, next item. Owen Creek is the first major drainage east of Mt. Wilson.

This formation occurs in two patches in the eastern main ranges and front ranges. The northern one runs from about Poboktan Creek (Sunwapta Warden Station on the Icefields Parkway) to just north of Kicking Horse Pass. The southern patch is small and narrow, a band running along the continental divide from Spray Lake west of Canmore to the upper reaches of the White River some 60 km farther south. A stiff climb up Mt. Wilson gets you to the type section, but you can see this rock more easily north of Mt. Wilson, where the Icefields Parkway runs steadily up through the Ordovician section. Owen Creek strata can be seen at a distance under the Mt. Wilson Quartzite on Mt. Wilson, and up close in Wilcox Pass, a scenic alpine area in southern Jasper National Park. The formation also outcrops in the hillside south of Cirrus Mountain Campground, along with the Skoki and Mt. Wilson formations.

The Owen Creek is not fossiliferous. Westward, it merges with the Glenogle Shales, page 96.

## Mount Wilson Quartzite
*Middle or Late Ordovician (447–450 Ma), up to 450 m*

White quartzite, weathering gray on gentle surfaces and yellowish on steep or overhanging surfaces, sometimes dazzlingly white, with dark stains where water runs down. Named for Mt. Wilson, where it forms a spectacular yellowish cliff on the skyline above Saskatchewan Crossing.

Note that the name is Mt. Wilson *Quartzite*, not Mt. Wilson *Formation*. And it's formally spelled *Mount* Wilson. To use the rock type in the formation name is British geologic practice, favored by some North American geologists. Other Canadian Rockies formations named in the British style include the Monkman Quartzite, the Tipperary Quartzite and the Glenogle Shales.

The Mt. Wilson Quartzite occurs in two separate patches in our area. They were originally connected, but mild uplift not long after deposition allowed erosion to remove most of the formation. Only the two isolated patches remain.

The northern patch is centred at Mt. Wilson, where it is 167 m thick. It is found north from there in the eastern main ranges and western front ranges to about Tangle Ridge, and south nearly to Hector Lake. Outcrops close to the highway are in the hillside one-half kilometre south of Cirrus Mountain Campground, along the Icefields Parkway 25 km north of Saskatchewan Crossing. Another good place to see the formation is in southern Jasper National Park, where it occurs with the other hard-to-get-to Ordovician units in Wilcox Pass, a trail approach from Wilcox Campground.

*The Mt. Wilson Quartzite (big pale cliff) on Mt. Wilson*

The other portion of this formation runs through the western ranges from Golden south to Radium Hot Springs, then into the western main ranges to a point south of Top of the World Provincial Park. From there the unit hooks back north in the eastern main ranges to Mt. Sir Douglas. It crosses Highway 93 about 2 km east of the aquacourt at Radium Hot Springs, where the canyon is narrow.

It took 30 years for geologists to realize that the quartzite at Mt. Wilson and the quartzite near Radium were the same formation. Charles Walcott had described the Radium beds in 1924 and named them "Wonah Formation." Even though he had named the Mt. Wilson Quartzite a year earlier, he didn't realize that the Wonah was actually the Mt. Wilson. This was an easy mistake to make: until the Lyell/Ottertail equivalence was worked out, no other Cambrian or Ordovician formation in this part of the Rockies was known to go all the way across from the front ranges to the western ranges. So it seemed unlikely to him that the two quartzites were the same, even though they looked similar. F.K. North and G.G. Henderson corrected the mistake in 1954, using "Mt. Wilson" for both.

This is the purest sandstone in our area, 99 percent quartz grains in most outcrops. At Moberly Peak, near Golden, it is mined for making high-quality glass and sold to golf courses desiring the very whitest sand traps. Sandstone this quartz-rich is so rare that one wonders what the source of the Mt. Wilson was. It could have been derived from eroding Mesoproterozoic sandstone on the Canadian Shield to the northeast, just as the Gog may have been derived a hundred million years earlier (see page 72).

This big pulse of sand covered the continental-shelf carbonate platform, page 81, and spread westward beyond it, over a part of the seabed that had accumulated nothing but shale, with the exception of the Ottertail limestone, since at least the beginning of the Middle Cambrian. The sand layer also marks the end of the Cambrian and Ordovician limestone/shale cycles found in the rock of the carbonate platform. The Mt. Wilson is the last sandstone in our area to get its material from the northeast, off the main part of the continent. Younger ones received theirs from the west, during the mountain-building phase of western Canada's geological history.

## Beaverfoot Formation
*Late Ordovician and Early Silurian (432–446 Ma), up to 540 m*

Pale-brown-weathering dolomite and limestone in medium and thick beds, resistant and cliff-forming. Named for the Beaverfoot Range, which forms the east wall of the Rocky Mountain Trench for a 50-km stretch south of Golden.

There was patchy uplift and erosion after the Mt. Wilson Quartzite (previous item) was laid down. When the sea covered the region again after a million years or so, Beaverfoot beds were deposited on rock that had been worn down to Late Cambrian layers in some places and not worn down at all—left below sea level, in other words—elsewhere.

The current distribution of the Beaverfoot Formation roughly follows the two-part arrangement of the Mt. Wilson, reaching the Peace River in the northern segment and Top of the World park in the southern segment. But that isn't the original extent of the formation. The sea covered most of western Canada during Beaverfoot time; patches of the formation can be found under various names farther north, through the Mackenzie Mountains to the Arctic Islands and as far east as Hudson Bay. It is a remarkably widespread unit.

Silicified fossils are common in the lower part of the Beaverfoot dolomite, and the limestone layers can be richly fossiliferous. Look in the lower part of the formation for some interesting things: the giant sponge *Aulacera* (tree-trunk-like fossils up to 20 cm in diameter), the warty-looking trilobite *Encrinurus,* the corals *Bighornia* and *Paleofavosites,* the brachiopods *Dinorthis* and *Rhynchotrema,* echinoderms, cephalopods, snails—a paleontological smorgasbord that shows the great variety of life that had evolved by this time.

Beaverfoot rock caps the great cliffs of Mt. Wilson seen above Saskatchewan Crossing, and it comes close to the Icefields Parkway in the hillside just south of Cirrus Mountain Campground. The easiest approach is along Highway 93 east of Radium Hot Springs, where the Beaverfoot Formation, stained red by iron oxide, forms a cliff beside the road just east of the hot pool.

### Nonda Formation
*Early Silurian (432–440 Ma), 210–305 m*

Mostly dark-gray cherty dolomite, weathering buff, with sandstone at the base and the earliest appearance in the Canadian Rockies of stromatoporoids, page 103, which became common in the Devonian Period.

The Nonda is found from about halfway between Pine Pass and the Peace River north to at least the Liard River. It outcrops at Summit Lake along the Alaska Highway. The highway crosses it again farther west, along the Toad River, and also at the south end of Muncho Lake.

Nonda rock is sparsely fossiliferous and rather uninteresting-looking, but in some places it rests above the greatest unconformity (not counting Pleistocene or Holocene deposits) exposed in the Canadian Rockies: below is the Chischa Formation, page 60, a Mesoproterozoic unit probably laid down around 1400 Ma. So the gap in the record here spans a billion years. In other places the Nonda lies above the Kechika group, page 96.

Another interesting thing about the Nonda dolomite is that it merges rather abruptly with the Road River shale to the west, like the change-over from limestone to shale in the main ranges of the central Rockies. The top of the Nonda is the sub-Devonian unconformity, page 98.

### Tegart Formation
*Early Silurian (430–432 Ma), up to 75 m*

Dark-gray and brownish shaly limestone, thin-bedded but without much texture in the beds. This is a deep-water formation. It is named for Mt. Tegart, which borders the Rocky Mountain Trench east of Windermere Lake.

The Tegart is thin and the area covered is small: Radium to Top of the World Provincial Park. There are no easily identifiable outcrops along roads; you have to hike up Windermere Creek to Pedley Pass to see it. But this is the only strictly Silurian rock in the southern part of the Canadian Rockies, so for some geologists it's worth the hike. Above the Tegart lies the sub-Devonian unconformity, discussed on page 98. Fossils in the Tegart are mostly graptolites and trilobites.

## *The shale belt*

While organisms were busily producing limestone during the Cambrian, Ordovician and Silurian periods on the shallower portion of the continental shelf, deeper water next door to the west was collecting mud that hardened and compacted to shale. This is the shale belt of the Canadian Rockies, found west of the continental divide in the western main ranges. The formations there are the same age as the neighboring limestones and dolomites of the eastern main ranges—just a different **facies,** meaning a different rock type. The shale facies is also much thicker.

The transition from limestone/dolomite to shale is abrupt. A good place to see this is on the TransCanada Highway in Yoho National Park. From the park information centre at the turnoff for Field, look past the townsite across the river. The big peak on the left is Mt. Stephen. The mountain on the right is Mt. Dennis. The rock in Mt. Stephen is mostly limestone and dolomite of the eastern main ranges, but the rock in Mt. Dennis is shale of the western main ranges. Try following individual beds from Mt. Stephen across to Mt. Dennis; they lose their identity in the shale.

If you have struggled through the description of the welter of Cambrian to Silurian formations discussed thus far, you may be pleased to hear that their shale-belt equivalents can be handled by only three names for the central and southern Rockies: Chancellor, McKay and Glenogle. For the northern Rockies there are only two: Kechika and Road River. Together, these units represent the mud that accumulated in the deeper-water area off the carbonate platform of the continental shelf, page 81. They either abut or tongue into the whole packet of limestones and dolomites in the eastern main ranges, from the Mt. Whyte Formation all the way up through the Cambrian and Ordovician to the Owen Creek Formation. The Ottertail Formation, page 84, is exceptional; it is a thick Late Cambrian limestone that lies between two of the shales, the McKay and the Glenogle.

The shale belt begins near Fernie, widens east of Golden, then angles out into the Rocky Mountain Trench where it is lost from sight under the Purcell thrust sheet. The belt picks up again farther north at Pine Pass, in the form of the Kechika Group and the overlying Road River Group. The shale belt existed into the mid-Devonian and longer in the northern Rockies, if you count the overlying Besa River Formation, which continued to collect shale through the Early Carboniferous.

*Mt. Stephen, as seen from the TransCanada Highway at Field, marks the edge of the eastern main ranges. If you follow the light-colored limestone and dolomite layers to the right (west), they change to dark-colored shale of the western main ranges.*

## Chancellor Group
*Middle and Late Cambrian (508–520 Ma), 2500–3000 m*

A thick sequence of brown or gray shale/slate and thin shaly limestone found west of the continental divide in the western main ranges between Fernie and the Peace River. The Chancellor is the western equivalent of the Mt. Whyte, Cathedral, Stephen, Eldon, Pika, Arctomys, Waterfowl and Sullivan formations, as described previously. The name comes from Chancellor Peak in southern Yoho park.

The Chancellor accumulated as fine mud on the continental slope, in water more than 200 m deep next to the edge of the carbonate platform. Occasionally pieces of the edge would break away and slide down the slope, leaving fragments behind that were then covered with mud. The "pieces" we're talking about could have been tens of kilometres in length and width, so the "fragments" found in the Chancellor slate are large: up to 60 m across. Geologists expect to find much bigger chunks. See page 83 for a diagram.

The break-offs may have been slow-moving events, with the pieces creeping slowly along the incline, but another form of slide movement was faster: underwater mudflows carried fine-grained material off the rim and out into the deep-water basin. Such flows are called turbidity currents (see page 82 for details); in the Chancellor they are responsible for great thicknesses of alternating shale and shaly limestone beds that can be called turbidites.

There are three units in the Chancellor. The lower part—1000 m of shaly limestone/dolomite, no fossils—is equivalent to the interval on the carbonate platform from the Mt. Whyte Formation to the Pika Formation. The middle part (600 m, shaly low and limy higher), matches up with the Arctomys and Waterfowl formations, and the upper part (1000–1400 m of greenish shale with a few *Cedaria* trilobites) corresponds only to the Sullivan Formation. Picking out the three units takes some experience, because Chancellor rock looks much the same—monotonous—to the untrained eye. Most of the shale in it has been converted to slate or silvery phyllite through heat and pressure.

Thick and wildly contorted from folding, this great wad of mildly metamorphic rock is on display for 15 km along the TransCanada Highway west of Field. It is also exposed in road-cuts west of Marble Canyon on Highway 93 to Radium. Structural geologists have worked hard to understand this tortured strata. Go and see for yourself; any road-cut demonstrates what pressure will do to material that we ordinarily think of as rigid. Some of the outcrops show that the sediment slumped into chaotic masses while it was still soft, long before folding distorted it further during the building of the Rockies.

The Chancellor Group forms dark-colored, irregularly shaped mountains that are not as high as peaks just to the east, where the tougher limestone equivalents mark the Kicking Horse Rim. But the group is often cliffy nonetheless.

Atop the Chancellor Group lies the Ottertail Formation, a limestone unit that is described on page 84, with the other carbonate-shelf formations.

*Kinked beds of Chancellor Group rock along the TransCanada Highway west of Field. Dark bands are limestone; light bands are shale.*

## McKay Group
*Late Cambrian and Early Ordovician (490–509 Ma), 400 m to approximately 2100 m*

Mostly calcareous shale and limestone, with a gray-green shale reminiscent of the Survey Peak Formation, page 88, and cherty beds like those of the Outram Formation, page 88, appearing near the top. "McKay" (long "a,") is from John McKay Creek, water supply for the town of Radium Hot Springs.

The TransCanada Highway runs through good McKay exposures in the canyon of the Kicking Horse River. Look for the shale along the 15-km stretch east from Golden. Like the other western-slope shales, this one is smashed up beyond belief; from the highway you can see a couple of contorted limestone beds in the slaty-looking shale that show just how deformed the unit is. For this reason, no one has ever been able to measure the thickness of the McKay Group precisely.

The beds are not very fossiliferous, either, but they do contain graptolites (page 97), trilobites and brachiopods that date the McKay as Late Cambrian and Early Ordovician, making it the deep-water, shaly equivalent of the shallow-water Bison Creek, Mistaya, Survey Peak and lower Outram formations of the eastern main ranges. To the west, in the area covered by the McKay Group, the water was deeper and bottom-dwelling life sparser. Still, there are limestone beds in the McKay, particularly evident near the head of Kicking Horse Canyon.

## Glenogle Shales
*Early and Middle Ordovician (452–490 Ma), 140–700 m*

Mostly black or dark-gray shale with lots of graptolite fossils and thin limestone layers. The upper quarter is silty, sandy and dolomitic shale, fossil-poor, weathering brownish. The whole formation is soft, eroding back into slopes.

This formation name uses the rock type rather than "Formation," so it is properly Glenogle *Shales,* not Glenogle *Formation.*

The Glenogle is the third division in the great stack of beaten-up shale and slate that makes up the western ranges of the central Canadian Rockies. A deep-water deposit, it is the western equivalent of several formations found in the eastern main ranges: upper Outram, Tipperary, Skoki, and Owen Creek. The Glenogle is topped off by the sands of the Mt. Wilson Quartzite.

Almost everywhere you find the McKay shale, previous item, you will find Glenogle rock overlying it. But the two rock units are so tightly folded and intricately thrust-faulted that it can be hard to tell which is which when looking at a particular bed. Color is a helpful criterion: Glenogle shale is always darker than that of the McKay Group, and never greenish.

Both units are well exposed in road-cuts along the TransCanada Highway east of Golden, in the eastern 10 km of Kicking Horse Canyon. "Glenogle" comes from Glenogle Creek, near the head of the canyon.

*A good exposure of the Glenogle Shales along the TransCanada Highway in Kicking Horse Canyon, 10 km east of Golden*

## Kechika Group
*Late Cambrian and Early Ordovician (472–508 Ma), about 1800 m*

A northern-Rockies unit named for the Kechika River, merging southward with the Survey Peak Formation, page 88, of the central Rockies but somewhat younger at the top. The Kechika also includes rock of the same age as the upper part of the Lynx Group, page 87. The formation is limy in the east and shaly in the west, like the Middle and Late Cambrian and Ordovician formations to the south. It lies on an erosion surface atop uplifted and bevelled Atan Group beds, page 75, so it shows that the ocean moved back into the north end of the Rockies area after mid-Cambrian uplift pushed it away for a while.

Renewed uplift and tilting of the eastern Rockies area in the Middle Ordovician caused another retreat, which lasted until the sea returned in the early Silurian. The intervening period of erosion bevelled off the tilt, so the Kechika underlies the next unit, the Nonda Formation, page 93, at an angle. There are particles of volcanic rock in the Kechika south of Tuchodi Lakes, which shows that the area probably lay close to the western continental edge at this time, for volcanism is common along the boundaries of crustal plates. Dykes of diabase, page 68, cut through the Kechika south of Redfern Lake.

The Alaska Highway just touches a large area of Kechika rock in the Terminal Range, west of the road when it turns north to Muncho Lake after Kilometre 710.

## Road River Group

*Early Ordovician to Middle Devonian (381–472 Ma), probably about 10 km*

A very thick unit of dark shale, not well known, with limestone, dolomite, chert and some volcanic material in the lower half. Found mostly in the Cariboo, Omineca and Cassiar mountains west of the Rockies, but in the Rockies proper it can be seen from about halfway along the northern arm of Williston Lake to the Liard River and beyond. It's the shale-belt equivalent of the Skoki, Beaverfoot, Nonda, Muncho-McConnell, Wokkpash and lower Stone formations. The Road River is recessive and usually heavily vegetated, with no highway access in the Rockies; however, west of the Rockies the northernmost 60 km of Highway 37 is continuously in shale-belt rock, including that of the Road River Group.

## *Graptolites*

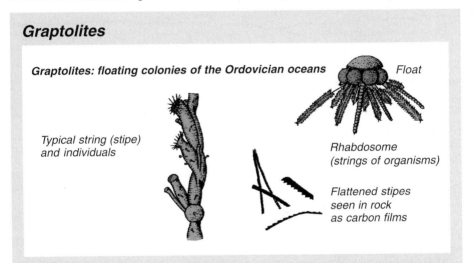

*Graptolites: floating colonies of the Ordovician oceans*      Float

*Typical string (stipe) and individuals*

*Rhabdosome (strings of organisms)*

*Flattened stipes seen in rock as carbon films*

The Glenogle Shale is loaded with graptolites: peculiar fossils that are common in Ordovician and Silurian black shales but scarce at other times and in other rock types (range: Cambrian to Mississippian). The only living things resembling graptolites are the pterobranchs, a class of the phylum Protochordata, whose members have a primitive notochord and thus may bridge the evolutionary gap between the chordates and the invertebrates.

Under a magnifying glass, graptolite fossils look like little pieces of hacksaw blades. They are the flattened, broken remains of linear colonies, preserved as films of carbon. The teeth of the hacksaw blade are the individual cups of the organisms. Each cup was made of chitin: the material of which the exoskeletons of modern insects and crustaceans are made. A colony member beat the water around it with a couple of fleshy plumes that it used to snag microscopic swimmers, which it would then draw toward its mouth as the corals do. When something wanted to eat *it,* a graptolite could pull itself inside the cup and hide.

Entire colonies are seldom found, but occasional whole specimens demonstrate that hundreds of these little animals were attached in strings to gas-filled floats of the kind that jellyfish use. The colonies drifted about the sea, well offshore; hence their preservation in black shale, a deep-water rock type.

Graptolites spread rapidly around the world and evolved quickly. This makes them good index fossils, because each species spans only a short period of time, meaning a couple of million years to a geologist, and is often found worldwide.

# *Something turned up missing*
The sub-Devonian unconformity, and what came after

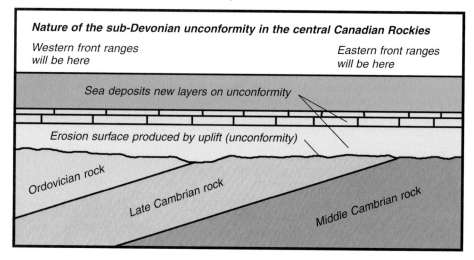

**Nature of the sub-Devonian unconformity in the central Canadian Rockies**

Western front ranges will be here

Eastern front ranges will be here

Sea deposits new layers on unconformity

Erosion surface produced by uplift (unconformity)

Ordovician rock

Late Cambrian rock

Middle Cambrian rock

In the eastern front ranges of the central Rockies, Devonian rock rests on Middle Cambrian rock. There is a gap in the geological record here of about 150 million years. The layers that should have been laid down during that time are missing.

Such gaps are called **unconformities** (see the boxed item on the opposite page for more information on conformities), and this one is well known to Rockies geologists, who call it the "sub-Devonian unconformity" because it always lies under Devonian strata.

Gaps of 150 million years are not common in the Canadian Rockies, but the peculiar thing is that some 20–30 km west of the mountain front the Devonian beds rest on Ordovician rock, which means that the gap is 60 Ma *less* than at the mountain front. Farther west the Devonian formations rest on Silurian beds, closing the gap even more, to about 50 Ma.

The illustration above displays the situation: the older units underlie the Devonian layers at a slight angle.

Here is how this came to be. For a very long time the Canadian Rockies region had been underwater collecting sediments, except for occasional short-lived emergences in some places, since the Early Cambrian. But at about 425 Ma, in the middle of the Silurian Period, sea level dropped significantly, exposing the whole region to erosion. Most of the Silurian sediments were washed back into the sea.

In the Early Devonian, at about 390 Ma, the sea began making its way back, advancing from the north and leaving sediments in the northern Rockies to mark its path.

Meanwhile, two regions of western Canada were experiencing uplift. One of these highlands lay west of the Rockies area and is known as the Purcell Landmass. The other lay east of the Rockies area and is known as the West Alberta Ridge, with a bulge at its northern end called the Peace River Arch. The West Alberta Ridge connected at its south end with Montania, a large highland area running farther south, into the United States.

The nature of the Purcell Landmass is not well understood. It was probably a lot of sediments washed off the continent and deposited out at the edge of the continental plate, now raised up enough to become a large island or group of islands. Later on the area underwent severe deformation and dislocation during mountain-building, which has obscured the evidence. But the West Alberta Ridge and the Peace River Arch lay farther east, beyond the later disturbance, and their history is clear.

The ridge and the arch rose perhaps a thousand metres above sea level, forming a long peninsula jutting north from Montania. (The term "arch" refers to a gentle bend in the layers running across it.) As this peninsula rose it was attacked by the sea, of course, and the sea eventually won, abetted by some subsidence of the land.

When the sea marches inland it knocks down everything in its path, battering down the headlands with waves and carrying the debris offshore with currents. This is a slow process, but what the ocean has accomplished over the course of geologic time is startling. Grinding away the low hills of the West Alberta Ridge took only a few million years. The Peace River Arch, though, the northern end of the ridge, resisted the waves longer, remaining an island until about 370 Ma.

Eventually everything was eroded board-flat and covered with a shallow sea in which the famous Late Devonian reefs of western Canada grew, as discussed on page 103.

Consider those slightly bowed formations dipping gently off either side of the West Alberta Ridge. Consider the western side, where the central and southern Canadian Rockies are now. Everything was planed at a low angle by the advancing sea; first the younger layers, then older and older ones as the waves chewed their way eastward into the ridge. Once underwater, the flat erosion surface was blanketed with Devonian sediments, producing the configuration seen today.

A terrific place to see the sub-Devonian unconformity is at Cold Sulphur Spring, 20 km east of Jasper along Highway 16. Walk east from the spring along the base of the glacially-

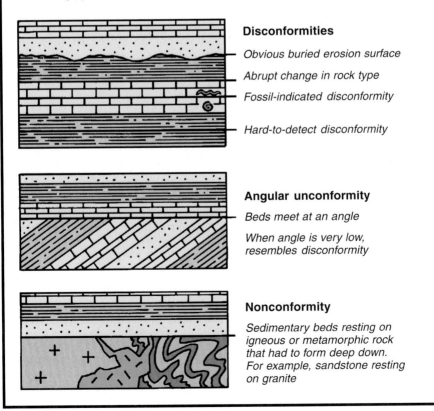

## Types of unconformities found in the Canadian Rockies

*An unconformity is almost always a buried erosion surface, where deposition was followed by uplift and then by renewed deposition. There is a gap in the rock record.*

**Disconformities**

*Obvious buried erosion surface*

*Abrupt change in rock type*

*Fossil-indicated disconformity*

*Hard-to-detect disconformity*

**Angular unconformity**

*Beds meet at an angle*

*When angle is very low, resembles disconformity*

**Nonconformity**

*Sedimentary beds resting on igneous or metamorphic rock that had to form deep down. For example, sandstone resting on granite*

smoothed cliff, which at this point is in steeply dipping Flume Formation dolomite bearing scattered white *Amphipora* stromatoporoids, brachiopods and other fossils. You cross the unconformity at the spot where the fossils end. A thin zone rich in gold-colored pyrite marks the base of the rock deposited on the erosion surface. Below the pyrite zone the rock looks fairly similar, but close inspection shows that it is fossil-free dolomite of the Late Cambrian Lynx Group (page 87).

## Muncho-McConnell Formation
*Latest Silurian or Early Devonian (401–414 Ma), up to 565 m*

Light gray fine-grained dolomite, with some shaly and sandy beds. Fairly resistant; weathers into cliffy slopes. This, with its shaly western equivalent the Road River Group (page 97), is the oldest Devonian rock in the Canadian Rockies. The unit occurs from the north end of the Rockies to about 25 km south of the Peace River. It is named partly for Muncho Lake, where there are good exposures along the Alaska Highway a kilometre from the south end; other outcrops occur near Summit Lake. The Alaska Highway crosses it a few kilometres east of the lake and again a few kilometres farther west.

The area covered by the Muncho-McConnell lay north of the West Alberta Ridge and just to the northwest of the Peace River Arch. Following the Late Silurian emergence of the whole Canadian Rockies region, the northern section was again covered by the sea, so sediments built up here while they were still eroding farther south. Farther north the water was deeper. This has led geologists to think of the area as a **platform:** a region of shallow seawater next to a region of deeper water, rather like the carbonate platform described in the preceding section, page 81.

The shoreline here was not far to the south, and occasionally mild uplift would push the sea northward, out of the area, and some erosion would occur. Then slight subsidence would allow the sea back in, and with it would come more sediment. So in the northern Rockies there are several minor Early Devonian unconformities instead of the single, major sub-Devonian unconformity that one finds in the central Rockies.

The Muncho-McConnell is not very fossiliferous, but the bluish phosphatic plates of Early Devonian fish have been found in it, as has the brachiopod *Kirkidium*, a Late Silurian fossil.

## Wokkpash Formation
*Early Devonian (about 401–405 Ma), 50 m*

Yellowish sandstone and dolomite, with **anhydrite,** a sulphur-rich mineral ($CaSO_4$) similar to gypsum but lacking gypsum's water content. Anhydrite and gypsum are both **evaporites:** minerals produced when seawater evaporates. So the Wokkpash anhydrite indicates that the sea was drying up in the northern Rockies area.

The Wokkpash is thin and rather easily eroded, with a disconformity at the top. The formation occurs along the mountain front and through the main ranges from the north end of the Rockies to about the Halfway River; south of there it is included in the Stone Formation, next item. You can see Wokkpash rock with the other Early Devonian units of the northern Rockies around Summit Lake on the Alaska Highway. "Wokkpash" is from Wokkpash Creek, the second big valley southwest of Summit Lake. No fossils are known from the formation.

## Stone Formation
*Early Devonian (387–394 Ma), up to 590 m*

Banded gray dolomite, resistant and cliff-forming. Contains **barite** ($BaSO_4$), a heavy mineral left occasionally by evaporation of seawater. South of Pine Pass a sandstone layer at the base of the Stone marks an unconformity atop Ordovician rock. To the west, Stone dolomite merges with the shale-belt rock of the Road River Group.

The Stone Formation runs from north of the Rockies to Monkman Pass. The middle slopes of Mt. St. Paul, the peak just north of Summit Lake along the Alaska Highway, display the formation well. The name comes from Stone Mountain, a peak 15 km north of Summit Lake. The formation name has an amusing aspect: the stone of the Stone Formation is named for

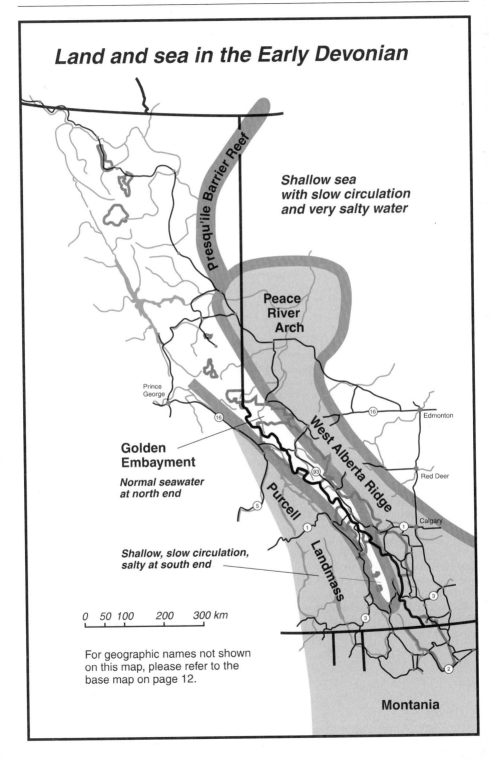

# Land and sea in the Early Devonian

*Shallow sea with slow circulation and very salty water*

Presqu'ile Barrier Reef

Peace River Arch

West Alberta Ridge

Prince George

Edmonton

Red Deer

## Golden Embayment

*Normal seawater at north end*

Purcell Landmass

Calgary

*Shallow, slow circulation, salty at south end*

0    50  100        200        300 km

For geographic names not shown on this map, please refer to the base map on page 12.

**Montania**

Stone Mountain, which is not named for its stone but rather for a biologist named Stone, for whom Stone's sheep, page 657, is also named.

Stone Formation stone contains the coral *Roemeripora spelaeana.* It also contains **conodonts,** tiny fossils that are the remains of tooth-like chewing structures in marine worms.

## Dunedin Formation and other rock of the Golden Embayment
*Middle Devonian (378–385 Ma), up to 300 m*

The Dunedin ("Dun-EE-den") is the most widespread of the Middle Devonian formations in the Rockies. There is a disconformity at its base. Dunedin rock is pale sandstone and siltstone in its lower quarter, and largely yellowish-gray limestone higher up that is fairly resistant to erosion and forms cliffs. The name comes from a river in the northern Rockies.

Like the underlying Early Devonian formations, the Dunedin extends north beyond the Canadian Rockies. It thins southeasterly to an erosional edge at Mt. Buchanan in Willmore park. The formation outcrops along the Alaska Highway near Summit Lake; accessible exposures are 5–6 km west of the lake, just west of the point at which MacDonald Creek intersects the road. Fossils to look for: stringocephalid brachiopods, abundant in some beds.

In Dunedin time, a long barrier reef ran northeast from the Peace River Arch. Called the Presqu'ile ("Press-KEEL") Barrier Reef, this feature prevented ocean currents from circulating freely across it. The water between the reef and the shore became very salty, leaving evaporite deposits—mostly salt and gypsum—under northern and eastern Alberta. Dunedin-type sediments were deposited on the northwestern, seaward side of this barrier reef, and in a bay reaching south through what is now the central Rockies between the West Alberta Ridge to the east and the Purcell Landmass to the west (see map on previous page). This long arm of the sea was called the Golden Embayment, named for the town of Golden, B.C. Erosion has since removed much of the rock deposited in the Golden Embayment, but near the south end of the bay the Harrogate Formation remains, looking very Dunedin-like. You see it in the western main ranges between Golden and Fernie; it is named for a small community in the Rocky Mountain Trench.

South of Radium one finds the Cedared ("See-der-RED") Formation, comprising shallow-water, light-gray or brown sandy dolomite and limestone that help to delimit the southern end of the Golden Embayment. On the other side of the Rockies the similar Yahatinda ("Yah-ha-TIN-duh") Formation, marks the eastern shore, while a very sandy deposit marks the western shore: the Mount Forster Formation, named for a peak on the west side of the Rocky Mountain Trench. Although probably part of the same deposit, the Cedared and Yahatinda segments occur on opposite sides of the Rockies, were studied independently and have kept different names. "Cedared" is from Cedared Creek, on the eastern side of the Rocky Mountain Trench south of Golden. There are good exposures in the ridge behind Fairmont Hot Springs, where you can also see the Harrogate and Mt. Forster formations. "Yahatinda" is from the Yahatinda Ranch, along the eastern mountain front north of the TransCanada Highway; Yahatinda rock can be viewed above Canmore under the hydroelectric penstocks (large pipes) accessible from the Spray Lakes Road.

The Cedared grades into a bed of gypsum known as the Burnais Formation, named for Burnais Creek near Windermere—a good place to see the unit. It shows that the sea was very shallow here and cut off at times from the rest of the ocean, so that evaporation concentrated the minerals in the seawater enough to cause gypsum to crystallize on the seabed.

Harrogate fossils include conodonts, corals and the brachiopod *Desquamatia;* the Cedared holds fish fragments, as does the Yahatinda, which also includes fossil marine plants. No fossils have been reported from the Burnais.

# *Devonian reefs*
## Riches in the rock of the Fairholme Group

Gentle uplift of western Canada occurred near the end of the Middle Devonian. This exposed the seabed for two or three million years and caused a widespread unconformity between Devonian layers called the Watt Mountain Break. This should not be confused with the sub-Devonian unconformity, page 98, which underlies all the Devonian rock in the Canadian Rockies. After the Watt Mountain Break the shoreline marched southward and the sea returned to the central and southern regions.

By this time the West Alberta Ridge was almost gone, leaving only the Peace River Arch—a northern remnant of the ridge—as an island east of the region where the Rockies would one day rise. The Purcell Landmass persisted to the west, although it, too, suffered some erosion.

In the northern Rockies the water deepened quickly and stayed deep, as shown by the great thickness of shale that accumulated there: the Besa River Formation. But farther south the water was shallower, as indicated by the limestone of the Fairholme Group.

Western Canada was in the tropics back then. The climate was warm, the water was clear, and the sunlit seabed was swarming with life. These conditions produced biological reefs: buildups for which the organisms themselves were responsible. The rock therein has kept Alberta geologists busy for several generations. Their labors have made some of them rich, because they have found a lot of oil and gas in those reefs.

From the Berland River in Willmore Wilderness Park, where the northernmost of the major reefs grew, south to Crowsnest Pass, the Late Devonian outcrops of the Rockies have become world-famous among geologists as places to study the reef rock, collectively called the Fairholme Group. The name comes from the Fairholme Range, part of the front ranges east of Banff.

Formation details begin on page 106, but here is an outline to help make sense of some complicated stratigraphy.

In the beginning, these were not coral reefs. In the Devonian Period the main reef-builders were stromatoporoids (see boxed item below).

## *Stromatoporoids*

Pronounce it "strome-uh-TOP-or-roids" or "strome-at-oh-PORE-oids," as you prefer. Hollywood should make a film called *Attack of the Stromatoporoids*. These things were bizarre, they took over everything, and then they died in a cataclysm.

It has taken many years to figure out exactly what the stromatoporoids were. Nature had a fondness for turning them into dolomite, which destroyed the fine detail; what remains is fist-sized gray blobs with hollow centres. Lucky fossil finds have enabled paleontologists to learn that the blobs were, in fact, colonies of sponges. They often grew in limy crusts and layers, thus the "stromato-" (scientific Greek for "bed," or anything spread out) and "-poroid" ("with pores").

*Gray stromatoporoids in black dolomite of the Cairn Formation*

There were tough, encrusting stromatoporoids that preferred the zesty ocean side of a reef; blobby-looking stromatoporoids that liked the side away from the big waves, and fragile, spaghetti-like stromatoporoids that sheltered in the protected central lagoon.

# Life and death of a typical Devonian reef

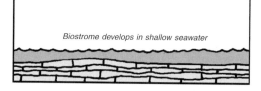

Biostrome develops in shallow seawater

1. A continuous limestone reef (Flume Fm. biostrome) is built by stromatoporoid sponges in warm, shallow, clear seawater.

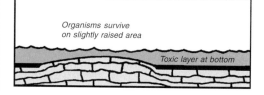

Organisms survive on slightly raised area

Toxic layer at bottom

2. An influx of mud (shale of Perdrix Fm.) and toxic water along the bottom kills most stromatoporoids, but some survive at slightly higher spots on the seabed.

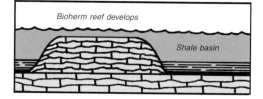

Bioherm reef develops

Shale basin

3. Deepening water forces the organisms to grow upward rapidly, producing a mound-like reef (Cairn Fm. bioherm). Fine mud accumulates slowly in the shale basin around the reef (shale of upper Perdrix Fm.).

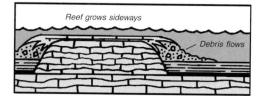

Reef grows sideways

Debris flows

4. Material slides down the reef slopes, into the shale basin. The reef grows sideways over the debris (limestone of lower Southesk Fm.).

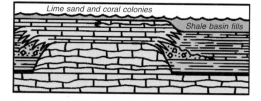

Lime sand and coral colonies

Shale basin fills

5. An influx of limy mud (Mt. Hawk Fm.) fills the shale basin. Stromatoporoids are replaced by corals and lime sand (upper Southesk Fm.). Clearing water allows stromatoporoids to start again (Simla Fm. biostrome).

Ronde Fm.    Simla Fm.    Sassenach Fm.
Southesk Fm.
Mt. Hawk Fm.
Cairn Fm.
Perdrix Fm.
Flume Fm.

6. However, a mass extinction event wipes out most reef life. Another influx of muddy water arrives (silt of Sassenach Fm.), covering the reeftops.

*Many thanks to Helmut Geldsetzer and Eric Mountjoy for help in producing this diagram*

Here is how the reefs got started, lived and died.

As usual in the tropics, cyanobacteria and calcareous algae were living in the sunlit water and, as they died, producing a goodly supply of lime crystals that settled on the seabed as soft, oozy lime mud. The tide moved in and out, channelling the mud with currents, carving into it here, piling it up there, and it was on the piles that the reefs began to grow. First a few brachiopods and calcareous algae would set up shop, then some stromatoporoids and corals would move in with the brachiopods, then some bryozoans would move in with the corals, then the clams would arrive, and the crinoids and the fish and ... you know how it is. Another unspoiled spot discovered by the masses—especially by the stromatoporoids, which comprised about 90 percent of reef life in the Devonian.

Sea levels fluctuated, but the water was never very deep at this time—often just a few metres under the tides—so the reefs had little space in which to grow upward. They spread *outward* instead, and pretty soon the seabed was virtually covered with intergrown reefs, home to innumerable creatures all eating one another, dying and leaving their hard parts to be incorporated into the reef/debris layer. That layer was a **biostrome,** the technical term for such a widespread accumulation, now called the Flume Formation in the central Rockies, the Hollebeke Formation in a geographically separated exposure in the southern Rockies, and the Starbird Formation along the Rocky Mountain Trench.

After a few million years this lively scene was threatened. Sea level rose enough (or the continental shelf sank enough) to bring oxygen-poor water into the area from the west, where rock of that age—black shale—shows the water to have been low in oxygen and probably poisonous with dissolved hydrogen sulphide gas. This water moved along the bottom, creating a zone so hostile that few organisms could live in it. An alternative explanation is that lime mud carrying fine silt and clay particles (Maligne and lower Perdrix formations) spread thinly across the seabed from the north and east. Either way, most stromatoporoids of the Flume/Hollebeke/Starbird biostrome would have been killed, because stromatoporoids seem to have required clean, clear, high-oxygen water to survive.

However, some spots on the seabed were havens for bottom-dwellers. The toxic water can be thought of as a thin sheet moving along the bottom. Higher-standing spots rose out of this zone into the normal seawater above. Here the stromatoporoids survived.

The sea continued to deepen, so the reef-builders had room in which to grow upward, producing the **bioherms** (mound-like reefs) of the Cairn Formation and the lower Southesk Formation. Fine mud—the rest of the Perdrix Formation—continued to accumulate around the reef bases, but the rate of deposition was slower than the rate of subsidence, so the water between the reefs gradually deepened. The reefs grew tall, especially northern ones such as the Miette and Ancient Wall reefs in eastern Jasper park, the tops of which stood up to 150 m above the seabed. Few life forms could survive off the reefs, on the intervening muddy bottom where the water was deep, dark and unhealthy. Geologists refer to these areas as the "shale basins" between the reefs.

Jarred by earthquakes or exposed to the weather by a drop in sea level, portions of the reefs broke up and slid down into the shale basins. The upper, sunlit parts of these slides had the effect of spreading the reefs sideward, because calcareous algae could grow on them, producing the rock of the lower part of the Southesk Formation, the Peechee Member.

A further rise in sea level was accompanied by another influx of muddy water that gradually filled the basins between the reefs with limy shale and siltstone, the Mt. Hawk Formation. Only scattered brachiopods, crinoids and other creatures able to tolerate the muddy water survived; they lived on the shallowing seabed as the reefs were surrounded nearly to the top with Mt. Hawk sediments. Few stromatoporoids grew on the reefs at that time; without active reef-building to counteract erosion, waves pounded the reef-tops into sandy shoals (Arcs Member of the Southesk Formation), while the quieter water of the central lagoons held coral colonies that remain as white fossils in black limestone (Grotto Member of the Southesk Formation).

The mud influx ended with a temporary drop in sea level, exposing the reef-tops to a short period of erosion. Higher water brought in a silty limestone (Ronde Member of the Southesk formation), with no further biostrome or bioherm development south of the Ancient Wall Reef in Jasper park. North of there, however, the Ronde is replaced by a limestone that is mainly silt-free, the Simla Formation, which in places is a stromatoporoid biostrome rather like the Flume and Hollebeke formations. This might have been the beginning of a comeback by the stromatoporoids, but for them the end was near.

Something seriously disturbed the sea worldwide about 367 million years ago. Cold, low-oxygen water welled up from the depths and spread over the continental shelves. Most of the temperature-sensitive and oxygen-sensitive plankton that make up the base of the oceanic food chain were killed, and many higher organisms—about 50 percent of known species—died out as a consequence. The world's biodiversity was cut in half. Stromatoporoids ceased to be important in the fossil record, here or anywhere else.

This disaster is known as the **Late Devonian mass-extinction event.** It occurred at the boundary between the Frasnian and Fammenian divisions of the Devonian Period.

Such mass-extinction events are well-known in the fossil record; see the black triangles on the geological charts, pages 192–194. Some of these cataclysms are very impressive, such as the one in the Late Permian that wiped out 85 percent of the world's species, or the one at the Mesozoic/Cenozoic boundary that caused the extinction of the dinosaurs (except the branch that exists today as birds) and some two-thirds of other species. See page 134.

Now that the Late Cretaceous event has been linked to the impact of an object from space— an asteroid, most likely—geologists are looking for evidence of similar impacts associated with other mass extinctions. Thus far, results are inconclusive for the Late Devonian event. The cause of the deadly upwelling is still unknown.

Three hundred and sixty-seven million years later, oil trapped in a Devonian reef gushed from an exploratory well drilled through the thick accumulation of younger sediments at Leduc, Alberta, south of Edmonton. Humans suddenly took a keen interest in the spongy centres of the long-gone stromatoporoids.

Glaciers have carved cross-sections through the Late Devonian reefs at several spots in the Rockies. Each reef is a little different, but the one near Miette Hot Springs, in Jasper park, is perhaps the most-studied. Small patches of exposed reef rock can be seen beside the highway at several locations in the southern and central Rockies. See the Cairn Formation item, page 108.

## Flume, Maligne and Hollebeke/Starbird formations (lower Fairholme Group)
*Late Devonian (373–375 Ma), 30–250 m*

Massive limestone/dolomite in the lower part, often with rice-like *Amphipora* fossils and bits of brachiopods. A thin sandstone lies at the base, marking the sub-Devonian unconformity. Sand is often a near-shore deposit, laid down as the sea moves back into a region that had been above the waves and thus eroding. Higher up the rock is dolomite, with lots of chert, page 119, in irregular masses, lenses and even beds. There are blobby stromatoporoids in this layer, as well as the brachiopods *Atrypa, Allanaria, Athyris* and corals such as *Thamnopora* and *Alveolites*.

The Flume Formation is a good one to know, even though it's not very thick. The unit is a classic biostrome: a layer of limestone built by organisms. It is the base upon which the Devonian reefs grew.

In many places the Flume Formation is overlain by a shaly limestone known as the Maligne Formation (pronounced "Muh-LEEN," not "Muh-LINE"), the name coming from the Maligne River in Jasper park. The Maligne Formation marks a deepening of the sea, and the first arrival of the fine mud that may have choked much of the biostrome. "Flume" is from a creek near Roche Miette, along the Athabasca River east of Jasper.

The Flume Formation proper is found from northern Willmore park to Crowsnest Pass. Roadside outcrops occur along Highway 16 near Disaster Point in eastern Jasper park and at Cold Sulphur Spring farther west. In northern Banff park along the Icefields Parkway, cross Nigel Creek on a high bridge and pass through a two-sided road-cut; just beyond that the North Saskatchewan River has eroded a very narrow gorge in Flume dolomite under a bridge over the old road. The Flume also outcrops one kilometre south of the Weeping Wall viewpoint.

South of Crowsnest Pass, Flume-like rock is known as the Hollebeke Formation, named for Hollebeke Mountain at the head of the Carbondale River south of Crowsnest Pass. The

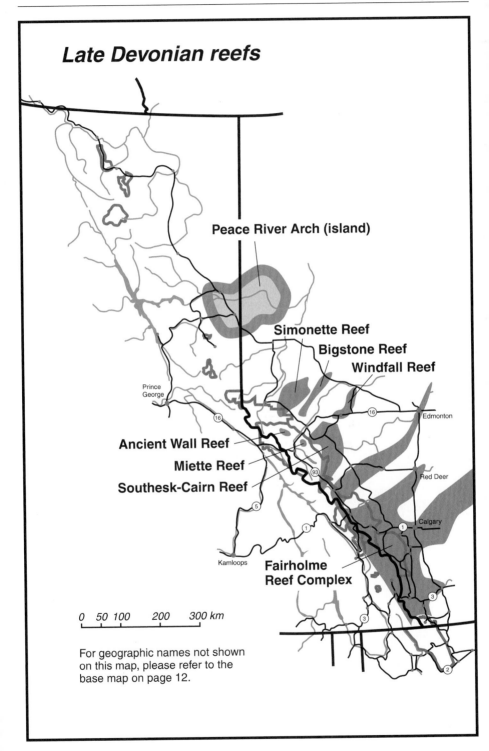

# *Late Devonian reefs*

Peace River Arch (island)

Simonette Reef

Bigstone Reef

Windfall Reef

Prince George

Edmonton

Ancient Wall Reef

Miette Reef

Red Deer

Southesk-Cairn Reef

Calgary

Kamloops

Fairholme
Reef Complex

0  50 100    200    300 km

For geographic names not shown
on this map, please refer to the
base map on page 12.

same rock appears on the west side of the Rocky Mountain Trench, where it is called the Starbird Formation. The Hollebeke/Starbird is siltier and less fossiliferous in the lower part than the Flume, and not cherty in the upper part. The best and most accessible Hollebeke exposures are on the north side of North Kootenay Pass, reached via the rough road up the Carbondale River. This is also a renowned place to look at the western margin of the Fairholme Reef Complex, the largest Devonian reef mass in Alberta.

Throughout the front ranges of the central Rockies, Flume and Hollebeke beds rest directly on the sub-Devonian unconformity. The gap is marked above by the sudden appearance of fossils, for the underlying beds are Cambrian or Ordovician and typically unfossiliferous.

### Cairn/Borsato and Southesk formations (upper Fairholme Group, reef facies)
*Late Devonian (370–373 Ma), up to 400 m*

The Cairn and Southesk formations go together; where you find the Cairn you will usually find the Southesk on top. They outcrop in the front ranges from the Peace River south to the Waterton area, where a unit similar to the Cairn and Southesk is called the Borsato Formation.

Cairn/Borsato rock is distinctive: poorly bedded black or dark-brown dolomite up to 300 m thick and full of blobby gray stromatoporoids, often with hollow centres. Little white rods, like grains of rice in the dark rock, are the oddball stromatoporoid *Amphipora*—definitely a fossil to learn, for it is easy to recognize and it instantly labels the rock as Devonian. *Amphipora* also occurs in the Middle Devonian Dunedin Formation of the northern Rockies, page 102. The organisms were actually long and stringy, like spaghetti, but they look rice-like in the rock.

This is reef rock. It is black with dried petroleum and loaded with organic compounds. When you break a piece it smells like a refinery.

"Cairn" comes from the Cairn River in eastern Jasper park. "Borsato" is from Mt. Borsato, near North Kootenay Pass in the Waterton area. There are three massive and well-studied Cairn reefs in Jasper park. One is the Ancient Wall Reef, in the northern part of the park; another, in the southern and eastern part of the park, is the Cairn-Southesk Reef, a branch of the huge

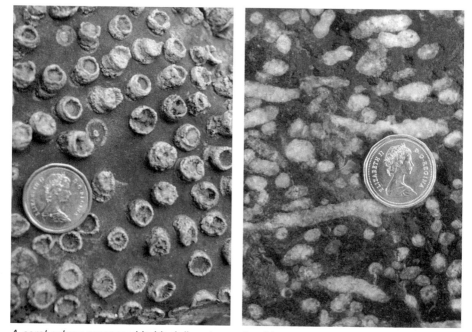

*A coral colony preserved in black limestone of the Grotto Member, Southesk Formation*

Amphipora *stromatoporoids from the Cairn Formation*

Fairholme Reef Complex of southern Alberta; and the third is the Miette Reef, found just south of Miette Hot Springs. At the springs the bed of the Sulphur River (a creek, really) is studded with beautifully stream-worn boulders of the rock that have come from the slopes of Utopia Mountain upstream, where the reef is exposed.

The Southesk Formation is mostly light-gray dolomite and limestone, resistant to erosion and 150–200 m thick. Often it can be identified at a distance by a dark-colored band 5–25 m thick—the coral-rich Grotto Member—that runs across the formation about halfway up. Southesk rock forms the upper part of the Devonian reefs in our area; the Cairn Formation makes up the lower part.

"Southesk" is from the Southesk River in eastern Jasper park. Distribution follows that of the Cairn. Heavily studied by oil-industry geologists, the Southesk Formation has been divided into three members: a lower light-gray limestone/dolomite with stromatoporoids (Peechee Member), a middle limestone coral bed (Grotto Member) and an upper pale-gray limestone made of lime sand (Arcs Member). "Grotto" and "Peechee" are from peaks in the Fairholme Range east of Banff and Canmore; "Arcs" is from Lac des Arcs ("Lack-days-ARK") in the same area. The Grotto bed is usually about 15 m thick and richly fossiliferous; common corals include *Alveolites, Syringopora, Thamnopora* and *Acinophyllum*. The other members of the Southesk are not as obviously fossiliferous, but they contain similar corals, stromatoporoids, and, in addition, sand-size **foraminifera:** tiny chambered animals. This group has been evolutionarily successful, with many descendant foraminiferan species living today. Fossil algae are also found in the Southesk.

The TransCanada Highway passes by an excellent Cairn-and-Southesk road-cut at the mountain front, just west of the white-weathering Eldon Formation outcrops. A little farther west, where the road curves north around the west end of Lac des Arcs, there is more Cairn. Another good place to examine Cairn and Southesk rock is along the Icefields Parkway below Cirrus Mountain, where some of the Cairn-Southesk Reef is exposed in the mountainside. Park at Cirrus Mountain Campground and scramble up the hillside to the southeast.

Farther north, just past the high bridge over Nigel Falls, a two-sided road-cut displays very dark Southesk strata, showing the Peechee-Grotto-Arcs sequence. The trail up Parker Ridge, a few kilometres toward Jasper, displays the flashy white-on-black coral beds very well. Collecting there is illegal, and thanks to the honesty of park visitors the outcrops have not been spoiled. For legal collecting, take Highway 11 east from Saskatchewan Crossing to the Cline River Bridge. The coral beds are a short walk upstream.

If you can't get to the mountains for a look at this interesting rock, drop by the Institute of Sedimentary and Petroleum Geology in Calgary at 3303 33rd Street NW, where the Geological Survey of Canada has a goodly chunk of Cairn dolomite on display outside the entrance. The hollows in the stromatoporoids of this specimen are impressively large. I once found a bat sleeping in one—a little flying mammal curled up inside a sea creature that lived 300 million years before bats appeared on the earth.

## Besa River and Perdrix formations (upper Fairholme Group, off-reef facies)

*Late Devonian to Early Carboniferous for Besa River (330–370 Ma), up to 500 m*
*Late Devonian for Perdrix (370–373 Ma), up to 200 m*

Both formations are black to grayish-green limy shale, the darker beds containing pea-sized blobs of gold-colored pyrite that weather into rusty streaks. These are recessive units, eroding back into slopes and typically hidden under soil and scree.

The Besa River Formation spans the time from the Late Devonian through the Early Carboniferous (Mississippian) periods. It is the deeper-water shale laid down in the north at the same time that the shallower-water limestones of the Fairholme Group (Flume, Cairn and Southesk formations, previous items) and the Rundle Group (page 116) formed to the south. Besa River shale is up to 500 m thick at the Liard River; 245 m at the Peace River. The Besa River, for which the formation is named, is a tributary of the Prophet River of the northern Rockies.

The Perdrix Formation is named for Roche à Perdrix, where the unit was first studied near the eastern boundary of Jasper National Park. Although included in the Fairholme Group, the

Perdrix can be thought of as a thin tongue of the lower Besa River shale that extends south into Fairholme Group country. The unit is found in the front ranges between Pine Pass and the international boundary. South of Crowsnest Pass it is mainly western-slope, lying above the Borsato Formation. The Perdrix shale looks a lot like the Exshaw Formation, page 115, but the Perdrix is older, thicker, and lacks the cherty beds and siltstone layer found in the Exshaw.

In the Late Devonian the central and southern Rockies area lay in shallow water spotted with reefs. Perdrix clay and silt were deposited between the reefs. At this time the northern Rockies area lay in deeper water where there were no reefs, so just Besa River shale accumulated. The water there stayed deep during the Early Carboniferous, so Besa River rock continued to build up, while to the south the Early Carboniferous formations are mainly limestone.

Large fossils are scarce in Perdrix and Besa River beds, probably because of the low oxygen levels associated with black shales. Spores and conodonts occur, though, and an organism called *Tentaculites*: a small phosphatic cone-like fossil that has no known living relatives and remains a mystery to paleontologists. Possibly the cone held a worm of some kind.

Good exposures of Perdrix or Besa River rock are difficult to find because the shale is so recessive. There is a small Perdrix outcrop just east of Jasper townsite, a half-kilometre east of the Maligne Road turnoff on Highway 16, but the site is close to a major fault (the Pyramid Thrust) and badly deformed. Better exposures are found in eastern Jasper park, a short distance south of Highway 16 along the west bank of the Fiddle River. The Alaska Highway crosses Besa River shale at One Ten Creek, which is the first drainage coming in from the south after the road descends from Summit Lake into the valley of MacDonald Creek.

*Perdrix shale seen along the Fiddle River, in eastern Jasper National Park*

## Mount Hawk Formation (upper Fairholme Group, off-reef facies)
*Late Devonian (369–370 Ma), up to 220 m*

Shaly black limestone that weathers gray; upper part nodular. Usually occurs above the Perdrix Formation, previous item, as the upper part of basinal fill between the reefs of the Fairholme Group.

The Mt. Hawk is limier and tougher than the Perdrix shale that underlies it. Typically it forms steep slopes and rotten cliffs. Distribution: in the front ranges from Pine Pass south to the international boundary. The Mt. Hawk becomes limier and more resistant to erosion as it is traced north; in Jasper park it looks much like the Palliser Formation from a distance and is often part of the same cliff.

The name should really be "Hawk Mountain Formation," not "Mount Hawk"; the peak for which the formation is named is Hawk Mountain, along the Athabasca River east of Jasper. There are good exposures on the slopes above Highway 16 east of the bridge 20 km east of Jasper. Highway 11 crosses the Mt. Hawk about 3 km west of Windy Point, near the mountain front, where the shaly Mt. Hawk beds are richly fossiliferous. Typical fossils for this formation are the brachiopods *Atrypa, Devonoproductus, Nudirostra, Gypidula, Cyrtospirifer* and bryozoans: tiny coral-like animals in colonies that resemble bits of window screen.

## *Pyrite*

Iron sulphide ($FeS_2$) to a chemist, pyrite is at its best in veins of ore, where crystals of the mineral have grown large and brassy, befitting their folk name "fool's gold." In the Canadian Rockies, where ore veins are few, pyrite is usually found in gray, metallic-looking blobs in black shale, such as that of the Besa River, Perdrix and Fernie formations. Pyrite is also common in quartzite and Rockies limestone, where it occurs in small crystals scattered through the rock.

Sedimentary pyrite is produced by bacteria that extract iron and sulphur from their surroundings (seawater and organic-rich bottom muck), combining the two to form the mineral. Energy is given off in the reaction, which sustains the bacteria. Such bacteria do not require oxygen—in fact, to most sulphide-producing bacteria oxygen is a poison—so the presence of pyrite in a sedimentary layer is evidence of oxygen-poor conditions on the seabed during deposition. Pyrite can also be formed later, inorganically, as hot water carries dissolved pyrite, quartz and other minerals among the grains and along the joints of hardened rock. The minerals crystallize out of the solution.

When pyrite weathers, the iron portion goes black or purplish, then turns to iron oxide (rust, in other words), which stains the rock yellowish-orange if the iron oxide is goethite ("GUR-tite," $HFeO_2$, also called limonite) or crimson-red if it is hematite ($Fe_2O_3$). These minerals often intermix on the rock surface, staining it streaky reddish-orange.

## Simla and Ronde formations (top of Fairholme Group)
*Late Devonian (367–369 Ma), up to 100 m*

These are two very different units that grade into each other. The Simla is light-gray massive limestone, often a biostrome, page 105, of stromatoporoids and other fossils; it weathers into a pale cliff that is rather easily identified among the other Devonian formations. The Ronde ("Rond") is thin-bedded silty and sandy limestone, not biostromal, but with scattered small coral buildups.

Simla beds are found from the Ancient Wall Reef in northern Jasper park (Mt. Simla is nearby) north to Monkman Pass, where they pinch out from erosion. To the south, the Simla meets the Ronde Formation, named for Roche Ronde in eastern Jasper park. Relationships between these two units are complex; the Ronde limestone shows that silty lime mud spread across the Devonian reef-tops from Jasper park as far south as Kananaskis Country. The Simla records a clear-water interval during which colonies of stromatoporoids flourished. Perhaps the Simla colonies might have continued to grow, but the Late Devonian extinction event at the Frasnian-Fammenian boundary (see page 106) snuffed nearly all of them out. That event is marked by an oncoid bed; above, the rock contains only a few brachiopods and conodonts.

No roadside outcrops of Simla rock are known, but Ronde beds are easy to get to via Highway 11, at a point 43 km east of Saskatchewan Crossing along the Cline River, west of the highway and downstream from the gorge.

### Sassenach Formation
*Late Devonian (366–367 Ma), up to 200 m*

Mostly fine-grained, thin-bedded, buff-weathering silty dolomite, siltstone and sandstone found from the Ancient Wall in Jasper park south to Elko, in the southern Rockies near the international boundary.

The Sassenach is patchy and varies a lot in thickness because of the way it was deposited. Sassenach silt filled rather local depressions in the otherwise shallow seabed of the time. Up to 150 m deep beside the Miette Reef, the depressions lay along the west side of the Devonian reefs, in the lee of the prevailing currents and facing away from the source of the mud of the Mt. Hawk Formation. Mt. Hawk sediment did not accumulate on the west side of the reefs, but it did on the east side, so the depressions resulted. The Sassenach came from the west, filling the depressions. The westerly source demonstrates that the Purcell Landmass, page 98, existed west of the Rockies region throughout the Devonian Period in western Canada.

There is a good Sassenach exposure 20 km east of Jasper along Highway 16, at the bridge over the Athabasca River, where tan Sassenach rock is exposed just east of the overlying Palliser Formation. A classic locality, but requiring a stiff scramble, is at the southern tip of the Colin Range, along the ridge separating Medicine Lake from the valley of Beaver Lake. The low gray cliff with a spring at its base 3 km east of Jasper along Highway 16 is Sassenach rock, and the formation also outcrops along the Cline River at the Highway 11 bridge.

# The late Paleozoic sandwich
## Things are falling apart, but the centre is still holding

There are two well-known geological sandwiches in the Canadian Rockies: the Cathedral-Stephen-Eldon sandwich of the Middle Cambrian (page 76), and this one, the Palliser–Banff–Rundle sandwich, with the thin Exshaw Formation as the lettuce leaf. It's a cliff-slope-cliff combination, easy to spot all over the front ranges between Crowsnest Pass and Jasper. The name recalls the age of the rock, which is latest Devonian to Permian (245–363 Ma), covering the final part of the Paleozoic Era. Seeing this sandwich tells you immediately where you are in the overall stratigraphic pile of the Canadian Rockies: near the top of the middle carbonates, which is the third great unit of the four introduced on pages 45–47.

*The late Paleozoic sandwich seen in Mt. Rundle, near Banff. Lower cliff is Palliser Formation; middle slope is Exshaw and Banff formations; upper cliff is Rundle Group.*

The geological history recorded in the late Paleozoic sandwich is complicated, but the general idea is that to the north and south of the Canadian Rockies area, plate collisions along the northern and western edges of North America were building mountain ranges across the Arctic (Ellesmerian Orogeny) and through Idaho into the west-central United States (Antler Orogeny). Between these two active regions, the Canadian Rockies area was less disturbed. It lay underwater most of the time, collecting marine sediments from lowlands to the east, the aforesaid mountains rising to the north and south, and chains of islands in deeper water to the west. Another deep spot was at the latitude of the Peace River. See the map on page 107. A mass-extinction event is recorded in this rock, not the Frasnian/Fammenian event discussed already (page 106), but another one that occurred as the Devonian Period closed some 360 million years ago.

At the very end of the Paleozoic, in the Permian Period, the island chains west of the Canadian Rockies began to crumple under impact with landmasses yet farther west, harbingers of the great plate collisions of the Mesozoic, which built mountains across western North America and produced the Canadian Rockies.

## Palliser Formation
*Late Devonian (366–363 Ma), up to 620 m*

Gray-weathering, very massive limestone mottled with buff-weathering dolomite. The Palliser forms big cliffs in the front ranges. Named for the Palliser Range of southern Banff park. In the front ranges the Palliser is easily confused with the Eldon Formation, page 79, which is also massive, gray-weathering and about the same thickness. The two also look alike on fresh surfaces: dark gray, with white calcite and dolomite veins. If you know the order of overlying and underlying formations, you can quickly figure out whether it is Palliser or Eldon you are looking at, but a quick way to differentiate the two is to look around the outcrop for fossils. If you find fossils, you have the Palliser; if you don't, you have the Eldon. The Palliser is not richly fossiliferous, but a few minutes' hunt will usually turn up some brachiopods, coiled snails or crinoid plates. The Eldon, on the other hand, is barren through most of its thickness.

*Slabs of Palliser limestone give the front ranges of the central Rockies their rugged character. This is the north end of the Queen Elizabeth Range, seen from Jacques Lake in eastern Jasper National Park.*

The Palliser Formation makes its southern-most appearance at Trail Creek in the Whitefish Range west of Glacier park, a few kilometres south of the international boundary. It becomes more widespread on the western slope around Fernie. East of Fernie at North Kootenay Pass, which is the head of the Carbondale River, the Palliser appears right along the divide, expanding east and west to outcrop throughout the front ranges and main ranges north to Kananaskis Lakes, where it then sticks to the front ranges all the way to Jasper. North of Jasper it becomes less resistant to erosion, even though the rock is still limestone/dolomite and not shale, and it thins to nothing near Hook Lake, between Monkman Pass and Pine Pass. Here it merges with black shale of the Besa River Formation, which was accumulating in deep water there at the same time the shallow-water Palliser lime-stone was forming to the southeast. There was also deep water to the southwest, for the Palliser goes to shale in that direction as well. There are two thick spots in the Palliser that represent de-pressions in the seabed: one at Phillips Peak, northwest of Fernie (620 m) and the other at Jarvis Lakes, northwest of Willmore Park (530 m).

*The Palliser Formation as you find it, in such great cliffs as this one, the Weeping Wall along the Icefields Parkway in northern Banff National Park*

The Palliser Formation is the most massively layered, most homogeneous limestone in the Rockies. Runners-up: Eldon and Cathedral formations. Palliser rock was laid down as lime sand and lime mud on a shallow seabed densely populated with worms and other burrowing organisms. They constantly moved the soft sediment around, churning it so much that in many layers neither the natural bedding nor the burrows can be seen. In other layers the burrows are beautifully displayed as a lacework of buff-weathering dolomite against gray-weathering limestone—the "mottling" mentioned earlier. The formation records deepening water, then shallowing, as the shore moved farther away from the Rockies area and then closer again. Much of the region was under very shallow water at the end of the Devonian, with minor erosion occurring near the top of the Palliser in places where the seabed was exposed. At the very top of the Palliser, a worldwide rise in sea level is recorded.

Common Palliser fossils include snails (mostly *Euomphalus*), the brachiopod *Camarotechia* and crinoid debris in upper layers. *Labechia palliseria* encrusting stromatoporoids are found in the Palliser—survivors of the Frasnian/Fammenian extinction event that wiped out most stromatoporoid species (see page 106).

Palliser cliffs are both common and spectacular. Along the TransCanada Highway, watch for Wind Tower, which sits in front of Mt. Lougheed as you pass the Deadman Flats turnoff 10 km east of Canmore. All the peaks on the west side of the highway between Wind Mountain and Cascade Mountain, including the Three Sisters and the lower cliff on Mt. Rundle, have Palliser cliffs. The dog-tooth spire of Mt. Louis, visible to the northwest from the Banff interchange, is a single vertically-tilted slab of Palliser rock. There is a road-cut in Palliser rock along the TransCanada at the west end of Lac des Arcs.

Along Highway 11 there are impressive Palliser cliffs in the vicinity of the Cline River, which has cut through the formation in a spectacular gorge. Such Palliser gorges are common in the Rockies; Maligne Canyon is another. The Weeping Wall, beside the Icefields Parkway, is a huge cliff of Palliser limestone striped here and there with ribbon-like waterfalls that freeze into lovely blue curtains of ice in the winter (photos this page and page 165).

Along Highway 16, between Jasper park's east gate and the townsite, the Palliser is prominent and grandly folded. Bedson Ridge, on the north side of the Athabasca River at the mountain front, has a particularly wonderful fold (photo on page 198) that looks like a squashed *Z*. The big cliff on Roche Miette, seen south of the highway, is also Palliser Formation. At the bridge over the Athabasca River 20 km east of Jasper, a glacially rounded Palliser hump locally called "River Rock" shows excellent exposures, both fresh and weathered, and a few fossils. The Palliser Formation is well known for caves; see page 168.

## Exshaw Formation
*Latest Devonian and Early Carboniferous/Mississippian (358–363 Ma), up to 100 m*

Named for a small community along Highway 1A near the eastern mountain front, the Exshaw Formation is thin but important. It has two parts. The lower unit is jet-black shale, often cherty and with marble-sized blobs of gold-colored pyrite, page 111, that weather as rusty streaks. The black color is from organic carbon, and under the prairies east of the Rockies the Exshaw contains oil. Like the Perdrix Formation, page 109, the Exshaw is thought to have been an important source of western Canada's Devonian oil, which moved from the shale into other rock. The upper unit, thicker than the lower, is tan, silty, sandy and dolomitic. It was deposited in shallower water than the black-shale portion.

The Exshaw is easily eroded and thus normally covered with soil or debris, but often exposed in stream gullies and bare slopes at high elevations. It has the same general distribution as the underlying Palliser Formation, but is patchy north of the Athabasca River.

Exshaw-like rock is remarkably widespread, found under various names from the Rockies to Manitoba, and in the United States as far away as Tennessee, where it is called the Chattanooga Formation. In fact, black shales such as the Exshaw are extraordinarily common worldwide at the end of the Devonian. There was a mass-extinction event at this time. Are the two related?

Quite possibly they are. The black shales seem to represent a rapid deepening of the sea, bringing oxygen-poor water from far offshore over the seabed quickly and thus killing most bottom-dwelling organisms. Or the shale may have resulted from increased erosion on the continents, caused by a new biological group—plants with roots—that broke down rock more quickly. This could have flooded the seabed with continent-derived, nutrient-rich nitrates and phosphates and created a huge algal/cyanobacterial bloom that used up enough oxygen to cause the mass extinction. Or perhaps an extraterrestrial impact was involved, as has been shown to be the case with at least two other evolutionary cataclysms.

Whatever the cause, this black shale is the gravestone of the Devonian Period. The upper part of the Exshaw Formation shows a rapid return of life in our area as the Carboniferous Period opened. These silty, sandy beds are not very fossiliferous, but they are extensively burrowed, showing that the seabed was busy indeed.

## Banff Formation
*Early Carboniferous/Mississippian (350–360 Ma), up to 820 m*

The Banff Formation and the underlying thin Exshaw Formation make up the filling in the late Paleozoic sandwich. As seen in the central Rockies between Banff and Jasper, at the base of the Banff Formation there is a dark-colored, deep-water phosphatic shale unit that looks a lot like the Exshaw shale, previous item. The Banff shale is limy, though, while the Exshaw is generally not; test with acid to find out. A layer rich in volcanic dust shows that eruptions were going on, but far away.

The next unit up is a thick, repetitive sequence of **spiculite**—rock made of sponge spicules— and coarse/fine beds that could be turbidites, page 61, representing a period of repeating underwater mudflows. Above that there is a gray-weathering limestone member up to 100 m thick that produces a cliff in the middle of the formation, a good identifier. Above the cliff an upper unit is mostly shaly limestone and dolomite, with stromatolites (page 58) and mud cracks near the top that show the water to have been very shallow. In places, there are the remains of land-based plants. As a whole, the Banff Formation records a deep-water phase followed by a shallow-water phase; that is, a time when the sea moved farther inland, then retreated.

The formation weathers brown from a distance but is strikingly banded gray and brown close up. It is easily eroded and thus recessive, except for the cliffy middle band. Distribution: from Trail Creek in the Whitefish Range west of Glacier park to the Sukunka River south of Pine Pass, where it merges with shales of the Besa River Formation, page 109. The Banff Formation is seen mostly in the front ranges, but it also reaches the surface in the western foothills at Moose Mountain southwest of Calgary and at Folding Mountain west of Hinton. It can be found in the main ranges south of Kananaskis Lakes, and farther north above the Weeping Wall along the Icefields Parkway in northern Banff park. South of Kootenay Pass, in the Waterton area, the Banff Formation lies west of the divide only. "Banff" is from the town of Banff.

*Typical banded beds of the Banff Formation, as seen near Disaster Point along Highway 16 east of Jasper*

The formation appears as a light-brown band running through the peaks of the front ranges, very conspicuous along the TransCanada Highway between Canmore and Banff, especially so in Mt. Rundle and in Cascade Mountain. Highway 16 passes by a good exposure of crumbly Banff beds about 23 km east of Jasper, near Disaster Point.

The upper Banff can be quite fossiliferous, loaded with brachiopods and crinoid fragments (see fossils, page 200). If you find yourself out on a steep, rubbly slope of Banff Formation rock—the usual way you meet this unit—then you may see large, well-preserved specimens of the brachiopod *Spirifer rowleyi*. Remember: no collecting in the national and provincial parks.

## Rundle Group and Spray Lakes Group
*Carboniferous (Mississippian and Pennsylvanian, about 300–350 Ma), up to 1100 m*

The Rundle Group is mostly gray-weathering limestone and dolomite, with layers of shale, siltstone and sandstone. Topping the Rundle Group in the front ranges between Kananaskis Country and Saskatchewan Crossing is the thinner Spray Lakes Group, which is mostly dolomitic sandstone, non-dolomitic sandstone and cherty dolomite.

Thick and resistant to erosion, the Rundle Group forms big gray cliffs rather like those of the Palliser Formation, page 113, but dark-banded at a distance and ledgier. Some Rundle units, especially the Mt. Head Formation, are very fossiliferous, full of corals, brachiopods and crinoids (see the fossil illustrations, page 200). A rule of thumb is that if you're in the front ranges between Banff and Jasper, any outcrop with lots of crinoid bits in it is likely to be Rundle rock. The group is named for Mt. Rundle, the much-photographed front-range mountain near Banff.

The Rundle Group is easy to pick out from a distance: it's the upper slice of bread in the late Paleozoic sandwich. The group generally follows the distribution of underlying Palliser and Banff beds, appearing west of Waterton/Glacier, running through the main ranges north to Kananaskis Lakes, then staying in the front ranges all the way to the north end of the Rockies. Rundle rock also reaches the surface here and there in the foothills closest to the mountain front, as in Moose Mountain west of Calgary or Folding Mountain west of Hinton.

Rundle-type rock is widespread in western North America. The Mission Canyon Formation of Montana and Wyoming resembles the Rundle Group, as does the Redwall Limestone of the Grand Canyon in Arizona.

Highway 40 passes through classic Rundle exposures in Kananaskis Country and south to Crowsnest Pass. Much of what you see along this road is the late Paleozoic sandwich, with the Rundle Group forming the jagged upper parts of many rugged peaks.

The Rundle Group is very complicated, with eleven formations that relate to each other in complex ways, beyond the scope of this book. As a whole, the group provides a record of waxing and waning seas on a west-facing continental shelf tilted and gently warped by the stresses of mountain-building to north and south, and by the presence of a string of unstable islands off the shelf to the west. The overall trend was toward shallower water. If you want to know more, read the technical discussion that begins on page 219 of *Geology of the Cordilleran Orogen in Canada,* or on page 221 in *Geological Atlas of the Western Canada Sedimentary Basin* (see "Further reading," page 202).

Briefly, in the central Rockies between Kananaskis Country and Jasper, where most people see the Rundle Group, it has an eastern set of formations that grade into a western set of formations. The eastern set, from bottom to top, includes the Pekisko, Shunda, Turner Valley and Mt. Head, total thickness up to 300 m. The western set includes the Livingstone (equivalent to the Pekisko, Shunda and Turner Valley), the Mt. Head, and the Etherington Formation, total thickness up to 900 m. Natural gas comes from Rundle strata in the foothills and eastern prairies, which has prompted geologists to study the group intensively.

The overlying Spray Lakes Group, total thickness up to 200 m, looks much like the Rundle Group from a distance and is usually found in the same cliff. It includes the sandy, dolomitic Tyrwhitt, Storelk, Tobermory and Kananaskis formations.

The Opal Range in Kananaskis Country: the Rundle Group at its ripsaw-ridge best

Fossil corals from the Rundle Group

## Pangea

Pangea ("Pan-GEE-uh") is the geological name of a supercontinent that at one time included nearly all the land on the planet. Its major components began assembling as early as the Ordovician, about 475 million years ago, and it reached its greatest compactness at about the end of the Paleozoic Era 245 million years ago, when it was shaped roughly like a letter "C." A landmass this large produced a climate of extremes: the annual summer high temperature in the northern temperate zone was calculated to have been 54°C. Pangea began to break up late in the Triassic, about 200 million years ago.

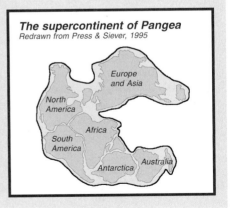

**The supercontinent of Pangea**
Redrawn from Press & Siever, 1995

## Ishbel Group
*Permian (258–286 Ma), up to 660 m*

The Ishbel Group is usually thin, under 200 m in most locations, with an erosion surface on top, but in spite of this it correlates in time and general rock type with the widespread Phosphoria Formation of the United States. "Phosphoria" brings to mind "phosphate," and indeed there is phosphate-bearing rock in the Ishbel Group, especially in the Johnston Canyon Formation, the lower member of the Ishbel Group in the southern and central regions.

**Phosphate,** chemical formula $PO_4$, occurs in nature mainly as the mineral apatite, which combines calcium (as $Ca_5$), with varying proportions of phosphate and usually some fluorine. Apatite forms today in shallow seawater as nodules on the bottom. The source of the phosphate is thought to be the bones, scales and teeth of fishes, all rich in phosphorus, and the shells of ostracods (small crustaceans).

Much of the Johnston Canyon Formation is silty dolomite, with black phosphatic blobs up to 5 cm across in the upper layers. The unit is thick in the southern part of the central Rockies (215 m southwest of Fernie), thinning northward to 30 m at Banff. It tapers to a thin edge at the Athabasca River. The formation is named for Johnston Canyon, near the junction of Highway 1A and Highway 93 between Banff and Lake Louise.

In a small area along the Elk River north of Fernie, the upper part of the Johnston Canyon Formation is replaced by the Telford and Ross Creek formations. North of Jasper, between Willmore park and Pine Pass, the Johnston Canyon is replaced by the Belcourt Formation.

Above the Johnston Canyon and its equivalents lies a weird and wonderful formation. I met it in the following way. Along the Maligne Road in Jasper park, between Medicine Lake and Maligne Lake, there lies a cabin-sized boulder of dark-brown rock. I had driven by that boulder many times on my way to Maligne Lake, where Parks Canada used to send me once a week, but when I stopped to look at it closely, I was astounded: it was made entirely of chert.

Chert occurs in blobs and lumps—proper term **nodules**—scattered through many Rockies limestones and dolomites, but seldom in the massive quantity required to produce a huge block of it. Where did that boulder come from?

It came from the mountain east of the road, as part of a huge rockslide. (See page 164 for more on the Maligne slides.) The boulder was originally part of a layer of chert about 50 m

*Boulder of massive Ranger Canyon chert along the Maligne Road in Jasper National Park*

thick that is present, although typically much thinner, all over the front ranges of the central and northern Rockies: the Ranger Canyon Formation.

**Chert** is a type of quartz that forms in seawater. Most seawater contains silica (another word for quartz) in solution, and many species of sponges are able to extract dissolved silica to form needle-like protective and supportive **spicules** in their tissues. Tiny **radiolaria,** which are marine protozoans, use silica to form their minute shells. When sponges and radiolaria die, most of the silica redissolves, but under the right chemical conditions it remains to become hard nodules of chert.

In the Canadian Rockies the rock gets more and more cherty in the Early and Late Carboniferous (American terms: Mississippian and Pennsylvanian periods), reaching a peak in the Permian. Massive beds of blue-gray chert, which appear dark-brown or black from a distance because they tend to be covered with dark-brown lichens, appear in the Ranger Canyon Formation, the source of that boulder along the Maligne Road.

The Ranger Canyon chert is thin but easy to identify because it is so dark against the pale formations below. In the front ranges between Banff and Jasper, the tough chert often lies in steeply tilted patches on the southwestern slopes of ridges, looking like the shadows of clouds. It is found between the international boundary and Wapiti Lake (east of Monkman Park). North of Pine Pass, similar rock is known as the Fantasque Formation, up to 70 m thick. A widespread unconformity is found at the base of both units, an erosion surface that can be traced over an area of 155,000 km² in Canada and the western United States.

Above the Ranger Canyon there is another unconformity, which represents the top of the Permian sequence—except between Monkman Pass and the Athabasca River, where there is a thin sandstone: the Mowitch Formation, 3–22 m thick, which escaped erosion in this area. You can see Mowitch sandstone at Mt. Greenock, along the Celestine Lakes Road in Jasper park.

Generally speaking, erosion was the norm in western Canada during the Permian period, here on the restless edge of the Pangean supercontinent. The layers are thin. Elsewhere in North America, thick, easy-to-sort-out sediments were laid down at this time. We shouldn't complain; the Canadian Rockies have one of the more complete and orderly geological records in the world.

And that's the top of the Paleozoic stack in our area, meaning also the top of the late Paleozoic sandwich and the great middle carbonate unit (see page 46). Above lie the siltstone, sandstone, shale and coal of the last great sequence of rock in the Rockies: the young clastics of the Mesozoic Era.

Before wading in, however, consider the only known sizable patch of igneous rock in our area.

## Ice River Alkaline Complex
*Late Devonian (about 368 Ma) igneous intrusion*

Aside from scattered diatremes, page 70, the only true **pluton**—mass of once-molten rock that crystallized deep underground—exposed in our area is the Ice River Complex. It covers 29 km² in the southern end of Yoho National Park and makes up the peaks immediately south and east of Mt. Goodsir; they have names such as Zinc Mountain and Manganese Mountain, hinting at the geology there. Access is by a good gravel road up the Beaverfoot River, then by a logging road up the lower Ice River to the park boundary, and finally by a half-day hike farther up the Ice River. Sodalite Creek is in the heart of the intrusion.

The Ice River intrusion is famous among geologists as one of the better exposures in the world of some rare rock types with appropriately alien names: jacupirangite, ijolite and urtite. These are all varieties of nepheline syenite: a grainy igneous rock that is mostly augite (chemical formula $Ca(Mg,Fe,Al)(Al,Si)_2O_6$) and nepheline ($NaAlSiO_4$), usually with a good percentage of orthoclase feldspar ($KAlSi_3O_8$). In the Ice River complex the augite is a peculiar variety called titanaugite; as the name indicates, the mineral contains the element titanium. There is also a fair proportion of magnetite, the magnetic iron mineral, in this rock. "Zinc Mountain" is misnamed; zinc is not significant in the complex. Manganese Mountain does contain some manganese, but there isn't enough to be worth mining, and in any case mining isn't allowed in the national park.

The "alkaline" in "Ice River Alkaline Complex" is a geochemistry term referring not to alkali (mineral salts left after evaporation of water) but to rock that is rich in orthoclase feldspar yet lacking in quartz. This is an unusual combination, for normally orthoclase and quartz go together. Granite, for example, is about 90 percent orthoclase and quartz. But the nepheline syenite in the Ice River complex is very low in quartz. This suggests that the Ice River magma probably came up from beneath the North American plate, where many a strange rock type is born through intermelting with the very different minerals of the mantle.

A blob of magma worked its way up from great depths into the overlying sedimentary strata here, where it spread out between the layers to form a sill (lens-shaped horizontal mass). It cooled slowly, so the minerals grew into large grains. Minerals crystallizing out of the molten pool floated upward or sank downward according to their densities, resulting in zones of different rock types. The weathered zones look layered from a distance, but the rock is not sedimentary.

After this first intrusion there was another, the second one a spreading vertical column that cut through the ceiling of the first. The second magma may have reached the surface, but if it did, then Devonian beds in the front ranges nearby ought to contain bits of material blown out of the resulting volcano, because alkaline volcanoes are usually explosive, like Mt. St. Helens. However, no such evidence has been found. If there was a volcano, the ejected material may have been lost to erosion.

Sodalite, $Na_8(AlSiO_4)_6Cl_2$, is found in the area. Sodalite is a bright-blue gem mineral, known to occur in the Canadian Rockies only at this site. But take heed, rockhounds: you risk a heavy fine if you are caught removing specimens from the national park, and working sodalite produces poisonous dust.

During the building of the Rockies, the Ice River complex behaved like a hard nut embedded in soft clay. The sediments surrounding the complex crumpled under the stress, but the complex itself, which was made of stronger rock, survived with only moderate folding and faulting.

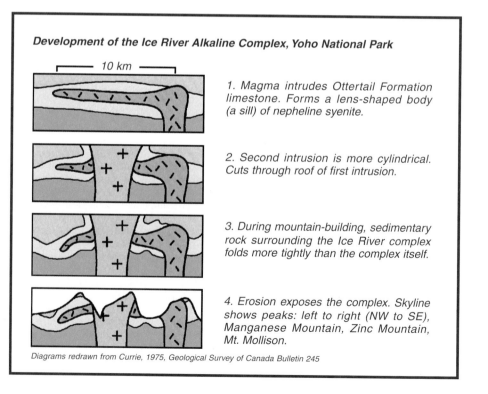

**Development of the Ice River Alkaline Complex, Yoho National Park**

10 km

*1. Magma intrudes Ottertail Formation limestone. Forms a lens-shaped body (a sill) of nepheline syenite.*

*2. Second intrusion is more cylindrical. Cuts through roof of first intrusion.*

*3. During mountain-building, sedimentary rock surrounding the Ice River complex folds more tightly than the complex itself.*

*4. Erosion exposes the complex. Skyline shows peaks: left to right (NW to SE), Manganese Mountain, Zinc Mountain, Mt. Mollison.*

*Diagrams redrawn from Currie, 1975, Geological Survey of Canada Bulletin 245*

# The muddy Mesozoic, and a tad of the Tertiary
## Triassic, Jurassic, Cretaceous and Paleocene

We are now dealing with the young clastic unit, the uppermost of the four great layers of the Canadian Rockies introduced on pages 45 and 46. Most of the rock in the young clastic unit is made of particles worn from nearby landmasses; limestone and other made-in-place rock is uncommon. The young clastics are found mostly in the foothills and front ranges, although in the southern Rockies some of the formations are also found west of the divide, in a region of coal-bearing rock that geologists call the Fernie Basin, and in the Rocky Mountain Trench.

Mesozoic sediments in our area record interesting features and exciting events: an inland seaway linking the Gulf of Mexico with the Arctic; a volcano in the southern Rockies, and the collision of groups of islands with North America, creating the mountains of western Canada.

Mesozoic geological history around the world has been worked out in fine detail, thanks to excellent index fossils. Among these are the **ammonite cephalopods,** a distinctive group of Cretaceous squid-like animals in coiled shells. (See photo on page 127.) The ammonites evolved from one species to another very quickly, and they can be identified to the species level easily— by experts, of course. Thus, ammonite-containing beds are routinely dated to within half a million years. Some units have been pegged to within 10,000 years, astonishing accuracy in dating sedimentary rock a hundred million years old.

Widespread uplift in the Late Permian or Early Triassic (245–250 Ma) left an erosion surface atop the Paleozoic formations of the Rockies. When the sea returned a few million years later, the shoreline pushed east, although not very far, so Triassic sediments in our area are mostly shallow-water types, silty and sandy. They belong to the Spray River Group and its northern equivalents. Toward the end of the Triassic the shoreline moved westward, exposing those sediments to erosion. Sea level rose again late in the Early Jurassic, at about 190 Ma, and the black shale of the Fernie Formation was laid down. The upper Fernie is silty and sandy, and the source of the particles is from the west. That is significant: it marks the impact of a large landmass with North America at about 175 Ma. With the collision came the accordioning of the continental margin into mountain ranges west of the Rockies, such as the Columbias, Ominecas and Cassiars. For more on that, see the next section, page 135. These new ranges started shedding sediment as soon as they rose above the sea, and some of the material spread far eastward across the Rockies area, which was still underwater and as yet undisturbed by the mountain-building.

Paradoxically, the same forces producing mountains west of us were causing subsidence of the crust here. The growing stack of folded, overthrust rock was heavy, and it pushed the edge of the continent down into the mantle. The continental basement rock was stiff enough to include our area in the downward bend, so a trough-like feature, covered with the sea, was formed between the rising mountains to the west and the main continental shore to the east. Long and deep, it is called the Rocky Mountain Trough. Note that this is different from the Rocky Mountain *Trench,* which is a valley in the modern landscape bordering the Rockies on the west.

The trough lay about where the front ranges and foothills of the Rockies are now. As the floor of the trough sagged down, erosion kept it filled with bits and pieces of the eroding highlands to the west. The Rocky Mountain Trough received sediment at rates of up to 300 cm per thousand years—torrential compared with the 5 cm per thousand years of, say, the Devonian Palliser Formation. Thanks to the sediments accumulated in the Rocky Mountain Trough, we have a record of the whole mountain-building sequence.

The Rocky Mountain Trough filled throughout the rest of the Mesozoic and into the Paleocene Epoch of the Tertiary Period. It did so in three episodes, discussed here informally as episodes I, II and III. Each ended in a period of erosion. Thus, there are three layers of sediments in the trough, each separated from the others by an unconformity. The deepest point in the basin holds nearly 7 km of rock.

## The Rocky Mountain Trough —
## a moving foredeep in front of the Rockies

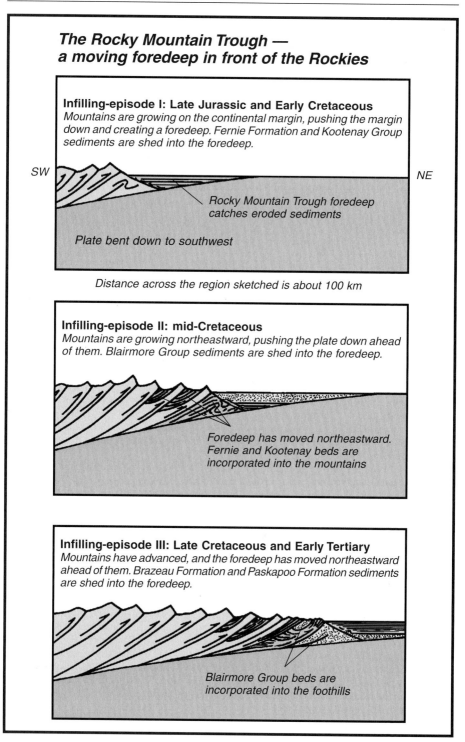

**Infilling-episode I: Late Jurassic and Early Cretaceous**
*Mountains are growing on the continental margin, pushing the margin down and creating a foredeep. Fernie Formation and Kootenay Group sediments are shed into the foredeep.*

SW

NE

*Rocky Mountain Trough foredeep catches eroded sediments*

*Plate bent down to southwest*

*Distance across the region sketched is about 100 km*

**Infilling-episode II: mid-Cretaceous**
*Mountains are growing northeastward, pushing the plate down ahead of them. Blairmore Group sediments are shed into the foredeep.*

*Foredeep has moved northeastward. Fernie and Kootenay beds are incorporated into the mountains*

**Infilling-episode III: Late Cretaceous and Early Tertiary**
*Mountains have advanced, and the foredeep has moved northeastward ahead of them. Brazeau Formation and Paskapoo Formation sediments are shed into the foredeep.*

*Blairmore Group beds are incorporated into the foothills*

## Infilling episode I

Counting the upper Fernie Formation as the beginning of deposition, because that is when the Rocky Mountain Trough first appeared, infilling episode I continued with the Kootenay Group of the southern region (Late Jurassic to Early Cretaceous), and its northerly equivalents-in-time, the Nikanassin Formation and the Minnes Group.

The lower Kootenay contains detritus from formations seen in the Columbia Mountains, the range immediately west of the Rockies, and in the main ranges of the Rockies themselves, meaning the part of the Rockies west of the continental divide. To have produced eroded sediments, this area must have stood above sea level in the late Jurassic, meaning that the rock of the main ranges was buckling upward above the waves 140 million years ago. Think of the mountains rising as lines of low islands that grew rather quickly to good-sized mountain ridges, forcing the sea away to the east.

The soft upper layers of sediment must have eroded quickly at first. In the northern Rockies area, which was still under the waves but close to the rising Cassiars and Omineers, sand and mud went quickly into the sea. Farther south the sea retreated earlier and much of the sediment wound up in immense deltas that grew seaward into heavily vegetated, swampy coastal plains. Remains of this vegetation formed the coal seams for which the Kootenay Group is noted.

Between 125 Ma and 135 Ma there was a lull in mountain-building activity. Erosion overtook upward growth; the Columbia Mountains and Rockies main ranges began to wear down. Over the next 10 million years this relieved the western continental margin of some of its burden, and the crust sprang back up. This was not mountain-building; it was just gentle uplift. But it raised the surface of the Rocky Mountain trough above sea level, ending infilling episode I and allowing the first major erosion of sediments in the trough.

## Infilling episode II

The plates took another crunch at about 125 Ma. The rate of mountain-building exceeded the rate of erosion and the mountains began growing again. As before, the crust responded by sinking deeper into the mantle, the Rocky Mountain Trough sagged and a second round of deposition began. In this episode, material eroded from the main ranges of the Rockies and other mountain chains to the west poured into the trough to become the rock of the Blairmore, Bullhead and Fort St. John groups.

Like the Kootenay Group, material in these units includes fragments from older formations. The presence of Gog Group quartzite, page 71, which is main-range rock, suggests that the main ranges of the Rockies, which could have been worn down considerably during the ten-million-year stall in mountain-building, were again standing high by 115 Ma. Volcanic eruptions farther west loaded rivers flowing into the southern and central parts of the basin with volcanic particles, giving the Blairmore Group its characteristic greenish color. Late in episode II some fireworks went off in the southern end of our area, where the Crowsnest Formation records flows of volcanic mud from vents in the Crowsnest Pass area (see page 131).

Another period of crustal quiet followed, with erosional loss in the western mountains and a corresponding upward adjustment in the continental plate. The second batch of sediments in the Rocky Mountain Trough suffered minor erosion, leaving about 2100 m of rock within the trough.

## Infilling episode III

At about 85 Ma, a change in the pattern of plate impact (see page 138) increased the pressure on the western edge of the continent, rejuvenating mountain growth. In the Late Cretaceous and Early Tertiary (45–85 Ma), the front ranges and foothills of the Canadian Rockies formed. As described in the section that follows, the main-range thrust sheets kept moving and stacking as younger ones developed eastward; it was during this period that the Rockies probably reached their greatest height.

In response to this new load of mountains, the crust sagged a third time and the Rocky Mountain Trough sagged with it, receiving a third and final batch of sediments: the shaly Alberta/Smoky Group, followed by the Brazeau Formation and its equivalents, which are sandy and coal-bearing. This rock includes detritus from formations seen in the front ranges, which means that the front ranges were well above sea level by about 80 Ma. Atop a minor unconformity lies the youngest unit in the Rocky Mountain Trough: the freshwater sandstone and shale of the Paskapoo and Porcupine Hills formations.

There is an interesting angle here. As the Rockies developed eastward, the sediments they shed were themselves caught in the eastward-moving disturbance. The deepest part of the Rocky Mountain Trough moved along, too, jumping eastward about 20–30 km during each of the three episodes of infilling. Thus, sediments deposited in the trough were uplifted, eroded, and redeposited eastward. Recalling that Kootenay Group rock includes fragments of older Rockies-area formations, it is interesting to think of the Kootenay Group itself eroding in the front ranges and feeding sediment to the Brazeau Formation, which was later exposed in the foothills and shed fragments into the Paskapoo Formation. Now, *that's* recycling.

## The Cretaceous seaway

Sea level was generally higher during the Cretaceous Period than it had been earlier in the Mesozoic, and it fluctuated markedly at least three times. Couple with this the subsidence of the continent along the front of growing mountain ranges in western Canada and the United States, which kept the western Interior Plains low-lying from the Gulf of Mexico to the Arctic, and the result was widespread inundation of the region.

Following a couple of advances and retreats during infilling episode I, the greatest of these marine invasions occurred at about 98 Ma, toward the end of episode II. The sea crept into western Canada from the north and joined a tongue lapping up from the south—the Kiowa - Skull Creek Sea—to produce a shallow seaway through the centre of North America. This was an inland sea far larger than any currently existing on earth, including the Mediterranean.

Size notwithstanding, this and the other Cretaceous floodings were ephemeral, coming and going in spans of a few million years. The rock record in the Rocky Mountain Trough documents no fewer than 11 cycles of deepening and shallowing. The last advance occurred at 75 Ma, when the Bearpaw Sea reached up from the south as far as Edmonton, depositing a layer of black shale called the Bearpaw Formation.

The front ranges of the Rockies were standing at the western shore of the Bearpaw Sea, but the area that would become the foothills belt was still submerged, receiving the Bearpaw shale. By 50–60 Ma the foothills were above sea level, and the Bearpaw Shale was caught in the folding and thrust-faulting.

East of the foothills, the Rocky Mountain Trough still existed, but it was no longer covered by the sea. It existed as a vast swampy area to which rivers delivered the mud and sand of the Brazeau and Paskapoo formations. The foothills grew eastward, folding and faulting western parts of the Brazeau Formation, but the Paskapoo Formation was little disturbed. Early Tertiary in age, about 60 Ma, it tops the stack of formations along the eastern edge of the foothills. On the western slope, though, there are some younger formations. For more on that, see page 142.

Herewith the details, formation-by-formation, from the beginning of the muddy Mesozoic.

### Spray River Group and northern equivalents
*Triassic (208–245 Ma), 90–740 m*

Often erroneously called the "Spray River *shale*," much of this rock is actually siltstone and fine sandstone.

The Spray River Group includes two formations in the southern and central Rockies: a lower reddish-brown-weathering dark-gray siltstone called the Sulphur Mountain Formation, 100–500 m thick, and an upper buff-colored silty dolomite called the Whitehorse Formation, up to 420 m thick, with gypsum beds in it. Both are marine.

These two formations are found from the upper Flathead drainage south of Crowsnest Pass to Monkman Pass, where the Triassic sequence thickens to about 1500 m and changes

*Bow Falls, where the Bow River has cut into siltstone of the Sulphur Mountain Formation near the Banff Springs Hotel*

somewhat, taking on new formation names. North of the Liard River, meaning north of the Rockies, Triassic rock has been eroded away.

"Spray River" and "Sulphur Mountain" are familiar names to Banffites. The Spray River joins the Bow River just east of the Banff Springs Hotel, which sits at the base of Sulphur Mountain. The road to Bow Falls passes by outcrops of Sulphur Mountain siltstone, and the falls themselves are cut into the formation. Sulphur Mountain rock is thin-bedded and laminar; it makes excellent building stone and has been used extensively in Banff townsite. Both the park administration building and the Banff Springs Hotel are faced with it. The Whitehorse Formation is named for Whitehorse Creek, in the front ranges south of Hinton.

The Spray River Group typically lies along the southwestern sides of tilted front-range ridges, where it is readily identifiable above treeline as a softly contoured reddish-brown zone that supports lush, brilliantly green vegetation.

Whitehorse Formation beds are easily eroded and thus seldom exposed. They usually occur with the very soft Fernie Formation, next item, in tree-covered front-range valley bottoms.

Interpreting the Spray River Group is straightforward: a shallow, muddy sea advanced inland from the west, laying down the Sulphur Mountain Formation. The lower part of the unit records daily tides: very thin pairs of coarser and finer beds that show how sediment was moved by the tidal current and settled out once the tide was in, the coarser particles at the bottom of each thin layer and finer particles higher up. The upper part of the Sulphur Mountain also has rhythmic bedding, but this is from undersea mudflows (turbidites; see page 61). During Whitehorse Formation time the sea became restricted, meaning the water in it didn't mix much with the rest of the ocean. Evaporation at a few locations produced the gypsum and other evaporites, page 100, of the Starlight Member of the Whitehorse Formation. At Helmet Mountain in eastern Jasper park there is a bed of gypsum 44 m thick. Few life forms can survive in water that is this heavily charged with minerals, so there aren't many fossils in Whitehorse rock. The water was muddy during Sulphur Mountain time, but fish did live in it, leaving black or bluish, phosphatic fossils of fish fins and scales in the siltstone.

North of Pine Pass the Triassic sequence acquires different formation names, but the geological history is fairly similar. An eastward movement of the shoreline deposited mud of the Grayling Formation, 35–395 m thick, and silt of the Toad Formation, 275–825 m. Then an influx of sand—the Liard Formation, 415 m—was followed by shallowing conditions, producing the Charlie Lake Formation dolomite and evaporites, up to 400 m thick. The water deepened enough to produce the limestone of the Baldonnel Formation, up to 145 m thick. Liard, Charlie Lake and Baldonnel rock all grade westward into the somewhat deeper-water limy/dolomitic siltstone and sandstone of the Ludington Formation, up to 900 m thick. After Baldonnel time, possible deepening is indicated by the Pardonet Formation's shale and siltstone, 137 m thick. At the top of the Triassic stack we find the Bocock Formation, a limestone 65 m thick occurring only in the Peace River area between Williston Lake and the Pine River. Caves have developed in Bocock rock; see page 168 for more on Rockies caves.

In the late Triassic, the sea withdrew. Losses to erosion were small in the west, greater to the east, and the sea soon returned, laying down the widespread Fernie shale of the Jurassic Period, next item.

Fossils in the northern formations are more common than in the southern Spray River Group. They include the coiled shells of ammonoid cephalopods, squid-like animals such as *Prionolubus, Wasatchites* and *Anagymnotoceras* in the Toad Formation; *Protrachyceras* and *Paratrachyceras* in the Liard Formation, and *Discotropites, Himavatites* and *Malayites* in the Pardonet Formation. The Pardonet is also well-known for the pelecypod *Monotis.*

And so into the Jurassic, near the end of which the Rocky Mountain Trough appeared, page 122, with its episodes of infilling.

## *Siltstone and shale*

Siltstone is made of silt-sized particles, which are about 0.002-0.06 mm in diameter, intermediate in size between clay and sand. Clay, particle size less than 0.002 mm, compacts to form shale. Sand goes to sandstone, in which the grains of sand are large enough to see easily. Silt goes to siltstone, which can look much like shale. To tell the difference between shale and siltstone, look at the rock through a magnifying glass. If it sparkles as you tilt it, then it is siltstone. The tiny grains of quartz—the main component in sandstone and siltstone—flash tiny reflections, especially when tilted toward the sun. A piece of shale, on the other hand, doesn't sparkle because the grains are too small. Also, they are often of clay minerals, which aren't as shiny as quartz.

**Fernie Formation** (Rocky Mountain Trough appears and infilling-episode I begins)
*Jurassic (135–208 Ma), 300–600 m*

Mostly dark, very soft shale in the lower half, with thin beds of orange-weathering gray siltstone. Gray or brown silty shale, siltstone and sandstone in the upper part, with ripple marks. Fernie shale is recessive (easily eroded) and thus seldom exposed in mountain slopes. Places to find outcrops are in gullies and along streams that have cut down to bedrock.

Fernie strata are found from just north of the international boundary to the Prophet River in the northern Rockies. Despite this long north-south distribution, the Fernie doesn't go very far east; it thins out quickly under the Interior Plains, barely reaching Edmonton and Calgary. The formation is best-developed west of Crowsnest Pass; look for outcrops of it along Highway 3, especially where the road crosses Alexander Creek and Hartley Creek. North of Crowsnest Pass Fernie shale commonly makes up the bottoms of front-range valleys and is sometimes exposed along streams. Good outcrops occur just east of the Banff interchange on the TransCanada Highway—the unit is upside down there—and about midway along the road to Miette Hot Springs in eastern Jasper National Park.

Fernie exposures are fascinating to look at: thin orange-weathering siltstone beds follow the contorted folding in the dark shale. The underlying and overlying siltstone and sandstone formations are usually much less disturbed, showing how different kinds of rock reacted to the stress that built the mountains. This also demonstrates that shale is quite malleable between upper and lower bounding units that are more rigid.

*Giant ammonite fossil found in the Fernie Formation near, of all places, Fernie.
Photo by David McIntyre.*

Apparently monotonous, there is more to the Fernie shale than meets the eye. There are four unconformities (gaps in the record from erosion). The formation coarsens upward, with silt and sand common in the upper part. These are the famous Passage Beds of the Fernie, which are the first evidence for the mountain-building phase of western Canada's Mesozoic history.

The Passage Beds are turbidites: sediments carried in on muddy currents originating at or near the shore (see page 61 for more on turbidites). These sediments arrived from the west as well as from the east, showing that there was new land to the west, where mountain ranges were rising above sea level.

Fernie shale is not very fossiliferous in the darker layers, although some contain abundant belemnites: the cuttlebone-like remains of a group of cephalopods. The silty/sandy layers are richer. One of these is known for its small clams as the "*Corbula munda* bed." Also present are ammonoid cephalopods, oysters and snails.

A good site for Fernie fossils is along Ribbon Creek at the base of Mt. Allan in Kananaskis Country, where the Fernie Formation is exposed in a small quarry for Spray River flagstone. The Fernie here is loaded with snails and clams; some 38 different species have been collected at this site over the years. But collection is illegal now, for the site is within a provincial recreation area. Other common Fernie Formation fossils include the ammonites *Chondroceras* and *Stemmatoceras*, and the clams *Inoceramus ferniensis*, *Gryphaea* and *Oxytoma*. The Passage Beds contain fossilized logs and stumps that floated out to sea—driftwood 145 million years old.

The upper Fernie Formation represents the start of infilling in the Rocky Mountain Trough, page 122. This first round included also the overlying Kootenay Group and more northerly formations of Late Jurassic and Early Cretaceous age, described next.

## Kootenay Group, Nikanassin Fm. and Minnes Group (infilling-episode I, cont.)
*Late Jurassic to Early Cretaceous (97.5–142 Ma), 600–1200 m*

These three units are all the same age, but they vary in rock type from south to north. The Kootenay Group, 100–1100 m thick, is mostly reddish-brown-weathering siltstone and sandstone, with shale and coal beds. It was named by G.M. Dawson in 1886 for the "East

Kootenays," meaning in those days the coal-bearing region around Fernie. See the history section, page 697. The geographic name is still in use, applied mainly to towns in the southern Rocky Mountain Trench such as Cranbrook and Kimberley.

The Kootenay Group runs north through the front ranges and foothills to the Brazeau River, on the southern boundary of Jasper park. A classic place to study Kootenay rock is on Mt. Allan in Kananaskis Country, where the entire unit is exposed. Other good outcrops occur along the TransCanada Highway between the eastern gate of Banff National Park and the Banff interchange, where the Kootenay Group and the Fernie Formation are exposed.

Bottom to top, Kootenay strata include the Morrissey Formation, which is fine- to medium-grained gray marine sandstone, 20–80 m thick; the Mist Mountain Formation, 25–665 m of interbedded nonmarine gray siltstone, sandstone and coal, and the Elk Formation in the upper part, up to 590 m thick and similar to the Mist Mountain but with little coal. The Elk includes chert-pebble conglomerate. The names come from the Kananaskis area, except for "Morrissey," which is a rail siding south of Fernie.

Except for plant fragments impressed in the coal, large fossils are not common in the Kootenay Group. Those that exist consist mostly of worm burrows in the Elk Formation. The group has been dated mainly from fossil pollen and spores in the Mist Mountain Formation.

Overall, the Kootenay Group seems to have been deposited as a huge delta that spread northwestward along the Rocky Mountain Trough.

Significant in the Kootenay are pebbles and grains of chert that could have come only from Canadian Rockies units such as the Banff Formation, page 115. Sand, limestone and dolomite fragments in the group have likewise been traced to older units now exposed in the Rockies. Those formations had to be above sea level to be eroding and providing sediment, and they had to be fairly close by, judging from the coarseness of the sand in the Kootenay. This evidence shows that the main ranges of the Canadian Rockies were on the rise in the Late Jurassic, 140 million years ago.

The Kootenay Group is famous as a coal producer between Canmore and the Crowsnest Pass region, including mines near Banff.

## *Coal in the Canadian Rockies*

Coal begins as **lignin**: the rigid ten-carbon and four-oxygen chain molecule (polymer) that spirals through the cell walls of plants to strengthen the soft cellulose, which is mostly carbon dioxide and water. When a plant dies, bacteria quickly rot the sugar-bearing cellulose, leaving much of the lignin framework intact. If the material can be protected from further bacterial attack—as it is when it has been covered quickly with sediment and the oxygen in that sediment has been used up rotting the cellulose—the tough lignin molecule compacts with time and loses one of its four oxygens, forming brown coal (lignite). With further aging, heat and pressure, the other three oxygens are lost along with any water in the material, producing bituminous coal. Even greater heat and compacting pressure produce anthracite coal, which is nearly pure carbon. The purer the coal, the hotter it burns.

*The Luscar open-pit coal mine, at the mountain front south of Hinton*

What? Coal-mining in Banff National Park? Yes; go and see the exhibits at Bankhead, along the road to Lake Minnewanka from the Banff interchange. See also page 697.

Like most of the coal in the Rockies, the deposits at Bankhead were of semi-anthracite, which is about 95 percent carbon. This kind of coal gave off very little smoke, so it was used in huge quantities in World War One for fueling troop-ships, which didn't want to give their positions away over the horizon. After the war a depression in the Canadian coal market resulted in the permanent closing of the mine at Bankhead, along with most other underground coal mines in the Rockies region. A few, though, continued to operate until more recently, including the large mine at Canmore, which closed in 1979.

Open-pit mining is cheaper, and since the early 1960s a boom in Japanese steel-making has provided a market for the low-sulphur coal of the Rockies as **coke** (coal from which impurities have been driven off by heating in the absence of oxygen) used in the blast-furnace smelting of iron ore. Open-pit coking-coal mines in the Fernie area, Hinton area, at Grande Cache and at Tumbler Ridge are still in operation in 1995, supplying mainly Asian markets. But new blast-furnace technology can use cheaper bituminous coal from Australia instead of expensive semi-anthracite coal from Canada. Decreasing demand could close most Canadian coking-coal mines in the next five or ten years. (See also thermal coal, page 134.)

Between the North Saskatchewan and Brazeau rivers, the Kootenay Group interfingers with the Nikanassin Formation, 300–600 m thick, named for the Nikanassin Range just east of Jasper National Park. Nikanassin beds are mostly orange-weathering sandstone and dark mudstone, with a few thin coal seams in the upper part. A fine place to view this beautiful rock is along the road over the Cardinal Divide south of Cadomin.

North of Jasper park the Nikanassin grades into the Minnes Group, named for Mt. Minnes northeast of Kakwa Lake. The Minnes Group thickens to the north to a maximum of about 2000 m and carries on to the Sikanni ("Sick-KAHN-ee") Chief River, north of which the group has been eroded away.

Lowest in the Minnes is the Monteith Formation, which is mostly fine-grained marine sandstone, with turbidites (material carried in bottom currents, page 61). Both sides of the Rocky Mountain Trough are preserved in the formation, showing that the trough was narrow at this stage. The Monteith is also important for its grains of green, radiolarian-rich chert. Such chert is not found in rock derived from North America; it must have come from an oceanic-based landmass colliding with the continent. The presence of the chert in the Monteith Formation dates the arrival of that landmass to latest Jurassic or earliest Cretaceous time, 135–140 Ma.

Above the Monteith lies the Gorman Creek Formation, about 1300 m thick in the Kakwa/Smoky River area. This formation is coarse and coaly, a river-bed and delta deposit. North of Pine Pass the Gorman Creek breaks into three smaller units. The mudstone of the Beattie Peaks Formation, 500 m thick, indicates deepening; above that, sandstones of the Monach Formation, 300 m, indicate shallowing, followed by a short period of fluctuating water levels represented in the marine-and-nonmarine Bickford Formation, 400 m, which is coaly sandstone and shale. Look for the clam *Buchia* in the Beattie Peaks and Monach.

Above that there is an unconformity, marking the end of deposition in this first infilling of the Rocky Mountain Trough.

## Cadomin Formation (basal Blairmore Group, start of infilling-episode II)
*Early Cretaceous (97.5–140 Ma), up to 200 m, usually 10–20 m*

Cadomin is a small community at the mountain front southwest of Hinton. The name comes from "*Ca*nadian *Do*minion *Min*ing," which built the coal-company town in the early part of the century.

The Cadomin Formation is a tough, erosion-resistant conglomerate. It looks like concrete, with pebbles, cobbles and even head-sized boulders in it. Found from south of Fernie to just north of the Peace River, Cadomin rock often caps ridges in the western foothills. It is thickest around the Peace. There are no outcrops along the TransCanada Highway, but the Lusk Creek Road in northern Kananaskis Country takes you through excellent exposures. Punchbowl Falls in Jasper park, not far off Highway 16 along the road to Miette Hot Springs, pours over the

Cadomin at a spot where the formation is steeply tilted. Cadomin conglomerate is also prominent around Grande Cache, where you can see it twisting through the folded Mesozoic strata there.

Beyond its ability to make hogback ridges, the Cadomin conglomerate is significant for the large size of its pebbles and cobbles, which are derived from the Paleozoic formations of the Canadian Rockies—especially the Gog quartzite, page 71. Fragments this large show that the peaks of the main ranges were close by, perhaps less than 20 km away in Cadomin time, 115 million years ago near the end of the Early Cretaceous.

The Cadomin is strangely thin for a formation covering this much area, a fact that has led geologists to think it may be a pediment: a thin veneer of gravel over bedrock. Pediments form in dry climates, when storms move massive amounts of material in flash floods.

*The concrete-like conglomerate of the Cadomin Formation*

## *Big doings in the Cretaceous*

Earth's climate warmed by about 15°C in the Cretaceous, from 100–120 Ma, due to an influx of carbon dioxide—the famous greenhouse gas—into the atmosphere. The $CO_2$ buildup was rapid, geologically speaking, occurring over a period of three to four million years. Temperatures during the Cretaceous rose high enough to make polar latitudes temperate and forested. Oceanic plankton growth increased, owing to the additional carbon and nutrients available, producing the great quantities of hydrocarbons found in the world's many Cretaceous oilfields.

Where did all that carbon dioxide come from? Out of volcanoes, most likely, which spilled enormous quantities of basalt into the western Pacific in the middle Cretaceous. The ocean floor also bulged upward there, accounting for a worldwide rise in sea level. The cause of the bulge may have been a huge plume of magma that peeled off the core/mantle boundary deep in the earth and reached the surface. This would have set off other plumes elsewhere, spreading under the world's plates generally and lubricating their movement, thus speeding them up. The result: more plate collisions and faster subduction, giving the world the burst of mountain-building activity and volcanism for which the Cretaceous is so well known. That wasn't all. The Cretaceous ended with a bang, as described in the boxed item on page 134.

### The rest of the Blairmore Group, the Bullhead and Fort St. John groups, and the Dunvegan Formation (infilling-episode II, continued)
*Mid-Early Cretaceous to early Late Cretaceous (93–124 Ma), 400–2000 m*

The Blairmore Group outcrops from southwest of Fernie through the foothills and front ranges north to the Highwood River, beyond which it is found in the foothills only. It includes the Cadomin conglomerate at its base, previous item, then alluvial sandstone and shale of the Gladstone Formation, 75 m thick, named for Mt. Gladstone north of Waterton park. There is a limy zone in the Gladstone Formation with abundant snails, clams and little nut-like ostracods, freshwater representatives of which live in the ponds of the Canadian Rockies today. See page 437.

Overlying the Gladstone is the salt-and-pepper sandstone of the Beaver Mines Formation, a freshwater deposit 200–2000 m thick, named for a small Waterton-area community. Red and green shales containing particles of volcanic material are also found in the Beaver Mines Formation, evidence of violent events to the west.

South of Burnt Timber Creek the Blairmore Group is topped by the Mill Creek Formation. About 100 m thick, the soft Mill Creek is composed of sandstone and red/green shale beds. It contains interesting plant fossils.

In and about Crowsnest Pass, lying atop the Mill Creek and occurring nowhere else, is the unusual Crowsnest Formation, one of only two units of volcanic rock known in the Canadian Rockies; the other is the lava flow capping the Siyeh Formation in Waterton/Glacier, page 57. The Crowsnest Formation is mudflow rock about 160 m thick, made up of pinkish fragments of **trachyte**: a kind of lava rich in feldspar and mica.

Trachyte is typical of violent eruptions; it emerges with the consistency of toothpaste, then quickly stiffens and tends to block the vent from which it issued. This causes a buildup of pressure underneath and an explosion, like the one that blew the top off Mt. St. Helens in 1980.

The larger fragments are found closer to the centre of such eruptions, and geologists have used this principle to locate three explosive centres: one under the town of Coleman, one southeast of Coleman, and a third at Ma Butte, 10 km north-northwest of Coleman—not far from Crowsnest Mountain, which looks rather like a volcano but is not. This discovery will cause a lot of confusion, I fear.

The Crowsnest Formation has been dated by its radioactive mineral content to 93 Ma. Small amounts of gold occur in some units. There is too little to be worth mining, and that's okay with me. Having dug up the Crowsnest area once for coal, it would be a shame to wreck it all over again for gold.

Blairmore strata are common in the southern foothills. The group is perhaps best viewed along Highway 3 on the eastern approach to Crowsnest Pass. The town of Blairmore itself, now part of the larger municipality of Crowsnest Pass, sits mostly on Fernie shale, but there are also outcrops of Blairmore strata, looking characteristically pale greenish. This color is from the mineral chlorite, originating as volcanic dust that blew in almost constantly from major eruptions to the west. Chlorite cements the grains in Blairmore Group sandstones; conglomerate layers hold pebbles of volcanic rock.

The Blairmore Group contains more and more coal as you follow it north through the foothills. Beyond the North Saskatchewan River it is so coal-rich that it acquires a different name: Luscar Group, with a maximum thickness of about 1000 m. North of Grande Cache the Blairmore/Luscar thins considerably as the overlying units thicken; it is known here as the Bullhead Group, 210 m thick.

Within the Blairmore/Luscar, the Gladstone continues to Grande Cache, where it becomes coal-bearing and is known as the Gething Formation (100–550 m); the Beaver Mines merges northward with the Gates Formation (400 m). "Gething" and "Bullhead" are from mountains that overlook the Bennett dam on the Peace River. The Gladstone/Gething and Gates are separated by shale: the Moosebar Formation (100 m), which appears south of the main Bullhead region at Burnt Timber Creek. The Gething Formation includes grains eroded from metamorphic rock found to the west in the Omineca Mountains, which were growing tall at that time.

Both the Gething and the Gates have been mined for coal; the Gates at Nordegg, Cadomin, Luscar—where the formation is exposed in open pits along the road between Hinton and Cadomin—and at Pocahontas in eastern Jasper park. A convenient place to see a bit of the Gething Formation is near Pocahontas, at Punchbowl Falls on the way to Miette Hot Springs. There are thin seams of coal in basal Gething beds at the lower viewpoint. Both the Gething and the Gates are currently mined at Grande Cache, where dinosaur tracks have been found in the rock. Farther north, in northeastern British Columbia, the Gates is mined at Tumbler Ridge and from there to the Peace River.

Beyond the Peace River the coal peters out. There are only thin seams at the Sikanni Chief River, where the strata go to marine sandstone and shale of the Fort St. John Group, 1000–1500 m thick. "Fort St. John" is from the British Columbia town to the east. This unit includes several formations above the Gates that were eroded farther south but remained underwater here: the Hulcross shale, Boulder Creek sandstone/conglomerate, Hassler shale, Goodrich sandstone and Cruiser shale. From the Halfway River north, the Buckinghorse Formation replaces everything from the Moosebar up, with Sikanni sandstone equivalent to the Goodrich Formation, but a little older, and the Sully shale taking the place of the Cruiser. Yet farther north, along the Toad River, the Buckinghorse shale is interrupted by two sandstones and the names change yet again, to Garbutt Formation shale at the base, through the Scatter Formation (which contains the sandstones), to the Lepine shale and over that the Sikanni and Sully.

As you might guess from all these names, stratigraphic relations among the Blairmore, Bullhead and Fort St. John groups are complicated, beyond the scope of this book. But their geological significance is fairly straightforward. All this rock documents another invasion of the Rocky Mountain Trough by the sea. Bullhead beds are mostly those of swampy, heavily vegetated deltas built out into the sea from the west. The strata carry plant fossils, while those below include the molluscs *Gastroplites* and *Posidonia*. Meanwhile the Blairmore Group accumulated above sea level, on land that was west of the sea's southward advance. To the east, though, on the Interior Plains, the sea reached south into Montana.

The sea withdrew early in the Late Cretaceous, at about 93 Ma, when the floor of the Rocky Mountain Trough rose slightly. At the same time, sea level dropped worldwide. As the inland sea shallowed, a vast delta/alluvial plain built eastward along the front of the northern Rockies. This is the Dunvegan Formation, up to 120 m of cliff-forming sandstone, which can be seen capping the foothills around Chetwynd and Hudson's Hope. Dunvegan rock lies atop the escarpment at the western edge of the Interior Plains farther north, where you see it from the Alaska Highway. Fossils include the ubiquitous clam *Inoceramus.*

The fast-building Dunvegan delta, coupled with a drop in sea level, divided the Cretaceous seaway into northern and southern segments. The Dunvegan Formation was eroded somewhat, and that unconformity marks the top of the second great packet of sediments in the Rocky Mountain Trough and thus indicates the end of infilling-episode II.

*Vertically tilted coal-bearing beds of the Luscar Group seen along Highway 11, at the mountain front west of Nordegg*

## Alberta Group and Smoky Group (start of infilling-episode III)
*Late Cretaceous (80–93 Ma), up to 1600 m*

The Alberta Group includes two thick units of dark, soft marine shale: the Blackstone Formation, 250–500 m thick, and the Wapiabi Formation, 300–500 m thick. A marine sandstone bed called the Cardium Formation, 10–75 m thick, lies sandwiched between. These three range from south of the Waterton/Glacier area to about the Athabasca River, where rock similar to the Alberta Group thickens considerably and continues north as the Smoky Group. The name changes because the Dunvegan sandstone (previous item) replaces the lower part of the Blackstone, the Kaskapau shale stands in for the rest, and above the Cardium the Muskiki shale, Badheart sandstone and Puskwaskau shale/sandstone top things up. Along the Toad River in the far northern end of the Rockies, the Kotanelee shale takes the place of the Puskwaskau. The Smoky Group is found mainly in the foothills, as is the Alberta Group, but Alberta Group beds also appear in the front ranges south of the Bow River and in the Mesozoic exposures southwest of Fernie.

Recessive and usually covered, Alberta/Smoky rock is best seen in the bedrock gorges along foothills streams. Two good places to view the Alberta Group are at the Kananaskis Dam along the Bow River west of Cochrane along Highway 1A, and below the Bighorn Dam, near the mountain front west of Rocky Mountain House along Highway 11. These sites expose the interesting, lumpily-bedded Cardium sandstone.

Blackstone beds outcrop where the TransCanada highway crosses Jumping Pound Creek west of Calgary, and also at the Oldman River bridge along Highway 22 north of the Crowsnest area. Look for black Wapiabi strata beside the TransCanada Highway where it crosses the Kananaskis River, just east of the Highway 1X turnoff near the mountain front. There is a sizable quarry in Wapiabi rock beside Highway 1X, and a sandstone bed in the Wapiabi called the Chungo Member is being quarried nearby, at the foot of Yamnuska Mountain. The quarry is accessible by taking 1X to 1A and turning north off 1A about one kilometre east.

The Alberta Group is marine, not quite the last marine rock in our area—that's the Bearpaw shale—but the last major unit. The Blackstone Formation holds fossils of lovely Late Cretaceous mother-of-pearl ammonites that swam the sea where prairie wheat grows now. The Cardium sandstone resulted from a shallowing phase, including a complete withdrawal of the sea north of the Peace River for about four million years. The Cardium is oil-bearing west of Edmonton, having sopped up from the surrounding shale the hydrocarbons of countless planktonic organisms. Atop the Cardium, the Wapiabi shale records a readvance of the sea, followed by yet another retreat a few million years later.

Fossils in this group include *Inoceramus* and *Watinoceras* in the Blackstone, tracks and burrows in the Cardium, *Scaphites* and *Inoceramus* in the Wapiabi.

### Brazeau Fm., Paskapoo Fm. and equivalents (infilling-episode III, continued)
*Late Cretaceous to Paleocene (60–80 Ma), up to 4000 m*

The Brazeau Formation, up to 1600 m thick, is a central-Rockies unit of nonmarine pebbly sandstone and river-carried shale, the sandstone beds full of dark and light grains that give them a salt-and-pepper look like that of the Blairmore Group. Also like the Blairmore, the Brazeau has a greenish cast from westerly derived volcanic dust and rock particles. North of Grande Cache the unit is called the Wapiti Formation, which is similar in thickness and rock type.

Deposition of the Brazeau and Wapiti formations was so fast that even though the Rocky Mountain Trough was sinking, it was kept filled with sediments. The sea was forced out of this area, which can be envisaged as a big, gradually subsiding marsh. Thus, Brazeau and Wapiti sand, mud and clay are freshwater deposits.

*Greenish Brazeau Formation sandstone and shale in a road-cut along Highway 16 west of Hinton*

There are road-cuts through tilted Brazeau strata along Highway 16 between the Obed railway overpass and Hinton, and an excellent natural Brazeau outcrop occurs at the turnoff to the Jasper-Hinton Airport. Shaly beds are visible in road-cuts nearby. Fossils in all these units are mainly those of plants.

Swampy conditions near the end of Brazeau time were right for the formation of low-rank lignite coal, also called **thermal coal** or **steaming coal** because it is used mainly in heating boilers. Seams of the Coalspur Formation are the youngest commercial deposits in the Canadian Rockies, currently mined in the eastern foothills for use in coal-burning power stations as far away as Ontario. Open-pit mining continues at Sterco, along Highway 40 near the Pembina River, and at the newer Obed mine northeast of Hinton.

South of the Bow River, Brazeau-equivalent sediments are more complicated. The nonmarine Belly River Formation, over 600 m thick, and the St. Mary River Formation, 250 m, resemble the Brazeau, but they are split by the marine Bearpaw Formation shale, 180–490 m, which represents the last advance of the sea into our area. You can see the Bearpaw shale in the eastern foothills southwest of Calgary; it holds the ammonite *Placenticeras*.

Above the St. Mary River comes the soft Willow Creek Formation, 1200 m of buff, pink or greenish sandstone and shale. The Willow Creek is the western equivalent of the upper Edmonton Group, which is famous for dinosaur fossils in the Drumheller area of south-central Alberta. The big reptiles did very well in the thickly vegetated swamps fringing the last of the Cretaceous sea, but for some reason dinosaur bones are seldom found in the Rockies foothills. You can see the same sort of pastel-hued beds that hold the big bones farther east if you travel Highway 22 north of Crowsnest Pass, where the road runs along the west side of the Porcupine Hills.

Topping the stack in the Rocky Mountain Trough is the Paleocene Paskapoo Formation and its southern equivalent the Porcupine Hills Formation: up to 1500 m of buffy sandstone and gray shale. The shale is rich in plant fragments and contains many freshwater snails. A good place to see this unit is anywhere in the Porcupine Hills (north of Crowsnest Pass), in the Calgary area and along Highway 16 west of Edson. From Hinton north, the Paskapoo is out on the Interior Plains, east of Highway 40, so there is no Paleocene rock on the eastern slope of the northern Rockies. The youngest rock found in the foothills there is the Late Cretaceous Wapiti Formation.

Is this the top of the whole collection of layers in the Canadian Rockies? Not quite. There are some formations on the western slope, in and around the Rocky Mountain Trench, that are younger than the youngest material in the Rocky Mountain Trough. (Again, keep in mind that the *trench* and the *trough* are two different things; see page 121.) Most of these trench deposits came after the mountain-building period in western Canada, and they exist because of events late in the disturbance. So they are best described *after* going into the mechanics of the upheaval.

## *The Cretaceous Period: out with a bang*

The end of the Cretaceous at 66.4 Ma has long been known for the sudden disappearance of the dinosaurs. However, the cause wasn't identified until the 1980s, when the discovery of a worldwide **iridium**-rich zone at the Cretaceous/Paleocene boundary led geologists to speculate about a catastrophe: the impact of an asteroid-sized object with the earth (iridium is common in space objects but rare on our planet), producing a pall of dust that blocked the sun's warmth for months or even years, upsetting the world's ecology so much that about two-thirds of all known species died out.

I should add that in western Canada the dinosaurs were already losing ground when the extinction event occurred. Climatic change and other factors had reduced Alberta dinosaur populations considerably in the Late Cretaceous; the astrophysical disaster seems to have been the capper. A number of other mass-extinctions are noted on the geologic charts that begin on page 192.

# *Orogenous zones*
## The building of the Rockies

The crust of the earth is divided into 14 interlocking pieces called **plates,** and the world's plates move. Tugged from below by currents of hot, nearly molten rock in the earth's mantle, the plates jostle at their edges, collide and slip past each other. At the mid-oceanic ridges the sea floor spreads sideways and makes the plates wider, yet the amount of surface area on earth is fixed, ensuring that collisions and overlaps will occur.

This is all taught in first-year geology classes these days, but when I was at university we learned the geological history of a world without continental drift. The explanations were difficult to follow and full of contradictions, because, as it turned out, they were wrong. Since then the science of **plate tectonics**—the study of plate interactions—has explained things in a way that makes sense. Western Canada, for example, is at the edge of a plate, and that plate has collided with another plate, pushing up mountains.

Beyond that the complications set in. They are amazing and fascinating. For example, the plate collision that built the Rockies was not a simple edge-to-edge impact; the floor of the Pacific Ocean slipped under the edge of North America. Some of it is still there, melting away, and magma from it has risen up to produce the volcanoes of central British Columbia. Landmasses riding on the Pacific floor did not go down with their plate; they were scraped off by the continent and added on to the western edge of North America, giving the residents of B.C. somewhere to live. Incredibly, much of central and western B.C. is land that formed along the western continental edge, then was carried southward to the position of Baja California, then back northward to approximately its present position. Much of B.C. is made of strips of land that continue their northerly trek to this day.

## *The time-lapse-movie account*

Imagine that we are high in the sky over what will eventually become the eastern foothills of the Rockies. The time is 200–220 million years ago in the Late Triassic or the Early Jurassic. The Rockies area is under the sea, part of a shallow continental shelf several hundred kilometres wide, attached to the mainland to the northeast. There are two parallel chains of islands lying off to the southwest. Let's call the inner chain of islands, which is about 100 km across, "landmass A." The outer chain of islands, which is much wider, say 500 km, we'll call "landmass B." Island chains such as landmass A and landmass B have been present intermittently along the edge of the continent for half a billion years. Some of the islands are fragments of North America left behind in its wanderings; others have been built by volcanoes. They are all stuck to the ocean floor, off the edge of the continent.

We notice that landmass A and landmass B are both getting closer, at a speed of something like 5–10 cm per year. We see that the North American continent is moving northwest while the island chains are moving northeast. This amounts to a collision course, at an angle.

The islands encounter the edge of the continent. They are scraped off the oceanic crust and added to North America, while the oceanic crust slides down under the edge of the continent. This is a geologically violent event in which mountain ranges are built, volcanoes go off and lots of earthquakes occur. An **orogeny,** in other words.

The orogeny continues for 55–75 million years. By 140 million years ago at the end of the Jurassic, the landmass-B islands, the outer chain, have crushed in on the landmass-A islands, the inner chain, creating a continuous strip of mountainous land several hundred kilometres wide that had been added to the west coast. The strip is moving inland, up over the edge of the continent, pressing toward us, bulldozing the sedimentary rock of the continental shelf ahead of it and narrowing the distance eastward to the mainland shore. We are overlooking a strait perhaps 200 km wide, aligned northwest to southeast.

On the southwest side of the strait are parallel ranges of Himalayan-size peaks: landmasses A and B. Reaching from them down to the shore are lower mountains: the continental-shelf

## The building of the Canadian Rockies

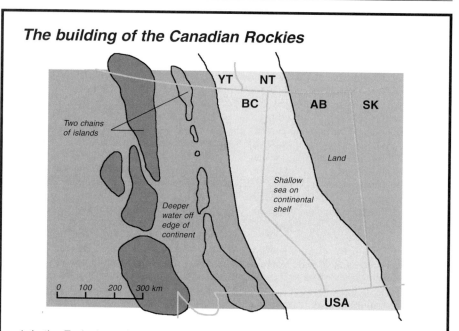

1. In the Early Jurassic, 200 million years ago, the Rockies area lies under shallow seawater on the western continental shelf. Two chains of islands exist in deeper water offshore. These landmasses are mostly volcanic, resting on the ocean floor.

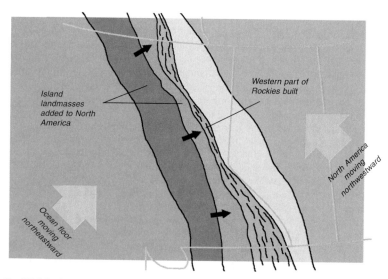

2. In the Middle Jurassic, 175 million years ago, North America moves northwestward. The oceanic floor is moving northeastward, so the two plates collide. The island chains are added to British Columbia. The impact builds mountain ranges across B.C., including the westernmost Rockies by about 140 million years ago.

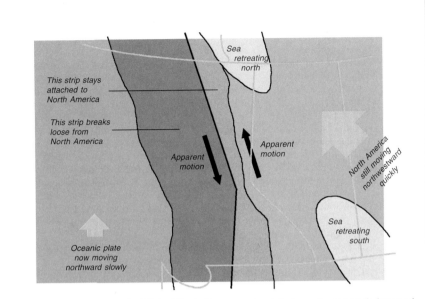

3. At the end of the Jurassic (135 million), the oceanic plate has slowed and changed its movement to northward. The continent is moving relatively faster. It slides past the outer landmass strip until the strip is opposite Baja California. Mountain-building stalls and the Rockies wear down for 10–20 million years.

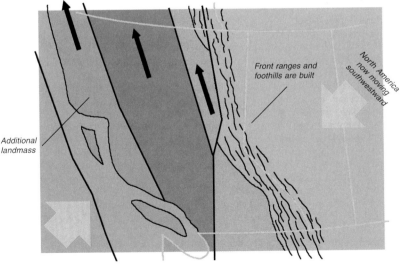

4. In the last stage, the oceanic plate moves northeastward again. The outer strip slides back northward, bringing a third landmass. This increases the plate squeeze. Mountains rise farther east, including the front ranges (85 million) and foothills (60 million). By this time the continent is moving southwestward.

sediments pushed ahead by the landmasses. Not as high as the peaks of landmass A and landmass B, these are the young main ranges of the Canadian Rockies, the westernmost part.

On the other side of the strait lie the coastal lowlands of the North American mainland. Rivers are carrying sediments into the sea from both sides of the strait, providing a geological record of all these events.

Ten million years later, the main ranges of the Rockies have grown considerably, although they are not as tall as the mountains of landmass A. We look over the top of the landmass-A peaks toward those of landmass B, and we see something startling: the mountains of landmass B appear to be moving southward. Landmass A is solidly attached to the western edge of North America, but not landmass B. A big fault has developed between landmass A and landmass B. The North American plate has continued northwest, taking landmass A with it, but not landmass B. Landmass B lies on the far side of the fault, on the oceanic plate, and the movement of the oceanic plate has changed. It is now headed north instead of northeast, and it has slowed down. It can't keep up with the continental plate. In effect, North America is passing landmass B in the righthand lane. From our perspective in the righthand lane, landmass B is going backward.

The parade of landmass B mountains goes by us from northwest to southeast for 10–20 million years, long enough for the peaks at the head of the parade to slide down the coast all the way to Baja California. While this is happening, the plates are slipping by each other rather than converging much, so the orogeny is stalled and the mountains are not growing. They are eroding, losing height.

Then, in the middle of the Cretaceous Period about 100–120 million years ago, the parade stops. The motion of the oceanic plate has changed back to what it was. It is now moving northeastward again, and it is speeding up, while the North American plate continues to move northwestward at its usual pace. This combination does two things:

• The oceanic plate carrying landmass B presses harder against landmass A and the continent, forcing landmass A farther inland to the northeast and bulldozing up more of the sedimentary rock of the continental shelf, building the main ranges of the Canadian Rockies higher and extending them northeastward into the strait.

• The parade reverses. In effect, the vehicle in the left lane (landmass B) now moves ahead of the vehicle in the right lane (landmass A). To us, it looks like landmass B is moving back up the coast along the big fault.

Landmass B goes by for 15–20 million years. Then we notice that it is growing wider on its seaward side, for it has picked up yet another strip of islands (we will call them "landmass C") while it was down in California. Meanwhile North America is gradually changing its direction of movement to the southwest, more directly against the motion of the oceanic plate. Landmass C is anchored to the oceanic plate, and is offering additional resistance to the edge of the continent. The orogeny intensifies; bulldozed mountains are being built farther northeastward, first the front ranges of the Rockies about 85 million years ago, and then the foothills 65 million years ago, at the end of the Cretaceous. The strait has dwindled away and western Canada is all land.

Forty million years after that, we look over to landmasses B and C sliding by and recognize some of the landmarks of landmass B that we saw when the parade started. They have come all the way back from Baja. And they keep going northwestward until the present time, when we note that they are up to 750 km northwest of their original locations. Meanwhile the strip of landmass-C mountains, the one farthest west, is galloping ahead even faster, reaching Alaska. British Columbia is breaking into other strips, and these are sliding northwestward, too. Every strip, although it is pressed against the continent, is moving independently in its own slot.

Watching this is giving us a headache. Having overseen the development of the entire Western Canadian Cordillera, we call it a day.

Here are the modern geographic names and approximate locations of the landmasses. Landmass A is the western part of the Columbia Mountains (western Selkirks, southwestern Monashees, western Cariboos), the western Omineca Mountains and the western Cassiar Mountains. Landmass B is everything west of that to the Coast Mountains. Landmass C, the additional strip picked up far to the south, is mostly underwater off the west coast, but Vancouver Island and the Queen Charlotte Islands stick up.

In geological terminology, landmasses A, B and C are **terranes,** meaning areas of land that have moved from their original locations to somewhere else. British Columbia is made up mostly of terranes; some 42 have been identified. Landmasses A and B together make up a collection of terranes known as Intermontane Superterrane (doesn't that roll off the tongue?). Landmass C is known as Insular Superterrane.

Please note that the timing of the events given above is still under debate, as are some of the scenes I have described. Some geologists are convinced that the Canadian Rockies are less than 120 million years old. Landmass B's trip to Baja and back is a new idea.

## Not uplift, but up-piling. And an accompanying down-sag

It is important to understand that the Canadian Rockies grew taller from a buildup of folded and overthrust rock, not by uplift from below. Geologists estimate that the once-horizontal sedimentary layers in the central Canadian Rockies have telescoped at least 300 km, perhaps as much as 500 km. That rock had to go somewhere, and it couldn't go down, for the thick basement rock of the continent (page 45) underlay it. So the sediments stacked up.

Thus, the Western Canadian Cordillera stands tall not through uplift but through up-piling. In fact, the opposite of uplift occurred: the growing pile of heavy rock pushed the underlying western margin of the North American plate down into the mantle. Continental crust is not very flexible, and the bend in the western margin extended for several hundred kilometres beyond the northeastern edge of the mountain mass, creating a long trough along the mountain front called a **foredeep,** meaning a deep place beside a mountain range. A foredeep subsides gradually, filling with sediments as it deepens. As the mountains are bulldozed ahead, the foredeep moves along in front of them. See the diagram on page 122.

Such a foredeep developed in front of the Rockies. Long known to geologists as a region of thick sedimentary deposits, this feature is named the Rocky Mountain Trough, not to be confused with the Rocky Mountain *Trench,* a modern valley on the west side of the Rockies. Jurassic, Cretaceous and Tertiary layers in the foredeep record the building of Canada's western

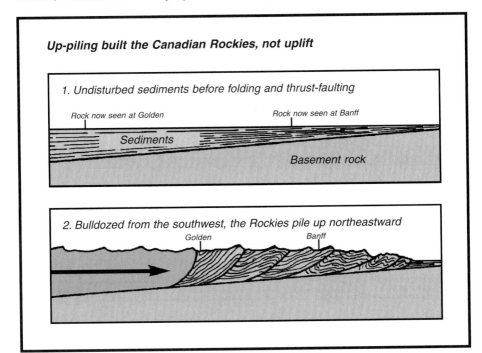

**Up-piling built the Canadian Rockies, not uplift**

*1. Undisturbed sediments before folding and thrust-faulting*

Rock now seen at Golden          Rock now seen at Banff

Sediments

Basement rock

*2. Bulldozed from the southwest, the Rockies pile up northeastward*

Golden          Banff

mountain ranges, but that is not why geologists first became interested in the rock of the foredeep. Early in the century, long before concepts such as "foredeep" had been considered, those western Canadian geologists were looking for coal, natural gas and oil. They found them in the foredeep, and they found them in abundance.

Next: the way in which the rock of the Rockies moved.

## Stacking from west to east

When a region of sedimentary rock is squeezed from the sides, it tends to split into slabs that ride up over one another, a process called **thrust faulting.** Thrusted slabs of rock in the Canadian Rockies are anywhere from a few centimetres thick to many kilometres thick, and the distance they have moved relative to the rock below is anywhere from a few centimetres to 60 or 70 km. A single slab, called a **thrust sheet,** can be many kilometres long and wide. Thrust-faulting occurred repeatedly from west to east in the Rockies, for millions of years, so the result has been a whole series of stacked thrust sheets, rather like shingles on a roof.

Most thrust faults in the foothills and front ranges are typically steep at the surface, but followed downward they flatten out and join one another, so that they all tie in to a stupendous horizontal fault along the buried surface of the basement rock some 5–10 km down. This is a general rule of Canadian Rockies geology, a defining characteristic of the Canadian Rockies

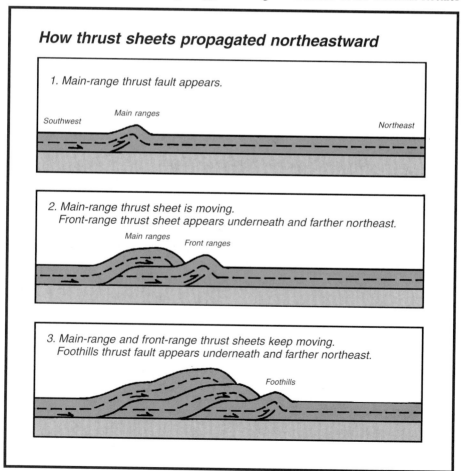

### How thrust sheets propagated northeastward

1. Main-range thrust fault appears.

Southwest    Main ranges    Northeast

2. Main-range thrust sheet is moving.
   Front-range thrust sheet appears underneath and farther northeast.

Main ranges    Front ranges

3. Main-range and front-range thrust sheets keep moving.
   Foothills thrust fault appears underneath and farther northeast.

Foothills

demonstrable wherever deep drilling has reached the basement. It applies throughout the range, except at the extreme western edge where the basement itself was thrust-faulted.

The geological consequence of this configuration is that the entire Canadian Rockies must have moved northeastward along that big thrust fault at the base of the heap. It's like pushing the skin on the back of your hand along with your thumb, causing wrinkling ahead of the thumb. The skin slides on the ligament layer underneath, just as the sedimentary rock of the Canadian Rockies has come loose and slid on the basement rock beneath. The geological term for this is French: **decollement** ("day-coal-MONT"), meaning "to come unstuck."

The record is clear: decollement and thrust-faulting in the Canadian Rockies proceeded from west to east. The diagram on the facing page puts this sequence together graphically. It shows a concept that is difficult to grasp: that each thrust fault formed *under and ahead of* the previous one, even though thrust-faulting is an up-and-over action.

Since deformation proceeded from west to east, and because the thrust faults of the Rockies were known to flatten out westward as they were traced deeper, geologists theorized that the faults of the front ranges had formed under and ahead of the main ranges. Likewise, it seemed impossible to escape the conclusion that the faults of the foothills had developed under and ahead of the front ranges. Fieldwork and drilling have shown this to be true. The thing to keep in mind is that as the thrusted area expanded to the east, *the whole works kept moving*. This maintained the up-and-over motion as new thrusts originated below and east of old ones.

You can model this process in the nearest sandbox, despite the difference in scale. Smooth out a patch of damp sand about a metre square. Now step firmly into it, with a forward motion of your foot. The sand will form rings ahead of your toes. These rings are actually thrust faults. Cutting a cross-section in the sand will show the same upward-curved fault planes you find in Rockies thrusts. The more force you apply, the more faults you get, and the farther they spread from the toe of your foot, just as the thrust faults of the Rockies spread outward from the zone of the crunch, from southwest to northeast. Thus, the main ranges, which are the most southwesterly ranges, are the oldest, followed by the front ranges and finally the foothills. The sedimentary record in the Rocky Mountain Trough agrees with this, and even provides the timing of the events.

## Big slips, and some back-sliding

There is a little more to this story, and it relates to that fascinating feature, the Rocky Mountain Trench. Again, be careful not to confuse it with the Rocky Mountain *Trough*.

As described in the previous section, during the building of western Canada's mountains some big faults developed between adjacent landmasses. These were not thrust faults; they were **transcurrent faults,** in which landmass B moved against landmass A, and so on. Thin and easily fractured, these oceanic-crust terranes split lengthwise and were tugged northward in strips. The lengthwise faults between them are transcurrent faults similar to the San Andreas Fault in California.

Two plates move horizontally along such a fault, sliding past each other. The plates move smoothly at depth, where the rock deforms plastically, but nearer the surface, where the rock is cool and brittle, the motion is jerky, causing the earthquakes for which the San Andreas and other transcurrent faults are famous.

There are several major southeast/northwest transcurrent faults in British Columbia, and one of them follows the northern Rocky Mountain Trench. West of the Northern Rocky Mountain Trench Fault, British Columbia has moved northwestward a distance of at least 400 km relative to the rest of the continent, and perhaps as much as 750 km. Rock that might otherwise be part of the central Canadian Rockies is found 400 km north in the Cassiars.

It is important to realize that the Northern Rocky Mountain Trench Fault does *not* follow the suture between landmass A and the North American plate. That boundary lies 50–100 km west of the fault, within landmass A. The northern Rocky Mountain Trench formed after landmass A had attached to the continent.

Given the maximum 50-million-year period of motion along the Northern Rocky Mountain Trench Fault (Late Cretaceous to Eocene), the annual slippage must have averaged nearly a centimetre per year. This would have produced strong and frequent earthquakes. One imagines the little fox-like horses that lived in western Canada getting knocked off their feet from time to time. The big slips of the Canadian Cordillera still move today, as evidenced by earthquakes in western British Columbia and Alaska.

## *Block-faulting in the southern Rocky Mountain Trench*

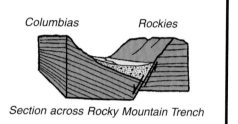

*Crustal stretching across southern British Columbia causes block-faulting along the southern Rocky Mountain Trench, dividing the Columbia Mountains from the Rockies. Similar faults define the Flathead Valley and Elk Valley. Streams fill these half-grabens with debris.*

Columbias     Rockies

*Section across Rocky Mountain Trench*

The northern section of the Rocky Mountain Trench runs straight as a die from the Yukon boundary southeast to the end of Williston Lake, where it begins to lose its clean lines. In the Prince George area, there is no trench. The main transcurrent fault has broken into a number of smaller faults—has **splayed**—and these angle southwesterly in a wide zone of weakness.

But southeast of Prince George the southern portion of the trench begins. In this section the faulting is quite different from that of the northern trench: up-and-down instead of sideways. Layers seen low in the trench around McBride match up with the edges of layers exposed a thousand metres higher on the northeastern wall. Here the trench is a **half-graben** ("half-GRAH-ben"), a strip of rock that has dropped down relative to the rock on one side, like a long, skinny door opening downward. The hinge would be on west side of the trench. "Trench" is an appropriate name for the valley here; the Rockies overlook a natural ditch in the crust.

This kind of faulting is called **block-faulting**. It is caused by crustal stretching, which occurred here from 35–55 million years ago in the Eocene Epoch of the Tertiary Period. The Rocky Mountain Trench from Prince George south seems to reflect only block-faulting, not transcurrent faulting. The rock on either side matches fairly well, indicating that little or no sideways motion has occurred along this segment.

Near the international boundary the trench breaks into several half-graben valleys and loses its linear character. Coarse sediments (the Kishenehn and St. Eugene formations of the Tertiary Period) filled these half-grabens as they formed. There are also Tertiary sediments in the northern Rocky Mountain Trench (the Sifton Formation) suggesting that some block faulting occurred here, too, even though this section shows predominantly transcurrent slippage.

One other block-fault valley in the Rockies worthy of mention is the Flathead Valley, at the far southern end of the range. This is a half-graben 6 km deep. It forms the western edge of Glacier National Park, Montana and continues north into Canada as the Elk River valley. The Flathead Fault lies along the eastern wall of both valleys; followed westward by seismic exploration, this major fault flattens at depth and merges with the Lewis Thrust, the big thrust fault that underlies the Waterton/Glacier area.

## *After mountain-building and before the Ice Ages*

The entire Rockies region has been above sea level since the early Tertiary, which means that erosion rather then deposition has been the rule here for about 60 million years. An exception occurs on the western slope, in the Rocky Mountain Trench and other deep valleys. Sediment worn from the mountains has accumulated here, in half-graben valleys formed by faults that became active at about 45 Ma in the Eocene Epoch.

One of these accumulations is the Sifton Formation, which occurs in the northern Rocky Mountain Trench between the Ingenika River, near the north end of Williston Lake, and Sifton Pass, which is a slight rise in the trench floor. (Sifton Pass divides the Kechika River from the Finlay River.) There is also a patch of Sifton sediment farther south on the west shore of Williston Lake opposite the Peace River outflow. An outcrop of similar but unstudied rock occurs yet farther south along Reynolds Creek east of McLeod Lake, and Sifton-like deposits dated as Oligocene occur nearby along Highway 97 at the bridge over the Parsnip River.

The Sifton is a little-studied nonmarine sequence of limestone-pebble conglomerate with beds of finer clastic rock and coal. The thickness is undetermined. Some of the sediments are known from plant fossils to be Paleocene and Eocene. They were derived in part from the east, which is to say from the Rockies of 35–45 million years ago. The trench deposits are tilted, showing that earth movements were still occurring in the northern Rocky Mountain Trench at this time.

Two better-known Tertiary units in the south end of our area mark the tapering-off of mountain-building more closely: the Kishenehn Formation and the St. Eugene Formation. Both occur on the western slope, in and about the trench. They are tilted but not bent into folds, showing that the main event was over by the time they were laid down.

## Kishenehn Formation
*Late Eocene to Oligocene (24–40 Ma), 300–2500 m*
Pronounced "KISH-en-en," from Kishenena Creek (note variant spelling), which flows from South Kootenay pass into the Flathead Valley just north of the international boundary. Mostly very coarse conglomerate, with boulders up to 2 m across, overlain by Oligocene lake silt. Includes **marlstone** (freshwater limestone) beds, oil shale and coal. The Kishenehn is found along the Flathead Fault from the southern end of the Canadian Rockies north to Packhorse Peak along the continental divide northwest of Waterton Park. There are good exposures beside the Flathead River, reached via the Flathead Road along the western border of Glacier National Park.

Following the piling-up of the Canadian Rockies, the Flathead Fault formed as a result of stretching. This is a big normal fault running from the Elk River valley north of Fernie to beyond the southern end of Glacier park. Land west of the fault dropped some 6000 m in the Eocene and Oligocene, and the resulting deep depression picked up a great deal of material eroded from the young Rockies beside it. That material is the Kishenehn Formation, essentially a collection of **alluvial fans:** sand and gravel spread out over the valley floor. Following Kishenehn beds upward illustrates the erosional stripping of the Rockies. The lower layers are full of pebbles that could have come only from the cherty Rundle limestones. The upper ones contain Palliser pebbles, equally easy to identify, that were washed in after the Rundle Group and the underlying shaly Banff Formation had been eroded away, exposing Palliser rock beneath. Atop the coarse conglomerate beds, fine-grained lake deposits show that erosion proceeded more slowly later on.

Kishenehn beds are tilted, indicating that the Rockies were still somewhat restless during the Oligocene.

## St. Eugene Formation
*Middle and Late Miocene (5.3–16.6 Ma), up to 1500 m*
The St. Eugene is mostly **colluvium** (coarse, angular, unconsolidated material that has moved downhill only a short distance), **fanglomerate** (hardened mudflows and alluvial-fan material), silt, sand and coarse gravel. Found in the southern Rocky Mountain Trench, it is overlain by Pleistocene glacial deposits. Best seen on the western side of the trench between Kimberley and Cranbrook along Highway 95A. A good exposure is located just off the highway on the north bank of the St. Mary River, 1.5 km northwest of the highway bridge over it, below a fenced picnic site. The unit is also found along Gold Creek north of Newgate, and on the east side of the trench along the Elk River south of Elko.

St. Eugene sediments are the youngest pre-glacial deposits known in the trench; they, and perhaps other, unexposed sediments filled the half-grabens of the extreme southern section.

The St. Eugene was deposited as the faults moved, so the sediments themselves are faulted. Detritus derived from a distinctive layer of volcanic rock in the neighboring Galton Range (the Purcell Lava, page 57), should be present in the St. Eugene but isn't—suggesting that the eastern wall of the Rocky Mountain Trench was *uplifted* 600 m after the St. Eugene was laid down. Block uplift is rare in the Canadian Rockies, where mountain-building has been accomplished through the stacking of thrust sheets. But block uplift late in the Miocene was common in the American Rockies to the south. Maybe some occurred here, too. Plant fossils and pollen preserved in the St. Eugene suggest a warmer, wetter climate in the area during the Miocene than at present.

*The St. Eugene Formation near Wycliffe, along Highway 95A south of Kimberley*

## Pre-glacial gravel on the eastern slope

*Pleistocene or older (1.9–2.5 Ma), up to 30 m*

Rivers have been carrying the Rockies bit-by-bit to the sea for ages. Here and there in the eastern foothills, and quite commonly on the prairies, one can find gravel deposits from the rivers that carried these sediments just before the major glacial advances of the last two million years disrupted river courses throughout most of Canada. Pre-glacial gravel deposits are the only sediments on the eastern slope that assuredly postdate the building of the Rockies—they cross folds and faults with no sign of disturbance—and they predate the arrival of ice from the Canadian Shield, because there are no Shield-type stones included.

Heavy glacial erosion seems to have removed all pre-glacial gravel from the western foothills, front range and main ranges (but see page 151).

*Pre-glacial gravel exposed in a pit atop Broadcast Hill in Calgary. Photo by Cia Gadd.*

# *Ice in the Rockies*
## The Quaternary Period (Pleistocene and Holocene epochs)

In reading this section you may see some glacial-geology terms that are not familiar. Or you may want a more general introduction to the topic. If so, turn to the section on modern glaciers, which begins on page 159. The diagrams and photos in that section explain many glacial features.

What caused the Ice Ages? This is one of the great questions of geology, and no single answer is universally accepted. Something, though, caused the earth's climate to cool markedly about 2.5 million years ago, near the end of the Pliocene Epoch of the Tertiary Period. The ensuing Pleistocene ("PLICE-tuh-seen") Epoch of the Quaternary Period, meaning the last 1.87 million years, has been the coldest, snowiest period on our planet in many millions of years. Even in the middle latitudes of the northern and southern hemispheres, snow that had previously melted away each summer remained year after year to accumulate into huge, continent-straddling glacial ice sheets. Many explanations have been offered for the Ice Ages, none entirely satisfactory, but one factor correlates well: the amount of carbon dioxide in the atmosphere has been high during warm periods in the earth's history and low during cold periods. Given that mankind has increased the amount of atmospheric $CO_2$ by 21 percent since the industrial revolution, this is food for thought.

Within the Pleistocene, there were many glacial advances and retreats. In 1938 Yugoslavian astronomer and mathematician Milutin Milankovitch linked these to regular, predictable changes in the earth's orbit and spin axis. He calculated cycles in the not-quite-circular path the earth takes around the sun (91,800 years), the angle between earth's spin axis and its orbital path, from 21°58' to 24°36' off perpendicular (40,000 years), and the precession of the equinoxes, meaning the wobbling of the planet on its spin axis (21,000 years). These cycles have correlated reasonably well with the timings of major glacial advances and retreats during the Quaternary. There is no reason to doubt that glaciers in the Rockies responded much as those elsewhere in the world did, and there is abundant evidence here of past glaciation far more extensive than we see now.

Some of this evidence is in the form of **till,** the essential glacial product. Glaciers move. They pick up rock, carry it, grind it up and dump it out as an unlayered mixture of mud and scratched-up stones eroded from outcrops anywhere upstream in the glacial flow. These are the essential characteristics of till. Nothing else seems to make till except glaciers. Other processes—landslides, mudflows, even turbidity currents—can produce deposits that have some characteristics of till but not all of them. So till is undeniable evidence of glaciation. It is often in the form of **moraines:** landforms made of till.

Till is found sporadically throughout the geological record as **diamictite,** also called **tillite:** till hardened to rock. There is good evidence for glaciation near the end of the Precambrian in the Rockies area, where the Paleoproterozoic Misinchinka Group has strikingly till-like diamictite units about 750 million years old (see page 68).

During the Pleistocene, the main ice centre for the mountains of western Canada was in central British Columbia, well west of the Rockies, where an ice sheet over a kilometre thick built up during each major glacial episode.

*Till seen near the Athabasca Glacier, with a raven for scale*

From it glaciers flowed in all directions. The Rocky Mountain Trench collected ice from both the Columbia Mountains, under the icecap, and from the Rockies, where there was another buildup. Ice in the deep Rocky Mountain Trench escaped not only by flowing out the southern end of the trench; it also overtopped the continental divide and flowed eastward across the Rockies. It may have taken the same routes during each major glacial advance, deepening the gaps more and more.

Today those gaps remain as the major Rockies passes—Crowsnest, Kicking Horse, Howse, Yellowhead, Pine and so on—including the largest and deepest of them all, which doesn't even have a name. It is the gap through which the Peace River flows.

Far to the east, another centre of glaciation was on the Canadian Shield west of Hudson Bay. Ice would spread out from this centre during glacial intervals, deepening enough to overcome the gentle uphill grade southwest across the prairies. Eastern glaciers reached the mountain front during at least one of the Pleistocene ice buildups. Which one (or ones) is currently a matter of debate among glacial geologists. It had been thought that the biggest

*These terraced deposits on the northern flank of Mt. St. George in Stone Mountain Provincial Park probably relate to the glacial history of the area, but how? This is just one of many unanswered questions on the Quaternary of the Canadian Rockies.*

ice buildup in or near the Rockies was the Illinoian advance of about a quarter-million years ago, but recent work is favoring the late-Wisconsinan advance of only 25,000 years ago, which had previously been thought to be minor. If this proposed revision is accepted, it will be a major change in the glacial chronology of the Rockies. Until the matter is sorted out, I'm speaking rather generally in this chapter.

Glaciation has been mainly an erosional process west of the mountain front, not a depositional one. The thickest ice buildup, whenever it occurred, would have scraped away most of the evidence of earlier glacial advances. It does appear that one glacial advance outdid all the others in ice depth and glacier length, leaving deposits that were untouched by lesser advances. It was called …

## The Great Glaciation

During the Great Glaciation, mountain ice flowed east through the foothills and onto the Interior Plains. At the mountain front, each valley poured forth its stream of slow-moving glacial ice as a spreading lobe that mingled with others. The scene might have looked like the Arctic Islands today, where glaciers now empty from the mountain valleys and spread out on the flats beyond.

River valleys of the foothills and eastern prairies were overrun by ice that unloaded till into them. This was fortunate, for it preserved evidence of the Great Glaciation along the eastern margin of the Rockies. In southern Alberta, the Oldman, Castle and St. Mary rivers have since cut down into these deposits. There seem to have been at least two Great Glaciation advances, about equally strong, each one involving mountain ice from the west, out of the Rockies, and prairie ice from the east, carrying stones from the Canadian Shield.

Did the eastern and western ice sheets meet? Yes. From Calgary north, mountain ice was deflected southward against the prairie ice front. South of Calgary, though, the two lobes seem never to have touched, although they crossed overlapping territory. Mountain ice flowed out first, maintained itself there for a while, then retreated to the mountain front before the far-travelled prairie ice arrived. Whether this happened more than once is unknown.

# The Canadian Rockies before, during and after the Great Glaciation

1. Before the glacial advances of the Pleistocene, the Canadian Rockies may have looked something like this. The topography is generally rounded. Slopes are convex, with broad summits and long, gentle ridges. Rivers flow in winding, V-shaped valleys. There are few lakes or waterfalls.

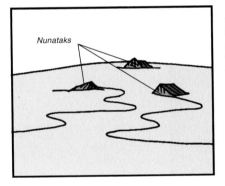

Nunataks

2. At the height of the Great Glaciation, the ice is over a kilometre thick. The Rockies are ice-capped: so deeply covered that only the higher summits stick through as **nunataks.** All this ice is moving. It grinds away at the peaks, removing a great deal of rock very quickly.

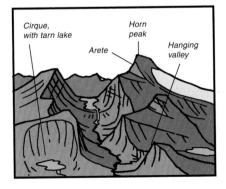

Cirque, with tarn lake
Horn peak
Arete
Hanging valley

3. Climatic warming melts most of the ice, revealing the glaciated landscape. The peaks have been carved into rugged **horns,** with bowl-shaped **cirques** in their sides. The ridges are sharp-edged **aretes** ("ah-RETTS"). The valleys are now straighter, and U-shaped in cross-section. Side valleys meet the main valley at a higher level; they are **hanging valleys.** There are many waterfalls. **Tarn lakes** lie in bedrock basins carved out by the ice.

The crest of the Porcupine Hills, which lie along the mountain front north of Crowsnest Pass, was not touched by ice from either direction, as shown by the absence of till. That makes the upper slopes and summits of the Porcupine Hills, and a few spots about 15 km west near the continental divide, the only places known in the Canadian Rockies that definitely have never been glaciated. Elsewhere, glacial landforms and deposits of till are ubiquitous. There are also large deposits of material that looks like till but isn't. Read on.

## The till that wasn't

Originally identified as till, surficial deposits in the Bow Valley between Banff and Canmore have troubled glacial geologists for a long time. The deposits are very stony, with faint layering that is normally lacking in till. The same sort of material, and there is a lot of it, can be found at low elevations in many of the major valleys in the Rockies, including the Rocky Mountain Trench. What is this stuff? Research in the 1980s has shown that it was deposited by **debris flows,** as follows.

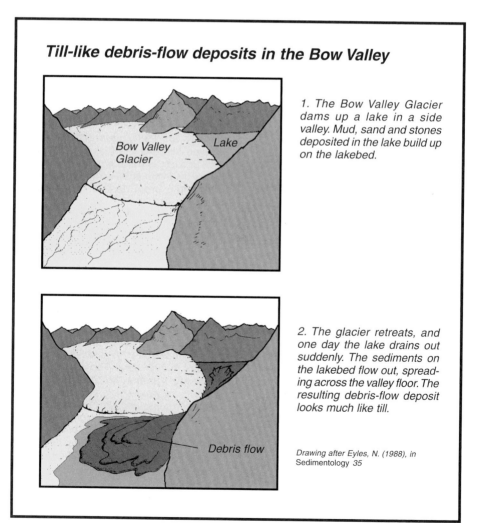

### Till-like debris-flow deposits in the Bow Valley

*1. The Bow Valley Glacier dams up a lake in a side valley. Mud, sand and stones deposited in the lake build up on the lakebed.*

*2. The glacier retreats, and one day the lake drains out suddenly. The sediments on the lakebed flow out, spreading across the valley floor. The resulting debris-flow deposit looks much like till.*

Drawing after Eyles, N. (1988), in Sedimentology 35

It's the end of a major glaciation in the Rockies. Around Banff and Canmore, the ice has melted back several kilometres in the side valleys, but the wide, thick glacier in the Bow Valley has taken longer to retreat, and its ice front lies somewhat east of the modern location of Banff. The big glacier acts as a dam, blocking the flow of water from the Cascade River and Lake Minnewanka. A large lake backs up into these valleys.

Gravel, sand and silt flow into the lake. Also, the water is deep enough to cover moraines along the sides of the valleys. These moraines, made of till, become saturated. The ice front of the Bow Valley glacier retreats slowly up the valley, getting closer and closer to the lake …

Suddenly the lake spills past the ice, releasing all its water in a matter of hours. Sediment on the lake floor is picked up and carried along in the drainage rush. The water-soaked moraines are highly unstable, and they slump into the lake as it withdraws. The resulting thick slurry of mud and gravel becomes a massive debris flow that covers much of the Banff and Canmore area with up to 30 m of mud and stones.

It turns out that this sort of spectacular event is common in mountainous areas in the late stages of glaciations. Ice-bursting floods can be seen today in Iceland and Greenland.

Surficial deposits around Jasper look much like the debris flows of Banff, as do those seen between Golden and Radium in the Rocky Mountain Trench. Lime in these debris flows, and in many other till-like deposits in the Rockies, has hardened somewhat, strengthening them. In the first 5 km of the trail up Forty Mile Creek near Banff, there are scattered till-like blobs along the trail that are cemented so well with calcite that they have become rock—diamictite—as have similar deposits along the opening stretch of the trail to Altrude Lake, near Vermilion Pass. Between Carrot Creek and the Banff hydroelectric plant along the TransCanada Highway you can see vertical walls 20 m high of debris-flow material that is similar but softer. It is easy to recognize: pale-buff and studded with cobbles and boulders.

The material forms **hoodoos.** "Hoodoo" is an African word having to do with witchcraft, in which humans are turned into pillars of earth. In the geological sense, hoodoos are pillars that form in surficial deposits. In most cases, the pillar has formed because something harder has protected the deposit under it from erosion. That "something" could be a hard layer of sandstone in shale, or boulders scattered through till—the hoodoos wear the boulders like hats, until they fall off—or hard patches in any sort of soft deposit.

For a close look at hoodoos, follow the Tunnel Mountain Road from Banff townsite to a marked viewpoint overlooking a group of classic hoodoos. No hats here; either they all fell off or these hoodoos are the hard-patch type. To see hoodoos with hats, hike to the Leanchoil ("Lee-ANN-coil") hoodoos in western Yoho National Park. Another impressive set of hoodoos lies right beside Highway 93 in the Rocky Mountain Trench, a few kilometres south of Fairmont Hot Springs, where the road crosses Dutch Creek. The first viewpoint along the Cavell Road in Jasper park overlooks a set of developing hoodoos, complete with their boulder hats. Perhaps the best hoodoos in the Rockies are found at the northern end of the range, in the valley of Wokkpash Creek. Access requires a full-day hike up the creek from the Alaska Highway near Summit Lake.

*Hoodoos near Banff, as seen from a marked viewpoint along the Tunnel Mountain Road*

## The drumlins of Morley Flats

Along the TransCanada Highway west of Calgary you can see a couple of classic **drumlins.**
Look for them a few kilometres east of the junction with Highway 40, near the turnoff for Morley.
Steep at one end and gently sloping at the other, drumlins are enigmatic landforms found only on
glaciated terrain. Rather than being sculpted by ice, they may actually be deposited by water.
Large amounts of water can build up under glacial ice, and sometimes it all escapes at once, in a
burst. Such a burst can erode drumlin-shaped cavities in the ice at the base of the glacier. These
cavities then fill with gravel or till, which remains as the drumlin after the ice melts.

*Drumlin seen from the TransCanada Highway on Morley Flats. The blunt end once faced
upstream into a flow of ice—or was it a flow of water?*

## The Big Rock, and other foothills erratics

The Foothills Erratics Train is a collection of boulders strung out in a line along the western
prairie margin from the Athabasca Valley south all the way into northern Montana. The boulders
are angular and sharp-edged—they look like they were quarried yesterday—and they are all of
coarse pink-and-white quartzite, with thin layers of greenish siltstone. Beyond a doubt, this is
Gog quartzite from the main ranges of the central Canadian Rockies.

Their consistent similarity, their apparent freshness and their distribution have led to specu-
lation that all these **erratics** came from one or more large rock slides that fell onto the Athabasca
Valley glacier, perhaps from the big quartzite peaks west of Jasper. Mt. Edith Cavell is in this
area, as are the Ramparts. It is also possible that glaciers from other Gog-rich valleys farther
south—those of the Brazeau and North Saskatchewan, for example—could have contributed
some of the rock. Whatever its source(s), the debris rode along on top of the glacier or near the
surface, thus escaping the rough treatment accorded materials carried deeper in the ice.

Once out of the mountains, the erratic-bearing ice seems to have been deflected south
against the edge of the eastern ice sheet. Erratic blocks up to the size of houses were deposited
in a zone about 10 km wide that passes a few kilometres west of Edson and Rocky Mountain
House, and right through Sundre, Calgary and Okotoks. South of Crowsnest Pass the erratics
are spread eastward as far as Coutts on the international boundary. They are also found in
northern Montana, where the southern edge of the prairie ice sheet lay. By this time the deflected
mountain ice had mixed with eastern ice, so the erratics sit in eastern-type till.

The Big Rock at Okotoks ("OH-kuh-tokes"), south of Calgary, is the biggest and best-known foothills erratic. You can see the Big Rock sitting in a field 8 km west of Okotoks on Highway 7. Now split into three parts, the block originally measured 9 m tall, 18 m wide and 41 m long. Its mass is about 16,300 tonnes. No bigger erratic is known to geologists.

"Okotoks" means "big rock" in Blackfoot, and the Blackfoot of southern Alberta tell a story about the Big Rock. In this tale the rock is rolling around, chasing people and squashing them. Naapi ("NAH-pee"), the Blackfoot mythical hero, shoots an arrow up into the sky. It comes down on the Big Rock, splitting it into the three pieces and thus bringing it to a halt. (For another legend about Naapi, see page 259.)

*The Big Rock, perhaps the largest glacial erratic in the world, is located near Okotoks in the eastern foothills south of Calgary.*

## Strange stones on front-range summits

While mapping geology in the eastern front ranges along the North Saskatchewan River in 1970, I noticed that the mountain summits were sprinkled with pebbles, cobbles and even boulders of pink and buff quartzite that were unmistakably from the Gog Group, page 71. These stones were lying 1500 m above the valley floors and on limestone and shale that was decidedly un-Gog. The sites were many kilometres away from the nearest Gog outcrops. Later I found that these stones had been reported occasionally in the geological literature of the Canadian Rockies since the 1930s, but never studied. The simplest explanation is that they are all erratics carried by thick, valley-filling glaciers to places where they would not otherwise be found. The source area is to the west, in the Gog peaks of the western front ranges and main ranges.

Gog erratics of this sort are found from east of Banff north to at least Pine Pass, where they have been reported on the summit of Sentinel Mountain at an elevation of 2515 m. I have seen similar erratics of Atan Group quartzite, page 75, on the peaks above Summit Pass at the north end of the Rockies, so probably they occur everywhere with a source of quartzite to the west. A typical deposit is on Roche Miette, where there are many pebbles and boulders scattered over the summit uplands, which have a maximum elevation of 2377 m. Looking for these erratics is good mountain-top entertainment; there always seem to be a few.

Many of the erratics are blocky, but others are well-rounded, indicating that they have been moved by water. This suggests several possible origins:

- They may be the deposits of preglacial rivers. This is unlikely, for they lie on glaciated terrain.
- They have been carried by water flowing on and beside glaciers thick enough to reach such elevations. This is a reasonable idea.
- They are all that remains of till deposits. This is also reasonable, if the till included water-worn stones, which Rockies tills usually do.

The erratics are nearly all quartzite. I have found a few that are siltstone or dolomite, but I have never found a limestone erratic at such elevations in the eastern front ranges, even though there are plenty of limestone boulders in glacial deposits lower down. It is highly unlikely that any till or outwash deposit as widespread as the Gog erratics would include only quartzite; there must have been limestone pieces mixed in when the erratics arrived. Where has the limestone fraction gone?

Taking the simplest explanation again, maybe the limestone portion has weathered away, leaving the practically insoluble, slow-weathering quartzite behind. Dolomite weathers more slowly than limestone, which may explain why there are some dolomite erratics left; the few dolomite fragments I have found among the quartzite erratics have been small and deeply weathered. If the degree of weathering is any indication, then the quartzite erratics must be old. How old? I'll leave that to the geologist who will soon, I hope, do a Ph.D.-level study of the high-elevation erratics of the Canadian Rockies. The fieldwork will certainly get that person into shape.

*An erratic of Gog quartzite (boulder between person and camera) resting on weathered limestone high on Roche Miette in eastern Jasper National Park*

## Holocene glaciation and the Little Ice Age

The last 10,000 years are known as the Holocene Epoch. No major glaciation has occurred during this time; the climate seems to have been remarkably stable. Still, there have been several minor glacial advances during the Holocene, the most recent of which corresponds to the Little Ice Age of Europe.

The world's climate has been warm during the Holocene, warmer at times than it is now. Logs preserved in alpine meadows and bogs show that between 9100 and 5200 years ago treeline was up to 100 m higher than at present. This corresponds to a worldwide warm period known as the Hypsithermal. Pollen in lakebed cores shows that in the central Canadian Rockies there were two temperature peaks during the Hypsithermal, during which plants made advances into places too cold for them now.

No one knows how far back the glaciers of the Rockies melted in the Hypsithermal, but it is unlikely that major glaciers such as the Columbia Icefield disappeared.

### Tephra

Holocene researchers in our area have a couple of very good time-lines to use in their studies: layers of tephra. Tephra is dust ejected in great quantities from erupting volcanoes. Another term for tephra is "volcanic ash," although it is not ash in the usual sense.

Tephra is common in the Canadian Rockies from Grande Cache south. To find some, locate a river cut-bank exposing fine-grained material and check the top metre or so. You may see a whitish band a couple of centimetres thick. Dig a bit out with the end of your finger; if it is uniformly white or pinkish in color and gritty in texture—a *layer* in other words, not just a concentration of white calcite in the soil—then probably it is tephra.

Prevailing winds from the big volcanic eruptions in the Cascades and Coast Mountains carried tephra into our area several times during the last 12,000 years. The approximate date of each eruption has been determined by isotopic techniques, and each tephra has a distinctive chemical fingerprint that can be determined in the laboratory. Tephra collects over a period of only a few days or weeks, so a better time-marker could hardly be found.

There are four tephra layers in the Canadian Rockies. The oldest is from an eruption of Glacier Peak, Washington, about 12,000 years ago. Glacier Peak tephra is found south of Crowsnest Pass. The thickest, easiest to recognize and most widely distributed tephra is from two closely spaced eruptions of Mt. Mazama (now Crater Lake, Oregon) 6850 years ago. Between Jasper and Saskatchewan Crossing there are two other tephra layers: Mt. St. Helens "Y" (3400 years) and Bridge River (2400 years). These two, plus the Mazama tephra, may be seen at the Crossing, in an exposure close to the northwest corner of the Icefields Parkway bridge over the river. It is a pity that tephras older than 12,000 years don't occur in the Canadian Rockies—they do on the prairies and closer to the west coast—for they would help to sort out problems in under-standing older glacial events here.

*A layer of Mazama tephra (volcanic dust) found along the Maligne Road 8.5 km south of Maligne Canyon in Jasper National Park*

## Late Pleistocene and Holocene minor glacial advances in the Canadian Rockies

Between 10,000 and 11,000 years ago, at the end of the last major glaciation, a minor advance occurred: the Crowfoot advance, named for Crowfoot Glacier near Bow Lake. It corresponds to a similar event in Europe, termed there the "Younger Dryas." The glaciers of the Rockies retreated, then grew again 2500–3100 years ago in the Peyto advance, named for the Peyto Glacier.

The most recent advance, called the Cavell advance because it was first documented at Mt. Edith Cavell, began about 950 years ago. By the 1700s the fronts of most glaciers had reached a couple of kilometres farther down their valleys than their present positions. After a slight retreat, the ice fronts reached practically the same point again in the mid-1840s. By the beginning of the 20th century the Cavell advance was definitely on the wane. It was the Rockies equivalent of Europe's Little Ice Age, when old records show that the summers became cooler and wetter. The Cavell advance got a bit farther than the Crowfoot advance, so Crowfoot moraines were mostly overridden and are thus difficult to detect. They were discovered in the late 1970s.

Photos taken of Rockies glaciers at the turn of the century show them nearly at their maximum Cavell extent. In the years that followed, warming and drying caused the loss of about a third of the glacial ice in the region. In 1843 the Athabasca Glacier reached nearly to the site of today's Icefield Centre. By 1994 the front of the glacier had withdrawn over 2 km. Other glaciers, such as the Robson Glacier, have melted back so far in recent years that they are uncovering forests smashed by advancing ice 3100 years ago.

In the 1970s a visitor to the Columbia Icefield area was so concerned about glacial retreat that he wrote to Parks Canada in Jasper and suggested that the Athabasca Glacier be refrigerated to prevent further loss! His company, he wrote, could supply the necessary equipment, tastefully hidden behind the moraines.

*Pair of photos taken from approximately the same point showing recession of the Angel Glacier at Mt. Edith Cavell, near Jasper. Left photo shows the glacier as it appeared in 1922, when the ice was still close to its Little Ice Age maximum extent. Right photo shows the glacier in 1971. Today the angel's robe has become a mini-skirt. Historical photo by F.M. Slark, courtesy Mrs. D. Guild.*

### Ever date a lichen?

A fine place to appreciate Holocene glaciation is on the Path of the Glacier Trail at Mt. Edith Cavell. You step out of your car at the edge of a heavy, dark subalpine forest that has been growing there for 10,000 years. Then you climb up a few metres onto a low ridge running across the valley, which is the 1840s moraine of the Cavell advance, and get a sudden, shocking view of the wasteland on the other side. Most of it was covered with ice less than a century ago. (The 1730s moraine, which lay just outside the 1840s moraine and was the actual terminal moraine at Cavell, was bulldozed away in the 1970s to make room for the present parking lot. Someone should have asked the scientists first.)

The slow, steady growth of long-lived lichens on the rocky moraines here has made it possible to date the melt-back of the Cavell Glacier. *Rhizocarpon geographicum,* which is called the map lichen, page 409, is a green-and-black lichen common on quartzite boulders; it grows at a known rate and colonizes the boulders soon after they are exposed by glacial withdrawal. One can see large patches of map lichen on the moraine near the parking lot, where the Edith Cavell Memorial is; as you walk south, toward the north face of the peak, the patches become smaller and smaller. By taking hundreds of lichen measurements—enough to get statistically significant results—geologists have worked out the melt-back sequence here, showing where the ice front had been at different dates.

### What's next: glacial advance or glacial retreat?

The retreat of most Rockies glaciers slowed in the late 1940s, and some glaciers actually began to advance in the 1950s, in response to a worldwide cooling trend that matched the natural cycle represented by the Milankovitch climatic curve (see page 145). The Columbia

Glacier, which drains the northwest side of the Columbia Icefield, advanced over a kilometre between 1950 and 1981.

But that minor fluctuation is now over, and the retreat of Rockies glaciers seems faster than ever. This comes despite the cooling trend expected from the earth's position in the Milankovitch cycle. Are we seeing the effect of human-caused global warming, due to increasing levels of atmospheric carbon dioxide from burning fossil fuels? The evidence for global warming continues to accumulate, and there are few doubters left in the scientific community. Since 1850, the world's $CO_2$ concentration has increased from 290 ppm to 350 ppm, enhancing the earth's natural greenhouse effect and holding in more heat than normal. If the warming is as much as recent predictions indicate—up to 5°C in the next hundred years—then the world is going to lose a lot of its glacial ice.

How much? A study of the retreat of a large icefield in the Peruvian Andes shows a 43 percent loss since 1963, with ice-front retreat accelerating from 8 m per year between 1973 and 1983 to 14 m per year more recently. The projection is for all glacial ice on high peaks at tropical latitudes to be gone in the next 50 years. This may be true for Rockies glaciers as well, because warming at our latitude is expected to be greater than it will be close to the equator.

On that disquieting note we conclude this geological history of the Canadian Rockies. Coming up: notes on some interesting features of the *modern* Rockies landscape.

# *Looking at the modern landscape*
## Features and erosional processes

How is erosion turning the peaks of the Rockies into prairies? Let me count the ways:

- **Chemical weathering:** breakdown on the molecular scale, as one mineral changes to another.
- **Solution.** Calcite, the main mineral in limestone, dissolves fairly easily in water. Dolomite is another soluble mineral, although less so than calcite. Like calcite, it is very common in the Canadian Rockies.
- **Mechanical weathering:** expansion and contraction of rock as it heats and cools. Most active on south-facing slopes in summer.
- **Spalling and exfoliation:** rock splitting away in sheets to release internal pressure. Common in massive limestone and quartzite cliffs.
- **Freeze-and-thaw.** Water from rain and snowmelt gets into cracks and freezes, expanding nine percent, which wedges bits of rock loose. Another name for this is **frost-wedging.** Also causes a slow churning of the soil (see next item). Freeze-and-thaw processes are most active in spring and fall, on north-facing slopes and at high elevations.
- **Soil-churning** in permafrost areas, which tends to sort out larger and smaller particles into areas of **patterned ground.**
- **Earthquakes:** rare around here, but with cumulative effects over time. In the late 1970s the north face of Mt. Clemenceau lost a great deal of its glacial cover in a massive ice avalanche that may have been earthquake-triggered.
- **Biological action:** very important; everything from root expansion and biochemical breakdown of minerals to the work of burrowing animals, goat-hooves and human machines.
- **Impacts** by falling rock or ice, causing breakage or dislodgement.
- **Rock slides** and rock falls move masses of bedrock down-slope, breaking up the rock and aiding disintegration.
- **Slides of soft material** (soil slumps, mudflows) move downhill when unconsolidated sediments are saturated with water. Common along moraines and in stream-cuts or road-cuts through lakebed sediments and glacial till.
- **Soil creep:** constant downhill motion near the surface in soft materials.

- **Solifluction** occurs in sloping alpine meadows underlain by permafrost: ground that does not thaw completely every year. Partial thawing in summer saturates an upper layer of soil with water, but the soil doesn't slump or flow because the roots of plants hold it together. Rather, lobes typically the size of a city lot move 3–30 cm downhill annually..
- **Avalanches** bring down rock and soil torn loose by the sliding snow.
- **Snow creep:** snow lying on a slope will move slowly downhill, tending to pull vegetation and loose soil down with it.
- **Glaciation** scrapes away rock particles. Glaciers undercut cliffs and dip slopes, page 157, causing slides. Glaciers not only erode material, they transport it down-valley and feed it into rivers.
- **Raindrops, sleet** (frozen raindrops), **snowflakes, graupel** (snow pellets) **and hail** loosen soil and mineral grains, especially when hurled against surfaces by wind.
- **Wind** transports silt-size particles, especially out of front-range valleys; moves sand grains in hops of a metre or two. Flings precipitation and rock particles at surfaces.
- **Wave-lapping** gradually washes the finer particles from the shoreline into a lake or stream. Sand and gravel near the shore grind together as they are washed back and forth.
- **Running water** washes across rock and soil surfaces, removing particles and soluble minerals.
- **Streams and rivers** remove materials in gullies, streambeds and along river banks. The bed load of a stream includes sand, gravel, cobbles and boulders that grind together, wearing away as they move down the streambed. This and the suspended load (silt and clay) and dissolved load (minerals in solution) are all carried out of the Rockies.

This long list of erosive agents suggests an interesting question: *How long will the Rockies last?* By measuring the amount of sediment in a sample of river water and doing some arithmetic, it is possible to figure that out. One must also assume that the rate of erosion is going to remain the same, which, when averaged over many millions of years, has been the case in the past.

The watershed of the North Saskatchewan River is typical of others in the Rockies: a mix of sedimentary rock types, about 5–10 percent covered with glaciers. The North Saskatchewan River carries off its portion of the Rockies at the rate of 60 Bubnoffs. (The "Bubnoff" should be nominated for Funniest-sounding Unit of Measure Ever Invented. It represents 1 mm of land-surface reduction per thousand years.) This means that, overall, the surface of the North Saskatchewan drainage basin is getting worn down about 6 cm every thousand years, or 6 mm in a hundred years, or 0.06 mm each year. That turns out to be the average for the whole area. Calculating our Bubnoffs forward, we find that the summit of Mt. Robson, highest point in the Canadian Rockies, will lie at the elevation of Edmonton in exactly 54,766,666 years and eight months.

*This rock slide occurred just after a light snowfall in November of 1987. View is from the Icefields Parkway near Nigel Falls.*

## *Why are some peaks higher than others?*

The big peaks of the Canadian Rockies—such as Mt. Assiniboine, Mt. Temple, Mt. Forbes, Mt. Columbia, Mt. Alberta, Mt. Robson—all have one thing in common: sedimentary bedrock that is flat-lying or only gently sloping. The age of the rock, its type and hardness vary considerably among the higher summits of the Rockies, but the angle of the bedding is in all cases close to horizontal.

The Canadian Rockies landscape has been carved into its present form by glaciers, and glaciers cannot erode flat-lying layers as quickly as they can erode sloping layers. A glacier flowing down a valley carved in tilted rock cuts away at the sides of the valley. The bedding that slopes *toward* the valley loses support as the down-dip edges of the beds are eroded away by the glacier. Large slabs, some of them reaching right to the ridgeline, slide down into the valley. This effectively reduces the height of the ridge, and thus the height of the summits along it. With a minimum of work on the part of the glacier, a great deal of rock is broken up and moved into the valley, thanks to the assistance of gravity.

On the other side of the valley, however, the glacier must carve directly into the upturned ends of the beds. The rock comes down mainly in small rock falls rather than large slides, so erosion on that side of the valley is much slower.

Now consider a valley carved in flat-lying rock. The glacier must cut directly into the edges of the beds on both walls. The big-slab slide mechanism is unavailable; only minor rock falls occur as the glacier cuts the valley sides back. The rate of erosion is thus slower in an area of flat-lying rock. Over time, this leaves the peaks there standing taller than those in surrounding areas of tilted bedding.

*This view of the Mt. Robson massif demonstrates how the angle of the bedding controls the height of the peak. Layers in Mt. Robson, at left, are nearly flat-lying. Layers of identical rock in Resplendent Mountain, at right, are dipping. Glacial cutting in the great cirque between the two has caused large slabs to slide down the dip slope from the summit of Resplendent Mountain, lowering the height of the peak. This kind of slide cannot occur in the flat-lying layers of Mt. Robson.*

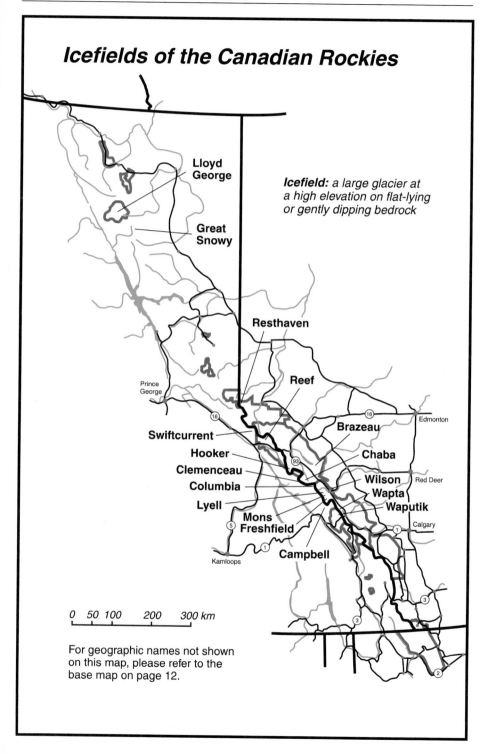

# Icefields of the Canadian Rockies

**Icefield:** *a large glacier at a high elevation on flat-lying or gently dipping bedrock*

Lloyd George

Great Snowy

Resthaven

Reef

Prince George

Swiftcurrent

Brazeau

Hooker

Chaba

Clemenceau

Columbia

Wilson   Red Deer

Wapta

Lyell

Waputik

Mons

Freshfield

Campbell

Edmonton

Calgary

Kamloops

0   50 100   200   300 km

For geographic names not shown on this map, please refer to the base map on page 12.

## Icefields and glaciers

In the eastern front ranges, and in the southern and northern ends of the Rockies generally, the glacial cirques, aretes and horns are fossil features. The ice that carved them is now largely gone. There is too little ice here to be doing much work on the landscape. Glacial erosion is still going strong, though, in the central Rockies along the continental divide, where there are **icefields:** large glaciers covering upland areas at high elevations. There is a string of icefields along the divide between Kicking Horse Pass and the northwest corner of Jasper park. The Columbia Icefield is the largest at 300 km². Fewer glaciers are found north of the Peace River, but in the northern Rockies the Lloyd George Icefield is the centrepiece of Kwadacha Lakes Provincial Park, and there is a large unnamed upland glacier around Great Snowy Mountain near the headwaters of the Akie River.

Some of the Alberta icefields are visible from the aptly named Icefields Parkway. But views from the road don't do them justice; like a toddler looking up to the dinner table, one sees the edges, not the surfaces of the ice-covered plateaus. Still, peering up the valleys of the glaciers draining the icefields gives the odd glimpse. Look for the Waputik ("WAH-poo-tick," Stoney for "mountain goat") Icefield at the head of Hector Lake and the Wapta ("WAHP-ta," Stoney for "river") Icefield above Bow Lake. From the north side of Bow Summit there is a grand view up the valley of Peyto Lake to Peyto Glacier and the north end of the Wapta Icefield. A small icefield covers the gentle eastern slope of Mt. Wilson, the big peak just north of Saskatchewan Crossing.

The Columbia Icefield is the most accessible. The Icefields Parkway passes near the Athabasca Glacier, one of six named glaciers—there are many unnamed ones—that carry the flow from the central ice mass down to lower elevations. The icefield itself is mostly out of view at the head of Athabasca Glacier, but the edge can be seen atop the cliffs of nearby peaks such as the Snow Dome and Mt. Kitchener.

The other main-range icefields—Freshfield, Mons, Lyell, Clemenceau, Chaba ("CHAH-ba"), Hooker, Reef, Swiftcurrent and Resthaven—are well off the highway, although you can get distant views of them here and there. There is also an icefield in the front ranges: the Brazeau Icefield, at the head of Maligne Lake.

*View southwest from the Snow Dome (3460 m) across the Columbia Icefield to Mt. Columbia (3747 m), highest peak in Alberta. Photo courtesy Jasper National Park.*

These icefields exist because the layered rock they rest upon is flat-lying or nearly so. As explained in the boxed item on page 157, areas of flat-lying rock erode more slowly than do areas of tilted rock, so they remain as high-altitude, cold uplands upon which more snow falls each winter than melts each summer. The resulting ice buildups feed the major valley glaciers of the Canadian Rockies. Hundreds of smaller glaciers dot the peaks.

### Glacial budget and flow

At higher elevations on the Columbia Icefield, 5–10 m of snow may fall each winter. Some of it **sublimates**—evaporates directly from ice crystals to water vapor, bypassing the liquid stage—but much remains for the sun to melt between May and October. As you might expect, melting is slow on the icefield, and more snow falls than melts. This, then, is the **zone of accumulation,** where each annual layer of snow is buried under the next.

The accumulated layers gradually turn into ice by spontaneous recrystallization over the years, aided by compaction. The crystals intergrow, becoming 1–2 cm across after about 150 years. If you start digging in the centre of the Columbia Icefield you will have to fetch the jackhammer when the hole becomes 10–20 m deep, because everything from there on down is ice. This is, truly, a *field of ice.*

Ice is brittle stuff in the refrigerator tray, but stack up 30–40 m of cubes (if that is possible) and the lower layers will start to squeeze out to the sides, toothpaste-like. So ice will flow, albeit slower than molasses in January, when pressure is put on it. It flows downhill, of course, from the heights of the icefield into the valley below.

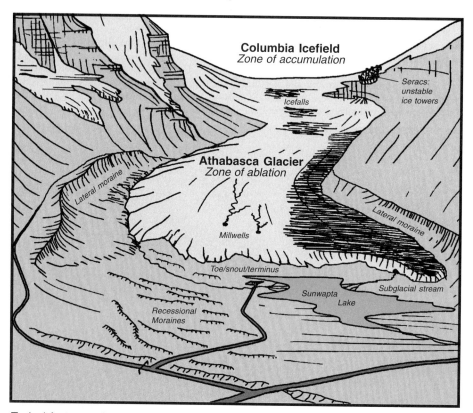

*Typical features of glaciers in the Canadian Rockies, as seen at the Athabasca Glacier. Sketch adapted from Kucera, 1981.*

At lower elevations, down in the valley, the glacier starts to meet its end. Summer temperatures are warmer down there, and the snowfall season is shorter. The annual snow layers melt off the glacier, exposing deeper, older layers the farther down-valley you go. This is the **zone of ablation,** where deposits made on the icefield are withdrawn. Only the flow of the glacier maintains the ice here. On the lower reaches of the Athabasca Glacier bare ice is exposed in July, August and into September.

At a point low enough in the valley, the forward flow cannot supply enough ice to overcome the rate of melt, and here you have the front of the glacier, also called the **snout** or the **toe.** If the rate of melting and the rate of supply exactly balance, then the toe stays in the same place. Although the speed of glacial flow is fairly constant (it's a little faster in summer than in winter), the melting rate changes hour by hour, day by day and season by season, so the glacial front is seldom stationary—although the position changes so slowly that it *looks* stationary.

Glaciers in the central Rockies move forward at an average rate of about 15 m per year. In the winter, when there is hardly any surface melt, the front forges ahead a few metres, pushing up a line of bouldery muck called an **annual moraine.** In the July heat, the glacier does not supply ice fast enough to keep up with melting, so the front melts back, leaving the annual moraine to show how much loss is occurring as the days go by.

Now: given a number of snowy winters and cool, cloudy, rainy summers, the rate of supply can exceed the rate of melt. In this case the front moves forward to a lower elevation, one at which summer melt and forward motion are again in balance. Conversely, a series of dry winters and hot, clear summers can force the front back to a higher elevation. These are the main factors in glacial advances and retreats.

*The glacial ice seen here is moving from right to left. The coat of mud on the extruded-looking, striated ice surface cannot last more than a few days when exposed to summer air temperatures, because the ice under it will melt away. This gives some idea of the speed of flow. Photo by Cia Gadd.*

*Stones embedded in the base of a glacier grind against the bedrock as the glacier moves, producing smoothed rock surfaces covered with scratches that all run the same direction. This striated* **glacial pavement** *in the Rockies near Tête Jaune Cache was covered by ice a few years before. Similar surfaces can be seen on bedrock outcrops in New York City's Central Park, and in many other places in the world, showing that glacial ice once flowed there, too.*

## Sub-glacial streams

It may surprise some readers to learn that the rock under Canadian Rockies glaciers is not below the freezing point. Snow and ice are insulating substances; heat moving upward from deep in the earth keeps the temperature at the base of a Rockies glacier slightly above freezing, so there is always a thin film of water there. The film is also sustained by pressure-melting, as under a skater's blade. That water has to go somewhere, and it does, moving steadily downhill as a sheet.

Surface meltwater in the ablation zone also finds its way under the ice through vertical conduits called **millwells,** which connect with horizontal tunnels at the base of the glacier. The sub-glacial film of water finds its way into this system, swelling the flow through the network.

That is why a sizable stream of meltwater pours out from *under* the toe of a large glacier. The water is gray with tiny particles of rock—**rock flour**—scraped away by glacial flow. In contrast, surface meltwater on a glacier is surprisingly clean.

## Ice-cored moraines and glacier caves

Scrambling over the moraines beside Rockies glaciers, one often comes across patches where a thin veneer of till or other rock debris is underlain by ice. Often you can't tell when you are on one of these **ice-cored moraines,** until suddenly your footing fails and away you go, slipping down into a mucky mess of glacial glop and getting scraped-up on rocks embedded in the ice.

Ice-cored moraine is nasty stuff to contend with, but I've had some beautiful hours *under* ice-cored moraines in winter, venturing into **glacier caves** hollowed out by summer meltwater. If you ski along the snout of any central-Rockies glacier you are likely to find a glacier cave. In winter the innards of these are frozen, so they are not wet or muddy, unless there is a strong winter flow of water, as there is out of the big ice cave at the toe of the Athabasca Glacier. But in summer such caves are usually too wet to enter—and dangerous besides. The water level can rise quite suddenly and the roof is more prone to collapse than it is in winter.

Glacial features are fascinating, so let me recommend an excellent little book on the Athabasca Glacier that gives more detail. It is called *Exploring the Columbia Icefield,* by Richard Kucera. Pick it up in many shops in Banff or Jasper, or order from the publisher: High Country, Box 5000, Canmore, AB  T0L 0M0. The principles in Kucera's description can be applied to other glaciers in the Canadian Rockies.

*Glacier cave in the toe of the Vulture Glacier, near Balfour Pass north of Lake Louise*

## Crevasses

Flow in a glacier is smooth at depth, but near the surface, meaning within the top 40 m or so, the ice is brittle. At spots where the glacier flows over a convex slope in its bed, the upper zone is stretched. That upper ice is too brittle to stretch much, so cracks form. These are crevasses ("kreh-VASS-es," *not* "crevices"). Crevasses on the Athabasca Glacier have been found up to 32 m deep; they may reach 40 m in some Rockies glaciers.

**Warning:** *stay off a glacier* unless you have mountaineering training and equipment. Falling into a crevasse unroped is almost certain to kill you. Crevasses narrow downward gradually and they are miserably cold, so it is possible to simultaneously suffocate and die of hypothermia, never mind the broken bones. In July of 1990 a child died of hypothermia after falling into a crevasse near the toe of the Athabasca Glacier, a place where tourists unwittingly risk their lives in droves by ignoring signs that warn of the danger. Another fatality of the same type occurred there in 1994. See page 731 for a list of organizations offering proper instruction in glacier travel.

Crevasses are obvious on the lower part of a glacier, where last winter's snow has melted down to the ice and exposed them, but higher up, where the glacier is still snow-covered, crevasses lurk under a thin layer of snow that may support your weight in the morning, when the surface is hard, and break through in the afternoon, when the snow is slushy. The entire glacial surface is dangerous in winter, when snow covers all, and especially in the fall, when the snow-cover is thin.

*A crevasse on the snow-covered upper Robson Glacier. The roped mountaineering party is practicing crevasse-rescue techniques. The crevasse pictured is perhaps 30 m deep.*

## Rock glaciers

Rock glaciers are lobe-shaped masses of boulders that have crept downhill. There must be thousands of these in the Canadian Rockies; they are common at and above treeline, especially where the bedrock is Gog quartzite, page 71. Perhaps the most easily approachable rock glacier in the region is in Kananaskis Country, just north of Highwood Pass beside Highway 40. Interpretive signs here explain the landform.

Heavy lichen cover on rock glaciers at treeline shows that they are moving very slowly these days, if at all. At higher elevations, though, the fronts of many rock glaciers expose scratched, lichen-free boulders that must have moved in the last few years.

Some rock glaciers seem to have originated as ice-rich glacial moraines that continued to slip downhill for a while before the ice in them melted. Others are obviously rock-slide heaps. These may have collected ice between the boulders during Holocene glacial advances and moved a few hundred metres before they dried out. Perhaps most rock glaciers continue to move today—very slowly—through the boulderfield version of soil creep or snow creep.

## *Rock slides*

The Canadian Rockies are rock-slide country. In 1903, for example, a good-sized chunk of Turtle Mountain landed on the town of Frank, along the eastern approach to Crowsnest Pass. At least 76 people were killed. Highway 3 goes right through the slide heap, which is about 1.5 km wide and includes about 36 million cubic metres of Rundle Group limestone and Banff Formation shale. The rock of Turtle Mountain has a large, tight fold in it, lying over a thrust fault. This has left the peak unstable. Coal-mining at the base may have led to the disaster.

The largest measured rock-slide deposit in the Canadian Rockies—probably the largest in the Rockies, period—floors the Valley of the Rocks, near the headwaters of the Simpson River in the Mt. Assiniboine area. The slide heap, which may be the result of more than one slide, is roughly one billion cubic metres of Palliser Formation limestone. There may be larger unmeasured slides, of course.

Moraine Lake, near Lake Louise, is dammed by a rock slide of Gog quartzite, not till. But if the material came down when glacial ice was still in the valley, and if the debris was carried even a little distance before the ice melted out from under it, then it can be thought of as a moraine anyway. Or maybe we should think of it as a pile of erratics.

The Icefields Parkway passes through a slide heap of more Gog quartzite boulders in Jasper National park, between Jonas Creek Campground and the Sunwapta Warden Station. This rock slide was typical of mass-movements in the Canadian Rockies: a tilted slab, quarried at its base by glaciation, let go and coasted down. The slide heap is little overgrown, indicating that it may be only a few hundred years old.

Also along the Icefields Parkway, the first viewpoint north of the Icefield Centre looks out on a large slide that came from Mt. Kitchener. This slide blocked the valley, accounting for the gravelly valley fill upstream between the slide heap and the Athabasca Glacier. The Sunwapta River is cutting a ragged gorge through the Kitchener Slide deposits directly below the viewpoint. Impassable to horses, the gorge deterred turn-of-the-century explorers from following the Sunwapta through this section; they had to take the next valley east, which is known as Wilcox Pass. The story that Walter Wilcox, the Coleman brothers and other early travellers (see page 698) used Wilcox Pass to avoid the Athabasca Glacier is untrue; the gorge was the obstacle.

*An air view of the Frank Slide, near Crowsnest Pass. Photo by David McIntyre.*

Jasper's Maligne Valley displays textbook rock slides. From the big slide heap (89 million cubic metres) damming Medicine Lake south to Maligne Lake, the road runs largely through rock-slide debris that has come down from the northeastern valley wall. The Palliser Formation limestone bedrock there is tilted at 30–40°, which is just right for maximum slide activity. Maligne Lake itself is dammed by slide deposits from the Opal Hills and from the next peak to the south, which is called locally and aptly "The Sinking Ship." The lake is not dammed by moraines, as previously thought; perhaps by the time you read this the Parks Canada interpretive signs there will be corrected. The heap from the Sinking Ship slide totals half a billion cubic metres. The fascinating, rock-garden-like slide heap is crossed by hiking trails, including the Moose Lake Loop and the opening stretch of the Skyline Trail.

Organic deposits in a depression on the Opal Hills slide are at least 5500 years old, but whether this is close to the actual age of the slide is unknown. The other Maligne Valley slides are undated. They are old enough to support mature subalpine forest, meaning at least several hundred years old.

It is likely that most of these slides came down not long after the last major ice advance ended some 11,000 years ago. The glaciers had cut into the lower valley sides, sawing away at the down-dip ends of the tilted slabs here. When the glaciers melted away, there was no ice left to support the undercut slabs and down they came.

In light of this principle, consider the quarrying operation at the base of Grotto Mountain, along the Bow River near the town of Canmore. A cement company is stripping away limestone from the down-dip edge of the tilted slabs there, doing exactly what the glaciers did. I hope the engineers handling this operation have done their fieldwork. If they undermine the mountain, some of it could come crashing down into the Bow River. It wouldn't take much of a slide to block the river and flood the valley upstream—wherein lies Canmore, built on the floodplain.

## Waterfalls and canyons

In the Canadian Rockies the valleys are nearly all U-shaped from glaciation, not V-shaped from erosion by running water. Side valleys are often **hanging valleys,** meaning that they join main valleys at a higher level—another glacial hallmark. (See the diagram on page 147.) Followed upstream, valley floors often rise in a series of cliffy steps rather than smoothly.

Streams flowing from hanging valleys and down valley steps can form lovely waterfalls, the best-known of which is Takakkaw Falls in Yoho National Park (380 m). This isn't the highest waterfall in the Canadian Rockies; water flowing from under the ice at many spots along the rim of the Columbia Icefield plunges over a kilometre to the valley floor.

In the Canadian Rockies the term "canyon" does not mean the same thing that it does in the western United States. There, a canyon is a steep-walled valley such as the Grand Canyon, a V-shaped feature cut by running water over millions of years. In Canada, glaciers have left the valleys of the central Rockies wide and U-shaped. The ice melted away only about 11,000 years ago, which hasn't allowed enough time for stream erosion to have cut very deeply

*Summer visitors to the Canadian Rockies should return in the winter, to see frozen waterfalls such as this one, the Weeping Wall, found along the Icefields Parkway north of Saskatchewan Crossing.*

Tangle Falls, seen beside the Icefields Parkway north of the Columbia Icefield

into the valley floors. But the process has begun, resulting in spectacularly narrow-walled limestone gorges at many valley steps and hanging-valley edges. These are the "canyons" of the Canadian Rockies.

Maligne Canyon, near Jasper, is a classic example of a Canadian-style canyon. This one is up to 55 m deep and only a couple of metres across in places—so narrow that boulders have rolled in from the sides and jammed across the top. The upper section, near the parking lot, displays well-developed **potholes:** places where water has swirled gravel around and around, causing it to drill downward into the rock, which is Palliser limestone.

Such canyons are common in the Canadian Rockies. Typically segmented by impassable waterfalls, they seem to materialize whenever I'm trying to follow a creek down through a limestone step in the valley, thereby complicating that day's explorations considerably.

Besides Maligne, here are some other deep canyons with easy access. From north to south:

*Inside Maligne Canyon, a place one dare not venture during higher water-flow*

- The canyon at Athabasca Falls, the only major one I know of to be cut in Gog quartzite, not limestone.
- The canyon at Sunwapta Falls, south of Jasper on the Icefields Parkway. Not as deep or narrow as Maligne, but with wonderful torrents pounding through on hot summer days when the Sunwapta River is swollen with glacial meltwater. The rock is Middle Cambrian limestone of the Cathedral Formation.
- North Saskatchewan Canyon, beside the Icefields Parkway and spectacular, but unnoticed by travellers because there is no marked viewpoint. In the north end of Banff park, go 1.5 km toward Jasper from the bridge over Nigel Creek, which is about 3 km north of the Weeping Wall viewpoint. Just before you cross the gravel flats ahead at a big loop in the road, spot the old highway bridge down the bank. The canyon is under it, cut in Flume Formation dolomite and incredibly narrow. Warning: there are no railings, which is probably why Parks Canada has not publicized the place.
- Mistaya Canyon, a short walk down a marked trail from a widened pull-off on the parkway a few kilometres south of Saskatchewan Crossing. Cut in Eldon limestone, the canyon features a small natural bridge–a bedrock arch, not the jammed blocks common in other canyons—and some wonderful potholes on the east side.
- Johnston Canyon, between Castle Junction and Banff on the Bow Valley Parkway (Highway 1A). Wider than most; Parks Canada has installed a steel walkway on one wall. The rock through the developed portion is the Rundle Group.
- Marble Canyon, 17 km west of Castle Junction along Highway 93. The gorge is carved in Cathedral dolomite, not marble. It, too, has a natural bridge in it, at the upper end.
- Sinclair Canyon, just east of Radium Hot Springs. Highway 93 passes right through Sinclair Canyon, which has been blasted out and spoiled, but the reddish color of the rock—dolomite of the Beaverfoot Formation—is striking.

It is interesting to speculate on the ages of these gorges and on their origins. Evidence at Maligne Canyon suggests that it may have existed under the ice of the last major glaciation. Small gorges can be seen at the fronts of modern glaciers and moraines in the Rockies, so it is possible that larger ones carried sub-glacial meltwater during the major glaciations of the past. Also interesting is the intimate connection of Maligne Canyon with the Maligne Valley cave system. This suggests that parts of the canyon may be cave passages that have been laid bare by glacial erosion, as is the case just upstream, where a smaller canyon can be followed into a sizable passage. Geologists wanting to pursue this subject may contact me for more information.

## Caves and karst

The longest known cavern in Canada is Castleguard Cave, in northern Banff National Park, which has 20 km of explored passages formed in Middle Cambrian limestone of the Cathedral Formation. The limits of exploration lie several kilometres out under the Columbia Icefield and about 200 m below the base of the glaciers. Several passages end in plugs of glacial ice, a feature known in the world only from Castleguard Cave. The first kilometre of passage is subject to sudden flooding. Castleguard is dangerous for other reasons, too, and Parks Canada has put a gate on the entrance. Entry is illegal except to experienced caving groups receiving advance permission. Write to the superintendent, Banff National Park, Box 900, Banff, AB T0L 0C0.

The deepest cave known in North America outside Mexico is also in the Canadian Rockies. Arctomys ("ARK-toe-miss," the old scientific name for the marmot) Cave is in Mount Robson Provincial Park. It follows steeply tilted Mural limestone into the earth in a seemingly endless series of short steps, some requiring technical gear. Only 2.4 km long, it reaches a total depth of 522 m below the entrance. Recent discoveries in the Rockies and on Vancouver Island may soon eclipse this record.

*Deep in the Castleguard system under the Columbia Icefield*

There are countless shallow shelter caves in our area, most of them frost pockets: niches formed by freeze-and-thaw at seeps. The caves discussed here are proper caverns dissolved out of limestone by groundwater. They may be many kilometres long.

Of these there are surprisingly few, considering the large amount of limestone in the Canadian Rockies. Caves form most frequently in rock that is flat-lying or gently dipping. Most of the rock in the Canadian Rockies is more steeply tilted. Further, glacial deposits undoubtedly cover the entrances to many unknown caves.

In deference to the caving community I am not providing cave locations. Caves are easily damaged, even by people not intent on vandalism, and Canadian cavers are understandably protective. All the caves in the region are chilly; temperatures in most are just a few degrees above freezing, with little seasonal variation. Some retain year-round ice deposits just inside their entrances. Most are dangerous, with slippery slopes and deep holes to fall into, so it is just as well that inexperienced people stay out. If you are an experienced caver, or want to become one, contact me at the address given at the front of this book. I will put you in touch with the Alberta Speleological Society.

Caves in the Canadian Rockies have formed in limestone, as most caves do. Groundwater is slightly acidic, for it picks up carbon dioxide present in the soil and in the atmosphere to form weak carbonic acid. Pyrite and gypsum in the bedrock contain sulphur, which forms weak sulphuric acid as it contacts groundwater. All this acid reacts chemically with the limestone, dissolving it.

Dating of calcite stalactites and stalagmites in Rockies caves has shown that most caves were fully formed at least 350,000 years ago. This may be a gross underestimate; discovery of Miocene pollen in Castleguard Cave shows that the upper level may be 10–13 million years old.

Cavern entrances in the Rockies are often found 500–1000 m above the valley floors. Yet those caves, like most limestone caves, must have formed below the water table, at a time when the valley floors were much higher in elevation than they are now. The difference in elevation between perched cave passages and the present valley bottoms provides a rough measure of how much rock has been lost to erosion since the caves formed. By making some educated assumptions and doing the corresponding calculations, geographers have estimated that the valley floors of 6–12 million years ago were at the level of the ridges we see now.

*Medicine Lake in Jasper National Park, showing the annual cycle of filling (spring) and draining (autumn). Photos courtesy Parks Canada.*

What may be the longest cave system in Canada lies unexplored below the Maligne Valley in Jasper National Park, running through Palliser limestone, page 113. It certainly carries the most water: the entire Maligne River goes underground at Medicine Lake. The system has been traced by pouring red rhodamine dye into sinks at Medicine Lake and detecting the dye at the many springs in and about Maligne Canyon, 15 km away. This dye-trace work has shown that if only one passage were involved, it would have to be 11–16 m in diameter to carry all the water known to enter the system. Flow-through times in the summer are on the order of 12–24 hours; in winter on the order of 5–9 days.

The cave connection gives Medicine Lake a pronounced seasonal cycle. The lake has no surface outlet stream; all water flowing into the lake drains into the cave system. The lake level rises and falls according to the amount of water flowing into it from the Maligne River. In late summer, when the river flow is low, the cave can carry away all the water, so the lake level drops. By mid-October there is little water left in the basin and the river braids its way across mudflats to sinkholes located along the east side and at the north end. In June, snowmelt increases the inlet flow and the sinks can't handle it all; they back up and the lake starts to fill. In some years Medicine Lake overflows and runs on the surface as well as underground, usually in July; it did so in 1983, 1986, 1990, 1991 and 1999.

Water flow through the cave is greatly reduced in winter, probably rendering it at least partially air-filled and thus potentially explorable. Although several entrances to the system have been found in the canyon area, all are blocked by rubble after a short distance; the water can move between the blocks but humans are too large. Attempts to enter the cave by drilling and digging have failed.

This is terribly frustrating to cavers, of course. However, the usual history of these things engenders hope: long after the experts have given up, someone will blunder onto the entrance. I just hope that person stops by the park information centre in Jasper to pass on news of the discovery.

Any place in which the landscape is being altered markedly by solution, with or without caves, is called **karst**. Impressively deep dissolved cracks and shafts are sometimes found in the Canadian Rockies in flat expanses of limestone above treeline. These surface features sometimes connect with extensive caves below.

Thus far, karst has been found to develop in eight Rockies limestones, roughly in order of prevalence the Rundle Group, Palliser Formation, Cathedral Formation and Mural Formation. At least one karst area occurs in the mixed limestone/dolomite sequence of the Lynx Group. A couple of caves are known from the Snake Indian Formation and another from Triassic limestones just south of the Peace River.

The *oldest* known karst in the Rockies is found in the Ordovician Skoki Formation, page 89, in which caves developed not long after deposition of the limestone 458–488 million years ago. The passages have since been filled with sand, which has hardened to quartzite, so exploration is not possible.

*Rillenkarren. Photo courtesy Jasper National Park.*

Many of the limestone boulders found in slide heaps in the Rockies are marked with **rillenkarren** ("RILL-en-car-en"): tiny gullies dissolved in the rock by rain and snowmelt. These small karst features can be up to several centimetres deep and intergrown; they look like miniature mountain ranges.

*An example of karst in the Canadian Rockies. This deeply fissured limestone surface is found on Snaring Mountain, in the back country of Jasper National Park. Water has produced the fissures by dissolving the limestone along joints (small cracks) in the rock.*

## Springs, hot and otherwise

The largest spring known in the Canadian Rockies is Big Springs, found southwest of Castleguard Meadows in northern Banff National Park. This spring drains the lower levels of Castleguard Cave, page 168; the typical summer discharge is 300,000 l/min (5 m³/sec). The springs in Maligne Canyon, which drain the Maligne karst system, page 169, undoubtedly have a combined discharge much greater than that of Big Springs, but the total discharge at Maligne is unmeasured. Another very large spring emerges near Watridge Lake in Kananaskis Country; called Karst Spring, it can be reached by trail (4.7 km) from the Smith-Dorrien Road.

Smaller but more interesting to most people are the **hot springs** and mineral springs of the Canadian Rockies. Some of these tie into cave systems but most do not, and they may be found in rock other than limestone. Information on the major known hot springs and mineral springs is given in the table on page 174.

In the Rockies, hot springs and mineral springs seem to work the same way: as natural water pumps.

Water can move through solid rock that is permeable, meaning that it contains interconnected pores or fractures. Since most rock in our area is at least slightly permeable, surface water seeping into the ground can be pulled by gravity down to great depths.

The temperature underground in the Rockies increases about 1°C for every 30 m in depth. At depths of three kilometres or more the rock temperature is at or above the boiling point of water.

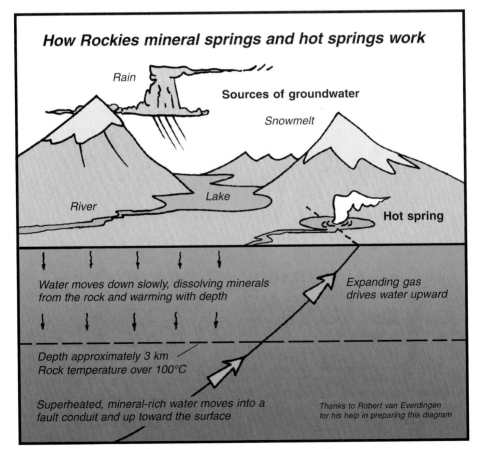

### How Rockies mineral springs and hot springs work

Rain

Sources of groundwater

Snowmelt

River

Lake

Hot spring

Water moves down slowly, dissolving minerals from the rock and warming with depth

Expanding gas drives water upward

Depth approximately 3 km
Rock temperature over 100°C

Superheated, mineral-rich water moves into a fault conduit and up toward the surface

*Thanks to Robert van Everdingen for his help in preparing this diagram*

Hot water is less dense than cold water, and expanding gases in it also decrease its overall density. If given the chance, hot water will rise over cold water. But normally the hot water at depth cannot force its way up through the rock fast enough to retain the heat, which is lost as it moves up into cooler layers, so it stops rising before it reaches the surface.

However, scattered through the earth's crust are long upward conduits to the surface—the hot-spring systems—that allow the hot water to rise rapidly. As it rises, replacement water is drawn in from the surrounding rock, keeping the hot-springs pump running. In the Canadian Rockies the water seems to move up along fault planes, for many of the springs are found at or close to faults.

The hot water cools on its way up, often mixing with normal groundwater near the surface. But it retains enough heat to provide warm soaks for eager humans who would much rather squeeze into crowded pools with dozens of strangers than have a hot bath at home.

An interesting point about hot springs is that they are partly nuclear-fueled. About a quarter of the earth's heat is generated by the slow decay of radioactive minerals throughout the planet. (The other three-quarters is mainly heat left over from the formation of the planet 4.6 billion years ago, solar heat, and heat from compression of gases under gravity.) Hot springs reach deep enough to tap a little of that heat. The water is slightly more radioactive than normal groundwater, probably because it has spent more time underground and thus has picked up greater amounts of radioactive minerals.

## Odors

The rotten-egg odor of hydrogen sulphide gas ($H_2S$) wafts from most of these pools. Where does it come from?

Gypsum (calcium sulphate, $CaSO_4 2H_2O$) is a common sulphur-bearing mineral that dissolves rather easily in warm water. Another is pyrite (iron sulphide, $FeS_2$), which is broken down and dissolved by sulphate-oxidizing bacteria. One or both of these minerals are present

*Cold Sulphur Spring, beside Highway 16 in eastern Jasper National Park. The water is cloudy with sulphates, and the spring smells strongly of hydrogen sulphide.*

in much of the bedrock in the Canadian Rockies region, so the dissolved sulphates are brought to the surface in our hot-springs systems. On the way up, further bacterial action, harmless to humans, often turns some of the dissolved sulphate into hydrogen sulphide.

Some of the gas remains dissolved in the water, which explains why rings made of silver tarnish if worn in a sulphurous hot pool. $H_2S$ also oxidizes to form microscopic sulphate particles that give the water flowing from most of our springs its characteristic milky look. Yellow elemental sulphur is deposited at some springs, such as Miette Hot Springs.

Springs that don't smell like rotten eggs, such as those at Radium and Fairmont, are those in which oxygen has mixed with the water on the way up. Odorless hot springs are not as common as stinky ones.

Heavy rainfalls sometimes dilute and thus cool the flow from hot springs. Such downpours also wash foreign material—plant matter, soil particles—into the systems. Earthquakes can dirty the water of Rockies springs by shock disturbance. The great Alaska earthquake of 1964 did this from a distance of 2300 km. However, the notable water-dirtying and cooling at Miette Hot Springs in Jasper park after the big eruption of Mt. St. Helens in 1980 was caused by a thunderstorm, not directly by the eruption, although the sudden onset of rainy weather throughout western North America that summer may have been related to the event. Water droplets condense around microscopic airborne particles, and the volcano ejected great quantities of tephra (volcanic dust) and sulphur compounds into the atmosphere. For more on tephra see page 152.

### Tufa

Surrounding most hot springs are deposits of **tufa** ("TOO-fuh"), not to be confused with **tuff,** a kind of volcanic rock. The tufa deposits in our area are lumpy, spongy-looking masses of crumbly calcite, with a little gypsum, that build up in layers as the hot water dribbles out. When hot-springs water reaches the surface, dissolved carbon dioxide escapes, reducing the water's capacity to hold calcium and magnesium compounds in solution, so tiny crystals form. These accumulate as the tufa deposit. Evaporation also causes some precipitation of calcite and gypsum, especially when the water flow is slow and the hot-spring stream doesn't join another water body for some distance.

### Life in a hot spring

Colonies of highly specialized algae and bacteria are present in sulphurous hot springs. Much of the soft, gray, pasty-looking material surrounding such springs is actually alive! Bright-yellow or purple coloring is from sulphur-dependent bacteria; stripes of brilliant green are usually from algae.

Deprived of a spring's unusual water chemistry and/or heat, these sensitive organisms die, as happens occasionally at the Banff springs due to influxes of normal water from heavy rain or rapid snowmelt.

Tropical fish are present in marshes warmed by one of the Banff springs. See page 497 for the details.

### Mineral springs

A mineral spring in the Canadian Rockies is simply a hot spring that flows cold. The hot water either cools a great deal on the return trip to the surface, perhaps by travelling farther or slower, or it becomes diluted with enough cold groundwater to lose its heat. Such springs tend to produce little tufa, but they often carry dissolved iron that precipitates as the iron-oxide mineral **goethite** ("GUR-tite," $HFeO_2$), which colors the surface around many mineral springs brilliantly red, orange and ochre.

The Paint Pots near Marble Canyon in Kootenay park are the most famous of these springs. The oxides there were used as pigments by the Stoneys and Kootenays. A geological study of the Paint Pots concluded that they probably lie over a deposit of lead and zinc sulphides, similar to the ones near Field. See page 697 for a description of the mines there.

# Hot springs and mineral springs of the Canadian Rockies

| Name and note number | Temp (°C) | Flow (l/min) | TDS[1] (ppm) | pH[2] | Remarks |
|---|---|---|---|---|---|
| 1. Turtle Mountain | 9.1 | 450 | 748 | 7.1 | Sulphur odor |
| 2. Fording Mountain | 25.9 | 325 | 2647 | 7.1 | Sulphur odor |
| 3. Sulphur Creek | - | - | - | - | Cool, sulphur odor |
| 4. Wildhorse River | 28.5 | 440 | - | 6.6 | Odorless |
| 5. Ram Creek | 36.6 | 225 | 225 | 7.6 | Beware poison ivy |
| 6. Lussier Canyon | 43.4 | 225 | 2708 | 7.1 | Sulphur odor, log pool |
| 7. Red Rock | - | - | - | - | Emerges in river bottom |
| 8. Fairmont | 48.9 | 2200 | 2069 | 6.8 | Odorless, developed |
| 9. Radium | 47.7 | 1817 | 706 | 6.8 | Odorless, developed |
| 10. Paint Pots | 10.7 | 330 | 3086 | 3.7 | Iron pigment; tasteless |
| 11. Canmore Creek | 6.1 | 5 | 1135 | 7.2 | Slight sulphur odor |
| 12. Banff (Upper) | 47.3 | 545 | 1029 | 7.2 | Sulphur odor, developed |
| 13. Banff (Kidney) | 39.2 | 91 | 1060 | 7.1 | Sulphur odor |
| 14. Banff (Middle) | 34.8 | 225 | 1100 | 7.1 | Sulphur odor |
| 15. Banff (Cave) | 32.8 | 500 | 963 | 7.2 | Sulphur odor, developed |
| 16. Banff (Basin) | 34.5 | 680 | 1677 | 7.1 | Sulphur odor, developed |
| 17. Banff (Pool) | 32.0 | 550 | 974 | 7.2 | Sulphur odor |
| 18. Vermilion Lake | 19.7 | 750 | 411 | 7.4 | Sulphur odor |
| 19. Stoney Squaw[3] | 6.5 | 1 | 584 | 7.4 | Slight sulphur odor |
| 20. Mt. Fortune | 14.0 | - | 1697 | 7.7 | Strong sulphur odor |
| 21. Panther River | 3.0 | 45 | 1146 | 7.4 | Slight odor, no tufa |
| 22. Forty Mile Creek | - | - | - | - | Small, lukewarm, odor |
| 23. Ink Pots | 4.8 | 1800 | 253 | 7.5 | Odorless karst springs |
| 24. Canoe River | 60.0 | 15 | 1540 | - | Odorless |
| 25. Cadomin | - | - | - | - | Cool, odor, also karst spring |
| 26. Miette | 53.9 | 800 | 1865 | 6.9 | Strong odor, developed |
| 27. Maligne River | - | - | - | - | Cool, odor |
| 28. Cold Sulphur | 9.0 | >500 | 724 | 7.4 | Strong odor |
| 29. Overlander | - | - | - | - | Flooded in summer, odor |
| 30. Shale Banks | - | - | - | - | Cool, iron pigment |
| 31. Mud Creek | - | - | - | - | Cool, mineral mounds |
| 32. Prophet River | - | - | - | - | Hot, good bathing |
| 33. Racing River | - | - | - | - | Sulphur odor |
| 34. Liard River | 54.0 | 2400 | - | - | Sulphur odor, developed |
| 35. Deer River | 32.0 | 4400 | - | - | Sulphur odor |
| 36. Portage Brûlé | 48.0 | 40 | 814 | 7.1 | Odorless |

Hyphens indicate data not available.

[1]"TDS" is abbreviation for "total dissolved solids," a measure of how mineral-rich the water is. "ppm" = parts per million. Normal drinking water usually has less than 400 ppm TDS.

[2]This is a measure of acidity. A value of 7 is neutral. Numbers under 7 are acidic; numbers over 7 are basic.

[3]No longer evident. See note 19.

## Sources

McDonald, J.; D. Pollock and B. McDermot (1978) *Hotsprings of Western Canada: a Complete Guide.* Labrador Tea Company, Vancouver.

van Everdingen, R. (1972) *Thermal and Mineral Springs in the Southern Rocky Mountains of Canada.* Environment Canada, Ottawa.

Personal observations and communications

## Location notes

1. Just west of Frank, Alberta. Follow Highway 3 across the Crowsnest River bridge, then note two gas stations a little farther on. Slow down and start looking for a trail south of the railway tracks with an old cabin beside it. Follow a short distance between rock outcrops and across a creek to the spring.
2. From Natal, take the Elk River Road 26.6 km north to springs and pools in a large meadow.
3. From about 6 km east of Fernie on Highway 3, take Hartley Creek Road over Hartley Pass and about 10 km down Sulphur Creek. Several cool springs are on the southeast side of the road, along the river bank in a clearing. Apparently unstudied.
4. From Ft. Steele, follow the road up Wildhorse River for 27 km, where a dirt track branches right; follow it down to the river. The springs (one warm, two cold) are on the other side.
5. Approach from Skookumchuck, via Lussier River Road (14.5 km), or as per Lussier Canyon springs (see note 6), continuing another 18.5 km past the Lussier springs and turning off on Hobonoff Road. Follow over a pass and down to the springs.
6. 6.5 km south of Canal Flats, follow White Swan Lake Road 18.5 km to a widened parking lot and short path to the river. Two springs, one with a bathhouse.
7. Follow the Kootenay River Road from Canal Flats 15.2 km northeast to the Red Rock site and tufa deposits.
8. Between Radium and Canal Flats along Highway 93. Resort.
9. A few kilometres east of Radium along Highway 93. Operated by Kootenay National Park; open year-round. 10.3 km south of Marble Canyon on Highway 93, in Kootenay park. Interpretive signs.
10. Located 20 km west of Castle Junction, off Highway 93 in Kootenay National Park. Walk 1 km on an easy trail.
11. From Canmore, take the Spray Lakes Road a few kilometres to Canmore Creek and follow a trail 800 m to a spring on the north side of the creek.
12. Follow Banff Avenue south across the river; follow signs 4.5 km up Sulphur Mountain to the aquacourt.
13. From upper Banff springs, follow Mountain Avenue back toward Banff for about 200 m; springs lie beside the road.
14. As per upper Banff springs, but park at the curve where the road turns south and follow a trail west 400 m to springs.
15. At the east end of the Cave-and-Basin Aquacourt, reached through a short tunnel.
16. At the west end of the Cave-and-Basin Aquacourt, in an artificial pool.
17. From the southeast corner of the Cave-and-Basin Aquacourt, take stairs to a trail and follow it past the hole in the top of the cave to the Pool Springs.
18. Follow Vermilion Lakes Drive from Banff west to Third Vermilion Lake, where there are springs beside the road.
19. Along the TransCanada Highway, on the northeast side of the Mt. Norquay interchange (western entry to Banff). During highway construction in 1985 the spring was covered with earth and forced to drain away underground, so there is no sign of it at the surface.
20. Follow Spray River Fire Road about 35 km to a warden cabin (or approach the same cabin more quickly if the Calgary Power road along the north side of Spray Lake is open). The springs are 360 m north of the cabin, on a trail.
21. Follow Cascade Fire Road 48 km to springs on both sides of the Panther River.
22. From upper Mt. Norquay ski area parking lot (near Banff), follow the Cascade Amphitheatre trail north 3.1 km to a crossing of Forty Mile Creek (keep right at the junction with the trail to Mystic Pass). Leave the main trail at the creek and follow the north bank of the creek, crossing a tributary. The spring is about half a kilometre farther, in the woods.
23. From Johnston Canyon, along Highway 1A between Banff and Castle Junction, follow a marked trail 6.4 km to several pools.
24. Jeep 15 km south of Valemount along the west bank of Kinbasket Lake. The springs are close to the shore.
25. About 4 km south of Cadomin, along the road to the Cardinal Divide.
26. From Pocahontas, 41 km east of Jasper, follow Fiddle Valley Road south to the springs at the end.
27. In the bed of the Maligne River just upstream of the Watchtower Trail bridge. Visible spring and fall.
28. 20 km east of Jasper along Highway 16, just east of the bridge over the Athabasca River. Marked by an interpretive sign.
29. From Cold Sulphur Spring (#28), find a trailhead 100 m west at the same parking area and follow Overlander Trail for about 6 km. Look for a faint path branching west down to the river. A small mineral spring flows out at the base of a short cliff at river level; it's covered by the river from June through August.
30. From Shale Banks warden cabin along Snake Indian Fire Road in eastern Jasper park, follow the east bank of the Snake Indian River about 1 km to a small orange-pigmented cold spring.
31. Just west of Mud Creek in northern Jasper park, on both sides of the North Boundary Trail. Marshy area of 1–2 ha (4–5 acres) with several flowing pools up to 5 m across, some in mounds of soft tufa. No odor, but strong mineral taste. Apparently unstudied.
32. Along the Prophet River in wilderness at about 124°55' N. Hot, good flow, good bathing.
33. Near the junction of the Toad and Racing rivers, northwest of the Alaska Highway. No other data.
34. After crossing the Liard River on Alaska Highway, continue to Liard Hot Springs Provincial Park. The springs are developed, no admission fee is charged. Interesting boardwalk approach across warm marshes.
35. Follow a trail 16 km east along the north bank of the Liard River from the Alaska Highway crossing at Kilometre 800, turning up the Deer River. It's 13 km farther to the springs, involving six river fords.
36. Eight springs and seeps in a 30-m strip along north bank of the Liard River about 3 km east of mouth of the Coal River. Approach unknown, but the Alaska Highway passes within a few kilometres of the site.

# *Rivers*

The eroded substance of the Rocky Mountains is exported mainly by rivers, but a fair bit also departs dissolved in groundwater, and a little leaves by air in the form of dust. The Liard is the biggest river in the region, with an average flow of 1350 m³/sec, measured near the northern tip of the Rockies. The Peace is next largest at 1050 m³/sec, measured at the mountain front. The others are much smaller; check the table on page 178.

River flow, properly termed **discharge,** varies greatly with the seasons in the Canadian Rockies. The lowest rate of discharge generally comes in March, although for a few rivers low water comes in February or even as early as January. The greatest discharge is reached at the peak of snowmelt, which usually comes in late June or early July. The average crest can be up to 100 times the average minimum flow, although a figure 15–30 times the minimum flow is typical. The champion trickle/flood river is the Kootenay, measured at Kootenay Crossing in Kootenay park. This is the one with the hundred-fold increase.

Note how the glacially fed main-range rivers of the central Rockies tend to peak in July while most of the others peak in June. Meltwater from the high-elevation uplands, with their glaciers, seems to contribute the most to the annual swelling of major central-Rockies rivers; discharge rises dramatically when summer hits the icefields along the continental divide.

Streams fed by meltwater also have a pronounced *daily* cycle. Hikers in the Rockies often learn about this the hard way. They cross a stream easily in the morning, hopping from rock to rock. But when they return in the late afternoon, the brook has turned into a roaring monster and crossing is quite out of the question. It may take hours to find a safe crossing point—or a long wait until the daily surge has gone by. The farther downstream you are, the longer it takes for the crest to pass. At Jasper, the Athabasca doesn't quit rising until the wee hours of the morning.

The Canadian Rockies are famous for **braided streams:** gravelly streams with multiple channels. The Sunwapta River at Beauty Creek, 87 km south of Jasper on the Icefields Parkway, is a classic example. The valley is wide and filled wall-to-wall with gravel. The river, which carries meltwater from the Columbia Icefield, splits up and wanders about the stony flats in many shallow separate channels that rejoin and diverge. "Braided" describes the river perfectly.

Braided streams and glaciers go together. Glacial meltwater is loaded with mud and stones that cannot be carried far unless the streambed is steep. In the case of the Sunwapta, the bed is steep enough for a while, but not across the flats at Beauty Creek. The speed of the river slows and thus its load-carrying ability diminishes. So the load gets dumped and the valley clogs with debris. Early in the morning at low flow, the Sunwapta finds its way at low speed among the gravel bars. At high flow in the afternoon, though, the river picks up some of the material it has dropped and carries it farther downstream. The number of channels that are used changes hour by hour, as the river level rises and falls. The positions of the channels change day by day, as the river cuts and fills.

Consider also the character of the water in that river. Like the Athabasca, or any glacial stream near its source, the Sunwapta is dishwater-gray with glacial muck. Much of this is **rock flour:** tiny bits ground from the glacier's bed. Included in the suspended load is pollen that landed on the glacial surface, particles of forest-fire smoke, and atmospheric dust that once formed the nuclei of the snowflakes that became the glaciers. See page 180 for the effect this material has on lakes downstream.

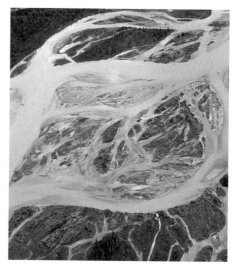

*Braided section of the Athabasca River*

*The Athabasca River east of Jasper, a typical glacially-fed river of the Canadian Rockies. Jasper Lake in the middle distance, and the cliff of Roche Miette beyond.*

# River discharge data for the Canadian Rockies (m³/sec)

| Name of river and station site | Watershed area (km²) | Mean daily | March min[1] | June max[2] | Record instant | Date of record |
|---|---|---|---|---|---|---|
| Athabasca near Jasper | 3880 | 87.8 | 10.2 | J265 | 722 | 29 Jun 84 |
| Athabasca at Hinton | 9780 | 173 | 30.6 | 501 | 1270 | 13 Jun 72 |
| Belly near Mountain View | 319 | 8.7 | J1.9 | 30.4 | 464 | 8 Jun 64 |
| Blaeberry below Ensign Ck | 230 | 7.5 | 0.9 | J21.2 | 74.5 | 24 Jun 74 |
| Bow at Lake Louise | 421 | 18.7 | 1.4 | 31.1 | 71.4 | 25 Jun 74 |
| Bow at Banff | 2210 | 39.7 | 7.64 | 127 | 399 | 14 Jun 23 |
| Bow at Calgary | 7860 | 90.9 | 44.2 | 231 | 2270 | 18 Jun 1897 |
| Brazeau below Cardinal R | 2590 | 56.4 | - | 93.0 | 668 | 4 Jun 80 |
| Brewster Creek near Banff | 109 | 2.2 | 0.04 | 5.2 | 20.5 | 28 May 86 |
| Bull R near Wardner | 1530 | 32.8 | F7.3 | 109 | 428 | 17 Jun 74 |
| Canoe R below Kimmel Ck | 298 | 14.3 | F1.7 | J42.8 | 119 | 13 Jun 87 |
| Cardinal near the mouth | 495 | 7.2 | - | 12.6 | 278 | 4 Jun 80 |
| Cascade near Banff | 664 | 8.0 | F3.7 | J16.4 | 39.4 | 24 Jun 38 |
| Castle near Beaver Mines | 823 | 15.9 | F2.8 | 60.8 | 736 | 20 Jun 75 |
| Clearwater above Limestone Ck | 1340 | 22.1 | - | 36.5 | 510 | 18 Jun 65 |
| Columbia near Fairmont | 891 | 10.5 | 3.6 | 34.6 | 99.4 | 11 Jun 72 |
| Columbia at Nicholson | 6660 | 108 | F23 | J320 | 504 | 30 Jun 90 |
| Columbia at Donald | 9710 | 174 | F31.9 | 522 | 1320 | 12 Jun 72 |
| Crowsnest near Frank | 404 | 4.8 | F1.3 | 15.5 | 73.9 | 9 Jun 53 |
| Elbow above Elbow Falls | 437 | 7.0 | 1.8 | 17.2 | 159 | 30 May 67 |
| Elbow at Bragg Ck | 791 | 7.1 | F2.6 | 24.2 | 283 | 31 May 67 |
| Elk at Fernie | 3110 | 46.5 | F12 | 161 | 446 | 30 May 86 |
| Finlay at Ware | 11100 | 190 | 29.5 | 720 | 1110 | 2 Jun 83 |
| Finlay at Finlay Forks | 43300 | 680 | 128 | 2360 | - | - |
| Flathead at Flathead | 1110 | 26.2 | F4.9 | M101 | 462 | 8 Jun 64 |
| Forty-Mile Ck near Banff | 133 | 3.5 | 0.5 | 7.2 | 20.5 | 17 Jun 74 |
| Fraser at Red Pass | 1700 | 46.7 | 5.3 | 157 | 402 | 12 June 72 |
| Fraser at McBride | 6890 | 198 | 31.3 | 578 | 1070 | 24 Jun 90 |
| Ghost near Black Rock Mtn | 211 | 3.2 | 0.5 | 8.4 | 126 | 13 Jun 53 |
| Halfway above Graham R | 3780 | 34.6 | F4.6 | 119 | 984 | 1 Jun 90 |
| Highwood near Diebel's Ranch | 774 | 12.3 | 1.7 | 38.2 | 283 | 9 Jun 53 |
| James near Sundre | 821 | 5.9 | J0.6 | 10.3 | 237 | 2 Jun 90 |
| Johnston Ck near mouth | 124 | 3.4 | - | 7.3 | 51.6 | 7 Jun 88 |
| Jumpingpound Ck near mouth | 571 | 1.4 | J0.1 | 5.4 | 138 | 29 Jun 69 |
| Kananaskis near Seebe | 933 | 15.4 | A7.2 | 40.6 | 337 | 2 Jun 32 |
| Kechika at mouth | 22700 | 246 | 47.3 | 771 | 1980 | 12 Jun 64 |
| Kicking Horse at Golden | 1850 | 41.3 | F5.5 | 130 | 367 | 30 May 86 |
| Kootenay near Kootenay Crossing | 420 | 5.0 | 0.2 | 20 | 42.5 | 26 May 81 |
| Kootenay at Canal Flats | 5390 | 87.8 | 18.2 | 301 | 876 | 29 May 86 |
| Kootenay at Newgate | 20000 | 298 | F72.4 | 1050 | 2780 | 28 May 48 |
| Kwadacha near Ware | 2410 | 50.9 | 6.3 | 162 | 489 | 1 Jun 90 |
| Liard above Kechika R | 61600 | 699 | 128 | 2440 | 550 | 3 Jun 72 |
| Liard above Beaver R | 119000 | 1400 | 273 | 4490 | 9510 | 16 Jul 74 |
| Maligne near mouth | 908 | 15.9 | 2.2 | J45.4 | 92.2 | 8 Jul 82 |
| McGregor at Lower Canyon | 4770 | 226 | F41.2 | 637 | 2090 | 12 Jun 72 |
| McLeod above Embarras R | 2560 | 20.1 | F2.4 | 56.7 | 1260 | 5 Jun 80 |
| Miette near Jasper | 630 | 10.5 | 0.8 | 40.5 | 123 | 29 Jun 84 |
| Mistaya at Sask Crossing | 249 | 6.4 | F0.6 | 20.8 | 65.4 | 15 Jul 53 |

| Name of river and station site | Watershed area (km²) | Mean daily | March min[1] | June max[2] | Record instant | Date of record |
|---|---|---|---|---|---|---|
| Moose near Red Pass | 458 | 14.5 | 1.3 | 48.7 | 189 | 18 Jun 67 |
| Murray above Wolverine R | 2410 | 56.8 | F10.1 | 193 | 872 | 13 Jun 90 |
| Muskeg near Grande Cache | 706 | 8.0 | 1.1 | 15.6 | 286 | 12 Jun 72 |
| Muskwa near Ft. Nelson | 20300 | 216 | F17.2 | J601 | 4620 | 28 Jun 75 |
| North Saskatchewan at Sask Xing | 1290 | 42.2 | 3.0 | J134 | 314 | 15 Jul 53 |
| N Sask at Saunders | 5160 | 98.7 | 11.7 | J254 | 1240 | 27 Jun 15 |
| N Sask near Rocky Mtn House | 11000 | 220 | 24.1 | J330 | 4110 | 27 Jun 15 |
| Oldman near Brocket | 4400 | 37.7 | J7.8 | 136 | 1560 | 20 Jun 75 |
| Parsnip above Misinchinka R | 4900 | 144 | F27.7 | 448 | 1380 | 13 Jun 72 |
| Parsnip near Finlay Forks | 20300 | 390 | 87.1 | 1280 | 2830 | 4 Jun 64 |
| Peace at Hudson's Hope | 69900 | 1080 | 728 | 2540 | 5580 | 12 Jul 72 |
| Pipestone near Lake Louise | 306 | 5.9 | 0.8 | 19.2 | 113 | 8 Jun 88 |
| Ram near mouth | 1860 | 14.9 | 3.1 | 44.5 | 951 | 27 Jun 15 |
| Red Deer above Panther R | 941 | 16.1 | - | 32.1 | 170 | 2 Jun 90 |
| Red Deer below Burnt Timber Ck | 2250 | 20.3 | 4.7 | 59.2 | 693 | 1 Jun 90 |
| Redearth Ck near mouth | 147 | 5.9 | - | 12.5 | 42.5 | 24 Jun 74 |
| Rocky at Hawes (near mouth) | 1140 | 14.8 | F1.7 | 50.8J | 168 | 27 Jun 15 |
| Sheep at Black Diamond | 595 | 4.6 | F0.9 | 18.2 | 207 | 26 May 90 |
| Siffleur near mouth | 515 | 15.2 | - | 25.2 | 126 | 8 Jun 88 |
| Smoky above Hells Ck | 3840 | 109 | 11.7 | 261 | 1380 | 12 Jun 72 |
| Snake Indian near mouth | 1580 | 51.2 | - | 87.6 | 564 | 12 Jun 72 |
| Spray at Banff | 749 | 8.7 | F2.6 | 26.1 | 181 | 19 Dec 72 |
| Sukunka above Chamberlain Ck | 927 | 24 | F3.0 | 76.8 | 289 | 22 May 81 |
| Sukunka near mouth | 2510 | 54.3 | F7.5 | 181 | 808 | 15 Jul 82 |
| Sunwapta at Athabasca Gl | 29.8 | 2.4 | - | 4.7 | 15.3 | 17 Jul 55 |
| Toad above Nonda Ck | 2570 | 43.9 | 7.5 | 132 | 762 | 28 Jun 75 |
| Trout at Km 783.7 (Muncho Lk) | 1190 | 16.8 | 5.8 | 44.2 | 411 | 28 Jun 75 |
| Vermilion at Mt. Verendrye | 951 | 21.6 | 3.0 | 72.7 | 191 | 5 Jun 56 |
| Waiparous near mouth | 334 | 1.8 | J0.4 | 5.0 | 150 | 2 Jun 90 |
| Wapiti near Grande Prairie | 11300 | 102 | F13.0 | 333 | 6300 | 15 Jul 82 |
| Waterton near Waterton Park | 614 | 18.3 | F3.6 | 77.0 | 728 | 9 Jun 64 |
| Whirlpool at mouth | 598 | 33 | - | J47.2 | 169 | 29 Jun 84 |
| Wood near Donald | 956 | 40.9 | F4.2 | J119 | 343 | 27 Jun 68 |

[1]Letter preceding minimum daily flow: minimum reached in month other than March (J = January, F = February, A = April, M = May)
Kananaskis minimum came in March before damming
[2]Letter "J" preceding maximum daily flow: river crests in July rather than June, indicating river heads at a major glacier. Kicking Horse crests in June despite glacial feed
Flathead crests in May
December maximum instantaneous flow for the Spray came from break-up of an ice jam

**Source**
*Historical Streamflow Summary, 1990,* published by Inland Waters Directorate, Water Resources Branch, Water Survey of Canada, Environment Canada, Ottawa (1991)

## Lakes: how do they get those colors?

Before answering that question, a few statistics. The largest natural water body in the Canadian Rockies is Maligne Lake, 22.3 km long, located in Jasper National Park. The deepest natural lake with a verifiable sounding is Upper Waterton Lake, at 148 m. The depth of Muncho Lake, along the Alaska Highway, is quoted in tourist literature as 223 m, even though the official depth, taken by the B.C. government in 1972, is 109 m. Maligne is third-deepest at 97 m. Williston Lake, the enormous human-made reservoir in the northern Rocky Mountain Trench, is by far the biggest water body in the Canadian Rockies. And it's an atrocity. Same with Mica Dam, which backs up Kinbasket Lake in the southern Rocky Mountain Trench, second-largest water body.

On to the question I get asked by visitors a hundred times every summer: what accounts for the brilliant hues of the lakes in our area?

It is not because the surface is simply reflecting the sky, although sky color can have a minor effect, and the amount of sun reaching the surface certainly makes a difference. Nor is it because lake-bottoms in the Rockies are coated with copper sulphate, an outrageous bit of misinformation regularly passed off on tourists.

Water is highly transparent, but it tends to absorb the longer wavelengths of light (yellow, red) more than it does the shorter wavelengths (blue, green). These blue and green hues are scattered—that is, reflected in all directions—and some of this light bounces back to our eyes, which is why pure water looks blue or bluegreen. It is the same for the blueness seen in well-crystallized ice, although the microscopic air bubbles commonly trapped in ice scatter all wavelengths, making most ice look bluish-white. The whiteness of snow is also due to light-scattering. Contaminants in glacial ice often give glaciers a dirty gray look.

Liquid water can produce a deep blue tone—if the water is very clear and relatively free of algae and other microscopic dwellers, which turn it greenish-brown, and if the water is not carrying much in the way of dissolved minerals.

When free of rock flour, Canadian Rockies river water meets all these criteria for clarity. It hasn't travelled very far from its source and it is quite cold, so there isn't much organic matter or dissolved material in it. That is why many Rockies streams—the ones that aren't glacier-fed—are wonderfully clear.

Suppose this clear water flows into a lake. When the depth reaches a couple of metres, then the beautiful blue color starts to show. Viewed from the upper terminal of the Jasper Tramway, the lakes on the valley floor across the river from Jasper townsite look brilliantly blue. The ones west of town lie in iron-rich rock, contain more dissolved minerals and more organic matter than the others, so they are darker.

Light is gradually absorbed with increasing depth, so that pure, deep water looks practically black—the midnight blue color seen in many of the deeper lakes in the Rockies that are not glacially fed.

Consider now the water that comes from a glacier. The meltwater stream carries boulders, rocks, sand, silt, pollen, atmospheric dust, soot from forest fires and rock flour. All this turns the water murky gray or brown as it departs the glacial snout.

Let's follow that glacial stream as it enters a lake. The boulders, gravel and sand drop out as the water slows, gradually building a delta out from shore. The silt gets somewhat farther into the lake, but soon it, too, sinks to the bottom. This leaves the rock flour and the other colloidal-sized particles (those less than about one micron in size), which are so small that they can stay in suspension in the water for months. The colloidal fraction spreads out in all directions and thus distributes itself evenly through the whole lake.

And that is when some magic occurs. A very tiny particle of any kind reflects most strongly the wavelength of light closest to its size. A mix of tiny particle sizes gives a whitish look to lake water because the particles are reflecting all the wavelengths. But as the larger particles settle out, the smaller ones remain in suspension. These strongly reflect the shorter wavelengths of light, that is, those in the blue and green parts of the spectrum. Fluorescence—emission of light by certain minerals—also occurs, but it is minor.

Thus, a lake loaded with various-sized rock-flour particles is gray. The meltwater pond at the toe of the Athabasca Glacier is a good example. A lake in which some of the rock-flour particles have settled out is pastel green, as Lake Louise often appears, and a lake in which only the finer rock-flour particles remain is bluegreen, like Maligne Lake.

The other part of the glacial-lake-color magic is the uniformity and brightness of the color. The whole lake is often the same brilliant shade. Why?

This is harder to explain—I could find nothing published on it—but here is a working hypothesis. Rock flour is by far the most common contaminant in the water of glacial lakes in the Rockies. In fact, rock flour is practically the only contaminant; the water between the particles of rock flour is surprisingly pure, having melted from snow and glacial ice only a few days or weeks before. Both the particles and the water molecules between them tend to scatter bluegreen light. So when you look down into Lake Louise, for example, you are seeing bluegreen light reflected back to your eyes by rock flour and the water itself. On a sunny day, a lot of light is reflected, and the color is strong. The uniformity comes from the even distribution of similar-sized rock flour particles in the lake. These particles are small enough to be kept in constant Brownian motion, and their electrical charges are similar, so they repel one another. They disperse quickly through the lake water, eventually distributing themselves fairly evenly, each particle as far away from its neighbors as possible.

A tiny copepod named *Hesperodiaptomus arcticus* (see drawing on page 437) takes in rock flour as it feeds. A study of the sediments flooring Bow Lake showed that nearly all the rock flour was deposited as copepod droppings. Same for other glacial lakes in the Canadian Rockies.

*Brilliant opacity, an oxymoron that applies to the water of glacial lakes such as this one, Peyto Lake, near Bow Summit on the Icefields Parkway*

## Sand dunes in the Canadian Rockies?

Yes, there are dunes here. Perhaps the best-developed set is at Jasper Lake, 20 km east of Jasper townsite along Highway 16. Jasper Lake is the first lake that the Athabasca River passes through on its way downstream, so it receives a great deal of glacial sand and silt each year. Jasper Lake also has an interesting annual cycle, and the cycle produces the dunes.

In the fall and winter Jasper Lake is a barren sand flat 8 km long and 2 km wide. Every spring, usually in late May, it fills—although the lake is less than a metre deep in most places, except along the Athabasca main channel, which lies near the north shore and is several metres deep. Thus, it is possible to wade far out into the lake before it gets even knee-deep. In late summer the lake shrinks again, exposing the silty, sandy floor to the westerly wind, constant and strong in this valley, which picks up the grains and carries them down the lake in dust storms.

The silt stays aloft for many kilometres, dusting the foothills to the east, but the sand grains are too heavy to rise more than about a metre above the surface; they proceed in short hops until they reach places where the wind speed lessens. There they form dunes up to 30 m in height.

You can see some of these dunes along Highway 16. The ones beside the road are small and mostly overgrown, but across the lake and farther west they are fresher and larger. During winter chinooks the wind howls through the Jasper Lake dunes at up to 100 km/h. Stones lying among the dunes have been eroded and polished on their upwind sides by sandblasting—like the faceted stones one finds in windy deserts.

*Dunes and blowing sand along Highway 16 beside Jasper Lake. The photo was taken in winter, when the lakebed was dry and the wind was picking up sand and silt from it. Photo courtesy Jasper National Park.*

# *Geology picture-pages*
## Time-line, block diagrams, maps, cross-sections, etc.

Major geological events in the Canadian Rockies are summarized in **time-line** form on the next page. The **block diagrams** on pages 186 and 187 help to visualize some of these events.

The regional extent of the four great layers of the Canadian Rockies is shown on the **geological maps,** pages 188–190. **Cross-sections** of the Rockies are given on page 191. **Geological columns** are presented on pages 192–194, showing the various formations and groups as if they were not folded or faulted; that is, the columns display the original order before mountain-building. You won't find the whole sequence in any particular mountain. Usually just a few formations are visible.

There are particular spots along main highways that offer good views of several formations in undisturbed order. Beginning on page 195, you will find **annotated photos** of some of these views.

**Pictures of common Canadian Rockies fossils** begin on page 199.

Sixty years ago, all these graphical items would have been sketchy, to say the least. There was simply too little geological information available about the Canadian Rockies. For the region north of the Peace River there is barely enough data even now, as I write this in 1995, and geological mapping of the Rockies at the preferred scale of 1:50 000 is still a long way from completion. Geologists are out there every summer, walking up and down the mountains with their hammers in their hands and their packs full of stones, filling in the white places on the geologic maps. They are lucky enough to be getting first crack at what remains of a scientific frontier.

Those who preceded them in the 1950s and 1960s, which was probably the golden age of Canadian Rockies geology, can reflect with pride that fieldwork was perhaps more exciting and certainly much tougher then. Entire ranges had not been explored, and the field parties travelled by horse rather than by helicopter. We owe these hardy folks a thank-you.

*A Geological Survey of Canada field party in the Canadian Rockies in the 1950s. Photo courtesy Geological Survey of Canada.*

## Time-line of major geological events

Millions of years ago

| Era | Millions of years ago | Event |
|---|---|---|
| Hadean | About 4600 | Earth forms from impacts of smaller objects |
| | 3500–4000 | Life (bacteria?) probably present<br>Atmosphere begins to develop |
| Archean | 3200 | Cyanobacteria appear, producing stromatolites |
| | 1800–2900 | Canadian Rockies basement rock forms |
| Proterozoic | 1700–1900 | Rodinian supercontinent amalgamates |
| | 900–1500 | Rodinia-rock sediments deposited |
| | 545–800 | Rodinia splits up, and area west of Rockies breaks away to become most of Antarctica and Australia<br>Old clastic unit deposited over new continental edge |
| | 545 | Major extinction event marks end of Proterozoic |
| Cambrian & Ordovician | 543 | Life diversifies rapidly, and organisms with hard parts (trilobites, brachiopods, etc.) appear |
| | 525 | Sea moves inland and Kicking Horse Rim develops<br>Deposition of middle carbonate unit begins<br>Burgess Shale fossils deposited |
| Silurian | 425 | Mild uplift raises most of Rockies area above sea level<br>Some of the middle carbonates erode away |
| Devonian | 375 | Sea returns, shallow and warm<br>Western Canada lies near the equator<br>Stromatoporoid reefs develop, holding oil and gas |
| | 367 | Cold, low-oxygen water upwells in the sea<br>Most reef-building organisms are lost |
| | 360–365 | Antler Orogeny raises land to west and south |
| | 360 | Another extinction event occurs<br>May have been caused by world-wide algal bloom |
| Carboniferous | 286–360 | Sea advances and retreats; crinoids common |
| Permian | 260 | Appalachian Mountains are built as North America collides with Africa and joins supercontinent of Pangea |
| | 255 | Biggest mass-extinction event known<br>85% of all species on earth disappear |
| Triassic | 245 | Young clastic unit begins to be deposited |
| | 200 | Pangea begins to break up<br>Atlantic Ocean begins to open<br>North America begins to move northwestward |

| Period | Million years ago | Event |
|---|---|---|
| Jurassic | 175 | North America overruns landmasses to west<br>Mountain-building begins in western Canada<br>Columbia, Omineca and Cassiar ranges are rising<br>west of the Rockies |
| | 140–145 | Westernmost Canadian Rockies begin to rise |
| Cretaceous | 125–135 | Plate motion changes and mountain-building stalls<br>Rockies lose height to erosion |
| | 120 | Rockies are on the rise again, main ranges tall |
| | 85 | Front ranges begin to rise |
| | 66 | A large object strikes the earth<br>Half of all species (dinosaurs, etc.) go extinct |
| Tertiary | 60 | Foothills begin to rise<br>Rocky Mountain Trench begins to form, dividing Rockies<br>from Columbias, Ominecas and Cassiars. Otherwise all four<br>ranges would be one. |
| | 45–50 | Mountain-building tapers off |
| Pleistocene | 1.9 | Earth's climate cools and Ice Ages begin<br>Glaciers sculpt the present Rockies landscape |

*Thousands of years ago*

|  |  |
|---|---|
| 200–300 | *Homo sapiens* appears in Africa |
| 128–240 | Illinoian glaciation |
| 64–75 | Early Wisconsinan glaciation |
| 11–25 | Late Wisconsinan glaciation |
| 12 | Humans have arrived in North America<br>Mastodons and many other species disappear |

| | |
|---|---|
| 4004 B.C. | World created, according to Archbishop James Ussher of Ireland (died 1656) |
| A.D. 1200–1845 | Little Ice Age leaves most recent terminal moraines |
| 1995 | Human overpopulation is causing extinction event |

"For utterly impossible as are all these events,
they are probably as like those which may have taken place
as any others which never took person at all
are ever likely to be."

— James Joyce, in *Finnegans Wake*

# Key phases in the geological history of western Canada

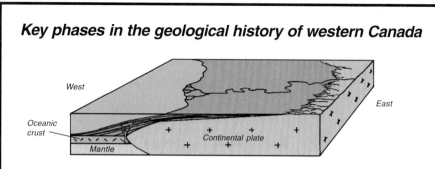

West

East

Oceanic
crust

Continental plate

Mantle

**1. Rodinia rock deposited** *(Mesoproterozoic, 900–1500 million years ago). Most of the world's continents have assembled into a supercontinent called Rodinia. In the area that will eventually become western Canada, rivers carry sediments into an inland sea.*

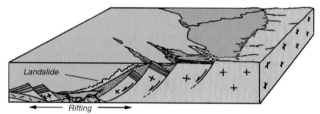

Landslide

←——— Rifting ———→

**2. Rodinia rifts (splits) away from North America** *(Neoproterozoic, 545–780 million years ago). Coarse sediments of the **old clastic unit** are deposited over a new continental edge. Undersea landslides carry these sediments out to sea as turbidity currents and sort them into gritstone and shale layers (turbidites). Near the end of this period a thick sandstone layer is deposited.*

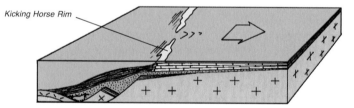

Kicking Horse Rim

**3. The sea moves inland,** *and living things deposit limestone and shale of the **middle carbonate unit** on a wide, very shallow continental shelf (Middle Cambrian to Middle Ordovician, 447–525 million years ago). The edge of the shelf runs through the area that will become the main ranges of the Canadian Rockies. The feature is called the Kicking Horse Rim.*

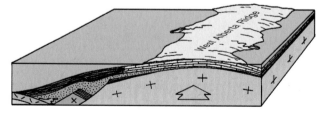

West Alberta Ridge

**4. Mild uplift raises the West Alberta Ridge and the Peace River Arch** *(Middle Silurian to Early Devonian, 390–425 million years ago), putting a gentle bend into the rock of the continental shelf. Some of the middle carbonates are eroded away.*

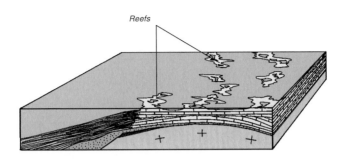

Reefs

**5. After the West Alberta Ridge is eroded away, reefs develop** *in a warm, shallow sea (Late Devonian, 366–373 million years ago). Planktonic organisms and cyanobacteria produce hydrocarbons, which remain to become oil and gas in the reef rock. All the world's major landmasses are assembling themselves into a new supercontinent called Pangea.*

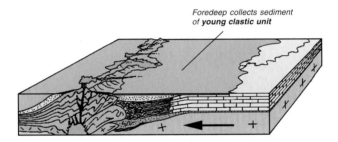

Foredeep collects sediment of **young clastic unit**

**6. Pangea starts to rift apart, and North America moves northwestward** *(Middle and Late Jurassic, 140–175 million years ago). The continent collides with two chains of islands riding northeastward on the oceanic floor. The islands amalgamate into a landmass strip that attaches to North America. The impact produces mountain ranges that spread northeastward. By 140 million years ago the westernmost Rockies are above sea level. The oceanic plate changes its direction of movement to southeasterly. Mountain-building stalls. The outer half of the added-on landmass is carried southeastward along the continental edge to Baja California. Later the oceanic plate resumes its northeasterly movement and the landmass strip slides back.*

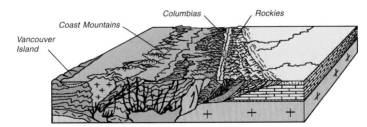

Coast Mountains    Columbias    Rockies

Vancouver Island

**7. Hauled in from the south along transcurrent faults, a third landmass presses against the west coast** *(Early Cretaceous to Early Tertiary, 85–45 million years ago). The pressure rejuvenates mountain-building across western Canada, raising the Rockies higher and extending them farther eastward. Toward the end, crustal stretching across southern British Columbia causes block-faulting that produces the southern Rocky Mountain Trench, dividing the Rockies from the Columbia Mountains. At present in the Rockies, after 45 million years of erosion, the old clastic unit is exposed mostly in the main ranges, the middle carbonates are exposed mostly in the front ranges, and the young clastics are exposed mainly in the foothills.*

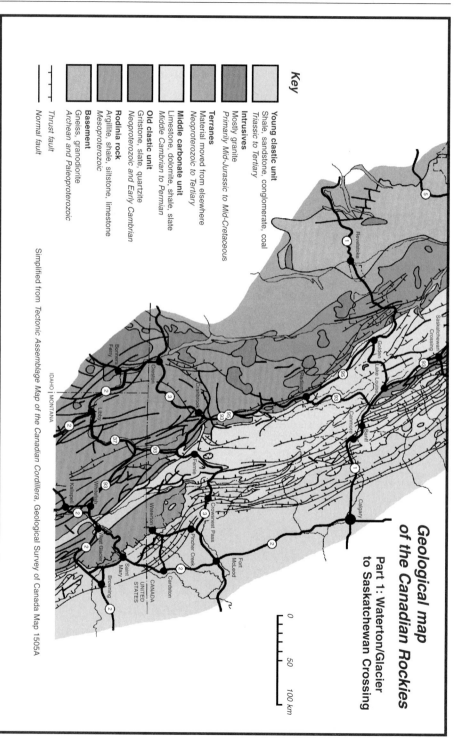

**Geological map of the Canadian Rockies**

Part 1: Waterton/Glacier to Saskatchewan Crossing

**Key**

**Young clastic unit**
Shale, sandstone, conglomerate, coal

**Intrusives**
Mostly granite
*Triassic to Tertiary*

**Terranes**
Material moved from elsewhere
*Primarily Mid-Jurassic to Mid-Cretaceous*

**Middle carbonate unit**
Limestone, dolomite, shale, slate
*Neoproterozoic to Tertiary*

**Old clastic unit**
Gritstone, slate, quartzite
*Middle Cambrian to Permian*

**Rodinia rock**
Argillite, shale, siltstone, limestone
*Neoproterozoic and Early Cambrian*

**Basement**
Gneiss, granodiorite
*Mesoproterozoic*
*Archean and Paleoproterozoic*

Thrust fault
Normal fault

Simplified from *Tectonic Assemblage Map of the Canadian Cordillera*, Geological Survey of Canada Map 1505A

0    50    100 km

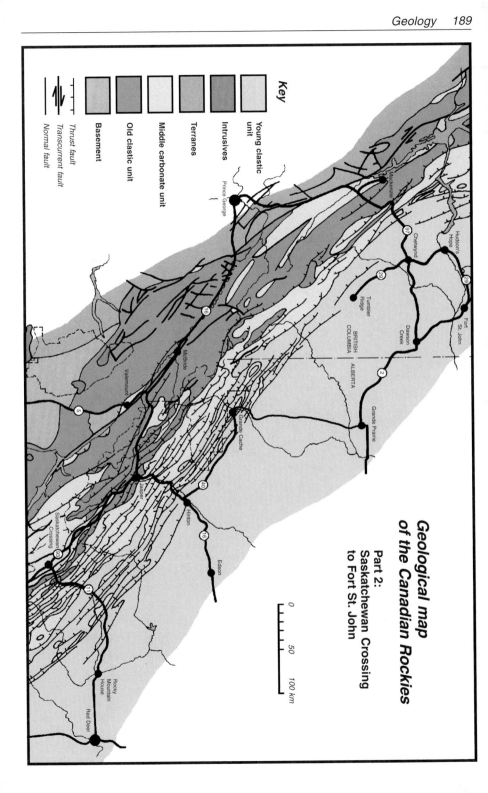

**Geological map of the Canadian Rockies**

Part 2:
Saskatchewan Crossing
to Fort St. John

Key

- Young clastic unit
- Intrusives
- Terranes
- Middle carbonate unit
- Old clastic unit
- Basement

Thrust fault
Transcurrent fault
Normal fault

0    50    100 km

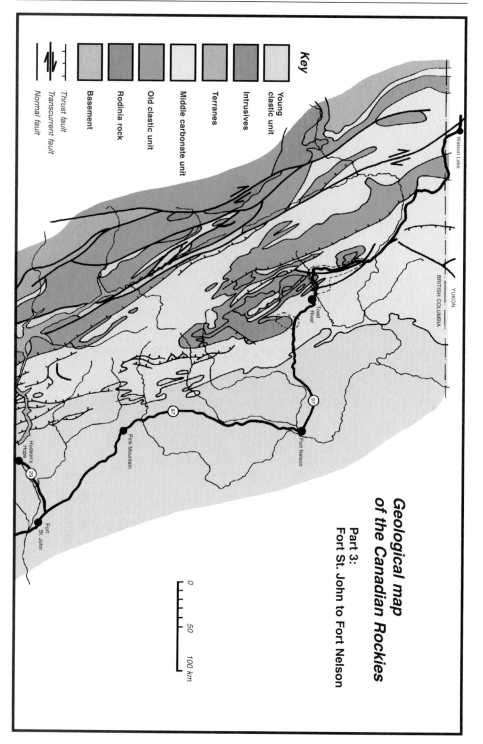

Geological map
of the Canadian Rockies

Part 3:
Fort St. John to Fort Nelson

Key

Young
clastic unit

Intrusives

Terranes

Middle carbonate unit

Old clastic unit

Rodinia rock

Basement

Thrust fault
Transcurrent fault
Normal fault

Watson Lake

YUKON

BRITISH COLUMBIA

Toad
River

Fort Nelson

Pink Mountain

Hudson's
Hope

Fort
St. John

0    50    100 km

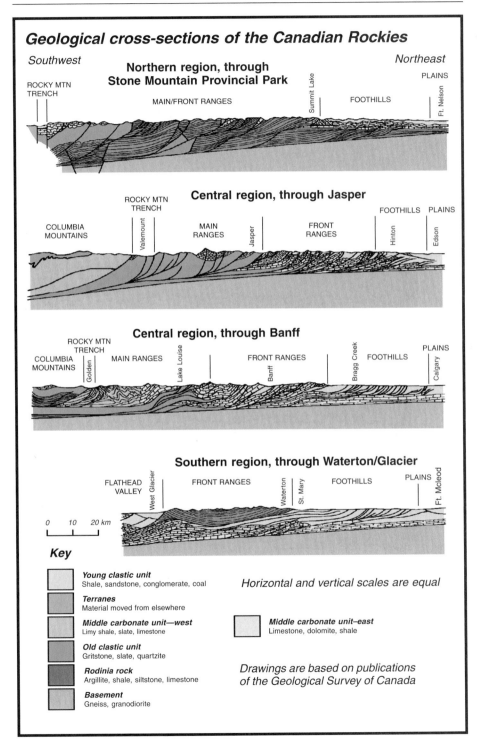

# Geological cross-sections of the Canadian Rockies

*Southwest*                                                                                  *Northeast*

**Northern region, through
Stone Mountain Provincial Park**

ROCKY MTN
TRENCH

MAIN/FRONT RANGES

Summit Lake

FOOTHILLS

PLAINS

Ft. Nelson

**Central region, through Jasper**

ROCKY MTN
TRENCH

COLUMBIA
MOUNTAINS

Valemount

MAIN
RANGES

Jasper

FRONT
RANGES

FOOTHILLS    PLAINS

Hinton    Edson

**Central region, through Banff**

ROCKY MTN
TRENCH

COLUMBIA
MOUNTAINS

Golden

MAIN RANGES

Lake Louise

FRONT RANGES

Banff

Bragg Creek

FOOTHILLS

PLAINS

Calgary

**Southern region, through Waterton/Glacier**

FLATHEAD
VALLEY

West Glacier

FRONT RANGES

Waterton

St. Mary

FOOTHILLS

PLAINS

Ft. Mcleod

0    10    20 km

## Key

*Young clastic unit*
Shale, sandstone, conglomerate, coal

*Terranes*
Material moved from elsewhere

*Middle carbonate unit—west*
Limy shale, slate, limestone

*Old clastic unit*
Gritstone, slate, quartzite

*Rodinia rock*
Argillite, shale, siltstone, limestone

*Basement*
Gneiss, granodiorite

*Horizontal and vertical scales are equal*

*Middle carbonate unit–east*
Limestone, dolomite, shale

*Drawings are based on publications
of the Geological Survey of Canada*

# GEOLOGIST'S CORRELATION CHART
Based on publications of the Geological Survey of Canada

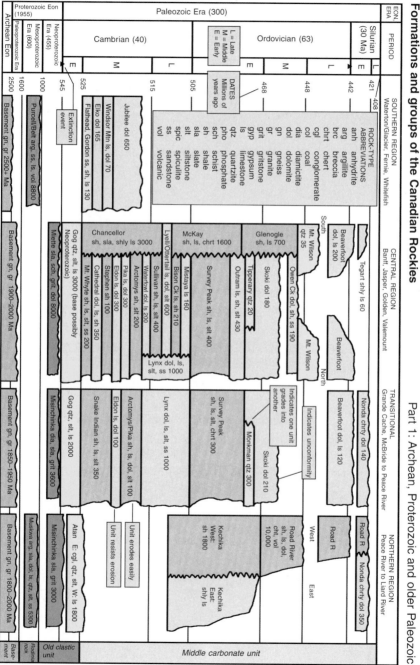

**Formations and groups of the Canadian Rockies**

**Part 1: Archean, Proterozoic and older Paleozoic**

Thickness of each rock unit is given in metres

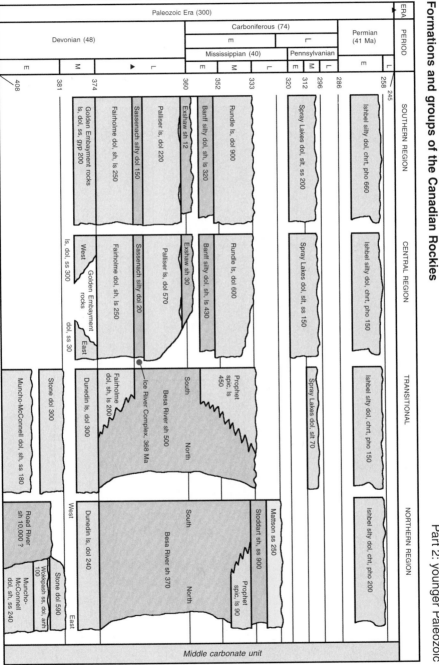

**Formations and groups of the Canadian Rockies**

**Part 2: younger Paleozoic**

*For meanings of abbreviations, see part one of the chart.*

**Formations and groups of the Canadian Rockies**

**Part 3: Mesozoic and Cenozoic**

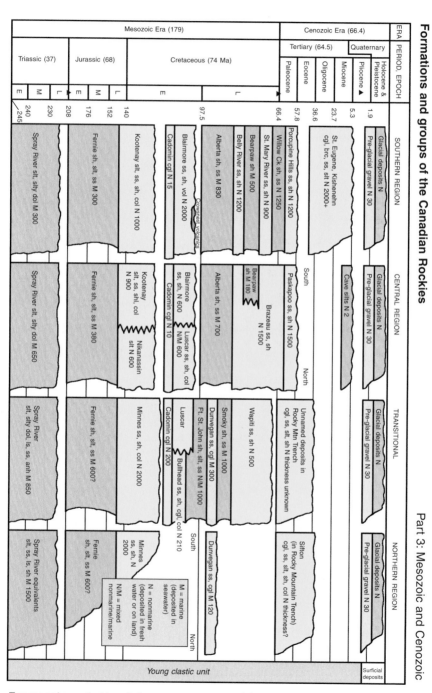

*For meanings of abbreviations, see part one of the chart.*

# Classic geological views

*Purcell Supergroup at end of Akamina Road, Waterton Lakes National Park*

Mt. Custer
Gateway
Sheppard
Purcell Lava
Siyeh
Cameron Lake
Photo: David McIntyre

*Purcell units in Vimy Peak*

Altyn
Mt. Crandell Thrust
Appekunny
Altyn
Waterton
Middle Waterton Lake
Upper Waterton Lake
Waterton Park
Photo: David McIntyre

*Crowsnest Mountain from Crowsnest Lake along Highway 3*

Rundle
Banff
Palliser
Rundle
Banff
Palliser
Lewis Thrust
Belly River
Photo: David McIntyre

View northward from Highwood Pass along Highway 40 in Kananaskis Country

Elpoca Mtn.

Ishbel and Spray Lakes

Rundle

Gap Mtn.

Rundle

Spray River

Rundle

Kootenay

Fernie

Lewis Thrust

Mt. Kidd from Highway 40 near Fortress Mountain ski area

Rundle

Anticline    Syncline

Northern end of Lewis Thrust

Yamnuska from the TransCanada Highway at the mountain front

Pika

Yamnuska

Eldon

Eldon

McConnell

Thrust

Belly River

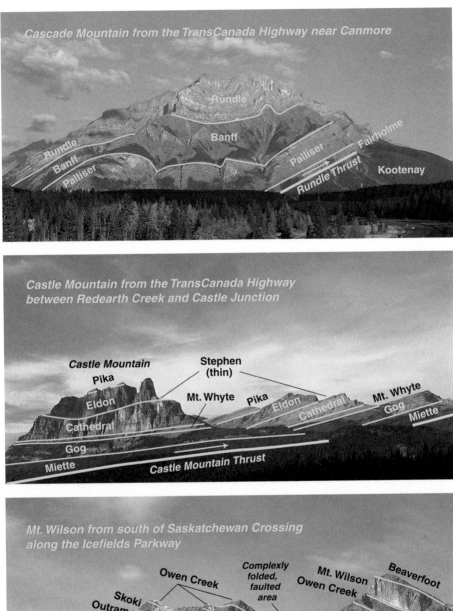

Cascade Mountain from the TransCanada Highway near Canmore

Castle Mountain from the TransCanada Highway between Redearth Creek and Castle Junction

Mt. Wilson from south of Saskatchewan Crossing along the Icefields Parkway

Folds in Bedson Ridge
from Highway 16 near the mountain front in Jasper National Park

Banff

Palliser

Roche Miette from Highway 16 east of Jasper

Nikanassin

Eldon and Pika

Arctomys

Flume

Sassenach

Palliser

Mt. Hawk

Perdrix

Miette Thrust

Mt. Robson from Highway 16

Lynx

Arctomys

Pika

# Common fossils of the Canadian Rockies

*Genus name, formation(s) in which it typically occurs, and age*

*E = Early, M = Middle, L = Late*

**Trilobites**

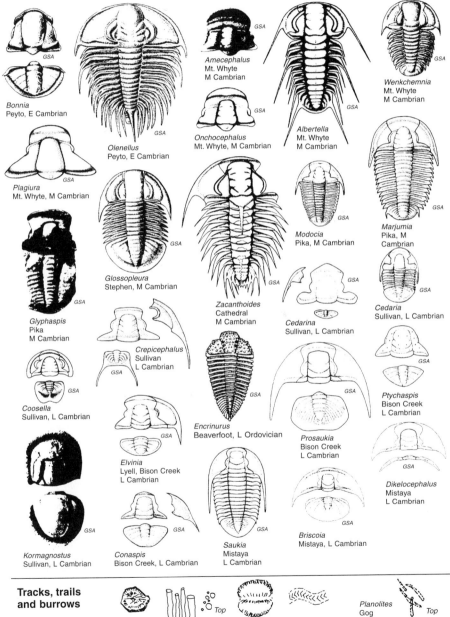

*Bonnia*
Peyto, E Cambrian

*Plagiura*
Mt. Whyte, M Cambrian

*Glyphaspis*
Pika
M Cambrian

*Coosella*
Sullivan, L Cambrian

*Kormagnostus*
Sullivan, L Cambrian

*Olenellus*
Peyto, E Cambrian

*Glossopleura*
Stephen, M Cambrian

*Crepicephalus*
Sullivan
L Cambrian

*Elvinia*
Lyell, Bison Creek
L Cambrian

*Conaspis*
Bison Creek, L Cambrian

*Amecephalus*
Mt. Whyte
M Cambrian

*Onchocephalus*
Mt. Whyte, M Cambrian

*Zacanthoides*
Cathedral
M Cambrian

*Encrinurus*
Beaverfoot, L Ordovician

*Saukia*
Mistaya
L Cambrian

*Albertella*
Mt. Whyte
M Cambrian

*Modocia*
Pika, M Cambrian

*Cedarina*
Sullivan, L Cambrian

*Prosaukia*
Bison Creek
L Cambrian

*Briscoia*
Mistaya, L Cambrian

*Wenkchemnia*
Mt. Whyte
M Cambrian

*Marjumia*
Pika, M
Cambrian

*Cedaria*
Sullivan, L Cambrian

*Ptychaspis*
Bison Creek
L Cambrian

*Dikelocephalus*
Mistaya
L Cambrian

## Tracks, trails and burrows

*Cyclomedusa*
Miette, Neo-
Proterozoic

*Irridinitus*
Miette, Neo-
Proterozoic

*Skolithos*
Gog, E Cambrian

*Rusophycus*
Gog
E Cambrian

*Cruziana*
Gog
E Cambrian

*Planolites*
Gog
E Cambrian
Miette
Neoproterozoic

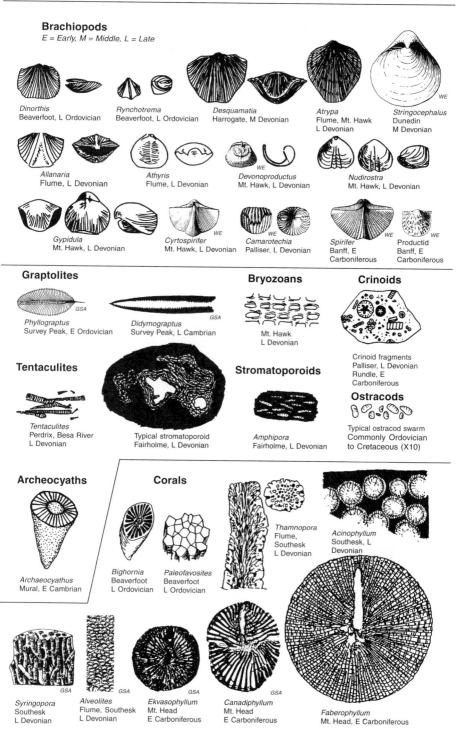

## Brachiopods
*E = Early, M = Middle, L = Late*

**Dinorthis**
Beaverfoot, L Ordovician

**Rynchotrema**
Beaverfoot, L Ordovician

**Desquamatia**
Harrogate, M Devonian

**Atrypa**
Flume, Mt. Hawk
L Devonian

**Stringocephalus**
Dunedin
M Devonian

**Allanaria**
Flume, L Devonian

**Athyris**
Flume, L Devonian

**Devonoproductus**
Mt. Hawk, L Devonian

**Nudirostra**
Mt. Hawk, L Devonian

**Gypidula**
Mt. Hawk, L Devonian

**Cyrtospirifer**
Mt. Hawk, L Devonian

**Camarotechia**
Palliser, L Devonian

**Spirifer**
Banff, E
Carboniferous

**Productid**
Banff, E
Carboniferous

## Graptolites

**Phyllograptus**
Survey Peak, E Ordovician

**Didymograptus**
Survey Peak, L Cambrian

## Bryozoans

Mt. Hawk
L Devonian

## Crinoids

Crinoid fragments
Palliser, L Devonian
Rundle, E
Carboniferous

## Tentaculites

**Tentaculites**
Perdrix, Besa River
L Devonian

Typical stromatoporoid
Fairholme, L Devonian

## Stromatoporoids

**Amphipora**
Fairholme, L Devonian

## Ostracods

Typical ostracod swarm
Commonly Ordovician
to Cretaceous (X10)

## Archeocyaths

**Archaeocyathus**
Mural, E Cambrian

## Corals

**Bighornia**
Beaverfoot
L Ordovician

**Paleofavosites**
Beaverfoot
L Ordovician

**Thamnopora**
Flume,
Southesk
L Devonian

**Acinophyllum**
Southesk, L
Devonian

**Syringopora**
Southesk
L Devonian

**Alveolites**
Flume, Southesk
L Devonian

**Ekvasophyllum**
Mt. Head
E Carboniferous

**Canadiphyllum**
Mt. Head
E Carboniferous

**Faberophyllum**
Mt. Head, E Carboniferous

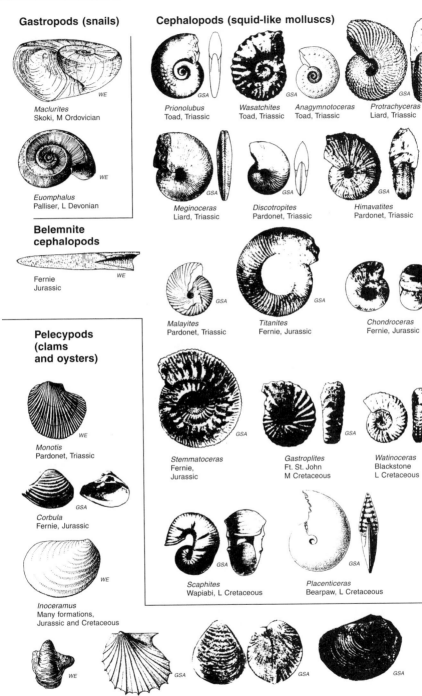

### Gastropods (snails)

*Maclurites*
Skoki, M Ordovician

WE

*Euomphalus*
Palliser, L Devonian

WE

### Belemnite cephalopods

*Fernie*
Jurassic

WE

### Pelecypods (clams and oysters)

*Monotis*
Pardonet, Triassic

WE

*Corbula*
Fernie, Jurassic

GSA

*Inoceramus*
Many formations,
Jurassic and Cretaceous

WE

### Cephalopods (squid-like molluscs)

*Prionolubus*
Toad, Triassic

GSA

*Wasatchites*
Toad, Triassic

GSA

*Anagymnotoceras*
Toad, Triassic

GSA

*Protrachyceras*
Liard, Triassic

GSA

*Meginoceras*
Liard, Triassic

GSA

*Discotropites*
Pardonet, Triassic

GSA

*Himavatites*
Pardonet, Triassic

GSA

*Malayites*
Pardonet, Triassic

GSA

*Titanites*
Fernie, Jurassic

GSA

*Chondroceras*
Fernie, Jurassic

GSA

*Stemmatoceras*
Fernie,
Jurassic

GSA

*Gastroplites*
Ft. St. John
M Cretaceous

GSA

*Watinoceras*
Blackstone
L Cretaceous

GSA

*Scaphites*
Wapiabi, L Cretaceous

GSA

*Placenticeras*
Bearpaw, L Cretaceous

GSA

*Gryphaea*
Fernie, Jurassic

WE

*Oxytoma*
Fernie, Jurassic

GSA

*Buchia*
Monach, E Cretaceous

GSA

*Posidonia*
Ft. St. John, M Cretaceous

GSA

## Further reading

There is little authoritative and up-to-date literature on the geology of the Canadian Rockies that is also non-technical, and I have included all of it here, plus a few essential technical publications.

Many geological reports on the Rockies and maps have been published by the Geological Survey of Canada (the "GSC"). These publications are available over-the-counter or by mail from the GSC's Institute of Sedimentary and Petroleum Geology in Calgary, at 3303 33rd St. NW, Calgary T2L 2A7. Topographic maps and satellite images are available as well. Phone 403-292-7000.

Bally, B. (1989) *The Geology of North America; an Overview.* Decade of North American Geology (DNAG) Volume A, Geological Society of North America, Boulder, CO. Technical and outstanding. Illustrated, fully referenced, including additional references on microfiche in a pocket on the inside back cover, indexed; 619 pages.

Beaty, C. (1975) *The Landscapes of Southern Alberta: a Regional Geomorphology.* University of Lethbridge Production Services. Non-technical, with info on the foothills and mountains. Illustrated, reading list, 95 pages.

Briggs, D; D. Erwin and F. Collier (1994) *The Fossils of the Burgess Shale.* Smithsonian Institution Press, Washington, D.C. Well-illustrated guide to the world-famous locality in Yoho National Park. Drawings, bibliography, index; 238 pages.

Conway Morris, S. and H. Whittington (1985) *Fossils of the Burgess Shale: a National Treasure in Yoho National Park, British Columbia.* GSC Miscellaneous Report 43. Every fossil fancier should have this inexpensive booklet on one of the world's more important paleontological sites. Outstanding fossil photos; 31 pages.

Gabrielse, H. and C. Yorath, editors (1992) *Geology of the Cordilleran Orogen in Canada.* GSC Geology of Canada Report 4. A technical, comprehensive, authoritative treatment, with accompanying volume of maps, cross-sections and correlation charts. Must-have for Canadian geologists. Illustrated, indexed, fully referenced; 844 pages.

Gould, S. (1989) *Wonderful Life: the Burgess Shale and the Nature of History.* W.W. Norton, New York. Stephen Jay Gould, the noted Harvard paleontologist, evolutionary theorist and essayist, has turned his lifelong interest in the Burgess Shale fossils into a fascinating, readable and important book. Illustrated, indexed, bibliography; 347 pages.

Harris, A. and E. Tuttle (1983) "Glacier National Park," in *Geology of National Parks.* Kendall/ Hunt, Dubuque, Iowa. Non-technical summary, 14 pages. The full book is an excellent resource on the American national parks.

Harrison, J. (1976) *Evolution of a Landscape: the Quaternary Period in Waterton Lakes National Park.* GSC Miscellaneous Report 26. Non-technical description of landforms and deposits in the park, with map. Illustrated, glossary, bibliography; 33 pages.

Kucera, R. (1999) *Exploring the Columbia Icefield.* High Country, Canmore. A terrific and well-illustrated non-technical booklet on Canada's favorite glacier, by the scientist who knows it best. Reading list, 72 pages.

McDonald, J.; D. Pollock and B. McDermot (1978) *Hotsprings of Western Canada: a Complete Guide.* Labrador Tea Company, Vancouver. Non-technical spring-by-spring compendium, with maps; 162 pages.

Morris, S. (1998) *The Crucible of Creation: the Burgess Shale and the Rise of Animals.* Oxford University Press, New York. The latest interpretations, and a point of view that differs with that of Stephen J. Gould, q.v. Illustrated, well-referenced, indexed; 242 pages.

Mossop, G. and I. Shetsen (1994) *Geological Atlas of the Western Canada Sedimentary Basin.* Canadian Society of Petroleum Geologists, Calgary. Technical, comprehensive, huge, gorgeous, expensive; 510 pages.

Muir, D. and D. Ford (1985) *Castleguard.* Canadian Government Publishing Centre, Ottawa. An entire book, and a beautiful one, devoted to Castleguard Cave and its surroundings, published as a Parks Canada centennial project (1885–1985). Co-author Derek Ford is an expert on the cave. Outstanding illustrations, 244 pages.

Raup, O. et al. (1983) *Geology along Going-to-the-Sun Road, Glacier National Park, Montana: a Self-guided Tour for Motorists.* Glacier Natural History Association, West Glacier, Montana. Well-done non-technical guide to the specially marked geology stops along the highway, with good fold-out map, glossary, reading list; 62 pages.

Robinson, B. and D. Harmon (1981) *Columbia Icefield: a Solitude of Ice.* Altitude Publishing, Canmore. Combination of geology and human history, with excellent photographs. Glossary, reading list; 104 pages.

Sedgwick, J. and W. Henoch (1975) *Peyto Glacier.* Inland Waters, Environment Canada, Ottawa. A terrific map of the north end of the Wapta Icefield, done in the style of Parks Canada's Columbia Icefield Map, with 30 pages of non-technical notes on the glacier and its surroundings.

Smith, D. (1987) *Landforms of Alberta.* Alberta Forestry, Lands and Wildlife, Land Information Services, Edmonton. A fascinating book of aerial photographs covering many mountain features, complete with a stereoscope for viewing them in 3-D. Bibliography, 105 pages.

Whittington, H. (1985) *The Burgess Shale.* Yale University Press and the Geological Survey of Canada. Semi-technical book on the famous fossils, with excellent photos and drawings. Index, technical bibliography; 151 pages.

Yorath, C. (1990) *Where Terranes Collide.* Orca Book Publishers, Victoria. An entertaining, non-technical look at the geological history of western Canada and the geologists who have studied it, written by one of them. Illustrated, glossary, reading list; 231 pages.

— (1997) *How Old Is that Mountain? A Visitor's Guide to the Geology of Banff and Yoho National Parks.* Orca Book Publishers, Victoria. Non-technical but thorough and up to date, with road logs. Illustrated, index, glossary, reading list; 146 pages.

— and B. Gadd (1995) *Of Rocks, Mountains and Jasper.* Dundern Press, Toronto. The geology of Jasper National Park, with road logs. Illustrated, index, glossary, reading list; 170 pages.

## What every geologist should know

**Mnemonic for remembering the names of the geological periods:**
*Camels often sit down carefully. Perhaps their joints creak. Perhaps early oiling might prevent permanent harm.* (Cambrian, Ordovician, Silurian, Devonian, Carboniferous, Permian, Triassic, Jurassic, Cretaceous, Paleocene, Eocene, Oligocene, Miocene, Pliocene, Pleistocene, Holocene)

The sailing on Maligne Lake was great, until that cloud turned into a thunderhead.

# Weather and climate
## When it's springtime in the Rockies, stay away

The **climate** of a place is described by its long-term averages of temperature, hours of sunshine, amount of precipitation (rain and snow), humidity, wind speed, wind direction and other elements. The **weather** is the status of these things at any given time.

Like the biology and the geology, the climate of the Canadian Rockies has an overall style. Here it is, in a one-paragraph summary:

The Rockies are hottest in July, with a typical daily maximum of 20° to 25°C in the valleys from one end of the region to the other. The coldest month is January, when the average overnight low is -15°C in the south and -30°C in the north. The higher the elevation, the lower the temperature (except during inversions, page 210) and the greater the precipitation. At subalpine and alpine elevations more moisture arrives in winter than in summer, while on the montane valley floors it is the other way around. The subalpine forests of the western slope (the mountains west of the continental divide) receive the most snow; the montane valleys in the eastern-slope front ranges get the least, along with the floor of the Rocky Mountain Trench south of Radium Hot Springs.

Climatologists would say that the Canadian Rockies have a "continental" climate, which means simply "inland." Such climates are marked by a great range in temperature over the year —a spread of 37°C between daily summer highs and winter lows at Banff, for example— coupled with a moderate amount of precipitation (468 mm at Banff). This contrasts with the "maritime" climate of Vancouver, for example, in which the annual temperature variation is less (22°C) and the precipitation is much more (1167 mm).

Under the Koeppen classification system, which is the climatologist's standard, our climate is "Dfc": a "cold, snowy forest climate with no distinct dry season and short, cool summers." The table on the next two pages provides essential climatic data for all public weather stations in the area that operate year-round.

These are long-term figures, most of them averaged over thirty years. But we are speaking of the mountains, which are notorious for climatic variety. The kind of weather we have, summer or winter, can vary considerably from year to year: warm and dry one summer, cool and wet the next; snowy and mild one winter, bare and bone-chilling cold the next. Further, the rough topography makes the climate of any particular hillside or valley a little different from that of its neighbors.

The daily weather also varies from valley to valley, and it changes quickly. As mountain residents are fond of telling visitors, "If you don't like the weather, just wait a minute." Corollary: "It may get worse." Even on a fine summer day, there is always a jacket in my pack to repel a sudden cold mountain shower or chilly high-country wind.

### Latitude and slope angle

This is a northerly mountain range, so the sun is lower in the sky than it is farther south. That means lower temperatures generally, because low-angle sunlight heats the ground less than high-angle sunlight.

Another effect of our high latitude is that the length of the day changes a great deal through the seasons. At Lake Louise, there are only eight hours of sunlight each day in December and January. This is precisely the same time that the sun angle is lowest, providing the least warmth. In June and July, the situation is the opposite: nearly 16.6 hours of sunlight and the highest sun angle of the year. So the days can become quite warm. In an average year, the temperature at Banff can range from -40°C in the dark, cold days of January to +30°C in the long, hot days of July.

## Climatic data for the Canadian Rockies

*The locations of most of the stations appear on the regional base map, page 12*

| LOCATION and years of data collection | Elev (m) | Mean temp (°C) | Days above 0°C[1] | Daily July high | Daily Jan low | All-time high | All-time low | Annl prec (mm) | Annl snow (cm) | Days with rn/snw |
|---|---|---|---|---|---|---|---|---|---|---|
| **ALBERTA** | | | | | | | | | | |
| Banff (61-90) | 1382 | 2.9 | 158 | 22.2 | -14.9 | 34.4 | -51.2 | 468 | 244 | 78/74 |
| Beaver Mines (61-90) | 1286 | 4.4 | 188 | 22.9 | -12.2 | 35.6 | -45.6 | 623 | 269 | 57/43 |
| Bighorn Dam (69-90) | 1341 | 2.6 | 150 | 20.9 | -15.3 | 33.3 | -44.5 | 484 | 167 | 65/45 |
| Bow Valley PP (67-90) | 1318 | 3.5 | 160 | 23.1 | -15.9 | 33.9 | -42.8 | 561 | 242 | 62/43 |
| Caldwell (61-90) | 1286 | 4.7 | 181 | 23.5 | -12.7 | 36.7 | -41.1 | 679 | 328 | 44/45 |
| Cardston (61-90) | 1193 | 5.3 | 185 | 24.9 | -12.6 | 38.9 | -41.7 | 547 | 229 | 46/38 |
| Carway (61-90) | 1359 | 4.1 | 168 | 23.0 | -13.4 | 36.7 | -43.9 | 503 | 237 | 40/41 |
| Castle RS (61-90) | 1360 | 3.0 | 149 | 22.9 | -15.7 | 34.4 | -43.9 | 866 | 459 | 67/67 |
| Clearwater RS (61-90) | 1280 | 2.0 | 125 | 20.9 | -17.7 | 32.8 | -41.7 | 653 | 213 | 73/54 |
| Coleman (61-90) | 1341 | 3.5 | 160 | 22.6 | -13.0 | 35.0 | -41.1 | 555 | 181 | 83/34 |
| Columbia Icefield (61-90) | 1981 | -1.8 | - | 15.0 | -18.1 | 26.1 | -41.1 | 963 | 712 | 62/111 |
| Edson Airport (70-90) | 921 | 1.9 | 138 | 21.7 | -18.5 | 33.3 | -47.3 | 568 | 180 | 88/61 |
| Elbow RS (61-90) | 1400 | 1.6 | 98 | 21.4 | -18.8 | 33.0 | -45.6 | 615 | 247 | 63/49 |
| Entrance (61-90) | 991 | 2.4 | 142 | 22.1 | -17.5 | 37.8 | -51.2 | 504 | 146 | 54/33 |
| Fort Macleod (61-88) | 950 | 5.6 | 190 | 25.7 | -13.9 | 42.8 | -45.0 | 425 | 137 | 48/36 |
| Ghost RS (61-90) | 1417 | 2.3 | 132 | 20.7 | -16.6 | 33.0 | -48.0 | 545 | 206 | 63/55 |
| Grande Cache (85-90) | 1255 | 2.1 | - | 20.5 | -17.5 | 31.0 | -40.0 | 602 | 278 | 79/71 |
| Grande Prairie (61-90) | 666 | 1.6 | 165 | 22.2 | -20.9 | 34.5 | -52.2 | 450 | 175 | 74/63 |
| Highwood RS (61-90) | 1493 | 1.6 | 125 | 21.2 | -19.3 | 34.4 | -45.6 | 633 | 319 | 52/51 |
| Hinton (56-76) | 1014 | 2.5 | 143 | 22.1 | -17.9 | 33.3 | -41.1 | 468 | 114 | 48/29 |
| Jasper (61-90) | 1061 | 3.1 | 164 | 22.2 | -15.6 | 36.7 | -46.7 | 394 | 144 | 83/61 |
| Jasper West Gate (74-90) | 1128 | 1.1 | 109 | 21.9 | -18.9 | 36.1 | -48.3 | 490 | 162 | 92/37 |
| Kananaskis (61-90) | 1391 | 3.1 | 152 | 21.6 | -14.4 | 33.9 | -45.6 | 638 | 279 | 64/54 |
| Kananaskis RS (62-87) | 1463 | 1.3 | 110 | 22.1 | -19.7 | 33.0 | -41.1 | 626 | 305 | 53/47 |
| Lake Louise (61-90) | 1524 | -0.4 | 94 | 20.4 | -21.4 | 34.4 | -52.8 | 602 | 329 | 69/63 |
| Nordegg RS (61-90) | 1320 | 1.0 | 102 | 20.5 | -19.2 | 32.2 | -47.2 | 596 | 191 | 67/50 |
| Pekisko (61-90) | 1439 | 2.1 | 129 | 21.2 | -16.3 | 36.1 | -46.7 | 683 | 320 | 54/58 |
| Pincher Creek (79-90) | 1189 | 5.2 | 198 | 24.2 | -9.4 | 35.6 | -41.7 | 466 | 204 | 61/52 |
| Prairie Creek RS (67-84) | 1174 | 0.4 | 93 | 20.5 | -23.0 | 32.8 | -46.7 | 606 | 154 | 58/44 |
| Robb RS (65-90) | 1130 | 2.2 | 132 | 21.4 | -17.9 | 33.0 | -45.5 | 636 | 197 | 76/42 |
| Rocky Mtn House (61-85) | 1015 | 2.7 | 156 | 22.0 | -18.5 | 33.3 | -43.9 | 566 | 199 | 70/65 |
| Sheep RS (63-76) | 1494 | 2.0 | 126 | 21.3 | -19.9 | 32.8 | -42.8 | 693 | 307 | 50/59 |
| South Wapiti RS (62-81) | 762 | 1.5 | 137 | 21.5 | -22.1 | 34.0 | -47.2 | 575 | 199 | 78/53 |
| Turner Valley (61-75) | 1238 | 2.3 | 142 | 21.3 | -19.0 | 32.8 | -45.6 | 573 | 238 | 48/46 |
| Whiskey Gap (65-85) | 1311 | 3.8 | 162 | 23.7 | -14.9 | 37.2 | -41.1 | 424 | 182 | 38/41 |
| **COMPARE WITH** | | | | | | | | | | |
| Calgary Intl Airpt | 1077 | 3.9 | 164 | 23.2 | -15.7 | 36.1 | -45.0 | 399 | 135 | 62/58 |
| Edmonton Intl Airpt | 715 | 2.1 | 153 | 22.5 | -19.8 | 35.0 | -48.3 | 466 | 127 | 72/57 |
| Lethbridge Airport | 929 | 5.6 | 190 | 25.9 | -14.2 | 39.4 | -42.8 | 398 | 160 | 53/54 |
| Revelstoke Airport | 443 | 6.7 | 215 | 25.3 | -8.7 | 36.7 | -29.4 | 950 | 445 | 135/71 |
| Vancouver Intl Airpt | 3 | 9.9 | 308 | 21.7 | -0.1 | 33.3 | -17.8 | 1167 | 55 | 159/13 |

| LOCATION and years of data collection | Elev (m) | Mean temp (°C) | Days above 0°C[1] | Daily July high | Daily Jan low | All-time high | All-time low | Annl prec (mm) | Annl snow (cm) | Days with rn/snw |
|---|---|---|---|---|---|---|---|---|---|---|
| **BRITISH COLUMBIA** | | | | | | | | | | |
| Canal Flats RS (62-82) | 817 | 5.7 | 187 | 26.8 | -13.7 | 38.0 | -41.7 | 383 | 124 | - |
| Chetwynd (82-90) | 609 | 3.0 | 165 | 22.5 | -12.5 | 34.4 | -42.8 | 456 | 155 | 75/52 |
| Cranbrook (68-90) | 939 | 5.6 | 153 | 25.7 | -12.8 | 38.9 | -41.1 | 385 | 148 | 78/49 |
| Dome Creek (70-90) | 648 | 3.5 | 153 | 22.4 | -14.1 | 34.4 | -46.1 | 853 | 301 | 120/56 |
| Elko (61-90) | 931 | 6.1 | 197 | 26.3 | -10.7 | 38.9 | -35.0 | 606 | 169 | 93/44 |
| Fernie (61-90) | 1001 | 4.9 | 177 | 24.6 | -11.7 | 36.1 | -41.7 | 1175 | 373 | 112/62 |
| Field (Boulder Ck) (71-90) | 1219 | 2.6 | 149 | 22.1 | -14.2 | 33.0 | -35.5 | 623 | 250 | 89/62 |
| Fording River (70-90) | 1585 | 1.0 | 118 | 20.9 | -15.3 | 37.5 | -49.0 | 677 | 366 | 61/69 |
| Fort Nelson (61-90) | 382 | -1.1 | 148 | 23.0 | -26.5 | 36.7 | -51.7 | 449 | 191 | 68/72 |
| Fort St. John (61-90) | 695 | 1.6 | 177 | 21.5 | -19.4 | 33.6 | -47.2 | 468 | 198 | 63/68 |
| Fort Steele (68-90) | 856 | 5.5 | 172 | 26.5 | -11.7 | 37.0 | -46.7 | 475 | 106 | 89/28 |
| Golden (61-90) | 785 | 4.6 | 175 | 24.9 | -14.4 | 40.0 | -46.1 | 491 | 184 | 80/41 |
| Grasmere (62-90) | 869 | 6.9 | 202 | 27.7 | -9.0 | 39.4 | -42.8 | 530 | 105 | 66/22 |
| Hudson's Hope (63-90) | 678 | 2.2 | 164 | 21.2 | -18.4 | 33.3 | -46.1 | 529 | 184 | 57/49 |
| Ingenika Point (72-84) | 680 | 0.8 | 155 | 20.5 | -21.2 | 30.5 | -47.0 | 466 | 176 | 101/71 |
| Kootenay Crossing (51-80) | 1170 | 1.7 | - | 23.4 | -18.1 | 36.5 | -42.8 | 505 | 193 | 64/48 |
| Kootenay Pass (74–90) | 1774 | 0.8 | 134 | 16.8 | -11.0 | 35.0 | -42.8 | 1529 | 1044 | 60/120 |
| Lower Post (61-90) | 583 | -3.4 | 128 | 21.2 | -32.2 | 35.0 | -52.8 | 436 | 188 | 61/61 |
| Mackenzie (71-90) | 695 | 2.2 | 151 | 21.8 | -15.6 | 35.0 | -45.1 | 653 | 330 | 95/84 |
| McBride (73-90) | 771 | 4.4 | 174 | 22.2 | -11.0 | 37.8 | -46.7 | 683 | 193 | 123/51 |
| McGregor (65-75) | 610 | 3.6 | - | 22.3 | -18.4 | 36.1 | -46.1 | 928 | 339 | 95/51 |
| McLeod Lake (63-71) | 704 | 2.1 | 155 | 21.1 | -19.1 | 33.9 | -44.4 | 712 | 333 | 82/67 |
| Mount Robson Ranch (75-90) | 869 | 3.4 | 165 | 22.7 | -12.8 | 34.0 | -36.0 | 595 | 222 | 105/57 |
| Muncho Lake (70-90) | 835 | -0.6 | 132 | 20.3 | -20.9 | 33.3 | -46.1 | 496 | 174 | 79/57 |
| Natal Harmer Ridge (71-90) | 1890 | 0.7 | 131 | 18.3 | -13.6 | 30.0 | -35.5 | 728 | 494 | 50/95 |
| Natal Kaiser (69-80) | 1128 | 3.8 | 155 | 24.3 | -15.6 | 34.4 | -40.0 | 619 | 234 | 80/50 |
| Pine Pass (62-81) | 945 | 1.0 | 149 | 19.1 | -16.6 | 31.1 | -40.0 | 1743 | 1120 | 78/94 |
| Pink Mountain (73-82) | 1204 | -0.2 | 144 | 18.6 | -17.5 | 28.5 | -40.0 | 489 | 156 | 43/29 |
| Prince George (61-90) | 676 | 3.7 | 173 | 22.1 | -14.1 | 34.4 | -50.0 | 615 | 234 | 105/74 |
| Red Pass (51-80) | 1059 | 1.7 | 135 | 21.7 | -18.4 | 32.8 | -39.4 | 743 | 405 | 86/69 |
| Radium Hot Springs (51-80) | 1088 | 3.8 | 208 | 24.0 | -14.1 | 36.7 | -32.8 | 547 | 190 | 66/37 |
| Sinclair Pass (51-80) | 1486 | 1.6 | 243 | 21.6 | -15.1 | 36.1 | -42.2 | 608 | 262 | 58/40 |
| Smith River (44-69) | 673 | 3.0 | 118 | 20.9 | -29.8 | 33.3 | -58.9 | 467 | 212 | 64/93 |
| Spillimacheen (61-80) | 818 | 4.4 | 169 | 24.8 | -14.1 | 36.7 | -40.0 | 445 | 163 | 75/42 |
| Valemount (71-82) | 793 | 3.6 | 168 | 22.9 | -15.4 | 40.6 | -51.1 | 498 | 170 | 83/45 |
| Ware (66-87) | 777 | -0.5 | 117 | 20.9 | -24.0 | 33.3 | -48.3 | 441 | 194 | 67/54 |
| Wonowon (73-90) | 914 | 0.9 | 155 | 20.0 | -16.5 | 28.9 | -40.0 | 544 | 193 | 62/52 |

[1]Temperature must stay above freezing for full 24-hour period
RS = Ranger Station
PP = Provincial Park
Source: Atmospheric Environment Service (1993) *Canadian Climate Normals, 1961–1990.*
Environment Canada, Ottawa

The dry mountain air cools quickly after sundown (moist air holds heat longer), so hot nights are rare throughout the region. That same dryness makes the winter cold feel more bearable than it would feel in a damp climate.

South-facing slopes in the Canadian Rockies are heated more strongly than north-facing slopes, because the sun lies at a fairly low angle throughout the year. Even at noon in summer, when the sun is highest in the sky, the rays hit a north-facing slope obliquely. At the same time, they hit a south-facing slope at a nearly perpendicular angle. So south-facing slopes are significantly warmer and thus drier than north-facing ones, an important factor in the ecology of northerly mountain ranges.

## Shading

Mountains create shade, locally delaying sunrise and hastening sunset. This reduces the number of hours of sunlight reaching shaded places, especially in winter when the sun's angle is low.

Regardless of the season, though, the east-facing slope of a valley feels the sun's touch sooner in the day than the west-facing slope, and the sun goes down later on the west-facing side. Given a perfectly symmetrical valley, one would think that these two factors balance, but they don't: the later sundown on west-facing slopes means that the sun is still shining there when the day has warmed. In contrast, the east-facing slopes receive their sun earlier, when the day is new and the air is cool. This tends to keep east-facing slopes cooler overall than west-facing ones.

## The Pacific influence

The western coast of Canada is one of the wetter places in North America, and the Rocky Mountains are close enough to the coast to receive a goodly dose of moisture each year from the prevailing westerly winds. However, mountain ranges west of the Rockies grab much of the rain and snow that would otherwise fall here. Typical annual valley-floor precipitation in the Rockies is 400–700 mm, compared with Revelstoke's 950 mm, in the next range west of the Rockies. The western slope of the Rockies is somewhat wetter than the eastern slope, receiving about 100 mm more precipitation at equivalent elevations—except for the southern Rocky Mountain Trench, the dry corner of the whole region: only 383 mm annual precipitation at Canal Flats.

A special case here is the region south of Crowsnest Pass. Here the western slope is wetter than it is elsewhere, especially on the western side of Glacier National Park, Montana, and around Fernie, B.C. The mountains west of the Rockies are lower here than they are farther north, which leaves more moisture in easterly moving airmasses to be precipitated upon reaching the Rockies. The peaks of Glacier park present a wall-like barrier, lifting the airmasses and capturing moisture moving in from the west. Further, the area lies along a well-known corridor for moist airmasses.

*Mt. Chephren, north of Bow Summit along the Icefields Parkway, sopping up the Pacific influence*

## The prairie influence

Although winds in the Canadian Rockies are mostly from the west, they tend to come from the east—that is, from the prairies—in early summer and during mid-winter cold snaps.

Summer easterlies often push prairie air into the mountains. The increasing elevation of the land forces the air upward, where it expands and cools. Atmospheric moisture condenses into clouds and rain starts to fall in the foothills and front ranges. This is **upslope weather.** It can go on for a week at a time. To beat it, head west, for the effect diminishes rapidly as you approach the continental divide. If Banff is cool and drizzly due to upslope conditions, look for better weather at Lake Louise, or west of the continental divide. Summers on the western slope are normally cloudier and rainier than summers on the eastern slope, but in summers with continuous upslope conditions, as in the summer of 1993, the situation is reversed.

During winter upslope episodes, the airmass moving in is usually quite cold, part of the huge arctic high-pressure cell that keeps the Canadian north frigid all winter. The increase in elevation often induces a constant precipitation of tiny ice crystals in the atmosphere. The mountains get overnight snow-dustings during winter upslope weather and ice-crystal haziness during the day. These light snowfalls can build up, especially at the mountain front. In the Waterton area, winter upslope can cause heavy snowfalls.

*Upslope weather, cool and cloudy. Air flow is from left to right.*

## Orographic weather

Upslope activity occurs at a smaller scale throughout any mountain range, regardless of wind direction. As long as air is moving at all, it will rise over ridges and fall over valleys. The rising motion produces clouds from cooling and condensation, which explains why a single mountain in the middle of a desert can have the only cloud in the area hanging doggedly over its summit. The proper term is **orographic lifting.**

In most mountain ranges there is a daily cycle operating on this principle. Called **orographic weather,** it is mainly a summer phenomenon and operates as follows. The day begins clear. Clouds start to form around the summits in mid-morning, building up in the afternoon and forming local thunderstorms. In the early evening the rain stops, the clouds disappear and the night is starry.

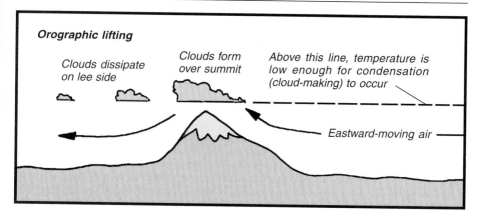

**Orographic lifting**

Clouds dissipate on lee side

Clouds form over summit

Above this line, temperature is low enough for condensation (cloud-making) to occur

Eastward-moving air

Such is the pattern in the Colorado Rockies to the south of us, where in summer one can confidently predict a thunderstorm at 3 p.m. if there are clouds in the sky by 9 a.m. We have orographic weather in the Canadian Rockies, too, but fast-moving airmasses and fronts influence the weather more strongly. So the rule about morning clouds and afternoon showers is not as reliable here as it is in the American Rockies—one of the differences between the two regions.

## Cold lows

Of all storms, the ones that produce the most precipitation in the Rockies are those termed **cold lows** by meteorologists. These storms can be 500–1000 km across, with a core of very cold air in the upper atmosphere. In a cold low the atmospheric temperature drops quickly with increasing elevation, and air warmed at the ground can rise very high, producing intense thunderstorms with a great deal of cold rain. I was caught in one of these events on a two-day rock-climb. Fortunately my partner and I had packed a couple of large plastic garbage bags, to use as emergency bivouac sacks. Without them, the situation might have been life-threatening. See the safety section, page 769, for more on dealing with rough weather in the Rockies.

## The mid-day clearing trend

One element in our weather picture seems to occur daily, winter and summer: a clearing trend at mid-day. No matter how bad the weather is, the cloud cover usually diminishes noticeably for an hour or so around noon. The day has warmed enough to heat the atmosphere, lowering the relative humidity and thus evaporating some cloud moisture. Later, the warm air rises enough to cool, and the clouds form again.

A friend refers to such partial clearing as a "sucker hole." Seeing a large gap in the clouds and figuring that the weather is on the mend, you're lured outdoors—only to wish, an hour or two later, that you had stayed inside.

## Effects of elevation

Any gas cools as it expands. The air temperature drops about 0.7°C for every 100 m of elevation gain due to thinning of the atmosphere. This is the **standard lapse rate.** The rate for air forced upward over a mountain range is greater, as much as 1°C. Thus, the temperature at the upper tramway terminal on The Whistlers is typically 10–15°C lower than it is at Jasper, 1400 m below. Valley-bottom elevations are 300–500 m lower on the western slope of the Canadian Rockies than on the eastern slope, so valley-bottom temperatures are normally a little higher west of the continental divide, other conditions being equal.

At times it can be *warmer* at higher elevations than at lower elevations. This can occur in any season, but most noticeably in winter, when the valleys are filled with very cold air from an arctic high-pressure system that has crept in from the prairies. The cold air is not very deep, often only 200–300 m. Overlying it is air that is perhaps 10–15°C warmer—a **temperature inversion.**

Skiers are familiar with this phenomenon. During cold snaps they can practically count on warmer conditions up on the mountain than down in the valley.

Not only is the air warmer above the inversion, it is often clearer as well. Below the inversion ceiling the cold, dense air is murky with ice crystals and trapped air pollution. Above the ceiling the sun shines brightly through drier, cleaner air. Of course, sometimes the cold air is so deep that it covers even the summits.

In the mountains, elevation has a great effect on precipitation as well as on temperature. This is especially obvious in checking the snow accumulation at different elevations. At 1850 m, not far below treeline on the slopes of Marmot Basin ski area above Jasper, the average snow depth on April first is 120 cm. Down in the townsite there is often none on that date. Summer or winter, there is more precipitation at higher elevations than there is on the valley floors.

A characteristic of the mountain climate is that the valleys get the bulk of their annual precipitation in the warm months, while the peaks get theirs mainly in the winter. A little thought turns up the reason for this. At cold temperatures, clouds are made of snow rather than mist. Thus, any spot swathed in winter clouds is usually receiving snow. Summits and upper mountain slopes are frequently cloud-covered during the cold months, so they get far more snow than the valleys, which lie below the cloud bases, except during storms. Both the uplands and the valleys get watered in summer, when storms are the main moisture suppliers.

In the front ranges and foothills, east of the continental divide, the maximum snow depth usually occurs in early March, while in the Rocky Mountain Trench, at the western edge of the Rockies, it is reached in mid-February. The snow lies deepest just below treeline, in the upper subalpine forest, and it reaches its greatest thickness there in late March or early April. Measurements are traditionally taken by governments on April 1; from these the amount of spring runoff can be projected.

Although more snow falls higher up, in the alpine zone, the unbroken wind there blows the snow over ridges and into leeward valleys. Drifts fill the gullies and extend downwind behind rocks. The alpine zone in winter is a mosaic of drifts and bare patches, impossible to measure accurately for snow accumulation.

The snowiest region in the Canadian Rockies is along the continental divide between Lake Louise and Jasper, where the mountain wall is continuously high (see page 160 for the reason) and thus very effective in capturing moisture moving across it. Several large valleys cut across the Columbia Mountains west of this region, allowing extra precipitation to reach that wall. The result is the chain of icefields one sees along Highway 93, the Icefields Parkway. Although Lake Louise is only 150 m higher than Banff, Lake Louise lies close to the heavy-snow section of the divide and gets considerably more snow: 329 cm per year at Lake Louise; 244 cm at Banff. See page 159 for more on icefields.

East of the icefield chain, the front ranges lie in a **rain shadow:** a dry area downwind of a wet one. Having dumped moisture over the main-range glaciers, the descending air has little rain or snow left for the front ranges. At lower elevations there is often bare ground in mid-winter along affected valleys such as that of the Athabasca River between Jasper and the eastern park gate, or the North Saskatchewan River at Kootenay Plains. In most winters the light and infrequent snowfalls in these valleys are carried away by strong westerly winds (chinooks, page 213) keeping windward slopes bare. Those slopes are essential winter range for bighorn sheep. In other places the snow is too deep for them to scrape down to the grasses they depend on. Chinooks are frequent here, too. In the foothills south of Crowsnest Pass, west-facing slopes are usually snow-free. The windblown snow piles up in huge drifts on the lee sides of hills.

## Wind

The predominant wind direction in the Canadian Rockies is southwesterly, perpendicular to the northwest-southeast alignment of ridges. This has two effects. The first is that winds in most valleys are light and shift frequently in direction, while winds in the few cross-cutting, southwest/northeast-aligned valleys are steadier and stronger. The second effect is that snow blows off the southwest-facing, windward side of ridges and accumulates on their northeast-facing leeward slopes.

Those northeast-facing slopes receive little sun in winter, and they are cool and shady in summer, so snow landing there tends to melt slowly. This combination of greater accumulation and less melt aids glacier development on northeast-facing slopes.

Wind can have catastrophic effects locally, in the form of forest **blow-downs.** Normally caused by gusts that flatten tree-groves a hectare or less in size, blow-downs sometimes are much larger. In late January of 1989, a blizzard with four days of continuous strong northerly winds uprooted many thousands of lodgepole pines around Jasper. This species carries most of its foliage on the upper half of the tree; the wind came with wet snow, which loaded the tops of the pines, then the trees rocked in gusts until, one by one, the roots snapped and trees blew over. The damage was most apparent around Jasper Park Lodge, but the greatest effects could be seen southwest of Pyramid Lake, where patches up to a kilometre long and 200 m wide were flattened. On November 21, 1993 a major blow-down in Yoho park felled 200 ha of trees, mostly lodgepole pine. Such events are unusual, but not unique; walking over the Athabasca Valley floor, I have noted many old, downed trees that fell toward the southeast, in alignment with the valley and with the strong northwesterly winds that funnel down it during storms.

*Who has seen the wind? You're looking at the shape of it here, made visible by these clouds around Mt. Robson.*

## Glacial winds and frost hollows

In summer, large glaciers cool a layer of air over their surfaces. This makes the air denser. It flows downhill, producing a breeze that is noticeably chilly. People walking up to the toe of the Athabasca Glacier often run back to their cars for jackets when they get within 50–100 m of the ice and feel the glacier's frigid breath. It is frequently 10° cooler at the snout than at the Icefield Centre nearby, where the air may be warm and still. Meteorologists call such winds **katabatic.** On days with a westerly breeze, the whole area between the toe and the visitor's centre is kept refrigerated by katabatic wind. Glacial winds can be particularly strong at night— a point forcibly impressed upon climbers who have pitched their tents near a glacial front.

Another kind of katabatic wind is felt more generally in the mountains in the evening, when cool air moves down the slopes. At the same time, the regional wind flow slackens, so the cool descending air collects in glacial cirques and valley bottoms, forming small temperature inversions. Such inversions occur at all elevations and during all seasons, but they are most noticeable in the winter and in the upper subalpine zone, just below treeline. The effect is so pronounced in this zone that ecologists credit katabatic winds with producing subalpine meadows. A classic example is the subalpine meadow that stretches from Sunwapta Pass, on the Banff/Jasper park boundary, to the Icefield Centre (photo on page 239).

Low temperatures through much of the winter in these **frost hollows** combine with a high water table to restrict the species of plants that can grow there. Trees do poorly, while shrub-size willows, grasses and sedges can withstand the severe microclimate. In this sense, subalpine frost hollows are little alpine patches among the forest.

Skiing down into a frost hollow can be a brutal experience. You hit the low-temperature air suddenly, and your forward motion adds wind chill. The result can be frostbite. Bow Lake and the gravel flats east of the Saskatchewan Glacier are notorious as large, extreme frost hollows.

Winter campers suffer if they've selected a frost hollow in which to bed down on a cold night. Moving only 10–20 m up the slope, where the overnight low may be several degrees higher, can mean the difference between shivering the hours away or sleeping soundly.

## Effect of the continental divide

The Canadian Rockies present a long, tall barrier to airmasses moving across them. The effect is most noticeable in winter, when a pool of cold arctic air on the eastern slope may keep valley-floor temperatures in the -30°C to -40°C range, while on the western slope the thermometer might be reading -10°C.

Another factor in the cross-divide temperature difference is that valley-floor elevations on the western slope are lower by several hundred metres. Compare Golden's elevation, 787 m, with that of Banff, 1382 m. The temperature is correspondingly higher in Golden.

Low spots in the divide direct Pacific air through the mountains, making the eastern sides of major passes such as Kicking Horse and Yellowhead wetter than they would otherwise be. The Peace River gap is the biggest and lowest of these breaks in the range; moist air moving through it spreads into the foothills to the east, supporting anomalous stands of devil's club around Chetwynd and Hudson's Hope. (Note that the continental divide actually lies west of the Rockies at this point, but the eastern-slope/western-slope concept still applies.)

Cold prairie air also drains west through these low spots a few times every winter. The town of Field, some 20 km west of Kicking Horse Pass, is famous for this. The wind suddenly comes in from the east at about 30 km/h and -25°C—invigorating, to say the least. Residents of Field call this the **Yoho Blow.** Kalispell, Montana, reports similar cold winds spilling through Marias Pass.

## Chinooks

A chinook is a warm westerly wind encountered in winter along the eastern slope of the entire North American Cordillera, from Alaska to New Mexico, but perhaps most frequently in the eastern-slope foothills of the Canadian Rockies. Chinooks usually occur here 5–10 times each winter, more often than that in the Waterton/Glacier region, heart of the chinook belt, where chinook winds blow for 30 days out of 120 in an average winter. Chinook conditions can also arise during summer, but the warm wind feels like any other summer breeze and goes unnoticed.

A similar warm wind is felt in western Europe, where it is called a **foehn** wind ("Foehn" is German, pronounced about halfway between "phone" and "fern.")

Typically, a chinook occurs when the eastern slope is very cold, submerged under an arctic high-pressure cell. To the west and northwest, in the Gulf of Alaska, a low-pressure system develops; its counter-clockwise spin sends winds eastward across the mountain ranges of British Columbia. After bringing rain to the coast, this weak flow of warm Pacific air skips across the dense, frigid air below, offering no relief. However, when a chinook is about to begin, the Pacific flow strengthens. It floods across the mountains, producing standing waves downwind of the easternmost range—the Rockies—much as a stone in a river produces standing waves on its downstream side. These waves are enormous: the crests can reach 10,000 m in elevation.

East of the continental divide the wind encounters the dome of cold, dense arctic air lying over the prairies. Moisture in the Pacific flow condenses, forming a cloud—the **chinook arch** familiar to foothills residents—up to 1000 km long, paralleling the Rockies. People in Calgary see the edge of the cloud band to the west, stretching from the northwestern horizon to the

*Chinook arch seen from Calgary*

southeastern horizon in a gentle, arch-like shape that follows the curve of the earth; thus the term "arch." Narrow at first, the cloud band can spread eastward for hundreds of kilometres as the chinook strengthens.

A wave has a trough as well as a crest, and it is the trough of this great standing wave, where air is rushing downward, that causes the surface wind felt as a chinook. The air descends the eastern slope, touching down at high speed in the foothills and pushing the cold air back across the prairies for 100–200 km. Typical wind speeds during a chinook are 30–50 km/hr; they can reach 100 km/hr.

The effect on the ground is sensational: the temperature can rise 30°C in only a few hours. The chinook wind is warm and quite dry (from gas compression as the air descends the eastern slope), so it laps up the snow very quickly through melting, evaporation and sublimation. Given a strong chinook lasting several days, valley floors and southwest-facing slopes in the foothills and front ranges can lose their entire snowpack. Unseasonably warm conditions can continue for a week or more, often ending in a storm. Clear, cold weather then follows the storm, completing the cycle.

While the foothills are basking in the sun, in the main ranges along the continental divide the weather during a typical mid-winter chinook is anything but pleasant. Although the temperature will have risen somewhat, the residents of places such as Lake Louise and Field experience variable gusty winds and twenty-minute blizzards that alternate with patches of blue sky. The clouds roil about uncertainly. This is the "rotor" effect of chinooks: the smooth westerly flow of air at higher elevations induces turbulent flow near the ground in the rough topography of the mountains. You can see this turbulence from Calgary on a chinook day as a line of swirling storminess at the mountain front. Pilots of light planes avoid it; meteorologists refer to it as the **foehn wall.**

Predicting a chinook a day or two in advance requires a weather map to see the configuration of high-pressure and low-pressure areas. The chinook arch often appears a few hours ahead. In the mountains proper the arch is not usually visible; however, the appearance of **lenticular clouds** (see photo on page 212) indicates a strong westerly flow of air—and suggests that chinook conditions are developing. The chinook flow moves overhead for some hours, gradually working its way down into the pool of cold air it is displacing.

Many people become irritable or restless a few hours before a chinook hits. Studies have documented mood changes among ground-dwellers just before a chinook. A jump in the number of auto accidents, crimes and suicides is associated with chinook weather. There may be a sound physical reason for this: absorption of positive ions causes a change in the body's level of **serotonin**, a known mood-affecting hormone that also raises the blood pressure.

One hears stories of cattle dying in the fields when powerful chinooks strike the southern foothills. I have my doubts about this, but other effects on the biota of the Rockies are well-demonstrated. For example, the warm chinook wind can dry lodgepole-pine needles to the point of killing them, for in winter the flow of sap is too slow to replace the lost moisture quickly enough. As a result, west-facing slopes in the foothills often show stands of brown-needled trees the following summer, a condition known as **red-belt**. (See also the item on lodgepole pine, page 253.)

The chinook zone is the winter home of most of the elk and bighorn sheep in the Rockies, for the wind removes snow from west-facing slopes, exposing the grassy feed these animals prefer. The floors of major valleys that cut through the front ranges and foothills are swept practically free of snow most of the winter; here the herds are largest.

### Wind through Crowsnest Pass and in the Waterton area

The southern region of the Canadian Rockies, especially the section from Crowsnest Pass to the international boundary, is famous for wind—and not just in winter, when chinooks there are frequent and strong. Winter or summer, there is often a **pressure gradient** over the mountains south of Calgary: a band of high pressure lying just west of the Rockies, next to a band of low pressure over the southern Alberta foothills. This is a wind phenomenon independent of the regional eastward-high/westward-low configuration associated with chinooks, previous section. Prevailing westerlies tend to compress slightly as they strike the Rockies and slow down, causing the increase in pressure on the western slope; then they expand and speed up on the lee side of the range, causing the decrease in pressure on the eastern slope. Wind blows from zones of high pressure to zones of low pressure, which partly explains why the front ranges and foothills of the Rockies so often feel a westerly breeze.

An additional factor in the Crowsnest/Waterton area is the lower elevation of the continental divide there, relative to its elevation in Glacier National Park to the south and along the section to the north. This amounts to a major gap in the range, and the wind finds it. Valleys in the Waterton/Glacier area tend to run perpendicular to the divide, and this also funnels wind. Missing in this area are the wind-slowing parallel northwest-southeast ridges of the foothills, so typical of the Rockies farther north. Check the satellite photo on page 15; it shows that the lay of the land in the Waterton/Glacier area is less strongly northwest/southeast than it is in the central and northern regions.

### Recent climatic change

Long-time residents of Jasper and Banff will tell you that the summer weather has changed over the years, from warmer and drier before the 1970s to cooler and wetter through the mid-1980s. Glaciers are good indicators of climatic trends, and their behavior also suggests a short period of cooling, followed by rapid warming. In the Rockies a general glacial retreat that had gone on since the maximum of the Cavell Advance ("Little Ice Age") in the mid-1840s slowed or stopped in the 1970s. Most glaciers—but not that best-known of Rockies glaciers, the Athabasca—actually readvanced; aerial photos taken in 1950 and again in 1981 showed that the Columbia Glacier had reached a kilometre farther down the valley. But in the mid-1980s, retreat set in again. I've been watching Rockies glaciers since 1968, and the rate of ice loss seems very fast indeed. Glaciologists have noted the same thing elsewhere in the world, which comes as no surprise to those climatologists convinced that a buildup of atmospheric carbon dioxide caused by burning of fossils fuels has been warming our planet unnaturally. See page 155 for more.

### Annual weather pattern in the central Rockies

In comparing one year's weather records with the next, it seems that in the Canadian Rockies between Banff and Jasper the weather in any particular year is different from the rest. But an average seasonal weather pattern does exist. You just can't rely on it. With that in mind, here is the weather pattern for the central Rockies during a typical year.

Spring comes in early April to the Rocky Mountain Trench, in mid-April to the eastern-slope montane valleys. Sunny days reaching highs of 10–15°C trade off with blustery days mixing rain and snow. This is frustrating weather, pretty unpleasant; not what the once-popular song *Springtime in the Rockies* extols. However, between flurries the skiers can enjoy their sport in teeshirts.

By late May the snow has gone from the valleys, although cold fronts can leave snow on the ground in late June. Snow falls and sticks at lower elevations in every month except July. Normally the last hard frost at Jasper occurs in early June.

*Springtime in the Canadian Rockies*

In the central Rockies there is often a week of warm, clear weather during May. The snowline moves quickly up the slopes and the rivers rise suddenly; the valleys become instantly green and the temperature soars. Out come the short pants.

Then, when it seems that summer has arrived prematurely, the clouds roll in, the temperature drops, the rain falls and so do the spirits of people wasting their holidays here in June. You see them huddling in picnic shelters at the campgrounds, watching wet flakes of snow covering their tent-trailers. Much of their discomfort comes from the upslope weather prevalent in the Rockies in early summer (see page 209).

But there is often a spectacular improvement in the first week of July. I have seen this many times. The sun comes out and stays out for several days—sometimes for over a week. The temperature climbs to summer normals and the rivers rise again, reaching their highest levels of the year. Floodplains get flooded. The days are long. The sunburn season is on.

The rest of July is likely to be warm, with afternoon showers. The wildflower season is at its height and the mountains are full of tourists. And bugs. Late July and early August bring the summer's more spectacular thunderstorms.

Late summer is less predictable. In some years August has provided weeks of wonderfully clear, warm weather, but in others a succession of Pacific low-pressure systems has kept the Rockies soggy and cool. You take your chances coming to the mountains in August, whereas in July you have a good chance of getting at least a few good days, and in June you are practically assured of rain. Foul weather in August is more common from Jasper north than it is from Jasper south.

Throughout western North America, autumn often enters with a week of bad weather. This frequently happens in late August in the northern Rockies, in the first week of September between Jasper and Waterton/Glacier, and in late September or early October in Colorado. As the rain falls, so does the temperature, until one morning there is snow on the ground.

Then the weather often clears, bringing fairly warm days, with highs of 15–20°C, and cool nights that drop below freezing. The Rockies are famous for long, beautiful autumns, both in Canada and in the United States. During a good one the sky is deeply blue for weeks on end, the aspen are golden and the bugs are gone. This weather pattern can last from mid-September to the end of October; it has the spooky habit of finishing right at Halloween, when the kids often go door-to-door in falling snow. In the Rockies north of the Peace River, the Halloween snowfall often comes a week or two earlier.

In November the temperature drops steadily and so does the snowline. In many years a windy arctic front blasts through late in the month—earlier north of the Peace—leaving little snow but freezing everything up for the winter.

The first half of December is a prime time for one or two major Pacific storms that lay down 50 cm of powder in the high country and 10–20 cm in the valley bottoms. This is an important period in the central Rockies, where most of the skiing in the Canadian Rockies occurs. It sets the pattern for the rest of the winter, for there is seldom another big snowfall until February or March. If the snow comes early, say in mid-November, then it falls on ground that is still warm from the summer. There is a fair bit of melting, leaving thin snow-cover for the rest of the winter. That's bad news for skiers, not only because there is less snow to ski on, but because the avalanche hazard can become extreme. A contradiction? Not at all; turn to the section on avalanches of depth-hoar, page 765.

Following the Pacific-storm period, frigid arctic air moves in, bringing cold, clear weather to the eastern slope in late December and January. Valley-bottom temperatures dip to -40°C, sometimes reaching -45°C or even -50°C along major valleys in the front ranges. The western slope suffers less, because the cold, heavy eastern airmass is not very thick and little of it crosses the continental divide. However, see the Yoho Blow, page 213.

The unexpected sometimes occurs during this extremely cold period: warm, moist air wafts through the mountains from the west coast. The deeply frozen eastern slope of the Rockies gets rain in January, which coats everything with ice.

The Jasper area is famous for this. When I was new in Jasper I wondered why so many of the locals walked in the street, winter and summer, instead of on the sidewalks. After my first ice storm, which left the sidewalks treacherous for a month, I knew the reason: the streets, at least, are sanded. Using them becomes habitual.

Merely inconvenient for humans, mid-winter ice-ups can be the undoing of ungulates such as sheep, deer and elk. Freezing rain forms a tough crust on the snow, making winter feed more difficult for these animals to reach. Their predators, on the other hand—especially wolves—can often travel atop the crust, giving them an advantage at a time when the prey are weakened.

In December of 1981 a flock of 120 bighorns in Jasper National Park lost 17 of its members to a bizarre accident caused by iced ground. The sheep tried to escape a pack of wolves by running to ledges just below the top of Cinquefoil Bluff, a hill that overlooks Talbot Lake. This would ordinarily have foiled the wolves, for dog-family members are notable acrophobes, but in this case the steep slope was glazed with ice and many of the sheep lost their footing. They fell over a cliff onto the ice of the lake, where the wolves found a banquet waiting.

North of the Peace River the Rockies often lie under arctic air for the rest of the winter, gathering little snow until March or even April. The snow is only 20–30 cm deep for most of the winter. The temperature hovers between -20°C and -40°C. The days are very short, with little solar heating, and the snow is generally nothing but sugary depth hoar.

South of the Peace River in the central Rockies, temperatures are more moderate (highs in January average -10°C to -20°C; lows -25°C to -35°C) and there are more frequent snowfalls, especially from mid-February through April.

Chinooks can come at any time in the Canadian Rockies, disrupting this pattern, but by February the region is almost certain to have one. The first chinook after a cold December and January provides a welcome thaw on the eastern slope. The ice fog disappears; the sun shines warmly; the air feels sweet on one's face and everything that has survived the desperate days of the post-Christmas cold snap gets a touch of spring giddiness.

A storm follows the chinook and winter returns. But there is another chinook a couple of weeks later, a shorter cold snap, yet another chinook—longer this time—and no cold snap, then suddenly it is April and maybe spring has arrived. "Boy; it's early this year," I think. "Look, the grass is turning green and the birds have returned!" Ah, such short-memoried fools we are. Mother Nature stirs up a blizzard in May, just to show us who is really in charge.

On the western slope the winters are milder and shorter, although the snow accumulation is up to 50 percent greater at any given elevation. The temperature difference is particularly evident in late March or early April, when a trip over the continental divide from Banff to Golden is a trip into spring. The grass greens and the flowers bloom a couple of weeks earlier at the lower elevations found in the Rocky Mountain Trench. Also, arctic air keeps the lid on spring longer on the eastern slope.

In a winter with **el Niño** ("ell NEEN-yo"), which is Spanish for "the Child," referring to the appearance of this weather-wackifying ocean-current phenomenon off the west coast of Peru around Christmas, temperatures are markedly higher than usual in the Canadian Rockies and snowfall is less. Winter seems like one long chinook.

## Predicting the weather

In summer the regional forecasts are accurate for the mountains only when large airmasses are involved. If you hear that British Columbia has washed away, then prepare for some wet days at Banff, with low clouds and shivery temperatures. If B.C. is basking, then probably the Rockies are going to be hot and dry shortly. But smaller systems do unexpected things here. I recall climbing Mt. Forbes in murk that arrived black and nasty the evening before, despite a fair-weather prediction on the radio. As the wind came up and the tent shook us awake, my partner took a peek outdoors, sighed and said, "Another unknown, uncharted storm system hits the Canadian Rockies."

Few of us carry a barometer around, but any Compleat Climber has an altimeter, which is essentially the same thing. The new wristwatch models are much less expensive than the old mechanical altimeters; many climbers and hikers now have them. If you are going to be at the same elevation for a while, keep an eye on the instrument. If the reading rises, so that you seem to have gained elevation, then the pressure is falling and the weather will probably deteriorate. If you seem to lose elevation, the pressure is rising and the weather should improve. But the pressure remains high during rainy upslope conditions, page 209. Further, normal summer-afternoon storminess can arrive without much change in pressure.

The clouds can also help you forecast the weather. Most of our rough weather comes from the west, and it usually announces itself in the form of cirrus (high, wispy clouds) fingering in from that direction. If the cirrus wisps go to a solid overcast within an hour or two, the rain/snow will probably start only a few hours later—sooner than expected, if you are used to the weather on the prairies. Out there, one can see the edge of a moist airmass when the mares' tails are still a hundred kilometres away. In the mountains one doesn't see them until they are practically overhead, because the alignment of ridges in most places blocks westerly views.

Clearing trends are indicated by cloud-lifting and thinning (obviously). The sky looks as if it were drying out, which is exactly what is happening. Lenticular clouds, meaning high clouds that are lens-shaped and smooth-edged, indicate a strong westerly flow at high elevations; they often precede a chinook.

Readers who reach high points in the mountains—climbers, especially—may want to turn to the section on storms and lightning, which begins on page 763. Skiers should take to heart the section about avalanches, page 764.

## Northern lights

There you are, camped in the back country in August. It's a clear night with no moon. Around ten o'clock you chance to look upward, and—what's this? Searchlights shining up from the other side of the ridge? A town lighting up the sky in that direction?

It's the **aurora borealis,** the scientific name for the northern lights. First you see a diffuse ethereal glow on the northeastern horizon, followed by shafts of light that mark the beginnings of the famous curtain-like shapes. On a good night for the aurora, the curtains will appear to rise higher and higher (they are actually spreading southwestward toward you), until the wavy lower edges may be seen and the whole spectacle stands clear of the ridge. Glowing blue-white or greenish, or sometimes pink, the curtains fold and swing gracefully as if moved by the wind. Indeed, they are moved by the wind—the solar wind, which powers the aurora.

Protons and electrons flung out from the sun's thermonuclear reactions blast past the earth at hundreds of kilometres per second. Some of these charged particles fall into our planet's magnetic field, especially on the side facing away from the sun, which is, of course, the dark, night side. The particles accelerate toward the poles, slamming into the thin atmospheric gases of the ionosphere 100–300 km up. As in a neon tube, the energy absorbed is given off as light: greens and reds from atomic oxygen, purple from molecular nitrogen, blue-white in combination.

At two or three in the morning the aurora is at its best. A radiant band 1000 km wide circles the earth along the latitude of Yellowknife. The northern lights ripple, flash and pulsate directly overhead, throwing a million amps of electromagnetic energy into Canada's fragile power grids and electronic circuits. Be glad, as you lie there snug in your sleeping bag under all this, that your bodily systems have evolved over billions of years to cope with it.

*Aurora over Pyramid Mountain, near Jasper*

## *Further reading*

Atmospheric Environment Service (1993a) *Canadian Climate Normals, 1961–1990: Temperature.* Atmospheric Environment Service, Environment Canada

— (1993b) *Canadian Climate Normals, 1961–1990: Precipitation.* Atmospheric Environment Service, Environment Canada

— (1982) *Canadian Climate Normals, 1951–1980: Volume 5: Wind.* Atmospheric Environment Service, Environment Canada

Christison, Tim (1986) "Snow-eater: the chinook turns winter into spring in an hour" *Nature Canada.* Spring, 16-22. The most readable discussion of chinooks I have seen.

Dightman, R. (undated) *Climate of Glacier National Park, Montana.* National Weather Service, Great Falls, Montana

Janz, B. and D. Storr (1977) *The Climate of the Contiguous Mountain Parks.* Atmospheric Environment Service Project Report No. 30, Environment Canada. Technical, but still fairly accessible to lay readers.

The foothills of the Rockies, a view westward from near Edson, Alberta. There's a big difference between the botanical community seen here and that found at higher elevations in the front ranges, seen in the distance.

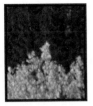

# Ecoregions and life zones
## What is growing on here?

Many plant species occur from one end of the Canadian Rockies to the other, and on both sides of the continental divide. That kind of biological integrity is a lucky thing for those of us with an interest in botany; if one learns the wildflowers in the Waterton/Glacier area, then one will also know many of them at Banff, at Jasper, and even along the Alaska Highway in the far northern end of the Rockies.

There is regional variation, of course. Two main east/west ecological divisions are separated by the crest of the range: the **eastern slope** and the **western slope.*** There are three north/south ecological divisions: **southern,** from Marias Pass to Crowsnest Pass; **central,** from there all the way to Pine Pass and the Peace River, and **northern,** to the Liard River.

The map on the next page shows the three divisions. The southern-central boundary is fairly clear, because Crowsnest Pass forms a sort of botanical divide. More on that later. The central-to-northern transition is gradual.

Going east to west there are more abrupt differences. Along the TransCanada Highway west of Calgary, for example, you pass from the grassy prairies into the wooded but meadowy foothills and front ranges, then into the thick forests of the main ranges near the continental divide. These differences are based mostly on elevation, for you are climbing higher into the mountains.

You cross the divide at Kicking Horse Pass and begin to descend the western slope. Through middle elevations the forest thins, and by the time you reach the Rocky Mountain Trench near Golden the landscape looks noticeably drier.

The same trip west from Edmonton creates a different impression. The foothills are solidly forested, broken only by cleared patches. The front ranges seem rather bare and dry in comparison. The continental-divide forests are familiar—thick and dark—but in descending the western slope one finds the forest thickening rather than thinning, with groves of tall red-cedar trees around the base of Mt. Robson.

Now take a ride west from Fort Nelson at the northern end of the Rockies. In the foothills the plant community is a low-elevation type on the south-facing side of the road and a higher-elevation type on the north-facing side, a function of the low angle of the sun this far north.

Finally, compare that with a transect at the other end of the Canadian Rockies west of Lethbridge. On this trip the forest is generally light on the eastern slope and heavy on the western slope.

The lesson here is that in the Canadian Rockies there are two kinds of ecological variety: variety based on **elevation** and variety based on **geographic location.** How can this be described? There are various approaches.

Naturalists discovered long ago that different kinds of plants grew at different elevations in any mountain range. They thought of mountain ecology in terms of elevational **zones.** Perhaps the simplest of these systems comes from Colorado, where one finds the "plains zone" for plants growing on the flats surrounding the mountains, the "foothills zone" and "montane zone" for the lower mountain slopes, the "subalpine zone" for the upper mountain slopes and the "alpine zone" for areas above treeline.

As an ecological overview this idea works pretty well in the American Rockies, so it has been carried north to the Canadian Rockies. The alpine and subalpine designations serve the same purpose here as they do there, and on the eastern slope south of Crowsnest Pass one can recognize a northern version of the grassy plant communities of the American plains zone.

*North of the Peace River, all of the Rockies lie east of the continental divide, so in this area "eastern slope" refers to the eastern slope of the Rockies, not of the continent.

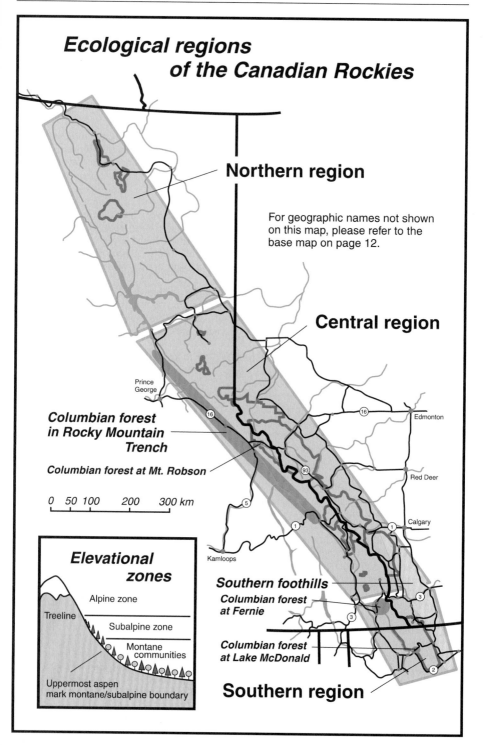

# Ecological regions of the Canadian Rockies

**Northern region**

For geographic names not shown on this map, please refer to the base map on page 12.

**Central region**

Prince George

*Columbian forest in Rocky Mountain Trench*

*Columbian forest at Mt. Robson*

16

16

Edmonton

93

Red Deer

0   50  100      200      300 km

5

1

1

Calgary

Kamloops

**Elevational zones**

Alpine zone

Treeline

Subalpine zone

Montane communities

Uppermost aspen mark montane/subalpine boundary

*Southern foothills*

*Columbian forest at Fernie*

3

3

*Columbian forest at Lake McDonald*

2

**Southern region**

But the foothills and montane zones do not correspond. Below the subalpine zone in the Canadian Rockies, it is not how high up you are, it is *where* you are that counts. A patchwork quilt of various plant communities is spread out over the foothills and lower mountains slopes.

Let's go in for a closer look. There is open, grassy forest in the Alberta foothills south of the Bow River and dense, heavy forest to the north. Same elevation, different vegetation. On the western slope there are no foothills at all. Tall peaks rise right out of the Rocky Mountain Trench.

The trench is a strange place botanically. The dry section from Radium Hot Springs south to the international boundary supports grassy woods of ponderosa pine and Douglas-fir, while north of Golden there is an abrupt change to dense forests of red-cedar and hemlock—an extension of the wetter Columbia Mountains to the west. Again, same elevation but different vegetation.

What we are seeing here are the effects of *differences in climate.* The table on pages 206 and 207 shows the variation in temperature and precipitation throughout the region. The discussion of the annual weather pattern on page 215 will also help to explain.

Is it any wonder that ecologists working in this part of the world have always had trouble stating that such-and-such a plant grows in one elevational zone or another? Elevation is important, yes, but ecological and climatic variation in the Canadian Rockies is regional as well as elevational. Thus, Alberta ecologists have divided the province into seven "ecoregions." Getting beyond the buzzword reveals a sensible idea based on differences in plant communities, climates and soils.

For most of Alberta the ecoregion system applies nicely, but in the mountains the system has its shortcomings. The term "montane," for example, has been restricted to apply only to the Douglas-fir woods lying mainly along the floors of certain major valleys, while the rest of the lodgepole/spruce/aspen woods that characterize much of the Rockies have been lumped in with the very different forest of the subalpine zone. Ecoregion divisions in the mountains are too coarse, and they seem rather arbitrary.

If you are trying to identify a flower by checking whether it is growing in the right sort of place, neither the elevational system nor the ecoregion system alone is very helpful.

Rather than setting forth an alternative system, which would be even more confusing (and I am not qualified to do it), I have borrowed from both the older zone system and the newer ecoregion system to present a practical view of the gross ecology of the Canadian Rockies, as follows.

There are three large ecological regions, as described previously: the **southern, central** and **northern** regions. Each of these can be divided into the **montane ecological communities** at lower elevations, the **subalpine zone** at middle elevations and the **alpine zone** at the top. The main montane ecological communities are the **eastern-slope montane forest** and the **western-slope montane forest.** The eastern-slope montane forest contains a special area: the **southern foothills.** The western-slope montane forest contains two special areas: the **southern Rocky Mountain Trench** and the **Columbian forest.**

The rest of this chapter explores all these places.

# *Ecoregions*
## Variety that is geographic

The three very general north/south divisions reflect differences in soil, overall elevation and climate. Here is a comparison.

### *Central region: Crowsnest Pass to the Peace River*

Here we find the regime of temperature, sun angle, precipitation, weather pattern and chinook influence to which other parts of the range can be compared. Elevations are higher than in the northern and southern regions, with icefield development along the continental divide and rain shadows—dry areas downwind from the divide—in the front ranges. There is a good deal of limestone bedrock. Lime neutralizes acids, so the soils here are not very acidic.

## Southern region: Marias Pass to Crowsnest Pass

The climate is warmer and somewhat drier than it is farther north, with strong and frequent chinook winds in winter. The sun angle is higher than in more northerly areas. There is less limestone here than in the central Rockies, so the soils in the southern region are more acidic.

Eastern-slope lands in the southern region are perhaps the most botanically interesting part of the Canadian Rockies. Some plants make their only eastern-slope appearance in this area; beargrass and ninebark, for example. Yet others that are common elsewhere, such as crowberry, twinflower and monkshood, are strangely rare or absent.

## Northern region—Peace River to Liard River

Elevations are lower and glaciers are fewer here than in the central region. The climate is cooler and wetter in summer than it is in the other areas, colder and drier in winter. Chinook influence is similar to that of the central Rockies. The lower sun angle has a strong effect on local ecology; north-facing slopes are much colder than south-facing slopes. The shaly rock is not as lime-rich as that of the central region. Soils tend to be more acidic.

# Life zones
## Variety that is elevational

Having considered differences among the southern, central and northern ecological regions, we can now deal with ecological variety by elevation. Let's start at the bottom and work our way up.

*The greatest elevational difference in the Rockies, and thus the best example of ecological variety controlled by elevation, occurs west of Jasper in the Valemount area. Here the floor of the Rocky Mountain Trench lies at 800 m above sea level. The summit of Mt. Robson, visible as the highest peak on the skyline, reaches almost 4000 m. Photo was taken from Canoe Mountain, looking northwest along the trench.*

# Montane ecological communities

In this book the term "montane" is used to describe various plant communities that cover the lower slopes and foothills of the Rockies. The term is used properly as an adjective, not as a noun. I don't speak of "the montane." It's "montane forest," "montane meadow," "montane species," and so on. The same applies to the words "alpine" and "subalpine," because they are adjectives, too.

To deal with ecological variety at montane elevations, which is the result mostly of forest fires and a patchy climate, I think of the montane part of the Rockies as having several subsets. They are described below. All of them have a common upper boundary: the elevation above which aspen do not grow.

## Eastern-slope montane forest

The eastern-slope montane forest is extensive, covering the lower mountain slopes, the valley floors and much of the foothills belt. The main tree species are lodgepole pine, white spruce and aspen, with buffaloberry, juniper, cinquefoil, wild rose and kinnikinnik the characteristic shrubs. From Jasper south, Douglas-fir stands dot south-facing and west-facing slopes along major valleys. The foothills south of Calgary are rich in Douglas-fir.

The montane woods get generally damper as you go north from Calgary, most noticeably in the eastern foothills, which some ecologists call the **boreal foothills.** To the non-botanist, the most obvious change north of the Bow River is the decrease in the number and size of clearings. The forest becomes denser and more continuous.

South of the Bow River the foothills are so rich in aspen, and so grassy, that they form a special part of the eastern-slope montane forest: the **southern foothills.** The foothills east of Glacier National Park, Montana are included in this region.

## Western-slope montane forest

Generally speaking, the western-slope montane forest is simply a wetter version of the eastern-slope montane forest. It is somewhat heavier and shrubbier, with the addition of species such as western larch and the Columbia lily, which are confined to the western slope. But the differences are more of degree than of kind, and it seems reasonable to continue calling this region "montane forest," adding "western-slope" to show that there *is* a difference.

Ecological differences that have little to do with elevation are best seen at lower elevations in the **Rocky Mountain Trench,** which is part dry, part wet and part in-between. This is an exceptionally varied place, botanically.

In spite of the overall wetter character of the western slope, the floor of the trench between Golden and the international boundary is the driest place in or adjacent to the Canadian Rockies. You can even find cactus growing in here. Douglas-fir is common, and there are stands of sun-loving ponderosa pine from Columbia Lake south. As you approach the Montana border there is a marked increase in western larch.

Between Golden and Prince George the floor of the trench is heavily treed in a mixed forest of Douglas-fir, spruce, western red-cedar, western hemlock and black cottonwood. In the dense undergrowth lurks spiny devil's-club. This is the **Columbian forest,** which is a spillover from the wet, warm Columbia Mountains to the west. Columbian forest is normally not found east of the trench, but storm tracks carry sufficient moisture to sustain red-cedar groves well into the Rockies at Mt. Robson and near Fernie. The Fernie groves have been wrecked by logging, but Robson's red-cedars are protected in a provincial park. Another patch of Columbian forest grows along the western boundary of Glacier National Park, Montana; it has crept eastward along the shores of Lake McDonald.

North of Prince George the Columbian forest gives way to typically montane species, although the influence of Williston Lake may change this. The lake is a huge reservoir in the northern Rocky Mountain Trench, created by damming the Peace River at the mountain front in 1967. Perhaps Williston Lake will moderate the climate there and increase the humidity, encouraging the expansion of Columbian forest to the north.

## "The montane" = montane wildlife wintering areas

"The montane" is a term I'm hearing often these days. I have put it in quotes because other people use it, not me. Not yet, anyway; it's not good grammar, as explained previously, and as a part-time English teacher I can't abide it. But the concept it represents is valid. "The montane" refers to the montane valley floors along major eastern-slope rivers such as the Bow, the North Saskatchewan and the Athabasca, which are essential winter habitat for elk, deer and bighorn sheep. Wolves and coyotes depend on these animals as prey, so they, too, winter on the eastern-slope montane valley floors and in adjacent parts of the foothills.

A better name for these places would recognize their exceptional importance to wildlife. I think of them as **montane wildlife wintering areas.** For more detail, see pages 234–236 in the photos of ecological communities.

As essential as they are, montane wildlife wintering areas make up only a small part of the landscape. They cover between two percent and ten percent of the Canadian Rockies, depending on how these areas are defined. And it is within that two-to-ten-percent that humanity has established itself within the mountains. Our roads, our railways, our resorts and campgrounds and towns—most of them have been built in wildlife wintering areas. From the townsite of Waterton Park through the communities of Crowsnest Pass, to Banff and Jasper, Grande Cache and Tumbler Ridge, we have taken over land that once sustained the elk, the deer, the bighorn sheep and the wolves. At one time the southern Rocky Mountain Trench might have been the greatest wintering area in the Rockies, but now it is thoroughly settled. Most of the wildlife there is gone.

Fortunately some large montane wintering areas lie in the national parks. Unfortunately the tourist industry wants them for convention centres and golf courses. The future of "the montane" is anybody's guess, and it is a hot issue these days in the never-ending political wrangle between developers and environmentalists. You can probably guess whose side I'm on.

*The town of Jasper is built in a montane wildlife wintering area. Humans and elk coexist here, but uneasily. Cars and trains hit the elk; the elk eat the residents' shrubbery and gardens, and they occasionally chase people.*

*Exploring the upper subalpine zone near Exshaw Pass, in the Fairholme Range east of Canmore.*

## Subalpine zone

In these pages the subalpine zone is considered to extend upward from the highest-growing aspen to treeline. These are the middle elevations on the mountain slopes, covered with a dark, heavy forest of tall subalpine fir and Engelmann spruce. Crowberry, grouseberry and Labrador tea are common on the mossy forest floor.

The subalpine climate is cool and damp. This is the zone of heaviest snow accumulation—the **snow forest,** much the same up and down the Rockies, regardless of which side of the divide you are on. In Europe and Asia this kind of forest is termed **taiga.**

Trees of the snow forest become shorter as you move up the slope. In the upper subalpine woods the fir and spruce are packed together in **tree islands,** dense clumps of evergreens in the flowery meadows (see photo above and on page 240).

Farther upslope the tree-islands flatten. The trees are shrub-like, growing only waist-high and often on the eastern, leeward side of rocks and ridges. In so doing these trees hide under the snow and thus escape the terrible winds of winter storms. Such trees are called **kruppelholz,** pronounced "KRUPPEL-holts," which means "crippled wood" in German.* The kruppelholz patches get smaller and more scattered as you climb higher, until the highest-growing trees are reached, tiny and stunted, barely surviving on this botanical frontier.

This is **treeline.** Here the ground is thawed for the minimum number of days a tree needs to gain its yearly supply of soil moisture and minerals. Here the air temperature is just high enough, for enough days, to permit the growth of tiny amounts of new foliage. At treeline, summer growth barely replaces needles and twigs killed in winter.

Note that treeline has nothing to do with absolute elevation. It depends on elevation and latitude combined. Treeline is at 3600 m in New Mexico at the south end of the Rockies, where the climate is considerably warmer than it is at the north end of the Rockies. There, treeline is down to 1500 m.

---

*Many people who should know better, including me, have referred to kruppelholz as **krummholz,** which is incorrect. See page 286 for the difference between the two terms.

The transition from solid forest to highest-growing kruppelholz takes a couple of hundred metres vertically. So exactly where on the slope should we draw the treeline? At the absolute upper limit of tree growth? Such a line would zigzag uphill and downhill between patches of kruppelholz. Should we draw it somewhere lower?

I have heard botanists arguing heatedly about the location of treeline, using tree heights, tree spacing, soil temperatures, air temperatures, climatic data and other esoteric stuff to tighten up an annoyingly imprecise element in their science. At least it gives them something to talk about while strolling uphill. My conclusion: treeline is a rather *thick* line.

By the way, I prefer "treeline" to "timberline." After I had used "timberline" for many years, someone pointed out to me that "timber" refers to trees that have been, or are going to be, cut down.

*Treeline appears well-defined from a distance, but when you're actually on the mountain it's anything but. Photo is of Mt. Murchison, near Saskatchewan Crossing in Banff National Park.*

## Alpine zone

The alpine *zone* of past days and the alpine *ecoregion* of the present are the same thing, but the term "ecoregion" seems poorly applied to alpine areas, which are scattered over the mountains rather than forming a single region. So in this book I am retaining the older term **alpine zone,** which means, simply, the land above treeline, whether it is meadow, bare rock or glacier.

True to the biological rule that nasty environments have less biodiversity than gentle ones, fewer kinds of plants and animals survive in the alpine zone than live lower down. Further, the list of alpine-zone flora and fauna is consistent all over our area. At any given latitude, you will find nearly all the same alpine species on either side of the continental divide, and many of the wildflowers, birds and mammals seen above treeline in Waterton Lakes National Park are also found in alpine meadows above the Alaska Highway in the northern Rockies.

## Practical matters

The foregoing has a practical purpose in this book. The various zones and regions described in this chapter are used in the plant listings that follow, to match species with their usual environments, and the same terms appear later in the book to describe animal habitats as well. If you become familiar with these terms, they will prove useful.

Next: a pictorial tour of some common and interesting ecological communities at various elevations and places in the Canadian Rockies.

## Further reading

Arno, S. and R. Hammerly (1984) *Timberline: Mountain and Arctic Forest Frontiers.* Douglas & McIntyre, Vancouver. The definitive treatment, with examples from various mountain ranges, including the Canadian Rockies. Drawings, maps, index; 304 pages.

Canadian Forestry Service (1974) *Ecotour of the TransCanada Highway, Calgary-Golden.* Information Canada, Ottawa. Non-technical booklet briefly describing ecological variety along the route. Illustrated, 18 pages.

Demarchi, D., et al. (1990) "The environment," pages 55–142 in *The Birds of British Columbia, Volume One.* Royal British Columbia Museum, Victoria. Summary of ecoregions in British Columbia, including the Rockies area, with maps.

Hardy, W., ed. (1967) *Alberta: a Natural History.* McClelland and Stewart, Toronto. General ecological guide to the province. Illustrated, indexed, bibliography; 343 pages.

Rowe, J. (1972) *Forest Regions of Canada.* Canadian Forest Service, Department of Environment, Ottawa. General ecology. Illustrated, indexed, bibliography; 172 pages.

Spalding, A., Ed. (1980) *A Nature Guide to Alberta.* McClelland and Stewart, Toronto. Mapsheet-by-mapsheet guide to the province, with good introductory material and mountain coverage. Illustrated, indexed, bibliography; 368 pages.

Strong, W., and K. Leggat (1981) *Ecoregions of Alberta.* ENR Technical Report T/4, available free of charge from Alberta Energy and Natural Resources, Seventh Floor, 9915 108 Street, Edmonton T5K 2C9. Summary of a major land-classification project; illustrated with photos and maps, 64 pages.

Zwinger, A. and B. Willard (1972) *Land Above the Trees: a Guide to American Alpine Tundra.* University of Arizona Press, Tucson. Detailed examination of high-country climates, species and ecology. Written mainly for mountain ranges in the U.S., but generally applicable here, too. Illustrations, glossary, index; 487 pages.

**See also** the general botanical bibliography on page 403.

*Subalpine meadow along the Whitehorse Pass Trail in eastern Jasper National Park. Grizzly bears eat the cow parsnip (large-leaved, white-flowered plant) that is abundant here. Other wildflowers in the photo: valerian (also white, close to the camera), fleabane (pink and daisy-like), ragwort (yellow).*

# Ecological communities
## *A photographic tour*

Here are 30 important, interesting, easily recognized biophysical communities found in the Canadian Rockies. The arrangement is roughly from low-elevation to high-elevation, with some special communities grouped at the end. A few species characteristic of each community are given. Some very common species are not listed because they occur in so many environments. One or two roadside or otherwise easy-to-get-at locations are given in italics.

This is by no means a complete discussion of ecological communities in the region. For more information, consult the reading list on page 403.

**Aspen grove.** Common montane community, on gently sloping, gravelly soil. Trembling aspen with minor spruce and white birch; Bebb's and Scouler's willows; water birch, bracted honeysuckle, buffaloberry, mertensia, wild rose, common juniper, buckbrush; wild pea, red paintbrush, Solomon's seal, twisted stalk, cow-parsnip, clematis. Thrushes, flycatchers, warblers; thirteen-lined ground squirrels (southern region), mule deer. Wildlife wintering area for elk. *Many locations.*

**Columbian forest.** At low elevations on the western slope; see map on page 222 for distribution. Cool, rainy summer; snowy winter with moderate temperatures. A heavy mixed-wood forest of red-cedar, hemlock, black cottonwood, Douglas-fir, white spruce, lodgepole pine, white pine and black spruce, with western larch in the southern end. Pacific willow, green alder, thimbleberry, devil's-club, sarsaparilla, orange honeysuckle, goat's-beard, lace flower, heal-all, *Lobaria* tree lichen. *Kinney Lake Trail, Mount Robson Provincial Park; Lake McDonald, Glacier National Park.*

**Southern-foothills meadow or grassland.** Dry and windy in winter from frequent chinooks, but large snow-banks accumulate in lee spots. Silty soils. Lodgepole pine, Douglas-fir, aspen, balsam poplar, limber pine, silver-berry. Many grasses: timothy, junegrass, fescue, bluegrass, brome, needle-and-thread, sweetgrass. Wildflowers like those of montane meadow, with horsemint common south of Crowsnest Pass. Meadow voles, thirteen-lined ground squirrels, Richardson's ground squirrels, northern pocket gophers, coyotes; red-tailed hawks, prairie falcons, meadowlarks, mourning doves, nighthawks. *The foothills from the Bow River south.*

**White-spruce woods.** In the eastern front ranges and western foothills, along floors of major valleys where extreme chinook conditions and the high water table prevent growth of lodgepole pine. White spruce is the only common tree; there are a few aspen. Shrubs: kinnikinnik, willows, shrubby potentilla, wild rose. Soil crusts (see page 399) between shrubs and tufts of grass. Important as wildlife wintering areas. *Floors of Bow, North Saskatchewan or Athabasca valleys near the mountain front.*

**Southern Rocky Mountain Trench floor.** Driest part of the Canadian Rockies, with Douglas-fir, lodgepole pine, ponderosa pine, Rocky Mountain juniper, sagebrush, snowbrush, Oregon grape, cactus, white mariposa lilies; yellow pine chipmunks. Paradoxically there are extensive wetlands here; species list is similar to montane wetlands, with more Columbian plants (see previous page), more amphibians and the only turtles in the range. *Wilmer Wildlife Refuge, north of Invermere.*

**Montane feather-moss forest.** On north-facing slopes at low elevations from the Bow River north. At higher elevations, this is part of the subalpine forest. Feather mosses cover the ground under closely spaced lodgepole pine, white spruce and black spruce. Gooseberry, wild rose, common juniper, bunchberry; few wildflowers. Mushrooms, *Peltigera* and *Cladonia* lichens. Ruby-crowned kinglets, winter wrens, red squirrels. Offers shelter from storms in wildlife wintering areas. *Hiking trails around Jasper.*

**Montane lodgepole-pine woods.** Mostly lodgepole pine, with white spruce, Douglas-fir (central and southern areas), aspen and white birch. Shrubs: buffaloberry, common juniper, wild roses, low-bush cranberry; thickets of Scouler's and Bebb's willows in damp spots, alder and Rocky Mountain maple. Wildflowers: red paintbrush, arnica, calypso orchid, yarrow, goldenrod. Grasses: ryegrass, ricegrass, spike trisetum, common timothy. *Cladonia* and *Peltigera* lichens. Branch-tip spiders, carpenter ants, beetles; woodpeckers, ruffed grouse, sharp-shinned and Cooper's hawks, owls, goshawks, thrushes, chickadees, juncos, pine grosbeaks, crossbills; deer mice, red squirrels, snowshoe hares, martens, black bears, coyotes, wolves, mule deer, white-tailed deer, elk, moose. Important wildlife wintering habitat for elk and deer. *Environs of Banff and Jasper.*

**Douglas-fir woods.** Grassy woods with ryegrass and fescue; moderately spaced Douglas-fir, with small, tight patches of white spruce and lodgepole pine. Not much shrub growth—some common juniper, buffaloberry, wild rose—and few wildflowers. Red-breasted nuthatches, juncos, chickadees; elk, mule deer, white-tailed deer, coyotes. Important as wildlife wintering areas. *Radium Hot Springs area, southern foothills, environs of Banff and Jasper.*

**Montane meadow.** Typical of open dry places on valley floors in the front ranges and foothills. Cold in winter, but chinooks warm it suddenly and remove much of the snow; moisture comes mainly as summer rain. Trees: same species as in montane lodgepole-pine woods, previous page, and Douglas-fir woods, previous item, but forest cover not continuous. Shrubs: common juniper, shrubby potentilla, buffaloberry, silverberry, wild rose, saskatoon. Many wildflowers: pasque flower, pasture sage, daisy fleabane, showy androsace, aster, stonecrop, gaillardia, yarrow, wind flower, harebell, *Antennaria* species, showy locoweed, ragwort, goldenrod, three-flowered avens, silverweed. Many grasses: montane timothy, trisetum, ryegrass, junegrass, brome, fescue, bluegrass, ticklegrass, foxtail barley. Wood ticks, ants, butterflies; ravens, sparrows, robins; Richardson's or Columbian ground squirrels, snowshoe hares, elk, deer, bighorn sheep, coyotes, wolves. Essential winter habitat for many ungulates and their predators. *Environs of Banff and Jasper.*

**Dryas flats.** Central and northern regions, mostly eastern slope, where yellow dryas covers gravel along streams and on highway shoulders. Broad-leaved willow-herb also common. *Along the Icefields Parkway north of Athabasca Glacier.*

**Montane or subalpine wetland.** Ponds, slow-moving streams. Very rich, diverse community. White spruce, black spruce, tamarack (foothills from the North Saskatchewan River north), alder; many willows, especially *Salix commutata, S. discolor, S. planifolia, S. rigida and S. candida;* Labrador tea, shrubby potentilla; bulrushes, bur-reed, cattail, water hemlock, bog orchids, elephant-head, swamp laurel, cotton grass and other sedges, rushes, horsetails, peat mosses. Mosquitoes, dragonflies, water insects and larvae; long-toed salamanders, chorus frogs, spotted frogs, western toads, garter snakes; dabbling ducks, snipes, soras, blue herons, red-winged blackbirds, hummingbirds, northern waterthrushes, yellow warblers, yellowthroats, sparrows; water shrews, meadow voles, water voles, beavers, muskrats, mink, moose, wolves. In wildlife wintering areas, frozen wetlands provide dried sedges and willow-browse for elk and moose. *Fenland Trail or Vermilion Lakes near Banff; Cottonwood Slough near Jasper; William A. Switzer Provincial Park near Hinton (photo).*

**Montane or subalpine river.** Banks and islands often with sandbar willows such as *Salix exigua* and *S. caudata,* mountain alder, cow parsnip, yellow paintbrush, white camas. Rainbow trout, brook trout, brown trout, whitefish; western toads, wood frogs; yellow-rumped warblers, ospreys, bald eagles, kingfishers, swallows; water shrews, mink, moose, black bears. Important predator and scavenger travel routes in winter. *Many locations. Photo of the Athabasca River courtesy Jasper National Park.*

**Montane or subalpine lake.** Shoreline vegetation as per montane or subalpine wetlands, previous page, with horsetails and chives. Water plants: mare's-tail, bladderwort, water smartweed, pondweed, pond lily, water hemlock. Leeches, water insects and larvae in water, dragonflies near shore; snails and fingernail clams; rainbow trout, brook trout, lake trout, suckers; loons, grebes, Barrow's goldeneye and other diving ducks, ospreys, bald eagles, sandpipers, yellow-rumped warblers, swallows; beavers, muskrats, moose. *Many locations. Photo of Christine Lake near Jasper by Cia Gadd.*

**Montane or subalpine canyon (gorge).** Damp, shady environment. Black spruce, white spruce, white birch, alders, willows, water birch, Labrador tea, menziesia; ferns, clubmosses, feather mosses, *Hygrohypnum* and *Scouleria* mosses by the water. Least chipmunks, red squirrels, ravens, black swifts. *Maligne Canyon, Johnston Canyon. Photo of Maligne Canyon courtesy Jasper National Park.*

**Lower subalpine forest.** Cool, short growing season; heavy snowfall. Subalpine fir, Engelmann spruce, lodgepole pine, whitebark pine; Barclay's and Drummond's willows, Labrador tea, menziesia, Rocky Mountain rhododendron, crowberry, mountain cranberry, bunchberry, arnica, larkspur, monkshood, columbine. Rich in tree lichens such as *Usnea, Bryoria, Hypogymnia* and *Letharia;* ground lichens also common from Banff north (*Cladonia, Peltigera, Cladina, Stereocaulon*). Clark's nutcrackers, gray jays, spruce grouse and blue grouse, three-toed woodpeckers, merlins, goshawks, hawk owls, Townsend's solitaires, shrikes; red-backed voles, red-tailed chipmunks, snowshoe hares, ermine, martens, fishers, porcupines, lynx, cougars, moose, grizzly bears. Wintering area for moose and caribou. *Lake Louise, or Mt. Edith Cavell Road.*

**Larch grove.** Subset of the upper subalpine forest, found from Bow Summit south. Grows just below the kruppelholz zone. Main species: subalpine larch and white heather. *Going-to-the-Sun Road; Highwood Pass along Highway 40. Photo taken at Opabin Plateau, Lake O'Hara area.*

**Subalpine meadow.** Moist soil and a cool, short growing season; very cold in winter. Bluegreen willow, Barratt's willow, rock willow, dwarf birch; valerian, western lousewort, Drummond's anemone, larkspur, monkshood, saussurea. Grasses: trisetum, bluegrass, fescue, alpine foxtail, mountain timothy. Horse flies, butterflies, mosquitoes; Brewer's sparrows, Savannah sparrows, northern harriers; pygmy shrews, heather voles, northern bog lemmings, Columbian ground squirrels, ermine, marmots, grizzly bears, elk, moose (wintering area for moose). *Bow Summit, or Sunwapta Pass (photo).*

**Upper subalpine woods and treeline.** Cool, very short growing season; cold, snowy, windy winters. Kruppelholz (page 286) and island-like patches of subalpine fir and Engelmann spruce, with loosely spaced subalpine larch from Bow Summit south. Grouseberry, crowberry, heather; beargrass in Waterton/Glacier area. Golden-crowned sparrows, fox sparrows, robins, blue grouse, warblers, gray jays; grizzly bears, elk and mule deer in summer, caribou in winter. *Bow Summit or Parker Ridge along Icefields Parkway; Going-to-the-Sun Road.*

**Avalanche track.** Green alder, willows, kruppelholz at higher elevations; cow parsnip, grizzly bears, moose. *Going-to-the-Sun Road; TransCanada Highway near Kicking Horse Pass; Icefields Parkway near Parker Ridge.*

**Alpine meadow/alpine tundra.** Cool, very short growing season; highly variable snow depth; very windy. Many small communities in this environment, but two main ones are meadow (fairly dry, grassy, with many wildflowers) and tundra (damper, carpets of heather, ponds). White, pink and yellow heather, willows (bluegreen, alpine, rock, snow), dwarf birch; forget-me-not, moss campion, white dryas, western anemone, alpine anemone, blue-bottle gentian, yellow paintbrush, arctic poppy, Lyall's saxifrage, head-shaped and alpine louseworts; alpine bluegrass, trisetum, alpine foxtail, mountain timothy; *Cladina* and *Stereocaulon* ground lichens. Rosy finches, ptarmigan, pipits, horned larks, northern harriers, golden eagles; brown lemmings, Columbian ground squirrels, marmots, grizzly bears, wolverines, caribou, bighorn sheep (summer), mountain goats (winter). *Logan Pass, The Whistlers via Jasper Tramway.*

**Summit.** Highest community, near tops of peaks. Very cool, extremely short growing season; very cold, extremely windy winters with patchy snow accumulation. Lichens such as *Xanthoria, Rhizocarpon, Umbilicaria, Thamnolia,* encrusting types, mosses among rocks, three-point saxifrage, purple saxifrage, mountain sorrel. Snow worms, springtails and hill-topping insects; ravens (year-round), golden eagles, golden-mantled ground squirrels, mountain goats, wolverines, marmots. *Top of The Whistlers near Jasper, just a short walk from upper terminal of Jasper Tramway. Photo: east face of Mt. Assiniboine.*

**Burn.** Young lodgepole pines, fireweed, corydalis, strawberry blite, *Marchantia;* woodpeckers, hawk owls, Townsend's solitaires, voles, deer mice, mule deer, moose. *Vermilion Pass, along Highway 93 in Kootenay park. Photo by Don Beers of Amiskwi Valley in Yoho National Park.*

**Blow-down.** A windstorm or powerful gust blows down a stand of trees covering an area that can be as large as a mountainside. Like a burn or avalanche, a blow-down occurs quickly and changes an existing community. Happens mostly in montane lodgepole and aspen stands, primarily on the eastern slope and especially south of Crowsnest Pass. Provides excellent habitat for carpenter ants, woodpeckers, grouse, wrens, snowshoe hares, porcupines. *Opening stretch of Maligne Road near Jasper (trees uprooted in 1989 winter storm); highways in southern Alberta.*

**Cliff or rocky slope.** Straggly white or Engelmann spruce, Douglas-fir, limber pine, whitebark pine; creeping and common juniper, kinnikinnik, shrubby potentilla, gooseberry, wild roses; white camas, pasture sage, silver plant and other buckwheat-family members, alpine potentilla. Kestrels, mountain bluebirds; wood rats, least chipmunks, golden-mantled ground squirrels, bighorn sheep, mountain goats. *Disaster Point along Highway 16 east of Jasper, Highway 40 in Kananaskis Country.*

**Talus or rock slide.** Lichens on the boulders, mosses on and between them; prickly saxifrage, gooseberry, sorrel. Long-tailed weasels, least chipmunks, golden-mantled ground squirrels, pikas, marmots. *Maligne Valley; Moraine Lake.*

**Glacial melt-back area (glacial forefield).** Recolonization of bare ground by young Engelmann spruce, white dryas, willows, river beauty, mountain sorrel, yellow saxifrage, sedges, rushes. *Forefield of Athabasca Glacier (photo), or road's end at Mt. Edith Cavell.*

**Scree slope.** Scree—small rock fragments that have come from cliffs above—is too unstable for most plants, but in spots that have not been covered for a few years there may be raspberry, bladder locoweed, dwarf hawksbeard (inset photo) and Chinese lantern. *Many locations.*

**Dunes.** White spruce, silverberry, creeping juniper, kinnikinnik, grasses and other dry-habitat montane species overgrowing stable sand dunes; active dunes tend to cover vegetation on leeward side and expose new (but difficult) growing places on windward side. *Jasper Lake shoreline along Highway 16 in eastern Jasper park; Jackman Flats Natural area near Valemount. Photo courtesy Jasper National Park.*

**Summer snowbank.** There is an interesting ecological community here, based on red algae living in the snow. See page 474 for more information. *High points along mountain highways. Photo by Cia Gadd.*

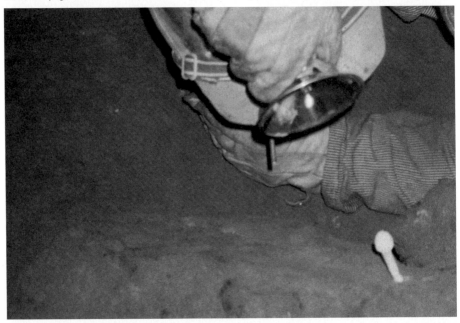

**Cave.** Molds and sometimes mushrooms on organic matter such as pollen, dead animals, wood rat and bat feces, human waste and trash. Blind, eyeless crustaceans such as *Salmacellus steganothrix,* an isopod, and *Stygobromus canadensis,* an amphipod known only from Castleguard Cave (page 168); ice insects (see page 476); wood rats near entrances and bats throughout. Essential hibernation sites for several species of bats (page 593). Martens travel far into mountain caves, perhaps seeking bats as prey; I have found marten skeletons over a kilometre beyond the entrance of Cadomin Cave. *No easy access.*

*The calypso orchid,* Calypso bulbosa *with guest. This flower plays a trick on the golden northern bumblebee. See page 333. Photo by Barry Giles.*

# Plant listings
*Brute force works, but finesse saves time*

Some 660 plants are pictured and described in this book—about half of all Canadian Rockies flora. The listings include all the common species, plus some uncommon ones that are bound to attract your attention if you happen to see them.

The first line in a species listing gives the English common name. For the convenience of French-speaking readers, the French common name is given in italics. Below that are the genus and species names, with the common name of the family to which a particular plant belongs. If you'd like to know the scientific family name, on page 401 I have listed them with their common equivalents. The list is in the order botanists use. The last line in a species listing gives the blooming period and whether a plant is annual, biennial or perennial (see page 287 for an explanation of these terms).

To make look-ups easier for amateurs, the plant listings in this book don't follow botanical order. Trees are placed first, then shrubs and wildflowers. The wildflowers are divided into those that grow mainly below treeline and those that grow mainly above, then by blooming color. Grasses, sedges, ferns and so on are placed last. Lichens and fungi, which aren't actually plants, have their own chapters.

For our purposes, a **tree** is a tall plant, normally 5 m high or taller, with a single woody stem—the trunk—although there may be more than one trunk per plant.

A **shrub** is any woody plant that is not a tree. Most shrubs have multiple stems. Some are vines.

Strictly speaking, wildflowers are **forbs:** the seed-bearing non-woody plants, excluding grasses, sedges and rushes. But most wildflower books include flowering shrubs as well as forbs.

Grasses, sedges and rushes have a wonderful collective name: the **graminoids,** meaning the "grass-like" plants.

The forbs plus the grass-like group comprise the **herbs.** So an herb is something different to a botanist than it is to a cook.

Next come the **ferns, clubmosses** and **spikemosses,** which are tricky to identify because they don't bloom.

Finally there are the **bryophytes,** which include the mosses and liverworts. These are the simplest organisms with cellulose and chlorophyll in their tissues, but they are not **vascular,** meaning that they have no roots or fluid-carrying conduits.

## *What is that flower, anyway?*
### How to look up the plants described in this book

Non-botanists, and I am one of them, can have a lot of trouble identifying plants. Perhaps you do your identifications like I do them: by brute force, looking at picture after picture until—aha!—there's the little beggar on page 373.

A botanist gets around this by using a **key system,** which requires knowledge of plant families and plant parts. There is nothing mysterious about keying plants, but who has the time to learn how to do it? Especially when there are other ways.

In these pages you will find some of those "other ways," as used in non-technical botany books. They work.

The idea is to go right to the section where your plant is likely to be, thus eliminating most of the page-turning. To use the listings, ask yourself the questions on the next two pages.

## 1. What sort of plant is this?

Is it obviously a **tree**? A **shrub**? A **wildflower** of some kind? Does it look to be at home in the **water**? Is it a **fern** or a **horsetail**? Does it look rather like **grass**? Or is it a **moss**? A **lichen**? Perhaps a **mushroom,** or some other kind of fungus?

Each of these groups has its own section, and most readers should get to the right section without any trouble. Just in case, though, the fern look-alikes are cross-referenced ("see also") and the little low-growing shrubs that look like wildflowers are stuck in with the wildflowers. Once you are in the right section, it probably won't take long to find the mystery plant—unless it is a wildflower. There are a *lot* of wildflowers listed in this book.

Suppose it is a wildflower. You can get two steps farther in the identification game before the page-turning starts. Check your surroundings and ask yourself the next question:

## 2. Am I above or below treeline?

The section on wildflowers has been split into those below treeline and those above. Sometimes it may be hard to tell if you are above or below treeline. Maybe the terrain is so rough and rocky that few trees are growing there. When in doubt, you can save time by checking the alpine flowers first, for that list is shorter. Then go to the below-treeline section.

## 3. What color is the bloom?

The wildflower listings have been further divided by color. There is no need to be precise here, because most wildflowers fall into one of six color groups:

- **White**
- **Green or greenish**
- **Yellow or orange**
- **Red or pink**
- **Blue or purple**
- **Brown, reddish brown or otherwise drab**

Having decided on the color, find the appropriate section and *then* start turning the pages. There won't be terribly many to turn.

But what about the greenish-white flowers, or the purplish-pink ones? There are certainly a few in-betweens, and there also can be a lot of variation in the color of a single species. Well, if you can't find a particular flower under one color, then try another color. To help with troublesome species, all possible colors are mentioned and some cross-referencing has been done.

## 4. What part of the flowering season is it?

The listing for each flowering plant shows the time of year during which it normally blooms. I have gathered blooming-date information for some years on common species in the Jasper area and have given the typical date of onset for these.

Willows are the earliest plants to bloom in the Canadian Rockies. The fuzzy **catkins** (pussy-willows) are the flowers, and on some species the catkins appear in late February. I have even seen them in late *January* during a warm winter at Jasper. A few wildflowers and shrubs begin to bloom in March on the western slope, and sometimes pasque flowers appear in March in the eastern-slope foothills, but don't expect to find many flowers on either side of the divide until the latter half of May, when frosts at the lower elevations are nearly finished and the growing season is on.

Deciduous trees leaf out in mid-May at Jasper, about a week earlier in the southern section and in the Rocky Mountain Trench, a week later north of the Peace River.

Most shrubs bloom in June, many of them with white flowers.

The montane valley floors are showiest in early July. Mid-July to the end of the first week in August is the height of the wildflower season anywhere higher, spectacular at all elevations but especially so in subalpine meadows at the July/August boundary. This is the warmest time of year in the Rockies, when pollinating insects are the most active.

The show has wound down noticeably by mid-August. By the end of the month there are few flowers to be seen. The first week in September often brings a killing frost, although the odd showy aster, gentian or harebell doggedly blooms through the middle of September, and sometimes you will find a flower in early October. Shrubby cinquefoil, page 275, sometimes puts out a batch of flowers *after* the leaves have turned!

If you are interested in **mushrooms,** you probably know that there are two seasons for looking: in early spring, meaning late April through mid-May in the Canadian Rockies, and again in early fall, from mid-August through September. Of the two seasons, the fall one is far richer in the number of mushrooms and in the diversity of species.

Of course, the time that a particular plant blooms depends on its elevation, the weather, and the blooming site—whether north-facing or south-facing, sheltered by rocks, open and windy, and so on. A flower that blooms early on the montane valley floor may bloom in midsummer up near treeline.

The Canadian Rockies are 1450 km long, covering nearly twelve degrees of latitude, so one would expect a pronounced lag in blooming time from south to north. But the difference isn't great. Given equivalent plant communities at Banff and west of Fort Nelson, the more northerly community will be about a week behind. During late July, widely distributed species are at the same stage of development throughout the Rockies. Fall color creeps over the whole range at once, beginning in early September.

The big north-south difference is not so much a matter of time as it is a matter of elevation: Banff is at an elevation of 1387 m, but the same plant community west of Fort Nelson occurs at only 650 m above sea level. A given plant grows at a lower elevation farther north.

So check the blooming period when looking up a plant. During the first week in June you can safely ignore the entries that are supposed to bloom in August.

### 5. Finally, if the illustration looks close to what you've got, read the item, checking the ecological information first.

You can close in on the correct identification by using the ecological data: the elevational zone or region the plant grows in (see two chapters back for an explanation) and the sort of environment it likes: wet, dry, wooded, open, etc. This information has been placed at the beginning of each item so that you can skim it and decide whether it fits. Following that, the key features of the plant are described, which should clinch the identification.

These listings are *mainly* for identification. There is a lot more to learn about Rocky Mountain botany, of course. If you want more detail, be it on certain species or certain ecological relationships, then it is time to head down to the library—preferably a university library. Easily obtainable publications on Rocky Mountain botany, technical and nontechnical, are listed on page 402.

Another source of detailed information is the government. The libraries of the national parks contain unpublished checklists, studies, copies of journal articles and theses. The Alberta Regional Office of Parks Canada in Calgary also holds duplicate copies of much of this material.

In the listings that follow, the blooming date is given at the end of the line with the scientific name and family. If no blooming date is given, then the species does not produce flowers.

## *Record-setting trees: tallest, shortest, oldest*

What is the tallest tree in the Canadian Rockies? There is no documented record that I could find. One would think that it would have to be a conifer of some kind, perhaps a red-cedar or a Douglas-fir, but until the record is known, I'll put my money on one of the immense **black cottonwoods** of the western slope. The grand specimens along Lake McDonald in Glacier National Park seem outstandingly huge.

The western red-cedar is the tallest of the tree species in western Canada, up to 60 m, but the red-cedars in the Rockies seem considerably shorter than their counterparts farther west, where the trees are generally taller. After decades of logging, there are precious few big red-cedars left. Yet the loggers have often ignored the cottonwoods. A strange but common sight in British Columbia is a large clear-cut area, everything reduced to rubble except a few giant cottonwoods.

The *shortest* mature trees are undoubtedly **kruppelholz** trees: subalpine firs and Engelmann spruces found at treeline. See page 286 for more on kruppelholz. In extreme cases, such trees spread flat on the ground.

Now: how about the *oldest* tree? If you consider that most aspen groves are groups of root-joined clones—that is, the whole grove is really a single plant—then this species holds the record, for some of these groves may have lived since the end of the last major glaciation 11,000 years ago, or even longer in the northern end of the Rockies, parts of which may have escaped glaciation for 64,000 years.

Currently the non-aspen champion is a whitebark pine found on the west side of the Ramparts in Mount Robson Provincial Park, with 873 countable annual growth rings. That tree would have started growing around A.D. 1110. On the eastern slope of the Rockies, the verifiably oldest tree is an Engelmann spruce in a subalpine grove just northeast of Icefield Centre along Highway 93, with an age of 680–720 years. The grove is known as the **Ancient Forest.**

A Douglas-fir just east of Banff has been dated to over 685 years. That is not very old in comparison with the Douglas-firs of Vancouver Island, one of which has been ring-counted to 1306 years. In the White Mountains of eastern California there are bristlecone pines 4600 years old—the world record for trees. These are treeline trees, which have grown very slowly. Treeline trees in the Canadian Rockies are mostly subalpine fir, which usually live only a couple of hundred years.

Limber pine is a close relative of bristlecone pine, and one would think that the gnarled limber pines of the southern Alberta foothills are old. Few live more than 200 years. An exception is a limber pine found at Whirlpool Point along the David Thompson Highway east of Saskatchewan Crossing. This tree may be the oldest non-aspen in the Canadian Rockies. As reported by Peter Murphy, author of *Alberta Trees of Renown,* it is too decayed at the centre to count the growth rings accurately, but they probably total over 1000. J.W. Campbell, of the Research Council of Alberta, reports larches with decayed centres estimated at 650 years old in Kananaskis Country and perhaps 800 years old farther south.

Some species of lichens are also probably quite old. See page 405.

*Oldest known Douglas-fir in Alberta, found near Banff. It began growing about A.D. 1310. Photo by Les Jozsa.*

# *Evergreen conifers*
## Meaning most of the trees in the Canadian Rockies

There are only 14 needle-leaved, cone-bearing tree species that grow in the Rockies, so learning them all is easy. Pine, spruce, fir, hemlock, Douglas-fir and larch are all members of the pine family (Pinaceae), while red-cedar belongs to the cypress/juniper family (Cupressaceae). Most of these species are evergreen, meaning that they keep their needles year-round, but the larches are deciduous.

### Lodgepole pine *Pin tordu*
*Pinus contorta* (pine family)

A characteristic montane tree, with a straight, gradually tapering trunk, useful for making tipi poles, hence the name "lodgepole"—although the species name "contorta" is something of a misnomer, for it comes from twisted specimens of the tree found where it was first identified along the California coast. Mature height 5–20 m, with the foliage mainly in the upper third. Needles 2–5 cm long, in bunches of two, the only pine in the Canadian Rockies with needles in twos. The bark is brown and scaly.

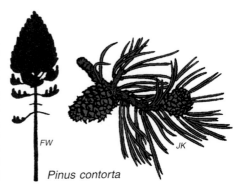

*Pinus contorta*

Non-botanists often call lodgepole pine **jack pine**, which is actually a separate species, *Pinus banksiana*. Jack pine grows east of the Canadian Rockies, not here, but if you think you may be looking at a jack pine, there's an easy way to tell the difference: the cones of jack pines grow at an angle to the branch, with the cone tips pointing *away* from the trunk. The cones of lodgepole pines also grow at an angle, and they point *toward* the trunk.

Lodgepole pine is the most common tree in the montane forest, perhaps the most common tree in the Canadian Rockies. It is the official tree of Alberta. In late June and early July, often beginning around June 25 at Jasper, lodgepole pollen drifts through the mountains in greenish-yellow clouds, accumulating as a yellow scum on any quiet water body. People sometimes ask if the scum is somehow related to acid rain. The answer is no. Nor is pine pollen very allergenic.

In all members of the pine family, the male and female cones are found together on the same tree. The soft, yellowish male pollen-cones are about 1.5 cm long; they wither and drop off after the pollen has been released. The female seed-cones are 2–5 cm long, egg-shaped, hard, and may take many years to open for seed release and germination. More commonly, though, the cones open quite suddenly, by the thousand, during a forest fire, when the air temperature exceeds 45°C.

Solid stands of lodgepole pine mark areas that have burned. The trees grow quickly, forming a dense **dog-hair forest** in which all members are the same age. Dog-hair forest gradually thins itself out. The faster-growing trees reach above the slower ones, which weaken and die because the needles of lodgepole pines cannot tolerate shade. In winter, snow overloads the tufts of foliage atop the long, skinny trunks of the weaker trees; they bow over to the ground and die. Disease also attacks weaker trees. As the years go by a lodgepole forest becomes open and sunny.

Eventually one of two things happens: (a) another fire goes through, repeating the process, or (b) over the course of 150 years or so most of the lodgepoles become rotten inside, succumb to disease and blow over, to be replaced by shade-tolerant spruce or Douglas-fir that have been patiently growing under the pines. These species owe their success to the low reproductivity of lodgepole in the absence of fire.

Fire suppression through the twentieth century has blanketed the Rockies with old lodgepole forests. In the national parks, fire is now recognized as a normal and essential part of forest ecology. It will be allowed to occur more often there, mainly in the form of controlled burns.

South of Crowsnest Pass over half the lodgepoles have been killed by the **mountain pine beetle** *(Dendroctonus ponderosae,* page 454) during a population explosion of the insect that peaked in the mid-1980s.

The trunks and branches of lodgepole pine are sometimes marked by swellings that collectors call **burls** and forest-disease specialists call **galls.** They are commonly caused by insect or fungal parasites, all evoking the same response from the tree: it quickly grows tissue at the infected or damaged site, walling off the intruding organisms and thus forming the gall. Perhaps the most common gall-causing organism is **western gall rust** *(Endocronartium harknessii).*

**Pine dwarf mistletoe** is a parasitic plant *(Arceuthobium americanum)* that grows along the branches of lodgepole pine. It does not produce galls, although the branches can become somewhat thickened, and it does not infect spruce, fir or other pine species in the Canadian Rockies. It does attack jack pine, which grows east of the Rockies.

Pine dwarf mistletoe

Mistletoe has greenish-yellow or yellowish-brown stems up to 10 cm long, with no leaves. The roots reach into the host-tree's bark and sap-wood for nutrients. The bud-like blooms take two years to mature into the seeds, which are spread by exploding from their cases. The seeds can travel several metres, lodging in other parts of the tree and spreading the infestation through the forest.

Look for mistletoe in old stands of lodgepole, where it does best. You can often spot it from a distance because some branches of the infected trees grow in dense bunches, called **brooms,** that look different from the rest of the tree. Perhaps the best place in the Rockies to observe mistletoe is at the Jackman Flats Natural Area just north of Valemount on Highway 5, where the pines are rife with it. See also "witches' brooms" on spruce and fir caused by *Chrysomyxa arctostaphyli,* a fungus that is sometimes mistakenly called mistletoe, page 258.

## Valley of the Crooked Trees

Not a "valley" by any means, this small stand of twisted lodgepole pines is found along Highway 93A south of Jasper. There is nothing obviously odd about the site, and saplings are affected as well as older trees, so I suspect that the condition is genetic.

**Red-belt** is another lodgepole affliction. This one is caused by the weather. Warm chinook winds in winter (page 213) cause the needles to dry, but the rest of the tree is frozen and sap movement is too slow to replace the moisture. The needles turn reddish-brown and drop off. The condition can affect whole mountainsides, producing reddish streaks of forest—thus the term "red-belt."

Red-belt may be the cause of an anomaly in the occurrence of lodgepole pine. Common at montane elevations throughout the Canadian Rockies, the species is surprisingly scarce close to the mountain front in the major cross-cutting valleys such as those of the Athabasca and Bow rivers. These valleys experience the most sudden rises in temperature during chinooks and the greatest wind velocities. White spruce and Douglas-fir, the two common conifers in these lodgepole-free areas, are not as prone to red-belt damage, which may explain why they survive here in place of the pines.

## Ponderosa pine *Pin ponderosa*
*Pinus ponderosa* (pine family)

Grows at low elevations in the southern Rocky Mountain Trench from Radium Hot Springs south. Can reach 30–40 m in height. The trunk is straight, but the crown, meaning the overall shape of the tree, is rather irregular. Easiest identifier: long needles (7–20 cm) in bunches of three. Cones are hard and prickly, 7–15 cm long. Reddish bark, with large, plate-like scales. The bark flakes with age, becoming smoother and exposing more of the pinkish-orange undersurface. Trunks of old ponderosas are quite pale and smell like vanilla.

Heavily logged, the ponderosa pine is a beautiful tree that needs protection in its few remaining stands. Unfortunately much of what remains has fallen to the mountain pine beetle (page 454).

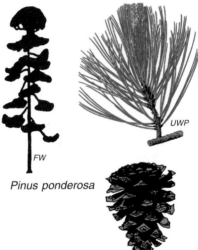

*Pinus ponderosa*

Of the three versions of this tree, the one found in the Canadian Rockies is the **Pacific ponderosa**, subspecies *P. p. ponderosa*. In southern Montana, Wyoming and northern Colorado, the **Rocky Mountain ponderosa**, subspecies *P. p. scopulorum*, looks like a cross between ponderosa and lodgepole. It grows mixed with lodgepole and is difficult to tell apart, for it has two or three needles in a bundle rather than always three. The needles are intermediate in length between the two species, and the bark is brown rather than reddish. For that reason, scattered Rocky Mountain ponderosa may be present in the southern part of the Canadian Rockies, where "three-needled lodgepoles" have been reported. The other variety of ponderosa, *P. p. arizonica* or Arizona ponderosa, is limited to southeastern Arizona.

## Western white pine *Pin argenté*
*Pinus monticola* (pine family)

Occasional in Columbian forest as far north as Valemount, perhaps most common along Lake McDonald in Glacier National Park. A few eastern-slope specimens have been reported between Crowsnest Pass and the international boundary, but otherwise not in Alberta. Grows 30–40 m tall, but mature individuals are uncommon and most of the trees seen are only 5–10 m in height.

Note how more live branches are present lower on the trunk than in lodgepole pine, and that there are five needles per bundle, rather than two or three. The bark is gray, roughening with age.

*Pinus monticola*

Differentiate from whitebark pine and limber pine by habitat, size, and shape—the other two trees are subalpine, shorter and squatter—and by the cones: western white pine cones are long (12–20 cm), narrow, and tend to curve.

### Whitebark pine *Pin à blanche écorce*
*Pinus albicaulis* (pine family)

Fairly common, found throughout the Rockies in the subalpine zone from the Peace River south. Does best in windswept, cliffy locations, away from other tree competitors, but also occurs in the forest. The bark is smooth and light gray in young trees, becoming brown and scaly with age. Mature height seldom over 10 m; the trunk tapers rapidly. Needles in bunches of five.

How do you tell whitebark pine from similar-looking limber pine? Whitebark cones are squat and egg-shaped, like lodgepole cones, and 5–10 cm long; limber pine cones are much larger (15–20 cm long). The large seeds of both are favorite foods of Clark's nutcracker, page 557. Whitebark pine is the oldest tree species known in the Canadian Rockies. See page 252.

*Pinus albicaulis*

### Limber pine *Pin flexible*
*Pinus flexilis* (pine family)

Mainly western-slope montane and subalpine, between Golden and Radium. On the eastern slope, scattered individuals and small stands grow at treeline in Waterton/Glacier and at much lower elevations in the southern foothills around Crowsnest Pass. The species has been reported as far north as Saskatchewan Crossing.

Limber-pine needles grow in bunches of five. The smooth gray branches are, indeed, very flexible, making the species well-adapted to windy locations. Distinguish from similar-looking whitebark pine by the cones: limber pine to 20 cm long; whitebark never longer than 10 cm. You may see limber pines in the Rockies diseased with **white-pine blister rust** *(Cronartium ribicola),* which produces large orange galls.

*Pinus flexilis*

### Engelmann spruce and white spruce
*Épinette d'Engelmann, épinette blanche*
*Picea engelmannii* and *P. glauca* (pine family)

These are the more common spruce species in the Canadian Rockies, sometimes difficult to tell apart because they interbreed.

Mature size 20–30 m; cone-shaped and symmetrical when young, becoming less so with age. Brown, shreddy bark. The papery cones are 2–6 cm long, carried mostly near the top of the tree—often so densely on mature white spruce that the tops look brown from a distance. The needles are 1–2 cm long and prickly; they are square in cross-section and can be rolled between your fingers. Fir needles are flat and will not roll.

Thus the naturalist's jingle, **"Fir is flat and friendly; spruce is square and sharp."** Pine needles are longer and form a round bundle when held together.

If you are determined to differentiate white spruce from Engelmann, providing the specimen you are looking at is not a hybrid, then consider first your location. White spruce grows throughout the Rockies, but Engelmann peters out north of Grande Cache. South of there, check your elevation. Except in cliffy places, Engelmanns grow higher on the mountain, mostly in the subalpine zone. White spruce is more common at lower elevations, never found in the upper subalpine tree islands or kruppelholz (page 286).

Check the needles and cones. Engelmann needles tend to curve upward; white spruce needles grow straighter and more evenly around the twig, and are somewhat less prickly. The cones are the key to positive identification of a pure-strain tree: the scales of Engelmann cones are thin and flexible, with wavy edges, while those of white spruce are stiffer and smooth-edged. Pure Engelmann scales are shaped rather like the blade-end of a screwdriver, while pure white-spruce scales are as neatly rounded as a manicured fingernail.

At the latitude of Jasper, I have observed an interesting east/west difference in elevation for pure Engelmann spruce. In the foothills the species is pure only at treeline. In the front ranges the species is pure at elevations down to the mid-subalpine range, while in the main ranges pure Engelmann can be found lower than that.

White spruce and Engelmann spruce are so common in the Canadian Rockies that they send greenish clouds of pollen through the valleys on windy days in late May. Lodgepole pine produces similar clouds, but about a month later.

**Swollen, salmon-colored branch tips,** very common on white and Engelmann spruce and sometimes on Douglas-fir, are caused by the **Cooley spruce gall adelgid,** *Adelges cooleyi.* The galls look a little like cones, but closer inspection shows them to be new-growth twigs and needles gone wrong. Fresh, greenish galls form in May. Breaking one off the tree and tearing it open will reveal tiny black larvae, one in each chamber of the gall, surrounded by a thin cottony layer. These are nymphs: immature insects. Later, the blue-gray adults fill the chambers, then leave the galls to suck plant juices from needles. When the females reproduce, they lay eggs along the twigs, each brood covered under a cottony speck. Sometimes the branches are practically white with these specks. Surprisingly, Cooley spruce-gall adelgids do little damage to the trees. They are important as food for insect-eating birds.

*Picea engelmannii*

*Picea glauca*

*Spruce gall*

## Witch's broom

Many spruce trees support strange, bushy growths among their branches that many people take to be squirrel nests. But a witch's broom is part of the tree: it's a dense mass of needles on twisted twigs that spring from a single point, often along the trunk. Some trees are afflicted with several witches' brooms, yet they don't seem to kill these trees, nor even to damage them much. The cause is a parasitic fungus called *Chrysomyxa arctostaphyli,* and what it does is the stuff of science fiction.

There is a yearly cycle. From the mass of twigs, bare of needles and seemingly dead—looking very much like some kind of nest—the short yellowish needles come out in May and June. The color is from masses of spores, which produce a musty, semen-like smell that can be quite strong but difficult to place. I have seen people on all fours under an infected spruce, hunting for what they assume to be a malodorous wildflower of some kind. The odor diminishes as summer passes. By October the needles have dried and fallen out, to regenerate next spring.

In some books, *Chrysomyxa* witches' brooms are called mistletoe, which is a mistake. Pine dwarf mistletoe is a very different plant. See page 254.

Chrysomyxa *broom on a spruce in Maligne Canyon, Jasper National Park*

### Black spruce *Épinette noire*
*Picea mariana* (pine family)

A short spruce (10–15 m), reaching 25 m occasionally, growing in bogs and damp places at montane and lower subalpine elevations. Look for it on the eastern side of the divide from Calgary north, and on the western side from Valemount north. This is the easiest spruce to identify from a distance: the top is often a dense, pointed tuft, while the rest of the crown is more open. The tree is slim throughout, with short branches. The twigs are hairy; the needles are short (1–1.5 cm) and straight, darker than other spruce needles (hence the name), and softer—not prickly. The bark is shreddier than Engelmann- or white-spruce bark, exposing a dark, purplish layer underneath. Black-spruce cones are typically 2–3 cm long in the Canadian Rockies, noticeably smaller than those of other spruces, and they don't open as widely.

### Subalpine fir/alpine fir *Sapin subalpin*
*Abies lasiocarpa* (pine family)

Characteristic of the subalpine forest throughout the Rockies, at home along with Engelmann spruce in both the heavy growth of the lower subalpine zone and the tree-islands higher up. Subalpine fir can sneak quite far down the hill on the north sides of steep-walled east/west valleys, which are cold and dark in winter. For example, there are tall subalpine firs only a few kilometres west of Jasper along the Miette River.

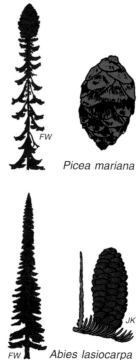

*FW*

*Picea mariana*

*JK*

*FW*   *Abies lasiocarpa*

The species also does well in heavy-snowfall areas of the Columbian forest; there is a grove below Mt. Robson, and you will find them at low elevations on the western slope from Prince George north.

This is the only true fir common in the Canadian Rockies; Douglas-fir is an imposter (see next item). **Balsam fir** *(Abies balsamea)* has been reported in the eastern foothills between the Peace and North Saskatchewan rivers, and near Jasper. Differentiating balsam fir from subalpine fir is tricky. The best way is to check the cone scales. A subalpine-fir scale is somewhat longer than it is wide, while a balsam-fir scale is noticeably wider than it is long. **Grand fir,** which has longer needles (3–5 cm) than subalpine fir, is found at low elevations in western Glacier National Park.

The subalpine fir is high-spired to shed the deep snow of the upper-elevation forest. Fir needles are soft and flat; they don't roll between your fingers. Young trees have smooth gray bark that becomes rougher with age. The cones are distinctive: purple and sticky, sitting *upright* on the upper branches rather than hanging down like those of other conifers. The cones don't fall off whole; instead, the scales drop off one by one, leaving little candle-like rods on the branches.

My favorite characteristic of the subalpine fir is its aromatic resin, which gives the subalpine forest a delightfully bracing balsam-like fragrance.

The less-than-delightful-looking stuff you sometimes find stuck on the lower branches of subalpine fir is **black-felt snow mold,** *Herpotrichia juniperi.* It's a fungus; see page 431 for more about it.

## Douglas-fir *Douglas taxifolié*
*Pseudotsuga menziesii* (pine family)

*Pseudotsuga menziesii*

Increasingly common at montane elevations as you follow the Rocky Mountain Trench south from McLeod Lake, perhaps the predominant tree in the trench south of Golden. Douglas-fir also grows at low elevations on the eastern slope along the Athabasca, North Saskatchewan, and Bow rivers. The most northerly stand on the eastern slope is at Brûlé Lake, just east of Jasper National Park. South of the Bow River the species forms scattered stands in the southern foothills, becoming common from Waterton south.

Smooth-barked, symmetrical and delicate-looking when young, Douglas-fir becomes gnarled and picturesque as it grows old. Mature trees have deeply furrowed bark (usually pocked with woodpecker holes) and heavy limbs. This species lives a long time—some have been ring-counted to over 1300 years—mainly because it withstands forest fire. Look for blackened bark on the trunk, especially around the base.

Persons familiar with the enormous Douglas-firs of the Coast Mountains (subspecies *P. m. menziesii*) will hardly recognize the interior Douglas-fir of the Rockies (subspecies *P. m. glauca*). It is much shorter, although still a good-sized tree for the Canadian Rockies: 30–40 m tall at maturity. The trunk often has a gentle curve, so the tree leans a little.

Douglas-fir resembles both fir and hemlock, but is actually neither; thus the "pseudo-" part of the scientific name. It has the flat needles characteristic of both groups. The cones are unusual: pick one up and note the bracts (little spiny flaps) that stick out between the scales, like the tails and hind legs of tiny mice. There is a Blackfoot story that ends with mice hiding in the cones to escape the wrath of Naapi, a legendary figure. Cones of larch, page 261, also have spiny bracts.

The Douglas-fir is picky about sunlight, temperature and soil moisture. In the southern Rockies of Colorado and New Mexico it grows on north-facing slopes; farther north, in Wyoming and Montana, it does equally well on either side of the mountain, while in Canada it grows mainly on south-facing exposures. See the Douglas-fir beetle, page 454.

### Western hemlock *Pruche occidental*
*Tsuga heterophylla* (pine family)

*Tsuga heterophylla*

Western slope only, at low elevations in the Columbian forest between Golden and Prince George; also around Fernie and in western Glacier National Park..

Hemlock is often easily identified by looking at the top of a mature tree: the tip, properly called the riser, nods limply over to the side. The needles of the hemlock are small (1–1.5 cm long), soft, flat and dark green, growing on short, hair-like stalks. The cones are also small (2 cm long), the scales tightly closed at first, then opening widely and showing a rectangular shape. Bark is reddish brown when young, darker and rather deeply furrowed when old; always scaly.

Hemlock becomes irregular in shape and ragged-looking as it grows older. This relaxed-looking tree isn't very strongly rooted, and it doesn't last long in windy places. Like red-cedar, the wood of the hemlock is valued for its resistance to rot; it contains tannin. Unlike red-cedar, western hemlock is also quite strong.

A population explosion of the western hemlock looper moth has killed about half the hemlocks between McBride and Prince George. See page 472 for more.

### Western red-cedar *Cèdre de l'Ouest*
*Thuja plicata* (cypress/juniper family)

*Thuja plicata*

Along with hemlock, red-cedar is a characteristic species of the Columbian forest. It is found mainly on the western side of the Rocky Mountain Trench, crossing to the eastern side from Golden north and fading out north of Prince George. Farther east in the Rockies the tree occurs wherever storm tracks lay down enough moisture for it; there are red-cedar groves at Mt. Robson and near Fernie, now mostly logged. The best remaining Rockies stands are along Lake McDonald in western Glacier National Park, Montana. Small specimens occur at the continental divide in Fortress Pass south of Jasper, and similar stunted red-cedars have been reported in Alberta just east of the divide in Crowsnest Pass, and at the headwaters of the Alexandra River in northern Banff park. A true anomaly is the single red-cedar specimen found 15 km northeast of the divide beside the North Boundary Trail in northern Jasper park, on the slopes of Twintree Mountain.

Identifiers: the straight, vertically lined gray trunk and scaly needles that look rather like juniper. Folk names often confuse juniper and red-cedar; they are also called "cypresses" in some regions.

Western red-cedar is a tall tree, commonly reaching 40 m. It has been heavily logged for its redwood-like lumber, which resists rot. Rapidly disappearing in British Columbia, the trees are not being replanted. Some red-cedar groves fall within national and provincial parks and are thus protected, but like the giant California redwoods, the western red-cedars of British Columbia will soon be scarce unless the government protects them generally.

# The larches
## Conifers that aren't evergreen

Larches, also called **tamaracks,** are peculiar conifers. In mid-September the needles turn golden, and in late October they fall. Through the winter the trees appear dead and skeletal—until the following May, when new needles emerge. You can tell a wintering larch from a leafless broad-leaved tree by checking the branches. On a larch, they are covered with little nipple-like needle bases, from which 10–40 soft needles emerge in the spring.

### Subalpine larch/Lyall's larch *Mélèze subalpin*
*Larix lyallii* (pine family)

Subalpine larch grows just below treeline, in open stands. Mature trees are branching and scraggly, 5–10 m tall, thinly clad in very soft, pale-green needles. Found mainly on the eastern slope, the current northern limit of this species in North America is Clearwater Pass, in the front ranges east of Bow Summit. A long-dead *L. lyallii* found near the toe of the Athabasca Glacier shows that this species once extended at least 95 km farther north; it lived from about A.D. 1000–1250, when the climate was somewhat warmer than it is now. Subalpine larch becomes less common south of Crowsnest Pass.

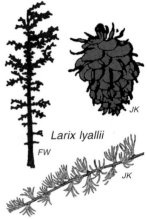

*Larix lyallii*

The trees are most conspicuous in the fall, when the needles turn golden and give the upper subalpine forest some fall coloration to match the aspen groves far below.

### Western larch *Mélèze occidental*
*Larix occidentalis* (pine family)

This is the western-slope larch, common at low elevations from Canal Flats south, patchy as far north as Golden. In Alberta it is found in the first 20 km east of Crowsnest Pass, with one report in the Kananaskis area.

Western larch is tall: up to 30 m in the Canadian Rockies. This sets it apart from the much-shorter tamarack, next item, which is restricted to the eastern slope. Unlike subalpine larch, previous item, western larch is fairly symmetrical, with a single, straight trunk; it grows at much lower elevations than subalpine larch. The leaves of all three larches are the same: soft, pale-green needles that turn golden in mid-September and drop off in mid-October. Western larch seldom grows in pure stands; usually it mixes with pine and spruce.

*Larix occidentalis*

### Tamarack/eastern larch *Mélèze laricin*
*Larix laricina* (pine family)

Eastern-slope montane, common in the foothills north of the Red Deer River, sharing boggy places with black spruce. Tamarack is symmetrical and short, 5–10 m tall in the Rockies, with pale green needles that turn golden in the fall and drop off. For a superb display of fall tamarack color, drive west from Rocky Mountain House on Highway 11 in the first week of October.

*Larix laricina*

**See also** the yew, page 274.

# Leafy trees
## Definitely in the minority in this part of the world

The four species of broad-leaved trees native to the Canadian Rockies are all described here, plus the Manitoba maple, which isn't native but seems determined to stay. If you see a tree that you can't identify, it may be another non-native species that has been planted by someone, or one that has escaped into the wilds.

**Trembling aspen** *Tremble/peuplier faux-tremble*
*Populus tremuloides* (willow family)
Pollen mid-April to early May

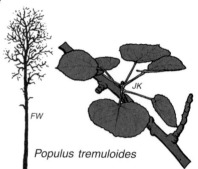

*Populus tremuloides*

Most common leafy tree in the Rockies, found everywhere at montane elevations and characteristic of that ecosystem. Smooth, white bark; gray and furrowed only near the base or not at all.

The bark of most Rockies trees has a tough, dead outer cortex. But not the bark of aspen; the surface is alive and photosynthesizes. A powdery white material on the trunks of aspens is produced by the tree as a defense against ultraviolet radiation. If the powder doesn't rub off easily, it is probably a species of lichen growing on the bark.

Stark black scars mark points of past injury to aspen bark. A common one is from the aspen-borer beetle, which keeps a slit open as it tunnels through the wood. Fungal infections introduced at this wound frequently cause death of the branch or trunk higher up.

Aspen bark is an attractive food for elk in winter. (See page 648 for the reason.) In any grove frequented by elk the trunks of aspen are typically scarred to a height of about 2 m, which is as high as the animals can reach, lacking upper incisors. Mule deer rub small trees with their antlers. Bears claw their way up when danger threatens, and they also scratch the trunks to head height, apparently to mark territory. Beavers cut down aspens for food and dam-building material, while small mammals such as the snowshoe hares eat aspen bark from branches and twigs bent near the ground under heavy loads of ice and snow.

**Frost cankers** are common on aspen in the Rockies. I see them on nearly every tree. Sections of bark up to 5 m long can be so badly frozen during cold snaps that they discolor and peel away in spring. If a canker doesn't heal, the bark sloughs off, leaving a brownish/blackish sickly-looking scar. Frost damage can continue year after year, enlarging the scar and eventually exposing the heartwood. Somehow the trees survive hideous frost cankers, in part by growing heavy, ribbed bark on the uninjured side of the tree, which strengthens it.

Aspen branches are fairly short. Foliage is sparse, concentrated near the top of the tree. The leaves are 3–5 cm across, rounded, pointed at the tip, finely toothed and waxy green; they rustle on their thin, flat stalks in the slightest breeze—hence the name "trembling aspen"—and in the fall turn brilliantly yellow, gold or reddish.

Aspens leaf out in mid-May in the Jasper area. The leaf buds and young leaves exude a nectar that attracts ants; the ants kill many of the forest tent caterpillars, page 472, that would otherwise defoliate the tree at this sensitive time. Later in the summer, look for other caterpillar species inside leaves they have rolled into tubes by sticking the sides together with silk.

In early spring, typically April 15th at Jasper, the trees produce willow-like catkins; there are male catkins and female catkins, and they are on separate trees. By early July the female catkins have become seed pods. They burst, ejecting downy seeds that travel by air and water.

Differentiate aspen from white birch, page 264, by the bark: peeling and often pinkish on the birch, solidly attached on the aspen. You can tell aspen from balsam poplar or black cottonwood by the leaves: smaller and rounder on the aspen. In winter, check the buds. Those of balsam poplar and black cottonwood are large, sticky and fragrant, while those of aspen are smaller and not sticky.

Aspens commonly grow in groves of **clones** (genetically identical individuals) formed by propagation along roots. The world's largest, heaviest organism may be a clone grove of 47,000 individuals in the Uintah Mountains of Utah. The total weight of this plant is estimated at about six million kilograms. Aspen are also found singly.

While aspen individuals are the shortest-lived of the poplars, averaging less than 80 years, aspen clone groves sprout constantly from the existing root system, especially after fires. Aspen groves are effectively immortal as long as a few members survive, making them the world's oldest known living things. Some clone groves in the western U.S.A. may be *millions* of years old.

The species does very well on gravelly places such as alluvial fans. Looking across to a slope heavily treed with conifers, you can often spot a fan by noting the triangular shape of a nearly pure stand of aspen growing on it. Most aspen groves in the Canadian Rockies include scattered white spruce, and clumps of white birch may be present as well.

Mature trees vary considerably in height, from only 5 m high in rough locations to 30–40 m in protected places. The wood is soft and brittle when dry. It easily makes a roaring fire, but gather a lot; aspen burns rapidly.

## Balsam poplar *Peuplier baumier*

*Populus balsamifera,* subspecies *balsamifera*
(willow family) Pollen in early May

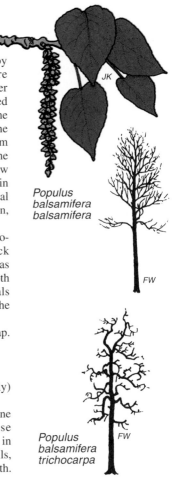

Populus
balsamifera
balsamifera

Populus
balsamifera
trichocarpa

This is the common eastern-slope poplar, replaced by black cottonwood on the western slope. Larger, more elongated leaves than aspen, dark glossy green on the upper surface and paler underneath. The bark is gray and furrowed well up the trunk, smooth and yellowish-white only near the top or when the tree is young. Balsam poplar prefers montane and lower subalpine streamcourses, where it can grow to 30 m in height. But any gravelly spot will do; in such locations the tree is usually stunted, with a bent-looking trunk and a few twisting branches. Unlike aspen, balsam poplar will grow in rather nasty places; I have found it within 100 m of glacial snouts. The species is prone to the same afflictions as aspen, previous item.

In July, balsam poplar produces cottony seeds in two-parted pods. This is how to differentiate it from black cottonwood, next item, which is practically identical but has three-parted pods. The fragrant buds appear in the fall on both these trees, large and sticky, providing food for animals through the winter. Black bears climb up to get them in the spring, when the odor is particularly strong.

The word **balsam** refers to any pleasantly aromatic sap.

## Black cottonwood/plains cottonwood
### Peuplier de l'Ouest

*Populus balsamifera,* subspecies *trichocarpa* (willow family)
Pollen late April to early May

Common on the western slope, in stands along montane and lower subalpine streamcourses, and in the dense Columbian forest of the Rocky Mountain Trench. Scarce in the eastern-slope mountains, except in the southern foothills, where it is common along streams from Crowsnest Pass south. Interbreeds with balsam poplar.

This tree closely resembles balsam poplar, previous item, and it's just a variety of the same species, but black cottonwood is usually larger and heavier-looking: up to 40 m tall, with the trunk up to 2 m in diameter. The leaves are somewhat bigger and broader, but otherwise similar. Male black cottonwood catkins contain 40–60 stamens; those of balsam poplar 12–20. The pod-like fruits are also diagnostic: black cottonwood pods split open in three parts; those of balsam poplar in two parts.

As the name implies, cottonwoods are prolific producers of cotton-fluff seeds. Groves become ankle-deep in the stuff, which can trouble people with allergies.

### White birch/paper birch *Bouleau à papier*
*Betula papyrifera* (birch family)

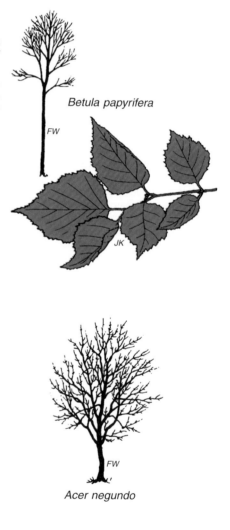

*Betula papyrifera*

Common at lower elevations, except in the southern Alberta foothills and in the Waterton/ Glacier area, where the species is less common. The bark is white, sometimes discolored to gray, always reddish on the smaller branches, and usually peeling off the trunk in sheets—hence the name "paper birch."

In the Rockies, birch is not a very tall tree: 10–20 m. It looks rather like aspen, and grows in mixed groves. Tell the two apart by the peeling birchbark and the leaves: birch leaves are smaller, with coarsely toothed margins, while the teeth on aspen leaves are finely, bluntly toothed. Willow-like catkins appear in spring, before the leaves come out. Both male and female flowers bloom on the same tree; female flowers are much thinner than male flowers. The small seeds have tiny wings that help to scatter them over the winter snow.

### Manitoba maple/box elder *Érable négundo*
*Acer negundo* (maple family)
Blooms in early May

A small tree, usually less than 10 m high and often reduced to shrub size. Eastern slope only, where it occurs west of its normal range on the prairies.

Seen mainly near the towns in which it has been extensively planted, the Manitoba maple seems to be escaping from cultivation. Recognize it by the leaves, which are in groups of seven leaflets. The tree is squat, with spreading branches that break in heavy snowfalls. The bark is gray-brown and furrowed. Drooping clusters of small yellowish-green flowers with pink stems come out before the leaves; the seeds, a favorite food of the evening grosbeak, are in twos, with back-sloping wings. See also Douglas maple, page 271.

*Acer negundo*

**See also** Scouler's willow, wild choke cherry, pin cherry, mountain alder, water birch and Rocky Mountain juniper, all of which can reach the size of small trees.

# Shrubs
## Never to be formally addressed as "bushes"

Shrubs are multiple-stemmed woody plants too small to be called trees. In the Rockies some species grow to tree height, 5 m or taller; others are so low-growing that they form ground cover. In this book the dwarf shrubs are listed with the wildflowers, because non-botanists tend to think of them as wildflowers. The reverse applies as well: tall, shrubby-looking wildflowers such as goat's-beard are listed with the shrubs. But in each case the true nature of the plant, woody or non-woody, is noted.

All the shrubs that grow in the Rockies are included in this section. A look through the listings will show that the western slope has more species. Shrubs tend to grow taller on that side of the divide, too, which is not surprising; it is warmer and wetter there. The next time you are thrashing through some Columbian-forest green hell, be sure to have this book along for looking up the head-high horror plant that just poked you in the eye. Another reason to learn the shrubs is that many of them produce edible berries.

The listings below are divided by height into a section for tall shrubs and one for short ones. This is rather arbitrary, for shrubs vary greatly in size from one location to the next. If you can't find a plant in the tall section, then check the short section. The willows, a tricky group, are listed together.

For shrubs that flower, blooming periods are given. I have collected blooming-date information on some Jasper species for up to seven years. The average date of onset of flowering for these is given after the blooming period, in parentheses.

## Willows *Saules*

*Salix* spp.* (willow family), flowering from late February to June

Most willow species grow in dense clumps near water, or even in it, and have elongated leaves. Beyond that, they are all different. At least 25 species grow in the Rockies, of which perhaps six are easy to identify. The rest are difficult, requiring in some cases a specialist.

So, what can the non-botanist do? Rather than merely presenting a few species, which causes identification errors because others are overlooked, a big problem in any condensed guide like this one, I have included them all—but not with exhaustive descriptions or complicated keys, which would take up too much space, as would illustrations of all species. Instead, I have worked out the summary list and quick key on the next page. Using it carefully will get you to the correct identification in many cases, or at least to a choice of only two or three species. Where possible, the common name is given as well as the scientific one.

Willows produce **catkins,** which non-botanists call "pussy-willows." Despite the lack of petals, catkins are true flowers; cottony seeds appear later. Willows are wind-pollinated, and on many species the catkins appear in winter—as early as fall in some cases—protected under sheaths until spring. Catkin buds are essential winter foods for grouse, ptarmigan and deer mice. Moose also receive nourishment from the buds when they browse the ends of willow twigs, where the bark is surprisingly nutritious in winter.

### Galls on willows

Bright-red galls are common on willow leaves. They are caused by insect larvae that live within the gall. Try cutting open a gall; you will probably find a little white worm-like larva inside it. Large, cone-like galls on the ends of willow branches are caused by the larvae of the gall midge *Rhabdophaga strobiloides.* See also galls on roses, page 277.

---

*"Sp." and "spp." stand for "species name(s) not given here," meaning that the species are listed individually, as in the willows, or that it was not practical to provide individual species names.

# A quick key to willow species in the Canadian Rockies

- **Tall (usually 2 m or more), lower montane, in bogs or beaver ponds**
  Dark, hairy twigs: *S. commutata*
  Purplish-brown bark: *S. maccalliana*

- **Tall, lower montane, near water, but not in it**
  Drooping branches: *S. amygdaloides*, **peach-leaf willow** *Saule à feuilles de pêcher*
  Reddish twigs, netted leaf veins, earliest catkins: *S. discolor*, **pussy willow** *Chaton*
  Purplish twigs, leaves only 2–3 cm long: *S. planifolia*
  Yellowish-brown branches, finely toothed leaves: *S. rigida*

- **Tall, lower montane, in thickets or open woods**
  Gray-brown bark, hairy leaves: *S. bebbiana*, **Bebb's willow** *Saule de Bebb*
  Yellow twigs, bark on branches fissured: *S. lasiandra*, **Pacific willow** *Saule du Pacifique*
  Reddish-brown bark, rather broad leaves: *S. monticola*
  Club-shaped leaves, early catkins: *S. scouleriana*, **Scouler's willow** *Saule de Scouler*
  Silvery-gray branches and leaves, tiny yellow flowers: see silverberry, page 268.

- **Tall, low-elevation montane, on sand and gravel. Long, narrow leaves**
  Spreading, droopy branches: *S. caudata*, **whiplash willow** *Saule-fouet*
  Gray-brown bark: *S. exigua*, **sandbar willow** *Saule des bancs de sable*

- **Tall, upper montane and subalpine, any habitat**
  Reddish-brown bark: *S. barclayi*, **Barclay's willow** *Saule de Barclay*
  Smooth, purplish-brown bark: *S. drummondiana*, **Drummond's willow** *Saule de Drummond*
  Gray bark, shiny yellowish-brown twigs: *S. serissima*, **autumn willow** *Saule très tardif*

- **Medium-sized (50–150 cm tall), lower montane, usually in water**
  Gray bark, narrow leaves: *S. candida*, **hoary willow** *Saule tomenteux*
  Brown branches, green twigs, wider leaves: *S. myrtillifolia*

- **Medium sized, subalpine**
  Purplish-brown bark, leaves 4–7 cm: *S. barrattiana*, **Barratt's willow** *Saule de Barratt*

- **Low-growing (under 50 cm tall), subalpine and alpine**
  Leaves 1–3 cm, felty both sides, branches gray: *S. brachycarpa*
  Leaves 4–10 cm, felty beneath, twigs felty, too: *S. alaxensis*
  Leaves 2–5 cm, branches reddish brown: *S. glauca*
  Yellowish twigs, prefers boggy places: *S. farriae*
  Leathery, heavily veined leaves: *S. vestita*, **rock willow** *Saule soyeux*
  Toothed leaves: see dwarf birch, page 276.

- **Alpine, creeping (less than 10 cm tall)**
  Club-shaped leaves, 2–3 cm, woody stem visible: *S. arctica*, **alpine willow** *Saule arctique*
  Round leaves only 0.5–1 cm, in groups of three right on the ground, woody stem not visible: *S. reticulata*, subspecies *S. r. nivalis*, **snow willow** *Saule des neiges*

The tree-size willow with the lovely yellow branches and twigs seen in the southern Rocky Mountain Trench is *Salix alba vitellina*, **golden willow**. It's a variety of **white willow**, a European import.

**See also** silverberry, page 268.

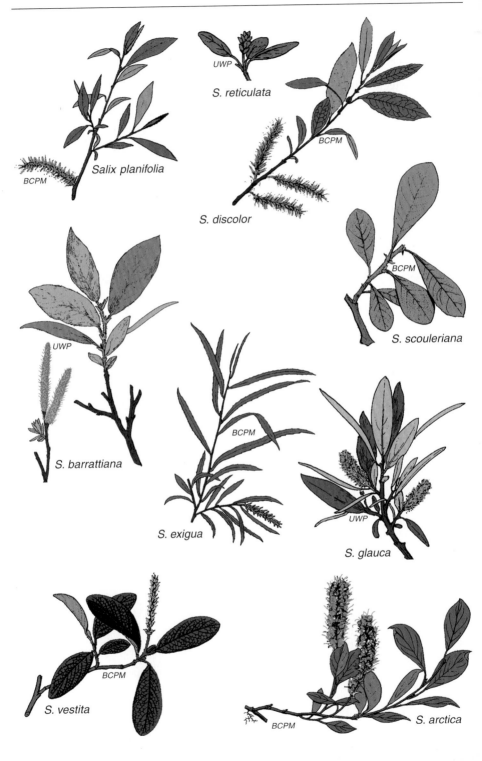

UWP

*S. reticulata*

*Salix planifolia*

BCPM

BCPM

*S. discolor*

BCPM

*S. scouleriana*

UWP

*S. barrattiana*

BCPM

*S. exigua*

UWP

*S. glauca*

BCPM

*S. vestita*

BCPM

*S. arctica*

# Tall shrubs

The plants in this group grow typically 1.5 m high or taller, sometimes to tree size.

### Silverberry/wolf willow
*Chalef changeant*
*Elaeagnus commutata* (oleaster family)
Late May to late June (Jasper: June 1)

Montane, at low elevations. Silverberry thrives in rough, gravelly places and on disturbed ground. Look for it on road shoulders. Resembles a willow, but isn't; is more closely related to buffaloberry (next item). Immediately identifiable by the coating of pale gray, silvery-looking scales that cover all parts of the plant: stems, leaves, even the berries. Hence the name. The tiny yellow four-parted flowers have a heavy, sweet smell—fragrant to the point of pungency for some sniffers. Following the scent will take you to either a silverberry thicket or a department-store perfume counter.

*Elaeagnus commutata*

### Canadian buffaloberry/soopolallie/soapberry *Shepherdie du Canada*
*Shepherdia canadensis* (oleaster family)
Late April to mid-May (Jasper: 20 April)

Most common shrub in the montane woods. Usually about 1.5 m tall. Shiny dark-green leaves are pale and fuzzy beneath, where there are also tiny brown dots. The tiny greenish flowers come before the leaves and barely show on the branches. Male flowers have several rod-like anthers, while female flowers have a central pistil. The sexes are on separate plants.

Soopolallie (pronounced "soap-uh-LAY-lee" or "soap-uh-LAL-ee") is a word in the Chinook language, which incorporates many English forms. It means "soap-berry." The berries arrive in July, brilliantly red and thus very conspicuous, even though they are carried close to the stems. Some plants have yellow berries, a form that is especially common from Sparwood to the southern boundary of Banff National Park. The juicy berries taste sweet at first, then leave a bitter, soapy aftertaste. Bears love them.

You can make an interesting aboriginal dish from this plant by beating the berries and whipping up the juice until it becomes foamy. Compare this species with buckbrush, page 281.

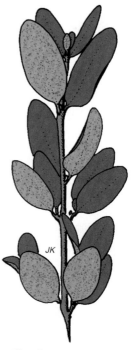

*Shepherdia canadensis*

### Red-osier dogwood
*Cornouiller stolonifère/hart rouge*
*Cornus stolonifera* (dogwood family)
Mainly late May to mid-July (Jasper: June 10),
but continues flowering all summer

Montane, along streams and other damp
places. Red-osier dogwood resembles white
spirea, page 283, but the leaves of red-osier
dogwood are not toothed and the flowers have
four petals, not five. Smooth red twigs and
shiny green leaves, arranged in typical
dogwood fashion. They turn dark red in fall.
The flowers are small and greenish white, in
little clusters at the ends of the stems. Green
berries appear in mid-July, turning bluish, then
white. They're not very tasty. See also
bunchberry, page 295.

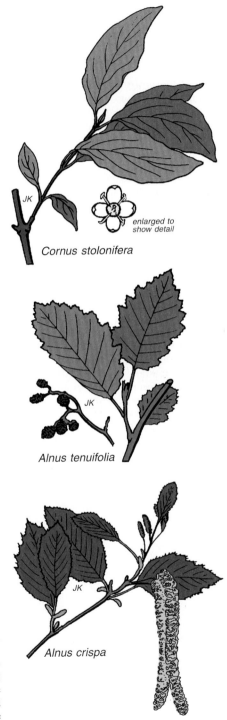

enlarged to
show detail

*Cornus stolonifera*

### Mountain alder/thinleaf alder
*Aulne rugueux*
*Alnus tenuifolia* (birch family)
Early April to late May

More common in western-slope montane
forest than on the eastern slope; grows along
stream courses in drier, more southern areas,
spreading onto moist slopes farther north. Can
reach 10 m in height; commonly 3–4 m. Grows
densely and makes for rough going wherever
you find it. Leaves are dull green above,
notably paler, slightly fuzzy and often
brownish underneath. Small blunt teeth along
the margin, superimposed on larger teeth.
Twigs are hairy; branches gray or light brown
with small white horizontal lines called
**lenticels.** The bark flakes off with age. Long,
willow-like male catkins; shorter female
catkins that become small, cone-like fruits.
Alders add nitrogen to the soil and are thus
important pioneer species. Compare with green
alder, next item.

*Alnus tenuifolia*

### Green alder/speckled alder *Aulne crispé*
*Alnus crispa* (birch family)
Late May to early June

The avalanche-track alder, growing
densely in mountain gullies. Mainly subalpine,
but sometimes higher or lower. Similar to
mountain alder, previous item, but with
smooth, shiny, sharp-toothed dark-green leaves
rather than dull, blunt-toothed ones. Twigs are
warty; bark has speckles rather than lines. Long
male catkins; short female catkins; cone-like
fruits. Subspecies *A. crispa crispa,* described
here, is common on the eastern slope; on the

*Alnus crispa*

western slope, subspecies *A. crispa sinuata* is very common, especially in the Rocky Mountain Trench from Golden north. It has broader leaves and more irregular leaf edges than the eastern-slope variety.

### Beaked hazelnut/filbert
*Noisetier à long bec*
*Corylus cornuta* (birch family) March
　　Mainly Columbian forest. Spreading, 2–3 m tall; grows in both woods and meadows. Toothy, alder-like leaves. Yellow catkins appear in early spring—the female flowers look like tiny red sea anemones—replaced by conspicuous green husks in July, each enclosing an edible nut.

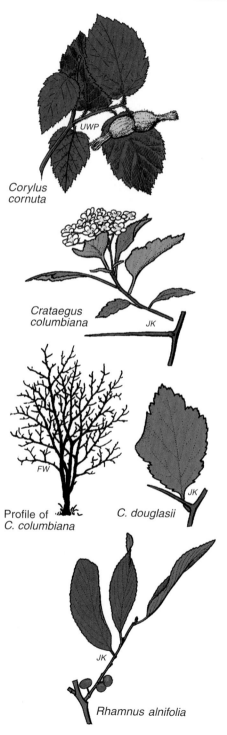

*Corylus cornuta*

*Crataegus columbiana*

JK

Profile of
*C. columbiana*

FW

*C. douglasii*

JK

JK

*Rhamnus alnifolia*

### Columbian hawthorn and black hawthorn
*Aubépine de Colombie, aubépine noire*
*Crataegus columbiana, C. douglasii*
(rose family) May
　　Contrary to what the name implies, Columbian hawthorn is not particularly common in the Columbian forest; black hawthorn is. Columbian hawthorn is more common in the southern Rocky Mountain trench from Golden south, and on the eastern side of the trench generally.
　　Small trees elsewhere in British Columbia, these two species seldom grow more than 5 m high in the Rockies. The leaves of both are toothed and alder-like; the bark is dark gray and very rough. The smaller branches and twigs are covered with sharp, woody spines 1–3 cm long, which make identification easy: hawthorn is the only tall shrub in the Canadian Rockies that has thorns.
　　Growing mainly on the western slope, both types of hawthorn have been reported as shrubs from Crowsnest Pass south on the eastern slope. Where the two are found together, mostly in the Golden area, differentiate by the thorns. Those of Columbian hawthorn are longer.
　　Clusters of unpleasantly scented flowers in May are followed in August by apple-shaped fruits called "haws." These are purplish on black hawthorn, scarlet on Columbian. Both kinds of haws are edible but seedy.

### Alderleaf buckthorn
*Nerprun à feuilles d'aulne*
*Rhamnus alnifolia* (buckthorn family) June
　　Lower montane, western slope south of Golden, eastern slope south of Crowsnest Pass, in marshy areas; sometimes in aspen groves.

Spreading, gray-brown branches, sparsely leaved, no thorns. Alder-like toothed leaves. Very small, greenish flowers carried inconspicuously along the stems; black one-seeded berries. Not terribly common, but often in large patches when you find it.

### Snowbrush/deer brush *Céanothus velu*
*Ceanothus velutinus* (buckthorn family) June

Dry lower montane slopes, south of Radium on the western slope and south of Crowsnest Pass on the eastern slope. Shiny evergreen leaves; rounded and with the finest of teeth. Compare with buffaloberry, page 268. Sticky fragrant yellowish-green twigs. Small white flowers in sprays, each flower on a hair-thin stalk. Seeds can live two centuries in soil, germinating after a fire.

### Water birch/ground birch
*Bouleau occidental*

*Betula occidentalis* (birch family)
Pollen in late April or early May

Scattered clumps in well-drained, gravelly places from valley floors to treeline (mostly montane). Shiny reddish branches with wart-like glands; small, dark-green toothed leaves. Can become quite tall (up to 10 m), and may hybridize with white birch, page 264. See also dwarf birch, page 276. Water-birch catkins are capsule-shaped and coarse, 2–3 cm long.

### Rocky Mountain maple/Douglas maple
*Érable nain*

*Acer glabrum* (maple family) June

Primarily a western-slope montane shrub that occurs sporadically east of the continental divide in the Athabasca, Bow and Crowsnest drainages. Up to 10 m tall, but stunted on the eastern slope. Prefers rocky places. Reddish-brown bark, roughened and patchy-looking with age, typically maple-shaped leaves. Inconspicuous flowers, but the buds and new twigs are bright red—as are the leaves in fall. The seeds have wings. Compare with high-bush cranberry, next item. The only other maple in the Canadian Rockies is Manitoba maple, page 264.

### High-bush cranberry/pembina *Pimbina*
*Viburnum opulus* (honeysuckle family)
Late May to mid-June

Occasional in moist places in western-slope montane woods. Known from the eastern slope south of Crowsnest Pass, but rare. Low-bush cranberry, page 283, is much more

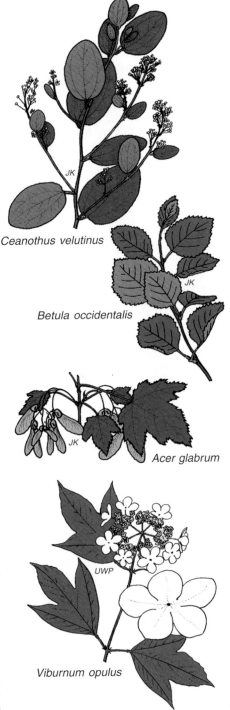

*Ceanothus velutinus*

*Betula occidentalis*

*Acer glabrum*

*Viburnum opulus*

common in the Rockies. High-bush cranberry reaches 4 m in height; usually 1–2 m. Not a true cranberry, like the mountain cranberry, page 331, but the red fruits are edible and used in making jam once the large flat seeds are removed. Sweeter after a frost. Has maple-like three-lobed leaves, (an older name for this plant was *V. trilobum),* but differentiate from Rocky Mountain maple, previous item, by high-bush cranberry's showy flat-topped clusters of white flowers at ends of stems, which are not red. An outer circle of large sterile flowers surrounds the smaller fertile flowers in the centre.

*Prunus virginiana*

## Wild choke cherry *Cerisier de Virginie*
*Prunus virginiana* (rose family)
Late May to early June
    Montane, throughout the Rockies, in sunny places at low elevations, bordering woods. On the western slope, wild choke cherry is often a small tree less than 10 m tall. On the eastern slope it is usually shrub-sized. As an ornamental it reaches tree height on both sides of the divide. Shape: squat and spreading, often with multiple trunks. The bark is dark and purplish-brown. Leaves are fairly broad and finely toothed. White flowers are carried in dense popsicle-shaped clusters up to 10 cm long, followed in fall by small purplish-black sour cherries. Compare with pin cherry, next item.

## Pin cherry
*Cerisier de Pennsylvanie/petit merisier*
*Prunus pensylvanica* (rose family)
Early May through June
    Montane, more common than choke cherry on the western slope, at lower elevations, usually in clearings bordering woods. Extensively planted in towns. Reddish-brown bark, marked on older specimens with powdery horizontal orange lines (lenticels). Shiny yellowish-green lance-shaped leaves taper to a point; they are finely round-toothed. White blooms in small open clusters of 4–12 flowers; small, sour red cherries on long stalks in August. Choke cherry has many more blossoms, in long cylindrical clusters; broader leaves that are sharp-toothed, and darker fruits on shorter stems.
    On the western slope between Radium and Valemount you may find the occasional **bitter cherry,** *P. emarginata.* It is very similar to pin cherry, but has grayish-brown bark and *dull* yellowish-green leaves that have fine *blunt* teeth.

*Prunus pensylvanica*

## Ninebark *Bois à sept écorces*
*Physocarpus malvaceus* (rose family)
Mid-June to early July

Columbian forest; occasional in the Waterton/Glacier area and through Crowsnest Pass. Spreads from a tight cluster of stems, growing 2–4 m tall. Very shreddy bark, in many layers; hence "ninebark." Sharply lobed leaves, white flowers in clusters. No berries; reddish seed cases instead.

## Mountain ash *Sorbier*
*Sorbus* spp. (rose family)
Late June and early July

Upper montane and lower subalpine, in meadows and sunny openings. Can grow to 4 m tall, but is usually chest-high in the Canadian Rockies. The leaves are distinctive: dark green above, pale below, in 7–13 toothy leaflets. Bark is dark brown. Blooms in dense clusters of small white flowers. The berries are very showy, bright reddish-orange, in large bunches. They attract flocks of waxwings, page 565. We have two species: **western mountain ash** *(S. scopulina)* with slightly larger leaves, 9–13 leaflets, and **Sitka mountain ash** *(S. sitchensis),* central and southern areas only, with smaller leaves, 7–11 leaflets.

## Red elderberry *Sureau rouge*
*Sambucus racemosa* (honeysuckle family)
Late May to early July (Jasper: June 20)

Common in Columbian forest clearings; occasional elsewhere. Five leaflets, dark branches, creamy white flowers carried in upright clusters. Berries small, round, and red or black. They are edible, but the seeds and other parts of the plant are toxic. In the southern Rocky Mountain Trench, look for **blue-berry elder** *(S. cerulea),* distinguished by its flat-topped flowerheads and bluish berries.

## Ocean spray/mountain spray *Embrun*
*Holodiscus discolor* (rose family) June

Dry areas at low elevations in the Rocky Mountain Trench from Golden south. Can reach 4 m, but usually about head-high. Small white flowers in long drooping plume-like clusters; no berries. Leaves both toothed and notched; green above, pale and hairy below.

## Goat's-beard *Barbe de la chèvre*
*Aruncus dioicus* (rose family)
Late June to late July

Columbian forest, in damp, shady places; on the eastern slope reported only from Pine

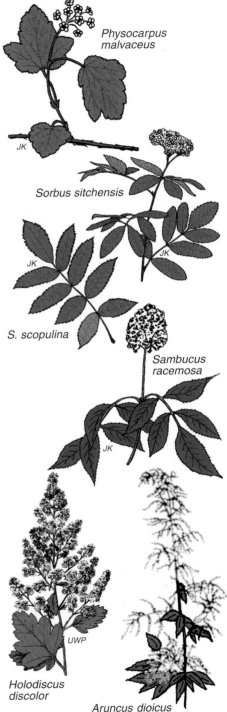

*Physocarpus malvaceus*

JK

*Sorbus sitchensis*

JK

JK

*S. scopulina*

*Sambucus racemosa*

JK

*Holodiscus discolor*

UWP

*Aruncus dioicus*

Pass. Up to 2 m tall; usually less, with lance-shaped, toothed leaflets along tough, ribbed stems that regrow each year. So it's not a true shrub, but it looks enough like one to include here. Distinctive blooms: long, pencil-shaped white or yellowish flower clusters at right angles to the stems. Strings of brown seeds later. Also known as *A. sylvester.*

### Devil's-club *Bois piquant*
*Oplopanax horridum* (ginseng family) June
Common in Columbian forest, occasionally western-slope montane, rarely reported on the eastern slope except in Waterton/Glacier, in the Peace-area foothills and east of the mountains in the Fox Creek/Valleyview area. Stands 1–2 m tall, growing in patches in red-cedar groves and other damp, shady places. The name of this plant says it all. The stout stems are covered with long poisonous spines; contact causes inflammation. The very large, deeply notched, pale green leaves are spiny on the underside. Greenish-white flowers bloom in clusters; brilliantly red berries are carried in upright bunches that are quite pretty.

### Rocky Mountain juniper/scopulorum juniper *Genévrier des Rocheuses*
*Juniperus scopulorum* (cypress family)
Mainly western-slope montane and Columbian forest. On the eastern slope, common through Crowsnest Pass; occasional north to Banff and south through Waterton/Glacier. The farthest north I have seen it on the eastern slope is at the Hoodoos Viewpoint near Banff. Easily identified as a juniper by the needle-like scaly leaves, small bitter blue or pale green berries and shreddy brown bark. Compare with prickly juniper (page 285), with which Rocky Mountain juniper interbreeds. Rocky Mountain juniper grows taller than prickly juniper—up to 5 m—sometimes symmetrically but more often raggedly, and it is not prickly.

### Western yew/Pacific yew *If de l'Ouest*
*Taxus brevifolia* (yew family) May
Western-slope montane from Valemount south, most common on the west side of Glacier park. Primarily a Columbian-forest species, yew grows at a few eastern-slope locations in Glacier park and along the Bertha Lake trail in Waterton park. This is a tree that stays shrub-size in the Rockies, with spreading multiple trunks. The bark is reddish and scaly. The sharp-pointed,

*Oplopanax horridum*

*Juniperus scopulorum*

*Taxus brevifolia*

flat needles are dull-green above and two-tone pale green below. Male flowers are very small cones 2–3 mm long among the needles. Seeds are more conspicuous: bright-red berry-like cups 4–5 mm across, each holding a brown or bluish seed. The seeds are poisonous, as are the branches and leaves of this plant.

## Short shrubs

How tall is short? The shrubs in this section grow about 1–1.5 m tall.

### Shrubby potentilla/shrubby cinquefoil
*Potentille frutescente*
*Potentilla fruticosa* (rose family)
Early June to early September (Jasper: June 7)
　　Common montane-to-lower-subalpine shrub, growing nearly anywhere, wet or dry. Shreddy brown stems and small leaves that are deeply divided, almost needle-like. The plant looks prickly but isn't. Most easily recognizable by the many yellow blossoms, which are five-petalled, showy, and bloom all summer. I have seen this species blooming in early October, when its leaves had turned.
　　There are many potentilla species in the Rockies, but this is the only woody one. It closely resembles garden-variety potentilla, bred from this species.

### Labrador tea/trapper's tea
*Thé du Labrador*
*Ledum groenlandicum* (heath family)
Early June to early July (Jasper: June 5)
　　Upper montane and subalpine forests, in wet, shady places. More common north of the Bow River; absent at Waterton/Glacier, but see next paragraph. A short shrub, 1 m or less, easily recognized by the leaves: 2–6 cm long, oblong but usually strongly curled-under along the edges and thus narrow-looking. They are evergreen. Undersides of new leaves are fuzzy white, becoming brown and furry after their first autumn. The flowers are small and white, with five petals; they bloom in dense tufts at the stem ends.
　　South of Crowsnest Pass, another Labra-dor-tea species is prevalent: *L. glandulosum,* which is very similar but with broader leaves that are not furry underneath and less curled-under. Labrador tea to the north and west of Waterton is usually hybridized *L. glandulosum/ groenlandicum*, and similar hybrids have been reported in Banff park.

*Potentilla fruticosa*
JK

UWP

*Ledum groenlandicum*

There is yet another Labrador-tea species, this one limited to the northern Rockies: *L. palustre*, whose range overlaps with *L. groenlandicum*. Differentiate by *L. palustre's* size (shorter: 10–50 cm), shorter leaves (1–4 cm) and more stamens (*L. palustre* 8–11; *L. groenlandicum* 5–7).

### Dwarf birch/swamp birch/bog birch
### Bouleau glanduleux
*Betula glandulosa* (birch family)
Late May to late June

Near water at any elevation, but especially common in subalpine and alpine meadows, where it is less than a metre high. Up to 6 m tall at lower elevations. Small (1–2 cm) round, toothed shiny green leaves turn brilliantly red or orange in autumn. The bark is black and warty. Flowers are oval catkins about a centimetre long, carried upright along the stems. Dwarf birch and rock willow (page 266) often grow together above treeline.

### Sagebrush *Absinthe/armoise grande*
*Artemisia tridentata* (composite family)
Mid-September to late September

Common western-slope montane shrub, found on the eastern slope through Crowsnest Pass and south. I have also seen it on dry hillsides along the Peace River near Hudson's Hope. Grows at low elevations, in open, dry places. Can reach 2 m, but is usually waist-high or lower. Easy to recognize by the sage fragrance of the gray-green leaves, which are unusually shaped: widening toward the tip, which is toothed. Shreddy, gnarled gray-green bark. Small yellowish flowers are inconspicuous on their short spikes; bloom at summer's end. No berries. See also pasture sage, page 323.

### Antelope brush/greasewood *Bois-gras*
*Purshia tridentata* (rose family) April

Western-slope montane, at low elevations. A sagebrush look-alike, but not even in the same family. The leaves are similar, but greener, and they lack the sage fragrance. They grow close to the stems, which are widely spaced. Can grow to 3 m tall, but usually chest-high. Small yellow flowers in spring.

### Rabbitbrush *Broussailles du lièvre*
*Chrysothamnus nauseosus* (composite family)
Late August to mid-September

Western-slope only, in the driest parts of the Rocky Mountain Trench around Wasa and

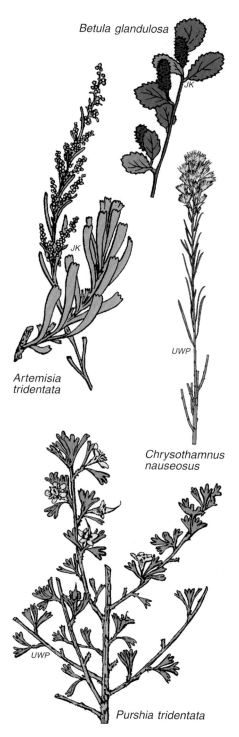

Betula glandulosa

Artemisia
tridentata

Chrysothamnus
nauseosus

Purshia tridentata

Fort Steele. Another sagebrush look-alike, but smaller–usually less than half a metre tall–and greener, with erect stems and thin, pointed leaves. Masses of tiny yellow flowers atop the stems make the plant showy in late summer and early fall. Resembles broomweed (page 319), which also has yellow flowers, but broomweed's stems are not woody and its flowers are larger, the ray-flowers larger and more petal-like.

### Wild roses *Roses*
*Rosa* spp. (rose family)
Late May to early August (Jasper: June 5)

Mostly montane. At their best in the open, wild roses are also very common in lodgepole and aspen forests. Small, toothed leaves grow in bunches of seven or nine, and large pink (sometimes purple or white) five-petalled flowers bloom with the typical rose fragrance.

The three eastern-slope species grow together and sometimes interbreed. The **common wild rose/thorny wild rose** *(R. woodsii)* can be identified by the combination of clustered flowers (rather than single flowers) and spines mainly at nodes along the stems rather than everywhere along the stems. Stems of the other two species are densely spiny. One of these, **dwarf prairie rose** *(R. arkansana,)* is rare on the eastern slope, found mostly in Waterton/Glacier. It is short (less than 40 cm tall), with clustered flowers. The stems die back each year. The other is **prickly wild rose/spiny wild rose** *(R. acicularis),* the provincial wildflower of Alberta and common throughout the mountains. It has single flowers and is taller than dwarf prairie rose, head-high sometimes.

To complicate things for western-slope rose-fanciers, two additional species occur there. **Nootka wild rose** *(R. nutkana),* is tall (up to 3 m), with spines at nodes and single flowers. **Baldhip rose** *(R. gymnocarpa),* is shorter. The stems are spiny throughout, and no sepals adhere to the back of the fruit. The leaves are doubly toothed.

In the fall, all these species produce **rose hips:** fleshy fruits that are rich in vitamin C. Rosehips make tasty jam or tea.

**Strawberry-like galls** on rose leaves are caused by the larvae of small cynipid wasps of the genus *Diplolepis.* See also the larval galls on willows, page 265.

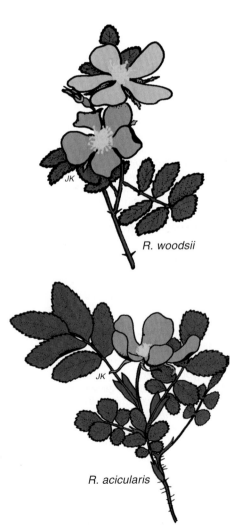

*R. woodsii*

*R. acicularis*

## Wild raspberry *Framboisier*
*Rubus idaeus* (rose family)
Late May to early July (Jasper: June 1)

Very prickly shrub found in gravelly places and on disturbed ground (often grows along highways) in montane areas. Grows 1 m to 2 m tall, but can be quite short—less than 10 cm—in damp places. Flowers white, about 5 cm across, with five petals like other rose-family plants. Dull-green leaves in threes are reminiscent of poison ivy, but the spiny stems prove otherwise. Tasty red berries appear in mid-August. Keep an eye out for bears in raspberry-rich places.

## Thimbleberry
*Ronce à petites fleurs*
*Rubus parviflorus* (rose family)
Late June to mid-July

Common Columbian-forest plant, found throughout the western-slope montane woods. Fairly common on the eastern slope from Crowsnest Pass south, at Pine Pass and along the Peace River; occasional elsewhere, close to the continental divide. A handsome shrub, with big three-lobed leaves up to 20 cm broad and large white flowers. Can be mistaken for devil's-club, but thimbleberry is not prickly or spiny, although it can be rather hairy. Fruits are raspberry-like, but seedy and not as juicy.

## Cloudberry/baked-apple *Mûrier nain*
*Rubus chamaemorus* (rose family) Mid-June

An uncommon plant of the eastern-slope Rockies north of the Athabasca River, found in boggy places where it often grows from a mossy bed. Stems are smooth and brown, the leaves lobed and toothed, 2–7 cm wide. Flowers are white and showy, about 2 cm across. The large fruit is red or yellowish; soft, juicy and sweet.

## Wild gooseberry and black gooseberry/swamp gooseberry
*Groseiller sauvage, gadellier lacustre*
*Ribes oxyacanthoides* and *R. lacustre*
(currant/gooseberry family) Late May to mid-June

Moist places in montane and lower-subalpine woods, growing up to a metre tall, open and ragged-looking.

Leaves of these species are coarsely toothed and three-lobed, although some leaves are so deeply notched they look five-lobed. The small flowers are white or greenish-yellow in

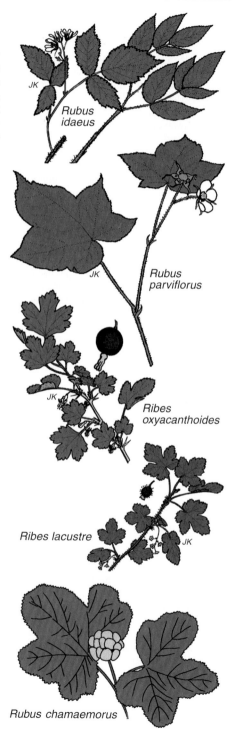

*Rubus idaeus*

*Rubus parviflorus*

*Ribes oxyacanthoides*

*Ribes lacustre*

*Rubus chamaemorus*

wild gooseberry, often pinkish/greenish-white
in black gooseberry. Wild gooseberries are pale
green and striped at first, turning dark red to
purple later. Black gooseberries become quite
dark, and they are hairy.

The way to differentiate gooseberries and
currants is to check the stems. Gooseberries
have spines and currants (next item) don't.

In the southern Rocky Mountain Trench
and at Waterton/Glacier there is another
gooseberry species: *R. inerme*. The stems are
less spiny than those of the other two.

### Skunk currant and sticky currant
*Gadellier glanduleux, gadellier collant*
*Ribes glandulosum* and *R. viscosissimum*
(currant/gooseberry family) Late May to early July
Montane and subalpine, found throughout
the Rockies but most common in Columbian
forest. Open, sparse shrubs up to about a metre
tall. Small bunches of white or pinkish/
greenish flowers are carried on a stalk.
Compare with gooseberry, previous item.

*Ribes viscosissimum*

Both these currants have a disagreeable
odor. Skunk currant is found mainly on the
western slope, and on the eastern slope from
the Bow River north; its odor is especially strong
when the plant is damaged. The fruits are dark
red, bristly and unpleasant-tasting. Sticky
currant grows in the Waterton/Glacier area. The
leaves are more pointed, in 5–7 lobes. The fruits
are blue-black and hairy, very sticky and
unpalatable. In the Mt. Robson Columbian-
forest area, look for *R. laxiflorum*, which has
reddish/purplish flowers and purplish-black,
hairy berries. Disagreeable odor and taste.

One genuinely tasty currant that grows in
the Rockies is *R. triste*, **red swamp currant.**
The berries are red and hairless, pleasant-
tasting when sweetened.

### Blueberry/bilberry/huckleberry/
### whortleberry *Airelle*
*Vaccinium* spp. (heath family) June and July
At all elevations, but mostly upper montane
and subalpine. Common on both slopes but
especially plentiful on the western side. Patch-
forming plants, sometimes blanketing open
valley bottoms and lower slopes. All species but
one have smooth stems and spring-green, finely
toothed leaves, often with yellow spotting. Small
white or pink bell-shaped flowers come in
clusters. The fruits are dark blue (except for

grouseberry, page 331), with a characteristic circular rim on the bottom. Look for berries about the middle of August; they are excellent raw or baked.

Discovering that all the common names above are applied mainly to one species (*V. caespitosum*), I thought I had broken the mystique of blueberry-group names. Then I found out that there were other species of blueberries and got mixed up all over again. Here is how to sort them out:

*V. caespitosum:* commonest species, 20–30 cm tall. The only one with reddish twigs. Prefers lightly wooded upper montane and subalpine slopes.

Vaccinium caespitosum

*V. membranaceum:* greenish twigs, leaves 2–5 cm long; tallest one on eastern slope, up to 150 cm, and with the largest berries (8–10 mm). Upper montane and subalpine, in open woods. Berries almost black when ripe.

*V. myrtilloides:* only one with velvety-looking hairy leaves and similarly hairy stems. Up to 40 cm tall; flowers greenish/pinkish rather than plain pink. Rocky Mountain Trench from Prince George south. Berries in clusters at the ends of branches.

*V. myrtillus:* dwarf subalpine and alpine species less than 30 cm tall, but producing berries 5–8 mm thick. Leaves only 1–2 cm long. Prefers open slopes.

*V. occidentale:* in bogs on the western slope, southern region; up to 30 cm tall, with yellowish-green stems; berries 4–5 mm across and very dark blue to black.

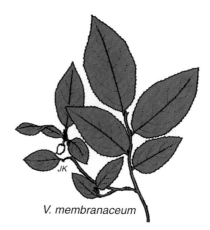

V. membranaceum

*V. ovalifolium:* in subalpine woods from Prince George south on the western slope, from the Bow River south on the eastern slope. Up to 150 cm tall (shorter on eastern slope), with rounded leaves. Berries have a bluish-whitish coating.

**See also** grouseberry, page 331, mountain cranberry, page 331, and small bog cranberry, page 335.

## Saskatoon/serviceberry/Juneberry
*Amélanchier à feuille d'aulne*
*Amelanchier alnifolia* (rose family)
Late May to early June (Jasper: May 18)

Montane, forming patches in dry clearings. Usually less than 1 m tall on the eastern slope, but frequently 2 m on the western slope. Purplish-brown twigs and gray branches. Leaves oval, lightly toothed, strongly veined; tend to fold upward along the centre. Flowers with five

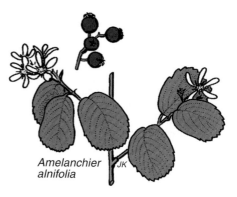

Amelanchier
alnifolia

well-separated white petals. Fruits appear in late July and August; they are round and purple when ripe, about 1 cm in size, with a characteristic mouth-like feature at the end. Bears stuff saskatoons into their own mouth-like features. Most humans prefer their saskatoons sweeter than they come naturally, in pies.

### Buckbrush/wolfberry/snowberry
*Symphorine de l'Ouest*
*Symphoricarpos occidentalis*
(honeysuckle family) July

A common montane shrub of dry, open areas, often bordering aspen and poplar groves. Usually knee-high, but can get taller. Thick leaves are 3–7 cm long, rather hairy beneath, oval and wavy or toothy, growing opposite one another on the grayish-brown stems, each pair set at 90° to the ones above and below, a common arrangement but especially visible on this plant. Small, funnel-shaped flowers are pinkish-white, blooming in clusters at points where the leaves attach to the stems. Greenish berries darken with age; not tasty. Note the other snowberry, next item, which has white berries.

### Snowberry *Symphorine commune*
*Symphoricarpos albus* (honeysuckle family)
Late June to early August

Knee-high montane shrub of dry hillsides, often growing with saskatoon. Most easily recognizable by the snow-white berries, which are about 5 mm thick and round, with a brown dot on the bottom. They are bitter and possibly poisonous. Leaves are oval, 2–3 cm long, pale and hairy beneath. Small, bell-shaped white flowers with a bit of pink, blooming in small clusters. The stamens don't stick out from the bell, as they do in *S. occidentalis,* previous item.

### Spreading dogbane
*Apocyn à feuilles d'Androsème/herbe à la puce*
*Apocynum androsaemifolium*
(dogbane family) July

Dry montane hillsides, often with saskatoon and snowberry. Knee-high or lower. Leaves are in pairs; dark glossy green on top and pale below, prominently veined, drooping like those of poison ivy. Clusters of pretty white bell-shaped flowers with pink tips; long seed pods later. Broken stems or torn leaves exude milky sap. Some people experience a poison-ivy-like reaction to this plant.

*Symphoricarpos occidentalis*

*Symphoricarpos albus*

*Apocynum androsaemifolium*

## Poison ivy
*Herbe à la puce/sumac vénéneux*
*Rhus radicans* (sumac family) June and July

Rare in the Rockies, but it does occur here, at low elevations in the Rocky Mountain Trench from Radium south. Occasionally poison ivy is reported from the eastern slope, in southern Glacier National Park; there are a few records in Waterton.

Leaflets in threes, each 10–15 cm long, glossy, drooping, dark green, heavily veined with wavy edges. Stems are reddish at junctions. Enough information to identify without touching? A maddening rash follows the slightest contact if you are sensitive, and most people are. Clusters of small yellowish-green flowers; photogenic white berries against red leaves in the fall. Never burn poison ivy; the smoke is dangerous to breathe.

*Rhus radicans*

## Bracted honeysuckle/black twinberry
*Chèvrefeuille à involucres*
*Lonicera involucrata* (honeysuckle family)
Late May to early July (Jasper: June 17)

Upper montane and subalpine, usually in aspen woods along streamcourses. Waist-high at low elevations; shorter near treeline. Nondescript-looking, with dull green wavy-edged leaves, but easily recognizable when in bloom or bearing fruit. The small flowers are yellow, in twos. Dark-purple berries arrive in mid-June, very popular with bears but rather bitter for humans. Berries form in twos, held in a pair of large red or purplish bracts (modified leaves) that curve back.

*Lonicera involucrata*

## Red twinberry/Utah honeysuckle
*Chèvrefeuille rouge*
*Lonicera utahensis* (honeysuckle family)
Late May to mid-July

Lower subalpine, from Crowsnest Pass south on the eastern slope and farther north on the western slope. Resembles bracted honeysuckle, previous item, but is usually shorter and with smaller leaves that are rounder. Similar yellow flowers; the fruit, though, is red rather than purple, and hangs in twos without the bright bracts typical of *L. involucrata*.

*Lonicera utahensis*

## Twining honeysuckle and orange honeysuckle
*Chèvrefeuille dioïque, chèvrefeuille orange*
*Lonicera dioica* and *Lonicera ciliosa*
(honeysuckle family) Early June to early July

Twining honeysuckle is common in Columbian forest, fairly common on the eastern slope, occasional in the Waterton area, strangely not reported in nearby Glacier. Messy-looking clusters of showy yellow or orange trumpet-shaped flowers darken just before they fall. Very fragrant, sweet smell; popular with hummingbirds. The leaves immediately below the flowers fuse into a cup-like shape that holds a cluster of red berries—not just a pair, as in bracted honeysuckle, which has very dark berries.

Orange honeysuckle is a high-climbing vine that resembles twining honeysuckle, but is limited to Columbian forest. It has a chalky coating on the leaves, orange flowers and orange berries.

## Squashberry/mooseberry/low-bush cranberry
*Baise d'orignal/viorne comestible*
*Viburnum edule* (honeysuckle family)
Late May and June (Jasper: June 8)

Montane and lower subalpine, common everywhere except in the southern foothills and the Waterton/Glacier area, where it is scarce. Prefers open spots in damp woods. Looks very much like pembina, page 272, but is shorter, often under a metre. Large glossy-green three-lobed leaves with toothed margins turn brilliantly red in the fall. Blooms in clusters of small star-shaped white flowers. Berries are red with a large flat seed in each.

## White spirea/white meadowsweet
*Spirée blanche*
*Spiraea betulifolia* (rose family)
Late June to early August

Montane, bordering woods. Up to 1 m tall, usually shorter. Gardeners recognize this plant immediately by its showy clusters of tiny white blooms, similar to the domestic bridal-wreath spirea. Leaves are distinctive: plain oval shape, but growing more deeply toothed toward the tip. Stems are smooth and reddish, with flowerheads atop them rather like red osier dogwood (page 269), which can be differentiated by the smooth-edged leaves. There is also a pink-flowering form—**pink spirea,**

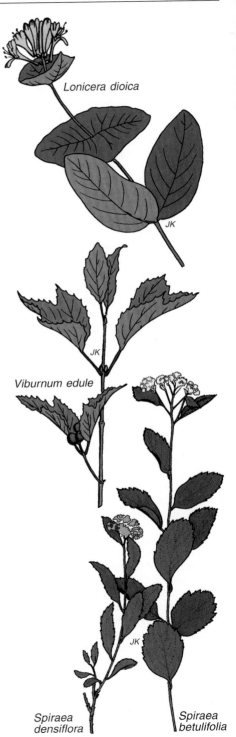

*Lonicera dioica*

*Viburnum edule*

*Spiraea densiflora*    *Spiraea betulifolia*

*S. densiflora*—which is similar but subalpine and found mainly south of Crowsnest Pass. Spirea produces seedpods rather than berries.

### Mock orange/syringa *Fausse-orange*

*Philadelphus lewisii* (hydrangea family)  July

Occasional in the Rocky Mountain Trench south of Elko and on the eastern slope from Crowsnest Pass south. Up to 2 m tall, but usually much shorter. Large, four-petalled white flowers in small clusters at stem-ends. Light-green leaves 2–5 cm long, each with three prominent veins and scalloped edges. Compare with Rocky Mountain rhododendron, next item.

*Philadelphus lewisii*

### Rocky Mountain rhododendron/white rhododendron

*Rhododendron à fleurs blanches*

*Rhododendron albiflorum* (heath family)

Early July to mid-August (Jasper: July 15)

Very common in damp Columbian-forest clearings, where it reaches 2 m in height; occasional and half that height elsewhere, in upper montane and subalpine areas. Broad white five-petalled flowers are cup-shaped and 2–3 cm across, in floppy clusters of two or three along the stem. The flowers drop off whole. Leaves are narrow and oblong, rather diamond-shaped, spring-green and glossy. Compare with menziesia, next item, which grows in the same places.

*Rhododendron albiflorum*

### Menziesia/false azalea/false huckleberry *Menziézie ferrugineuse*

*Menziesia ferruginea* (heath family)

Late May to early July (Jasper: June 15)

Pronounced "men-ZEE-see-uh" or "men-ZAY-see-uh." A common subalpine species in moist forest, also found at much lower elevations in Columbian-forest areas. Blueberry-like leaves, but slightly hairy, with rather irregular margins and sunken veins. The leaves form fan-shaped clusters. The bark is brown and shreddy. The flowers are small peach-pink bells (no white on them) in drooping, long-stemmed clusters; they have a sharp, rather skunky smell, pungent when a large patch is blooming. No berries; seeds are enclosed in dry capsules. When not in bloom, menziesia strongly resembles Rocky Mountain rhododendron (previous item), but menziesia leaves are not glossy and often are stained red at the tips by disease.

*Menziesia ferruginea*

## Mountain-lover/false box/myrtle boxwood *Pachistime*

*Pachistima myrsinites* (bittersweet family)
May and June

 Southern montane, mostly western slope but also eastern slope from Crowsnest Pass south. An evergreen shrub 20–60 cm high, growing in the woods. Thick, bright-green leathery leaves are opposite, oval and toothy, 1–3 cm long on squared, ridged stems. Small reddish/greenish four-petalled flowers bloom along the branches.

## Prickly juniper/common juniper and creeping juniper *Genévrier commun, genévrier horizontal/Savinier*

*Juniperus communis* and *J. horizontalis* (cypress family) Pollen late May to early June

 Very common, easily recognized montane and lower subalpine shrubs. **Prickly juniper** grows up to a metre tall in roughly circular knee-high patches, the branches drooping outward from the centre, while **creeping juniper** lies on the ground in irregular patches. The two species are not supposed to interbreed, but I have often seen specimens with intermediate characteristics.

 Both species have needle-like leaves that are prickly in prickly juniper and scaly in creeping juniper, both with the distinctive juniper odor. Brushing against prickly juniper in early June produces yellow smoke: pollen from the inconspicuous brown flowers. The berries are green in their first summer and blue or purple when mature in their second summer. They are very bitter—the original flavoring used in gin—but in spite of that I have seen squirrels eating them. Grouse like them as well, and Bohemian waxwings need them for winter survival.

 Brown-needled, sickly looking prickly juniper is probably afflicted with a rust of the genus *Gymnosporangium*, an internal fungus. It becomes visible in very wet weather, when it produces striking flame-like, yellowish-orange fruiting bodies along the stems. The fruiting bodies last only overnight, and they don't seem to be produced every year. See also page 426.

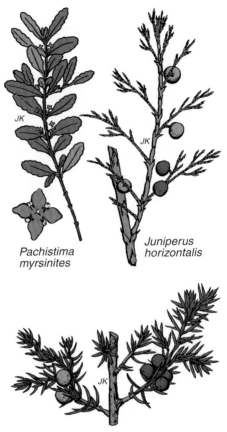

*Pachistima myrsinites*

*Juniperus horizontalis*

*Juniperus communis*

*The fruiting bodies of* Gymnosporangium *on common juniper*

## Kruppelholz spruce and fir

**Kruppelholz** ("KRUPPEL-holts") means "crippled wood" in German. The name fits perfectly the scrubby, shrub-like patches of evergreens that mark treeline. Not shrubs at all, these are trees stunted in their extreme environment to knee-high size. Any part that grows tall enough to poke up above the protective winter snow is likely to die, so the foliage thickens below. Thus, patches of kruppelholz indicate places in which the snow tends to accumulate.

**Krummholz** is a term often improperly applied to kruppelholz. I used the wrong word for many years, until treeline ecologist Kevin Timoney straightened me out. Krummholz means "crooked wood" in German, and it refers to trees that grow stunted and bent for genetic reasons, not because of their environment. Perhaps the lodgepole pines in the Valley of the Crooked Trees near Jasper (see page 254) could be called krummholz, if their affliction is actually genetic, but the typical high-country tree-mats of the Canadian Rockies are kruppelholz, not krummholz.

The two tree species that commonly produce kruppelholz in the Canadian Rockies are subalpine fir *(Abies lasiocarpa),* with flat needles and smooth gray bark, page 258, and Engelmann spruce *(Picea engelmannii),* with square, prickly needles and rough brown bark, page 256.

Sometimes there will be the odd whitebark pine *(Pinus albicaulis),* with needles in bunches of five and squat cones, page 256, or in southern areas limber pine *(Pinus flexilis),* similar to whitebark pine but with longer cones, page 256.

Some kruppelholz trees have two parts: a dense, sprawling lower part and a more normal-looking upper part. Between the two, the trunk is usually bare on the side facing the prevailing wind. Such trees, called **flag trees,** have been able to grow higher than their protective snow cover would ordinarily allow. The bare zone on the trunk marks the height at which cold, abrasive ice crystals blow across the snow surface, killing branches that would otherwise grow there. Higher up, perhaps half a metre above the top of the snowpack, the foliage of a flag tree assumes the normal-looking conical spruce or fir form.

So how does a flag tree manage to grow through that deadly blowing-snow zone? The tree tries to send a new leader—a new tip—upward each summer. In most winters the leader dies, but a string of winters with deeper snow than usual, or lighter winds and warmer temperatures, can allow the leader to survive and push upward into the safe zone above.

**Flagged trees can also be seen beside highways in deep-snow areas,** where the plows throw snow at them. The short branches face the flow of traffic, so the trees standing on one side of the road are flagged oppositely from those standing on the other side of the road.

Like the alpine meadowland, kruppelholz has a fragile beauty that is easily destroyed. When walking at treeline, I try to go around the dense kruppelholz patches rather than thrashing through them, for a small branch might have taken fifty years to grow. Even the dead branches have a job here: to protect the living wood from the bitter alpine gales.

# Wildflowers below treeline
## If you can't find it here, try the alpine wildflowers or the shrubs

Wildflowers may be **annual** (grow from seed, bloom, set seed and die, all in the same year), **biennial** (grow from seed in the first summer, die back to the roots, then grow, bloom, set seed and die the next summer) or **perennial** (live year after year, regrowing from roots each summer). This is indicated for each species listed. Individuals of some species can be annual *or* biennial, or some other combination, as noted.

Since the publication of the first edition of this book in 1986 I have collected up to seven years of blooming-date information for wildflowers common at Jasper, which is located roughly in the centre of the Canadian Rockies, both north/south and east/west. Thus, for species with fairly consistent blooming periods I have given the date of onset.

## White wildflowers below treeline

Or cream-colored, or champagne ivory, or bleached-poodle blonde.

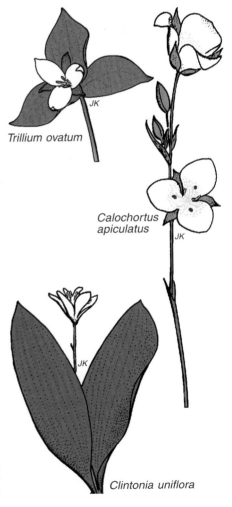

Trillium ovatum

Calochortus apiculatus

Clintonia uniflora

### Trillium/wake-robin
*Trille blanc de l'Ouest*
*Trillium ovatum* (lily family)
Mid-April to late May, perennial

Western-slope montane and subalpine, from Radium south, in moist, shady places. Has been reported from eastern-slope Waterton/Glacier. A large flower with three narrow white petals, going pinkish or purplish with age, offset against three green sepals underneath. Three broad leaves, 10–15 cm long.

### White mariposa lily/sego lily
*Lis de mariposa*
*Calochortus apiculatus* (lily family)
Late June to early July, perennial

Western-slope montane south of Radium, eastern-slope montane from Crowsnest Pass south. Prefers dry, open slopes. Very showy three-petalled flower; white or yellowish, more yellow toward the centre. The long, thin leaves grow only at the base. Like other large-flowered lilies, it makes a big three-sided seed capsule after blooming. Unlike the others, the mariposa capsule hangs down.

There is a pale-purple mariposa lily in the southern Rocky Mountain Trench. See page 341.

### One-flowered clintonia/queen's-cup/beadlily *Clintonie uniflore*
*Clintonia uniflora* (lily family)
Early June to mid-July, perennial

Western-slope montane and lower subalpine shady forest. Most common in Columbian forest; on the eastern slope mainly from Crowsnest Pass south.. A low plant, usually about 10 cm high, with two to four glossy green leaves at the base. The flower is reminiscent of Easter lily but smaller, in six parts with long yellow anthers. Has perhaps the most beautiful fruit in the mountains: a single bead-like bright-blue berry, not edible, atop the stem.

### Wild lily-of-the-valley
*Maïanthème du Canada/faux-muguet*
*Maianthemum canadense* (lily family)
Mid-June, perennial

Western-slope montane and Columbian forest, from Valemount north. Tiny white flowers in a single spike above two heart-shaped leaves, the whole plant 10–20 cm tall. Red berries are possibly noxious. This is a boreal woodland plant, uncommon in the mountains but easily identified. See it along the Kinney Lake Trail in Mount Robson Provincial Park.

UWP

*Maianthemum canadense*

### Star-flowered Solomon's-seal/ "western" Solomon's-seal and three-leaved Solomon's-seal
*Smilacine étoilée, smilacine trifoliée*
*Smilacina stellata* and *S. trifolia* (lily family)
Mid-May to mid-June, perennial
(Jasper: highly variable, April 20 to May 30)

Montane and subalpine, mostly on wooded north-facing slopes. *S. stellata* stands 20–40 cm tall. Seven or so smooth, spring-green pointed leaves angle upward off the stem. A few delicate snowy white six-petalled flowers are carried near the top. Fruit is an inedible striped green berry that becomes red, then black. Three-leaved Solomon's-seal (*S. trifolia*) is similar, but has only three leaves.

Confusing names department: true Solomon's-seal belongs in the genus *Polygonatum,* which resembles *Smilacina* but grows in eastern North America and not here. So the Canadian Rockies version is false. But we also have our own false Solomon's seal, *S. racemosa* (next item), which is a close relative of *S. stellata,* the one that many people think to be true Solomon's seal but really isn't. I suppose we could call *S. stellata* "false Solomon's seal" and *S. racemosa* "false-false Solomon's seal," but teachers of logic tell us that something that is false-false is true. Which in this case is false, if you see what I mean.

Clear as mud. Try this. I have taken to using "western Solomon's-seal" for both the *Smilacina*s and "eastern Solomon's seal" for *Polygonatum,* calling the false-false version (*S. racemosa*) by its commonest common name, just "false Solomon's-seal."

JK

*Smilacina
stellata*

*Smilacina
racemosa*

Incidentally, Solomon's seal itself is a star symbol with six interlocking points, thought to ward off disease. It does not ward off lexicological confusion.

### False Solomon's seal
*Smilacine à grappes*
*Smilacina racemosa* (lily family)
Late May to mid-June, perennial

Moist montane woods. The largest of the three *Smilacina*s, up to 60 cm tall, and the showiest, with puffy clusters of small fragrant white flowers. The leaves have wavy edges rather than straight ones, as in *S. stellata* (previous item). Berries with dark spots on them. This plant is sometimes confused with false hellebore, page 311, which is taller—up to 2 m—with straight-edged leaves and cascades of green flowers. False hellebore is more common at higher elevations.

### White camas/death camas/smooth camas *Zygadène élégant*
*Zygadenus elegans* (lily family)
Mid-June to mid-August, perennial
(Jasper: June 25)

A common montane plant throughout the Canadian Rockies, 20–30 cm tall, preferring open areas or light woods at lower elevations. Sometimes found much higher, growing in dwarf form above treeline. Long, narrow, pale-green leaves rise gracefully from the base. The flowers are creamy or greenish, carried on a loose spike above the leaves.

As indicated by one of its common names, this plant is very toxic.

### Death camas *Zygadène vènèneux*
*Zygadenus venenosus* (lily family)
Late May to mid-July, perennial

Common from the Bow River south, less common on the western slope, in montane meadows. Resembles white camas, previous item, but is shorter, with greener leaves and smaller flowers in a tighter head. Death camas is appropriately named; the bulb is quite poisonous. See also beargrass, page 302.

### Fairy bells *Dispore à fruit velu*
*Disporum trachycarpum* (lily family)
Late May to mid-June, perennial
(Jasper: May 25)

Fairly common, growing knee-high in montane aspen woods; fading out north of Grande Cache. Drooping white flowers,

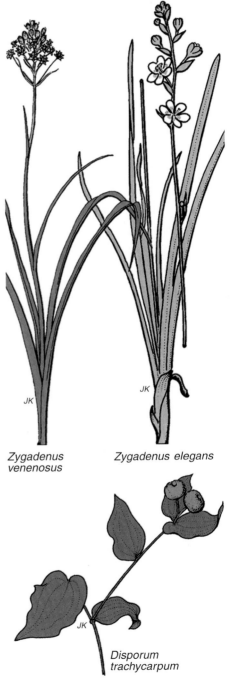

JK

JK

*Zygadenus venenosus*

*Zygadenus elegans*

JK

*Disporum trachycarpum*

sometimes tinged yellow or green, in groups of one to four at the ends of stems. The flowers are bell-shaped at first but soon split into separate petals and wilt, becoming ragged-looking. The large reddish-orange lumpy berries grow in twos; they are velvety looking and sweet-tasting but contain large seeds. Slightly zig-zagging stems and wavy-edged leaves resemble those of twisted-stalk, page 310.

Clematis
ligusticifolia

Claytonia
lanceolata

Geranium
richardsonii

### Western clematis/traveller's joy
*Clématite de l'Ouest*
*Clematis ligusticifolia* (buttercup family)
July, perennial

Southern montane, not common, usually in thickets. A woody vine—a shrub, in other words—that likes to grow on other shrubs. Leaflets are lance-shaped, often notched, always toothy. Showy white flowers with four sepals and long, spread-out centre parts. See also blue clematis, page 341.

### Western spring beauty
*Claytonie lancéolée*
*Claytonia lanceolata* (purslane family)
Late April to late June, perennial

Montane to alpine, in meadows, open woods and even scree slopes well above treeline. Common in southern areas. Grows 10–20 cm tall, with two broad leaves partway up the stem. One or more white or pale-pink flowers about 1 cm across, with pink or purplish lines. Can bloom very early at low elevations. There is a strictly alpine version, page 357.

### Star-flower *Trientale d'Europe*
*Trientalis europaea* (primrose family)
Early June to mid-July, perennial

Western-slope montane and lower subalpine woods, near water. A striking little plant, known in Alberta only from one location near Jasper. Small white flowers with five to seven petals (usually six) above a whorl of dark-green leaves partway up the stem. No picture.

### Wild white geranium
*Géranium de Richardson*
*Geranium richardsonii* (geranium family)
Late May to early July, perennial

Montane woods, common in the southern region but less so farther north. Grows up to a metre high; usually about 50 cm. Easily recognized as a geranium by the deeply divided, lightly hairy leaves. Showy white or pale-pink flowers with pink to purple lines in them that probably guide bees to the nectar. See also the pink/purple geraniums, page 345.

### Sweet-flowered androsace/rock-jasmine *Androsace des rochers*
*Androsace chamaejasme* (primrose family)
Mid-May to early July, perennial
(Jasper: June 10)

Montane and higher, in open places. One of those striking little flowers that makes you say, "Awww ..." Straight, warty stems that reach up about 5 cm from a tuft of small overlapping leaves. A fragrant cluster of several small white flowers—1 cm or less—tops each stem. Each flower has a hole in the centre with a yellow rim. Compare with fairy candelabra, next item.

*Androsace chamaejasme*

### Fairy candelabra/pygmy flower *Androsace septentrional*
*Androsace septentrionalis* (primrose family)
Late April to early June, annual (Jasper: May 1)

Tiny, delicate montane plant that prefers open, rocky locations and blooms early. Rosette of narrow basal leaves. Straight wire-thin reddish stems reach up 5–20 cm, dividing near the top; each one carries a tiny white flower at the end.

This plant shows a lot of variation, which seems to depend upon the blooming time. In April the stems are short, sometimes un-branched, and bear very small flowers. Plants blooming later in the season, in June, have longer stems and the flowers are somewhat larger. Differentiate from *A. chamaejasme* (previous item) by the branching in fairy candelabra and its single flower at the end of each thin stem.

### Rock cress *Arabette*
*Arabis* spp. (mustard family)
Late April through July, biennial or perennial

Montane to subalpine, in grassy meadows and rocky places. Eleven species in the Canadian Rockies, difficult to distinguish from one another. Each has a tuft of short, lance-shaped basal leaves; the stem is 10–20 cm tall, usually hairy and clasped by small leaves. The four-pet-alled flowers are on short stalks at the top and vary from cream or pale pink to pale purple. Most species bloom early, in May or June.

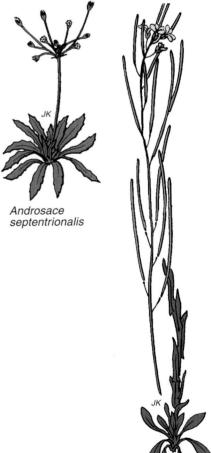

*Androsace septentrionalis*

*Arabis drummondii*

In July and August long, pod-like seed cases typical of the mustard family are carried erect in some species, drooping in others. Individual identification is tricky; the most common species in the Canadian Rockies is *A. drummondii*—yet another Rockies plant bearing the name of Thomas Drummond, page 692. It grows mainly in montane meadows, and individuals can be either biennial or perennial.

Like *Draba*, next item, *Arabis* can become infected by a **fungal rust.** The first tiny leaves to appear in spring are colored yellowish by the dot-like rust colonies. The diseased plants don't grow much and seldom bloom.

See also the alpine *Arabis* species, page 371.

### White draba/whitlow-grass
*Drave blanche*
*Draba* spp. (mustard family)
May to early June, mostly perennials

Mainly western-slope montane and the Waterton/Glacier area; less common elsewhere on the eastern slope. Most of the drabas are yellow, but a few are white. All are difficult to identify to the species level. General characteristics: four-petalled flowers, each petal in two lobes, carried in a small cluster atop a stem 10–20 cm long. Small basal tuft of little lance-shaped hairy leaves. Elliptical seedpods. See also rock cress, above, and *Smelkowskia,* page 359.

### Chickweed/starwort *Stellaire/céraiste*
*Stellaria* spp. and *Cerastium* spp. (pink family)
May to August, perennials—but see below

At all elevations, but when below treeline mostly montane in exposed places. See also the alpine species, page 357. More common south of the Peace River, especially in the Waterton/Glacier area. Look for the cleft petals, sometimes so deeply indented that they look like double petals.

*Stellaria* species in the Canadian Rockies have three styles (pointed female parts in the flowers), while *Cerastium* species have five. **Common chickweed,** *Stellaria media,* is an introduced species that is, yes, very common. Unlike the other chickweeds and starworts, it is an annual. See also mountain sandwort, page 360, and dwarf epilobium, page 338.

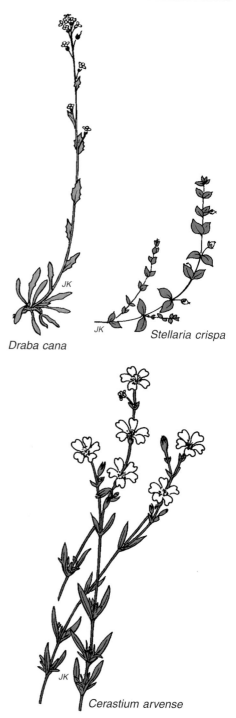

JK

JK    *Stellaria crispa*

*Draba cana*

JK

*Cerastium arvense*

### Fringe-cup
*Lithophragma à petites fleurs*
*Lithophragma parviflora* (saxifrage family)
Late April to early June, perennial

Western-slope montane, in open areas. Flowers resemble chickweed, but the petals are notched in threes rather than twos and the leaves are different: spreading, five-lobed and bluntly toothed rather than lance-shaped.

### Windflower *Anémone multifide*
*Anemone multifida* (buttercup family)
Late May to late June, perennial
(Jasper: May 21)

Common montane plant of dry meadows and open woods. Ankle-high, with a fuzzy stem and a fringe of fern-like leaves partway up the stem, which is capped by 1–3 flowers. Flower color quite variable; usually white, tinged with purple on the back. Sometimes purple on the front, too—or even red. Produces a dense, woolly ball of downy seeds. The seedhead opens for distribution by the wind.

Windflower resembles **Drummond's anemone** *(A. drummondii),* page 356, which lacks the fringe, produces a single flower, and is mostly alpine/subalpine rather than montane. See also alpine anemone, page 356.

### Prickly saxifrage/common saxifrage/ spotted saxifrage *Saxifrage épineuse*
*Saxifraga bronchialis* (saxifrage family)
July to early August, perennial
(Jasper: June 5, but variable)

Rocky places at all elevations. Wire-thin reddish stems growing 10–20 cm above a cushion of prickly needle-like leaves. The small white flowers are exquisite up close: each petal is marked with a pattern of tiny red and/ or yellow dots. See also three-point saxifrage, page 358.

### Leather-leaved saxifrage
*Leptarrhéna à feuilles de pyrole*
*Leptarrhena pyrolifolia* (saxifrage family)
July, perennial

Subalpine and alpine, along mossy stream banks. Numerous small white flowers clustered near the top of a hairless stem 10–20 cm tall. Shiny, broad, evergreen toothed leaves are clustered at the base, but there is usually one along the stem. Compare with western saxifrage, next page.

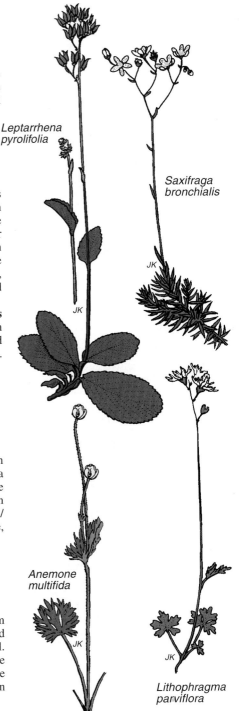

*Leptarrhena pyrolifolia*

*Saxifraga bronchialis*

*Anemone multifida*

*Lithophragma parviflora*

## Western saxifrage/false leather-leaved saxifrage *Saxifrage de l'Ouest*
*Saxifraga occidentalis* (saxifrage family)
Early May to mid-August, perennial
At all elevations, in nearly any habitat; most common saxifrage in southern sections. Closely resembles leather-leaved saxifrage (previous item), but has no leaf on the short-haired stem and is not evergreen. Flowers very early at low elevations, much later in the alpine zone.

## One-flowered wintergreen/single delight *Monésès à une fleur*
*Moneses uniflora* (wintergreen family)
Mid-July to early August, perennial
(Jasper: July 13)
A small plant, growing under evergreens in montane and subalpine forests. One nodding flower, waxy white with a green ovary in the middle surrounded by yellowish stamens. The rounded leaves are glossy green with finely toothed edges. Fragrance is like that of lily-of-the-valley, page 288.

## Grass-of-Parnassus *Parnassie*
*Parnassia* spp. (grass-of-Parnassus family)
July and August, perennial
Mostly subalpine, but also montane and sometimes above treeline. Grows in wet places. Looks rather like a straightened-up one-flowered wintergreen, with prominent ovary and stamens, but is not even in the same family. Glossy, round, basal leaves, plus one leaf low on the stem on *P. palustris* (lower elevations, beside streams; July to early August) and one leaf higher and smaller on *P. fimbriata* (**fringed grass-of-Parnassus,** the most common species, high-subalpine and alpine, late July to mid-August). The other species in the Rockies, *P. kotzebuei,* page 356, lacks the upper leaf.

## Moss phlox *Phlox de Hood/phlox mousse*
*Phlox hoodii* and *P. alyssifolia* (phlox family)
Late April to early June, perennials
Southern foothills and the Waterton/Glacier area, in dry, open places. Looks like an alpine cushion plant, and there is an alpine phlox of similar appearance (**white phlox,** *P. multiflora,* found farther south in the Wyoming and Colorado Rockies); however, moss phlox grows at low elevations. A cushion of prickly green leaves is dotted with showy white flowers, sometimes a bit pink or purple, with yellow centres; the petals are squared at

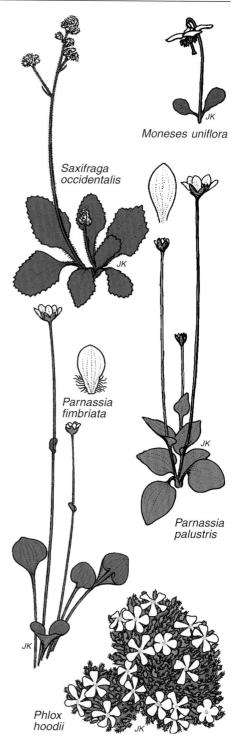

Moneses uniflora

Saxifraga occidentalis

Parnassia fimbriata

Parnassia palustris

Phlox hoodii

the ends. *P. alyssifolia* is very similar, but the leaves and flowers are a little bigger and often pink. It grows in similar locations and blooms slightly later; has been reported from Glacier but not from Waterton, although one was reported a kilometre northeast of the Waterton boundary. See also moss campion, page 368, and *Phlox diffusa*, page 369.

### Western Canada violet and kidney-shaped violet *Violette du Canada, violette réniforme*
*Viola canadensis, V. renifolia* (violet family)
Late May to mid-July, perennials

Montane woods, in shady places. Western Canada violet is the taller of the two, typically 10–30 cm, with large, wrinkled heart-shaped leaves at the base, becoming more oval higher up; indented veins and lumpy margins. Flowers are white or pale purple, with dark veining and yellow centres. Kidney-shaped violet is short stemmed and small-flowered, with kidney-shaped leaves. Upper montane to lower subalpine, aspen woods and mossy places, Kananaskis Country north, absent in Waterton. Both species bloom about the same time.

### Bunchberry/dwarf dogwood
*Quatre-temps*
*Cornus canadensis* (dogwood family)
Early June to late July, perennial
(Jasper: June 10)

Common in montane and subalpine evergreen woods, but less common on the eastern slope south of Crowsnest Pass. Often mistakenly identified as the provincial flower of British Columbia, but the official flower is the bloom of the dogwood *tree (C. nuttallii),* not the wildflower. Low-growing, usually in patches; leaves in a bilaterally symmetrical grouping of four or six. Distinctive bloom: four petal-like bracts turn from green to white, surrounding the tiny, greenish flowers that look like the central part of a single flower. Cluster of pretty red berries in August; bland taste.

### Wild strawberry *Fraisier de Virginie*
*Fragaria virginiana* (rose family)
Early May to late July, perennial
(Jasper: May 8)

Montane and lower subalpine, usually in dry open woods. Easily recognized by the three-parted toothy leaflets and the red stems running across the ground. Small but showy white

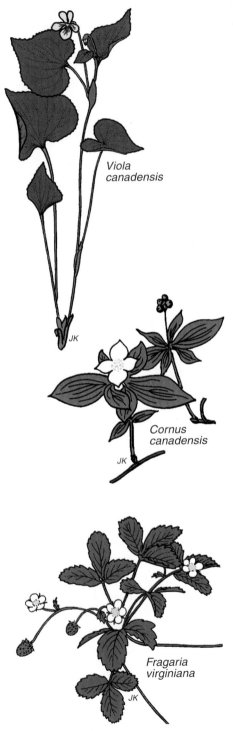

*Viola canadensis*

*Cornus canadensis*

*Fragaria virginiana*

flowers, yellow-centred; berries in July and August. All the flavor of a big grocery-store strawberry is concentrated in the wild version, which is about as big as the end of your little finger. Can be confused with trailing raspberry, next item. See also sibbaldia, page 366.

### Five-leaved bramble and trailing raspberry
*Framboisier rampant, ronce pubescente/ catherinettes*
*Rubus pedatus* and *R. pubescens* (rose family)
June and July, perennials

Montane and subalpine, mostly from Jasper park north but also reported from Lake Louise. Five-leaved bramble is a trailing vine, resembling strawberry but with leaflets in fives and thin dark woody stems. Produces a few large bright-red tasty raspberries in September.

In Columbian forest areas, you may see *Rubus pubescens,* another white-flowered, low-growing raspberry vine. This one has leaflets in threes, not fives; it's also a little taller, but with somewhat smaller flowers. Makes sour red raspberries.

*Rubus pedatus*

### Kinnikinnik/bearberry *Raisin d'ours*
*Arctostaphylos uva-ursi* (heath family)
Early May through July, perennial
(Jasper: May 1)

Common ground-covering shrub; grows best on dry, south-facing montane slopes. A mat of small, thick, glossy oval leaves on woody stems. Leaves are evergreen but may become purplish through the winter. Blooms in small inconspicuous white flowers that are urn-shaped, with out-turned pink lips. Berries are bright red, rather mealy and bland, but edible. Can be confused with mountain cranberry, page 331, which has pink flowers without lips, and twinflower, page 330, before it blooms.

Pronounced "KINNY-kin-ick" or "kin-ICK-kin-ick," Algonquin for "smoking mixture." The leaves were mixed with tobacco. The berries were an aboriginal staple food, pounded up with saskatoons, page 280, and animal fat to make **pemmican.** Kinnikinnik is a close relative of California's manzanita, *Arctostaphylos columbiana.* See also red bearberry, page 361.

*Arctostaphylos uva-ursi*

### White pussytoes/small-flowered everlasting *Patte de la chatte*

*Antennaria microphylla* (composite family)
June and July, perennial (Jasper: May 19)

Eastern-slope montane, in patches on dry slopes. The tight flowerhead is off-white and fuzzy; looks like the underside of a cat's paw. It takes a long time for the incipient, floppy flowerheads to firm up into the distinctive pussytoes look. The small leaves are pale green or gray, fuzzy, and spreading at the base. Compare with molecule plant, next item, and pearly everlasting, this page. There is also a red- or pink-flowered *Antennaria,* page 332.

### Few-flowered everlasting/racemose pussytoes *Antennaire à grappes*

*Antennaria racemosa* (composite family)
Mid-May to early July, perennial
(Jasper: May 20)

Montane and subalpine woods; 10–30 cm tall. Up to a dozen ball-like white flowerheads are arranged on bare stems; reminds me of a molecular model. The leaves are mostly basal, green and glossy on the top, gray and felty underneath, broadly lance-shaped, not toothed.

### Pearly everlasting *Immortelle*

*Anaphalis margaritacea* (composite family)
Early July to early August, perennial

Montane and lower subalpine, in moist meadows. More common on the western slope. Resembles pussytoes and few-flowered everlasting, previous entries, but is larger, standing up to 60 cm tall, with bigger, more-expanded heads of round, ball-like flowers. Leaves felty and green on top, furry underneath. "Everlasting" refers to the longevity of cut flowers in this genus. Many *Antennaria*s are also called "everlasting," and for the same reason, but none looks quite like *Anaphalis margaritacea.*

### Coltsfoot, white lettuce and brickellia *Pétasite, prenanthe, brickellie*

*Petasites, Prenanthes* and *Brickellia* spp. (composite family)
Late April to early May, perennials

Damp places at low elevations—or sometimes alpine. Coltsfoot has two personalities. The tufted flower-bearing stem comes out of the ground earlier than the large leaves, which come up next to the stem but do not appear to be joined. The small leaves on the flower stem bear no resemblance to the large, notched or deeply cleft leaves of the rest of the plant. It's

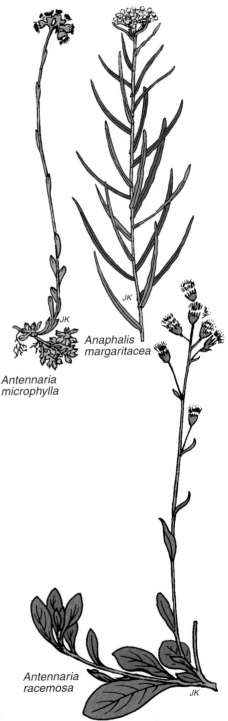

*Anaphalis margaritacea*

*Antennaria microphylla*

*Antennaria racemosa*

easy to think you're looking at two different plants. The blooms have no disk flowers; they form conspicuous white tufts as the ray flowers expand.

Broad, deeply lobed leaves are of *Petasites palmatus,* known previously as *P. frigidus. Petasites palmatus* also grows in the alpine zone. Toothy, woolly leaves are of *Petasites nivalis,* known previously as *P. hyperboreus.* These species both grow 15–20 cm high and bloom very early—often before the leaves are out. Very fragrant. Along the eastern slope the species is mostly *P. palmatus.*

Another type, **arrowleaf coltsfoot** *(Petasites sagittatus),* has toothed but not notched leaves. It grows in wet meadows and marshes, such as the lovely wetlands at the head of Moose Lake along Highway 16 in Mount Robson Provincial Park. Look for the striking cottony seedheads among the sedges.

In the Waterton/Glacier area there is a similar-looking plant called **white lettuce** *(Prenanthes sagittata)* that has smaller leaves 2–3 cm long. And, just to confuse things thoroughly in that part of the mountains, there is yet another, called *Brickellia grandiflora,* that can be distinguished by arrow-shaped leaves that are toothy at the base and smooth toward the tip. Yellowish flowers. This species avoids the damp sites favored by coltsfoot and white lettuce.

## Wild sweet pea/vetchling
*Gesse jaunâtre*
*Lathyrus ochroleucus* (pea family)
Late May to July, perennial (Jasper: June 1)

A montane vine, often found in aspen woods or in thickets. The most pea-like pea, with tendrils at ends of stems and edible peapods. Smooth oval leaflets 2–3 cm long. Cream-colored to pale-yellow flowers in clusters of a few. Compare with milk-vetch, next item.

## Milk-vetch *Astragale*
*Astragalus* spp. (pea family)
Late May to mid-June, perennials
(Jasper: May 24)

Southern and central montane. Showy white or yellowish-white blooms, sometimes with a line of pink or purple along the back. Small leaflets are very narrow and set along the stem like sawteeth (typical vetch arrangement). Pea-family members, the vetches produce small

Petasites
sagittatus

Brickellia
grandiflora

Astragalus
americanus

Lathyrus
ochroleucus

pods. There are many species, difficult to differentiate; *A. americanus* is a common one. Compare with wild sweet pea, previous item.

### White clover/Dutch clover
*Trèfle rampant/trèfle blanc*
*Trifolium repens* (pea family)
Late June to early August, perennial

Montane and lower subalpine. Most common form of clover, an introduced species. Grows in low patches in meadows, lawns, roadsides and grassy places everywhere. Familiar-looking clover-type leaflets in threes—sometimes fours, of course—and honey-fragrant white or pinkish ball-shaped flowerheads, popular with bees.

### White sweet clover
*Mélilot blanc/trèfle d'odeur*
*Melilotus alba* (pea family)
Late June and July, annual or biennial

Montane, usually on disturbed land such as roadsides, where it has been seeded. Can grow to 2 m high, but usually a metre or less in the Rockies. Bushy plant with curving stems; toothy leaflets in threes; small white strongly scented flowers in cylindrical clusters. See yellow sweet clover, page 326, for picture.

### Sundew *Rossolis*
*Drosera* spp. (sundew family)
Mid-June to mid-July, perennial

Strange little montane/Columbian-forest plants of wet, mossy streambanks and bogs. Absent at Waterton but present in western Glacier. Reddish rosette of sticky, hairy leaves attracts and holds insects; a leaf folds in and the plant digests the bugs. Tiny white flowers bloom at the top of a bare 15–cm stem growing up from the centre. **Round-leaved sundew** (*D. rotundifolia,* round leaves) is found on both slopes. Two long-leaved species (*D. anglica,* leaves 1–3 cm long and 3–4 mm wide, and *D. linearis,* with longer, even narrower leaves) are mainly western-slope. Other insectivorous plants in the Canadian Rockies: butterwort, page 348, and bladderwort, page 376.

### Ghost flower *Monotrope uniflore*
*Monotropa uniflora* (ghost-flower family)
Mid-July, perennial

Shady places in moist montane woods. Never common, absent at Waterton but known from Glacier. Instantly recognizable, this dead-

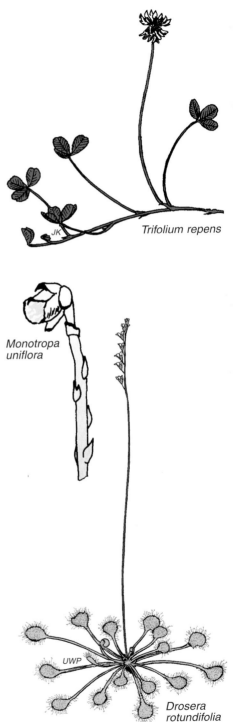

*Trifolium repens*

*Monotropa uniflora*

*Drosera rotundifolia*

white plant has no chlorophyll; it is a saprophyte, rooting in decaying matter. But it is also a proper flowering plant, not a fungus. See also clustered broomrape, page 326.

### Sparrow's-egg orchid/Franklin's lady's-slipper/northern lady's-slipper
*Sabot-de-la-vierge-des-oiseaux*
*Cypripedium passerinum* (orchid family)
Mid-July, perennial (Jasper: June 10)

Western-slope montane and Columbian forest, occasionally eastern-slope montane north of the Bow River, in shady protected places. Grows 15–30 cm tall, usually in small groups. Finely hairy stem and leaves; pure-white egg-like flower partly covered with green sepals. Look for purple dots inside. Compare with mountain lady's-slipper, next item.

### Mountain lady's-slipper
*Cypripède des montagnes*
*Cypripedium montanum* (orchid family)
July, perennial

Western-slope montane, at low elevations in damp places; uncommon. Found at somewhat higher elevations in Yoho. On the eastern slope found only in Waterton/Glacier. A tall orchid, up to 50 cm; leaves broader and fewer than sparrow's-egg. Closely resembles the yellow lady's-slipper, page 314, but is white rather than yellow, although it has a yellow tongue.

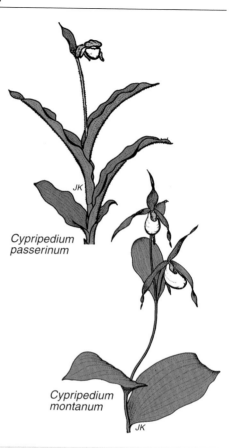

*Cypripedium passerinum*

*Cypripedium montanum*

## Gee, that would look nice on the picnic table ...

Picking wildflowers is an absolute no-no. Wildflowers are protected by law throughout the Canadian Rockies, and for a very good reason: experience has shown that even light picking of some species can wipe them out. Plants must maintain an adequate density of individuals for successful fertilization and maintenance of ongoing generations, and the rarer ones are often right on the threshold of survival. Why should we destroy anything lovely and natural simply because we wish to possess it? When identifying wildflowers, I bring my eye down to the flower, not the flower up to my eye.

*Detail of* Habenaria orbiculata, *an uncommon orchid—not in a vase*

## Bog orchids/rein orchids
*Habénaires*
*Platanthera/Habenaria* spp. (orchid family)
June and July, perennials

Damp places in montane meadows and woods. Seven species, all with the same general form: a spike 20–70 cm high of many small white or greenish flowers. Long leaves grow up from the base; sometimes there are a few on the stem. Called "rein orchids" because the lip—the petal that hangs down in the centre—is narrow and strap-like.

The genus name *Habenaria* has long been used in North America for these plants, but *Platanthera* is now replacing *Habenaria*.

**Tall white bog orchid/white rein orchid** *(H. dilitata)* has the whitest flowers. Perhaps the most common species; delicious fragrance of vanilla.

**Northern green bog orchid** *(H. hyperborea)* is another common one. Also the tallest one, up to 70 cm, with brown stamens in the flower and two small yellow anthers.

**Blunt-leaved bog orchid** *(H. obtusata)* is small, with a single broad leaf, sometimes two.

**Bracted bog orchid** *(H. viridis bracteata)* has long bracts under the greenish flowers. Also known as *Coeloglossum viride*.

**Alaska bog orchid/slender-spired bog orchid** *(H. unalascensis)* is unusual because it blooms in dry places. Scale-like bracts up the stem; greenish flowers sometimes marked with purple.

**Round-leaved orchid** *(H. orbiculata)* is a large orchid, up to 60 cm tall, with two or three large, patterned leaves lying flat on the ground. See also *Goodyera oblongifolia*, drawing on this page, description on next page.

## Hooded ladies'-tresses
*Spiranthe de Romanzoff*
*Spiranthes romanzoffiana* (orchid family)
July and August, perennial

By running water or in bogs, montane and lower subalpine forest. Tell it from the bog orchids by the larger, somewhat showier flowers, always white, not greenish, and by their spiral arrangement on the flower spike. Sweet-scented.

### Rattlesnake plantain
*Goodyérie à feuilles oblongues*
*Goodyera oblongifolia* (orchid family)
August, perennial (drawing on previous page)

Montane, southern area. Unlike most orchids, this one prefers fairly dry locations in coniferous woods. Spike of greenish-white flowers. Easily recognized by the leaves, which are basal, broadly lance-shaped, with a distinctive white pattern against the dark-green surface that resembles rattlesnake markings. Compare with round-leaved orchid in the previous bog-orchid listings. Another white-on-green pattern is found on freshly emerged leaves of toadflax, page 308.

### Northern coral-root orchid/pale coral-root orchid *Corallorhize trifide*
*Corallorhiza trifida* (orchid family)
May and June, perennial

Damp places, montane woods. The most distinctive feature is the lack of leaves: the plant is a saprophyte. It roots in dead material, symbiotically sharing its substrate with fungi that further break the food down, releasing nutrients. The stubby roots look rather like branched coral; hence the name. The flowers are a combination of yellow, green and white. See also clustered broom-rape, page 326.

### False asphodel *Tofieldie glutineuse*
*Tofieldia glutinosa* (lily family)
July, perennial

Northern montane, at edges of bogs and ponds. Rare south of the Bow River. Tuft of tiny white flowers, sometimes greenish or yellowish, atop a green stem 10–40 cm tall. Warty glands roughen the stem and make it sticky. Narrow leaves reach up from the base about half the length of the stem.

**Dwarf false asphodel** (*T. pusilla*) grows in wet upper subalpine and alpine areas in the northern Rockies. It is shorter, under 25 cm tall, with shorter, broader leaves that form a basal tuft. See also bistort, page 360.

### Beargrass *Xérophylle*
*Xerophyllum tenax* (lily family)
Late May to mid-July, perennial

South of Crowsnest Pass only, in open woods and meadows at subalpine and low alpine elevations, but sometimes much lower. Very long 40–50 cm olive-colored grass-like leaves reach up from the base; shorter leaves clasp the stem, which can be up to a metre tall. Large,

*Corallorhiza trifida*

*Tofieldia glutinosa*

*Xerophyllum tenax*

easily recognized bloom: a dense, club-shaped tuft of tiny white flowers that trail down the stem. Often the lower part of the club is in bloom before the upper part has opened. A big patch of beargrass looks for all the world like a grassy meadow, but in fact it is a field of lilies. The plant blooms roughly three times in ten years, and like arnica (page 317) most of the plants in a particular location bloom at the same time. See also death camas, page 289.

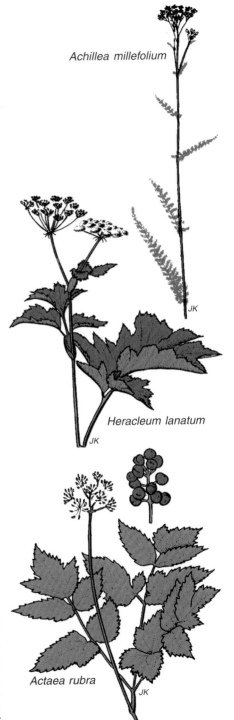

*Achillea millefolium*

*Heracleum lanatum*

*Actaea rubra*

JK

### Yarrow/milfoil/tansy
*Achillée millefeuille/herbe à dindes*
*Achillea millefolium* (composite family)
Early June to early September, perennial
(Jasper: June 7)

Very common throughout the Rockies up to treeline, and well known in Europe, too. One or more flat clusters of small white flowers with pale yellow or white centres atop a stem 20–50 cm tall. Characteristic sage-like smell, although it is not a sage. The frilly, fern-like gray-green leaves are narrow and tend to clasp the stem. They speed up blood-clotting when crushed and placed on a wound.

### Baneberry
*Pain de couleuvre/poison de couleuvre*
*Actaea rubra* (buttercup family)
Late May through June, perennial
(Jasper: June 8)

Montane woods, often among aspen. Can grow to a metre tall; leaflets droop in threes or fives, with deeply toothed margins. Dense, conical heads of tiny white flowers with 4–10 petals carried above the plant. Beautiful clusters of large, bright red—sometimes white—shiny berries; attractive but poisonous, so don't keep them around the house where little kids might eat 'em.

### Cow parsnip
*Berce laineuse/berce très grande*
*Heracleum lanatum* (carrot family)
Mid-June through July, perennial

Tall, very common montane/lower-subalpine plant growing beside running water, frequently in aspen woods. Thick, hairy stems grow up to 2 m high on the western slope, shorter on the other side of the divide. Heavy, flat flowerheads atop the plant are dense with tiny white flowers that give off a musty smell. Very large leaves sit lower down in threes; they are deeply lobed, toothed, dark green and hairy underneath. The leaves resemble those of devil's-club, page 274, which you will sometimes find lying in wait for you among otherwise-innocuous cow-parsnip patches on the western slope.

*Caution:* bears, especially grizzly bears, eat a lot of cow parsnip. As you approach a subalpine meadow full of cow parsnip, make plenty of noise.

### White angelica *Angélique blanche*
*Angelica arguta* (carrot family)
July to early August, perennial

Montane and subalpine, southern area. Resembles cow parsnip and grows in similar locations, but it is not hairy and the flower clusters are ball-shaped rather than flat.

From Crowsnest Pass south, look for **yellow angelica** *(A. dawsonii),* a subalpine species.

### Caraway *Caraway*
*Carum carvi* (carrot family)
Late June and early July, biennial

Montane and lower subalpine, an agricultural plant introduced from Europe that tends to escape cultivation and grow along roadsides and in meadows. Caraway is a white-angelica lookalike (see previous item), but the leaves are divided more finely and the flowerheads are flatter and less showy.

### Pathfinder/trail plant
*Adénocaule bicolore*
*Adenocaulon bicolor* (composite family)
July, perennial

Western-slope montane south of Golden and the Waterton/Glacier area. Small tufted flowers on long stalks, reminiscent of coltsfoot, page 297, but coltsfoot flowers bloom earlier. Compare also with arrowhead balsam root, page 317. When you walk through a patch of pathfinder the leaves turn over, marking your path with the light-colored, hairy undersides. The seeds catch on clothing.

### Lace flower/foam flower/false mitrewort/Nancy-over-the-ground
*Tiarelle monofoliée*
*Tiarella unifoliata* (saxifrage family)
Early June to late July, perennial

Western-slope montane and subalpine, very common in Columbian forest. On the eastern slope most common in the Waterton/Glacier area, occasional near the continental divide at least as far north as Jasper. Height

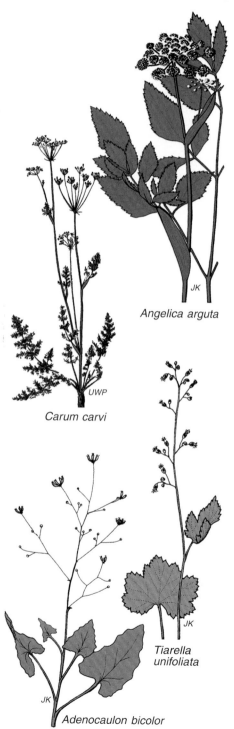

*Angelica arguta*

*Carum carvi*

*Tiarella unifoliata*

*Adenocaulon bicolor*

10–30 cm. Maple-shaped leaves about 8 cm across; tiny white flowers on drooping stalks in a showy open cluster atop the plant. If the leaves are very deeply divided, the plant is *T. trifoliata.*

### Three-tooth mitrewort/mauve mitrewort *Mitelle mauve*
*Mitella trifida* (saxifrage family)
Late May to early July, perennial

Mainly western-slope upper montane and subalpine, and Waterton/Glacier, in damp woods. Has been reported as far north as Jasper. Delicate plant up to 40 cm tall with toothy heart-shaped basal leaves on rather long stems and one or more leafless flower stalks. Near the top there is a line of 10–20 small white flowers. They are not as frilly as those of *M. pentandra* or *M. nuda,* page 309.

The name "mauve" gives the wrong impression. The flowers can be purplish, but they are usually white.

### Alum-root *Heuchère à petites feuilles*
*Heuchera parvifolia* (saxifrage family)
Late May to early July, perennial

Columbian forest, western-slope montane around Fernie, and in the Waterton/Glacier area. At all elevations, on rocky outcrops and cliffs. Leaves are all basal, 2–3 cm wide on long stems and deeply divided into three or five lobes. The reddish flower stalk, 30–40 cm tall, is hairy; the small flowers may be yellowish as well as white. See also *H. cylindrica,* page 323.

### Wild buckwheat *Renouelle subalpine*
*Eriogonum umbellatum* (buckwheat family)
Early June and July, perennial

In sunny, fairly dry places at all elevations. Tall, up to 40 cm, the leaves all basal except for a set just below the flowerheads. These are cream-colored or yellowish, often tinged with pink; the color is from the sepals, not the flowers, which have no petals. See also the yellow buckwheats, page 328.

### Valerian *Valériane*
*Valeriana* spp. (valerian family)
Late June to mid-August, perennial

Subalpine meadows to a little above treeline. Stout square stem up to a metre tall, with large, deeply lobed and toothed leaves; those of *V. dioica* are more delicate than those of *V. sitchensis.* Dense tuft of small flowers at the top, purplish at first, turning white later.

*Heuchera parvifolia*

*Eriogonum umbellatum*

*Mitella trifida*

*V. dioica*

*V. sitchensis*

After a frost this plant spreads a strong, rather unpleasant odor. The seed-like fruits have feathers.

Valerian is sometimes called "wild heliotrope"—a poor name, for it is not a heliotrope (genus *Heliotropium)* at all. Valerian is the original source of the tranquilizer and muscle-relaxant diazepam, known commercially as **Valium.**

### Northern bedstraw *Gaillet boréal*
*Galium boreale* (madder family)
Mid-June to early late August, perennial
(Jasper: June 14)

Common in open montane woods. Calf-high plant with narrow dark-green leaves and showy tufts of tiny white four-parted flowers. Leaves are in fours, too, growing symmetrically from each node.

### Fleabane *Vergerette*
*Erigeron* spp. (composite family)
April to August, perennial

If it looks like a daisy, but it's growing a long way from the roadside, then it is probably a fleabane. That is the general rule in the Rockies, where real daisies (*Chrysanthemum* spp., see next page) are not native.

There are many fleabane species in the Canadian Rockies, some very difficult to identify, and to make matters worse the asters, page 351, are quite similar. I am content just to be able to tell a fleabane from an aster. Try this, ahem, simple procedure. Look at the little green cup under the flower—the scaly **involucral bracts.** If the bracts are all the same length it is a fleabane. If some bracts are obviously shorter it is an aster.

Having got that far, here are two fleabanes that are fairly easy to know. See also the alpine varieties on page 359.

**Daisy fleabane** (*E. compositus*), mid-April through June, is common at all elevations throughout the Rockies, very common on grassy montane slopes, where it is one of the early spring flowers. Frilly, hairy leaves at the base are each divided into three lobes at the end. Stem has narrow, clasping leaves or leaflets, 10–20 cm tall. One flower—flowerhead, really, for in members of the composite family the petal-like parts are all individual flowers, as are the little bumps that make up the centre—per stem, 2–3 cm across. This plant may or may not have petal-like white **ray-flowers.** The ones that lack ray flowers have only

Galium boreale

Erigeron caespitosus

Aster    Fleabane

involucral bracts

Erigeron compositus

mustard-colored **disk flowers** (the ones in the centre). When both forms are blooming together they look like different species. In July and August they all produce fuzzy round seedheads the size of marbles.

**Common fleabane** *(E. caespitosus)*, late May to late July, is montane, often in large patches. Ankle-high, very daisy-like plant with narrow, undivided leaves covered in fine hairs, as are the stems. The ray-flowers are usually white, sometimes pinkish or bluish, and rather wide compared with those of other fleabanes; the disk-flowers are the color of hot mustard.

**See also** townsendia, page 339.

*Aster hesperius*

### Western willow aster
*Aster des saules de l'Ouest*
*Aster hesperius* (composite family)
Mid-June to late July, perennial

Low-elevation montane, in moist grassy meadows. Most asters are purple or blue; this is one of the few white or pinkish species in the mountains. Up to a metre tall but usually much shorter. The leaves are narrow and lack stalks, but the most distinctive thing about the plant demands that you get your eye close to the stems: they have thin white lines of hair running down them.

### Ox-eye daisy
*Marguerite/chrysanthème leucanthème*
*Chrysanthemum leucanthemum*
(composite family)
June to August, perennial (Jasper: June 15)

A true daisy, unlike the fleabanes and asters, and thus not native to the Rockies. Look for this species around towns, where it has spread from gardens, and along roadsides. At 40–60 cm it is taller than any white fleabane, with bigger flowers 4–6 cm across. The basal leaves are paddle-shaped and cleft, becoming narrower and more pointed up the stems.

The flower is easily confused with that of **scentless chamomile,** *Matricaria perforata,* but scentless chamomile leaves are so finely divided and less frilly, and *M. perforata* is usually a prairie plant.

Like a lot of plants, daisies produce chemical toxins in their tissues to repel attackers. The daisy's defense is particularly gruesome: having eaten from the leaves, an army worm dies quickly as ingested polyacetylenes react to sunlight, turning the worm bright blue. Then it blackens, shrivels and dies.

*Chrysanthemum leucanthemum*

# Greenish wildflowers below treeline

The flowers listed in this section often display other colors, such as white or pink, but they are mostly greenish. See also the bog orchids, page 301.

### One-sided wintergreen
*Orthilie unilatérale*
*Orthilia secunda* (wintergreen family)
Mid-July to early August, perennial
    Montane and lower subalpine woods. A small plant 10–20 cm tall with rounded basal evergreen leaves and small ball-shaped greenish-white flowers hanging in a row beneath the arching stem. The styles stick out.

### Green pyrola/green wintergreen *Pyrole verdâtre*
*Pyrola chlorantha* (wintergreen family)
Late June to mid-July, perennial
    Montane, usually in dry lodgepole woods. Very similar to pink pyrola, see page 370, but with green flowers and stems rather than pink ones. Green pyrola is also smaller, 10–20 cm rather than 20–30 cm for pink pyrola, and it flowers a little earlier. See also lesser wintergreen, page 333.

### Northern false toadflax/bastard toadflax/comandra
*Géocaulon livide/géocaulon du Nord*
*Geocaulon lividum* (sandalwood family)
June, perennial
    Montane woods. A single stem per plant, 10–20 cm tall, with smooth lance-shaped leaves, often stained brown. Most of the new plants are sickly-looking, afflicted with the **comandra blister rust,** a fungus that patterns the crinkly leaves yellow and green. They become smooth and more evenly pale-green later. But in late summer the leaves become splotched with brown. Look for tiny greenish flowers along the stem, at leaf nodes. Showy red berries in fall are inedible.
    Northern false toadflax is parasitic on strawberry, mountain cranberry and tree/shrub roots generally. It also produces some of its own food. Once known as *Comandra livida,* northern false toadflax is often confused with **pale comandra,** *Comandra umbellata* (also called **bastard toadflax),** which is taller, with branching stems and narrower leaves. True toadflax is the genus *Linaria,* page 327. See also rattlesnake plantain, page 302.

Orthilia
secunda

JK

*Pyrola chlorantha*

*Geocaulon lividum*    UWP

### Meadow-rue *Pigamon*

*Thalictrum* spp. (buttercup family)
Late May to late July, perennial
Montane and subalpine, in damp sheltered places. Up to a metre tall, with leaves the shape of yellow columbine, page 322, but smaller, bluegreen and veined. Male flowers are greenish and nodding; female flowers are purplish and star-shaped. The two common species are difficult to differentiate, even for botanists. Leaves of *T. venulosum* are more heavily veined than those of *T. occidentale*.

### Mitrewort/bishop's-cap *Mitelle*

*Mitella* spp. (saxifrage family)
Mid-June to early August, perennial
Southern montane and subalpine, in damp shady places. Small plants of the forest floor; easy to pass by. But the flowers are distinctive: yellowish-green stars, with strange frilly petals that extend well beyond the petal-like sepals. The fruit opens to show a shallow cup with tiny black seeds in it. We have three species that are similar, of which the commonest one is *M. nuda*, about 10 cm tall. Its leaves are broadly heart-shaped, with rounded scallops along the edges. *M. pentandra* is up to 25 cm tall, and the leaves are toothier. The other *Mitella* has white flowers that are not as frilly; see page 305.

### Northern twayblade *Listère boréale*

*Listera borealis* (orchid family)
July and August, perennial
Mostly subalpine, in the woods. Small orchid 5–20 cm tall, with two wide, warty-looking leaves partway up the stem. The flowers are small and greenish but distinctive: the tongue-like lower lip is long and notched at the end. If the lip is markedly narrower at the base than near the end, with two tiny teeth at the base, then it's *L. caurina*, less common than *L. borealis*. In the southern area, you may see *L. convallarioides*, with the same characteristics as *L. caurina* but no teeth at the base of the lip. If the lip is reddish and deeply forked, like a snake's tongue, it's heart-leaved twayblade, page 334.

### Peppergrass *Lépidie densiflore*

*Lepidium densiflorum* (mustard family)
Mid-June to early August, annual
Montane forest, on disturbed ground. Spikes of tiny greenish flowers up to 50 cm tall. Narrow, toothed leaves up the stem to the

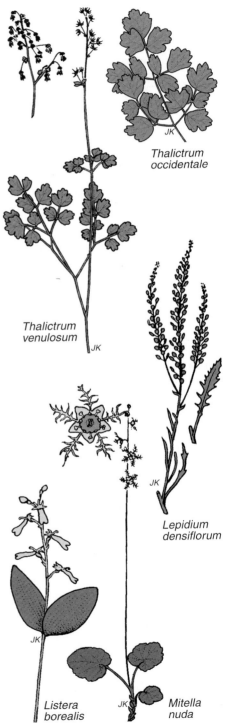

Thalictrum
occidentale

Thalictrum
venulosum

Lepidium
densiflorum

Listera
borealis

Mitella
nuda

point at which the flowers begin. There are usually no petals, only sepals. Showy sprays of small pods in fall.

### Western sweet cicely
*Osmorhize de l'Ouest*
*Osmorhiza occidentalis* (carrot family)
Late May to early July, perennial
   Eastern-slope montane, from Crowsnest Pass south. Up to 1 m tall, with toothy leaflets in threes. Tiny greenish flowers in upright clusters on very thin stems, carried above the leaves. See also the antenna plant, next item.

### Antenna plant/sweet cicely
*Osmorhize antenne-télé*
*Osmorhiza depauperata* (carrot family)
Late June to early July, perennial
   Montane and subalpine. Fairly tall, up to 60 cm, with peculiar branching stems at the top that *do* look rather like television antennas, especially when the plant is in seed. Indented, carrot-like leaflets grow below the antenna-like part. Blooms are inconspicuous and white. Seeds taste like licorice. See also western sweet cicely, previous item.

### Wild sarsaparilla *Salsepareille*
*Aralia nudicaulis* (ginseng family)
Early June to mid-July, perennial
   In deep montane woods. Common on the western slope; fairly common in central and northern sections of the eastern slope. Absent at Waterton and eastern-slope Glacier. Distinctive-looking: the leaves are carried flat on three stems atop the plant, like an umbrella. The leaflets resemble poison ivy, especially when they are young and in threes, but they later go to fives, and the leaves of wild sarsaparilla are dull, while those of poison ivy are shiny. Small, greenish-white flowers bloom in ball-like clusters, usually three to a plant. Dark-purple berries, not tasty.
   This plant spreads through **rhizomes:** long, food-storing roots. Individuals in the network can nourish each other through the rhizomes.

### Twisted stalk *Streptope amplexicaule*
*Streptopus amplexifolius* (lily family)
Late May to late June, perennial
   Montane, in shady places near running water. Up to a metre tall. The stems zig-zag slightly. Wavy-margined leaves are rather like those of fairy bells, page 289, but often with

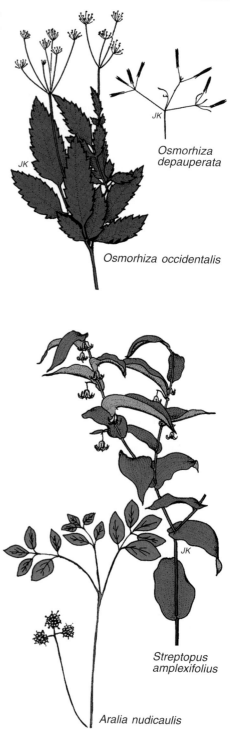

*Osmorhiza depauperata*

*Osmorhiza occidentalis*

*Streptopus amplexifolius*

*Aralia nudicaulis*

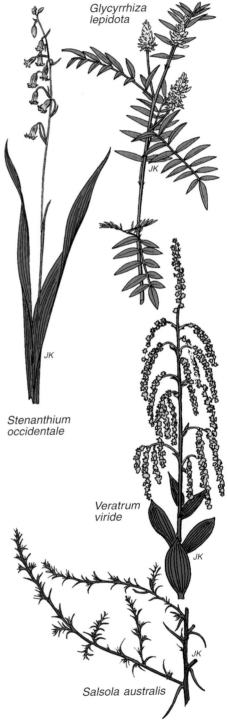

Glycyrrhiza
lepidota

JK

yellow spots. Small greenish-white flowers
hide underneath, hanging from twisted stalks.
The red berries are oval-shaped, also hanging
from twisted stalks.

### Bronze bells/western stenanthium
*Stenanthium de l'Ouest*
*Stenanthium occidentale* (lily family)
Late June to early August, perennial
  Moist montane and lower-subalpine
woods, southern and central sections. Delicate
plant 20–40 cm tall, with 6 to 10 small greenish
or brownish, or even purplish bell-shaped
flowers hanging from a thin stalk. The sides
of the bells have purplish streaks and there is a
yellow clapper. Narrow leaves grow up from
the base.

### Wild licorice *Réglisse sauvage*
*Glycyrrhiza lepidota* (pea family)
July, perennial
  Southern montane, in dry places. Grows
up to a metre tall, with vetch-like sawtooth
leaves. Flowers are small and greenish or
yellowish-white; inconspicuous. The seed pods
are distinctive: 1–2 cm long and covered with
prickles. Roots taste weakly of licorice.

### False hellebore *Varaire/faux hellébore*
*Veratrum viride* (lily family)
July and August, perennial
  Montane and subalpine woods, often near
running water. The tallest lily in the Rockies,
often head-high, with very long parallel-veined
leaves. Often called skunk-cabbage, page 378,
by non-botanists, although the two plants look
quite different. Compare also with false
Solomon's seal, page 289. Flowers of false
hellebore are small and yellowish green; lots
of them hang in streamers atop the plant.
  *Caution:* all parts of false hellebore are
quite poisonous. They contain the alkaloid
protoveratrine, which slows heartbeat and
breathing. True hellebores, of the European
genus *Helleborus,* cause digestive upsets.

### Russian thistle/tumbleweed
*Chardon de Russie/soude roulante*
*Salsola australis* (goosefoot family)
June and July, annual
  An introduced weed found in disturbed
places at low elevations, common in the
southern region. Not a true thistle, but prickly
when dead and dry. The stiff, rounded plant

Stenanthium
occidentale

JK

Veratrum
viride

JK

Salsola australis

JK

breaks off at the root and goes tumbling along with the wind, spreading its seeds. The plant is prickly when alive, too; the leaves are narrow, hard and pointed. Look (carefully) for the tiny greenish flowers along the stems. Plant used to be known as *S. kali.*

### White thistle *Chardon blanche*
*Cirsium hookerianum* (composite family)
Mid-July to mid-August, biennial or perennial

Montane and lower subalpine meadows, mostly eastern slope from the Athabasca River south. Unlike the purple thistles in the Canadian Rockies, this one is native. Up to a metre tall, white thistle is the prickliest, hairiest plant in the Rockies, covered so thickly with assorted armaments that it looks to be wrapped in spiderwebs. Even the *flowers* are spiny.

### Stinging nettle *Ortie dioïque*
*Urtica dioica* (nettle family)
Late June and July, perennial

Montane, mainly on disturbed ground; more common on the western slope. Usually about a metre tall, but can grow larger.

*Avoid this plant:* merely brushing it lightly will cause a burning sensation that can last an hour. The toothy, lance-shaped leaves have small spines that break off in the skin and discharge an irritant. You can spot stinging nettle by noting the small green flowers in drooping strings; otherwise it looks much like wild mint, page 350, which is immediately differentiated by the minty smell, which stinging nettle lacks.

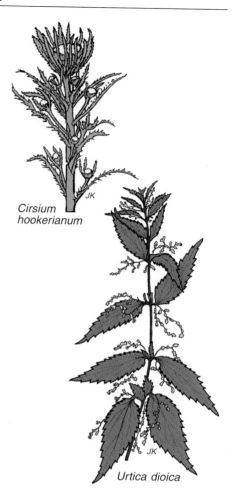

*Cirsium hookerianum*

*Urtica dioica*

## Yellow or orange wildflowers below treeline

For "the golden poppies blooming on the banks of Lake Louise," see page 363.

### Glacier lily/snow lily/avalanche lily/dogtooth violet
*Erythrome à grandes fleurs*
*Erythronium grandiflorum* (lily family)
Mid-May to mid-July, perennial

Upper montane to subalpine, common in southern areas of both slopes; scarce north of Bow Summit on the eastern slope but found at least as far north as Valemount on the western slope. Unmistakable, large brilliant-yellow flower that follows the snowline up the mountains. Usually two upstanding, in-curling leaves 10–15 cm long, with the single flower, sometimes two, nodding atop a slightly higher stem.

### Western wood lily *Lis de Philadelphie*
*Lilium philadelphicum* (lily family)
Mid-June to mid-July, perennial (Jasper: June 15)

On south-facing open montane slopes and aspen woods; also found in Columbian forest. The large, very showy orange flower has black dots inside and black-ended stamens. It faces upward, unlike the orange flower of the Columbia lily, next item, which faces downward. Western wood lily's narrow leaves grow from the stem, not from the base like most other lilies. Height is 5–50 cm. Often mistakenly called "tiger lily," which is *Lilium tigrinum,* an Asian species.

The western wood lily is the floral emblem of Saskatchewan. Despite protected status throughout Canada, it is always a picker's target. And picking kills it, for the bulb cannot generate two sets of leaves in the same summer. That explains why it is becoming scarce along highways and in populated places, except in the national parks, where visitors generally follow the no-picking rule.

### Columbia lily/tiger lily
*Lis de Colombie/lis tigré*
*Lilium columbianum* (lily family)
June and July, perennial

Western-slope montane and subalpine from Prince George south, in moist places. There are only a few short, narrow leaves, but several large orange flowers nod over on stems 20–70 cm tall. The black-dotted petals bend backward, exposing long anthers.

This is not the true tiger lily, *Lilium tigrinum.* See previous item.

*Erythronium grandiflorum*

*Lilium columbianum*

*Lilium philadelphicum*

## Yellow mountain violet and evergreen violet *Violette jaune, violette toujours-verte*
*Viola glabella* and *V. orbiculata* (violet family)
Late June to early July, perennial

Both grow in damp, mossy montane and subalpine woods. Rounded, bluntly toothed leaves are notched in at the stem. Bright yellow flowers with purple veins, five-petalled and not radially symmetrical. Differentiate the two species by the short stems in the low-growing evergreen violet. The yellow mountain violet can reach 30 cm.

## Yellow prairie violet
*Violette jaune des prairies*
*Viola nuttallii* (violet family)
Early to mid-May, perennial

Mainly western-slope southern montane, but also in the southern foothills. Prefers dry, open spots at low elevations, but sometimes grows in alpine scree slopes. Note the long, scalloped leaves, not like those of most violets. Flowers are yellow with purple veins and a purple tinge on the backs of the upper two petals. Sometimes called "Johnny jump-up," a name applied to various garden violets and pansies. Compare with yellow monkey-flower, next item.

Like golden corydalis, page 326, yellow prairie violets enlist ants to help disperse the seeds. Each seed has an oily blob on it called an **elaisome**; the ants carry the seed home, eat the elaisome and discard the seed.

## Yellow monkey-flower *Mimule jaune*
*Mimulus guttatus* (figwort family)
July to September, annual/perennial

Mainly western-slope, montane to subalpine; eastern slope in southern Banff National Park and south. Grows in wet, open spots. Up to 30 cm tall, with large blooms and toothed, pointed leaves. Look for dots on the lower lip of the flower. Individuals can be either annual or perennial.

## Yellow lady's-slipper/moccasin flower
*Sabot-de-la-vierge jaune*
*Cypripedium calceolus* (orchid family)
Mid-June to early July, perennial

Shady montane woods, all areas, although scarce on the eastern slope north of Jasper and south of Crowsnest Pass. Large, very distinctive bloom: a bright yellow bag—attractive to bees—with a brown sepal above and two more on the

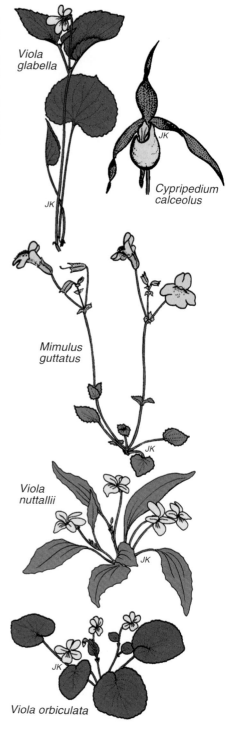

*Viola glabella*

*Cypripedium calceolus*

*Mimulus guttatus*

*Viola nuttallii*

*Viola orbiculata*

side, spiralling. Grows about 20 cm high. Several smooth, parallel-veined leaves at the base. Very similar to mountain lady's slipper, page 300, except for the flower color.

### Yellow penstemon/yellow beard-tongue *Penstémon jaune*

*Penstemon confertus* (figwort family)
Early June to August, perennial

Central and southern regions, common from Lake Louise south—very common from Crowsnest Pass south—in dry montane and sub-alpine meadows. The only yellow penstemon in the Canadian Rockies, and thus easily identified. Plants mostly on single stems less than 30 cm tall with lance-shaped leaves. Radial clusters of small yellow trumpet-shaped flowers, the lower lip three-lobed and the upper lip two-lobed in characteristic penstemon fashion.

### Dandelion *Pissenlit*

*Taraxacum officinale* (composite family)
Early April to late September, perennial

The common, lawn-variety dandelion. Usually the first yellow flower of spring, found in every grassy, clovery place. Very familiar: ragged leaves, all basal; large, brilliant-yellow bloom with no central disk; round, fluffy seedhead that blows away in the wind. But don't confuse with the look-alike false dandelion and goat's-beard, next items, or with seedheads of the anemone group, or seedheads of white dryas, page 357, and yellow dryas, page 322. *T. officinale* is an introduced species, along with the similar *T. laevigatum*, but there are native dandelions in the Rockies, including an alpine-zone species. See page 365.

This plant's French name refers to dandelion's sometimes-unwelcome diuretic qualities. It means "pee in the bed."

### False dandelions

*Agoséride/faux pissenlits*
*Agoseris* spp. and *Microseris nutans* (composite family)
Mid-June to August, perennial

In meadows and open woods. The **large-flowered false dandelion** (*A. glauca*, montane, mid-June to early July) is a good imitation, but the petals are fewer and broader, and the leaves are narrow and not toothy. A related species, **orange-flowered false dandelion** (*A. aurantiaca*, all elevations, July), has a

Penstemon confertus

Taraxacum officinale

Agoseris aurantiaca

Agoseris glauca

showy reddish-orange bloom. The leaves have a few broad, cuspy teeth. *A. lackschewitzii* is a pink-flowered false dandelion.

In southern western-slope montane meadows and at Waterton/Glacier there is yet another false dandelion: *Microseris nutans*. The leaves are long and very narrow, often with backward-pointing teeth. The blooms are 1–2 cm across and yellow, often with purple lines; they nod before they bloom. See also goat's-beard, next item.

### Goat's-beard/yellow salsify/oyster plant/giant dandelion Salsifis majeur
*Tragopogon dubius* (composite family)
Late June to mid-July, perennial

Low-elevation montane, usually on disturbed ground. Looks rather like a dandelion but is much larger, up to 60 cm tall. Leaves are long and grass-like, rather than broad and toothy like a dandelion. Bloom is bright yellow; the petal-like ray flowers are rather sparse and blackish toward the centre; sharp-looking green bracts extend beyond the edges. Seedhead is dandelion-like but much larger. You will see this plant in gardens, along with a purple species, *T. pratensis*.

### Hawkweed Épervière
*Hieracium* spp. (composite family)
July and August, perennial

Common montane and subalpine plants, growing in dry open areas and often forming patches. About a dozen species, difficult to differentiate and easily mistaken for sow thistle, next item. All hawkweeds have bright-yellow, dandelion-like blooms 2–3 cm across, with no central disk, a few to a dozen per plant. The flowers bloom on stalks rising from the places where the leaves join the stem; look for dark hairs under the blooms, another hawkweed identifier.

Two low-elevation hawkweeds to look for are **narrow-leaved hawkweed** (*H. umbellatum*), with leaves that are shallowly toothed at the base, becoming narrower and less toothy up the stem, and **prairie hawkweed** (*H. cynoglossoides*), which has club-shaped leaves and is very hairy. At subalpine elevations look for **slender hawkweed** (*H. triste*). This one can be mistaken for arnica, next page, but in slender hawkweed the blooms are smaller—less than 3 cm across—and they lack a central disk.

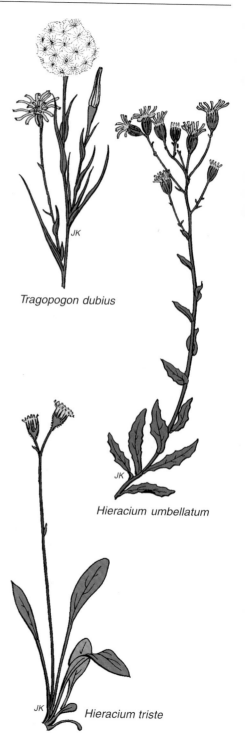

*Tragopogon dubius*

*Hieracium umbellatum*

*Hieracium triste*

## Perennial sow thistle
*Laiteron des champs*
*Sonchus arvensis* (composite family)
Late July and early August, perennial

Montane, along roadsides and in disturbed, dry, sunny places. Common in most places but absent at Waterton, although present at Glacier. Looks like a hawkweed stuck onto a nettle. Tall—up to 2 m—with large 10–20 cm toothy, prickly-edged leaves. If you see a sow thistle with leaves that are not prickly, it is *S. asper*, **annual sow thistle,** which is, indeed, annual, not perennial.

## Arnica *Arnica*
*Arnica* spp. (composite family)
Late May through August, perennial

Montane and subalpine, usually in evergreen woods. Even though it's a perennial, arnica imitates biennial plants by blooming every other year. Like beargrass, page 302, most of the individuals of a particular arnica species in a particular place bloom at the same time, so that in one summer there are very few arnica flowers, while in the next the woods are full of them.

Large, bright-yellow ray flowers curl a bit at the edges, with small teeth at the petal ends. Small yellow centres. Fifteen species, sometimes interbreeding. Some common ones:

**Heart-leaved arnica** *(A. cordifolia)* is upper montane and subalpine; has the broadest leaves. They're usually scalloped along the edges. Compare with broad-leaved arnica, next item.

**Broad-leaved arnica** *(A. latifolia)* resembles *A. cordifolia,* but the leaves are not quite so heart-shaped and the petioles (stems) are wider.

**Narrow-leaved arnica** *(A. fulgens)* has narrow leaves, mostly basal. Look for brown hairs at the point where the leaf comes off the stem.

**Leafy arnica** *(A. chamissonis)* is tall, up to 80 cm, common in aspen groves around Jasper. Look for tiny white hairs at the tips of the involucral bracts (small leaves cupping the flowerhead).

**See also** alpine arnica, page 364.

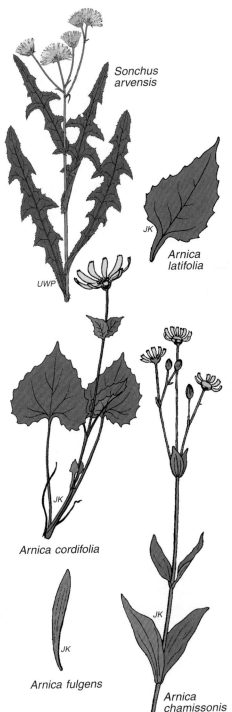

*Sonchus arvensis*

*Arnica latifolia*

UWP

*Arnica cordifolia*

*Arnica fulgens*

*Arnica chamissonis*

### Arrowhead balsam root/spring sunflower *Racine baumière*

*Balsamorhiza sagittata* (composite family)
Mid-May through June, perennial

Low-elevation western-slope montane from Golden south, and the southern foothills. Arnica-like flower but with very different leaves: up to 20 cm long and all at the base, arrow-shaped and fuzzy underneath, rather like those of pathfinder, page 304. But pathfinder blooms white and grows in the woods, not on dry open slopes.

### Wild gaillardia/brown-eyed Susan *Gaillarde aristée*

*Gaillardia aristata* (composite family)
Early July to September, perennial
(Jasper: June 11)

Common plant of dry, grassy montane meadows and road shoulders. Up to 50 cm tall, with scalloped leaves and hairy stems. The blooms are large (5–10 cm across) and very showy: domed brown centres with long yellow petals that often droop backward, each getting wider toward the tip, which is divided into three small lobes that give the illusion of many more ray flowers (petal-like parts) than there actually are. Brown-eyed susan is a relative of the *black-eyed susans (Rudbeckia* spp.) that grow in the southern and eastern U.S.A.

### Golden aster *Aster doré*

*Heterotheca villosa* (composite family)
July to late August, perennial

Southern montane, in dry meadows at low elevations. Not really an aster—there are no yellow asters—but close enough. A sprawling plant with hairs on stems and leaves, and somewhat sticky. Flowers are showy; they bloom at the ends of the stems.

### Gumweed *Herbe collante*

*Grindelia squarrosa* (composite family)
August and early September, biennial/perennial

Western-slope montane from Golden south at low elevations, and in the southern foothills. Prefers dry, open places. An unkempt-looking plant, despite the pretty yellow blooms. It exudes a sticky harmless juice. The central disk is paler than the surrounding rays. Individuals can be either biennial or perennial.

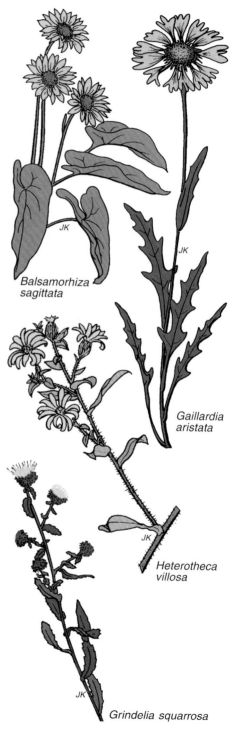

*Balsamorhiza sagittata*

*Gaillardia aristata*

*Heterotheca villosa*

*Grindelia squarrosa*

## Broomweed/snakeweed
*Herbe en forme de balais*
*Gutierrezia sarothrae* (composite family)
Late August and early September, perennial

A southern Alberta prairie plant that creeps into the foothills, although it hasn't made it into Waterton or eastern-slope Glacier. Look for it also around Cranbrook. Looks rather like rabbitbrush, page 276, but has very thin, hairy leaves 1–3 cm long on slender dark-green stems 30–40 cm long. Lots of small yellow blooms cover the top in showy clusters.

## Yellow puccoon/woolly gromwell/
## lemonweed *Grémil jaune*
*Lithospermum ruderale* and *L. incisum* (borage family)
Late May to Mid-July, perennials

Mostly southern montane, in open places. Seen at Jasper. A showy, bushy plant 20–50 cm tall with hairy dark-green leaves. Clusters of yellow flowers with dark centres.

Puccoon is a prairie plant found in the mountains where horses use the trails (figure that out). The flowers of *L. incisum* are bright yellow, with fringed petals; those of *L. ruderale* are paler, without fringes. Both species bloom twice each summer; the flowers described are from the first blooming. The second set of flowers often lacks petals and is self-fertilizing, giving the plant a second chance at reproducing.

## Creeping mahonia/Oregon grape
*Berbéris rampante*
*Berberis repens* (barberry family)
Late May and June, perennial

Western-slope montane, eastern slope only in the Waterton/Glacier area, in open woods and rocky places. The holly-like leaves of this shrub are distinctive, as are the sour blue berries. Blooms are small and yellow, in tight clusters near the centre of the low-growing plant. *B. nervosa*, also called Oregon grape, has leaves that are even more holly-like; grows in open areas of the Columbian forest.

## Pineapple weed *Matricaire odorante*
*Matricaria matricarioides* (composite family)
July and August, annual

Pineapple weed is common on disturbed ground at low elevations throughout the Rockies. This is a small plant 10–20 cm tall; very lacy leaves emit the odor of pineapple, especially when crushed. The blooms are

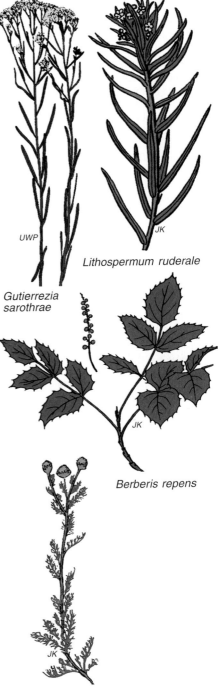

Lithospermum ruderale

Gutierrezia
sarothrae

Berberis repens

Matricaria matricarioides

mustard-colored, lacking ray flowers (no petal-like parts). Scentless chamomile, *M. perforata,* is a relative that looks like the ox-eye daisy, page 307.

## Potentilla/cinquefoil *Potentille*

*Potentilla* spp. (rose family)
May through August, mostly perennials

At all elevations, in various habitats. This genus is familiar to gardeners, but there are many wild forms as well. Good identifiers: five-fingered leaflets and brilliant-yellow, five-petalled flowers, often indented at the petal-ends and alternating with five smaller green sepals. There are a lot of potentilla species, some of which are easily confused with one another and with certain buttercups and avens. The common potentillas are listed below, followed by the buttercups and avens, for comparison.

**Early potentilla** *(P. concinna)* is perennial, early May through July. Eastern-slope montane, on south-facing hillsides. Very early starter; leaves come out in April and early May. Typical potentilla flowers set close to a ground-hugging mat of rather small, hairy five-pointed leaves, pale-green on the top and light-gray beneath.

**Silverweed** *(P. anserina)* is perennial, late May to early August, growing on dry montane slopes. Grows with early potentilla and looks like it, but the leaves are different: larger, with rows of leaflets; silvery hairy both top and bottom (can also be smooth and green on top).

**Montane potentilla** *(P. gracilis)* is peren-nial, late June to early August. Most common low-elevation species; grows everywhere. Spreading, geranium-like toothed leaves are slightly hairy underneath and 4–7 cm across at the plant's base, becoming smaller and less numerous up the reddish stems, which can reach 60–70 cm in height, topped by typical potentilla flowers with indented petal-ends.

*P. diversifolia* is perennial and closely resembles *P. gracilis,* but grows at higher elevations and has smaller leaves that are only lightly hairy.

**Subalpine potentilla** *(P. glandulosa)* is perennial, mid-May through July. Subalpine and alpine, in open dry spots. Grows 20–30 cm tall, with rounded, toothy leaflets and petal ends that are not indented.

**See also** shrubby potentilla, page 275, yellow avens, next page, the alpine potentillas, page 364, and water potentilla, page 381.

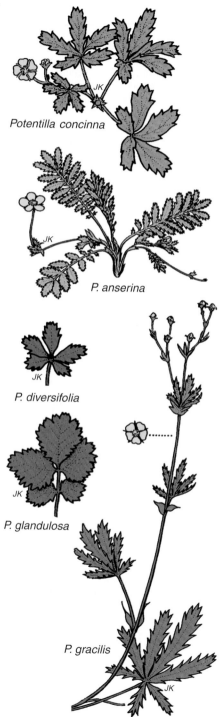

*Potentilla concinna*

*P. anserina*

*P. diversifolia*

*P. glandulosa*

*P. gracilis*

### Buttercup *Renoncule*
*Ranunculus* spp. (buttercup family)
See below for blooming dates, perennials

There are many members of this genus, and they run the gamut of Rockies habitats. They look rather like some potentilla species and often grow with them. Differentiate by the shiny, varnished-looking petals and green centres in buttercup flowers; potentillas have yellow centres and less-glossy petals. Buttercups closely resemble yellow avens, next item. Differentiate by the small leaves that grow just below an aven's flowers, and their absence in buttercups. Here are some common buttercups:

**Western buttercup** *(R. occidentalis),* April through June, is the most common western-slope buttercup, found everywhere at low elevations. Three-lobed toothed leaves, stems 5–50 cm tall.

**Hairy buttercup** *(R. uncinatus),* May through July, grows in shady western-slope montane and Columbian forests, central region. Occasional on the eastern slope from Saskatchewan Crossing south. Three-lobed leaves as above, but narrower; hairy stems and smaller flowers.

**Macoun's buttercup/hairy buttercup** *(R. macounii),* June and July, is found in montane meadows. The hairiest buttercup. Resembles and grows with tall buttercup, next item; has larger leaves but smaller flowers. Named for Irish-Canadian botanist John Macoun, who collected a lot of Canadian Rockies plants in 1872 and 1875.

**Tall buttercup** *(R. acris),* June to mid-August, grows in damp meadows at low elevations. Hairy stems; similar to Macoun's buttercup, previous item, but with smaller leaves and larger flowers.

As you can see, identifying buttercup species is a job for botanists. Thankfully, I'm a geologist. See also yellow water crowfoot, page 380, and the alpine buttercups, page 364.

### Yellow avens *Benoîte d'Alep/jeune éclaire*
*Geum aleppicum* (rose family)
Early June to early August, perennial

Montane meadows, in wet ground. Strikingly similar to tall buttercup, previous item, and sometimes growing with it, but note the cone-shaped green centre in the flower and small leaves growing not far below it. Tall buttercups have long, hairy flower-stems that lack the small leaves high up.

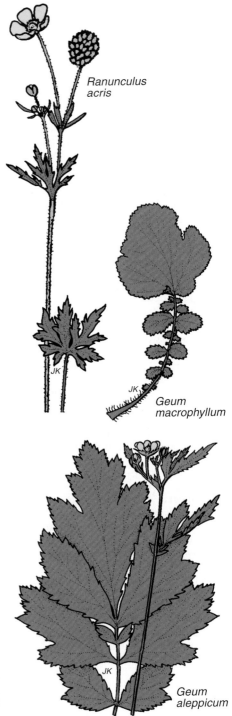

*Ranunculus acris*

*Geum macrophyllum*

*Geum aleppicum*

**Large-leaved avens** *(G. macrophyllum)* is another common species; differentiate from *G. aleppicum* by the rounded leaflets at the end of each basal leaf.

### Yellow columbine Ancolie jaune
*Aquilegia flavescens* (buttercup family)
June to early August, perennial (Jasper: June 12)

Mainly eastern-slope subalpine meadows, but also at lower elevations in moist woods. Up to 1 m tall, with large, very showy, complicated flowers. These are normally pale yellow, but often tinged with pink in plants near the continental divide, where they hybridize with the red western-slope species, page 336. Flower stems emerge from a bushy growth of distinctive leaves: dark green, a few centimetres across, with rounded lobes. See also meadow-rue, page 309.

### Purslane Pourpier gras
*Portulaca oleracea* (purslane family)
July, annual

Montane, on disturbed ground. This is a low-growing weed everyone has seen, but hardly anyone knows. Easily identified by the glossy, fleshy green leaves that resemble those of kinnikinnik. Look closely—the small white-and-yellow flowers are lovely.

### Yellow dryas/yellow mountain avens
Dryade de Drummond
*Dryas drummondii* (rose family)
Mid-June to early July, perennial

Montane version of white dryas, page 357, very common on the eastern slope of the central region; less so elsewhere. This mat-forming shrub quickly covers stony ground such as glacial outwash flats, front-range streambeds and roadsides. It's a pioneer plant that adds nitrogen to the soil, an essential nutrient for species that follow. The leaves are green above, gray or brown below, and blunt-toothed; flowers on stalks 5–10 cm tall, nodding over, with 8–10 short yellow petals. As the flowers go to seed they gradually straighten up, sending a twisted cone of plumes out from the centre. The cone expands into a dandelion-like seed head. See also three-flowered avens, page 332.

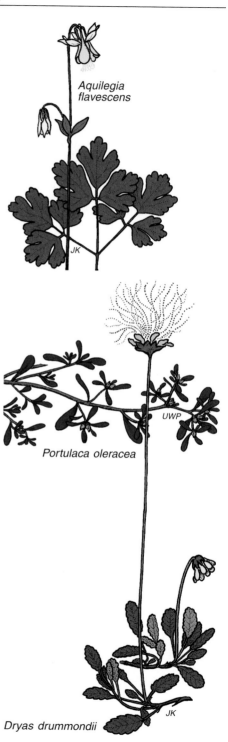

*Aquilegia flavescens*

*Portulaca oleracea*

*Dryas drummondii*

## Pasture sage/pasture wormwood
*Armoise des pâturages*
*Artemisia frigida* (composite family)
August, perennial

Montane, in dry places on sandy soil. Most easily identified by the strong sage fragrance of the leaves when crushed. They smell like the deserts of the American southwest. Tufts of finely divided, fuzzy gray-green leaflets with inconspicuous small flowers hidden along the stems. Blooms late. Yellow centres; no ray flowers (petals).

## Stonecrop/sedum *Orpin*
*Sedum* spp. (orpine family)
June, perennials (Jasper: June 13)

Throughout the Rockies at all elevations, in exposed places. **Succulent** (fleshy) plants, easily identified by the stout pinkish stems and short, fat leaves. Flowers are about 1 cm across, yellow with green centres and long stamens.

There are three species of stonecrop in the Canadian Rockies. *S. lanceolatum* is the most common and widespread, growing in dry, sunny spots at any elevation, with stems 5–15 cm tall and leaves about 1 cm long. *S. divergens* is alpine, found from the Athabasca River north; it tends to lie on the ground in mats and has shorter leaves. *S. stenopetalum* is up to 20 cm tall, found in rocky alpine locations in the southern region; the leaves are 1.5–2.5 cm long.

## Oval-leaf alumroot
*Heuchère à feuilles ovales*
*Heuchera cylindrica* (saxifrage family)
Early July to mid-August, perennial

Montane to alpine, in dry, rocky locations. Small yellow upright bell-shaped flowers in a spike atop a leafless stem, often sticky and hairy. Leaves are all basal, notched, toothy and also sticky/hairy. Flowers are near the top of the stem and fixed closely to it. Compare with *H. parvifolia,* a whitish species, page 305.

*Artemisia frigida*

JK

*Sedum lanceolatum*

*Heuchera cylindrica*

UWP

JK

## Mustard family
*Famille de la moutarde/crucifères*
(Various genera)
May to July, mostly perennials

Small plants, all with small four-petalled flowers that embody the word "cute." The seed pods are often distinctive, as shown in some of the illustrations. There are many species; differentiating them is best left to botanists, but here are a few easy ones.

**Draba/whitlow-grass** *Drave (Draba* spp.), early May through July. Rocky, stony places at all elevations. Several species, all low-growing and similar-looking, with the same small yellow four-petalled flowers—white in some species—and finely hairy, mostly basal gray-green leaves. Seeds are in small upright pods. *D. incerta* is probably the most common species in the Rockies; *D. aurea* is the tallest, 20–30 cm, preferring dry montane locations.

**Flixweed** *Sagesse des chirurgiens (Descurainia sophia),* June and July. A common montane weed. The tallest mustard, up to 1 m, with finely divided, frilly-looking leaves and slender pods.

**Wallflower/small-flowered rocket** *Vélar aux petites fleurs (Erysimum inconspicuum),* late May to mid-July. Montane, at low elevations; common in the southern region. Loose clusters of small but showy bright-yellow flowers atop a stem 40–60 cm tall. Narrow, slightly hairy leaves. Long skinny pods in fall. There is also a purple alpine version, page 371.

## Ragwort/groundsel *Séneçon*
*Senecio* spp. (composite family)
June to August, perennials

Montane and subalpine, in open places. Often growing with mountain goldenrod, next item, and rather similar-looking, but ragwort blooms occur in clusters of a few right at the top of the plant, while goldenrod blooms are smaller and trail partway down the stem. The ray flowers (petal-like parts) of the head sometimes come out later than the disk flowers at the centre, which vary from red to orange on the same plant. There are 18 ragwort species in the Rockies, some of which have no ray flowers at all. Here are three easy-to-identify ragworts:

**Prairie ragwort** (*S. canus*), late May to mid-June. Eastern-slope montane, in dry places; 10–20 cm tall, with smooth-edged basal leaves and irregularly toothed stem leaves.

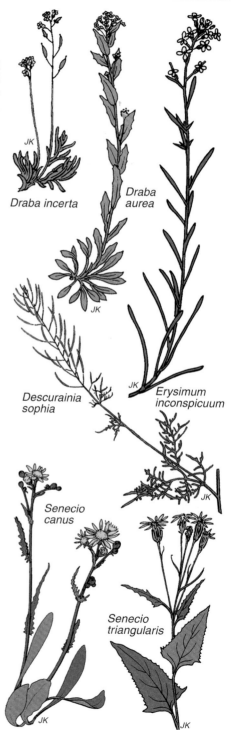

Draba incerta

Draba aurea

Descurainia sophia

Erysimum inconspicuum

Senecio canus

Senecio triangularis

**Triangular-leaved ragwort** *(S. triangularis)*, mid-July to mid-August. A tall 1–1.4 m subalpine species with large, coarsely toothed arrow-shaped leaves.

**Small-flowered ragwort** *(S. pauciflorus)*, mid-July to mid-August. Mostly subalpine, 10–60 cm tall, usually with only disk flowers. They range from yellow to reddish-orange. Leathery oval basal leaves.

**See also** alpine goldenrod, which looks like ragwort, page 368.

## Mountain goldenrod
*Verge d'or des montagnes*
*Solidago spathulata* (composite family)
Late June to early September, perennial
(Jasper: June 23)

Montane, in dry places, blooming throughout the summer. Grows 10–30 cm high, often in small patches. Showy tufts of small all-yellow flowers in a loose spike atop erect stems with long oblong leaves.

Mountain goldenrod is the most common species in the Rockies. There are eight others, and they aren't easy to differentiate. A couple of easy ones: **giant goldenrod** *(S. gigantea,* up to head-high, with multiple open flower clusters) and **Missouri goldenrod** *(S. missouriensis,* with dense, plume-like branching flower clusters). See also alpine goldenrod, page 368.

## Golden bean/buffalo bean/false lupine
*Haricot d'or*
*Thermopsis rhombifolia* (pea family)
May and June, perennial

Handsome plant of eastern-slope montane meadows, from the Bow River south to Waterton. Glacier reports *T. montana,* which is similar but taller, with larger leaves. *T. rhombifolia* grows 15–45 cm tall in sandy, open spots. Clusters of rich yellow pea flowers against contrasting green leaflets in threes, hairy on close inspection. Makes curved, hairy gray pods about 5 cm long holding poisonous seeds.

## Early yellow locoweed *Oxytropis jaune*
*Oxytropis sericea* (pea family)
Early May through June, perennial
(Jasper: May 12)

Southern and central montane, in dry places at low elevations; common along highway shoulders. Not a tall plant, but showy in bloom. Compact mat of gray-green hairy leaves, with tufts of pale yellow pea-type flowers above it on stems 15–40 cm high.

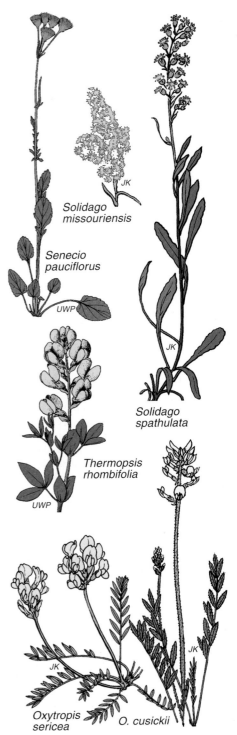

*Solidago missouriensis*

*Senecio pauciflorus*

*Solidago spathulata*

*Thermopsis rhombifolia*

*Oxytropis sericea*

*O. cusickii*

Poisonous to grazing animals. If selenium is present in the soil, this plant picks it up and concentrates it. A smaller subalpine and alpine species, *O. cusickii,* blooms later in the summer. Interbreeds with *O. sericea* and can be difficult to differentiate.

### Yellow hedysarum *Sainfoin jaune*
*Hedysarum sulphurescens* (pea family)
Early June to early July, perennial
Subalpine meadows and open woods, central and southern areas. Fairly tall plant, 20–50 cm, with rows of dark-green leaves that tend to fold in. Multiple pointy spikes of yellow pea-type flowers. See also the other *Hedysarum* species in the Rockies.

### Yellow sweet clover/yellow alfalfa
*Mélilot officinal/trèfle d'odeur jaune*
*Melilotus officinalis* (pea family)
Mid-July to September, annual or biennial
Introduced, common on disturbed ground at low elevations. A tall plant with narrow cylindrical flower clusters like white sweet clover, page 299, but with bright yellow flowers. Individuals can be annual or biennial.

### Golden corydalis *Corydale dorée*
*Corydalis aurea* (fumitory family)
Late May to early July, biennial
Montane, on south-facing dry hillsides; often on disturbed ground and in burns. Easily mistaken for a sprawling pea-family plant; the flowers are rather similar and so are the pods produced later. But note how the leaves are different.

The seeds each have an **elaisome:** an exterior bulge that attracts ants. The ants carry the seed to the nest, eat the elaisome and discard the seed, aiding in plant dispersal. The yellow prairie violet also attracts ants in this way.

### Clustered broomrape
*Orobanche fasciculé*
*Orobanche fasciculata* (broomrape family)
Mid-June to mid-July, perennial
At low elevations in sandy places, from the Athabasca River south. Uncommon. A strange little plant 3–10 cm tall, with three or more yellowish, purplish or pinkish pipe-shaped flowers on scaly, sticky, hairy stems. See also northern coral-root, page 302, and ghost flower, page 299.

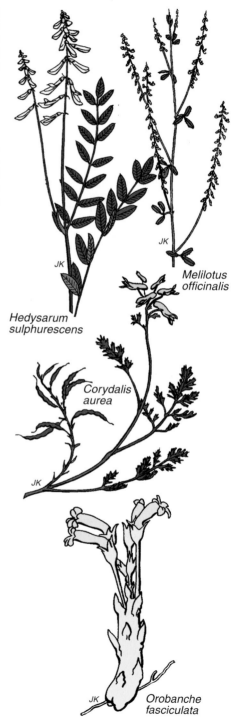

*Melilotus officinalis*

*Hedysarum sulphurescens*

*Corydalis aurea*

*Orobanche fasciculata*

### Yellow rattle
*Rhinanthe crête-de-coq/claquette*
*Rhinanthus minor* (figwort family) July, annual

Fairly common upper montane to high-subalpine plant, in moist meadows and open woods. Pouch-like flowers show just the tips of the yellow petals at the opening of the pouch. Opposite leaves, toothy and deeply veined. Yellow rattle takes some of its nourishment from the roots of surrounding plants. The name "rattle" describes the seeds. They dry inside the pouch and rattle in it when you shake the plant.

### Yellow paintbrush *Castilléjie jaune*
*Castilleja lutescens* (figwort family)
June and July, perennial (Jasper: June 9)

At low elevations, in meadows and in gravelly places along streams. Yellow version of the familiar red paintbrush, page 329. Color tends to be pale and greenish. See also alpine yellow paintbrush, page 367, and compare with owl clover, next item.

### Owl-clover *Trèfle d'hibou*
*Orthocarpus luteus* (figwort family)
July to early September, annual

Southern montane at low elevations, occasional north to Jasper. Erect hairy stems 10–30 cm high; short leaves. Small yellow tubular flowers along the upper two-thirds of the stems. The leaves continue through the flower spike. Resembles western lousewort, next item, but the leaves are different.

### Western lousewort/bracted lousewort/ wood betony *Pédiculaire de l'Ouest*
*Pedicularis bracteosa* (figwort family)
July and August, perennial

Subalpine and alpine meadows. Plant stands 20–40 cm high, with fern-like leaves that range from green to olive-drab. Dense spikes of small, tubular yellow flowers, often with a pinkish or purplish tinge, and green bracts. *P. labradorica* is a similar species with fewer flowers per head.

### Butter-and-eggs and yellow toadflax
*Linaire vulgaire, linaire à feuilles larges*
*Linaria vulgaris* and *L. dalmatica*
(figwort family)
Late June through July, perennial

In patches along montane roads and on disturbed ground. *L. dalmatica* is a tall plant—a metre or more—with long gently curving stems. Fleshy, pale-green leaves contrast

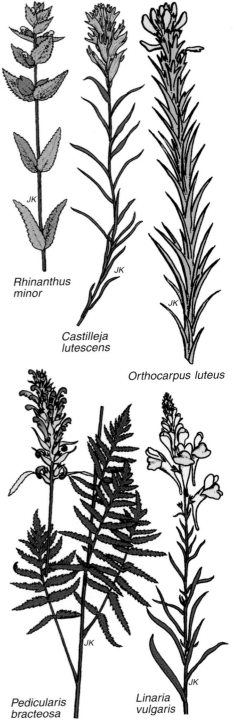

*Rhinanthus minor*

*Castilleja lutescens*

*Orthocarpus luteus*

*Pedicularis bracteosa*

*Linaria vulgaris*

sharply with a long spike of brilliant yellow-and-orange flowers. Looks rather like a snapdragon, and is in the same family. The plant is an introduced weed, disliked in agricultural circles, but it is beautiful. *L. vulgaris* is similar but shorter, with thinner, darker-green leaves.

## Sulphur plant/umbrella plant/wild buckwheat *Renouelle*

*Eriogonum* spp. (buckwheat family)
June to August, mostly perennials

In rocky places at all elevations everywhere. A large group of small plants, all having the same half-round, umbrella-shaped flowerhead. Oval or lance-shaped basal leaves, with a leafless stalk rising from the centre to support the dense flowerhead of tiny petal-less flowers. The sepals provide the color. A common species to know is the **sulphur plant** *(E. flavum)*, mid-June to early August. It's eastern-slope, quite hairy, with a bright-yellow, less-compact flowerhead.

See also silver plant, page 366, and the white *Eriogonum* on page 305.

## Prairie parsley/biscuit root *Lomatium*

*Lomatium* spp. (carrot family)
Mid-May to early July, perennial

Southern montane. Several clusters of tiny, mustard-yellow flowers blooming close together to form a loose canopy. Many small, carrot-like leaflets spread out around the base. Edible stems and taproot. Four species in the Rockies; some larger, some smaller, all similar.

## Mullein/miner's-candlestick *Molène vulgaire/tabac du diable*

*Verbascum thapsus* (figwort family)
Mid-July through August, biennial

Pronounced "MULL-in." Common at low elevations in the southern Rocky Mountain Trench; on the eastern slope mainly in the foothills from Crowsnest Pass south. But mullein is an introduced species that can pop up anywhere; I have seen it along the railway just west of Jasper. Prefers disturbed ground. Spends its first summer putting down a big root, then in the second year sends up a ramrod-straight flowering stem often a metre or more tall; coarse and stout, with large oblong soft fuzzy olive-colored leaves that get smaller up the stem. Flowers are bright yellow, 1–2 cm across, packed in a spike atop the plant, which turns brown and stiffens in the fall.

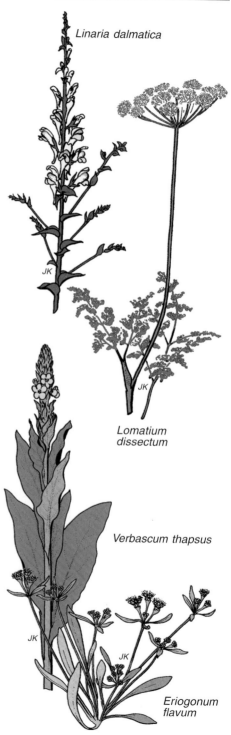

*Linaria dalmatica*

*Lomatium dissectum*

*Verbascum thapsus*

*Eriogonum flavum*

### Fragile pricklypear/brittle cactus
*Crapaud vert*
*Opuntia fragilis* (cactus family)
Mid-June to mid-July, perennial

Fairly common in sunny, dry places in the southern Rocky Mountain Trench from Radium south. Small and inconspicuous compared to the large cacti of the American southwest, but still easily identified as cactus: spiny greenish or salmon-colored fleshy joints each a few centimetres long, lying on the ground. They break off easily. Showy yellow flowers develop into reddish/purplish fruits.

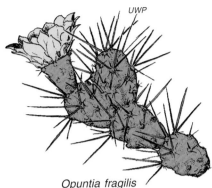

UWP

*Opuntia fragilis*

### Other flowers to check
- Wild sweet pea and milk-vetch, page 298
- *Brickellia,* page 298
- Skunk-cabbage, page 378
- Yellow water crowfoot, page 380

## Red or pink wildflowers below treeline

If it's not here, try the section for drab or reddish/greenish/brownish flowers, page 353.

### Red paintbrush *Castilléjie rougeâtre*
*Castilleja* spp. (figwort family)
Mid-may to late August, perennial

Montane and subalpine meadows, some-times above treeline. Perhaps the best-known flower of the Rockies and very easy to identify. A close look shows that the color, which ranges from reddish-orange to purple, is not carried on the petals—they are green—but on the bracts. Another little-known fact about paintbrush is that the plant is a parasite, attaching its roots to those of other plants to gain part of its nutrients.

There are many species and keying them out is difficult. The most common red species is *C. miniata;* its color varies from reddish-orange to crimson. Purplish flowers are usually *C. rhexifolia,* which interbreeds above treeline with alpine yellow paintbrush, page 367. Along the Alaska Highway you may see one with purplish stems: *C. raupii.*

See also yellow paintbrush, page 327. There are also red/yellow hybrids.

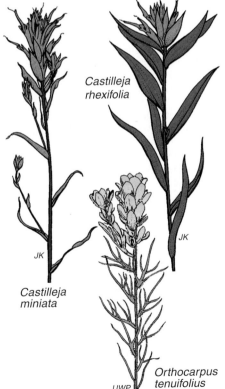

*Castilleja
rhexifolia*

*Castilleja
miniata*

JK

JK

*Orthocarpus
tenuifolius*

UWP

### Thin-leaved owl-clover
*Trèfle d'hibou aux feuilles minces*
*Orthocarpus tenuifolius* (figwort family)
June and July, annual

Low elevations, western-slope montane from Radium south. Colored bracts like paintbrush, but also tiny trumpet-shaped flowers hidden among them. The leaves are very narrow, hairy and divided into threes.

## Pale sweetvetch/pale hedysarum
*Sainfoin alpin*
*Hedysarum alpinum* (pea family)
Late June to early August, perennial
(Jasper: June 13)

Montane, in clearings. Pale pink flowers on tall, pointy spikes; rows of small paired leaves. Compare with wild vetch, page 342, and purple sweetvetch, page 343. Members of this genus have jointed pods, which distinguishes them from the other pea-family plants. See also yellow hedysarum, page 326.

## Red clover *Trèfle des prés/trèfle rouge*
*Trifolium pratense* (pea family)
Mid-June to early August, biennial/perennial

Montane, in open grassy places and on disturbed ground. Most individuals are biennial; some are perennial but live only a few years. The leaves of red clover are noticeably larger than those of lawn-variety white clover, as are red clover's flowerheads, which are pale pink or reddish, not white. Differentiate from similar **alsike clover**, *T. hybridum*, by red clover's toothy leaves with whitish markings, and the small leaves under the flowerhead.

## Horsemint/wild bergamot *Monarde fistuleuse/monarde à feuilles de menthe*
*Monarda fistulosa* (mint family)
Mid-July to mid-August, perennial

Southern montane and lower subalpine, occasional as far north as the Columbia Icefield, in meadows. Showy flowerhead looks like the frayed end of a pink or mauve rope; flowers are tube-like with stamens sticking out. The square stem is straight, about 50 cm tall, with pairs of toothy leaves. Just below the flowerhead the leaves are smooth-edged.

## Twinflower *Linnée boréale*
*Linnaea borealis* (honeysuckle family)
Late June to late July, perennial (Jasper: May 14)

Montane, subalpine and in Columbian forest. A ground-covering shrub with small round leaves rather like kinnikinnik, page 296, or mountain cranberry, next item, and often growing with them. But the leaf tips of

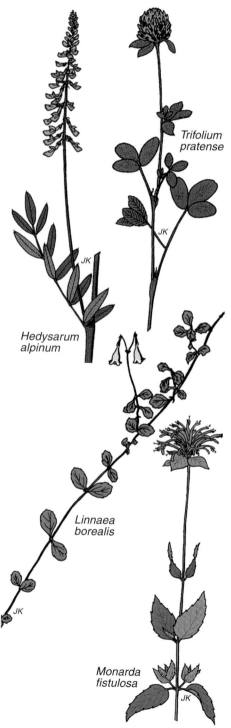

Trifolium
pratense

Hedysarum
alpinum

Linnaea
borealis

Monarda
fistulosa

twinflower are toothy. Common except in the Waterton/Glacier area and easy to identify by the two pale-pink bell-shaped flowers hanging from bent stalks. Fragrant.

This plant was the favorite of Carl von Linné, known to science as **Carolus Linnaeus,** the Swedish botanist and medical doctor who established the binomial (genus-and-species) classification system in 1753. His official portrait shows him holding a specimen of twinflower.

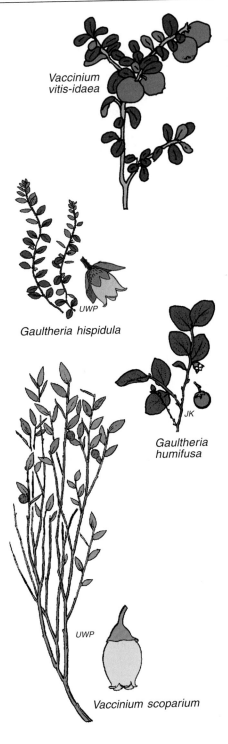

*Vaccinium vitis-idaea*

*Gaultheria hispidula*

*Gaultheria humifusa*

*Vaccinium scoparium*

### Mountain cranberry/lingonberry/cow-berry *Airelle de montagne*
*Vaccinium vitis-idaea* (heath family)
June, perennial

In subalpine and damp montane woods, common from the Bow River north, absent at Waterton/Glacier. A ground-covering shrub that resembles kinnikinnik (page 296) and largely replaces it in subalpine forest. The two species grow together in the northern foothills. The leaves are smaller than kinnikinnik and have tiny black glands underneath; the plant blooms in small clusters of little pale-pink bell-shaped flowers without the out-turned lip of the kinnikinnik flower, which is mostly white. The red cranberries are tart, sweetening after several frosts. See also creeping wintergreen, next item.

### Creeping wintergreen/creeping snowberry *Gaulthérie hispide/petit thé/oeufs de perdrix*
*Gaultheria hispidula* (heath family)
July, perennial

Damp spots in montane evergreen woods; absent at Waterton/Glacier. Low-growing, with tiny oval leaves that are dark above and hairy brown beneath. Even tinier pinkish flowers only 2 mm across are cup-shaped, hidden among the leaves. Produces small white berries flavored like wintergreen mints. *G. humifusa* has white flowers and red berries. It grows at subalpine elevations from Waterton/Glacier at least as far north as the Kakwa River.

### Grouseberry *Airelle à fruits roses*
*Vaccinium scoparium* (heath family)
Mid-June to mid-July, perennial

Upper-subalpine shrub, common in open woods of the central region. Low-growing and straggly, with pale-green stems and a thin foliage of small, pointed pale leaves. Flowers appear at places where the leaves join the stem; they are small, urn-shaped and pink. The red-to-purple berries are BB-sized and flat-ended—like tiny blueberries, which is what they are. Delicious.

### Pink pussytoes/rosy everlasting
*Antennaire rosée*
*Antennaria rosea* (composite family)
June to August, perennial
    Meadows and open montane forest, usually in small patches. A tight cluster of small, rounded flowers on short-leaved stems above larger, finely divided felty gray-green basal leaves. Each flower in the cluster has a white centre with a narrow red border, making the whole flowerhead appear pink. *A. rosea* may be a subspecies of white pussytoes. See page 297 for picture.

### Three-flowered avens/prairie smoke/ old-man's whiskers *Benoîte à trois fleurs*
*Geum triflorum* (rose family)
Mid-May through June, perennial
    South-facing open montane slopes, more common on the eastern side of the Rockies. Strange-looking plant: three round red closed blooms with bright-red hairy sepals hiding cream-colored petals within, nodding on reddish stems over finely divided leaves. Stands only 10–15 cm tall. Flowers turn upward when going to seed, like dryas; they produce wavy filaments. A field of seedheads looks like smoke when seen from a distance.

### Pipsissewa/prince's pine
*Chimaphile à ombelles/herbe à peigne*
*Chimaphila umbellata* (wintergreen family)
July, perennial
    Montane forests, mostly in the southern area and on the western slope. Small plant with leaves near or on the ground; several flowers on stalks radiate from a central leafless stem 10–20 cm tall. Flowers red and globe-shaped at first, later opening out in pale-pink petals with pink centres. The leaves are distinctive: rather holly-like, glossy green, oblong and toothy, in basal whorls.

### Common pink wintergreen/pyrola
*Pyrole à feuilles d'Asaret*
*Pyrola asarifolia* (wintergreen family)
Mid-June to mid-August, perennial
(Jasper: June 12)
    Montane evergreen woods. Striking plant: a greenish-pink, leafless stem, 10–20 cm high,

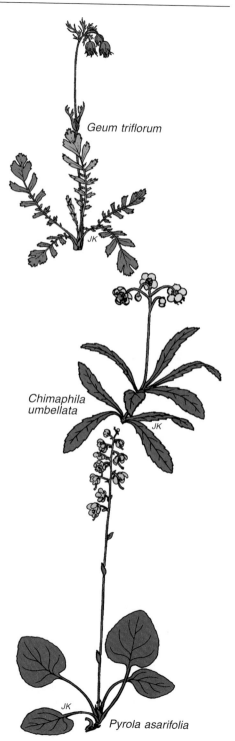

Geum triflorum

Chimaphila umbellata

Pyrola asarifolia

with about a dozen nodding pink flowers. If they are greenish-white, see green pyrola, page 308. The leaves are round and glossy green, lying at the base.

None of the wintergreens listed in this book smells of wintergreen oil, although the berries of creeping wintergreen, page 331, taste of it. The wintergreen for which the fragrant oil is named is *Gaultheria procumbens,* native to southeastern Canada and the northeastern U.S.

### Lesser wintergreen *Pyrole alpine*
*Pyrola minor* (wintergreen family)
July, perennial

On moist ground in mossy woods up to treeline; sometimes above, in sheltered places. More common in northerly sections. Has glossy basal leaves, a bare stalk and pale-pink, white or greenish flowers. Resembles common wintergreen, previous item, and green wintergreen, page 308, but the pistil of *P. minor* is straight and does not extend past the petals. This is a dwarf species, growing only about 10 cm tall; the others are 20–30 cm.

### Elephant-head/little elephants
*Pédiculaire du Groenland*
*Pedicularis groenlandica* (figwort family)
Late June to early August, perennial

Montane and subalpine, in wet places. A spike of small pink flowers, each of which looks like the head of an elephant, complete with trunk and ears. Leaves are frilly and drab purplish-green.

### Calypso orchid/fairy's-slipper/ Venus's-slipper *Calypso bulbeux*
*Calypso bulbosa* (orchid family)
Mid-May to early July, perennial
(Jasper: May 8)

Shady montane woods. The most beautiful of the Rocky Mountain orchids; once seen, always remembered. See photo on page 248. Upper part of flower pink to pale-purple; below, bright-yellow stamens with black tips hang over the purple-marked white lower lip of the flower. Often in small patches, each plant with only one basal leaf, round and dark-green.

The flower's shape, colors, fragrance and early blooming time are all designed to attract bumblebee queens, which accidentally pick up sticky pouches of pollen from one flower and unknowingly deliver them to another. Such good service is not rewarded, however: the

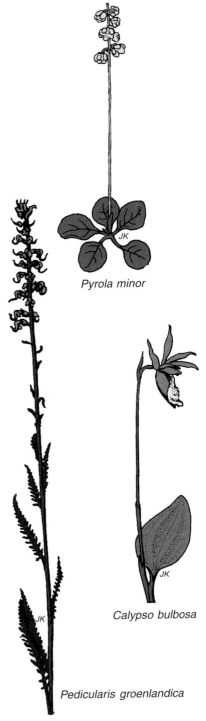

*Pyrola minor*

*Calypso bulbosa*

*Pedicularis groenlandica*

plant produces no nectar. The bumblebees soon learn this, but enough young, naive queens fall for the ploy each year to ensure that pollination occurs and *Calypso bulbosa* endures.

### Heart-leaved twayblade
*Listère à feuilles cordées*
*Listera cordata* (orchid family)
July and August, perennial

Subalpine, in shady woods. Can range in color from green to purple, but most often red. Two round leaves, pointed at the tip and indented at the back, are paired partway up the stem. At the top of the plant, which is only 10–15 cm tall, are five to ten small flowers, each with a long split lower lip and a canopy of five petals. See also the other twayblades, page 309.

### Spotted coral-root and striped coral-root
*Corallorhize maculée, corallorhize striée*
*Corallorhiza maculata* and *C. striata*
(orchid family) Mid-June to mid-July, perennials

Moist montane woods. No leaves; these plants are saprophytes that send their coral-like roots into buried dead plant matter. Associated fungi help take up nutrients. Strikingly colored: spotted coral root has droopy reddish flowers, with white tongues marked by red spots and blotches. The striped coral-root has larger flowers that are marked with thin red lines. See also northern coral-root, page 302.

### Pine drops *Ptérospore andromède*
*Pterospora andromedea* (ghost-flower family)
July and August, perennial

Low elevations in the Rocky Mountain Trench at least as far north as Valemount and Tête Jaune Cache; on the eastern slope found only south of Crowsnest Pass. Easily identified: a tall, skinny reddish or purplish sticky stalk with no leaves—it's parasitic on roots of pines—and small round pale flowers. The stem can be shoulder-high; it dries out and stands through the winter, distributing seeds.

### Red monkey-flower *Mimule de Lewis*
*Mimulus lewisii* (figwort family)
Mid-July through August, perennial

Subalpine to low alpine, along streams; common in southern areas and on the western slope, scarce north of Crowsnest Pass on the eastern slope. Large, showy pink or red flowers that are sometimes mistaken for violets, but

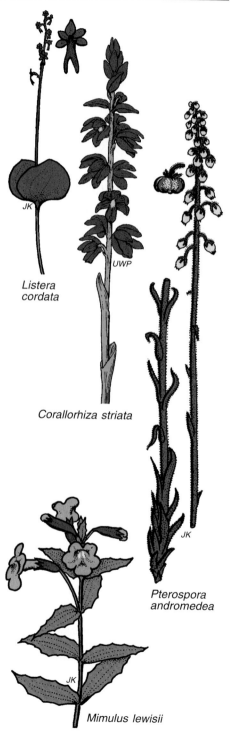

*Listera cordata*

*Corallorhiza striata*

*Pterospora andromedea*

*Mimulus lewisii*

there are no red or pink violets known in the Canadian Rockies. Yellow flower centres with dark dots. Leaves grow in pairs on stems 30–50 cm tall; they are pointed and scalloped.

### Lyall's beard-tongue *Penstémon de Lyall*
*Penstemon lyallii* (figwort family)
June to early August, perennial

Upper montane and subalpine, sometimes alpine, found mainly south of Crowsnest Pass. Large, showy pink-to-purple flowers seem too heavy for the weak stems, which let the plant flop untidily on the ground. Narrow leaves. See also the purple penstemons, page 344.

### Shooting star/peacock/roosterhead
*Giroselle*
*Dodecatheon* spp. (primrose family)
Late May to late June, perennial
(Jasper: May 23)

Mostly montane, but also subalpine and low alpine, in meadows and along lakeshores. Large, very striking flower: the deep-pink or purple petals bend straight back, exposing yellow stamens and dark, pointed anthers. Don't confuse with the small bog cranberry, next item, which is similar but much smaller.

We have two species of shooting stars, best differentiated when in seed. In *D. conjugens,* which grows in dry places, the pod opening has squared edges; in *D. pulchellum,* which needs moister soil, the opening is saw-toothed. Both species are equally common in southern areas; *D. conjugens* is unreported north of Saskatchewan Crossing on the eastern slope.

### Small bog cranberry *Atocas à petits fruits*
*Vaccinium oxycoccos* (heath family)
June, perennial

Swamps, streambanks and lakeshores, montane and subalpine, central and northern areas. More common on the eastern slope, but absent at Waterton/Glacier. Often growing with Labrador tea. It's actually a shrub, because it has a woody stem, but it grows right on the ground. The stems are covered with tiny needle-like (but soft) green leaves that resemble crowberry, page 374, or heather, page 361, until the plant blooms. The small flowers are readily identifiable: each has four pale-pink petals bent backward, like a miniature shooting-star—see previous item—leaving the yellow anthers exposed. The berries are tasty, true cranberries, sweeter after a frost or two. Also known as *Oxycoccos microcarpus.*

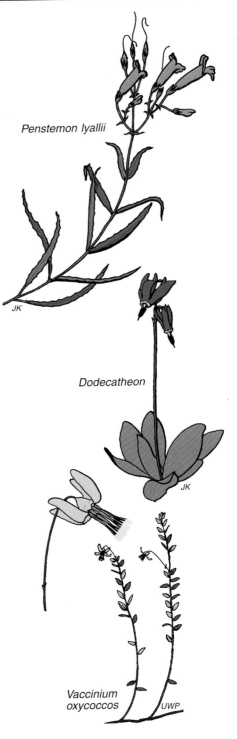

Penstemon lyallii

JK

Dodecatheon

JK

Vaccinium oxycoccos

UWP

### Swamp laurel/mountain laurel
*Kalmia à petites feuilles*
*Kalmia polifolia* or *microphylla* (heath family)
Late June and July, perennial

Subalpine, sometimes alpine, beside streams and in bogs; rare in southern areas. An ankle-high shrub with thick evergreen leaves that are dark green on top, paler beneath and often rolled under like those of Labrador tea, but not fuzzy underneath as in Labrador tea. The five-lobed pink flowers are small but showy, with an elongated style sticking out.

Botanists disagree on the species name, listing one as a variety of the other. Certainly the *microphylla* species/variety is shorter, with smaller leaves, and grows at higher elevations than the *polifolia* species/variety.

### Red columbine *Ancolie rouge*
*Aquilegia formosa* (buttercup family)
Early June through July, perennial

Western-slope montane to alpine; occasional on the eastern slope in central sections. Bushy plants up to a metre tall. Large, very showy flowers with characteristic nectar-laden spurs in the back. Color ranges from crimson to orange. Typical columbine leaves: broad but deeply indented, with rounded edges. Compare with leaves of meadow-rue, page 309.

This plant hybridizes with yellow columbine, page 322, especially through mountain passes in the central section, where many flowers are both pink and yellow.

### Fireweed and river beauty/broad-leaved willow-herb
*Épilobe à feuilles étroites/bouquets rouges, épilobe à feuilles larges*
*Epilobium angustifolium* and *E. latifolium* (evening primrose family)
mid-July to late-August, perennials

Montane and subalpine. Showy plants with large four-petalled pink flowers. Be sure you get the right one; at time of writing, an interpretive sign along the Icefields Parkway near Beauty Creek misidentifies river beauty as fireweed.

**Fireweed** *(E. angustifolium)* is a tall plant, up to 1.5 m, with dozens of flowers carried on a tall spike with many rod-like seed pods. It grows best on disturbed ground, such as roadsides, logged areas and recent burns. Official floral emblem of the Yukon.

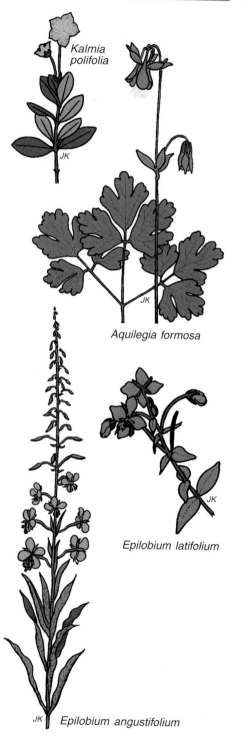

*Kalmia polifolia*

*Aquilegia formosa*

*Epilobium latifolium*

*Epilobium angustifolium*

**River beauty** (*E. Latifolium*) has somewhat larger flowers, but there are fewer on the spike—typically half a dozen—and the whole plant is lower-growing than fireweed, seldom more than 30 cm tall. Broad-leaved willow herb likes gravelly places such as alluvial fans, especially the outwash flats downstream from glaciers. It is common from the Bow River north. Both species produce long, cottony seeds in late summer.

## Collomia *Collomia*
*Collomia grandiflora* (phlox family)
Mid-June to early July, perennial
Western-slope montane, at low elevations. Grows 15–20 cm tall, with narrow leaves along the stem and a cluster of large, trumpet-shaped flowers at the top. *C. linearis* grows in the Waterton/Glacier area; is similar but with smaller flowers. Collomia is sometimes mistaken for scarlet gilia/skyrocket, *Gilia aggregata,* which borders the Canadian Rockies on the south and west.

## Bird's-eye primrose and mealy primrose *Primavère de Mistassini, primavère farineuse*
*Primula mistassinica* and *P. incana*
(primrose family) Late May and June, perennial
Montane and subalpine, near water. Common in northern areas and occasional south to the Bow River; absent at Waterton/Glacier. Bird's-eye primrose is a small plant 10–15 cm tall, often overlooked. Small, toothy basal leaves and a leafless erect stem bear one or more flowers with five distinctive notched pale-pink or purplish petals. There is a pit in the flower centre, surrounded by a yellow rim.

Mealy primrose is similar but taller, up to 40 cm, with a larger number of smaller flowers and smooth-edged basal leaves. See also dwarf raspberry, next item, and dwarf epilobium, next page.

## Dwarf raspberry/arctic raspberry/dewberry *Ronce arctique*
*Rubus arcticus* (rose family)
Late June to mid-July, perennial
Montane and lower subalpine, in moist meadows. Scarce in Waterton/Glacier, fairly common north of Banff. Close relative of the raspberry, page 278, with similar leaves, but dwarf raspberry is a wildflower, not a shrub, because it dies back to the roots each year.

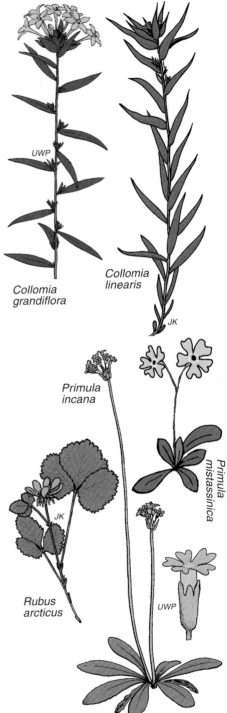

*Collomia grandiflora*

*Collomia linearis*

*Primula incana*

*Primula mistassinica*

*Rubus arcticus*

This plant grows low to the ground. Pink, widely separated petals are interspersed with green bracts that quickly become ragged, giving the flowers a wilted appearance. Insipid-tasting raspberries in August. In Columbian forest this species is absent; in its place is the smaller, white-blooming *R. pedatus,* trailing raspberry, page 296.

### Dwarf epilobiums *Épilobes naines*
*Epilobium* spp. (evening primrose family)
Late June to early August, mostly perennials

Subalpine and alpine, sometimes at low elevations but nearly always beside running water.

There are 11 species of *Epilobium* in the Canadian Rockies, and except for fireweed and river beauty, page 336, few are known to anyone but botanists. Most of these plants are small and difficult to differentiate. The flowers are typically only a centimetre or so across, but they are often eye-catching: the four petals of most meet at right angles like an X. On many individuals each petal is deeply notched, so that it looks like a double. *E. anagallidifolium* is perhaps the most common form in the Canadian Rockies, and it has these characteristics.

The color of the dwarf epilobiums varies a lot. Most plants are pink, but I have seen pure white ones at Vermilion Pass, at Waterton, and in northern Jasper park.

*Epilobium anagallidifolium*

*Iliamna rivularis*

### Mountain hollyhock
*Rose trémière des montagnes*
*Iliamna rivularis* (mallow family)
June through September, perennial

At low elevations, western-slope montane and at a few locations in Waterton/Glacier. A tall plant up to 2 m, bushy and showy, with large pale-pink flowers 5–10 cm broad in spikes. The leaves are large and maple-shaped, with toothed margins.

### Showy milkweed *Asclépiade éclatant*
*Asclepias speciosa* (milkweed family)
June and July, perennial

Found mainly in the driest part of the southern Rocky Mountain Trench around Wasa and Fort Steele, on sunny slopes. Reported from Glacier and the southern Alberta foothills but not from Waterton. Large rounded clusters of star-shaped pink or purplish flowers atop stems with lance-shaped leaves showing distinctive white veining. Milky juice. Large pods split

*Asclepias speciosa*

open, spilling cottony seeds; the stalks dry and remain upright for much of the winter.

Milkweeds are pollinated by insects that get little horseshoe-shaped pollen-carriers called **pollinia** clipped onto their legs as they enter the flower. They must break the pollinium free to leave; many cannot and are trapped. Escapees fly to other milkweeds, where the pollinia catch, come off, and fit perfectly into the proper spot for fertilization.

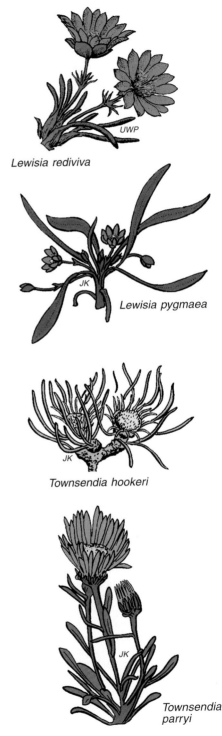

*Lewisia rediviva*

### Bitterroot/rock rose *Racine-amère*
*Lewisia rediviva* and *L. pygmaea*
(purslane family) April and May, perennials

Both species are low-growing but showy. *L. rediviva* is southern western-slope montane, with reports from the eastern-slope foothills around Crowsnest Pass. Prefers dry, rocky places. It has pink flowers 4–6 cm across with 10–15 petals that are often paler toward the flower centre, which is orange or yellow. State flower of Montana. The leaves are thick and narrow, succulent in spring but then drying up as summer goes by. The thick taproot is distinctive, often wedged in rock.

*L. pygmaea* looks similar, but has 6–8 petals on a smaller flower. It's mainly a southern, western-slope subalpine and alpine species. Also reported from Waterton/Glacier.

*Lewisia pygmaea*

### Townsendia *Townsendie de Hooker*
*Townsendia hookeri* (composite family)
Early May, perennial

In dry meadows in the southern foothills and eastern parts of Waterton/Glacier, but also found sporadically at least as far north as Jasper and possibly on the western slope south of Radium. At first glance this short, stout-stemmed, showy flower looks like a pink fleabane, but it belongs to a different genus; all the fleabanes are *Erigeron,* and most are paler; see page 306.

Townsendia varies in color from pure white to purplish; there is a purplish-blue species in the Rockies from the Red Deer River south *(T. parryi).* Usually at least one bloom on *T. hookeri* will have pink-tipped petals. Hairy leaves with upturned margins, mostly at the base. Large flowers on short stalks, only 2–5 cm high.

*Townsendia hookeri*

### Strawberry blite *Arroche-fraise*
*Chenopodium capitatum* (goosefoot family)
June–August, annual

A Eurasian weed found at low elevations in disturbed places, especially in burns. In the

*Townsendia parryi*

Rockies usually 20–50 cm tall, with triangular leaves and eye-catching flowerheads that look like ripe strawberries set along the stem.

### Bladder campion *Silène cucubale/pétards*
*Silene cucubalus* (pink family)
August, perennial

An introduced species, common in the southern area, found north at least as far as Cadomin. Typically knee-high and bushy, with lance-shaped leaves. The blooms are interesting: a swollen pink sepal tube—the "bladder"—is showier than the actual petals, which are white and barely protrude. No picture.

### One-toed baby's-bottom *Faisses-bébé*
*Infansdorsum unidactyl* (baby's-bottom family)
Mid-July, perianal

Exceedingly rare but interesting, known only from one location halfway up the Palisade cliff near Jasper, growing on a wood-rat nest. Bulbous pink two-part flower carries a single toe-like pediatric pistil, always on the right lobe. Leaves are opposite and deeply cleft. Striking odor.

### Other pinkish flowers
- Lyall's saxifrage, page 358
- Windflower, page 293
- Showy locoweed, page 343
- Moss phlox, page 294
- Buckbrush, page 281

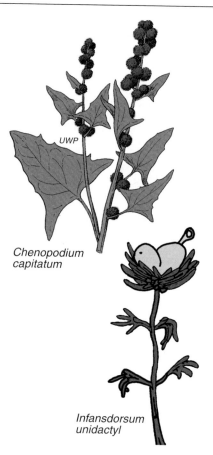

*Chenopodium capitatum*

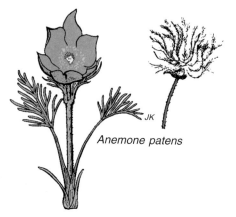

*Infansdorsum unidactyl*

## Blue or purple wildflowers below treeline

This section includes such favorites as the harebell and the early blue violet.

### Pasque flower/prairie crocus
*Anémone des prairies*
*Anemone patens* (buttercup family)
Late March to mid-May, perennial
(Jasper: April 7)

Montane, usually on south-facing slopes. Widely thought of as the earliest wildflower in the Rockies, although the pussy willow, page 266, is actually the earliest. Look for pasque flowers only a few days behind the melting snow.

The prairie crocus is not a crocus, it's an anemone, but the shape is crocus-like. "Pasque flower" is a better name; it refers to the beginning of blooming around Easter. Flower is pale-blue or pale-purple, occasionally white, with a yellow centre, open by day and closed by night. Grows close to the ground on a short,

*Anemone patens*

very fuzzy stem; leaves are frilly, also fuzzy, and appear beneath the flower after it has come up. As in all anemones, the plant is taller when in seed.

The name of this plant is often mis-pronounced. It's "a-NEM-oh-nee," not "a-NEN-oh-me." Same with the anemone that lives in the sea. Keep the syllables straight by remembering that "any money is better than an enemy."

*Calochortus macrocarpus*

### Sagebrush mariposa lily/green-banded mariposa *Mariposa mauve*
*Calochortus macrocarpus* (lily family)
Late May to early June, perennial

Rocky Mountain Trench floor from Radium south, on dry slopes. Easily identified: one, sometimes more large lavender flowers, each with three broad petals marked by a central green band. The stem stands 20–50 cm tall, with one long, narrow leaf at the base. See also the white mariposa lily, page 287.

### Blue-eyed grass *Herbe-aux-yeux-bleus*
*Sisyrinchium montanum* (iris family)
Mainly June; again in August, perennial (Jasper: June 15)

Montane, in open places near water. Grass-like leaves 10–40 cm tall, with star-shaped, yellow-centred blue flowers individually on stems as long as the leaves. Blooms early, then repeats in August, although in lesser numbers.

### Blue clematis *Clématite bleue*
*Clematis occidentalis* (buttercup family)
Late May and June, perennial (Jasper: June 1)

Most any pronunciation is acceptable. Take your pick: "KLEM-uh-tiss," or "klem-AH-tiss," with long or short *a*. A woody vine, clematis twines among the shrubbery in montane woods and brushy places, central and southern sections. Down-turned flowers each have four long sepals, blue to purple, that tend to twist near the ends. They look like petals. Leaves 3–8 cm, lance-shaped, with indented veins. Plant is also known as *C. columbiana*.

### Blue camas *Quamassie*
*Camassia quamash* (lily family)
Late May to early June, perennial

Eastern slope only, in a few locations in the southern region. Deep blue, showy flowers with six parts and long stamens. Grows 30–60 cm tall, with long, narrow leaves reaching up from the base. Short blooming season.

*Camassia quamash*

*Sisyrinchium montanum*

*Clematis occidentalis*

### Nodding onion *Ail penché*
*Allium cernuum* (lily family)
Mid-July to early August, perennial

Central and southern montane and subalpine, in open places and often near water. Distinctive flowerheads: many lavender, purple or even pink bell-shaped flowers on long stalks that radiate from the top of the stem. Long, very narrow leaves smell of onion if crushed. Grows 15–50 cm tall; bulb is edible and strongly flavored.

However, you might wish to pass such edible plants by in favor of the grocery-store varieties. All native wildflowers need protection—and many of them get it, in the form of no-picking laws.

### Wild chive *Ciboulette*
*Allium schoenoprasum* (lily family)
Late June and July, perennial

Montane, in moist ground; often along lakeshores. Another kind of wild onion, this one with a tuft-like flowerhead that varies from pink to purple, usually mauve. Long thin hollow leaves grow upward from the base. Seeds are in small dark pods.

### Purple milk-vetch *Astragale pourpre*
*Astragalus dasyglottis* (pea family)
Late May to early June, perennial

Dry montane meadows, central region. A small, hairy plant with fairly compact clusters of pea-type pale-purple or purple-tinged white flowers on stems 5–20 cm tall. Common around Jasper.

### Wild vetch/American vetch
*Vesce d'Amérique*
*Vicia americana* (pea family)
June and July, perennial

A montane vine—but not a shrub—hanging onto its neighbors. Common in Yellowhead Pass on the highway shoulders. Oval leaflets in rows, and tendrils at stem ends like wild sweet pea, page 298, but with bluish-purple flowers rather than cream or yellowish ones. Pea-pods in August. This is the only native vetch that is common in the Canadian Rockies, although many other pea-family plants are called "vetch." Compare with sweetvetch, next item.

Allium
cernuum

Allium
schoenoprasum

Astragalus dasyglottis

Vicia americana

### Sweetvetch/Mackenzie's hedysarum
*Sainfoin de Mackenzie*
*Hedysarum boreale* (pea family)
Late May to early July, perennial

The dictionary pronunciation is "hee-DISS-uh-rum." A common montane and lower subalpine species, in dry clearings. Very fragrant reddish-purple pea-type flowers in floppy clusters. Small dark-green leaflets in rows. Bears dig up and eat the roots of this plant in spring. See also pale sweetvetch, page 330.

*Hedysarum boreale*

### Showy locoweed *Oxytrope brillant*
*Oxytropis splendens* (pea family)
Late June to mid-July, perennial

Montane, in dry open places; often on disturbed ground such as highway shoulders. Common on the eastern slope; occasional on the western slope.

This a hard one to group by color. Both pink and purple occur on the same plant; some people think of it as pink, perhaps because the plant is so white-hairy that the purple is diluted. It looks purple to me. At any rate, it blossoms in dense spikes above fuzzy gray-green leaves. Not tall, 10–20 cm, but easy to spot and identify. Unlike some other locoweeds, this one is not harmful to cattle.

*Lupinus sericeus*

### Wild lupine *Lupin*
*Lupinus* spp. (pea family)
Late June to early August, perennial

Montane and subalpine, common on the western slope but on the eastern slope common only in Waterton/Glacier and north of the Peace River. Occasional elsewhere, usually in lower subalpine forest.

With its pea-like flowers, lupine would be difficult to tell from the other pea-family members were it not for the leaves, which spread out in frondy leaflets rather than looking like rows of teeth.

There are many lupine species, varying in minute ways. Most are blue or lavender, although the flowers of **arctic lupine** (*L. arcticus*), a common form along the Alaska Highway in the northern area, are blue with white tips. From Jasper northward, and from farther south on the western slope, look for the very showy *L. nootkatensis*, which has white and yellow patches at the bases of the large blue petals. *Lupinus sericeus* is a common species in the southern region; it has the typical lupine leaf shape and flowerhead.

*Oxytropis splendens*

### Spotted orchid/round-leaved orchid
*Orchide à feuille ronde*
*Orchis rotundifolia* (orchid family)
Mid-June to early July, perennial
(Jasper: June 10)

Eastern-slope montane, central and northern regions, usually in spruce woods; rare in Waterton/Glacier. Not common but worth hunting for: the small flowers look like angels in purple-dotted white robes, with mauve hats and wings—really! One rounded leaf at the base.

### Penstemon/beard-tongue *Penstémon*
*Penstemon* spp. (figwort family) .
May to August, perennial

At all elevations, but mainly montane and subalpine, in a variety of habitats. Many species, difficult for the non-botanist to differentiate. All have showy spikes of tubular flowers with asymmetric lips: two petals above, three below. Shades of color differ inside and outside. Hairiness within the flower accounts for the name "beard-tongue." Here are five common species, easier than some others to tell apart.

**Slender blue beard-tongue** *(P. procerus),* late May to July (Jasper: June 10). Perhaps the most common penstemon in the Rockies north of Crowsnest Pass. Its flowers are only 1 cm long, smaller than the others, and carried in a tiered spike. The plant stands 10–20 cm tall. Look for it in moist, open places, montane and subalpine.

**Smooth blue beard-tongue** *(P. nitidus),* May to June. Limited to the southern foothills/ Waterton/Glacier area in dry, sunny places. Easily identified by the fleshy bluegreen foliage, with basal leaves narrow and ones on the stem broader, and interestingly colored trumpet-shaped flowers: blue inside, with a long yellow stamen; pink or pale purple outside. Tall for a penstemon: 20–30 cm.

**Lilac-flowered beard-tongue** *(P. gracilis),* June and July. A dainty-looking species with pale-lavender or even white flowers, 2–3 cm long. Grows 10–20 cm tall in grassy places in the southern foothills, although it is absent at Waterton/Glacier.

**Crested beard-tongue** *(P. eriantherus),* June. Known mainly from the southern area. Husky, colorful lavender to deep-purple blooms (pink inside) that seem to overweigh their stem. The throat of each flower is very hairy.

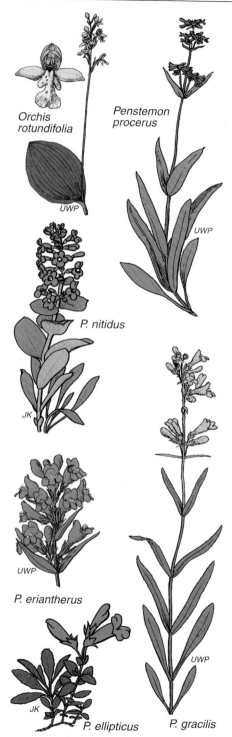

*Orchis rotundifolia*

*Penstemon procerus*

UWP

UWP

*P. nitidus*

JK

UWP

*P. eriantherus*

JK

*P. ellipticus*

*P. gracilis*

UWP

**Elliptical-leaved penstemon** *(P. ellipticus)*, late June to August. A low-growing penstemon with bluntly toothed, rather broad leaves and large lavender flowers on short, hairy stems. Subalpine and alpine.

### One-flowered broomrape/cancer-root
*Orobanche uniflore*
*Orobanche uniflora* (broomrape family)
April and May, perennial

Western-slope mostly, from Prince George south; on the eastern slope from the Bow River south. Like paintbrush or toadflax, broomrape is a root parasite. It has no green leaves. Hosts include stonecrop, saxifrages and pasture sage. Normally low-elevation montane, it sometimes grows well above treeline in moist places where saxifrages live. Small 2 cm penstemon-like, violet-like flower varies in color from yellow to mauve; usually blue. Always yellow inside. One flower atop each hairy stem, 5–10 cm long. See also clustered broomrape, page 326, and butterwort, page 348.

### Sticky geranium and Bicknell's geranium/crane's-bill
*Géranium visceux, géranium de Bicknell*
*Geranium viscosissimum* and *G. bicknellii* (geranium family)
Late May to August, annual or biennial

Montane meadows and open woods. Both plants have spreading, deeply divided leaves like those of cultivated geraniums, but the flowers are smaller, purple or pink-purple with reddish lines in the petals. These lines reflect ultraviolet light strongly and guide UV-seeing insects, such as bees, to the nectar. Sticky geranium grows from Saskatchewan Crossing south; is tall, 20–60 cm, sticky and blooms from June to mid-August. Bicknell's/crane's-bill, found in all regions, has smaller blooms about 1 cm across, is shorter, 15–25 cm, not sticky and flowers from late May to early July. See also wild white geranium, page 290.

### Montane speedwell/montane veronica
*Véronique*
*Veronica* spp. (figwort family)
July to early September, mostly perennials

Montane, in moist places. Various sizes, but usually less than 50 cm tall. The flowers bloom in sprays from leaf junctions; they are small, four-petalled and pale-blue to violet.

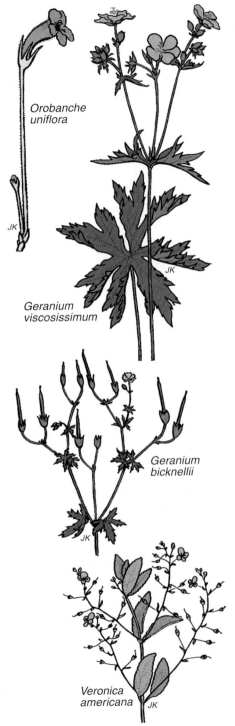

*Orobanche uniflora*

*Geranium viscosissimum*

*Geranium bicknellii*

*Veronica americana*

Look closely: the petals are unequal in length. *V. americana* is low-growing, with bluntly fine-toothed leaves; *V. catenata* often grows in water; *V. peregrina,* an annual species, has its flowers tucked up against the stem. See also alpine speedwell, page 370, a common alpine and upper-subalpine plant. Compare with forget-me-not, page 370, and next item.

### Blue-bur/stickseed *Bardanette bleue*
*Lappula squarrosa* (borage family)
Late June and early July, annual
    Montane meadows and disturbed ground. A wiry knee-high weed, but with pretty yellow-centred blue flowers very much like those of forget-me-not, page 370, a much smaller plant that grows above treeline—although there is a rare introduced forget-me-not, *Myosotis arvensis,* that may be present to confuse you. In August, blue-bur loads up your socks and shoelaces with tiny barbed seeds, which forget-me-not wouldn't think of doing.

### Jacob's-ladder *Polémoine très belle*
*Polemonium pulcherrimum* (phlox family)
Late May to mid-July, perennial
    Mostly montane but sometimes much higher; common in southern areas, occasional elsewhere. Prefers dry, open places. Looks like a taller, larger-flowered forget-me-not, page 370, but the leaflets are small and fern-like, arranged in sawtooth rows on reddish stems 20–30 cm high. See also western Jacob's-ladder, next item, and sky pilot, page 372.

### Western Jacob's-ladder
*Polémoine de l'Ouest*
*Polemonium acutiflorum* (phlox family)
June and July, perennial
    Clearings in dry montane woods, common from the Peace River north, occasional south to Cardinal Divide near Cadomin. An eye-catching plant: showy blue flaring bells ride in clusters atop tall (20–30 cm) wire-thin stems with incongruous sawtooth, pea-like leaves. Taller than *P. pulcherrimum,* previous item. Harebell, next item, has different leaves, as does wild blue flax, next page.

*Lappula squarrosa*

JK

JK

*Polemonium pulcherrimum*

UWP

*Polemonium acutiflorum*

## Harebell/bluebell
*Campanule à feuilles rondes*
*Campanula rotundifolia*
(harebell/bluebell family)
Mid-June to late September, perennial
(Jasper: June 15)

Very common in grassy eastern-slope montane meadows and open woods; also common on the western slope. Easy to recognize: several large sky-blue bells on a skinny stem 10–40 cm tall. But sometimes confused with Jacob's-ladder (previous item), wild blue flax (next item), and mertensia, next page.

The name is puzzling. If it were "*hair*bell," referring to the thin stems, that would be sensible, but it is *hare*bell, as in bunnies. The Scots seem to have done this to us. The plant is common in Scotland, where it is variously "bluebell" or "harebell." Further confusing the issue is Robert Burns's famous "Bluebells of Scotland" poem and song. These refer to *Endymion nonscriptum,* a wild hyacinth. "Harebell" is an old term, perhaps having something to do with witches turning themselves into hares, for an even older name is "witch's thimble." On the other hand, some sources say that harebell is just a phonetic spelling of the way people used to say "heather bell" in Britain long ago. The species does indeed grow in the heather over there.

People use "bluebell" for so many plants that I think we should stick to "harebell" for this one. There is only one genus called "harebell" in the Canadian or American Rockies, although there are two species: an alpine one, page 371, and the common one growing below treeline.

## Wild blue flax *Lin de Lewis*
*Linum lewisii* (flax family)
Late June to late July, perennial (Jasper: June 3)

Montane meadows and open woods. Fairly tall plant, up to 1 m, covered with individual showy blue flowers, yellow-centred, on slender stalks with small narrow leaves. The flowers are flatter than harebell, previous item, and the leaves are not sawtoothed like those of Jacob's-ladder, previous page. Each flower blooms but a day. Close relative of cultivated flax.

*Campanula rotundifolia*

*Linum lewisii*

### Mertensia/bluebell/tall lungwort
*Mertensie paniculée*
*Mertensia paniculata* (borage family)
Late May to late July, perennial (Jasper: June 2)
Common in montane woods, especially in aspen groves, through northern and central areas. Absent in Waterton/Glacier. Bushy plant up to a metre high, but not a shrub. Dark-green, heavily veined leaves and clusters of small nodding bells that are pink in the bud and blue upon opening. In the Waterton/Glacier area *M. paniculata* is missing, replaced by a smaller, less-bushy version: *M. longiflora.*

### Early blue violet/dog violet
*Violette bleue printanière*
*Viola adunca* (violet family)
Late April to early July, perennial (Jasper: Mayday)
Montane meadows and open woods, often in grass. A low-growing violet, usually in patches. Typical violet flower, often more purple than blue, with a white centre marked by dark lines. You may find an albino. Many small rounded leaves 1–3 cm long with blunt teeth, indented at the stem.
This plant may bloom again in the fall. In Jasper, early blue violets flowered *after* a hard frost in September of 1984, carrying on gaily in my lawn until October 16, when several centimetres of snow finally shut them down.

### Butterwort *Grassette vulgaire*
*Pinguicula vulgaris* (bladderwort family)
June and July, perennial (Jasper: June 3)
Montane and subalpine woods, near water. A small plant with pale-green slightly in-curled glossy basal leaves covered with the bugs that it traps and digests; like sundew, page 299, butterwort is insectivorous. It can grow in nitrogen-poor locations because the bugs provide the nitrogen. The bloom is pretty and blue, a violet-like flower with a spur on the back, nodding on a stalk 10–15 cm high. Another insectivorous plant in the Rockies is bladderwort, page 376.

### Brook lobelia *Lobélie de Kalm*
*Lobelia kalmii* (lobelia family)
Mid-August to early September, biennial
Occasional in wet places, central and northern montane woods, usually on sites with limestone bedrock. Small but distinctive blue or purple flowers: two narrow petals on the

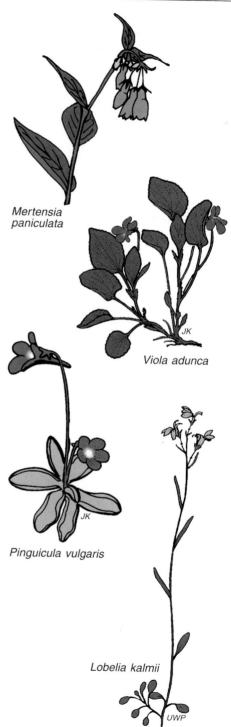

*Mertensia paniculata*

*Viola adunca*

*Pinguicula vulgaris*

*Lobelia kalmii*

upper part, with a bump between them, and three wider petals below. White and yellow in the centre. Plant is only 10–20 cm tall. If you find a lobelia growing in shallow water of a lake or pond, it is *L. dortmanna.*

### Northern blue columbine
*Ancolie bleue/gants de Notre-Dame bleues*
*Aquilegia brevistyla* (buttercup family)
Mid-June to early July, perennial

Occasional in montane and subalpine meadows or open woods from the Bow River north; absent at Waterton/Glacier. Large, showy flowers like yellow columbine, page 322, or red columbine, page 336, but blue, mauve or purple with white trim.

Northern columbine is bushy, with spreading, deeply divided round-edged leaves. The flowers of northern blue columbine look rather like those of their southern-Rockies kin *A. coerulea,* the Colorado columbine, but *A. brevistyla* flowers are smaller. Hybridization of northern blue columbine with yellow columbine and red columbine can produce some odd color combinations. See also alpine columbine, page 372.

### Tall larkspur/tall delphinium
*Dauphinelle glauque*
*Delphinium glaucum* (buttercup family)
Mid-July to mid-August, perennial

Subalpine meadows, central and northern areas; not found at Waterton/Glacier. Tall, very showy spikes of deep blue or purple flowers, each with a spur on the back. Leaves are dark-green, spreading and finely divided. Poisonous; animals do not eat it. A much shorter version, *D. bicolor,* mid-May to late June, grows at all elevations from the Bow River south; it's most common in the Waterton/Glacier area; the flower has white on it as well as blue. In the southern Rocky Mountain Trench look for a shaggy version, *D. menziesii.* See also monkshood, next item.

### Monkshood/aconite *Aconite*
*Aconitum delphinifolium* (buttercup family)
Late June and July, perennial

Subalpine meadows, northern and central areas. Not found south of the North Saskatchewan River. Monkshood often grows with larkspur, previous item, which it resembles in size, color and leaf shape—but the flowers are different. Like larkspur, monkshood is poisonous.

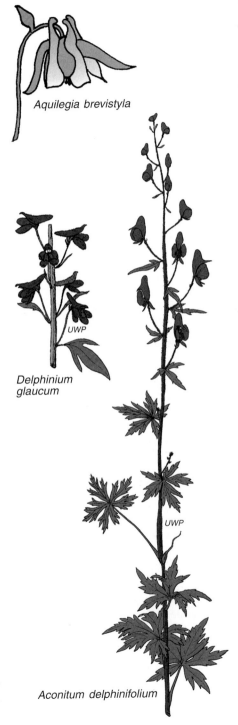

*Aquilegia brevistyla*

*Delphinium glaucum*

UWP

UWP

*Aconitum delphinifolium*

### Purple alfalfa/lucerne *Luzerne*
*Medicago sativa* (pea family) July, perennial

Dry montane meadows, fields and disturbed ground. Introduced. Not as tall as white sweet clover, page 299, or yellow sweet clover, page 326, but with the same pea-family leaves. The purple flowers are in small clusters rather than long cylindrical ones; the pods are coiled. This plant shows an incredible range of color: from golden yellow through green and blue to purple.

### Wild mint *Menthe sauvage*
*Mentha arvensis* (mint family)
July and August, perennial

Montane, near water. Knee-high, in bushy patches. Dark-green color and coarse toothy leaves make it resemble stinging nettle, page 312, but you can tell the two apart without having to touch the plant: smell the strong fragrance given off by all parts of the mint. Mint is shorter, and its small mauve or purple flowers snuggle against the stem, while stinging-nettle flowers hang in greenish strings.

### Hedge nettle
*Épiaire des marais/crapaudine*
*Stachys palustris* (mint family)
June, perennial

In damp, open places at low elevations. A tall plant that resembles wild mint, previous item, but the leaves are spiny/hairy and the flowers are larger and trumpet-shaped. Strongly scented, but not as pleasant as mint.

### Heal-all/self-heal *Prunelle vulgaire/brunelle*
*Prunella vulgaris* (mint family)
Mid-June to mid-August, perennial

Western-slope montane, in moist places; rare on the eastern slope outside Waterton/Glacier. A strange-looking plant about 20 cm tall. Small orchid-like blue or pale purple flowers protrude from a heavy, dense club at the top. The flowers don't all bloom at once; the non-blooming portions of the club are green with brown-tipped sepals. The pointed leaves are yellowish-green, in pairs. Heal-all is medicinal: an extract helps to stop internal bleeding.

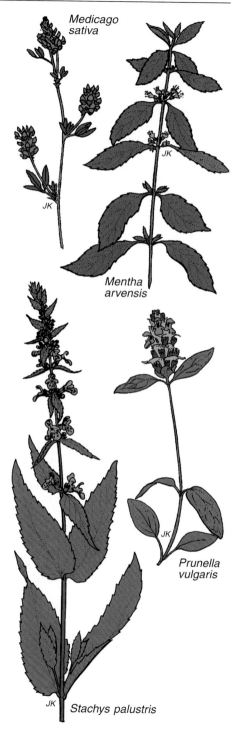

*Medicago sativa*

*Mentha arvensis*

*Prunella vulgaris*

*Stachys palustris*

### Showy aster/large purple aster and Siberian aster
*Aster remarquable, aster de Sibérie*
*Aster conspicuus* and *Aster sibiricus*
(composite family)
August and September, perennials

Of the 18 species of asters found in the Canadian Rockies, 12 can be blue or purple. They are difficult even for botanists to differentiate, and easily mistaken for the equally prolific fleabane tribe, so they are really beyond the scope of this book. However, two very common species are easy to identify as asters: showy aster and Siberian aster. These two look rather alike and often grow together.

**Showy aster** is up to 70 cm tall, with rather wide, coarsely toothed leaves that are rough to the touch. Low-elevation montane, very common in clearings and meadows. It blooms late in the summer; the flowers are purplish-blue or violet, with yellow or pinkish/reddish centres. The ray flowers (petal-like parts) are rather thin and sparse, not toothed at the ends like those of showy fleabane, next item.

**Siberian aster** is a little smaller and less bushy, with thinner leaves that are seldom toothed. The flowers are similar to those of showy aster. Found mostly from the Athabasca River south at montane and lower subalpine elevations.

See page 306 for how to tell asters from fleabanes.

### Showy fleabane/tall purple fleabane
*Vergerette voyageuse*
*Erigeron peregrinus* (composite family)
July, perennial

Montane to alpine, but mostly in subalpine meadows, often in large patches. A tall, common fleabane with one or more blooms per plant that range from pale blue or purple—sometimes almost white—to pastel shades. Large yellow centre with upturned ray flowers. Smooth-edged leaves, toothed ray-ends, plant not sticky—all of which serve to differentiate from showy aster, previous item. But there are similar fleabanes, and if you have ever tried to identify fleabanes you can understand why I'm ending this item right here.

### Gentians *Gentiane*
*Gentiana* and *Gentianella* spp. (gentian family)
June to September; annual, biennial or perennial

All elevations, but mostly subalpine. Gentians are known for the beautiful saturated blue color of their flowers, which are mostly

Aster conspicuus

Erigeron
peregrinus

Gentianella
crinita

Gentianella
amarella

in the form of upright bells. There are many species, including several alpine ones, page 373. Two that are easy to recognize and grow below treeline are given below.

**Fringed gentian** *(Gentianella crinita,* annual), July and August. A montane species 15–40 cm tall, occasional at lower elevations in moist places. A single, large flower, deep blue, at the top of the plant and well above the very narrow leaves. Petal edges are fringed. Also known as *G. detonsa.*

**Northern gentian/felwort** *(Gentianella amarella,* annual or biennial), late June to early September. Mostly montane, in the woods, but reaching well above treeline on occasion and often growing out in the open. Don't confuse alpine specimens with blue-bottle gentian or four-parted gentian, page 373.

Felwort is the only common gentian with flowers that may be other than blue; they range from pink to purple and tend to bleach out as the flower ages. Each plant has several/many straight stems up to 50 cm tall. Leaves and flowers arranged along the stems in tiers, each composed of two leaves with several small flowers clustered just above the leaves and next to the stem. Individuals can be annual or perennial.

### Bull thistle/Scottish thistle and Canada thistle *Chardon vulgaire/ piqueux, chardon des champs*
*Cirsium vulgare* and *C. arvense*
(composite family) Late July and early August
*C. vulgare* biennial, *C. arvense* perennial

Montane meadows and disturbed ground, often in patches that one learns to avoid. Very coarse-looking introduced plants with extremely prickly leaves and flowerheads. Blooms of the bull thistle/Scottish thistle are large rose-purple tufts 5–7 cm across, anchored in a bulbous calyx; Canada thistle blooms are smaller, 1–2 cm across, and lighter-colored. Canada thistle is usually less than a metre tall, shorter than bull thistle. See also white thistle, page 312.

### Spotted knapweed *Centaurée maculée*
*Centaurea maculosa* (composite family)
July and August, biennial/perennial

Western-slope montane, eastern slope mainly south of Crowsnest Pass, but introduced and likely to turn up anywhere. Can be biennial or short-lived perennial. Thistle-like, but not

*Cirsium vulgare*

*Cirsium arvense*

*Centaurea maculosa*

prickly. Purple flowerheads at ends of stems branch from a central stalk up to a metre tall. The leaves are narrowly divided, and the entire plant is hairy. Feathery seeds in autumn. Farmers don't like knapweed, and the Alberta government asks all citizens to pull it up where found.

### Other purplish or bluish flowers
- Rock cress, page 291
- Windflower, page 293
- Bronze bells, page 311
- Pine drops, page 334
- Three-tooth mitrewort, page 305

## *Drab wildflowers below treeline*

These oddball blooms are brown, reddish-brown, greenish-brown or even black. If you haven't found it anywhere else, check here.

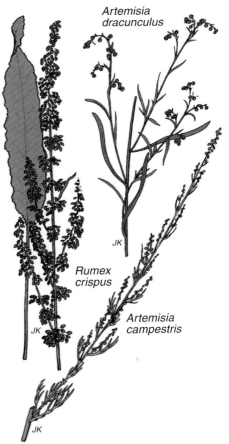

Artemisia
dracunculus

Rumex
crispus

Artemisia
campestris

### Curled dock *Rumex*
*Rumex crispus* (buckwheat family)
July, perennial
    Eastern-slope montane, occasional western-slope; a European import found usually on disturbed ground such as highway shoulders. Up to a metre tall. Long, finely toothed leaves that tend to curl along the edges. Bloom is reddish/yellowish, in long spikes of tiny flowers, but these plants are better known for their showy streamers of reddish-brown seeds. Each is carried in a round envelope that looks like a cap-gun cap. There are other low-elevation weedy species of *Rumex* in the Rockies. See also mountain sorrel, page 363.

### Dragon sagewort/false tarragon
*Armoise dragonne*
*Artemisia dracunculus* (composite family)
August, perennial
    Low-elevation montane, southern Rocky Mountain Trench and Waterton/Glacier, in dry, open places. Often aromatic like sage, but not always. Narrow, dull-green leaves set rather sparsely on the stems, which are smooth, woody, and grow to a metre tall. Tiny brown or olive-drab ball-shaped flowers hang from drooping stems on the upper part of the plant.
    On the eastern slope, as well as on the western slope, look for *A. campestris,* which has frilly gray-green leaves but no strong sage smell.

**Cudweed sagewort/prairie sagewort**
*Armoise de Louisiane*
*Artemisia ludoviciana* (composite family)
August, perennial
    Low-elevation montane, in southern sections. Silvery, fairly narrow leaves angle upward along the single stem, which can be a metre tall. The small blooms are upright and brown, cupped by hairy white bracts.

*Artemisia ludoviciana*

**Black henbane** *Jusquiame noire/potelée*
*Hyoscyamus niger* (nightshade family)
July and August, biennial or annual
    Occasional in the southern Rocky Mountain Trench and the southern foothills, but not reported from Waterton/Glacier. Can be up to 1.5 m tall, but usually 20–40 cm. Hairy all over, with ragged-edged drab-green leaves. Large bell-shaped flowers are carried along the stem; they are greenish-yellow with purple veining that directs insects to the pollen. The plant is malodorous and poisonous, an unloved European weed.

*Hyoscyamus niger*

## *Nature discovered the parabola long ago*

I used to wonder why so many alpine plants have large, cup-shaped flowers rather than the flower clusters or nodding blooms one sees more often at lower elevations. Now I know the reason: concave, up-turned flowers collect solar heat. The parabolic shape concentrates that heat on the reproductive parts in the centre. Having attracted insects by color and fragrance, these plants also offer a bit of warmth, encouraging bugs to linger. They tramp about in the pollen longer and thus carry more of it from plant to plant than they otherwise would, aiding fertilization.

    Many alpine plants have reddish leaves and stems. The color is from iron-rich **anthocyanins,** the pigments seen in some leaves in the fall. Anthocyanins not only look lovely; they convert light into heat, a useful property up there in the freezing mists. Anthocyanins also function as antifreeze. Everything is smarter than we think it is.

*Globeflowers keeping themselves pointed at the sun*

# Alpine wildflowers
## What's a nice plant like you doing in a place like this?

Postcard scenes to the contrary, the high country is actually a rather nasty place. Go there on a warm morning in late July; you may catch a few hours in the meadows before the rain starts and the wind comes up.

When everything is perfect, though, when the day is calm, the skies are clear, the hummingbirds are about and the fragrance of a hundred nectars drifts through the heather—when all clichés are in gear—then you know why people get silly over the alpine zone.

Strictly speaking, an alpine plant is one that grows above treeline. But some typically alpine species, such as white dryas, may grow well below treeline on cliffs, in scree and talus, among rock slide blocks and so on, in places that are bare, rocky, windy and alpine-*like*.

Summer comes late to the alpine zone, and it is very short: most flowers bloom between late June and the middle of August. Further, the blooming dates for a particular species can vary a great deal, depending on the date at which the snow melts.

Flower-learners, here is good news: at high elevations in the Canadian Rockies there is little difference between eastern-slope botany and western-slope botany. In fact, you are likely to see many of the same species anywhere above treeline in western North America.

## White alpine wildflowers

Unlike white wildflowers below treeline, few of these are on the greenish side.

Anemone
occidentalis

Trollius
albiflorus

### Western anemone/chalice flower
*Anémone occidentale*
*Anemone occidentalis* (buttercup family)
Late June and July, perennial
In grassy alpine and subalpine meadows. Blooms early, poking up behind retreating snowbanks and sometimes even through their edges. In this it even outdoes its close and familiar relative of lower elevations, the pasque flower, page 340. Large, creamy white cup with a yellow centre. Each flower is on a furry stem 15–40 cm tall, with a collar of frilly, fuzzy leaves partway up the stem. Basal leaves are also frilly; they grow taller after blooming. Distinctive shaggy seedheads. Compare with globeflower, next item.
Remember: it's "a-NEM-oh-nee," not "a-NEN-oh-me."

### Globeflower *Trolle à fleurs blanches*
*Trollius albiflorus* (buttercup family)
June to mid-July, perennial
In damp places, often near water. Resembles western anemone, previous item, and grows with it, but the stem is not furry and the flower has a cone of green pistils at the centre, surrounded by yellow stamens, while the anemone centre is all yellow. The leaves are different, too: smooth, not as finely divided as those of the anemone. Blooms later than the anemones.

### Alpine anemone/northern anemone
*Anémone parviflore*
Anemone parviflora (buttercup family)
Early May to mid-August, perennial

On exposed alpine and high subalpine slopes, sometimes much lower, flowering early at low elevations and much later higher up. Flower 2–3 cm wide, smaller than the western anemone or globeflower, previous entries, with yellow stamens and a green pistil. Single flower has petal-like sepals, often bluish on the back; it sits upright on a slender hairless stem above glossy basal leaves, each divided into three lobes and notched as well. Similar leaves in a fringe about halfway up the stem. Round, tight seedhead is dark-colored, but with white wool. See also windflower, page 293.

### Drummond's anemone
*Anémone de Drummond*
Anemone lithofila (buttercup family)
Early June to mid-July, perennial

Very similar to the windflower, page 293, but growing mainly above treeline and in subalpine meadows. The single flower is 2–3 cm across, creamy white, with petal-like sepals that are often blue-tinged underneath. To differentiate from windflower, which sometimes grows in subalpine meadows and even above treeline, note that there is just one flower on Drummond's anemone, not two or more as on windflower.

### Alpine grass-of-Parnassus
*Parnassie alpine*
Parnassia kotzebuei
(grass-of-Parnassus family) July, perennial

In damp places, often near streams and in patches; fairly common in northern and central areas, scarce in the south. Glossy green, oval basal leaves with parallel veins. One small white flower per leafless stem, carried 10–15 cm high. Finger-like stamens. Strictly an alpine/high-subalpine species, but often mixed with fringed grass-of-Parnassus, page 294, which also grows at lower elevations. Differentiate by the unfringed petals on the alpine version.

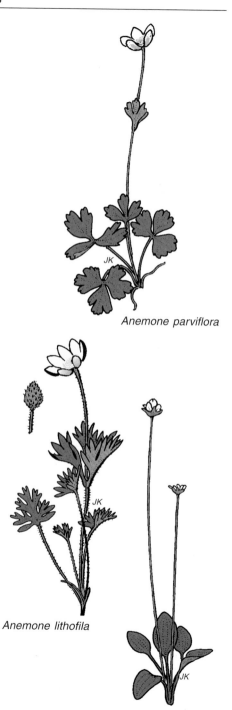

*Anemone parviflora*

*Anemone lithofila*

*Parnassia kotzebuei*

### Alpine spring beauty
*Claytonie à gros rhizome*
*Claytonia megarrhiza* (purslane family)
Mid-July to early August, perennial

Mainly from Highwood Pass south, but reported as far north as the North Saskatchewan River, on scree slopes and rocky, exposed places. A small, fleshy plant with red-rimmed leaves in a rosette. Small white flowers bloom around the edge of the plant rather than in the middle as you might expect; the petal ends are toothed. Compare with double bladder-pod, page 366.

### Alpine starwort and chickweed
*Stellaire, céraiste*
*Stellaria monantha, Cerastium* spp.
(pink family) May to mid-August, perennials

On scree slopes, among rocks and along ridges. Alpine starwort has small white flowers on short 5 cm stems and lance-shaped bluegreen leaves, very common in Waterton/Glacier, where it grows in big white patches that are showy against the red argillite slopes. In chickweed patches the leaves are not bluegreen. The petals of most species are so deeply cleft that the five petals look like ten. If the patch is small, with tiny pure-white flowers having petals that are not notched or cleft, you may be looking at sandwort, page 360.

### White dryas/mountain dryas/white mountain avens *Dryade blanche*
*Dryas octopetala* and *D. integrifolia* (rose family)
Mid-June to early August, perennial

Very common alpine ground-covering shrubs of stony, rocky places. Occasionally found much lower, even on the valley floors, in windswept places such as cliffs and lakeshores. Nitrogen-fixers. Small, bluntly toothed leaves, green above and dull brown or gray below. Short-stalked showy white flowers up to 2 cm across, with 8–10 petals; they look straight up at you and beg not to be stepped on. Seedhead forms a twisted plume that later opens, looking like a dandelion. Compare with yellow dryas, page 322.

*D. octopetala* is a southerly species, found from Jasper National Park south, while *D. integrifolia* is a northerly species, found from Jasper National Park north. In the park itself, where they overlap, differentiate the two by the leaves, which are wide and scallop-edged in *D. octopetala*, narrow and smooth-edged in *D. integrifolia*. The flowers are similar.

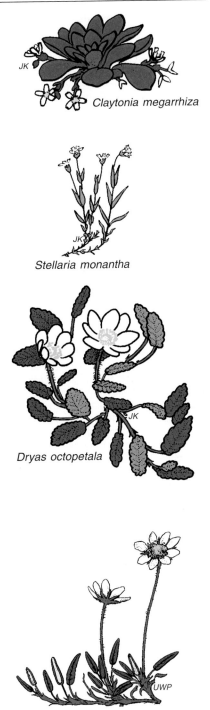

*Claytonia megarrhiza*

*Stellaria monantha*

*Dryas octopetala*

*Dryas integrifolia*

## Alpine marsh marigold
*Populage à fleurs blanches*
Caltha leptosepala (buttercup family)
June to August, perennial

On wet ground, often growing with globe-flower and buttercups. Common elsewhere, this plant is absent in the Waterton/Glacier area. Showy white flowers with yellow centres have 6–12 petal-like sepals, resembling mountain dryas, previous item, but the oval leaves are large and glossy. Stems 5–10 cm tall, smooth and purplish.

## Three-point saxifrage
*Saxifrage à trois points*
Saxifraga tricuspidata (saxifrage family)
Late June and July, perennial

Alpine, on rocky ground, from the North Saskatchewan River north. Identical to prickly saxifrage, page 293 (see for picture), except that the leaves of *S. tricuspidata* end in three small points, and the flower stems are usually green instead of red. In the Canadian Rockies the plant is nearly always alpine, while prickly saxifrage is found at all elevations. Three-point saxifrage prefers non-limy soils.

## Lyall's saxifrage  *Saxifrage de Lyall*
*Saxifraga lyallii* (saxifrage family)
Early July to late August, perennial

Near running water, often in large patches that look reddish from a distance. Each plant has several small white flowers, each with a prominent reddish pistil but no dots on the petals like three-point saxifrage, previous item, or prickly saxifrage, page 293. The stem of Lyall's, up to 30 cm tall, is also reddish.The leaves are fan-shaped and toothed on the ends. Compare with wedge-leaf saxifrage, next item.

## Wedge-leaf saxifrage
*Saxifrage ascendante*
*Saxifraga adscendens* (saxifrage family)
July, perennial

On moist slopes and rocky ledges, scarce south of Crowsnest Pass. The leaves resemble those of Lyall's saxifrage, previous item, but they are hairy. The flower stem is shorter and greenish; the flowers are white, but have green lines in them.

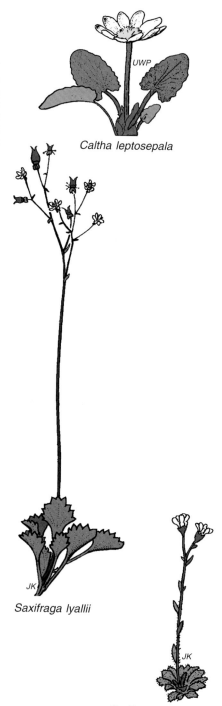

*Caltha leptosepala*

*Saxifraga lyallii*

*Saxifraga adscendens*

### Nodding saxifrage and pygmy saxifrage
*Saxifrage penchée, saxifrage petite*
Saxifraga cernua and *S. hyperborea*
(saxifrage family)
Mid-July to early August, perennials

In protected places. These two plants are quite similar, with small but broad, toothy leaves. Mostly basal, they also grow on the stem. The flowers are single, on green stalks 10–15 cm tall. The leaves have three to five teeth.

To differentiate, check the flowers. *S. cernua* has flat or indented petal ends, while those of *S. hyperborea* are round. Note also the presence of more than one flower on a stem in *S. hyperborea*. *S. cernua* frequently carries little bulblets, which are parts that drop off to form new plants, in the spots where the leaves join the stem. See also romanzoffia, next item.

*Saxifraga cernua*

*Romanzoffia sitchensis*

### Romanzoffia/mistmaiden
*Romanzoffie de Sitka*
Romanzoffia sitchensis (waterleaf family)
Mid-June to mid-August, perennial

Looks very much like the two saxifrages above, especially like *S. hyperborea,* and it grows in similar moist, ledgy locations. But romanzoffia has more than one flower per stem, and the leaves normally have more than five teeth, which are not as well formed. The flower petals are fused, while those of *S. hyperborea* are separate from one another.

*Smelkowskia calycina*

### Smelkowskia *Smélkowskie d'Amérique*
*Smelkowskia calycina* (mustard family)
Late May to early August, perennial

Mostly eastern slope, on alpine scree slopes and in rocky places. A hairy plant, on which clusters of small white four-petalled flowers grow on short stems with frilly gray-green leaves at the base. Tends to form cushions. Typical mustard-family seedpods later on.

### Alpine fleabane and woolly fleabane
*Vergerette alpine, vergerette laineuse*
Erigeron purpuratus and *E. lanatus*
(composite family) July and August, perennials

There are many fleabane species, but only a few white-flowered alpine ones, all rather rare. These two are both quite woolly, with flowers that can be pinkish as well as white. Separate them by the leaves: alpine fleabane

*Erigeron lanatus*

*Erigeron purpuratus*

has notched leaf-ends, but woolly fleabane does not. As well, the flower of woolly fleabane is larger—about 2 cm across, while alpine fleabane is rarely more than 1 cm across.

### Contorted lousewort
*Pédiculaire entortillé*
*Pedicularis contorta* (figwort family)
June and July, perennial

In sunny alpine and subalpine locations; fairly common between the Bow River and Crowsnest Pass. A tall plant by alpine standards: 20–30 cm, with drab fern-like leaves. Showy cream-colored or yellowish-white flowers in an open spike atop the stem, each flower in the shape of a down-curled tube.

### Mountain sandwort *Sabline*
*Minuartia* and *Arenaria* spp. (pink family)
Mid-May through July, annuals or perennials

Mainly alpine, but can grow higher or lower on dry, rocky slopes or ridges. Height 10–15 cm, with very narrow, hair-like leaves, mostly basal; the edges are yellow and minutely spiny. Small star-shaped flowers have narrow petals and 10 stamens. *M. austromontana* looks like moss campion, page 368, but is white.

### Luetkea/meadow spirea/partridge-foot
*Luetkéa pectinée*
*Luetkea pectinata* (rose family)
Late July to late August, perennial

Alpine and high subalpine, fairly common north of the North Saskatchewan River. Grows in damp meadows that are not limy; common on quartzite terrain. Rod-like clusters of small creamy-white flowers, five-petalled with lots of stamens, atop a short 10 cm stem with small frilly leaves, each part cleft into two or three at the tip. More frilly leaves at the base, forming mats when the plant grows in patches. See also bistort, next item, and false asphodel, page 302.

### Bistort/viviparous knotweed
*Renouée vivipare*
*Polygonum viviparum* (buckwheat family)
Late July to early August, perennial

Usually alpine and subalpine, in meadows, but sometimes much lower, near water. A small plant with a column of tiny white flowers. Compare with luetkea, previous item, and false asphodel, page 302, which grows by water at lower elevations and has a rounder flowerhead.

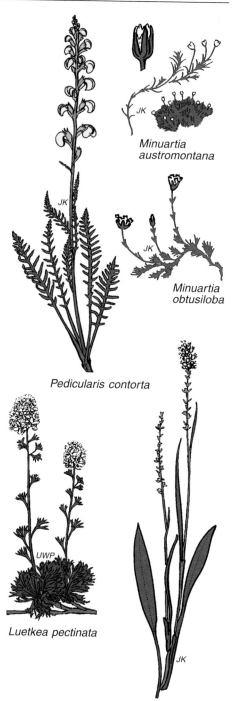

*Minuartia austromontana*

*Minuartia obtusiloba*

*Pedicularis contorta*

*Luetkea pectinata*

*Polygonum viviparum*

In addition to the usual flowers-and-seed method of reproduction, bistort can reproduce asexually by forming little purple bulblets—miniature plants—that drop off the lower end of the flower cluster and take root. The bulblets sometimes sprout leaves while still on the parent plant.

**Alpine pussytoes** *Antennaire*
*Antennaria alpina* and *A. lanata*
(composite family)
July, perennial
   In dry meadows. Less than 10 cm tall and rather hairy, with a cluster of very short, diamond-shaped woolly leaves at the base. They continue up the stem. Dishwater-white flowers on top, not densely packed. *A. lanata* is similar to *A. alpina* but 10–20 cm tall, with larger, longer leaves, mostly up the stem, and a denser flowerhead.

**Alpine coltsfoot** *Pétasite des neiges*
*Petasites nivalis* (composite family)
Late June and July, perennial
   Alpine, in wet, well-vegetated meadows. Looks rather like *P. palmatus,* page 298, but the leaves are more arrowhead-shaped and not as deeply lobed. Same fuzzy white flower, very fragrant.

**Alpine bearberry/red bearberry**
*Raisin d'ours rouge*
*Arctostaphylos rubra* (heath family)
Late June and July, perennial
   An alpine and high subalpine relative of kinnikinnik, page 296, but you wouldn't know it to look at this plant. Grows in central and northern areas. The leaves are netted-looking, larger, thinner, and much brighter green than those of kinnikinnik. Unlike kinnikinnik, which is evergreen, in mid-August the leaves of *A. rubra* turn brilliantly red—the first plant to show autumn coloration in the high country—and die. The berries are large and semi-transparent.

**White heather** *Cassiope blanche*
*Cassiope tetragona, C. mertensiana*
(heath family)
Late June to early August, perennial
   Similar-looking alpine and high subalpine dwarf shrubs, common in central and northern areas but absent in Waterton, although reported from Glacier. Both species form large patches

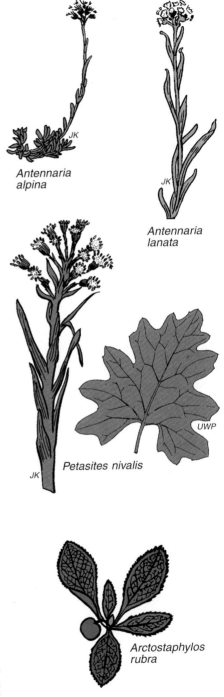

*Antennaria alpina*

*Antennaria lanata*

*Petasites nivalis*

*Arctostaphylos rubra*

of upward-curving dark-green scaly stems 10–20 cm long. The scales are actually tiny leaves lying close to the stem.

White heather often grows with pink heather, yellow heather and crowberry, all of which look rather alike until they bloom. But these three look thicker and fuzzier than the two white heathers, because their leaves are a little longer and stick out from the stem at right angles. In bloom, the white heathers are easy to tell from the others: they are the only ones that have pure white flowers. These are small but numerous and showy, little nodding white bells on which the petals turn outward at the lip. No berries.

*C. mertensiana* has no groove on the back of the leaf. It forms bright-green mats. *C. tetragona* has a groove on the back of the leaf and grows in dark-green tufts.

*Cassiope tetragona*

## Yellowish-green and reddish-green alpine flowers

If you can't decide what color it is, look here.

### Yellow heather/green heather/yellow heath *Phyllodoce jaune*
*Phyllodoce glanduliflora* (heath family)
June and July, perennial

Alpine and high subalpine, common in central and northern areas, scarce south of Crowsnest Pass. A ground-covering shrub that often grows with pink heather, page 370, and white heather, previous item. Stems 5–10 cm long, covered with needle-like leaves that are not prickly. Flowers are urn-like, with out-turned lips, in small nodding clusters atop the stems; the color ranges from pale yellowish green to pale yellow. No berries are produced. See also crowberry, page 374.

### Longstem greencaps/alpine wormwood *Armoise alpine*
*Artemisia norvegica* (composite family)
August, perennial

In alpine and subalpine meadows, central and northern areas; absent at Waterton/Glacier. Frilly bright-green leaves, mostly at the base of a hairy stem 30–60 cm tall, with a dozen or so odd-looking blooms at the top. Each is a nodding flattened green ball about 1 cm across with dark-green ribs on it, like lines of longitude. The flowers look like they are going to open further, but they don't. See also Chinese lantern, next item.

*Phyllodoce glanduliflora*

*Artemisia norvegica*

### Chinese lantern/bladder campion/ alpine campion/nodding pink
*Lanterne Chinoise*
*Silene uralensis* (pink family)
June and July, perennial

On stony, high-alpine scree slopes and moraines. Rare in southern sections, not common anywhere, but with an arresting bloom that looks like a greenish oriental lantern with purple stripes. This is actually the calyx, not the flower; to see the petals, which are purple, look inside the mouth of the calyx. The plant is only 5–10 cm tall and lightly fuzzy all over; the leaves are lance-shaped and mostly basal. Known previously as *Lychnis apetala*.

*Silene uralensis*

### Mountain sorrel *Oxirie de montagne*
*Oxyria digyna* (buckwheat family)
July, perennial

In protected spots, often among boulders. Leaves round, reddish brown to olive drab and indented at the stem. Atop the stem, 20–30 cm tall, there is a spray of tiny reddish/greenish flowers, each on the thinnest of stalks. The small seeds are typical of sorrel or dock: each in a little circular envelope, carried by the hundred in reddish-brown plumes.

*Oxyria digyna*

## Yellow or orange alpine wildflowers

You haven't seen a poppy at its best until you've seen an alpine poppy.

### Alpine poppies *Pavots alpins*
*Papaver kluanensis, P. pygmaeum*
(poppy family) July and August, perennial

In rocky, exposed places well above treeline. Not common, but unmistakable: frilly basal leaves and a few skinny, black-haired stems 10–40 cm tall that kink below the showy poppy-like flowers, one per stem. Hairy pods later on.

North of Crowsnest Pass the main species is *P. kluanensis*, 20–40 cm tall and greenish yellow. *P. pygmaeum*, 6–12 cm tall, is limited to Waterton/Glacier and yellow to apricot-colored. Differentiate by the hairiness: *P. kluanensis* is densely hairy on both the tops and undersides of the leaves, while *P. pygmaeum* is fuzzy, not hairy, and mainly on the undersides of the leaves. A red-blooming species, *P. freedmanianum*, has been reported from Jasper National Park.

These plants amaze me. Often I have come upon a half-dozen fragile-looking poppies flopping about on some forlorn, wind-raked col. This is heart-rending—they are so *brave*.

*Papaver pygmaeum*

The taller orange/reddish poppy you see growing in gardens in the Canadian Rockies, such as the plantings at Chateau Lake Louise, is the **Iceland poppy,** *P. nudicaule,* which is not native. Sometimes it escapes, as at Bow Summit along the Icefields Parkway.

### Alpine potentilla/alpine cinquefoil
*Potentille des neiges*
*Potentilla nivea* (rose family)
Early June to mid-July, perennial

A cushion plant with brilliant yellow flowers blooming on a mat of silvery green fuzzy leaflets in threes, with teeth. One of the showier alpine plants; look for it in rocky, windy places both above and below treeline. It's part of the climber's rock garden. See also the other potentillas, page 320.

### Alpine buttercup/snow buttercup
*Renoncule des neiges*
*Ranunculus eschscholtzii* (buttercup family)
Late June to early August, perennial

Alpine and subalpine, in sheltered damp places. The only common buttercup that grows at high elevations, which solves the usual problem of differentiating species in this complex genus. Look for the shiny-yellow buttercup flower with its green centre, and the bright-green, deeply cleft leaves. The **yellow anemone,** *Anemone richardsonii,* is a buttercup-like flower seen at treeline from Kananaskis Country north. No leaves high on the stem.

### Alpine drabas/whitlow grass
*Draves alpines*
*Draba* spp. (mustard family) July, perennial

In sunny, rocky places. Several hard-to-tell-apart species of small plants, often growing in tufts or mats. Most have gray-green felty leaves and small yellow four-petalled flowers. A common species is *D. paysonii,* illustrated here. Another is *D. incerta,* page 324, which also grows at lower elevations in similar habitat.

### Alpine arnica *Arnica alpin*
*Arnica angustifolia* (composite family)
July and August, perennial

Prefers dry spots that are sandy or gravelly. This is the most common high-country arnica, identified as such by the showy all-yellow arnica bloom, which has three teeth on the end of each ray. Low-growing for an arnica species, 20–30 cm, with lance-shaped leaves and a woolly stem.

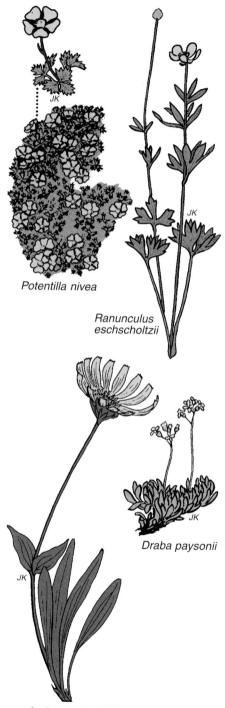

*Potentilla nivea*

*Ranunculus eschscholtzii*

*Draba paysonii*

*Arnica angustifolia*

## Alpine dandelion *Pissenlit de montagne*
*Taraxacum ceratophorum* (composite family)
June through August, perennial

Yup, the lowly dandelion grows way up here, at least from the Athabasca River south. And it's a native. Easily identified as dandelion by the ragged-looking leaves spreading from the base, the brilliant yellow blooms made of ray-flowers only—no central disk—and the fluffy, round seedhead. All these parts are smaller in the high-country version than they are in the lawn varieties. If the flowers are right but not the leaves, see hawksbeard, next item.

## Alpine hawksbeard *Crépis nain*
*Crepis nana* (composite family)
Mid-July and August, perennial

In exposed places, among scree and broken rock; prefers limy soil. A tiny plant with a big taproot, but please don't rip it out to look. Small, flat rosette of smooth, spoon-shaped leaves 1–2 cm across, dark bluegreen or slightly purplish, rather like those of mountain sorrel, page 363. A cluster of purple tubes at the centre of the rosette opens into little dandelion-like flowers. This is my wife's favorite plant; the Latin for it translates as "crackling dwarf."

## Golden fleabane *Vergerette dorée*
*Erigeron aureus* (composite family)
July and August, perennial

The only yellow fleabane at any elevation, but can be confused with Lyall's goldenweed, next item. Golden fleabane grows in alpine and subalpine meadows; it is found between the Brazeau River and Crowsnest Pass. The bloom is 1–2 cm across, all-yellow, with rather wide ray-flowers (petal-like parts) for a fleabane. Stem is hairy and leafless; basal leaves are also hairy.

## Lyall's goldenweed/Lyall's iron-plant
*Haplopappus de Lyall*
*Haplopappus lyallii* (composite family)
July and August, perennial

Habitat and appearance similar to golden fleabane, previous item, but the bloom is larger, up to 3 cm across, and the stems have small leaves on them that are sticky as well as hairy. This plant and golden fleabane are the only yellow daisy-like flowers you are likely to see in the high country.

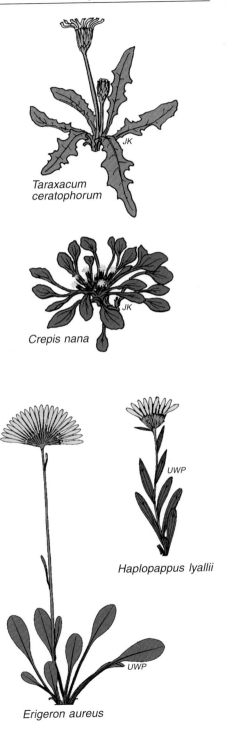

*Taraxacum ceratophorum*

*Crepis nana*

*Haplopappus lyallii*

*Erigeron aureus*

## Sibbaldia *Sibbaldie couchée*
*Sibbaldia procumbens* (rose family)
Early June to early July, perennial

A mat-forming plant; grows in rocky places. The three-parted leaves are rather like those of strawberry, page 295, but smaller (1–2 cm long) and toothed only at the ends of the lobes, which tend to fold inward along the centreline. Distinctive flowers: star-like, with small yellow petals alternating with larger, pointed green sepals. Sibbaldia leaves turn beautifully red in fall—meaning late August in the alpine zone.

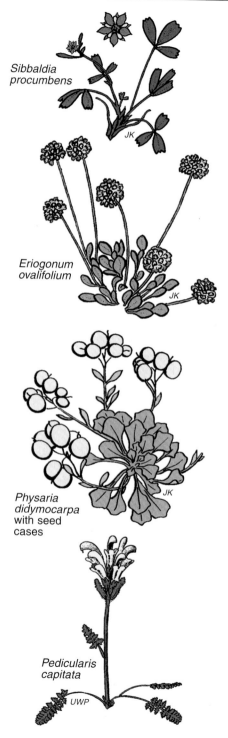

*Sibbaldia procumbens*

## Silver plant *Renouelle à feuilles ovales*
*Eriogonum ovalifolium* (buckwheat family)
June and July, perennial

Mostly south of Crowsnest Pass. Prefers rough, rocky places at high elevations, but can be found much lower at alpine-like sites. Plant is a cushion of silvery-looking felty leaves with several hairless stalks rising about 10 cm and each carrying a tight, rounded cluster of tiny cup-shaped flowers that are yellowish green, turning reddish with age.

*Eriogonum ovalifolium*

## Double bladder-pod *Cosse-jumelle*
*Physaria didymocarpa* (mustard family)
Late May through June, perennial

From the Athabasca River south, in exposed places at any elevation, but mostly alpine and always on limy soils. Not a large plant, but conspicuous for its shape: spokes of prostrate flowerheads radiating from a central rosette of gray-green diamond-shaped hairy leaves rather like those of alpine pussytoes, page 361. Small bright-yellow flowers have the four petals typical of mustard-family plants. The seed cases are interesting: transparent round inflated pods. See also bladder locoweed, page 372, and alpine spring beauty, page 357.

*Physaria didymocarpa* with seed cases

## Head-shaped lousewort
*Pédiculaire capité*
*Pedicularis capitata* (figwort family)
July and August, perennial

Prefers stony places. The shortest lousewort, often rising only a few centimetres above the ground. A central and northerly species, not reported from Waterton/Glacier. Leaves small and fern-like. Striking flowers: 3–4 cm long, each a curved pale-yellow tube with brown lips and a tiny tongue hanging out. See also western lousewort, page 327.

*Pedicularis capitata*

## Alpine yellow locoweed
*Oxytropis jaune de montagne*
*Oxytropis campestris* or *cusickii* (pea family)
July, perennial

On sparsely covered ground, alpine and subalpine. Looks much like its montane relative early yellow locoweed (see *O. sericea,* page 325, for picture) and interbreeds with it, so in-betweens can be found at low elevations. *O. campestris* is slightly smaller in every dimension, has black hairs on the stems and lies on the ground. Also known as *O. cusickii,* sometimes as *O. gracilis* or *O. monticola.*

## Yellow mountain saxifrage
*Saxifrage jaune*
*Saxifraga aizoides* (saxifrage family)
Late June and July, perennial

Alpine, on moraines and other barren, stony places with limy soil. Central region, from Kananaskis Country north on both slopes. Absent at Waterton. A small, fleshy-leaved plant, easily identified as the only yellow flower in the high country with orange spots on the petals, very faint or missing on some specimens.

The only other alpine yellow saxifrage is *S. flagellaris,* the **spider plant,** a northerly species found as far south as Sunshine Meadows west of Banff, but rare anywhere south of Jasper. Easily identified by its tufts of tiny, pointy saxifrage leaves joined by red runners.

*Saxifraga aizoides*

## Alpine yellow paintbrush
*Castilléjie occidentale*
*Castilleja occidentalis* (figwort family)
Late June to mid-August, perennial

Alpine and subalpine meadows, usually in small patches. Pale yellow or greenish-yellow blooms on reddish or purplish stems 10–20 cm tall. Narrow leaves climb the stems, becoming denser near the top, where they merge with the flowerhead. Like the yellow paintbrush of lower elevations, page 327, the yellow alpine paintbrush carries its color on petal-like bracts that surround the spiky green flowers. The whole plant is lightly hairy.

This species interbreeds with red paintbrush species such as *C. rhexifolia,* page 329, to produce interesting hybrids with reddish-tipped yellow bracts, pinkish colors and so on.

*Castilleja occidentalis*

### Alpine goldenrod
*Verge d'or à plusieurs rayons*
*Solidago multiradiata* (composite family)
August, perennial

Mostly alpine, but also subalpine. The only common high-country goldenrod. A cluster of about a dozen small yellow flowers atop a leafy stem 10–20 cm tall. Often mistaken for one of the ragworts (see page 324).

### Other flowers to check in the below-treeline listings
* Stonecrop, page 323
* Western lousewort, page 327

**See also** yellow heather, page 362.

*Solidago multiradiata*

## Red or pink alpine wildflowers

Including that all-time favorite:

### Moss campion *Silène acaule*
*Silene acaulis* (pink family)
Mid-June to early August, perennial

Alpine, in open rocky places. One of the better-known alpine wildflowers, common throughout the Rockies, moss campion is a classic **cushion plant:** tiny bright-green leaves packed into a domed mat that looks a lot like moss, but studded with small pink or (rarely) white flowers. Mosses don't have flowers. Compare with spreading phlox, next item.

If you see what looks like *white* moss campion, it may be *Minuartia austromontana,* page 360.

*Silene acaulis*

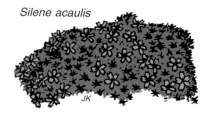

## Keep those boots off the botany

Moss campion is one of the faster-growing alpine plants, yet it still takes ten years for the first flower to appear. The cushion is only 20 cm across at 25 years. One misplaced step can wreck this amazing organism. The same is true of many other delicate alpine plants, so please stay on the trail on the tundra.

*Illustration courtesy of Parks Canada*

## Spreading phlox/carpet pink
### Phlox diffus
*Phlox diffusa* (pink family)
June to August, perennial

Alpine and subalpine, in open rocky places. Absent at Waterton/Glacier (see moss phlox, page 294). A pink moss-campion look-alike, see previous item, but rare and found only in British Columbia—one of the few high-country plants with a preference for one watershed or the other. Differentiate from moss campion by the less-compact character of spreading phlox, and by the leaves, which are longer.

*Phlox diffusa*

*Telesonix heucheriformis*

*Pedicularis arctica*

*Tolmachevia integrifolia*

## Telesonix *Télésonix*
*Telesonix heucheriformis* (saxifrage family)
June and July, perennial

Mostly alpine and subalpine, but at any elevation with the right location. Mostly eastern-slope, fairly common from the Columbia Icefield north; absent at Waterton/Glacier. Dense colonies in crevices on limestone or dolomite outcrops, often under overhangs. Round leathery leaves 3–5 cm across, with toothy edges; early in the summer they smell like turpentine. Reddish-purple bell-shaped flowers a centimetre across, carried erect on prominent red stalks. Bristly flower bases and red sepals. Imagine: a wildflower with a name like an electronics company.

## Alpine lousewort *Pédiculaire arctique*
*Pedicularis arctica* (figwort family)
Early July to early August, perennial

Alpine, central and northern regions, in rocky spots; not found south of the Oldman River. A short plant with small fern-like leaves and woolly white hair. Showy spike 5–15 cm tall with purplish-pink flowers, each an upward-curved tube. Also known as *P. langsdorfii*.

## Rose-root *Orpin rouge*
*Tolmachevia integrifolia* (sedum family)
June and July, perennial

Normally alpine, but can be found much lower in exposed rocky places. A small plant, less common on the western slope, identifiable immediately as a sedum by the fleshy leaves. The stem is about 10 cm long, carrying a dense cluster of small red or reddish-purple flowers at the top. Also known as *Sedum roseum*.

### Pink heather/pink heath
*Phyllodoce à feuilles de camarine*
*Phyllodoce empetriformis* (heath family)
July and August, perennial

Alpine and high subalpine meadows, in ground-covering patches. A dwarf shrub. The stems are 5–10 cm long and covered with needle-like but soft leaves. The flowers are small pink bells in clusters atop the stems. Compare with alpine laurel, next item. When not in bloom, pink heather is difficult to tell from yellow heather, page 362, or crowberry, page 374. Unlike crowberry, pink heather does not produce berries.

### Alpine laurel *Kalmia à petites feuilles*
*Kalmia microphylla* (heath family)
Late July to early August, perennial

On moist tundra and in high subalpine forest, central and northern areas. Resembles pink heather, previous item, but the flowers are larger and more open, ribbed like an umbrella. The stems have fewer, larger leaves. Please see *Kalmia polifolia*, page 336, for a picture.

### Other species to check
- Lyall's beardtongue, page 335
- Lyall's saxifrage, page 358
- Red monkey-flower, page 334
- Lapland rosebay, page 372

*Phyllodoce empetriformis*

## Blue or purple alpine wildflowers

Starting with the other all-time favorite. Can you guess what the first one is? See page 368.

### Alpine forget-me-not *Myosotis alpin*
*Myosotis alpestris* (borage family)
July, perennial

Alpine and high subalpine, in open areas throughout the Rockies. A small plant 10–20 cm high, with fuzzy lance-shaped leaves. Well-loved for its small yellow-centred, sometimes white-centred, sky-blue flowers borne in small clusters atop the plant. Can also be pink. Prefers limy soils. Compare with alpine speedwell and alpine rock cress, next items.

### Alpine speedwell/alpine veronica
*Véronique alpine*
*Veronica wormskjoldii* (figwort family)
Late June to August, perennial

Subalpine and alpine, in moist meadows. Flowers are rather like alpine forget-me-not, previous item, but smaller and four-petalled rather than five-petalled, deeper blue—

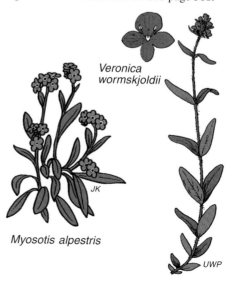

*Veronica wormskjoldii*

*Myosotis alpestris*

sometimes almost purple—and without a yellow or white centre. A single stem 10–30 cm tall, with paired hairy oval leaves. Flowers in a small cluster at the top. Plant is also known as *V. alpina*. Compare with moss gentian, page 373, and see also the other veronicas, page 345.

### Alpine rock cress
*Arabette de Lyall, arabette de Lemmon*
*Arabis lyalli, A. lemmonii* (mustard family)
June and July, perennials
    Alpine and subalpine, in exposed places. Small, deep-purple flowers with four petals, carried in a small cluster atop a 10–20 cm stem. Leaves are small and shaped like elongated arrowheads; plant is hairiest at the base. *A. lemmonii* is not as hairy as *A. lyalli*. Both species produce long slender seed pods.

### Alpine harebell *Campanule tomenteuse*
*Campanula lasiocarpa*
(harebell/bluebell family)
July and August, perennial
    Alpine, on stony ground, rare south of the Columbia Icefield. Showy, bell-shaped bloom like that of its montane relative, page 347, but a much shorter plant, restricted to the high alpine zone and not nearly as common. Absent at Waterton/Glacier. A single flower on a short stem 2–10 cm tall with mostly basal leaves; look for a little furriness just behind the flower.

### Purple saxifrage *Saxifrage pourpre/ saxifrage à feuilles opposées*
*Saxifraga oppositifolia* (saxifrage family)
Early May to late July, perennial
    Common on rocky alpine slopes, except in Waterton/Glacier where it is strangely absent. This low-growing plant looks nothing like the other members of the genus. Bright-violet bell-shaped flowers stare up from a mat of tiny scraggly leaves—they look like miniature hen-and-chickens—set close to the spreading stems. Very early bloomer, for an alpine species, flowering only a few days after the snow goes.

### Alpine purple wallflower *Vélar alpine*
*Erysimum pallasii* (mustard family)
Mid-June to mid-July, biennial or perennial
    Alpine, in stony, shaly places, occasional from the Bow River north. Four-petalled lavender flowers in a ring-like cluster above a

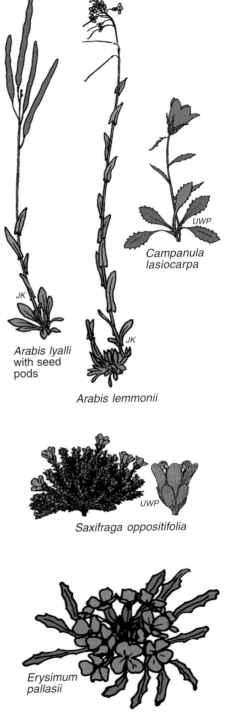

Campanula
lasiocarpa

Arabis lyalli
with seed
pods

Arabis lemmonii

Saxifraga oppositifolia

Erysimum
pallasii

rosette of narrow leaves that tend to fold inward. Blooms early; the flower cluster grows taller as the days go by.

### Lapland rosebay
*Rhododendron de Laponie*
*Rhododendron lapponicum* (heath family)
June, perennial
   Northern area, occasional as far south as the North Saskatchewan River, in rocky places and tundra, usually on limy soil. A dwarf shrub, ground-hugging to 30 cm tall. Large, brilliantly purple or pink flowers in low clusters. The leaves are small, oval, drab and leathery-looking, with rust-colored scales underneath. Spicy scent.

*Rhododendron lapponicum*

### Sky pilot/skunkweed *Polémoine viscide*
*Polemonium viscosum* (phlox family)
June and July, perennial
   Rocky alpine areas and scree slopes south of Crowsnest Pass, fading out to the north. A striking plant: blue flowers 2–4 cm across, with contrasting yellow stamens. The leaflets, which are tiny, give off a strong, unpleasant odor. See also Jacob's-ladder, page 346.

*Polemonium viscosum*

### Alpine columbine *Ancolie de Jones*
*Aquilegia jonesii* (buttercup family)
June, perennial
   Waterton/Glacier only, in limestone scree slopes at high elevations. A rare plant with tufted, un-columbine-like leaves, but instantly recognizable as columbine when it blooms: a single large, deep-blue or blue-and-cream flower with five spurs, carried on a short stem.

### Bladder locoweed
*Oxytrope à gros fruits*
*Oxytropis podocarpa* (pea family)
Early June to late July, perennial
   Rocky places, often in scree slopes. Common in northern and central sections, and found just south of Crowsnest Pass, but missing at nearby Waterton/Glacier. A low-growing plant, forming a scraggly rosette; the only blue or purple locoweed at high elevations, identifiable as such by the pea-type blossoms and leaves. After blooming, the plant produces large, eye-catching reddish inflated seed pods lying on the ground at the ends of long stalks.

*Aquilegia jonesii*

*Oxytropis podocarpa*

### Alpine milk-vetch *Astragale alpin*

*Astragalus alpinus* (pea family)
Late June and July, perennial

In meadows and on scree slopes. Fragile-looking and fairly small, 10–20 cm tall, blooming in dense clusters on straight leafless stalks that rise above the straggly stems bearing hairy leaves. Pea-type flowers are pale blue with purplish or pinkish tips.

### Alpine gentians *Gentianes alpines*

*Gentiana* and *Gentianella* spp. (gentian family)
July and August, annual to perennial

Like their montane relatives, the flowers of the high-country gentians listed below have beautiful shades of blue and bluegreen.

**Mountain gentian/explorer's gentian** (*Gentiana calycosa*), July and August, perennial. A subalpine and alpine species that is fairly common in the Waterton/Glacier area and reported just north of Crowsnest Pass. Grows 10–20 cm high, with small but broad, pointed leaves in pairs up the stem. The deep blue flower is the largest gentian bloom—very lovely—with dots inside against a white background.

**Blue-bottle gentian/smooth alpine gentian** (*Gentiana glauca*), mid-July to mid-August, perennial. In alpine and subalpine meadows; absent at Waterton/Glacier, occasional through Banff and common from Jasper north. Low-growing but erect, with several waxy bluegreen flowers atop each stem, which bears pairs of rounded leaves. All parts of the plant quite glossy-looking. Resembles four-parted gentian, next item, but that plant has tiers of small flowers while smooth alpine gentian bears its flowers only at the top.

**Four-parted gentian** (*Gentianella propinqua*), July and August, individuals annual or biennial. In subalpine and lower alpine meadows. Resembles blue-bottle gentian, previous item, but the lavender-blue flowers occur farther down the plant as well as on the top. Strongly resembles felwort, which is a montane relative.

**Moss gentian** (*Gentiana prostrata*), July to early August, biennial. A ground-hugging alpine species with small sky-blue flowers and small paired leaves. The flowers close in cloudy conditions, or when touched. Compare with alpine speedwell, page 370.

**See also** northern gentian, page 352.

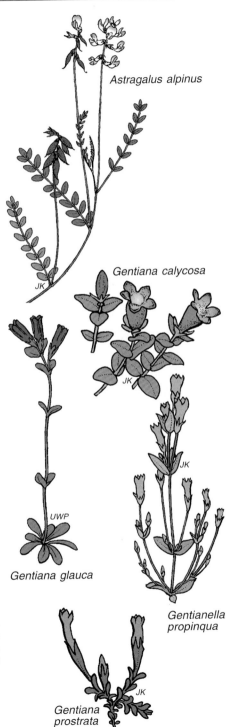

*Astragalus alpinus*

*Gentiana calycosa*

*Gentiana glauca*

*Gentianella propinqua*

*Gentiana prostrata*

### Scorpionweed/silky phacelia/purple bee-plant

*Phacélie soyeuse, phacélie de Lyall*
*Phacelia sericea, P. lyallii* (waterleaf family)
Late May to mid-August, perennials

Sheltered alpine spots and subalpine meadows, but sometimes growing at much lower elevations. Striking plants, unlikely to be confused with anything else. They stand 15–40 cm high, the upper part of the stem crammed with small purple flowers from which project long stamens, hairs and whatnot. The leaves are long and frilly; they tend to droop.

*P. lyallii* occurs only south of Crowsnest Pass. Its flowers occur in clusters rather than spikes, and the leaves are not quite so finely divided. A similar cream-colored species with smooth-edged leaves, *P. leptosepala,* is found south of the Bow River.

*Phacelia sericea*

*Phacelia lyallii*

### Saw-wort/saussurea *Saussurée dense*

*Saussurea nuda* (composite family
July and August, perennial)

Alpine scree slopes and subalpine meadows from Crowsnest Pass north. May grow fairly tall, up to 40 cm, but is usually 5–20 cm. Thistle-like at first appearance, but lacking spines. Large, heavy, hairy purple flowerheads above a ground-hugging rosette of scallop-edged hairy leaves.

Waterton/Glacier has another saw-wort species: *S. americana,* which is a much taller species with finely toothed leaves.

*Saussurea nuda*

### Crowberry *Camarine à fruits noirs*

*Empetrum nigrum* (crowberry family)
June, perennial

Another fuzzy-stemmed ground-covering shrub of subalpine and alpine meadows, common everywhere except in the southern area; absent at Waterton/Glacier. Short needle-like leaves, very similar to yellow heather, page 362, and pink heather, page 370. The flowers, though, are quite different: small and purplish, carried close to the stem. Juicy berries appear in August, dark purple to black. They are sweet—the flavor seems apple-like to me—but seedy.

### Other plants to check

- Western lousewort, page 327
- Chinese lantern, page 363
- Rose root, page 369
- Elliptical-leaved penstemon, page 345

*Empetrum nigrum*

# Water plants
## Evolutionary success despite over-watering

Many plant species can tolerate occasional flooding, and some prefer soil so damp that it is nearly saturated. Still, this chapter is reserved for plants that normally grow in water, whether it be a puddle, a pond, a marsh, lake, stream or river.

Believe it or not, there are plants from tropical-fish aquariums growing outdoors near Banff Hot Springs. Turn to page 497 to find out about the tropical fish there.

## Higher water plants

These are flowering plants, with plumbing.

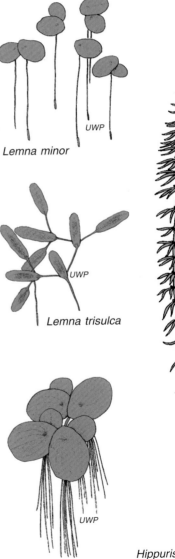

**Duckweed** *Lenticule*
*Lemna* and *Spirodela* spp. (duckweed family)
In bright-green floating colonies on shallow, warm ponds at low elevations, often covering a good deal of the surface. Each plant is a small leaf-like pad called a **thallus,** 2–8 mm across, with one or more tiny roots hanging down. Duckweed reproduces mostly by budding, but occasionally it puts forth microscopic flowers. In the fall, tiny bulblets drop off the thalli to overwinter at the bottom; in spring they rise to the surface and begin covering the pond anew.

There are three duckweed species in the Canadian Rockies. **Common duckweed** *(Lemna minor)* is by far the most common one; the thalli are oval, 2–5 mm across and not connected. They float at the surface. In **ivy duckweed** *(L. trisulca)* the thalli are elongated and interconnected in mats that float below the surface. **Larger duckweed** *(Spirodela polyrhiza)* is not really much larger— it's 4–8 mm across and oval—but has several tiny roots hanging off the thallus rather than just one.

*Lemna minor*

*Lemna trisulca*

**Mare's-tail** *Hippuride/queue de cheval*
*Hippuris* spp. (mare's-tail family)
July and August, perennial
In or beside shallow water at low elevations, rooted in the mud. A segmented plant resembling horsetail, page 392, but with flat leaves rather than round horsetail-type stems. As well, mare's-tail produces tiny green flowers along the stem where the tiers of leaves join, while horsetail does not flower. Easily confused with milfoil, next item, when the plants are not young, because they float just below the surface in the same way and acquire a coating that makes the leaves look frillier under the surface than they are. Carefully lift a stem above the water and look closely.

*Spirodela polyrhiza*

*Hippuris vulgaris*

There are two species in the Canadian Rockies: *H. vulgaris,* with stems 5–30 cm long, and *H. montana,* with stems only 1–10 cm long. The latter prefers moving water rather than lakes and grows from Saskatchewan Crossing north.

### Eurasian water-milfoil
*Myriophylle blanchissant*
*Myriophyllum exalbescens*
(water-milfoil family)
July and August, perennial

In quiet water up to 2 m deep at low elevations. A very frilly plant, reaching up a metre or so from roots in the bottom and floating just below the surface. Usually a single stem per plant. Tiers of little green flowers stick up a few centimetres above the surface. Compare with bladderwort, next item.

Eurasian water-milfoil is considered to be a weed by the government of Alberta, even though it is native, because it spreads quickly in the shallows of calm lakes when carried there accidentally on someone's boat.

### Bladderwort *Utriculaire*
*Utricularia* spp. (bladderwort family)
Late June and July, perennial

A floating, unrooted plant, growing in tangled masses below the surface in shallow water at low elevations. Stems up to a metre long with very frilly leaves and little dark bladders that not only support the plant at its proper depth but also feed it in an interesting way. Like its relative butterwort, page 348, bladderwort is insectivorous. The bladders are sensitive to the slightest touch, opening when tiny water creatures bump into them. The animals are swept in, where they die; their remains are ingested by the plant. Bladderwort has one to several showy flowers, yellow and snapdragon-like, carried above the water on a stem.

Three species in the Canadian Rockies, all rather alike. *U. vulgaris* is by far the most common. See also water-milfoil, previous item, which looks rather similar but is rooted and doesn't have bladders.

### Common cattail *Quenouille*
*Typha latifolia* (cattail family)
Late June to early July, perennial

Montane, at low elevations; often in roadside ditches. Common colonial marsh plant, rooting in water less than half a metre deep. Stands up to 2 m tall, with fat stems. Very long leaves, often with dried-out papery tips.

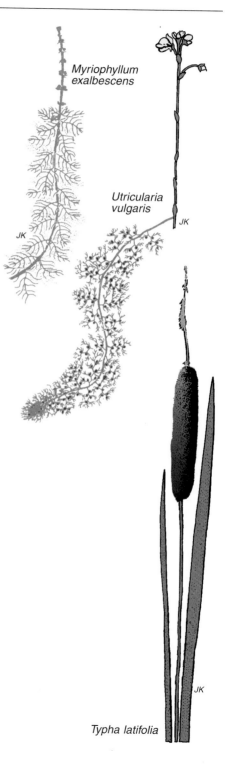

*Myriophyllum exalbescens*

*Utricularia vulgaris*

JK

*Typha latifolia*

Most people recognize the hot-dog-shaped brown seedheads of the cattail, but what about the flowers? Check the plant in early summer; you will find that the hot-dog part is made up of umpteen thousand female flowers, each nothing more than a hairy pistil. There are no petals. The male flowers occur on the same plant; they make up the spike atop the hot-dog. When cattail goes to seed the male flowers dry up and the spike hardens. The female flowers become fluffy seeds that disperse in the wind after birds break up the heads.

### Common great bulrush/tule
*Scirpe vigoureux*
*Scirpus validus* (sedge family)
June to July, perennial

Montane, fringing lakes in colonies. Stands 1–3 m tall; all parts dark green or drab. What you notice are the stems. The leaves grow down near the base, underwater, and they look like loose parts of the stem. The flowers are also drab; they spring from a point near the top of the stem, forming a loose cluster on stalks.

There is also a small bulrush: *S. caespitosus,* 10–50 cm tall, which looks like any other sedge (page 386) except for the tuft of very short, needle-like leaves at the base of the plant. Most sedge leaves are much longer and wider. Common in bogs and fens.

### Bur-reed *Rubanier à feuilles étroites*
*Sparganium angustifolium* (bur-reed family)
July and August, perennial

At low elevations in water up to half a metre deep. True reeds *(Phragmites australis,* over 2 m tall, leaves up to 4 cm wide) are very rare in the Canadian Rockies; the bur-reed, though, is common. Long grass-like leaves clasp the stems, often floating on the surface of the water; leaves are flat on one side and slightly rounded on the other. Fluffy round pinkish male flowerheads and spiky green ball-like female flowerheads, producing greenish fruits up to 2 cm across. There are several other species of bur-reed, similar-looking and sometimes hybridizing with this one, which is the most common.

### Reed canary grass *Phalaris roseau*
*Phalaris arundinacea* (grass family)
June and July, perennial

Montane, in shallow water at edges of ponds and marshes, and in roadside ditches. May be native to Canada, but probably

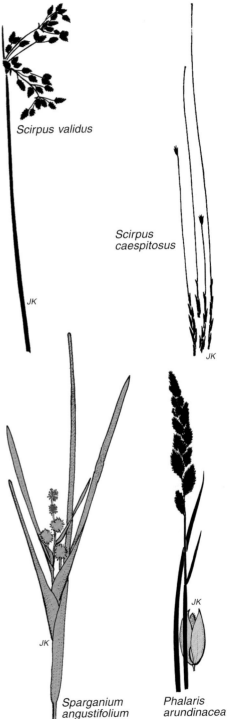

Scirpus validus

Scirpus caespitosus

JK

Sparganium angustifolium

Phalaris arundinacea

introduced in the Rockies. Becoming more common. One of the few grasses that grows right in the water, this one is tall enough—up to 1.5 m—and stout enough to be mistaken for a reed *(Phragmites;* see previous item). Leaves of canary grass are 1.5 cm across. Note the heavy seedheads.

### Yellow skunk-cabbage
*Chou de mouffette*
*Lysichitum americanum* (arum family)
Late April and early May, perennial

Western slope only, in Columbian forest marshes and wet spots, often among red-cedars. Huge, broad leaves often a metre in length or longer spread out from the centre; they give off a pungent odor when crushed.

This plant can be mistaken for false hellebore, page 311, before the skunk-cabbage has grown very large. But skunk-cabbage leaves have stalks and false hellebore leaves do not. Further, false hellebore is far more widespread, and it prefers a drier habitat. Yet many people call false hellebore "skunk-cabbage." This can be a fatal mistake if you eat false hellebore; it is quite poisonous.

The tiny yellow flowers of skunk-cabbage crowd along a club-shaped structure partly wrapped in a sheath-like bract called a **spathe.** Inside the spathe the temperature is a constant 22°C during the early-spring blooming period. This may attract pollinating insects. The leaves come later, edible after boiling to remove stinging calcium oxalate crystals. The large rootstock was an aboriginal staple, made into flour.

If you're in the northern foothills, you may see **water arum** *(Calla palustris),* also called **wild calla,** which is another member of the arum family. It grows in montane marshes and shallow ponds. The glossy green heart-shaped leaves each have a prominent yellow central rib. This plant tries hard to hold its leaves up out of the water, and it mostly succeeds. The flower resembles that of skunk-cabbage, with a large leaf-like spathe—but white, not yellow—partly surrounding a club of tiny yellowish-green flowers.

### Arrow-grass *Troscart maritime*
*Triglochin maritima* (arrow-grass family)
July, perennial

Montane, fringing marshes. Thin plant about half a metre tall, drably colored and not very noticeable until it blooms, when it makes

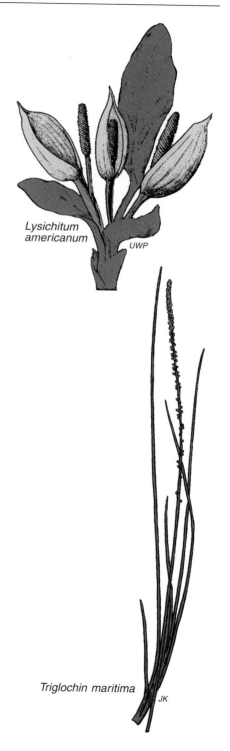

*Lysichitum
americanum*  UWP

*Triglochin maritima*  JK

a spike of small green flowers. These look like little bumps on the lower part of the spike, becoming a dense head farther up. Plant contains glycosides that produce cyanide in the stomachs of animals making the mistake of eating it.

See also pondweed, this page.

### Water smartweed/water knotweed
*Renouée amphibie*
*Polygonum amphibium* (buckwheat family)
Mid-June to late July, perennial

At low elevations in shallow water, often rooting on the sides of beaver channels. Glossy green leaves, prominently white-veined, float on the water. One large pink-to-red flower cluster stands 5–10 cm above the water, with one or more smaller clusters lower on the stem.

### Broad-leaved water-plantain
*Alisma-commun*
*Alisma plantago-aquatica*
(water plantain family) July, perennial

Western-slope and Waterton/Glacier, in marshes and along the shores of shallow lakes at low elevations. Leaves 10–30 cm long with parallel, ladder-like veins. Has a pretty bloom: small white three-petalled flowers, each at the end of a stalk, starburst-like.

### Pondweed *Potamot*
*Potamogeton* spp. (pondweed family)
Early July to August, perennial

Rooted in montane ponds, in the shallows of lakes and in slow-moving streams. Most of the plant is submerged, but the leaves usually float. In some thin-leaved species, these indicate the direction of water flow. The flowers always stick up out of the water; they are tiny, in club-shaped greenish clusters a couple of centimetres long. When not in bloom, pondweed can be differentiated from water-plantain or water smartweed, previous entries, by the translucent sheaths along the stems at the bases of pondweed leaves. Plant can also be covered by a thin, crunchy coating of calcium carbonate.

There are nine species of pondweed in the Rockies, most of them difficult to differentiate. The most common is *P. richardsonii,* illustrated.

*Polygonum amphibium*

*Alisma plantago-aquatica*

*Potamogeton richardsonii*

**Buck-bean** *Herbe à canards/trèfle d'eau*
*Menyanthes trifoliata* (buck-bean family)
June and July, perennial

In shallow standing water at montane elevations. Erect leaves held above the water are each divided into threes. A spike of showy white-to-purplish fringed flowers is carried higher still; the anthers are bright red or purple.

**Yellow pond lily**
*Grand nénuphar jaune/pied-de-cheval*
*Nuphar variegatum* (water lily family)
Mid-June to mid-July, perennial

Occasional on low-elevation ponds and sometimes slow-moving streams. Easily identified by the large round floating leaves. Strongly rooted in the bottom mud, the plant produces large yellow flowers with red-fringed centres. The flowers are carried singly atop stems that stick up above the surface.

Pond lily is a very salty plant: 9375 parts per million in its tissues, which is about 1000 times saltier than vegetation is typically. Porcupines, salt-cravers that they are, seek it out. Of course, they must swim to get it.

**Arrowhead**
*Sagittaria cuneata* (water-plantain family)
July, perennial

Common at low elevations in ponds and shallow lakes on the western slope to at least as far north as Golden, on the eastern slope to the Bow River. Has two kinds of leaves: long, very narrow ones under the water and larger, arrowhead-shaped leaves that break the surface. White three-parted flowers.

**Yellow water crowfoot**
*Renoncule de Gmelin*
*Ranunculus gmelinii* (buttercup family)
June and July, perennial

In shallow ponds or sluggish streams. Yellow water crowfoot is fairly common on the western slope and at Waterton/Glacier, occasional elsewhere. It has weak stems, so it either floats or lies on the shoreline mud when the water is low. Divided leaves 1–2 cm across, forming tangled mats. Typical buttercup flowers.

Two other buttercup species sometimes grow in water. Both of them have tiny yellow flowers. *R. cymbalaria* has rounded, toothy leaves. *R. flammula* has thinner leaves. Both plants have a sprawling stem that roots.

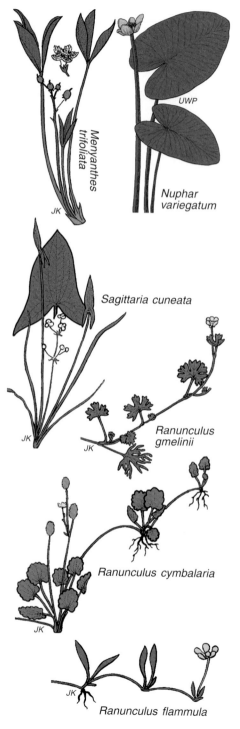

*Menyanthes trifoliata*

UWP

*Nuphar variegatum*

*Sagittaria cuneata*

*Ranunculus gmelinii*

*Ranunculus cymbalaria*

*Ranunculus flammula*

### White water crowfoot
*Renoncule aquatique blanche*
*Ranunculus circinatus* and *R. aquatilis*
(buttercup family)
July and early August, perennial

These are two very similar-looking, frilly-leaved, white-flowered water buttercups. In *R. circinatus* the leaves divide very close to the point of attachment, while in *R. aquatilis* they divide farther along the leaf-stem.

### Water hemlock *Cicutaire maculée*
*Cicuta maculata* (carrot family)
July and August, perennial

In wetlands up to treeline, often in standing water. Up to 2 m tall; usually less than a metre, with prominently veined sawtooth leaves. The flowers are tiny and white, carried in clusters above the plant like cow parsnip, page 303, which is a relative. Water hemlock is very poisonous, especially the lower parts and the roots; cattle die after eating only a few plants. Compare with water parsnip, next item.

### Water parsnip *Berle douce*
*Sium suave* (carrot family)
July and August, perennial

Western slope mainly, on the eastern slope from the Bow River south. Grows in marshy places, often with water hemlock, previous item, which looks like it. Differentiate by the simpler form of the leaves on water parsnip, compared with the doubly compound arrangement on water hemlock. Water parsnip is also reportedly poisonous, although supposedly not as dangerous as water hemlock.

### Water potentilla/marsh cinquefoil
*Potentille palustre/argentine rouge*
*Potentilla palustris* (rose family)
July, perennial

A northern species, south to the Athabasca River in ponds and sedge marshes. Not readily identified as *Potentilla* because the flowers are reddish purple, not yellow. But it has the classic five-part toothy potentilla leaf, which it holds up out of the water.

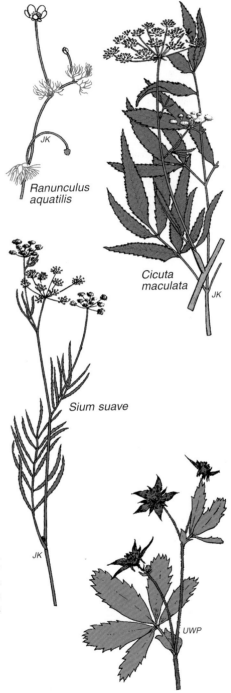

*Ranunculus aquatilis*

*Cicuta maculata*

*Sium suave*

*Potentilla palustris*

**Purple loosestrife** *Salicaire*
*Lythrum salicaria* (loosestrife family)
Mid-July to September, perennial

Southern area, in marshes, by the edges of shallow ponds and along streams. Not yet common, but inclined to spread rapidly. A tall, showy plant with stems often over a metre tall and lance-shaped downy leaves up to 10 cm long. Purple or pink five-petalled flowers bloom among the leaves on the upper part of the stem.

Introduced from Europe, this plant pushes out native vegetation and is a dangerous wrecker of wetlands ecology. But it's beautiful, and gardeners unwittingly spread it. For this reason the plant has been made illegal to cultivate in Alberta.

*Lythrum salicaria*

# Grasses and grass-like plants
## All that looks like grass is not grass

What is a "grass," anyway? It's something that looks like … well, *grass,* you know. Grasses, sedges and rushes all fit the non-botanist's image of grass: anything with skinny leaves. Nothing in biology is that easy, of course; each of these three groups is in a different family.

True **grasses** are round-stemmed and hollow. They grow in joints rather than as single, continuous, tubular stems. Bamboo is a grass. Grass leaves may be very narrow or perhaps curled inward, but essentially they are flat.

In **sedges** both the stems and the leaves are triangular in cross-section, although the leaves are often flattened so much that they look flat.

**Rushes** have round stems that are hollow, like grass. But they don't grow in joints; the stems are continuous tubes. And the leaves, rather than being flat, are usually round.

The botany student's way of remembering all this is to repeat, over and over before the exam, **"Rushes are round, sedges have edges, and grasses have joints."**

All these plants produce flowers, but they are tiny brown or purplish parts, not very colorful. Actually, there *is* a little color in the flowers of grasses and sedges: the tiny anthers are bright yellow. Not so in the rushes.

## Grasses

There are over a hundred grass species in the Canadian Rockies, of which 21 species have been selected for this book. All are in the grass family, the Gramineae, so the family is not given in the listings. The blooming date is not particularly important—the same picture suffices for both bloom and seedhead in grasses—so it isn't given in the listings either.

How does one identify grasses? By getting acquainted with their morphology, especially all the little parts of the flowerheads, then sitting on the ground for hours with a magnifying glass and a botanical key. This is too much trouble for me; I am content to casually pick out the few species described below, which besides being very common can be identified mostly by shape, size and color. But for confident identification that magnifying glass will be required.

In the listings that follow, note that "broad leaves" means broad *for a grass leaf:* 3–5 mm. Narrow is *really* narrow: 1–2 mm. Few grasses grow singly as just a stem and a few leaves; most grow in tufts, with many stems and leaves growing from a single point. Very large tufts become **tussocks,** which are especially common in high-subalpine and alpine meadows. Only a few species form **sod,** meaning lawn-like patches.

## You've got to be sharp, out there in the field

The seeds of some grass species are self-planting. Sharp-pointed on one end, with a long spine on the other, they fall to the ground and tend to land point down, sticking in like spears. Whenever the wind blows, the spine vibrates, sending the seed deeper and deeper into the soil. For another interesting self-planting mechanism, see needle-and-thread, page 386.

### Timothy *Phléole*
*Phleum* spp., perennial

Grows in sparse tufts 10–50 cm tall, usually in moist meadows. The two Rockies species of timothy occur at different elevations. **Common timothy** *(P. pratense),* an escapee from seed mixes, is mostly montane, although it may grow higher. Note the hot-dog-shaped flowerhead, which is purplish green. **Mountain timothy** *(P. commutatum)* is mostly alpine, but also subalpine; similar head, but shorter, as is the whole plant.

Timothy is easily confused with foxtail, next item, and can be reliably differentiated only with a magnifying glass. Check the tiny parts of the head, called **spikelets;** in timothy, each spikelet has a fringe of coarse bristles on the sides, while in foxtail the spikelets have scattered hairs all over them.

### Foxtail *Vulpin*
*Alopecurus* spp., perennials

Up to 80 cm tall. We have two species in the Rockies:

**Water foxtail** *(A. aequalis)* is lower montane, most common in the southern region, often growing singly; it prefers muddy places and can stand shallow water, while its look-alike, common timothy, previous item, will grow in damp places but not in water.

**Alpine foxtail** *(A. occidentalis)* grows in tufts, often with mountain timothy, in moist subalpine meadows. Alpine foxtail is usually a few centimetres taller than mountain timothy, but the only way to differentiate for sure is with a magnifying glass, as described in the item on timothy.

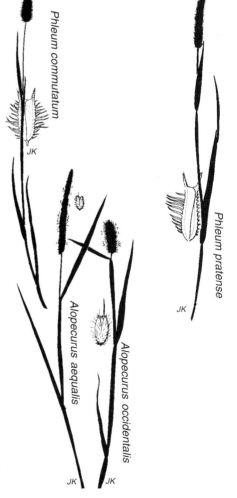

### Spike trisetum *Trisète à épi*
*Trisetum spicatum,* perennial
Upper montane and higher, in tufts with narrow leaves. The purplish-to-silvery heads look like lumpy timothy, with longer hairs.

### Smooth ryegrass *Élyme lisse*
*Elymus glaucus,* perennial
Tufts up to a metre tall in montane woods. The leaves are broad and tend to droop. Compared with the heads of the foregoing grasses, rye is coarser but still compact, and green rather than purplish. **Hairy wild rye** (*Elymus innovatus*), is also common in montane woods. The heads are purplish or grayish, very soft and, yes, hairy.

### Marsh reed grass/bluejoint reed grass and purple reed grass
*Foin bleu, calamagrostis pourpré*
*Calamagrostis canadensis* and *C. purpurascens*
Perennials
Marsh reed grass grows tall—up to 120 cm—and is common along fringes of montane marshes and lakes. The heads are large and feathery; each part is small, only 3–4 mm long, with a spray of fine hairs at the base.
Purple reed grass is shorter, 30–70 cm; has a similar but much tighter head. Grows in dry, often rocky montane and lower-subalpine locations in the central and southern regions.

### June grass *Keulérie*
*Koeleria macrantha,* perennial
Common in dry, grassy montane meadows. Grows 20–50 cm tall, in tufts; the narrow leaves are mostly basal. Note the divided head, which is usually purplish-green.

### Awnless brome/smooth brome/ northern brome *Brome inerme*
*Bromus inermis,* perennial
Montane, on dry slopes, growing singly or in loose colonies. This is a typical brome, the most common of six species in the Canadian Rockies. Note the dozen-or-so parts in the head, each about 1 cm long. The leaves are broad.

### Fescue *Fétuque*
*Festuca* spp., perennials
Montane and subalpine, in dry meadows. Nine species, all growing in tufts with narrow leaves and coarse, branched heads. Two

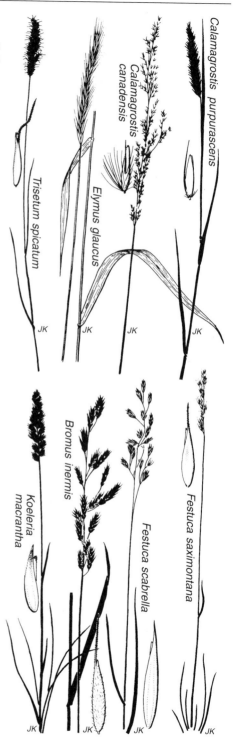

common species: **rough fescue** *(F. scabrella),* common in the southern region, 50–100 cm tall, and **sheep fescue** *(F. saximontana),* common throughout the Rockies and 10–50 cm tall.

### Bluegrass *Pâturin*
*Poa* spp., mostly perennials

Bluegrass is native to the Rockies, where it grows at every elevation in meadows. There are 19 species in the Canadian Rockies, very tricky even for botanists to tell apart. Here are two species to know:

**Kentucky bluegrass** *(P. pratensis)* is all over the Rockies at low elevations, and in nearly any lawn you see. It forms sod under good conditions; otherwise it grows in tufts. The heads are denser and heavier than the other two common Rockies bluegrasses. But you will have to leave the lawn uncut to check this out.

**Alpine bluegrass** *(P. alpina)* is common above treeline, growing in tufts or small patches 10–30 cm tall. The heads are well-branched and mostly green, the leaves wide.

### Ticklegrass/hairgrass
*Agrostis scabre/foin fou*
*Agrostis scabra,* perennial

Montane meadows. Grows in dense tufts up to 50 cm tall. Medium-wide erect leaves and very thin stems. The heads tickle, all right; they are small purple parts on long, skinny stalks.

### Sweetgrass *Foin d'odeur/herbe sainte*
*Hierochloe odorata,* perennial

Most common in the southern foothills, in dry meadows, but found at least as far north as Jasper. Grows 30–60 cm tall, with short leaves 2–3 cm long that are also broad. The head is well divided on long stalks, and the plant gives off the sweet smell of **coumarin,** especially when it burns. The Blackfoot hold sweetgrass especially dear; they use it in religious observances.

### Foxtail barley *Orge queue d'écureuil*
*Hordeum jubatum,* perennial

Montane, usually growing in tussocks and often on disturbed ground. Foxtail barley has the largest, fluffiest head of any Rockies grass. This is a beautiful plant; the winds of late summer and early autumn set fields of it nodding in coppery-hued waves.

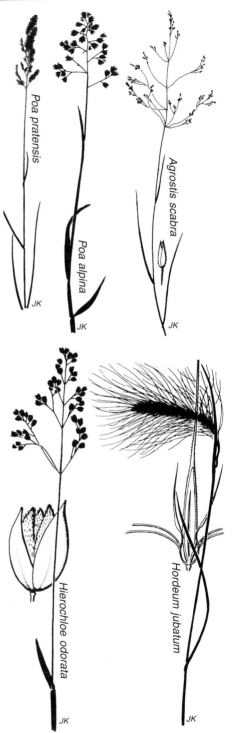

### Needle-and-thread/spear grass
*Stipe comateuse*
*Stipa comata,* perennial

On dry slopes at low elevations, mostly south of the Bow River but also found at Jasper and perhaps farther north in montane meadows. The species grows in spreading tufts. When you see it up close, you realize that needle-and-thread is aptly named, for the seeds look like small threaded needles. The thread is twisted; rain causes it to uncoil, screwing the very sharp seed into the ground. Pick these off the dog; they can go deep under the skin and infect.

### Woodland oatgrass
*Danthonie de Californie*
*Danthonia californica,* perennial

Dry montane meadows and gravelly places, sometimes subalpine. Grows in dense tufts 10–50 cm tall. The leaves are moderately broad and often hairy, but this grass is easy to identify by the very large parts that make up the heads.

### Ricegrass *Oryzopsis à feuilles rudes*
*Oryzopsis asperifolia,* perennial

Open montane woods, common from Banff south, in tufts. The leaves are mainly basal, reaching upward along the stems. Distinctive heads with rice-like parts on short stalks.

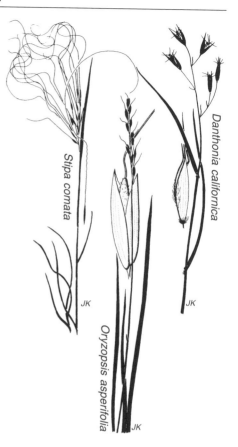

# Sedges

Sedges belong to their own family, the Cyperaceae. They are perennial grass-like plants, but their stems are triangular in cross-section, not round, and typically solid rather than hollow. Sedge leaves are often triangular as well, although more flattened than the stems. They have tiny, sharp teeth along the edges, all pointing the same way. If you run your fingers against the grain of those teeth, they can cut you.

Green with brownish or yellowish heads, sedges have grass-like flowers—tiny, no petals, with brownish or purplish parts—which means that they are not at all showy. Most prefer soggy places, although some species grow where it is dry. You can find sedges at all elevations.

The intimidating thing about the sedges is that there are about 80 species in the Rockies and nearly all belong to only one genus: *Carex.* Thus they are extremely difficult to identify because they look so much alike. Even professional botanists agonize over them. Job Kuijt, who produced a weighty tome on the flora of Waterton Lakes National Park, summed it up well when he introduced the 70 *Carex* species known from Waterton as "an extraordinarily large and difficult genus," the identification of whose members requires "a special kind of courage and devotion." (Kuijt, 1982, page 207)

That explains why, in so many botanical checklists for various places in the Rockies, one finds the sedges under "*Carex* spp.," with nary a species name given.

What if, like me, you are not even a botanist? You give up early in the game. For this book I have simply picked out a few common, representative sedges and stuck them in. The idea is not to try to identify species, but just to see what sedges look like.

Here are a couple of things to look for in sedges:

- The peculiar, beaked, flask-like **perigynium,** the seed-carrying part of the sedge, which is important in identification.
- The difference between male and female flower spikes on the same plant. Male flowers are usually the upper ones, in narrow spikes with lots of stamens dangling out; female flowers are usually below, in fatter-looking spikes.

### Dark-scaled sedge
*Carex atrosquama,* perennial

A classic mountain sedge, found in moist subalpine meadows. Grows 2–80 cm tall, in tufts.

### Beaked sedge
*Carex utriculata* (also known *as C. rostrata),* perennial

Montane marshes, in the water, where it grows in clusters or singly. Up to a metre tall, with fat female flower-clusters below and skinny male ones above. Leaves are rather wide and flat, for a sedge: up to a centimetre. In the fall, when they're dry, they look netted and lumpy.

### Water sedge
*Carex aquatilis,* perennial

Another tall water-sedge, but not as tall as *C. utriculata,* with narrower leaves. Has similar male/female flower setup. Leaves are usually bent-over at the top; when dry, they're smooth and plain-looking.

### Black alpine sedge
*Carex nigricans,* perennial

A small alpine species, growing in patches on tundra. Easy to spot: the heads are very dark, giving patches a blackish look.

### Rush-like sedge
*Carex scirpoidea,* perennial

This one is quite common on grassy montane and subalpine slopes, usually growing singly. The leaves are leathery, with very rough edges. Male and female flowerheads are on separate plants.

### Holm's Rocky Mountain sedge
*Carex scopulorum,* perennial

This species grows densely enough to form sod. Found at all elevations, in both wet and dry locations.

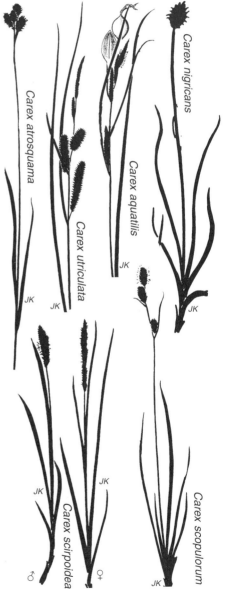

## Cotton grass *Linaigrette*
*Eriophorum* spp., perennials

Finally, here are sedges that are fairly easy to identify. These grow by the hundred in tundra ponds and at the water's edge in marshes, bogs, ponds and along slow-moving rivers, standing 1–30 cm tall with narrow basal leaves and cotton-puff heads. Of the five cotton-grass species in the Rockies, *E. polystachion* and *E. viridi-carinatum* are common from Jasper south; they have multiple heads. *E. chamissonis* is a common single-headed species found in all areas at subalpine elevations.

*Eriophorum chamissonis*

JK

# Rushes

Rushes belong to the family Juncaceae. They are nondescript green-and-brown plants with tiny purplish flowers that have three petals and three sepals, like those of the lily family. They fall mostly into the genus *Juncus,* which (get ready) resembles the *Carex* sedges.

Fortunately it is easy to tell the sedges and rushes apart: rushes have hollow, round stems like grasses, but no joints, while sedge stems are usually solid and triangular in cross-section. Further, rushes have round leaves, not flat ones like grasses or flattened triangular ones like sedges. The flowering parts of rushes are usually larger, so the heads look coarser.

## Common rushes *Jonc*
*Juncus* spp.

These are mostly short, easy-to-miss plants. They are typically 10–20 cm tall, although some grow to 60 cm, usually found singly or in small groups—not densely colonial like some of the lakeside sedges. Only a few are tufted. Here are some common representatives from the 15 species in the Canadian Rockies.

**Wire rush** *(J. balticus)* prefers mud or shallow water at low elevations. Rigid, wire-like stems 20–60 cm tall, with a few brownish clasping leaves near the base.

**Toad rush** *(J. bufonius)* is a lower-montane plant, found in wet places. Tufted, but not colonial, 10–20 cm tall. The heads are at the ends of branches.

*J. mertensianus* grows in subalpine bogs. Note the solitary head.

## Small-flowered wood rush
*Luzule à petites fleurs*
*Luzula parviflora*

Wood rushes are rushes that prefer drier places than *Juncus* rushes. So they grow in meadows and among the trees. Of the six Canadian Rockies species, this one is both the commonest and the easiest to identify. Note the many small nodding or drooping heads on branched stalks. The leaves are wider and flatter than those of other rushes.

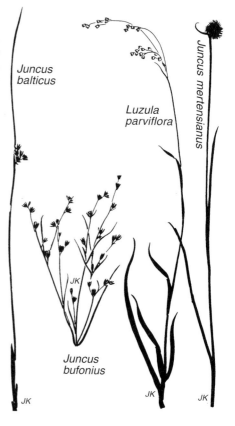

*Juncus balticus*

*Luzula parviflora*

*Juncus mertensianus*

*Juncus bufonius*

JK

# Non-flowering plants
## Ferns, horsetails and clubmosses/spikemosses

These plants do not bloom. They produce spores instead of seeds, like the mushrooms, mosses and lichens.

Lacking flowers, members of this group are perhaps harder to identify than the flowering plants—although the ferns have a lot of variety in their leaves, and that helps. Eleven common species are included here. The horsetails are trickier to differentiate, while the clubmosses and their close relatives, the spikemosses, are intent on remaining anonymous to anybody but a botanist. Still, there are two clubmosses that are fairly easy to pick out, and one spikemoss that is unmistakable.

## Ferns

Ferns are moisture-loving plants, which means that one finds many more of them, and more species, on the western slope than on the eastern slope. The best places are in Columbian-forest areas of the Rocky Mountain Trench.

Note how some species have two distinctly different kinds of leaves: fertile ones, which carry the spore cases, and sterile ones, which do not. They look different.

A fern pokes out of the ground in a wheel-like roll called a **fiddlehead.** The fiddlehead unrolls and grows. Fiddleheads are tasty, but at least one species—bracken, next page—has been shown to cause cancer in cattle.

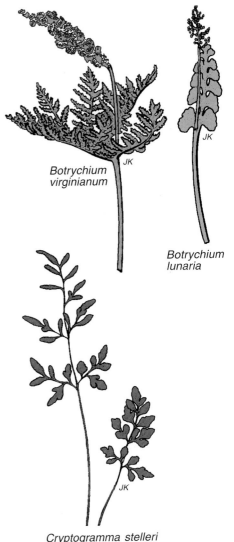

*Botrychium
virginianum*

*Botrychium
lunaria*

*Cryptogramma stelleri*

### Grape fern/moonwort *Botrique*
*Botrychium* spp. (adder's-tongue family)
Perennial

Montane and lower subalpine meadows, but sometimes above treeline. Only 5–20 cm tall, but striking: the spore cases are carried above the leaves on a stalk, rather like a bunch of tiny grapes. Several species, difficult to tell apart, except for *B. virginianum,* which is the easiest to identify because it has frillier leaves than other members of the genus. This is also the most common grape fern. Of the others, moonwort, *B. lunaria,* is also fairly common.

### Steller's rock brake
*Cryptogramme de Steller*
*Cryptogramma stelleri* (common fern family)
Perennial

Western-slope montane, central and southern regions; occasional on the eastern slope from Banff south. Prefers mossy cliffs. Sparsely leaved and pale, it's not much to look at, but rock brake is interesting for its two kinds of leaves: narrow fertile leaflets and oval sterile ones. The fertile frond is taller, and the fertile leaflets have translucent edges that roll inward. The stems are yellowish. Compare with parsley fern, next item.

### Parsley fern *Cryptogramme persil*
*Cryptogramma crispa* (common fern family) Perennial

Alpine and high subalpine, among rocks; sometimes much lower. Similar to Steller's rock-brake, previous item, but the sterile leaflet edges are toothy and the fertile leaflets, which point upward, do not have translucent edges. Plant has more foliage and often grows taller, 20–30 cm, than Steller's rock brake. Also known as *C. acrostichoides*.

### Lady fern *Fougère femelle*
*Athyrium filix-femina* (common fern family) Perennial

Montane and subalpine, in moist, shady protected places; common in Columbian forest. One of the larger ferns you are likely to see in the mountains: fronds up to 2 m long. Note how each frond has short leaflets at the base and the tip; there are longer ones between.

### Bracken *Grande fougère*
*Pteridium aquilinum* (common fern family) Perennial

Montane woods, western slope and occasional in Waterton. Another big fern, up to a metre tall in the Rockies. Simple shape: branches and leaflets along a stem—a single leaf, actually, growing from the rootstock. Feathery, delicate appearance.

### Fragile fern and northwestern woodsia
*Cystoptéride fragile, woodsia nord-ouest*
*Cystopteris fragilis* and *Woodsia oregana* (common fern family) Perennial

Fragile fern is the most common fern in the mountains, growing everywhere, in almost any situation. Small and delicate, with easily broken fronds 20–30 cm long. The stem is shiny and translucent.

This plant is easily confused with northwestern woodsia but is much more common. The only reliable way to distinguish the two is to look at the spore cases: the brown dots under the leaflets. In fragile fern, small veins pass under the spore cases and continue to the edge of the leaflet; in northwestern woodsia the veins end at the spore cases.

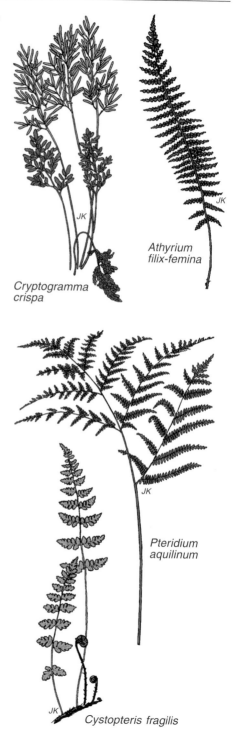

*Athyrium filix-femina*

*Cryptogramma crispa*

*Pteridium aquilinum*

*Cystopteris fragilis*

**Oak fern** *Fougère du chêne*
*Gymnocarpium dryopteris*
(common fern family)
Perennial
    In deep forest, mostly lower subalpine. A medium-sized, rather delicate-looking fern, standing 20–40 cm tall. The frond branches into three, each branch roughly equal in size.

**Cliff woodsia** *Woodsia des falaises*
*Woodsia scopulina* (common fern family)
Perennial
    A small fern, growing at all elevations but mostly subalpine and alpine, among rocks in sunny places. More common on the eastern slope. Prefers soil derived from sandstone and shale rather than from limestone or dolomite; common on quartzite. Stems are dark-brown at the base and yellowish near the ends. The leaves are sparsely hairy but the stems are smooth.

**Northern holly fern/Christmas fern**
*Polystic*
*Polystichum lonchitis* (common fern family)
Perennial
    A western-slope plant, rare north of the Bow River on the eastern slope, often found among broken rock and talus; sometimes growing in meadows. Easy to identify: tough shiny green prickly leaves. Several erect fronds 20–40 cm tall; stems covered with brown scales. Leaflets are not symmetrical, and they stay green all winter.

**Other plants with fern-like leaves**
- Lousewort, pages 327 and 366
- Yarrow, page 303
- Jacob's-ladder, page 346

*Gymnocarpium dryopteris*

*Woodsia scopulina*

*Polystichum lonchitis*

## *Horsetails*

Like ferns, horsetails reproduce by shedding spores rather than seeds. There are no leaves; photosynthesis goes on in the central stem and side branches, if any. The reproductive structure is called a **cone,** found at the tip of the main stem. More common in the Canadian Rockies than one might think, there are nine species you are likely to see here. Identification isn't easy in most of these. In addition to the short descriptions, pay close attention to the enlarged drawings of the stem joints, which are diagnostic features.

### Common horsetail and other horsetails with side branches
*Prêle des champs*
*Equisetum arvense* and others (horsetail family)
Perennial

*Equisetum arvense* is very common along montane and lower subalpine roadsides, in meadows and woods. Can manage in ground that is rather dry; need not grow in wet places. Common horsetail normally stands 10–30 cm tall in the Rockies. It is medium green and has lots of side branches that give it a frilly look. After the first hard frost of fall, these plants lose their color and fall over, looking like fish skeletons before the silica in their bodies turns to dust.

Common horsetail produces two kinds of shoots: brown-sheathed flesh-colored un-branched fertile ones, which come up in early spring, and branched green sterile ones lacking cones, which come up later. Here are the other two horsetails in the Rockies that usually have side branches:

*E. pratense,* found in the same habitat as *E. arvense* and often growing with it, but less common. Grows 20–50 cm tall. Distinguish by the fertile shoots, which are branched in *E. pratense* and unbranched in *E. arvense*.

*E. sylvaticum,* found from Jasper north, in the woods; 30–60 cm tall. The branches curve down, and the branches branch again— unique in the Rockies. Like *E. pratense,* this species produces both sterile and fertile plants, and both are branched.

### Dwarf scouring-rush/sedge-like horsetail *Prêle faux-scirpe*
*Equisetum scirpoides* (horsetail family)
Perennial

Common in damp montane and subalpine woods of the central region, usually growing in patches bordering marshes. Easily identified by its short size: 5–15 cm. It is jointed and has no side branches; the skinny stems are wavy rather than straight. From a distance, a patch of this plant looks very much like grass.

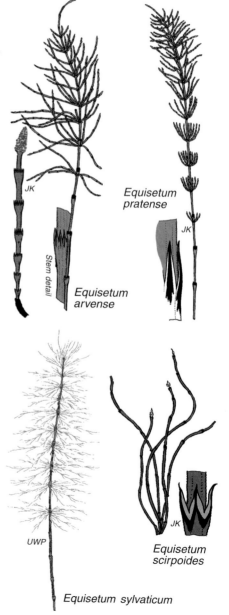

*Equisetum pratense*

Stem detail

*Equisetum arvense*

*Equisetum scirpoides*

*Equisetum sylvaticum*

## Scouring-rush group *Prêle*

*Equisetum* spp. (horsetail family) Perennial

These species match the standard image of a horsetail: straight dark-green hollow jointed stems without side branches, although side branches are sometimes present.

*E. variegatum* is fairly short, 10–40 cm, montane and subalpine, in moist meadows and on gravelly stream flats or along lakeshores. Stems are evergreen, meaning that they remain green under the snow, and have 5–10 fine ridges. This is the most common unbranched species in the northern and central Canadian Rockies, less common in the southern region.

*E. fluviatile* is central and southern montane and subalpine, usually growing in water. Up to 1 m tall, sometimes with side branches; stems delicately ribbed.

*E. palustre* is 20–60 cm tall, in marshy spots at low elevations. Resembles *E. fluviatile,* previous item, but with a smaller central stem cavity of less than one-third the diameter of the stem.

*E. hyemale* is central and southern montane, on streambanks and lakeshores, but sometimes in very dry locations, such as the Jackman Flats dunes (see page 399). Up to 1 m tall, with tough gray-green evergreen stems that have 18–40 very rough ridges.

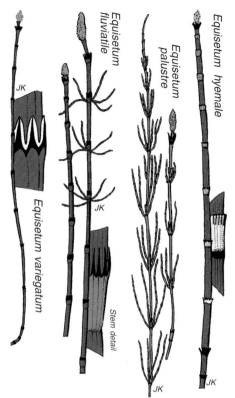

*Equisetum fluviatile*

*Equisetum palustre*

*Equisetum hyemale*

*Equisetum variegatum*

*Stem detail*

## *Clubmosses and spikemosses*

The clubmosses and spikemosses look like heather, page 361, or crowberry, page 374: short stems covered with needle-like leaves. The way to tell them from heather or crowberry is to look for the cone-like spore cases on the clubmosses. You won't find anything resembling a cone on heather or crowberry. Further, clubmosses and spikemosses are much less common than either heather or crowberry, so if you are strolling through heathery meadows there is no need to worry that you may in fact be strolling through clubmossy/spikemossy meadows. There may be patches of clubmoss/spikemoss to look at if you keep an eye open for them.

By the way, these are ancient plant forms. *Lycopodium*-type clubmosses appeared in early Devonian times, about 400 million years ago. (The earliest land plants, the extinct psilophytes, evolved in the late Silurian, some 10 million years before that.)

## Stiff clubmoss *Lycopode innovant*

*Lycopodium annotinum* (clubmoss family) Perennial

Montane and subalpine, in damp, shady places. Look for this plant growing among feather mosses, page 395, on north-facing slopes. Erect spring-green stems 10–20 cm tall with sharp-ended leaves; yellowish cones at the stem ends. Of the several other species of *Lycopodium* in the mountains, *L. dendroideum* is the easiest to differentiate: the stem has so many branches that the plant looks like a tiny evergreen shrub.

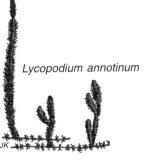

*Lycopodium annotinum*

**Ground-cedar** *Lycopode aplati*
*Lycopodium complanatum* (clubmoss family)
Perennial

Mainly western-slope montane, in the woods; common in Columbian forest, occasional on the eastern slope. Looks very much like little fronds of red-cedar growing up out of the mossy forest floor. Scaly olive-drab stems branch repeatedly from the creeping rootstock.

**Spikemoss/prairie selaginella**
*Sélaginelle dense*
*Selaginella densa* (spikemoss family)
Perennial

Mostly low-elevation montane, but occasional to treeline, in open dry places. Looks very much like some sort of coarse moss: fuzzy olive-drab stems, silvery near the tips, reaching up a couple of centimetres. But a close look will often reveal little cones at the ends of the stems, which would never be found on moss. During rainy periods this plant brightens up considerably.

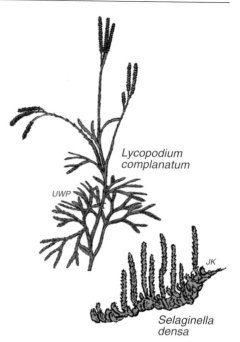

*Lycopodium complanatum*

UWP

JK

*Selaginella densa*

# *Mosses and liverworts*
## No plumbing, no flowers

Mosses are largely anonymous to most of us. They are not flashy like wildflowers, possibly poisonous like mushrooms or conspicuous like trees. Yet the mosses—especially the feather mosses—cover a lot of the forest floor in the Canadian Rockies. One might as well get to know a few species.

Mosses and liverworts, the two branches of the phylum Bryophyta, are not vascular plants; they have no roots and little means of moving water around in their bodies—no plumbing at all, really, which means that they quickly suck up any moisture that comes their way and hold onto it for as long as possible. Moss leaves are very small, while some liverworts are merely one large leaf-like body. Both groups stay green all the time, winter and summer, although they dull down a bit under the snow or during dry spells.

This dependence on incidental moisture leads mosses and liverworts to favor damp places in which to grow: along streams, at springs and seeps, or in bogs. To cut losses by evaporation, many bryophytes live in the shade. The cool, damp subalpine forest is just right, as are Columbian-forest areas of the western slope.

Still, a few species are good enough at hoarding moisture to make a go of it on the driest of bare-rock cliffs and sunbaked slopes. Cold is not a particular problem; mosses can spend a good part of the year frozen to some high-country crag, revving up the photosynthetic factory whenever there is liquid water about.

Most bryophytes are colonial, living shoulder-to-shoulder (well, gametophyte-to-gametophyte) with many others of their own kind.

Bryophyte sex is interesting. These plants can grow sexual organs, contribute sperm and egg, then send up a sporophyte and release spores. If that is too much trouble they can create little reproductive packets called **gemmae,** which fall off and germinate. If all else fails, this group has the choice of going to pieces: fragmenting, each bit starting anew.

Except to the specialist, mosses and liverworts are difficult to identify. It's all done through a magnifying glass (or a microscope). And, of course, there are many species. For the purpose of this book it seems adequate to introduce the more common groups in the Rockies, illustrating them with species likely to catch your eye. The many nondescript ones—the Little Green Mosses—can be left for the bryologists to sort out.

## Mosses of the forest floor: the feather mosses

Easily the most obvious and perhaps also the most common bryophytes of the Rockies, feather mosses cover the shady ground in montane and subalpine coniferous forests. They don't do well in deciduous woods, where the falling leaves tend to bury them. We are speaking here of very frilly mosses, the tiny leaves growing along branching stems 5–10 cm long.

Stepping off a dusty, hard-packed trail into pillowy feather moss is a treat for tired feet—although not particularly kind to the moss. The thing to do is to lie down on your tummy and get nose-to-moss, preferably with a magnifying glass. Don't worry; there are no tiny beasties in this micro-jungle to bite you, although in spring you should check yourself for ticks (page 457) when you get up.

There are four kinds of feather mosses you are likely to see in the Canadian Rockies, and three other moss species that aren't feather mosses proper but live with feather mosses.

**Stairstep moss** *(Hylocomnium splendens)* is the most common feather moss on the eastern slope. Tiers of curving branches come off the main stem, each tier representing a year's growth; these stair-like tiers give the plant its common name. The tiny leaves stay pressed tightly together. The branches have branches.

**Big red-stem** *(Pleurozium schreberi)* is the most ordinary-looking feather moss, but still easily differentiated by the red stem; all the others have green stems. The leaves are larger than those of most feather mosses, although smaller than those of *Rhytidiadelphus* (next item), growing on the stem and on branches that stick out from the stem at right angles. The upper stem often nods to one side.

*Hylocomnium*   *DV*    *Pleurozium*   *DV*

**Goose-neck moss** *(Rhytidiadelphus triquetrus)* has the largest leaves but the fewest branches. It looks very fuzzy; the leaves grow on the stem as well as on the branches, and the tips hang over, goose-necked. The color is spring green. On the western slope this is the most common feather moss.

**Knight's-plume** *(Ptilium crista-castrensis)* is the featheriest feather moss. The many branches are regularly arranged left and right along the stem like an ostrich feather, becoming gradually longer farther down. The tiny leaves curl downward, each like a sickle.

*Rhytidiadelphus*   *DV*    *Ptilium*   *DV*

*Dicranum* spp. are also common among the feather mosses of the subalpine forest floor. They are coarse and fuzzy, standing erect with no side branches. If it is possible for a moss to look windswept, these do.

*Barbilophozia lycopodioides* is another plant you may find in this community. It's an olive-green single-stemmed liverwort (moss relative; see page 400) that looks a lot like a moss. The tiny four-pointed leaves are arranged in two opposite rows along a single unbranched stem; they are translucent and a little slimy-looking.

*Polytrichum commune* hides among the feather mosses and humus. This is the largest moss in the mountains, easily identified by the heavy stems, which are up to 3 cm thick and 30 cm long. No photo.

*Dicranum*  DV   *Barbilophozia*  DV

## Peat mosses

In the central and northern Canadian Rockies there is a special kind of swamp called **muskeg:** a heavily vegetated black-spruce bog with hummocks and hollows. Sometimes the surface will support your weight. Breaking through puts you up to your knees in smelly black muck, which is mostly the remains of many, many little peat mosses.

It takes dedication to be a peat-moss bryologist.

One would expect the mosses growing in Rockies peat bogs to be species of the genus *Sphagnum,* which is the only true peat moss, in the botanical sense. *Sphagnum* is common elsewhere in the world and does grow here, but not abundantly. Instead, we have mainly *Drepanocladus* species, which prefer the soggy hollows, and *Tomenthypnum nitens,* which forms the hummocks. Both are golden-brown, long-leaved and frilly looking; tell them apart by the curving, overlapping leaves of *Drepanocladus* and the fuzzy stems of *Tomenthypnum.*

*Sphagnum*   B. Zimmer   *Drepanocladus*   DV   *Tomenthypnum*   DV

## Peat

What exactly is peat, and how does it form? Peat is the first stage of what eventually becomes coal.

The slow-moving water in wetlands is low in dissolved oxygen, so the decay process is very slow. It can take hundreds of years for the cellulose that makes up the plant fibres to break down into its main components: carbon, hydrogen and oxygen.

The freed-up oxygen is quickly used by other organisms, while the hydrogen combines with sulphur, always present in living tissues, to be released as stinky hydrogen sulphide ($H_2S$) or tied up in the sulphide minerals found as a black undercrust at the bottom of most Rockies ponds. Some of the carbon winds up in the other common swamp gas, methane ($CH_4$), but much of it simply collects as peat, becoming purer as time goes by. After several thousand years the stuff is concentrated enough to burn, once it has dried out. Ask any Scot.

On our side of the Atlantic we don't burn peat; we wait a hundred million years or so until it has become nearly pure carbon, i.e. coal. But we destroy our muskegs anyway, digging them up to get at the blackened bottom layers of dead peat moss, which go into our gardens and around our potted plants. The next time you see a bulldozed-out bog in the foothills, you will know what happened.

Beyond commerce, peat has value to science. Swamp and lake bottoms can be cored, yielding peat records of the recent geological past and telling us what the weather was like thousands of years ago.

## Mosses along streams and at springs

Small perennial streams and springs with steady water levels are terrific places for bryophytes to grow, so there will be lots of anonymous Little Green Mosses there, many of them species of the genera *Bryum*, *Pohlia* and *Philonotis*.

If the water level varies a good deal, which is typical of front-range streams, you may find *Hygrohypnum luridum*, a coarse brownish-green moss that grows in the narrow zone between high and low water (the splash zone). In winter, anyone walking up the dry streambed of Maligne Canyon between Fifth Bridge and Fourth Bridge can easily locate the summer water level, which is marked along the canyon walls by *H. luridum*.

On the western slope, look for *Scouleria aquatica* on wet rocks just above the water line. This moss prefers to stay soggy all the time.

*Bryum*   DV   *Philonotis*   DV   *Scouleria*   DV   *Hygrohypnum*   DV

# Mosses on cliffs and in other rocky places; alpine mosses

The north side of any rocky outcrop is likely to be mossy in the Canadian Rockies. Cliffs at any elevation mimic the alpine-zone environment: they are extremely variable in surface temperature, alternately wet and dry, with little or no soil.

The mosses that live in this difficult environment depend on rain and snowmelt for water, but as bryophytes they are good at conserving it—especially on the shady side of the rock. Vascular plants such as wildflowers, which have roots, require soil in which to grow; they fare poorly on vertical rock. But mosses don't have roots, don't need much soil (if any), and thus fit the cliffside ecological niche quite nicely. Bryophytes do well on the stony ground above treeline for the same reasons.

*Grimmia* species are small and tufted, often very dark green or even black. Look for tiny white hair points sticking up above the surface. This genus is the aridity champion, growing in amazingly dry spots. The drier the conditions, the blacker the moss. *Grimmia* survives on south-facing rocks in the hot summer sun and on the ground on sunny, open slopes at low elevations. It luxuriates in the relative comfort of a cool north-facing cliff.

*Orthotrichum* species look a lot like *Grimmia* (previous item) and grow in similar places, but are larger and lack hair points. The surface sometimes has a whitish look. **Capsules** (spore cases) are often present, peeking up from the leaves.

*Thuidium abietinum* is frilly and branched, rather like a small feather moss. It is thready when wet and fluffy when dry.

*Tortula ruralis* is fuzzy-looking, with white hair points. It takes up water very quickly, swelling noticeably in only 10 or 15 seconds; the leaves clasp the stem when dry, but stand off it when wet.

*Encalypta* species are easily identified by the prominent dunce-cap-like structures that stick up from the surface on wire-like red stalks. Called **calyptras,** they cover the plant's spore-bearing capsules. How modest.

*Tortella tortuosa* has very narrow leaves arranged spirally around the stem. The leaves resemble those of *Distichum capillaceum,* which has two rows on a shiny stem. Both species grow in sheltering limestone or dolomite crevices that seep slowly. Here they get a little moisture.

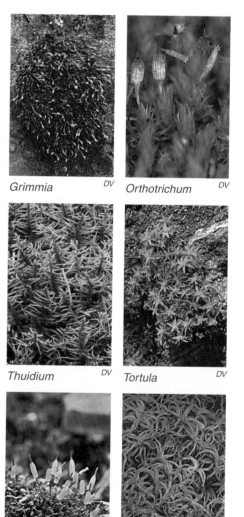

Grimmia          DV   Orthotrichum      DV

Thuidium         DV   Tortula           DV

Encalypta        DV   Tortella          DV

*Hypnum revolutum* and *H. vaucheri* are creeping and branched. All the tiny leaves curl the same way, and they are tightly pressed together along the stem.

*Polytrichum* and *Pogonatum* are called the **hairy-cap mosses.** Low and round, they resemble tiny pincushion cacti—especially when wet, which causes the radially arranged leaves to spread out. When dry, these mosses close up. They grow singly or in small groups on the ground, preferring non-calcareous soil and usually choosing sandy places among rocks at high subalpine and alpine elevations. A good place to see hairy-cap mosses is along the Path of the Glacier Trail at Mt. Edith Cavell. In *Polytrichum juniperinum* the leaves are shiny with red tips; in *Polytrichum piliferum* the tips are white. *Pogonatum alpinum* is similar but with dull leaves and green tips.

*Hypnum*    DV    *Polytrichum*    DV

## Soil crusts

Mosses can combine with lichens and other fungi to produce patches of crust on the ground that are technically termed **cryptogamic soil,** from "crypto-" meaning "hidden" and "-gamic" meaning "life," or **microbiotic crust.** These tiny ecological communities are often the first to colonize bare ground. They were first recognized in the arid lands of the American southwest, where they had long been thought to be mineral deposits. Soil crusts are surprisingly widespread, from the equatorial desert sands to the arctic tundra, and they are common in the Canadian Rockies, especially on sand or silt in dry, open, windy places.

*Typical lichen-rich soil crust seen in the Canadian Rockies. Photo taken on Syncline Ridge, Jasper National Park, by Toby Gadd.*

# Liverworts

Liverworts resemble some lichen species. But liverworts are not fungi, so they are not lichens.

*Marchantia polymorpha* is a common and interesting liverwort. It looks like green plastic that someone poured onto the ground. The thallus (technical name for a plant body that has no stem or leaves) is bright green, thick and leathery, somewhat scaly and thready underneath. It gets 4–6 cm long.

Note the eye-catching reproductive structures: umbrella-like female and male organs, and cup-like green or brown holders for gemmae that are scattered by raindrops. The gemmae grow into new plants. Look for small colonies of *Marchantia* in damp spots at any elevation—especially in areas that burned a year or two ago.

The only plant likely to be mistaken for *Marchantia* is the lichen *Peltigera aphthosa,* page 408, which is white underneath, rather than green, and lacks umbrellas or gemmae cups.

Other liverworts are more moss-like. *Barbilophozia lycopodioides,* a leafy liverwort described on page 396, is a good example.

*Marchantia*　　　　　　　　DV

# Algae

These are protists, not plants, but since they are found mostly in water they are discussed briefly here. Few are very conspicuous, even though there are thousands of microscopic species in the Canadian Rockies. Lichens, which *are* conspicuous, also contain algae or cyanobacteria; see page 405.

### Plankton

All Rockies lakes have plenty of planktonic (free-floating) algae in them. Even the clearest lake water carries plankton. Some lakes are murky with it. The normal plankton in Canadian Rockies waters are not harmful to drink, but human pollution with intestinal bacteria and the protozoan *Giardia lamblia* (page 773) has rendered all surface water in the southern and central regions suspect.

### Attached algae

The other kind of algae that you may notice are those species that can send you headlong into the creek if you step on a boulder or a log coated with them. Beware the slippery surfaces early in the day, when water levels are low in the mountains.

How can you tell attached forms of algae from similar-looking mosses? Look closely; they really aren't similar at all. Mosses are far more complicated plants than algae. If the thing you are looking at is nothing more than green slime or filaments in water, then it is a species of algae. But don't be fooled by *Chara,* which is a very common algal species that looks like a moss or small underwater horsetails. It has tiers of leaf-like filaments. *Chara* grows in very shallow water, completely submerged. Viewed from a boat, colonies of *Chara* look like miniature dark-green forests.

There are algae that live in snow. See page 474 for these and other interesting snow-and-ice organisms in the Canadian Rockies. See also cyanobacterial colonies on the ground, page 430.

# Plant families
## Scientific names and their common equivalents

All plant families known or likely to occur in the Canadian Rockies, whether or not a representative is described in this book, are listed here in the botanical order given in *Flora of Alberta,* second edition (1983), by Moss and Packer, or in *Flora of the Pacific Northwest* (1976), by Hitchcock and Cronquist. Where the two disagree on family designations, botanical order or species names, I have used *Flora of Alberta* because it is newer.

| | | | | |
|---|---|---|---|---|
| Lycopodiaceae — Clubmoss | Gramineae — Grass | Ranunculaceae — Buttercup/crowfoot | Celastraceae — Bittersweet | Menyanthaceae — Buck-bean |
| Selaginellaceae — Spikemoss | Cyperaceae — Sedge | Berberidaceae — Barberry | Aceraceae — Maple | Apocynaceae — Dogbane |
| Isoetaceae — Quillwort | Araceae — Arum | Papaveraceae — Poppy | Rhamnaceae — Buckthorn | Asclepiadaceae — Milkweed |
| Equisetaceae — Horsetail | Lemnaceae — Duckweed | Fumariaceae — Fumitory | Malvaceae — Mallow | Convolvulaceae — Morning-glory |
| Ophioglossaceae — Adder's-tongue | Juncaceae — Rush | Capparidaceae — Caper | Hypericaceae — St. John's-wort | Polemoniaceae — Phlox |
| Polypodiaceae — Fern | Liliaceae — Lily | Cruciferae — Mustard | Violaceae — Violet | Hydrophyllaceae — Waterleaf |
| Marsileaceae — Marsilea | Iridaceae — Iris | Droseraceae — Sundew | Loasaceae — Loasa | Boraginaceae — Borage |
| Salviniaceae — Water-fern | Orchidaceae — Orchid | Crassulaceae — Stonecrop | Cactaceae — Cactus | Verbenaceae — Verbena/vervain |
| Cupressaceae — Cypress | Salicaceae — Willow | Saxifragaceae — Saxifrage | Elaeagnaceae — Oleaster | Labiatae — Mint |
| Pinaceae — Pine | Betulaceae — Birch | Parnassiaceae — Grass-of-Parnassus | Lythraceae — Loosestrife | Solanaceae — Nightshade/potato |
| Taxaceae — Yew | Cannabinaceae — Hemp | Hydrangeaceae — Hydrangea | Onagraceae — Evening-primrose | Scrophulariaceae — Figwort |
| Typhaceae — Cattail | Urticaceae — Nettle | Grossulariaceae — Currant/gooseberry | Haloragaceae — Water-milfoil | Orobanchaceae — Broomrape |
| Sparganiaceae — Bur-reed | Santalaceae — Sandalwood | Rosaceae — Rose | Hippuridaceae — Mare's-tail | Lentibulariaceae — Bladderwort |
| Najadaceae — Water-nymph | Loranthaceae — Mistletoe | Fabaceae — Pea | Araliaceae — Ginseng | Plantaginaceae — Plantain |
| Potamogetonaceae — Pondweed | Polygonaceae — Buckwheat | Geraniaceae — Geranium | Umbelliferae — Parsley/carrot | Rubiaceae — Madder |
| Zannichelliaceae — Horned pondweed | Chenopodiaceae — Goosefoot | Linaceae — Flax | Cornaceae — Dogwood | Caprifoliaceae — Honeysuckle |
| Juncaginaceae — Arrow-grass | Amaranthaceae — Pigweed | Polygalaceae — Milkwort | Pyrolaceae — Wintergreen | Adoxaceae — Moschatel |
| Lilaeaceae — Flowering-quillwort | Nyctaginaceae — Four-o'clock | Euphorbiaceae — Spurge | Monotropaceae — Ghost-flower | Valerianaceae — Valerian |
| Scheuchzeriaceae — Scheuchzeria | Portulacaceae — Purslane | Callitrichaceae — Water-starwort | Ericaceae — Heath | Campanulaceae — Harebell/bluebell |
| Alismataceae — Water-plantain | Caryophyllaceae — Pink | Empetraceae — Crowberry | Primulaceae — Primrose | Lobeliaceae — Lobelia |
| Hydrocharitaceae — Waterweed | Nymphaeaceae — Water-lily | Anacardiaceae — Sumac | Gentianaceae — Gentian | Compositae — Composite/aster |

## Further reading

Alberta Forestry Association (1986) *Alberta Trees of Renown: an Honour Roll of Alberta Trees.* Alberta Forestry Association, #311, 10526 Jasper Avenue, Edmonton T5J 1Z5. Catalogue of notable trees in the province: record-holders, unusual, historical. Illustrated, 32 pages.

Clark, L. (1974) *Wild Flowers of Forest & Woodland in the Pacific Northwest.* Douglas & McIntyre, Vancouver. Handy guide to the western-slope forbs and shrubs. Photo illustrations; 80 pages.

—, completed by J. Trelawney (1974) *Lewis Clark's Field Guide to Wild Flowers of Marsh and Waterway.* Gray's, Sidney, BC. Good treatment of wetland forbs and shrubs; photographs, 64 pages.

Conard, H., and P. Redfearn, Jr. (1979) *How to Know the Mosses and Liverworts.* Wm. C. Brown, Dubuque, Iowa. Good introduction to North American mosses. Keyed, illustrated; 302 pages.

Cormack, R. (1977) *Wild Flowers of Alberta.* McClelland and Stewart, Toronto. Good descriptions of many eastern-slope wildflowers, with so-so photo illustrations; 415 pages.

Goward, T. (1974) *20 Plants of Interior Parks.* Free illustrated booklet available from British Columbia Parks and Outdoor Recreation, #308, 1011 Fourth Avenue, Prince George, BC V2L 3H9.

Hitchcock, C.; A. Cronquist and J. Janish (1976) *Flora of the Pacific Northwest.* University of Washington Press, Seattle. The five-volume botanist's authoritative compendium, totalling 2977 pages. Technical. There is also a one-volume version that covers all species, but with a reduced number of illustrations, which are quite small. 730 pages.

Johnson, D., et al. (1995) *Plants of the Western Boreal Forest & Aspen Parkland.* Lone Pine Publishers, Edmonton. Detailed guide to over 1000 species, including mosses and lichens. Color photos, drawings, index; 392 pages.

Kuijt, J. (1982) *A Flora of Waterton Lakes National Park.* University of Alberta Press, Edmonton. The best illustrated guide for both amateurs and professionals interested in Canadian Rockies botany, because Waterton has most of the species found in the region. But out of print; check the library. Illustrated; 684 pages.

Lyons, C., and B. Merilees (1995) *Trees, Shrubs & Flowers to Know in British Columbia & Washington.* Lone Pine Publishing, Edmonton. New edition of a very popular lay guide to over 600 species. Drawings, color photos, index; 375 pages.

Lauriault, J. (1989) *Identification Guide to the Trees of Canada.* Fitzhenry & Whiteside. Replaces Hosie's old *Native Trees of Canada* as the authoritative guide. Good black-and-white drawings, range maps, tree profiles, lists of rare trees; indexed, 479 pages.

Little, E. (1980) *The Audubon Field Guide to North American Trees, Western Region.* Alfred A. Knopf, New York. Comprehensive and pocketable. Photographic illustrations, range maps; 640 pages.

MacKinnon, A.; J. Pojar and R. Coupé, eds. (1992) *Plants of Northern British Columbia.* Lone Pine Publishing, Edmonton. Excellent, all-round field guide to the botany of the western slope of the Rockies (eastern slope, too, north of Willmore Wilderness Park), with detailed descriptions of 615 species from lichens—no other fungi—through bryophytes, ferns and horsetails, to trees. Good photos, keys, glossary, index—wow! 352 pages.

Moss, E. and J. Packer (1983) *The Flora of Alberta.* University of Toronto Press, Toronto. The standard guide for Alberta. Very technical and not illustrated; range maps for most species; 687 pages.

Parks Canada (1982) *Wild Flowers of Waterton Lakes National Park.* Illustrated 32-page booklet with brief descriptions of 104 species, available from Waterton Lakes Natural History Association, Box 145, Waterton Park, AB T0K 2M0.

Porsild, A. and D. Lid (1974) *Rocky Mountain Wildflowers.* National Museum/Parks Canada. Excellent illustrations of 325 eastern-slope plants, but the choice of species seems arbitrary and the text is skimpy; 454 pages.

Scotter, G. and H. Flygare (1986) *Wildflowers of the Canadian Rockies.* McClelland and Stewart, Toronto. My first choice for the common Rockies wildflowers and flowering shrubs, covering 228 species on both eastern and western slopes. Index, glossary, excellent color-photo illustrations; 170 pages.

Shaw, R. and D. On (1979) *Plants of Waterton-Glacier National Parks and the Canadian Rockies.* Mountain Press Publishing Company, Missoula, MT, and Summerthought, Banff. Very good photos of 220 species, including both flowers and fruits of species that make berries. Non-technical text; 160 pages.

Trelawney, J. (1983) *Wildflowers of the Yukon.* Gray's; Sidney, BC. Excellent guide to common northern species; covers 332 forbs and shrubs. Good text and unusually good photo illustrations; 214 pages.

Underhill, J. (1979) *Guide to Western Mushrooms.* Hancock House, Surrey, BC. Handy booklet on 45 common western-slope fungi. Photo illustrations; 32 pages.

— (1980) *Northwestern Wild Berries.* Hancock House, Surrey, BC and Blaine, WA. Short guide to western-slope shrubs, with information on edibility and suggested preparation. Photos; 96 pages.

Vitt, D.; J. Marsh and R. Bovey (1994) *Mosses, Lichens & Ferns of Northwest North America.* Lone Pine Publishing, Edmonton. The second edition of an excellent field guide to these often-overlooked but interesting groups. Full-color photos, range maps, glossary, index; 296 pages.

*Pixie-cup lichens. Photo by Barry Giles.*

# Lichens
## *A fungus took a likin' to some algae*

Lichens are not plants. They are members of the fungal kingdom, grouped with the cup fungi in the division Ascomycota. Like mushrooms, lichens do not contain cellulose; their cell walls are made mainly of **chitin,** the same substance that insects use for their exoskeletons. The difference between lichens and mushrooms is both subtle and profound: a mushroom extends its thread-like network to secure external sources of food, while a lichen gets its nourishment from algal and cyanobacterial cells held within itself.

These cells contain chlorophyll, so they photosynthesize sugars and other carbohydrates. In many lichens, tiny straw-like structures called **haustoria** penetrate the algal or cyanobacterial cell walls and remove some of this food—a form of internalized, carefully controlled parasitism. In most species the parasitized organism is a green alga of the genus *Trebouxia,* which seems unable to live without its fungal captor, so there is an element of mutualism in the relationship.

To reproduce, a lichen must maintain its algal/fungal association. Simple fragmentation works well for this; the bits of lichen clinging to your shoes after a walk in the woods contain both the fungal and algal/cyanobacterial components. A single fragment can start a new colony somewhere. See the item on lung lichen, page 407, for another method of reproduction used by lichens.

Many lichen species are antibiotic, perhaps to help them compete with surrounding fungi and bacteria, and they have been used medicinally. Lichens tend to concentrate pollutants such as sulphur dioxide and heavy metals. This hurts them, of course, and many species cannot grow in polluted places. As a rule, tree-lichens are the most sensitive—especially the hair lichens and beard lichens described in the next section.

Sometimes it can be difficult to tell a moss from a lichen, especially in the case of the stringy lichens that hang from trees. Many people mistakenly call these "Spanish moss." True Spanish moss is neither a moss nor a lichen; it is an epiphyte (rootless plant) of the genus *Tillandsia.* It grows from the southern U.S. to Peru, not here.

If the object in question is found any higher than about a metre up a live tree in the Canadian Rockies, it is always going to be a lichen. You might find a few mosses huddling around the base of the trunk, but they don't get more than a little way up.

What about mosses and lichens growing on rocks and on the ground? How do you tell *them* apart? Mosses have leaves, no matter how tiny, while lichens do not. Lichens consist of crust-like lobes, worm-like tubes, or other definitely un-mossy structures. Further, mosses are nearly always green, although *Grimmia,* page 398, can be quite dark, practically black, while lichens are usually other colors: gray, yellow, red, black, white—although there are a few lichen species that are quite green. And many fluoresce under ultraviolet light.

Here's something to consider as you hop from one lichen-covered boulder to the next: the age of the organisms you're walking on. Growing outward slowly and steadily, colonies of some lichen species in the Rockies can be several hundred years old.

Lichenologist Trevor Goward has used this discovery as a stepping stone to another one. People who study forests have always wondered how long an old-growth forest has existed in a particular place. Such forests may be much older than their individual trees, so coring the trees won't tell you how many years have passed since the forest became established. But looking at the lichens will, because lichens have their own form of ecological succession. Other things being equal, the more species of lichens an old-growth forest contains, the older it is. Goward is now in the process of working out a system for dating old-growth forest by looking at its lichen assemblages.

# Lichens on trees

Lichens that grow on wood are plentiful in Rockies forests, especially in subalpine stands. They hang in hair-like masses, encrust the bark and tuft the trunks and branches of both living and dead conifers. Do arboreal lichens kill or otherwise damage the trees they grow on? Apparently not; there are only a few lichen species known to penetrate their hosts to take nourishment from them.

*Usnea*                                    DV

*Usnea* ("UZ-knee-uh," **old-man's beard)** and *Alectoria* (**witch's hair**) species are commonly misidentified as Spanish moss. *Usnea* is pale grayish-green, hanging from twigs in coarse hair-like masses. It is never dark brown or black like *Bryoria*, next item. Gently pulling a strand of *Usnea* apart reveals a central cord that is just a little stronger than the sheath. *Alectoria sarmentosa*, the only *Alectoria* likely to be found in the Canadian Rockies, is yellowish green and lacks the elastic central cord.

*Bryoria*

*Bryoria* species, which used to be included in the genus *Alectoria*, are called **horsehair lichens.** They hang from trees rather like *Usnea* and *Alectoria*, but are much darker in color and thinner, like wisps of black horsehair hanging from dead twigs and branches. There is no central cord. The genus is especially common in subalpine forests, where the average height above ground of the lowest hair lichens shows the maximum winter snow depth in an average year.

*Hypogymnia*                               DV

*Hypogymnia physodes* and *Parmelia sulcata* are scaly, covering the surfaces of twigs with gray-green lobes. In color and form they closely resemble each other, but pulling apart a lobe of *Hypogymnia* shows that it is hollow, while *Parmelia* is solid.

*Parmeliopsis ambigua* resembles *Parmelia sulcata*, previous item, but is smoother, with smaller lobes that are more tightly attached. It grows mainly on the lower trunks of trees rather than on branches and twigs, never much higher than the portion covered by snow each year.

*Parmeliopsis*                             DV

*Vulpicida pinastri* is another twig-encrusting lichen. The thallus is yellowish green with yellow edges.

**Wolf lichen** *(Letharia vulpina)* is brilliantly greenish yellow. It grows in showy tufts on dry wood that has lost its bark, most plentifully in the high-subalpine woods. Contains the toxin vulpinic acid, once used in Europe for poisoning wolves.

**Frogskin lichen** *(Lobaria pulmonaria,* also known as **lung lichen),** is instantly recognizable: large and papery, loosely swaddling the lower limbs of trees in Columbian forest. The upper surface is pale gray-green, bright green on a rainy day or within a minute of wetting, and coarsely ridged. The back side is quilt-like, with white lumps against light-brown channels. White **soredia** and **isidia,** which are powdery clumps of algae and fungal threads that break off and spread the lichen, cluster along the edges.

    This weird organism looks vaguely evil, like something out of the science-fiction film *Aliens.* But it does good work in the woods: the cyanobacteria in the lichen acquire nitrogen from the air, store it in the form of ammonia and other nitrogen-bearing compounds, then make that nitrogen available to green plants as the lichen decays on the ground. Lichens containing cyanobacteria are important sources of soil nitrogen in old-growth forests.

## Lichens on the ground

The farther north you go along the Rockies chain, the more lichens you will find on the ground, especially above treeline. There is some sort of lichen divide at the latitude of the Columbia Icefield; north of there the ground-growing lichens are markedly more common—and so are the caribou that feed on them.

*Cladonia* species are the commonest forest-floor lichens in the Canadian Rockies. The many species are mostly greenish gray, sometimes pale tan, and always erect. Most produce **podetia:** hollow structures up to 10 cm tall in the form of worm-like rods, irregular branching rods that end in knobs, or cupped structures that look like little gray golf tees.

*Vulpicida*

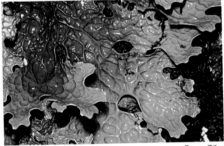

*Letharia*

*Lobaria*

*Cladonia*

If the podetia are rather irregular and tipped with bits of brilliant red color, the species is probably *C. borealis,* a common one here. Worm-like ones are often *C. cornuta.* The very golf-tee-like ones are likely to be *C. chlorophaea, C. gracilis* or *C. pyxidata,* all going by the common name **pixie cups.**

*Thamnolia vermicularis,* **rock worm,** is a tundra lichen. It produces worm-like rods that are bone white. Each rod is a separate organism; it is not attached to anything and simply lies on the ground, or sometimes on rock surfaces, reproducing vegetatively, without spores. One wonders how it got started in the first place.

Thamnolia

Yellow rods 2–3 cm tall in tundra are *Dactylina arctica,* **baby-fingers.** They look rather like coral fungi, page 426.

*Cladina* species are the **reindeer lichens,** consumed by caribou and known to model-railroad buffs as the miniature shrubs they use in their layouts. The hobby-shop variety, usually *C. stellaris,* has been dyed; the natural color is a pale yellowish gray. Sponge-like and rounded, 5–10 cm across, the species prefers alpine tundra. The other common species are more irregular. In this latter group we have gray-green ones *(C. rangiferina)* and yellow-green ones *(C. mitis* and *C. arbuscula.)*

Dactylina    *DV*

*Stereocaulon* species, called **coral lichens** or **froth lichens,** are steel-gray masses up to 8 cm tall, tightly convoluted and reminiscent of sea corals.

*Peltigera* species are common on the forest floor, often growing with feather mosses. Two species are easily identified:

*P. canina,* the **dog-ear lichen,** is flat and spreading, wrinkly at the edges, growing to 20 cm across. The color is dull olive-drab on top, from the cyanobacterial component—this lichen is an important nitrogen-fixer—and it is white or tan underneath, with rootlike threads called **rhizines** that anchor the lichen to the soil. Tiny dark-brown **apothecia** (spore-spreaders) stick up from the surface and resemble dog's ears.

Cladina    *DV*

*P. aphthosa* is similar but green—brilliantly green when wet—because of the green alga it contains. But there are dark, warty dots called **cephalodia** scattered on the surface

Stereocaulon    *DV*

that are colonies of the cyanobacterium *Nostoc.* *Nostoc* turns up in many other places, including on the ground. See page 430.

*Vulpicida tilesii* is the most common yellow tundra lichen. It resembles peeling paint, and it prefers calcareous soil. *Cetraria nivalis* is a cream-colored peeling-paint lichen, as is *C. cucullata,* which has greater in-turning at the edges.

*Solorina crocea* is a small but distinctive alpine ground lichen that prefers acidic (non-limy) soil and commonly grows along trails used by horses. It is flat, like *Peltigera,* but smaller: only 4–6 cm across. The top surface is nondescript pale greenish brown, but check the edges: they are usually turned up, showing the brilliantly orange lower surface.

*Icmadophila ericetorum* is also easy to recognize. It looks like patches of powdered sugar with pinhead-sized, salmon-colored apothecia.

In the 1980s a bryology student at the University of Alberta gave *Icmadophila* the perfect common name: **fairy upchuck.** Look for it on the cut banks of trails in moist forest, where it is often found overgrowing mosses.

## Lichens on rocks

These are mostly **crust lichens,** a large group whose members are notoriously hard to identify. Most are gray or black, in various shades, and they require laboratory work with microscope and chemicals to differentiate to even the genus level. Thus, we have Little Gray Lichens to go with our Little Green Mosses, Little Brown Mushrooms and Little Gray Birds.

Some rock-encrusting lichens actually live within the rock itself. They etch the rock surface with acids and send their tissues down into the upper few millimetres.

*Rhizocarpon* species, the **map lichens,** are easily identified. They are yellowish green with black mottling. Crust lichens, they grow only on non-calcareous substrates such as quartzite, which they colonize extensively in the main ranges.

*R. geographicum,* a common map lichen, lives a very long time: up to 9600 years in the

Peltigera                                                          DV

Cetraria                                                          DV

Icmadophila

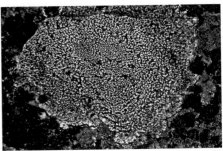

Rhizocarpon                                                     DV

Arctic. In the central Rockies it grows about 0.42 mm/yr for the first 110 years, 0.114 mm for the next 140 years and perhaps even more slowly from then on. By measuring the diameter of map lichens on the boulders of glacial moraines, geologists have established the history of glacial advances and retreats over the last few hundred years in quartzite-rich parts of Jasper and Banff parks. The Path of the Glacier interpretive trail at Mt. Edith Cavell develops this topic.

Even more map-like are the intergrown colonies of crust lichens one commonly finds on quartzitic streambank cobbles and boulders. The many species—too numerous and too taxonomically difficult to be covered here— look much like varicolored maps, complete with black dividing lines between colonies. Some common genera in the Canadian Rockies are *Bacidia, Buellia, Lecanora* and *Lecidea.*

*Crust lichens on quartzite*

*Xanthoria* is the only common orange lichen of its size in the Canadian Rockies, reaching 5 cm across and often intergrowing to form wider colonies. *Caloplaca* lichens are also orange, but the colonies are usually much smaller.

*Xanthoria* looks to be a crust lichen, but close inspection shows that it is a **leaf lichen:** lobes are lumpy, fairly thick and rather easily removed from the rock. There are a half-dozen species in the Canadian Rockies, colonizing limestone, sandstone and shale from the lowest elevations to the highest rocky summits; the most common is *X. elegans.*

*Xanthoria* gets its nitrogen by growing where small animals and birds regularly excrete. That is why one so often sees orange lichens on high points where hawks and eagles perch, on cliff walls below ledges where ravens have nested, or anywhere that wood rats or chipmunks scurry about the rock. My kids call *Xanthoria* the "poop lichen."

*Xanthoria*                                    DV

*Umbilicaria* is a leaf lichen that should be familiar to anyone who has crossed a quartzite boulderfield in the rain. These dark-brown lichens swell when wet, becoming gelatinous and amazingly slippery underfoot. Each plant is anchored at only one point, so not only is it slippery, it breaks loose when you step on it.

*Umbilicaria*                                  DV

## Further reading

Goward, T.; B. McCune and D. Meidinger (1994) *The Lichens of British Columbia: Illustrated Keys.* B.C. Ministry of Forests Special Report Series 8, Part 1, Foliose and Squamulose Species. Available from Crown Publications, 546 Yates St., Victoria, BC V8W 1K8. Technical reference, fully illustrated, indexed; 181 pages.

Hale, M. (1979) *How to Know the Lichens.* Wm. C. Brown, Dubuque, Iowa. The best book for amateurs on North American lichens, with textbook material at the front. Keyed, illustrated; 246 pages.

MacKinnon, A.; J. Pojar and R. Coupé, eds. (1992) *Plants of Northern British Columbia.* Lone Pine Publishing, Edmonton. Mainly botany, but also includes some 40 lichen species. Photos, drawings, keys, glossary, index; 352 pages.

Vitt, D.; J. Marsh and R. Bovey (1994) *Mosses, Lichens & Ferns of Northwest North America.* Lone Pine Publishing, Edmonton. The second edition of the best lichen field guide for our area, covering 154 species. Full-color photos, range maps, glossary, index; 296 pages.

Is this mushroom poisonous, or is it not? Only its mycologist knows for sure. Photo by Barry Giles.

# Mushrooms
## *From the eyelash cup to the earth star*

Mushrooms grow all over the Rockies, from the wooded valley floors to the barren heights. I have seen them popping up in patches of white dryas on the rocky summit of Yamnuska Mountain and growing on discarded food deep in Cadomin Cave. You'll see more fungi in spring and fall than in mid-summer.

Mushrooms, puffballs, shelf fungi and the like do better on the warmer, wetter, shadier western slope than they do on the cooler, drier, sunnier eastern slope. One sees more fungi and more fungal variety in Columbian-forest areas (see map on page 222) than anywhere else.

We are speaking here of organisms that are not plants. The fungi are in their own kingdom.*

Unlike plants, mushrooms lack chlorophyll and thus do not manufacture their own food. They must get it somewhere else. Where? From dead organic matter, from soil, from feces, from living things. From rotting logs, elk droppings, dead animals, live insects—but most often, surprisingly, from the roots of living plants. The notion that mushrooms are all saprophytes is quite wrong. The vast majority are **mycorrhizal.** Their **hyphae**—strands of cells thinner than a human hair—surround and penetrate the tiniest rootlets of green plants, taking nutrients (sugars and starches) from them.

In doing so, the fungi provide water directly to the roots, and at the same time release enzymes into the soil that break down phosphorus-bearing and nitrogen-bearing molecules, making these essential elements more easily available to the green plants. Further, mycorrhizal fungi confer some protection from bacterial disease: they seem to release antibiotics into the soil. And, speaking of the soil itself, mycorrhizal fungi produce a polysaccharide cementing agent that helps to form granules, loosening the soil—non-granular soil packs hard—and allowing water and air to move through it more easily.

In the case of lichens, page 405, specific fungi and algae combine to prosper where neither organism could manage alone, and the same is doubtless true of many mushroom/green-plant associations.

While we are dealing with misconceptions, it is important to say that toadstools and mushrooms are the same thing. But just as geologists don't have any use for the word "dirt," so botanists in Canada and the United States seldom use "toadstool." They use "mushroom."

Mushroom life takes place mostly out of sight. Inside a host organism such as a tree, or often underground, is the **mycelium:** a collection of soft, thready hyphae that spread through or around the food source. If you have seen mold, you have seen a mycelium. The net of hyphae grows a **carpophore**—the mushroom proper—which emerges into the air and sun. The carpophore is the reproductive equipment of the fungus. It produces spores that grow new mycelia.

Spore dispersal is so effective that many mushroom species are distributed worldwide. The same mushroom species you see at Bow Lake might turn up in the Alps, the Andes, the Himalayas—or in your yard, if the growing conditions are right.

---

*The kingdoms of life keep increasing in number. At time of writing we are up to at least five: plants, animals, fungi, one-celled life forms with nuclei in their cells (algae and protozoa) and one-celled life forms without nuclei, meaning mainly bacteria. The vanishingly small viruses and prions, which straddle the boundary between living things and the inorganic world, inject genetic material into other kinds of cells to reproduce, so some biologists place them in yet another kingdom, bringing the count to *six*.

## Edibility

Dare you *eat* the mushroom in your yard? Many mushrooms are tasty, but some are poisonous, even life-threatening. Others will make you crazy for a while. If the squirrels eat a particular species, is it safe for us? If the juice discolors silver, is it poisonous? Do the poisons disappear if the mushroom is cooked or dried?

Reject these folksy notions, for they are all false. The only safe way to eat mushrooms is to know exactly what you are eating—that is, *you've got to know exactly what species you have picked.* When in doubt, don't eat.

In line with the outlook of this book, I'm not encouraging mushroom-picking. Like everything else in the Rockies, it is better to leave the fungi alone. Although less sensitive to mass picking than wildflowers, some mushroom species—particularly the boletes—will disappear in heavily picked places.

## Intoxicating and poisonous mushrooms

We have *Amanita muscaria* here, which will make you sick as well as high, although this magic mushroom is reportedly much less potent in North America than it is in Europe and Asia. I seldom see the hallucinogenic *Psilocybe* species, which are at least easy on your body if not on your mind. They prefer the wet, mild climate of the west coast—especially Vancouver Island and the Queen Charlottes—over the drier, colder climate of the Rockies.

Neither do we have many really poisonous species. The deadly *Amanita virosa* can turn up here, though. *Amanita pantherina,* which is supposedly toxic enough to kill small children, is fairly common, as is false morel, another nasty one. Fungi in the Canadian Rockies known or thought to be poisonous are noted as such in the text.

## Identifying mushrooms

Making positive identifications of mushrooms is tricky. Mushrooms are fairly simple in structure; thus, there are few diagnostic features. Further, mushrooms can change considerably in appearance over a matter of a few days. The general pattern is this: the cap is rounded and brightly colored (if a colored species) when coming up, then it flattens, dries and becomes paler, finally blackening and shriveling.

A solid identification requires that you correctly determine:

• The texture, color and size of the cap surface. Shape is not as important in most species as these other factors, for mushroom caps tend to be rounded when new, flattening and turning upward at the edges later.

• The texture of the stalk, and whether rings are present.

• The gill type, arrangement and color.

• The color of the spores, as revealed in a **spore print.** To make a print, set the cap on a piece of white paper. You might set a part of the cap on black paper, to see the spores if they are white. Put a cup over the mushroom to keep the tiny spores from drifting away. After an hour or two, preferably overnight, lift the cap and look at the color of the spores left on the paper. In most species the color is unvarying and thus a reliable characteristic—although using a specimen that is too young or too old may give a spore print that is too light, or no spore print at all.

Many identifications can be made without spore prints, but until you get to know a particular species you shouldn't neglect this step, particularly if eating is the goal. Making a print need not mean picking the mushroom. If you remove only part of the cap, leaving most of it and the stem intact, the mycelium will not be overly damaged and the mushroom will be back next year.

## Ordinary capped mushrooms

Herewith the common, normal, mushroom-like mushrooms of the Canadian Rockies.

### King bolete
*Boletus edulis*
August to October, choice edible

Very common in montane spruce/pine/aspen woods, found in soil and usually singly. A large mushroom, the cap buff to reddish-brown and often resembling a nicely browned bun. Smooth in dry weather, sticky in wet. Can be large: up to 30 cm across, usually 10–20 cm. Under the cap, but easily visible from the side, is a sponge-like mass of white to greenish-yellow pores instead of gills. The stalk is usually white, although sometimes brown, with a net-like texture. It thickens downward. King bolete goes buggy very quickly. Spore print: olive brown.

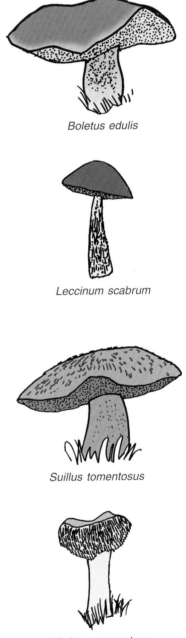

*Boletus edulis*

### Rough-stemmed bolete
*Leccinum scabrum*
July to August, edible

Look for this bolete around birch trees, sometimes near dwarf birch in high subalpine and alpine situations. It's a northern species on the western slope but fairly common all along the eastern slope. Looks like the other boletes described, but with a rougher stem marked by lines of raised black dots. The cap is large (up to 20 cm), grayish-brown to yellowish-brown and tends to be flatter than that of the other boletes. Spore print: brown.

*Leccinum scabrum*

### Woolly pine bolete/suillus
*Suillus tomentosus*
August to November, edible

In lodgepole pine forest. Bolete-like mushroom, 5–10 cm across, differentiated by its scaly, rather slimy cap—especially slimy in wet weather—with brown flecks on a yellow background, a yellow stem with brown dots and a barely noticeable ring. Edible, although not particularly tasty. Spore print: dark olive drab.

*Suillus tomentosus*

### Hedgehog mushroom
*Hydnum repandum*
July to November; often quite late, edible

Tends to grow in groups or fairy rings under conifers in mixed-wood forests. Small to medium-sized mushroom, easy to recognize by looking under the cap: instead of gills or spongy pores, it has soft fragile white spines.

*Hydnum repandum*

The cap is creamy white and 5–15 cm across, usually with a depressed centre and a fold on one side. Stem always white and usually thickening upward. The hedgehog mushroom resists bugs and thus lasts a long time. New ones are good eating. Spore print: white.

### Scaly tooth/shingle-top

*Sarcodon imbricatus*
August to October, edible

Common in montane forests, usually in groups. A larger version of the hedgehog mushroom, up to 25 cm across the cap. Easily recognizable by the very rough cap surface, which is tiled with large brown scales. White spines underneath go gray to brown with age; the stem is pale brown and fairly smooth. Long-lasting like its relatives, the cap of scaly tooth gradually turns upward, becoming almost funnel-shaped as the days pass. Tasty when new; older ones become tough and acrid. Spore print: reddish-brown. Also known as *Hydnum imbricatum.*

*Sarcodon imbricatus*

### Shaggy mane

*Coprinus comatus*
August to September, choice edible

In dense groups on disturbed ground, common in grassy places or pushing out of hard-packed earth—even paved road shoulders. Yet the plant is very delicate. Easily identified by the bullet-shaped, scaly white cap that gets speckled with black as the gills underneath deteriorate. Eventually, only the stalk is left. Shaggy mane tastes rather like asparagus. But eat it soon; like inky cap, page 421, it soon liquefies. Unlike inky cap, shaggy mane won't make you ill if you have an alcoholic drink after eating it. Spore print: black.

*Coprinus comatus*

### Shaggy parasol

*Macrolepiota rhacodes*
September to October, CAUTION

On disturbed ground, compost heaps, along roads, single or in groups and fairy rings. Covered with large cinnamon-to-pink scales, the white cap shows more and more as the mushroom flattens. There is always one big scale at the centre. Stem smooth and white with a ring near the top. Gills are white at first; darken later. A choice edible mushroom and not likely to be confused with any other in the mountains, *except* poisonous **green-spored lepiota** *(Chlorophyllum molybdites),* which

*Macrolepiota rhacodes*

looks similar—the scales are lighter-colored—and gives a green spore print. Spore print of shaggy parasol is white.

### Russet-scaly trich
*Tricholoma vaccinum*
July to November, not palatable

Usually under pine or spruce. Scaly reddish-brown mushroom with lighter gills and a rough stem. Cap is 2–8 cm across, conical at first, flattening somewhat later; has cob-webby veil bits stuck to the edge. Spore print: white.

*Tricholoma vaccinum*

### Fly agaric
*Amanita muscaria*
June to August, **POISONOUS,** mind-altering

Fly agaric is fairly common in montane woods, under conifers or birches—and on your lawn if you have these trees. This is a very beautiful gilled mushroom up to 30 cm across, frequently bright red but sometimes pink, orange or yellow. Bits of the white veil that covers the mushroom as it emerges adhere to the cap, although rain can wash them off. The cap is rounded at first, flattening out later as it grows larger. The stem is always white, with a skirt-like ring near the top and cup at the base.

Fly agaric is famous as a dope mushroom, especially in Siberia, although the drug content is extremely variable and differs between North American and Asian specimens. The effects of our version are not pleasant: dizziness, uncoordination, muscle cramps and delusions, although without hallucinations. Intense activity, often violent, is followed by deep sleep. Three alkaloid drugs: ibotenic acid, which goes to muscimol and muscazone, all apparently used by the fungus as insecticides. Milk in which a cap is sitting will kill flies attracted to it. Spore print: white.

**Panther agaric** *(A. pantherina,* April to September) is similar in form and habitat to fly agaric, but pale brown or greenish rather than red or yellow. Same adhering bits of veil on the cap and rings on the stem. Similar woodsy locations. Similar sort of poisoning, too, but worse; is reputed to have killed children. Spore print: white.

*Amanita muscaria*

### Giant leucopax
*Leucopaxillus giganteus*
August to October, edible

Favors disturbed ground and open woods, singly or in groups and fairy rings. A big mushroom, 10–45 cm across, with a smooth

*Leucopaxillus giganteus*

white cap that tends to lift at the edges, exposing white gills that run a little way down the short, smooth, white, ringless stem. Edible but sometimes foul-smelling and bad-tasting. Spore print: white. Formerly called *Clitocybe gigantea,* the giant clitocybe.

### Silvery-violet cort/silvery cortinarius
*Cortinarius alboviolaceus*
August to October, edible

In mixed woods, solitary or a few at a time. There are many *Cortinarius* mushrooms, most of them hard to differentiate, but this one stands out: it is shiny-gray with a violet cast. Cap is 3–6 cm wide, bell-shaped at first and flatter later, silky-textured with the edge turned under. The stem is thick and smooth or a bit gnarly, with that silvery-violet tinge. Gills are pale violet at first, becoming rusty brown later. Confirm the rusty spore print before eating.

*Cortinarius alboviolaceus*

### Tacky green russula
*Russula aeruginea*
July to September, edible if cooked

Common under aspen and lodgepole pine in montane woods. Slightly sticky, faintly radially lined cap 5–8.5 cm across, greenish at least near the centre, which becomes depressed. Gills and stalk yellowish white. No rings on stalk. Not recommended for eating raw. Spore print: pale yellow.

*Russula aeruginea*

### Emetic russula/the sickener
*Russula emetica*
August to September, **POISONOUS**

Boggy places in montane and subalpine woods, often among mosses in small groups. Slimy, sticky, bright-red cap 2.5–7.5 cm across, flat or concave; yellowish-white gills and stem. The cap color fades in time, as if washing away. Stem is dry and without rings. This mushroom tastes hot and makes you throw up. Spore print: white.

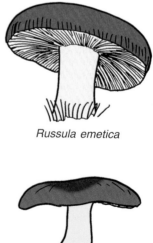

*Russula emetica*

### Shellfish russula/woodland russula
*Russula xerampelina*
August to September, not tasty

Fairly common in Columbian forest, but found everywhere under spruce, Douglas-fir and hemlock. Cap purplish-red to brown, 2.5–15 cm across, smooth in dry weather, slimy in wet; radial lines along the edge. Stem white to pink and unringed, gills pale yellow. Smells fishy. Spore print: pale yellow.

*Russula xerampelina*

## Meadow mushroom
*Agaricus campestris*
August to September, choice edible

In grassy meadows, where it can be quite abundant. Medium-sized mushroom 3–10 cm across, convex cap white to gray-brown, dry; fat stalk same color; one ring at the top. Gills pink at first, then darkening to brown. A close relative of the common commercial mushroom, but with more flavor.

Be careful, though, that you are not gathering a deadly *Amanita virosa* by mistake. All the poisonous amanitas have a skirt-like ring on the stem and a cup or bulb at the base; *Agaricus* species have the ring but lack the cup or bulb. Spore print is dark brown. See also poison pie, this page.

*Agaricus campestris*

## Bleeding agaricus
*Agaricus haemorrhoidarius*
July to October, CAUTION

In moist mixed-wood forest, single or a few at a time. Cap is 5–15 cm across, brown-flecked and scaly; white or pinkish stem has one ring on the upper part. Gills are white at first, becoming pinkish and then purplish-brown. Main feature: flesh instantly turns bright red when injured. Edible for most people; upsetting for some. Spore print: dark brown.

*Agaricus haemorrhoidarius*

## The prince
*Agaricus augustus*
July to September, choice edible

Prefers to grow singly in disturbed ground; often found along montane roads and paths. A big mushroom: cap up to 35 cm across, unfolding flat, with down-curved edges, yellowish with circular rows of brown scales. Flesh bruises yellow. Whitish gills turn pink, then brown. Stem is thick and short, scaly and white, with a ring at the top. This mushroom gives off an odor of anise and almond; it is renowned for taste and meatiness. Spore print: dark brown.

*Agaricus augustus*

## Poison pie
*Hebeloma crustuliniforme*
September to November, **POISONOUS**

In mixed-wood forests, often in fairy rings on disturbed ground. Fairly small cap (3–9 cm), buff at centre and paler at edges, usually convex, but sometimes flat or with uplifted edges. Stem white, flaky near the top, no ring.

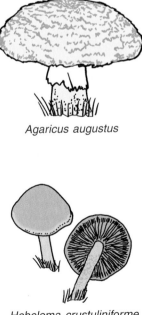
*Hebeloma crustuliniforme*

Odor of radishes. Most common of the *Hebeloma* species in the Canadian Rockies; there are others, but difficult to differentiate. All have that sharp, radishy odor. Spore print: brown to rust.

## Blewit
*Lepista nuda*
August to November, CAUTION

In deep woods, common in Columbian forest, found everywhere and usually in small groups or alone. Also called *Clitocybe nuda.* Cap convex to flat, with in-rolled or at least down-turned margins, 10–15 cm across, uniformly gray-brown with a purplish cast and dry, silky feel. Rough violet stem, often thick, no ring. Gills notched where they meet the stem. Tasty but not recommended by mycologists because some similar *Clitocybe* species are poisonous. Spore print: peach.

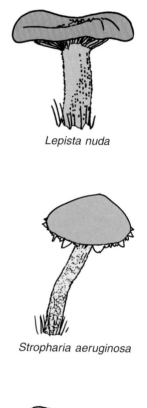
*Lepista nuda*

## Bluegreen stropharia
*Stropharia aeruginosa*
September to October, CAUTION

Occasional in Columbian forest, standing singly. Small mushroom, easily identified by the cap: less than 7 cm across, greenish/bluish and slimy, with bits of white veil adhering to the edge. Top gets yellowish with age. Stalk is long and thin, quite rough, also blue-green, with a ring near the top. Gills are gray at first, purplish later. Not tasty, and one of its relatives, *S. coronilla,* is poisonous. Spore print of bluegreen stropharia: purplish-brown.

*Stropharia aeruginosa*

## Honey mushroom
*Armillariella mellea*
August to November, CAUTION

In clusters on living or dead trees; often very common. Tends to kill its host. Quite variable in appearance because of variable stalk thickness. Cap usually light brown, convex with in-rolled white edge, 2–10 cm across and sticky with erect dark hairs at the centre, becoming scaly toward the edge. Gills white, stem same color as cap toward base but white and often thickening abruptly at the top, where there is a ring.

The honey mushroom produces black **rhizomorphs** (runners) from its base; these may be up to 100 m long.

Boil this mushroom first or risk upset. Further, there are some nasty look-alikes around, so be sure of identification. Spore print of *A. mellea* is white.

*Armillariella mellea*

## Fawn mushroom/deer mushroom

*Pluteus cervinus*
May to October, edible

Common on and over rotting wood, in mixed-wood forest, present all summer and well into fall, especially after rain. Cap is 3–12 cm across, smooth or a bit rough and brown to light gray. Stem smooth and white. Gills creamy, pale yellow or pink. Radishy odor; tasty when freshly emerged. Spore print: salmon-pink.

*Pluteus cervinus*

## Anise-scented clitocybe

*Clitocybe odora*
July to September, edible

Montane and subalpine woods, more common on the eastern slope. Medium-sized (2–10 cm) rough gray-green cap, aging paler with a dark bump in the centre. Gills white to greenish, no ring on the stalk. Strong odor of anise (licorice). Spore print: pale pink to white.

*Clitocybe odora*

## Slimy-sheathed waxy cap

*Hygrophorus oliveaceoalbus*
September to October, CAUTION

Near Engelmann spruce, subalpine zone. An unappealing mushroom: slimy gray cap 3–12 cm across, white gills underneath, and a slimy white stalk with scabs of dark gray ick on it. Bland and slimy, yet some people eat it. Spore print: white.

*Hygrophorus oliveaceoalbus*

## Inky cap/alcohol inky

*Coprinus atramentarius*
May to September, CAUTION

In clusters near buried wood. A common and easily recognized mushroom: droopy, vertically lined gray cap 5–6 cm wide; slender pure-white stem with one ring at the base. Nipple-like touch of brown atop the cap; often pale brown or darker gray at the pleated cap margin. The gills of inky caps self-destroy in a few days by turning into a black liquid.

If you want to eat this mushroom, do so before it starts to liquefy and don't drink alcohol *for several days* before or after. Inky caps take away the body's ability to break down any alcohol in the bloodstream; if you mix booze and inky caps you will probably have flushing of the face and neck, tingling in the extremities and an instant hangover—rather like the effects of drinking after taking the alcoholic-treatment drug Antabuse (disulfiram). Symptoms last a few hours. Spore print: black.

*Coprinus atramentarius*

## Fuzzy foot

*Xeromphalina campanella*
May to November, not tasty

In clusters on well-decayed wood, most common on hemlock in Columbian-forest areas but found everywhere. Small orange mushroom only one or two centimetres across but easily identified by the hairy tuft at the base. Cap has radiating lines, is smooth and usually moist; stem yellowish at the top and unringed; gills cross-veined. Spore print: pale buff.

*Xeromphalina campanella*

## Buttery collybia

*Collybia butyracea*
July to September, not tasty

Under conifers. The cap feels greasy and looks buttery; this is one of the few mushrooms that is lighter in the centre and darker toward the edges. Looks like butter melted over the top of it, and even smells rancid. Cap 1–5 cm across; stem is gray to yellowish, narrowing upward, ringless. Spore print: white.

*Collybia butyracea*

## Dung-loving psilocybe

*Psilocybe coprophila*
June to October, hallucinogenic

On dung, especially that of domestic cattle. Sticky brown cap 1–3 cm across, with a yellowish stalk; very umbrella-like mushroom. A widespread psilocybe and not strongly psychoactive, but in quantity it will turn your mind into something like its substrate. Spore print: brownish-purple.

*Psilocybe coprophila*

## Fairy-ring mushroom

*Marasmius oreades*
May to September, CAUTION

In lawns or other grassy places, many at a time in the shape of a ring. This is an anonymous-looking small mushroom, cap 1–4 cm across and cream to pale brown with most color near the centre, where there is usually a knob. Long, thin, rubbery stems; creamy gills.

Like other fairy-ring species, this one sends up mushrooms from the edge of a mycelium that grows steadily outward from the original growing site. Fairy rings can be quite old: up to 500 years. Eating *Marasmius* won't do you any harm, but there are several poisonous ones (notably *M. cystidosius*, *Clitocybe dealbata*, and *Inocybe umbratica*) that can do a nasty number. If you have little kids, keep their play spots clear of fairy rings. Spore print of *M. oreades*: white or buff.

*Marasmius oreades*

## Little brown mushrooms (LBMs)

Speaking of fairy rings: if you're interested in them, you will have many species of small mushrooms to learn. Every biological branch has its plain little something-or-others; these are the mushroom versions. Some of them, such as the common lawn-growing *Galerina* species, are deadly, and there are other poisonous ones. Unless you are a real or aspiring mycologist, you may, like me, be happy to label the whole crowd LBMs and let them go at that. And not eat them.

## Chanterelles and chanterelle look-alikes

If the cap is irregular and strongly turned up at the edges, so that the gill-like underfolds are easily visible, check this group.

### Golden chanterelle
*Cantharellus cibarius*
September to October, choice edible

   Montane, fairly common in Douglas-fir woods and brushy areas, in soil. Egg-yolk yellow to pale orange, medium-sized mushroom (10–15 cm across); vase-shaped, with a crinkly-edged cap and prominent coarse gill-like folds that are cross-veined between the ribs. Often smells like apricot. The flesh is white and solid. This is a spicy, peppery mushroom; very popular in Europe—in Germany they call it the "Pfefferling," pepper mushroom. Spore print: pale yellow or buff.

   Be careful not to confuse these with the possibly poisonous **false chanterelle** *(Clitocybe aurantiaca)*, which is smaller, gives a white spore print and has true gills instead of folds.

*Cantharellus cibarius*

### Orange-latex milky/delicious lactarius
*Lactarius deliciosus*
October to November, CAUTION

   Singly in pine and Douglas-fir forests, where it may be abundant. Another chanterelle-like mushroom, this one with smooth margins and zones of lighter/darker orange color around the cap. As it gets older, it becomes green-stained. The *Lactarius* group ooze a milky fluid when cut; in this species it is orange. Eat with caution, for some of the group members are poisonous. Spore print: cream.

*Lactarius deliciosus*

### Apricot jelly
*Phlogiotis hellevoides*
May to July; August to October, edible

   Under conifers, sometimes on rotting trees. Translucent funnels 1–7 cm across and up to 10 cm tall; reddish-orange to pink. This species resembles a chantarelle, but there are no gill-like folds. Edible, but with rubbery texture and little taste. Spores are white.

*Phlogiotis hellevoides*

# True and false morels

In these species the spores are carried on top of the cap rather than underneath, an arrangement that produces weird-looking and thus readily identifiable mushrooms. An easily recognized group and common on the western slope, the morels are tricky to identify to the species level. But all are edible and some are choice. Just be careful that you haven't got a false morel, for they can be quite poisonous.

### Yellow morel/sponge mushroom
*Morchella esculenta*
April to June, choice edible

The yellow morel is perhaps the most common morel, coming up a few days behind the last spring snows in aspen/birch woods and bushy places. Note the strange cap: deeply pitted, with raised ridges between the pits. Cap is pale yellow to medium brown, 4–5 cm across. The white stem attaches at the base of the cap, and the whole thing is hollow—which means you have to slice it open and check well for bugs before cooking. Very tasty; dries well. Spores are white.

*Morchella esculenta*

### Black morel/narrow-capped morel
*Morchella elata/angusticeps*
April to May, CAUTION

This species prefers mixed woods and can be plentiful in areas that have recently burned. Similar to yellow morel above, but more pointed and with a darker cap. The stem is often deeply grooved or even divided. This is perhaps the tastiest of the morels, but may be upsetting if eaten with alcoholic beverages. Spores are white.

*Morchella elata/angusticeps*

### Conifer false morel
*Gyromitra esculenta*
April to June, **POISONOUS**

Here is a potentially lethal mushroom that looks rather like the prized morels: lumpy brown cap with a white stem. Further, this species of false morel appears at the same time of year as the true morels, although it prefers to grow under conifers rather than broadleaf trees. Differentiate by the cap: wrinkly in false morel (3–10 cm across) rather than pitted as in true morel.

False morel poisonings are caused by monomethylhydrazine (MMH); symptoms are severe gastrointestinal upset followed by muscle cramps and uncoordination. In the worst cases there is fainting, convulsions, coma and death. Spores are white. See also saddle-shaped false morel, next item.

*Gyromitra esculenta*

### Saddle-shaped false morel/ hooded gyromitra
*Gyromitra infula*
August to October, CAUTION
   Singly or a few at a time on disturbed ground. This false morel has a distorted-looking pale-brown cap 10–15 cm across. The stem is pale and often inward-folded. Some people eat the saddle-shaped false morel with no ill effects; others experience upsets. The problem is in differentiating from the poisonous conifer false morel (previous item). Spores of *G. infula* are pale yellow.

*Gyromitra infula*

### Fluted white helvella
*Helvella crispa*
September to October, CAUTION
   Montane woods. Rather similar to saddle-shaped false morel (previous item), but white, with a ribbed, holey stem. Cap 1.5–6 cm across. Fairly tasty, although some people tolerate it poorly. Always cook it first. Spores of *H. crispa* are white.

*Helvella crispa*

## Club-like fungi

These look like mushrooms that have lost their caps. That is not the case; in the club fungi there is no cap. The spores are on the exterior surface, although usually colorless and thus not very obvious.

### Strap-shaped pestle/strap fungus
*Clavariadelphus sachalinensis*
August to October, unpalatable
   Common eastern-slope mushroom of montane woods. Swollen-ended rods, with ends that are somewhat wrinkly and club-shaped, flattened or depressed. Orange, ochre or yellowish, 2–8 cm tall. Bitter taste. Spores are buff-colored.

*Clavariadelphus sachalinensis*

### Pestle-shaped coral
*Clavariadelphus pistillaris*
July to October, unpalatable
   In lodgepole woods, in groups. Yellow to salmon-pink clubs, sometimes branching, 5–20 cm tall with swollen ends. Pale and hairy near the base of the stalk. Bitter taste. Spores white.
   **Cudonia** (*Cudonia circinans,* July to September) looks rather like pestle-shaped coral, but it's browner and smaller, with more expansion at the top; looks a bit like it's wearing a shower cap. Spores white.

*Clavariadelphus pistillaris*

**Dead-man's fingers**
*Xylaria polymorpha*
June to October, edibility unknown
   On rotting wood. Dark-gray fingery clubs
2–8 cm long, whiter in early stages. Spores are
very dark.

*Xylaria polymorpha*

## *Coral fungi*

Usually on the ground but sometimes on wood, there are many coral-fungi species, mostly of the genus *Ramaria* or *Clavaria,* which all look rather alike. Colors range from yellow-tipped orange to bright red and run evenly along the branches.

   The coral-like lichens *Cladonia, Thamnolia,* and *Dactylina,* page 408, resemble the coral fungi, but the fungi last only a few weeks and disappear, while the lichens remain for many years.

   The **cauliflower fungus** *(Sparassis crispa)* looks leafy. It is huge—sometimes half a metre across—and yellowish/whitish, going brown as it ages. Watch for it in Columbian-forest areas in September and October.

   In wet weather you may see the **bright orange, tongue-like fruiting bodies** of *Gymnosporangium* sp. on junipers (illustration on page 285). This fungal rust has a two-host life cycle: it alternately infects junipers and members of the rose family. I have seen the fruiting bodies on both common juniper and creeping juniper.

*Ramaria*

*Clavaria*

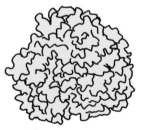

*Sparassis crispa*

# Shelf fungi

When one thinks of a mushroom one thinks of a round-capped thing with a central stem. But if the stem is off to one side of the cap, then you have the basic structure of many shelf fungi. Eliminate the stem entirely and you have the rest. Most shelf fungi, also called **bracket fungi,** grow on wood and are members of the polypore family; they have pores on their under surfaces rather than gills. Shelf fungi are hardier than most other fungi, maintaining their carpophores longer than mushrooms do, even through the winter in some cases.

A shelf fungus requires something to make a shelf on. This is usually rotting wood—often a stump—but can also be live wood. Polypores tend to spread through a stump or a log in ever-expanding tiers; the mycelium within can cause a lot of damage in live trees. Like insect infestations, shelf fungi are natural eliminators of old, weak trees.

Although some shelf fungi are edible, and even choice, I leave them where they be. They are lovely to look at; many take a long time to grow and their mycelia are badly harmed when the carpophores are ripped off their moorings.

Included with this bunch is the smoky polypore, page 428, an encrusting fungus that resembles a lichen.

## Oyster mushroom
*Pleurotus ostreatus*
April to May; September, edible

Damp places, on decaying broadleaf trees. Colonies of very pale, wavy-edged delicate mushrooms 5–20 cm wide with short off-centre stems—or none at all. Is it a mushroom or is it a shelf fungus? Only its mycologist knows for sure. Spore print: white to violet-gray.

The oyster mushroom has a taste for the nematodes (microscopic worms) that live in dead wood. A toxin released by the mushroom paralyzes any nematode venturing into the mycelium. Hyphae then grow down the worm's throat and digest it from inside out—while it is still alive.

*Pleurotus ostreatus*

## Angel wings
*Pleurocybella porrigens*
September to October, edible

In colonies on rotting conifers. Common in Columbian forest, on hemlock and red-cedar. Angel wings look rather like the oyster mushroom (previous item), but thinner and whiter. Spores are white.

*Pleurocybella porrigens*

## Birch bracket-fungus/birch polypore
*Piptoporus betulinus*
Year-round, unpalatable

On live or dead birch trees; in the Canadian Rockies on white birch. A fleshy, tough semicircular growth with concentric rings in varying shades of tan and brown, pale underneath, where there are pores instead of gills. Spores are white.

*Piptoporus betulinus*

## White spongy polypore
*Spongiporus leucospongia*
August to November, unpalatable

On stumps of subalpine-zone conifers. Rough brown top 3–10 cm across and rather irregular, with distinctive white, cottony underside. Spores are colorless.

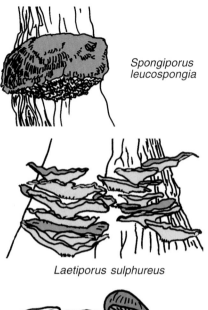

*Spongiporus leucospongia*

## Chicken mushroom/sulphur shelf
*Laetiporus sulphureus*
May to November, CAUTION

In closely spaced tiers on stumps and logs; sometimes on living trees. Smooth-surfaced wavy-edged reddish-orange tops 5–30 cm across, often turned up at the edge and displaying brilliant yellow tubes underneath. Tastes like chicken, but eat it when it is young or risk swollen lips, a common allergic reaction. Spore print: white.

*Laetiporus sulphureus*

## Jelly crep
*Crepidotus mollis*
June to October, unpalatable

In tiers on rotting deciduous trees. Brown to reddish-brown hairy/scaly shelves 1–8 cm across with lighter margins; brown gills underneath. A stalkless mushroom, really. Spore print yellowish-brown.

## Violet toothed polypore
*Trichaptum biformis*
May to November, unpalatable

Common in damp forests, sometimes by the hundred in open tiers on dead deciduous material. Tough, semicircular, mostly detached shelves 1–7 cm wide, concentrically zoned in grays and browns, becoming more violet toward the edge. Creamy violet pores underneath that get tooth-like with age. Spores are white.

*Crepidotus mollis*

## Turkey tail
*Trametes versicolor*
May to December unpalatable

On dead wood or at injured spots on live trees. A very beautiful, fan-like fungus of closely spaced tiers 3–10 cm across, each member with concentric zones of warm browns and tans; contrasting white margin. White to yellow pores underneath. Spores are white.

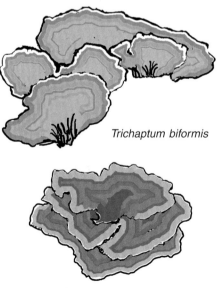

*Trichaptum biformis*

## Smoky polypore
*Bjerkandera adusta*
July to November, unpalatable

Usually parasitic on living trees, often in drier locations. This species is inclined to kill the host, so you may also find it on dead wood.

*Trametes versicolor*

A smoke-colored encrustation, sometimes shelf-like, paler gray around the edges. Actually it is a colony; on most specimens you can see concentric zones that show where the organisms, individually 1–7 cm across, have grown together. Spores are white.

If the encrustation is white, it may be **conifer parchment,** *Peniophora gigantea,* also known as *Phlebia gigantea.*

*Bjerkandera adusta*

## Cup fungi

Cup shaped, with the spores carried on the top of the plant rather than underneath. They scatter in wind and rain.

### Yellow donkey's ears
*Otidea onotica*
August to September, edibility unknown

Single or in small groups on soil in coniferous woods. Each cup is elongated and tilted upward, so that it resembles a donkey's ear. Smooth, 1–3 cm across, varying in color from deep yellow to pale orange. Spores are larger than those of most fungi; each contains two tiny droplets of oil.

*Otidea onotica*

### Eyelash cup
*Scutellinia scutellata*
June to November, edibility unknown

In dense colonies on and around rotting wood. Easily recognized: small red or orange cups 1–2 cm across with dark hairs around the edges that look just like eyelashes. Underneath, the cups are short-hairy. The spores are oily.

### Bird's-nest fungi
*Nidula, Cyathus,* and *Crucibulum* spp.
September to November, edibility unknown

On plant debris and on the ground, often in the dung of browsing (twig-eating) animals. Tiny cups a centimetre wide or less, with egg-like spore packets inside, waiting in gel to be tossed out when hit by a raindrop. The airborne packet trails an adhesive thread that catches in nearby vegetation, often wrapping onto a twig like a bolo. When an animal eats the vegetation the spores pass through, starting a new bird's-nest fungus in the droppings.

There are many species of bird's-nest fungi in the mountains. They are allied more closely with the puffballs, page 431, than with the cup fungi, but placed here because they look rather like cup fungi.

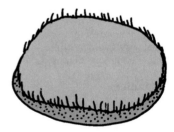

*Scutellinia scutellata*

*Cyathus*

### Tree-ear
*Auricularia auricula*
May to June, September to November, edible

In coniferous forest, a few at a time to many in colonies. Fairly large (3–15 cm across) and, as the name says, ear-like, translucent brown and rubbery with wart-like bumps. Spores are white.

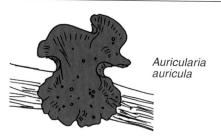

*Auricularia auricula*

## Slime molds, witch's butter and non-fungi that look like fungi

Here we have a collection of weird-looking organisms that most people react to by saying "yecch." But precisely because they are strange, they are also interesting. Most of them are simple fungi without gills or stems.

### Slime molds: fungi that move
Subdivision Myxomycotina

Yes, they move. A slime mold produces the usual fungal mycelium, spreading its network of nutrient-gathering threads through a great variety of living or nonliving things, then it assembles itself above ground as a **plasmodium,** typically an amoeba-like mass of protoplasm that flows slowly. This is when people notice slime molds. The plasmodium stops, changes form to something that can distribute spores (clusters of small balls, for example) and fruits. Look for slime molds in mid-to-late summer, in wet weather.

I photographed the slime mold shown here in my back yard in Jasper, where it appeared in three different spots in the grass. Perhaps it was **tapioca slime,** of the genus *Brefeldia,* a common slime mold.

*Slime mold*

### Witch's butter
*Tremella mesenterica*
Year-round, edible

Montane and lower subalpine, on alder branches, page 269. Bright yellow or orange lumpy blobs, soft and jelly-like in damp weather, tougher when dry. A similar fungus, *Dacrymyces palmatus,* is orangish and grows from a single point. It, too, is edible.

### Cyanobacterial colonies on the ground

During rainy weather, you may see rubbery-looking yellowish-brown blobs lying loose on hard-packed ground in grassy places. These are not fungi; they are colonies of **cyanobacteria** (once known as "bluegreen algae") of the genus *Nostoc.* The colonies are quite common. Present year-round, in dry

*Tremella mesenterica*

weather they look dark-colored and ropy or papery—rather like old animal droppings. When the ground is well-saturated, the colonies swell and become easily visible.

### Black-felt snow mold
*Herpotrichia* sp.
Year-round, edibility unknown
    This is the black stuff that looks like feces smeared on the lower branches of conifers, especially on subalpine firs at treeline. It parasitizes needles under the snow surface. Snow mold looks slimy but is actually dry to the touch and, yes, felty.

*Black-felt snow mold*

## Puffballs and earthstars

This chapter ends with the only group of fungi that is any fun to play with: the puffballs. Once a puffball has dried out inside, and a small hole has opened in the top, it begs to be squeezed, which will eject the spores in little puffs of dark-colored dust. This is most amusing for kids, although inhaling the spores is rumored to be unhealthy.
    Puffballs are renowned for flavorful eating. Why am I saying this? Humans shouldn't be eating up all the fungi in the Rockies. Here is a reason to leave an unknown puffball alone. It may be a poisonous amanita mushroom, page 417, still in the bud stage. Further, don't eat a puffball that is anything but white inside. Other colors indicate that it is either past the palatable stage or unsafe.

### Gem-studded puffball
*Lycoperdon perlatum*
July to October, edible
    On the ground at practically any elevation. A little egg-shaped ball 2–6 cm across; white with soft, short spines that tend to disappear as the puffball ripens. The white spore masses inside become olive-drab about the same time the covering becomes papery and the hole opens. Tasty in the early stages. If it is purple inside, or any color other than white, don't eat it; it may be a poisonous puffball-like fungus called *Scleroderma citrinum* that has a tan pigskin-like cover and splits open rather than puffing.

*Lycoperdon perlatum*

### Western giant puffball
*Calvatia booniana*
July to August, choice edible
    In meadows; seen more on the western slope than on the eastern slope. A great big puffball 20–60 cm across, with buff warts. White inside at first; later it goes olive brown as the spores mature. Rather than exiting through a hole as in most other puffballs, the

*Calvatia booniana*

spores expand until the ball cracks open. Don't eat if there is any internal structure—the protocap and gills of a potentially poisonous mushroom—or if not white inside.

### Buried-stalk puffball
*Tulostoma simulans*
April to December, edibility unknown
    In sandy soil, sometimes growing up through feather mosses. Usually as a cluster of small puffballs only 1–1.5 cm across on long, mostly buried stalks. The hole in each protrudes a bit. Spores are pinkish-yellow, leaving a brown stain around the hole.

*Tulostoma simulans*

### Barometer earthstar
*Geastrum* sp.
September to November, edibility unknown
    What's this? A little puffball with *petals?* Looks like it, but the rays are the outer skin of the puffball that has curled back and cracked in a star-shaped pattern 2–4 cm across, revealing an inner sac of spores that puffs through a central hole. The rays lie out on wet days and curl inward when it is dry—thus the common name: barometer. A charming, terribly intelligent fungus and my favorite. Look for earthstars in sandy places, in groups, talking about the weather.

*Geastrum*

## *Further reading*

Arora, D. (1986) *Mushrooms Demystified: a Comprehensive Guide to the Fleshy Fungi.* Ten Speed Press, Berkeley, CA. Perhaps the best single book on North American species, and fun to read, too. Fully illustrated, with keys, index, bibliography; 959 pages.

— (1991) *All That Rain Promises and More: a Hip Pocket Guide to Western Mushrooms.* Take-it-with-you guide, written in Arora's friendly syle. Fully illustrated, basic key, 264 pages.

Bandoni, R., and A. Szczawinski (1964) *Guide to Common Mushrooms of British Columbia.* British Columbia Provincial Museum Handbook No. 24. Photographs, non-technical; 179 pages. Order from the Provincial Museum, Victoria.

Lincoff, G. and C. Nehring (1981) *The Audubon Society Field Guide to North American Mushrooms.* Alfred Knopf, New York. Comprehensive, with good photographic illustrations; 928 pages but still pocket-sized.

Schalkwijk-Barendsen, H. (1991) *Mushrooms of Western Canada.* Lone Pine Publishing, Edmonton. Covers 550 species, many of them found in the mountains, and features the author's charming watercolor illustrations. Indexed three ways: by common names, by genera and by species. 415 pages.

*The spider and the fly:* Chrysops *meets* Misumena *in* Chrysanthemum. Misumena *is hungry. Photo by Barry Giles.*

# Bugs
## Insects, spiders and other arthropods

How are the bugs in the Canadian Rockies? Doing just fine, thank you. We have lots: mosquitoes, flies and ticks to bite you, bees and wasps to sting you, giant ants that plod over your bare feet. What we don't have are the really nasty ones: no black widows, no scorpions, no fire ants. Nor are we likely to acquire any in our cold northern climate.

In the insect awards presentation, the mosquito wins, hands down, in the Most Annoying category. Bald-faced hornet gets Most Painful. Horse fly receives Most Persistent. The award for Most Maddening Itch goes to the black fly, which shares honors with the Rocky Mountain wood tick for Sneakiest Mode of Attack. Most Frightful-Looking goes to the huge, wasp-like horntail, which is harmless.

But never mind all that. Insects are beautiful. Their strange, alien lives are quite interesting. And remember this, while you are slapping and swearing: if it were not for the bugs the wildflowers wouldn't get pollinated and we mountain-dwellers would be up to our knees in unprocessed elk poop.

Insects have six legs and spiders have eight. They are all arthropods. Of the 100,000 or so species of arthropods in North America, there are perhaps 20,000 species found in the Canadian Rockies—far too many to present in any sort of detail. Rather, I have singled out a few individuals and groups that are bound to attract your attention (in one way or another). To help in looking up the myriad species that are not covered here, the scientific family name is given with each item rather than just the common family name.

Getting your hands on insect specimens is surprisingly easy, and I'm not talking about swatting mosquitoes. Just walk or bicycle along any highway shoulder. So many bugs are killed by auto traffic that a goodly number are always lying beside the driving lanes, many in un-crunched condition.

Another place to look for insects is at the top of a hill. It need not be high; any fairly prominent point will do. Plan to arrive at about 10 a.m. on a June morning, when you will probably find plenty of varied buzzers, flutterers and droners **hill-topping,** which is the entomologist's term for swarming around a high point, mating. Hill-topping is especially common among the flies. Only on hill tops are you likely to see the males of many fly species.

But be prepared for a little interest from the bugs, particularly if it's a rocky prominence and *you* are the highest point. A sting or bite isn't likely; just a mass landing. While sitting on the tip of a rock spire in Colorado, my climbing partner and I were "hill-topped" by literally thousands of winged beasties, all vying for the choicest places on which to alight: on eyelids, inside ears, etc. The situation was so outrageously funny that we could not get the ropes set up for the descent, and we might have rolled off the rock in hysterics if we hadn't been tied in.

The listings in this chapter begin where many bugs begin their lives: in water. Later sections deal with insects that normally live on land or fly over it, from houseflies and spiders to butterflies and moths. At the end there is a special section on cold-adapted arthropods such the snow crane fly and the ice insects, page 474.

So, naturalists observe, a flea
Hath smaller fleas that on him prey;
And these have smaller fleas to bite 'em,
And so proceed *ad infinitum.*

—Jonathan Swift, 1733

# Bugs in, on or over water
## Including a whole lot of things that aren't insects

There are thousands of tiny animals in the lakes and streams of the Canadian Rockies, most so small you need a microscope to see them: **hydrozoans, rotifers, tardigrades, roundworms, flatworms, gastrotrichs, rhizopods, suctorians** ... and everything is eating everything else. A few of the tiny eaters and eatees are illustrated on the next page.

Next up the ladder we have the **crustaceans** (arthropods of the class Crustacea), known popularly as "freshwater shrimp." You can leave your microscope at home for these, but bring a finely woven dip net and a magnifying glass if you want to catch some for a look-see. They are water arthropods, freshwater versions of their much-larger marine relatives the lobsters and shrimp. Crustaceans are year-round water dwellers, going about their lives under a metre of ice in winter. The ones illustrated are all common around here, especially in warm, low-elevation lakes in spring. Scooping up a handful of bottom mud will usually get you a few **amphipods**, also called "scuds," and "sideswimmers," and some seed-like **ostracods.** Sweeping a net through the water just off the bottom will often bag **fairy shrimp** (anostracads), **water fleas** (cladocerans) and **copepods.** In the southern Rocky Mountain Trench you may find **crayfish.** Water closer to the surface gives up **plankton,** including **diatoms**, algae and algae-eating **copepods, water fleas** and **fairy shrimp.**

There may be other things in your net, of course. Consider the possibilities on the next few pages.

## Snails, clams and leeches

There are very few species of molluscs in the mountains, which is not surprising when you consider that most molluscs are sea creatures. Nonetheless, the floors of shallow montane lakes and ponds are sometimes covered with **snails** (order Gastropoda) of the genus *Lymnaea*. You can also find **fingernail clams** (order Pelecypoda, genus *Pisidium*) in the same habitat, although they are not as plentiful.

You can thank the snails for **swimmer's itch:** attacks by microscopic parasites of the genus *Trichobilharzia.* These trematodes, which are flatworms, infest snails first, then blood vessels of warm-blooded animals. At one stage in the life cycle, the tiny **cercariae** swim out of the snail in great numbers, looking for waterfowl, their next host. But they sometimes hit swimming humans instead. They quickly penetrate the skin, only to find that they have invaded the wrong organism, man rather than duck. This mistake is fatal for the flatworms—they soon die—but only annoying for us.

Swimmer's itch begins after you get out of the water. You feel an itching sensation all over, or just on the legs if you only went wading, often followed a few days later by a rash as the parasites die and fester out. The rash clears up and that is the end of it in our part of the world. But elsewhere, in the tropics, there are human-specific trematodes of the genus *Schistosoma* that can kill.

See also *Giardia lamblia,* page 773, a waterborne human parasite that does occur in the Canadian Rockies.

Finally, among the miscellaneous water dwellers of the mountains we must not forget the **leeches** (phylum Annelida, class Hirudina). These live in shallow montane ponds and sluggish streams. Leeches are black worms, half-round in cross-section and up to 10 cm long.

There is a sucker at each end. Of the many species of leeches in the Rockies, none are likely to do the thing that leeches are famous for: attaching to your body and sucking blood. They do that to other creatures, usually fish. Leeches spend most of their time stuck onto rocks or submerged pieces of wood near the bottom, their bodies held vertically. Occasionally you may see one swimming through the water. It does so like a snake, undulating along most gracefully. Like many other worms, leeches are hermaphroditic: male and female at the same time. Think of the advantages.

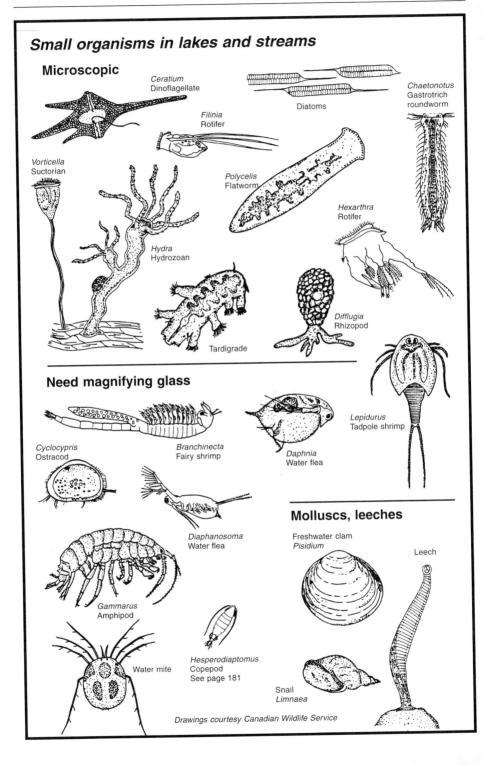

# Small organisms in lakes and streams

## Microscopic

*Ceratium*
Dinoflagellate

Diatoms

*Chaetonotus*
Gastrotrich
roundworm

*Filinia*
Rotifer

*Vorticella*
Suctorian

*Polycelis*
Flatworm

*Hexarthra*
Rotifer

*Hydra*
Hydrozoan

*Difflugia*
Rhizopod

Tardigrade

## Need magnifying glass

*Lepidurus*
Tadpole shrimp

*Cyclocypris*
Ostracod

*Branchinecta*
Fairy shrimp

*Daphnia*
Water flea

## Molluscs, leeches

*Diaphanosoma*
Water flea

Freshwater clam
*Pisidium*

Leech

*Gammarus*
Amphipod

Water mite

*Hesperodiaptomus*
Copepod
See page 181

Snail
*Limnaea*

*Drawings courtesy Canadian Wildlife Service*

# Insect larvae

Many airborne insects begin life under water. Here are a few common insect larvae found in mountain water bodies. Note that larvae of stoneflies, mayflies, damselflies and dragonflies are called **naiads,** but they are larvae all the same.

## Mosquito larvae
(Diptera, family Culicidae)
April to August

Montane to alpine, in still water. Very common in shallow lakes and temporary water bodies during June, but also found in any spot of water as long as its surface is not oily: in buckets, tin cans, tree holes, pitted stumps, you name it. Mosquito larvae are up to 15 mm long. They hang from the water surface upside down, each breathing (well, *respiring;* insects don't breathe) through a tube that breaks the surface. Oil kills a mosquito larva because it keeps the tube from reaching air. The larvae constantly curl and uncurl; they are known to fishermen as "wrigglers." Adult form: page 443.

## Midge larvae (bloodworms and phantom midges)
(Diptera, families Chironomidae and Chaoboridae)
Year-round

Montane to alpine, in lakes and sluggish streams. Hemoglobin in the otherwise-transparent larval bodies of midge species colors them red; thus the name **bloodworms,** although they aren't really worms. The larvae of **phantom midges** such as *Chaoborus* lack hemoglobin and are practically invisible underwater. Other midge larvae are dark-colored. They are all 10–20 mm long and very active, bringing their front and back ends together and then snapping them apart. They eat small organisms and decaying matter. See page 445 for the adult form.

## Black fly larvae
*Simulium* spp. (Diptera, family Simuliidae)
May to September

In vigorous montane and subalpine streams. Small (2–5 mm long), living under rocks, attached by a rear-end sucker disk and eating microorganisms. Adult form: page 447.

## Predaceous diving beetle larvae (water tigers)
(Coleoptera, family Dytiscidae)
Year-round

In montane and subalpine water bodies of any kind. Small to very large (5–50 mm), slim and agile, patrolling up and down in the bottom waters in search of other insect larvae. These things can catch tadpoles or even small fish with their hefty front-end pinchers.

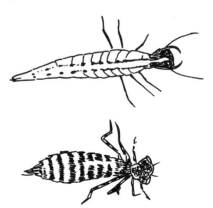

## Dragonfly naiads
(Odonata, suborder Anisoptera)
Year-round

In montane lakes and streams, on the bottom or clinging to water plants. One of the larger insect larvae to be found in mountain water, up to 50 mm long, distinguished from the other naiads by the absence of a tail. The abdomen is fat and the eyes are large. Like diving beetle larvae, previous item, dragonfly larvae are voracious predators, attacking nearly anything. Mosquito larvae are staple foods.

These naiads have an interesting modus operandi. The lower lip (if insects can be thought of as having lower lips) suddenly flicks out, snaring the prey and dragging it back. Then the lip retracts under the head.

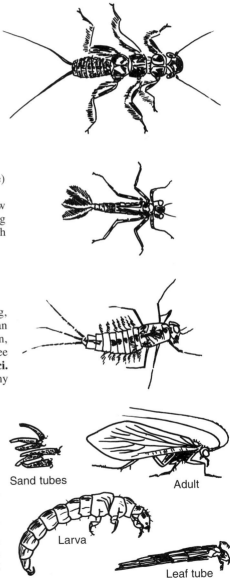

### Stonefly naiads
(Plecoptera, various families)
Year-round

In streams and well-oxygenated montane and subalpine lakes, on the bottom. Length up to 40 mm, the body yellowish or brown, with strong-looking legs, large eyes and two harmless spine-like sensory organs sticking out the back. The head and next three segments are handsomely patterned in contrasting tones.

Most stonefly naiads putter about the bottom, shredding detritus. Some are predators, gobbling up other bottom-dwellers. They live up to three years before changing to adults.

### Damselfly naiads
(Odonata, families Coenagrionidae and Lestidae)
Year-round

Montane to alpine, on bottoms of shallow ponds. Length to 30 mm. Brown body resembling stonefly naiads, previous item, but slimmer, with three large leaf-like gills at the tail. Predatory.

### Mayfly naiads
(order Ephemeroptera)
May to August

Montane and subalpine, in fast-flowing, rocky streams. Length to 15 mm, smaller than similar stonefly and damselfly larvae. Green, brown or transparent body has slim legs and three filaments on the end; two are sensors called **cerci.** Mayfly naiads feed on plant material and tiny animals. They can live up to four years before metamorphosing to adults.

### Caddisfly larvae
(order Trichoptera)
Year-round

Montane and subalpine, in lakes and streams. Caterpillar-like larvae live in cylindrical cases up to 50 mm long made of sand, twigs or leaves held together with silky glue secreted from salivary glands. Caddisfly larvae extend their heads and front legs to crawl about the bottom, dragging the cases with them. It takes a year for them to reach the adult stage; they pupate in the cases.

Sand tubes

Adult

Larva

Leaf tube

# Water bugs, water beetles

Some of these are true bugs, meaning that they are members of the order Hemiptera. True bugs have leathery forewings. They feed by sucking through a piercing beak. Immature bugs, called **nymphs,** are smaller, wingless versions of the adult forms.

## Backswimmers

(order Hemiptera, family Notonectidae)
July to October

In montane and subalpine ponds and streams, often at the surface in shallow quiet water. Length 10–15 mm. Backswimmers live belly-side up (black side up); the other side is white to green, often with prominent red patches. Covered wings are used only in spring, to fly from one pond to another. One pair of legs is long, sticking straight out to the side and propelling this bug—a true bug, in the scientific sense—like oars. The front legs, also fairly long, are used to grab prey, small insects mostly, held in the tension of the surface water. Although small, this bug can bite you. Compare with water boaters, next item.

## Water boaters

(order Hemiptera, family Corixidae)
June to September

Montane and subalpine ponds, puddles and other small or very small water bodies—even discarded cans that hold water. And open septic tanks. Length 5–15 mm. Resembles the backswimmer, previous item, but lives right side up. Body is brown with fine white or gray parallel wiggly lines; the hind pair of legs are long and do the rowing; the shorter legs help. Since the minute water bodies they use often dry up, water boaters fly from one stagnant pool to the next. They eat mostly algae, but some are predaceous. None bites.

## Giant water bug

*Lethocerus americanus* (order Hemiptera, family Belostomidae)
June to September

Shallow, montane ponds and sloughs, often just under the surface among underwater vegetation. Largest water insect in the mountains, up to 60 mm long, brown and flat, with thick front legs to seize prey up to the size of a small salamander. The giant water bug grabs and stabs, thrusting a sharp beak into the victim. It can do the same to your foot if you step on it while wading, the reason for its folk name, "toe-biter." The nymphs tend to eat each other, thus keeping the number of giant water bugs in any one pond fairly small. Good.

## Whirligig beetles

*Gyrinus* spp. (order Coleoptera, family Gyrinidae)
May to September

Montane and subalpine, at the surface in quiet water. Whirligig beetles in the Canadian Rockies are 3–7 mm long, oval and black, often shiny, with lines of dots and orangey legs. The name comes from peculiar group behavior. Lots of whirligig beetles will congregate, each one whirling round and round—but seldom colliding because they can sense one another's ripples.

This probably is a way of avoiding predators; have you ever tried to *catch* one of these? Larvae eat small organisms, crawl out of the water to pupate and return in the adult, whirligig form. See also the diving beetles, next item.

### Diving beetles
(order Coleoptera, family Dytiscidae)
May to September

Montane ponds and slow streams, in weedy shallow water. Many species; small ones are less than 10 mm long in our area, with brown bodies that have yellowish markings and yellow, bristly back legs. The larger species, up to 40 mm, are often of the genus *Dytiscus;* their oval bodies are shiny black with a yellow rim.

Your typical diving beetle grabs a bubble of air on its butt and dives to the bottom, grubbing about there among the insect larvae and whatnot until the bubble is gone, at which point it returns to the surface for another one. The bubble actually extends up under the beetle's elytra (wing coverings), so there is more air there than it would seem. The beetles fly from pond to pond at night, feeding on mosquito larvae and anything else they can catch; the large ones also kill tadpoles and small fish.

Like the whirligig beetles, previous item, diving beetles pupate in damp soil. They return to the water as adults that overwinter and live three years or more.

### Giant water scavenger beetle
*Hydrophilus triangularis*
 (order Coleoptera, family Hydrophilidae)
August and September

Montane and subalpine ponds and sluggish streams. Length 25–40 mm. Resembles a large diving beetle, previous item, but lacks the yellow rim around the body and has a pair of long **palps** (mouthparts) sticking out the front. Predatory, feeding on snails; also scavenges along the bottom for dead stuff. At night these beetles fly around. They are attracted to lights. You can also sometimes find their floating egg cases: silky cocoons 20–25 mm across, each with one projecting point. The larvae live underwater, pupate in damp soil by the shore and re-enter the water in late summer. They are active under the ice all winter.

### Water striders
(order Hemiptera, family Gerridae)
June to September

Montane to alpine, on still water surfaces. Body 10–15 mm long, dark brown. Long, skinny middle and hind legs snap forward and back, propelling these bugs (true bugs) across the water very quickly. They eat mostly insects stuck in the surface film, especially mosquito larvae, and they talk to one another by making ripples. Really! Adults overwinter on the shore, under leaves buried beneath the snow. Texans, creators of wonderful folkisms, call them "Jesus bugs" because they walk on water. In Canada, true to northern form, we often call them "pond-skaters."

# Mayflies (order Ephemeroptera)

Mayflies are found in hovering swarms above lakes and fast-flowing montane and subalpine streams from May to August. There are hundreds of species, differing mainly in size (5–15 mm long) and color (white, yellow, brown, greenish). Body layout is similar throughout: slender, with gently up-curved abdomen, clear or smoky wings held together vertically above the body, and two or three long filaments extending from the tail.

This is an ancient animal, little changed in 280 million years. The males form the swarms, attracting females into the throng. A male seizes each female and they mate on the wing. Within an hour the females drop eggs into the water, where they lodge under stones. The naiads cling to rocks, eating small organisms and/or algae; they emerge from the water and molt to dark-colored nearly mature adults called **subimagos** or "duns." Subimagos molt again a few hours later to join the dancing adults, living only a day or two and not eating at all.

Mayflies represent all that is giddy about the short northern summer.

# Dragonflies and damselflies (order Odonata)

Dragonflies and damselflies are readily identified by the long, slender abdomen and two sets of wings. These are Carboniferous insects; they have done well on this planet for some 280 million years. The secret of their success: possibly their helicopter-like flying ability. Up, down, forward, back, sideways, hovering—these flyers can do it all, making them extremely agile hunters. They catch prey with their feet.

The difference between the dragonflies and damselflies is mainly in the eyes, which are larger on dragonflies, covering most of the head, and in the wings, usually folded back when at rest in damselflies, held out horizontally in dragonflies. Further, the forewings and hindwings of damselflies are equal in size, while those of dragonflies are not.

Dragonfly/damselfly sex is interesting. The male produces a little bag of sperm from the tip of his abdomen, then curls the abdomen under to place the packet in a special chamber under the second segment back from the thorax. When a female comes along, the male grabs her around the neck with special claspers. As they fly along united, she bends the tip of her abdomen up to take the sperm bag from its compartment, later depositing the fertilized eggs in the water or on plants nearby. Some females dive underwater to glue their eggs to rocks.

The naiads (larvae) spend one or more years eating mainly mosquito larvae before crawling out of the water and changing over a few hours into adults, which live along the shores of lakes, ponds and streams at all but the highest elevations. They may be seen throughout the summer, patrolling a little way out from shore. Some species prefer to do their hunting in the woods.

Here are some dragonfly species to know:

**Darners** (family Aeschnidae): seen over montane ponds and lazy streams. Large, with bodies 60–80 mm long and wingspans to 100 mm, brilliantly blue, green and/or brown with clear wings.

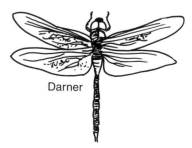

Darner

**Emeralds** (family Corduliidae): seen over cold montane and subalpine marshes, bogs or slow-moving streams. Medium-sized (40–60 mm), with iridescent green eyes, metallic green or greenish-bronze thorax and a dark abdomen, sometimes with white rings. Common ones are *Somatochlora* spp. and *Cordulia shurtleffi*.

**Whitefaces** *(Leucorrhinia* spp., family Libellulidae): seen over montane and subalpine marshes and bogs. Small (25–40 mm), black with red or yellow markings and white faces.

**Meadowhawks** *(Sympetrum* spp., family Libellulidae): seen over montane and subalpine marshes. Usually red or golden all over. One common species *(S. danae)* is black like *Leucorrhinia,* previous item, but has a dark face. Meadowhawks like to land on white-colored things: rocks, bleached logs, tan pantlegs.

**Four-spot skimmer** *(Libellula quadrimaculata,* family Libellulidae): montane to subalpine, seen over lakes and slow-moving rivers. Length 70–80 mm; olive-brown with yellow stripes along the sides, yellow face. Each wing has two smoky spots along the leading edge.

**Clubtails** (family Gomphidae): montane, over small, fast-flowing streams. In the Rockies we have mainly the **pale snaketail,** *Ophiogomphus severis,* 45–52 mm long, thorax pale greenish-yellow with dark markings, abdomen black with yellow spots. The eyes of gomphid dragonflies do not meet atop the head.

Here are some damselflies to watch for:

**Bluets** (family Coenagrionidae), June to September: montane to alpine, common over ponds and lakes. Length 30–40 mm. Sky-blue with black markings and clear wings.

**Spreadwings** (family Lestidae), June to August: montane and subalpine, near small ponds. Length 35–40 mm, the thorax bright metallic green or bronze, abdomen darker and vaguely banded, wings clear and held out from the body at rest, like those of a dragonfly.

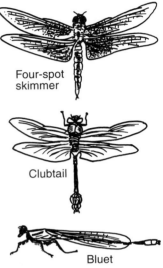

Four-spot skimmer

Clubtail

Bluet

# Bugs on land and in the air
Meaning most insects you see in the Rockies each summer

Let's start this section with the flies (order Diptera), including two universal favorites, houseflies and mosquitoes.

## Mosquitoes (family Culicidae)

There are some 28 species of mosquitoes in the Canadian Rockies, of which four common ones are described here. They are all flies, order Diptera. The eggs hatch in spring and the larvae are all water-dependent, staying just under the surface and feeding mostly on algae, floating pollen and decaying plant matter. The pupal phase is interesting: while the pupae of most insects are motionless, well-hidden in their capsules as they change to adults, mosquito pupae float openly at the water's surface and can swim away to the bottom when threatened.

Mosquito larvae and pupae are a common food of other pond dwellers, who are faced with such a sudden glut that they cannot eat them all in the small time—a week or two—that it takes for the larvae to metamorphose to adults. This is the mosquito's survival strategy.

The adults use their slender, piercing probosci to feed on plant juices. Male mosquitoes have very feathery antennae; females have skinny ones.

After mating, the male dies. In some species the fertilized female hibernates, but in most species she lays eggs in the summer or fall and then dies. In either case she must have a blood meal to obtain proteins necessary for successful egg production. She homes in on metabolic waste products in your breath, not your body warmth or clothing color, although clothing color is important during final approach. Repellents work by jamming the ladies' $CO_2$ detectors with the wrong molecule, in most cases N, N-diethyl-metatoluamide, commonly abbreviated **DEET.** Formulations that are 40 percent or more DEET work for several hours and are effective against black flies and other biting flies as well as mosquitoes.

Recent tests have shown that DEET concentrations of more than 40 percent are not notably more effective. Since DEET is a smelly solvent that attacks most kinds of plastic, minimal use is advised. Whenever I use it to go birdwatching in buggy places, my binoculars get tacky to the touch. This leads me to wonder what the stuff is doing to my body. Like any other chemical, we should use bug repellents cautiously, only when (buzz, whine, ouch!) one must either smear up or go indoors. Two layers of upper-body clothing and long pants will keep the vulnerable areas small. Wear a turtleneck shirt under a tightly-woven outer layer. If you can't wear repellent, or don't want to, just slip on some light gardener's gloves and one of the head nets available at outdoor equipment stores. Some shops sell anti-bug anoraks made of netting; these are great for hot days, because they can be worn with no shirt. You keep the anorak in a bag impregnated with repellent.

Mosquito season in the southern and central Canadian Rockies is mercifully short. Except in prime breeding sites, such as marshes, shallow ponds, sluggish streams, which are buggy all summer, the worst time for mosquitoes comes in late June or early July and lasts only a couple of weeks in the valleys, where most dwellings are. Higher up, though, in the subalpine forest and above treeline, mosquitoes are a bother throughout July and well into August. The wetter, warmer western slope is worse than the cooler, drier eastern slope. The northern region is the worst of all.

**To get instant relief** from a swelling, itching mosquito bite, try using your fingernail to indent the skin over the bite. Apply lots of pressure, making two marks that cross each other. The annoyance will subside for a while. For sensitive individuals who get big lumps from mosquito bites, an antihistamine insect-bite ointment provides relief through the I-can't-stand-it stage.

## House mosquitoes

*Culex* spp. (family Culicidae)
April to September

Southern and central regions mainly. Uncommon only at very high elevations, where the temperature dips below freezing nearly every night. In hordes near shallow ponds and marshes, where they breed. Length 4–5 mm. Worst time is mid-June through mid-July. The most abundant mosquito genus in the mountains; members are light brown all over with faintly banded abdomens. Not very hairy. They keep all legs down when inserting the proboscis. *C. tarsalis* is a common species; she overwinters in talus slopes, caves and rodent burrows, emerging in May to bite and lay eggs. Most active at night. Transmits the virus of western equine encephalitis, mainly a disease of birds but also a killer of horses. Humans get it occasionally.

## Malaria mosquito

*Anopheles earlei* (family Culicidae)
May to August

Montane and subalpine, in woods and near towns; more common on the western slope. Length 4 mm. Same size and similar to house mosquito, previous item, but the abdomen is not banded. Easiest way to identify one of these is to let it light on you; the malaria mosquito raises its tail nearly straight up, hind legs in the air, as it inserts the proboscis. As the name says, these mosquitoes may carry malaria—and other diseases, too. Although malaria is supposedly not present in Canada, it is wise *not* to let these ladies under your skin. They overwinter by hibernating in animal burrows, beaver lodges and such, emerging in May.

### Snow mosquito
*Aedes communis* (family Culicidae)
July and August

At all elevations, near small pools of water. This is a little yellowish mosquito that reaches its greatest numbers in midsummer. Eggs are laid the previous summer under leaves or in evergreen-needle duff in low places that hold water for a while in spring, frequently beside a melting snowbank. Neither sex survives the winter. The young may hatch under the snow, but they develop very slowly until early spring brings the meltwater they need.

*Aedes vexans* is a similar species, reddish brown rather than yellow. It is known for persistence in attacking and for population explosions, both of which are reflected in the species name.

## *Other kinds of flies (order Diptera)*

In the typical fly life cycle, the worm-like larvae metamorphose into winged adults that exist mainly to mate and lay eggs, often dying soon after. Many fly species in the Rockies go through their larval stage in water.

### Crane fly
*Tipula* spp. (family Tipulidae)
May to August

Montane and subalpine, often near water. Looks like a great big mosquito, with long, dangling legs, but it is not. Brown body with clear wings. Poor flyer; bumbles through the air. Often winds up indoors for some reason. Despite its size and appearance, the crane fly is harmless—it doesn't even eat, existing only to mate and die. Males are smaller than females and have skinny abdomens with a ball on the end; females have cigar-shaped abdomens.

### Midges
(Chaoboridae and Chironomidae families)
July and August

Montane and subalpine, along lakeshores and in the woods, hovering in compact swarms that are often just at head-level (cough, choke). To most people, they are "gnats," although true gnats are rare around here while midges are plentiful. Midges are very mosquito-like in appearance, but they either have short prosboci or none at all. The ones we have don't bite—which is a good way of telling a cloud of midges from a cloud of mosquitoes. Midges sit with their wings held out to the side rather than folded parallel as mosquitoes do. There are lots of species, some very specialized. One type lives in limestone cave openings. Some species have red larvae that wiggle about in the water; see bloodworms, page 438. What fisherfolk call "black gnats" are actually midges.

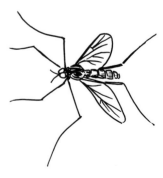

## House fly

*Musca domestica* (family Muscidae)
June to October

In any habitat and at any elevation, although especially common around garbage, human food and mammal feces. Scarce above treeline. This is the common fly that walks around on the rim of your teacup with its dirty feet. Length about 7 mm, body gray with four black stripes on the **thorax,** the part with wings. Behind that is the **abdomen.** This is the typical layout of any insect. House flies have reddish eyes. The clear wings are folded parallel to the body.

House flies do not bite; they vacuum up liquids that are sweet or decaying. While vacuuming you, a house fly may be transferring such things as typhoid, cholera, dysentery and various parasitic worms. So brush a fly off; don't squash it on your skin.

Intensely reproductive, house flies produce 5–6 broods a year of 75–120 eggs that hatch within 12 hours. The **maggots** live in poop, dead stuff and garbage. They reach adulthood in only 12 days, living for 15–26 days and making more flies as fast as possible. Support your local birds.

## Blue bottle flies

*Calliphora vomitoria, C. cadaverina* (family Calliphoridae)
June to September

Montane, around dead animals, meat and garbage. The possessors of these charming species names are large flies of the blow-fly group, about 13 mm long, with dark-gray bodies, red eyes and metallic blue abdomens. Bristly all over. They buzz around the house, attracted to meat.

The life cycle of the blue bottle fly is wonderfully attractive. Eggs laid on decaying or festering flesh hatch almost immediately. The maggots suck decay juices, crawl off to pupate in a drier place, then emerge after 2–3 weeks in adult form to feed on carrion and in wounds. Only the female adults feed; the males mate and die.

Despite their eating habits, blue bottle flies are not known as disease transmitters. In fact, an infected open injury or sore attacked by the larvae or adults of these blow flies will become sterile, although it may take longer to heal.

## Green bottle fly

*Lucilia illustris* (family Calliphoridae)
June to September

Montane, found around dead fish, carrion and garbage. Large, 10–14 mm long, with brilliantly metallic green thorax and abdomen; black head with red eyes; clear wings. A blow fly, with a life cycle like that of the blue bottle fly, previous item. Green bottle flies hang around garbage cans and carrion, eating rotten meat. One of their favorite things is trout guts thoughtfully left out for them by people fishing.

## Dung fly

*Scathophaga stercoraria* (family Scathophagidae)
June to August

Montane, common around stables and domestic animals. Easily recognized by the color: coppery or yellowish, especially on the abdomen. Bristly all over, with red eyes and clear wings that are yellowish near the front. A bit larger (10 mm) than the house fly, which is the prey of the adult dung fly. Thus, dung flies are friends, not foes. The larvae are the dung-eaters, tunneling in from eggs deposited there.

## Deer flies
*Chrysops* spp. (family Tabanidae)
June to August

Montane and subalpine, usually in the woods. More common on the western slope. They look rather like house flies, but the difference is obvious when they land: they bite.

Ten millimetres long, the common **callidus deer fly**, *Chrysops callidus*, is a little larger than a house fly and sits with its wings held out a little to the side, while the house fly folds its wings pretty well straight back. Deer fly wings are darkly banded. There is a bit of yellow on the thorax and head, and the eyes are patterned greenish or gold.

The larvae live in water, preying on small insects that they kill by injecting venom. They pupate in mud along the shore. Like the mosquito, only the female adult deer fly bites, sometimes transmitting tularemia to snowshoe hares, which can then infect us if we eat them. DEET repellents work on deer flies, which is good, because they are too quick to swat.

## Horse flies
*Hybomitra* spp. (family Tabanidae)
June to August

At all elevations, but particularly common in subalpine meadows. A large fly, up to 20 mm long. Gray head with enormous iridescent striped green eyes that are beautiful; rest of body gray, sometimes gray and orange; wings clear.

The horse-fly larva lives in water, eating other insects for up to three summers and overwintering in bottom mud. One spring it pupates, emerging a few weeks later as either a pollen/nectar-eating adult male, which mates and dies, or a female, which lives until fall, taking blood from large mammals and laying eggs in plants that hang over water into which the larvae drop.

A horse fly will follow a back-packer for hours, occasionally landing to attempt a bite. The mandibles work like a pair of scissors, opening a wound that bleeds freely because the fly's saliva contains an anti-clotting agent. Repellent works, but horse flies are also rather slow on takeoff and thus vulnerable to swatting. They have been known to carry disease, but not ones transferable to humans, so swat away. And swat hard; horse flies can survive knocks that would do in most other kinds of insects.

## Black flies
*Simulium* spp. (family Simuliidae)
July and August

Montane and subalpine, along streams. Black flies are uncommon south of Lake Louise, gradually increasing in numbers as you go north. These are small flies, only 2–4 mm long. There are many species in the Canadian Rockies; most are gray, some with yellow banded legs and abdomens. There is an interesting life cycle: eggs laid next to running water, often in a spring, hatch in October; the small black larvae wiggle into the water and can sometimes be seen clinging by the hundred to stones under the surface. They overwinter there, pupating in silk cocoons, then pop out in midsummer as adults, riding bubbles of self-produced gas to the surface and flying away. The males eat only nectar, but the females of most species also require blood from birds or mammals to reproduce.

That's bad news for us humans. Black flies are voracious. And sneaky: you don't notice them biting. They usually go for the back of the neck, just under the hairline from ear to ear, or around the eyes. You feel an itch there, bringing away a spot of blood on your finger that shows you are too late; the fly has struck and gone. The wound swells to a lump about a centimetre across, with a red dot in the middle. It itches for several days, making crusts, and takes a week or more to go away. Treatment: don't scratch; that only makes it worse. Insect-bite ointments help. In sensitive people, especially if bitten around the eye, the spot may swell hugely, becoming an eye-closing purple egg that infects. Go to the doctor.

Fortunately, black flies do not bite at night. They are busiest around sunset. During the day, a little insect repellent applied around the hairline will keep them away. Use a brand that is at least 40 percent DEET. Wearing light-colored clothing helps, for they prefer to land on dark colors.

In late summer black flies like to come indoors, where they seldom bite and can be observed up close as they scramble around the window panes.

Although black flies transmit blindness-causing parasites in the tropics, they are not known as vectors for human disease in the Rockies. Birds suffer from them, though; ducks, geese and swans in our area can contract **waterfowl malaria** from black fly bites, and it is often fatal.

✤ **Punkies,** also called **"no-see-ums,"** are tiny flies of the family Ceratopogonidae. The females of some species bite, inflicting surprisingly painful and itchy wounds. ✤

## Bees, wasps, hornets and their mimics (order Hymenoptera)

Here is the don't-mess-with-me crowd, most of them sporting bright-yellow bands of warning. Maybe this is where we humans got the idea to use yellow as a caution or safety color.

### Honey bee

*Apis mellifera* (family Apidae)
June to August

Montane, in open areas with wildflowers or cultivated legumes such as alfalfa. The honey bee is the most common bee in the world, but it is rivalled here in numbers by the golden northern bumble bee, next item.

The honey bee is 11–15 mm long, with a furry yellowish-brown head and thorax, black eyes, banded ochre-and-black abdomen, black legs; lower parts often covered with pollen. Honey bees live in very large colonies of 60,000–80,000 members that build hives of wax in tree holes, attics, woodpiles and other dry, woody places.

Of all the bees and wasps, the honey bee exhibits the most complex social behavior and has perhaps the most interesting life cycle. Eggs in waxy cells hatch to larvae that remain there, pupating into various physical forms: queens, which are reproductive females; drones, which are reproductive males, and workers, which are non-reproductive females. Control of types is through feeding of larvae. The amount of **bee-bread** (pollen/honey mixture) consumed and intake of special foods such as royal jelly controls who grows up into what. Adults eat nectar and honey, live a year or less, except for the queen, who lives 3–5 years, overwintering within the hive while layers of workers surround her, the outer workers perishing in the cold at this latitude. The queen leaves in early spring, taking with her a swarm of remaining workers to start a new colony. New queens emerge in the old hive, killing one another until only one remains. She then flies about, mates and produces replacement eggs for the swarm that left. The honey bee has a barbed stinger that lodges in human flesh, thus killing the bee when it stings.

Amazing Bee Facts Department: as it moves from flower to flower, a worker marks the ones it has milked with a short-lived repellent scent that informs it, or other workers approaching that flower, that the nectar there has already been gathered. When a worker returns to the hive after finding a good source of nectar, it moves in a figure-eight-shaped pattern that tells the others of the direction and distance to the source, and even of its relative food value. Other bees will find the flowers there marked with a long-lasting *attractive* scent.

## Golden northern bumble bee
*Bombus fervidus* (family Apidae)
June to September

Montane and subalpine, in flowery meadows. A large bee 20–30 mm long, easily differentiated from other Rockies bees by its size and by its very furry, broad bands of yellow and black. Legs are black with orange pouches; wings are small and smoky-looking.

Bumble bees fly sluggishly from flower to flower, eating nectar and gathering pollen to take home to the nest, which is in the ground or in the wall of a building. They seem to eat other things, too; one of these bees once landed on my bare leg and licked it (they have little red tongues) for fifteen minutes straight.

When caught by cool, rainy weather away from the nest, golden northern bumble bees become dormant and hang upside down beneath flowers. Perhaps they seek out flowerheads in order to get a kick-start shot of nectar when coming out of their torpor.

Like yellow-jackets and hornets, next item, only the mated females survive the winter, starting a new nest and feeding honey to the first brood of larvae, which become under-sized workers not much bigger than honey bees. In July and August, subsequent broods of full-size adults enlarge the nest until cold weather kills all but the young, newly mated queens, who overwinter to start new colonies. The seasonal death of these bees is touching. One can see them on late summer mornings, torporous on the upper surfaces of asters. One morning, covered in frost and snow, they do not wake.

See also the thetis clearwing moth, page 470.

## Western yellow-jacket
*Vespula* spp. (family Vespidae)
June to September

Montane, common in dry open woods. Often in campgrounds. Gaudy yellow-and-black banded body 10–15 mm long; yellow legs, clear wings. Hairy face; compare with bald-faced hornet, next item.

Most yellow-jackets in the Canadian Rockies nest in the ground, often under common juniper, page 285, but there is at least one species here that builds papery, wasp-like nests under building overhangs (and my lawnmower; see photo). Yellow-jackets are renowned for attacks if the nest is disturbed. However, I have stumbled on many ground nests over the years without getting stung, so maybe they are less easily aroused here than elsewhere. One hot afternoon I guzzled most of a can of juice left all morning on a campground picnic table, then put the can down when I noticed a buzzing feeling on my lips—at which point several yellow-jackets zipped out. None stung me.

Life cycle: emerging from forest litter and soil in spring, a young mated female digs a shallow nest and produces eggs, feeding the larvae pre-chewed insects or a variety of other foods, including stuff scavenged from picnics. The young hornets are all female workers, who forage to support subsequent broods. Adults eat only nectar. At summer's end, males develop from infertile eggs laid by workers. (Nature is amazing.) The males mate with new queens, who are the only ones to survive the winter.

*Any dry spot will do for a hornet nest. This gives you some idea of how often I cut my lawn.*

## Bald-faced hornet
*Vespula maculata* (family Vespidae)
June to August

Montane, in meadows; fairly common in towns, around flower gardens, where they sting with very little provocation. The bald-faced hornet looks a lot like a yellow-jacket, previous item, but it is bigger (15–20 mm long), and patterned differently: black and white rather than black and yellow, the face white and bald rather than hairy like a yellow-jacket, the abdomen unstriped.

Hornets make papery gray nests of chewed wood pulp that hang under tree branches or other woody supports; larvae in cells inside are fed insect pulp by adults. The life cycle is like that of the yellow-jacket.

## Hover flies
(order Diptera, family Syrphidae)
July and August

Montane and subalpine, near shrubbery where the larvae can eat aphids and other small insects. Hoverflies are non-bees in disguise. They mimic yellow-jackets and hornets, but cannot sting. They are also smaller, about 10 mm, with brown eyes rather than black.

Hover flies hover, all right, hanging around people in a rather too-interested way. Yet they are not after blood; the adult drinks mainly nectar and other sweet stuff. It may vacuum your skin with its proboscis, in the manner of a housefly. Doesn't seem to spread disease.

## Black-and-yellow mud dauber
*Sceliphron caementarium* (family Sphecidae)
June to September

Occasional at low elevations, Banff south. Easily recognized as a wasp by the long thread-like waist. Body length 25–30 mm; wings not as long as body, folded straight back. Mostly black, with yellow legs, yellow patches on head and thorax, yellow waist and yellow spot on abdomen at connection. This wasp packs a wallop; beware.

The female builds a nest of mud under any over-hang (rocks, eaves); places a stung spider, alive but immobile, in each cell and lays an egg on it. Larvae eat the spiders, remaining in the cells through pupation to adult stage, when they emerge to drink nectar and mate.

## Western giant ichneumon
*Megarhyssa nortoni* (family Ichneumonidae)
June to August

Montane, often in deciduous woods. Females very large, 35–75 mm long; males 25–40 mm. A very elegant wasp, with an extra-long waist, long yellow antennae, long yellow legs, and in females a very long, two-part black **ovipositor** (egg-laying tube) hanging from the abdomen. Head is yellow around black eyes; there are also yellow and/or red markings on the body.

Ichneumons are parasitic wasps. The egg-laden female listens with her antennae for horntail larvae, next item, boring in dead wood. Then she works her long, sharp-ended ovipositor into the wood at several sites, laying her eggs in the tunnels. The eggs hatch and the ichneumon larvae enter the horntail larvae, feeding inside them until the ichneumon larvae are grown, at which point the hosts die. The western giant ichneumon is active by day, feeds on nectar and cannot sting. But there are short-tailed nocturnal species of the family Ophionidae that *do* sting.

### Smoky horntail

*Urocerus* spp. (family Siricidae)
July and August

Montane, around dead wood in forests; often seen around lumber piles in towns. Big, scary-looking wasp-like insect up to 40 mm long. Dark-brown body with yellow or ochre head, black eyes and yellow/ochre bands on the thorax and abdomen. No thread-like waist, though. Female has a prominent ovipositor sticking out the back; she uses it to lay eggs under the surface of dead wood. Despite the nightmare-bug appearance, horntails are harmless.

The larvae bore galleries, sometimes becoming victims of ichneumon wasps, previous item, which parasitize them. The adults live on nectar, and they are attracted to campfires.

### Sand wasp/digger wasp

*Ammophila* or *Podalonia* spp. (family Sphecidae)
May to August

Montane meadows, on bare earth; often seen digging in dusty trails. Body 15–20 mm long and all black, with clear wings; short thread-like waist identifies it as a wasp.

Interesting to watch; you can get quite close without disturbing it. The female digs quickly into bare soil, disappearing for a moment into the vertical burrow and then emerging. Usually she flies to another site and repeats the process. What she is doing is looking for the perfect spot in which to dig a deeper burrow, which will have a chamber at the end. She drags an immobilized insect (usually a caterpillar) to the chamber and lays an egg on it, then departs, sealing the entrance and also the fate of the prey, which is to become food for the larva.

## *Stings of bees, wasps and hornets*

To avoid getting stung, stay away from hives and nests, and don't run around barefoot in flowery meadows. A sting of this group is mildly venomous and thus feels fiery, although the pain subsides quickly, especially if the site is numbed with ice. Insect-bite ointment can reduce any follow-up itching. The wound will be tender for a day or two, and it may swell. If a honeybee stinger comes off in the skin, it should be removed.

You may be allergic to the venom and not know it until you are stung. The symptoms are rapid swelling at the site, general feeling of weakness and discomfort, and in severe cases an asthma-like restriction of the bronchial tubes that makes it hard to breathe. For some people, this airway blockage can be fatal if untreated. A simple allergy test by a doctor can determine whether you are allergic and to what degree. Very sensitive people carry medication to take after a sting.

# Ants (order Hymenoptera, family Formicidae)

Like wasps, ants have a bend in their antennae and a slender waist—a **pedicel**—between the thorax and abdomen.

## Red ants

*Formica* spp. (family Formicidae)
May to September

Montane and subalpine, southern and central sections, very common in dry lodgepole woods from Banff/Golden south, less so as one goes north. Several species, all similar: body length 5–10 mm, reddish-orange head and thorax, black abdomen.

The most common ants in the Canadian Rockies, red ants nest underground, building up extensive heaps of soil particles around the entrances. Red ants are aphid farmers (see item at bottom of page), finding aphids and stroking them to receive "honeydew," which is sweet stuff secreted from the aphid's anus. Sometimes red ants carry aphids to more convenient locations, but they don't take them underground. Red ants also eat enough other things—flower nectar, small insects, human food and garbage—to make a go of it nearly anywhere, which accounts for their success.

The life cycle is typical of ants. Each colony, which can number many thousands, has one queen. She stays underground in the complex nest, producing eggs. The larvae remain in the nest until they pupate and mature as one of two castes: workers, which are wingless sterile females, and winged reproductive females and males, which number only a few in each nest. The young reproductive females and males go on mating flights to other colonies, then the males die. Each mated female flies to a suitable site for a new nest, tears her own wings off and starts digging. She produces the first brood of larvae, feeding them herself until they pupate. They emerge as workers who will serve her for the rest of their lives. Red ants can bite. They also spray defensive **formic acid** into the wound, which causes a stinging sensation.

## Giant carpenter ant

*Camponotus herculeanus* (family Formicidae)
May to October

Montane and subalpine woods, on the ground or on dead wood. Very large ant, up to 20 mm long. Body looks black at first glance, but may actually be dark reddish brown. Antennae have elbows, as in all ants.

Carpenter ants make their nests in dead trees, both fallen or standing, chewing out long galleries. They don't eat the wood; they merely carry the sawdust outside and dump it. They eat fungi grown in their galleries, insects and anything sweet, which will draw them to your picnic. Despite their size, carpenter ants seldom bite; at least, they have never bitten me while exploring my body. But they'll bite hard if you grab them. Life cycle is similar to that of red ants, previous item.

# Aphids (order Homoptera, family Aphididae)

Aphids are very common on willows, roses, pea-family plants, aspen, poplar—you name it; it seems to have an aphid that eats it. There are thousands of species, all designed to do the same thing: suck the juice from the plant. Aphids are mostly quite small, 2–3 mm long, and wingless, although at one point in their complicated life-cycle winged females appear. Only the eggs overwinter, but each summer there are many generations, producing zillions of tasty, defenseless aphids that become staple foods of other insects and birds. Some aphid species coexist symbiotically with many species of ants, which practice agriculture on them. See the item on red ants, previous page.

## Beetles (order Coleoptera)

There are thousands of species of beetles in the Canadian Rockies—30,000 species in North America, 300,000 in the world—which are far too many to detail here. So I have written up just a few, very common ones, plus a couple that you may find interesting, common or not. If you want to know more about Rockies beetles, see "Further reading," page 477.

A beetle on the ground looks wingless, but it does have wings; two sets, in fact, like a butterfly. The forewings are called **elytra.** These are stiff and hard, running down the beetle's back and serving as covers for the hindwings underneath, which are clear and do the work of flying. What looks like a beetle's abdomen from above is actually the two elytra, closed and fitting together down the midline with the precision of Italian sports-car bodywork. When a beetle flies, the elytra open to the side while the hindwings buzz.

Beetle larvae are properly termed **grubs.** They look worm-like, but they have legs. Equipped with biting mouthparts, they chew plants, including the underbark of trees, or they attack prey. The grubs pupate, often in the ground or under tree bark, emerging as adults at various times through the spring and summer.

### Black ground beetles
(family Carabidae)
July to September

Montane and subalpine, often in moist woods under rocks or logs lying on the ground. The most common beetles in the mountains, probably because they are the most common beetles in North America: more than 3000 species, according to the Audubon guide. Black ground beetles are indeed black, and shiny. They are about 15 mm long, with many parallel grooves down the back, meaning on the wing covers. Mostly active at night, they sometimes venture out during the day, hunting busily for caterpillars; they like their food *soft.* Eggs laid in late summer soon hatch to larvae that overwinter in the ground, growing, pupating, and reaching the adult stage in midsummer.

### Ladybirds/ladybugs
(family Coccinellidae)
May to September

Montane, in woods and brushy places. There are many genera and species of these beetles in the Canadian Rockies, all pretty similar: small (about 5 mm long), with a black-and-white front end, rounded orange back with black spots, and black legs. Differences among species are reflected in the number of spots, which vary from 13 to none (all orange or all black) and in the pattern on the thorax.

The **nine-spotted ladybird** (*Coccinella novemnotata*) is perhaps the most common one in the mountains; we also have the **three-banded ladybird** (*C. trifasciata;* three black bands across the back) and two two-spotted versions (*Adalia bipunctata;* one spot on each side, and *A. frigida,* with two faint spots and a bar near the back). The **convergent ladybird** (*Hippodamia convergens*) is the 13-spotted one; it also has converging white stripes on the **pronotum,** the head-end.

Ladybirds eat mainly aphids, which are usually plentiful in the Canadian Rockies. These beetles are also prolific, producing several generations in the short mountain summer. Adults overwinter, snug below the snow under bark and leaves. The word "ladybird" comes from "Our Lady," an old European name for the beetles that honors their ability to keep the aphids under control in vineyards. Here in somewhat-colonial Canada, entomologists prefer the British "ladybird" to the American "ladybug."

## Black pine sawyer beetle

*Monochamus oregonensis* (family Cerambycidae)
July and August

Montane, in lodgepole pine woods. A large black beetle up to 30 mm long, instantly recognizable by the extremely long antennae on males; on females the antennae are only about half as long, and furry. These are gnawing insects. The female chews a hole into the bark of a lodgepole pine and deposits eggs there. The larvae eat inward, almost to the heartwood, then start back out, reaching the bark layer again a couple of years after starting, just as they are about to pupate. The emerging adults eat their way out through the bark, continuing to feed on bark as they seek mates.

## Engraver beetles

*Ips, Dendroctonus* and other genera (family Scolytidae)
July and August

Montane and subalpine forests. Small, 5–10 mm long, and black or brown, you may never see them, but they are very common, perhaps the leading killers of conifers. In midsummer the female tunnels under the bark of a pine, spruce or Douglas-fir, laying eggs. The larvae hatch in about two weeks. They excavate tunnels just under the bark, in the nutrient-rich cambium layer. Trees that have died from heavy infestations soon lose their bark, exposing the crisscrossing galleries that look like engravings on the wood. After overwintering under the bark, the larvae continue eating until June of the following year, when they pupate and emerge over the next two months as adults that have chewed their way out through the bark. Flying about the woods for a couple of weeks, they mate, reproduce and die.

The **mountain pine beetle** *(Dendroctonus ponderosae)* is a particularly well-known member of this family. In the late 1970s and early 1980s, a population explosion of mountain pine beetles in montane pine forests occurred south of Banff on the eastern slope and south of Valemount on the western slope. About half the lodgepole pine, and a good bit of ponderosa and western white pine, were killed south of Crowsnest Pass on the eastern slope and south of Golden on the western slope. Farther north, colder winter temperatures inhibited larval survival and limited the infestation.

The **Douglas-fir beetle,** *Dendroctonus pseudotsugae,* kills trees the same way its mountain-pine-beetle relative does, by chewing larval galleries at right angles to the nutrient flow under the bark. *D. pseudotsugae* can survive lower temperatures than *D. ponderosae.* Spreading northward from a population explosion in Colorado in the 1980s, the beetle is now common in British Columbia and has reached the northern limit of Douglas-fir in Alberta: Jasper National Park, where, sensibly, Parks Canada does not plan to fight it.

Why is this bug such a potent tree-killer?

The galleries of most engraver beetles tend to run up and down the trunk, the way the nutrient-bearing sap tubes (the **xylem** and **phloem** bundles) run. These galleries tend to fill with fungus behind the larvae, so the sap flow is diminished somewhat but not cut off. Thus, it takes a great number of larvae to kill a large tree—although small trees succumb rather easily, as do old trees that cannot drown the invaders in toxic **resin,** a defensive substance produced by conifers. The mountain pine beetle, on the other hand, chews galleries that go *around* the trunk, across the flow of sap. This interrupts the flow, introduces fungus and kills the tree.

We humans must blame ourselves for pine-beetle population booms. The bug does best in stands of old, mature lodgepoles, of which there are many in the Rockies, the result of 70 years of fighting forest fires.

But trying to stop the beetle is doomed to failure, rather like the ill-conceived spruce-budworm poisoning campaigns in New Brunswick. Years of costly, polluting aerial spraying there have served only to keep the

*Beetle-killed pine stands in Waterton Lakes National Park. Photo courtesy Parks Canada.*

budworm population from reaching its limit and crashing naturally back to pre-explosion levels. That crash would take a good bit of timber with it, which the forest industry of New Brunswick is unwilling to surrender to the bugs. Insecticide manufacturers are enthusiastic allies in this battle.

Something is going to destroy the unnaturally old pine stands of the Canadian Rockies, be it fire or disease. Rather than compound the harm by trying to intervene, we might as well let insect attacks run their boom-and-bust courses. The mountain pine beetle is unlikely to advance much farther north, for temperatures of -35°C to -40°C kill the overwintering larvae, and such temperatures are reached nearly every winter in central and northern regions. Further, genetic weakness due to excessive inbreeding tends to limit any exploding population.

With insect attacks comes something that the logging industry calls "salvage logging." Bug-killed trees, and to some extent fire-killed trees, can still be turned into lumber and paper, so loggers go into affected areas and clear-cut tracts of forest that would otherwise recover naturally by ecological succession. Often permits are given for "salvage logging" in environmentally sensitive places that would otherwise be off-limits to loggers. How strange: little insects that selectively and neatly kill only certain tree species, opening up the woods naturally, without removing the nutrients or damaging the soil, are used as an excuse by humans to wreck an entire ecosystem.

## *Grasshoppers and crickets (order Orthoptera)*

Orthopterans are not as common in the Canadian Rockies as they are to the south and east, in the grassland of the prairies, but we have a few species.

### Pallid-winged grasshopper
*Trimerotropis pallidipennis* (family Acrididae)
June to October

Montane, in dry, grassy places. Length 30–40 mm. A well-camouflaged beast, the pallid-winged grasshopper seems to disappear against the yellowish-brown foliage of late summer, the season when adults of this species are most common. Identify them by the two black bars across the white-to-yellow wings. They feed on wildflowers and grasses, mating in late fall and dying around Halloween in the first cold weather. Eggs laid in the soil overwinter, hatching in early June. The nymphs are small versions of the adults, but lack wings.

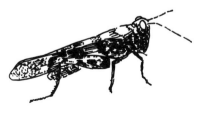

### Alpine grasshopper
*Melanoplus alpinus* (family Acrididae)
June to October

A montane species of low elevations despite its species name, found in dry, grassy places. Length 20–25 mm. Gray to yellowish-brown and shiny, as if the parts were made of plastic. There are black V-shaped markings on the back legs, the lower parts of which are blue with black spines. This grasshopper eats grasses and has a life cycle like that of the pallid-winged grasshopper, previous item.

### Field cricket
*Gryllus pennsylvanicus* (family Gryllidae)
June to October

Montane, in woods or moist stony places, seen mainly at night. Length 15–25 mm, black. Grasshopper-like, but more compact and with long antennae. Two spine-like, harmless **cerci** (sensors) stick out the back. Females also have a prominent ovipositor positioned between the cerci. A male is illustrated. Hiding by day in thick foliage and under rocks, crickets emerge at dusk to feed on seeds, plant fruits, young growing plants or dead insects.

This species sings by **stridulating:** rubbing the rows of raised veins at the root of one wing against a similar organ on the other wing. The sound is amazingly loud for a creature so small.

The adults die at the first heavy frost; eggs laid in soil overwinter. The nymphs, which look like tiny adults, emerge in early June and grow steadily through the summer to maturity in August. You may find adults and immatures in your basement when September rolls around, hoping to spend the winter with you.

## Cicadas (order Homoptera)

Cicadas make themselves known in July, in montane woods, where they cling to trees, sometimes to shrubs or wildflowers. You will hear these insects before you see them; they make a loud, continuous buzzing that is unmistakable. Finding the cicadas themselves, which are large (20–30 mm long), is surprisingly difficult. They hold very still, and they are often the color of the bark they sit on.

Our cicadas are mostly *Okanagana* and *Platypedia* species, greenish or brownish and quite fat, with large eyes and large clear wings. Often what one finds is the empty shell of the nymph stage, which looks a lot like the adult but lacks wings.

The life cycle is interesting. Eggs are forced into tree bark in late summer by the female's strong ovipositer. They soon hatch, the nymphs dropping to the ground right away to burrow down among the tree roots, which they eat for one to three years (some eastern species spend as long as 17 years underground) before emerging in midsummer to shed their exoskeletons and fly about on new wings. Finding trees of the right species, they sing loudly, attracting mates. Most species don't eat anything in the adult stage; rather, they are eaten themselves by birds and small mammals, for whom the annual cicada banquet must be a highlight of summer.

## Thrips (order Thysanoptera)

Have you ever looked at a flower closely and noticed dark-colored bugs only a millimetre or two long crawling around in it? Those were probably thrips, the singular of which is also "thrips." There are many groups; the ones that people notice are usually adults of the banded-thrips family (the Aeolothripidae). Eggs inserted into plant tissues hatch as wingless nymphs, which look much like small adults and prey on aphids, mites and other tiny plant-eating insects. The nymphs overwinter in the soil and emerge as adults to gather in flowers for mating. They often arch their abdomens up as they move.

## Ticks (class Arachnida, order Acarina)

Placed in the same class as spiders, but in their own order, ticks are not insects. Most of the ticks in the Rockies are small and seldom noticed by humans, although they parasitize most birds and mammals. One species, described below, is particularly troublesome for humans as well as for wildlife.

### Rocky Mountain wood tick
*Dermacentor andersoni* (family Ixodidae)
Usually seen from April to June, but present year round

Montane, as far north as Grande Cache on the eastern slope and perhaps farther on the western slope, common in grassy places frequented by small mammals such as ground squirrels. There are other species of ticks in the Rockies, but this one is of particular interest to humans because it can parasitize us.

A wood tick looks like a little flat spider: triangular body about 5 mm long, with eight legs. It is in the same class as the spiders, but in a different order, which also includes the mites. Female is reddish brown with a white patch behind the head; male is reddish brown with gray mottling. Ticks move slowly, one leg at a time. They are easy to grab and they cannot sting. If you are in the Rockies in the spring, you may have occasion to do some grabbing.

Adult ticks and near-adults climb up grasses and other low-growing plants in the spring, hanging on with two legs while leaving the other six extended. Hooks on the ends catch in the hair of any passing animal—or on the pantlegs of certain kinds of passing animals. Note that ticks do not drop out of trees; they climb only a few centimetres. They also crawl toward their would-be hosts, attracted by exhaled carbon dioxide and perhaps other metabolic byproducts.

Once on the host, the tick then climbs higher, seeking tender skin that can be penetrated easily by its mouthparts. These are inserted very gradually, so the host doesn't notice.

Note that only the mouthparts go into the skin. The rest of the tick, including the tiny head, stays outside. The notion of Rocky Mountain wood ticks burrowing under the skin is false.

The tick begins to feed, taking in blood under capillary pressure and injecting an anti-clotting agent to keep the blood flowing. As it feeds, the tick's body swells. Mated females bloat to many times their unfed size, looking like large gray kernels of corn when full; males take much less blood and swell only a little.

If immature, the tick then drops off, grows a bit, molts (splits out of its exoskeleton, which has become too small), and in so doing reaches maturity. It then finds another host on which to take one more meal and look for a mate.

After mating, the male dies. Mated females drop off and lay masses of 5000–10,000 eggs under rocks, leaves or logs. The eggs overwinter, hatching in June and July. The tiny larvae are also parasites; they feed on blood from small rodents. Then they metamorphose to nymphs (the immature stage mentioned in the previous paragraph), which can become adults that same summer if more blood is obtained; if not, the nymphs overwinter under the snow and emerge in early spring as adults, ready to renew the cycle.

Amazingly, an adult tick can remain unfed for up to three years before it expires.

Ticks are seen often in the Canadian Rockies from early April to early June, when the elk are crawling with them and hikers resting in spring-green meadows are picking them up without knowing it. Not to worry (yet); ticks don't attach right away. Like the camper seeking the best site in the campground, a tick walks slowly over a human host for several hours before settling down to feed.

Elk, moose and other large mammals may carry thousands of wood ticks. This is possible because large mammals frequent the same places year after year, lying about in swarms of well-fed parasites. Humans sometimes sit or lie in these same places; grassy clearings in the woods are particularly inviting spots for lunch and a snooze or a bit of lovemaking. It happens often: the amorous couple, oblivious to the hordes of ticks closing in, jump up in panic when they see several crawling on them. "Eeeeeee! Ernie, get it *off* me!"

A tick remains on its host for at least a couple of days and sometimes a week or more. The wound left by a tick after it drops off is small and soon heals, but ticks can do you harm in other ways.

For example, compounds in the anti-clotting fluid injected to keep the blood flowing are toxic to the human nervous system, and a tick left on the back of the neck for several days sometimes causes bizarre symptoms as the toxin affects the upper spinal cord and brain: numbness in arms and legs, loss of coordination, drowsiness and personality changes. Yikes! All this from a bug smaller than the tip of your little finger.

That is not all. The symptoms above clear up within a few hours after the tick is removed, but ticks on the eastern slope of the Rockies can also carry a nasty disease that, if you get it, will wreck your summer at the very least and may possibly kill you. This is **Rocky Mountain spotted fever,** also called **tick fever.*** The cause is *Rickettsia rickettsii,* a tiny organism that falls phylogenetically between the viruses and the bacteria. A small percentage of the ticks in the mountains carry these rickettsiae in their bodies, transferring them to humans through the mouthparts. The females are on the body longer than the males and thus are more likely to infect the host. Other mammals seem unaffected.

Infection begins a few hours after feeding starts. Three to 12 days later the symptoms come on suddenly: severe headache, chills and muscular pain. You definitely know that you are sick. Fever begins, reaching 39.5–40°C by the second day and remaining high for as long as two weeks. A cough develops, followed on the fourth day of fever by a rash that appears on wrists, ankles, palms, soles of feet and forearms, spreading to neck and face, rear end and trunk. The rash gets nasty, becoming infected-looking. If untreated, the disease goes on to delirium, coma, brain and heart damage, and death in about 25 percent of cases.

Treatment is by the antibiotics tetracycline or chloramphenicol; the idea is to get to the doctor fast if you find a well-attached tick on your body and start showing the symptoms above. Even when treated early, tick fever hangs on for a long time, leaving you feeling run-down for weeks. Children living in Rocky Mountain communities are most commonly struck; they are outdoors a lot in spring, often on the ground, and they don't notice the beasties. Their parents had better.

Insect repellents that contain at least 40 percent DEET (check the label) will keep ticks away. If you know you are going to be passing through tick-infested places, a bit of repellent applied around the ankles and lower pantlegs will discourage hangers-on. However, you would have to bathe in the stuff to really ensure protection, so inspection for ticks each evening is still required. I don't bother with repellents, except when the mosquitoes are utterly maddening. Once-a-day tick-picking is quick and easy, avoids the use of chemicals, with their attendant odor and plastic-eating properties, and thus is almost certainly healthier as well as more convenient.

---

*****Lyme disease** is unreported in the Canadian Rockies at time of writing but may appear soon. A long-term, debilitating disease of the joints and nervous system, it is caused by the bacterium *Borrelia burgdorferi.* The organism is usually transmitted by pinhead-sized **deer ticks** of the genus *Ixodes,* but it has also been found in other species. Mice and white-tailed deer carry ticks associated with Lyme disease. White-tailed deer are increasing in numbers in the Rockies; see page 646 for the reason.

*If the tick has attached,* remove it by pulling *gently and steadily.* Unless the tick is well-glued-on, mouthparts firmly imbedded, it will come off intact. Folk remedies such as burning the tick's rear with a match or lighted cigarette, or pouring gasoline or whiskey on it, serve only to kill the tick while it is still hooked in. But applying a little DEET repellent may encourage the tick to let go.

If the mouthparts stay in the wound, they should be removed. Tease them out with a flamed needle or knifeblade. Then wash the wound well with soap and sterilize it with antiseptic if you have any. A bit of that whiskey will do.

See also the winter tick (afflicts elk, not humans), page 647.

## *Pick that tick before it sticks*

Each day you are out in the mountains during April and May, strip down before supper and check yourself over well, especially in your hair (and in other hairy places). Ticks often go for the nape of the neck or behind the ears, where there is plenty of hair and the skin is thin. They will also attach beneath a belt or brassiere strap, or under the elastic band in your underwear—anywhere that clothes fit tightly, which may help a tick to dig in on our sparsely haired bodies. Get somebody to look at your back.

In the late afternoon, any ticks you picked up during the day will probably still be crawling around. Grab them and either flush them down the toilet or burn them up. They are hard and flat, difficult to squash, and people have contracted tick fever by handling crushed ticks. If you are camping, you must kill every one you find; any let go alive around a campsite will make their way back to you.

Check your pets, too. On dogs, wood ticks usually wind up behind the ears and under the collar. Cats don't seem to get them.

Dermacentor andersoni *looking for a campsite. Photo courtesy Jasper National Park.*

# Spiders (class Arachnida, order Araneae)

Spiders, like ticks, have eight legs, so they are not insects. They live in every habitat, from valley-floor marshes to alpine boulderfields, and not all of them spin webs to obtain their food.

Large, hairy spiders such as the tarantula do not live in the Canadian Rockies. Neither do any dangerously poisonous ones, such as the black widow or the brown recluse—although you never know what will turn up in your basement or heated garage. Eggs imported from south of the border can hatch anywhere warm enough.

## Branch-tip spiders

*Dictyna annulipes* (family Dictynidae)
April to October

Montane woods. If you have ever walked along a mountain trail in the morning, then I'll bet you've brushed through dozens of straggly, nearly invisible webs produced by this very common, harmless little spider. By afternoon most of the webs have been ripped down by passing animals and birds. They will be rebuilt that evening.

The branch-tip spider's body is only a few millimetres long, buffy brown all over with a tiny **cephalothorax** (in spiders the head and thorax are combined), longish legs and round abdomen marked on top by a series of nested brown "W"s. The female hangs her white egg-case in the web, which is why you may find odd little white balls on your pants and shirt after a day in the woods. The spiderlings mature by fall and overwinter under the snow.

## American house spider

*Achaearanea tepidariorum* (family Theridiidae)
All year, indoors

In houses, barns, garages—any sheltered places, for these spiders do not like the outdoors. Small and harmless, they are yellowish brown, the round abdomen much bigger than the head and decorated with brown, black and white squiggles. Males have orange legs, females black-banded yellow ones. Both sexes produce irregular webs in the corners of windows and ceilings, catching bugs that might otherwise annoy the human occupants. The female hangs little brown pear-shaped egg cases in her web, from which spiderlings venture. She may live more than one year.

House spiders are very tolerant of humans. If you are tolerant of them as well, you will find them interesting to watch—as my whole family did one year.

Our house spider would run over to a struggling fly stuck in the web (or placed there by my children, heh heh), sting the fly a couple of times to paralyze it, then wrap it up in a bit of silk. Retiring to a corner of the web, the spider would wait a few minutes for the fly to liquefy inside, another nice property of spider venom. Then it would tenderly hold the fly, piercing it with its mouthparts at various points to suck up what my wife referred to as a "fly shake."

We thought it impolite of our spider to merely toss the empties onto the window-ledge when it was finished with them, although leaving the fly-shells in the web was kind of ugly, too, so occasionally we would clean up the mess.

## Long-jawed orb weaver

*Tetragnatha* spp. (family Tetragnathidae)
June to September

In tall grass and shrubs along streams or other water bodies. Easily identified by the skinny abdomen, up to 10 mm long and pale yellowish green or silvery with a few black dots. This spider keeps its long, nearly transparent legs bundled together ahead of it and behind it, as if it were living in a straw. It builds a web for catching small insects; when disturbed, it drops out and runs away.

### Goldenrod spider
*Misumena vatia* (family Thomisidae)
May to September

Found hiding in yellow or white flowers, or among green leaves. I have noticed it only at montane elevations. Fairly small (body less than 10 mm long), this member of the crab-spider family matches its color to that of its shelter, so it varies from pale white or greenish to bright yellow. Always, though, there will be a red stripe on each side of the abdomen. The spider waits, legs folded, until a small insect visits the flower or plant in which it hides.

Then, zap! It grabs, bites and eats. Check the photo on page 434.

### Wolf spiders
*Pardosa* spp. (family Lycosidae)
May to September

Common in montane woods, where they poke about on the forest floor or beside streams; also common among talus and scree at any elevation. Body 10–15 mm long, grayish brown with a ragged gray stripe along the front part and moderately long brown legs. Females are bigger than males.

Often seen in the daytime, wolf spiders are even more active at night. They have good eyesight for a spider: a few inches. They move quickly and pounce on insect prey rather than spinning a web, although they use a lifeline of silk to catch themselves when they fall. There is no nest. Females carry around a white egg-case attached to the abdomen; when the spiderlings hatch they ride on mum's back, subsisting on their yolk-sacs until they drop off a few weeks later to go their own ways and begin eating. Wolf spiders overwinter under the snow, in pine needles and other litter.

### Jumping spiders
*Phidippus* spp. (family Salticidae)
June and July

Fairly common in dry montane places, often seen along dusty trails. Not large; 5–10 mm long. The immatures are easily spotted by their quick movements and bright red or reddish-orange coloration with lovely iridescent green mouthparts. The legs are short and black. The adults are drably black and gray, much more difficult to see.

Jumping spiders do just that when hunting (or being hunted); they have the best vision of any spider, which you can test by bringing a finger toward one and finding the distance at which it takes notice. *Phidippus* lives in a little silken nest under a stone, fallen branch or leaf. It may move in with you; is harmless.

### Boulderfield spider
*Aculepeira carbonarioides* (family Araneidae)
July to September

Common on alpine talus slopes, this member of the garden-spider family is fairly large, with a dark-colored body and light-and-dark-banded legs. It makes a very strong, wind-resistant web that typically has two thick white strands strung between boulders. The spider sits in the centre, and it drops like a rock when disturbed.

## Harvesters/daddy-long-legs

*Phalangium* and *Leiobunum* spp. (order Opiliones, family Phalangiidae) June to October

Montane, common on trees or on the ground, often sunning themselves low down on south-facing building sides. Small, round brown bodies (4–8 mm) and eight very long, extremely skinny brown legs.

Harvesters look like spiders but are not; they are in a separate order. They have only two eyes, rather than the eight (more or less) of true spiders. *Phalangium*'s eyes are stuck on a tiny black bump on the harvester's head, while *Leiobunum*'s eyes are mounted low and in front. The latter is a little larger than the former, and a little lighter in color.

Harvesters eat small bugs, decaying stuff and plant juices. They don't produce silk. After mating in late summer, the female lays eggs in the soil; they overwinter and the young emerge next spring, very tiny at first, becoming large enough to notice in June—for *Phalangium;* the young of *Leiobunum* show up about a month later. Most adults cannot survive the Canadian Rockies winter, but they try to hibernate en masse. I know of one overwintering spot: a small chamber at the back of a short limestone cave along the Maligne River. The entrance is small, and when I crawled in and stood up I was nose-to-spider with patches of clustered harvesters on the walls.

*Hibernating harvesters*

# *Butterflies, skippers and moths*
## "The butterfly in the light-laden air ..." —Richard Jefferies, 1883

Somehow, butterflies are *not* bugs. We say "Oh, look, John—there's a blue butterfly sitting on your shoulder!" Not "John, look out—there's some kind of icky *bug* on your shoulder!"

Butterflies are not icky; to human eyes they are the most beautiful of the insects. Better yet, they are harmless. Thus we refrain from harming *them*—except when they are in the larval stage, as caterpillars. These we squash and poison just as fiercely as we do anything else that strikes us as ugly or alien.

Moths are, well, not as attractive as butterflies. Mostly drab-looking night-flyers, they are inclined as larvae to eat up the crops and make holes in our clothes. They are *almost* bugs.

Between the moths and the butterflies there are the skippers, looking rather like each group.

The life cycle of all these creatures is in four stages: egg, caterpillar, **chrysalis** (pupa: the insect motionless inside a case, undergoing metamorphosis), and adult butterfly, skipper or moth. In most species the cycle lasts one year. The caterpillar feeds mostly on leaves—the "host plants" mentioned in the descriptions below—while the adults either feed on flower nectar or don't eat at all. Except for a few species that overwinter as adults, they fly about for a couple of weeks, mate, produce eggs and die.

Butterflies have a way of moving on just as you get close enough to identify them, so binoculars are useful for watching butterflies as well as for watching birds. I think it's better to enjoy butterflies from a distance, which doesn't harm them, rather than capturing them.

## Butterflies (order Lepidoptera)

There are some 90 species of butterflies known from the Canadian Rockies. Here are a few common and easily identifiable ones.

### Mourning cloak

*Nymphalis antiopa*
(brush-foot family, Papilionidae)
April and May, again in early autumn
    Common in montane aspen/poplar woods and adjoining meadows. Host plants: willows, aspen, balsam poplar. A large butterfly (75–85 mm), easily recognized by the gold margin on the dark-brown, velvety wings. Note also the line of deep blue or purple dots, the rough wing edges and the stubby tail on the hindwing. Underneath, the wings are woody-looking with a whitish border. Listen to this butterfly as it leaves its perch; you may hear it make a clicking sound.
    Mourning cloaks overwinter as adults, which explains why they are the first butterflies you see in spring and the last in fall.

*Nymphalis antiopa*

### Faunus anglewing

*Polygonia faunus*
(brush-foot family, Papilionidae)
April to September
    Common in montane woods. Caterpillar feeds on willows, birch, alder and currant. Wingspan 45–55 mm. Like the mourning cloak, the adult faunus anglewing overwinters, so you see it early in the spring. Orange and black like the fritillaries, page 466, but the pattern is less complicated and the trailing edges of the wings are scalloped.

*Polygonia faunus*

### Milbert's tortoiseshell

*Aglais milberti*
(brush-foot family, Papilionidae)
April to October
    At all elevations, in any habitat. Host plants: nettles. Wingspan 45–50 mm. Milbert's tortoiseshell has an unmistakable yellow-and-orange band along the wing. The rest is dark brown, except for reddish-orange bars along the leading edge, a small white crescent near the wingtip and bluish flecks along the irregular trailing edge. Underneath, the wings are drab brown with a lighter zone under the bright topside band.

*Aglais milberti*

# White admiral

*Limenitis arthemis*
(brush-foot family, Nymphalidae)
June to September

Common in and bordering aspen and poplar groves. Host plants: birch, willow, poplar and aspen. Large (75–80 mm), black except for a broad white band across the wings, both above and below. Note also the red spots behind the band, and the blue crescents along the trailing edge.

Watch for the **red admiral,** *Vanessa atalanta,* which is the only butterfly in the region with a broad red band on the wings.

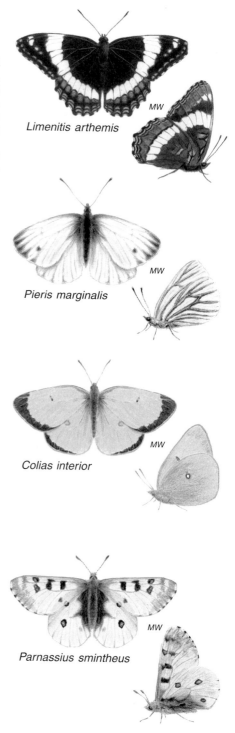

*Limenitis arthemis*

# Veined white

*Pieris marginalis*
(whites/sulphurs family, Pieridae)
April to August

Montane and subalpine, in shady, damp places. Seeks mustard-family wildflowers such as rock-cress. Small, 30–40 mm. Black body, white wings with a bit of black along edges. Males often have one black spot on each fore-wing; females, two. Wings white underneath, hindwing with brown or greenish veins that are heavy in northern populations and often un-noticeable in southern ones. Similar **cabbage white,** *Pieris rapae,* has yellow patches be-neath hindwing and no veining. Veined white is also known as *Artogeia napi.*

*Pieris marginalis*

# Pink-edged sulphur

*Colias interior*
(whites/sulphurs family, Pieridae)
June to September

Eastern slope, in montane and subalpine meadows, often found on asters, although the host plants for the caterpillars are blueberries. There are at least nine other species of sulphurs in the Rockies.

*Colias interior*

# Phoebus parnassian

*Parnassius smintheus*
(swallowtail family, Papilionidae)
June to September

Eastern-slope, found only where stonecrop *(Sedum* spp.) grows, in open, meadowy places at all elevations. A large (55–75 mm) white, dusky or transparent-looking butterfly. Note black markings at the wingtips and red markings in a bar along the leading edge. Red also in a black-edged circle on the hindwing and in three spots underneath. Males are less transparent-

*Parnassius smintheus*

looking than females. Species is smaller and darker at higher elevations. Also known as *Parnassius phoebus.*

## Canadian tiger swallowtail

*Papilio canadensis*
(swallowtail family, Papilionidae)
May to October

Moist montane woods and meadows; host plants are willows, aspen, balsam poplar and birches. Can be quite large, up to 140 mm, but in the Canadian Rockies usually 80–90 mm. Lots of yellow showing, with black trailing edge and black stripes, two of which intersect at the back to form a vee. Bit of red at the back. Underneath, the hindwing has red and blue spots along the trailing edge, which differentiate the Canadian tiger swallowtail from the **western tiger swallowtail,** *Pterourus rutulus,* which has red only between the tails.

*Papilio canadensis*

## Northern blue

*Lycaeides idas*
(gossamer-wings family, Lycaenidae)
June to August

Subalpine and alpine, often around sub-alpine bogs with host plants laurel, labrador tea and crowberry. Span 20–30 mm. Males blue with black margin, plus a row of vague black dots on the hindwing, and silvery fringe; females brown with orange dots next to the fringe. Below, both sexes are buffy gray with numerous white-rimmed spots and a line of interesting black-orange-black bars along the wing edge. Also known as *Lycaeides argyrognomon.*

*Lycaeides idas*

## Mariposa copper/Reakirt's copper

*Lycaena mariposa*
(gossamer-wings family, Lycaenidae)
June to September

Southern and central montane and subal-pine, near bogs, ponds and in other damp places. Caterpillar may feed on knotweed. Wingspan 25–30 mm. Male is illustrated; or-ange with brown wing margins and black spots on forewing; hindwing sooty orange with row of black crescents at the rear and white fringe. Female very dark, with bright orange spots. Underneath, forewing of both sexes is similar to upper surface, orange and black, but female hindwing is sooty/silvery. Also known as *Epidemia mariposa.*

*Lycaena mariposa*

## Anicia checkerspot

*Euphydryas anicia*
(brush-foot family, Nymphalidae)
May to September

At all elevations, but most common in dry montane meadows and woods. Host plants are mainly paintbrush and penstemons. Wingspan 30–50 mm. Confusingly variable topside, but more uniform below: three bands of white on the orange hindwing, with black netting and an orange margin. Also known as *Occidryas anicia.*

*Euphydryas anicia*

## Field crescentspot

*Phyciodes campestris*
(brush-foot family, Nymphalidae)
June to August

In subalpine and alpine meadows; caterpillar eats asters. Wingspan only 30–35 mm, smaller than the checkerspots. Identify by the dotted row of orange spots on the upper hindwing. Otherwise checkered pale-yellow and dark brown (often black in the Canadian Rockies.) Underneath, the wings are patterned in varying shades of burnt orange.

*Phyciodes campestris*

## Titania's fritillary

*Boloria chariclea*
(brush-foot family, Nymphalidae)
June to September

Common butterfly, found nearly anywhere at montane and subalpine elevations. Host plants are willows and bistort. Boldly marked but small (30–45 mm). On the underside, the hindwing is diagnostic: purplish or reddish and densely patterned, with several pairs of pale yellow opposed black chevrons bordered in yellow or white, making interesting, X-like figures. Also known as *Clossiana titania.*

*Boloria chariclea*

## Chryxus arctic

*Oeneis chryxus* (satyr family, Satyridae)
May to August

In pine forest and small clearings, mostly northern but found throughout the mountains. Host plants: grasses. Wingspan 45–50 mm. Topside, the pattern is a brown yoke with an orange zone near the trailing edges, which are marked by black dots and a dark border. Underneath there is a jagged band crossing the hindwing, plus an eyespot.

*Oeneis chryxus*

## Common alpine

*Erebia epipsodea* (satyr family, Satyridae)
June to August

At all elevations, in damp meadows or boggy places. Host plants: grasses. Wingspan 45–55 mm. A distinctive butterfly, mostly drab brown, but with orange patches near the wing margins and white-dotted black eyespots in the orange. Lower wing surfaces are likewise drab, although the forewing is orangey, with repeated eyespots.

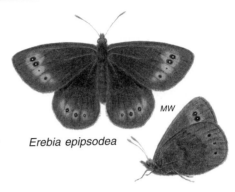

*Erebia epipsodea*

# Skippers (order Lepidoptera, family Hesperiidae)

What was that? Looked like a moth, sort of. More like a butterfly, but the wings seemed too small for the body. Aha—it was a skipper.

Skippers are furry-looking and drably colored, like moths. Yet, unlike most moths they are active in the daytime, and their bodies are much more butterfly-like than moth-like. A reliable way to differentiate between moths and skippers is to check the antennae: thickened and hooked at the end in skippers, whip-like or furry in moths.

The name "skipper" comes from the way these things fly: quickly, darting up and down.

## Common branded skipper

*Hesperia comma*
(skippers family, Hesperiidae)
June to August

Alpine and subalpine meadows. Host plants: grasses. Wingspan 20–25 mm. Streaky orange and black on top. Underneath, the wings are burnt-orange to brown with unconnected angular white spots that are well defined.

## Arctic skipper

*Carterocephalus palaemon*
(skippers family, Hesperiidae)
June and July

Central and southern subalpine streams, bogs, meadows and forests. Not usually alpine, despite the name. Host plant: reedgrass. Wingspan 20–30 mm. Orange and black, rather like a fritillary, see previous page, but with smaller wings relative to body size.

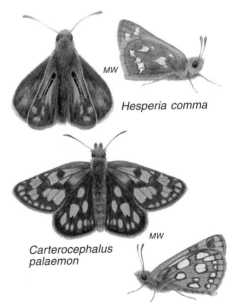

*Hesperia comma*

*Carterocephalus palaemon*

# Moths (order Lepidoptera, various families)

There are far more moth species in the Rockies than butterfly species, but moths are generally small and drab, fly mainly at night and thus are not noticed as much by humans, who are mostly daytime seekers of the bright and beautiful. Still, moths have a soft beauty all their own.

Given a rather drab butterfly, a skipper and a moth, pick out the moth by the way it holds its wings when not flying: usually folded down over its back, tent-like, rather than folded upward or spread out. Note also the antennae, which are commonly whip-like or very furry, not thickened at the ends like those of skippers or true butterflies.

### Acraea moth
*Estigmene acraea*
(tiger-moth family, Arctiidae)
June and July

In open areas at low elevations. Host plants: poplar, choke cherry, alder, wildflowers. Wingspan 45–50 mm. Forewing mostly white, spotted with contrasting black markings; hindwing yellow in male and white in female. Black legs, and black antennae that are comb-like under a magnifying glass.

*Estigmene acraea*

### Meal moth
*Pyralis farinalis* (pyralid family, Pyralidae)
Anytime indoors; summer outdoors

At low elevations, around dwellings, but also in the wild. Caterpillar eats mostly grain, especially the processed grains humans eat. Very small, wingspan 15–25 mm, but fairly easy to identify: V-shaped at rest, rusty brown with creamy shoulders.

*Pyralis farinalis*

### Forest tent caterpillar moth
*Malacosoma* sp.
(tent-caterpillar family, Lasiocampidae)
June and July

Montane, in aspen or balsam poplar groves. The caterpillar, page 472, is a voracious eater of aspen and poplar leaves. The adult is 30–40 mm across and pale brown, lightly furry all over, with darker oblique bands near the middle of the forewing. The wings are held loosely spread, although drooping in typical moth fashion.

*Malacosoma*

### White-marked tussock moth
*Orgyia leucostigmata*
(tussock-moth family, Lymantriidae)
May to September

Eastern slope, in aspen or mixed woods. Common small moth, wingspan 30–35 mm, woody looking, with zones of brown across the wings. The male has big, feathery antennae; the wingless female is smaller, with whip-like ones.

*Orgyia leucostigmata*

*An underwing moth (Catocala sp., family Noctuidae) on a Douglas-fir. It hopes, with some justification, that you haven't noticed it. Photograph by Barry Giles.*

## Big poplar sphinx
*Pachysphinx modesta*
(sphinx-moth family, Sphingidae)
May to August

Active at night in montane aspen groves and mixed aspen/pine woods. An enormous moth—wingspan 90–140 mm—readily identifiable by its size and simple color pattern: light brown across the head and forward part of the wings, chocolate brown in a band farther back, and mottled brown toward the trailing edges. In the middle band there is a small white crescent on the forewing.

*Pachysphinx modesta*    MW

## Cerisy's sphinx/eyed hawk-moth
*Smerinthus cerisyi*
(sphinx-moth family, Sphingidae)
May and June

Montane and subalpine, near water and often in willow thickets. Host plants: willows and poplars. A large moth, wingspan 60–85 mm, with a very distinctive eyespot on the hindwing. The forewing pattern varies.

*Smerinthus cerisyi*    MW

## Thetis clearwing/bee hawk-moth
*Hemaris thetis*
(sphinx-moth family, Sphingidae)
July and August

In montane forest clearings, southern and central regions, flying by day. Wingspan 30–35 mm. Mimics a bumble bee: yellow and black, complete with transparent sections in the wings. But note the rusty color near the wing-roots, the tiny head and elbow-less antennae; these show that it isn't a bee at all. Harmless. The caterpillar eats several montane plant species: snowberry, honeysuckle, lowbush cranberry and hawthorn.

Another member of this genus is the **hummingbird moth,** *Hemaris thysbe.* With its green head and reddish abdomen, it looks very much like a small hummingbird.

*Hemaris thetis*

## Parthenice moth
*Apantesis parthenice*
(tiger-moth family, Arctiidae)
May to August

Montane. This is the family of the woolly bear caterpillar, very familiar as a larva but less so in the adult form. Wingspan 20–30 mm. Black-on-tan pattern on the wings, showing orange when opened.

*Apantesis parthenice*    MW

# Caterpillars (order Lepidoptera)

A caterpillar is not a worm; it is the larval stage of a butterfly or moth. Worms are all grown up just the way they are. Caterpillars, unlike their attractive adult forms, evoke in humans such responses as "yuck," or "don't touch it!" This is partly sensible; there are many poisonous caterpillars in the world, and lots of prickly ones.

To tell a caterpillar from any other insect larva, check the legs. With few exceptions, there will be three pairs of real legs on the front end and up to five pairs of knob-like **prolegs** farther back.

A caterpillar is all business. Typically hatching from eggs that have overwintered, the larva must eat its way through many times its body weight in very specific plants before it is time to spin a shell around itself—the chrysalis, or pupa—and emerge as a winged adult, whose job it is to find a mate, lay eggs and die. A few species overwinter.

Here are some common, easily identified Canadian Rockies caterpillars. The sizes given are maximums, for caterpillars grow steadily larger until they pupate.

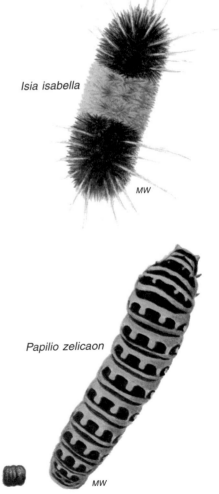

## Woolly bear caterpillar
*Isia isabella* (tiger-moth family, Arctiidae)
August and September

Mostly montane, often around dwellings, but can be found even at alpine elevations. Eats mostly willows. Maximum length 50 mm. This must be the best-known caterpillar in North America; it occurs everywhere at summer's end. Black, with a reddish band in the middle, and very furry. Like some other brightly marked caterpillars, this one is toxic to birds. Amazing caterpillar facts: the woolly bear lives in the Arctic, where it can take up to 14 years to reach pupation. Survives temperatures of -70°C, the cytoplasm in the cells remaining unfrozen due to the large amount of glycerol antifreeze the thing generates.

But does a small red band mean a hard winter and a large red band a mild one, as folklore has it? According to the Audubon guide, a small reddish band means that the caterpillar is not mature yet. And does a large crop of woolly bears tally with a rough winter ahead? Not necessarily, although it does mean that the little darlings had a good summer.

*Isia isabella*

MW

## Anise swallowtail caterpillar
*Papilio zelicaon*
(swallowtail family, Papilionidae)
June and July

Subalpine and montane, feeding mostly on cow parsnip. Length 50 mm. Smooth and green, with fancy yellow-and-black stripes. When very young, the caterpillars resemble bird droppings.

*Papilio zelicaon*

*Papilio zelicaon*
Droppings

MW

## Forest tent caterpillar

*Malacosoma* spp.
(tent-caterpillar family, Lasiocampidae)
May to July

Montane, in groves of aspen, balsam poplar and white birch. Maximum length 50 mm. Body dark brown with blue sides and white or yellowish spots along the top; long white hairs sprout from the sides. Appearing in early spring, the caterpillars produce tent-like silky mats in the trees.

Forest tent caterpillars indulge in cyclic population explosions. They can become so numerous that one can't help but walk on them; they denude entire trees, which leads acreage owners to douse the caterpillars with pesticide. This is unnecessary—most trees recover from losing all their leaves—and it is ill advised, for it has the paradoxical effect of delaying the peak of the caterpillar boom. Instead of getting the inevitable population crash, followed by several years of low numbers, the chemical warrior has to fight the caterpillars in large numbers every year. Meanwhile the toxic residues accumulate.

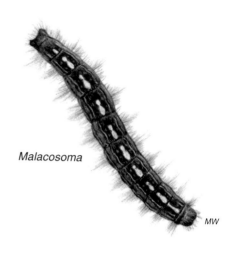

*Malacosoma*

MW

For a view of the adult moth, see page 468.

## Western hemlock looper

*Lambdina fiscellaria*
(looper/inch-worm family, Geometridae)
Late May to August

Columbian forest, mainly in western hemlock but also in other conifers during population explosions, such as the one that occurred from 1991 to 1994 in the Rocky Mountain Trench between McBride and Prince George, killing about half the hemlock there. Maximum caterpillar length 35 mm. Body beige/gray, with brown to black markings. Adult is small and brown.

*Lambdina fiscellaria*

MW

This is just one of a very large family, all of which move by grasping with the front legs, hunching the body upward—"looping"—to bring the back end to the front, then letting go with the front legs and reaching forward to the next hold. When threatened, the larvae of many looper species hold themselves straight out from the branch, mimicking small twigs. They also hang from silken threads like the leaf miners, next item.

## Leaf miners and leaf-blotch miners
(families Lyonetiidae and Gracilariidae)
July

Widespread group of small larvae that chew sinuous tracks in leaves, such as the "mined" aspen leaf illustrated. ("Hot diggety! A really massive chlorophyll vein!") The birch-leaf miner is my favorite; it hangs from trees by silken threads, each strand having either a caterpillar on the end or crawling up a strand affixed to the ground. Hundreds from the same tree; very decorative.

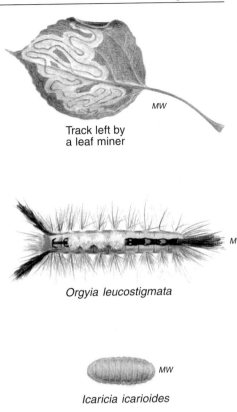

MW

Track left by
a leaf miner

## White-marked tussock-moth caterpillar
*Orgyia leucostigmata*
(tussock-moth family, Lymantriidae)
June and July

Eastern slope montane. Maximum length 35 mm. Another long-haired caterpillar. Yellow body with a black top line set with red dots; the head is brilliantly red. It eats the leaves of many kinds of deciduous trees and shrubs.

ML

*Orgyia leucostigmata*

## Common blue caterpillar
*Icaricia icarioides*
(gossamer-wings family, Lycaenidae)
June and July

Subalpine, mainly on lupines. Tiny, stubby caterpillars only 10 mm long, green with many short hairs and diagonal markings. Well-disguised; see if you can find one.

MW

*Icaricia icarioides*

## Cabbage white caterpillar
*Pieris rapae* (whites family, Pieridae)
May to August

Montane and subalpine, on mustard-family plants. Length 20 mm. Skinny, finely haired and spring green. Look for the thin yellow stripes along the back and sides. Also known as *Artogeia rapae*.

MW

*Pieris rapae*

# *Life in the snow*
## Yes, Virginia; there *are* ice worms

Consider the Columbia Icefield, a singularly snowy place. Cold and lifeless? Cold, yes; lifeless, no. On a sunny day in July, every square metre displays refrigerated insects.

Flies, beetles, butterflies and moths arrive on updrafts and storm winds, buzzing or fluttering across the rolling whiteness. Blanketing the surface there is a metre of chilled air that is deadly to warm-weather bugs. A moth comes too close to the surface. The wingbeat slows, and it drops onto the snow.

A pair of ravens cruise by. They descend for lunch. Their big black feet step among the numb and dying insects as the birds pick at their leisure.

*Watermelon snow*

## Watermelon snow

*Chlamydomonas nivalis*
(Chlorophyta, green algae)
June to September

Everyone likes to play on a roadside snowbank in the middle of summer, an activity not possible in, say, Ontario but quite normal at high points along the Icefields Parkway. A word of caution, though: sliding on a steep snow patch can easily put you in hospital, for it is easy to get out of control and crash into the rocks at the bottom.

But what's this? *Pink* snow? Yes, indeed. The red color in the snow is caused by millions of one-celled algae, each with a bit of red hematochrome pigment. Sometimes the algae are so abundant in a snowfield that the snow acquires a pinkish hue.

Most often you don't notice the color until the algae are artificially concentrated, which happens when you slide down a slope or walk across it. Your rump-track or boot-tracks stand out, watermelon-pink.

How does anything live in the snow? The cell content of *Chlamydomonas,* which like all protoplasm is mostly water, resists freezing through a little elementary chemistry. Minerals and other substances dissolved in water depress the freezing point a few degrees. Photosynthesizing among the snowbanks, the algae get their mineral supply from dust in the snow.

In turn, watermelon-snow algae support populations of other creatures: snow worms (next item), little bugs that eat the snow worms, birds that eat the bugs, etc., etc. All it takes is some food-producing plant at its base, and the ecological pyramid grows—in the *weirdest* places.

For some reason, watermelon snow is seldom seen in the Waterton/Glacier region. Elsewhere, look for it in the alpine zone from early June through early August. And be careful on those sloping snowpatches.

## Snow worms/ice worms
*Mesenchytraeus* spp. (class Oligochaeta)
May to August

Alpine, wriggling on top of melting snowbanks that have a high concentration of watermelon-snow algae, previous item, which seems to be the primary food of the worm.

There are perhaps a dozen snow-worm species in the Canadian Rockies, most of them on the western slope. They are up to 2 cm long and yellowish-brown to dark reddish-brown, often curled up in little dark balls. Not much is known about them, but they seem to live only on snowbanks that melt entirely each summer, and only on snowbanks lying over soil, not on snow lying over glacial ice or rock.

Eggs laid in soil hatch in early spring. The worms work their way up through the snow to the surface and stay there until melting of the snowbank returns them to earth in late summer for production of next year's crop. Adults may overwinter under the snow.

## Springtails/snow fleas
(order Collembola)
Winter and early spring

There is a "Mt. Collembola" in the Kananaskis area near Ribbon Creek. I had always wondered what the name meant, then learned one day that collembolans are tiny wingless insects—springtails. Mt. Collembola is well named, for the normal habitat of many springtail species is well above treeline, under rocks and among the shallow litter of tundra plants, where they eat pollen, molds and decaying vegetation. Denizens of incredibly hostile places, they even live in Antarctica.

Springtails are only 2–6 mm long, with a water-sucking tube sticking out of the abdomen. The **furcula,** an abdominal plate, cocks forward, held by a tiny catch. When a springtail decides to leap, the catch lets go and the furcula snaps back, flipping the springtail 10–15 cm into the air. Wheeeeee!

Hatching from eggs laid in soil, the tiny nymphs mature so late in the year that they reach the adult stage in winter. Adults climb up vegetation and rocks to reach the snow surface, where they mate in a swarm, a sort of arthropod orgy in which thousands of them gather on the thin, early-winter snow of November and December. You may also see them in February and March. The largest swarms I have seen occur at subalpine elevations, where countless black springtails pepper the snow over areas measured in square kilometres.

## Small winter stoneflies
(order Plecoptera, family Capniidae)
March and April

Found swarming over the snow near streams. These stoneflies are 5–10 mm long, larger than springtails, previous item. One of my sources says the larvae feed on plants and the adults feed on cyanobacteria; another says the adults eat lichens.

## Snow crane fly
*Chionea* spp. (order Diptera, family Tipulidae)
October to April

Seen singly in subalpine forest, but sometimes at lower elevations, picking its way slowly across the surface of the snow. A dark-colored wingless bug 5–12 mm long that looks at first like a spider, but on closer inspection turns out to be an insect: it has six legs rather than eight. (I have seen live spiders on the snow, too.)

Snow crane flies start to appear with the first snows of fall. In the central Rockies I see them all winter, sometimes at outrageously low temperatures, down to about -20°C, although they are most active at temperatures between -5°C and 3°C.

For most of their lives, snow crane flies live in the burrows of ground squirrels and other small rodents, eating the tiny organisms—fleas and such—that infest these animals. The larvae metamorphose to adults in early autumn and disperse, looking for mates. They reach the snow surface by climbing up the trunks of trees and branches of shrubs. After a few weeks of mating, the males die and the females go back under the snow to lay eggs in the soil.

Most insects that survive winter in the larval form flood their tissues with glycerol, which is natural antifreeze, but at temperatures well below freezing it is thought that the body fluids of a snow crane fly are supercooled. This means that the insect is subject to instant and complete freeze-up if jolted—which may explain why it walks so carefully.

Compare with the snow scorpion fly, next item.

## Snow scorpion fly
*Boreus* spp. (order Mecoptera, family Boreidae)
February and April

In mossy montane and subalpine forests, seen on the snow surface in late winter and early spring. Snow scorpion flies and snow crane flies, previous item, look rather alike, but the snow scorpion fly (3 mm long) is smaller than the snow crane fly (5–12 mm), so small that you may not notice the scorpion flies, even though they can be quite numerous on a warmish day in April. They mate in the snow, after which the male dies and the female lays eggs in feather mosses at the base of the snowpack. Both the caterpillar-like larvae and the flightless adults are scavengers, working their way through the deep beds of moss in search of dead insects. They may also eat the moss itself.

## Ice insects
*Grylloblatta* spp. (order Grylloblattodea)
June to September

Found under stones, wood fragments and other debris in cold, north-facing locations at all elevations, on glacial ice near its margins, and in caves that contain ice. Length 15–30 mm, light brown, with long antennae on the front and cerci (more sensors) on the back.

These creatures actually live in contact with ice as well as snow, although the eggs must be laid in soil. A primitive and thus probably ancient order related to the earwigs, the ice insects were discovered in Banff National Park in 1914. Only ten species have been discovered worldwide, six of them in North America. *Grylloblatta campodeiformis* is shown here. Little is known of their lives, except that the adults feed on bugs trapped on the cold snow surface. They are nocturnal and cold-seeking, unable to tolerate temperatures greater than 8°C. Placed in a warm hand, they die.

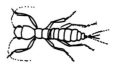

## *Further reading*

There is little literature for the lay public specifically about the arthropods of the Rockies, and the technical literature is enormous and difficult. So I refer to the items listed below, which tell me what family—sometimes genus, rarely species—that a particular bug belongs to. When I need detailed information, I call up experts in government and at universities.

Acorn, J. (1993) *Butterflies of Alberta*. Lone Pine Publishing, Edmonton. Covers all 156 species known from Alberta, in a handy field guide. Illustrations, range maps, glossary, index; 144 pages.

Arnett, R., Jr. (1980) *How to Know the Beetles*. Wm. C. Brown, Dubuque, Iowa. 1500 species, 900 illustrated with line drawings. Introduction, key, index, glossary; 416 pages. Also in this series, but not listed here: books on mites and ticks, aquatic insects and immature insects.

Bird, C., et al. (1995) *Alberta Butterflies*. Provincial Museum of Alberta, Edmonton. Definitive guide to the 181 species known to occur in the province. Fully illustrated with color photographs, plus B&W drawings of host plants. Range maps, extensive bibliography, index; 349 pages.

Bland, R. (1978) *How to Know the Insects*. Wm. C. Brown, Dubuque, Iowa. Keyed tour of all families, with line drawings. Introduction, key, index, glossary; 409 pages.

Borror, D. and R. White (1970) *A Field Guide to the Insects of America North of Mexico*. Peterson series, Houghton Mifflin, Boston. Text is minimal but drawings are very good, including color section. Index; 404 pages.

Kaston, B. (1978) *How to Know the Spiders*. Wm. C. Brown, Dubuque, Iowa. All known North American spiders (519 species) except the Micryphantidae. Line drawings, introduction, key, index, glossary; 272 pages.

Milne, L. and M. (1980) *The Audubon Society Field Guide to North American Insects and Spiders*. Knopf, New York. Information-packed; the best all-round layman's publication on arthropods. Covers 550 common species, illustrated with very good color photos. Index, 989 pages.

Pyle, R. (1981) *The Audubon Society Field Guide to North American Butterflies*. Knopf, New York. Comprehensive treatment of butterflies and skippers, with information on caterpillars and eggs. Color photo illustrations; special index of host plants; 914 pages.

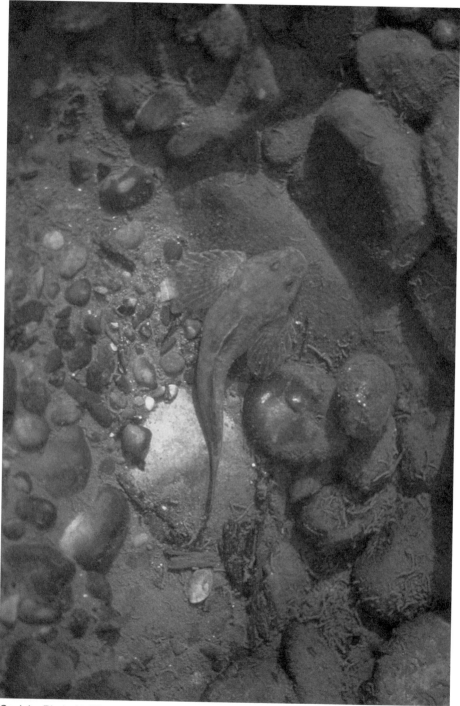

Sculpin. Photo by Wayne Roberts.

# Fishes
*There's more to fish than just fishing*

Fish belong to the phylum Chordata, subphylum Vertebrata, superclass Pisces. Only 41 species of fishes are known to swim in and about the Canadian Rockies, plus three special-case species at the Banff hot springs and a number of named hybrids, so they are all included here. That is not to say that you won't come across other species, because governments and individuals are forever trying to transplant fish from one drainage to another.

This practice is on the wane. It upsets watershed ecology, often eliminating native species. As well, the number of lakes and streams without fish—interesting to study and essential for survival of organisms that cannot coexist with fish—has shrunk considerably since stocking began in the region at the turn of the century. The entire Maligne River basin in Jasper park, for example, was originally fish-free, probably because of a high waterfall near the mouth of the river. Brook trout were introduced into Maligne Lake by the government in 1928, and rainbow trout were introduced without authorization in the 1960s. To a person who enjoys fishing, a lake without fish is a lake that needs stocking. To a naturalist, anything wild is fine just the way it is.

This book is mainly for naturalists, so this chapter is mainly about fish, not fishing. There is plenty of literature available on how and where to catch this and that; the idea here is to present the kind of information seldom found in fishing guides.

What kind of information? Well, how about the answer to this intriguing question: what became of the fish in the Canadian Rockies during the Pleistocene glacial advances? Practically the entire region has been under ice at one time or another in the last two million years, which means that the fish must have been forced out. Obviously, they came back—but from where?

At the end of the Late Wisconsinan glaciation some 11,000 years ago, it seems likely that our native species spread up the Missouri-Mississippi system on the eastern slope to the Waterton/Glacier area, and up the Columbia system on the western slope. Both these great drainage basins were unglaciated in their southern portions, providing **refugia** (literally, safe places) for fish during the ice ages. There may also have been a refugium to the *north*, strangely enough, for large parts of the Yukon were never glaciated, and at least one of those regions connects with the Rockies via the Liard River.

So far so good, but how did fish return to the Fraser, Bow, North Saskatchewan and Athabasca systems? These rivers drain much of the Rockies, and they all lie well within the area that was covered by ice.

As it turns out, the ice probably helped them to return. Glaciers in the mountains melted back more quickly than the huge icecap on the prairies, and meltwater streams running out of the mountains collected in large, deep lakes dammed up against the easterly glacial mass. This chain of temporary lakes stretched along the mountain front, at various times connecting one watershed to the next. Thus, it was possible for fish to move across the low divides of the foothills and prairies, advancing north.

At the same time, on the other side of the Rockies, a chain of glacially dammed lakes in the Rocky Mountain Trench undoubtedly provided connections between the Columbia and Fraser drainages over the low divide in the trench floor between Golden and Valemount. To the north, the Fraser and Peace systems were probably joined for a time around McLeod Lake. This would have provided an Arctic-Pacific link, for the Peace cuts right across the Rockies and drains into the Athabasca-Mackenzie system to the Arctic Ocean. There were other north–south links farther west, in the Okanagan-Shuswap area.

Yet another east–west link may have existed: the lower passes of the Canadian Rockies. At the end of the late-Wisconsinan glaciation (maybe at the end of the early-Wisconsinan glaciation in the northern Rockies), a lake was impounded at the summit of each pass by the interaction of retreating ice and reactivated streams. Some of these lakes, reduced in size and depth from 11,000 years of sediment infilling and erosion at their outlets, can still be seen today: Crowsnest Lake at Crowsnest Pass, Wapta Lake at Kicking Horse Pass, Cinema Lake at Thompson Pass, Fortress Lake at Fortress Pass, Moat Lake at Moat Pass, Yellowhead Lake at Yellowhead Pass and so on. Depending on the changing positions of ice fronts during deglaciation, the outlets of these lakes could have switched from one watershed to the other and back, perhaps repeatedly, opening the way for fishes to move up a stream on one side of the continental divide and, as the lake's outlet reversed, down a stream on the other side.

One must keep in mind that all these watershed connections need not have been open for very long. Theoretically, a single season would have been enough to allow a particular species to cross. Nor did they all have to be open at the same time. Fish could have moved across one temporary drainage link after another, their bridges burning behind them, so to speak. Research continues.

In describing foods eaten by fish, the word "invertebrates" is used in a special sense to include all the insect larvae, crustaceans and non-flying adult arthropods that live in the water or on its surface. Other invertebrates, mentioned separately, include flying insects, molluscs (snails and freshwater clams), worms such as leeches, and **plankton:** the tiny animals and plants that live suspended in the water or floating on the surface. For our purposes, microorganisms can be considered plankton as well.

Fish sizes vary a lot, mainly because fish continue to grow throughout their lives. The figures given here are for average-size adults in the Canadian Rockies; you may see individuals that are much larger. Records are noted when I have been able to find them.

A note on reproduction in fish. All the species described in this chapter lay eggs, except for two live-bearing species: the mosquitofish and the sailfin molly, both present only at Banff Hot Springs (see page 497).

Egg-style reproduction in fish is called **spawning.** The female produces gelatinous eggs, either simply broadcasting them over the bottom or laying them in a shallow nest scooped out of the bottom. The male emits sperm (termed **milt**) that fertilizes them. Often the pair lie side-by-side as this occurs; they quiver, mouths gaping open—fish sex must be exciting. Spawning is so similar in most species that I have not described it repetitively in the individual entries. Some species, though, have different and interesting ways of spawning, and these are described in a little detail.

**Fishing regulations** vary considerably from place to place in the Rockies. Be sure to obtain the latest rules, available at fish and wildlife offices and sporting goods shops in Alberta, British Columbia and Montana. Regulations in the national parks may differ from provincial or state regulations. Allowing fishing in the parks is strange, because all other wildlife is protected. You can't hunt or harass a bird or mammal in a national park, but you can kill a fish or abuse it by catching it and letting it go.

On to the listings. With the exception of the lamprey, page 489, all of the species described here belong to the class Osteichthyes, the bony fishes. For the convenience of French-speaking Canadians and European visitors, fish names are also given in French.

## Salmon, trout, grayling and whitefish

The word "salmon" is applied to those species in the family Salmonidae that normally hatch in fresh water and then head downstream to spend most of their lives in the sea, returning inland at the end to spawn. This life cycle is termed **anadromous.**

Trout, on the other hand, seldom venture into salt water. They do not make the journey down-river as fry, and they may spawn many times before dying. This makes evolutionary sense: why go through the trauma of switching from fresh water to salt water and back again if you can manage just fine in one medium or the other? And why expend all your reproductive capacity in one shot? The probable answer: food is available in the ocean in far greater quantities than it is in lakes and streams.

Some species within the salmon family can occur in either a freshwater (trout-type) form or an anadromous (salmon-type) form. Rainbow trout and steelhead, for example, are the same species, yet steelhead are anadromous, while rainbows are not.

The anadromous form usually grows much larger than the equivalent freshwater form. The freshwater kokanee, for example, averages about 22 cm long, but the anadromous sockeye attains 80 cm out in the Pacific. Both are *Oncorhynchus nerka.*

The only ocean-going salmon species that spawns regularly in the Canadian Rockies is the chinook, which migrates up the Fraser as far as Mt. Robson. There used to be a tremendous salmon run up the Columbia-Kootenay system, but this ended in 1939 when the Grand Coulee Dam was built on the lower Columbia in Washington state. A fish ladder—a series of artificial steps in the river to bypass the dam—failed to work. Salmon experimentally netted and trucked around the dam continued to their spawning grounds, but the young were killed in the turbines on their way downstream to the sea. This error has never been corrected, many more dams have been built on the Columbia, and it now seems that we humans have destroyed one of the world's great salmon runs. Fortunately, the Fraser remains un-dammed.

### Chinook salmon/spring salmon *Saumon chinook*
*Oncorhynchus tshawytscha* (salmon/trout family)

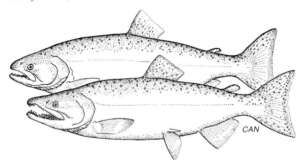

Seen in the Rockies only along the Fraser River and its tributaries between late August and mid-September during the spawning run. Most adults are 83–92 cm long and weigh 8–10 kg; maximum 160 cm and 57 kg. Identification: during spawning the fish are dark red, almost black in some individuals, with greenish heads and patches of white fungus on places where they have been injured while struggling up rapids and waterfalls. Males have distinctive hooked jaws and slightly humped backs.

About 18 months after they hatch, chinooks head for the sea, remaining there for up to five years, two or three years on the average. They normally return inland to spawn when four or five years old.

No one can fail to be impressed by the sight of enormous red chinook salmon writhing in water that barely covers their bodies as they spawn in small streams feeding the Fraser. They have come over 1000 km upstream in pursuit of the thready chemical flavor of the water in which they first swam. They haven't eaten a thing in ten weeks.

Each female fans her tail to produce a shallow depression in the gravel called a **redd.** A male takes one or more females as mates, preventing other males from spawning with those females. Or a female may choose a particular male. The female lies on her side and quivers, releasing eggs; the male releases milt at the same time, the act repeated until 500–700 eggs are laid. The female covers the fertilized eggs with gravel, then moves on to make another redd until several thousand eggs are laid. When the females are finished, so are the males; all adults die a day or two after. Birds and bears clean up the remains.

So strong, so elemental, so sad, the salmon run is a great event to witness. You can see the spawning chinooks up close on the northern outskirts of Valemount, where Highway 5 crosses Swift Creek. There is a special viewing bridge there.

Another spot is at Rearguard Falls, near Mt. Robson, where the fish attempt to pass the falls—a tremendous rapid, really—by jumping from step to step. It had been thought that Rearguard Falls was the upper limit of the salmon run on the Fraser, but several hundred chinooks have been seen in the past several years spawning above Rearguard Falls at Swiftcurrent Creek. Six-metre Overlander Falls, a few kilometres farther upstream, is truly impassable to the fish and thus the end of the line.

Pacific salmon species are declining in numbers, the blame placed largely on destruction of spawning streams by clear-cut logging, overfishing, chemical pollution from mining, smelting and pulp mills, and damming of rivers. Spawning salmon are protected by law upstream from Prince George, and they are not particularly good eating, anyway, this far from the sea.

## Kokanee *Kokani*
*Oncorhynchus nerka* (salmon/trout family)

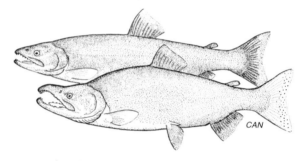

Native in western-slope lakes, but now absent through much of the Columbia system due to dam-building. Present in the Fraser drainage and Williston Lake, and downstream along the Peace River in Alberta, but other attempted eastern-slope introductions have failed. Adults 20–23 cm, 0.3 kg; maximum about 70 cm and 4 kg.

Kokanee look much like rainbow trout, next item, with the pink line along the side, but kokanee are bluish rather than greenish along the back and lack spots. Spawning adults are redder all over, with greenish heads; the males develop the curved jaws and hump typical of salmon. Both sexes carry patches of white fungus when spawning.

The kokanee is simply a landlocked sockeye salmon, similar in all ways except smaller. The species feeds mainly at the surface, on zooplankton such as copepods (see page 437), which they strain from the water through their long, fine **gill rakers:** rod-like projections on the gill supports. The fish reach maturity in three years. Introduced extensively in western Canada as an easily caught and tasty game fish, kokanee are present in the Fraser drainage, and in some of the lakes in the Columbia system.

Kokanee once thrived in Flathead Lake, just west of the Rockies near Kalispell, Montana. In this case they were introduced accidentally with other salmon in 1916. The kokanee prospered enough to go through an annual spawning run upstream, just as if the lake were their ocean home. They laid eggs in Glacier park's McDonald Creek, where the gravelly bed was sufficiently aerated and at the right temperature for successful reproduction. Park staff reported runs of 100,000 fish in mid-September. All adults died shortly after spawning, providing a sudden protein glut that attracted up to 600 bald eagles. Gulls, ravens, magpies, bears and even deer came to eat the dead and dying fish.

This all ended in 1987, when the kokanee population crashed. Montana fisheries officials had introduced a small non-native crustacean named *Mysis relicta* into the watershed in the mid-1970s. Kokanee and other trout had done well on *Mysis* all over the Pacific Northwest, but in deep lakes such as Flathead and Kootenay, the unexpected occurred. *Mysis* retreated to deep water during the day, when the kokanee were feeding. This was not a problem; the kokanee were not depending on *Mysis* for food. But *Mysis* was coming to the surface at night, when the kokanee did not feed, consuming most of the zooplankton that the kokanee normally ate.

Meanwhile, bottom-dwelling lake trout, another introduced species, increased in numbers by feeding on *Mysis* hiding from the kokanee. Result: the adult kokanee starved, and many of the fry were eaten by lake trout. Thus, one introduced species (kokanee) was wiped out by two other introduced species (lake trout and *Mysis relicta*). At time of writing, there seem to be no kokanee left in Flathead Lake.

With the kokanee went their remarkable spawning run, the gathering of the eagles, the tourist dollars the run attracted, etc. Officials of Montana Fish, Wildlife and Parks have learned a difficult lesson in ecology. I hope they can apply it in looking after Flathead Lake's native populations of cutthroat trout and bull trout.

### Rainbow trout/steelhead *Truite arc-en-ciel*
*Oncorhynchus mykiss,* formerly known as *Salmo gairdneri* (salmon/trout family)

M. Paetz

Native on the western slope, and in the upper Peace and Athabasca drainages; introduced elsewhere and now common at all elevations in streams and lakes. Average size 35–40 cm and 400–600 g; Alberta record 9.7 kg, from one of the tiny Five Lakes near Jasper, 1980. Identification: pale bluish or greenish back, the color often extending down the sides, which become silvery or yellowish lower down. Fish is black-spotted all over except on the belly. Pink or reddish band on the sides, starting at the gills, is prominent on spawning males.

This fish has two forms: freshwater/saltwater migrant, or freshwater only. There are no major physical differences. The ocean-going form, called **steelhead,** is native to B.C. and the Pacific states. It hatches mainly in coastal streams and moves to the sea after 2–4 years, then returns inland about three years later to spawn, thereafter migrating annually between stream and sea and living 6–8 years. There may be steelhead in the Fraser portion of the Rocky Mountain Trench, but probably not many.

Rainbow trout spawn in spring, in early summer at high elevations; they reach sexual maturity at 3–5 years. Although few live beyond their first spawning, it is not uncommon to find 12-year-old individuals. Primary foods are flying insects, leeches, snails, invertebrates and small fish. The most popular game fish, rainbow trout are easily raised in hatcheries and tolerate warm water, although they do better in cool water. Rainbows often hybridize with cutthroat trout, this page.

### Golden trout *Truite d'or*
*Oncorhynchus aguabonita,* formerly *Salmo aguabonita* (salmon/trout family)
Eastern slope only, successfully stocked in the high-elevation Barnaby Ridge Lakes of the upper Castle River system in the Waterton area, and in Coral Lake of the Cline River drainage. Average size about 20 cm, 0.5 kg; Alberta record 2 kg, Barnaby Ridge Lakes, 1965. Identification: very similar to rainbow trout (see previous item for illustration), but even more colorful: yellowish body, larger spotting and orange fin tips. The spots are confined to the tail region and back.

Golden trout are native to the Kern River in the Sierra Nevada mountains of California. They live on flying insects and invertebrates; spawn in midsummer.

### Cutthroat trout *Truite fardée*
*Oncorhynchus clarki,* formerly *Salmo clarki* (salmon/trout family)
Native to headwaters lakes and streams from the Bow River south on the eastern slope (one record on the upper Wapiti) and from the Columbia south on the western slope. Introduced

in the headwaters of Alberta streams from the Athabasca river south. Average size 25 cm, 0.2 kg. Alberta record weight 4.3 kg, South Castle River. Identification: yellowish-green to beige on the back, sides paler; black spotting along the back also covers the sides; tail fin spotted, too. Usually reddish on the belly. All cutthroat show a red line in a crease along the lower jaw; it fades when the fish is caught and dies.

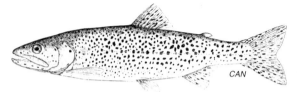

Cutthroat trout readily hybridize with introduced rainbows, and as a result pure cutthroat are becoming rare in the Canadian Rockies. In an attempt to preserve the inland form (there is also a sea-run cutthroat that spawns in coastal B.C. streams), the Alberta government has introduced cutthroat, and only cutthroat, in the Ram River above David Thompson Canyon, which has waterfalls that have kept the watershed upstream previously free of fish.

Cutthroat do well in high, cold mountain lakes and streams, eating flying insects, invertebrates and small fish. Mature in two to four years, cutthroat spawn in spring and early summer and live about 4–7 years.

**Brown trout** *Truite brune*
*Salmo trutta* (salmon/trout family)

An introduced species, now fairly common on the eastern slope in the North Saskatchewan, Red Deer and Bow drainages, and also in the upper Athabasca River, mainly in cool but gentle foothills streams with well-vegetated banks. Rarer, but present on the western slope in the Kootenay River. Average size 20 cm, 1 kg; Alberta record weight 7.96 kg and length 87 cm from Swan Lake, in the foothills southwest of Caroline, 1991. A 78-cm specimen has come from Lake Edith at Jasper. Identification: golden-brown to olive-drab along the back, lighter colored along the sides with black spots and orange-to-red spots on the body that are less prominent on the fins. Spots have white halos. Tail is unforked.

Brown trout are European and Asian, introduced in the eastern-slope national parks in 1924–1925 and in coastal B.C. rivers in the 1930s. Active both day and night, they eat mostly flying insects and invertebrates, although large adults take other fish, amphibians and even mice. During the day, brown trout often hide under banks, around rocks and in vegetation; they are difficult to catch and not as tasty as the other trout. Spawning time is late fall; age at maturity is 4–5 years and lifespan may reach 13 years. Brown trout hybridize with brook trout, next item.

**Brook trout/speckled char** *Omble de fontaine*
*Salvelinus fontinalis* (salmon/trout family)

Introduced, now common in eastern-slope streams and lakes between the Athabasca and Bow rivers, and on the western slope from Valemount south. Average size 25–30 cm, 0.5 kg; Alberta record 5.9 kg, from Pine Lake in Wood Buffalo National Park, 1967. Identification: olive-green back with yellow worm-like markings, paler green on sides, with light spots, plus red spots that have blue halos. Lower fins are pink to red, with white front edge and black stripe just behind.

CAN

Brook trout are native to eastern Canada, where coastal dwellers migrate between inland and marine waters. Prized for fishing, they have been stocked throughout the continent, with most success in upland regions. They eat mostly caddisfly larvae, midges, mayflies and water invertebrates, living about five years and spawning every fall when two to four years old.

Brown trout and brook trout are known to hybridize occasionally, producing a fish with intermediate characteristics called a **tiger trout.** Brook trout also hybridize with bull trout and lake trout (see splake in next item).

### Lake trout *Touladi*
*Salvelinus namaycush* (trout family)

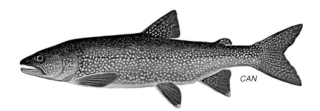

CAN

Native throughout the Rockies on the eastern slope, from Valemount north on the western slope, in deep, cold lakes. Average size 30 cm, 1.5 kg; Alberta record weight 23.9 kg, from Cold Lake in northeastern Alberta, and length 91 cm from Pyramid Lake, near Jasper. A giant 1.3 m long and weighing 46.3 kg was caught in Lake Athabasca, just outside Alberta in northwest Saskatchewan, in 1961. Identification: lighter-colored than other trout, olive to gray-green or brownish above and lighter on the sides, speckled or mottled with white. Deeply forked tail.

Lake trout seek water 15°C or colder, staying deep in the summer and feeding on small organisms; in winter they move closer to the surface and eat mainly other fish. Juveniles feed on invertebrates. Spawning begins at age 6–10. Lifespan has not been established, but if the spawning age is any indication, it may be the longest of any trout. Spawning time is fall.

**Splake** are fertile hybrid trout produced at the Banff hatchery in 1946 by artificially crossing male brook trout and female lake trout. Natural hybridization of these two is not known. Splake were introduced in many lakes in Banff and Jasper parks, but only Lake Agnes, a small tarn above Lake Louise, is known to have an established splake population.

### Bull trout and the Dolly Varden *Omble des montagnes, Dolly varden*
*Salvelinus confluentus* and *S. malma* (salmon/trout family)

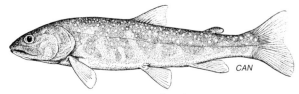

CAN

*Salvelinus confluentus*

Native to the western slope and once common on both sides of the Rockies, especially from Bow River south, bull trout have been over-fished and are now scarce. Better protection measures are now in place, and the species has been declared Alberta's provincial fish emblem.

Bull trout have been confused with the northern Dolly Varden, which gets its name from a character in the Charles Dickens novel *Barnaby Rudge* who dressed in pink-spotted calico that looked rather like the coloration of this fish. But true Dolly Varden trout, which are a coastal species also found in Asia, are present in the Canadian Rockies only at Chester Lake in Kananaskis Country, where they were introduced in 1974 from native populations in the Mackenzie River or the Firth River of the Yukon.

Bull trout eat mainly invertebrates and fish. They mature in their fifth year and spawn in autumn. They can live up to 20 years, 10–12 years on average.

### Arctic grayling *Ombre arctique*
*Thymallus arcticus* (salmon/trout family)

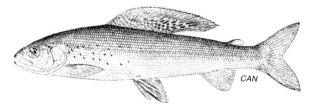

Native to cold lakes and streams, fairly common from the Athabasca River north on the eastern slope and in the Peace River drainage. Also found much farther south, where they seem to have been native but are now represented, at least in the Flathead and Belly River drainages, with introduced varieties. Average size in the Canadian Rockies 20–30 cm, 0.2–0.8 kg. Identification is easy: look for the very large, white-spotted dark dorsal (top) fin. In spawning males, the fin becomes quite reddish. Back is iridescent green or bluish gray, lighter on the sides, with a few dark spots on the front half.

Arctic grayling need clean, cool water. They are very sensitive to pollution, especially stirred-up silt. They eat mainly insects and other invertebrates, sometimes feeding on bottom-dwelling species. Occasionally they eat the fry of other fish. Grayling reach maturity in 4–6 years and spawn following ice breakup, meaning mid-April to early June at various elevations in the Rockies. The fish live as long as 8 years.

### Mountain whitefish *Ménomini des montagnes*
*Prosopium williamsoni* (salmon/trout family)

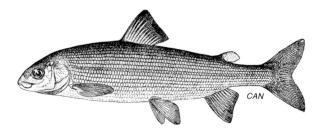

Native to cold lakes and streams, fairly common from the Athabasca River north on the eastern slope and in the Peace River drainage. Also found much farther south, where they seem to have been native but are now represented, at least in the Flathead and Belly River drainages, with introduced varieties.

Whitefish are bottom feeders, eating mostly invertebrates—especially insect larvae—snails and small fish. They prefer the main watercourses and the lakes that lie along them. Sometimes called "grayling" in southern areas, they look rather similar to immature arctic grayling, previous item; differentiate by the large dorsal fin on the grayling. Age at maturity 3–4 years; maximum lifespan 29 years from Spray Lakes Reservoir. Spawning is in the fall.

## Pygmy whitefish *Ménomini pygmée*
*Prosopium coulteri* (salmon/trout family)

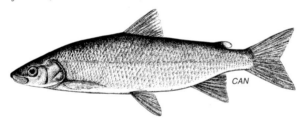

Occasional along the western slope, on the eastern slope in the Peace River, in Waterton Lakes, and in the upper Athabasca River near Jasper. Typically 10 cm long. Similar to mountain whitefish, previous item, but smaller and slimmer, with smaller adipose fins. Habits and life history also similar.

## Lake whitefish *Grand Corégone*
*Coregonus clupeaformis* (salmon/trout family)

Probably native in larger, deeper lakes and rivers, but now reported only from the Athabasca drainage (including, surprisingly, Talbot Lake, which is shallow) and Upper Waterton Lake. Average size 45 cm, 1 kg. Resembles mountain whitefish, previous page, but is larger, darker and more heavily built. Small mouth and dark fins.

Lake whitefish feed near the bottom, sometimes higher, eating mainly invertebrates, snails and plankton. They mature in 4–6 years, spawn in the fall and live about 10 years; maximum 28 years.

**Cisco,** *Coregonus artedi,* were successfully stocked in Lake Minnewanka near Banff in 1916–1917, and in the Spray Lakes Reservoir near Canmore in 1953. They look like miniature lake whitefish, with a longer lower jaw. Sometimes hybridize with lake whitefish. Often found at mid-depth, but come to the surface to eat plankton and small fish.

# Big fish: pike and sturgeon

One of these acts like it looks. The other doesn't.

### Northern pike/jackfish *Grand Brochet*
*Esox lucius* (pike family, Esocidae)

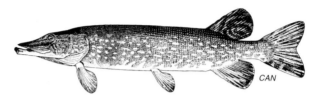

Eastern slope mainly, but also in Peace and Liard drainages, occasional in low-elevation lakes along the larger rivers. Average size 40 cm, 3 kg; Alberta record 122 cm, 19.5 kg, from Lake Newell, 1953. Identification: large size, dorsal fin far back on the body and long snout with a big mouth full of nasty-looking teeth. Fisherfolk beware: it bites! Color pattern varies considerably, from rather plain bluish to spotted and striped, with orange or yellow fins.

Northern pike are large, yet they live in shallow lake water, hunting the weedy fringes for fish—90 percent of the diet—frogs, mice, young muskrats and ducklings. Pike spawn in early spring. There is no nest; four or five males follow one female about, releasing milt as she releases eggs. Juveniles eat mainly invertebrates and small fish. Maturity comes at 2–3 years for males, 3–4 years for females. Lifespan is about 10–12 years, maximum 26 years.

### White sturgeon *Esturgeon blanc*
*Acipenser transmontanus* (sturgeon family, Acipenseridae)

Uncommon but present in the Fraser as far upstream as Longworth, east of Prince George, possibly to McBride, and in the Kootenay River to at least Lake Koocanusa in the southern Rocky Mountain Trench; possibly in the upper Columbia as well.

This is by far the largest fish species found in the Rockies—the largest in North America, in fact. Record weight in the lower Fraser is 548 kg, and individuals reaching 270 cm and 150 kg have been caught near Prince George. But white sturgeon are seldom seen upstream from Prince George, and they are usually comparatively small, about 120 cm long on the average. Regardless of size, sturgeon are readily identifiable by their shape, and especially by the rows of pointed bony plates along the back and belly.

Despite their formidable appearance, sturgeon are toothless bottom feeders. They use their sucker-like mouths to pick up anything edible there. Not only are sturgeon our biggest species, they are also the oldest: the females spawn first at 26–34 years and the males at 11–22 years. Large ones are 60–70 years old. They don't die after spawning, and they may reach the age of 100!

Sturgeon can be anadromous (saltwater/freshwater), moving up the Fraser from the Pacific in early spring to spawn and returning to the sea in late summer, but individuals above Prince George seem to be strictly freshwater dwellers.

**Lake sturgeon** *(Acipenser fulvescens),* darker than white sturgeon and somewhat smaller (Alberta record 1.7 m, 33 kg) have been reported close to the foothills from the North Saskatchewan River south, with an unconfirmed report below the Bighorn Dam near Nordegg.

# Codfish and lampreys in the Rockies?

Yes, me b'y.

## Burbot/ling *Lotte*
*Lota lota* (codfish family, Gadidae)

Native in lakes and occasionally in rivers and foothills streams. Average size 30–40 cm; a 6.1 kg specimen 1.0 m long was taken from the Red Deer River. Burbot look eel-like, long and round, with continuous fins on the back and under the long tail; compare with Pacific lamprey, next item. Like other codfishes—burbot is the only true freshwater cod—there are two short protuberances on the nose and a long, wispy barbel (sensory organ) under the chin. Coloration: dark brown with yellowish mottling.

Bottom feeders, burbot eat invertebrates when young and mostly other fish when older. Spawning is unusual: under ice in winter, at night. Ten or twelve fish spawn together, writhing, in a ball-shaped clump that moves along the bottom spewing milt and eggs. Burbot are tasty if skinned, but often rejected as eels or catfish. However, there are no eels in the Canadian Rockies, and no catfish, although the 15-cm **stonecat**, *Noturus flavus,* could show up in the southern foothills, in the Milk River system. Burbot reach maturity at 3–4 years and may live to 10–15 years.

## Pacific lamprey *Lamproie de Pacifique*
*Entosphenus tridentatus* (class Cephalaspidomorphi, the higher jawless fishes; family Petromyzontidae, the lampreys)

Present in the upper Columbia system of the Rocky Mountain Trench, but not common; present in the Fraser below Prince George, but not reported above. Eel-like, with a prominent round disk-like mouth, no lower fin and no fin behind the gills. Average adult length 20 cm.

Lamprey are dark-colored, brown to blue-black, and unpatterned; they are parasites, attaching to other fishes by means of a sucking mouth. Small teeth rasp off scales and skin to reach the tissues beneath, from which the lamprey withdraws blood. About a third of the host fish die.

Lamprey young spend 5–6 years buried in river-bottom mud, eating mostly microorganisms. When they grow up they move downstream to the sea, or, in the case of the Columbia-system lampreys, which are landlocked by dams, to one of the large lakes or reservoirs. There they feed parasitically for several more years, eventually heading back upstream in late summer to lie under stones along the bottom until the following year, when they spawn (April to July) and die within two weeks. Apparently they eat nothing during the entire 9–10 month migration/resting/spawning period.

# Suckers (family Catostomidae)

Suckers are the most widespread and perhaps the most numerous fish in the Canadian Rockies. We have four species. Mostly bottom feeders in lakes, they eat algae, invertebrates and snails. Fisherfolk don't care much for suckers, but they ought to. Sucker fry are a staple food of the trout they catch, and suckers clean up dead fish eggs that would otherwise spread fungal fish diseases. Besides, suckers are interesting in their own right—and quite watchable as they spawn in spring, the males colorfully orange-striped, at the water's edge in mountain lakes. Juveniles patrol the shoreline in large schools, going round and round the lake. They don't reach maturity until age five, and can easily live ten years.

The species described are all present in the Rockies. An additional one, the **bridgelip sucker** *(Catostomus columbianus),* is present in the Fraser River below Prince George and might make it into the Rocky Mountain Trench.

## Longnose sucker *Meunier rouge*
*Catostomus catostomus* (sucker family)

CAN

Common throughout the Rockies at all elevations, mostly in the deeper lakes. Average size elsewhere 40–50 cm, but somewhat smaller in the mountains; 31 cm in Pyramid Lake near Jasper; larger ones reported from Lower Kananaskis Reservoir. Readily identified as a sucker by the round, sucking mouth; differentiate from other suckers in the Rockies by the longer snout of the longnose and the small scales. Body is round, dark olive to brown on the back, lighter down the sides, with dark top and tail fins, pinkish lower fins. Hybridizes with the white sucker, next item, and also with the largescale sucker, next page. Spawns in the Jasper area in late May, usually in creeks.

## White sucker *Meunier noir*
*Catostomus commersoni* (sucker family)

CAN

Another common sucker, tolerant of environmental variation and thus widely distributed. Average size 40 cm elsewhere but only 20–30 cm in the Canadian Rockies. Often found in lakes with the long-nosed sucker, previous item, and hybridizes with it; differentiate by the paler color of the white sucker, the blunter head and larger scales. Also hybridizes with the largescale sucker. White suckers feed on the bottom, eating invertebrates and algae. Highly adaptable, these fish spread farther than any other species during deglaciation of the Rockies. For more on that interesting story, see page 479. White suckers spawn from early May to mid-July, often in lakes. Mature at age 5 or 6; longevity 14–17 years.

**Largescale sucker** *Meunier à grandes écailles*
*Catostomus macrocheilus* (sucker family)

Fairly common in the upper Columbia, Fraser and Peace drainages, at montane elevations. The largest sucker, typically 30–45 cm long and reaching 60 cm in the larger rivers. Seldom found in lakes. Dark above, pale below; during spawning, adults acquire a golden look on the back and sides, and often sport a greenish side band. Good identifier: ahead of the top fin, there is a low ridge along the back that is not present in our other suckers. Foods: snails, invertebrates and algae, all taken from the bottom. This species spawns in May and June, usually in small creeks, and matures at age 5. Hybridizes with white suckers.

**Mountain sucker** *Meunier des montagnes*
*Catostomus platyrhynchus* (sucker family)

In swift eastern-slope streams from the upper North Saskatchewan River south, often at high elevations. Smaller than the other suckers in the Rockies, averaging only 10–15 cm long. Body olive drab or brown, lighter down the sides, often with three brown bands and scattered black speckles. Looks like the longnose sucker, but has a shorter nose and a cartilaginous sheath behind the upper lip, useful for scraping algae off rocks, and distinct notches at the corners of the mouth. Mountain suckers mature in about two years and spawn in early summer. Longevity unknown, but probably less than that of other suckers.

## Little silvery fish: the minnows (family Cyprinidae)

We are speaking here of a taxonomic group of fishes, not just any little fish (juvenile fish are properly called **fry**). True, most of the minnows are small—the little silvery fish of the mountains—but some grow nearly as large as the average trout. None has teeth in the jaw, but there are **pharyngeal teeth:** tooth-like projections on curved arches of bone beside the gills. Many minnows have **barbels,** tiny projections of flesh near the corners of the mouth. Barbels are sensory organs, responsive to smell and touch.

**Northern pikeminnow** *Sauvagesse du Nord*
*Ptychocheilus oregonensis* (minnow family)

Mainly western-slope, in lakes of the Columbia and Fraser systems, but also occasional on the eastern slope in the upper Peace system. Average size 25–30 cm, large for a minnow; a 43.5-cm specimen has been reported from Peace River, Alberta. Round body like most minnows, dark gray to brown along the back and silvery down the sides. Young pikeminnows often have a prominent black spot at the base of the tail. Juveniles eat plankton and invertebrates; adults eat small fish. Squawfish spawn at six years in May to July and may live to be 20, the most geriatric of the minnows in this region.

### Peamouth chub *Méné deux-barres*
*Mylocheilus caurinus* (minnow family)

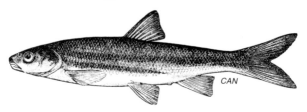

In the weedy shallows of western-slope lakes and slow-moving rivers at low elevations from the Peace River south; eastern-slope only in the Peace. Average size 10–25 cm; reported to 36 cm. Small fish, pointed at the front with a small mouth; olive-brown along the back and often partway down the side, where there is a prominent dark stripe from front to base of tailfin. Sometimes there is another stripe below the first one, reaching from the gills about halfway to the tail. Peamouth chub are often seen in schools, feeding on invertebrates; they also spawn en masse, right at the water's edge, in May and June. Lifespan up to 13 years.

### Flathead chub *Méné à tête plate*
*Platygobio gracilis* (minnow family)

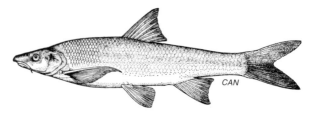

A northerly species, common in the Peace system; also known from the Athabasca River. Prefers muddy rivers with gravelly bottoms. A large minnow; average size 15–20 cm, maximum 32 cm, faintly brownish above and white below, silver-sided with no other markings. Good identifiers: barbels at the corners of the mouth, sickle-shaped fins and small eyes. Foods: mainly surface fare such as water striders, beetles and flies; adults also take small fishes and have been known to eat the young of aquatic rodents. Spawning is probably in summer; lifespan unknown but may be many years.

### Lake chub *Méné de lac*
*Couesius plumbeus* (minnow family)

Throughout the Rockies over gravelly bottoms, common at low elevations but sometimes found in treeline lakes and streams. Average size 5–10 cm. Small greenish-silver fish, nearly round in cross-section, with a prominent dark line along the side from nose to base of tail. Lake chub eat invertebrates, plankton and algae; they spawn at 3–4 years and live about five. In early spring this species begins to move upstream, spawning near headwaters in late June and July. It

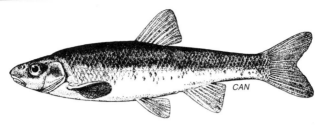

is probable that most die after this run. Hybridizes with longnose dace, this page, in Upper and Lower Kananaskis reservoirs.

Lake chub can survive higher water temperatures than any other fish in the Rockies except the tropical species at Banff Hot Springs (see page 497); lake chub are the only fish living in the warm-water marshes below Liard Hot springs.

### Pearl dace *Mulet perlé*
*Margariscus margarita* (minnow family)

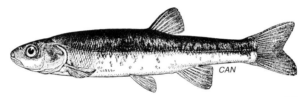

Eastern slope only, in foothills lakes and sluggish streams from Peace River south. Average size 6–11 cm. Very similar to the lake chub (previous item): olive along the back, with a dark stripe along the side. In adults the stripe fades toward the front, which is a way of telling this fish from other single-striped minnows, whose stripe is either solid all along the body or tends to fade at the back rather than the front. Male pearl dace have a bright red stripe below the dark one from November to July; spawning is in spring. Lifespan is short, probably just a couple of years maximum. Foods for this species include algae and invertebrates.

The **spottail shiner** *(Notropis hudsonius)* is a common minnow in eastern Alberta, but not reported in the Rockies except in Talbot Lake, Jasper National Park. Rather similar in shape to the pearl dace or lake chub, previous items, the spottail shiner is bluish on top, silvery below, with a small dark spot on either side, at the base of the tail.

### Longnose dace *Naseux de rapides*
*Rhinichthys cataractae* (minnow family)

Bottom-dwellers in lakes and rivers, often in small, fast-flowing streams, where they manage to stay on the bottom by deflating their air-bladders. Most common small fish in the Canadian Rockies. Average size 5–10 cm; reported to 18 cm. Easily recognized by the long, nose-like upper lip and dark, dirty-looking mottling on the back and sides. Fins are white; body is rounded. There are barbels just ahead of the eyes. Longnose dace feed on invertebrates, especially aquatic insect larvae, and live about five years. They spawn in June and July and are known to hybridize with lake chub, previous page.

**Leopard dace** *Naseux léopard*
*Rhinichthys falcatus* (minnow family)

Occasional on the western slope around Prince George, in small, sluggish streams. Average length 5–10 cm. Identified by the large dark spots on the cream-colored sides. Head is rather dark, with barbels on the nose; fins are yellowish. Breeding males have orange lips. Food is mainly fly larvae and other invertebrates when very young; mainly flying insects later. Spawning is thought to occur in July; lifespan perhaps four years.

**Redside shiner** *Méné rose*
*Richardsonius balteatus* (minnow family)

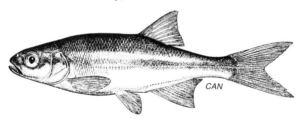

Throughout the western slope; on the eastern slope only in the Peace system. Mainly in rivers but occasionally in lakes, usually in large schools in shallow water. Small, thick-bodied silvery fish, average size 4–10 cm, dark olive along the back with a dark side stripe beginning at the front and fading out toward the rear. There are often scattered black spots along the stripe. Breeding males are colorful: the stripe is bright yellow, there is a crimson patch behind the gills, and the belly is pink. Redside shiners feed mainly on plankton and algae, the larger ones also taking insects at the surface, fish eggs and small fish. Spawning is in midsummer and lifespan about three years.

**Northern redbelly dace** *Ventre rouge du nord*
*Phoxinus eos* (minnow family)

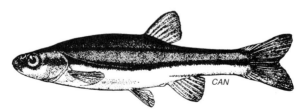

Eastern slope only, in the foothills portions of the Peace, Athabasca, North Saskatchewan and Red Deer rivers. Not common. Preferred habitat: quiet, shallow ponds with brown-colored muddy bottoms and dark-stained water, such as one finds in beaver ponds. Average size under 5 cm. Eats algae and plankton. Resembles other minnows; differentiate by the two dark bands along the side with yellowish color between them. Breeding males are reddish. This species spawns in summer, laying eggs in algal masses. Adults live up to six years.

**Finescale dace** *Ventre citron*
*Phoxinus neogaeus* (minnow family)

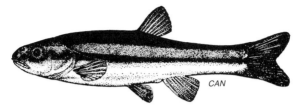

Eastern-slope only, from Peace River south, in shallow quiet water like that favored by northern redbelly dace, previous item, with which it shares habitat. Physically similar, too; differentiate by the larger mouth of the finescale dace and its single dark stripe rather than double one. Finescale dace eat surface insects, plankton and invertebrates, but there is little life-cycle information available on this species. It seems to spawn in June, and interbreeds with other minnows so much that entire schools of hybrids are seen.

**Fathead minnow** *Tête-de-boule*
*Pimephales promelas* (minnow family)

Eastern-slope only, from Athabasca River south, in warm, shallow streams and lakes; common in the Waterton/Glacier area. Small—average size 5–7 cm—thick and yellowish. Spawning males are easily identified by the large, blackish head with prominent tubercles (horny bumps) on the face and chin. Fathead minnows feed mainly on algae and invertebrates; they are resistant to extremes in pH and salinity, and tolerant of low oxygen levels.

Spawning in this species is well-studied and interesting. In spring the male herds a female to a log, branch or stone; he nudges her up sideways against the undersurface of the object, and she sticks eggs to it with a special ovipositor. He squirts milt over the eggs, chases that female away and attracts another for the same performance. He defends the nest himself. The fry mature in only a few months, but life is short for this species: a couple of years.

# *The rest of the kettle*

Here in the miscellaneous section you'll find the brook stickleback and some odd-looking little fish that most of us associate with the B.C. coast, not the mountains: sculpins.

## Brook stickleback *Épinoche à cinq épines*
*Culaea inconstans* (stickleback family, Gasterosteidae)

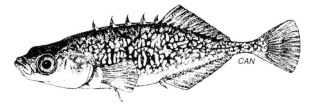

Eastern-slope only, from Peace River south, in the well-vegetated shallows of streams and lakes; often in beaver ponds. Average length about 3–6 cm; 9 cm maximum. Usually dark olive with creamy mottling; sometimes just the reverse. Good identifier: 4–6 prominent spines along the back.

More tolerant of high-pH, high-salt and low-oxygen conditions than other species, brook sticklebacks and fathead minnows (previous page) make a go of it where other species fail. Sticklebacks eat mainly invertebrates, fish eggs and worms, hunting for them among aquatic vegetation. When spawning in May and June, the male builds a round nest about 2 cm across; it's made of plants and algae held together by a special glue he secretes from his kidneys. The male herds a female into the nest by nipping and nudging, then butts her under the tail until she lays the eggs. Afterward he chases her away and looks after the egg-guarding and fry-rearing himself, then dies. The young mature in about a year. Females may live 2–3 years.

## Sculpins *Chabots*
*Cottus* spp. (family Cottidae)

Small but interesting-looking, sculpins are known more as marine fish than freshwater species. Yet there are sculpins in and about the Canadian Rockies—at least six species, maybe seven. They are all quite small (5–10 cm), with disproportionately large, broad heads, very fat lips and bulbous eyes. The side fins are large and feathery. Adults tend to stay on the bottom, hiding under rocks, so they are seldom seen. They eat mainly bottom-dwelling invertebrates such as insect larvae, aquatic plants and tiny fish. Spawning is in the spring. A female places her eggs under a rock guarded by a male, who fans the water with his fins until the eggs hatch in a few weeks.

**Slimy sculpin** (*Cottus cognatus*) is mainly a western-slope species, present on the eastern slope in the Peace system and north. It has been found in the Smoky River.

**Spoonhead sculpin** (*C. ricei*) is common in eastern-slope streams from the Wapiti River south to the Red Deer, and occasional in the Bow and the Oldman.

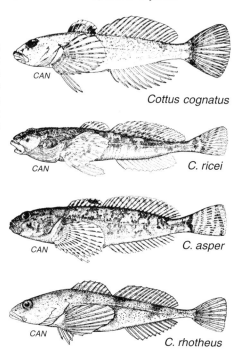

*Cottus cognatus*

*C. ricei*

*C. asper*

*C. rhotheus*

**Prickly sculpin** *(C. asper)* is found in the Fraser, Columbia and Peace drainages.

**Torrent sculpin** *(C. rhotheus)* is a Columbia-drainage species.

In the southern area, a sculpin that resembles *Cottus confusus* but is not closely related lives in the Flathead drainage on the western slope and in the St. Mary River on the eastern slope. Of undetermined species, it is identified as just *"Cottus sp."*

**Deepwater sculpin** *(Myoxocephalus thompsoni)* is known in the Rockies only from Upper Waterton Lake.

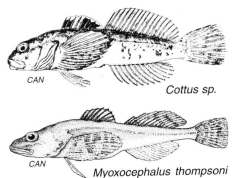

CAN

*Cottus sp.*

CAN

*Myoxocephalus thompsoni*

## Tropical fish in the hot springs at Banff?

No, not in with the bathers, but yes, in the springs that feed the Cave and Basin Centennial Centre, and in the abnormally warm marsh nearby. Go down to the Parks Canada boardwalk, where you will see hundreds of little tropical fish dependent on the warm water for survival in a climate that would otherwise kill them. They eat the stringy white bacterial masses in the springs—certainly not typical fish food. In 1924 the parks service introduced larvae-eating **mosquitofish** *(Gambusia affinis),* and local aquarists have illegally introduced many other species, of which only the the dark-colored **sailfin molly** *(Poecilia latipinna)* and the colorful **jewelfish** *(Hemichromis bimaculatus)* have survived.

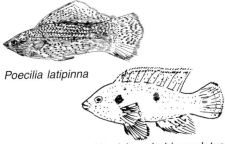

*Poecilia latipinna*

*Hemichromis bimaculatus*

## Further reading

Boschung, Jr., H.T. et al. (1983) *The Audubon Society Field Guide to North American Fishes, Whales and Dolphins.* Knopf, New York. Comprehensive, with good photographic illustrations, short entries, no range maps; 848 pages.

Butler, J. and R. Maw (1985) *Fishing Canada's Mountain Parks: the Fish and Their Environments.* Lone Pine Press, Edmonton. An unusual fishing guide, with natural-history information. Illustrated, indexed, 126 pages.

Carl, G., W. Clemens and C. Lindsey (1967) *The Freshwater Fishes of British Columbia,* fourth edition. Royal B.C. Provincial Museum, Victoria. The standard for the western slope, 192 pages.

Nelson, J. (1983) "The tropical fish fauna in Cave and Basin hot springs drainage, Banff National Park, Alberta," *The Canadian Field Naturalist,* vol. 97, no. 3, pp. 255–261. Not as readily available as other sources listed here, but interesting reading.

— and M. Paetz (1992) *The Fishes of Alberta.* University of Alberta Press and University of Calgary Press. Lots of detail, with color photo illustrations and range maps; 438 pages.

Scott, W. and E. Crossman (1973) *Freshwater Fishes of Canada.* Bulletin 184, Fisheries Research Board, Environment Canada, Ottawa. Illustrated, 966 pages.

*The amazing wood frog, page 501, which freezes solid in the winter. Photo by Barry Giles.*

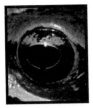

# Amphibians and reptiles
## Or, as those in the know call them, "herptiles"

Here is a division of science in which two major categories of organisms—the class Amphibia and the class Reptilia—require one scientist, because the scholar of reptiles is usually a scholar of amphibians, and vice versa. From this comes the term "herpetology," coined to refer to the study of amphibians and reptiles both.

As you can see from the small size of this section, there are not many herptiles in the Canadian Rockies—only 15 species. No reptiles live north of the Peace River, but a couple of frogs do just fine all the way to the Liard River and beyond. Some species live at high elevations in the mountains; it always amazes me to find frogs in a tundra pond, where the climate allows them only four months of the year in which to grow and reproduce. Then they have to survive through the other eight months of hibernation.

There is such variation within species of reptiles and amphibians that many species have subspecies names, included here where applicable. Subspecies identifications are difficult in places where subspecies overlap, but this is not the case in the Canadian Rockies. Most species are near the northern limits of their ranges. Only one subspecies is present.

## Salamanders, toads and frogs
### Subphylum Vertebrata, class Amphibia

Most amphibians have two-phase lives, in which there is an aquatic larval stage (tadpole) followed by a terrestrial adult stage (salamander, toad, frog). The skin is not scaly, the eggs have no shell, and fertilization occurs externally. These characteristics can be used to separate the amphibians in the Rockies from the reptiles.

### Tiger salamander *Salamandre tigrée*
*Ambystoma tigrinum melanostictum* (order Caudata, family Ambystomatidae)
April to September

Present in the eastern-slope foothills in the Bow River corridor and in the Waterton and eastern-Glacier areas, but you are unlikely to see it except in the morning after a rainy night. Adult length 14–18 cm. Identifiers: stout shape, glossy, wet-looking skin, black spots on a brown or gray back, or yellow and black blotches. The long-toed salamander, which is the only other salamander in the mountains (next item), is smaller and skinnier, with a yellow or greenish stripe down the back. No apparent vocalizations.

HM

Salamanders live near water, but they spend a surprising amount of time out of it, hunting in the woods at night for earthworms, insects and one another, for they are cannibalistic. Like most amphibians, they return to their natal pond to reproduce. They spawn in water during early spring, sometimes even before the ice is off the ponds, laying eggs attached to vegetation in temporary pools. The male leaves a gelatinous mass of sperm in or by the entrance to the female's **cloaca,** the single egg-and-waste exit chute in amphibians, reptiles and birds. Each egg is fertilized as it moves down the cloaca or exits from it.

Salamander larvae have external gills but otherwise look much like tadpoles at first. Later on they acquire all four limbs and the gills become quite large. They eat invertebrates (in the fish-food sense, see page 480) at first, then larger prey such as tadpoles and small fish. The larvae transform to adults either in late summer or the following spring. Some individuals do not transform; they remain mud-puppies. The adults hibernate out of water in burrows they dig or borrow from small mammals. But life is short for amphibians, and they rarely live even a year.

When overpopulation occurs among tiger salamanders, one or more in a pond can become **cannibal morphs** in the larval (**axolotl**, or "mud-puppy") stage. A cannibal morph is larger, has an armored head and sharp teeth. It attacks and eats other larvae. After the population is greatly reduced—in a laboratory tank, the monster eats everybody else—the cannibal morph reverts to normal larval form and the adult looks and acts like any other salamander.

### Long-toed salamander *Salamandre à longs doigts*
*Ambystoma macrodactylum* (order Caudata, family Ambystomatidae)
April to September

Scattered, but locally common near montane ponds or small marshes along major river valleys from the Peace River south on the western slope and from Jasper south on the eastern slope. Not known from the upper Red Deer or upper North Saskatchewan drainages. Normally active only at night and thus seldom seen. Adult length 8–12 cm. This salamander is slender, with brown or dark-green glossy skin, a yellow-to-green stripe down the back and scattered white flecks on the sides. Differentiate from the tiger salamander, previous item, by the long-toed's smaller size and different coloration. Habits and life cycle are similar.

### Boreal toad *Crapaud de l'Ouest*
*Bufo boreas boreas* (order Anura, family Bufonidae)
May to September

Found in moist montane and subalpine woods and meadows, usually near water, from the Peace River south. Adult sitting length 4.5–11 cm. A very toad-like toad, mottled olive and warty, with yellow eyes and a pale throat. There is usually a prominent creamy stripe along the back, and often it runs right up onto the head. In the Canadian toad the stripe is less prominent and usually doesn't reach the head. The Canadian toad has a bony-looking plate between the eyes, but the boreal toad doesn't.

The boreal toad is active in the early evening in hot, clear weather and all day in cool, showery weather, eating mostly beetles, ants and other insects, along with worms and slugs. This critter is easily caught and observed, but don't try to keep it; it dies. It sings rather weakly, with a sound like peeping chicks.

Spawning is from April to June. Like other toads and frogs in the Canadian Rockies, mating is done in the water. Males call to the females, then cling to their backs in amplexus; the water carries the sperm to the eggs as they are laid. The eggs wind up scattered in strings on aquatic vegetation; the tadpoles transform to adults in late summer and overwinter in burrows, either of their own digging or borrowed from rodents. The toads also move into vacant beaver lodges.

If you handle a toad, wash your hands afterward. Toads don't cause warts, but the large glands on the head produce a toxin intended to irritate the mouth of a predator.

### Canadian toad *Crapaud du Canada*
*Bufo hemiophrys* (order Anura, family Bufonidae)
April to September

Eastern slope only, occasional at low elevations in the Bow River corridor east of the mountain front. Small; adult sitting length 4–7.5 cm. Very similar to the boreal toad, previous item, but the stripe along the back does not reach the head, which has a distinctive plate on it between the eyes. And the throat is darker.

Quicker than the boreal toad, the Canadian toad plops into water when threatened, swimming fast and far. This toad is a good burrower. On each hind foot it has two spur-like digging tubercles. The song is a trill, low-pitched and not very loud. Life cycle and habits like those of western toad. A prolific reproducer: egg counts reach 16,500 per female.

## Fewer frogs

When Rachel Carson wrote *Silent Spring* in 1962, she predicted a world without birdsong. Indeed, there are fewer birds today than there were then. Frogs sing, too, and since the late 1970s amphibians have been suffering an even more alarming drop in numbers than birds have. This global population crash has affected many species. It may be a natural cycle of some kind, and some herpetologists think it may be bottoming out, but such a cycle has not been documented before. Scientists are looking primarily for human-related causes: global warming, habitat loss, water pollution or an increase in ultraviolet radiation caused by thinning of the ozone layer. If one or more of these possibilities bears out, the implications for our own species are ominous. This is the stuff of science fiction. "First the frogs died ..." But it may be all too true.

### Wood frog *Grenouille des bois*

*Rana sylvatica* (order Anura, family Ranidae)
May to September

HM

Still fairly common at low elevations in moist woods near water; occasionally subalpine or even alpine. Has always been scarce at the southern end of its range in Glacier National Park. Small: adult sitting length only 3–6 cm. The wood frog is easily identified by the dark mask-like shading behind the eyes. Compare, though, with the Pacific treefrog, page 503. The color varies from dark brown through pale brown and gray to pale green; there is sometimes a creamy stripe down the back. The song is a high-pitched, repetitive quack. If attacked, this frog screams.

The wood frog is the most northerly frog on the continent, ranging beyond the arctic circle. It lives in damp places and marshes with good vegetation cover, spending more time out of the water than in it, catching worms and insects. Adults overwinter out of water, under logs and in leaf mats below insulating snow cover, where the temperature stays just a few degrees below freezing all winter. In the fall, the frog pulls its back legs up under it, puts its front legs over its head, and dozes off.

Then it freezes solid. Yes, *solid;* it goes clunk if you tap it. There is no heartbeat, no respiration, no detectable brain activity. Yet if you remove the frog from the cold and set it in a warm place, it soon thaws and hops away.

How does it survive? No one is sure, but when the temperature reaches -2°C, and the frog starts to freeze, the liver pumps out glucose—a sugar—in amounts that would kill other living things. The glucose floods into the cells, where it sucks up moisture. This keeps the cells from losing too much water during freezing. Freezing cells ordinarily dump their water into the bloodstream, dehydrating themselves and thus killing the organism. Despite this water-fixing mechanism, 50 percent of the body fluid in a hibernating wood frog is ice.

This species comes out of hibernation and spawns just as the ice is melting in the marshes. It spawns by amplexus, like our other frogs and toads. Male wood frogs struggle so hard with one another in holding onto females that some of the males die, apparently from exhaustion. Masses of eggs are left attached to plants or simply floating in the water.

### Northern leopard frog *Grenouille léopard*

*Rana pipiens* (order Anura, family Ranidae)
March to October

HM

Occasional as far north as the Columbia Icefield on the western slope. Used to be present on the eastern slope, but no longer, except for a remnant prairie population just west of Calgary. Lives in cold montane and subalpine streams and ponds with thick vegetation. Adult sitting length 5–10 cm. This is the froggiest-looking frog in the mountains, smooth and green to yellowish or brownish with sharply defined black spots all over and pale ridges running from the eyes back to the tail. The song is varied and interesting, like a snore or a motor, mixed with clucks and grunts; Peterson's guide describes it as sounding like a balloon being rubbed. Like the wood frog, the leopard frog screams while being attacked, which can startle a predator into releasing it.

Mainly nocturnal, this frog stays in water by day but may go on land at night to hunt for insects. It dodges and leaps quickly back into the water if threatened. Spawns in the water from April to early June, by amplexus, with masses of eggs placed on the bottom or stuck to water plants.

### Columbian spotted frog *Grenouille maculée*
*Rana luteiventris* (order Anura, family Ranidae)
April to October

A mountain species, found scattered throughout the region in montane and subalpine streams or ponds without much vegetation sticking up above the water. Adult sitting length 4.5–10 cm. Same shape as the preceding *Rana* species, but different coloration: dark greenish brown, with scattered blurry light-centred dark spots, and a reddish tummy and nose. It makes fast, low-pitched calls that get louder in series—rather like the sound of a helicopter—but the voice is seldom heard. The male is smaller than the female and has extra-large thumbs (frog machismo).

Spotted frogs are active in the day, mainly staying in the water. They often move upland in spring to higher ponds; in the fall they return to lower elevations to hibernate underwater. The species spawns very early, often in March while there is still ice on the water; amplexus leads to masses of 700–1500 eggs.

### Tailed frog *Grenouille-à-queue*
*Ascaphus truei* (order Anura, family Ascaphidae)
April to September

Occasional in cold, swift montane streams south of Crowsnest Pass on the western slope. Adult sitting length 3–4 cm. Rough-skinned, the color varying from olive to gray, usually with dark spots and mottling; there is a triangular yellow spot on the snout.

Rather similar in color and pattern to the spotted frog, previous item, the tailed frog is usually more mottled, and the male has a tail-like extension of the cloaca that is used like a penis in copulating, while the spotted frog does not. No voice reported.

### Boreal chorus frog *Rainette faux-grillon*
*Pseudacris maculata* (treefrog family, Hylidae)
April to September

In shallow marsh ponds at low elevations on the eastern slope at least as far north as the Peace River. This is a small frog, adult sitting length 2–4 cm, but very loud, especially during the early-spring mating time. You can hear it as soon as the ponds are free of ice—although not in the large numbers I recall from the Jasper area in the early 1980s. The song is a loud trill, like the sound of a fingernail run along the teeth of a comb. The animal is olive-green to brown, with bumpy skin, but it's not warty like a toad. Three khaki stripes or rows of spots run down the back; the upper lip is white.

Chorus frogs are mostly nocturnal, when they leave water to hunt for insects on the ground, sometimes climbing up on plants to reach them. They spawn by amplexus and hibernate in burrows out of water. They freeze in the same manner as the wood frog, previous page.

**Pacific treefrog** *Rainette du Pacifique*
*Pseudacris regilla* (treefrog family, Hylidae)
April to September
    Occasional at low elevations on the western slope of Glacier National
Park and possibly around Fernie. Small; adult sitting length 2–5 cm. Plain
green, brown or yellowish, and capable of changing its color in a matter
of a few minutes. It always has a broad dark stripe through the eye, though,
rather like the mask of the wood frog, page 501. The Pacific treefrog has

HM

knobs at the ends of its fingers and toes, the skin is rough, and it never ventures to higher
elevations. Preferred habitat: up in shrubs and small trees beside water. The song is a loud, two-
part rasp, the second note higher than the first, familiar to nearly anyone as the sound of night
you hear in films and on television.

# *Snakes and turtles*
## Subphylum Vertebrata, class Reptilia

Reptiles have scaly skin and amphibians have smooth skin. Other differences: reptiles do not
undergo transformation from a larval stage to an adult stage. They just grow bigger. Fertilization
is internal—they copulate—and the eggs have shells. Some of our species bear their young
without shells.
    Ophidiophobes can relax in the Canadian Rockies. Snakes are scarce this far north, and
we haven't any poisonous ones. Well, any *really* poisonous ones. They are so small they can
hardly bite you. Except for one. Read on.

**Wandering garter snake** *Couleuvre de l'Ouest*
*Thamnophis elegans vagrans* (order Squamata, family Colubridae)
April to October
    Scattered populations in montane wetlands and woods in the Banff area,
Golden area, Jasper area and the Peace River Valley. Usually found in or near
water. A small snake: adult length in the mountains 30–80 cm. The illustration
shows the coastal variety of this snake, and the colors of Canadian Rockies
specimens are not exactly as illustrated. There is a prominent narrow pale stripe
down the back and yellow stripe along each side. Upper sides are dull olive or
gray, often with black spots; the lower sides and belly are lighter, with a bluish
tinge. Differentiate from the red-sided garter snake, next item, by the red-sided's

HM

black, red-spotted sides.
    The wandering garter snake catches tadpoles and small frogs, rodents and baby birds,
fish, slugs and worms. Like other garter snakes, it swallows its prey whole. If caught by a
predator, or by a person, it excretes nasty-smelling feces spiked with repellent compounds. Its
bite is slightly venomous from toxins secreted in the mouth, but harmless to humans. The
snake hardly ever bites anyway.
    Garter snakes are solitary most of the time, but they gang up for sex and hibernation.
During the spring mating, 5–10 males wrap themselves around a female, all of them trying to
get close enough to impregnate her. A male coils about the female and inserts a **hemi-penis,** of
which he has a pair, into her cloaca. The hemi-penis has barbs on it to prevent withdrawal until
the job is done. Garter snakes are **ovoviviparous:** the shells hatch inside the female, then the
young are born. The snakelets are 10–15 cm long at birth; they soon crawl away on their own.
    In September or October, garter snakes seek communal hibernating quarters in abandoned
rodent burrows, among boulders or deep in bedrock cracks. There they snooze the winter away
by the dozen. They can survive temperatures only down to -3°C. Emerging in April, they are
sluggish in the cool spring weather. The few I see around Jasper are often lying right in the
middle of a trail, immobile, soaking up the sun; I have had to step over them. One allowed my
wife to stroke it down the sides.

### Red-sided garter snake *Couleuvre rayée*
*Thamnophis sirtalis parietalis* (order Squamata, family Colubridae)
April to October

Occasional in or near montane streams and marshes, but sometimes found at much higher elevations. Most northerly reptile in North America, ranging to Fort Smith in the Northwest Territories. Found in the Rockies from the Peace River south. Adult length 45–130 cm. Colors not exactly as illustrated. On Canadian Rockies specimens, there is a prominent narrow cream stripe along the back, and a yellow stripe along each side. The snake typically has black upper sides, often with red spots; the lower sides are dark. There can be a lot of color variation in individuals, some of which may be markedly duller and thus very similar to the wandering garter snake, previous item; note differences in the wandering garter's belly color and somewhat smaller eyes.

The red-sided garter snake hunts mainly in the water, taking tadpoles, frogs, salamanders, small fish and leeches, but it also searches on land for small rodents, slugs and insects. The bite is mildly toxic, like that of the wandering garter snake, but harmless to humans, who are unlikely to be bitten at all. The habits and life cycle are essentially the same as that of the wandering garter. The young are born eggless in late summer or early fall, depending on the temperature; they take two or more years to mature and may live up to ten years.

HM

### Bullsnake/gopher snake *Couleuvre à nez mince*
*Pituophis catenifer* (order Squamata, family Colubridae)
April to October

Rare, but reported in the Waterton/Glacier area and in the eastern foothills south of Calgary. Could be present on the Rocky Mountain Trench floor from Golden south. Bullsnakes prefer grassy, sandy or rocky open woods.

This is by far the longest snake in the region, thick and heavy-looking with a small head; adult length 90–250 cm. It is sandy colored, with contrasting earth-brown regular patches along the back, becoming smaller toward the tail. The sides are mottled in the same amazingly protective color scheme, the head sandy and unpatterned.

The bullsnake hunts by day, especially at dawn and dusk, eating mostly rodents it kills by constriction. At night it hides in rodent burrows or among rocks. It fights back if threatened, hissing and shaking its tail in imitation of a rattlesnake, even striking like one. But there is no rattle and no poison. Still, this snake can bite hard. Don't pick it up.

HM

Bullsnakes mate in spring, laying eggs in sandy burrows or under rocks and logs; the eggs hatch 2–3 months later, in late summer. The adults hibernate in burrows, either taken from rodents or dug themselves.

### Rocky Mountain rubber boa *Boa caoutchouc*
*Charina bottae utahensis* (order Squamata, family Boidae)
May to September

Nocturnal, rare and thus seldom seen, but present in damp montane forests and meadows of the western slope from Radium south. The rubber boa ranges farther HM north in the Columbia Mountains just west of the Rockies, so it may be present in the Columbian forest area north of Golden. But unreported. Adult length 35–80 cm. It really does look like it's made of rubber: unpatterned, glossy olive to chocolate brown above, yellowish below.

This primitive snake has a very blunt tail; from a distance, it's hard to decide which end is which. On adult males, two spurs—vestigial hind limbs—near the anus are prominent. Females have them but they do not protrude as much.

The rubber boa burrows under rocks, logs and forest litter; at night it emerges to hunt small mammals, birds and lizards, often by swimming in shallow water or climbing into shrubs or partway up trees. It kills its prey by wrapping around it and squeezing, allowing exhalation but not inhalation. So it's a boa constrictor, but a wimpy one, harmless to humans. Two to eight young are born each year in early fall, without eggs. Presumably they overwinter in burrows.

## Western painted turtle *Tortue peinte*
*Chrysemys picta belli* (order Testudinata, family Emydidae)
April to October

Occasional in shallow, gentle streams and lakes at low elevations on both slopes of Glacier National Park; north in the Rocky Mountain Trench to Golden; reported from the Crowsnest Pass area and Bow River in Banff National Park. Adult shell 10–25 cm long. The shell is olive-brown on top, often with red or orange at the plate junctions; underneath it is brilliant red to yellow, with a dark pattern down the centre. The head, legs and tail have yellow stripes against a dark-olive background.

The only turtle in the Canadian Rockies, the painted turtle basks on mud, logs or rocks in shallow, weedy water with a muddy bottom. It eats aquatic insects, small fish, tadpoles and amphibians, becoming more vegetarian and scavenging as it grows older. It mates in spring, producing eggs in a bottle-shaped nest in shoreline sand; the young take a long time to grow up (males 2–5 years, females 4–8 years) and may live for several years more. Young turtles are freeze-tolerant and often hibernate in the nest. The adults usually hibernate underwater, in the bottom mud, although they have been known to stay active all winter under the ice.

Keeping painted turtles captive is usually unsuccessful. They need lots of clean water and the right natural foods; otherwise they die of various diseases. We have so few turtles in the mountains that they deserve every chance they can get. So please leave 'em be. The same can be said of our other reptiles and amphibians.

## *Further reading*

Behler, J. and F. King (1979) *The Audubon Field Guide to North American Reptiles and Amphibians.* Knopf, New York. Comprehensive and portable, with photographic illustrations and continental-scale range maps; 719 pages.

Green, D. and W. Campbell (1984) *The Amphibians of British Columbia.* Royal British Columbia Museum Handbook No. 45, Victoria. Slim and inexpensive, with good illustrations and range maps; 100 pages.

Gregory, P. and R. Campbell (1984) *The Reptiles of British Columbia.* Royal British Columbia Provincial Museum Handbook No. 3, Victoria. Companion guide to Green and Campbell's amphibian book, this one with a species index; 101 pages.

Russell, A. and A. Bauer (1993) *The Amphibians and Reptiles of Alberta.* University of Alberta Press and University of Calgary Press. A new guide, with excellent illustrations. Range maps, bibliography, index; 265 pages.

*A goshawk. (It's "GOSS-hawk," by the way, not "GOSH-hawk.") Photo by Barry Giles.*

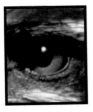

# Birds
## *Dinosaurs of a feather*

Yes, birds are dinosaurs. They're not classified that way yet; birds still occupy their own class (Aves) in the subphylum Vertebrata. But recently it has been shown that birds are so similar in form and life cycle to the thunder lizards that they might as well be included with the subclass Archosauria dinosaurs in the class Reptilia. Thus, you can now tell your kids that (a) the trees are full of dinosaurs, and (b) you're going to serve them dinosaur for dinner tonight, in the form of chicken.

Of the 650-odd species of birds in North America, we have 277 in the Canadian Rockies, of which 211 are seen frequently enough to be detailed in this book. The rare list is on page 588. Common and scientific names of bird families in the region are listed on page 589.

Birds do interesting things. They fly about, eat stuff, squabble with each other, throw their little heads back and sing amazingly. It's really not so surprising that bird-watching is the most popular outdoor activity in Canada and the United States. You can do it practically anywhere, and to any degree from casually observing birds in the park or on the feeder to full-blown, travel-anywhere-to-get-that-species obsession. I like to stop in places that seem birdy and wait quietly for a few minutes, binoculars in hand. The birds soon forget that I am there and go back to doing whatever they were doing when I arrived.

By the way, this technique—sitting very, very still until you become part of the woods—works for observing all sorts of animals. Called **Seton-watching,** after the Canadian naturalist Ernest Thompson Seton, who did it a lot, the method produces astounding results. Birds will land on your head; mice will walk over your shoes. I have heard of one case in the Rockies in which a beaver climbed out of a pond and curled up in a woman's lap while she was Seton-watching.

In the Rockies, water birds are the easiest to identify. They are boldly patterned and usually stay in male/female pairs. There is little or no vegetation to block the view, and the birds sometimes paddle close by if you are quiet. So beginners often learn the ducks, geese and other waterfowl first. You may also see osprey and bald eagles, fish-eaters both, around lakes and rivers. Valley-bottom lakes or ponds are the most productive; subalpine and alpine water bodies are less frequented. Getting there early (at dawn is best) will reward with the most bird business: flopping about in the water, diving and **dabbling**—which means tilting end-up to reach food on the bottom in the shallows—singing, flying about, doing mating displays, fighting and whatnot. But any time of day is okay. Best time of year: spring, from first open water in late April or early May until most of the breeding is over in mid-June. Except for the Waterton/Glacier area, the Rockies do not lie along a major waterfowl flyway,* so we don't get the enormous lakefuls of birds found farther east. However, the variety here is pretty good.

A sad note on waterfowl: their numbers, about 32 million for North America, are half what they were in the 1970s. Loss of habitat, drought on the prairies and overhunting have all been hard on them. Songbirds that winter in the tropics and subtropics are also in decline. See the boxed item on neotropical migrants, page 570.

Forest birds are more difficult to find and watch as they flutter among the trees or scrabble in the undergrowth. Except for the grouse family they are mostly smaller than waterfowl and often rather drab. Beginners usually learn the common, clearly marked ones first (black-capped chickadee, raven, magpie, gray jay) and get to the sparrows, warblers and flycatchers later. The best forest locations are around the edges of marshes, where there is the most activity and

---

*The Rockies do lie along a major eagle migration route. See page 541.

variety. Dry, grassy clearings are good, too. Again, morning is the best time and spring the best season. After mid-July the courtship displays and singing are over; to quote one Jasper birder, "Everybody just shuts up."

Open slopes at montane elevations are home to most of the mountain hawks and falcons. You'll see others, such as the merlin and the goshawk, mainly in the woods. Be prepared for frustration in identifying hawks; they are notoriously variable in color pattern. Ours are inclined to be dark.

Owls are woodland birds, active mainly at dawn and dusk. A knowledgeable owler goes mainly by the calls, which are distinctive and easy to learn. Listen in April and May.

The Rockies are famous for alpine-zone birds: ptarmigan, pipits, golden-crowned sparrows, horned larks and gray-crowned rosy finches. The ptarmigan is a curiously fearless and thus readily approachable high-country grouse. Northern harriers may pass close by as they fly low looking for ground squirrels, which are plentiful in the high country. Golden eagles sometimes do the same.

Recommended bird guides for the Rockies: George Scotter's excellent *Birds of the Canadian Rockies* and Kevin Van Tighem's *Birding Jasper National Park*, with its habitat-based approach. See "Further reading," page 591, for details on these books and information on checklists.

*Hunters:* be careful what you shoot. Nearly all birds in the Canadian Rockies are protected. The game laws keep changing, so I can't list them here; you should contact the Alberta and British Columbia wildlife departments before killing anything. Likewise, it is illegal to live-trap many species or to possess them even if you find them dead. You can't just pick up a road-killed hawk or keep an eagle feather found on the trail, for example.

# *Try these places first*
## Good birding localities in the Canadian Rockies

People accustomed to the tremendous numbers of birds seen in more temperate regions—the United States, for example, or along major flyways—may be disappointed when they come to the Canadian Rockies, for there are far fewer birds here. This is a difficult environment for birds. Perhaps the greatest problem for them is the mountain weather, which varies so much from year to year during the early-summer breeding season. A week of cold rain in late June can kill many a nestling, and the rest of the summer is too short for most species to manage a second brood.

Here are some of the better places in which to see birds. The numbers key to the map on the opposite page.

**1. The Waterton area** is on the Trans-mountain and Central waterfowl migration routes, so look for a good variety of ducks, other water birds and shorebirds in spring and fall. **Maskinonge Lake** and the adjoining marshes in Waterton are the best locations. Also, the prairies abruptly meet the mountains here, so you can find grassland species not seen farther north.

**2. The woods around Lake McDonald** in western Glacier National Park have species that prefer the deep Columbian forest found there.

**3. Wilmer Wildlife Refuge,** just north of Wilmer in the southern Rocky Mountain Trench, offers a fine assortment of wetland and lake species, with many tundra swans in spring. For more on this interesting place, see page 716.

**4. Kananaskis Country** is home to front-range species such as the mountain bluebird, which are regularly seen from Highway 40. A viewpoint near **Mt. Lorette** is the most famous in the Rockies for watching the eagle migrations of spring and fall (see page 541). Off the main access road in Kananaskis Lakes Provincial Park, the scrubby meadows along **Pocaterra Creek** are particularly recommended. The lakes themselves are notable for shorebirds, and black swifts are seen there.

**5. The foothills west of Calgary** are known for red-tailed and Swainson's hawks, kestrels and prairie falcons. Check the hogback ridges west of **Jumping Pound Creek** along the TransCanada Highway.

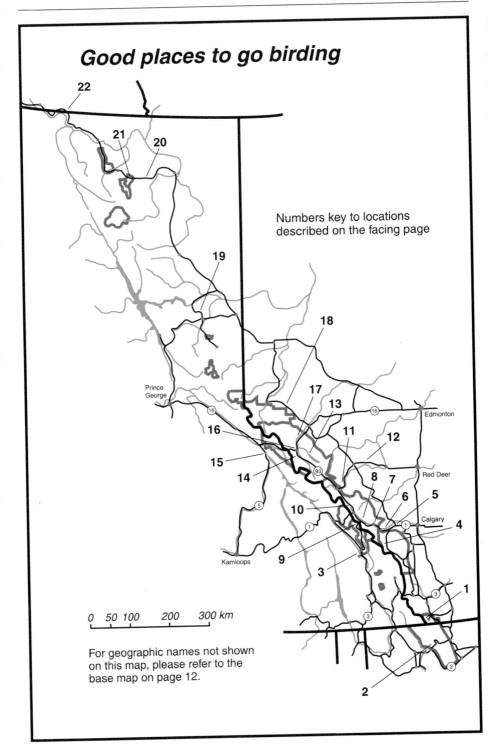

# *Good places to go birding*

Numbers key to locations
described on the facing page

Prince
George

Edmonton

Red Deer

Calgary

Kamloops

0  50 100  200  300 km

For geographic names not shown
on this map, please refer to the
base map on page 12.

**6. Lac des Arcs,** along the TransCanada Highway just west of the mountain front, has concentrations of ducks, Canada geese and tundra swans in spring and fall. Across the valley on Highway 1A, **Gap Lake** is another prime eagle-watching site during the migrations.

**7.** In Banff National Park, **Banff townsite** offers perhaps the best variety of woodland birds in the park. Nearby, **Fenland Trail** leads through old-growth spruce forest (woodpeckers, nuthatches, pygmy owls) and warbler-rich wetlands with shallow ponds well known for dabbling ducks. **Vermilion Lakes Drive** gives clear views over larger water bodies in the same area, and a boardwalk with a viewing blind has been built into the marshes below the **Cave and Basin** hot springs.

**8.** The **Bow Valley Parkway** in Banff park (Highway 1A) passes through prime mixed-wood habitat for chickadees, juncos, flycatchers, kinglets, thrushes and woodpeckers. Black swifts nest at **Johnston Canyon,** which is along this route.

**9. The Vermilion Pass Burn** along Highway 93 in Kootenay park is an area of ecological succession well known for northern hawk owls, pygmy owls, Townsend's solitaires and woodpeckers.

**10. Bow Summit,** north of Lake Louise along the Icefields Parkway, is an upper-subalpine area with easy walking access to alpine-zone birds. The trail up **Parker Ridge,** in the northern tip of the park, passes through similar habitat.

**11. The Kootenay Plains** lie along Highway 11 (the David Thompson Highway) east of Saskatchewan Crossing. This is a dry, grassy, aspen-rich region that attracts prairie species. Take a stroll around **Two O'clock Creek Campground.**

**12. The foothills between Rocky Mountain House and Nordegg** offer perhaps the best birding in western Canada. The boreal forest, aspen parklands and montane forest overlap here, so species from all these habitats may be seen.

**13. The Maligne River** in Jasper National Park, especially where it exits Maligne Lake, is the best locality in North America for observing courting harlequin ducks (late May to end of June).

**14.** Clark's nutcrackers are very common at the end of the road to **Mt. Edith Cavell,** and golden-crowned sparrows sing on the **Cavell Meadows** tundra reached by trail from here.

**15. Cranberry Marsh** near Valemount is famous for its black terns.

**16. Jasper townsite** offers a good variety of montane forest birds, with many ravens, white-crowned sparrows and swallows. Merlins nest in the town. The lakes surrounding Jasper are good for Barrow's goldeneye and red-necked grebe. **Cottonwood Slough,** located beside the road to Pyramid Lake, is good for warblers, snipes, soras and hummingbirds. Ospreys nest just east of town along the Athabasca River. It takes birders only seven minutes to reach the alpine zone on **The Whistlers** via the touristy Jasper Tramway. Walking down the trail to the mountain's base allows birding in every life zone.

**17. Eastern Jasper National Park** has large wetlands at low elevations along Highway 16; the marshes at **Pocahontas** and **Talbot Lake** are good spots. This is one of the few places in the Rockies for seeing yellow-headed blackbirds.

**18. Highway 40 between Hinton and Cadomin** is renowned for great gray owls and other boreal species, as is Highway 40 north to Grande Cache, which passes through the wetlands of **William A. Switzer Provincial Park.**

**19. Moberly Lake,** found between Chetwynd and Hudson's Hope along Highway 29, is a good location for waterfowl. Sapsuckers and other birds of the northern aspen parklands live along the shore.

**20. The Alaska Highway west of Fort St. John** is a good place to see flocks of snow buntings in winter, and short-eared owls.

**21. Summit Lake** in Stone Mountain Provincial Park is on the crest of the northern Rockies, where you may see the northern variety of the white-crowned sparrow. See page 583.

**22. The Liard Hot Springs marshes** along the Alaska Highway at the north end of the Rockies are bird-rich, and famous for mew gulls that buzz people.

## Species listings
### Binoculars at the ready, bird-book close at hand

The order of the listings here is essentially that of most bird books, modified in places so that look-alike birds can be more easily compared.

**Bird names.** In North America, ornithologists have been able to agree on standard common names. The standard English name is given first for each bird listing in this book. Then, for French-speaking readers, the common French name is given in italics. The Latin genus-and-species name is next, also in italics, followed by the common name of the family in parentheses. See the list on page 589 for scientific family names.

**Time of occurrence.** Seasonal bird arrival and departure dates given here are those noted in the national parks, where the best records are kept. Same for the abundance data. Because there are no national parks in the Rockies north of Jasper, the entire northern section lacks this degree of documentation and birders there will no doubt find errors in my abundance figures and dates for arrival/departure and nesting. Please let me know, so that corrections can be made in the next edition. My address is at the front of the book.

**Habitat descriptions** are based on field observations. The habitat preferred in the Canadian Rockies in summer is often different from that preferred in wintering areas far away. The ecological terms used, such as "montane," "subalpine" and "Columbian forest," are explained in the chapter on vegetation patterns. See page 221.

**Relative abundance of species.** In this book, *very common* means that a good birder will usually see or hear more than 25 of that species on a given day-long trip to the right habitat in the right season. *Common* means between 6 and 25, *fairly common* means 1 to 5, and *occasional* means perhaps one or two of that species over the course of the season. *Rare* means that the species has been reported in the national parks fewer than five times over the years. Rare birds aren't written up individually here, but on page 588 there is a list of rare and accidental (well-out-of-range) species.

**Voice.** For many species I have tried to describe in words what a particular bird sounds like. This is risky; birds don't speak English. A duck's call might sound something like "quack" "quack" to us, but of course it's actually saying, "Helluva big fish off your port bow, Roy."

My wife is convinced that all those chickadees and other cute little forest birds are trading warnings and insults back and forth; stuff like "My terr-i-tor-EEE!" and "Get out! Get out, nest fouler!"

Most woodpeckers **drum:** they bang their bills on resonant wood. This has nothing to do with drilling for bugs. It is a way of proclaiming territory and of announcing themselves to rivals and potential mates.

**Foods.** In the listings, the word **invertebrates** is used as it is in the section on fish. It refers mainly to water-dwelling insect larvae and crustaceans. Worms, snails, clams and flying insects are mentioned separately.

**Breeding dates** given here are intentionally vague. Experience has shown that in the mountains a particular species can nest over a rather long period, depending mostly on elevation. The snow melts up to a month earlier in the valleys than it does at treeline, and nesting frequently begins soon after the snow leaves. Birds in the south end of the range generally nest about a week earlier than birds in the north end. Further, a species that nests in mid-May in a normal spring might nest three weeks later if the winter has been snowy and the spring late. With a complicated formula like that, it is amazing that the birds know when to do their thing at all.

Speaking of which, you may be wanting to know how they actually do it. Answer: birds are one-holers. Everything—urine, feces, eggs—comes out the **cloaca.** Birds mate by briefly touching cloacas. The male passes sticky semen to the female, and the sperm move up her cloaca.

**Nesting records.** Seeing a bird on its nest is not an everyday occurrence. Even finding a nest takes some work. And identifying a species by looking at the nest is more difficult yet. Still, birders always want to know whether a given species nests in a given region. For nesting records in the Canadian Rockies I have had to rely on those kept by the national parks. If you see "No nesting record here" in the text, it means that there is no nesting record in the park checklists. The species may nest elsewhere—just outside the park boundary, for example. Please let me know if you find one of these "no-nesting-record" birds nesting in the Rockies.

**Nest construction:** cup-like unless otherwise indicated. Common nesting materials are twigs, shredded bark, moss, rootlets, grass and leaves; linings are usually feathers, hair and/or moss. When unusual materials are used they are mentioned.

**Eggs and nestlings.** The number of eggs given is the usual number; there can be more or fewer. Except as noted, all birds in the listings lay just one clutch of eggs each year. Egg colors don't seem to vary much in a particular species, but egg markings—speckles, blotches, scrawls or whatever—can vary a lot, so much so that providing detail on markings would take up too much space in a guide like this. The **incubation period** is the number of days between laying and hatching. To **fledge** is to fly, and usually is the time when a young bird leaves the nest—but not always. Ducks, grouse and sandpipers stay just a short time in the nest, often leaving as soon as they dry after hatching. These birds are **precocial,** meaning that they hatch fully feathered, able to see and to feed themselves immediately. Fledging dates a week or more past hatching mean that the bird is **altricial:** it comes into the world practically or completely naked, blind and helpless, requiring feeding and parental warmth for some time. Most birds in the Rockies are altricial.

**Range.** The complete summer range of a species seen here is not given for lack of space, but a brief note on the winter range is included because people want to know where the birds go. Likewise, the summer range is given for those birds that winter here.

## Ducks and duck-like water birds

See also the phalaropes, page 531.

### Common loon *Huart à collier*
*Gavia immer* (loon family)
Early April to early November

Common on montane and lower subalpine lakes, in ones and twos; doesn't like sharing territory. Length 60 cm, wingspan 150 cm. Sexes look alike. Head black. Neck has one wide white collar and one wide black one. Prominent white front, the rest patterned black and white. Red eye.

Loons ride lower in the water than ducks, and they carry their long bills tilted upward while swimming. They fly with the head and neck low, feet clasped together. Song is instantly recognizable: one or more loud "whoo-EEE-ooo"s followed by an insane-asylum laugh. Thus the phrase "crazy as a loon." The birds sing in flight, occasionally at rest. They dive frequently and may swim 50–100 m underwater before surfacing. Diet: mostly small fish, plus aquatic insects, snails and leeches.

*MW*

Breeding is in mid-spring. The nest, a raised heap of vegetation in light cover at the waterline on an island or close to shore, is used year after year by the same pair. Two brown-spotted olive eggs hatch in about 29 days. The young ride on their parents' backs for a couple of weeks, not flying until 70-77 days after hatching. When an adult pair is approached, one bird often comes toward you, singing; you are supposed to be distracted while the other bird swims off with the children. Loons winter along the west, east and Gulf coasts, and on the Great Lakes. **Pacific loons** use Pine Pass as a migration corridor through the Rockies, at least in autumn, when they have been reported in large flocks.

These birds cannot take off from land, but must start from water. If you find a loon or a grebe (next item) flopping about on a highway that it has mistaken for a river, just take it to the nearest body of water over 100 m long so that it can get airborne again.

### Red-necked grebe *Grèbe jougris*
*Podiceps grisegena* (grebe family)
Early April to early November

On lakes with shoreline vegetation, in ones and twos or small flocks. Common in central area, fairly common in the north, locally common south of Crowsnest Pass. Most often seen in May and June. Length 30 cm; wingspan 80 cm. Sexes look alike. Fairly long neck, rusty red, with prominent gray throat and lower head, black toupee. Sharp yellow bill, red eye. Back is mottled brown.

MW

The song of this bird is loud, squawky and frantic-sounding. The species dives for fish and invertebrates, and like the other grebes eats clams shell and all. Eats its own feathers, too, perhaps to line the stomach and aid in casting up hard parts. Like loons, previous item, grebes must take off from water and can become stranded if they light on land by mistake.

Every October I see a couple of grebes stuck in the thin lake ice of autumn. These birds have failed to migrate in time. Ice has built up around the shore, creeping out toward the centre until one day there has not been enough open water for takeoff. Trapped, the grebes are frozen in. Rescue is very risky over the thin ice; coyotes appreciate the waterfowl dinner.

Red-necked grebes nest in May/June, the nest a floating heap of rotting plants anchored in shallow water among vegetation; 4–5 white eggs hatch in 22–25 days. The young birds ride piggy-back and get fed invertebrates (plus adult feathers); don't fly until at least 10 weeks old. Wintering grounds: west and east coasts.

### Western grebe *Grèbe élégant*
*Aechmophorus occidentalis* (grebe family)
Early April to early June, again in September and October

On lakes; fairly common in flocks at a few locations; occasional elsewhere. The largest grebe: length 46 cm, wingspan 100 cm. Sexes look alike. Very long white-fronted neck, black on the back of the neck, white cheeks, long yellowish beak, red eye, dark mottled back. Rides low in the water. Song is surprisingly high and screechy, like fingernails on a blackboard.

MW

The western grebe runs on the water when taking off, and it has a wonderful courtship display: both sexes run along the surface together, necks arched, bills tilted up and wings held out. Diet: mostly fish, invertebrates and its own feathers. No nesting records. Winters along the west coast from Alaska to Baja California.

### Horned grebe *Grèbe cornu*
*Podiceps auritus* (grebe family)
Early April to early November

Occasional on lakes and marsh ponds, usually in small flocks; seen mostly in May and September. Length 25 cm, wingspan 60 cm. Short neck for a grebe, rusty-red, with front and underparts also rusty, black head and back. Prominent orange tufts run from the red eye to the upper back of the head; differentiate from similar eared grebe, next item, by the neck, all black on eared, and orange tufts lower on head of eared.

MW

Song resembles that of red-necked grebe, previous item, but squeakier. Dives for small fish and bottom-dwelling invertebrates. Rarely nests in the Canadian Rockies; reported from a marsh near Bragg Creek. Winters on the west coast.

### Eared grebe *Grèbe à cou noir*
*Podiceps nigricolli* (grebe family)
Late April to mid-May

Occasional; look for it on lakes and marsh ponds, in small flocks or among horned grebes. Length 23 cm, wingspan 58 cm. Resembles the horned grebe, previous item, but the neck is a little longer and black rather than red. Front is also black. The "ears" are tufts of orange feathers that sweep back from the red eye; feathers on the head form a dark topknot. On the horned grebe, the orange feathers ride higher, obscuring the top of the head. Song of the eared grebe is a series of quick reedy whistles, each one low-high.

MW

Unlike the other grebes, this one feeds mostly at and just below the surface, eating few fish but lots of water invertebrates, water boaters and dragonflies. No nesting records. Winters on lakes from Colorado south.

### Pied-billed grebe *Grèbe à bec bigarré*
*Podilymbus podiceps* (grebe family)
Late April and May, again in September

Occasional on lakes and wetland ponds at low elevations, usually alone. Rare in northern region. An odd-looking grebe; small (length 23 cm), with a disproportionately large head, large brown eye, and heavy bill with a dark line across it. Dark throat and light rump; the rest is plain brown with a little mottling down the sides.

MW

This grebe makes the sort of sounds one imagines coming from a flying saucer: rhythmic "wah-wah-wah" for a bit, then "ee-oo, ee-oo, ee-oo" for a bit. Dives for water invertebrates and small fish. Builds a small nest in late spring, the nest floating in tall vegetation near the shore of a lake or pond. Four to seven white eggs hatch in 23 days; the young are precocial, ride on parents' backs. Flying age unknown. Winter range: west coast from Vancouver Island south, through the southwest to the Gulf coast, up the east coast to New York.

### Mallard *Canard colvert*
*Anas platyrhnchos* (waterfowl family)
Year-round; common April through November

The most common duck in the mountains, found in flocks on lakes, marsh ponds and slow-moving streams. Readily identified by the large size (length 40 cm, wingspan 90 cm) and the male's coloration: green head with yellow bill, white stripe at base of neck, rusty front, white sides with blue patch on each side near the rear, dark back with a couple of cute curls on the rump. Compare with northern shoveler, next item, which is smaller, with white front and rusty sides—just the reverse of the

MW

mallard—and long black bill. The female mallard is mottled brown with an orange bill and the same blue patch on the side near the back. This is actually part of a band of color along the trailing edge of the wing, seen folded. Called the **speculum,** this band is useful in identifying the otherwise drab-looking females of many duck species as they fly.

Male mallards are mostly silent, sometimes rattling a little; the female song is "quack-quack-quack," very familiar. Mallards don't dive under water; they are dabblers, meaning they tip up and down in the shallows snapping up bulrush seeds, snails and invertebrates from the bottom, grabbing the odd tadpole and sometimes scavenging dead fish.

Nesting is in early spring to mid-spring, the nest a plant-lined mud hollow at the water's edge (although up to a half-kilometre inland on occasion); 8–10 pale-green/bluegreen/white eggs are hidden under down. They hatch in 26–29 days, the young heading for the water with mum as soon as they are dry. First flight is at 7–8 weeks. Mallards can live a long time; the record is 29 years. Some of our mallards overwinter in the southern Rocky Mountain Trench; most fly southwest to lakes in Washington and Oregon. However, the species will overwinter anywhere that has shallow open water, such as at a spring-fed pond with a good food supply.

### Northern shoveler *Canard souchet*

*Anas clypeata* (waterfowl family)
Late April to early June, again late August to late September

Fairly common on lakes and ponds, often with wigeons, next item. Length 35 cm, wingspan 80 cm. Very mallard-like duck, with green head and lots of white, but smaller, with a long black bill rather than a shorter yellow one and a white front rather than a rusty one. Sides are brown or rusty. Females are also mallard-like: mottled brown, but again the long bill differentiates. Voice: "cluck-luck, cluck-luck," like the tick of a large clock.

Shovelers skim the surface with their big bills, scooping up floating bugs, water boaters and floating seeds; they also tip up and down in shallow water, getting seeds and invertebrates off the bottom. No nesting records here. Wintering is from the B.C. coast to Baja California, across American southwest, Gulf states and Caribbean.

### American wigeon *Canard siffleur d'Amérique*

*Anas americana* (waterfowl family)
Early April and May, again August through October

Fairly common when on migration, seen on lakes, sloughs and gentle streams, in flocks. Length 35 cm, wingspan 85 cm. Male easily identified by the green band from eye to nape of neck; the rest of the head is brown-speckled white, top whiter than the rest. Green-winged teal, next item, also has a green band, but the rest of the head is rusty red, not white.

Female wigeons are mottled brown; check for black on the end of the gray bill to differentiate from similar teal species and gadwall, page 517. Ring-necked females, page 518, have a similar bill, but they are bigger, with a white eye-ring and stripe; some other female ducks are even more similar, but their heads are never mottled with white like the wigeon. Scaup females, page 519, have white around the bill base. Female ducks are tricky to identify, but fortunately they stick with the readily identifiable males.

The male wigeon has an endearing voice, like the squeak of a bath-toy rubber duck. Females quack. Pairs and groups dabble in the shallows, calling frequently and sometimes walking along the shore. They eat mostly pondweed, grasses and sedges. Breeding is in late spring, in a poorly concealed mound of vegetation lined with down, well out of the water. Eggs 9–11, white/buff, hatch in 25–26 days. Young leave nest same day, fly at 6–8 weeks. Wintering grounds are along the west coast from Vancouver Island south.

Male **Eurasian wigeons**, *Anas penelope*, have been showing up in spring in the Jasper area since the early 1990s. This species looks much like the male American wigeon, but the male's head is reddish, with no green band, and his sides are gray, not pinkish. Fronts of both species are pink. No female Eurasian wigeons have been reported yet; they are practically identical to female American wigeons (may have somewhat darker heads). This bird does not nest in North America, but in recent years it has been *wintering* on the west coast in ever-greater numbers, flying across the Bering Strait from Asia and south as far as Baja California. The ones we see are probably trying to return to their summering grounds in Siberia.

### Green-winged teal *Sarcelle à ailes vertes*
*Anas crecca* (waterfowl family)
Late March to late October

Fairly common in marshes, on lakes and rivers, in small dabbling groups. Length 27 cm, wingspan 60 cm. Like the male wigeon, male green-winged teal is easily identified by the shiny green band from eye to nape of neck. But the head is rusty red, not mottled white like that of wigeon, and lacks the broad white over-the-head stripe. Female is mottled brown, nondescript except for the iridescent green speculum in the wing, part of which often shows even when the wing is folded. Wigeon female has this too, but the band is quite small and the head is whiter.

MW

Song is a very high "ka-peet, ka-peet, ka-peet." Breeding is in late spring, the nest well concealed at the water's edge, sometimes farther ashore, lined with down. Eggs 10–12, elliptical and matte white; they hatch in 23–24 days. Birds leave the nest a few hours later and fly at 44 days. They winter in the western and southern United States.

### Cinnamon teal *Sarcelle cannelle*
*Anas cyanoptera* (waterfowl family)
Late April to late July

Occasional on small lakes and in marshes, southern and central regions, singly or in pairs. Length 28 cm, wingspan 64 cm. Male is the only all-over reddish duck in the Canadian Rockies; the back is red-mottled black. Female teal of all three species are difficult to tell apart: cinnamon has a broad white line on the side, ahead of the green speculum; female blue-winged has a pale blue to gray stripe in the same location, while green-winged has a brownish stripe.

MW

Male cinnamons make a rattling noise. The species dabbles in the shallows, eating mainly seeds of aquatic vegetation; also snails and invertebrates. No nesting records. Winters in California, Nevada, Mexico and South America.

### Blue-winged teal *Sarcelle à ailes bleues*
*Anas discors* (waterfowl family)
Late April to early October

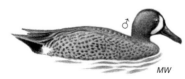

Fairly common on lakes and slow rivers in small flocks, always at the end opposite your viewing point. A small, shy duck that flies away at the slightest alarm. Length 28 cm, wingspan 60 cm. Male has beautiful head coloring: white crescent moon between bill and eye, rest of head blue with black top. Body mottled brown with a bit of the blue wing often showing along the upper side,

MW

just ahead of the green speculum, and a white patch low at the back. Female is mottled brown, with the same blue stripe along the side and a prominent brown eye-line. Both sexes show the blue wing color in flight. Squeaky-toy song, with high-pitched quacking.

This duck dabbles in the shallows, sometimes tipping to reach the bottom for snails and invertebrates but mostly skimming with its bill at and just under the surface for seeds. Nests in mid-spring, usually by a small marsh pond, the down-lined, basket-like nest well hidden on the ground. Eggs 9–11, cream to pale olive, hatching at 23–24 days; like other teal species, the young hit the water a few hours after hatching. Wintering: far to the south, in Mexico or the Gulf states, some along the coast of southern California.

### Gadwall *Canard chipeau*
*Anas strepera* (waterfowl family)
Late April to mid-June, again August and September

Occasional; look for gadwalls in pairs, often with wigeons, page 515, or pintails, next item, on lakes and marsh ponds. Length 37 cm, wingspan 80 cm. A drab duck; even the male has no bright coloration. This can be an easy identifier: any pair of ducks in which both partners are drab is probably a pair of gadwalls. Male has a thin white curved line on the side, near the front, and there is a small white patch farther back. Female is similar, lacking the curved white stripe, with a lighter bill and brown eye-line. Song is simple and quacky.

*MW*

This duck mainly dabbles for stems, leaves and roots of aquatic vegetation, but it also ventures into deeper water to dive for small fish and leeches, going to the bottom for invertebrates and worms. Nests east of the Rockies; winters in the southern and southwestern states and in Mexico.

### Northern pintail *Canard pilet*
*Anas acuta* (waterfowl family)
Early April through October

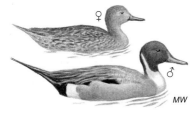

Occasional to fairly common on lakes and marsh ponds, a few pairs at a time, usually dabbling among wigeons. Length 47 cm, wingspan 90 cm. Easily identified by the long, sharp-looking tail feathers of the male; compare with oldsquaw, next item. Pintail also sports a white front and neck, the white continuing up onto the brown head in a finger-like stripe. There is a white patch low on the side, near the rear. Female is mottled brown, plain-Jane until she flies, when the

*MW*

speculum (stripe of colored feathers along trailing edge of wing) shows rainbowy orange, green and white. Male song is a small but insistent "NIN-yee, NIN-yee"; the female quacks.

Pintails dabble in the shallows for seeds along the bottom, also getting snails, invertebrates, leeches and the odd minnow. Occasionally they nest in the mountains, in mid-spring, along the shores of lakes or marsh ponds in thick vegetation. Eggs 7–9, in various pale colors in a down-lined mound. Hatching is at 25–26 days, leaving nest right away; the young fly at 7 weeks. The birds winter on the west coast.

### Oldsquaw *Canard kakawi*
*Clangula hyemalis* (waterfowl family)
Mid-April to mid-May

Occasional on lakes, passing through on their way to summering grounds in the Arctic. Length 38 cm, wingspan 75 cm. Long, sharp tail like the pintail, previous item, but smaller body with different markings: black head and neck with large white patch

*MW*

on face; white sides and dark back. Female lacks the long tail, has white face with dark spot below and behind the eye. Male says "ah, ah-oo-ah"; female quacks.

Feeding is mainly by diving, sometimes as deep as 60 m, for bottom-dwelling invertebrates and freshwater clams; also eats aquatic vegetation. Fast flyer, 120 km/h. Oldsquaws winter along the coasts, often well out to sea.

### Canvasback *Morillon à dos blanc*
*Aythya valisineria* (waterfowl family)
Mid-April to late May, again mid-August to late September

Fairly common on lakes and ponds, seen mostly in the foothills. Rather large duck: length 38 cm, wingspan 86 cm. Easily picked out among other birds by the dark-red head and neck, black front and light-gray body with black tail. But closely resembles the redhead, next item. Differentiate by the canvasback's longer, flatter, blacker bill that curves smoothly up into the forehead; redhead's bill is gray with black tip and stubbier. Female canvasback is gray with light-brown front and head. Male canvasback song is a turkey-like gobble; female quacks.

This duck dives for bottom-growing aquatic vegetation; also eats seeds, invertebrates, snails and small fish. Nests east and west of the Rockies, but not here. Flocks migrate in V-shaped pattern to/from the west coast, Vancouver south.

### Redhead *Morillon à tête rouge*
*Aythya americana* (waterfowl family)
Mid-April to mid-June

Occasional on lakes in spring, during migration to nesting areas east and west of the Rockies. Sighted a few times in the fall. Length 37 cm, wingspan 85 cm. Male closely resembles canvasback, previous item, and this species often swims with canvasbacks, but the redhead bill is stubbier and gray, with a black tip. Head is rounder. Female is plain brown with light cheeks and underparts. Male call is a short siren-like sound, repeated over and over; female quacks.

Feeding is by diving for stems and leaves of water plants, skimming duckweed and snatching bugs. No nesting records. Wintering is along the west coast from Vancouver south.

### Ring-necked duck *Morillon à collier*
*Aythya collaris* (waterfowl family)
Early April to mid-October

Common in pairs and small flocks on southern and central lakes and marsh ponds, less common in the northern area. Length 30 cm, wingspan 72 cm. Males are dark purple or black on the head and neck, with yellow eyes. Eyes of female are brown. A low tuft of feathers on the head makes a rounded point; black-tipped gray bill is similar to redhead. White line behind the black tip is more prominent, and there is a narrow fringe of white at the bill base.

Differentiate from scaup, next item, by the dark back and the black-and-white bill markings on the male ring-necked, and by the prominent white bill base on the female scaup. Female ring-neck is brown with pale cheeks and black-and-white-tipped bill like that of male; she also sports a white eye-ring and line leading back, like a pair of spectacles without the nose-bridge. Soft male song is seldom heard; he whispers sweet nothings. Female's voice is low and quacky.

This is a shallow-diving species, picking up seeds, invertebrates, worms and snails from the bottom. Breeding is usually in small marsh ponds in mid-spring, the nest a down-lined hollow by the water with 6–12 greenish eggs that hatch in 26 days. Birds are precocial. First flight at 49–56 days. Wintering is along the American west coast and through the south to Mexico.

### Lesser scaup *Petit morillon*
*Aythya affinis* (waterfowl family)
Late March through October

Fairly common on lakes and marsh ponds, in flocks. Length 30 cm, wingspan 75 cm. Male very similar to ring-necked duck, previous item, but the head-bump is not as prominent and the bill lacks the white markings. Scaup head is purplish, although it often looks black from a distance. Female is brown, rather dark on the head, with a prominent white ring around the base of the bill. Both sexes have yellow eyes.

Males coo softly; females say "scaup, scaup, scaup." They feed by diving for small fish, tadpoles, snails and aquatic insects; they eat seeds and aquatic plant parts as well. Breeding time is late spring; 8–12 dark-olive eggs in a down-lined hollow near the water hatch in 26–27 days; young leave nest right away, fly at 49 days. Winter range: west coast, Mexico and the Gulf states.

### Barrow's goldeneye *Garrot de Barrow*
*Bucephala islandica* (waterfowl family)
Early March to mid-November

On lakes and rivers, in pairs. Very common from Banff north, less common to the south. Length 33 cm, wingspan 80 cm. Male is strikingly black and white, with a prominent white crescent on the cheek. Female is mottled gray, brown-headed or sometimes rusty, with a white ring on the neck. Eyes of both sexes are bright yellow. Compare with very similar common goldeneye, next item; note smaller facial spot on the common, larger white spots on the back, and more white on the female common. Male Barrow's hasn't much of a voice—he grunts and whistles softly during courting—but makes a characteristic "woo woo woo" sound with wings when flying.

When approached, goldeneyes are inclined not to fly. They usually just paddle away a short distance. These ducks dive for dragonfly and damselfly larvae; they eat a lot of pondweed and get the odd small fish. Interesting courtship display: male swims toward female, moving his head forward and then *way* back. Nesting is in mid-spring, in hollow stumps and woodpecker holes in the woods; 8–14 greenish or bluegreen eggs hatch in 30 days. The young jump out of the nest soon after and follow mum to water; they stay with her for a month or two before they can fly. Wintering is on the west coast; this species may be found year-round in central B.C. and south along the American Rockies.

## Common goldeneye *Garrot à oeil d'or*
*Bucephala clangula* (waterfowl family)
See below for seasons

On lakes and rivers, seen from November to March wintering on any open water. During breeding season they are occasional in central areas, where they are seen in April and May headed north. In November and December they can be seen again. Look for them through the summer north of Peace River. Length 33 cm, wingspan 80 cm.

Male very similar to Barrow's goldeneye, previous item, but the facial spot is smaller and the head greenish and shaped a little differently; the body is whiter, without the plunging black mark on the shoulder. Females are whiter than Barrow's females. Males say "jeep, jeep," and their wings go "woo woo woo" when flying. Females quack. Feeding and diet like that of Barrow's.

Common goldeneyes breed in the late spring, nesting in tree cavities in the woods near water; 6–11 greenish eggs hatch in 30 days. Young birds jump from the nest, follow the female to water and swim with her until they fly at about 60 days. Winter on the west coast, through southern B.C. and most of the U.S.A.

## White-winged scoter *Macreuse à ailes blanches*
*Melanitta fusca* (waterfowl family)
Early May to mid-June, again mid-August to late October

Fairly common on large lakes during migration, usually in flocks. Length 40 cm, wingspan 97 cm. A large, very dark duck, with an apostrophe-like white eye patch on the male and another white patch on the upper side near the rear. Bill is diagnostic: small and bright orange, with a prominent black bump at the base. Female's bill is black and lacks the bump; she has two white facial patches and a white patch near the rear; looks much like female surf scoter, next item, which lacks the white rear patch. Male white-winged is more easily told from male surf scoter by head pattern and bill shape. The male croaks but is seldom heard.

These are diving birds. They subsist mainly on invertebrates and small fish, but also eat freshwater clams, shell and all. No nesting records here. They work their way into northwestern Canada from winter homes along the west coast from Alaska to Baja California, in the Great Lakes and along the Gulf/east coast from Alabama to Newfoundland.

## Surf scoter *Macreuse à front blanc*
*Melanitta perspicillata* (waterfowl family)
Early May to mid-June, again late September to early November

Occasional during migration on lakes from Banff north, in ones and twos. Length 35 cm, wingspan 83 cm. Very dark, like the white-winged scoter, previous item. Male identified by the interesting pattern of white and black spots on the head—somewhat variable and often difficult to make out in poor light—and the heavy

orange bill. No prominent bump at the bill base, as in male white-winged scoter. Female surf scoter is very similar to female white-winged, but lacks the white patch on the upper side, near the back. Habits and range similar to white-winged; no nest records here.

### Bufflehead *Petit Garrot*

*Bucephala albeola* (waterfowl family)
Early April to mid-November
　　Fairly common on lakes, marsh ponds and rivers. A small duck, length 25 cm, wingspan 60 cm. Both male and female are easily identified by their white head patches: male has a large, broad one and female a smaller, oval one. Lots of white on the male; female is grayer. Male whistles softly; female quacks harshly.

　　This species dives for insect larvae and bottom invertebrates, snails, small fish and seeds. Breeds on the western slope in late spring; nests in flicker holes near water. Eight to twelve cream/buff or pale-olive eggs in the unlined cavity, hatching in 29 days; the young jump to the ground soon after, following mother to water. First flight at 50–55 days. This species winters along the west, east and Gulf coasts and through the western U.S.A.

### Ruddy duck *Canard roux*

*Oxyura jamaicensis* (waterfowl family)
Early April to mid-June, again early August to late October
　　Occasional on lakes and marsh ponds, during migration. Length 28 cm, wingspan 58 cm. Courting male has a good identifier: fan-shaped black tail held stiffly upward. Body is reddish, with prominent white patch on lower face and black upper head with low crests over the eyes. Bill is blue. Female fairly similar, but drab rather than red, with dark line through the light facial patch. She carries her tail down. Male song: several quick chips, followed by "braaak."
　　Feeding: ruddies dive for seeds and bottom-dwelling vegetation; go especially for midge larvae. No nesting records here, although the Canadian Rockies lie within their summer range. Winter range: west coast from Vancouver Island south, across Mexico and along the Gulf and east coasts.

### Harlequin duck *Canard arlequin*

*Histrionicus histrionicus* (waterfowl family)
Early May to mid-August
　　Occasional on swift rivers and around lake outlets/inlets, usually in pairs or a few at a time. Small, length 30 cm, wingspan 66 cm. Gaudy. Male is bluish-black, with white stripes outlined in black, and red patches. Compare with wood duck, next item. Female is drabber, browner, with white facial patches. Voice seldom heard; male squeals, female croaks.
　　This species lives in the torrents; it dives in the rapids and works its way along the bottom, eating larvae of mayflies, stoneflies and caddisflies. Known to eat fish eggs. Females nest in early summer, mostly on islands in the same rivers where breeding occurs; males head for coastal B.C. after breeding. Four to eight

creamy eggs are laid in a downy hollow in the ground, hatching in 27–33 days. Young fly at 40 days. Wintering is in heavy surf along the coast, although some stay on open water in the Rockies.

An endangered species in eastern North America, the harlequin duck is losing ground in the west, too. Hydroelectric development, which turns its habitat into reservoirs, is one cause. The other is the growth of fly-fishing, recreational kayaking and especially commercial whitewater rafting, which puts so many boatloads of hollering humans down the river that the ducks are disturbed too often to breed. The Maligne River in Jasper National Park and McDonald Creek in Glacier National Park are closed to boating throughout the summer to protect the ducks during courting and nesting. But elsewhere there is no such protection. If you want to see this amazing little duck before human greed and ignorance extirpate it, go to the outlet of Maligne Lake in late May or early June and look downriver from the bridge, where harlequins will be courting in the waves and resting on the boulders.

## Wood duck *Canard branchu*
*Aix sponsa* (waterfowl family)
April to mid-June, a few seen all summer

Occasional from Waterton/Glacier to Jasper. Length 34 cm, wingspan 71 cm. To many the most beautiful duck in North America: male is multi-colored red, brown, white, blue, green—even fancier than the harlequin, previous item—with a prominent drooping crest at the rear of the head. Red eyes. Female is much less colorful, although she, too, is elegant: crest, spectacles (eyes are black), lacy pattern on neck, front and lower sides, and blue patch running onto the tail. Males whistle; females say "wok."

MW

Wood ducks spend more time on land than other species in the mountains, running about the shore for plant fruits and seeds in addition to their staple, duckweed. Sometimes the birds perch in trees. The few wood ducks that visit the Canadian Rockies also breed here, in mid-spring, nesting in tree holes. Eggs 8–10, cream-colored, hatching in 29–32 days. The young jump out of the nest, sometimes from 10–20 m up (!), then follow their mother to water. Fly 63 days later. Wintering grounds: not far away in western Washington and along the coast, where wood ducks live year-round.

## Common merganser *Gran Bec-scie*
*Mergus merganser* (waterfowl family)
Late March to late October

Properly pronounced "MER-gan-zer," although many people say "mer-GAN-zer." Fairly common in pairs and small flocks on lakes and rivers; very common in the south end of the Canadian Rockies. Large: length 45 cm, wingspan 95 cm. Male is green-headed, with long orange bill that is hooked on the end; female is rusty-orange on the head with a crest down the back of the neck and similar bill. To differentiate from male red-breasted merganser, next item, note crest and spotted brown front on the red-breasted; the male common lacks the crest and is white-fronted. Females of the two species are trickier to tell apart: common's head coloration ends abruptly on the neck; red-breasted's color changes more gradually downward. Male voice sounds like a plucked musical string; female says "ruff, ruff, ruff."

MW

Mergansers swim along with their heads down in the water looking for small fish to dive after; they also eat frogs, salamanders, snails, leeches, worms—nearly any water animals they can get. Breeding is in mid-spring; 7–14 cream or yellowish eggs in a down-lined tree-hole or plant-lined hollow among shoreline rocks. Hatching is in 28–32 days; nest is left a day or two later. The ducklings paddle around with mum for about five weeks before they can fly. Wintering is on inland lakes throughout much of the United States; some overwinter on open water in southern B.C.

### Red-breasted merganser *Bec-scie à poitrine rousse*

*Mergus serrator* (waterfowl family)
Late April to early June, except summer resident in north end of the Rockies

Occasional on northern lakes and rivers, rare from Jasper south. Length 40 cm, wingspan 85 cm. Very similar to common merganser, previous item; differentiate males by crest and spotted brown vest on the red-breasted, which the common lacks, and fuzzy color edge on female red-breasted's neck. Males go "yeow, yeow"; females quack.

Habits are like those of common merganser, but red-breasted apparently doesn't nest here, except possibly at the far northern end of the Rockies. It holds the speed record for ducks in the range: 160 km/h. Wintering is along the west and east coasts.

MW

### Hooded merganser *Bec-scie couronné*

*Lophodytes cucullatus* (waterfowl family)
Early April to end of May, again from late July to early November

Occasional migrant, seen on lakes, gentle rivers and marsh ponds. Smaller than the other mergansers; length 33 cm, wingspan 66 cm. Males have a distinctive crest. Raised, it produces a large white patch on the head; lowered, it can still be seen as a narrow white triangle or broad white line. Compare with bufflehead, page 521. Females look very much like the other merganser ladies, but the bill is shorter and dark rather than orange. Males make a noise like a ship creaking; females are silent.

This species dives for invertebrates, insect larvae and small fish. Occasionally it nests in the Rockies from Banff south, in cavities of dead trees near water. Winters in southwestern B.C. and in fresh water along the west, Gulf and east coasts.

MW

### American coot *Foulque d'Amérique*

*Fulica americana* (rail family)
Early April to early November

Very common in flocks on southern-area lakes and marsh ponds, especially in spring and fall, becoming less common as you go north. Length 30 cm, wingspan 65 cm. A drab bird, except for its large bone-white bill and red eye. Easily recognized by the way it paddles: the head moves back and forth, pigeon-like. Males and females look the same.

MW

Voice is cackly and chicken-like, as is the bird, for coots are not really ducks, even though they act like ducks. Coots have lobed toes rather than webbed feet. They feed both on the shore and in the water, energetically leaping up when they dive, mainly for aquatic vegetation but also for seeds, small minnows, tadpoles, snails, worms and invertebrates. This species rarely nests in the Canadian Rockies. There is one definite record, for a pond in the Jasper area.

## Geese and swans

Canada geese steal each other's children. Read on.

### Canada goose *Bernache du Canada*
*Branta canadensis* (waterfowl family)
Early April to end of October

Locally very common, overall less so, on lakes, gentle rivers and marsh ponds. Big, but quite variable in size: length 40–65 cm, wingspan 125–170 cm. Our birds are as large as they come. Easily identified by the long black neck with the white patch at the top. The body is brown, lighter on the front, with black tail feathers and white underparts. Males and females alike. The voice is instantly recognizable: "a-honk, a-honk, a-honk," an aural image of the north.

MW

Canada geese sometimes dabble in shallow water for roots, leaves and seeds of aquatic vegetation, but mainly they graze on land. They especially like the tender grass of golf greens, where they coexist uneasily with the golfers and presumably consume a lot of weed-killer.

Nesting is in mid-spring, usually on a small island or overgrown beaver lodge. Arriving adult pairs, which mate for life, fight for these sites, calling loudly, biting, and beating each other with their wings. Eventually the territories get sorted out, and each nest holds 5–6 large white eggs that hatch in 25–30 days. At any particular nesting locality, which might have several pairs of adults living fairly close to one another, the eggs all hatch at the same time. The goslings leave the nest the same day, swimming after the parents until able to fly at about nine weeks.

The more aggressive adults lure goslings away from their natural parents and keep them, forming **gang broods** of up to 250 birds, with multiple pairs of adults. In a species as aggressive as the Canada goose, this behavior makes sense; a gang brood is a strong brood, better able to compete for feeding sites during migration and wintering. Parents who lost their young to these gangs often fly well north in May, along with other failed breeders and yearling birds, to lakes not frequented by gang-gatherers. This amounts to a minor second migration.

Some Canadian Rockies birds spend the winter close by in northern Idaho, while others fly to the west coast (B.C. to California) or overwinter inland from California's big San Joaquin Valley to Colorado. During migration the birds fly in a V-shaped pattern that has been shown to reduce the effort for all birds except the leader, which is usually a female. In any particular gaggle, though, the gander of the pair with the most goslings, their own offspring or recruited, is the dominant bird. Canada geese can fly at speeds of 90 km/h, and they can live a long time: the documented record is 33 years, unverified to 80 years.

### Snow goose *Oie des neiges*
*Chen caerulescens* (waterfowl family)
Late April to early May, again in September

Uncommon, resting on lakes with Canada geese during spring and fall migrations. Length 48 cm, wingspan 150 cm. The snow goose is mostly white and thus easily mistaken for the all-white domestic goose. But check the wingtips: if they are black, it is a snow goose. Males and females look alike. Call is similar to Canada goose, previous item, but a little higher-pitched.

Like the Canada goose, the snow goose is a grazer: it eats the tender young shoots of grasses and marsh vegetation. Also digs out shoreline tubers and sprouts with its bill. Breeds in the Arctic, not here. Winters along the west coast, from Washington to Mexico.

MW

### Tundra swan and trumpeter swan *Cygne siffleur, cygne trompette*
*Cygnus columbianus, C. buccinator* (waterfowl family)
Late March to late May,
again early October to mid-November

The tundra swan was formerly called "whistling swan," *Olor columbianus.* Occasional flocks rest on lakes during spring and fall migrations; perhaps most common in the southern Rocky Mountain Trench. Trumpeter swans are seen occasionally in tundra-swan flocks. Tundra swan length 90 cm, wingspan 200 cm; trumpeter length 115 cm, wingspan 225 cm, second-largest bird in the Canadian Rockies after white pelican, next page.

Identification: swans are all white, with a very long neck and a big black bill. The tundra swan has a yellow spot at the base of the bill, by the eye, which the trumpeter swan does not. Check carefully; the spot can be very small. Males and females look alike. Voice of the tundra swan is an oboe-like honking, rather like the Canada goose or snow goose, previous items, but more musical and higher-pitched. Trumpeter swan is aptly named; very loud, with one low note followed by several higher ones.

MW

Swans are dabblers that eat mostly water plants, using their long necks to reach the bottom in water up to half a metre deep. Sometimes dabbling ducks such as mallards and wigeons will stay close by them, sharing food stirred up by the swans in water too deep for the short-necked ducks. Swans also come on land to graze as geese do. Breeding is in the Arctic. The birds winter in huge flocks at scattered places in the United States. Site nearest us is in western Washington.

## *Weird birds that live in the swamp*

Except as noted, in this section males and females look the same. See also the blackbirds, page 574.

### Great blue heron *Grand Héron*
*Ardea herodias* (heron family)
Early August to end of September

Fairly common in southern area, occasional in central section, rare in the north end. Look for this bird in marshes, along lakeshores and slow-moving rivers. It is very large: length 97 cm, wingspan 175 cm. Easily recognized by the bluish color, long S-shaped neck and big orange bill. Head is white with a black line extending off the back in a long crest. Flies with neck folded back, extending it only when landing or taking off. This habit can be used to differentiate from **sandhill crane,** *Grus canadensis,* a prairie species that is sometimes seen in southern or northern areas, which flies with neck extended. Sandhill is also lighter, has red crown, white cheeks and no crest. More closely related to the heron is the **great egret,** *Casmerodius albus,* heron-like in build but pure white with black legs and lacking a crest. Rare, but seen occasionally as far north as Jasper. And speaking of white birds, the **American white pelican,** *Pelecanus erythrorhynchos,* is seen every spring in Waterton and Chain Lakes Provincial Park. The trailing edges of the wings are black, and the long, heavy bill is orange. Largest bird in the Rockies, wingspan 274 cm.

*Ardea herodias*

*Grus canadensis*

MW

Herons stand in the water on their long legs, stabbing for fish with their sharp bills. They also eat frogs, salamanders, small water mammals and aquatic insects. Breed east and west of the Rockies, but supposedly not here. Herons in the Canadian Rockies area fly *north* to winter along the west coast in northern B.C. and Alaska.

## American bittern *Butor Américain*
*Botaurus lentiginosus* (heron family)
Early May to September

Occasional in marshes, and quite large—length 58 cm, wingspan 114 cm—but rarely seen because it hides so cleverly among the tall vegetation. The camouflage coloration is terrific: stripy/mottled brown and white. The bird holds its head vertically and freezes in that position when you approach; you can walk right by and never notice it. But then comes the startling song, usually uttered at dawn and dusk: "gunk-swish, gunk-swish," or "ka-GUNK," like the sound of a pebble dropped in a bucket of water, followed by a sound like something passing by one's head at high speed. Bizarre and unmistakable.

MW

Bitterns tramp slowly about the swamp on their long green legs, snapping up little water creatures. They breed in spring, the well-hidden nest a large stack of plants on the ground or raised above the water, with 2–5 large buff-to-olive eggs that hatch in 24–29 days. The young leave the nest at about two weeks. Bitterns winter in fresh water along the west coast, through the American southwest and south into Central America.

## Sora *Râle de Caroline*
*Porzana carolina* (rail family)
Early May to early September

A fairly common but shy marsh bird that you rarely see. Listen for it at dusk and dawn. Length 17 cm, wingspan 32 cm. Body mostly gray, with brown atop the head and down the back; the black face and throat patch are good identifiers, as are the yellow bill and the long greenish or yellowish legs. Voice is loud and distinctive: "ah-WIP, ah-WIP, ah-WIP," followed by a high-pitched laugh that trails off at the end.

MW

Soras act like shorebirds, picking food from the mud; diet mostly seeds, plus snails and aquatic insects. They've been known to walk underwater. Breeding is in mid-spring, the coarse nest just above the water, well-hidden among the bulrush stems that support it. Lots of eggs (8–12), buffy or olive and spotted with red or purple; they hatch in 16–20 days and the young leave the nest after only a day or two, returning at night. They can fly at 36 days. Soras winter in salt marshes along the coasts, from southern California and Virginia south through Central America and the Caribbean to Peru.

### Common snipe *Bécassine des marais*

*Gallinago gallinago* (sandpiper family)
Early April to mid-October; sometimes year-round in the southern Rocky Mountain Trench.

Common in central and northern marshes; less common in the southern area. Length 23 cm. A sandpiper-like bird that prefers the dense growth of marshes to the open shoreline. Feeds by sticking its bill into the mud for worms and insect larvae. Also seen in meadows.

MW

Snipes perform a wonderful spring mating display known as **winnowing.** The male suddenly flies up out of the swamp to about 100 m, then plunges down at speeds up to 160 km/h, spreading his tail feathers, which show orange and vibrate in the wind to produce a strange "woo-woo-woo" sound. The female loves this, sometimes doing it herself, and lays 3–4 brown-blotched greenish eggs in a mud nest that hatch after 18–20 days. The snipelets leave the nest as soon as their down is dry; they are fed for 19–20 days, then fly away. Wintering grounds: southwestern B.C. and most of the U.S.A.

## *Sandpipers and other shorebirds*

See also the snipe, previous item.

### Killdeer *Pluvier kildir*

*Charadrius vociferous* (plover family)
Early March through September; sometimes year-round

In almost any open habitat below treeline, but in our area usually not far from water. Length 20 cm. A type of plover, larger than the semipalmated plover, next item, with two black neck rings; semipalmated has only one. Rusty rump patch, red eye-ring. Flashy white stripe along the rear of the wing.

Killdeer make a variety of high-pitched calls, some of which sound rather like "kill-dee-deer," "kill-dee-deer." I don't know what they have against deer. You may sometimes hear this call at night. Food: beetles, grasshoppers, caterpillars, other insects. This bird is famous for faking a broken wing to lead you, or whatever else it figures to be a predator, away from the nest. Breeds in the open, the nest a simple scrape lined with whatever is handy— grass, bits of wood, or nothing at all—holding four brown-marked buff eggs. The young hatch at 24 days and immediately head for water, flying at 40 days. Our birds winter from Vancouver south along the coast, across the southwest and through the American Rockies from Yellowstone south.

MW

### Semipalmated plover *Pluvier semipalmé*
*Charadrius semipalmatus* (plover family)
Mid-August

Occasional flocks on shorelines around Jasper and north, passing through from arctic summering grounds. Like the killdeer, previous item, but smaller (length 13 cm), with one broad neck ring instead of two; rump is plain brown rather than rusty. The bill is orange with a black tip. Says "pee-wit" and twittery things; runs quickly about on the mud, stabbing for invertebrates and grabbing grasshoppers. No nesting records here. Winters in coastal marshes from northern California south, along the Gulf of Mexico and up the east coast to Maryland.

*MW*

### American avocet *Avocet Américaine*
*Recurvirostra americana* (avocet family)
Mid-April and mid-August

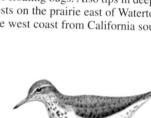

Occasional along open shorelines, central and southern areas. Length 38 cm. Easily identified by the long, upturned bill, rusty head and neck, white body with broad black wing markings. Call: "wee-wee-wee-wee."

An avocet runs along in very shallow water, sweeping its bill back and forth near the bottom to stir up aquatic insects and larvae. Skims surface for floating bugs. Also tips in deeper water, and sometimes dives. No nesting records here, but nests on the prairie east of Waterton/Glacier, so might be found in the foothills. Winters along the west coast from California south to Guatemala, and along the Gulf of Mexico.

*MW*

### Spotted sandpiper *Chevalier branlequeu*
*Actitis macularia* (sandpiper family)
May to mid-October

Most common sandpiper in our area, seen along shorelines of lakes and rivers at all elevations. Length 16 cm. Several identifiers: coarsely spotted throat, front and underparts (they go plain in the fall); orange-and-black bill, and especially its habit of bobbing its tail up and down. Compare with solitary sandpiper, next item. Calls "burbledy-WEET" repetitively as it flies; flutters with wings down-curved. Sometimes dives under water from the air to escape attack.

*MW*

Spotted sandpipers catch insects on the wing or on the ground rather than probing for them in the mud. They eat a lot of grasshoppers. This species breeds in late spring, nesting on the ground in forested wetlands. Four creamy, brown-spotted eggs in an unlined nest-hollow on the ground; the female often produces more than one clutch, her assorted male mates looking after the extra nests. Hatching is in 20–24 days, the young up and running about immediately. Winters along the west coast from Washington south into Mexico.

### Solitary sandpiper *Chevalier solitaire*
*Tringa solitaria* (sandpiper family)
Early June to mid-October

Fairly common beside stagnant pools, along streams and lakeshores in central and northern areas, less common farther south. Seldom seen with others of its own kind but shares habitat with spotted sandpiper, previous item, which it rather resembles. Similar in size—length 18 cm—but not

*MW*

spotted; bobs head as well as tail. Lack of white eye-line differentiates from other sandpipers; note also the gray-green legs. Gives typical sandpiper "pee-weet" as it flies.

Snatches flying and crawling bugs; probes in the mud, stirring up shallow water with forward foot. Breeds in late spring, the female finding a tree nest abandoned by another species, usually in mossy woods near water. Four brown-splotched pale-green eggs; little known about incubation and fledging, but the species is precocial and the young probably jump out of the nest into the moss below. Wintering grounds: west and east coasts of Mexico.

### Least sandpiper *Bécasseau miniscule*
*Calidris minutilla* (sandpiper family)
Early August to early September

Seen mostly during the fall migration, at marsh ponds and along lakeshores, northern and central areas, eastern slope; uncommon west and south. The smallest—"least" in the biologist's quaint usage—sandpiper, a tiny, unwary, endearing bird only 12 cm long and nearly invisible, even within a metre or two, as it picks among the multi-colored pebbles of a typical Rockies shoreline, chasing silverfish and probing for invertebrates in the sand. Mottled brown back and breast with white underside. Dark bill, quite skinny; white curved eye-line and yellowish/greenish legs. Compare with very similar semipalmated sandpiper and Baird's sandpiper. Call: cute, high-pitched rising "peeep." Breeds in the Arctic; winters down the west coast of the U.S.A. and along the Gulf of Mexico.

### Semipalmated sandpiper *Bécasseau semi-palmé*
*Calidris pusilla* (sandpiper family)
Late July to mid-September

Fairly common shorebird during the fall migration, seen in eastern-slope central and northern areas; rare elsewhere. Closely resembles least sandpiper, previous item, but slightly larger (length 13 cm), with black legs rather than yellowish/greenish and white front rather than brown. Short neck, curving eye-stripe. Cry is cheepy-peepy. Runs about snapping up invertebrates, probing occasionally. No nesting records here; summers in the Arctic. Winters along the Gulf of Mexico and Florida's east coast.

### Baird's sandpiper *Bécasseau de Baird*
*Calidris bairdii* (sandpiper family)
Mid-August to mid-September

Occasional, mostly along eastern-slope alpine lakes and ponds, a high-arctic migrant stopping in on its annual fall journey to Chile. What a trip for such a small bird! Still, at 15 cm long, Baird's is noticeably bigger than the semipalmated or least sandpiper; otherwise it is very similar. Good field marks: dark legs like the semipalmated and brown breast like the least, a combination that effectively differentiates it. Says "kreep"; snatches insects on the ground rather than probing in the mud for them. No nesting records here.

### Pectoral sandpiper *Bécasseau à poitrine cendrée*
*Calidris melanotos* (sandpiper family)
Late July to late September

Fairly common in eastern-slope alpine marshes and grassy meadows, rare elsewhere. Length 20 cm but can be quite a bit smaller. Like the least sandpiper, the pectoral has yellowish/greenish legs and a brown breast, but it is nearly twice as large, and the breast pattern is herringbone rather than dark-spotted chestnut. The "peep" is quite raspy. Feeds in grassy places, eating mostly flies, beetles, grass seeds. No nesting records; breeds in the Arctic. Flies to Mexico and Central America for the winter.

### Stilt sandpiper  *Bécasseau à échasses*

*Calidris himantopus* (sandpiper family)
Mid-to-late August

Common in flocks from Jasper park north during the fall migration; rare or unreported elsewhere in our area. Look for it along marsh shorelines. Length 20 cm, about the same size as the pectoral sandpiper, previous item, which it resembles, but the neck, bill and especially the legs of the stilt sandpiper are longer. Very similar to lesser yellowlegs, next item, but a little smaller; the stilt has ruddy streaks or patches on the head, which the lesser and greater yellowlegs lack. Voice is frog-like.

*MW*

The stilt feeds in tight groups standing in water; the heads dip under as the birds probe the bottom mud for worms, insect larvae, seeds and roots. They summer along the Arctic coast, winter from Central America to Chile.

### Greater yellowlegs and lesser yellowlegs

*Grand chevalier à pattes jaunes, petit chevalier à pattes jaunes*
*Tringa melanoleuca* and *Tringa flavipes* (sandpiper family)
Greater: early May to mid-October
Lesser: May and September

Greater yellowlegs are common shorebirds in the central and northern areas; uncommon farther south and on the western slope. Lesser yellowlegs is occasional, passing through. Next to the avocet, page 528, these are the largest shorebirds in the Canadian Rockies, and the only yellow-legged ones. They are nearly identical, so one drawing suffices for both. The lesser, length 22 cm, has a proportionately shorter bill and whiter face than the greater, length 28 cm. Compare also with stilt sandpiper. Greater calls "cheep-cheep-cheep" in flight; lesser says "pew" or "pew-pew," rather quickly. I have watched a greater yellowlegs standing at the top of a spruce tree—the last place you would expect to see a sandpiper—calling and calling. A short distance away, another yellowlegs was doing the same thing.

*Tringa melanoleuca*

*MW*

These birds wade. The greater picks up floating bugs and tiny fish near the water surface, while the lesser probes in the mud. Greater breeds near water at high subalpine and alpine elevations; four blotchy buff eggs in a hollow on the ground, sparsely lined with grass or dead leaves. Incubation: 23 days; precocial young fly 18–20 days later. Lesser breeds north of the Rockies. Winter range of greater: coastal U.S.A. from California south, Texas, Mexico, Gulf coast, east coast up to New England. Lesser: both Mexican coasts.

### Long-billed dowitcher and short-billed dowitcher

*Bécasseau à long bec, bécasseau roux*
*Limnodromus scolopaceus* and *L. griseus* (sandpiper family)
Long-billed: fairly common in flocks on mudflats in northern and central areas from mid-July to October, scarce in the south.
Short-billed: seen occasionally during migration in May.

These are large sandpipers up to 25 cm in length, with long, heavy bills for their short necks. Unlike other sandpipers, they are ruddy underneath. Greenish-yellow legs, rather long. Separating the species is very difficult; bill lengths overlap. Most short-bills have a fair amount of white on the belly, and long-bills have very little. Call: "keek," either singly or in frantic repetition. They pick insects and seeds out of the mud, the long-billed often sticking its head into pools to probe the bottom. Long-billed breeds on the northwest coast of Alaska; short-billed not far northeast of the northern Rockies. Both species winter along the east and west coasts south of Oregon and Virginia, and on the Gulf.

MW

### Wilson's phalarope *Phalarope de Wilson*
*Phalaropus tricolor* (sandpiper family)
Early May to mid-June, all summer at Waterton

Occasional on marsh ponds and lakes, swimming. This sandpiper acts like a duck and has lobed toes like a coot, page 523. Length 20 cm. Distinctive markings: black eye-line gets thicker toward the back of the head, then turns down the side of the neck, becoming a red stripe over the back. Another red back stripe parallels the first one. Gray atop the head, with

MW

white front and underparts; very sharp, long bill. Compare with red-necked phalarope, next item. Says "rope, rope," and makes buzzing noises. Feeds mostly along muddy shorelines, poking its head into pools for mosquito larvae. Also spins round and round in the water, using its feet to pump up small invertebrates. Follows dabbling ducks, getting larvae the ducks stir up.

Female phalaropes are bigger and more colorful than males. In a case of sexual role reversal, the female displays to attract the male, lays the eggs, then the male incubates them. Wilson's breeds in marsh ponds; nests reported in the Rockies only from Waterton. Winters along the Mexican Gulf coast.

### Red-necked phalarope *Phalarope hyperboré*
*Phalaropus lobatus* (sandpiper family)
Mid-May to late May, again from early August to mid-September

Occasional migrant seen on montane and subalpine lakes, ponds and rivers; sometimes seen near treeline. Rare in the south. Length 15 cm, noticeably smaller than Wilson's phalarope, previous item, the only other bird with which it is likely to be confused. Both species are sandpipers that swim about like ducks rather than sticking to the shore. Sex-role reversal as in Wilson's.

MW

Generally darker than Wilson's, the red-necked has a dark-gray head with no white above the eye and a shorter neck. The red in the neck continues across the breast as a colorful bib, instead of running onto the back as per Wilson's. In late summer we see the red-necked in its gray-and-white fall plumage. Voice: quick "wip-wip-wip." Both phalaropes in our area stir up the bottom mud with their long legs, turning in the water and snapping up the insect larvae they have disturbed. Unlike Wilson's, the red-necked phalarope seldom comes to shore. Breeds in the Arctic; winters on the ocean off southern California and south of the equator.

### American pipit *Pipit spioncelle*
*Anthus rubescens* (pipit family)
Mid-May to mid-November, less common after September

Very common above treeline, usually around ponds or hopping about on summer snow patches, in small flocks. Length 14 cm. A plain little bird, the American pipit looks sparrow-like and flashes junco-like white tail feathers when it flies. Bobs like a dipper or a spotted sandpiper. But there is one sure way to know that it's a pipit: it tells you so, saying "pip-it." Also makes other calls in the same squeaky tone. Previously known as "water pipit," *A. spinoletta*.

MW

Pipits are bug-eaters, getting them at the water's edge or refrigerated in snowbanks. They also eat seeds, both on the ground and in seedheads. In fall pipits come down to lower elevations, walking along the mudflats exposed by autumn's low water levels. They breed in early summer, nesting among talus boulders or back in the natural earth cavities that form along tundra streams. Four to six heavily brown-blotched white or gray eggs are laid in a cup sheltered under a bank or grass tussock; they hatch in about two weeks, the young leaving the nest 14–16 days later. Winter range: west coast from Washington south, through the southern U.S.A. and northern Mexico, up the east coast.

## Seagulls in the Rockies?

Sure. Gulls live everywhere. Although they normally winter along the seashore, many species nest inland. Only the mew gull nests in the Rockies; the others we see breed north or east of the mountains.

Gulls can eat practically anything: live fish or dead, carrion of all kinds, the eggs of other species, seeds and grain—you name it. This group is smart, too. Gulls open clams by dropping them on rocks from the air. A golf course in Ontario had to be closed when the gulls kept stealing the balls and dropping them on the highway next door, resulting in broken windshields.

Gulls take up to four years to mature. The juveniles are typically darker than adults, usually brown-mottled in the first two years. The descriptions and drawings here are of adults. The sexes look the same.

### Ring-billed gull *Goéland à bec cerclé*
*Larus delawarensis* (gull family)
Late April to mid-November

Common around low-elevation lakes, rivers and especially garbage dumps; very common in August and September. Length 40 cm, wingspan 125 cm. Typical gull coloration: white head and tail, gray body and wings, black wingtips, yellow legs. Identify by the black ring around the tip of the bill. California gull, next item, has a red and a black spot on the tip; mew gull has no spot or ring on the bill; herring gull has pink legs. Ring-billed says "yeah, yeah," and makes a rather plaintive, sheep-like "baa."

MW

Omnivorous like other gulls, this species has a taste for dead ground squirrels and has been known to choke to death trying to swallow them whole. No nesting records here; prefers northern lakes. Winters along the North American coasts from Vancouver and New York south.

### California gull *Goéland de Californie*
*Larus californicus* (gull family)
Late April to end of October

Common around low-elevation lakes, rivers and garbage dumps, especially in August and September. Similar to ring-billed gull, previous item, but a little bigger; length 43 cm, wingspan 132 cm. Has a small red spot next to a small black spot on the bill. The eyes are black rather than yellow. Call includes various screechy, gull-like tones, including one like the wheezy beginning of a donkey's bray.

Habits similar to the ring-billed, although the California gull prefers prairie marshes for nesting rather than northern lakes. Eats a lot of grasshoppers and other agricultural pests; farmers like it. The Mormons built a statue in Salt Lake City to honor this bird.

MW

The California is very dark when immature, with a black bill-tip. It doesn't get adult coloring until its third summer. The other gulls in our area are lighter than the California when immature, and they tend to be spotted. Wintering: west coast from Vancouver south.

### Herring gull *Goéland argenté*
*Larus argentatus* (gull family)
Mid-April to mid-May,
again late June to early October

Fairly common in central and northern sections as they cross the mountains between their west-coast wintering grounds and their boreal/prairie summer range east and north of us. Our biggest gull: length 50 cm, wingspan 140 cm.

Very similar to California gull, previous item, but nonetheless easily differentiated by the legs—pink, not yellow—and the yellow eye color of the herring gull, rather than black. Voice: "karrr," with assorted squeaks and whistles; the sound of the sea, right at your local dump.

### Mew gull *Goéland cendré*
*Larus canus* (gull family)
Mid-May to mid-September

Common in the north end, occasional at Jasper, rare in the south. Smallest of the gray-and-white gulls in our area (length 35 cm, wingspan 107 cm), but otherwise similar except for three things: black eyes, no mark on the bill, and a voice you must hear to believe. "Mew" is simply too mild; this thing cries like a Siamese cat. And it does it non-stop.

Diet: heavy on bugs and worms. Breeds in late spring, nesting in spruces sticking up from swamps. The parents are very protective; people strolling along the boardwalk leading to Liard Hot Springs are routinely dived-at by shrieking mew gulls nesting nearby.

Three brown-marked pale-green eggs hatch in 22–27 days; the young leave the nest in only a day or two, sticking nearby until flying at 4–5 weeks. Wintering: Gulf of Alaska and down the west coast to the Mexican border.

### Bonaparte's gull *Mouette de Bonaparte*
*Larus philadelphia* (gull family)
Month of May, again (rarely) from mid-August to mid-September

Named for a French biologist, not for Napoleon. Fairly common in spring, northern and central areas; rare in the south. A small gull (length 28 cm, wingspan 80 cm), easily identified by the black head and bill, but can be confused with **Franklin's gull,** *Larus pipixcan,* which is seen occasionally in the southern foothills. Check the wings: in Bonaparte's the tips are white with black trim; in Franklin's the tips are black with white trim. Both birds have bright-orange legs.

Bonaparte's gull quacks softly, like a duck; eats a lot of insects. It breeds in northwestern Canada but apparently not in the Rockies; winters along both west and east coasts of the United States.

# Birds that dive into water from the air, and the dipper

See also the osprey, page 539.

### Common tern *Sterne pierrigarin*
*Sterna hirundo* (gull family)
Mid-May to late June, month of September

Occasional over lakes during spring and fall migrations, diving from the air for fish. Length 35 cm, wingspan 80 cm. Black cap and split tail are immediate identifiers; note also reddish-orange bill, usually with black tip, and reddish legs. Says "BEE-yert," with lots of buzz. Nests east of us on the big prairie lakes. Wintering: along Baja California and the southeastern/Florida/Gulf coasts of the U.S.A.

MW

### Black tern *Guifette noire*
*Chlidonias niger* (gull family)
Mid-May to mid-June

Occasional over lakes and marsh ponds, mostly scooping up airborne bugs rather than diving for fish. Length 23 cm, wingspan 90 cm. The angled wings are tern-like, but the tail is not deeply split. Dark all over, except for white under the tail. Says "ee-ah," sometimes just "ee" or just "ah." Breeds mainly east and west of the mountains, with only a few records here (Waterton, Valemount). Flight speed 50 km/h—not very fast, but this bird travels a long way each year: winters from Panama to Chile.

MW

### Belted kingfisher *Martin-pêcheur d'Amérique*
*Ceryle alcyon* (kingfisher family)
Year-round; seen most often late April to mid-September

Fairly common at low elevations around rivers, lakes and ponds. Length 30 cm. With its disproportionately large head, big bill and crest, the kingfisher is likely to be mistaken only for Steller's jay or the blue jay, page 558. But the kingfisher has a broad white neckband, which Steller's lacks. Blue jay has a white throat and face, but the coloration does not go all the way around the neck. Kingfisher females have a rusty band across their middles that the males lack. In flight they produce bursts of tuneless rattling, like the sound of a scratch-gourd in a Latin band.

♀

MW

Kingfishers perch in trees along the water, suddenly diving in headlong after fish. They also catch tadpoles, frogs, toads, mice and insects. Breeding is in early spring. The birds tunnel 1–2 m, sometimes 4–5 m, into a soft bank by digging with the bill and kicking the dirt out. The burrow emits a powerful fishy odor. Six to eight white eggs in a clutch, hatching at 23–24 days; the young fledge at 30–35 days and are taught to fish by the parents, who drop meals into the water for them to dive after. Most kingfishers in the Rockies probably winter not far to the west, in the Columbia Mountains of B.C. and along the coast, where there is open water all winter. Some remain at the few open spots to be found in the Rockies.

### American dipper *Cincle d'Amérique*
*Cinclus mexicanus* (dipper family)
Year-round

Common along fast-flowing streams; a classic species of North America's western mountains. In Europe there is a similar species called **water ouzel**, *Cinclus cinclus*, a name sometimes applied to our birds. Length 14 cm. The dipper is a round gray bird with a very short tail. It trills in flight and sings beautifully at rest, cheeping, buzzing, whistling and warbling. It does so all year round. I'll be skiing up a snowy, frozen stream on a deathly cold day in January, when the song erupts. There, at a small patch of open water, is a dipper. It plops in, stays under a moment hunting the aquatic larvae, snails and tiny fish it eats, then jumps back up on a rock, bobbing up and down like a kid needing the bathroom. It sees me and flies, squirting a line of blackish poop into the snow on takeoff, then lands at the next open spot. I have never seen dipper tracks in the snow.

MW

These birds have evolved interesting anatomical features for living year-round in cold water: enormous oil glands to waterproof their feathers; little flaps to seal their nostrils; heavy **nictitating membranes** (transparent extra eyelids) to cover their eyes. The species breeds in early spring, building a wren-like domed nest of feather mosses in a rock crevice in a streamside cliff, usually under an overhang and often behind a waterfall. There are 4–5 eggs; they hatch in 16 days. The young enter the water at 18–25 days, before they can fly. Non-migratory in the Canadian Rockies area. Canmore and Kananaskis Country hold the North American records for the most wintering individuals.

## Hawks, falcons and a perching bird that acts like a hawk

These are hunting birds, called **raptors** by ornithologists, from the Latin *raptus,* meaning "to seize, rob or plunder." Owls are also raptors.

Hawks and falcons migrate along the foothills and mountain front, where birdwatchers look for them in spring and fall. Recently a migration route for eagles has been found within the front ranges. See the boxed item on page 541.

### American kestrel *Crécerelle d'Amérique*
*Falco sparverius* (falcon family)
Early April to mid-October

♂

Used to be called "sparrow hawk." Fairly common in open places, especially at the edges of dry, sloping meadows at low elevations. Hangs around marshes, too. Smallest hawk-like bird in the mountains: length 22 cm, wingspan 53 cm. A falcon; has pointy wings and a long, narrow tail. Identify by the size and coloration: male has red tail with black terminal band and bars—but much smaller than red-tailed hawk, page 538. Red back, red crown, black line leading down from base of beak. Female is barred reddish-brown with similar face. Voice is high and squeaky; says "killy-killy-killy."

MW

Eats mostly insects, knocking off mice, bats, frogs and small birds when it can. Slope-soars at tree-top height; often circles and hovers before dropping on prey. Not terribly shy; one often sees kestrels on phone lines and fences along the highway. They also frequent towns. Nests in mid-spring, using an abandoned tree-hole. Four or five brown-blotched white/pinkish eggs hatch at 29–30 days; young birds fledge at 30 days. Wintering is along the west coast from Prince Rupert south, and through much of the U.S.A. and Mexico.

### Merlin *Faucon émerillon*
*Falco columbarius* (falcon family)
Early April to early September

Formerly called "pigeon hawk." Occasional in forest clearings and along lakeshores; likes the subalpine zone. A small falcon (length 30 cm, wingspan 58 cm), the male dark on the back like the rare **peregrine falcon,** *Falco peregrinus,* but smaller, lighter-colored on the head, without the clearly defined black cowl of the peregrine. Has several black bands on the tail, which the peregrine doesn't. Female resembles kestrel, but larger and more solidly dark on the back. Call is rather like that of the kestrel, high and squealing. Not shy; can be closely approached.

Merlins hunt at tree-top level, snatching small birds out of the air; they do not stoop or soar. Also take shorebirds, squirrels, mice, bats, insects. Nests in Jasper townsite, with its good supply of house sparrows, and perhaps in other Rockies towns; otherwise in deep woods east of the mountains. Flies at 75 km/h. Winters on the west and east coasts, through the southwest states and Mexico, along the Gulf of Mexico and through the Caribbean islands to South America.

MW

### Prairie falcon *Faucon des prairies*
*Falco mexicanus* (falcon family)
Late May to late September

Normally a prairie bird, but occasionally seen in the foothills and above treeline in the mountains from Jasper south. Length 40 cm, wingspan 102 cm—significantly larger than the merlin, previous item, which it resembles. A light-colored falcon; compare with female northern harrier, facing page. Best in-flight prairie-falcon identifiers: a dark zone under the wing, right at the root, giving the bird a sweaty-armpit look (sweaty-wingpit look?), and one obvious black band under the tail. The merlin has several bands, while the rare peregrine, another large falcon, has none. The prairie falcon says "yee-yee-yee," rather like an osprey on the nest.

MW

Prairie falcons in the Rockies eat mainly ground squirrels. The bird comes in fast and low, often less than 2 m from the ground, hitting an unsuspecting squirrel and sometimes rolling with it on the ground after impact. Prairie falcons also snatch a few small birds and will drop to the ground to eat grasshoppers. This species nests on cliffs, but apparently not in the Canadian Rockies. Winters in the western U.S.A. and down into Mexico.

### Sharp-shinned hawk *Épervier brun*
*Accipiter striatus* (hawk family)
For season see below

Occasional at the forest fringes or in the woods. Seen most frequently from mid-August to the end of September, but has been reported year-round. Length 27 cm, wingspan 53 cm. Resembles the merlin or American kestrel, especially in the narrow, banded tail, but the wings are broader and more rounded. Differentiate from similar Cooper's hawk, next item, by the sharp-shin's smaller size and straighter end of tail. Voice: high-pitched, rapid "pew-pew-pew."

MW

A sharp-shinned hunts swiftly through the woods, picking off small forest birds from their perches, sometimes grabbing a bird in mid-air or coming in low to get one on the ground. Kills by working its talons in and out. Breeds in early spring. Large nest of twigs in the woods holds 4–5 brown-blotched white eggs; hatching is at 34–35 days, fledging 23 days later. Wintering: along the B.C. coast and through much of the United States. Sometimes overwinters in central and southern Canadian Rockies.

## Cooper's hawk *Épervier de Cooper*
*Accipiter cooperii* (hawk family)
Early May to early October

Occasional in or over the woods, catching small birds and snatching rodents. Length 40 cm, wingspan 70 cm. Very much like the sharp-shinned hawk, previous item, with dark back, mottled underside and banded tail, but much bigger. The tail is rounded at the end, not squared off. Head looks larger and heavier; black cap more prominent. To differentiate from merlin or peregrine falcon, page 535, note broad, rounded wings; falcons have sharply pointed, angular wings.

Cooper's hawk says "awk-awk-awk," quite rapidly. Like the sharp-shinned, it hunts at low levels in the woods, catching mostly squirrels, chipmunks and robin-size birds. Has a taste for domestic chickens. Sometimes dunks prey in water to drown it. Cooper's breeds in mid-spring, nests in old aspen groves 10–20 m up. The male builds a platform of twigs, covering it with bark flakes. Four eggs normally, whitish/bluish, hatching in 36 days. Fledging is 30–34 days later; the young are independent at eight weeks. Wintering is on the west coast and through the U.S.A.

MW

## Northern goshawk *Autour des palombes*
*Accipiter gentilis* (hawk family)
Year-round central, summer in the north, winter in the south

Occasional in old-growth forest, or soaring along sparsely timbered slopes. Length 48 cm, wingspan 107 cm, the largest of the **accipiters** (members of the genus *Accipiter)* and very impressive. Distinctively dark-colored back with silvery breast; more uniformly colored than our other hawks and falcons. At close range, check the white eye-stripe. Voice is rather like Cooper's: repetitive "eck-eck-eck-eck," but a good bit higher.

Voracious hunters, goshawks blast through the woods at high speed, taking mostly grouse; also snowshoe hares, squirrels, chipmunks, ducks, other hawks and owls—most anything that moves, it seems. Killing is by hitting with the talons open, driving them in, then quickly clenching. Breeding is in mid-spring. The male builds the nest and supplies the food; the female broods and changes the nest lining of conifer needles and leaves. She is very protective; will attack people near the nest—and sometimes sends them to hospital for stitches in the scalp. Here is one good reason to wear a hat in the woods. Two or three bluish-white eggs hatch in 36–41 days. The young fledge 40 days later and are particularly bloodthirsty, often killing each other and even attacking their parents, who abandon them as soon as they can feed themselves.

MW

The northern goshawk, although reclusive and rarely seen, is still widespread through the Canadian northern forests, but its winter habitat in the western U.S.A. is quickly disappearing. The Coast Mountains of B.C., once a vast winter refuge for this bird, are being ravaged by clear-cut logging.

## Northern harrier *Busard Saint-Martin*
*Circus cyaneus* (hawk family)
Late April to late May, again early July to late September, sometimes all summer

Formerly called "marsh hawk." Fairly common at any elevation, often over wetlands, subalpine meadows and tundra, flying low in search of ground squirrels and other rodents, small

♀

MW

birds. Length 42 cm, wingspan 107 cm. Fairly large hawk, easily identified from above—which you often are, because the bird flies so low—by the white patch on the lower back. Male is gray on top and pale beneath, with banded tail and black wingtips; female same but streaky brown; immatures have reddish breasts. Holds wings in an upward vee while gliding, slides side to side. Often hovers, fluttering its wings. Makes a sound you can imitate by loudly kissing the back of your hand, quickly and repeatedly.

Occasionally nests here at high subalpine elevations, close to the ground in willow thickets; 4–9 bluish or spotted eggs brooded by both sexes. Winter range: southeastern B.C. and most of the U.S.A., possibly the southern Rocky Mountain Trench.

### Red-tailed hawk *Buse à queue rousse*

*Buteo jamaicensis* (hawk family)
Early April to mid-September

Fairly common in open country, especially in the eastern-slope foothills. Large: length 46 cm, wingspan 122 cm. Body color and pattern can vary considerably, from very light to very dark, but the tail is always a good identifier: red above, pink below, spread wide in flight. Dark-phase individuals have a yoke of brown under the wing, which is lighter elsewhere with black-tipped feathers at the tips. Compare with Swainson's, next item, which is much less common.

MW

The red-tail's call is distinctive: a long, whistling scream—"SHEEEE-ahhhh!"—repeated frequently, with a little space between blasts. Startling and spooky. This hawk slope-soars low along meadowy ridges or sits on a tree, post or pole; glides coolly down to surprise ground squirrels, mice and other rodents. Occasionally takes birds in the air by stooping; drops on frogs, salamanders, even fish. Will eat worms.

Mates for life; breeds very early in spring, the nest a mass of twigs on a ledge or in a tall tree. One to three brown-blotched off-white eggs hatch in 28–32 days; the young fly at 6–7 weeks. Long-lived: 14–16 years in the wild, up to 29 years in captivity. Can dive at over 160 km/h. Winter range: most of the U.S.A., Mexico, south to Nicaragua.

### Swainson's hawk *Buse de Swainson*

*Buteo swainsoni* (hawk family)
Early April to mid-September

Occasional in the foothills and on the western slope. Mainly a prairie bird. Length 45 cm, wingspan 125 cm. Shape and size much like red-tailed, previous item, but Swainson's is darker, with a broad, banded tail. The coloration of this species varies considerably from bird to bird. There is usually a distinctive dark area on the trailing half of the underwing—just the reverse of the red-tail's dark leading-edge yoke—a brown or reddish bib and a white throat. Soars with its wings in a shallow vee; red-tailed holds them flat. Call is much like that of red-tailed, but screamier and less whistling: "eee-yaaa," the sound you are supposed to make when falling over a precipice.

MW

One would imagine this impressive hawk diving on bunnies. Instead, it hops along the ground, eating mostly insects and mice; waits at entrances to ground-squirrel burrows to grab them in talons; catches bats. Seldom takes other birds; sits on fencelines and other low perches rather than soaring. Swainson's breeds in early spring, preferring the intermountain valleys and the prairies, but reported to nest in the southern foothills and in Waterton park. Bulky nest, often easily seen in a lone tree; two lightly brown-marked white eggs hatch in 28 days. Young fly 4–5 weeks later. Age data: 6–9 years. Wintering grounds are in Argentina, requiring a very long migration in which the birds soar up several thousand metres and then glide long distances.

### Rough-legged hawk *Buse pattue*

*Buteo lagopus* (hawk family)
Mid-November and December in southern and central areas, April in the north

Occasional, during migration; the only hawk you are likely to see in the snowy months, for some individuals spend the winter in the far southern foothills, along with a few red-tails. Length 48 cm, wingspan 132 cm; a little larger than red-tailed or Swainson's but similar. Differentiate by the broad black band across the tail, which is longer and narrower than red-tailed or Swainson's; by the dark body, especially from the waist down, and prominent black trailing edge under the wing, sometimes with black leading-edge yoke. Call is very similar to Swainson's, although shorter; it is seldom heard.

MW

In its arctic breeding grounds, the rough-legged hawk eats lemmings and ptarmigan. In the Rockies it picks off mice and grouse, plus the odd ptarmigan while passing over alpine areas. Winters through much of the U.S.A.

### Osprey *Balbuzard*

*Pandion haliaetus* (hawk family)
Early March to late September

Fairly common along lakeshores and rivers, flying to and from a massive nest atop a tree. Large: length 57 cm, wingspan 137 cm. Easily identified at short range by the white head with black eye-stripe and black bill. Brown back and upper wings, black-and-white underside with prominent black patches at the wing joints. Flies with drooped wingtips. Calls: plain whistles, and a worried "yee-yee-yee" if you get near the nest.

MW

This is the fish-hawk, gliding over water and swooping down to grab anything finny with its talons. Occasionally takes rodents, frogs, sandpipers, ducks. The mated pair returns year after year to the same huge nest, built of sticks atop a tree at the water's edge. Breeding is in mid-spring; three cream/yellowish, brown-blotched eggs hatch in 32–33 days. The young birds and female are fed by the male until fledging occurs at 7–8 weeks. Wintering: along the west coast from California south, east coast from Florida south, and well into South America.

### Northern shrike *Pie-grièche grise*

*Lanius excubitor* (shrike family)
Early March to late May, again early October through November

Occasional in montane and subalpine forest, at openings atop a conifer. Length 20 cm. This bird summers mainly north of the Rockies and winters from about Lake Louise south. Identifiers: large, curved bill, black tail, black wings and black bandit's mask against gray head. Compare with gray jay and Clark's nutcracker, page 557. Waterton/Glacier region is also summer home of the **loggerhead shrike**, *L. ludovicianus*, which is quite similar but has a shorter bill and broader eye-mask. Loggerhead goes "tir-bzzt, tir-bzzt" and "bzzt-tir, bzzt-tir"; northern shrike says very little.

MW

This is the hawk-pretender mentioned in the section head, a songbird gone bloodthirsty, with a hawk-like tearing bill but little songbird feet. Shrikes catch small birds, rodents and insects, killing by biting into the neck. They carry the prey in the bill—the legs are too weak—often sticking it on a thorn or barbed wire fence, or hanging it in a forked branch to eat it. Shrikes are very territorial, chasing others of their kind away. They nest in a conifer in mid-spring, building a large cup of twigs and moss, lined with feathers, roots and hair. Eggs 5–7, greenish-white with brown speckles, hatching at only 15 days and fledging 19–20 days later.

# *Eagles*

There are two species seen in the Canadian Rockies: golden and bald.

## Bald eagle *Pygargue à tête blanche*
*Haliaeetus leucocephalus* (hawk family)
Mid-May to mid-September, sometimes year-round

Fairly common along rivers and lakes, sitting atop a tree or soaring. The third-largest bird in the Canadian Rockies; length 82 cm, wingspan 203 cm. (Largest is white pelican, page 526; second-largest is trumpeter swan, page 525.) Very impressive in its unmistakable brown-and-white plumage. Voice is out of character: wheezy and high-pitched.

The bald eagle feeds primarily by fishing, like the osprey, but also eats carrion and takes the odd muskrat or injured duck. Breeds in mid-spring. During the mating display a pair sometimes lock feet in flight and tumble earthward, releasing at the last moment. Two white eggs are laid in a perennially used nest like the osprey's: a great big clump of sticks well up in a conifer, but seldom at the top. The first nestling to hatch (35–36 days) usually kills the other or starves it by taking all the food. It fledges comparatively late: 10–11 weeks.

MW

Longest-lived bird in the region: up to 48 years in captivity. If open water is available, this species will sometimes spend the whole winter in the mountains; usually it flies to the west coast from the Alaskan panhandle south, or to various locations inland throughout the United States. Avoids Washington, D.C.

## Golden eagle *Aigle royal*
*Aquila chrysaetos* (hawk family)
Late May to early October

Occasional at high elevations and over the tundra, a soaring alpine bird that always impresses. Nearly as big as the bald eagle, the golden is 81 cm long with a wingspan of 198 cm. Dark brown all over, often with light patches under wings and tail; "golden" refers to the neck, which looks golden only up close. Voice is small and twittery; quite incongruous.

A golden eagle soars for hours, seldom flapping. When the ground squirrels forget that it's up there and venture out of their burrows, the eagle dives to pick one off. Also goes for snowshoe hares and marmots. Sometimes seen eating dead sheep or goats, and has been known to strike bighorn lambs repeatedly, apparently trying to kill them.

Nests in mid-spring, sometimes every other year. The life-mated pair build an enormous perennial stick nest up to 3 m across and a metre thick, usually on an alpine cliff-ledge; sometimes they use very little nesting material. There are two white eggs, blotched/streaked reddish-brown and gray, hatching at 43–45 days but a couple of days apart. The older one usually kills the younger one. Juveniles have white rump patches and pale patches under the wings. Flies leisurely, 50 km/h, but can do nearly 200 km/h if chased. Wintering grounds: west coast from Alaska panhandle south and through much of the U.S.A.

MW

## The great Canadian Rockies eagle migration

In 1992 naturalist Peter Sherrington discovered a previously unknown major bird-migration route. From early March to early May, 6000–8000 golden eagles move north through the front ranges of the Rockies, flying in groups of 10–40. They are joined by much smaller numbers of other raptors, including bald eagles, hawks and falcons. From mid-September to early December they return.

This is the Canadian leg of a route that may stretch from northern Mexico to Alaska; a bird banded in Denali National Park has been recovered in eastern Colorado. It's different from the well-known raptor-migration corridor in the foothills, which concentrates hawks and falcons along the mountain front.

At the height of the eagle migration in the latter half of March and the first week in April, about 200 golden eagles can be seen each day. The record is over a thousand. The height of the fall migration comes in late September and early October, over exactly the same route.

If you want to watch, contact local birders in eastern-slope towns for *exact* spotting sites. The best locations are where the birds cross a major valley, such as at Bellevue near Crowsnest Pass, at Livingstone Gap on the Oldman River, at Mt. Head on the Highwood River, in the Kananaskis Valley at Mt. Lorette (the classic site; stop at the Barrier Lake information centre along Highway 40 for details), at Gap Lake along Highway 1A east of Canmore, at the Lake Minnewanka dam near Banff, at the western end of Abraham Lake along Highway 11, or at Pocahontas in eastern Jasper National Park. Look for the eagles above ridges and peaks. They are most visible against a high, thin cloud-cover. The birds fly high; bring good binoculars and a telescope.

## Owls

These famous night-hunters of the dark forests home in on sounds with some special equipment: offset ears that tell the birds very accurately where the sound is coming from. One ear-hole is lower on the skull than the other, so the timing of sound-wave arrivals relates to the angle above or below the head. An owl follows a sound straight to its prey, even unseen beneath snow, much as human pilots follow their electronic glide-paths to night landings.

Highway 11 between Rocky Mountain House and Nordegg is the best place in the Rockies to listen for owls. Go in late February or early March, when many species are courting.

### Great horned owl *Grand Duc d'Amérique*
*Bubo virginianus* (typical-owl family)
Year-round

Fairly common in the woods, but seldom active during the day and thus infrequently seen. Very large owl: length 50 cm, wingspan 140 cm. This is the only owl you are likely to see in the Canadian Rockies area with horn-like tufts of feathers. Horned owls hoot loudly, saying "hoo, hoo-oo-oo, hoo, hoo"—one of the more familiar night sounds throughout North America. They hunt mostly at night, although sometimes during the day, coasting silently down on prey located mainly through sound. They catch and kill with their talons, bringing the meat home to eat it. Prey: mainly snowshoe hares and skunks when available, but also mice, tree squirrels, ground squirrels, chipmunks, bats, frogs, insects, waterfowl, perching birds, hawks, other owls—and fuzzy caps worn in the woods at dusk.

Nests late in winter or early in spring, usually in a borrowed hawk-nest, sometimes in a rock cleft or tree cavity. Very protective; don't come close. Two or three white eggs hatch in 30–35 days. The owlets flop out of the nest in 4–5 weeks; they are fed on the ground for a while and fly poorly until 9–10 weeks. They follow mum and dad around for months afterward, begging food. Don't breed until two years old; record lifespan in captivity 29 years. Non-migratory. Provincial bird of Alberta.

North of the Peace River you may see another owl with ear-tufts: the **short-eared owl,** *Asio flammeus*. Once on the rare list for the Rockies, this species is becoming more common in the foothills, but is still seen mainly on the prairies. This is the only owl species in the Rockies that migrates. It turns up in the Edmonton Christmas bird counts, wintering from central Alberta across the United States and south to Mexico.

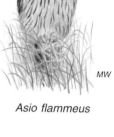

MW

*Asio flammeus*

## Great gray owl *Chouette lapone*
*Strix nebulosa* (typical-owl family)
Year-round

Occasional in northern areas, scarce farther south. The largest owl in North America: length 70 cm, wingspan 152 cm. More brown than gray in the mountains, but the facial disk is quite gray, large and concentrically ringed around the eyes, which are yellow. No horns. Larger than the similar barred owl, next item, which has black eyes.

The great gray speaks in very low hoots; the furry creatures listen. So does the owl: it can hear the mice under the snow. The big bird dives softly, the feathers making no noise. It punches through the crust with its long legs to reach the little snowy tunnel. The warm mammal within barely has time to shriek as the talons close, penetrating heart and lungs. Also hit: hares, tree squirrels and sometimes small birds.

MW

Often active during the day and strangely unwary, this bird will let you approach rather closely. Breeds in early spring, taking over a crow's nest or hawk's nest in a large conifer; sometimes nests in a snapped-off hollow tree trunk. Eggs 3–5, white. Incubation time varies from egg to egg; all birds leave the nest at 3–5 weeks but fly weakly and require parental attention for months. Non-migratory.

## Barred owl *Chouette rayée*
*Strix varia* (typical-owl family)
Year-round

Occasional in the woods; more commonly heard than seen. Large: length 43 cm, wingspan 112 cm. Hornless; the eyes are black, not yellow, and there is a large barred ruff below the bill and down the breast. Brown-streaked buffy front. The call is an easy one to know: a low-toned "hoo-hoo-hoo-HOO-aww" ("Who cooks for YOU-all?"), unlike any other. Listen at dusk, when barred owls are most active; if there is one around, it will call back to you.

Barred owls eat mainly mice, voles and other small rodents, also taking birds, insects, frogs and sometimes grabbing fish. They like to nest in wetland tree cavities, sometimes in the unused nests of hawks or other large birds. Breeding is in late winter or early spring; 2–3 white eggs hatch in 28 days, the young fledging at 4–5 weeks but staying close to the nest until the sixth week. Non-migratory.

MW

### Northern hawk-owl *Chouette épervière*
*Surnia ulula* (typical-owl family)
Year-round

An uncommon bird of wetlands in the northern foothills; occasional in subalpine forest and burned areas farther south; rare south of Banff. Length 35 cm, wingspan 85 cm. The hawk-owl's face is reminiscent of the great horned owl's, page 541, but hornless; the top of the head is speckled white on brown and the bill is yellow. The bird is most easily identified by the long, hawk-like tail, which it raises and lowers when perching. Finely barred all the way down the front, which serves to differentiate from boreal owl and northern saw-whet owl. Voice is a lovely warble given only in flight and rarely heard.

MW

This owl is active in the daytime. Unwary; can be closely approached. Watches for mice and other small rodents from a tall vantage point, dropping on them. Breeding is in mid-spring, the nest usually in a natural tree cavity or in a large woodpecker hole. Sometimes manages two broods in a year. Eggs 3–10, white, hatching in 25–30 days; the young fledge at 23–27 days.

### Boreal owl *Nyctale boréale*
*Aegolius funereus* (typical-owl family)
Year-round

Fairly common in older mixed-wood forest, especially in the northern region. Seen most often from mid-April to mid-May. Smallish: length 25 cm, wingspan 60 cm. Resembles the northern saw-whet owl, next item, which is smaller, more colorful, and has a darker bill. Boreal owl has a black-rimmed facial disk. Front is mottled rather than barred. Call is distinctive, associated with the northern woods at night: rather high-pitched, quick, "hoo-hoo-hoo-hoo-hoo-hoo," rather like the winnowing of the snipe, page 527.

MW

After a hard night of gobbling up mice, voles and shrews, the boreal owl dozes away the day on a branch. You can get quite close when it's asleep. Nesting: mid-spring, in tree cavities, often those made by woodpeckers. Eggs 3–6, white, hatching in 26–36 days. Fledging is 30–36 days later. Non-migratory.

### Northern saw-whet owl *Petite Nyctale*
*Aegolius acadicus* (typical-owl family)
Year-round

Occasional year-round, seen most often from mid-April to mid-May, in the woods. Scarce in the north end of the Rockies. Small owl: length 18 cm, wingspan 43 cm. Resembles boreal owl, previous item, but is smaller, with a streaky head rather than a spotted one, no eye-line, and streaky front rather than mottling or barring. Calls in hoots and whistles, and sings by making a short, sharp, whistling sound like that of a file on a saw blade; thus "saw-whet." Does so at less frequent intervals than boreal owl; faster than pygmy-owl.

MW

Hunts at night, mostly for insects, sometimes for little rodents and small birds. By day this species is fast asleep and easily approached at its low roost. Nests in late winter or early spring, often using a flicker hole. There are 5–6 white eggs—a lot for an owl—hatching at 26–28 days; young leave the nest 27–34 days later. The young look very different from the adults: white eyebrow-like vee over eyes, rest of head uniformly brown.

### Northern pygmy-owl *Chouette naine*
*Glaucidium gnoma* (typical-owl family)
Year-round

Occasional year-round, seen most often from early April to late May, in the woods. Often hangs around towns in winter, knocking off house sparrows. Our smallest owl: length 15 cm, wingspan 38 cm. Another long-tailed owl, but so much smaller than the hawk-owl, previous page, that confusion is unlikely. Resembles saw-whet owl, previous item, but has a longer tail and a darker face—it's rather fierce-looking—and diagnostic dark markings on the back of the neck, outlined in white.

MW

Gives forth cute little hoots, but over and over, monotonously, every 3–5 seconds; calls in the daytime and under moonlight. Active at dawn and dusk, more diurnal than most other owls; it perches above a clearing and swoops down on mice and insects, hitting also ground squirrels and small birds. Breeds in mid-spring, usually taking a woodpecker hole. Three to four white eggs hatch in 28 days; the young owls fledge at 29–32 days. Non-migratory.

## Chickens of the mountains: grouse and ptarmigan

Grouse and ptarmigan are in the order Galliformes, along with the domestic chicken, *(Gallus gallus,* family Gallinaceae), turkeys both domestic and wild (family Phasianidae) and quail, partridges and pheasants (subfamily Phasianinae). Grouse and ptarmigan belong in the subfamily Tetraoninae. See page 589 for more on bird families.

### Ruffed grouse *Gélinotte huppée*
*Bonasa umbellus* (grouse family)
Year-round, seen most often early March to end of October

Common in montane woods, often in aspen groves and near the edges of small clearings. Length 35 cm. Of the three grouse you are likely to see in the Canadian Rockies, this is the only one with a crest, present on both sexes, and thus the easiest to identify. Note also the black-banded tail. Males seldom show their characteristic red spot above the eye. On females, the middle two feathers in the tail are mottled brown at the end, producing a fuzzy-looking break in the band.

Grouse don't say much; they make little soft sounds to their children and sometimes squawk when frightened. But the male ruffed grouse **drums:** standing on a log, he beats his wings up and down to produce a very low thumping sound that is repeated for eight to ten seconds, slowly at first, then faster near the end. It sounds much like a big diesel engine starting up somewhere in the woods, then stopping.

MW

Slow-motion photography has shown that the noise is not made by thumping the body, whacking the wings together or hitting the log. It is simply made in the air. This is a mating call; despite its low frequency of 40 Hz, which makes it hard for humans to pinpoint, the female finds her lover. He puts on a wonderful display: fluffs out the dark feathers on his neck (the ruff), and fans out his reddish tail.

Ruffed grouse eat insects and most above-ground parts of a great variety of plants during the warm months; in winter they subsist on seeds and twig-ends until February, when many shrubs and trees are producing nutritious buds. Although grouse are folk-named "fool-hens" because they can often be approached so closely, the ruffed grouse is nonetheless the most skittish of the family and will suddenly fly up under your feet with a loud, startling blast of wings. Surprise! How's your heart?

This species breeds in early spring, among the last snowbanks in the woods. The nest is a small scrape on the ground, lined with whatever is nearby. The eggs, 9–12, white or buff, sometimes brown-speckled, take 23–24 days to hatch—a long time, considering the dangerous nesting site—but like all grouse and ptarmigan the young are precocious and leave the nest just a few hours out of the shell. Almost immediately they are pecking for seeds and bugs. They are able to fly up to a little security in small trees at only 10–12 days.

Baby grouse is a favorite food of many predators, which explains why so many eggs are laid. If one clutch gets snapped up, the pair usually produce another. The birds don't migrate.

## Blue grouse *Tétras sombre*
*Dendragapus obscurus* (grouse family)
Year-round

MW

Fairly common on brushy avalanche slopes and in upper subalpine forest. At lower elevations, often seen in pine forests and burns. Length 43 cm; our largest grouse. This grouse has no crest. Males have dark breasts rather than brown/white mottled ones like the other grouse species—the throat is mottled, though— and a black tail. Our birds are the northern Rockies variant, with little or no terminal gray band on the tail. The male has a yellow spot above the eye, sometimes red. The females are plain mottled brown but have the black tail. The female spruce grouse, next item, also has a dark tail, but with small cinnamon spots, and with or without a cinnamon terminal band. The tail of the female ruffed grouse, previous item, is black-banded at the end, not black all over.

Like other grouse, in autumn the blue grouse grows little horny **pectinations**: short spines on its toes, which help it move in the snow. Blue grouse live on fruits, berries and bugs when they can get them; mostly on evergreen needles during the winter.

Breeding time: mid-spring. The male hoots softly during courting, five hoots per call. The sound is made as the bird draws back its neck feathers and exposes twin patches of skin on either side of the neck. These patches are typically bright reddish-orange, sometimes purplish. They bulge out as the esophagus inflates. Five to ten brown-speckled pink/buffy eggs are laid in a concealed plant-lined hollow on the ground. Hatching at 26 days, the young quickly start feeding themselves, following momma as she picks and pecks about—the pattern for all our grouse. Fly weakly in 7 days. By late summer the kids have grown up and left. Migrates altitudinally: down in winter and up in spring for birds that breed in subalpine zone, or in reverse for birds that breed lower down.

## Spruce grouse *Tétras du Canada*
*Dendragapus canadensis* (grouse family)
Year-round

MW

Common in pine forests and upper-subalpine woods. Unwary; you can walk to within a few metres of this bird, at which point it might flop up into a tree, if it isn't there already; spruce grouse are more arboreal than their relatives. It sits there at eye-level, an easy target for hunters. Length 33 cm. No crest. The male is easily identified by his black breast patch and black throat bordered by a white line; there is sometimes a spot of bare red skin showing above the eye. South of the Peace River, the birds are the variety called **Franklin's grouse,** with white spots in the male's tail feathers, as shown. North of the Peace, Franklin's males lack the white spots and both sexes have reddish-brown tail-tips. The female looks a lot like the female blue grouse, previous item, but female spruce grouse has reddish-brown spots on her tail (look closely), which may also have a cinnamon terminal band.

The male spruce grouse doesn't have a fancy expanding neck patch like the blue grouse, nor does it hoot. (The Cornell bird recordings include a low hoot for the spruce grouse, but this is an error. The recording was of a blue grouse.) Males of the Franklin's variety of spruce grouse display by fanning their tails and clapping their wings together loudly as they take little jumps.

Diet: mostly spruce needles, one of the few animals to eat conifer needles. Also berries, seeds and other plant parts, mushrooms, ferns, insects. Nesting is in mid-spring, the nest on the ground but well-hidden. Seven or eight buffy or pale pink speckled eggs hatch in 24 days, the downy chicks leaving the nest right away to feed themselves. They can fly after only a week. Locally migrates altitudinally.

### White-tailed ptarmigan *Lagopède à queue blanche*
*Lagopus leucurus* (grouse family)
Year-round

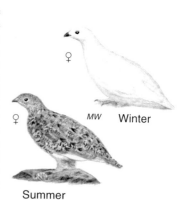

*MW*    Winter

♀    Summer

Pronounced "TAR-mi-gun." Common on alpine tundra, but so well-camouflaged that you practically have to step on a ptarmigan to see it—which the bird may almost let you do, it is so unwary. Length 25 cm. Ptarmigan plumage changes with the seasons; they are mottled brown-and-white in the summer, turning all white in the winter except for the small black bill and eye, and red patch ("comb") above the eye in both sexes, all seasons. A good way to tell a summer-plumage ptarmigan from a grouse is to check the tail: it is neat and narrow on a ptarmigan, wider on a grouse. Further, ptarmigan have white feathers on their feet and lower legs at all times of year, while the feet of grouse are unfeathered. Of our three ptarmigan species, the white-tailed is the one with no black at all in the tail, winter or summer. The other two, discussed in the next item, have black outer tailfeathers.

Ptarmigan don't say much, mostly clucking and making other soft sounds. But sometimes you may hear white-tails scolding, shouting "boo-OW-oo" at one another. During the summer, ptarmigan move slowly through alpine meadows and boulderfields in family groups of four to eight birds, nibbling shoots, buds, flowers, fruits and seeds, and catching bugs. In the winter they flock more numerously—a dozen or two together—and subsist on seeds, twig-ends and early buds at or above treeline, often moving to higher elevations at night. This may seem odd—conditions are harsher there—but the birds can dig into the snow for shelter (see boxed item), and the predators are few.

White-tails breed in early summer, nesting on the ground in the open. There are usually 3–9 brown-speckled/spotted pinkish or buffy eggs; they hatch in 22–23 days and the young leave the nest right away, wonderfully camouflaged as they follow mom about the tundra, peeping. You can follow her, too; she doesn't get very upset. Once, when I was resting on a high-country trail near Jasper, a family of ptarmigan passed right by me, stepping over my feet and even walking under my bent-up legs. Endearingly unwary, these birds. If not picked off by hawks or other chicken-loving predators, ptarmigan can live up to 15 years. The white-tailed is non-migratory except in very lean winters, when it moves down to the intermountain valleys in B.C. and out onto the prairies looking for food.

### Willow ptarmigan *Lagopède des saules*
*Lagopus lagopus* (grouse family)
Year-round

Occasional above treeline from Jasper north, usually near willow mats. Length 33 cm, noticeably larger than white-tailed ptarmigan, previous item, and easily differentiated if you get a look at the tail: the outside feathers are black, not white. The rest of the summer plumage is mottled brown and white. In winter the bird is all white, except for the black outer tail feathers, bill and eye. Like other ptarmigan species, willow ptarmigan have white feathers on their feet. Males have a red spot above the eye in the spring and early summer.

These birds are not very vocal, normally clucking and cooing quietly, but sometimes they come out with long, loud conversations, making a variety of quacky sounds. They walk about in small family groups, eating mostly willow leaves. In winter you may see their tracks, as well as those of white-tailed ptarmigan, previous item, going from bush to bush. At this time of year they eat mainly the buds, which willows are kind enough to bring forth in early February. These buds are amazingly rich in proteins and sugars, just the thing to get a bird through the tough alpine winter. During storms the birds burrow into the snow.

MW

The species nests in early summer among its beloved willows, laying 6–11 yellowish or reddish, heavily marked eggs in a cup on the ground. Hatching is at 20–26 days, the chicks leaving the nest right away and following the parents to the willows, which they are dependent on for the rest of their lives. Like white-tailed ptarmigan, willow ptarmigan prefer not to migrate, but they move to lower elevations when the alpine food supply runs low.

In the northern section of the Rockies, from Pink Mountain north, you may see the **rock ptarmigan**, *Lagopus mutus*. It resembles the willow ptarmigan but is a little smaller. In winter the male rock ptarmigan has a broad black line from bill to eye, and a narrow black line behind the eye. In summer the male is mottled while the male willow ptarmigan is more evenly brown, except for the white wings characteristic of all our species. In summer the female willow ptarmigan has a light line behind the eye, while the rock-ptarmigan female has a dark line.

## What made these droppings?

A ptarmigan, most likely, if the droppings are curved and appear to be made of sawdust, deposited in a little snow pit in the high country. The birds hunker down into the snow at night, and they leave their calling cards behind when they leave the next morning. If bad weather has kept them pinned down for a couple of days, the dropping collection will be larger. You can also see these dropping piles on the tundra in summer.

In a severe winter storm the ptarmigan dig in deeper. The wind leaves the snow surface smooth, with no trace of the birds underneath. On one occasion I unknowingly skied through a flock of such dug-in ptarmigans, and their heads all popped up at once to look at me.

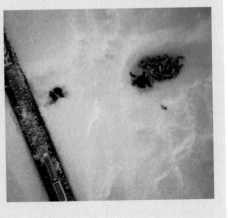

# A lark in the high country

See also the other classic alpine species in the Canadian Rockies: ptarmigan, pipit, rosy finch and golden-crowned sparrow.

### Horned lark *Alouette cornue*
*Eremophila alpestris* (lark family)
Mid-April to mid-October

MW

Fairly common in the alpine zone, even though this is mainly a bird of the prairies. Length 17 cm. Plain brown body with a black breast-band. Very distinctive head: black line just above the bill that crosses the forehead and hooks downward, broadening at the eye. There are two little black feather-tufts on the crown—the "horns," often inconspicuous on our birds. The face is mostly yellow, sometimes quite pale or white. Voice is cheepy, with bubbly/gurgly sounds. In flight the bird folds in its wings after each flap.

Horned larks flit about the tundra eating flies, mosquitoes, seeds and fruits. During late-spring courtship the male flies up 200–300 m, sings lustily while circling, then dives earthward, pulling out at the last moment. The female is impressed and builds a nest on the ground, protected in a hollow behind a rock or shrub. Often there are goat/sheep poops or pebbles spotted around it. Four brown-speckled greenish/grayish eggs hatch in 10–14 days; the young leave the nest 9–12 days later but don't fly for another 3–5 days. Winter range: U.S.A. and Mexico.

# Swallows, swifts and nighthawks

Not as closely related as they seem—they are in different orders—all these birds do look rather similar, eat bugs and spend most of their waking hours on the wing. So I have grouped them together here.

### Barn swallow *Hirondelle des granges*
*Hirundo rustica* (swallow family)
Mid-May to late August

Very common, although subject to large fluctuations in numbers from year to year. Often common in towns. Length 15 cm. Easy to recognize: bluish-black with a brown front and a deeply split tail. Tails of the other swallow species are forked, not split like this.

MW

Swallows put on a constant summer airshow for people in mountain communities, swooping about at street-level for bugs—they feed on the wing—and perching by the dozen along wires. The barn swallow is endearing in many ways, but its voice sounds like someone loudly rubbing squeaky glass and then giving the Bronx cheer. The birds call constantly, starting at first light, meaning five in the morning in midsummer.

Diet: strictly flying insects. Barn swallows drink by skimming water in flight. They nest in mid-spring, building mud cups under any sort of overhang and often inside buildings. If you construct a little platform for them under an eave by a window, a pair may move in and keep you entertained for months. The feather-lined nest holds 4–5 small red-speckled white eggs; they hatch in 14–16 days, the female sitting on the eggs while the male guards nearby. The young fledge 17–24 days later. This short reproductive cycle allows two broods a year in the southern section, one or two centrally and north.

The altricial nestlings lie out of sight, below the rim of the nest, until one of the parents arrives with a throat full of masticated insects. All the little heads pop up at once. One or two birds get fed; the others have to wait a couple of minutes until next time. The nestlings sink back slowly, as if deflating. Newly fledged birds are particularly fun to watch. They teeter on wires and fences, fluttering their wings and begging plaintively whenever an adult cruises by. The nestlings stay together for a few weeks, crowding back into the nest at night and on rainy days.

Swallows are famous for geographically precise and punctual migrations, arriving and departing in the same week year after year. Yet they travel farther than any other perching birds, some of them round-tripping annually between Alaska and Argentina. (The water-based arctic tern travels even farther, from the high Arctic to the southern tip of South America.)

### Cliff swallow *Hirondelle à front blanc*
*Hirundo pyrrhonota* (swallow family)
Mid-May to late August

Common, especially around towns and under bridges, and nearly as tolerant of humans as the barn swallow. Length 13 cm. Resembles the barn swallow, but the tail is not as deeply forked. There is a prominent white patch on the forehead. Back is lighter, with a brown patch on the rump. Compare with bank swallow, next page.

MW

These swallows live in colonies, flying out over water for mosquitos and such. The calls are like those of barn swallows, but higher-pitched and less strident. They seldom perch on wires, preferring instead to sit on the edges of their nests, which are little bottles made of mud stuck onto sheltered vertical or overhanging surfaces. You may see the nests on buildings, under bridges and culverts, on cliffs and under thick treelimbs. These summer condos are reused year after year if left intact.

Breeding is in mid-spring, again in midsummer in the southern section where there are often two broods each year. There are 4–5 small pinkish eggs, reddish/brownish-speckled, incubated 16 days by the female only. The young birds are fed by both parents, fledging at 23 days. Returns regularly from wintering in South America.

### Violet-green swallow *Hirondelle à face blanche*
*Tachycineta thalassina* (swallow family)
Late April to late August

Common in the main ranges and front ranges, especially around towns; less common through the foothills. Length 12 cm. This swallow and the tree swallow, next item, both have white breasts and greenish backs; on the violet-green swallow the white region extends up onto the back and above the eye, while on the tree swallow it is less extensive. The tree swallow is also seen less frequently in the Rockies.

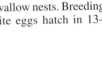

MW

Violet-greens behave much like barn swallows, perching in rows along wires and aerobatically chasing bugs. Their call is twittery rather than raucous, and they nest more secretively, in crevices, tree holes and nest boxes, or even in unused cliff-swallow nests. Breeding time: mid-spring. Mud is not used in the nest. Four or five small white eggs hatch in 13–15 days; fledging is at 23–25 days. Wintering is in Central America.

### Tree swallow *Hirondelle bicolore*
*Tachycineta bicolor* (swallow family)
Late April to mid-September; less common after July

Common, but stays mainly in the woods and is thus not as obvious as the swallows listed above. Length 13 cm. Very similar to violet-green swallow, previous item, with a white tummy and green or blue back, but the white does not extend up onto the back, nor does it curl behind the eye. Voice is twittery/cheepy. Differs in some ways from

MW

our other swallows: not colonial; will sometimes feed on the ground, taking seeds and berries as well as insects. Nests in mid-spring, usually expropriating a woodpecker hole near water, with 4–6 small white eggs that hatch in 13–16 days. The young fledge 13–24 days later. Where possible, this bird lines its nest with white chicken feathers! Winters along the coasts from California/Virginia south, often in huge flocks.

## Bank swallow *Hirondelle des rivages*
*Riparia riparia* (swallow family)
Mid-May to mid-August

Locally common, in colonies along vertical silty/sandy river banks. Length 12 cm. Brown on top and white below, most easily identified by a brown bar across the breast. Voice is quite nasal and buzzy. Diet: flying insects taken in the air.

The bank swallow, the northern rough-winged swallow and the kingfisher are the only birds in the Canadian Rockies area that burrow. The large river valleys of the Canadian Rockies are generally floored in glacial silt and loess (very fine wind-blown sand). River-cut banks or road-cuts in these materials, complete with an overhanging root mat at the top, make fine sites for bank-swallow colonies. The holes are reoccupied year after year in late spring, usually with lots of territorial squabbling upon arrival. "Number 32? Look; we don't *want* Number 32. We *always* take Number 33!" New burrows are dug by hacking with the bill and kicking soil out with the feet. The burrows are 2–5 cm in diameter, widening somewhat inside for the nest-mat made of plant parts, wool and feathers, which may be placed more than a metre back. Rodent burrows that open when banks collapse are used as well.

Breeding is in May; 4–5 small white eggs hatch in 12–16 days. As in other swallow species, only the female sits on the eggs, but both parents feed the young. Bank swallows fly to South America for the winter.

## Northern rough-winged swallow *Hirondelle à ailes herissées*
*Stelgidopteryx serripennis* (swallow family)
Mid-May to mid-August

Fairly common in southern and central regions, swooping above lakes and streams. Length 12 cm. Rather similar to the bank swallow. Differentiate by the lack of a brown breast-bar on the rough-winged. Named for tiny hooks along the primary wing feathers, which give the wing a rough feel.

These birds sound rather like nighthawks, facing page. The call note is a buzzy "preet." Diet is like that of other swallows: insects scooped up by the wide mouth while in flight. Unlike most other swallow species, though, rough-wings are seldom colonial. They nest mostly by burrowing in silty earth, like the bank swallow, but they also move into rock crevices, drill-holes in dynamited road-cuts or the little pipes that drain bridges. Breeding time: mid-spring. A pair produces 6–7 small white eggs—a lot for a swallow—that hatch in 15–16 days. Young leave the nest 15–16 days later. Wintering is in Central America and South America.

## Black swift *Martinet sombre*
*Cypseloides niger* (swift family)
Early June to mid-October

Fairly common but rather reclusive and high-flying for such a small bird. Seen less on the western slope than on the eastern slope. Two good spots: Johnston Canyon, between Banff and Lake Louise on the Bow Valley Parkway (Highway 1A), and Maligne Canyon, near Jasper. Length 18 cm, larger than any of our swallows, but otherwise rather swallow-like in design.

The body of a swift is short in comparison to the wingspan, and the wings are narrow. The birds look like little fat cigars with flittery curved wings. The plumage is black, with a small bit of white on the face that doesn't show except at close range. Compare with Vaux's swift, next item, which is common only south of Crowsnest Pass.

Swifts fly constantly all day. They take a few quick, fluttery wingbeats—once thought to be alternate, but since shown to be together—then glide. I often see them around dusk, cruising home in formation several hundred metres above the ground. Usually travelling in small flocks, they cover hundreds of kilometres daily, seeking the most delectable insect swarms.

Not deigning to perch in the usual way, swifts hang from some sort of edge, usually the edge of the nest, which is hidden away in a cool, drippy gorge, often behind a waterfall. I have also found their nests high above treeline in north-facing cave entrances on cliffs. There is but one egg in a mossy cup; it is white and rather elongated. Black swifts are so secretive that little is known of their lives; in the Canadian Rockies the birds breed in midsummer. The egg hatches in late July, and the young bird grows slowly, probably because it is fed only once or twice a day. It fledges 45 days later, meaning in early September—long after other birds have fledged. Baby swifts can survive several days unattended by going into torpor. This can happen often, for swifts avoid bad weather and the adults will fly long distances to reach sunny skies and the swarms of flying ants they relish before returning to feed the children. Like the swallows, black swifts head for Central America and South America in the fall.

### Vaux's swift *Martinet de Vaux*

*Chaetura vauxi* (swift family)

August

Common in the western-slope portion of Glacier National Park, nesting in stands of red-cedar, and occasionally seen elsewhere in the southern region, mostly in Columbian-forest areas. Vaux's swift (pronounced "vox," not "voe") is small, length 11 cm, more easily confused with the swallows than with the black swift. It is dark, with a white throat and breast. The call is a squeaky "chip-chip."

In mid-spring a pair of Vaux's chooses a hollow tree or some other deep shaft-like structure—sometimes a chimney—and sticks a cup of twigs onto the inside with salivary glue as the chimney swifts do. In Asia this glue is boiled from swifts' nests, forming a protein-rich broth: the famous bird's-nest soup. The eggs (4–7) take 18–20 days to hatch; the nestlings leave the nest at 20–21 days and cling to the wall beside it for a few days more before flying. Vaux's swift winters from Mexico to Panama.

MW

### Common nighthawk *Engoulevent de Amérique*

*Chordeiles minor* (nightjar family)

Early June to early October

Occasional, flying over openings in dry woods. Length 23 cm, wingspan 58 cm. Usually active at dusk, cruising in pairs for bugs, these dark-colored birds are not easy to see. They look somewhat like large swallows or swifts: narrow-winged, with a diagnostic white bar across each wing about two-thirds

MW

of the way to the end. Males have a white tail band; females don't. Note also the pale throat and the enormous flat head. An easy identification is by sound: nighthawks say "beer!" in a buzzy way. The male displays by diving very fast, then producing a roaring sound ("booming") as it pulls out close to the ground.

Nighthawks are not hawks; the owls do any night-hawking that comes along. Nighthawks are members of the nightjar family, a group of nocturnal or twilight birds that includes nighthawks, whip-poor-wills and nightjars proper. These birds sit longwise on their perches instead of crosswise.

Some of them, but apparently not the common nighthawk, go into a deep, hibernation-like torpor on their wintering grounds.

Nighthawks nest in late spring, laying the eggs right on the ground, sometimes on a gravelly roof. There are two eggs, whitish/greenish and heavily marked; they hatch in about 19 days and the young fly at 23 days. Wintering is in southern Mexico and South America.

MW

# Woodpeckers

Although they are roughly the size and shape of songbirds, woodpeckers are in their own order, the Piciformes. Within that order, all the woodpeckers in the Canadian Rockies belong to the family Picidae.

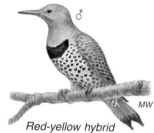

### Northern flicker *Pic flamboyant*
*Colaptes auratus* (woodpecker family)
Late March to mid-October

Common in the woods, especially in aspen groves. Length 27 cm. Used to be called "common flicker," and is probably the most common woodpecker in the Canadian Rockies, best identified on the wing by the barred brown back and white rump patch. Perches by clinging to a tree trunk. Note the spotted breast with black throat bar and black tail feathers.

MW

*Red-yellow hybrid*

There are three different flicker varieties, of which we have two: **red-shafted** and **yellow-shafted.** "Shafted" refers to the shaft of the wing feather, where the color is most pronounced. Flicker varieties can best be differentiated in flight. The red-shafted flicker, more common on the western slope, has pink underwings. The yellow-shafted flicker, more common on the eastern slope, has yellow underwings. The heads are also different: yellow-shafted has gray crown with red band across the nape, brown cheeks and a black mustache; red-shafted has a *brown* crown with no nape patch, *gray* cheeks, and a *red* mustache.

Now the kicker: the different forms interbreed, producing all sorts of odd combinations. All varieties say "wick-wick-wick," and "kee-arr," the flicker calls, loud and ubiquitous in the forest. The birds drill, but they don't drum. They eat mainly ants, using their long, sticky tongues to reach into anthills and carpenter-ant galleries. Other foods: other insects.

Flickers nest in large cavities they hack out of either live or dead trees, the rounded entrance 7–10 cm across. Begun in mid-spring, this is a three-week effort, but, as is true for other woodpeckers, it is repeated every year—and often in the same tree. The resulting surplus of nesting holes provides chickadees and other small cavity-nesters with lodgings far larger and more solid than they could hope to produce themselves. Flickers lay 6–8 white eggs on a nest-mat of wood chips; they hatch in 11–12 days. The young are fed regurgitated insects and fly away 22–26 days later. The yellow-shafted variety winters in the eastern United States. The red-shafted variety stays west of the Mississippi; some overwinter in southern B.C.

### Pileated woodpecker *Grand Pic*
*Dryocopus pileatus* (woodpecker family)
Year-round

Occasional in older montane woods. Although many birders say "PILE-e-ated," as suggested by the American Ornithological Union, the word seems to come from the Latin *pileum,* a "cap worn by freemen." Change to *pileatus,* meaning "having the shape or character of," and you've got the name of the woodpecker, for which the normal Latin pronunciation would be "pill-e-ATE-us." This leads to "PILL-e-ated," which sounds better to me.

This is a great big woodpecker, length 38 cm, the largest in the Canadian Rockies. But it's shy and tries to avoid detection. Aside from the size, it is easily identified by the red crest on both sexes; this bird is the model for Woody the Woodpecker. No other woodpecker in our area is crested. The female's crest is smaller than the male's. Males have a small red cheek patch as well. Voice is like that of the flicker, previous item: "wick-wick-wick." The species drums loudly, 3–5 seconds at a time, which the flicker does not.

Pileated woodpeckers eat carpenter ants, page 452, the big black

MW

ants that live in dead or dying trees, fallen logs and stumps. Apparently, the bird can *hear* the bugs inside the tree. (Mother ant to her children: "Quit chewing with your mandibles open, or the woodpecker will come.") The bird drills deeply into the ant galleries and drags the bugs out with its long sticky tongue. It also chops out several large cavities that are used strictly for roosting. For this it prefers dead wood in big poplars and cottonwoods, 10–20 m up. A square or rectangular entrance 8–12 cm across, diagnostic for this species, leads into a cavity up to 60 cm deep and 20 cm wide. You can always tell where a pileated woodpecker has been at work: the chips are many and large.

Nesting is in a similar cavity in mid-spring. Three to five white eggs hatch in about 18 days; the young fledge 22–26 days later. Nonmigratory.

### Hairy woodpecker *Pic chevelu*
*Picoides villosus* (woodpecker family)
Year-round

♂

Fairly common in the woods, often in mixed conifer/leafy growth and in damp places. Length 20 cm. A black-and-white woodpecker with a white back; male has a red spot on the back of the head. Very similar to the downy woodpecker, next item. Differentiate by size: the downy is noticeably smaller, with a disproportionately smaller bill. Differentiate female hairy or downy from three-toed woodpeckers, next page, and female black-backeds, next page, by the white backs of the hairy and downy. Voice: "pweet," "pweet." Drums in short bursts. Hairy woodpeckers eat mainly wood-boring beetle larvae, cutting into their galleries under the bark, and also ants, other insects on the ground, berries, and sap at sapsucker wells, page 555.

MW

Breeds in early spring, whacking out a cavity in a dead trunk or limb on a live tree. The rectangular entrance is about 4 cm across and 5 cm tall. Four eggs on a mat of chips hatch in 11–12 days; the young can climb to the entrance for feeding after 17 more days—most woodpecker nestlings are fed at the entrance, all the little heads sticking out at once—and fly at 28–30 days. Nonmigratory.

### Downy woodpecker *Pic mineur*
*Picoides pubescens* (woodpecker family)
Year-round, but seen mainly from early May to end of September

♂

Fairly common in willow thickets, aspen woods or on poplars. Hangs around river banks. The smallest woodpecker: length only 15 cm. Black and white; male has red nape. Nearly identical to hairy woodpecker, previous item, but markedly smaller, especially the bill, and less wary. You can get quite close. Female told from other black-and-white woodpeckers by the white back; others are black except for hairy, which is larger than female downy. Voice: quick "weet"s, trailing off at the end. Drums in short bursts.

MW

Diet is like that of hairy woodpecker. Excavates a winter roosting cavity as well as a nesting hole. Breeds in early-spring, drilling a cavity in dead wood; entrance hole is round, about 3 cm in diameter. Four or five small white eggs hatch in 12 days; the young leave the nest 20–22 days later but are fed by adults for another 2-3 weeks. Nonmigratory, but seldom seen in the winter.

### Three-toed woodpecker *Pic tridactyle*
*Picoides tridactylus* (woodpecker family)
Year-round

Fairly common in subalpine forest on the western slope and on the eastern slope from Jasper north; scarce on the eastern slope farther south. Seen most often in April and May. Length 20 cm. Yet another black-and-white woodpecker, but the males are easily identified by the yellow crown—that is, if you haven't got a black-backed woodpecker, next item, which also has a yellow crown. Females lack the yellow. In these cases, check the back. If it is barred black and white, then it's a three-toed woodpecker, which, sure enough, has only three toes. All other woodpeckers except this one and the black-backed have four toes.

Voice: a very short "pert." The three-toed also drums, the hits getting quicker as they trail off. Unwary and easily watched, this bird eats mainly wood-boring beetle larvae and other under-bark bugs, sometimes sampling the cambium layer itself. Nests in mid-spring, excavating a cavity in a dead conifer. Four or five white eggs hatch in about two weeks; fledging date unknown. Most woodpecker children will make sounds if you tap the tree holding the nest. In this species, they set up quite a row. Nonmigratory.

MW

### Black-backed woodpecker *Pic à dos noir*
*Picoides arcticus* (woodpecker family)
Year-round

Occasional on dead or dying conifers, seen most often in burned or bug-damaged stands. Uncommon on the eastern slope south of Jasper. Length 21 cm, a little bigger than the three-toed woodpecker, previous item, which it closely resembles. Check the back: the black-backed is all black, while the three-toed is barred—birders say **laddered**—black and white. Like the three-toed, the black-backed has only three toes. Males are yellow crowned; females not. Voice: very short "pert," like that of the three-toed.

Most woodpeckers drill for their food, but the black-backed *peels the bark* instead, a subtle behavioral difference that gives the black-backed its own ecological niche. Nesting is in mid-spring, the cavity in dead wood with an oval entrance 4 cm by 5 cm. Four white eggs hatch in about two weeks; fledging date unknown. Nonmigratory.

MW

### Williamson's sapsucker *Pic de Williamson*
*Sphyrapicus thyroideus* (woodpecker family)
Mid-May to late August

In montane pine forest, occasional in the southern Rocky Mountain Trench, reported from the eastern slope at Waterton and Glacier. Length 21 cm. This bird is a little larger than the closely related yellow-bellied sapsucker, next item. Williamson's is even brighter-yellow on the belly; this, and the lack of the red forehead mark on the Williamson's male, distinguish it from the yellow-bellied. The female is quite unlike the male: she has a brown head, black spot on the breast, but again a bright-yellow belly.

This species is normally silent but sometimes lets go with a scream like that of the red-tailed hawk, page 538, which must shake up the neighbors. It drums in very short bursts like those of the yellow-bellied sapsucker. Breeding is in late spring. The nest is in a dead conifer trunk; like the flicker, this species seeks the same tree each year and produces a new hole each time. Five or six white eggs are laid in late May; the incubation time is not known. The bird winters from Nevada and Arizona into Baja California and northern Mexico.

MW

### Yellow-bellied sapsucker *Pic maculé*
*Sphyrapicus varius* (woodpecker family)
Late April to late August

Fairly common in aspen and poplar groves, but shy. Length 20 cm. Yet another black-and-white woodpecker, this one differentiated by red patches on the forehead and throat—female has a white throat—and the tummy, which is buffy or yellowish rather than the usual white. There is a large white patch on the surface of each wing, near the body, and a white patch on the rump. The bird says "keer" every now and again.

Between the Peace River and McBride, you may see the **red-breasted sapsucker,** *S. ruber,* which resembles the yellow-bellied or Williamson's but has a brilliantly red head and a white mustache. If the breast is also bright red, and the mustache does not go past the eye, it is the subspecies *S. r. ruber;* if the breast is pink and the mustache goes past the eye, it is *S. r. daggetti.*

In the Rockies south of McBride, watch for the **red-naped sapsucker,** *S. nuchalis,* which has a red spot on the back of the head but is otherwise the same as the yellow-bellied. The throat of the female is white right under the bill and red lower down.

MW

All these varieties drill in very short bursts, sometimes just a couple of taps at a time. They drum a lot, though, a few taps at first, then a roll, then a few disconnected taps at the end.

True to its name, the sapsucker does drink sap. It has a special brush on the end of its tongue for licking up the stuff. Partly insectivorous, it also eats bugs that are attracted to the feeding holes, called **wells.** Wells are easily recognized as small holes in rows across the trunk, usually in birches, aspens or poplars, but also in conifers. Some people don't like sapsuckers; they say that sapsuckers damage trees. Maybe so, but trees and sapsuckers have coexisted for a very long time, and both are still here, so they must have made an evolutionary deal. I suspect that the sapsucker gives something back to the tree.

Sapsuckers nest in mid-spring, drilling out a dead section in a live aspen or poplar. The entrance hole is round, 3–4 cm across. Five or six white eggs hatch in 12–13 days. The young leave 25–29 days later. Unlike most woodpeckers, sapsuckers migrate, wintering from western Oregon south to Texas and Mexico, east into the midwest and eastern United States.

### Lewis's woodpecker *Pic de Lewis*
*Melanerpes lewis* (woodpecker family)
Mid-March to September

Occasional in open or brushy areas of the foothills and southern Rocky Mountain Trench; sometimes seen in Banff National Park. A large woodpecker, length 23 cm, that doesn't act like its relatives. It perches in trees rather than clinging to the bark. It also sits on fenceposts and wires, from which it flies for bugs. Readily identifiable by the red face and pink belly. The back is greenish black. Sexes are alike.

MW

This bird makes little kissing noises rather than the usual flicker-like woodpecker cries, but it nests like a woodpecker, in a cavity carved in dead wood. Six or seven eggs are laid in late spring. Incubation is 12–13 days; the young fledge at about 21 days. Wintering is from Oregon and California to New Mexico.

## Ravens, crows and their kin

These are the Corvidae, as in "twa corbies," newly slain knights, etc. In the Canadian Rockies we have a goodly representation of this whip-smart family, with resident ravens, crows, magpies, gray jays, Steller's jays, blue jays and Clark's nutcrackers.

### Common raven *Grand Corbeau*
*Corvus corax* (corvid family)
Year-round

One of the more common birds in the Canadian Rockies, found in nearly any habitat but most often in montane lodgepole-pine woods, in towns and at very high elevations. Unwary and approachable. Large—length 53 cm—and completely black, unlikely to be confused with any bird in the Rockies except the American crow, next item.

Ravens are usually larger than crows, with heavier bills. The end of the raven's tail is bluntly pointed, while the crow's is flat or slightly rounded. Raven plumage is shaggier than that of crows, especially on the neck. Crows flap steadily as they fly; ravens often coast and soar. Most crows leave the mountains in winter, while ravens stay.

I have noticed something else that seems diagnostic: watch the bird walk. If it moves its head briskly back and forth like a pigeon, then it is a crow; if it moves its head only slightly back and forth, often from side to side, then it's a raven.

Skulking about, big and dark, ravens are the image of malevolence in literature. They are not cute; not well liked. But I think they are the most interesting birds in the mountains. They live everywhere and eat almost anything. I have seen one swoop down on a fledgling house sparrow and swallow it whole. Consummate scavengers, they cluster by the dozens at dumps and are quick to converge on a wolf kill. They are surprisingly agile for their size. A raven will suddenly fold its wings and make a twisting somersault in the air, dropping several metres before pulling out of the stunt with a "rawk" that sounds self-satisfied to human ears. The bird uses the same maneuver as defence against harassing kestrels.

The ravens of Jasper townsite, which seem typical, spend most of the day in ones or twos. They perch atop the street lights, keeping an eye out for anything edible. The birds talk to one another from their posts, saying "croak," "tock" and many other things. Sometimes one will bark like a dog, or make little mewing sounds like a kitten. In the late afternoon the ravens gather and flap off together to one roost or another. They are terribly smart—most intelligent of the perching birds—with a complex social structure that Bernd Heinrich has written about in his best-selling *Ravens in Winter* and *Mind of the Raven*.

Ravens mate for keeps, usually in their third year. They breed in late winter, preferring a cliffside niche when they can get one, otherwise nesting in a tree. Both sexes work on the nest, carrying up substantial sticks and twigs to the site. Not just any stick or twig will do; it must be old and bare of bark. A fair bit of the building material gets chucked overboard. It doesn't seem to be clumsiness—it's pickiness.

The nest is lined with moss, grass and leaves, then with an inner layer of hair, often bighorn wool. The 4–6 eggs are large, variously greenish or bluish and often heavily scrawled with other pigments. For some unknown reason there is frequently one egg in the nest that is plain blue. The nestlings hatch in 20–21 days, are brownish/purplish/blackish with patchy feathers; only their parents could love them. Fed regurgitated or piecemeal foods, they leave the nest five or six weeks later, following the parents about and begging piteously, even when grown nearly to full size. Nonmigratory, but can travel many kilometres, perhaps seasonally.

## American crow *Corneille d'Amérique*
*Corvus brachyrhynchos* (corvid family)
Mid-March to early November

Very common birds at lower elevations, in open areas and in the woods, usually in small flocks. Length 43 cm. Very similar to the common raven; see previous item for ways to differentiate. Not as talkative as ravens, crows caw rather than croak; they eat most anything, including the unattended eggs and newly hatched young of other species, as do most corvid-family birds.

*Corvus corax*          MW          *Corvus brachyrhynchos*

Nesting is in early spring, the nest usually in a dead tree, although sometimes on a utility pole and often near other crows' nests. A large cup of sticks is lined with mud, grass, leaves and hair; 4–5 greenish/bluish, variably marked eggs hatch in 18 days. The young leave the nest 35 days later.

Crows are most common from early spring to late September; after that they slip away south and west for the winter, some of them going no farther than the Rocky Mountain Trench south of Golden.

## Black-billed magpie *Pie bavarde*

*Pica hudsonia* (corvid family)
Year-round

Locally common to occasional in small family flocks in and around towns at lower elevations; irregularly distributed (some places have many; others have none) and quite variable in population from year to year. Length 45 cm. For its size, the magpie has the longest tail of any bird in the region (but see also mourning dove, page 564). That, and the bold black-and-white wing pattern, make it easily identifiable.

Magpies say "hack-hack," and make soft mewing sounds; they fly very low, often just above the ground, alternately flapping and gliding. These birds are decorative but not particularly popular; like other jays, they have a taste for eggs and baby birds. They are noisy, too. Early in the morning. On the other hand, magpies eat lots of insects, especially caterpillars and grasshoppers, endearing them to farmers.

Magpies are highly social, living in small, carefully ordered flocks. They breed in mid-spring, nesting colonially in brushy places near water. Each nest is a bulky igloo of sticks with one or two entrances; a mud-lined cup within holds lots of eggs, usually 5–9, maximum of 12, hatching in 17–18 days. The young leave the nest 22–28 days later. Nonmigratory.

## Clark's nutcracker *Casse-noix d'Amérique*

*Nucifraga columbiana* (corvid family)
Year-round, but mainly April to November

Common in subalpine woods in southern and central sections, less so farther north. Especially common in upper subalpine campgrounds and picnic sites. Length 28 cm. Gray body with flashy black-and-white wings. The beak is long and black, an easy way to tell it from the gray jay, next item, a similar bird that lives in the same habitat.

A folk name for Clark's nutcracker is "camp robber," which aptly describes its behavior around people. Calling all day long in harsh, loud voices—"KRAW! KRAW!"—the birds fly from tree to tree, folding their wings between flaps. They frequently drop to the ground or onto picnic tables looking for seeds, bugs, crumbs or other goodies. They will also drop unexpectedly onto whatever is dangling at the end of your fork.

Clark's favorite natural foods in the Canadian Rockies area are the large, fatty, nut-like seeds of the whitebark pine and limber pine. The long, strong bill is just the tool for breaking into the tough cones. It also uses the bill like a woodpecker does, for going after beetle larvae and ants in rotten wood. Like the gray jay, Clark's nutcracker hides its food, tucking it behind flakes of bark, poking it among conifer fronds and sticking it into the ground. Studies of this behavior have shown that the bird actually *remembers* where each item is—and there can be thousands of items. It must forget sometimes, because whitebark pine are spread mainly through misplaced seeds.

Nesting is often in April, when the subalpine forest is still deep in snow; the mated-for-life pair builds a typical bulky jay-style nest of sticks on a stout conifer branch. Two or three brown-speckled greenish eggs hatch in 16–18 days; the young leave the nest 22 days later and follow the parents about, hounding them mercilessly for food. This noisy begging goes on dawn to dusk in high-country campgrounds.

Supposedly nonmigratory, the birds largely desert the main ranges in late fall, moving to good pine-nut supplies in the southern foothills and southern Rocky Mountain Trench. You seldom see them in Jasper or Banff parks between early November and late April.

### Gray jay *Geai du Canada*
*Perisoreus canadensis* (corvid family)
Year-round

Common in the upper montane and subalpine forest, gliding from tree to tree. It shares that environment with its look-alike, Clark's nutcracker, previous item. Both birds go by the folk names "camp robber" and "whiskey-jack." The latter is from the Cree "Weesakejac," a figure in aboriginal mythology, anglicized to "whiskey-jack." An older birder's name for the gray jay was "Canada jay."

The gray jay is smoky-colored, with lighter head and dark nape; Clark's nutcracker is uniformly gray on the body, with black-and-white wings. Bill is short on gray jay and long on Clark's nutcracker. Gray jay is slightly smaller, length 25 cm, stays in the mountains all winter and is much more endearing. It arrives just as you are getting out the sandwiches. It sits atop your ski pole and waits quietly to be offered some lunch. The patience lasts a couple of minutes, then the bird simply jumps on the sandwich and takes what it wants.

All fluffed up on a cold day, gray jays evince softness. They usually speak softly, too, saying "wheer-ooo." But underneath that gentle exterior lurks the rowdy soul of the jay tribe. It bursts out from time to time, when the birds squabble loudly, steal eggs, that sort of thing. Perhaps you will be lucky enough to hear a gray jay sing. It sits atop a conifer and whistles, warbles, cheeps—an amazing production.

Gray jays eat most anything: seeds, bugs, carrion, unattended nestlings; they have been known to do in the odd mouse in distress. They hoard food for the winter, coating it with sticky saliva and pasting it to conifer branches, making large stores in unused woodpecker nesting cavities and remembering where everything is stashed.

Breeding is in late winter. The life-mated pair builds a warmly lined cup nest in a conifer, producing 3–4 brown-spotted greenish/grayish eggs that hatch in about 15 days. The young leave the nest a couple of weeks later, begging from the parents for two or three weeks more. When you see one gray jay you will often see three. These are usually young birds, perhaps nestmates staying together until maturity. Nonmigratory, although bad winters will send gray jays to better foraging grounds at lower elevations.

## Jays that are blue, and blue birds that aren't jays

Birds included in this section are diverse, but they're all blue.

### Steller's jay *Geai de Steller*
*Cyanocitta stelleri* (corvid family)
Year-round, but mostly from early October to end of April

Fairly common in coniferous woods on the western slope and south of Crowsnest Pass on the eastern slope, occasional elsewhere. Length 28 cm. Heretofore Steller's was the only crested jay likely to be seen in the Rockies, but the **blue jay**, *Cyanocitta cristata*, is becoming more common, apparently moving into the foothills in growing numbers and now seen frequently in the front ranges. A nesting pair of blue jays has been reported on the western slope, from near Radium Hot Springs in the Rocky

*Cyanocitta stelleri*

Mountain Trench. Steller's is mostly dark, shiny blue, with a smoky black crest, head and upper back; it has frosty-looking eyebrows and other small white markings on the forehead and throat. Blue jay is much lighter, with white breast and face, blue crest and white wing bars. The call of Steller's jay is easy to recognize: a loud, "Shack! Shack! Shack!" rather like that of the magpie, page 557.

*MW*

*Cyanocitta cristata*

Habits and life history of Steller's jay are much like those of other jays, but it makes a specialty of imitating the calls of red-tailed hawks and thus scaring other birds. There must be a reason for this; perhaps it causes other birds to drop their food and fly to safety—whereupon the jay makes off with the loot. Diet: mostly pine seeds, fruits and bugs. Rather shy, for a jay; not a camp-robber. Nesting is in early spring, the mud-lined cup of sticks holding four bluish/greenish eggs that hatch in about 16 days. Fledging date not known, but the young follow their parents around for several weeks after. Nonmigratory, but seen more in the winter months, when it comes down from the high country to visit bird feeders. Provincial bird of British Columbia.

### Mountain bluebird *Merle-bleu azuré*
*Sialia currucoides* (thrush/kinglet family)
Mid-March to mid-October

Fairly common in the eastern front ranges, in dry, open montane areas; occasional farther west and at higher elevations. Length 15 cm.

The mountain bluebird is robin-like in shape, part of the same family. The male is quite blue on top, grayish beneath with a white belly. Females are mostly gray-brown, with blue in the wings and tail, and on the rump. Song is varied, with soft cheeps and trills. Of the other birds in the Canadian Rockies that are blue, Steller's jay and the blue jay are conspicuously crested, and the lazuli bunting, next item, is smaller, with an orangey breast.

♂

*MW*

Mountain bluebirds are bug eaters, zooming from a low perch, gobbling, then flying back. Sometimes they hover. The birds nest in old woodpecker holes and other tree cavities, sometimes in borrowed bank-swallow lodgings, rodent burrows or rock crevices. They will move into bird boxes erected in open places for them. These boxes are important in protecting the species. Breeding is in mid-spring, 5–6 pale blue eggs hatching in 13–14 days, but the fledging date is unknown. Winter range: Vancouver area, down the coast to California, then a broad area encompassing most of western U.S.A. and northern Mexico.

The Rocky Mountain Trench south of Golden lies at the eastern range limit for the **western bluebird**, *Sialia mexicana*, which has been seen there a few times.

### Lazuli bunting *Passerin azuré*
*Passerina amoena* (finch family)
June to August

Fairly common in the foothills from Bow River south, occasional north to Jasper, and in the southern Rocky Mountain Trench, where it sometimes is seen in Kootenay National Park. Prefers aspen groves and deciduous shrubbery. Length 11 cm. Likely to be confused only with the mountain bluebird, previous item, the lazuli bunting is smaller, has an orange-and-white breast, white wing bars and a heavier beak.

♂

*MW*

It eats mainly insects and seeds, the male flying up into aspens to sing his varied cheepy song. Breeding is in June; the nest is in low shrubbery, with three pale blue or greenish eggs that hatch in 12 days. The young birds fledge at 10–15 days and are attended for a few days longer by the male. Winter range: American southwest and Mexico.

## Robins and their relatives

These are the thrushes. See also the mountain bluebird, previous page.

### American robin *Merle d'Amérique*
*Turdus migratorius* (thrush/kinglet family)
End of March to end of October, but see below

Common in any wooded habitat. Length 22 cm. The best-known bird in North America lives in the Canadian Rockies, out on the lawn, but also way up at treeline, nesting in the kruppelholz (dense stands of dwarf fir and spruce, page 286). Easily identified by the gray back and wings against the orangey breast. Females have a dark bill and are a little paler on the head.

Robins make a familiar burbly cheeping that is not easily imitated; it goes something like "cheer-ee-er-i-lee." They also utter a sharp alarm call and make other sounds that don't seem robin-like at all. Robins spend a lot of time on the ground, intent on worms, grubs and bugs.

Does the red, red robin go bob-bob-bobbing along, as in the old popular song? No; the bird runs a few steps, then stops suddenly and holds stock-still for a moment, head turned to the side. Studies show that it is not really listening, as commonly supposed; it's looking down at the ground for food.

MW

Nesting is in early spring, usually in a conifer; four light-blue eggs in a cup made of mud and grass hatch in 11–14 days; the young fledge about two weeks later. Robins winter not far south of the Canadian Rockies, through much of the U.S.A. South of Crowsnest Pass they arrive a month earlier and leave up to two months later than they do farther north. Sometimes they stay all winter in the southern Rocky Mountain Trench.

### Varied thrush *Merle à collier*
*Ixoreus naevius* (thrush/kinglet family)
Mid-March to mid-November

Common in spruce forests, very common in the Columbian forest of the western slope, but secretive. Seen most often from early April through August. Length 20 cm. Robin-like in size and shape, the varied thrush is decked out for Halloween: black and orange. The orange eye-stripe and black bar across the breast are good field marks; the only other orange-and-black bird in the Canadian Rockies is the American redstart, page 572. But one seldom sees the varied thrush. Rather, one hears it at dawn and dusk. A long buzzy note is followed a moment later by another, a little higher pitched, then a third, again higher pitched. People who can whistle while humming can imitate it.

MW

Like its relatives, the varied thrush scuttles about the forest floor eating insects and worms. It breeds in early spring, nesting low in a conifer, and is extremely secretive at this time; there are three light-blue eggs, but the hatching and fledging times are not known. Winter range: west coast from Prince Rupert south to the Mexican border.

## Swainson's thrush *Grive à dos olive*
*Catharus ustulatus* (thrush/kinglet family)
Early May to mid-September

Common in coniferous woods, heard for about a half-hour at dawn and dusk. Length 16 cm. Secretive and thus infrequently seen, Swainson's is built like a robin, but a little smaller, with a dark olive-brown back. The front is buffy and spotted/streaked with black—very much like the hermit thrush, next item. Differentiate by the reddish-brown tail and rump of the hermit thrush. See also northern waterthrush, page 572.

*MW*

Swainson's has a beautiful, flute-like song, clear and liquid, rising up the scale in a slow trill. Once heard, easily recalled—but similar to the song of the hermit thrush, which usually begins with a single note, then the rising trill. The birds also say "whit."

Swainson's feeds in the trees rather than on the ground, eating beetles, flies, ants and caterpillars. It also likes berries. The species breeds in mid-spring, laying 3–4 brown-speckled light-blue eggs in a cup-like nest made of plant matter and mud. The nest is low but well hidden 1–2 m up in a conifer. Hatching is at 10–13 days; fledging 10–12 days later. Winter range is from southern Mexico to Argentina. As with the other neotropical migrants, this bird is rapidly declining in numbers. See page 570 for the reason.

## Hermit thrush *Grive solitaire*
*Catharus guttatus* (thrush/kinglet family)
Early May to end of September

Common in coniferous forest, but secretive. Length 15 cm. Has also been reported to nest among rocks above the treeline. Looks very much like Swainson's thrush, previous item, but the tail and rump are rusty or cinnamon-brown rather than dark olive. The bird raises its tail often, something the other thrushes don't do. The song is like that of Swainson's, but preceded by a single note.

*MW*

Hermit thrushes pick for bugs, worms, fruits and berries on the ground, usually under concealing shrubbery. However, you can see them when they fly up into the lower branches of aspens to sing. Nesting is in mid-spring, in a well-hidden cup on the ground; 3-4 light blue eggs hatch in 12–13 days. The young leave the nest 10 days later. Wintering is along the west coast from Vancouver south to Guatemala, across the Gulf states and up the east coast to Boston.

## Veery *Grive fauve*
*Catharus fuscescens* (thrush/kinglet family)
Mid-May to early-September

Occasional in deciduous groves, southern area; rare farther north. Length 15 cm. The veery closely resembles the hermit thrush, previous item, but is brown or rusty all over rather than just on the rump and tail. And the veery is uncommon in the mountains. It says "veet—veer, veer, veer" and spends most of its time on the ground in pursuit of creepy-crawly food. The species nests on the ground too, mostly farther east of us, but occasionally in the Waterton/Glacier area. Goes to Central America and Brazil for the winter.

*MW*

## Townsend's solitaire  *Solitaire de Townsend*
*Myadestes townsendi* (thrush/kinglet family)
Mid-April to end of September, but may stay through the winter

Common in open subalpine forest, usually sitting atop a conifer; seen at much lower elevations in spring. Length 17 cm. Drab-colored, but still rather easily identified by the long tail outlined on each side by a white feather. There is also a white eye-ring and some thin white barring on the wings, which have a bit of burnt-orange in them. Song is loud, beautiful, burbly and robin-like, but much longer, a little higher-pitched and crisper. Also makes a soft "peet."

*MW*

Townsend's acts like a flycatcher, leaping nimbly off its tree-top perch to grab insects out of the air. Also eats bugs on trees and descends for fruits, berries and worms. But it nests on the ground, often among rocks or at the base of a big spruce or subalpine fir, where there are often natural cavities in the soil around the roots. You may find Townsend's nesting in road cuts, too.

Breeding time: late spring. There are four white/pinkish/bluish eggs, heavily marked in darker colors. The incubation time is not known; neither is there any information about the nestlings or fledging date. Townsend's solitaire winters just south and west of us, in the western mountains of the U.S.A. and in south-central B.C. Some birds winter in the southern Rocky Mountain Trench, and the species has been recorded several times in the Jasper Christmas bird count.

# Hummingbirds

Because hummingbirds eat sweet flower nectars, it is easy to attract them to feeders that dispense sugar water. Once you start feeding these birds, though, they become dependent on the supply and you must keep feeding them until they migrate at the end of the summer. Watch for the growth of black mold in the feeder, and clean it thoroughly if this develops. Don't put food-coloring into the sugar solution, and never use honey; it can go bad.

## Rufous hummingbird  *Colibri roux*
*Selasphorus rufus* (hummingbird family)
Mid-May to end of August

Common in nearly any habitat with wild-flowers, above or below treeline; often seen flying from a dead snag in or beside a pond. Length 9 cm. This is the most northerly hum-mingbird species on the continent; it reaches the southern Yukon.

*MW*

The problem in identifying hummingbirds is that they don't sit still for very long. However, there are only two common species in the Canadian Rockies, the rufous and the calliope. The rufous male is easy to identify. Much of the body is red, especially the brilliant **gorget,** a patch of shiny feathers wrapped around the front of the neck of many hummingbird species, sometimes covering the head as well. The female rufous is green on the back and mostly white underneath with a reddish vest, much like the calliope hummingbird, next item; however, the rufous female is larger, with red spots on the throat and red in the tail.

Rufous males make short buzzing sounds, with voice as well as with wings. They put on a wonderful courtship display: vertical loops in the air, sometimes over and over, each loop 5–10 m in diameter.

Hummingbirds have the fastest metabolisms in the bird world. They need a lot of sugar, which they get from flower nectar, the bulk of their diet. They feed by sticking their long, brush-tipped tongues out the ends of their needle-like bills and lapping away. Protein comes from tiny bugs picked off the flowers. The birds eat constantly, carrying extra food in their crops to live through the night; if they run out of gas, which happens during bad weather, hummingbirds become dormant for a day or two and thus survive. Rolling their shoulder joints back and forth enables them to hover, even to fly backward. No other group of birds does this.

Rufous hummers are strongly attracted to red flowers—paintbrush, penstemons, columbine—or anything else that is red. A friend who was trying out a new red sleeping bag in a flowery alpine meadow was beset by hummingbirds trying to get in with him. ("Wow! If this thing is fulla juice, my summer's made!")

The rufous breeds in late spring, the tiny nest low down in a conifer or shrub, made of plant down wrapped up in spiderwebs and camouflaged with lichens. There are two itsy-bitsy white eggs, incubation period about 14 days; the young birds fledge about 20 days after hatching. Flight speed of hummingbirds can reach 80 km/h. The rufous winters in Mexico.

### Calliope hummingbird *Colibri de Calliope*
*Stellula calliope* (hummingbird family)
Late May to end of August

Fairly common in any flowery habitat. Length only 7 cm, the smallest bird in North America. (The bee hummingbird of Cuba is about 20 percent smaller, the smallest bird in the world). Emerald green on top and white below, the male calliope has a streaky reddish-purple gorget. Females are similar but lack the gorget; they have green-freckled throats. Compare with female rufous, previous item.

Male calliopes sound a loud, long "SEE-REE" when doing the display flight, which is a series of climbs and dives. One hears this often in the mountains, sometimes without seeing the tiny bird that makes it. It zooms from flower to flower, drinking nectar and nabbing small bugs in the blooms.

The calliope hummingbird, like its relatives, is outrageously aggressive for its size, chasing much larger birds away from its nesting site or food. Feeding and breeding habits are like that of the rufous hummingbird. Incubation time is 15 days, fledging date 21–23 days after hatching. Wintering: Mexico.

There is a now a third hummingbird in the Canadian Rockies: the **black-chinned hummingbird**, *Archilochus alexandri,* reported fairly often since the 1980s in the southern area. It's mostly green and looks a lot like the calliope, but is larger, the same size as the rufous. The female has no rusty color on her breast, as the female calliope does, and the male has a black patch below the eyes and bill. The gorget is smaller, neater, and less conspicuous than that of calliope males.

## *Familiar feathered friends (sometimes enemies)*

See also the house sparrow, page 581.

### European starling *Étourneau sansonnet*
*Sturnus vulgaris* (starling family)
Present year-round from Jasper south; a summer resident farther north

Common around towns, in flocks. Length 15 cm. Starling plumage changes with the season. The birds are dark brown all summer; in good light you can see a purplish/greenish iridescence on head and breast. Good identifiers: longish yellow beak, short tail and constant squeaky chatter. In winter starlings become spotted, especially on the breast and head. The beak becomes black. Young birds, newly fledged, look different again: brown above, gray below, with black bills.

Not native, starlings have done all too well in North America since 100 of them were released in New York City in 1890. They have pushed native species out of their habitats. In the Canadian Rockies the flocks are currently small—usually a couple of dozen birds—and the species is not a problem, but elsewhere they eat up crops and spread disease around their communal roosts.

Starlings are sociable and quite interesting to watch. Their tinkly, whistling calls are pleasant to my ear, and wonderfully varied; they imitate other bird calls, too. When alarmed they say "veer!" Diet: insects, fruits and seeds, taken mostly on the ground. Starlings nest in all kinds of cavities—woodpecker holes, hollow trees, rock crevices, attics, birdhouses—beginning in early spring. Five to seven white, light-blue or greenish eggs hatch in 12–15 days; the young fledge 20–22 days later and beg food from the parents for several weeks more. Northern Rockies birds may move into central and southern areas for the winter.

## Rock dove *Pigeon biset*
*Columba livia* (dove family)
Year-round

Fairly common in small flocks around towns, farms and ranches, although scarce in the south end of the Canadian Rockies. Length 28 cm. This is an introduced species, formerly called "domestic pigeon." Most rock doves in the Canadian Rockies are the wild, as-introduced form: mostly gray with black banding, a white rump patch and purplish/greenish iridescent feathers on the throat. However, mating with domesticated showy strains produces birds with wildly varying plumage: white to brown, red or black, variously mottled and streaked.

MW

Rock doves coo, usually in a series that starts low, gets higher, and ends low. At the same time they often turn round and round. When a rock dove takes off, its wingtips hit noisily together and whistle; when the bird glides, the wings are held in a vee. Doves and pigeons pick about on the ground for seeds and fruits; as they walk, their heads snap back and forth.

This species nests in groups, preferring holes in buildings to natural sites in cliff crevices. They can breed almost any time from early spring to the end of summer, sometimes producing two broods in a summer if they start the first one early enough. Two white eggs are laid in a minimal nest of twigs or roots; in towns, bits of wire are often used. Hatching in 17–19 days, the nestlings fledge 30–35 days later—rather late in comparison to other songbirds. The young are fed in their first few days on **pigeon milk:** thick mucus secreted in the adult's crop. Rock doves are long-lived songbirds: 16 years for sure, possibly as long as 32 years. They are quite fast on the wing, up to 150 km/h. Nonmigratory.

## Mourning dove *Tourterelle triste*
*Zenaida macroura* (dove family)
Mid-April to end of August

In open areas at low elevations, fairly common in Glacier, scarce farther north. Usually seen in pairs. Length 27 cm, about half of which is tail, like the magpie, page 557. Mourning doves are rather plain birds, light brown above, paler below, with sooty gray wings that are spotted in black. A close look reveals pink iridescence

MW

behind the neck, a black patch low on the head, and blue rings around the eyes. The song of the mourning dove is a very soft and, yes, rather mournful "coo, coo, coo-WOO-oo." The birds are hunted in the U.S.A., but protected in Alberta and British Columbia.

Mourning doves live almost entirely on seeds, feasting in foothills grain fields. They breed in early spring, sometimes raising two broods a year. Nest is a rough platform in a tree or tall shrub; it is built by the female from twigs supplied by the male. There are only two eggs, which are white; they hatch in 14–15 days and the young fledge 13–15 days later. The species is nonmigratory throughout much of the U.S.A., but our birds move south onto the central great plains or west to the Pacific states for the winter.

# Waxwings

Sleek and colorful, these two species rate their own section.

### Bohemian waxwing *Jaseur des boréal*
*Bombycilla garrulus* (waxwing family)
Year-round, most common late August through April

Common in fall, in flocks—sometimes quite large flocks—at low elevations, especially around towns. Length 16 cm. Sleek-looking crested birds, mostly buffy gray, with a distinctive yellow terminal band on the tail, black mask and a small but brilliant red spot on each wing, like a bit of sealing wax. Differentiate from similar cedar waxwing, next item, by the Bohemian's larger size, white markings on the wings, gray abdomen and rusty coloring under the tail. Both species talk constantly; Bohemians say "zirrr," high-pitched and twittery. When the flock perches, most birds face the same direction.

Waxwings are insect-eaters and berry-gobblers, with a particular craving for the fruit of the mountain ash, page 273. After a summer of secretive nesting in boggy woods, when you rarely see them, the birds flock to town in late September to eat the red-orange berries of the ornamental mountain-ash trees planted there. Some 2000 (yes, two thousand) waxwings at a time have settled on my neighbor's rowan tree, stripping all the berries in a couple of hours. The birds wolf down six or seven berries, then fly off and circle back for another round, pooping red berry-bits all over the place and sometimes breaking their necks by flying into my windows, even though I keep them shaded. When no berries are left on the tree, the birds swarm over the ground, picking up dropped ones. During one of these feeding frenzies my twelve-year-old boy walked out among the waxwings. They scuttled over his shoes and perched on his head and shoulders, calling constantly in their whispery voices.

But the annual pig-out soon ends for these birds, and they must switch to juniper berries to survive. As winter drags on, the flocks of waxwings shrink and shrink. Many birds head east onto the prairies, where big flocks arrive in Edmonton in time for the Christmas bird count. By spring perhaps only 10–15 percent are left in the mountains. These days the numbers in autumn seem considerably fewer, too.

Waxwings breed in late spring, laying five sparsely spotted bluish eggs in a cup-shaped nest in a conifer or birch. Very fond of string and hair for nest-lining, waxwings will pick at clothes hanging out to dry and steal strings from a mop left outside. Hatching is at 13–14 days, fledging 15–17 days later. Their winter flights to better sources of berries are not true migrations.

### Cedar waxwing *Jaseur des cédres*
*Bombycilla cedrorum* (waxwing family)
Early June to end of September

Fairly common in the southern section; less so farther north. Length 15 cm, a little smaller but otherwise very similar to the Bohemian waxwing, previous item. To differentiate, note how little white there is in the cedar's wings. But under the tail it is white, not rusty brown like the Bohemian, and the lower breast of the cedar waxwing is yellowish. Voices are similar: high, thin whistles, trills and soft notes.

Cedar waxwings have much the same life cycle as Bohemians, but we see them only in the summer rather than year-round and never in great numbers. They winter not far south of the Canadian Rockies through most of the United States and into Mexico.

# Little gray birds: the flycatchers and vireos

"LGB"s for short, these species are tough to identify. Bring your best binoculars and a good ear.

### Eastern kingbird *Tyran tritri*
*Tyrannus tyrannus* (flycatcher family)
Early May to late September

Common in open places, often at ponds, perched on a snag. Less common north of Peace River. Length 17 cm. Here is one of the few flycatchers that is easy to identify: black-and-white, with a white band at the end of the tail. No other perching bird in the Canadian Rockies has this. The Latin name says it all: *T. tyrannus* is fierce. A pair of kingbirds will chase much larger birds away from their territory.

MW

Kingbirds sit on a tree top or snag with a good view, flying off after bugs and intruders. At dawn the species gives a raspy call frequently and loudly; the song is different, chittery and more subdued. Breeding is in late spring, the nest often out on a rather low branch over water. Three or four scrawled-up white or pinkish eggs hatch in 12–13 days; the nestlings fledge a couple of weeks later, but they beg food from the parents for another month. Wintering: South America.

### Least flycatcher *Moucherolle tchébec*
*Empidonax minimus* (flycatcher family)
Mid-May to mid-September

Usually in aspen groves. Common on the eastern slope from Banff north; uncommon on the western slope, rare at Waterton/Glacier. A small flycatcher, length 11 cm, but typical: mostly olive-gray, with darker wings that have two white wingbars. Belly is lighter. Head large and slightly crested; there is a light eye-ring. As with other flycatchers, the best identifier is the song: a quick, rather high-pitched "che-BECK," just like the French name for this bird, repeated often and accompanied by a sneeze-like twitch.

MW

Least flycatchers flit actively among deciduous trees, eating flying insects and caterpillars. They are quite aggressive, chasing other small birds away. Breeding is in late spring. The nest is typical for this genus: compact and deep, made of shredded bark and other fibrous plant matter, lined with grass, hair, and feathers. Spider webs and cocoons add strength. Four creamy eggs hatch in 14–16 days; the young leave two weeks later. Winter range: Mexico, Central America.

### Hammond's flycatcher and dusky flycatcher *Moucherolle de Hammond, moucherolle sombre*
*Empidonax hammondii* and *E. oberholseri* (flycatcher family)
Mid-May to mid-August

Look for Hammond's in mature coniferous forest; dusky in dry open woods or shrubbery at lower elevations. Length 11–12 cm. Both species small, very much like least flycatcher, previous item, but with yellow-tinged bellies. Hammond's and the dusky flycatcher are nearly identical, but Hammond's is found at higher elevations than dusky. Hammond's is fairly common; says "pee-WIT, cha-lirp." Dusky is occasional in the montane woods; says the same thing but the second part is higher-pitched, often inaudible.

MW

Both species perch on the upper branches of a conifer and fly out after bugs. They also chase other small birds away. Breeding: dusky in late spring, Hammond's in early summer. Three or four creamy eggs are laid in a nest like least flycatcher's, usually in a conifer, well up for Hammond's; 2–3 m up for dusky. Hatching is at 12–15 days; fledging is 17–18 days later. Young birds are fed by the parents for another 20 days. Winter range: Mexico, Central America.

### Willow flycatcher and alder flycatcher *Moucherolle des saules, moucherolle des aulnes*

*Empidonax traillii* and *E. alnorum* (flycatcher family)
Mid-May to mid-August

Common in brushy places and willow marshes. Alder flycatcher is more common from Jasper north; willow is more common from Banff south, always at montane elevations. Length of both 12 cm. Another case of nearly identical flycatchers. The two species were formerly one, known as "Traill's flycatcher," but they are now separated because the songs and breeding habits are different. Identification: small birds with large pointed heads, mostly olive-gray but greenish/yellowish on the breast with darker wings and yellowish wingbars. This combination, plus a white throat, helps to differentiate from other flycatchers. Mainly, though, go by the voices: willow flycatcher says "fitz-bew"; alder flycatcher says "free beer." If the bird isn't singing, it is proper to call it Traill's.

These birds stay in the shrubbery, hopping about and grabbing bugs. They nest in late spring, 3–4 white eggs with tiny brown speckles on one end, laid in a neat nest among dense foliage. Hatching is at 13-15 days, fledging 12–15 days later. Wintering is from Mexico south to Argentina.

### Pacific-slope flycatcher *Moucherolle du Pacifique*

*Empidonax difficilis* (flycatcher family)
Early June to end of July

Fairly common in southern region and in the Rocky Mountain Trench from Golden south; occasional central and northern in older mixed-wood stands and along rivers. Length 13 cm. Typical flycatcher layout: large, pointy head; olive-gray body with black wings and white wingbars, distinguished from the rest by the yellow throat. Lower half of bill is also quite yellow, and it has a yellowish belly. Voice is squeaky, higher-pitched than other flycatchers; the bird says "pretty-pretty-pretty." In northern areas, the similar **yellow-bellied flycatcher**, *Empidonax flaviventris*, has an orange lower bill and loudly calls "chew-EEE."

The Pacific-slope flycatcher flits about, bug-hunting in the shade of large trees. Probably breeds on the western slope, in mid-spring, the nest in a tree-hole or rock crevice; four brown-marked creamy eggs hatch in 14–15 days. Fledging is at 14–18 days. The birds winter from Baja California to Honduras.

### Western wood-peewee *Pioui de l'Ouest*

*Contopus sordidulus* (flycatcher family)
Mid-May to mid-August

Fairly common in damp montane woods and wetlands. Length 16 cm. Yet another nondescript flycatcher, although not of the genus *Empidonax*. The difference is very small, but it is one you can often see clearly: there is no eye-ring. Song is whistling and nasal, with a loud "cheee" call on the end.

The bird often perches at the edge of a clearing, flying out after bugs and returning to a different branch. Nesting is in late spring, the nest of plant matter placed midway up a conifer and wrapped with spider webs. Three cream or pale-yellow brown-spotted eggs hatch in 12–13 days. Young birds fledge 15–18 days later. Winter range: Panama to Bolivia.

### Olive-sided flycatcher *Moucherolle à côtés olive*

*Contopus borealis* (flycatcher family)
Late May to mid-August

Common in open coniferous woods, near water. Often seen at treeline and in burned places. Length 16 cm, large for a flycatcher. Typical flycatcher shape and olive-gray plumage, but with two good identifiers: dark, vest-like coloring alongside the lighter breast and small white tufts on the back, visible in flight and tending to overlap the wings at rest. The song is distinctive, too: olive-sided flycatchers say, "Quick, THREE beer!" and "pip-pip-pip." They sit high up in a conifer, darting after flying insects and returning.

Nesting is in late spring, three creamy or pinkish, brown-spotted eggs in a nest made mostly of greenish *Usnea* tree lichens, page 406. Incubation: 16–17 days; fledging: 15–19 days. Wintering: South America.

### Warbling vireo *Viréo mélodieux*
*Vireo gilvus* (vireo family)
Late April to end of August

Very common in aspen and poplar groves, especially near marshes, sometimes among pines and Douglas-firs. Length 12 cm. An LGB with a vague white eye-stripe and a slightly hooked bill, no wingbars. Go by the song, heard in the same spot for a long time: "Bring it here, bring it here, bring it." Calls "kwee," rising and harsh. Stays high in the trees, eating caterpillars, insect eggs and bugs that live on branches and leaves. Breeds in mid-spring, the deep nest slung in the fork of a branch high up. Four sparsely speckled white eggs hatch in 12 days; the young fledge about 12–14 days later. Winter range: central Mexico and Central America.

### Solitary vireo *Viréo à tête bleue*
*Vireo solitarius* (vireo family)
Early May to mid-September

Common in deciduous stands and in pine/Douglas-fir woods. Length 12 cm. An LGB that resembles the warbling vireo, previous item, but with white wingbars and a white line running from bill to front of eye. This is the **plumbeous** or Rocky Mountain version, found in southern and central areas. Farther north and east the bird has a yellow vest and olive back **(blue-headed vireo)**.

Like the other vireos, this one sings beautifully, usually in two-note or three-note phrases that rise and fall. It patrols the treetops for caterpillars, moths and walking/crawling insects, also eating some flying types. Moves slowly, making it hard to pick out.

Breeds in mid-spring, a typical vireo hanging cup built low in a deciduous or coniferous tree. Very reclusive, this bird stays on the nest when approached. One can usually come right up to it, even touch it, pick it up and peek at the eggs. But disturbing any nesting bird to this extent seems unfair. Four speckled white eggs hatch in about 11–12 days. Winters from Arizona through the American south and Mexico, to Nicaragua and Cuba.

### Red-eyed vireo *Viréo aux yeux rouges*
*Vireo olivaceous* (vireo family)
Mid-May to end of August

Fairly common in deciduous groves. Length 13 cm. Brown on top with a gray crown, white underneath; best field marks are the red eye—the only obviously red-eyed perching bird in the Canadian Rockies—and the white eye-stripe bordered by thin black lines.

This bird sings a great deal, the song warbling and robin-like: "Way up, tree top, here I am, see me?" It carries on all day, all summer, continuing after the nesting season is over; it even sings at night. Eats mostly caterpillars and sleeping moths on tree branches and leaves; will occasionally take flying insects, including bees and wasps. Also likes berries. Breeds in late spring; four finely speckled white eggs in a deep cup hanging in a fork 2–3 m up a deciduous tree. Incubation: 11–14 days; fledging: 12 days. Winters in the Amazon basin of South America.

# Little yellow birds: the warblers

All the birds in this section belong to the wood-warbler family, the Emberizidae. Within this family are several subfamilies, including the Parulinae, which are the warblers proper, as listed below. Confused? Refer to the bird-families listing on page 589.

### Yellow warbler *Paruline jaune*
*Dendroica petechia* (wood-warbler family)
Late April to late September

Common in marshy places, in the shrubbery. Length 10 cm. This is the only North American bird that is essentially yellow all over. It's a bit greenish on top, and the breast of the male is streaked with cinnamon. Female is paler yellow on the breast and a little grayer all over. Voice is rather high-pitched, the song a series of regular cheeps at the start and quick warbled ones later.

MW

Yellow warblers go mainly for caterpillars and other insect larvae that live on shrubs and trees. The birds are not very shy and tend to stay in one place for a minute or two, which makes them fairly easy to see. Breeding is in mid-spring, the urn-like nest usually low in a shrub fork. Four or five white/greenish/bluish eggs, brown/olive-speckled on one end, hatch in 11 days. Warblers are altricial, but they grow quickly, fledging only 9–12 days after hatching. Winter range: Mexico, Central America, Peru and Brazil.

### Wilson's warbler *Paruline à calotte noire*
*Wilsonia pusilla* (wood-warbler family)
Early May to late September

Common on subalpine avalanche slopes, in willow marshes and scrubby coniferous growth. Length 11 cm. Nearly all-yellow, but with a black cap. Breast is pure yellow; compare with yellow warbler, previous item. Olive on the back; wings are dark and without wingbars. Song: a short series of slow warbles, rather like that of a yellow-rumped warbler but without the speeded-up warbles at the end.

MW

Wilson's warbler feeds low in the shrubbery, catching both flying and walking/crawling insects. Twitches its tail as it hunts. Breeds in mid-spring, nesting on the ground, usually in dense shrubbery or hidden in a tall grass tussock. Five white, finely brown-speckled eggs hatch in 11–13 days; fledging is 10–11 days later. Winter range: Mexico, western Gulf coast south to Panama.

### Common yellowthroat *Paruline masquée*
*Geothlypis trichas* (wood-warbler family)
Late April to end of September

Very common in wetlands, in the bushes; the only warbler known to frequent cattails. Length 11 cm. Easily identified: a little yellow bird with a raccoon-like black mask. Back, wings, tail and top of head are olive. Song is also easy to recognize: loud "witchity, witchity, witchity." Also calls "chat, chat." Female lacks mask; is grayer.

MW

Yellowthroats flit and hop through shrubbery, usually near the ground. They catch mostly flying insects—small dragonflies and grasshoppers are favorites—as well as insects and larvae on leaves. Breeding is in mid-spring. The cup nest, low in a dense shrub, is sometimes built up along one side of the rim, hood-like. Four brown-speckled white eggs hatch in 12 days; fledging is 9–10 days later. Wintering: west, east and Gulf coasts from California/New York south through Mexico to Panama and the West Indies.

### MacGillivray's warbler *Paruline des buissons*

*Oporornis tolmiei* (wood-warbler family)
Mid-May to late September

Common southern and central in dense brushy places, often in wetlands and along streams; also in aspen groves, avalanche slopes and logged places. Length 12 cm. An odd-looking warbler: yellow body, olive on the back, with a gray hood on the head. Note also the white eye-ring broken by black eye-line. Says "ta-weet, ta-weet, ta-weet" and then "peachy peachy peachy," or some other trill. Stalks elusively about in the shrubbery, getting beetles and caterpillars. Nests in mid-spring, low in a thicket; four brown-marked white eggs hatch in 11 days. The young fledge 8–9 days later. Winters from central Mexico to Panama.

### Townsend's warbler *Paruline de Townsend*

*Dendroica townsendi* (wood-warbler family)
Early May to end of August

Very common in tall coniferous forest, but usually up high and thus difficult to see. Length 11 cm. Yellow and black on the head, back and breast; black wings with white wing patches, white belly. Voice: high and wheezy, in a variety of cheeps and trills.

Townsend's warbler sticks to the woods, picking bugs off spruce and subalpine firs. It breeds in late spring, usually nesting high in a conifer but sometimes only 2–3 m up; lines the nest with moss spore-cases and hair. Three to five brown-speckled white eggs; hatching and fledging times not known. Winter range: west coast from Vancouver south, spreading east into Mexico and south as far as Nicaragua.

### Orange-crowned warbler *Paruline verdâtre*

*Vermivora celata* (wood-warbler family)
Late April to end of September

Very common in brushy woods and wetlands up to treeline, but hides in the bushes. Length 11 cm. Greenish-yellow bird, gray on the upper parts, with a pale white eye-line. The orange spot atop the head is usually covered. Sings in trills with cheeps at the end.

Orange-crowns flit through the bushes eating caterpillars, other larvae and insects. They nest in late May, when they can find dry spots on the ground among shrubs; sometimes the nest is a half-metre up. There are five red/brown-spotted white eggs in a rather large cup for a bird this size. Incubation time and fledging date unknown. Winters across the American southwest and south, through Mexico to Guatemala.

## *The plight of the neotropical migrants*

North American birds that winter in Central America and South America, meaning most of our warblers, thrushes, flycatchers, swallows and hummingbirds, even some of our shorebirds and sparrows, are in serious trouble. Their numbers are about half what they were in the 1960s, and dropping fast. The cause is habitat loss through deforestation, both here in Canada and in the birds' wintering areas. We humans are taking too much land for our own use and leaving too little for other species.

Neotropical migrants are bug-eating birds. They help to control insect population explosions. What will happen to human agriculture—ironically the cause of much tropical and subtropical deforestation—without the neotropical beetle-eaters, aphid-eaters, caterpillar-eaters and grasshopper-eaters? What will happen to the trees, shrubs and wildflowers of the Rockies when the insects that eat them are out of control? What will the mountains be like with ten times as many mosquitoes, horse flies and ticks?

Clearly, it's time to stop cutting the world's trees. There are alternatives.

# *Warblers that are not mainly yellow*

These are true warblers, of the subfamily Parulinae, even though yellow is not the major color of their plumage.

### Yellow-rumped warbler *Paruline à croupion jaune*

*Dendroica coronata* (wood-warbler family)
Mid-April to mid-September

Very common in the woods, along shorelines and in wooded marshes. Length 12 cm. Our most common warbler, mainly bluish-black and white but readily identified by yellow patches in at least three places: top of the head, bend in the wing and on the rump. Compare with magnolia warbler, next item.

If the bird has a yellow throat, then it is the **Audubon** variety, which used to be called "Audubon's warbler." If the throat is white, then it's the **myrtle** variety, which used to be called "Myrtle warbler" and was once thought to be a separate species. You may see in-betweens, one of the reasons for combining the two species into one. The song is high, with regular cheeps; begins with several "tsip"s.

Yellow-rumps eat mainly flying insects, but also creepy-crawlies and ants; the birds often perch on snags hanging over rivers or lakes and dart out over the water for flies, returning to the same perches between runs.

Breeding time is variable; mostly in mid-spring here. Four brown-marked eggs laid in a feather-lined or hair-lined nest anywhere from 1–15 m up in any sort of tree hatch in 12–13 days, the young fledging 12–14 days later. In August the upper subalpine forest is full of immatures, grayish and not easily identifiable if not for the bright-yellow rump patch that already shows. Winter range: the midwest, southeastern U.S.A., Mexico and the west coast from Oregon south.

### Magnolia warbler *Paruline à tête cendrée*

*Dendroica magnolia* (wood-warbler family)
Mid-May to end of June

Occasional in open woods and black-spruce bogs, more common in the northern region, seen on spring migration. Length 11 cm. Resembles the yellow-rumped warbler, previous item, but has a black-streaked yellow breast, yellow throat and white eye-line. There is no yellow crown spot, but the rump is yellow. Note also the white tailband and broad white wingbar. Voice: like that of yellow warbler, page 569, but softer and less complicated. Magnolia warblers eat beetles, larvae, aphids, spiders and other bugs that live on or just under the bark of conifers. Probably doesn't breed in the Canadian Rockies. Wintering: Mexico and Central America.

### Tennessee warbler *Paruline obscure*

*Vermivora peregrina* (wood-warbler family)
Mid-May to mid-September

Fairly common in montane woods, especially in aspen groves and clumps of spruce in marshes. Length 11 cm. Greenish-yellow on the back, but otherwise not yellow. Gray crown, white breast, faint white eye-stripes. Compare with the vireos, page 568. Song is long but rather easily recognized: high-pitched "ticka-ticka-ticka-ticka-ticka, whit-whit-whit-whit-whit," finishing with a trill.

Tennessee warblers search the branch-ends of trees and tall shrubs for bugs, dropping to the ground occasionally for seeds, berries and fruits. Breeding is in late spring; the nest is on the ground. Four to six brown-speckled white eggs in the cup; no information on incubation or fledging. Winters from southern Mexico to northern South America.

## Blackpoll warbler *Paruline rayée*
*Dendroica striata* (wood-warbler family)
Early May to end of August

Occasional to fairly common in montane and subalpine spruce forest bordering wetlands, more common in the northern region. Length 12 cm. A black-and-white warbler, the best male field marks being the black cap, white cheeks, black moustache and streaked vest. Females are greener and lack the white cheeks. Both sexes have white patches under the tail feathers. Song is very high and thin, a monotone of quick "tsit"s, becoming louder, then softer.

Blackpolls stay fairly low in conifers, eating a lot of aphids and other tree-crawlers as well as flying insects. They breed in the dwarf forest at treeline, sometimes above treeline in willow mats, in early summer. Four or five brown/purple-speckled white or greenish eggs in a low cup hatch in 11 days. Fledging is 10–12 days later. Species winters in South America.

In the northern Rockies you may see the **black-and-white warbler,** *Mniotilta varia,* which resembles the blackpoll warbler but is more heavily marked, with a broad black stripe over the eye. It acts like a nuthatch, searching the branches and trunks of conifers for bugs.

## Northern waterthrush *Paruline des ruisseaux*
*Seiurus noveboracensis* (wood-warbler family)
Mid-May to mid-August

Fairly common in marshes and along the shores of woodland ponds. Length 13 cm. Identifiers: olive-brown back, streaked pale breast and light-brown eye-line. Song is a loud "sweet-sweet-sweet-sweet" and then some warbles.

This bird walks on the muddy ground and out on floating logs, bobbing along like a spotted sandpiper. It eats water insects and flying bugs, turns over leaves to find slugs and crawly bugs, and even grabs the odd tiny fish.

It breeds in early summer, nesting among the roots of a fallen tree, in a streambank hollow or in a cavity in rotten wood. There are four or five brown-marked white/buff eggs; incubation time and fledging time unknown. Winter range: western Gulf coast, southern Florida, Mexico, central America and northern south America.

## American redstart *Paruline flamboyante*
*Setophaga ruticilla* (wood-warbler family)
Early May to mid-September

Locally common in alder and willow thickets, wetlands and bushy places. Length 11 cm. Males are black with flashy orange trim on the wings and tail; compare with varied thrush, page 560, the only other bird in the mountains that is orange and black. Females are quite different: gray-headed with a white eye-ring, olive-brown back, dark wings and tail with yellow patches. Song: "wee-wee-wee-wee," a little warbling and strongest at the middle.

Redstarts perch in the woods, waiting for flying insects. They usually let their wings droop and fan their tails before leaping into the air after a bug. Breeding is in early summer, the nest 2–4 m up in a vertical Y of a small deciduous tree or shrub. Four brown-speckled cream/greenish eggs lie in a tidy cup lashed with spiderwebs and often ornamented with *Usnea* tree lichens. Hatching: 12 days; fledging: 9 days later. Winter range: central Mexico and southern Baja California through the West Indies to northern South America.

## Yellow birds that are not warblers

Most of the species listed in this section belong to the large wood-warbler family, the Emberizidae, but they are not members of the subfamily Parulinae, the true warblers. I have provided both family and subfamily names where required to make the taxonomy clear.

### Western tanager *Tangara à tête rouge*
*Piranga ludoviciana* (family Emberizidae, subfamily Thraupinae)
Early May to end of August

MW

Fairly common in montane forests on the fringes of wetlands, often among aspens or Douglas-firs. Length 16 cm, larger than the warblers. The western tanager is not a warbler, but it looks like one: female all yellow except greenish on the back, with black wings and white wingbars. Males have red heads. A good identifier for both sexes is the bill, heavier and paler than any warbler's. Song is three quick rising rasps traded off with two rasps and a chirp.

Mainly bug eaters, tanagers relish wasps and ants, working both the treetops and the ground. They also eat berries. Western tanager breeds in late spring, nesting in conifers. There are 3–5 brown-marked light-blue eggs; they hatch in 13 days, but the fledging date is not known. Winter range: Mexico to Costa Rica.

### Evening grosbeak *Gros-bec errant*
*Coccothraustes vespertinus* (family Fringillidae, subfamily Carduelinae)
Year-round

MW

Fairly common on the eastern slope, less so on the western side, mainly in lower subalpine forest. Flocks often spend the winter in town. Length 18 cm. A chunky yellow-and-black perching bird with a very heavy, stubby pale bill. Males have a big yellow eyebrow and are more brightly colored than females; both sexes have white wing patches, but the male and female patterns are different. Song is twittery/whistling, sung often in the flock.

Evening grosbeaks eat mostly conifer seeds, also grabbing any bugs that happen to be sitting nearby. In winter they head for lower elevations and easier pickings: fruits, berries and especially the winged seeds and buds of the Manitoba maple, an ornamental tree that attracts these birds into yards. Evening grosbeaks are also fond of the sand and salt spread along highways, where they get run over.

The birds breed in early summer, nesting in either conifers or deciduous trees. A large, rather untidy-looking nest is made of sticks, with lichens woven in. Three or four light-blue or greenish eggs hatch in 12–14 days; the young fledge about two weeks later. Evening grosbeaks winter throughout the Canadian Rockies, but they will leave when food is scarce here, moving down into the central and southern United States.

### Yellow-headed blackbird *Carouge à tête jaune*
*Xanthocephalus xanthocephalus* (family Emberizidae, subfamily Icterinae)
Mid-April to mid-May

MW

Occasional in wetlands, southern and central areas, mostly eastern-slope. Sometimes seen in towns. Length 22 cm. The male of this species is the only North American bird that is half yellow and half black. Note the white in the wing. Females are quite different: orange/ochre-colored breast with unique white lace along the bottom, ochre cheeks, white throat, brown back and crown. Song: a variety of chirps, buzzes, and whistles, fascinating to listen to. The birds make a sound very much like a cat's meow.

Yellow-headed blackbirds are seen here during the spring northward migration, picking up worms and bugs along the edges of marsh ponds and lakes. A few nest in the Rockies, with recent records from Talbot Lake east of Jasper and Cranberry Marsh near Valemount. Winter range: west coast from San Francisco south through Mexico.

### Western meadowlark *Sturnelle de l'Ouest*

*Sturnella neglecta* (family Emberizidae, subfamily Icterinae)
Mid-April to end of May

Occasional in the eastern foothills, front ranges and Rocky Mountain Trench, in large grassy meadows. Length 22 cm. A yellow-breasted bird with brown-and-black mottled back, easily identified by the broad black necklace on the breast. Long bill, yellow and white eye-line, white outer tail feathers. Song is well-known, although difficult to describe; an up-and-down trill/warble that some people can imitate by whistling.

Meadowlarks feed on the ground, picking up such insects as beetles, grasshoppers, weevils and sow bugs; they also eat worms, snails, grain and carrion. No nesting records here. We see them during the spring migration north and east; they winter from Vancouver south, throughout the desert states, plains states and Mexico.

MW

## Blackbirds, cowbirds

These are wood-warblers (family Emberizidae) of the subfamily Icterinae. See also the yellow-headed blackbird, previous page.

### Red-winged blackbird *Carouge à épaulettes*

*Agelaius phoeniceus* (subfamily Icterinae)
Mid-March to mid-August

♂

Very common in marshes, especially those with cattails, page 376. Length 18 cm. Males are glossy black with a brilliant red shoulder patch bordered in gold; females are streaky brown and sparrow-like, the streaking extending all over the breast and abdomen, unlike any of our sparrows. Male red-wings have a wonderful, indescribable song that sounds something like "konk-la-REEE-ah."

MW

The birds nest communally, yet the males are very territorial and aggressive, constantly bickering with others in the flock, chasing other birds away and making aerial dives at anything else venturing near the nest—birdwatchers, for example. Blackbirds feed together in flocks, eating mainly seeds, also bugs, berries and other fruits. Breeds in mid-spring, the nest a deep, bag-like cup woven between cattail stems or willows growing in water. Four pale-blue eggs, often scrawled with black/purple, hatch in 10–12 days; the young are out of the nest 10–11 days later, but hang around another 10 days for feeding. Winter range: most of the U.S.A. and Mexico. Red-winged blackbirds have been reported in Banff park through December, so a few may overwinter in the marshes of the southern Rocky Mountain Trench.

### Brewer's blackbird *Quiscale de Brewer*

*Euphagus cyanocephalus* (subfamily Icterinae)
Early April to mid-October

♂

Fairly common in the foothills, often in shrubby meadows and along roads, in small flocks. Length 20 cm. Appearing all black, the male Brewer's is actually slightly greenish and has a purplish, iridescent head. The yellow eye is sufficient to differentiate from male cowbird, next item. Females are plain brown, nearly identical to the female cowbird. Differentiate by the bill: longer and thinner on the blackbird, shorter and thicker on the cowbird.

MW

Brewer's blackbird makes a sound like a rusty gate-hinge, also calling "chack." It walks about picking up bugs and leaping at flies, snapping its head forward as it moves; also eats grain and weed seeds. Breeds in early spring, the nest often near water but otherwise quite varied in location: high up in trees, low in shrubs, in tree cavities, or under grass tussocks and overhanging banks. Nest includes conifer needles and mud with the usual plant matter. Five or six gray/brown-marked pale-blue or greenish eggs hatch in 12–13 days; the young fledge 13 days later but continue to be fed for another 12–13 days. Wintering: from southeastern B.C. through much of the western and southern U.S.A., Mexico.

The **rusty blackbird,** *E. carolinus,* migrates through the Canadian Rockies in spring to nesting areas north of the Rockies and is seen here occasionally. It has been known to nest in Jasper park. It looks just like Brewer's, but lacks the purplish/greenish iridescence. The female has yellow eyes.

### Brown-headed cowbird *Vacher à tête brune*
*Molothrus ater* (subfamily Icterinae)
Mid-April to mid-September

Common around ranches, following cattle. In the wilds it follows herds of elk and sheep. Also follows hiking and horseback-riding humans; frequently seen in campgrounds and towns. Length 13 cm. Males are greenish-black like Brewer's blackbird, but the brown head is plainly visible in good light; further, the eye of the cowbird is brown, not yellow like that of Brewer's, and the cowbird is much more common. Females are more difficult to tell from Brewer's; note the stubbier, heavier cowbird bill. In his courtship display the male hunches up and spreads his tail, meanwhile uttering a rising squeak. The birds also gurgle and say "chuck" to one another.

Female cowbirds are bizarrely unwary of humans, walking among groups of hikers having lunch, hopping over their feet and flying up to catch bugs. If there are a lot of mosquitoes buzzing around you, and you are not moving about, a cowbird may light on your head or shoulder to get closer to the swarm. Still, this bird eats more seeds than anything else.

Their nomadic lifestyle prevents cowbirds from building a nest and raising their young in the normal avian way. Instead, the species is parasitic, leaving its eggs in the nests of other birds to be raised unknowingly by foster parents. It breeds from late April through much of the summer. The cowbird deposits 10–12 brown-speckled white or greenish/bluish eggs in the egg-laden nests of other species, one egg per nest, usually throwing one of the host's clutch overboard—or eating it—to keep the number the same. Many species are parasitized in this way, and about half of them accept the cowbird egg. Robins are among the species that reject it; some birds get rid of a cowbird egg by removing it, while others build a new nest over the whole clutch and lay another.

Hatching in 11–12 days, the young cowbird is often larger than the host's offspring and manages to get the most food, sometimes starving the other nestlings or throwing them out of the nest. It fledges after about 11 days, staying near the nest to beg food from the hosts for another two weeks. In the fall the young cowbirds find their own kind and flock south into the U.S.A. and Mexico.

# Red/pink birds

These are finches, of the family Fringillidae, subfamily Carduelinae.

### Pine grosbeak *Durbec des pins*
*Pinicola enucleator* (finch family)
Year-round

Fairly common in coniferous woods at upper montane and lower subalpine elevations, taking to the valley bottoms and towns in the winter. Found in small flocks. Length 20 cm. Chunky bird with a heavy black bill, the males quite red on head, back and breast, with patches of gray; the females gray with brown crowns and rumps. Both sexes have black wings with white wingbars. Males look a good deal like male crossbills, next item, but are noticeably larger and have a heavier bill. The purple finch, facing page, is smaller, has no wingbars and the bill is buff rather than black.

Pine grosbeaks sing in a burbly, robin-like way. They live mostly on seeds of deciduous trees and shrubs (birch, alder, Manitoba maple), spruce cones, shrub fruits (rose hips, mountain ash, snowberries), spring buds and insects. The birds are on the ground a lot, yet not very shy. Breeding is in mid-spring; four black/purplish-marked light-blue/greenish eggs in a bulky nest of sticks hatch in 13–14 days. The nestlings fledge 20 days later. Pine grosbeaks are nonmigratory, but they often move to lower elevations and into towns for the winter.

### White-winged crossbill *Bec-croisé à ailes blanches*
*Loxia leucoptera* (finch family)
Year-round

Common in lower subalpine spruce forests, in small flocks. Length 15 cm. Compare with male pine grosbeak, red crossbill and purple finch, all in this section. In crossbills the bill is actually crossed: the upper mandible overlaps the lower, curving off to one side. This unusual asymmetrical arrangement helps in opening spruce cones to extract the seeds, an important food of this bird. It also eats many insects.

The white-winged crossbill sings in rapid cheeps, like a chipping sparrow, page 582, but varies the pitch and speed as it sings. Crossbills breed in late winter; they nest in conifers, building a platform of twigs supporting a cup made of grass, leaves, moss and lichens lined with hair and feathers. Three or four brown-spotted pale-blue eggs hatch in 13–16 days; the young fledge 17–22 days later and beg food from the adults for a month longer. The birds don't migrate regularly, but they do move around in the mountains in winter.

### Red crossbill *Bec-croisé rouge*
*Loxia curvirostra* (finch family)
Year-round

Common in lodgepole forest. Length 14 cm. Resembles the white-winged crossbill, previous item, but lives at lower elevations and lacks the white wing bars. Compare with male pine grosbeak as well. To tell a male red crossbill from a purple finch, note the buff, stubby bill on the finch and the black, crossed bill of the crossbill. Females are mottled reddish/brownish.

This species sings in short, high-pitched cheeps, slower than the white-winged. The red crossbill is a seed-eater, but goes mainly for pine cones rather than the spruce cones and insects eaten by the white-winged. Breeding habits are like those of the white-winged. Nonmigratory.

## Purple finch *Roselin pourpré*
*Carpodacus purpureus* (finch family)
Mid-April to late August

Occasional in open montane woods and around towns, where they come to feeders. Length 14 cm. Compare with the male pine grosbeak and the crossbills, previous items. Female purple finch is brown-streaked and sparrow-like, with a broad white line running back from the eye.

Purple finches are talkative birds, with whistling, warbling voices. They eat grass seeds, fruits, berries and buds. Breeding in mid-spring, they lay four or five black/brown-spotted light-blue eggs in a cup of twigs, grasses and tiny roots lined with moss and hair. Hatching is at 13 days, fledging at about two weeks. Wintering: through most of the U.S.A., excluding the Rockies.

## Rosy finch *Roselin brun*
*Leucosticte arctoa* (finch family)
Mid-February to early November

A common alpine bird, flying low over the tundra in flocks and often seen along rocky ridges. Length 15 cm. Our rosy finches are of the **gray-crowned** variety, diagnostically gray atop the head and with a black forehead patch. Other varieties have a larger or smaller gray zone on the head; they live south of the Canadian Rockies. The rest of the bird is reddish brown, with pink belly and wings; the bill is pale. Voice: simple repetitive cheeps, quicker when alarmed.

Rosy finches eat the seeds of tundra plants, often flocking on snowbanks and searching cliff bases where such food accumulates and is easy to see. The birds grab the odd insect and have a taste for snow worms, page 475, which is another reason they congregate on snow patches. Breeding is in early summer, 4–5 pear-shaped white eggs laid in a soft cup of grass or moss hidden back in a rock crevice or built on a ledge. Incubation period is 12–14 days; fledging is 18–20 days later. The young birds are fed by the adults for another two weeks.

Rosy finches form flocks of up to 500 in the fall, moving down to lower elevations as the snow arrives; with the onset of cold weather, many eastern-slope birds cross the continental divide to winter in the Rocky Mountain Trench and west.

## Common redpoll *Sizerin flammé*
*Carduelis flammea* (finch family)
Early November to end of April

Common winter resident in birch groves, alder thickets and weedy lots, usually in small flocks but sometimes numbering in the hundreds. Length 13 cm. A little round bird with a brilliant red patch on the forehead and a black chin. Most males are also red on the breast; females are not. Both sexes have pink rumps, something to remember because sometimes you may see a few **hoary redpolls,** *C. hornemanni,* in with a flock of common redpolls. The hoarys are white on the rump instead of pink.

Both species make a variety of sounds, calling "bzeee?" at the end, rather like the siskin's call, cheeping and warbling, especially when in flocks. They are seed-eaters, preferring birch and alder cones but with a taste for the weed seeds they find on disturbed ground in settled places and along highways. Redpolls aren't shy; you can get quite close. They nest just south of the northern treeline, equivalent to our high subalpine zone. But redpolls nest here only rarely.

Redpolls can survive colder weather than any other songbird; the Canadian Rockies in winter are a southern holiday spot for them. They leave in April.

## Little forest birds

Here we have the chickadees, kinglets, nuthatches, wrens and creepers.

### Black-capped chickadee *Mésange à tête noire*
*Parus atricapillus* (chickadee family)
Year-round

Very common in conifers or mixed woods, in small flocks; perhaps our most numerous species. Length 11 cm. Chickadees are little round birds with inordinately large heads and tiny bills. Black-capped is the most common chickadee. Has a black cap, all right, with white cheek patches and a black throat. Breast is gray/buffy, not white. Similar boreal chickadee has a dark-brown cap that looks black from a distance, with diagnostic white breast and cinnamon-colored vest. Mountain chickadee has a white eye-line.

On the western slope from Valemount south, and from Crowsnest Pass south on the eastern slope, you may see the **chestnut-backed chickadee,** *P. rufescens,* which looks like a black-capped with a reddish-brown back.

Call of all four species is "chick-uh-dee-dee-dee," but the sound is subtly different for each species. The black-capped's "chicka" is very clear, while that of the mountain and chestnut-backed is less so, and the boreal's sounds asthmatic. The number of "dee"s in the black-capped's call varies, and sometimes the "chicka" is missing. In spring one hears the plaintive song: three clear notes, the first higher and longer than the other two. Chickadees move energetically through the woods in groups, calling frequently. Woodsy lore: every flock has its own special *way* of saying "chickadee," which enables two different flocks crossing paths to keep themselves sorted out.

The birds search the branches for small bugs, insect eggs, larvae and seeds, often hanging upside down as they poke about with their little bills. Breeding is in early spring, the pair excavating a small cavity in a rotten tree low to the ground—often in a stump—or moving into an unused woodpecker nesting hole. They line the space with moss, plant down, feathers, spider cocoons, anything soft. Six to eight brown-speckled white eggs hatch in 12–14 days; the young fledge 16 days later. Chickadees are nonmigratory, staying at low elevations in winter and sometimes moving into towns.

### Boreal chickadee *Mésange à tête brune*
*Parus hudsonicus* (chickadee family)
Year-round

Fairly common in coniferous woods. Length 11 cm. Resembles black-capped chickadee, previous item, but the cap is dark brown and the breast is white with cinnamon-colored sides rather than plain gray with buffy sides. The call is similar to that of other chickadees but is a little lower-pitched and more guttural; it sounds wheezy. Song is sometimes heard in spring; it is shorter and a little more warbling than that of the others.

Habits are like those of black-capped, but the boreal breeds somewhat later than the black-capped, in mid-spring; 4–9 brown-speckled white eggs lie in a rotten-wood or woodpecker cavity low in a tree or in a stump. Incubation time 15 days; fledging is 18 days later. Nonmigratory.

### Mountain chickadee *Mésange de Gambel*
*Parus gambeli* (chickadee family)
Year-round

Common in montane and subalpine conifers, southern and central areas. Length 11 cm. Resembles the other chickadees in the Canadian Rockies, but with a white eyebrow in the black cap. Breast is white with gray sides. Call is a little squeakier and raspier than the other chickadee calls, not wheezy like boreal's or quite as clear as the black-capped's; says "uh-dee-uh-dee-uh-dee" rather than "dee-dee-dee." The spring song is similar to black-capped's, very wistful. Habits and breeding like that of other chickadees; 5–7 white brown-spotted or unspotted eggs, hatching dates and fledging dates unknown. Nonmigratory.

### Ruby-crowned kinglet *Roitelet à couronne rubis*
*Regulus calendula* (kinglet family)
Early April to mid-October

Very common in fairly open spruce stands to treeline, usually near water. Length 10 cm. A little gray bird, undistinguished and rather flycatcher-like except for two things: a bright red patch on top of the male's head (patch not always exposed) and the song, which is readily identified once it is heard.

In the Rockies the bird has a long, spectacular song. Here's the series: "tsip-tsip-tsip, chow-chow-chow, CHEEP, cheepa-cheepa CHEEP, cheepa-cheepa CHEEP," usually trailing off in more "tsip"s. This song is *loud;* a great performance for such a small creature.

Kinglets move through the lower branches of conifers in singles and pairs, looking for insects. According to a recent radio item the average Christmas-tree-sized spruce has about 60,000 mites, spiders, aphids and such on it, so there would seem to be plenty to pick at. The birds also take the odd bit of sap. Kinglets are unwary; you can get quite close.

Breeding in late spring. A pair builds a small, very cozy deep-dish nest made of plant fibers, *Usnea* tree lichens and grass. Lined with feathers, it hangs between twigs and is tied on with spider webs and hair. Seven or eight brown-speckled teeny white eggs hatch in about two weeks; the fledging date is not known. Winter range: southwestern B.C., south and east through the American southwest, Mexico, through the southern states and up the Atlantic seaboard to New England.

### Golden-crowned kinglet *Roitelet à couronne dorée*
*Regulus satrapa* (kinglet family)
Mid-March to end of December, most common from early May to end of September

Common in old-growth spruce. Length 9 cm. A very small bird, mostly greenish-gray. The male has a brilliant yellow crown with a red stripe down the middle; the female's crown is yellow only. Both sexes have a long white stripe just above the eye, which differentiates from the golden-crowned sparrow (no stripe; see page 584).

Pairs and small flocks of golden-crowned kinglets hunt for bugs and insect eggs in the upper foliage of spruce and Douglas-firs, sometimes pines, calling "tsip" constantly. The full song is fairly complicated but seldom heard. Instead, you find yourself surrounded by twittering kinglets that are maddeningly difficult to locate. One would think there were far fewer of these little birds than there really are.

Nesting habits are like those of the ruby-crowned, but there are usually 8–9 eggs instead of 7–8. The bird's winter range extends farther north than the ruby-crowned's; a fair number of golden-crowns hang around Jasper until New Year's, even later in the south end of the area and on the western slope.

### Red-breasted nuthatch *Sittelle à poitrine rousse*
*Sitta canadensis* (nuthatch family)
Year-round

Common in coniferous woods, especially on Douglas-firs. Length 10 cm. A little gray-backed bird with a rusty breast; black cap like a chickadee but no black bib on the throat. Long, wide white eye-line runs from bill to nape of neck. patches that show when the tail is flared.

Nuthatches say "ank" often as they scuttle about on the trunks and branches of conifers, especially old lodgepole pines and Douglas-firs.

These trees are good hunting spots for the beetles and other bark-dwelling bugs with which this bird supplements its staple diet of conifer seeds. It hacks open the cones with its light-looking but powerful bill; hence the name "nuthatch," meaning "nut-hacker."

This is the only bird you are likely to see that walks headfirst *down* the trunk; in this way it spots tidbits that the woodpeckers and other normal, head-up trunk-walkers miss. Red-breasted nuthatches breed in mid-spring, nesting in a cavity the pair have pecked out of rotten wood, sometimes with help from unmated birds, who may also help rear the young. The nest may also be in a natural wood shelter, unused woodpecker nesting hole or bird box. The birds wipe conifer resin around the entrance. Resin is toxic to insects—part of a tree's defence system—and perhaps the nuthatches use it to repel parasites trying to invade the nesting chamber.

Five or six brown-speckled white or pinkish eggs hatch in 12 days; the young leave the nest 18–21 days later. Nonmigratory, but seldom seen in winter; may move well south into the U.S.A. in some years.

The **white-breasted nuthatch,** *S. carolinensis,* used to be rare in the Rockies but is becoming more common, with frequent sightings from Tumbler Ridge south. The size and coloration are similar, without the rusty chest and white eyeline of the red-breasted. Prefers leafy trees instead of conifers.

MW

## Winter wren *Troglodyte des forêts*
*Troglodytes troglodytes* (wren family)
Mid-April to mid-August

Common but inconspicuous, in heavy, mossy-floored old-growth montane and subalpine forest and densely vegetated marshes—any place that is thickly vegetated. Very small bird, length 8 cm, with a short, sharply upturned tail that flicks up and down. Dark reddish brown, with vague black barring on top; lighter below. The barring is quite visible on the lower abdomen, which is a good way to differentiate from the very similar house wren, next item, in which the barring begins even farther back, under the tail. Throat of the winter wren is pale and there is a faint eye-stripe. Song: long and high, composed of thin insect-like trills, interspersed with whistles; scolds "tick-tick." It is hard to pinpoint. Don't look up into the trees; the bird will be on the ground, poking about among the deadfall, mosses and shrubbery for bugs.

The winter wren breeds in early spring, the male building one or more large, rough, domed nests hidden among tree roots and tangles on the forest floor. He is often polygamous, attracting several females to the various nests, which his mates line with feathers. There are 5–8 white eggs, sometimes minutely brown-spotted, in each nest; they hatch in 14–17 days. Males help with the feeding, which keeps them quite busy as first one clutch then another hatches. Fledging is at 15–20 days.

MW

"Winter wren" is a misleading name in the Canadian Rockies; the birds winter on the west coast and in the American east—although some stay here as late as January and then die.

## House wren *Troglodyte familier*
*Troglodytes aedon* (wren family)
Mid-May to end of September

Occasional in the bushes at low elevations. Length 11 cm. Very similar to winter wren, previous item, but larger, with a longer tail and black barring starting farther back on the belly. Up-cocked tail flicks down. Sings in trills and whistles, often at length; scolds "chak-chak-chak." Flits secretively among the shrubbery grabbing bugs, but sings so much and so often that it makes its presence known.

MW

Breeding habits are like those of the winter wren, but the house wren also nests in tree holes and birdhouses. Winters on the west coast from California south, through the Gulf states and up the east coast.

The **marsh wren,** *Cistothorus palustris,* has been seen nesting at Cottonwood Slough near Jasper, in the wetlands around Yellowhead Pass and at Cranberry Marsh near Valemount. Easily distinguished from the other wrens in our area by the light eye-line. The male produces multiple nests, most of them fakes, made of grass-like sedge leaves.

MW

### Rock wren *Troglodyte des rochers*
*Salpinctes obsoletus* (wren family)
Early May to end of August

Occasional on eroded till banks, dry cliffs and other sparsely vegetated places at low elevations, southern and central area. Length 12 cm. Uplifted tail and curved bill identify this bird as a wren; to differentiate from the other two wrens in the Canadian Rockies, note the buff terminal band on the tail, the very light belly and the finely streaked breast. Rock wrens say "chew-EEE," "ee-or," and many other things; the voice has a buzzy quality. The bird busies itself on dry slopes, chasing insects and spiders. Ought to nest here, but no reports. Winters in the American southwest.

MW

### Brown creeper *Grimpereau brun*
*Certhia americana* (creeper family)
Year-round

Fairly common in old-growth coniferous woods, southern and central sections; usually seen among recently fallen timber or walking up the trunks of live trees. Length 11 cm. The creeper is a reclusive little camouflaged bird that is more common than one might think. Brown with white streaking on top, white below, with longish down-curved bill and very short legs. The thin five-note song is seldom heard and hard to imitate, but it is distinctive and unvarying.

MW

Starting at the bottom of a tree, a creeper climbs up in a spiral, looking for bugs on the bark and under loose flakes. It also clings to the underside of limbs and fallen trees. Eats seeds, too. Breeds in late spring, building a horn-shaped nest that nearly fills a vertical crevice in live or dead wood. Six brown-dotted white eggs are laid in a cup at the top of the horn; they hatch in 14–15 days. The young climb out of the nest 14–16 days later.

My information sources disagree on migration; some brown creepers may move over to the warmer western slope and Columbia Mountains in winter, while others remain in the Rockies.

## *Sparrows and sparrow-like birds with unstreaked breasts*

Within the large wood-warbler family, the Emberizidae, the North American sparrows are in their own subfamily, the Emberizinae. The first species in this section, though, isn't North American.

### House sparrow *Moineau domestique*
*Passer domesticus* (Old World sparrow family)
Year-round

Very common in towns and other habitations at low elevations, in small flocks. Length 13 cm. Male easily identified: brown back and wings, gray head and breast with large black bib, black bill. Females look quite different, and the fact that they flock separately from the males leads to the illusion that they are a separate species. Females are all brown with a pale bill, lighter on the breast and often streaky gray on the abdomen, with a diagnostic dark-brown facial line that hooks down behind the eye. No other bird with an unstreaked breast has this.

♂

MW

House sparrows, formerly called "English sparrows," are European, introduced in Brooklyn in 1851. By 1900 the birds had colonized all of North America except the Arctic. One sees and hears them in any Rockies town, loudly calling "cheep, cheep" all day long. They eat mainly beetles, grasshoppers and other crawling/jumping bugs in the summer, switching to seeds and plant fruits in the winter.

When automotive transport took over from horses in North America, the number of house sparrows declined, for the birds had been getting many of their seeds from horse droppings. Nowadays one sees house sparrows picking bugs out of the radiators of parked cars and eating scraps in the parking lots of fast-food restaurants, so they seem to be quite adaptable.

Breeding begins variably in the spring, usually in May but sometimes much earlier, during warm periods in March or April. Several males gather about a female, usually on the ground, then fight for her, rolling about in the dust and mud in Hollywood-cowboy fashion. The winner then mates up to 14 times with his lady, who flutters her wings and says (no kidding) "tee hee."

The male builds most of the nest, a dome of twigs, sometimes a simple cup, under an eave, back in a crevice or in a birdhouse. House sparrows love to nest behind ivy. Sometimes two broods are raised in a summer. Three to five gray/brown-dotted white/greenish/bluish eggs hatch in 11–14 days; the young fledge 15 days later. The life span is very long for such a small bird: up to 23 years in captivity. Nonmigratory.

### Dark-eyed junco *Junco ardoise*
*Junco hyemalis* (sparrow subfamily)
Mid-March to end of December, most common from early April to end of August

Formerly called "slate-colored junco." Very common in the woods, from low elevations to treeline. Length 13 cm. On the eastern slope, juncos are mostly of the **slate-colored** variety, the grayest of little gray birds, marked only with a white belly, and—the main identifier—white outside tail feathers that are obvious only when the bird flies. Some other sparrows in the Canadian Rockies also flash white tail feathers, but none is otherwise gray. Throughout the area, and particularly in the spring, you may also see juncos belonging to the **Oregon race,** which has a gray cowl, sometimes very dark, contrasting with brown back and vest, white breast and belly, plus the same diagnostic white tail feathers. Regardless of race, the junco song is a long trill, very much like that of the chipping sparrow, next item, but a little slower and less buzzy; not heard as frequently as the chipping-sparrow's song.

Juncos flit among the lower branches of conifers, saying "tick" to one another. The white tail feathers flare out as a bird darts into a spruce and disappears. The species is secretive sometimes and approachable at others; it seldom sings from an exposed perch like a chipping sparrow does. Feeds on the ground, hopping after beetles and other bugs; also takes seeds and is easily attracted to feeders.

The species often rears two broods a year, starting in early spring. The nest is usually on the ground in a natural cavity of some kind among roots, under deadfall, under an overhanging bank or in a grass tussock, and the cup is always well hidden. Three to five sparsely brown- or gray-marked white or greenish/grayish eggs hatch in 11–12 days; the young fledge 10–13 days later. Some Rockies juncos winter at low elevations south of Crowsnest Pass, but most of the birds migrate west to the Columbia Mountains and Coast Mountains of B.C., and south through the United States.

### Chipping sparrow *Bruant familier*
*Spizella passerina* (sparrow subfamily)
Early May to mid-September

Very common in conifers. Length 12 cm. Brown on back and wings with white wingbars, unstreaked breast and face, reddish cap on the head—the only sparrow with a rusty crown likely to be seen in the Canadian Rockies. Black-and-white eye-line. An easy sparrow to identify by sight, the chipping sparrow is even easier to recognize by sound: a sustained one-note buzzy trill, usually sung from a conspicuous perch in a conifer or on a fencepost, often only head-high.

Despite its preference for the woods, this bird eats mainly grass seeds, supplemented with bugs. It breeds in mid-spring; four pale-blue, lightly brown/blue/black-marked eggs lie in a cup 1–6 m up in a conifer. Hatching is at 11–14 days; the birds leave the nest at 9–12 days, a few days before they are able to fly. Winter range: coast-to-coast in the southern quarter of the U.S.A., south to Nicaragua.

The **swamp sparrow,** *Melospiza georgiana,* is another red-capped sparrow, but with a gray face rather than a white eyeline. It has been reported from Cottonwood Slough near Jasper, and at Tumbler Ridge.

### White-crowned sparrow *Bruant à couronne blanche*
*Zonotrichia leucophrys* (sparrow subfamily)
Mid-May to mid-October

MW

Very common in small flocks in nearly any habitat, most often in open, shrubby places, including alpine meadows and towns. Length 15 cm. The white-crowned is one of two sparrows with three prominent white stripes through a black cap on the head. The other is the white-throated sparrow, next item, which has a spot of yellow ahead of the eye and is much less common in shared habitat. The white-crowned has no yellow anywhere on the head, which differentiates it from the golden-crowned sparrow as well as the white-throated. Song of the white-crowned is easily recognized and heard often: a musical, rising two-note beginning followed by a higher, buzzy "chee-zee-zee" and often a trill. ("Bring me Cheesies, please.") North of the Peace River, listen for the slightly different song of the **northern race:** "I wanna go wee-wee now."

White-crowns feed on the ground, scratching for seeds and bugs; they also eat moss capsules and willow catkins. But they fly up to sing, often from the top of an aspen or poplar. The birds are not shy; you can get within a couple of metres. Breeding is in mid-spring at low elevations, in June at treeline. The birds nest in mossy or bushy places on the ground, sometimes low in a dense shrub or up in a tree, the nest concealed in moss or undergrowth. Two to five reddish-speckled bluish/greenish eggs hatch in 9–15 days; fledging is 9–11 days later but the feeding tapers off over another 25–30 days. If one clutch is lost, the pair produce another. When a predator comes near the nest, the parents fly up nearby, calling "pwit" very sharply. Under this stimulus the babies make no sound or movement. Winter range: southeastern B.C., American northwest and Rockies from Wyoming south through most of U.S.A. and Mexico to Cuba.

### White-throated sparrow *Bruant à gorge blanche*
*Zonotrichia albicollis* (sparrow subfamily)
Early May to late August

MW

Common in the foothills, fairly common from Banff north in the mountains, usually seen in bushes and aspen groves, sometimes in small flocks. Length 15 cm. Very similar to white-crowned sparrow, previous item, with similar striped head, but has a small patch of yellow just ahead of the eye and a prominent white patch on the throat, bordered with a black line on each side. Unstreaked gray breast, pale bill. Song is clear and slow, like someone absent-mindedly whistling 5–6 notes, last few a little warbling. First two fall, next seven are lower yet, and all at same pitch. Has been described as, "Oh, me, Canada-Canada-Canada," or, in French, "Oo la, Frederik, Frederik, Frederik." (Americans have it as, "Old Sam, Peabody, Peabody, Peabody.") Call: "pick."

Like the white-crowned sparrow, this bird scuttles about the ground scratching for weed seeds and bugs. It breeds in mid-spring, nesting on the ground in dense shrubbery at the edge of a clearing; 4–6 reddish-spotted pale-blue/greenish eggs hatch in 11–14 days, the young leaving the nest 8–9 days later but not flying for 2–3 more. Winter range: American west coast, southern states, midwest, New England.

### Golden-crowned sparrow *Bruant à couronne dorée*

*Zonotrichia atricapilla* (sparrow subfamily)
Mid-May to early October

Common in subalpine forest from Bow Summit north, often at treeline or above. Length 17 cm. Yet another little brown bird with a gray breast, but this one has a black cap with a bright-yellow centre. Compare with golden-crowned kinglet, page 579. Immatures look somewhat like female house sparrows, page 581. Song is three slow and wistful notes: "O-ver there," like the first phrase of the First World War marching song or the beginning of the pastoral movement in *Peer Gynt,* followed by a short buzzy trill.

Like the other *Zonotrichia* species, the golden-crowned spends most of its time on the ground picking for seeds and bugs. The birds breed in early summer; they build their nests on the ground among treeline willows or under a grassy overhang, often incorporating ferns and moosehair. There are three to five eggs like those of the white-throated sparrow; incubation and fledging times not known. Wintering: west coast from Vancouver to Baja California, inland through Cascades and Sierras.

### Clay-colored sparrow and Brewer's sparrow *Bruant des plaines, bruant de Brewer*

*Spizella pallida* and *S. breweri* (sparrow subfamily)
Mid-May to mid-September

Common in open places, clay-colored are seen most often in wetlands at lower elevations, Brewer's frequenting shrubby subalpine meadows and also seen in the grassy southern foothills. Length 11 cm. The two species are nearly identical—brown back and wings, white wing bars, creamy unstreaked breast, same facial pattern—except for one thing: the clay-colored has a white line down the top of the head and Brewer's does not. The song of the clay-colored is simple and buzzy, but Brewer's can bring forth an amazingly eloquent song, reminiscent of a wren's, with cheeps and whistles added to the insect-like noises. Note also the difference in habitat.

Both birds feed on the ground, picking up seeds and bugs. Birds seen early and late in the Canadian Rockies are mainly clay-colored sparrows; Brewer's arrives about two weeks later and departs about three weeks earlier. Breeding is in mid-spring, both species nesting low in the shrubbery but Brewer's preferring high-subalpine locations, often in kruppelholz conifers, page 286. Three or four eggs are brown-blotched light-blue. Clay-colored's eggs hatch at 10–11 days and the young fledge only 7–9 days later. No information on Brewer's incubation and fledging. Winter range: Brewer's from southern California across to western Texas and down into Mexico, clay-colored mainly in Mexico.

### Snow bunting *Bruant des neiges*

*Plectrophenax nivalis* (sparrow subfamily)
Early November to early April

Very common winter resident in the central front ranges and foothills after October, in flocks along highway shoulders and other weedy places, sometimes in towns. Less common in the north end of the Canadian Rockies, which they pass through on their way south. These birds move as far south as Colorado, but for some reason they avoid the Canadian Rockies south of Crowsnest Pass. Length 15 cm. The whitest small bird in the mountains, round and big-headed with a small bill, like a parakeet. Males are mostly white, with black tail and black patches on wings, cinnamon back and crown, cheeks and collar. Females are generally browner, with rusty vests, but still look quite pale compared to other birds.

Song: whistles and trills, sung frequently as the birds move through a field or along a highway shoulder picking up seeds and the last of a summer's bug population. They feast on grain spilled along the railway. Look for the odd Lapland longspur, page 587, or horned lark, page 548, in the flock. Snow buntings spend a lot of time along highways but they pay little attention to the traffic, with predictable results. They nest in the high Arctic.

# Sparrows with streaky breasts, longspurs and siskins

Like the sparrows with unstreaked breasts, these are members of the wood-warbler family (Emberizidae) and sparrow subfamily (Emberizinae), except for one species, the pine siskin, which isn't a sparrow at all.

### Song sparrow *Bruant chanteur*

*Melospiza melodia* (sparrow subfamily)
Late March to early October, seen less often after July

MW

Common in shrubby montane meadows, wetlands, deciduous groves and towns. Length 14 cm. A little brown sparrow, well-known all over North America. It is told from its kin by the following combination: spot in the centre of the streaky breast, gray-on-brown face and round-ended tail. When it flies, the tail pumps up and down. The only other sparrows in the Canadian Rockies with central breast spots are the fox sparrow, which is noticeably larger, and the savanna sparrow, which has yellow in the eyeline and a notched tail.

Appropriately named, the song sparrow sings beautifully and at length, whistling, cheeping, buzzing and trilling. The first part of the typical song follows the famous first four notes of Beethoven's Fifth Symphony, although it is "tweet-tweet-tweet-BUZZ" instead of "dum-dum-dum-DOM." Be aware, though, that the song varies a great deal from place to place, and you may not hear this.

The bird picks and scratches on the ground for a while, then flits up into the shrubbery or even into the treetops; it eats bugs, seeds, fruits and berries. Not shy. Breeds in early spring, nesting on the ground under a grass tussock or sometimes low in a tree. Will nest twice if the first brood doesn't make it. Occasionally produces two healthy baby-bird batches in a summer. There are 3–5 reddish/brownish-marked pale bluish/greenish eggs; incubation time is 12–14 days; the young leave the nest 10 days later but don't fly well for another week. Winter range: west coast from Aleutian Islands all the way to Baja California, inland across the southwestern and southern United States, through much of the east up to the St. Lawrence River.

### Fox sparrow *Bruant fauve*

*Passarella iliaca* (sparrow subfamily)
Mid-April to late September

MW

Common at treeline during the breeding season; at other times occasional on brushy avalanche slopes and in dense subalpine alder and willow thickets. Length 16 cm, our largest sparrow. Generally darker than other sparrows, this one varies a lot through the Rockies in head and back coloration, from gray to brown. The breast is always heavily streaked with inverted vees, there is usually a central spot, and the rump and tail are typically reddish. Compare with song sparrow, previous item, and savanna sparrow, next item. Sings very beautifully from a concealed perch, chirping, whistling and trilling as well as the song sparrow. Seldom buzzes like song sparrow. Anglicization: "All I have is here, dear. Take it."

Breeding is in late spring, often in the kruppelholz, nesting on the ground in dense cover or low in a shrub or tree. Three to five heavily brown-marked bluish/greenish eggs hatch in about 12–14 days; fledging date unknown. Wintering is along the west coast from Vancouver Island south to Baja California, inland through the southwest and southern U.S.A., up the east coast to New England.

### Savannah sparrow *Bruant des prés*

*Passerculus sandwichensis* (sparrow subfamily)
Late April to early October

MW

Very common in open, grassy places and wetlands up to treeline. Length 12 cm. A little brown bird with a streaked breast that has, in our area, a small spot. Main identifiers: a touch of yellow in the light eye-line, pink legs and notched tail. Song: a few "tip"s, then a buzzy, insect-like section, with a couple of cheeps at the end. Compare with fox sparrow and song sparrow, previous items.

The savannah sparrow hops secretively through the grasses looking for seeds and bugs; in wetlands also eats snails. Stays put until you are almost on top of it, then darts out of the grass and nips back in a few metres away. It breeds in early spring, the nest in a hollow scratched out of the ground and lined with grasses/sedges, rootlets or hair, never with feathers. Four or five faintly greenish or bluish brown-spotted eggs hatch in 12 days; fledging date unknown. Winters along both coasts from the international boundary south, through the southwest, Gulf states, lower Mississippi valley, Mexico to El Salvador.

### Vesper sparrow *Bruant vespéral*
*Pooecetes gramineus* (sparrow subfamily)
Mid-April to early September

Fairy common in dry, grassy places at low elevations. Length 14 cm. This bird is a little larger than the savannah sparrow, previous item, which lives in same habitat and is generally similar except for the tail: vesper sparrow has junco-like white outer feathers that show in flight, the only streaky-breasted sparrow with this feature. No yellow in eye-line like that of savannah, and there is a patch of reddish-brown at the vesper's shoulder.

MW

Vesper sparrows forage on the ground for bugs and seeds. They like to take dust baths. Not secretive, the birds can be closely approached. The species sings from the highest perch it can find; song is cheepy and easily recognized: two low notes, two high ones, then a couple of trills. Often heard just after rain.

Breeding is in mid-spring. The bird digs a small hollow in the ground, usually sparsely concealed but sometimes in the open, and then builds a cup in it. Three to five speckled white eggs hatch in 11–13 days; the young leave the nest 9–13 days later but cannot fly for a few days more. They get fed for another 20–22 days. Wintering is through the American southwest and southern states, up the Atlantic seaboard to New England, south through Mexico.

### Lincoln's sparrow *Bruant de Lincoln*
*Melospiza lincolnii* (sparrow subfamily)
Early May to mid-September

Very common in shrubby wetlands and along grassy streams in the woods. Length 12 cm. Quite similar to the vesper or savannah sparrows, but check the tail: there are no white tail feathers like the vesper sparrow's, and the end is round, not notched like the savannah's tail. Nor is there the savannah's yellowish eye-line or breast-spot. Song is long and interesting; cheepy, buzzy, with trills. Named for Thomas Lincoln, an associate of John James Audubon, not for Honest Abe.

MW

A shy bird, Lincoln's sparrow prowls the undergrowth along the shoreline and sings from cover. It scratches with both feet together—picture that—to get bugs and seeds. Breeds in mid-spring, the cup on the ground and well hidden. Four or five pale-green brown-speckled eggs hatch in 13–14 days; fledging is 10–12 days later. Winters from coastal California south through the American southwest, northeast as far as Missouri, through Mexico into central America.

### LeConte's sparrow *Bruant de LeConte*
*Ammodramus leconteii* (sparrow subfamily) June

Occasional in eastern-slope marshes, rare south of Jasper. Length 11 cm. Still another little brown sparrow, this one differing from the others by the white stripe down the top of the head, ochre or orange eye-line and buffy streaked breast. End of tail looks ragged and sharp. Voice is also a good identifier: high insect-like buzz, with no birdy cheeps at all—the only one like it in the Rockies.

MW

LeConte's pokes furtively among dense shrubbery and grasses for bugs and seeds, prefers to hide or run along the ground rather than fly. When flushed, it flies a short distance and drops back into cover like the savannah sparrow. There are no nesting records for this species in the national parks, but it may breed in the foothills in late spring. The nest is on the ground or raised a few centimetres in a dry spot in a marsh, well concealed in dense cover and made of woven grasses. Four white, heavily brown-marked eggs hatch in 11–13 days; fledging date unknown. Winter range: the Gulf states and up the east coast to Georgia.

### Lapland longspur *Bruant lapon*
*Calcarius pictus* (sparrow subfamily)
Early September to early October

Occasional in fall, in grassy places at any elevation, sometimes seen migrating in large flocks, or mixed with snow buntings, page 584. Length 15 cm. Male looks like a cross between a sparrow and a horned lark, page 548, with the black breast-band of the lark and the face of a sparrow. Compare also with house sparrow, page 581. Note also the yellowish bill, streaky vest and cinnamon patches on back of neck and wing. Female Lapland longspurs are streaky brown, with a bit of cinnamon on the back.

♀

MW

*Calcarius pictus*

This bird changes plumage with the seasons, and in early autumn you may see it in summer dress, with its black breast, face and cap. At this time it resembles **Harris's sparrow,** *Zonotrichia querula,* seen occasionally in the fall and winter. But the longspur has a rusty patch on the nape of the neck, while Harris's sparrow has gray cheeks with a dark bar.

Breeding ♂

MW

*Zonotrichia querula*

The song of the Lapland longspur is squeaky/buzzy, reminiscent of red-winged blackbird, or western meadowlark, page 574. Longspurs passing through the mountains are fueling up on seeds and late-season insects as they head south from the Arctic to spend the winter across the middle United States.

### Pine siskin *Chardonneret des pins*
*Carduelis pinus* (finch family)
Early April to mid-December

Very common in small flocks at low elevations in the woods and in town. Length 11 cm. Pine siskins were once called "linnets," for which Linnet Lake in Waterton was named. They are streaky brown birds that look like some kind of sparrow, until you notice the yellow patches in the wings, which are flashy in flight. There is also yellow on the rump and under the tail. Siskins say "zeeeee?" The voice rises in pitch as if asking a question. They also jabber a lot in fussy-sounding squeaks.

MW

Although they are "pine" siskins, I see this species more often in birches and alders, picking apart the catkins in summer and the cones in fall. They eat many different foods: insects, seeds of all kinds—they relish dandelion heads in summer—buds, nectar, even oozing sap. Towns offer a smorgasbord for these unwary little birds, but they break their necks flying into windows.

Breeding is in early spring; 3–5 bluish/greenish purplish-speckled eggs lie in a nest halfway up a conifer. Hatching is at 13 days, fledging at 14–15 days. Most songbird parents remove droppings from the nest in the form of tidy capsules that are easily carried away, but siskins let the nest go foul after nine days. Winter range: west coast and most of the United States.

## Birds seen less often

Some birds on this list are truly rare, reported in the Canadian Rockies only a few times, while others are species that only a good birder is likely to see, and not very often. An asterisk beside a name indicates that the species is increasingly spotted.

*Pacific loon *Gavia pacifica*
Red-throated loon *Gavia stellata*
Double-crested cormorant
   *Phalacrocorax auritus*
Green heron *Butorides striatus*
Great egret *Casmerodius albus*
Brant *Branta bernicla*
Greater scaup *Aythya marila*
*Turkey vulture *Cathartes aura*
Broad-winged hawk *Buteo platypterus*
Ferruginous hawk *Buteo regalis*
Gyrfalcon *Falco rusticolus*
*Sharp-tailed grouse
   *Tympanuchus phasianellus*
Ring-necked pheasant *Phasianus colchicus*
*Gray partridge *Perdix perdix*
Virginia rail *Rallus limicola*
Yellow rail *Coturnicops novabonracensis*
Lesser golden-plover *Pluvialis dominica*
Black-bellied plover *Pluvialis squatarola*
*Long-billed curlew *Numenius americanus*
Eskimo curlew *Numenius borealis*
Upland sandpiper *Bartramia longicauda*
Wandering tattler *Heteroscelus incanus*
Ruddy turnstone *Arenaria interpres*
Sanderling *Calidris alba*
Western sandpiper *Calidris mauri*
Dunlin *Calidris alpina*
Buff-breasted sandpiper
   *Tryngites subruficollis*
Marbled godwit *Limosa fedoa*
Red phalarope *Phalaropus fulicaria*
Parasitic jaeger *Stercorarius parasiticus*
Long-tailed jaeger *Stercorarius longicaudus*
Thayer's gull *Larus thayeri*
Sabine's gull *Xema sabini*
Forster's tern *Sterna forsteri*
Band-tailed pigeon *Columba fasciata*
Western screech owl *Otus kennicottii*
Snowy owl *Nyctea scandiaca*
Burrowing owl *Athene cunicularia*
Long-eared owl *Asio otus*
Ruby-throated hummingbird
   *Archilochus colubris*
*Western kingbird *Tyrannus verticalis*
*Eastern phoebe *Sayornis phoebe*
*Say's phoebe *Sayornis saya*

Yellow-bellied flycatcher
   *Empidonax flaviventris*
Pygmy nuthatch *Sitta pygmaea*
Northern mockingbird *Mimus polyglottos*
Gray catbird *Dumetella carolinensis*
Gray-cheeked thrush *Catharus minimus*
Eastern bluebird *Sialia sialis*
Sprague's pipit *Anthus spragueii*
Philadelphia vireo *Vireo philadelphicus*
Nashville warbler *Vermivora ruficapilla*
Cape May warbler *Dendroica tigrina*
Black-throated gray warbler
   *Dendroica nigrescens*
Black-throated green warbler
   *Dendroica virens*
Bay-breasted warbler *Dendroica castanea*
Palm warbler *Dendroica palmarum*
*Ovenbird *Seiurus aurocapillus*
Canada warbler *Wilsonia canadensis*
Bobolink *Dolichonyx oryzivorus*
*Northern oriole *Icterus galbula*
Common grackle *Quiscalus quiscula*
*Rose-breasted grosbeak
   *Pheucticus ludovicianus*
*Black-headed grosbeak
   *Pheucticus melanocephalus*
Dickcissel *Spiza americana*
*Cassin's finch *Carpodacus cassinii*
House finch *Carpodacus mexicanus*
*American goldfinch *Carduelis tristis*
*Rufous-sided towhee
   *Pipilo erythrophthalmus*
Lark bunting *Calamospiza melanocorys*
Grasshopper sparrow
   *Passerculus sandwichensis*
Baird's sparrow *Ammodramus bairdii*
Sharp-tailed sparrow
   *Ammodramus caudacutus*
*American tree sparrow *Spizella arborea*
Chestnut-collared longspur *Calcarius ornatus*

## Bird families and groups in the Canadian Rockies

These are listed in the standard order used by the American Ornithologist's Union.

Loons: order Gaviformes, family Gaviidae
Grebes: order Podicipediformes, family Podicipedidae
Pelicans: order Pelecaniformes, family Pelecanidae
Herons and bitterns: order Ciconiiformes, family Ardeidae
Waterfowl (ducks and geese): order Anseriformes, family Anatidae
    Ducks: subfamily Anatinae
        Surface-feeding (dabbling) ducks: tribes Cairinini (wood duck) and Anatini (all others)
        Bay ducks: tribe Aythyini (scaup, ring-necked, redhead, canvasback)
        Sea ducks and mergansers: tribe Mergini
            (goldeneyes, harlequin, bufflehead, oldsquaw, scoters, mergansers)
        Stiff-tailed ducks (ruddy duck): tribe Oxyurini
    Swans and geese: subfamily Anserinae
        Swans: tribe Cygnini
        Geese: tribe Anserini
Hawks and falcons: order Falconiformes
    Hawks, osprey, eagles: family Accipitridae
    Falcons: family Falconidae
Grouse and ptarmigan: order Galliformes, family Phasianidae, subfamily Tetraoninae
Cranes and allies: order Gruiformes
    Rails and coots: family Rallidae
    Cranes: family Gruidae
Shorebirds and gulls: order Charadriiformes
    Plovers (including kildeer): family Charadriidae
    Avocets: family Recurvirostridae
    Sandpipers and phalaropes: family Scolopacidae
    Gulls and allies: family Laridae
        Gulls: subfamily Larinae
        Terns: subfamily Sterninae
Doves: order Columbiformes, family Columbidae
Owls: order Strigiformes, family Strigidae
Nightjars (nighthawk): order Caprimulgiformes, family Caprimulgidae
Swifts and hummingbirds: order Apodiformes
    Swifts: family Apodidae
    Hummingbirds: family Trochilidae
Kingfishers: order Coraciiformes, family Alcedinidae
Woodpeckers: order Piciformes, family Picidae
Perching birds: order Passeriformes
    Flycatchers: family Tyrannidae
    Horned larks: family Alaudidae
    Swallows: family Hirundinidae
    Crows, jays, magpies: family Corvidae
    Chickadees: family Paridae
    Nuthatches: family Sittidae
    Creepers: family Certhiidae
    Wrens: family Troglodytidae
    Dippers: family Cinclidae
    Kinglets, thrushes and bluebirds: family Muscicapidae
        Kinglets: subfamily Sylviinae
        Thrushes and bluebirds: subfamily Turdinae
    Pipits: family Motacillidae

Waxwings: family Bombycillidae
Shrikes: family Laniidae
Starlings: family Sturnidae
Vireos: family Vireonidae
Wood warblers: family Emberizidae
    Wood warblers: subfamily Parulinae
    Tanagers: subfamily Thraupinae
    Sparrows: subfamily Emberizinae
    Blackbirds, cowbirds: subfamily Icterinae
Finches: family Fringillidae, subfamily Carduelinae
Old world sparrows (house sparrows): family Passeridae

*White-tailed ptarmigan in summer camouflage plumage*

# Further reading (and listening)

Beck, B. & J. (1992) *Birds of Northern and Central Alberta.* A bird-song tape produced by Barb and Jim Beck of the University of Alberta. Includes some mountain species, and a tape specifically for the Rockies is in the works. Available at the University of Alberta Bookstore, nature shops in the region and the Friends of Jasper National Park shop in Jasper.

Ehrlich, P.; D. Dobkin and D. Wheye (1988) *The Birder's Handbook.* Simon & Schuster, New York. All the information that *isn't* in the identification guides: behavior, diet, conservation, and so on for each species, with a running series of short items on topics of general interest to birders. A must-have, illustrated, indexed, 785 pages.

Finlay, J. (1984) *A Bird-finding Guide to Canada.* Distributed by McClelland & Stewart, Toronto. Includes hot birding spots in the Canadian Rockies. Checklists, maps, 387 pages.

Godfrey, W. (1986) *The Birds of Canada.* National Museums of Canada, Ottawa. The authoritative source for the whole country; excellent color illustrations, range maps, indexed; 595 pages. Gives bird names in French as well as English, and a complete French edition is available.

Holroyd, G. and H. Coneybeare (1990) *The Compact Guide to Birds of the Rockies.* Lone Pine Publishing, Edmonton. Exactly as the title states, with full-color paintings of all species described. Checklist, index, 144 pages.

Kellogg, P. (1975) *A Field Guide to Western Bird Songs.* Houghton Mifflin, Boston. Three 60-minute cassette tapes in a plastic folder, with index. Excellent recordings of some 500 species, announced by Roger Tory Peterson.

Salt, W. and J. Salt (1976) *The Birds of Alberta.* Distributed by McClelland & Stewart, Toronto. Readable text, with interesting information on each species in the province. Hardbound, but small enough to be carried along. Mixed photos and painted illustrations; information and range maps sometimes don't agree with other sources; 498 pages.

Savage, Candace (1985) *The Wonder of Canadian Birds.* Western Producer Prairie Books, Saskatoon, SK. Up-to-date, interestingly written items on 55 species, including many in our area; emphasis on behavior. Excellent photo illustrations; index, species bibliographies; 209 pages.

Scotter, G., T. Urlich and E. Jones (1990) *Birds of the Canadian Rockies.* Douglas & McIntyre, Vancouver. This is *the* bird book to carry in the mountains, covering all the species you're likely to see. Photo illustrations, checklist, bibliography, index; 175 pages.

Semenchuk, G. (1992) *Atlas of Breeding Birds of Alberta.* Federation of Alberta Naturalists, Edmonton. Comprehensive for the province. Illustrated, range maps, bibliography, index; 391 pages. An associated tape of owl calls may still be available.

Thomas, R. (1994) *Making Connections: Alberta's Neotropical Migratory Birds.* Alberta Wilderness Association, Calgary. Interesting short item on birds that spend summers here and winters in the tropics. Explanation for decline of these species, with a well-informed and eloquent plea for habitat protection. Well-illustrated, checklist, 23 pages.

*Checklists* are available for Banff, Jasper, Kootenay, Yoho, Waterton Lakes and Glacier national parks, and for Kananaskis Provincial Park. Pick them up at information centres in the individual parks.

*Hoary marmot, the high-country woodchuck. Photo by Barry Giles.*

# Mammals
## Fur, hair, horns and hoofs

Members of the class Mammalia have hair, and the females have teats for nursing their young. Except for a few species such as the platypus, mammals are born, not hatched. These things are sufficient to differentiate mammals from other animal groups. In the Canadian Rockies there are 69 naturally occurring species of mammals, including *Homo sapiens.*

Mammals are mostly ground-dwellers and larger than many other creatures, so they leave **sign:** tracks, trails, droppings, the discarded remains of meals, the burrows and dens, the squirrel middens and pika haystacks. This messiness is handy for mammal-watchers, because many of their subjects are shy creatures of the night. In daylight you can tell who has been around the evening before if you know what to look for, especially in winter, when tracks abound. Check the tracks-and-scats pictures on pages 665 and 666.

Anyone exploring the woods is bound to find mammalian bones and antlers occasionally. See pages 660 through 664 for pictures of the skulls of most mammal species in the Canadian Rockies; antlers are illustrated in the drawings of deer-family members, pages 644–652.

Here is how the species listings work. In each listing the English common name is followed by the French common name. The next line gives the Latin scientific name in italics and the family to which that particular species belongs. The dates on the next line give the time of year in which a species or its sign is likely to be seen. Some mammals hibernate, while others stay under the snow in winter and are not seen, even though they are active.

The body measurements and weights are averages for adults in the Canadian Rockies. To save space the range of size and weight for each species is not given, although it can be considerable. The overall length includes the tail, the length of which is also given separately. The average height of the larger animals is measured at the shoulder. Among the larger mammals, males are usually 10–30 percent bigger than females and a good deal heavier.

Each year, most mammals go through two or more **moults:** loss of one coat of hair and its replacement by another, often of a slightly different color. Where the difference is eye-catching, it is indicated.

Much of each item is devoted to mammal behavior. Details of reproduction include mating behavior, breeding season, the length of **gestation** (time in the womb), what time of year the young are born, how many are in a litter and how they grow up. This is a lot to put in a field guide, so it has been kept brief. Longevity data is provided where possible, but information on lifespan is usually based on few records and should not be relied upon.

*Hunters:* many species of mammals are protected in Alberta, British Columbia and Montana. Be sure you know the game laws before you shoot.

## Bats: hung up about caves

This is the order Chiroptera, family Vespertilionidae, the evening-bat family. The only truly airborne mammals, bats fly with membranes of naked skin that stretch between their elongated finger-bones. The membrane is attached to the sides of the body, incorporating the back legs and extending along the tail. The wings are uniformly thin, not thickened in the centre to provide the sort of airfoil that gives lift to the wings of birds, but the jointed fingers create curvature in the bat's membrane to produce an airfoil anyway. Thus, bats fly essentially as birds do.

Bats have evolved sonar for navigating and for locating prey in the dark. (See also the shrews, page 597.) A bat squeaks at frequencies of 30,000– 100,000 hz, too high for humans to hear. As each pulse leaves the bat's nose and mouth, the ears seal off the sound so that the animal hears only the returning echo. The brain interprets the timing of the echos to give distance, direction and texture to whatever bounced the sound back. A bat forms a sonar image of its surroundings; it catches flying insects with ease, differentiating them from complex forest backgrounds. Bats also make audible noises.

Bugs are often caught on a wingtip, then passed down to a pocket formed by curling the interfemoral membrane (skin between legs and tail) inward, like the pocket of a baseball mitt. After the fly is fielded, so to speak, it is eaten immediately if small—the bat ducks its head down—or taken to a perch for eating if large. A bat typically catches one insect every seven seconds all night long. It consumes half its own weight in insects every 24 hours. Given the large number of bats on the evening air, consider the impact on the bug population.

Coupled with these skills is a prodigious memory for terrain and cave passages. Most bats overwintering in the Canadian Rockies travel deep into caverns for hibernation, flying through complex passages in complete darkness. They find their way home to the same cave each winter, although it may be hundreds of kilometres from where they spent the summer and the cave entrance may be tiny.

Bat coordination is terrific: bats have been known to escape from a locked laboratory room by flying unscathed through a turning ventilator fan. Bats have flown right past me in tight cave passages without brushing my clothing. And they don't get caught in your hair.

In this climate, bats can carry on their nightly foraging flights from early May to early September, when the evening temperature is above freezing and insects are plentiful. During the other seven months of the year they hibernate—even the species that fly south—and must survive without eating. Having put on a surprising amount of fat for an airborne animal, about one-third of their body weight, they become dormant, hanging head-downward in tightly packed underground colonies. Their body temperatures drop to that of the air temperature, which in Canadian Rockies caves is just a few degrees above freezing year-round. Their hearts beat only 2–3 times each minute, and they breathe only once each hour.

Most bats in the Rockies mate in late August or early September, but the females keep the male sperm alive in their uteruses until the following spring—a period of about eight months. Ovulation and fertilization occur at the end of dormancy, when a bat's metabolism increases. Only then does the embryo begin to grow.

Females of most species bear only one baby each year, sometime between mid-June and mid-July. Each mother bat carries her baby with her for the first week or so; it clings crosswise to her furry chest, often attached to one of two tiny nipples located like human ones. When the bat becomes too large to carry, its mother leaves it with others in a nursery roost. The young can fly on their own only three weeks after birth.

The lifespan of bats is amazingly long for such small mammals: up to 30 years, which explains how they survive with such a low rate of reproduction.

Bats can carry rabies, so it is unwise to touch them. If you get bitten by a bat, which is highly unlikely, you should see a doctor. But we need not fear bats. Just the opposite; as ravenous bug-eaters and biological marvels, bats deserve our respect and protection. When entering caves in winter, people should be careful not to disturb hibernating bats, causing them to fly around and use up precious fat reserves needlessly. This can kill them. It is illegal in both Alberta and British Columbia to disturb hibernating bats.

Bat measurements are important for determining species, so several measurements are given for each. They are averages. Length refers to the distance from the tip of the nose to the tip of the tail. Ear measurement is from base to tip.

## Little brown bat *Petite Chauve-souris brune*
*Myotis lucifugus* (evening-bat family)
May to September

Common from valley floors to treeline, seen from dusk to dawn flitting silently about the sky nabbing insects. They often hunt over water. In daytime, found roosting in colonies in tree hollows, rock crevices, caves and unused parts of buildings. Overwinters in the region, hibernating mainly in caves and

MW

abandoned underground mines. Length 8.6 cm (tail 3.7 cm), ear 1.3 cm, weight 6.2 g. Dark-brown back, lighter underside, dark face, ears, wings, legs and tail. Compare with big brown bat, California myotis and long-eared bat.

Little brown bats emerge from hibernation in early spring, when small flying insects, especially mosquitoes, become active. Mating occurs in autumn in the Rockies, just before hibernation begins, but fertilization is delayed until after hibernation. Gestation takes 50–60 days and delivery of the single young occurs from mid-May to July. Carried about in its first few days, the young bat gains weight quickly and soon flies; it matures during the first annual hibernation, which begins with the disappearance of flying insects in fall, usually by mid-September in the Canadian Rockies. The longevity of this species, up to 30 years, explains why I keep seeing bats banded in the 1970s hibernating year after year in Cadomin Cave.

### Big brown myotis/big brown bat *Grande Chauve-souris brune*
*Eptesicus fuscus* (evening-bat family)
May to September

MW

Fairly common from Jasper south, seen chasing flying insects in forests and meadows from dusk to dawn. Often seen in towns. Length 11.6 cm (tail 4.6 cm), ear 1.5 cm, weight 15.2 g. Similar to the little brown bat, previous item, but noticeably larger and furrier. Often rustier in color, the coat is glossier and the face lighter brown. Positive identifier: no extra-small tooth behind the canine.

Habits and life cycle are like those of the little brown bat, but the big brown bat is bolder and more urban, often hunting for insects around dwellings. It will sometimes come inside houses through open doors or chimneys. If you leave a window open, it will leave on its own. It seldom chooses attics for winter roosts, though; these are usually too warm, or the temperature fluctuates too much. Like the little brown bat, the big brown bat hibernates mostly in caves. Quite hardy, these bats become dormant later in the fall and emerge earlier in the spring than other bats in the area.

### California myotis/California bat *Chauve-souris de Californie*
*Myotis californicus* (evening-bat family)
May to September

Southern region of the western slope, reported from montane forest in Kootenay National Park. Length 8.0 cm (tail 3.6 cm), ear 1.3, weight 4.4 g, the smallest bat in the Canadian Rockies. Fur is a dark, dull rusty color; bare skin is black. Differentiate from the similar-looking little brown bat by the feet: small in the California myotis, with a little flap of skin extending off the wing-edge by the heel.

This species hunts mostly over water bodies from dusk to dawn, roosting in any handy place, natural or man-made. Diet is unstudied, but probably similar to that of little brown bat. Reproduction is similar. Hibernates in caves and mines.

### Long-legged myotis/long-legged bat/hairy-winged bat
*Chauve-souris à longues pattes*
*Myotis volans* (evening-bat family)
May to September

Occasional in dry woods and meadows from Grande Cache south, seen mostly at dawn and dusk. Length 9.4 cm (tail 4.3 cm), ear 1.2 cm, weight 7.2 g. Dark brown like most bats, differentiated by looking closely at the wings: the underside of the wing membrane is lightly furry between the elbow and the knee.

MW

This bat eats mainly moths and spends its time much as the little brown bat does. There is a hibernation record for Cadomin Cave, but most individuals seem to fly farther south to hibernate.

### Western long-eared myotis/western long-eared bat
*Chauve-souris à longues oreilles*
*Myotis evotis* (evening-bat family)
May to September

MW

Occasional from Prince George south in forest openings, emerging later in the evening than other bats. Length 9.2 cm (tail 4.2 cm), ear 2.0 cm, weight 5.5 g. Yet another brown bat with black wings. This one can be differentiated from the rest by the ears: they are noticeably longer. The western long-eared bat hunts over water less than the other *Myotis* species. It eats mostly moths, catching many of them as they sit in the shrubbery. It seems able to hear a moth flutter its wings as it warms up before taking off.

The rare **northern long-eared myotis** (*Myotis septentrionalis*) looks similar, but is a little shorter and at the same time heavier. Its ears are smaller (1.7 cm) and paler. Reported from Hudson's Hope on the Peace River, from Cadomin Cave and from Jasper National Park. Possibly found in Kootenay National Park.

### Silver-haired bat *Chauve-souris argentée*
*Lasionycteris noctivagans* (evening-bat family)
Late May and late August

MW

Occasional from Prince George south, usually seen in spring and late summer when bats are migrating to and from their winter ranges in the U.S.A. Length 10.0 cm (tail 4.1 cm), ear 1.2 cm, weight 9.0 g. Looks black from a distance; up close you can see the silver-tipped hairs.

Silver-haired bats appear earlier in the evening than other bats, sometimes in afternoon daylight. They often fly over water in wooded places, catching moths, mayflies and other insects that hover above the surface. Slower on the wing than other bats, and somewhat clumsy-looking, they have been known to crash into the water and then swim out of it. Daytime roosts are solitary in tree hollows, sometimes in large abandoned bird nests, so clear-cutting destroys this bat's habitat. Silver-haireds migrate south in the fall. Reproduction and life cycle are typical of bats, although two young are born annually instead of one.

### Hoary bat *Chauve-souris cendrée*
*Lasiurus cinereus* (evening-bat family)
Late May and late August

MW

Occasional to rare from Jasper south, flying well after dark in heavily wooded areas. Largest bat in the region: length 13.7 cm (tail 6.0 cm), ear 1.4 cm, weight 28.4 g. Silvery like the silver-haired bat, previous item, but the underlying fur of the hoary bat is much lighter, and the hoary is quite a bit larger and stouter. Typically it has tawny patches on the throat, shoulders, arms, around the ears and on the wings. The rear parts of the wing membranes are lightly hairy. Note the round ears.

Hoary bats are solitary, even during migration, which is mainly when we see them. They hibernate in the southern U.S.A. and Mexico. They usually feed over water, picking off the larger night-flying insects—mostly moths—and perhaps killing other bats. Roosts are mainly in tree cavities rather than in caves or human structures. The species mates in August and gives birth to twins in June, but little else is known of its life cycle.

# Shrews (order Insectivora, family Soricidae)

If it looks like a mouse with a long, pointy nose and a wire-thin tail, then maybe it's a shrew. But shrews are not rodents; they are insectivores, a primitive order of mammals.

Shrews are active year-round, in winter staying under the snow. Busiest just before dawn and just after dusk, shrews have incredibly fast metabolisms—their hearts beat up to 1200 times per minute—and they must eat at least their weight in food each day. Menu: insects (mostly moth and beetle larvae), slugs and snails, fungi, lichens and seeds. Shrews spend their waking hours rooting around in ground litter. They are hunted by many small predators, especially by weasels and owls, and they have been known to eat one another. They are fierce for their size, taking over the burrows of larger creatures—they don't seem to dig their own— and defending solitary territories. They have a musky odor.

Unlike most other small rodents, shrews are quite vocal, twittering away as they make their rounds. Why? Shrews have been shown to use echo-location, although the ability seems not to be as well-developed as in bats.

Mating is usually in the spring; sometimes in the fall. The nest is built of grass or willow leaves under a log or rock, usually with two entrances. Gestation time: about 18 days. There are one or two litters of 2–10 young, average 4–5, each year, the offspring reaching maturity in about four months and living at the most only two summers and the intervening winter. When travelling, a family of young shrews **caravans:** with mum in the lead, each latches onto the furry rump of another (not to the tail, as had been thought) and follows.

## Masked shrew *Musaraigne cendrée*

*Sorex cinereus* (shrew family)
Spring to fall

In damp meadows and forests, sometimes above treeline, usually near water. Probably our most common shrew, but secretive, normally foraging under leaf litter, concealing itself there and thus seldom seen. Length 10 cm (tail 4 cm); weight 4.1 g.

MW

Recognized as a shrew by the long, whiskery nose. Fur color: grayish-brown or sepia-colored, grayer below. Coat is much heavier in winter than in summer, and usually darker. Very small eyes, flattened ears almost hidden in fur. Long sparsely furred tail, pinkish feet with five toes on each foot. Mice, sometimes confused with shrews, have four toes on their front feet, five on the back. The masked shrew is a little smaller than the very similar dusky and wandering shrews. To differentiate confidently you have to check the teeth. In the upper jaw of the masked shrew the third and fourth **unicuspids** (the little sharp teeth between the incisors at the front and the molars at the back) are smaller than the first two. In the dusky and wandering shrews the third unicuspid is smaller than the fourth.

The **prairie shrew** *(S. haydeni)* has been reported along the southern mountain front near Cowley and Seebe. It resembles the masked shrew, but the prairie shrew's fur is paler, the tail is shorter and the tail-tip is not as dark. Sure identifier: total length of the row of unicuspid teeth is less than 2.3 mm.

## Dusky shrew and wandering shrew *Musaraigne sombre, musaraigne errante*

*Sorex monticolus* and *S. vagrans* (shrew family)
Spring to fall

Grassy/willowy shores of bogs and streams, montane to alpine. Dusky shrew fairly common from Crowsnest Pass north; wandering shrew in Waterton/Glacier. Length 11 cm (tail 5 cm), weight 5 g.

Both species closely resemble the masked shrew, but they are a little longer and heavier, with redder fur. See previous item for how to differentiate confidently. You can tell whether it is a dusky shrew or a wandering shrew by geographic range—the two species do not overlap— and by the deeper coloration on the upper incisors of the dusky shrew. Habits and life history are like those given in the introduction.

The **black-backed shrew,** also called **arctic shrew** *(S. arcticus)* is a boreal species that ranges close to the foothills from the North Saskatchewan River northward, and has been found along the Ram River just east of Highway 940. It is about 11.5 cm long (tail 4 cm) and weighs about 8.5 g. Resembles the other shrews, but it has a three-colored coat. In winter the coat is shiny black on the back, brown on the sides and gray underneath; in summer the back is brown, but a lighter tone than the sides. Positive identification: the unicuspids grow smaller toward the molars.

## Pygmy shrew *Musaraigne pygmée*

*Sorex hoyi* (shrew family)
Spring to fall

Occasional in grassy subalpine meadows; widespread, but never common. Prefers drier habitat than other shrews. The smallest mammal in the New World: length only 8 cm, of which 2.5 cm is tail. Weight about 3 g.

Typical shrew features: pointy whiskered nose, skinny scantily furred tail, pink feet. Coat sepia above, smoky below. Differentiated from other shrews in the Canadian Rockies by size, noticeably smaller; by the tail, proportionately shorter, and dentition: in the upper jaw, two of the teeth behind the incisors are so small that you need a magnifying glass to see them. Thus, at first glance, pygmy shrews appear to have only three teeth between the incisors and the molars, whereas the others clearly have four (and actually have five, for the fifth unicuspid is tiny).

Life cycle of the pygmy shrew is probably like that of other shrews, but the species needs more study. It seems even more frantically hungry than its relatives, eating about three times its weight each day in insects and carrion.

## Northern water shrew *Musaraigne palustre*

*Sorex palustris* (shrew family)
Summer and fall

In or at the edge of small mountain streams, often in heavy subalpine forest. Largest shrew in the Rockies: length 15 cm (tail 7 cm), weight 10–20 g.

Typical shrew-like pointy face with long whiskers. Coat is black or dark gray above, white below; the animal appears silvery in the water from bubbles adhering to the thick fur. The hind feet are unique among our shrews: bristly along the toes and partly webbed to help in paddling.

Water shrews swim well, and watching one is fascinating. It appears to run across the water's surface when swimming quickly. Paddling furiously to overcome its bubbly buoyancy, it dives to the bottom in shallow water to grab caddisfly, mayfly or stonefly larvae, or other invertebrates and fish eggs, sometimes taking small fish—and sometimes becoming a meal for a large trout. Emerging from a stream, a water shrew shakes the water off and quickly combs itself dry with its bristly hind feet. The species also hunts on land, searching the shoreline rocks for insects.

Mating begins in late winter. Two or three litters of about six young are raised before summer's end; gestation period unknown. Like other shrews, this one mates again shortly after giving birth. The nest is at the water's edge, often hidden among the sticks of a beaver dam or lodge. The animal is short-lived, going about its frantic life for only two summers. Shrews don't hibernate; this one survives the winter in the water, breathing from holes it keeps open and from the airspace that develops under the ice along the shore as the water level drops. During this time it hunts as little as possible. Mostly it rests and grooms itself—quite a change from its normal behavior.

# *Mice—and a rat*

These are all rodents (order Rodentia). All rodents in the Rockies belong to the family Muridae. Within that family, we have the New World mice and rats (subfamily Cricetinae), the Old World mice and rats (subfamily Murinae), and the voles (subfamily Arvicolinae). Most of the small rodents seen in the Rockies and called "mice" are actually voles. Mice have larger ears than voles and longer tails. Their teeth have roots like ours, while those of voles do not.

### Deer mouse *Souris-sylvestre*
*Peromyscus maniculatus* (New-World mice/rats subfamily, Cricetine)
Year-round

MW

Very common in any dry habitat; found from the valley floors to treeline and sometimes higher. Nocturnal. Size quite variable; in the mountains often large: length about 20 cm (tail about 10 cm), weight about 35 g. The deer mouse is reddish/grayish-brown above, with white tummy, chin, legs and feet. The eyes and ears are larger than those of the voles—the deer mouse was the model for Walt Disney's Mickey Mouse—and the long, lightly fuzzy tail is dark on top and white underneath.

Deer mice are nocturnal, thus seen less often than their numbers warrant. Quick and agile, using their long tails for balance, the animals travel widely on the ground, running about in overlapping one-hectare territories and crossing highways. This is the mouse that you see in your headlights. Deer mice climb trees to the top for buds and fruits. Other foods: mostly seeds, especially those of conifers, but also berries, insects (mostly larvae), lichens and an underground fungus called *Endogone* that is popular with most mice.

Although deer mice can become torporous when they would not otherwise survive, they are typically active year-round, leaving lots of tracks on the winter snow. If you follow the tracks, easily identified by the tail print, you may come to a little snow tunnel going down toward the nest, which is a ball of grass or feather moss about 10 cm across, hidden in a grass tussock or low tree cavity, in a hollow among roots, an abandoned burrow or (a favorite) an empty container. The mice store several litres of seeds nearby for winter use.

Given a low entrance hole, deer mice will move indoors with you, not so much to eat your food, which they *will* do, as to share accommodations—including your mattress stuffing. They are fond of nesting in cupboards and drawers; in 1980, users of the Hilda Creek Hostel along the Icefields Parkway near the Columbia Icefield opened and shut a silverware drawer many times, never pulling it out far enough to see the deer-mouse nest at the back.

If you sleep outdoors, a deer mouse may come up to your head, often walking on your sleeping bag or even on your face, to gently nibble loose a few strands of hair for nesting material. I have always found this amusing, but one time it gave the horrors to a British climber bivouacked with me under a boulder. "Bloody 'ell!!" he cried at 2 a.m. "There's a *raht* in me 'air!" And he started flailing with a piton hammer, somehow missing me as well as the "raht." A couple of fig bars flung into a corner of our kip distracted the beast, which was the size of a cat according to the hammer-wielder, and we went back to sleep listening to it going "tsit-tsit-tsit" as it ate. At dawn I awoke with crumbs rolling into my eyes. It was a deer mouse, perched on my forehead as it finished the last fig bar.

*Peromyscus maniculatus was here*

Seldom vocal, deer mice drum with their front feet when alarmed. They are prey for night-hunters such as weasels and owls, sustaining their numbers through prolific reproduction. The breeding period is March to October; there are normally two or three litters a year averaging four babies per litter. Gestation is 22–35 days, the nursing period the same length. Papa leaves when the young are born, then returns to help out with the washing and nest-tidying when they are a few days old. Mum weans the young'uns at 22–35 days, then chucks them out; they often move in with dad, who meanwhile is seeing mom again. In fact, female deer mice often mate within a day or two of giving birth; they can suckle one batch of young while gestating the next. Most mice and rats can do this.

Females mature at 32–35 days, males at 40–45 days. Lifespan in the wild is normally less than a year, although deer mice have lived for eight years in captivity.

## *Don't mess with mouse droppings*

Droppings and urine from deer mice can harbor a dangerous virus: **hantavirus,** from the Hantaan River of Korea, where the virus was discovered in the 1950s. Hantavirus causes fairly mild, flu-like symptoms at first, followed by shortness of breath, increased heart rate—and death from fluid-filled lungs in two-thirds of the untreated cases. If you are cleaning up after mice in the cabin or the hut or the hostel, wear a respirator with a HEPA filter. Put on protective goggles and use rubber gloves. Wet the area first with diluted bleach. Can house mice and other small rodents carry the virus? Yes, although the prevalence is less: about 10 percent of house mice test positive for it at time of writing, compared with 30 percent for deer mouse.

### House mouse *Souris commune*
*Mus musculus* (Old World mice/rats subfamily, Murinae)
Indoors year-round

Common in townsites, in dwellings with accessible food. Nocturnal. Length 17 cm (tail 8.5 cm); weight 20 g. Brown above, dark-gray below, with large dark ears, pink nose and feet, pale tail. Looks like the deer mouse, previous item, but smaller and not white underneath. The white mice used in laboratories and kept as pets are albino house mice.

MW

House mice are colonial; they evolved on the east-European steppes (grasslands, like those of the Canadian prairie provinces), then moved indoors for an easy life with the Russians of Turkestan. Like the Norway rat (only reported once in the Canadian Rockies, from Field, in 1953), house mice have spread throughout the world as stowaways.

They nest in walls, behind cupboards, under the floor—anywhere out of sight and safe from the cat. There are sometimes communities in grain and hay fields, for seeds are their natural foods; as human commensals they prefer cereals, flour and sugar, fruit, vegetables and whatever appeals in the garbage.

House mice come out at night, gnawing noisily into bags and boxes, leaving little rod-like droppings on the counters and carting off mattress stuffing, newspaper and hair for nesting material. Like the deer mouse, previous item, house mice can carry hantavirus. See boxed boxed item above. Given their reproductive rate of a litter of four to eight every couple of months, year-round, it usually becomes necessary to crack down on house mice with traps or feline help. Gestation is 21 days, maturity 35 days after birth.

## Bushy-tailed wood rat/pack rat *Rat à queue touffue*
*Neotoma cinerea* (New-World mice/rats subfamily, Cricetinae)
Year-round

MW

Common in coniferous woods, living in rock crevices, under boulders, in caves and under or in buildings. Nocturnal, most active just after dusk and before dawn. This is our largest mouse-like land rodent. Length 42 cm, half of which is tail; weight 400 g. The tail is so bushy that some people mistake the wood rat for a squirrel, but none of our squirrels has the large ears and beady, protruding eyes of the wood rat. The soft coat is brownish gray, with black-tipped hairs; sometimes it is quite pale. Feet are white.

One seldom sees a wood rat, for they are usually active after dark. Instead, one sees (and smells) their dwellings. Nearly any deep crevice in a rocky outcrop below treeline could be home to a solitary wood rat, the entrance piled high with old conifer needles and twigs. There are sludgy deposits of black feces nearby, and the rocks surrounding the nest are stained yellowish from urine.

But don't get the wrong idea. These animals are actually very clean and tidy. Protected behind the midden is the nest, made like a bird's nest of soft mosses and hair. Curled up asleep within it by day is the wood rat, often surrounded by a collection of shiny man-made objects: bits of glass, aluminum, coins, cutlery, bottle caps and so on. Wood rats living far from human activity collect colored rocks, crystals and feathers. Thus the folk-name "pack rat" for these creatures. Another folk name, "trade rat," comes from the animal's supposed practice of leaving one object in place of another. What actually happens is that the rat drops what it is carrying in favor of a more attractive item. Wood rats are excellent climbers. I have passed by their nests 50 m up on difficult rock-climbing routes. The species drums its hind feet when alarmed.

Main wood-rat food: foliage, mostly of deciduous shrubs and trees, but also of conifers. The rat often drags a leafy or needle-covered branch back to the nest, where it is dried for a while before being eaten. Fruits and seeds are also on the menu. In fall, wood rats stockpile cuttings in and near their dens; they are active all winter, mainly under the snow, but you sometimes see their tracks on the surface. They look like those of the deer mouse, page 599, but are larger.

Breeding begins in February, the males marking territory with their anal musk glands and fighting viciously among themselves as they search for females. But they are gentle with the ladies, nuzzling them and purring before mating. Gestation is 27–32 days; normally there are one or two litters of 3–4 (range 1–5) young each year, weaned at 26–30 days. Maturity, though, takes a long time by rodent standards: nearly a year. Daughters often set up house-keeping close to the dens of their mothers, or they may share a den. Maximum longevity of both sexes in the wild is about four years.

Longevity in someone's cabin is often considerably shorter. Wood rats make a stinky mess of borrowed lodgings, building large middens on the beds and in the stove and cupboards. All collectibles are dragged thereto. They eviscerate mattresses, shred up blankets and clothing, poop everywhere and piss on the walls—real party types, and quite noisy at night as they waddle clumsily about and send things crashing. Not nice to have indoors. But interesting!

## Western jumping mouse and meadow jumping mouse
*Souris sauteuse de l'Ouest, souris sauteuse des champs*
*Zapus princeps* and *Z. hudsonius* (jumping-mouse family, Dipodidae)
Spring to fall

Fairly common in moist meadows and grasslands at all elevations, usually near water. Mostly nocturnal. Length 25 cm (tail 15 cm); weight 30 g. The **western jumping mouse** has a brown back and tawny sides in the southern part of the Canadian Rockies; is overall gray in the north. Both races are cream-colored underneath, with a long skinny tail that is dark on top and light below. Big back legs, large ears.

From Valemount north on the western slope and Pine Pass north on the eastern slope, one also finds the **meadow jumping mouse,** quite similar but a little smaller (length 21 cm, tail

13 cm, weight 15 g), brown and tawny like the southern race of the western jumping mouse, but with a broad olive-brown band down the centre underneath. Neither species is very vocal, but adults sometimes rasp, chatter their teeth and drum with their tails. The babies squeak.

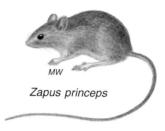

MW

*Zapus princeps*

Both the western and meadow jumping mice jump, all right: 1–2 m at a time, holding very still for a moment after landing. To predators, this combination makes the mouse seem to disappear. Then it goes quietly about its business in short hops, eating grass seeds, berries and other plant fruits, sometimes climbing grass stems. Jumping mice are good swimmers, diving over a metre deep on occasion. They can dig their own burrows or move into found ones.

Territories are about 100 m across, although jumping mice move around more than other small-rodent species and may finish life a kilometre away from where they were born.

True hibernators, these species practically double their weight in fall, curling up tightly inside a grass ball at the end of the burrow in September and not stirring until May. Then they mate, each female producing just one litter of 5 (range 2– 7) young in June. Gestation is probably 18 days. The tiny babies are born pink and hairless, blind and deaf, like those of most rodents. But they are on their own a month later and mature at two months. Few live more than a year.

## Southern red-backed vole/Gapper's red-backed vole and northern red-backed vole

*Campagnol a dos roux de Gapper, campagnol a dos roux boréal*
*Clethrionomys gapperi* and *C. rutilus* (vole subfamily, Arvicolinae)
Summer and fall

Common, although populations fluctuate markedly, in subalpine forest, usually near water. Length 14 cm (tail 4 cm); weight 24 g. Red-backed voles are easily identified by a broad stripe of reddish-brown to bright red fur running from head to tail-base. The two species are very

MW

*Clethrionomys gapperi*

similar, but their ranges divide at the Peace River with little overlap. The southern red-backed vole, found south of the Peace, has a browner stripe than the northern red-backed vole, found north of the Peace, on which the stripe is quite red.

Mainly nocturnal, red-backed voles sometimes come out during the day. The northern species eats all parts of many kinds of shrubs and wildflowers. The southern species is pickier; it prefers the petioles (stalks) of leaves, supplemented with berries when it can get them, and buds, twigs, seeds and even bark when leaves are scarce. Doesn't cache food. Both species will eat carrion, including their own kind, and inspections of stomach contents in the Cascade Mountains have shown a diet rich in truffles, a form of underground fungi. Lichens are eaten as well.

Neither species swims much, but they both climb up into shrubs and trees. Each vole ranges through 1–2 ha, tunneling in the feather mosses of the subalpine forest floor. There is a ball-shaped nest of grass, leaves and moss hidden under deadfall or in the natural hollows that one always seems to find among the roots of large trees in boggy subalpine forest.

Active all winter, voles build an extra nest right on the ground, under the snow, joined to the extensive tunnel network that rodents maintain in the sugary-textured depth-hoar at the base of the snowpack. Occasionally they come out on the surface, leaving the tiny tracks shown on page 665.

Everything seems to eat voles, so they reproduce prolifically. Two to four litters of 4–7 young are born from May to October each year. Gestation period 17–19 days; 18–21 days later the young are weaned and chased out of the nest to make way for the next batch. Maturity comes at four months, so females born early in the year can breed in their first fall. Others wait until the following spring to mate. Lifespan is unknown, but certainly not very long in the wild.

Vole populations vary enormously from year to year, a boom-and-bust cycle made worse by man's killing of weasels, wolves, coyotes and predatory birds. In years of overpopulation, cabin-dwellers, especially those living north of the Peace River, find themselves beset with waves of hungry voles. In other years they see very few.

## Meadow vole *Campagnol des champs*
*Microtus pennsylvanicus* (vole subfamily)
Spring to fall

Very common in damp montane meadows, grassy marshes, hay or grain fields and untended yards. Length 16 cm (tail 4.5 cm), weight 35 g. Its gray coat, brown-tipped in summer, gray feet and lightly hairy tail cause many people to mistake this animal for a mouse. Its folk name is "field mouse." But the small ears and eyes show that it is a vole, not a mouse.

This is the most common rodent of open areas at low elevations; it is active in the morning and late afternoon in habitat that humans use, so we see it frequently. Meadow voles live in runways among grasses and sedges, their usual foods. They also eat lichens. They are active year-round, but they seldom venture above the snow, preferring to forage in tunnels they dig easily in the loose depth-hoar snow found at the base of the snowpack. In summer they swim well, diving into marshes to escape predators—but sometimes they are eaten by trout or pike in so doing.

Like most small mammals, the meadow vole has a home territory when the population is low, 35–350 per hectare. But the population density often increases dramatically, up to 1000 voles per hectare, and when this happens the species becomes communal, sharing runways, toilet places and food caches. Despite this degree of social organization, the animals spend a lot of time fighting, and they maintain tiny inviolate territories around their individual nests. It's life in the city.

The nest is a ball of grass about 15 cm across, placed under a rock or down an unused ground-squirrel burrow when possible, in a grass tussock when not. The species is very clean; soiled bedding is discarded, and in winter new nests are built everywhere under the snow. In spring you can see the little abandoned nests and runs.

Female meadow voles pop out babies at such a rate that a single breeding pair would chain-produce a million descendants in a year if it were not for very heavy predation. And cannibalism in crowded conditions, when unattended children are often eaten by the neighbors.

Breeding starts in April and runs through October. The promiscuous females call squeakily to the males, who run about obliging one and all. There are three or four litters of about six each; gestation time is 20–21 days, weaning 12 days later and maturity at only 25 days. That quick growing-up is essential to meadow-vole survival: the average lifespan is only two months for the spring batch, with 90 percent mortality in the first month. Meadow voles born in fall are more likely to last the winter, when their predators find them harder to get, and thus the species survives until the following spring.

## Heather vole *Phenacomys*
*Phenacomys intermedius* (vole subfamily)
Spring to fall

Fairly common in shrubby montane and subalpine forest, and in shrubby alpine meadows from Pine Pass south; occasional north of the Peace River. Length 14 cm (tail 3.5 cm), weight 30 g. Resembles the meadow vole—see previous item for picture—but is paler and occurs in the same habitat as the red-backed voles. The heather vole is a little grayish-brown beast with a silvery tummy, small ears and eyes and a short wire-like tail. Unlike the other voles, this one has white feet.

More common than once thought, heather voles scuttle unnoticed through forest-floor debris, brush and shrub patches. They are active mainly at twilight, munching the leaves of many subalpine shrubs, chewing up wildflowers and eating berries. In winter they eat the buds and bark of willows, dwarf birch, blueberries and kinnikinnik, caching twigs under the snow for lean weeks. These caches can reach a couple of litres in volume. They also eat lichens. Life-cycle: breeding is from May through August, averaging five to the litter; gestation period is 19–24 days, weaning is 17 days later and sexual maturity is reached at six weeks. Lifespan probably less than a year in the wild.

## Long-tailed vole *Campagnol longicaude*
*Microtus longicaudus* (vole subfamily)
Spring to fall

Fairly common in several kinds of habitat: in grassy forest glades, along stream banks and in bouldery places such as talus slopes. A large vole: length 18 cm (tail 7 cm), weight 45 g. Closely resembles the meadow vole, previous page; long tail is a good identifier. The fur is brown on top, going gray down the sides; belly and feet are gray. Habits not well known, but probably similar to those of meadow vole: grass/sedge eater, diurnal, active under the snow, communal runways in grass or among rocks. Reproduction is unstudied, although this species is not as prolific as the meadow vole.

## Richardson's water vole *Campagnol de Richardson*
*Arvicola richardsoni* (vole subfamily)
Summer and fall

MW

Fairly common from Grande Cache south, in subalpine and alpine marshes, along stream banks and in wet meadows. Length 25 cm (tail 8.3 cm), weight 85 g; our largest vole, almost twice the size of the meadow vole. Easily identified by size when seen out of water. In water it looks like a miniature muskrat, page 616. Reddish-brown back, gray belly and feet; furry tail, dark brown above and light gray below. Very blunt head and small eyes for its size; long claws.

Water voles do spend a lot of time in the water, although they don't seem to feed there; they eat mainly subalpine and alpine wildflowers (especially valerian, lousewort, arnica and lupine). In winter they subsist on willow buds and twigs.

So what are they doing in the water? I have no information on this, except that it seems a good place to avoid predators; they are too large to be eaten by most fish. They are also burrowers, digging networks of shallow tunnels 5–10 cm in diameter in streambanks and along shorelines. The water vole creates a ridge of soil over the tunnel like a mole, the only animal in the Canadian Rockies to do so. (We have no moles. In the far south end, the northern pocket-gopher, page 611, also pushes up soil from underground, but in piles, not in ridges.)

Water voles construct runs at the base of the snowpack, building winter nests in them that are larger than those of other voles and caching vegetation; the nests litter the ground in spring.

Not much is known of the water vole's life cycle, but it breeds from mid-June to early September, producing at least two litters of five each year. Like the other voles, this species is prone to population explosions.

## Brown lemming *Lemming brun*
*Lemmus sibiricus* (vole subfamily)
Summer

MW

On alpine tundra and talus, and in subalpine bogs, from the Peace River north. Length 15 cm (tail only 2 cm), weight 70 g. A vole-like creature rather easily identified by the gray head with yellowish cheeks, gray shoulders, brown back with yellowish sides, buffy gray tummy and very short tail. Pikas, page 619, live in much the same habitat, but are larger and all gray, with much bigger ears.

This is the famous lemming that lives in the north and flings itself into the sea. Lemmings are colonial burrowers, active day and night, although less so on bright days. They dig shallow burrows down to the permafrost, one burrow per family, with a nesting room, an indoor toilet and a couple of bare chambers, function unknown. Lemmings eat grasses and sedges mostly, lichens sometimes, and one another occasionally. They are not true hibernators, but neither do they cache food for the winter; they nibble away at grasses, sedges and willows under the snow, producing snow-runs and grass-ball nests that are exposed when the snow melts.

Now the interesting part. This creature produces one to three litters of seven young (range 4–9) each year, breeding from June through August and sometimes all winter. Despite the best intentions of numerous lemming-devourers—hawks, eagles, weasels, martens, foxes, wolverines, wolves, bears; you name it, it eats lemmings—the population builds and builds, as becomes evident in May or June, when lemming business shuts down so that everybody can leave home and move to higher ground during the spring melt.

This is to avoid drowning in a flooded burrow, but it has the effect of reapportioning territory. When one of these emigrations occurs at the peak of the population cycle, meaning once every 2–5 years, the Arctic suddenly swarms with lemmings. The creatures swim quite well, so they plop into the ocean, probably figuring to be across the lake shortly. In the Canadian Rockies the lemming and vole population cycles are not as extreme.

Gestation: 23 days. Lifespan: less than a year for nearly all; up to 14 months for a few.

### Northern bog lemming *Campagnol-lemming boréal*
*Synaptomys borealis* (vole subfamily)
Summer and fall

Occasional in black-spruce bogs, grassy marshes and damp shrubby meadows at all elevations, but mostly subalpine. Scarce south of Crowsnest Pass. Length 13 cm (tail 2.5 cm), weight 33 g. Smaller than the brown lemming but similar (see previous item for picture), this species is differentiated mainly by features of the skull. This is hard on the subject; a peek in the mouth will tell the tale sometimes: if the incisors appear quite broad and have conspicuous lengthwise grooves, it's a bog lemming.

Bog-lemming foods include grasses and sedges, winter and summer. The animals are burrowers in summer and snow-tunnel dwellers in winter; they store food in runways and build winter nests of grass, like the voles do. Reproduction habits are little known; breeding is May to August, four to the litter (range 2–8). This species does not have mass emigrations and doesn't seem to suffer the boom-and-bust cycle of its relatives.

## Chipmunks and striped ground squirrels (Sciuridae)

Chipmunks are solitary, active only in daylight and not very shy; they run about nervously with their tails held upright, while ground squirrels let their tails droop. Chipmunks have stripes on their heads as well as on their backs, while striped ground squirrels do not have stripes on their heads.

During summer, most chipmunks like to spend their evenings in woody places: abandoned woodpecker tree-holes—they are good climbers—hollow logs and stumps. But in late summer each digs a winter burrow about 2 m long, with two entrances leading to a roomy nesting and storage chamber about a metre underground. One entrance is used to eject the soil; when the nesting chamber is finished, this hole is plugged well and the other one, which has no dirt around it, is used for going in and out. This is a clever bit of work, but it also leaves the animal no emergency exit in case a snake or weasel comes slithering down.

### Least chipmunk *Tamia mineur*
*Eutamias minimus* (squirrel family)
Spring to fall

Common along forest edges and in rocky places at any elevation, except between Golden and the Peace River on the western slope (the Columbian forest area); common again to the north. Length 22 cm (tail 10 cm), weight 43 g. Of our three chipmunks, this is nominally the smallest; the range of sizes overlaps. The least chipmunk is striped like the others, with two white lines on the face. One line runs from nose to ear above the eye, the other from lower eye to ear. There are four gray lines along the back, bordered in black, and burnt-orange patches on the shoulders and flanks. The belly is white. The tail is fluffy, dark-brown above and yellowish below. To differentiate positively from the very similar yellow pine chipmunk, next item, is nasty, requiring dissection, but note that the least chipmunk is grayish while the yellow pine chipmunk is, in fact, yellowish, and that the habitats are somewhat different.

The least chipmunk eats strictly seeds, especially those found in succulent fruits and berries. These it needs for the spring and early summer, before the year's new seeds are available. If you see a pile of discarded raspberry pulp, you know who has been there. Its fruit-eating neighbors must love this critter. It has pouches inside its cheeks, which it stuffs with food to be eaten later or carried home.

MW

A grassy nest is built in the burrow, right on top of a couple of litres of stored seeds. These it needs for the winter; the least chipmunk hibernates fitfully, awakening every now and again and heading to the larder for a bite to eat. Torpor begins in mid-October and ends in mid-April, which is breeding time. Gestation of 28–30 days produces 4–7 young once a summer in the Rockies; they hang around with mum for two months before leaving home. She sometimes carries them around by the loose skin on their tummies or necks.

The least chipmunk chatters noisily when threatened by a dog, but it does not seek much protection. It usually just runs under a shrub. The dog could easily reach into the shrub and catch it, but it doesn't. It keeps a little distance, turning its head. Chipmunk chirps have high-frequency harmonics beyond the range of human hearing; maybe this is a form of sonic defence.

### Yellow pine chipmunk *Tamia amène*
*Eutamias amoenus* (squirrel family)
Spring to fall

In dry montane forests from Grande Cache south, common in the Douglas-fir woods of the southern Rocky Mountain Trench. Length 22 cm (tail 10 cm), weight 50 g. Very similar to the least chipmunk (see previous item for picture), with same marking pattern, but brighter and with more yellow. South of the Bow River the yellow pine chipmunk tends to stay in dry forested areas at low elevations, while the least prefers moist forest openings and fringes at or near treeline. North of the Bow River the least chipmunk is mainly at *low* elevations, while the yellow pine chipmunk lives in upper montane and lower subalpine forests. Otherwise the habits and life cycle are quite similar, although the yellow pine chipmunk eats more than just seeds, taking flowers, fruits and roots as well.

### Red-tailed chipmunk *Tamia à queue rousse*
*Eutamias ruficaudus* (squirrel family)
Spring to fall

Fairly common in the Waterton/Glacier area, usually in subalpine forest but also at lower elevations. Length 23 cm (tail 10 cm), weight 60 g. A little larger and stockier than the yellow pine chipmunk, rather easily differentiated in the small part of the Canadian Rockies in which the ranges overlap because the red-tailed does indeed have a reddish tail, both top and bottom, while tails of the yellow pine and least chipmunks are brown above and tawny or ochre-colored below. The red is especially noticeable underneath.

There is little information available on the red-tailed chipmunk. It is diurnal like other chipmunks, known to spend much of its time scampering through the lower branches of Engelmann spruces and subalpine firs. It's inclined to be noisy, the chatter reminiscent of the red squirrel's scolding, page 611. Eating habits and life cycle unknown.

### Golden-mantled ground squirrel *Spermophile à mante dorée*
*Spermophilus lateralis* (squirrel family)
Spring to fall

MW

Common from Grande Cache south, in dry, rocky places, mainly at subalpine and alpine elevations. Length 30 cm (tail 10 cm), weight 230 g. Much bigger than any chipmunk, this ground squirrel nonetheless looks and acts rather like one. It has two white stripes running from neck to hips, bordered by black; the rest of the back is salt-and-pepper gray. The lower sides and tummy are buffy, while the head and shoulders—the "mantle"—are yellow-ochre, brown or reddish.

This species is gregarious, living in small groups and often in the company of chipmunks, hoary marmots or pikas. It is livelier than other ground squirrels, running quickly about by day to eat and gather the seeds, leaves, flowers and fruits of a wide variety of subalpine shrubs and wildflowers. Like the voles, it also eats underground fungi and grabs what insects it can.

What the golden-mantled ground squirrel likes best is anything coming from human hands. These are the junk-food junkies of the rodent world. At the roadside viewpoints that frequently fall within their rugged habitat they are out in force on any sunny summer day, boldly coming up to be fed, climbing onto the shoes of delighted humans and sometimes even climbing up their legs. This is cute, but it is not particularly healthy behavior. Most of the food the squirrels receive is either very sweet or very salty, and it's loaded with chemical preservatives. One wonders what happens to their body chemistry from accumulated Cheezie toxins and Ding-Dong byproducts unknown to nature. For years many a park naturalist, including me, told the listeners at the evening campfire program that human food would kill ground squirrels during hibernation. This was always part of the obligatory don't-feed-the-animals remarks. But a study of the effect of human foods on mice and voles (S. Gilbert and C. Krebs, 1981, *Oecologia* 51) suggests that these animals do better with junk food than without it! Whether the same can be applied to other ground squirrels and chipmunks is unknown.

This still leaves one very good reason for discouraging people from attracting ground squirrels to their hands and allowing them to scamper on their clothing: the animals often have fleas, and the fleas have been known to carry bubonic plague in the Rockies.*

Unlike the burrows of other ground squirrels, there is no mound of dirt to mark the entrance to a golden-mantled's rather simple workings. These are usually 1–2 m in length and only half a metre deep, with a single chamber at the back holding a bed of shredded vegetation and a litre or two of seeds. A couple of side passages serve for pissoir and additional storage.

Hibernation is deep but not continuous in the Canadian Rockies. Nodding off in September, the squirrels rouse themselves every few days to eat and urinate. They don't seem to drink anything all winter. The males emerge first, in mid-April. When the females come out a couple of weeks later the breeding season is on and one litter of 4–6 young is produced in early summer. Gestation time is probably similar to that of other ground squirrels, about 28 days. The kids leave home in mid-summer; they are ready to mate by the following spring. In captivity these animals have lived for 11 years, a very long time for a small rodent species.

### Thirteen-lined ground squirrel *Spermophile rayé*
*Spermophilus tridecemlineatus* (squirrel family)
Spring to fall

Occasional in the southern foothills from Calgary south, in shrubby areas and aspen stands not far from water. Length 27 cm (tail 10 cm), weight 150 g.

Much bigger than a chipmunk, but striped and thus often mistaken for one. However, there are no lines on the cheeks of the squirrel, the ears are small and the tail is not as bushy. The 13 lines include seven wide brown stripes with pale dashes in them; there are six pale stripes separating the brown ones.

MW

Like the golden-mantled ground squirrel, previous item, this one is diurnal. It eats far more insects—mostly grasshoppers, crickets and caterpillars—than greenery. Insects are salty,

*Although plague is not associated with the golden-mantled ground squirrel, it is with Richardson's, next page, and the Columbian ground squirrel, page 609. Plague is easily cured nowadays, but there have been deaths from it in the Rockies because the flu-like symptoms have not been recognized in time for treatment.

which explains why this species needs to drink water. The other ground squirrels do not. Further, it is the only one that would rather live in the shade than out in the open.

The thirteen-lined is fairly vocal, uttering shrill cries that are difficult to pinpoint among the shrubbery. It is solitary, digging a burrow up to 5 m long and 2 m deep. There is a large chamber at the end, with a ball-nest of grasses among hoarded seeds. A second entrance is dug from the inside under a grass tussock. The tailings are used to plug the first entrance and thus to provide a hidden entry point with no telltale dirt. There is a 90° bend a little way along to discourage excavation by badgers.

Hibernation begins usually in late September. Lab study shows that the body temperature drops from the normal 36–38°C to just above freezing; the pulse drops from 100–200 per minute to 1–15, which is typical for species of ground squirrels in the Canadian Rockies. The animal cannot be aroused by prodding, but wakes up voluntarily every week or two for a nibble and a pee.

In early April it is time to head outside for breeding. Because this species is solitary, the males must search widely for females. Males fight each other when they meet. The litters are large, average of eight, but there is just one litter each year. Gestation period is 27–28 days. The young venture above ground in early July, leaving about ten days later to dig their own burrows. They are sexually mature by the following spring.

## Unstriped ground squirrels, and the only true gopher

Many people call unstriped ground squirrels "gophers," but they are not. I have included the northern pocket gopher in this section, for comparison.

### Richardson's ground squirrel  Spermophile de Richardson
*Spermophilus richardsonii* (squirrel family, Sciuridae)
Spring to fall

Very common in the foothills from the Bow River south, in grassland, dry open places such as pastures and along roadsides. Length 28 cm (tail 7.5 cm), weight 300– 600 g. Identifiers: buff belly and flanks, black-tipped hairs peppering the head and back, and black streaks in the tail, which is furry but not lush. Large almond-shaped black eyes set high on the head, small ears, black whiskers.

There are various folk names for this beast. "Gopher" and "prairie dog" are commonly used, but both are erroneous, for we have no prairie dogs and only one species of gopher; see page 611. Another name, "picket pin," is more on the mark. It refers to the animal's habit of sitting up so straight that it looks from a distance like a wooden stake of the kind used to tie a horse out in pasture.

Richardson's ground squirrel is a creature of the open prairie, living at the northwestern limit of its range in the Canadian Rockies. It is active in the daytime, spends a lot of time above ground and is thus easy to watch, foraging for grasses and wildflowers, of which it eats all the parts, including the roots and seeds. From time to time the animal sits motionless on its heels atop the dirt pile at the main burrow entrance. This gives it a good view and makes it hard to see from above. When something threatens—a hawk, a coyote, a person—it cries "tweep!" as it twitches its tail once and pops underground. Because the squirrels are loosely colonial (they live near one another but don't share burrows or food stores), there is usually at least one squirrel on guard while the others are concentrating on food-gathering. Thus warned, all rush below ground, squealing.

The burrows are 7–8 cm in diameter, 4–15 m long and 1–2 m deep; they are maze-like, with interconnecting passages and several rooms. The main entrance is obvious, marked by a large pile of excavated dirt; there are also a half-dozen or so inconspicuous entrances called "funk holes," which the squirrel uses for quick escapes. The nesting chamber is lined with grass and seed hulls. There may also be seed-storage rooms, despite Richardson's reputation as a champion hibernator. Adult males often go into **estivation** (summer dormancy) in mid-July, not emerging until the first warm weather of late March or early April. Females go to bed in mid-August, while juveniles can remain active until November in a mild autumn. So why store extra food? It may help the squirrels get through the first unpredictable weeks of spring, when snow can arrive suddenly and cover the sparse spring vegetation for several days. Richardson's also eats insects and carrion, including its own dead.

Breeding occurs right after hibernation; one litter a year of 5–11 is born about the end of April (gestation 22–23 days). The young come above ground in late June and reach sexual maturity in time for next spring's mating. Late summer of its first year is the toughest time in a ground-squirrel's life. That is when the current crop of juveniles disperse, engaging in a deadly serious game of musical chairs in which too many squirrels compete for too few territories. Most of the youngsters get gobbled by coyotes and hawks, especially by red-tailed hawks.

In the spring, Richardson's ground squirrels are famous for flaunting themselves before that most wasteful of predators, the automobile. Ravens sit along the fencelines and wait for meals to be served. Driving west from Calgary or Lethbridge in spring, you may see dozens of squirrels along the highway shoulders, inching jerkily out into traffic and sitting upright in the middle of the road as the cars bear down. ("Hmmm . . . the ground's hard out here, but what the heck, it's unclaimed territory.") Any squirrel setting up shop on the TransCanada is doomed, of course, although it may survive a few encounters by coolly letting the monsters pass over.

Ranchers and farmers shoot, trap and poison Richardson's ground squirrel, blaming it for eating their grain and hurting their livestock, which sometimes break their legs by stumbling in its holes. But these same folks also kill the coyotes that would otherwise gladly keep the ground-squirrel population under control.

## Columbian ground squirrel *Spermophile du Columbia*

*Spermophilus columbianus* (squirrel family, Sciuridae)
Spring to late summer or early fall
Common on meadows at all elevations from Pine Pass south, except where replaced at low elevations by Richardson's ground squirrel, previous item. Length 35 cm (tail 10 cm), weight 400–1000 g. This may be an illusion, but it seems to me that the higher the elevation, the larger these squirrels become.

MW

In alpine meadows the squirrels are often mistaken for marmots, next item. This is understandable, for the salt-and-pepper back coloration of the two species is similar. But the Columbian ground squirrel is much smaller, and burnt-orange or reddish on the nose, chin, belly, legs and feet, while the hoary marmot is bigger and drably colored all over, except for some tawniness under the legs and in the tail. Its feet are black.

Columbian ground squirrels behave rather like Richardson's, active only in the daytime and living in small colonies in which each member has its own burrow. They graze nearby, eating the roots, stems and leaves of a great variety of wildflowers and shrubs. They are more arboreal than might be imagined; I have seen them climbing up into the lower limbs of subalpine larch trees to eat the needles. Like Richardson's, Columbians sit upright at their burrow entrances and dodge in when alarmed. They say "tweep" sharply and repeatedly, such that I have been fooled into thinking that I was hearing the alarm note of a robin—but where is the bird? Hikers on tundra trails will set off whole meadowfuls of these squirrels.

The burrow is wonderfully engineered. A main entrance with dirt mound angles downward for about a metre, then levels off and leads into a large central chamber about 75 cm across that contains bedding of grass or plant down. Radiating off are 3–20 m of tunnels that underlie the feeding area; placed along them are hidden entrances for quick dives underground. Disrespectful of this technology, grizzly bears rip up the workings to gobble the workers.

In August the squirrel digs a special tunnel to its solitary hibernation chamber, typically 40–80 cm deep in our area, which it lines thickly with dried grass. To drain away any water that might percolate down, just off the chamber there is a sump tunnel that goes up to half a metre deeper. Entering the winter den in late August, early October in the high country, the squirrel plugs the entrance of its chamber with soil and curls up tightly. In spring, it doesn't simply push out the plug and proceed through the house to the front door; it digs directly upward to the surface. Emergence is in early April in the valleys, as late as mid-June above treeline.

Then it is mating time, with lots of fighting among the males, who have been up and about for ten days already. They chase the females. The children arrive about 24 days later, one litter of four (range 2– 7) each year. They are weaned after a month, at which time you see them above ground for the first time; maturity and reproduction don't occur until the following spring at low elevations, in the second spring higher up. The average lifespan is five years, with a maximum of 11 years for males and 13 years for females—much longer than that of other ground-squirrel species. Unlike Richardson's, Columbian ground squirrels seldom play in traffic.

Occasional bubonic-plague cases in the mountains show that Columbian ground squirrels carry fleas that harbor the disease. Don't handle these squirrels or allow them to climb on you.

## Hoary marmot *Marmotte des rocheuses*
*Marmota caligata* (squirrel family, Sciuridae)
Summer and fall

Common in alpine meadows from the Bow River north, less common to the south. Length 72 cm (tail 21 cm), weight up to 5.8 kg. "Hoary" refers to the long, coarse, white-tipped coat. A dark patch on the light forehead continues as two smudgy lines over the ears and down the neck. There is a black line across the nose, and the feet are all quite black. The lower back and rump are brownish, and the short, bushy tail is often streaky tawny/black. Underneath, the animal is gray, usually tawny on the inside of the legs.

MW

Some people confuse the marmot with the Columbian ground squirrel, previous item, despite their differences in size and coloration. One need only look at the paws: if they are black, it is a marmot.

The **yellow-bellied marmot,** *M. flaviventris,* is smaller and yellower. It lives at low elevations near the Rockies in the southern area, and you just might see it in the southern foothills or the southern Rocky Mountain Trench.

Marmots whistle (well, vocalize) a loud, long note. Folk names include "whistler" and "whistle-pig." No matter what you call it, the marmot is a close relative of the **woodchuck/groundhog,** *Marmota monax,* which comes close to the Rockies from Rocky Mountain House north, but doesn't quite make it into the foothills. Woodchucks also live in the Columbia Mountains just west of the Rockies, and they cross the Rocky Mountain Trench occasionally, turning up in the Radium Hot Springs area and in Mount Robson Provincial Park.

Marmots have an enviable life. They seem to have little to do in the summer except loll about in lush alpine meadows, eating anything green. They also eat lichens. They have few predators. Golden eagles pick them off from the air, grizzly bears dig up their burrows in summer, and wolverines go after them underground at any time of year.

A marmot burrow is short and simple, dug among boulders with a grass-lined chamber at the end. Like most other ground squirrels, marmots are loosely colonial, nesting near one another; families sometimes share burrows. They end hibernation in late April or early May, digging their way out through the lingering high-country snow-cover. What do they live on until the meadows green up in June? Food squirreled away the previous fall, one would suppose, but there is no mention in the literature of marmots storing food. Here is a mystery waiting to be solved.

Marmots mate every other year. Four or five little marmots poke their noses above ground in July, and everyone goes back to bed in September.

**Northern pocket gopher** *Gaufre gris*
*Thomomys talpoides* (pocket-gopher family, Geomyidae)
Active year-round, but unseen

MW

Common in Waterton/Glacier and the southern Rocky
Mountain Trench, at low elevations in moist meadows with deep,
fine soil. Fossorial (living underground) and thus seldom seen. Length 23 cm (tail 6.5 cm), weight
140 g. Blunt-headed and mole-like, with strong clawed feet, this animal has tiny pink ears that
are visible under the short coat, which is inclined to mimic the soil color of the region in which it
lives. There are white patches under the chin, and large dark areas behind the ears. The eyes are
small, and the large yellow incisors always show because the lips close behind them.

This is the only true gopher in the Canadian Rockies; the other rodents people call "gophers"
here are actually ground squirrels.

Pocket gophers are so named because they have external cheek pouches: fur-lined pockets
on the sides of their faces, extending from cheek to shoulder, opening toward the back and not
connected through to the mouth. The gophers use their front feet to stuff these pockets with cut
plant stems and roots, emptying them later underground.

The species is solitary and subterranean, emerging seldom and then only at night, but you
can easily find its sign: low piles of soil pushed up from underground, with no hole to be seen.
The gopher digs its burrow by loosening soil with its front feet and kicking it back; after a
while it turns and bulldozes the lot out to the surface. Water voles, page 604, also push up soil
from underground, but in lines directly above their tunnels. Pocket gophers don't make these
ridges, although they burrow in the base of the snowpack like many other rodents, lining their
snow runs with soil that remains for a while after the snow has gone.

Main foods: grasses and wildflowers eaten mostly while burrowing. The incisors nip off
roots, and whole plants are pulled down from underground. The shallow feeding tunnels branch
off from a deeper system dug below the frostline. There are storage rooms for laying in winter
supplies of greenery and roots—the animals don't hibernate—and a chamber for the grassy nest.

Breeding is in May and June; the young are born in late June or early July. There is
usually just one litter of four (range 1–8). Gestation period: 19 days. The young are on their
own after 6–8 weeks and must leave mum's burrow, resulting in a fall gopher-feast for predators.
The average lifespan of those youngsters that get safely back underground is 3–4 years; sexual
maturity comes at 11–12 months.

## *In the trees: squirrels and sometimes a porcupine*

See also the marten, page 621.

### Red squirrel *Écureuil roux*
*Tamiasciurus hudsonicus* (squirrel family, Sciuridae)
Year-round

MW

Very common in montane coniferous forest, less common in
subalpine forest. Length 31 cm (tail 12.5 cm), weight 190 g.
Despite its name, the red squirrel is not particularly red in the
Canadian Rockies. The summer coat is olive brown with pale buff
or gray underparts; in winter the coat is thicker, finer and redder.
The tail, though, is usually reddish above and grizzled black/gray
below, with a dark tip. There is always a white ring (two crescents,
really) around the eye.

Ubiquitous, mostly diurnal and not at all shy, this is probably our most commonly seen
wild mammal, although the voles and mice outnumber it many times over. It is also the only
tree squirrel in the Canadian Rockies that one is *likely* to see; the northern flying squirrel, next
item, is nocturnal and much less common. Red squirrels are quite vocal, chattering loudly at
passersby. They sound rather like a kid's pull-toy noisemaker that is dragged quickly at first,
then slower and slower as the puller tires.

This species is mostly arboreal, but in the Canadian Rockies it nearly always nests in the ground, not in trees. Although summer nests of twigs are reported here, I have never identified one. People commonly confuse witches' brooms in spruce (see page 258) with squirrel nests.

Each squirrel maintains a territory of 1–2.5 ha that includes a large trash heap called a **midden.** The burrow lies in and under it; there are several entrances. These animals are cone-shuckers. They eat the seeds, discarding the scales in the midden, which can be 10 m across and a metre deep. It is the home of just one squirrel, or of a female and her babies.

Most middens are large and deep, with many years of rot evident in the lower layers. Inspecting these heaps, which are made up mostly of cone scales, shows that the favorite cone species in the Rockies seem to be white spruce and black spruce. Lodgepole pine cones are less popular, which stands to reason because they are quite hard. The animals collect few Douglas-fir cones, and I haven't seen the cones of subalpine fir in the middens, either. I often find lodgepole-pine galls (branch swellings; see page 254) on the middens, their bark gnawed away. I could find no reports on this, but the squirrels may chew the galls because the cambium layer just under the bark is full of sugars and plant substances created in the rapid growth of the gall.

Besides conifer seeds, red squirrels eat many other things: buds, bark, catkins and plant fruits, including the bitter berries of junipers, as well as lichens, insects, birds' eggs, nestlings, baby rodents and carrion. The squirrels hang mushrooms in the crooks of branches to dry, and they dig for subterranean fungi.

In exchange, lots of things eat squirrels. Their main predators are tree-climbing martens, page 621, and tree-raiding hawks such as Cooper's, page 537, with coyotes, wolves and lynx taking them on the ground. Forest fire is an obvious threat, although squirrels in the Canadian Rockies burrow among their middens and may survive minor fires in this way.

Red squirrels don't hibernate, but neither do they spend much of the winter in the trees. In fall they collect cones, piling them according to species on the midden. When the snow comes the piles are covered, and the squirrel connects them to its midden tunnels with short snow-runs. It stays below during very cold weather, drowsing the days away, but comes out on the warmer afternoons to patrol its territory.

Breeding occurs in either early spring or early summer, at which time the males chase the females noisily up and down tree trunks and from tree to tree. After gestation of about 35 days there is a litter of five or so, born naked and helpless. They quickly get furry and stay with mum for about 18 weeks. Then each must locate a new territory. Since the life span of an established adult can reach ten years, it is certain that the surviving proportion of each generation is quite small—or the mountains would be overrun with red squirrels. Population explosions do occur from time to time.

Red-squirrel behavior around humans is puzzling. Sometimes a squirrel that is busy on the ground will let me pass closely by with little interest, while at other times a squirrel 10 m up a tree and 10 m away will go shrieking farther up the trunk, scolding me until I'm out of earshot.

## Northern flying squirrel *Grand Polatouche*

*Glaucomys sabrinus* (squirrel family, Sciuridae)
Spring to fall

MW

Common in montane coniferous woods, yet seldom seen because the species is strictly nocturnal. Length 30 cm (tail 14.5 cm), weight 180 g. Easily identified in flight—in *glide,* really; they don't actually fly—by the thin furry membrane that stretches from the front paws to the back paws. It is gray, buff at the edges. The rest of the critter is brown. The eyes are quite large, and there is no eye-ring as in the red squirrel, previous item.

Becoming active well after dark, flying squirrels scramble about the conifers and jump from tree to tree in search of lichens, buds, seeds and fruits. Like the red squirrel and the voles, they have a taste for truffles and other underground fungi, the spores of

MW

which they help to spread. Flying squirrels are much less dependent on cones than red squirrels are, and they spend more time in shrubs. Occasionally they produce a chirping call.

In winter the squirrels remain in their nests, which they build in hollow trees or large woodpecker cavities. They fight the cold with lots of nesting material and stock other cavities with cached food. They don't go underground or use snow runs as the red squirrel does.

Winter or summer, flying squirrels live in family groups, male and female sharing the nest with the young. Breeding occurs in early spring, with one litter of three born each year in May. That is a low reproduction rate for the squirrel family; the chances of survival must be pretty good. Gestation period is probably about 40 days; weaning is at about 65 days and climbing/gliding ability is not well developed until 90 days—a long apprenticeship in the rodent world.

## Porcupine *Porc-épic d'Amérique*

*Erethizon dorsatum* (New World porcupine family, Erethizontidae)
Year-round

Fairly common in coniferous woods; usually seen at subalpine elevations. Mostly nocturnal, but also seen frequently in the daytime. Length 77 cm (tail 21 cm), weight 6.5 kg or more. Our second-largest rodent after the beaver, the porcupine is easily identified by its long yellow-and-black quills. The small blunt black face shows at the front of this peculiar armor; the short flat tail drags along behind. It may assist in climbing.

MW

Porkies are well-protected by some 30,000 sharp, stiff, hollow, barbed spines that are modified hairs. Native peoples throughout North America have sewn short sections of these quills onto apparel as decoration, sometimes dyeing them other colors. Besides the face, the only un-quilled parts of a porcupine are the legs and belly. Under attack the animal protects these places by turning its back on the assailant, when possible placing its head between two rocks, against a log, or in some other protective spot. It seldom curls up. The quills fluff out, covering the feet, and the tail flops back and forth—an effective weapon, for it swipes quickly and the quills detach easily. Successful enemies, which are mainly the fisher, lynx, cougar, wolverine and wolf, attack by biting the face. They hold the mouth and nose closed, killing the porcupine by suffocation, not by biting the underside as some people believe. Any would-be porky predator risks blinding, or starvation from a mouth full of quills, or a punctured gut from eating quills.

If stupid Spot gets quilled-up, veterinarians recommend that you bring him in as soon as possible, for the quills work their way in deeper and deeper until removed. If you must do the job yourself, don't cut the end off each quill; this only causes splintering. Muzzle the dog, grab the pliers and start pulling. Deep quills may have to be pushed out the other side of a pinched-up skin flap, which is not as painful as it sounds. Quills in the cheeks and lips can be pushed through rather easily, although

*Porcupine tracks are unmistakable. I saw these at treeline, as I often do in the winter. The animals gnaw the resinous bark of the subalpine firs that grow there.*

somebody wearing heavy gloves must keep the dog's mouth open. Any spines embedded around the nose are particularly painful to remove because they must be pulled, not pushed. Best advice: keep your pets tied up in porcupine country. Occasionally an unwatchful parent will let a toddler play with a porcupine, an early and unforgettable lesson that nature can be nasty.

Porcupines are solitary. They roam over territories less than a square kilometre, climbing shrubs and trees to eat leaves in summer and strip bark in winter. Porkies don't eat the bark; they remove it to gnaw the sugary cambium layer beneath. They eat Lyall's larch needles. They feed mainly at night; in the day they climb up high to sleep in safety.

And they crave sodium, meaning they crave salt. This leads them to gnaw outhouse seats to get the salty dried urine. Wooden-handled tools are also appealing. The animals have a taste for sodium-rich painted or varnished signs, which they edit randomly, e.g.

> *Danger! Hikers are warned that the . . .*
> *. . . in this area. Parks Canada.*

Porcupines chew up plywood and cardboard to get the glue (more sodium), and they love to gnaw rubber, including the road-salty tires and brake lines of vehicles parked overnight in the woods. Some people fence their cars with chicken wire to prevent this.

Porkies don't burrow. They use natural shelters such as boulder piles, cracks in cliffs and jackstrawed fallen trees. They use no nesting material, and they eject existing litter. Then they excrete in their dens. Predators have learned to look along highways for porcupines curled up in culverts. One night a porcupine simply walked right into my tiny one-person tent, stepping on me in my sleeping bag until I twitched. Then it turned around somehow (whew!) and walked back out. Now I keep my porcupine netting zipped. In winter the animals spend more time in their shelters, but they don't hibernate.

Breeding occurs in mid-to-late October in our area. Question: how do they do it? Answer: carefully. This is the oldest joke in biology.

Really, now: how *do* porcupines mate? A male locates a female in a tree and stays near, sometimes for days as he waits for her to become receptive. He grunts and hums sweet nothings. She squeals in reply. If other suitors come around, they fight for her, quilling each other. They must bite away some of their own quills and fur to remove imbedded enemy ones. Eventually the female comes down to the ground to mate. He hoses her with urine. Then she flips her tail up over her back (the underside of the tail has no quills) and he gets his reward, mounting her in the usual mammalian way.

Two-hundred and ten days later she produces only one baby, born in May or June. It weighs about 500 g, with fur and soft quills, and is able to see right away. This is all unusual; most rodents produce large litters of tiny, blind, naked babies after short gestations. Young porcupines nurse a long time: about 125 days. They follow mum around for four months, going on their own after that but not reaching sexual maturity until their second year. Females stay close to home for six months; males don't seek new territories for four years.

## *In the water: beavers, muskrats and sometimes an otter*

See also the northern water shrew (page 598), Richardson's water vole (page 604) and the mink (page 622).

### Beaver *Castor*
*Castor canadensis* (beaver family, Castoridae)
Active year-round, but not seen in winter

Fairly common in montane marsh ponds of its own creation, also in natural ponds and slow-moving streams. Length 105 cm (tail 44 cm), weight 20 kg. This is our largest rodent. Beavers are blunt-bodied and brown, with small eyes and ears, and a large flat hairless tail that is gray to dark-brown and

MW

appears scaly. It is used as a prop while standing up to gnaw and for whacking the water as an alarm before diving. Beavers are likely to be confused only with muskrats, next page.

That is just the start of an astounding list of adaptations: a dense undercoat of fur for insulation in the water; lips that close behind the incisors for underwater chewing; self-stopping ears and nostrils for diving; large back feet with webbed toes for swimming; two serrated claws on each hind foot for combing oil through the coat from large oil glands located by the anus; other glands that discharge **castoreum** for scent-marking; small, well-coordinated front fingers for delicate handling of objects.

Their behavior is as interesting as their bodies. Essentially nocturnal, beavers are also active in the early morning and the early evening, when there is enough light to watch them swimming slowly and smoothly about their ponds. As they make their way through marshes and along the shores, they squirt musky-smelling castor oil onto mud-pie scent posts and scratch the mud with their claws. This seems to be more than simple territory-marking; some biologists think that the communications are meant for group-members, all of whom do a lot of sniffing and squirting ("Gone for willows. Back in five minutes. —Al.") Females are dominant in beaver society.

Beavers are bark-eaters like porcupines, going for the nutritious cambium layer in willows, birch, balsam poplar, cottonwood and aspen, their favorite. They also eat leaves and twigs, and the seeds of some water plants. Conifers are the last resort. It takes half a hectare of medium-sized aspen to support one beaver for a year, so don't be surprised to walk into your favorite pond-side glade and find it gone. A beaver can bring down an aspen 25 cm in diameter in only a few minutes. Occasionally the tree-feller gets squashed in so doing.

Beavers are well-known dam-builders. Locating a narrowing in a gentle, marshy stream, a family of beavers builds up layers of sticks, logs, roots and stones, plastered together with mud and sod to dam the flow. As the water level rises the dam is extended to the sides and upward, until there is a sizable pond 1–3 m deep. This provides a safe medium for travel to and from the feeding grounds—beavers are slow and awkward on land—which become more accessible as the pond grows. A network of canals is dug through water too shallow for swimming.

When the pond reaches its limit a large **lodge** is built. Prior to lodge construction the animals live in bank burrows; these are maintained after the lodge is done and used for emergencies. The family builds its lodge on a small island or on a platform of sticks and mud in shallow water or against the shore. Placing heavy sticks and logs against a core of lighter vegetation, the animals construct a dome some 2–3 m tall and 3–6 m in diameter; the core is removed from the inside. The walls are heavily plastered with mud, except near the top, which allows ventilation between the sticks, and a couple of tunnels are dug down and out into the water at a level below the thickest winter ice. Inside there is a chamber about 150 cm wide and 75 cm high, dry quarters for the family. This fortified house in the pond amounts to a castle with a moat.

Existing ponds are given up when the food supply runs low, a cyclic occurrence. In the Jasper area, where I have watched beaver ponds for years, the animals usually breach the dam and drain the pond when they leave. This makes sense, because the roots of willows flooded by the pond quickly produce a new stand. In only a few years the beavers can return.

The animals are especially busy in fall, when they are cutting a great deal of vegetation and towing it out into deep water near the lodge. By sticking the ends of saplings and branches into the bottom mud, or simply by stacking under the floating mass, this **raft** reaches from the surface to the bottom and provides food all winter under the ice.

Beavers don't hibernate. When the pond freezes thickly, their predators—grizzly bears, wolves, coyotes, lynx and wolverines—can walk right over to the lodge, but by then it is a concrete-like mass of frozen mud and sticks. Should a foe persist in chewing its way in, bank burrows may provide emergency shelter. River otters, page 617, can enter beaver lodges and pick off the occasional young or feeble individual. Humans cut holes in the ice and stake traps on the bottom, drowning their prey to obtain its fur coat.

Beavers breed in January or February; the gestation time is 3.5 months, which is long for a critter this size. There is one litter every year of about four "kits" (range 1–8) born in late spring. Papa is banished to a bank burrow while the kits are nursing. Upbringing is also long by rodent standards; the young are not put to work until their second summer. You can recognize the juveniles by their white noses.

In summer there are normally three generations in a beaver pond: mum and dad, last year's kits and this year's kits, for a total of 6–8 residents. The following spring the yearlings are chucked out before the next litter arrives. Dispossessed, the juveniles of a family often travel together to a new location that may be up to 200 km away downstream, although it is usually much closer—about 10 km on the average, sometimes across a height of land to a different watershed. Lifespan in the wild: up to 12 years.

---

## *Those blasted beavers have flooded the highway again!*

As humans, our inclination is to blast them back, literally, using dynamite to wreck their dams. This seldom works for long; Canada's national symbol is just as industrious and persistent as it is reputed to be. But there is a solution, discovered in Gatineau Park, near Ottawa. After years of warring with beavers, park-employee Michel Leclair discovered a way of keeping the beavers under control that was effective, cheap, and best of all not hard on them.

Beavers are attracted to the sound of water running over their dam. At these places they build the dam higher. Leclair put a pipe at least a metre under the surface in the pond and drained the water over or through the dam, so that it made no sound leaving the pond. The beavers quit building it higher. A wire cage protected the upstream end of the pipe, and the downstream end could be adjusted to control the level of water in the dam. All that was required was to clean the wire cage from time to time, which the beavers, clever as they are, would plaster over with mud and sticks.

Leclair also discovered how to solve the beaver-vs.-culvert problem. Beavers will plug culverts, turning road embankments into dams and flooding highways. ("Nice of those humans to build this for us; we'll just close this leak, here.") He reasoned that beavers would build a dam *upstream* of a culvert if he started one there, as an enticement. The ploy worked. It was necessary only to make a very small dam, backing up just a little water; the beavers would then continue building the dam, and the water overtopping it would run over and through the culvert. Problem solved.

Now, this is enlightened treatment of animals. It's very different from what usually passes for "management," which is brutality.

---

### Muskrat/water rat *Rat musque*
*Ondatra zibethicus* (family Muridae, New World mice/rats subfamily, Cricetinae)
Spring to fall

Common in wetland ponds and lakes with marshy shores, sometimes in slow-moving streams with good cover along the banks. Length 57 cm (tail 25 cm), weight 1 kg. Muskrats and beavers are sometimes hard for people to differentiate in the water. They have a similar build: chunky and blunt-headed, with small eyes and ears. Both are brown.  But muskrats are half the size of beavers, with narrow, rat-like tails, while beavers have very wide, flat tails. This leads to a difference in swimming style. The muskrat tail whips back and forth, visible in the churning wake, while the beaver tail lies out flat, leaving a smoother wake.

Muskrats are essentially large water-dwelling mice. Well-adapted to their amphibious lives, they have been known to stay underwater for 17 minutes at a time. Their back feet are partly webbed for swimming. Their lips close behind the incisors for underwater gnawing and cutting. In the Canadian Rockies, muskrats eat mainly cattails, bulrushes, tubers, sedges, water milfoil and bladderwort; they have a taste for freshwater clams and take the odd frog or salamander. Having snipped, dug or caught its food, a muskrat takes it to a feeding platform made of mud and plant leaves surrounded by water. After eating it cleans the platform and grooms itself.

Like beavers, muskrats are lodge-builders. They also burrow in muddy banks and dig canals in marshes, which are other beaver-type activities. But they don't build dams. The animals maintain territories about 60 m in diameter, fighting savagely among themselves when challenged. However, I have seen more than one muskrat at work on the same lodge; perhaps the species is gregarious in winter. Muskrat lodges appear in fall, just before freeze-up. These structures are usually located on an emergent spot of land, sometimes a tussock or a log, next to water that is too deep to freeze to the bottom. A dome about a metre high is built up from layers of marsh vegetation and mud. The structure quickly freezes and becomes very strong. Tunnels out the bottom lead into the water. Muskrats also build **push-ups:** holes in the ice covered with vegetation brought up from the bottom. Push-ups are essentially air pockets that allow extended foraging trips under the ice to beds of submerged plants that provide winter food. Muskrats don't hibernate, nor do they store food as beavers do. I have seen them living in abandoned beaver lodges. Their main predators are minks, canids, otters and humans.

Breeding begins in spring. The males become extremely aggressive, occasionally battling each other to the death, which is rare in nature, and even attacking human observers. The females, too, get quite nasty as they compete for bank-burrow dens. During April and May it seems that all muskrats are fighting and bloody, coats and ears torn. Eventually everybody pairs off. Each couple stays together for the summer and following winter, producing two litters of 3–7 young. Gestation is 25–30 days. Births are in late spring or early summer, and weaning occurs in a month. The young muskrats are ready to breed by the following spring. Lifespan of those reaching adulthood is about three years, up to ten years in captivity. The water rat is trapped, drowned and shot for its lovely soft coat. See also Richardson's water vole, page 604.

## River otter *Loutre de rivière*
*Lutra canadensis* (weasel family, Mustelidae)
Year-round

MW

Occasional in lakes and the larger rivers, in clear water that is not silty or polluted; rare south of Banff. Length 110 cm (tail 42 cm), weight 7.5 kg. Otters are about the size of beavers and likewise dark brown, but they are easily differentiated by their swimming style: fast and undulating, alternately breaking the surface and going under. Beavers swim slowly and smoothly, head out flat. The tail of the otter is long, thick and pointed; the cheeks are very whiskery, and the throat is often pale or silvery. The toes are webbed.

Like the much-smaller mink, page 622, the otter is a water weasel. It lives in little family groups of 4–6. The species is mainly nocturnal, although sometimes active on cloudy mornings or afternoons. It generally avoids places frequented by humans, its major predator.

River otters eat mainly fish, with smaller catches of muskrats, small rodents, amphibians and insects; they also take young or enfeebled beavers. Like sea otters, they often float on their backs while dining. But they spend time on land, too, loping about after meadow voles.

Otters are famous for their love of *sliding.* It seems to be part locomotion and part play. They like to enter the water by flopping down well-used muddy runs, and they play on grassy banks or muddy slopes, tobogganing over and over. These slides give their presence away. In winter the animals have a unique way of travelling on snow: they alternately run a few steps and then slide 6–8 m on their tummies. They have been clocked doing this at 25 km/h.

Otters don't hibernate, but during cold snaps they stay in their dens, which are usually unused bank-beaver burrows or abandoned lodges.

Right after one batch of young are born, otters start another. This occurs variably in late winter or early spring, but the embryo doesn't implant in the womb for many months, resulting in a gestation period of up to a year. The single annual litter is small (1–4, usually 2–3). Mum kicks dad out while the kids are little; he returns in six months, by which time they are weaned and venturing out of the den, hunting and playing. Otter families are close, a rarity in the lonely, blood-and-guts world of the weasels, and they stay together a long time. Females are not ready to breed for two years, males not until they are six or seven.

## Hares and rock-rabbits, but no true rabbits

These animals are not rodents. They belong to the order Lagomorpha. Among the differences: lagomorphs have two sets of upper incisors, one behind the other; their front feet have five toes and their back feet have four; their tails are short or absent, and the caecum, which is a pouch in the large intestine near the point where the small intestine comes in, is spiralled. (Humans, too, have a caecum.)

### Snowshoe hare *Lièvre d'Amérique*
*Lepus americanus* (rabbit/hare family, Leporidae)
Year-round

Common in the woods, but mostly nocturnal. Length 48 cm (tail only 5 cm), weight 1.5 kg. "Snowshoe" from the large furry feet. Snowshoe hares moult twice a year; in the summer they are brown or grayish with white tummies; in the winter and spring they are white with black-tipped ears. Moulting animals are mottled.

MW

**Summer**

This is the only bunny you are likely to see in the mountains, although the **white-tailed jackrabbit,** *Lepus townsendii,* is reported occasionally in the southern foothills. It is larger, with very long, jackrabbit-style ears. Those of the snowshoe hare are shorter, 10– 12 cm.

By day this species sleeps fitfully in its **form:** a beaten-down spot under the drooping, thickly needled lower branches of a spruce, sometimes in dense brush or long grass, or under a log in a tangle of fallen trees. At twilight the bunnies emerge to patrol their run-laced ranges of 6–7 ha, often coming out early on a dim December afternoon. At night they stand transfixed in vehicular headlights and are just as likely to run right under the car as off into the bushes. Richard Adams, who wrote a great children's novel about rabbits called *Watership Down,* would say that they are "tharn."

**Winter**

MW

Summer foods: grasses, wildflowers—especially pea-family plants and clover—and new leaves of aspen, willow and birch. In winter they eat the leaves of plants that stay green, such as kinnikinnik and wintergreen, the twig-ends and buds of shrubs, and sometimes lichens. At any time of year they eat their own special fecal pellets, green and made of partly digested food. When the hares are many and starving, they strip bark and eat their own dead.

Breeding begins in mid-March and continues until mid-summer. The males **(bucks)** chase the females **(does)** about with very little fighting among rivals; after a gestation period of 37 days the first litter of 3–4 young **(leverets)** comes along in May. There is usually one more litter that summer, sometimes two. Baby rabbits are born blind and naked, but newborn hares are furry and precocious—a major difference between these two groups.

*Lest anyone doubt the exploratory zeal of the snowshoe hare, these tracks provide proof. The photo was taken close to the summit of Mt. Gordon, one of the peaks of the Wapta Icefield, in March.*

Hares are out of the nest and starting on solid food after only a week. This gets them off the blocks quickly in a race with death that is soon over for most; even among adults, the yearly survival rate is only 10–50 percent, depending on the stage of the population cycle. Principal eaters of our bunnies are owls, lynx, martens and other weasels, cougars, foxes, coyotes, wolves and man.

The reproductive rate in snowshoe hares is so high that there are never enough predators to gobble up the population explosions typical of this species. Surges can send the concentration to 1300 individuals per square kilometre. These booms end in mass die-offs from starvation and disease. At such times the animals harbor many parasites and carry diseases such as **tularemia**, a bacterial infection that is serious in humans. Don't handle wild hares.

### Pika/coney/rock-rabbit *Pica d'Amérique*

*Ochotona princeps* (pika family, Ochotonidae)
Spring to fall

Common from Jasper south, occasional north to Pine Pass, in alpine talus slopes and boulderfields with nearby vegetation; occasionally at lower elevations in slide heaps. Length 19 cm (no tail), weight 115 g. "Pika" is usually pronounced "PIE-ka," although the word is native Siberian and they pronounce it "PEE-ka," in imitation of the call.

MW

The pika looks like a guinea pig but is not closely related; it is a lagomorph like the hares and rabbits, while the guinea pig is a rodent. Pikas have unusual feet: the soles are covered with tiny hairs, good for traction on rocks.

This is a creature that you hear first and see later. Something in the boulders gives forth a nasal "eek." What was that? Not until the pika moves do you see it: a little gray beast with large round ears and no tail. The animal may be sitting on a rock only 5 m away, but it holds very still and the ventriloquistic voice could have come from anywhere.

Pikas eat grasses, sedges, lichens, many kinds of alpine wildflowers and the emerging leaves of alpine willows and dwarf birch. In late summer they collect vegetation and dry it on flat boulders, then take it down into their runs among the jumbled rocks. They also stash their hay under boulders that can be reached through snow burrows. A lot of supplies must be laid in, for winters are long in the Canadian high country and the pika does not hibernate.

Like rabbits and hares, pikas **refect,** meaning that they eat their own dung. This sounds disgusting to us primates, but only special pellets are eaten, soft and green, made of partly digested food. Normal droppings are not eaten.

Pikas live in loose colonies. Each animal has its own territory, perhaps 50 m by 50 m in size. Those members of the group not otherwise occupied act as sentries, moving about from one vantage point to the next and warning everyone of approaching enemies: golden eagles, northern harriers, weasels, wolverines and lynx. The most dangerous is the short-tailed weasel, page 620, which is able to enter pika runs.

A study in southwestern Alberta has shown that pikas there produce 3–5 babies in May. Often another batch arrives in July, but few of the second litter survive. The young are precocious, born furry and active; they are weaned in only 12 days and are nearly grown in a couple of months, although they are not sexually active for at least a year. Lifespan is about 3–4 years.

## Pika trivia

The first identification of a North American pika species was made in an 1828 publication by John Richardson, for whom Richardson's ground squirrel is named. Richardson said that the specimens were "collected near the headwaters of the Athabasca River," meaning probably Athabasca Pass in Jasper National Park.

# Various weasels, the skunk and the raccoon

Welcome to the order Carnivora, the carnivores. These are the smaller ones, which are mostly weasels (family Mustelidae), from the least weasel (45 g) to the most weasel, in our area, the wolverine. Plus the skunk and the raccoon, which aren't in the weasel family but sort of belong in this section, and minus the otter, which is a weasel but has been grouped with the muskrat and beaver (see page 617) because it lives in the water.

## Short-tailed weasel/ermine/stoat *Hermine*
*Mustela erminea* (weasel family)
Year-round

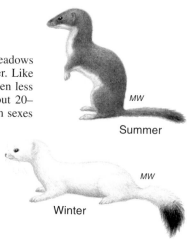

MW

Summer

MW

Winter

Short-tailed weasels are common in subalpine meadows and surrounding forest; less common lower and higher. Like most weasels they are primarily nocturnal and thus seen less frequently than their numbers warrant. Males are about 20–30 percent larger than females; average length for both sexes is 27 cm (tail 7.5 cm), weight 80 g.

Our most common weasel, this one is long and skinny, with large black eyes, a pointed whiskery face with a pink nose, and a fairly short, fuzzy, club-shaped tail. From April to October this species is brown on top and white underneath, with black-tipped tail and white feet; in the snowy months of November to March it is all white, except for the black tail-tip, and termed "ermine." Like the other weasels it has anal scent glands, which stain the fur yellowish under the tail.

Quintessential rodent-eaters, stoats are perfectly adapted to slip down burrows after their prey and to spread terror through the network of winter runs that small mammals make at the base of the snowpack. They are voracious night-time hunters, knocking off mostly voles and mice but also killing ground squirrels their own size and even young snowshoe hares. They have been known to climb trees and kill birds. Ermine swim readily, sometimes to catch fish but usually just to cross streams or to escape their own predators: owls, larger weasel-family members, coyotes and foxes.

Short-tailed weasels kill like other weasels, by quickly biting their prey through the neck vertebrae. Rather than eating the catch on the spot, an ermine usually carries it home to its burrow—which in most cases originally belonged to one of its victims—or to a storage burrow nearby. In winter they keep a few carcasses in the cooler for lean weeks. They also eat carrion.

Breeding begins in June and continues until August. Most females are impregnated in early summer. But the young aren't born until the following spring, in April or May, because the tiny embryo doesn't implant in the uterus and begin growing until March, for a total gestation that lasts up to ten months. Why the long delay? It allows mating to occur at the optimum time and raising of the young to occur at the optimum time, even when these would ordinarily be way out of sync. There are usually six in a litter (range of 4–9). The females grow up quickly: they are ready to reproduce in only 2–3 months. But the males are not sexually active until the next spring mating period, so weasel maidens go with older guys.

Stoats are tied to the boom-and-bust cycles that afflict their prey. When the woods are full of mice there are also a lot of stoats.

Like their cousin the marten, facing page, short-tailed weasels are very good at getting into unattended human dwellings and making off with goodies. They are not fearful of man, nor are they very smart about traps. In Canada some 30,000–40,000 are killed annually by the fur industry.

### Least weasel *Belette pygmée*
*Mustela nivalis* (weasel family)
Year-round

Occasional from the Columbia Icefield north, rare to the south, where it has been reported on the eastern slope in the foothills. Lives in meadows and mixed woods; active only at night. The smallest weasel: adult males are only 20 cm in length (tail 3.5 cm) and weigh only 45 g; females are 10 percent smaller.

The least weasel closely resembles the stoat, previous item, but is a third shorter, with smaller ears and the shortest tail in the weasel tribe. In summer the coat is dark brown above and white below; the feet are white—furry even on the soles—and there are often buffy patches on the cheeks. The winter coat is the whitest of any weasel, with the least black at the tip of the tail. Habits are like those of the stoat.

The smaller the animal, the more it seems to eat for its size. This one goes through about half its body weight in small rodents every day; main prey is the meadow vole. Least weasels also eat insects and amphibians. Burrows are taken in the usual weasel fashion, from their victims, and lined with fur from carcasses, something the stoat does also.

Least weasels breed once each year, anytime between February and December. With a gestation period of 35–37 days (no delayed implantation in this species), the young can be born any time between March and January. They are weaned at 24 days, but their eyes don't open until day 30. Sexual maturity comes at four months, when they leave home.

### Long-tailed weasel *Belette à longue queue*
*Mustela frenata* (weasel family)
Year-round

Occasional in open country, from low-elevation meadows in the foothills to the alpine tundra; perhaps most common above treeline. Nocturnal. Length of adult males 40.5 cm (tail 13.5 cm), weight 225 g; females are about 20 percent smaller.

This species looks very much like the short-tailed weasel, facing page, but it's somewhat larger, with a noticeably longer tail. The summer coat (April to October) is cinnamon brown above and white below, with a black tip on the tail; in winter the animal is all white except for the black tail-tip. Its diet and habits are like that of the short-tailed, but it is inclined to take somewhat larger prey and to eat more birds. Reproduction is also similar, with delayed implantation and litters of six (range 3–9).

Once I was lucky enough to stumble across a den of young long-tailed weasels right beside the trail, under a rock. As I sat and watched, they all came out to have a look at me, some of them coming up to sniff the toes of my boots. Their mother came home and shooed them indoors.

### American marten/American sable *Martre d'Amérique*
*Martes americana* (weasel family)
Year-round

Common in montane and lower subalpine forest; active day and night. Length 60 cm (tail 18 cm), weight 1 kg. Females 15 percent smaller. Typical weasel build, although not as long-bodied as the others and rather easily differentiated by the large ears and pale coloration. In the Rockies the coat is often reddish brown, with charcoal smudges on the legs and on the very bushy tail. The throat and chest of Canadian Rockies martens are often pale or dull orange; the underside is light brown. There is no drastic color change in the winter.

Most of the weasel family are occasional tree-climbers, but especially so the marten, not so much in looking for prey—it does hunt for sleeping birds and squirrels—but mostly for safe snoozing quarters after night-time hunts that take place largely on the ground. Sometimes the animal dens in squirrel middens. Besides the standard rodent-rich weasel diet (red-backed voles are a staple), martens eat many grouse, bugs and berries. They don't pass up carrion, either. And they seem to venture deep into caves, perhaps searching for bats. I have found three marten skeletons in Cadomin Cave, all farther in than 1 km. Not many predators will take on a marten, for they are quite nasty in the clinch. But fishers, lynx and great horned owls will.

Reproduction: martens breed in July and August. Implantation of the blastocyst (early embryo) is delayed until at least the following February, though, so the young are not born until March or April. There is just one litter a year, of 2–3 (range 1–4). The female dens in a leaf-lined tree cavity or among rocks. Development is slow: the eyes don't open until day 39 and weaning isn't until six weeks. It usually takes two years for martens to reach sexual maturity; owing to the timing of the breeding season most young adults don't mate until they are over two years old. Adults use temporary shelters, not burrows.

Martens are not very sociable, and when several converge on the same booty there is bound to be a scene. At Mosquito Creek Hostel a bold marten came down the chimney one early morning in February when I was there. It rattled around in the cold firebox of the wood-burning kitchen stove. The hostellers, snug in their sleeping bags, thought that someone had got up to start the fire, but no crackling ensued, so I investigated. Here was the marten trying to make off with half a chicken we had left out on the table the night before.

Quickly it dragged the bird off the table, across the floor and under the woodbox, where I could hear it crunching away, growling. This annoyed me: there went the chicken sandwiches. So I poked at it with a broom handle—and out came the marten, snarling. Yikes!

The other hostellers were now awake, enjoying the growing fiasco, and I yelled at one of them to open the front door, intending to lob the marten out with a flick of the broom. But the marten was way ahead of me. It quickly dashed back to the woodbox, grabbed the chicken and was out the door with it.

That wasn't the end of the story. Other martens arrived, surrounding the one with the chicken. His problems, it appeared, were just beginning. In the ensuing noisy fight (martens yowl and hiss at one another) the chicken changed hands, I mean mouths, several times, until it was in so many pieces that everybody must have got some.

Here is the woodsy-lore part. Do you know how the martens did their battling? By backing up to each other and *kicking with their hind feet!* The jaws of these beasts are deadly weapons, full of sharp teeth, and if the animals habitually bit one another the species would probably be in trouble. So they have adopted this relatively harmless kick-boxing instead. On occasion, though, they have been seen going at it head-to-head, with gory results.

## American mink   *Vison d'Amérique*
*Mustela vison* (weasel family)
Year-round

Fairly common along streams and lake-shores and in wetlands; seldom alpine. Nocturnal. Length of adult males 55 cm (tail 18 cm), weight 1.5 kg. Females are a little shorter and a good

MW

deal slimmer. Mink are about the same size as martens, but stockier and darker-brown, with shorter ears and blunter faces. As per martens, they don't change color in the winter.

Like otters, page 617, mink spend a good deal of time in streams and ponds, mostly at night, catching small fish, muskrats, water voles, water shrews, frogs and salamanders. They also venture well away from the wet, into grassy places full of sleeping meadow voles.

In winter the mink make use of a peculiar transport corridor: the space between water and ice that opens when stream levels drop after freeze-up. Mink usually live in bank burrows strong-armed from beavers or muskrats—which must not be easy, considering how tough these large rodents are—but sometimes dig their own.

Breeding: mink mate promiscuously in late winter or early spring, then go their separate ways. Implantation of the embryo is delayed such that all the babies, called "kits," arrive at about the same time in any particular region, usually late in April or early in May. The kits, five or so (range 2–10) in the annual litter, are born deaf and blind, not opening their eyes for three weeks. A few days later they are weaned. They follow their mother around until fall comes, when they go on their own. It takes the females a year to mature sexually, the males 18 months.

Despite the growth of mink-ranching, a lot of mink meet nasty ends in traps. (Not that mink-ranching is any less cruel, really.) Fortunately much mink habitat in the Canadian Rockies is either off-limits to trappers or inaccessible for their purposes, and most of the annual mink-kill, known to decimate populations, occurs elsewhere.

## Fisher *Pékan*

MW

*Martes pennanti* (weasel family)
Year-round

Occasional from Crowsnest Pass north, rare in Waterton/Glacier, in subalpine forest, usually near water. Length of males 95 cm (tail 35 cm), weight about 3.7 kg but variable, as in other weasel species; females 15 percent smaller. The fisher is the most sombre-colored weasel, ranging from chocolate brown to black. It is darkest underneath, lightest on the head and shoulders, while with the other weasels it is the reverse. Seen in the twilight or dawn dimness, a fisher looks a lot like a big black cat. Compare with the river otter, page 617.

This creature is misnamed; it seldom catches fish, if at all. Some sources suggest that the name was really meant for the mink, which fishes a lot. Fishers are solitary hunters, active at any time of day or night. They hunt primarily on the ground, often running along the fallen logs that litter the subalpine forest floor. Prey: red-backed voles and snowshoe hares, grouse, deer mice and other rodents. They kill porcupines by biting them across the nose and mouth and thus suffocating them. Fishers are also fond of blueberries and grouseberries, which are common in the upper subalpine woods. The species only has a few predators, mainly the larger hawks and owls and man, who traps it for its fur.

Fishers patrol territories some 15 km across, sheltering among fallen trees or rocks. They travel most actively during mating season in March or April. Implantation of the tiny blastocysts is delayed for about ten months. After a further two months in the womb, the young are born the following spring, between late March and late April, nearly a year after they were conceived. The total gestation is 338–358 days, the longest of any mammal in the Canadian Rockies. The females usually mate again immediately. Litters are small by weasel standards: 1–4 young, average 2–3. The helpless young don't even open their eyes for seven weeks, and they require two years to reach maturity.

In many years of tramping through fisher habitat I have seen two. This demonstrates the need to protect this sparsely distributed animal, which has been wiped out over much of North America by trapping, cutting of the old-growth forests it needs and the indiscriminate use of anti-predator poison.

## Striped skunk *Moufette rayée*

MW

*Mephitis mephitis* (skunk family, Mephitidae)
Late winter to fall

Fairly common south of Crowsnest Pass, becoming scarce farther north, in grassy or shrubby places at low elevations. Reported occasionally in the Rocky Mountain Trench as far north as McBride, and on the eastern slope as far north as Jasper. Mostly nocturnal. Length of males 57 cm (tail 22.5 cm), weight 2.5 kg. Females slightly smaller.

Skunks are boldly marked and readily identifiable, with good reason: that black-and-white pattern tells everyone in the woods to stand aside or suffer the consequences. Like weasels, skunks squirt musk to mark territory, but skunks have also turned the trait to defence. A pair of large musk glands empty into the anus through small spray nipples. When a skunk is threatened it raises its tail, everts the anus to expose the nipples and delivers a blast of oily greenish fluid that reaches out 5–6 m, misting as it goes. Sulphur compounds called **mercaptans** give the stuff such a strong and revolting odor that a predator must be very hungry to continue the attack. A squirt in the face causes momentary blindness, and a skunk can aim quite well by twisting its rump around. Contrary to popular belief, picking up the animal by the tail doesn't prevent it from squirting. Fortunately, skunks are loath to use their repellent in any but life-threatening situations.

Skunks waddle about with impunity, sometimes in daylight and often at dusk, eating nearly anything: grasses, leaves, buds, fruits and berries, insects such as grasshoppers and grubs, small rodents, birds' eggs, fish, snails, amphibians, snakes and carrion. And garbage out of cans in the alley. They are a natural reservoir for rabies.

Skunks live in borrowed burrows when they can, sometimes digging their own or simply sheltering in fallen trees or under buildings. They hibernate—skunks and badgers are the only weasel-like Rockies mammals that do—from early December to March. Often several females and youngsters will curl up together in a grass-lined nest. The males are less sociable and hibernate individually; they arise early, in late February and March, and go searching for females. These they awaken and pester for sex. Thus, for a couple of weeks the woods at night seem full of horny, heedless skunks. At this time the eggs of the great horned owl are hatching, and the owlets are fed largely on male skunk.

Gestation in skunks is about 62 days; the young are born black-and-white, for cradle-to-grave protection, and they acquire the fine art of musk-blasting by seven weeks. They follow mom about at night, staying with her through the ensuing hibernation and leaving in spring to find highways to cross. The rest you know.

## American badger *Blaireau d'Amérique*
*Taxidea taxus* (weasel family)
Spring to fall

Occasional from Valemount south on the western slope and from the Bow River south on the eastern slope, at low elevations in open grassy places. Length 70 cm (tail 14 cm), weight 7 kg. Unmistakable: a fat and flattened-looking animal with a grizzled buff/black back, black-and-white face and black feet with long white claws. Badgers are grassland weasels, uncommon in the mountains but reported a few times every summer, mainly south of Crowsnest Pass. They hunt mostly at night, digging out ground squirrels, pocket gophers and other small rodents, but they also emerge from their burrows in the morning to lie in the sun before the day gets too hot. Like skunks, previous item, badgers hibernate in winter. After an August or September mating, there is one litter a year of four (range 2–5) young in April or May, the long gestation caused by delayed implantation of the embryo, as is the norm in the weasel family.

## Wolverine *Carcajou*
*Gulo gulo* (weasel family)
Year-round

Occasional at subalpine or alpine elevations, in nearly any habitat. Length 100 cm (tail 23 cm), weight 15 kg. Females about 10 percent smaller. If you see something that is large, dark and too small-headed to be a bear, then it might be a wolverine. This beast is thickly furred, mostly dark brown, but with a light band across the forehead and a broad light stripe along each side, extending into the tail.

Wolverines are fierce and aloof, each male patrolling a territory that may cover 1000 km². Females range through 100–500 km². The species follows its nose from carrion-heap to carrion-heap, cracking bones and crunching cartilage between powerful jaws whose dentition resembles that of the African hyena. Wolverines are very protective of their food, supposedly standing their ground even against grizzly bears. When threatened, or doing the threatening, wolverines are quite vocal, snarling, hissing and yowling.

Wolverines hunt, too, readily taking any small mammal—including muskrats and beavers, which are renowned fighters—and they do in the odd porcupine, sometimes dying when ingested quills perforate their stomachs. In winter their favorite prey is marmots, caught by working their way down into the hibernation burrows, much as other weasel-family members go after smaller rodents. In Scandinavia, wolverines have been known to kill reindeer (caribou) in weakened condition, but researchers have not been able to document the taking of prey this large in North America.

These animals are constantly on the move. One winter I happened to ski up the same wilderness river a wolverine was following, always a day ahead of me for four days, covering 60 km before it out-distanced me. In another winter, from the summit of Mt. Balfour I was able to trace with binoculars the tracks of a wolverine that gained the Waputik Icefield from near Takakkaw Falls in the Yoho Valley, crossed it to the Niles/Daly Col and returned the same night to spend the day sleeping under a boulder not far from where it started its jaunt.

Wolverines visit simple shelters along their routes as fishers do, page 623, the females digging in among boulders or heavy fallen trees for the natal lair. The breeding season runs from April to early September. One male tends several mates and keeps other males away. Whether the males fight one another is unknown. Implantation of the embryo doesn't occur until January, delaying birth of the annual litter of 2–5 young until late February to mid-April. Development is quick; the little wolverines are able to leave the den in only a few weeks. They follow mum on her rounds through their first winter and go on their own about a year after birth. Age at mating seems to be about 15 months for females and 2–3 years for males; longevity and many other aspects of wolverine life history are unknown.

This amazing animal has only one predator: man. Humans trap it for its fur. The wolverine is large enough and fierce enough to get even with us, but it doesn't attack people. Instead it attacks human dwellings while no one is home, breaking in and savaging the interiors. An aboriginal name for this animal is "skunk bear," because wolverines mark their kills and their carrion with foul-smelling musk. If your cabin has had a visit from a wolverine, you will probably find that everything edible has either been gobbled up—"Gulo gulo," the Latin name for wolverine, means "Glutton glutton"—or squirted with Eau d'Unbearable. Bedding and mattresses are often ripped up and doused as well.

Mountain huts are sometimes hit by wolverines. Please, fellow climbers and skiers, latch the door well when you leave your high-country haven, or a wolverine may come in and turn it into a skunk-works.

## Raccoon *Raton-laveur*
*Procyon lotor* (raccoon family, Procyonidae)
Year-round

Rare in the Canadian Rockies, reported occasionally from Crowsnest Pass south, but possible anywhere in the foothills from the Peace River south, at low elevations along streamcourses. Not a member of the weasel family. Length 85 cm (tail 25 cm), weight 8.6 kg. Females slightly smaller than males. Raccoons are brownish gray, easily identified by the black mask around the large eyes, the mouse-like pale ears and the furry, black-ringed tail. "Cute" is the word that comes to mind, although raccoons can carry rabies and should not be handled or approached closely.

MW

Sometimes singly, sometimes in family groups, raccoons move along streambanks at night, grabbing fish, frogs and insect larvae out of the water, taking small rodents in the grass, catching insects on the ground and eating berries. They spend their days well up in big poplars and cottonwoods, often in large natural tree holes; in winter they confiscate the dens of skunks or other largish burrowers, going dormant during cold snaps but otherwise remaining active.

Mating can occur anytime between February and June, with peak activity in March; there is one litter a year of 3–4, born March or later. The little coons follow their mother around and stay with her until the following spring, when sexual maturity rends raccoon families just as it does any other.

## Cat family

The wild cats of the Rockies are in the order Carnivora, family Felidae. We have three species.

### Lynx *Loup-cervier*
*Lynx canadensis* (cat family)
Year-round

Occasional in deep subalpine forest in summer, sometimes seen above treeline, moving to lower elevations in winter. Nocturnal. Length of male 90 cm (tail 10 cm), weight 11 kg; females up to a third smaller. Lynx are gray and brown, buffy underneath, with black-trimmed ears that have long black tufts sticking up from the ends. The tail is black-tipped. Bobcats, next item, are similar in size and build, but the legs are a little shorter, the feet are smaller and the tail is a little longer. Differentiate mainly by the browner coat of the bobcat, which is vaguely spotted. The bobcat also has small black smudges on the legs and more black on the tail; the ear tufts are shorter.

MW

In my twenty-five years in the Canadian Rockies I have glimpsed one lynx for a few seconds, yet I see their tracks frequently in the winter. Intolerant of human activity, lynx prefer dense forest and brush. They become active at dark and head home an hour or so before sunrise, hunting alone through a territory of 12–50 km² (up to 240 km²) and usually keeping clear of settled places and highways. Based on 13 years of tracking in the foothills and mountains southwest of Calgary, researcher Ian Ross estimates that only 24–36 lynx live in the 800 km² of suitable habitat available there.

Snowshoe hares are the favorite item on the lynx menu; a single cat may eat 200 of them each year. So lynx populations follow the ups and downs of the hare cycle (see page 618). Other foods: grouse and perching birds, ducks, rodents, including mice, voles and ground squirrels/tree squirrels, and sometimes young hoofed mammals. Like other cats, lynx hunt more with their eyes and ears than they do with their noses; often they lie in wait for their dinner to come to them. They are good climbers, dropping on their prey occasionally from trees or ledges. Their own enemies are cougars and wolves, which kill them—particularly the kittens—as unwanted competition. Owls, foxes and coyotes pick off the kittens, too.

Lynx are not afraid of water and readily cross rivers. They mark their territories and leave messages for one another by scratching up the ground and urinating on it. Although they can yowl and cry like other cats, lynx seldom do. They need little shelter; a rough scrape under an overhang, among fallen timber or under the drooping lower branches of a big spruce will do, even for rearing offspring.

Little is known of this animal's life history beyond the essential facts. It mates in early spring, sometime from March to May. An annual litter of two or three young (range 1–5) are born about nine weeks later, from mid-May to mid-June, and they are tended by the female for about 12 weeks. The kittens are furry and playful; their eyes open at 12–17 days. They remain with their mother for the first 10 months, but the date of maturity is unknown. Few lynx live more than five years in the wild.

The lynx needs extensive forest and is thus losing ground steadily as land-clearing continues in North America. In Canada many thousands of lynx are killed every year so that people can look fashionable in their skins.

## Bobcat/wildcat *Lynx roux*
*Lynx rufus* (cat family)
Year-round

Occasional on the western slope from the Peace River south and in the southern foothills. Length of male 83 cm (tail 18 cm), weight 10 kg; females about 30 percent smaller. Bobcats look very much like lynx, previous item, and can be found in habitat also used by lynx, but they are less common than lynx in the Canadian Rockies. Bobcats are a bit smaller than lynx, and tawnier, with faint brown spotting and black smudges on the legs; the tail is longer, and it is white underneath for its entire length, black-barred at the end rather than just black-tipped. The ears are outlined in black like those of the lynx, but with shorter tufts.

MW

Lynx behavior and bobcat behavior are fairly similar. Both are hunters of small mammals. The differences seem mainly in the bobcat's vocalizations, which are louder and more frequent, and this cat's ability to live in open spaces where the lynx cannot. Thus, the bobcat survives longer after man has arrived and cleared the land. Population fluctuations among bobcats are less extreme than those in lynx.

The habits of the bobcat are better known than those of the lynx. Bobcats mate in early spring in the Rockies. Gestation is 50–60 days. The young are weaned at two months, after which the father helps to supply food. In January, eight months after they are born, the young are on their own. Bobcats have lived 12 years in the wild, 25 years in captivity. Their fur is not as popular as that of the lynx, so in Canada we lose only 3200 a year to trappers.

## Cougar/mountain lion/puma/panther *Couguar*
*Felis concolor* (cat family)
Year-round

Occasional at montane and subalpine elevations. Length of males 230 cm (tail 75 cm), weight 70 kg. Females are 25–30 percent smaller. Readily identified: a great big cat with a fairly short brownish/grayish coat that is essentially unpatterned. The belly is buff; chest, throat, chin and whiskers are white; the ears are black on the back, but not tufted like the lynx or bobcat, and there is a dark vertical smudge above each eye. Tip of the tail is black.

MW

When you see this animal you know it. But it is so shy that you may never see it. There are notable exceptions to this. In the late 1970s an aging female cougar moved in under a trailer in Jasper townsite and had her kittens there. Studies of cougars in the foothills and front ranges west of Calgary through the 1980s have shed some light on the habits of these animals in the Canadian Rockies. Our cougars are solitary, with a population density of 2.7–4.7 per 100 km$^2$, hunting from dusk to dawn and sometimes in the daytime through territories averaging 87 km$^2$ (summer) and 96 km$^2$ (winter) for females and 314 km$^2$ (summer) and 204 km$^2$ (winter) for males. The main prey species are mule deer, 60 percent of stomach contents, on average. The cats also take white-tailed deer and elk, which they must surprise at close range for a successful attack, for the cougar tires quickly in a chase. Male cougars have a taste for moose calves and yearling moose in spring.

Cougars typically kill their prey by biting the underside of the neck and clamping the windpipe closed. The canine teeth are long, so smaller prey may be killed by a bite through the skull. The teeth farther back are massive and very sharp; placed near the hinge line, they work like powerful shears. While cougars are capable of bringing down all the big-game animals, they seldom attack adult moose, bighorn sheep or mountain goats in the Canadian Rockies, and they hardly ever attack domestic livestock. Smaller prey include porcupines, snowshoe hares and beavers. These cats like their meat fresh, and they usually stay with a carcass until they are finished with it. Cougars sometimes cover their kills with leaves, forest duff or snow, which masks the odor.

Like other cats, cougars scratch up spots in their territories and mark them with urine. They groom themselves often, licking their coats, and they purr loudly. Except for females with kittens, cougars in our area do not use fixed dens. They sleep under sheltering conifers wherever and whenever they need to.

Unlike most other animals in the mountains, a female mountain lion can go into heat in any season; in Canada she often does so between March and June. A study in Kananaskis Country showed that May is the prime time in the central Rockies. She gets interested only every other year, normally, and goes searching for a male, often attracting more than one suitor. The rivals fight for her as only cats can. After mating, the male leaves. Gestation is 90–96 days, with a litter averaging two kittens (range 1–6) usually born between June and October, with a peak in August from May matings.

The kittens are spotted and striped, quite unlike the adults. The female keeps them in a litter-free den usually located among boulders. Weaning is gradual, normally complete at six months, when the little lions become plain brown. During their first year they are fed on mum's kills. Initially she brings parts home; later the cubs follow her to the carcasses. In our area the cubs stay with their mother for about 15 months. First mating is at about 30 months for both sexes. Longevity in the wild reaches 10–12 years; in captivity cougars have lived 18 years.

Is the mountain lion a dangerous beast? It can be. There have been at least 12 fatal attacks recorded in Canada and the U.S. since 1890, one so far in the Canadian Rockies (a cross-country skier killed near Banff in 2001), and the attack rate seems to be increasing. We are inclined to take after the species with dogs and guns. In some jurisdictions, troublesome cougars are caught and relocated rather than shot. Having lost much of their North American range to human occupation, and persecuted by bounty hunting until the 1960s, cougars are now protected in eastern parts of Canada and the United States. However, hunting cougars for sport continues in Alberta and British Columbia at time of writing.

The big cats seem reluctant to hunt us back, nor is the species known to attack people who have blundered on its babies. But in several documented cases starving cougars have killed children for food. It's something to think about when you're eight years old and sitting around the campfire with Uncle Al, who has been telling these really great cougar stories, but now you've got to go to the bathroom, and the outhouse is way over there, in the dark.

# Dogs

Here we have the coyote, wolf and fox, all members of the order Carnivora, family Canidae.

## Coyote/bush wolf/brush wolf *Coyote*
*Canis latrans* (dog family)
Year-round

Common in any montane setting, especially grassy places and open woods; sometimes in subalpine forest and occasional above treeline. Frequently seen around towns, picnic sites and campgrounds. Length of males 120 cm (tail 35 cm), weight 13–20 kg. Females a little smaller. Pronounced "KIE-yoat" or "kie-YO-tee."

Coyotes are grizzled gray on top, buffy brown down the sides and pale underneath. The eyes of coyotes are yellow. There are

MW

patches of cinnamon on the nose, behind the ears and on the legs. Coyotes are about one-third smaller than wolves, with proportionately longer and bushier tails that are carried low when running, with a slight curve upward at the end, while wolves carry their tails straight out when running. A coyote's face is foxier-looking, with larger ears and a sharper muzzle. Canadian Rockies wolves are highly variable in coloration, while coyotes are not.

When people report seeing a wolf or a "bush wolf," it is usually a coyote. Wolves are much less numerous and quite a bit more wary of humans. Anyone spending a few days in the Canadian Rockies is likely to see at least one coyote, particularly around Banff or Jasper, where the animals regularly patrol the townsite outskirts, the picnic spots and the campgrounds. In summer I see them in ones and twos, sometimes in families of 3–6; in winter they are inclined to run in packs of 3–8.

Coyotes are out and about in any season and at any time of day or night. They are most active at dusk and dawn, when I often hear them yipping, yapping and howling just out of town. They eat mainly small rodents—especially meadow voles—as well as carrion and showshoe hares. During spring they take many newborn deer. They seldom kill livestock, but in agricultural areas they have come to depend on the carcasses of dead cattle in winter. This can lead farmers to mistakenly believe that coyotes are killing their cattle.

In summer coyotes spend much of their time mousing in meadows. You may see a coyote snuffing about, then suddenly pouncing on a meadow vole, catching it between the front paws and gobbling it up. In the southern foothills a coyote will hang around while a badger digs into a ground-squirrel colony. Squirrels running out of their holes are snagged by the coyote.

In winter coyotes subsist mainly on carrion of ungulates killed by wolves. In the Rockies they shadow wolf packs, despite the danger of getting killed by the big guys. Occasionally coyotes will behave like wolves themselves, working together in groups of 2–8 to bring down a deer, sheep or elk struggling in deep snow. Sometimes the tables are turned and the prey species will be seen chasing the predator. Part of the coyote diet is vegetarian, and they eat lots of grasshoppers when available. Pups like them.

Hearing and especially sense of smell are keen in coyotes, but they don't see at a distance as well as humans, and they are colorblind.

While history has shown that human fears about wolves are unjustified, coyotes are another matter. In the national parks they approach humans quite closely, sometimes with nasty results. There were four coyote attacks in Jasper park during the summer of 1985, all involving young children. In three cases the coyotes had been or were being fed; they nipped and bit when no further food was offered. Such incidents show the wisdom of the strict anti-feeding laws in the mountain parks, especially when coyote populations are high and the animals are running short of natural foods.

The fourth incident of 1985 was more serious. A two-year-old child playing in her yard was attacked by a coyote that may have wanted to eat her. The child's mother came to the rescue as the coyote was dragging the toddler into the woods, but the child was badly bitten and required hospitalization. The coyote was killed and found to have a glove caught in its gut, which may have caused the desperate behavior. Keep an eye on the kids if there are coyotes about; toddlers should always be watched very closely when outdoors in wildlife-rich places.

In the 1970s a coyote on the Banff Springs Hotel golf course bit a player trying to retrieve her ball, which the coyote had stolen. No one knows why coyotes pick up the balls on the Banff and Jasper courses—maybe the animals mistake them for eggs—but it is a fairly common occurrence. Coyotes sometimes sit by park highways, waiting for cars to stop. They approach the windows, hoping for a handout, and may chase the car, yapping and snapping at the wheels as it pulls away.

This species mates for several years at a time; for life in some cases. The female comes into heat for just a few days sometime between late January and late March; after gestation of 60–63 days a litter of six pups (range 1–9) is born typically in late April or early May. The female digs the den, usually located in silty soil at the base of a rise near water. A tunnel 2–3 m long leads to a chamber at the end.

Coyote pups are dark tawny brown and look just like domestic-dog pups. Their eyes open at nine days. At three weeks they are venturing outside, and at 5–8 weeks they are weaned.

Like wolf pups, they are fed by both parents on vomit (doggy baby food) for a while. At one year they are fully grown and ready to mate. Maximum age in captivity: 18 years. A **coydog** is the hybrid offspring of a coyote/domestic-dog mating. It is fertile, as are **coywolves.**

Coyotes are trapped in Canada at the rate of 48,000 a year. Fearing for their calves and lambs, ranchers often kill coyotes. Grain farmers are inclined to be more tolerant, for coyotes are effective predators of crop-eating mice and voles. Whatever one's view of this animal, the records show that it is increasing in numbers throughout western North America.

### Gray wolf/timber wolf/arctic wolf *Loup*
*Canis lupus* (dog family)
Year-round

Fairly common from Jasper north, occasional to rare farther south, seen most often in summer in grassy montane woods and in winter on montane or subalpine frozen lakes. Length 175 cm (tail 45 cm), height at the shoulder 1 m, weight 35–60 kg. Females are slightly smaller and lighter.

*MW*

Unlike coyotes, previous item, wolves vary a great deal in color; I have seen black ones and white ones in the same pack. They are inclined to be browner in summer, after moulting their heavy winter coats. In the Canadian Rockies common colorings are often either a malamute-like black-on-pale-gray or dark brown with buffy trim. The eyes are always shades of yellow. Wolves are larger than coyotes, with tails that are relatively shorter and less fluffy, carried straight out when running rather than drooping as coyotes carry theirs. The face is blockier on the wolf, the ears shorter and the muzzle blunter. But even with all these differences, people still confuse wolves and coyotes. It is usually the coyotes that are reported; even inside the national and provincial parks, where wolves are protected, it may be some time before you see one.

Wolf populations and distributions are difficult to determine because the animals are secretive and move around a lot. Radio-collared wolves from Banff National Park have moved as far south as Pend Oreille Lake in Idaho—and back. (Cross-border shopping?) A single radio-collared wolf has been tracked from the Flathead Valley west of Glacier park on the Canada/U.S. border, to Fort St. John along the Peace River. Another in the same group was followed to Yellowstone National Park. Absent from Banff National Park since the 1950s, when the misguided government of the day exterminated them as vermin, wolves returned to the Bow Valley in the mid-1980s. Wolves have also reestablished themselves as far south as Waterton and Glacier national parks. There may be many living in isolated areas north of the Peace River.

Wolves eat big game, especially in winter when many of the smaller mammals are harder to get under the snow or hibernating in burrows. Wolf menu for the Canadian Rockies: elk and deer are about equally preferred, then moose, bighorn sheep, snowshoe hares, ground squirrels, beavers, muskrats, marmots and mice/voles. See also the item on caribou, page 651.

A single wolf can kill a deer rather easily, and lone wolves have been known to kill elk and moose, but the species routinely hunts in organized packs. They prefer to take isolated individuals. When attacking a herd or flock, the usual strategy is to separate one animal from the group and get it out in the open, where it can be chased to exhaustion. When it cannot run any more, the wolves close in. They usually kill deer quickly; larger prey they bring down by nipping and biting until the animal is subdued. The wolves then tear it to pieces, snapping and snarling. They go for internal organs and rib meat first.

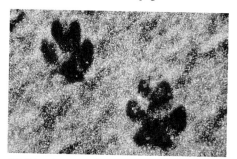

*Wolf tracks on a frozen lake east of Jasper. Rear foot at upper left, front foot at lower right.*

Seeing this sort of thing makes one shudder. It's no wonder that people are afraid of wolves. But we needn't be. There have been only three documented wolf attacks in Canada, and only one resulted in injury: a badly-bitten arm. Wolves are curious, and they will sometimes approach people quite closely. Perhaps they wish to see us clearly and catch our scent; once they do, they leave. Yet they are also surprisingly tolerant of non-threatening humans in their territories, as students of wolves have learned.

They are *not* tolerant of bears. A wolf was seen harrying a young male grizzly bear—actually biting it—along Highway 16 west of Jasper. It drove the bear away, perhaps in defence of pups nearby, for bears kill wolf pups. Likewise, wolves kill newborn bear cubs whenever they can.

Wolves in the Rockies live in packs of 4–7, sometimes more. These are essentially extended families. The toughest, smartest wolf, either male or female, is usually the leader, called the **alpha**. Dominant females lift their legs to urinate as males do, and the other pack members squat. The alpha is challenged from time to time by a younger wolf, with vicious fighting often the result. The pack leader carries its tail high, while the others carry theirs lower. The leader usually mates for life, and these two often are the only breeding pair in the group; they try to prevent the rest of the pack from mating.

A pack's home range in the Canadian Rockies might cover 1000–2000 km$^2$. That sounds like a lot of land, but typically only 25 percent is valley-bottom habitat usable for hunting. The pack members move freely about this area, individually or together, constantly marking selected spots with urine. Packs avoid each other; if they should meet accidentally there are aggressive displays and occasional fighting.

Each pack has a nursery site with one or more dens. In the Canadian Rockies these dens are often old beaver bank-burrows beside a small lake or marsh, the burrows now above water level because the dam has been breached and abandoned. Bone fragments and white, bony scats show who has been living there.

***Never handle wolf scats.*** They often contain the eggs of the **hydatid tapeworm** *Echinococcus granulosus,* which lives more-or-less harmlessly in the gut of dog-family members but invades the lungs and brains of other hosts, including accidental hosts such as humans. The wolves pick up the encysted worms by eating the infested internal organs of prey species such as elk and deer. The cysts develop into adults in the wolves' intestines, and eggs are shed with the droppings. The eggs hatch, and tiny larvae crawl onto vegetation, where they are eaten by ungulates, which in turn are eaten by the wolves.

Female domestic dogs usually go into heat twice a year, at any time, but wolves in the Rockies do so just once a year, and only in the winter. Estrus occurs over a few days between late February and mid-March. The female dens up to deliver and raise the pups. The other pack/family members hang around, supplementing their usual large-ungulate diet with the rodents that are plentiful at this time, including beavers. There is normally a litter of five pups (range 1–11) born in late April or early May after a gestation period of 60–65 days. The pups are dark gray, nearly black. Their eyes open at 5–9 days and they venture out of the den at three or four weeks, tussling about in typical doggy fashion. They are weaned at 6–8 weeks and fed for a while on regurgitated meals bummed from any adult in the pack. A pup gets fed by licking and nipping his relatives around the mouth. This is why domestic-dog pups lick the faces of people.

At about two months the female often carries the pups by the scruff of the neck to another den nearby, for reasons only she knows. It may be because the original den has become too dirty and/or buggy.

By late summer the pups are weaned and their mother can join the pack for big-game hunts. The pups remain with various pack members in a **rendezvous** area. Any members that have been away arrive at a particular meadow or lake to get organized for the winter. There is a lot of evening howling at this time, and if you know where a pack is located you can go out and howl to them. They will often howl back. Crisp moonlit nights from September on are best, around midnight. You need not howl convincingly; wolves will reply to anything from a moan to a noisy car radio. Once you have got them going, they often keep it up for several minutes at a time. Then maybe you will hear a bunch go off on the other side of the valley—which is what this must be all about. "We're the Pyramid Lake Pack. Who are you-oooooo?"

Few pups survive even for a year. Those reaching maturity typically live 5–7 years in the wild.

Humans are taught to fear and hate wolves, having grown up on *Little Red Riding Hood, The Three Little Pigs* and *Peter and the Wolf.* We learn that wolves are Bambi-killers, despicable savages that kill just for the fun of killing. Actually, wolves seldom kill more than they need, and they feed a host of scavengers on the remains. Unlike man, who hunts as trophies the strongest, healthiest animals in a herd, the wolf kills the old, the sick and the less-fit. This actually improves the viability of the herd by strengthening the gene pool.

Provincial and territorial wildlife agencies "manage wolf populations," meaning that they kill wolves. This is done at the request of ranchers who don't like wolves on their lands, and under pressure from hunters' organizations who would rather kill Bambi themselves. Studies suggest that wolves in Alberta may take more deer and elk than hunters do, which fish-and-game associations find upsetting.

In protected, hunter-free situations, the wolf population is known to control itself. When the number of hoofed animals is steady, so is the number of wolves. When there are too many wolves, pack fertility drops naturally and so do wolf numbers.

Unlike the coyote, the wolf does not laugh at its tormentors and prosper anyway; *Canis lupus* has lost most of its former range in North America. The animal is currently making a modest come-back, thanks to legal protection in many places, but the long-haul outlook for the species is not good. Here in the Canadian Rockies we still have wolves, thanks in part to their protection in the national and provincial parks. However, the packs routinely cross the boundaries into hostile territory, and in the northern half of the range the only protection wolves have is the isolation of the wilderness. This is scant refuge from incidental killing by trappers and fly-in hunting parties mainly after other game.

As I write this in 1995, there are still government-backed airborne wolf kills in western Canada. The Alberta government has gone along with a U.S.-instigated capture program to break up packs and dump their members far to the south in unfamiliar surroundings. The loud public outcry against such brutality shows growing appreciation of the world's greatest dogs. I can sometimes hear them singing from the hills above Jasper—the dogs without masters, the dogs who are free.

## Red fox *Renard roux*
*Vulpes vulpes* (dog family)
Year-round

Occasional in grassy places and open woods; nocturnal, shy and seldom reported. Length 1 m (tail 40 cm), weight 5 kg. If it looks rather like a coyote, page 628, but it is smaller and the tail is nearly half the body length, then it may be a fox.

Like the black bear, facing page, the red fox has "phases": different coat colors that are genetically determined and always present in the same proportions in any population.

The most common phase, 50–75 percent of individuals, is the **red fox,** brown or cinnamon above, white below, with black-backed ears, black on the fronts of the legs and a white tip on the tail. (The term "red fox" refers to the species overall as well as to this phase.) The **cross fox,** a quarter to a third of the population, is mottled buff and dark brown, rather like a tortoise-shell housecat. A line of black down the back meets a line of black across the shoulders, which forms a cross-shaped figure. The cross fox, too, has a white tip on the tail. The other phase, the **silver fox,** is less common; no more than 17 percent of the population. Silver foxes are essentially black, but with white-tipped guard hairs on the head, back and tail that give them a hoary, silvery look. The ears and legs are black, the muzzle is dark, and there are black circles around the eyes, golden as in all foxes but especially striking in this one. And there is the ever-present white tip on the tail.

Rockies foxes are solitary during late fall and winter, living without dens in home ranges of 3.5–8.5 km². At this time the main foods are small rodents dug out from under the snow.

Foxes also eat birds and snowshoe hares. When available, they eat carrion, including left-overs from wolf kills.

When the female comes into heat sometime between mid-January and mid-March, she chooses a mate from several suitors and the pair den up, usually in last-year's burrow. If it is unavailable, then they search for an abandoned burrow (beaver burrow, badger burrow) or dig a new one themselves. The **whelps,** sometimes called "kits," are born typically from late April to early May, after gestating 51–53 days. The usual litter is five (range 1–10).

Whelps are puppy-like; their eyes open in the second week and they are weaned at one month. By this time they are coming out of the den and feeding on fresh meat brought by both parents, who are themselves eating a lot of insects, vegetation and ground squirrels as summer rolls in. By 14–16 weeks the whelps are ready to leave home for good; they are sexually mature at 10 months, which is a short time in the dog family.

These facts may be of little use, for few people ever see a fox in this region. That is partly because they are nocturnal, prowling nervously about from dusk to dawn, sometimes active in the early morning or late afternoon on dark days. They are also quite shy—although surprisingly bold on occasion. One family lived under a building at Rampart Creek Hostel in 1979, the adults coming and going when people were around.

The species is large enough that it would be reported more frequently if there were many foxes in the Canadian Rockies. Inescapable conclusion: there aren't many.

## Bears

There are two species of bears in the Canadian Rockies, black bears and grizzly bears. Both are classified in the order Carnivora, family Ursidae.

### Black bear *Ours noir*

*Ursus americanus* (bear family)
Late April to early November
Fairly common in nearly any habitat below treeline, although most common in montane woods. Average length of males (boars) is 168 cm (tail 10 cm), height at shoulder 95 cm, weight 170 kg; females (sows) are about one-third smaller.

MW

Black bears are not always black. There are two common color phases in the Canadian Rockies: black, often with a white spot on the chest, and light reddish brown—the **cinnamon bear**—also with the white chest spot. Both types are usually tan on the sides of the muzzle. Like the phases of the red fox, previous page, black-bear phases are present throughout the population; black and cinnamon offspring (cubs) can be born in the same litter. Blacks outnumber cinnamons in the Grande Prairie area just east of the Rockies by 2.5 to 1; around Jasper I see brown-phase bears less frequently than this figure suggests.

To differentiate black bears from grizzly bears, next item, one need only see the front feet. The front claws of grizzly bears are long and straight; they are easily visible sticking out beyond the fur. Claws of black bears are shorter, and stick out only a little, if at all. Other differences: black bears are short and round, with long faces and large ears, while grizzly bears are rangier, with a prominent hump on the shoulder, flatter forehead and smaller ears. Black bears are usually evenly colored, while grizzly bears are usually multi-toned, in streaks and patches. Size is not a reliable criterion; large black bears are larger than small grizzlies.

Black bears are more tolerant of humans than grizzly bears are. Black bears are often seen beside highways, along trails, hanging around campgrounds and cabins, and sometimes in the alleys of towns. They are active day and night, shuffling along, nose to the ground, always

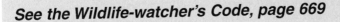

*See the Wildlife-watcher's Code, page 669*

looking for food. Although they see better than once thought, it is mainly their well-developed sense of smell that leads them to their meals. They hear well, too.

When a bear is trying to locate the source of a smell or sound, it often stands up on its hind legs. It turns from side to side, sniffing and grunting in what may appear to be a threatening posture but is actually not. Real attacks are made on all four feet, usually low to the ground. In standing, the bear brings its nose up from the interference of odors near the ground to sample the air moving by.

Despite the inability of bears to digest cellulose as hoofed mammals can, the black bear diet is about 75 percent vegetarian. Their guts are very efficient at wringing liquids from plants, squeezing the barely chewed intake as if it had been through the wringers of on old-style washing machine. In spring and summer the animals prefer sprouting plants and the buds or inner bark of shrubs and trees, all of which are low in cellulose, high in sugar and protein; in the fall they eat fruits and berries. In midsummer you may see black bears eating flowers; they are very fond of dandelions. They dig for roots and tubers, but not as much as grizzly bears do. Carrion accounts for 10–15 percent of their warm-weather diet in the Canadian Rockies, insects 5–10 percent and small mammals and fish less than one percent. Black bears occasionally take young deer, elk or moose. As explained on page 640, they have been known to prey on humans.

Tree-climbing is the black bear's usual defence against the grizzly bear, which is its main natural enemy. Probable reason: competition for food. Grizzlies have been known to drag hibernating black bears from their dens and kill them, as have wolves. These species also kill cubs when they can. To escape danger, a black-bear cub runs quickly up the trunk by hugging it, cat-style. This accounts for the short, strong, curved claws of black bears. Adult females climb as well, but large boars seldom do. Aspens are often used as getaway trees, although any tree will do; look in aspen groves for black-scarring scratches on the trees caused by bears. Horizontal or slanting scratches that go well up the trunk are caused by ascents; vertical ones a metre or two above the ground are thought to be communications to other bears.

Black bears are generally solitary, except for females with cubs. Siblings may remain together for a few months after leaving their mother's care in their second year, and may den together in their third winter. Less territorial than once thought, male black bears range through overlapping areas covering about 200 km² each in the mountains. This figure can vary a lot, depending on a bear's age, the population density and availability of food. The home ranges of sows are smaller and typically non-overlapping. There is little territorial conflict among black bears; several can share a productive berry patch, a scavenged carcass or a dump.

Black bears are usually silent, but they become vocal when agitated. They grunt, woof, growl and chop their teeth; the cubs cry to their mothers like human babies, and they can make a humming/purring sound when contented.

This species typically breeds every other year. Breeding takes place between June 20 and July 10, but the cubs don't arrive until mid-January or early February. This long gestation, about 220 days, is caused by delayed implantation of the embryo, as in the weasel family. The embryo floats free in the womb until October or November, when it attaches to the uterine wall and starts to grow. Normally there are 2–3 cubs per litter (range 1–5), born during the mother's dormant period. She usually awakens during birth, cleans her cubs, eats their afterbirths, then goes back to sleep.

The cubs are very small, about the size of newborn puppies. They nurse and crawl about as the mother sleeps. Their eyes open at six weeks, but they are not weaned until five or six months old. They follow the sow around for the remainder of that summer, den with her the following winter, and typically leave in their second spring, just before mating time.

In late summer, black bears experience a powerful hunger that drives them to become grossly fat. They take in 4.7 MJ (20,000 calories) of food per day at this time. For comparison, the normal human daily intake in Canada is about 0.5 MJ (2500 calories). When cold weather hits in October, the bears move up the slopes to subalpine elevations, where the snow will be deepest, although low-elevation denning occurs occasionally. Snow is good insulation, sufficient to keep the den temperature above freezing in the coldest weather. Each bear digs a simple shelter, usually under a tree or tall shrub, sometimes under an overhanging bank or among the roots of a wind-thrown tree. In the mountains the animals seldom burrow in more than a metre or two, and I have never seen a bear, or any bear sign, in a cave—a true cave, deeper than a few metres—in winter or in summer. However, wardens in Banff park report one instance of denning in a shallow limestone cave. In the Canadian Rockies, nearly all black bears are in hibernation by the end of October; they emerge in late winter or early spring—usually by mid-April in the central Rockies.

Bear hibernation is a biochemical marvel. If the definition of "hibernation" includes a low body temperature, then bears are not true hibernators, for their body temperatures don't drop much. They decrease from the normal 38°C to 34–31°C. Because their muscles are warm, dormant bears can become active very quickly if need be. The animals go through about 1 MJ (5000 calories) of energy per day during hibernation, which is nearly as much as they use when active. How can they keep up that high metabolic rate for over five months without eating or drinking? Large fat reserves provide the energy, and the bears convert their own urea, a byproduct of metabolism that mammals normally unload as urine, into proteins. This makes all the difference during dormancy, preventing toxic buildups of urea while maintaining muscle mass until spring. Water released from the metabolism of fat provides enough fluid to make milk for the cubs. It's very concentrated.

## Grizzly bear/brown bear *Ours brun*
*Ursus arctos* (bear family)
March to early November

MW

Once fairly common in any mountain environment, now only occasional; usually found at low elevations in spring and above treeline in summer. Length 190 cm (tail 8 cm), height at the shoulder 130 cm; in the Canadian Rockies males weigh 250–320 kg, females 200 kg or less.

This is a large bear, with a prominent shoulder hump and long claws that stick out beyond the fur on the front feet. The name "grizzly," which has fallen out of favor with some biologists because this animal is really the same as the brown bear of Europe, comes from "grizzled," referring to the white tips commonly found on the animal's hair. The loss of pigment in the ends of these hairs gives the bear a hoary look, especially over the shoulders and down the back. But there is a lot of color variation, from black to tawny; a white bear has been reported from Waterton. Unlike the black bear, previous item, which can also be black or tawny, the grizzly bear's color is not uniform: it is lighter here, darker there, often streaky. As well, the grizzly is larger and rangier, with big shoulders. The face is flatter, dished around the bridge of the nose, The muzzle is more pointed and the ears are smaller.

I have often heard it said that this animal was driven into the mountains from the prairies, where it lived before it was exterminated there. While it is true that grizzly bears once lived as far east as Ontario, the notion of them being forced westward into the Rockies is false. Grizzlies have always lived throughout the Canadian Rockies, and west to the coast.

The grizzly bear's habits are much like those of the black bear, but grizzlies are more active in daylight, and they do a lot of digging for roots and tubers. A favorite is sweetvetch. Sometimes grizzly bears dig out marmots and ground squirrels, tearing up alpine meadows. This is a lot of work for very little reward, meal-wise; the bears may crave ground squirrels for their high fat content.

Grizzly bears eat astonishing quantities of buffaloberries—often 200,000 per day—and leave characteristic red, seedy droppings along trails in late July and early August; see sketch on page 666. Blueberries are just as popular in the fall. The bears savor the fatty, nut-like seeds of whitebark pine and all parts of cow parsnip. They eat more fish than black bears do, piling on the calories during the late-summer salmon run up the Fraser River to Mt. Robson (see page 481). Renowned scavengers, grizzly bears are hunters, too, picking off weak or very young hoofed animals. Sometimes they kill cattle or horses, which has not endeared them to ranchers.

Despite this taste for fresh meat, grizzly bears almost never attack humans to eat them. The attacks are for other reasons, as discussed in the next section. Their only predator is man, although wolves will kill infant and juvenile grizzlies bears when they can.

Grizzly bears cache their meat, covering it with scratched-up plant material and soil. If they arrive at a kill made by another animal, they take it over. If you find a lot of bones scattered around a fair-sized excavation, then you know what did it. Don't hang around; some of the kill may still be buried and the bear may be near.

Except when the females have cubs, grizzly are solitary, moving about annual home ranges of at least 200 km$^2$. Over a lifetime, a sow may have lived in an area of 1800 km$^2$, a boar, 4000 km$^2$. The bears travel long distances, crossing high passes and traversing glaciers. A friend of mine saw one going over Abbot Pass, a glacial col between Mt. Victoria and Mt. Lefroy above Lake Louise, and grizzlies have been seen crossing the Columbia Icefield. They swim well, crossing swollen glacial rivers with ease.

Like black bears, grizzly-bear females mate every other year, sometimes every three years, in early summer, meaning late June to early July in the Canadian Rockies. Gestation is 229–266 days, with implantation delayed as

*Rear (upper) and front (lower) track of the grizzly. Photo by Cyndi Smith courtesy Jasper National Park.*

in black bears. A pair of cubs (litters range from one to four) are born between mid-January and early March, while the mother is hibernating. They are weaned at four or five months, but stay with mum through the following winter, sharing her den, then leave in their second spring as she prepares to mate again—although there have been many reports of two-year-old cubs still with their mothers. Like black bears, the cubs may den with each other in their third winter. They become sexually active at five or six years and may reach the age of 30.

A grizzly-bear sow is very protective while the cubs are with her, because a boar is inclined to kill them if he can. Although the cubs will climb trees to escape, grizzlies are often above treeline, where there are no trees to climb. Most often flight is the response to danger, but occasionally the cubs must count on mum to stand up for them, which she does, sometimes leading to nasty encounters with people. When the people have guns, the mother often gets shot; later, the cubs die, too.

Grizzly bears are winter-dormant in the manner of black bears, although grizzly hibernation is not as well-studied as black-bear dormancy. Grizzlies retire at the onset of cold weather, usually in late November or early December, preferring denning sites on rather steep slopes of 25–45° in high-subalpine meadows. They dig in more deeply than do black bears. In the Rockies they seem to emerge earlier than black bears do, often in March, when the snow is still deep in the high country. They stay near the den for a while, living on their remaining fat reserves, then move to lower elevations, hoping to find carrion or managing to kill winter-weakened hoofed animals. In April I have come across grizzly bears several times in the woods around Jasper. They were digging up roots, enjoying the new buds on shrubs, eating the spring grass and so on. They were much too busy to pay any attention to me. Of course, I was thinking rather a lot about *them*. Read on.

## People vs. bears in the Canadian Rockies

Bears and humans have never gotten along very well. Bears eat our unattended apple pies and make a mess of the garbage. They tear open our hives and eat the honey. They come into our campsites, intimidate us and steal our food. They are big enough to hurt us and sometimes do.

This last, especially, is not acceptable, so we have hunted bears to extinction in much of the world. But not in the Canadian Rockies, where our two species of bears have survived, if not flourished. When one is on foot in these mountains one knows that the grizzly bear is also out there, neither well-intentioned nor malicious, just out there. Just around the corner, maybe.

This adds a dash of fear to a mountain outing. A lot of people never venture into the woods because they are afraid of bears. Never mind that they are more likely to be hit by lightning than hurt by a bear, or that the German shepherd tied up in the next campsite is probably more dangerous to one's toddler than a bear is. In 35 years on foot and unarmed in the mountains I have never been attacked by a bear, but I have been attacked by several dogs. All the bears I have met on the trail, including grizzly bears, have either run away or watched me curiously until I passed by. Only once have I been charged, and it was an embarrassing incident for both the grizzly bear and me. We had been moving away from each other in the same direction (it was so bushy we couldn't see one another), and the bear, convinced that *I* was chasing *it*, figured that it was going to have to fight. I went up a tree and the bear ran away.

To those readers who worry about bears, the message in the next few pages is to relax. Respect bears, yes, for they are amazing creatures. Be wary of them, yes. Avoid them if you can. But don't *worry* about them. This is unnecessary and spoils an outing.

My bear worries are for *their* health and safety, not mine. Consider the hypothetical, but typical, chain of events outlined below.

A wild black bear follows its nose to a campground. There, left out on a table, is a loaf of bread. The bear eats it, plastic wrapper and all. Ooo, that was good. Any more around? Yes! Over there. Smells like *meat!* Gotta have it. Uh, oh; something big coming. Noisy, but not a grizzly. Got the meat. Run away now. Back tomorrow night.

The bear *does* come back the next night, to the same campsite at the same time. Bears have good memories that way. There is more booty; more easy pickings.

Night after night this happens. The bear becomes bolder and bolder. The campers are half-delighted, half-afraid; this is going to be memorable. Some of them feed the bear. Others throw things at it. Someone has a big dog; turns it loose on the bear. The bear runs away. Hah! Great show!

Later on, when everyone has gone to bed, the bear comes back. It breaks into an RV in which a bag of groceries was left sitting just inside the screen door. The occupants awake in terror, shouting. The bear, confused, tries to get out the wrong end of the vehicle. Thinking it's cornered, it bites one of the fleeing occupants. Somebody goes for the wardens. The wardens come and shoot the bear. Thus the wardens' sad rhyme, "A fed bear is a dead bear."

The lesson here is that **letting a bear get into human food or human garbage is much the same as killing that bear.\*** Eventually, whether it is shot by the authorities or hit by a car or strangled from the inside by a plastic bag snarled in its gut, that bear will probably die an unnatural death.

And rarely, very rarely, it may take a human with it.

---

\*While this is true in the Canadian Rockies, a case has been made by the Craighead brothers, world-renowned grizzly-bear experts, for allowing bears to eat garbage in Yellowstone National Park. Yellowstone can no longer sustain the bear population it used to, say the Craigheads, because of human settlement around it and heavy human presence in the park. Officials there closed the dumps to bears without realizing that the dumps were essential food sources. The bears became desperate, resulting in many destructive incidents and the killing of most bears in the park. The Craigheads warn that if grizzly bears are to survive in Yellowstone, and more than a handful of black bears, they must be *fed*. Such is not the case here, where populations seem to be self-sustaining, but the time may come.

I would rather that human not be me, as I'm sure you would rather it not be you. Humans and bears can coexist in the Canadian Rockies if we adjust our behavior to accommodate theirs. We must never, ever feed them or allow them to eat human food.

That means no garbage left around. No food left out on the picnic table. No fish guts dumped beside the stream. People who are fishing stand a greater-than-average chance of running into bears hanging around their fishing holes.

On the trail it means putting every bit of your food, including such bear-foods as toothpaste, soap, cosmetics and trash, at least 4 m off the ground at night, slung between two trees on a rope, or up on the special poles erected just for this purpose in many back-country campsites. Eat everything you cook, thereby avoiding the problem of garbage disposal.

Polar bears are attracted to used tampons and black/grizzly bears may be as well. Although attacks on menstruating women have been reported, menstruation has not been shown to attract bears. Still, on an overnight hike, women in their periods should change pads frequently and wash before going to bed. Do not simply discard pads in the woods. You may be long gone, but another person may happen by while a bear is investigating. Put used pads down outhouses or burn them.

*If you go down to the dump today, you're in for a big surprise. Photo: Parks Canada.*

For the sake of both bears and humans, I inform people whom I see breaking these rules. There is no need to be pedantic or authoritarian; if I see someone feeding a bear from the car window, I just say something like, "Hello. I noticed you feeding that bear, and I thought you should know that if the wardens see you doing that they'll fine you $500. Oops—I think I see a warden truck turning around! 'Bye!"

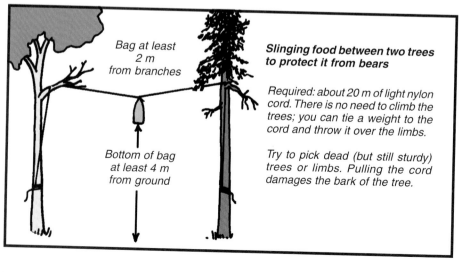

Bag at least
2 m
from branches

Bottom of bag
at least 4 m
from ground

**Slinging food between two trees to protect it from bears**

*Required: about 20 m of light nylon cord. There is no need to climb the trees; you can tie a weight to the cord and throw it over the limbs.*

*Try to pick dead (but still sturdy) trees or limbs. Pulling the cord damages the bark of the tree.*

# What to do in an encounter with a bear

Here is a summary of expert advice on what to do if you and a bear find yourselves sharing the same patch of the mountains. Much of the following is distilled from *Bear Attacks: Their Causes and Avoidance* (Herrero, 1985), which is recommended reading for any outdoorsperson.

If you see the bear at a distance of more than 10 or 20 m, just stop walking. This is automatic, right? Wow! A bear! Have a quick look around to see if there are any cubs, then walk away quietly without coming between mum and the kids. Black bears are fairly tolerant of people around their cubs, but grizzly bears are not. Loop widely around the whole scene, a kilometre or more if it is a female grizzly bear with cubs, and continue your hike. The bear(s) will likely do the same. End of a typical encounter.

If the way is narrow and you are going to have to pass closely by the bear—that is, you would like it to move out of your way—then stand beside a suitable escape tree and make some noise so that the bear realizes that you are there. It probably doesn't, or it would be gone by now. Chances are, it will now take off.

What if the bear doesn't run? If it just watches you, give it a wide berth as you go on. You may have to backtrack to get by.

What if it comes toward you? Possibly it's a garbage-addicted campground bear, used to people, not afraid of you and figuring to either beg or extort a handout. Or maybe there is a carcass nearby, and the bear is thinking that it may have to defend the meat from you. Either way, you need to leave. Walk quickly away, keeping an eye on the bear—but not staring it in the eye, for reasons coming up soon. Seldom will it follow.

What if it does follow? What if it starts to chase you? You are in trouble. **Climb a tree.**

Pick a sturdy one; bears have been known to bite off aspens 15 cm thick. *Climb high:* a grizzly bear will climb partway up after you if it is really intent, but not over 5 m in reported incidents. Black bears are tree-climbers, but they climb primarily for escape, not for attack, and will seldom follow a person up a tree, although sometimes they have.

If you have a pack on, drop it as soon as you decide to climb. The pack will slow down the bear, which will probably stop to check it, and climbing the tree will be easier without the pack. If the tree-climbing is strictly cautionary, meaning that you have plenty of time, you may want to take your pack up with you, to keep it from being damaged by the bear.

Getting up the tree does not end the encounter. There you are, up in the tree, and there is the bear, down there. It may just *stay* down there, perhaps for hours. However, if there is no carcass nearby that the bear is defending, it will probably amble away in a few minutes. Wait awhile longer, watching and listening to make sure the bear is gone, before you descend.

Suppose you come face to face with a bear, a surprise encounter for both parties. We are getting into a low-probability situation, here, but it has happened to me.

In a confrontation like this the instincts of both the bear and the person are to jump back and run. Again, end of encounter. But if it's a grizzly sow with cubs, or either sex at a kill, then the bear may hold its ground, considering a charge. Steve Herrero's excellent book covers the next few moments in detail. What he says can be applied just as well to a situation in which an aggressive bear has approached you above treeline, where there are no trees to climb.

If the bear snorts, makes other loud sounds and slaps the ground, then probably it is about to charge. There are three schools of thought on what to do next, each with statistical evidence of success.

One school suggests running like hell. That is a natural thing to do, and probably is what a charging grizzly bear hopes you will do. The usual reason for a charge is to drive away an intruder, and when you run, the bear may see that as submissive behavior not requiring further action. Most grizzly charges break off short of contact, when the bear decides that you have been sufficiently intimidated. However, a grizzly bear can easily catch a running human, going uphill or down; thus, if it wants to catch you, it will. Further, running may stimulate a curious bear to chase you as prey.

Assuming that the bear pursues and there are no trees, it seems wise to head for the nearest rocks or water. People have escaped attacks by jumping in lakes and climbing up cliffs. Or climbing *down* cliffs. But don't believe that old story about running quickly downhill, so that the bear will trip over its short front legs and stumble. This is nonsense; bears can run downhill faster than humans can.

You may want to dump your pack, hoping to distract the bear and increase your speed. But a pack offers some protection from injury to the back and can be used as a shield in a fight.

School-of-thought number two suggests that you **back off slowly and quietly, avoiding eye contact with the bear.** This tells the bear something important: that you are a powerful predator yourself, but that you're not interested in a fight just now. Among mammals, the larger solitary predators are inclined to leave one another alone in chance encounters. Humans behave as if we were in this category, something that gives us uncanny protection in the wilds. Statistically, it is often a good plan to show little interest when blundering into a bear. You recognize the bear's presence but show no alarm. Avoid eye contact, which can be construed as threatening, and move slowly away.

The third approach is to intimidate the bear. It is a normal human reflex to become noisy when threatened, and many people automatically shout at the bear, waving their arms, snarling, showing their teeth, picking up something heavy—looking dangerous in typical primate fashion. Fortunately this, too, often seems to work, especially on young bears.

But suppose the bear charges. Usually this is a bluff. It stops short, 2–3 m away. Even at this point the bear is inclined not to take you on. It must overcome its fear to approach you at all. Your instinct is the same, and during a charge you will probably be projecting universal signs of fear, which will tell the bear that you are not threatening, that you are just scared. Both parties can then back shakily away, ending the incident.

Given a charge that isn't a bluff, it is time to be sure of the species of bear and take action accordingly as it makes contact. **If it's a black bear, fight back. If it's a grizzly bear, play dead.**

Consider the black bear situation first. Black bears are less likely to charge humans than grizzly bears are, and their charges are much more likely to be false. But if a black bear continues the attack, then it may be trying to kill and eat you.

Black bears are actually more predatory on man than grizzly bears are. I know this sounds strange, but Herrero has shown conclusively that while grizzly bears are more likely to hurt humans than black bears are, black bears are more likely to prey on humans for food than grizzly bears are. Yet black bears are considerably less ferocious in the clinch.

This is not to say that black bears commonly prey on humans. Such attacks are extremely rare. But the possibility has important implications for your actions during an attack. If it is a black bear, then experience has shown that you should fight back. Use whatever comes to hand—a stick, your pack, a rock, a knife, your teeth. Kick and strike, struggle hard. Black bears are not as persistent in their attacks as grizzlies are, and showing determined resistance will often drive the bear away.

Playing dead in a black-bear attack is not a good idea, for in many cases the bear begins to eat, ripping flesh from the apparently incapacitated victim's arms and legs or disemboweling the person.

Here are some signs of predatory behavior in black bears: the bear keeps approaching despite an absence of food, moving closer as if stalking. It approaches quietly, without slapping the ground, and tries to get in behind you, then runs suddenly toward you, trying to knock you down. The animals can kill expertly, by biting the neck and shaking the victim until the neck breaks.

Grizzly bears are more aggressive than black bears, yet grizzlies seldom kill humans in order to eat them. They seem to injure us as enemies, not as prey. When victims of grizzly-bear attacks have lain very still, the attacks have nearly always ended. If a victim begins to move while the bear is still around, the bear often attacks again. So if it is a grizzly bear, the recommended action is to play dead immediately on contact, and play dead well. In many cases a bear has given a motionless human a few nuzzles and walked away.

Of course, there is a slim chance that you are being attacked by a grizzly bear as prey—something that will become apparent if the bear drags you some distance and starts to pull away flesh. At this point you had better fight back; you have nothing to lose, and grizzly bears have been successfully denied human meals. In one case near Banff in the 1970s, a six-year-old was dragged into the bushes by a grizzly bear. The boy's parents, an English couple who had never been in the Rockies, took their shoes off and flung them at the bear. Confronted by the characteristic valor of the British, the bear dropped the lad and ran off.

**Protective posture in a grizzly-bear attack:** the bear is inclined to bite your head, neck and shoulders. Curl up, knees drawn close to the chest and hands clasped over the neck. If possible, get your pack over your neck as well. Lying flat on the ground, again protecting the neck with the hands, also seems to be a good position.

## To avoid bear trouble, avoid bears

Stay alert in the back country. Look ahead and to the side for bears and bear sign: tracks and scats, evidence of digging, flipped-over rocks and ripped-up logs or stumps, tipped-over garbage cans. Are the signs fresh? Is the odor of rotten meat on the wind, or are there many ravens in the area? There could be a kill nearby.

Avoid places where bears are likely to be feeding: berry patches, stream banks rich in cow parsnip (page 303) and horsetail (page 392), brushy areas.

Hike with a group. According to Herrero, no group of six or more people has ever been attacked by a grizzly bear. Avoid hiking at night, when bears are most active. Pitch your camp well off the trail, for bears use trails at night. Sleep in a tent, not out in the open; bears often investigate people in sleeping bags, but seldom enter tents—unless they smell food in there. Before bed, search your clothing, and anything else going into the tent with you, for forgotten goodies. Check children's clothing and gear especially well.

Choose canned or dried camping food, which has little odor, and store it out of reach of bears, as shown on page 638. Take out only the food needed for the meal in preparation, leaving the rest safely stored. Cook at least 50 m downwind of your camp. Clean up well after cooking, putting slops down an outhouse, burning them or burying them. Try not to have leftovers; cook the right amount of food and eat it all. Any leftovers should go back into your food cache. Burying garbage is not a good idea; it will be dug up. Burn cans to remove odors and pack all non-combustibles out.

Camping above treeline poses special problems: no trees to use in caching food, no trees for escape and no fuel for a fire. So whenever possible, camp below treeline. If you must camp above treeline, you can cache food and garbage on the ground in several layers of sealed plastic garbage bags hidden under bushes or among rocks. Containers made of PVC pipe with screw-on caps have been found to be bear-proof.

Regardless of where you are camped, if a bear arrives and doesn't leave shortly, pack up and go somewhere else. The bear will hang around until it gets what it wants.

## Making noise

If you let the bears know that you are coming along the trail, then the chance of an encounter is quite small, for wild bears nearly always move well away from oncoming humans.

Mind you, everything else in the woods will clear out, too, which means that you won't see much wildlife when clanging, whistling or shouting along. I'm a naturalist, and my job is to see things in the woods. So I usually go quietly—thus far without ill effect, the incident described on page 637 notwithstanding.

But there are times when all signs point to the necessity of making my presence known. When I'm moving along a noisy stream, or walking quickly along a winding trail in berry season or through head-high brush that blocks the view, with the wind coming toward me, then I contact the bears every minute or two, bellowing something like, "HOO-HOO-HOO-HOO," meaning "Hello, bears! This is a human being, and I'm coming through! No harm intended; would you mind letting me by?" They have always been polite and quick to oblige.

Wearing a small bell on your pack, by the way, won't do the job. What the sporting goods shops sell as "bear bells" are not nearly loud enough. They serve only as talismans. If you want to use a bell, better get one off a locomotive.

Wildlife workers who spend time along streams during salmon spawning take the greatest risk of any group. They have found that frequent blasts from a gas-cartridge air horn eliminate bear encounters, even though many bears are in the area.

Loud noises—really loud noises, such as the sounds of firecrackers or guns—have successfully repelled charging bears. They have also failed.

## Chemical repellents and guns

One hears of putting moth balls around one's campsite to deter foraging bears at night, or of carrying squirt guns loaded with ammonia. Pen-sized flare guns available in safety supply shops have often been carried by people working in the wilderness, apparently with some success. But these flares can also start forest fires.

**Anti-bear sprays** have become widely available in the last few years. Such sprays are aerosol cans containing about one percent **capsaicin,** the skin irritant found in plants of the pepper family. Designed to fire a tight stream a distance of 5–10 m, anti-bear sprays have proven to be effective repellents. But some bears seem not to react. And there are other problems. You must use the spray at very short range, meaning that you must be ready, and you must aim accurately. If you release the spray into the wind, it will come back on you, probably incapacitating you and perhaps not driving off the bear. A can of anti-bear spray has gone off in a helicopter, immediately blinding everyone on board, including the pilot; fortunately the machine was still on the ground at the time.

Anti-bear spray is a weapon, dangerous to the wielder as well as to the intended target. As a guide I feel obligated to carry it, but I don't like the stuff—and neither do the police, who see it turning up more and more often in bar fights and muggings. I expect it to be restricted soon to people with a demonstrated need to carry it.

Then there are guns. Should a person carry a gun in bear country? In most of the Rockies area this is allowed, although not in the national and provincial parks. Certainly firearms have saved human lives in bear attacks. But toting a gun on the trail tends to make a person overly bold and under-attentive—a bad combination. The same can be said of people armed with anti-bear spray. Pepper spray won't hurt a bear, but twitchy fingers on the triggers of high-powered rifles have been the death of many bears.

Biologists who study bears in the field seldom carry firearms; in fact, most recommend against doing so. An adequate rifle, meaning at least a .30-06 with heavy slugs, is a tiresome burden, and a large-calibre pistol, which is illegal for most people to possess in Canada, is woefully inaccurate.

Aiming properly to kill a bear is difficult as it lunges forward. The shooter must be experienced with the weapon and the weapon must be ready. If you shoot a bear that is attacking someone else, you risk killing that person by mistake. My conclusion: firearms are dangerous, much more likely to hurt someone than a bear is. So I don't carry a gun in the mountains.

## Being realistic

Despite the unpleasant nature of the foregoing, I hope that it has shown how unlikely it is that you will be injured by a bear in the Canadian Rockies. Herrero could document only 53 injuries by grizzly bears reported in the national parks up to 1979, and 24 of those attacks were in Glacier Park, Montana, a small area of prime grizzly-bear habitat that is heavily visited by people. For black bear attacks, Herrero found only 23 documented fatalities in all of Canada and the United States from 1900 through 1980.

Will the number of bear-inflicted injuries increase in the Canadian Rockies in the years ahead? Back-country use has not grown as quickly as once seemed certain, although in the long run the number of people in bear habitat is bound to increase, with more frequent encounters and thus more frequent injuries. One way to interpret the unusually high injury rate in Glacier is to conclude that the back country there is saturated with people, from the bears' point of view, which induces a constant bear/human tension found nowhere else in the Canadian Rockies area. If this is the case, then perhaps the problem at Glacier may spread to other parts of the Rockies as back-country travel increases beyond the danger point. But bear-carrying capacity varies greatly from place to place, and it would be folly to predict that what has happened in Glacier will happen everywhere. What is needed is continued, careful monitoring of the bears-and-man situation over the years. Hasty judgments by park managers, often made under pressure from a fearful public, have resulted in actions against wildlife that were regretted later.

## Why we need the grizzly bear

Grizzly bears top the food chain in the mountain ecosystem, and without them the natural community is in trouble, but the grizzly is also an icon of something we Canadians hold dear: our wildlands.

Let me illustrate this with a scenario I have seen often in Jasper National Park. A busload of visitors is cruising along the Icefields Parkway when someone shouts, "A bear!"

There it is: a big, furry, brown-and-buff bear, turning over stones and licking up the bugs not 50 m off the highway. The bus driver stops. Everyone rushes to the windows, cameras clicking and whirring. Cars pull over. People are getting out of them. The driver refuses to open the door, but some of the passengers just push their way out.

A park warden shows up. He hustles everybody back onto the bus and instructs the driver to move on. He is more concerned about an accident on the highway here than he is about a bear attack. To him it is a "bear jam," quite routine.

And the bear? It just keeps on with its bearish business (eat! eat!), ripping open rotting logs, rolling over boulders, ambling along from one scent to the next. Its coat ripples in the sun; it is the strongest wild thing in the mountains of North America. It has little interest in the spectators along the highway. Just part of living in a national park, eh?

Indeed, this *is* part of the national-park experience, worthwhile and fine. Never mind the touristy aspect. *The bear is there, and it's not in a zoo.* If there were no bears here, if all the bears were gone, then it would be like back home in Toronto. Or New Jersey, or Frankfurt, or Tokyo. It is the bear that awakens us to the fact that this is not any of those places. This is the Canadian Rockies, where bears run free in the wilderness.

# Cloven-hoofed crew

This is the order Artiodactyla, including the family Cervidae (deer, elk, caribou and moose) and the family Bovidae (sheep, goats and bison). All these animals are **ungulates,** from the Latin *unguis,* meaning a claw or fingernail. They have hoofs, which are nails gone huge. They also have the **rumen,** the stomach compartment in which bacteria break down cellulose.

You and I get no nourishment from the cellulose that makes up most of the vegetable fibre we eat, and neither do the ungulates, directly. But by feeding the countless bacterial cells in their rumens plenty of grass, leaves and live bark, the ungulates keep a constant flow of microorganisms moving from the rumen into the part of the gut that can process them and their metabolic byproducts as food. So an ungulate is an animal that lives mostly on bacteria. Proteins, sugars, other non-cellulose carbohydrates and fats, all of which are found in plant matter, can be digested directly.

All members of the deer family lack upper front teeth, or, as in caribou, the upper incisors do not develop enough to stick out through the gums. Rather than biting off their feed, they pinch it between the lower incisors and the palate and tear it off or pull it out of the ground, consuming some of the roots. The stomach is divided into four sections, and the animals have no gall bladders. Most deer-family species have scent glands on their legs and faces; other glands in their hooves spread scent wherever they go. Moose and elk lack the hoof glands.

An obvious difference between the deer family and the bovids is that deer, elk, moose and caribou grow antlers that are shed each year, while bighorn sheep, mountain goats and bison have proper horns, which grow throughout their lives. None of the native deer or bovids in the Rockies has upper incisors.

Most of the wild-animal carcasses found in the Rockies are those of ungulates. If the animal has not been consumed, you can often tell whether it was killed by predators or died on its own: prey are normally stretched out, amid blood, hair and other signs of the struggle, while carcasses that are curled up are usually those of animals that died on their own. Predators and scavengers eat everything but bone and hair. Wolves, coyotes and wolverines crack the bones to get at the marrow. No species eats the contents of the rumen, although ravens and other scavenging birds will pick through it.

## Feast all summer, starve all winter

For an ungulate, life depends on getting fat enough in summer to survive the winter. The dead grass and leaves these animals must eat in winter are not as nutritious as live vegetation. Through the winter the feed deteriorates. Molds attack it under the snow; small rodents eat it; the process of decay begins. This happens at the coldest time of year, when a great deal of energy must be expended just to keep warm. Ungulates must use nearly all their waking hours eating, and even so they cannot take in enough food. They lose weight all winter.

The trick is to lay on enough fat beforehand to make up the difference. All the ungulates become as fat as possible in the late summer and fall—that's when ungulate meat is most attractive to us omnivores in this, the hunting season—so they can use that fat through the winter.

Early spring is the key period. If you observe elk herds in the mountains in April, you can see how lean the animals are. Many of them are on the verge of starvation. Scattered heaps of well-picked bones in the wintering areas are all that remain

*Do hoofed animals get fat? Yes; this bighorn sheep has survived three winters by getting fat in the previous summers.*

of those that starved already. A late spring, a bad year for ticks, a round of overpopulation, or even an afternoon of unintentional harassment by humans wanting to get close with cameras, can send a weakened ungulate over the edge.

## Mule deer *Cerf mulet*

*Odocoileus hemionus* (deer family, Cervidae)
Year-round

Common in montane woods and brushy meadows from the Peace River south; occasional farther north. Length of adult males (bucks) 180 cm (tail 20 cm), height at shoulder 100 cm, weight 80–120 kg. Females (does) about 15 percent smaller, up to 80 kg. About the same size as the white-tailed deer, page 646, but with larger antlers. Much smaller than elk, page 647. Mule deer are reddish-brown in summer and gray in winter, always with a white rump patch, black-tipped white tail, white chin and white throat; the ears are white inside, rimmed with black. There are large scent glands at the bend in the back legs, smaller ones ahead of the eyes on the face and at the bases of the antlers, and others between the hoofs.

MW

To differentiate mule deer from the rather similar white-tailed deer, check the tail, which is narrow and white with a black tip on mule deer; wide and brown on white-tailed, fringed with white, showing all-white only when it is flipped up. The ears are long on mule deer, shorter on white-tailed; the eyes are larger on mule deer. A mule-deer antler branches in twos, while a white-tailed deer antler is a forward-pointed beam with tines that stick up along it.

Mule deer are active both day and night, napping every now and again; you see them most often at dusk and dawn. They move timidly about the woods, bounding away in stiff-legged jumps when approached—except in the national parks, where they have been protected for many generations and are thus a good deal less shy. I often see them along the highways, in campgrounds and walking down the alleys of Jasper townsite. They come into my yard to nibble the grass and the shrubbery, often staying the night and leaving gifts of fertilizer.

Does usually stay at low elevations year-round, often in small herds of a couple of females and their young, seldom venturing far from a home range about 15 ha in size. The adult bucks are usually solitary in summer, moving up to subalpine elevations and returning to the valley floors in winter, where they often join the female herds or buddy up with one or two other males. When deer populations are high, bucks form male herds in summer and fall.

In spring and summer deer eat mainly grasses and wildflowers, favoring leaves at summer's end; in winter they are browsers, nibbling the twigs and late-winter buds of shrubs, aspens, poplars and evergreens. They also eat lichens. They are beset with heavy-duty predators: mountain lions, wolves, coyotes, grizzly bears, lynx and bobcats.

Breeding behavior starts in early fall, when the bucks get a big dose of testosterone. This period is called the **rut.** The necks of the bucks swell. They follow the does, sniffing female urine puddles and wrinkling their upper lips to stimulate the estrus-sensing Jacobson's organ (see page 655). They also become quite aggressive at this time and should not be approached. People have actually been killed by rutting deer.

A buck's antlers begin to grow 60–80 days after the last set drops off in late winter or early spring. The "velvet," which is the blood-rich tissue that deposits the bony antler material, dries in early September, and the bucks rake their new sets through the brush and against small trees to strip it off. When the velvet is gone, the animals rub the bark off willows and small aspens, leaving scent on the injured stems from glands on the fronts of their faces.

Mule deer don't bugle as elk do, but the bucks spar with each other, placing their antlers together and shoving back and forth. Common and frequent among mule deer throughout the year, this sparring reinforces the hierarchy and produces a form of male bonding between partners. It's a form of sport. Even though the antler tips are quite sharp, sparring seldom produces injuries. Fights during the rut, though, cause many injuries and even death from infection.

Mule deer do not gather harems as elk do. A buck locates a receptive female, mates with her, then finds another. Fights over females do occur, of course, when two equally matched bucks encounter the same doe. The older, more experienced bucks mate with most of the females, while the younger bucks are generally unsuccessful.

A successful buck will impregnate several does between mid-November and early December. After a gestation period of about 210 days, the fawns are born in early June, sometimes as early as March or as late as November, for deer will come into heat several times in order to get pregnant. A doe's first breeding usually gives her just one fawn; after that she normally has twins.

The fawns are spotted and odorless; they hide in the brush or under conifers for their first month, nursing. Later they follow the doe about, staying with her until the next spring. When separated from mum for a moment, the young bleat plaintively, saying "baaa" in a high-pitched voice. Fawns lose their Bambi suits in late summer, going gray for the winter. Sexual maturity comes at about 18 months, and mule deer have lived in captivity for 20 years.

It is surprisingly risky to approach or feed a deer. Even though some deer seem tame, they are still wild animals and easily spooked. If this happens close to a human they often strike out with their front hoofs, which are hard and sharp, capable of inflicting bruises, cuts and even broken ribs. Deer fed by hand can become dangerous; they impatiently paw their providers, sometimes striking out.

### White-tailed deer *Cerf de Virginie*
*Odocoileus virginianus* (deer family)
Year-round

MW

Fairly common in montane open woods on the western slope from the Fraser River south and on both slopes in Waterton/Glacier; increasing in numbers on the eastern slope as humans move into the foothills, breaking up the forest and creating the woodland-edge habitats that white-tails require. Length of bucks up to 190 cm (tail 30 cm), height at shoulder 100 cm, weight up to 130 kg. Does are about ten percent smaller and weigh up to 80 kg.

Reddish-brown in summer and gray in winter like the mule deer, the white-tailed deer doesn't seem at first sight to have a white tail; the outside surface of the tail is brown, with a narrow white edge. But when the deer is about to run away, it flips up the tail and, sure enough, the tail is white underneath. So is the exposed rump. The look-alike mule deer, previous item, has a much narrower tail that is white on both surfaces, with a black tip. The white patch on a mulie's rump is bigger, and so are the ears. Compare the antlers. Both species have the same set of scent glands in the leg and face, at the base of the antlers and in the hoofs.

The general habits, food preferences and predators of the white-tailed deer are similar to those of the mule deer, so check the previous item for details. One difference: while the female mule deer seldom moves out of its 15-ha montane territory, the white-tailed doe moves up the mountains in summer, from its winter range in the open montane woods, through the heavy subalpine forest, where there is little in the way of deer food, to the alpine meadows above.

In this species the antlers of the bucks begin to grow in May, requiring about 140 days to reach full size in September. Older males drop their antlers in December, immediately after the fall rut; the younger ones keep theirs until early February.

White-tailed deer mate from mid-November through mid-December. The does usually deliver their fawns in late May and early June, after gestation of 205–210 days. This means that most are impregnated in late November. The fawns, usually one in the first year and two thereafter, are reddish-brown with white spots, looking like dapples of sunlight on the conifer-needle duff of the forest floor. They lie very still. The mother caches each fawn separately, often under the lower boughs of spruce trees up to 100 m apart. The doe nurses first one, then the other. Deer-family newborns are odorless, so predators often walk right on by—although enough kills are made to eliminate about half the yearly production.

The fawns follow their doe around after three weeks and are weaned at four months. The bucks grow their first set of antlers in their second winter. Those reaching adulthood may live for ten years in the wild, up to 20 years in captivity.

## *Deer antlers*

The antlers of mule deer branch in twos. The antlers of white-tailed deer point forward, with the tines arranged along a beam.

Many rodents depend on antlers to supplement their diets, which means that we humans should leave antlers where they lie rather than decorating our dens with them. This obvious ecosystem-protection measure has been codified in the national parks, where it is unlawful to steal antlers.

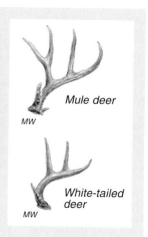

*Mule deer*

MW

*White-tailed deer*

MW

## *What happens to all the antlers?*

Deer, elk, moose and caribou grow and discard their antlers every year, and the bony antler material takes a long time to weather away. You'd think the woods would be full of antlers. However, small rodents and snowshoe hares help the process along considerably by gnawing antlers for the minerals—especially the phosphates—they contain. And there are lots more rodents and hares than there are deer.

Photo by Barbara Zimmer

### Elk/wapiti *Wapiti*
*Cervus elaphus* (deer family)
Year-round

Common on the eastern slope from Grande Cache south, in grassy places; on the western slope from Golden south. Occasional farther north. Within the national parks, elk tend to congregate in and around townsites and campgrounds. Length of adult males, often called "bulls" but properly termed "stags," is 230–270 cm (tail 14–17 cm), height at shoulder 140 cm, weight 330 kg. Females, often called "cows" but properly termed "hinds," are about ten percent smaller and weigh 250 kg.

MW

"Wapiti" is a Shawnee word meaning "white rump," a fitting name for this animal. The Blackfoot name is "ponoka," the name of a community in central Alberta. Using "wapiti" straightens out a mistake that won't go away: "elk" is the northern European name for the moose. I guess we are stuck with "elk," though; when I use "wapiti" no one knows what I'm talking about. Early British visitors to the Canadian west called the animals "red deer," because the same species, with slight differences, occurs in the British Isles, in other parts of Europe and across mid-latitude Asia. Our red deer came from northeastern Asia by way of the Bering Strait near the end of the late Wisconsinan glaciation about 12,000 years ago, when much of the shallow strait was land. They are practically identical to the Siberian elk.

Whatever you call them, elk are easily identifiable: large, with a long head on a long neck. The neck and head are dark brown, as are the legs and a halo around the buffy rump patch, which has the shape of a light bulb. The tail is small, the same color as the rump patch. The rest of the animal is light-brown to buff, lightest in winter—especially the males—at which time there is a shaggy mane on the neck. This mane looks tattered on some individuals. The neck hair falls off in patches that mark the sites of infestations of the **winter tick,** *Dermacentor albipictus.* Hairy scent glands are present on the hind legs, but not in the hoofs. There is an additional pair of scent glands at the base of the tail.

Elk are grazing and herding animals, able to live in forest, prairie or alpine habitats. A 1988 study of elk in the Bow Valley of Banff National Park showed that the animals move regularly through ranges averaging 15–30 km². About half the population there migrates annually from the valley floors, where they have spent the winter and spring, to the high country for the summer and back to low elevations in autumn. The same foods are eaten both in the valleys and above treeline; perhaps the change in range is to take advantage of the increased calorie content of higher-elevation plants.

Males predominate in this migration, but both sexes are involved, and so are many young of the year. Surprisingly, the same animals do not migrate every year. Some males even move to the valley floors for the fall mating period, then climb again to windblown clearings above treeline for much of the winter. Some Jasper-park stags that spend the summer in the eastern front ranges along Highway 16 regularly saunter—they rarely run—125 km west to the Rocky Mountain Trench after the rut.

In Banff and Jasper parks the males seldom join the females to form the large winter feeding herds noted in the American Rockies. Female/immature herds in Canada typically number 10–50 animals. The males are usually either solitary or in small groups of fewer than 20. Winter and summer, the females and young prefer meadows and open woods; in winter the males are often seen in heavier timber.

If the snow-cover is thin, which it usually is in the montane valleys, the animals continue to scrape through it to reach the grass that is their staple winter food, 75 percent of the cold-weather diet. They also eat aspen bark, the main reason that aspen are often black-scarred to about head-height. From this bark they get nitrogen, which the bacteria in their rumens require to break down the cellulose in the grass. Lodgepole pine needles, eaten even in years when grasses are abundant, may serve the same function. In summer, elk eat mostly willow leaves and wildflowers; grasses account for 20 percent of the warm-weather diet. They also eat lichens.

Elk are preyed upon by men, wolves, mountain lions and grizzly bears, ranked roughly by number of animals killed. The natural predators take mostly calves and, surprisingly, large bulls. The prime bulls grow weak during the fall rut, when they eat very little, making them easy prey in winter. The same is true for bighorn sheep, page 655. Many Rockies elk carry the large **American liver fluke**, *Fascioloides magna*, which is several centimetres long. This parasite produces a sizable cavity in the liver. An elk or deer can tolerate one or two, but heavily infected or otherwise weakened animals often die. See also the item on moose.

In the late nineteenth and early twentieth centuries the elk of the Canadian Rockies were almost wiped out by hunters, who shot them not only for their meat but also for their vestigial canine teeth—called "elk ivory," unique among the deer family in the Rockies—which sold for up to 75 dollars a pair to members of the Elks Club, and for their antlers, which were made into knife handles. Small populations in the Tuchodi Lakes and Muskwa River areas of the northern Rockies survived, and possibly a few animals escaped the hunters farther south as well. But elk had to be largely reintroduced into Banff and Jasper parks, in 1917 and 1920 respectively. Killing of wolves and other large carnivores, which was policy in the national parks at that time, had the effect of causing a population explosion among the ungulates, and soon the wardens were killing elk, too. This kind of wildlife management by rifle continued for many years; in Jasper park the predator/prey ratio is now in better balance, so numbers are more stable. In British Columbia, elk population densities are less, and elk have become solidly reestablished only in the southeastern corner of the province and in their northern stronghold.

The notion that elk are plains creatures, foreign to the mountains, is false; remains show that the species lived throughout the Canadian Rockies until the recent near-extermination.

Antler growth among elk stags begins in April, not long after last-year's set has dropped off in February or March. Young males, who herd with the females for a couple of years, grow peculiar-looking antlers at first: small and upright, like two-tined pitchforks; these animals are called "spike males." Among Bow Valley elk, the second-year set of antlers is surprisingly mature, with four or five points; the third-year set has the normal six tines, so from the third year on the antlers give no obvious indication of age. The rack of a stag in its prime is magnificent, often 150 cm long, reaching well down the back and weighing 12–17 kg.

Why would an animal grow and then lose these heavy structures *each year?* There is a good evolutionary reason for doing so. Antlers are biological indicators, growing large when an animal is strong and healthy, smaller when it is not. The bigger, healthier males, which have done well at foraging and thus usually have the larger antlers, are the ones that impregnate the females. Such animals are evolutionary successes, and their genes strengthen ongoing generations.

Rutting begins in late August, when the stags thrash the velvet off their antlers against shrubs and small pines. The necks of the stags swell. They urinate in the mud, then roll in it, and they "bugle": make a strange call that starts with a low "unnh," goes up the scale in a series of whistles and finishes with grunts and coughs.

All of this is most attractive to the hinds (pronounced like "rinds"). Each picks a favorite stag and hangs around him as part of a **harem.** Other stags challenge for possession of the harem. Rival stags lower their heads to bring their antlers together, then push and shove each other around. A successful stag might have up to 30 hinds in his harem, and he usually manages to impregnate them all.

But the other stags are not denied entirely. While the dominant stag is dozing or busy, the bolder rivals mount the hinds. By Christmas the hinds are pregnant and the rut is winding down. The stags have eaten very little since August, and they have lost a lot of weight.

In the national parks, elk rut along the highway shoulders and up and down the streets of Banff and Jasper. Drivers must be careful not to smash into heedless elk along the roads at night. Elk don't run across the road suddenly, like deer do; they just walk majestically out into traffic.

Stag-watchers on foot are warned to be wary. The big animals, which stand taller than a man, consider any other creature that is not a hind to be an adversary. If you get too close to a rutting stag—10 m or so—he will come toward you, throwing those enormous antlers up and down and pawing the ground. Time to get back in the car, fast.

The central meadow in Whistlers Campground, at Jasper, is the site of a 600-seat outdoor theatre where park naturalists present evening programs. In late August of most years that clearing also holds a stag and his harem. On some evenings the campers approach the theatre, carrying their blankets and flashlights, only to be driven back by the stag, who thinks they are after his females. But while the stag is threatening those campers coming from one side of the meadow, others sneak in from the opposite direction. Eventually everyone gets seated and the program begins.

Ah, but the stag is now patrolling the periphery of the theatre. Having resisted the intrusion into his meadow, he is not going to let anyone *leave*. The naturalist has a captive audience; if someone is overly bored, too bad. By the time the show ends, though, it is dark and the stag has settled down for the night. The campers go to their sites with a story to tell.

Each female elk usually bears one fawn each year, in late May or early June after gestation of 249–262 days. Often it is born on an island in a lake or river; it swims to shore with its mother only a few hours after birth. The fawn is white-spotted like a deer fawn, hidden by its mother in the brush for about ten days and nursed when safe to do so. Sometimes several mothers cache their fawns in the same spot. Weaning is in September, when the spots disappear. Already a third of the year's young have been lost to predators; two-thirds will be gone by the following spring. Maturity comes at 16 months (the second fall), but the females normally don't breed until their third year, and the males are not strong enough to gather a harem until they are four or five years old.

*An elk with her fawn is dangerous.* She is quite protective, especially during a fawn's first few weeks, when it is a favorite prey of large carnivores. From late May to mid-July, stay well away from any female elk.

The lifespan of a female elk may reach 24 years, but the males seldom live more than 13 years, owing mainly to predation and starvation during winter, which they enter exhausted from the rut, often wounded, and usually too lean from lack of eating. Often, prime males are taken by wolves at only seven or eight years. This explains the lop-sided sex ratio seen among elk: 30–40 stags for each 100 hinds.

## See the Wildlife-watcher's Code, page 669

## This is not a good idea

More visitors are showing up in the Rockies national parks in fall and spring these days, thanks in part to advertising campaigns intended to increase business in what the tourist industry calls the "shoulder seasons." And some of those visitors are having wildlife experiences they hadn't expected, such as being chased through the woods by an enraged rutting stag or getting kicked in the chest and trampled by a mother elk protecting her young from persistent wildlife watchers who are, as far as she is concerned, acting like predators. These animals are large and powerful; they can kill you. Keep your distance. Parks Canada has issued a pamphlet on the subject, and some problem spots around Banff and Jasper have been closed to the public seasonally. At time of writing the situation is getting worse. I wish the parks service would get enough people in uniform out there in the spring and fall to referee the situation.

## Moose *Orignal*
*Alces alces* (deer family)
Year-round

Fairly common in subalpine meadows and marshes, sometimes higher or lower; less common south of Lake Louise. Length 250 cm (tail 17 cm), height at the shoulder 181 cm, weight of Rockies moose typically 450 kg. Females are about ten percent smaller.

MW

The moose is the second-largest naturally occurring land animal in North America. The bison, page 653, is the biggest; horses are imports. Moose are brown all over, darker underneath, with no white rump patch as other deer-family members have. There are scent glands on the legs and at the bases of the antlers, but not in the hoofs. With its long head and dark color, the moose is hard to mistake for any other animal.

This creature is a product of the Pleistocene, well-designed for an ice-age existence in cold, snowy, marshy country. It survives low temperatures and deep snow, simply cruising through on its long legs. Those same legs are useful in summer, for wading out into bogs and reaching down under the water with that lengthy muzzle to pull up swamp vegetation. Despite the ungainly look, moose are quite agile, able to run at 50 km/h through the woods. Moose swim well, as do other deer, but moose also dive beneath the surface in lakes to reach vegetation as deep as 5 m.

The antlers of the bulls have palm-like blades with tines along the edges. Hanging under the chin is a long skin flap called the "bell," a scent-dispenser that the bull impregnates with urine. If the antlers are large, so is the bell. However, the bell often freezes off and does not regrow.

"Moose" means "twig-eater" in Algonquin, an apt name, for the animal does a lot of that very thing. Its favorite browse species are willows, red-osier dogwood and shrub-size aspen and poplar. These are winter staples; in summer moose spend much of their time belly-deep in marshes, gobbling water plants. They have been known to eat lichens.

In summer, moose are mostly loners, sharing overlapping ranges of a few square kilometres. You seldom see more than one at a time, except for a cow with her calf. Outside the rutting season they are quite shy, moving well away when humans are around. If you hold very still they seem to forget that you are there. They are active at any time, but mainly at dusk and at dawn.

In winter, when the other ungulates are down in the montane valley bottoms escaping the snow, the moose tend to stay at somewhat higher elevations, stepping through metre-deep drifts along shrubby streamcourses. They often kneel in the middle of the road in winter, licking highway salt, so watch out for them if you are driving at dusk. Their dark coloration makes them hard to see, even though they are huge.

The main predators of moose in the Canadian Rockies are packs of wolves and men. A grizzly bear is strong enough to take a weakened adult, as is a cougar. Moose don't tolerate liver flukes, page 648, as well as elk and deer do, and moose populations can be decimated when rising numbers of elk bring too many of these parasites into the grazing environment.

Moose antlers begin to grow in April. The velvet dies and dries in late August; by early September the hormones are flowing freely and both sexes are acting completely wacko. They lose their shyness, the cows bleating and thrashing in the brush to attract the bulls, who produce very sexy coughs and bellows.

Contests between bulls are largely bluffing matches: they posture and shake their antlers menacingly at each other, mentally comparing size and shape. Rather than getting down to rude pushing and shoving, one party will often decide that, golly, the rival's rack is just too wonderful, and bow out.

On the other hand, bull moose can fight viciously with their antlers. People are simply other suitors as far as the bulls are concerned, and one is well advised to keep clear in rutting season. There have been serious injuries and deaths from bull-moose attacks.

Valerius Geist, a well-known mammalogist from the University of Calgary, once attracted the wrath of a bull while filming it in the fall. The bull paid little attention to Val and his co-worker at first, so the two men decided to imitate another bull in order to get some action. Val rolled up his sleeves, exposing his bare arms—white like antlers—and he spread his arms out, tilting them as a moose does. This ploy was a little too successful; it provoked a charge. Fortunately the moose caught the human scent before making contact and veered away.

In light of that story, imagine some poor hiker in a teeshirt crossing a log or a beaver dam, arms out to keep in balance …

The females (cows) are impregnated between mid-September and late November. After gestating for 240–246 days, the cow bears one calf or twins—usually just one in the Canadian Rockies—in late May or early June. It is on its feet right away, depending on its mother for defence rather than on protective coloration and concealment.

A cow moose is quite protective, and thus dangerous to approach, when her calf is less than a month old. Cow moose have trampled to death humans whom they took to be possible predators. When the calf is a month old the cow expects it to follow her wherever she goes, even across raging rivers and into deep lakes, wherein it sometimes drowns. Weaning is at about three months, but the calf follows doggedly throughout its first year. The young moose stays with its mother until the birth of the next offspring, when mum chases the yearling away. For a few weeks it seems rather lost, an easy meal for wolves. If it survives this crisis, it might live for another 20 years.

## Caribou/reindeer *Caribou*
*Rangifer tarandus* (deer family)
Year-round

An endangered species found on alpine tundra in the summer and in subalpine forest in the winter between Pine Pass and the Siffleur Wilderness, which is south of the North Saskatchewan River. Despite its low numbers—probably under 500 in the Alberta Rockies, with an unknown number in B.C.—the species seems to be extending its range south,

MW

having been reported several times in winter along the Icefields Parkway just north of Bow Summit, and near Lake Louise in summer. Caribou are also present in the north end of the Rockies, from the Graham River north. Most Rockies caribou stay within the front ranges and main ranges year round, but some migrate northeast to the boreal forest of the foothills belt in winter. They return in spring.

Length of adult males, properly called "bucks or stags" but commonly termed "bulls," is 190 cm tail 15 cm, height at the shoulder 100 cm, weight 120–250 kg. Does, also called "cows," are about 25 percent smaller. These figures are from Jasper National Park. The name "caribou" comes from the French pronunciation of "xalibu," an Algonquin word meaning "the one that paws or scratches."

Caribou are about the size of mule deer but more heavily built, with thick necks, long, moose-like heads and big feet. Unlike the other deer-family ungulates in the Rockies, both sexes of caribou grow antlers. Male antlers are large and curved, with a palm-like section on one antler—seldom on both—that juts forward over the muzzle. Female antlers are smaller, and not all females grow antlers. Female antlers are out of phase with male ones; they grow from June to September and stay on through April or May, dropping when the fawns are born. Antler growth on bucks starts in May; the velvet dries up in September, ready for the short fall rut, and the antlers drop off right afterward. So in winter it is the females that have antlers, while the males do not. In summer it is usually possible to determine sex by antler size: mature males have larger ones. Caribou antlers become rubbery after they drop off, and their former owners are inclined to chew them up.

Our caribou are dingy brown in summer, with uneven patches of white on the rump, belly, backs of the legs and tip of the nose; there are bands of white just above the hoofs, like spats. The long winter coats are generally lighter-colored, with a mane of long white hair on the neck, especially pronounced on bulls.

Canadian Rockies caribou are but remnants of what must have been huge herds in the mountains at the end of the last big glacial interval 11,000 years ago, when treeline was lower and much of the region was unforested. The species has declined alarmingly since the 1950s, due mostly to logging of old-growth forests, road kills, human settlement and poaching. Even the herds in southern Jasper National Park and the Siffleur Wilderness, which stay within protected lands year round, are gradually losing numbers and are down to 100–150 animals at time of writing. The total for the entire Canadian Rockies is unknown, but it may be under a thousand.

In summer you have to get up above treeline to see caribou. In Jasper park there are some reasonably short routes to caribou country. One is to take the tramway up The Whistlers, walk to the summit of the peak and into the meadows on the other side. Another is to hike the trail to Cavell Meadows, which starts at the end of the road to Mt. Edith Cavell. In winter, caribou are often seen along the Icefields Parkway between the Jonas Creek Campground and Beauty Creek Hostel, at Silverhorn Creek, and along the Maligne Road not far from Maligne Lake. In spring they show up on the big alluvial fan at the head of Medicine Lake, where horsetails and sedges come up early.

The animals stay in small herds; they are easily spooked and seldom let a human get close, except along roads in winter and spring, when they are licking highway salt. They run like horses, prancing along with their necks out straight. Tendons snapping over bones in their feet produce a unique clicking sound. Not very vocal, caribou snort when surprised and occasionally grunt to each other.

The main caribou foods, summer and winter, are ground-growing lichens such as *Cladina*, page 408. In summer the animals also eat grasses, sedges and horsetails, and in winter when the snow is too deep for them to reach the ground lichens they eat tree lichens such as *Bryoria* and the twig-ends of shrubs. Caribou move down below treeline in winter, which puts the animals into deep-snow country, but nature has provided snowshoes. Caribou hoofs grow large and splay out in winter, with a thick growth of stiff hair underneath and around the sides.

Mountain caribou have few predators. Wolves seldom go above treeline in summer, nor do the packs hunt very often in the deep subalpine snow. Grizzly bears and mountain lions kill a few caribou, and migratory caribou can be attacked by wolves in the foothills in winter. Their main threat is from the clear-cutting of the large tracts of lichen-rich old-growth forests they need for survival. Plowed roads, snowmobile tracks and packed ski trails allow wolves to penetrate their deep-snow sanctuaries in winter; environmentalists have asked Parks Canada to quit plowing the road to Maligne Lake, to protect these animals in winter.

Rutting begins in early October and ends in early November. The stronger bucks try to gather harems of does, as elk do; in the mountains the herds are small and so are the harems, usually fewer than a dozen animals. Gestation is 7–8 months, and one calf is born between mid-May and July. The spotted fawn is up within 30 minutes and able to outrun a human by the next day, when it falls in with the herd. For the first month it lives on milk, then begins to eat vegetation, but it suckles occasionally throughout its first winter. In both sexes, the first set of antlers appears at 3–4 months. Females are sexually mature at 16 months and males later, as is typical of the deer family. A study of caribou mortality in Jasper park showed a mean age at death of 10.4 years for cows and 9.0 years for bulls, showing that male caribou may survive longer relative to the females than male elk do. The record geriatric caribou in Jasper is an 18-year-old cow.

## Bison/buffalo *Bison*
*Bison bison* (bovid family, Bovidae)
Year-round

MW

Properly speaking it is *bison,* not buffalo. The term "buffalo" is properly used for the true buffalo of Africa and Asia. The native bison of the Rockies is often called the "wood bison," but it is genetically identical to the more-familiar bison of the plains. The shaggier coat and other characteristics of the "wood" bison come out when any individual *Bison bison* lives in a cold, forested climate.

This is the largest land native animal in North America. Length of bulls 350 cm, height 170 cm, weight 700 kg. Some reach 900 kg. Females about 25 percent smaller. Easily identified: dark brown all over, shaggy from very large head to prominent shoulder hump, shorter-haired elsewhere. Upturned black horns on both sexes.

Bison once lived in montane meadows and open woods throughout much of the eastern slopes of the Canadian Rockies, and on the western slope from Golden south, but they were hunted to extinction throughout the region by the 1880s. After the species was reintroduced in Canada in 1906, from a herd kept in Montana, a few of the animals wound up in paddocks at Banff and Waterton. There is a small herd of non-native bison in a paddock in Waterton Lakes National Park, and until recently another herd was kept in a paddock near Banff. Other animals are found on bison ranches in the foothills. A herd of about 600 feral bison has become established in the northern foothills around Pink Mountain, having grown from 200 that escaped from a nearby bison ranch in 1962.

Concerned that the Banff paddock was really a kind of zoo, and worried that the fencing was impeding wildlife movements in the Valley, Parks Canada planned to send its bison to new homes in Saskatchewan in 1994. But Banff businesses successfully lobbied the government to retain the paddock as a tourist attraction for two more years.

Jasper National Park may have the best natural bison range in the Rockies, and in 1973 a small herd of about 28 animals was helicoptered from Elk Island National Park, east of Edmonton, to the remote northeastern corner of Jasper park. But nearly all the animals quickly moved out of the park and into the foothills. Twenty-two were recaptured and returned to the park, but in the end, most strayed and were lost. Two bulls stayed on, moving south to the grassy meadows around the old Jasper House site along the Athabasca River. Too bad the animals had not been a cow/bull pair! One disappeared soon after, and the other was last seen in the fall of 1984, so it must be long dead. In 1978 or 1979 seven or eight escapees from a bison ranch near Hinton entered Jasper National Park via Mystery Pass. All but one soon died, mostly in bison/train encounters, but the remaining cow hung on until 1995 or 1996. Her bones were found along the Rocky River in 1997.

Bison feed mostly on grasses and wildflowers. The sexes herd separately, coming together in July for rutting. The bulls charge each other, knocking heads—not horns—to achieve dominance of a harem. Gestation is 270–285 days; each female gives birth to one calf in May. It follows its mother right away. She protects it from intruders by charging, and the bulls can be ornery, too, so stay out of bison paddocks and keep clear of any bison you see in the wild. The calf nurses for up to seven months and is sexually mature in 2–3 years in the wild, sooner in captivity. These animals can live a long time, typically 25 years.

## Bighorn sheep/mountain sheep *Mouflon d'Amérique*

*Ovis canadensis* (bovid family, Bovidae)
Year-round

MW

Fairly common on the eastern slope from Pine Pass south and on the western slope from Golden south, on open hillsides with grass at any elevation. Length of adult males, called rams, is 172 cm (tail 12 cm), height at the shoulder 97 cm, weight up to 125 kg. Females, called ewes, are about 20 percent smaller and much lighter, averaging 65 kg. Both sexes have horns.

Shorter than a mule deer but stockier, the bighorn is mostly brown in summer and gray in winter, at all times with a large white rump patch, small dark-brown tail, white muzzle-tip and white line down the back of each leg. There are scent glands just ahead of the eyes, on the legs and between the two parts of the hoof. Dall's sheep, next item, is quite similar, but lives north of the Peace River. The two ranges do not overlap.

Female bighorn sheep somewhat resemble domestic goats, and thus many visitors to the Rockies think the ewes they see are mountain goats, page 657. But the two species really look quite different. The goats are completely white, rather than brown-and-white like bighorns. The goats' horns are shiny black, straighter and more slender than the gray-brown, rough-surfaced, well-curved horns of the sheep. The difference is most obvious in the rams, which have much longer, much heavier horns than the ewes do. Ram horns often spiral nearly 360°.

We are speaking here of true horns, which grow continuously from birth and are not shed and regrown annually as the antlers of the deer family are. Seasonal growth fluctuations in bighorns produce alternate grooves and swellings along the horn; by counting the major ones you can determine an animal's age.

In June the thick winter coat is shed. It often comes off in tattered hunks that give the animals a diseased look. While the animals may indeed be diseased, and most wild creatures have lots of skin parasites, the raggedness is quite normal at this time of year.

Bighorns eat mostly grasses, which make up 60 percent of their diet in summer, along with wildflowers, foliage and lichens. In winter they seek out windblown slopes where the grass is exposed, nibbling the shrubbery when grass is scarce or covered with snow. Bighorns are sociable, living in flocks of about 10–50 animals. They graze together on and near steep, rocky ground almost as precipitous as mountain-goat terrain, running to ledges when predators approach. Wolves, mountain lions and grizzly bears take lambs and adult sheep; lynx and possibly golden eagles are able to kill lambs.

This species prefers to be in the open and seldom travels more than a few hundred metres through the woods. Fire prevention in the past 100 years has greatly increased the forest cover of the Rockies, shrinking the suitable bighorn habitat. This has decreased the number of animals the mountains can support, and it is causing the flocks to become isolated from one another.

This is mostly negative, but the increased isolation confers some protection from fatal infestations of the **lungworms** *Protostrongylus stilesi* and *P. rushi,* which have caused mass die-offs of the sheep, and it also helps to slow the spread of **soremouth,** also called **orf,** a viral disease that turns the mouths and hoofs of afflicted bighorns into crusty messes and often kills them. Soremouth is similar in some ways to the hoof-and-mouth disease that afflicts domestic cattle, but it is caused by a different virus.

Surprisingly, cold winter air is essential to ungulate health, especially among sheep. Breathed in, it tends to kill parasites such as lungworm. Thus, overly mild winters are just as difficult for sheep as overly cold ones.

The geographic range of a typical bighorn flock in the Rockies is small, usually taking in a small number of grazing areas among which the sheep move only a few kilometres seasonally. Wherever a flock goes it leaves dusty bedding-down spots littered with black pellet-like droppings. In summer the rams separate from the ewes and immatures. The rams graze in flocks above treeline where possible, while the rest usually remain at lower elevations. In fall the sexes reconvene for the rut.

Bighorns are well-known for head-butting, and both rams and ewes engage separately in petty pushing and bumping to maintain the pecking order. The rams spend much of their time when not grazing one-upping each other in displays of machismo. All-out fights occur during the rut, which begins in early November and runs through most of December. The rams follow the ewes about, sniffing their rear ends and urine puddles for the odor of heat. A ram curls his upper lip, head raised—an action called "flehmen"—which allows odors to reach his estrus-sensing **Jacobson's organ,** which is located in the upper palate. When two rams court the same ewe, posturing usually intimidates the one with smaller horns, but if neither backs down the script moves on to the strange and violent ritual for which these beasts are famous. The animals back off 10–15 m and rear up on their hind legs, snorting loudly. They lower their heads as they charge forward, front legs pawing the air. The horns collide with an echoing crack; the combatants stagger away for a moment, shaking their heads. When the bells quit ringing they display their horns, back off and do it again, over and over—reportedly for up to 25 hours at a stretch—until one gives up and is chased off.

Bighorns hardly ever charge humans, thank heavens, but the species gets touchy during the rut and it is wise to keep well out of the way.

The toughest ram impregnates most of the ewes, maintaining the genetic strength of the flock. But the strength of that particular ram may be at a low ebb after beating his head for weeks, during which time he seldom eats. The coldest part of winter is just ahead, and the wolves are waiting for the least sign of weakness. He who most recently walked the halls of power may soon lie mangled in the snow. Among bighorns the position of chief stud changes every couple of seasons. Only the true herd leader, always an old ewe, abides.

The new lambs arrive in late May and early June; gestation is 175 days. Births are usually single. Each lamb lies hidden for its first week, then quickly learns to follow its mother on the precipitous terrain this species uses to evade its predators. Mum says "baa" to her lamb when it bleats. Weaned at five or six months, the young mature sexually at two to three years and may live for 14 years in the wild.

The provincial governments allow hunting of bighorns in the Rockies by people who wish to possess sheep-heads. The animals are quite shy in places where they are hunted, but in the national parks they have been protected for many generations and are frequently seen close beside the highway, or right in the middle of it, readily approachable. Poachers in Jasper park have been known to simply walk up to tame bighorns licking highway salt off the road and shoot them point blank. The wardens will go to any length, including long investigations in cooperation with the police forces of other countries, to catch the people who do this. The penalties used to be trivial, but amendments to the National Parks Act in 1988 raised the fine to $150,000, plus a prison term, for any sheep poached in the parks. Same for mountain goats, grizzly bears and several other important species. The bighorn sheep is Alberta's official mammal.

If you want to see bighorn sheep, the following places offer a good chance. Please be cautious as you drive by; the sheep can run out in the road suddenly. Some visitors still feed the sheep from the car window—a criminal thing to do, and punishable by a hefty fine.
- At Appekunny Creek along the Manyglacier Road in Glacier park.
- Near the trail to Crandell Lake, along the Akamina Road to Cameron Lake in Waterton park.
- Along the road to Red Rock Canyon in Waterton park.
- In Sinclair Canyon, along Highway 93 near Radium Hot Springs.
- In the first few kilometres west of the Mt. Norquay/Banff intersection on the TransCanada Highway. Vermilion Lakes Drive passes through the same area.
- At the Mt. Kitchener and Tangle Falls viewpoints along the Icefields Parkway in southern Jasper park, just north of the Columbia Icefield.

- Along Highway 16 east of Jasper. Good locations: at the junction with the Maligne Road, at Cold Sulphur Spring 20 km east of the townsite, at Cinquefoil Bluff (west end of Talbot Lake) and at Disaster Point, where there is a mineral lick frequented by mountain goats as well as sheep.
- At Miette Hot Springs in eastern Jasper park.

## The road-kill problem

Its craving for road salt costs the bighorn sheep dearly in the national parks. The animals often do not get out of the way when a car comes. Fast-moving trucks sometimes kill more than one sheep at a time.

Parks Canada is currently experimenting with calcium chloride in Jasper National Park as a substitute for the usual sodium chloride, but calcium chloride doesn't work as well in the sanding mix and will probably be abandoned. Considering the inestimable value of the park's bighorns, one would think that the government would be willing to pay for calcium-magnesium acetate (CMA), an expensive but truly effective salt substitute. However, this doesn't seem to be the case.

In Banff National Park most of the TransCanada Highway has been fenced. This keeps the animals off the road, but the fence is a real hindrance to normal wildlife movement and it allows predators to trap sheep, deer and elk against the fence and kill them. A better solution, more in line with the park's mandate to put wildlife first and human convenience second, is to slow the traffic down, enforce the speed limit, put on CMA in minimal amounts, and—my wife's suggestion—make the truckers, who routinely speed through the kill zones, go in hourly convoys behind a Parks Canada pilot car. This may sound silly, but the road-kill rate among bighorns along Highway 16 in Jasper National Park is now so high that over the long term it threatens the viability of the flocks.

MW

### Dall's sheep/Stone's sheep *Mouflon de Dall*
*Ovis dalli* (bovid family)
Year-round

   Fairly common from the Peace River north, in steep, rocky places with grass. Length 160 cm (tail 10 cm), height at shoulder 95 cm, weight 90 kg. Females are quite a bit smaller, as much as 40 percent. See drawing of bighorn sheep on page 654 for illustration.

   Dall's sheep are very similar to bighorns, previous item, but a little smaller and less ruggedly built, with pointier faces and smaller horns. In our area we have the race known as Stone's sheep, *O. dalli stonei,* named for, Andrew J. Stone, an American hunter/naturalist who supplied some to the American Museum of Natural History in the 1890s. Unlike the better-known pure-white *O. dalli dalli,* which lives in most of the Yukon, Stone's sheep is mostly dark-brown to black, with a gray head. The rest is bighorn-like: white rump with a black tail, white muzzle and white stripes down the backs of the legs. Habits are practically identical to those of the bighorn, including ignorance of predatory cars and trucks. The sheep are frequently out on the Alaska Highway around Summit Lake in Stone Mountain Provincial Park; please watch out for them.

### Mountain goat *Chèvre de montagne*
*Oreamnos americanus* (bovid family)
Year-round

   Fairly common on very steep, cliffy terrain, usually at high elevations. Unreported between Pine Pass and the Peace River. Males, called "billies," average 180 cm long (tail 12 cm), stand 106 cm at the shoulder and weigh up to 120 kg. Females, called "nannies," are about 30 percent smaller. The young are called "kids." All this terminology is off the mark, because mountain goats are not goats at all, as explained farther on.

   A mountain goat is easily identified by its long, thick white coat. Sometimes it is yellowish. No other large animal in the mountains is this light-colored. But note that when the goats cover themselves in dust the color becomes darker. The only really dark parts of the species are the jet-black horns, eyes, tip of nose and hoofs. Differentiating the sexes is difficult, except when the kids are with the nannies, but the horns of most nannies curve rather sharply at the tips, while those of most billies start curving farther down. Both sexes have scent glands at the horn bases.

   Rumors that this creature is not really a goat are true: it is related most closely to the **serows** *(Capricornis* spp.) and **gorals** *(Naemorhedus* spp.), which are mountain antelopes of Asia. A more distant relative is the **chamois** of Europe *(Rupicapra rupicapra).* The pronghorn antelope of the prairies, often compared with the mountain goat, is not even in the same family.

   Male mountain goats are solitary, but the nannies and young of both sexes are loosely social. Typically one sees them as a half-dozen white dots scattered over the gray limestone slabs of a front-range peak. Mountain goats are present in the main ranges as well. The foothills belt is generally too low in elevation to support mountain goats.

   These animals use communal shelters under big overhangs; I have often come across the dusty bedding spots amid accumulations of pellet-like droppings, which look just like sheep scats. While grazing in summer, nannies with kids tend to stay near other females. Despite this sociability the nannies do not tolerate the close approach of other nannies. They use their horns to intimidate one another. When billies are present, they are subservient to the nannies, except during the rut. Females become territorial in the winter, excluding all others from their chosen wintering spots.

   Mountaineers know that viewers looking up from below see nothing but the cliffs, while the climber or the goat, looking down from on high, sees the ledges. This kind of terrain keeps the goats safe from most predators. Mountain lions take a few, golden eagles may kill the odd kid, and humans get the most.

   Some goats are killed in falls despite their incredible climbing ability, but the main hazard to this species turns out to be avalanches. In winter the fierce high-country wind keeps grassy west-facing slopes clear of snow, and the goats, warm in their shaggy coats, prefer to stay up high while all the other ungulates are heading down to the valley floors. Steep gullies are routinely crossed, and sometimes the snow lets go. Several times I have come across the bodies of goats melting out of avalanche debris.

What do they find to eat up there in the barren rocks? Mostly grass—about 75 percent of the diet in summer—growing luxuriously on ledges. They also eat wildflowers, sedges and lichens. The windiness of this habitat tends to expose feed in winter, but the goats must sometimes depend upon the needles and twigs of subalpine fir.

Mountain goats moult in June, when shrubs along goat-paths become adorned with fluffy white hair. Goats losing their winter coats look just as ragged and terrible as do shedding bighorns, with big patches of purple skin showing through. People come to the park authorities, asking, "What's wrong with your goats?" Given a couple of weeks the new hair grows in and the animals look fine.

Mountain goats need sulphur, an essential element for growing the vast amount of hair they shed each year. They get their sulphur from the gypsum (calcium sulphate) content in limy glacial silt deposits, and from the breakdown of pyrite (iron sulphide) in black-shale outcrops. The animals seldom lick road surfaces for salt; I have seen this behavior only once.

Normally wary, mountain goats at a lick show surprisingly little fear of humans. Perhaps this is a measure of how desperate the goats are for the minerals they need. One can only assume that they are stressed, even though they may tolerate being approached within a few metres. Thus we must be considerate. Apply the wildlife-watching rules given on page 669.

Jasper park is fortunate in having two licks that are right next to the road. There is parking at both. The Goats-and-Glaciers Viewpoint is 38 km south of Jasper on the Icefields Parkway; the Disaster Point lick is 29 km east of Jasper along Highway 16.

Another well-known goat lick is on the southern boundary of Glacier National Park, along Highway 2 about five kilometres east of the Walton Ranger Station. Glacier has the greatest concentration of mountain goats in the Rockies. Anyone walking in the high country there is likely to see a few. The peaks, steep but ledgy, afford excellent habitat.

Mating among mountain goats takes place in November. One looks for bizarre behavior in ungulates during the rut, and the goats don't disappoint. The billies coat themselves well in urine-soaked dust. They thrash vegetation with their horns, which are encircled with scent glands at the base, and they strike heroic poses before the nannies. Competing billies circle each other, hunching their backs and throwing their heads up and down. They lie next to each other in dust wallows, pawing the ground with a foreleg. In fights, the billies spar with their horns, sometimes inflicting serious injuries or even killing each other. Harem-building can occur if the snow is deep, but usually the goats pair off as couples and scatter among the cliffs for mating.

A billy approaches his mate-to-be from behind, actually or ritually sneaking up until he can kick her sharply in the side in what must be construed as a sign of affection. There is usually one kid, sometimes twins, born in late May or mid-June after gestation of 178 days. The little goats are endearing: lively and playful, nursing on bended front knees with tiny wriggling tails, tripping after the nannies wherever they go, up and down the cliffs. The kids are usually present at the licks described above. They are weaned at six weeks and on their own by the following spring, although they stay in the parents' neighborhood until sexual maturity (27 months for nannies, 39 months for billies). Mountain goats may live 12 years in the wild.

## *Primates (order Primates, family Hominidae)*

In the Rockies we find only one species in this group.

### Human *Homme*
*Homo sapiens* (hominid family)
Year-round

Common in townsites and other inhabited places, fairly common on highways, occasional on trails, seldom seen in untracked places. Average length of adult males, called "men," 170 cm (no tail), height at the shoulder 145 cm, weight 75 kg. Females, called "women," are somewhat smaller. Easily identified: our only mammal that habitually walks on its hind legs.

This animal is sparsely haired over most of its body, but grows visible patches on the head, groin and under the front legs. Coat color varies considerably from individual to individual. Males and females are difficult to tell apart, for the species is inclined to cover its mammaries and genitalia, even in hot weather and when swimming. Vocalizations are frequent and varied.

Humans are predominantly migratory, arriving in the Canadian Rockies mostly in June and July—biggest influx: July 1—and leaving by the end of September. The summer visitors live in densely colonial campgrounds, staying in family groups in a bewildering variety of mobile temporary shelters. Popular forms include tents, towed hutches and motorized cottages. A few humans remain in the mountains year-round, building large heated dens for winter use, stocking them with food and bringing in entertaining possessions.

*H. sapiens* is omnivorous, consuming everything from raw fish and grains to foods that apparently have no nutritive value whatever. Eschewing naturally occurring foods, humans carry imported delicacies with them during their summer migrations. A favorite seems to be the meat of cattle *(Bos* spp.) cooked over an open fire until covered with ashes, then placed on stale bread and washed down with alcoholic beverages. ***Warning:*** the species is unpredictable and dangerous when intoxicated.

Human females are sexually receptive in any season, but Rockies residents rarely produce young—an average of only three or four in a lifetime. Gestation is about 280 days. The babies are born helpless, although not blind or deaf as among the rodents. Weaning is at six months to a year, followed by hand-feeding for about another year. Sexual maturity is reached at age 13 or 14, but successful mating is usually delayed for several more years. Humans have difficulty surviving in the wild, but they have been known to live well over 100 years in captivity.

MW

# Skulls of mammals in the Canadian Rockies
*Not to scale*

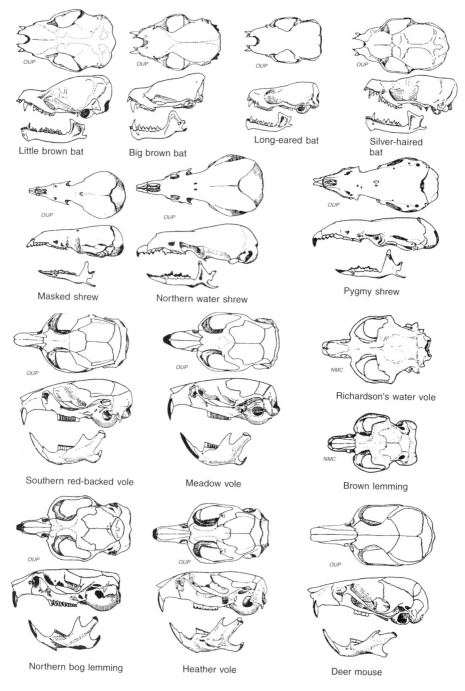

Little brown bat

Big brown bat

Long-eared bat

Silver-haired bat

Masked shrew

Northern water shrew

Pygmy shrew

Southern red-backed vole

Meadow vole

Richardson's water vole

Brown lemming

Northern bog lemming

Heather vole

Deer mouse

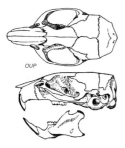

OUP

House mouse

OUP

Meadow jumping mouse

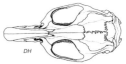

DH

Bushy-tailed wood rat

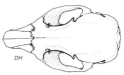

DH

Thirteen-lined ground squirrel

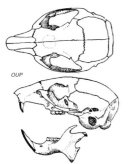

OUP

Least chipmunk

NMC

Richardson's ground squirrel

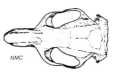

NMC

Northern pocket gopher

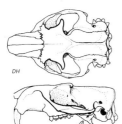

DH

Hoary marmot

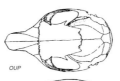

OUP

Red squirrel

OUP

Northern flying squirrel

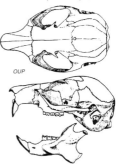

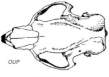

OUP

Porcupine

OUP

Beaver

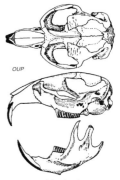

OUP

Muskrat

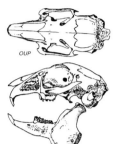
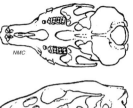
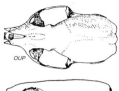

Snowshoe hare

Pika

Short-tailed weasel

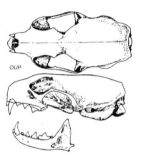
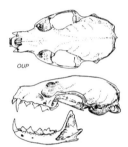

Least weasel

Long-tailed weasel

American marten

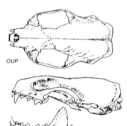
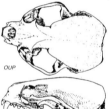
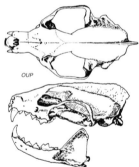

American mink

River otter

Fisher

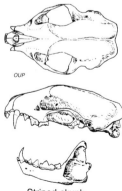
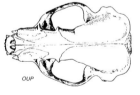
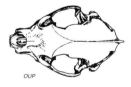

Striped skunk

American badger

Wolverine

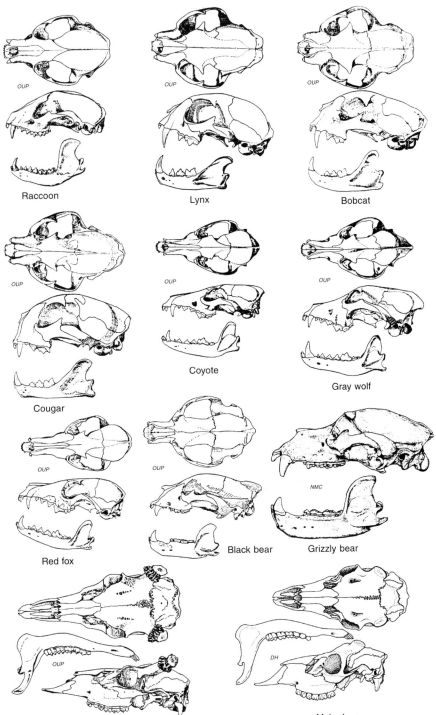

Raccoon

Lynx

Bobcat

Cougar

Coyote

Gray wolf

Red fox

Black bear

Grizzly bear

White-tailed deer

Mule deer

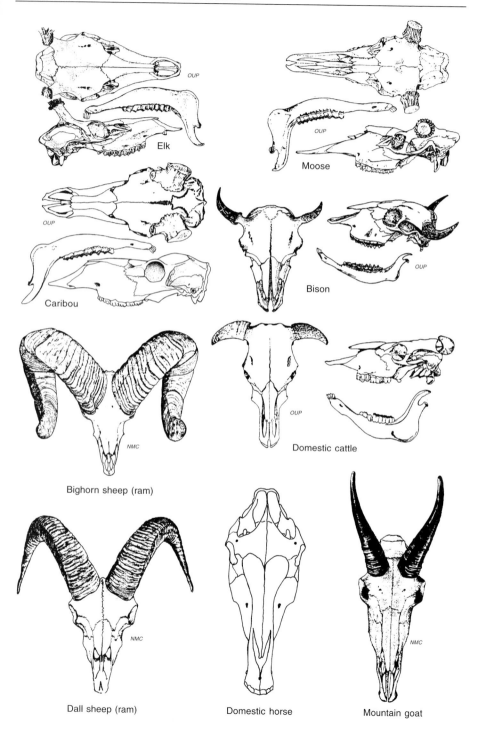

Elk

Moose

Caribou

Bison

Bighorn sheep (ram)

Domestic cattle

Dall sheep (ram)

Domestic horse

Mountain goat

# Tracks and scats in the Canadian Rockies

*Not to scale. Top of each track is forward direction. Walking gaits shown unless otherwise indicated.*

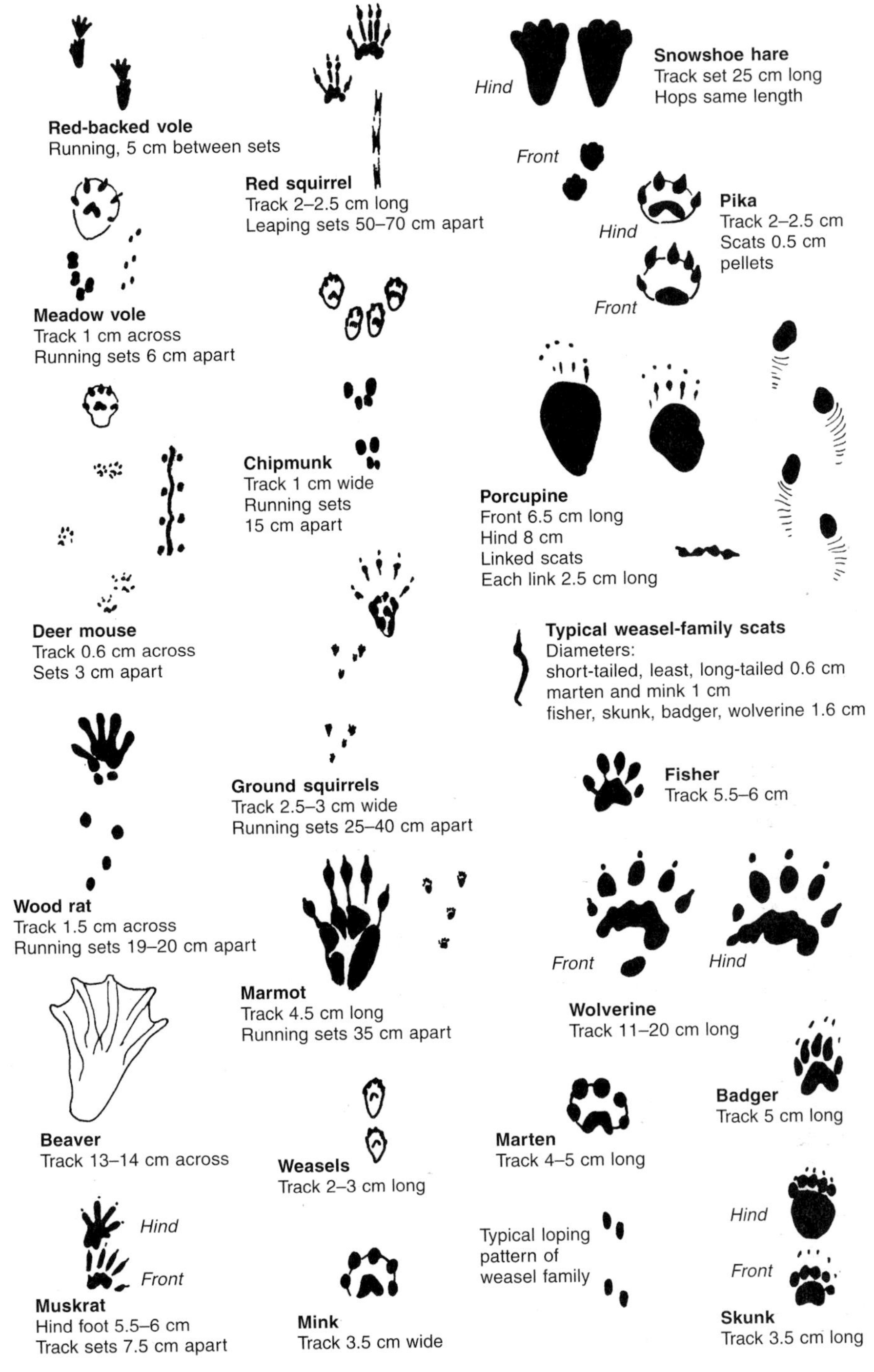

**Red-backed vole**
Running, 5 cm between sets

**Red squirrel**
Track 2–2.5 cm long
Leaping sets 50–70 cm apart

**Meadow vole**
Track 1 cm across
Running sets 6 cm apart

**Chipmunk**
Track 1 cm wide
Running sets
15 cm apart

**Deer mouse**
Track 0.6 cm across
Sets 3 cm apart

**Ground squirrels**
Track 2.5–3 cm wide
Running sets 25–40 cm apart

**Wood rat**
Track 1.5 cm across
Running sets 19–20 cm apart

**Marmot**
Track 4.5 cm long
Running sets 35 cm apart

**Beaver**
Track 13–14 cm across

**Weasels**
Track 2–3 cm long

**Muskrat**
*Hind*
*Front*
Hind foot 5.5–6 cm
Track sets 7.5 cm apart

**Mink**
Track 3.5 cm wide

*Hind*
*Front*
**Snowshoe hare**
Track set 25 cm long
Hops same length

*Hind*
*Front*
**Pika**
Track 2–2.5 cm
Scats 0.5 cm
pellets

**Porcupine**
Front 6.5 cm long
Hind 8 cm
Linked scats
Each link 2.5 cm long

**Typical weasel-family scats**
Diameters:
short-tailed, least, long-tailed 0.6 cm
marten and mink 1 cm
fisher, skunk, badger, wolverine 1.6 cm

**Fisher**
Track 5.5–6 cm

*Front*    *Hind*

**Wolverine**
Track 11–20 cm long

**Marten**
Track 4–5 cm long

Typical loping
pattern of
weasel family

**Badger**
Track 5 cm long

*Hind*
*Front*
**Skunk**
Track 3.5 cm long

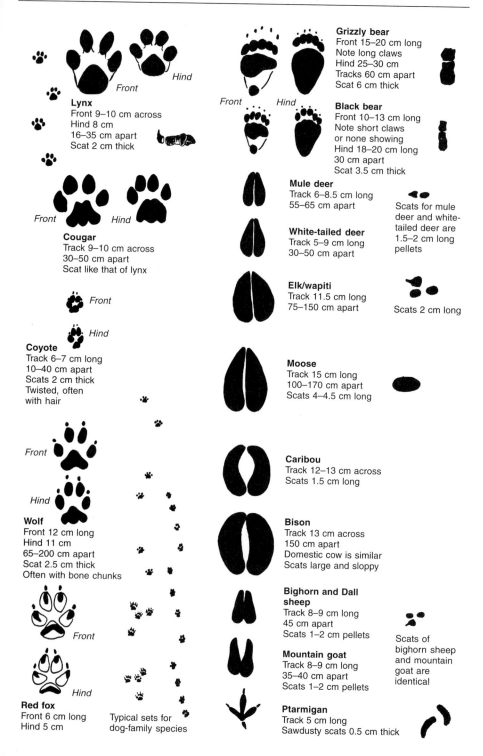

**Lynx**
Front 9–10 cm across
Hind 8 cm
16–35 cm apart
Scat 2 cm thick

**Cougar**
Track 9–10 cm across
30–50 cm apart
Scat like that of lynx

**Coyote**
Track 6–7 cm long
10–40 cm apart
Scats 2 cm thick
Twisted, often
with hair

**Wolf**
Front 12 cm long
Hind 11 cm
65–200 cm apart
Scat 2.5 cm thick
Often with bone chunks

**Red fox**
Front 6 cm long
Hind 5 cm

Typical sets for
dog-family species

**Grizzly bear**
Front 15–20 cm long
Note long claws
Hind 25–30 cm
Tracks 60 cm apart
Scat 6 cm thick

**Black bear**
Front 10–13 cm long
Note short claws
or none showing
Hind 18–20 cm long
30 cm apart
Scat 3.5 cm thick

**Mule deer**
Track 6–8.5 cm long
55–65 cm apart

**White-tailed deer**
Track 5–9 cm long
30–50 cm apart

Scats for mule
deer and white-
tailed deer are
1.5–2 cm long
pellets

**Elk/wapiti**
Track 11.5 cm long
75–150 cm apart

Scats 2 cm long

**Moose**
Track 15 cm long
100–170 cm apart
Scats 4–4.5 cm long

**Caribou**
Track 12–13 cm across
Scats 1.5 cm long

**Bison**
Track 13 cm across
150 cm apart
Domestic cow is similar
Scats large and sloppy

**Bighorn and Dall
sheep**
Track 8–9 cm long
45 cm apart
Scats 1–2 cm pellets

**Mountain goat**
Track 8–9 cm long
35–40 cm apart
Scats 1–2 cm pellets

Scats of
bighorn sheep
and mountain
goat are
identical

**Ptarmigan**
Track 5 cm long
Sawdusty scats 0.5 cm thick

# *Further reading*

Items in the short list below are representative, easily obtainable at time of writing and are specific to the Canadian Rockies.

Alberta Forestry, Lands and Wildlife (1990) *Alberta Wildlife Viewing Guide.* Lone Pine Publishing, Edmonton. A catalogue of good places to see mammals and birds, with information about other plants and animals, too. Illustrated, indexed, 96 pages.

Banfield, A. (1974) *The Mammals of Canada.* University of Toronto Press/Museum of Nature, Ottawa. The standard book, available in French, but getting old and in need of updating; with illustrations, range maps and index; 438 pages.

Barwise, J. (1989) *Animal Tracks of Western Canada.* Lone Pine Publishing, Edmonton. A pocket guide, but surprisingly complete and well-illustrated, with range maps and a comparative track-size chart at the back. Index, bibliography, 126 pages.

Carbyn, L., ed. (1983) *Wolves in Canada and Alaska.* Canadian Wildlife Service Report Series, Number 45; Canadian Government Publishing Centre, Ottawa. Collection of pivotal papers, with photos, maps and other graphics; 135 pages.

Chadwick, D. (1983) *A Beast the Color of Winter: the Mountain Goat Observed.* Sierra Club Books, San Francisco. The standard work on this heretofore little-understood species. Illustrations, bibliography, index; 208 pages.

Craighead, F. (1978) *Track of the Grizzly.* Sierra Club Books, San Francisco. The standard work on grizzly bears. Illustrated, referenced, indexed; 261 pages.

Dekker, D. (1994) *Wolf Story: from Varmint to Favourite.* BST Publications, 3819 112A St., Edmonton T6J 1K4. Good information and evocative essays about wolves, with special attention to their relationship with humans. Illustrations, index, reference list; 200 pages.

Geist, V. (1990) *Mule Deer Country.* NorthWord Press, Minocqua, WI. A large-format book combining detailed information about the natural history of this species, especially on life cycle and behavior, with many excellent color photographs; 176 pages.

— (1991) *Elk Country.* NorthWord Press, Minocqua, WI. The second in Dr. Geist's series on mountain ungulates, in the same format and style as the book listed above. More fine photos and insights on behavior; 176 pages.

— (1993) *Wild Sheep Country.* NorthWord Press, Minocqua, WI. The third in Dr. Geist's series on mountain ungulates, just as good as the previous two. Richly illustrated, 176 pages.

Glacier Natural History Association/National Park Service (1978) *Glacier National Park Mammals, Field Checklist.* Glacier National Park; West Glacier, Montana. Pocket checklist, good for the entire Canadian Rockies region if you add some shrews and bats, Richardson's ground squirrel, caribou, bison and Stone's sheep.

Herrero, S. (1985) *Bear Attacks: Their Causes and Avoidance.* New Century; Piscataway, New Jersey. The authoritative work on avoiding problems with grizzly bears and black bears. Completely referenced, quite readable, illustrated, indexed; 287 pages.

Kunelius, R. (1983) *Animals of the Rockies.* Altitude Publishing, Canmore. Interesting write-ups of 18 mammal species seen often in the Canadian Rockies, written by a Banff park warden who knows them well. Illustrated, 72 pages.

Langshaw, R. (1987) *Animals of the Canadian Rockies: a Finder's Guide.* Summerthought, Banff. Short guide to identification and habits. Illustrated, with glossary and bibliography; 62 pages.

Lopez, B. (1978) *Of Wolves and Men.* Charles Scribners Sons, New York. History of the wolf, including the whys and hows of human persecution. A renowned book; illustrated, bibliography, index; 309 pages.

Lynch, W. (1995) *Wildlife of the Canadian Rockies.* Alpine Book Peddlers, Canmore. Descriptions of common birds and mammals, with Wayne Lynch's incomparable photographs; 80 pages.

Marshall, L.; D. McIntyre and M. McIntyre (1992) *Crowsnest Pass Wildlife.* Sweetgrass Communications and Friends of the Frank Slide Assoc., Blairmore, AB. Inexpensive pocket checklist of common species from fishes to mammals, with additional information; 36 pages.

Mech, L. (1970) *The Wolf: the Ecology and Behavior of an Endangered Species.* University of Minnesota Press. Well-written compendium of information; illustrated, referenced, indexed; 384 pages.

Murie, O. (1954) *A Field Guide to Animal Tracks.* Houghton Mifflin, Boston. Peterson-series guide, old but comprehensive and well illustrated (line drawings), including scats. Enjoyable text with lots of anecdotes; 374 pages.

Nagorsen, D. and R. Brigham (1993) *Bats of British Columbia.* UBC Press, Vancouver. Covers all species that live in the Canadian Rockies in sufficient detail for experts, but quite readable for the general public. Illustrated, skull drawings, glossary, index, good reference list; 165 pages.

Province of British Columbia (1978) *Some Mammals of Interior Parks.* Ministry of Recreation and Conservation; Victoria, BC. Pamphlet on 13 western-slope mammals.

Roze, U. (1989) *The North American Porcupine.* Smithsonian Institution Press, Washington, D.C. The definitive book on this interesting animal, written with care and compassion. Illustrated, with glossary, index and extensive reference list; 261 pages.

Savage, A. and C. (1981) *Wild Mammals of Western Canada.* Western Producer Prairie Books, Saskatoon. Coffee-table book on 70 species. Interesting text, excellent photo illustrations in color, index and bibliography; 209 pages.

Scotter, G. and T. Urlich (1995) *Mammals of the Canadian Rockies.* Fifth House Publishers, Saskatoon. Like Scotter's other two Rockies guides, one on wildflowers and the other on birds, this one is well written, authoritative and beautifully illustrated with color photographs. Indexed, 176 pages.

Smith, H. (1993) *Alberta Mammals.* Provincial Museum of Alberta, Edmonton. Replaces Soper's outdated *Mammals of Alberta.* The authoritative guide for the province, with range maps, skull pictures and excellent color photos. Glossary, index, 239 pages.

Schmidt, D. and E. (1991) *Photographing Wildlife in the Canadian Rockies.* Lone Pine Publishing, Edmonton. Descriptions of common birds and mammals, with tips on how to photograph them. Illustrated, 192 pages.

Stelfox, B., ed. (1993) *Hoofed Mammals of Alberta.* Lone Pine Publishing, Edmonton. Mostly of interest to wildlife workers, with lots of info on distribution, management, hunting, disease, predation and game ranching. Well-illustrated, with glossary, index, many references; 242 pages.

— S. Wasel and L. Hunt (1992) *Field Guide to the Hoofed Mammals of Jasper and Banff National Parks.* Friends of Jasper National Park, Jasper, Alberta. Handy guide for lay readers and experts alike, with terrific color paintings of all eight species, range maps, skull drawings, info on life cycles. Glossary, index, detailed references list; 72 pages.

Van Tighem, K. (1992) *Wild Animals of Western Canada.* Altitude Publishing, Canmore. Descriptions of common mammals, including many in the Rockies, with interesting anecdotes. Bibliography, 96 pages.

— (1997) *Bears.* Altitude Publishing, Canmore. Well-written compendium of bear facts and fallacies, with emphasis on Rockies animals. Well-illustrated, indexed, 160 pages.

Winnie, J. (1996) *High Life: Animals of the Alpine World.* Northland Publishing, Flagstaff, AZ. Impressively researched, well-written guide to selected birds and mammals of the Rockies high country, illustrated with Winnie's remarkable photographs. Reading list, index; 130 pages.

Government libraries in the various national parks have hard-to-find reports on mammals. All reports produced for Parks Canada are available in the library of their Alberta Regional Office in Calgary.

## The Wildlife-watcher's Code

- When you see wildlife along the highway, *slow down.* If you want to stop, signal, then *park well out of the driving lanes.* You don't want to cause an accident.

- To be safe, and to inflict the least stress on the animal, *watch it from a vehicle.* This is especially important with bears, with female elk, deer or moose that have young, and with male elk, deer or moose during the autumn rutting season.

- If you are not within a vehicle, *watch the animal openly, where it can see you plainly.* Sneaking up on wildlife, predator-style, scares it.

- *If the animal moves away or looks nervous, you are too close.* Back off until it relaxes. Never pursue.

- *Be courteous to other watchers.* Don't come between them and the object of their attention. Stay out of other people's photos. Don't be the one to chase the animal away by getting too close.

*Pyramid Mountain and Pyramid Lake, near Jasper. This scene is more than just a list of rock types, climatic data and species—although that's one way to start understanding it.*

# Seasonal ecology
## *Putting it all together*

In any natural ecosystem, the plants and animals have evolved over a very long time to survive in that particular geological setting, in those weather conditions, and with each other. Throughout, the basic cycle has been the time it takes our planet to go once around the sun.

Interest leads to observation, which leads to experience, which leads to understanding. My way of understanding an ecosystem is to work out its **seasonal ecology:** what goes on there over the course of a year.

Seasonal ecology is a *method* as well as a category of information. Given some field guides and a bit of background knowledge—an interest in birds, say—nearly anyone can do seasonal ecology. You can use it to learn the natural history of a particular place—a forest, a marsh, a mountain meadow, the seashore, a city park, whatever. You look at the topography, the underlying geology, the weather and climate, the plants and the animals of that place, then you work out how each of these goes through its physical or biological cycle over the course of a typical year. In so doing, you get the big picture of what is going on in that ecosystem. This is reality. This is fascinating. You discover how different plants and animals interact, you see general ecological principles at work, and you come away with a deeper appreciation of the natural world.

I'm a geologist by training and a naturalist by experience; when I go to a new place I see it in a multidisciplinary way, mentally cataloguing the physical and biological environment from the bedrock up. I'm fascinated with seasonal changes, so I try to imagine what a particular place looks like in spring, summer, fall and winter. Then I consider what the flora and fauna—as many species as I can identify—are doing individually and with/to each other during each season.

When I'm in a region I know well, such as the Rockies, the current seasonal-ecology highlights pop out in only a few minutes of observation: "Hmm … here I am on a ridge covered with alpine tundra. Must have been a snow-patch here a day or two ago, because nothing has greened up yet and the western anemones are just opening. Bit of snow-mold left, so the last of the snow probably went yesterday. Amazing how those anemones can start themselves in frozen ground."

Sometimes I'll spend an hour doing a more careful job, checking around the site for things I might otherwise miss, looking up species in field guides and so on. I walk away with a pretty good picture of that particular ecosystem, gained with very little effort.

*Getting knee-deep into seasonal ecology in the Moose Lake Marshes, Mount Robson Provincial Park. The water was warm. Photo of Elderhostel group by Keith Miller.*

# How to do seasonal ecology
## Rocket science it's not

As presented here, seasonal ecology is an amateur activity. But the same approach can be used more rigorously to develop a proper biophysical inventory. Here is the basic sequence. You can do this alone, but it works even better in groups, especially if there are people in the group who live in the region under study.

## 1. Preparation

Bring field guides with you, a notebook, binoculars, a magnifying glass and perhaps a map. Collecting is not required; you look things up on the spot.

## 2. Start with the physical environment—the landscape and the climate

Let's assume a location in Alberta. Are you in the mountains? On the prairie? Next to a lake or river? Are you in a gully or on a hilltop? What is the elevation? (Check the map if you have one.) If the site is sloping, in which direction does it face? What underlies the vegetation? Rock? Gravel? Sand? Clay? Black soil?

The topography and geology of a place have a lot of control over what grows there. For example, consider elevation. A mountaintop may be covered with alpine tundra, quite different from the forested valley floor far below. In Canada, the direction a slope faces is very important, because it controls the amount of sunlight received and thus the ground temperature, which in turn affects the overall dryness or wetness of the soil. A bedrock surface supports little vegetation, while thick soil supports a lot. A dry, gravelly site supports a different plant community than a wet, clay-rich site does.

What about the weather? Is this a cold place? A warm place? Hot and humid in summer? Hot and dry? Would you expect a lot of snow to accumulate here in winter? Hardly any? Is it windy? Get a handle on the overall climate of the site.

## 3. Catalogue the plants

Go from the ground up, writing your findings in your notebook. What's growing right on the ground? Are there **mosses, lichens** or **fungi** there? Is there **cryptogamic soil** (tiny fungi, mosses and lichens growing tightly together to form a crust on the surface)? Are there **clubmosses** or **horsetails?** Is there **grass?** If you know the difference between grasses, sedges and rushes, you might look for each type, keeping in mind the botanist's rhyme: "Rushes are round, sedges have edges and grasses have joints."

Estimate how much of the ground is covered by each of these groups. You needn't be accurate; just write down "most," "some," "a little" or "none."

Are there **wildflowers,** meaning leafy seed plants that are not woody? Identify any species you know, and estimate the ground coverage. If you can, note whether the various wildflowers are annuals, which must grow from seed every year; biennials, which grow from seed in the first year, then bloom, bear seed and die in second year; or perennials, in which the roots produce a new stem and leaves each year.

Are there **ground-covering shrubs,** such as kinnikinnik, mountain cranberry or heather? These are frequently confused with wildflowers, but they have woody stems. Are there **taller shrubs,** such as willows or buffaloberry or saskatoons or blueberries or Labrador tea? Are there **evergreen shrubs,** such as junipers?

Are there **trees,** which are essentially tall shrubs with only one or two trunks? What tree species can you identify? Are there evergreens, deciduous trees or both?

## 4. Now do the animals

One can assume that there are many small animals in the soil, such as microscopic nematodes, rotifers and tiny arthropods, which are much more numerous than the larger, more visible worms and larvae. What kinds of **insects and spiders** can you see on the ground, on plants and in the air? Do you see flies (including mosquitoes), dragonflies, beetles, crickets, grasshoppers, ants, bees, butterflies, moths? Are there immature forms around, such as caterpillars on vegetation or dragonfly nymphs in the water? Are there **fish** in the water? How about **amphibians and reptiles,** meaning frogs, toads, salamanders, snakes, turtles or lizards?

What kinds of **birds** can you see? Common groups to consider: ducks and other water birds, sandpipers, gulls/terns, hawks/falcons/eagles, owls, grouse, woodpeckers, corvids (jays, crows, ravens, magpies, nutcrackers), hummingbirds, swallows, swifts/nighthawks, bluebirds, starlings, thrushes (robins, etc.), waxwings, flycatchers, warblers, blackbirds, finches, larks, grosbeaks, chickadees, nuthatches, wrens, sparrows.

And what about the **mammals?** Groups: bats, shrews, mice and other small rodents, chipmunks, ground squirrels, tree squirrels, porcupines, beavers, muskrats, weasels—there are lots of weasel species in western Canada, including the otter and the skunk—hares/rabbits, raccoons, the cat family, the dog family, bears, hoofed animals, and, of course, *Homo sapiens.* This last critter is a major habitat-modifier, like the beaver. Consider human impact at that particular site.

## 5. Finally, put it all together

Having studied the playing field and identified the players, analyze the game. This is the interesting part, the real *seasonal-ecology* part.

Start with the current season—spring, say. When does spring come to this spot, meaning in what part of what month does the snow melt? If you don't know, perhaps someone in the group does. If you're alone, take a guess. There's no need to be terribly accurate. For example, if you guess that the snow is usually gone by mid-April, that wildflowers are beginning to show in late April, and that by mid-May there are leaves on the trees, you would be right for most of western Canada.

What is happening in the physical environment in early spring? Temperatures are rising, along with the number of hours of daylight and the strength of solar radiation. Soil is thawing, with liquid water available during the day but frozen overnight. The ground is exposed to ultraviolet light, killing fungi and bacteria that had been living under the snow. The lengthening days are triggering hormonal responses in plants (seed germination, flow of sap, budding) and in non-dormant animals (annual migratory movements, reproductive urges).

Use your notes to help remember what plants and animals you found in the cataloguing part of the exercise. Consider the effects on each. This takes some time, but it's worth the effort because it establishes the method.

Keep the *when* aspect in mind: "The swallows arrive in early May." Then make ecological connections: "Sure, because that's when the insects are getting really numerous, so the swallows have plenty of food—and the same with warblers, because they're bug-eaters too." This is the *aha!* part, very pleasing.

When you've worked out enough of the spring seasonal ecology, move on to summer. You needn't define "summer" very closely; just think of it as the time of warm weather and green, growing vegetation. You might be able to split the summer into early, middle and late stages. Go over your notes, linking changes in the weather pattern with the activities of plants and animals: blooming or mating, setting seed or bearing young, etc.

Move on to autumn. When does fall come? When do the leaves drop from the trees? When does the first frost occur? When does winter begin, loosely defined as the time when the ground freezes and the snow stays? When is the coldest period? When is the time of deepest snow accumulation? Is it possible to think of early, middle and late winter for this site? And what are the indicators that winter is on the way out?

Do each part of the year this way, in as much detail as you desire. You'll need to look up the blooming and seed-setting periods for plants, and the mating and reproducing periods for animals; you'll need to look up what animals eat, and what eats *them;* where things live, what they do for the winter, and so on. You'll be learning what species do what things at what times and with whom, and thus you'll arrive at the insightful *why.*

# *Seasonal ecology's reward*
## Guaranteed to amaze and delight, or your money back

In doing seasonal ecology I have run across many demonstrations of the overriding ecological principle that everything depends on everything else, often in surprisingly specific ways. For example, many butterfly caterpillars in the Rockies eat only certain species of plants, tying these species together in time and place. The plants must be in a condition to be eaten—many species become less edible or even toxic as the summer wears on—and the caterpillars must be present and sufficiently advanced in their life cycles to do the eating. Some plant species, such as the beautiful calypso orchid that blooms around Jasper in May, must be fertilized by specific insects, in this case the golden northern bumblebee. It must be a queen bumblebee, for only the queens are alive this early in the spring; the workers and drones come later. Further, it must be a young, inexperienced bee, for the orchid manages to attract it and effect pollen exchange without providing any nectar. Wow! There are many more revelations waiting in the literature, with textbook examples available in one's backyard.

Going from the very specific to the very general leads to another truth, a truly astounding one: *everything you see around you is the product of 3.6 billion years of seasonal ecology.* Everything is smarter than we think it is. Every feature of every organism, every biological process and every behavior—all have been honed over a staggering amount of time. So there is a *reason* for everything found in nature. To discover a new reason, no matter how small, is to contribute to the body of ecological and evolutionary science, and there's nothing preventing the amateur from doing so. To merely speculate on these relationships is a delight.

So go out and give seasonal ecology a try. If you're a naturalist, it will get you beyond list-making and into something more profound.

*A seasonal ecologist busy discovering how the mountains work. The mountains here are the Ramparts, west of Jasper, with Amethyst Lakes below.*

# Seasonal ecology applied
## Looking at a typical Canadian Rockies ecosystem

Here is an outline of the seasonal ecology of the montane woods and meadows found at lower elevations on the eastern slope of the central Canadian Rockies. See page 235 for photos.

### Topography, geology, soil

Shaped by heavy glaciation, the landscape is one of steep mountains and broad, flat valleys lying at elevations of 1000–1500 m above sea level. The main rock types are limestone, shale and gritstone; bedrock is exposed mostly on the valley walls. The valley floors are thickly carpeted with a base layer of glacial till and/or mudflow debris, upon which rivers have deposited gravel and sand carried from glaciers upstream. Water moves through this material easily. The top layer is wind-blown silt, on which a thin layer of limy soil has developed in the 10,000–11,000 years that have passed since the last glaciation. The water table is high in most places, sustaining lakes, ponds, and extensive wetlands, but any location a few metres higher than its surroundings is dry, because rain and snowmelt drain downward so easily.

### Climate and weather

The eastern slope of the Rockies lies in a mild rain shadow downwind of the continental divide. Cold, dry winters are followed by fairly warm, fairly dry summers. There is a good deal of wind. Winter temperatures are often lower on the valley floors than at higher elevations because of temperature inversions, which puddle cold air near the ground. Snowfalls are light and the snowpack is thin, usually less than half a metre at lower elevations. Summers are longer here than at higher elevations; the air temperature is continuously above freezing from mid-June to late August or early September. The soil freezes very deeply in winter, because the snowcover is so thin, but the ground thaws entirely in spring and becomes quite warm. South-facing and west-facing hillsides dry out in the summer heat, which favors the growth of grassy meadows, while north-facing and east-facing hillsides remain moist, which favors the growth of moss-floored forests. As elsewhere in the mountains, there is much micro-climatic variation, depending on the angle of a particular slope and the direction it faces.

The weather is orographic, meaning typical of mountain regions, controlled mainly by the rough topography. In summer, there is a daily pattern of sunny mornings and stormy afternoons. In winter, periods of cold, clear weather are broken by occasional chinooks, each of which is usually followed by a storm. At any time of year, moist, warm, low-pressure airmasses come in from the west, with fronts. Cool, moist airmasses bring cold rain from the northeast in summer, while very cold, dry, high-pressure airmasses arrive from the northeast in winter.

### Plants and fungi

Lodgepole pine, white spruce and Douglas-fir are the main conifers. The most common leafy tree is aspen, usually in groves, with scattered balsam poplar and white birch.

Typical shrubs include pussy willows, Scouler's willows, alders, buffaloberries, silverberry thickets, dogwood, wild roses, wild raspberries, wild strawberries, shrubby potentilla, common and creeping junipers and kinnikinnik.

Common wildflowers include pasque flowers ("prairie crocuses"), harebells, wild gaillardia, western wood lilies, hawkweed, goldenrod, clover, fireweed, rock cress, wild blue flax, paintbrush, locoweed, Solomon's-seal, windflowers and violets. Fescue, ryegrass and spike trisetum are common in dry places; marsh reedgrass, foxtail and timothy are common in moist places. Highway shoulders support stands of foxtail barley. Wetlands are rich in pondweed, water smartweed, bulrushes, the plant-like alga *Chara* and aquatic sedges such as *Carex utriculata*.

Feather-moss species carpet the forested north-facing slopes, while cryptogamic soil crusts (page 399) containing such drought-tolerant moss species as *Grimmia* are common on south-facing slopes. The wetlands are rich in peat mosses. Lichens are common in trees and in soil crusts, less common on limestone outcrops, while gritstone outcrops are heavily covered. Bolete mushrooms and coral fungi are fairly common in moist, north-facing woods.

## Animals

Arthropods are abundant, including mosquitoes, ground beetles, butterflies, moths, grasshoppers, branch-tip spiders and ticks. The wetlands support many water insects, such as water bugs, water striders, dragonflies and damselflies. Rivers and lakes contain trout, minnows and suckers. Amphibians here include toads and frogs, but their numbers have dropped a great deal in the past decade. There are two species of garter snakes.

Typical birds seen in summer include waterfowl, sandpipers, marsh birds, gulls, kingfishers, hawks and falcons, osprey, several species of owls, ruffed grouse, swallows, flickers and pileated woodpeckers, the jay tribe (gray jays, ravens and crows are common), hummingbirds, waxwings, flycatchers, warblers, blackbirds, thrushes, chickadees, red-breasted nuthatches, wrens, creepers, juncos, many species of sparrows. Winter residents include the jay tribe, owls, chickadees, grouse, nuthatches and creepers.

Common mammals seen in summer include bats, shrews, meadow voles, deer mice, wood rats, least chipmunks, Columbian ground squirrels, red squirrels, flying squirrels, beavers, muskrats, snowshoe hares, martens, smaller species of weasels, lynx, wolves, coyotes, red foxes, black bears, mule deer and white-tailed deer (mule-deer bucks often at higher elevations), elk, bighorn sheep (mainly females; most males move to higher elevations). Large numbers of visiting humans drive the highways of the Rockies and congregate in towns such as Banff and Jasper in the national parks. Smaller numbers live in these places year-round.

## Early spring (late March, April)

Temperatures vary widely, and the weather is often cloudy and stormy, with snow falling at higher elevations. But the sun is bright and melting is rapid, so at lower elevations the snowpack doesn't get any deeper. The snow surface is hard-frozen in the morning, wet in the afternoon. It begins to lose depth and is gone on the montane valley floors by the end of April, when under-snow molds and in-snow algae/bacteria are exposed to ultraviolet light and complete their life cycles. The ground has thawed enough for plant growth on south-facing slopes.

Evergreen needles can photosynthesize during the mid-day thaw, so conifers and junipers get a head start on leafy trees and shrubs. As the snowcover melts, wintergreen species of plants ("wintergreen" simply means that the leaves are not lost in winter) are exposed and also begin producing food in their leaves. Grass grows new leaves quickly in south-facing sheltered places. Silverweed is the first common wildflower species to produce leaves. Dandelions leaf out and bloom quite early. Aspens and poplars produce catkins in April, before leafing out. Sap begins flowing in trees and shrubs.

Earliest flowers seen: those of willows (pussy willow is the earliest; it may have been blooming since February). Buffaloberry is also early; the tiny flowers lack petals and are easily missed. The earliest forb (wildflower) is the pasque flower ("prairie crocus," *Anemone patens*). Other early ones: daisy fleabane, fairy candelabra and whitlow grass. Most early-blooming plants do so in response to rising soil temperatures; later ones are controlled more by air temperature and the length of the day.

Flying insects that overwinter as adults appear, including midges (they look like mosquitoes), some species of mosquitoes and the mourning-cloak butterfly. Insect eggs hatch when thawed and begin to grow into larval forms. Rocky Mountain wood ticks become active in early April.

The ice on lakes melts, allowing oxygen and more light into the water. Water plants have been photosynthesizing all winter under the ice, producing some oxygen, but not as much as is available when the ice thaws; these plants can now increase their metabolic rate, as can water insects, fish and snails. Some fish species spawn.

Frogs and toads break hibernation as soon as the ponds thaw. How do they know? The increase in the oxygen level reaches them, perhaps, or they are sensitive to other changes brought on by open water above. They spawn right away, and the eggs soon hatch. The tadpoles swim about, providing easy food for fish and other predators. The wood frog awakens from its frozen state under leaf litter and hops to open water to mate. Chorus frogs croak loudly from the ponds, although I hear fewer frogs every year.

Owls and corvids (ravens, jays, magpies) have nested already, beginning in late February, and the young have hatched. Corvid nestlings are fed mainly on the carrion that is abundant in early spring, while owlets are fed mainly rodents that have been displaced (see next paragraph). The male ruffed grouse is drumming. Most woodpeckers nest from late-April to mid-May, and so do the chickadees; their eggs will hatch at the right time for feeding the young on plentiful insect larvae. Migratory waterfowl (ducks, geese) begin to arrive. The birds are in their breeding plumage, so this is the best time of year to identify them. They show courting behavior during migration; some stay and nest. Loons and grebes arrive last, when they are not likely to get frozen into the ice (see page 513 for more on this). Songbirds that don't require many flying insects—robins, juncos, wrens—arrive in mid-April and begin courting; the warblers, which eat mainly flying insects, arrive toward the end of the month and in early May.

Bats emerge from hibernation in caves in late April or early May, when enough bugs are on the wing to feed them. Even though they mated in the fall, female bats become pregnant only now. Migrating bat species begin to arrive. Shrews and non-hibernating rodents with runs at the base of the snowpack lose their protective snow covering late in April. A scramble for territory ensues. Weasels bear their young now, when the nursing mothers can sustain themselves on these plentiful, easy-to-catch rodents. Bears come out of hibernation from late March to mid-April; they move to lower elevations in search of the first green growth of spring, the roots of plants such as sweetvetch and kinnikinnik, and carrion. Rodents that hibernate emerge from their burrows and rock dens from mid-April to early May.

Lynx mate in late March or early April; wolves and coyotes have mated in February or early March. Cougars may mate at any time of year, but most do so in May, not now.

T.S. Eliot said that "April is the cruellest month," and it certainly is for ungulates. Moose, deer, caribou, elk, bighorn sheep and mountain goats are at their weakest in early April. For them the food supply is poor, with little nutrition left in last-year's leaves and grasses. The snow surface freezes and thaws daily, making it crusty and difficult to reach food through. All hoofed animals are thin; some are living on their last fat reserves: their bone marrow. On top of

*Early spring at Cottonwood Slough, along the Pyramid Lake Road near Jasper. Pyramid Mountain in the background.*

this, the females are pregnant. Thus weakened, many ungulates die in early spring or are killed by predators, most of whom are giving birth to young that will be fed, either directly or by nursing, on the bounty. Scavenging birds and mammals do well on the ample carrion supply. Respite for hoofed animals comes late in April, when the grass starts to grow.

Human visitors to the Rockies are fewest at this time of year, when the skiing season is ending and summer has not yet arrived. Town populations are reduced somewhat, as many people engaged in the tourist business take their holidays elsewhere. Wildlife harassment and human-caused stress are reduced.

## Late spring and early summer (May and June)

Mid-May in the montane meadows and woods of the central Canadian Rockies is inclined to be sunny, late May and June rainy. Daytime temperatures are rising rapidly. The very long days give plenty of sunlight, but the soil is still cool and the weather is often cloudy and wet, so plant growth is less rapid than might be expected. Some overnight frosts occur in May, but in June the temperature stays above freezing. All lakes and rivers are now thawed, but the water is still cold. The frost is out of the ground by mid-May.

Evergreens put on their annual growth quickly. New leaders (new branches and needles) start in late May and reach their maximum length in mid-July. Why so soon? New growth must have enough time to harden to wood before winter.

Many shrubs flower in May, before most wildflowers do. Insect-pollinated flowers bloom later than air-pollinated or self-pollinating ones. Deciduous trees (aspen, balsam poplar, white birch) leaf out, along with shrubs, providing food for deer and cover for birds, which are arriving in great numbers. Vegetation growth at this time is rapid, with new leaves and shoots rich in sugars and proteins providing excellent forage.

Warming of the soil brings worms and burrowing insects closer to the surface, where birds and shrews can eat them. Insects that have overwintered in soil (mainly beetles) emerge. The first generation of this-year's mosquitoes takes to the air in early June. Most insects that overwintered as adults mate, lay eggs and die. The eggs hatch quickly and develop into larvae.

Most species of fish in the Rockies, except for salmon and some species of trout, spawn in mid-spring or early summer. Their eggs soon hatch, and the abundant fry are a rich source of food for large water insects, diving ducks, shorebirds and water-dwelling predatory mammals such as mink. Garter snakes emerge from hibernation and mate. They don't lay eggs; the young are born as small versions of the adults.

The last migrant songbirds arrive in mid-May; these are the swallows and flycatchers, which live on the flying insects that are now abundant. All migrant species are courting, and there is lots of singing. Late arrivals construct nests in June; the non-migrants that haven't nested earlier (grosbeaks, crossbills, nuthatches) are now nesting.

Chipmunks and ground squirrels come out of hibernation in early May. They mate right away, heedless of predators such as coyotes, who catch them easily and feed them to their young, now eating solid food. Tree squirrels, which are non-hibernators, are also mating. Hawks catch them and bring them back to their nestlings.

Bear cubs born helpless in late winter are out of the den, following their mothers about. This explains why they are born so early: bears must move around a lot because their foods are found at different locations and different elevations through the summer and fall, and the cubs must be sufficiently advanced by this time to follow.

Ungulate females are heavily pregnant and give birth in May. Caribou females present at montane elevations in the foothills from Jasper north move back to the upper subalpine forest in the mountains, just below treeline, to give birth while snow is still on the ground there. This protects them from wolves, which have difficulty moving in deep snow. Grizzly bears, though, have come out of hibernation at these same elevations and are looking for caribou fawns. Mountain goats have their babies in cliffy places, often at alpine (above-treeline) elevations, safe from most predators. Bears, wolves, cougars and coyotes kill and eat many of the deer and elk babies born at lower elevations, in timing with the most rapid growth of their own young.

Tourists begin to arrive, taking advantage of the lower accommodation rates and cheaper tours available in the spring. They try to photograph elk and deer fawns, get too close and are sometimes chased and injured by the mothers, who see them as potential predators. Human-induced stress in wildlife populations is rising along with visitation.

## Midsummer (July and early August)

The cloudy, rainy weather of June often clears up dramatically in the first week of July. This is the warmest time of the year in the montane woods and meadows of the central Rockies, with the highest air temperatures reached in mid-July. Soil temperatures lag behind a week or two, but the long, warm days produce the fastest plant growth of summer.

Plants are growing and flowering as quickly as possible; they are rich in sugars and proteins. Some early-blooming species are already setting seed.

Most insects are in the larval stage, and many are plant-eaters, feeding most heavily at the time of year when plants are most nutritious. Fish fry and amphibian tadpoles are growing fast, feeding on water-insect larvae and water plants. Likewise, predators are feeding on them.

Birds such as geese, ducks and grouse, which bear precocial young (ready to leave the nest when only a day or two out of the egg), are leading their ducklings and chicks about. Songbirds, which bear altricial young (helpless in the nest for three weeks to a month) are scouring their territories for food for them.

Young ungulates are precocious, ready to follow their mothers or the flock between grazing sites, and ready to run when threatened. Non-ungulate mammals are slower to develop. They are usually reared in burrows or secure rock dens.

Human activity is at its height in the Canadian Rockies, with many thousands of people present in the montane ecosystem. Human-induced stress on wildlife is also at its seasonal maximum, and so is traffic on the highways, with increased accidental killing of wildlife. Traffic jams form wherever wildlife is spotted. Any large mammal revealing itself is instantly the subject of intense human attention. Trails near tourist centres attract many hikers, and humans are penetrating remote back-country valleys.

*Summer at Cottonwood Slough*

## Late summer and early fall (late August to early September)

A cooling trend is apparent, usually accompanied by unsettled, showery weather. A cold rainstorm goes to snow. This is a key weather event in the montane woods and meadows; temperatures drop below freezing for the first time since June.

Plants have gone to seed and berries are ripe, devoured by mammals and birds, which spread the seeds in their droppings. Leaves begin to turn. Yellow/orange carotenoids and brown tannins that have been masked by the deep green of chlorophyll all summer begin to show through. Red/purple anthocyanins are produced in fall from residual sugars left in the leaves. Day-length is the main control in defoliation; temperature and soil moisture are also important.

Most species of insects lay eggs in late summer, which will survive the winter and hatch in spring. The mild frosts of early fall kill most adult insects, but the adults of some species seek shelter in soil, under litter, in tree-cavities or among rocks to hibernate. Many larval forms also hibernate, metamorphosing in their pupal cases to emerge next spring as adults.

Chinook salmon arrive in the upper Fraser River on the western slope of the Rockies; they may be viewed spawning at Swift Creek just north of Valemount. The fish die after spawning, and many scavengers feed on the remains. Bears, eagles, weasels, rodents—even deer—eat the fish.

Insectivorous birds fly south. Swallows depart in mid-August; warblers, flycatchers and others leave later.

Small mammals gather and store food. Red squirrels sort evergreen cones by species and store them in and around their middens. Least chipmunks eat the seeds of fruits such as raspberries and wild roses. They discard the pulp. Strangely unwary in fall, chipmunks seem to prefer food-gathering to predator avoidance. This is an interesting survival tradeoff, indicating that more genes have been passed along from those chipmunks concentrating on food-gathering than from those chipmunks concentrating on not getting caught.

Ground squirrels enter hibernation early, in mid-August, removing a staple food source for coyotes. Coyote pups are now old enough to leave the den site and travel farther with the pack in search of food.

Wolf packs rendezvous in swampy meadows at low elevations. The pups are old enough to leave the den permanently; the pack gathers and builds solidarity for winter hunting patrols. Coyotes show similar behavior.

Bears fatten, consuming about 4.7 kJ/day (about 20,000 calories; compare with typical human intake of 0.5 kJ/day, which is 2000–3000 calories). Grizzlies typically eat 200,000 buffaloberries daily.

Ungulates are also fattening as much as possible, to prepare for the food-intake deficit they experience in winter. Elk begin rutting.

Human numbers drop in the Rockies as the vacation season ends. Traffic decreases on the highways. Visitors tend to be older than those of summer, often retired; they seldom venture far on trails. Outside the national parks, hunters selectively kill the better-looking male ungulates for trophies, and they take many animals for meat.

## Mid-fall (mid-September to mid-October)

The weather in the montane woods and meadows tends to be dry and stable, with frost at night but temperatures well above freezing during the day. Ice forms on shallow ponds on the colder nights, but it thaws the next morning. Snow may fall, but it soon melts.

Plant seeds are dropping, eagerly gathered by small rodents and birds. The leaves of deciduous trees and shrubs reach their brightest color and drop off.

Most insects have completed their life cycles or become dormant. Most amphibians burrow into the mud below lakes and streams to hibernate, but the wood frog leaves the water, moves under leaf litter and freezes. A massive release of sugars into the bloodstream during freezing prevents cell destruction. The spotted frog also hibernates out of water, in a burrow. Garter snakes seek deep cracks in rock outcrops or abandoned burrows, for mass hibernation.

The remaining migratory songbirds leave. Loons and grebes leave, even though the lakes are still open, because these birds are easily trapped in ice (they need extensive open water for takeoff) and can't risk staying any longer. Canada geese are forming flocks, preparing to leave.

The remaining small hibernators retire (bats, chipmunks, jumping mice). Elk are at the height of their rut, bugling night and day. The males eat and sleep very little as they gather and guard harems of females.

The human presence increases slightly as visitors arrive to enjoy the fall color and to watch the rutting elk, which are attracted to the large lawns, playing fields and golf courses in and near population centres in the national parks. The stags collect crowds of onlookers. Occasionally people are chased and property is damaged. Park wardens cut the antlers off elk stags deemed to be aggressive, and move some of them away from the townsites. The rutting animals pay little attention to cars and trucks, and the wildlife-collision rate in October is the highest for the year, even though traffic is light.

## Late fall (late October to early November)

The first snowfall that remains on the ground at montane elevations often occurs at Halloween. The temperature may dip below freezing all day. The ground surface is now frozen; small-mammal burrows must be finished by now or they cannot be dug. Shallow lakes freeze.

Water in lakes is now colder near the surface than it is at the bottom. The upper layer moves downward, causing circulation and mixing. Nutrients and toxins are redistributed.

Wildflower species that grow anew every year survive only as seed. Perennial wildflowers have died back to the roots. Deciduous shrubs and trees are dormant, but the needles of evergreens can still photosynthesize on the warmer days.

Most waterfowl migrate. Some grebes and loons become trapped in lake ice and are eaten by coyotes and the larger weasels. Snow buntings arrive from farther north; they eat seeds. Voles and lemmings prepare their winter runs at the base of the snowpack. They dig snow tunnels and line them with vegetation.

*Autumn at Cottonwood Slough*

Bears move up to subalpine elevations where the snow is deepest, thus offering the best insulation, and prepare dens. Grizzlies dig fairly deep dens on steep slopes. Black bears don't dig as deeply; in the central Rockies they often excavate a small den among the roots of a tree. Black bears go dormant in mid-November, grizzlies a week or two later.

Elk are nearing the end of the rut. Successful males have spent far more time rutting than eating, and they are now going into winter in weakened condition. Mule deer and white-tailed deer begin rutting at montane elevations; moose and caribou are rutting higher up. Bighorn sheep begin rutting in rocky areas at low elevations, mountain goats at higher elevations.

Visitation to the Canadian Rockies diminishes, and the small resident population takes a dip as people employed in the tourist industry leave the area for vacations. Traffic is lighter, although salt spread on the highways to melt snow and ice attracts ungulates, especially bighorn sheep. Now rutting, they are often hit.

## Early winter (late November to mid-December)

An arctic front arrives in mid-November, bringing the first really cold weather of the winter. Temperatures on the montane valley floors drop to the -20s and stay below freezing. The larger, deeper lakes freeze, along with the smaller streams. A major Pacific snowstorm arrives, usually early in December; this is often the biggest snowfall of the winter. It comes in warm and wet, but afterward an extremely cold arctic airmass settles in over western Canada. It can linger through Christmas, and on, and on.

Vegetation, both deciduous and evergreen, is now dormant. Wintergreen plants keep their chlorophyll under the snow but carry on little photosynthesis.

Few insects are seen. Most exist as eggs or pupating larvae. But cold-adapted arthropods such as springtails remain active in leaf litter under the snow. The remaining waterfowl migrate. Bohemian waxwings have been eating mountain-ash berries in towns; they now switch to their winter staple of juniper berries.

Small rodents and shrews depend on the arctic-front storm and the Pacific storm to bring protective snow. Many die if the ground is left bare before the temperature drops. Weasels begin to hunt rodents and shrews under the snow. Owls, using their 3-D sound sense, plunge their talons into the snow tunnels to catch their prey. Wolves are hunting in packs. Coyotes and ravens follow the wolves, scavenging.

Bighorn sheep are nearing the end of the rut in early December. Successful males are exhausted afterward, and vulnerable to attack by wolves. The sheep must try to regain lost weight on winter feed. Human activity is low.

## Mid-winter cold period (late December to late January)

This is the coldest time of the year in the montane woods and meadows of the central Rockies. Temperatures drop to -40°C. Most of Canada lies under an arctic airmass. The larger rivers freeze over and their water levels drop, leaving a dry strip under the ice along each bank. This protected corridor is travelled by shrews, otters and mink. The snowcover is not very deep, typically less than half a metre. The weather is clear, and there is not much wind. Frequent temperature inversions occur, in which the air at ground level is colder than the air higher up, so the subalpine slopes and ridges are often warmer than the montane valley floors.

Depth hoar—loose, sugary crystals formed by the recrystallization of snowflakes—is building up at the base of the snowpack, weakening it. This is good for grazers, who have less trouble pushing the snow aside with their hoofs, and small rodents and shrews find it easier to make snow tunnels. But depth hoar makes life more difficult for wolves and coyotes, which break into the collapsing snow as they try to travel over it. Depth hoar causes trouble for cross-country skiers; their skis break through, and the avalanche danger grows.

Life under the ice in lakes and ponds continues. Larvae of flying insects such as dragonflies and mayflies are developing through the winter as naiads. Fish conserve oxygen by minimal movement; none of the species in the Canadian Rockies spawns in winter except for one, the burbot. Amphibians are hibernating in the bottom mud.

Redpolls arrive from the north to eat the seeds in birch and alder cones. Grouse eat spruce needles, willow twigs and juniper berries. Ravens and jays survive mainly on carrion from wolf kills and winter-killed animals, and on what they can find in towns and at dumps. Small forest birds such as nuthatches and chickadees are eating mainly insect eggs, pupae and seeds.

Dependent on the forage in a few critical montane wintering areas (see page 226), all ungulates are now losing weight. They eat constantly, but cannot consume enough food energy to keep their body temperatures high enough in the extreme cold without using some of their fat reserves. Grass and dried leaves are becoming harder to reach under the snow, and the nutritional value of the feed is steadily decreasing as the vegetation is attacked by molds and consumed by rodents. Evergreen plants are toxic, eaten as a last resort.

Adult male ungulates are especially weak from rutting. They become prey for wolves, coyotes and cougars. Lynx kill mainly snowshoe hares. Wolves hunt by surprising a single individual, or by separating one animal from the herd/flock and chasing it into an open area with little snowcover, such as a frozen lake or river. Wolves can kill a deer in only a few minutes. Elk resist longer, and a single moose can fight off a pack for days.

Mid-winter rain chills the ungulates, causes crusting of the snow surface and icing of bare slopes. It becomes harder for hoofed animals to move, and feed is harder to reach. Such conditions favor their predators.

Humans are indoors much of the time, burning natural gas and wood for heat, which causes ice fog and air pollution on the colder days. Bird feeders help to sustain resident species such as chickadees and nuthatches, and non-native species such as house-sparrows. Most towns and settlements are located in the same critical montane wintering areas needed by ungulates. In the national parks, elk and deer tend to congregate in towns, eating ornamental shrubs and the non-native bluegrass planted in lawns. Wolves and coyotes seldom enter these towns, and the ungulates they hunt receive some protection there. But plowed highways, packed snowmobile tracks and cross-country ski trails leading from montane elevations to higher country allow wolves and coyotes to reach wintering moose and caribou that would otherwise be safe from attack. Highway conditions are frequently slippery, and road-salting is heavy.

*Winter at Cottonwood Slough*

## Late winter (mid-February, March)

Chinooks in the central Rockies are frequent, with generally warmer temperatures. The weather is cloudier than the previous period, with frequent snowfalls. This is the period of deepest snow at higher elevations, but here in the montane woods and meadows the snow is thinned considerably by chinooks. In some winters it disappears entirely in windier parts of the eastern front ranges and foothills. This is good for grazers, but it is deadly for small rodents and shrews.

Insects that have been active under the snow all winter, such as springtails and snow crane flies, now appear at the surface to mate. Corvids nest, in preparation for the carrion feast ahead. Male skunks emerge and are caught by owls, which are also nesting.

Ungulates continue to lose weight. Under-snow feed is becoming poorer and scarcer; elk may switch to browsing (eating twigs) and evergreen needles. They eat aspen bark to keep the nitrogen levels in their rumens high, for better bacterial breakdown of cellulose. But they gradually grow weaker, and the less-fit begin to die. Wolves and coyotes are doing fine; it's the mating season for them.

Bear cubs are born. Their mothers wake during delivery, then return to dormancy. The cubs do not hibernate; they nurse as their mothers sleep.

Some new foods become available, just in time: poplar and aspen buds, willow catkins. All are sweet and protein-rich, good food for hoofed animals, birds, rodents and hares. Humans emerge from their dens and take down the Christmas lights. The sun is strong enough to sunburn skiers. And on into spring.

This is by no means the complete seasonal ecology of even one ecosystem in the Canadian Rockies, but it presents some of the major cycles and species interactions in the ecosystem that is known best. The details are just as interesting as the overall picture, and there are many more fascinating interrelationships waiting to be discovered.

## Further reading

Most natural-history books and outdoor-activity guides emphasize the warm season. Here are three that deal primarily with winter.

Finlay, J. (1982) *Winter Here and Now.* Aspen House Productions, Box 8644, Station L, Edmonton, AB  T6C 4J4. Things to see and do in the Canadian winter, written for all ages but especially useful for school groups. Illustrated, with bibliography; 138 pages.

Halfpenny, J. and R. Ozanne (1989) *Winter: an Ecological Handbook.* Johnson Books, Boulder, CO. A serious but readable account of the winter environment and how living things respond to it, based on the work of Colorado's famed Institute of Alpine and Arctic Research. Illustrated, indexed, bibliography; 275 pages.

Hayley, D. and P. Wishart (1993) *Winter: a Guide to Nature, Activities and Fun.* Lone Pine Publishing, Edmonton. Thick spiral-bound book written for kids, organized mainly by species of wildlife, with plenty of fact, folklore and activities. Illustrated, bibliography; 170 pages. First in a series, one book for each season.

## *Some rules of natural history*

1. Everything is smarter than we think it is. Animals, plants, pond scum, everything.

2. Whatever an animal is doing, it's probably the right thing. Or it would be dead.

3. Wherever a plant is growing, it's probably the right place. Or it would be dead.

4. If you sit very still in the outdoors, keeping very quiet, the animals will forget that you're there and go on about their business. Or they'll come over to see if you're dead.

5. There is a reason for everything we see out there. Except in quantum mechanics, where probability prevails. And, uh, quantum mechanics governs everything.

6. Plate tectonics, the Milankovitch Cycle and random worldwide extinction events ensure that nothing on this planet stays the same for long. Thus, evolution is essential. Without it life would consist entirely of pond scum. Or maybe there wouldn't be any life at all.

7. The earth's present ecosystem represents four billion years of learning everything the hard way. Don't mess with that.

Mountaineers George Weed (left), J. Norman Collie and Hugh Stutfield camped near Waterfowl Lakes in 1902, en route to five first ascents in the Mt. Forbes area. Photo by Herman Woolley, one of the climbers, courtesy Jasper-Yellowhead Museum and Archives.

# History
## Who did what and when

Most of the readily available historical literature about the Canadian Rockies concerns events in the Canadian national parks, a bias reflected in this outline. But I have tried to include some essential information about other parts of the region, including Glacier National Park, Montana. Events of interest to naturalists and recreationists have been emphasized.

The current population of the region is given in the table on page 708.

### 11,000 BP

"BP" refers to years before the present. A radiocarbon-dated site at **Vermilion Lake**, on the southern slope of Mt. Cory, west of Banff, has yielded stone spear points, choppers and knives, along with many bones of butchered animals, mostly bighorn sheep. Possible evidence of a house, if verified, would make it the oldest known structure in the Rockies.

The discovery of some 950 prehistoric sites in the mountain national parks shows that the major eastern-slope valleys had been occupied, at least in summer, since the end of the late Wisconsinan glacial period at about 11,000 BP. In 1993 Parks Canada archeologists discovered a Clovis point—the oldest type known in North America, dating from between 10,500 BP and 12,000 BP—in Clearwater Pass, Banff park, above treeline at an elevation of 2330 m.

Human groups may have spread from Siberia to North America as early as 30,000 BP, if disputed evidence in South America turns out to be valid, and thus humans may have seen the Canadian Rockies during the period of ice retreat between the early and late Wisconsinan advances (25,000–64,000 BP). Even during the late Wisconsinan (11,000–25,000 BP), the Rockies formed the western wall of an **ice-free corridor** between mountain glaciers and a great ice sheet covering the prairies. The ice-free corridor connected unglaciated regions to the north, in the western Yukon and Alaska, with the southern limit of ice in Montana. If our species was present on the continent, it is possible that we lived in the corridor during most of the late Wisconsinan ice advance; the corridor was closed by glaciers for perhaps only a few thousand years, if at all. (Note: in light of recent glacial-history research, some geologists are beginning to doubt whether the "ice-free corridor" is a valid concept.)

In addition to the Vermilion Lakes bonanza, other major prehistoric sites in the Rockies include chert (flint) quarries near Crowsnest Pass and in Top of the World Provincial Park, B.C.; pictographs in Jasper National Park and in the Canmore area, and camps in Waterton Lakes National Park and in William A. Switzer Provincial Park, near Hinton, Alberta.

### Just before European contact

North of the Athabasca River, the Athapaskan-speaking **Déné** probably occupied both sides of the Rockies, although in small numbers. Main tribes: **Sarcee** between Jasper and Prince George, **Beaver** from there north to the Peace River and **Sekani** in the northern Rockies.

South of the Athabasca* River, the game-rich **Ya-Ha-Tinda** area (name means "Meadow in the Mountains") along the mountain front north of the Bow River was particularly attractive, winter and summer, to prehistoric peoples. Artifacts from there and from elsewhere in southern Alberta show that the most successful of these were the **Kootenays**—American spelling "Kootenais," tribal spelling "Ktunaxa," pronounced "Toon-AWK-ah," no "K"—who were

---

*"Athabasca," also spelled "Athabaska" and "Athapaska," is a Cree word meaning "the place where there are reeds." It refers to expanses of bulrushes (see page 377) growing in the delta of the Athabasca River at Lake Athabasca in northeastern Alberta.

linguistically and culturally unrelated to surrounding groups. The language of the Kootenays resembled the Uto-Aztecan tongues of Mexico; perhaps the Kootenays stayed in Canada while other aboriginals moved on to settle Central America.

Proper mountain-dwellers, the Kootenays occupied both the eastern and western slopes of the Canadian Rockies from the North Saskatchewan River south. In the southern foothills their easterly neighbors were the **Blackfoot** branch of the Plains nations and, on the south, the **Shoshoni,** sometimes called "Snakes." On the west they met the **Shuswaps,** an Interior Salish branch of the Plateau peoples, sometimes called "Carriers." Both groups fished the lakes and rivers of the Rocky Mountain Trench.

Relations among the various tribes were cordial, with constant trade and little conflict. Shuswap-style pit houses have been found on the Banff Springs Hotel golf course, suggesting that Shuswaps overwintered at least occasionally on the eastern slope, and there is evidence of Shuswap occupation in eastern Jasper park, near the site of Jasper House. As elsewhere in western North America, native populations reached an all-time high. Accordingly, game species in the Canadian Rockies were becoming depleted.

### Early 1700s

Pushed westward by European conquest of eastern North America, eastern aboriginals displaced a tribe of the Sioux group: the **Stoneys** (spelled with an *e),* named for their method of cooking by boiling with hot stones. Also called "Assiniboines," "Nakodas" and "Dakotas," the Stoneys came from Lake of the Woods on the Canadian Shield.

Desperately fleeing smallpox and fighting other tribes along the way, bands of Stoneys moved west along the North Saskatchewan to the western edge of the prairies, where dwelled the **Blackfoot, Blood** and **Peigan** tribes of the Blackfoot Confederacy. (Peigan is spelled "Piegan" in the U.S.A.) The Stoneys were tough, but so were the Blackfoot, American name "Blackfeet"; conflicts often resulted in killings, so they came to be resolved ritually, in the form of games. If not welcomed, the Stoneys were tolerated.

*Stoney band members Samson Beaver, his wife Leah and daughter Frances Louise at a camp on the Kootenay Plains near today's Two-O'Clock Creek Campground along Highway 11, in August of 1907. Photo by Mary Schäffer courtesy of the Whyte Museum of the Canadian Rockies (image V469/NG-1).*

The Stoneys preferred the mountains and foothills, home of the Kootenays—whom they attacked. About this time the Kootenays, Stoneys and Peigans acquired **horses,** brought to the New World in the 1500s by Spain and traded north.

## Mid-1700s

**Guns** came into use among the western First Nations, increasing the bloodshed. Horse-mounted, gun-toting Stoney and Peigan warriors pushed the Kootenays off the eastern slope and back to their safer western-slope lands. Fear of smallpox kept them there.

At about this time the Sarcees were moving south, pushed by the **Cree:** a James Bay tribe who had spread through much of northern Canada as middlemen and trappers working for whites. The Sarcees reached the Bow River in the early 1800s; they survived along the western plains margin in uneasy coexistence with the Stoneys, who had become the dominant tribe in the central Rockies.

## 1754

**Anthony Henday,** scouting for the fur-trading **Hudson's Bay Company,** saw the Rockies from near modern-day Innisfail, between Calgary and Edmonton. But he didn't reach the mountain front.

## 1780s

**Smallpox** killed three-fifths of the western aboriginal peoples. The fur trade arrived not long after, bringing more disease and more guns. There was now continuous warfare among displaced tribes. Wildlife populations rose in the Rockies as human numbers fell.

## 1792

Englishman **Peter Fidler,** an explorer/surveyor for the Hudson's Bay Company, was the first non-native person to verifiably enter the Canadian Rockies. In December of 1792 he met a group of Kootenays on the upper Oldman River south of Calgary. See also David Thompson, next page.

## 1793

Scottish fur-trader **Alexander Mackenzie,** a partner in the Canadian **North West Company,** which competed with the British-owned Hudson's Bay Company in the fur trade, followed the Peace River to the Rockies from Fort Chipewyan, which still exists on Lake Athabasca in northeastern Alberta. In his report on aboriginal peoples, he noted that the Beavers had been displaced by the Cree. By this time there were also scattered bands of **Iroquois, Algonquins** and **Nipissing** in the area, remnants of eastern tribes trying to keep ahead of white settlement and epidemics while working in the fur trade. Bloodthirsty by reputation, the Iroquois were hated by their western counterparts, who killed them at every opportunity. See the death of Pierre Bostonais, in the item for 1820.

Mackenzie followed the Rocky Mountain Trench up the Parsnip River to the Fraser, traveled south on it for a while, then was warned by his aboriginal guides of watery perils ahead and turned west, reaching the Pacific via the Bella Coola River. His was the first known overland trip across western Canada.

## 1797 or 1798

**John Finlay,** another partner in the North West Company, founded **Fort St. John** just east of the Rockies along Peace River.

## 1799

Farther south, **Duncan McGillivray** established **Rocky Mountain House,** a North West Company post, just east of the foothills on the North Saskatchewan River.

## 1800

English-born **David Thompson,** a trader with the North West Company at Rocky Mountain House, sent his scouts **La Gasse** and **Le Blanc** across the Rockies with a band of Kootenays to set up trade on the fur-rich western slope. That same year, Thompson and McGillivray traveled south to the Highwood River and scouted the Bow River as far west as the mountain front. Lacking local guides—the local Peigans were uncooperative—they turned back. McGillivray explored north along the front ranges, reaching Brazeau Lake and continuing to the Sunwapta River. But no suitable pass was found.

### Also in 1800

The Nor'westers built **Fort Nelson** near the site of the modern community. It soon fell into disuse, but was revitalized by the Hudson's Bay Company in 1865.

## 1805

**Simon Fraser,** another partner in the North West Company, built a fur-trade post at **Hudson's Hope,** where the Peace leaves the mountains. That community still exists; it is the oldest in the Canadian Rockies proper.

The following year Fraser followed the Peace through the northern Rockies and took the Rocky Mountain Trench south to found **Fort George** (now Prince George) in 1807. In 1808 he followed the Fraser to the Pacific and confirmed that it was too dangerous for regular travel. David Thompson named the Fraser River for its explorer, who had already named the Thompson River, a tributary from the Columbia Mountains, for his friend David, who didn't travel it.

### Also in 1805

**Merriwether Lewis** approached the Montana Rockies on the outbound, westward leg of the **Lewis and Clark Expedition.** He explored 50 km of the Marias* River, naming it after his cousin Maria Woods, but decided to cross the mountains farther south, along the route of today's Interstate 90. On the 1806 return trip, after crossing the Rockies from the west, Lewis again followed Marias River northward, hoping to establish an easy connection with the Saskatchewan River system of Canada. He took the Cutbank Creek branch and came within 15 km of what is now the eastern boundary of Glacier park. The Lewis Range and Clark Range are named for that expedition.

## 1806

**Pine Pass,** between Jasper and Peace River, was crossed by a couple of unnamed deserters from Simon Fraser's trip up the Peace.

## 1807

Guided by Kootenays, fur-trade explorer David Thompson followed the North Saskatchewan valley to **Howse Pass,** crossing it to reach the Columbia. He continued upstream and built **Kootenae House** [sic] at the Columbia headwaters near present-day Invermere. Having recruited the Kootenays as trappers, Thompson returned, but was harassed at Rocky Mountain House by the Peigans, who feared he would arm the Kootenays. He *did* arm the Kootenays.

## 1810

The Peigans had closed Howse Pass to David Thompson, so he looked farther north for an alternative. An Iroquois guide named **Thomas** led Thompson's group over **Athabasca Pass** in January of 1811 and down the Wood River to the Columbia. They wintered uncomfortably at **Boat Encampment** on the Big Bend of the Columbia (historic site now under Kinbasket Lake), then went up the Columbia in the spring to Kootenae House, down the Kootenay River to its junction with the Columbia and so reached the west coast in July, claiming Oregon (at that time

---

*The geographic pronunciation is "ma-RYE-us."

a vast territory that also included modern Washington state) for Britain and the North West Company.

However, **Astorians,** who were American fur-traders working for John Jacob Astor, had arrived first. This didn't faze Thompson; he had been told of a deal between the two companies. Little did he know that the deal had fallen through. After many years of legal haggling, dirty tricks and the occasional act of violence, the Americans got Oregon and the British got "British" Columbia.

### Also in 1810

Three of David Thompson's scouts made the first recorded crossing of **Marias Pass,** the southern boundary of Glacier park. **Finan McDonald, Michael Bordeaux** and **Baptiste Buché** were taken across from west to east by Kootenay guides. Ambushed in the pass by primitively armed Blackfoot warriors, the whites used guns against them, chasing the attackers east over the top.

### 1811

While Thompson was away exploring the Columbia basin, a few of his men were left behind to build **Henry House** on the Athabasca River somewhere across from the site of modern Jasper. Named for **William Henry,** head of the construction crew, this was the earliest permanent structure built by non-natives in the Canadian mountain national parks. Nothing seems to remain of Henry House, and the exact location is unknown. Perhaps it is somewhere on the present lease of Jasper Park Lodge. If so, then the site has been the location of first one kind of hotel, then another. The fur-trade posts of the Rockies were mostly for sheltering company employees on the trail and for keeping their horses, not mainly for trading.

Thompson paddled back up the Columbia to Boat Encampment that same year, proving the Columbia navigable to the west coast. He recrossed Athabasca Pass to Henry House in October and thus set the main route of trans-Rockies travel for the next 50 years.

A cartographer as well as a fur-trader, Thompson drew the first accurate map of the west—he had used sextant readings to determine locations—upon his return to Montreal. He never went back to the Rockies. By now a partner in the North West Company, he became rich as well as famous. But he invested his money badly and died poor in 1857.

The twice-yearly **fur brigades,** composed mainly of French-speaking **voyageurs** ("voy-ah-ZHOORS," meaning "travelers"), were a romantic part of Canada's history. Starting from Ft. William on Lake Superior in spring and fall, the voyageurs paddled and portaged northwest across the lakes and rivers of the Canadian Shield to the North Saskatchewan River. At Edmonton they portaged north to the Athabasca and followed it to the mountain front, where they quit paddling and took to horses, following the Athabasca valley to a large, snowy mountain they called **la montagne de la grande traverse**—"the mountain of the great crossing"—in reference to Athabasca Pass. Today the peak is called Mt. Edith Cavell (see 1916 item for the reason). Just beyond was the Whirlpool River, which led west to the pass. The objective of the eastern brigade was to meet a western brigade somewhere between the Athabasca River and the Columbia River. The western group exchanged its furs for trade goods from the east and each party headed back the way it came.

In 1821, after many years of bitter and sometimes violent competition, the Hudson's Bay Company absorbed the bankrupt North West Company. Going all the way to Lake Superior, the voyageurs took the furs to the HBC's port of York Factory, on Hudson Bay.

Many voyageur names survive in the Jasper area, the best known being **Roche Miette,** a landmark in the east end of Jasper park. "Miette" ("mee-YET" or "MY-yet") was once thought to be the name of an early fur-trade employee, but no such name appears in company records of the time. Instead, "Miette" is probably the French version of "my-et," Cree for bighorn sheep. Bighorns are quite common now at Roche Miette, just as they were in the fur-trade era.

### 1813

The North West Company built another "Rocky Mountain House" along the shore of Brûlé Lake, a widening in the Athabasca at the mountain front. This is the place at which the voyageurs became horse-riders for the upper-Athabasca part of the trip. The structure soon became known as "Jasper's House," named for **Jasper Hawes,** the person who ran it for the company.

In 1829 the post was moved farther upstream, to near the junction of the Snake Indian River and the Athabasca. The name "Jasper" settled over the whole district. "Jasper's House" became **Jasper House.**

## 1820

First reference to **Pierre Bostonais*** ("boss-tun-AE"), a fair-haired Iroquois trapper and fur-company guide more commonly known as **Tête Jaune** ("tet zhawn"), French for **Yellowhead.** Bostonais operated from **Tête Jaune Cache,** in the Rocky Mountain Trench at the western approach to **Yellowhead Pass** (1131 m). Yellowhead Pass didn't get much fur-trade use, for it connected with the surly Fraser River, not with the placid Columbia. However, shipments of leather goods through it to the Prince George district between 1826 and 1828 gave it the temporary name "Leather Pass."

Like many other eastern tribespeople trying to survive in the west, Bostonais and his family were killed by local natives, in this case by a band of Beavers in late 1827 or 1828.

## 1824

**Sir George Simpson,** a Scottish higher-up in the Hudson's Bay Company, crossed Athabasca Pass. At the summit he toasted other HBC officers at a small lake he named the **Committee's Punch Bowl.** Simpson continued to the Columbia and on to the coast.

In 1841, now governor of the entire company, Simpson passed through the Bow Valley on his way west, crossing **Simpson Pass** (near today's Sunshine ski area) to the Vermilion River, then down the Kootenay until turning west, crossing Sinclair Pass (see item for 1841) and emerging in the Rocky Mountain Trench near **Radium Hot Springs.** This was the first recorded pleasure trip in the Canadian Rockies, it would seem; the gentleman continued west, right around the globe and back to Britain.

## 1825

**Thomas Drummond,** a Scottish botanist, was the first naturalist known to visit the Canadian Rockies. He traveled from Edmonton to Jasper House, then up the Snake Indian River and along the front ranges to the **Grande Cache** area. Drummond wintered in the Rockies, visited Boat Encampment and returned to Edmonton in 1826 with 2000 specimens of plants, mammals and birds in his collection—including a number of species new to science that bear his latinized name *drummondii* after the genus designation.

## 1826

**David Douglas,** another Scottish botanist, traveled up the Athabasca. His discoveries included the Douglas-fir, page 259, and Douglas maple, page 271, now more commonly known as Rocky Mountain maple.

Douglas crossed Athabasca Pass and claimed to have climbed Mt. Brown, the western pass buttress, giving its height and that of McGillivray Ridge, the eastern buttress, which he mistook for Mt. Hooker, as 16,000–17,000 feet (4800–5100 m). This would have made Brown and Hooker far higher than any other peaks in the Rockies, north or south. His report attracted climbers/explorers for the next 70 years. See page 698 for more.

If Douglas reached the summit of Mt. Brown, which is rather unlikely given the circumstances (he was using snowshoes, which were new to him), it would have been the first recorded ascent of a major peak on the continental divide in the Canadian Rockies. In 1835 Douglas died nastily in Hawaii, trampled to death in a pit used to catch wild cattle.

---

*Historian David Smyth has shown that Yellowhead's last name was not Hatsinaton, as had been believed previously *(Alberta History,* winter 1984).

**Some time between 1835 and 1840**
Twenty-four of 37 Shuswaps, known locally as "Snakes" or "Snaring Indians," camped near Jasper House were killed by Stoneys at the mouth of Snake Indian River. One of the survivors was a 17-year-old girl—name not recorded—who lived alone for 18 months in the foothills east of Grande Cache before she was taken in by the Iroquois Metis community there. A domestic job at Jasper House led to reunion with a group of her people five or six years after the massacre.

**1835**
**Colin Fraser** was placed in charge of Jasper House. Beginning his fur-trade career as a company bag-piper, this Fraser, no relation to Simon Fraser, was well known in the Jasper area for 15 years; the **Colin Range** is named after him.

**1841**
On behalf of the Hudson's Bay Company, freelance fur-trader **James Sinclair** took a group of 200 settlers, mostly Metis, from Manitoba across the Rockies via **White Man Pass** and **Sinclair Pass** to relocate in Oregon and thus to support Britain's claim to it. The group survived the trip, but Oregon became American territory anyway—with the blessing of the settlers, who had become disillusioned by the company's unfulfilled promise of land distribution. Sinclair was killed in Oregon by natives in 1856.

**1845**
**Father Pierre-Jean de Smet** (a Flemish name and thus pronounced as spelled, not "de SMAY"), a Jesuit missionary from Belgium, crossed the Rockies from the west, via White Man Pass, to make peace among the First Nations and to convert them to Christianity. In 1846 he returned over Athabasca Pass. He was well received on his journeys, a jovial fat man who gave away white shirts, including the one off his back when he ran out of the gift supply.

De Smet kept a witty journal. In it the name **Maligne** ("muh-LEEN," French for "wicked") first appears, used to describe a tricky crossing of an Athabasca tributary near Jasper. The name was applied to that river, and later to the now-famous gorge and lake upstream.

De Smet was the first to record the presence of **coal** in the Canadian Rockies, in 1845, noting exposures along Elk River in the Fernie/Crowsnest area.

**Also in 1845**
British soldiers **James Warre** and **Mervin Vavasour** crossed White Man Pass on their way to Oregon to spy on the Americans. They posed as traveling gentlemen; Warre painted views of the Rockies, including a picture of Jasper House done on the return trip over Athabasca Pass.

**1846**
**Paul Kane,** a well-known painter and genuine traveling gentleman, ventured through Athabasca Pass with a fur brigade. Later, he published the first printed illustrations of the Canadian Rockies in his popular 1859 travelogue. The educated world noticed the mountains of Canada.

**1847**
**Robert Rundle,** a Wesleyan Methodist missionary, held Sunday service with a small congregation of Stoneys near the site of modern Banff. That town's postcard-famous peak was later named for him.

**About 1850**
The Hudson's Bay Company decided to ship furs to its beaver-hat factories from the west coast rather than by the overland route, and thus the fur-brigade days ended. Athabasca Pass was seldom crossed in the years ahead and Jasper House was staffed less often; in the 1860s it was abandoned.

## 1858

**John Palliser,** who was Irish, organized a joint British/Canadian exploratory trip across the Canadian west to see whether the land there could be settled. The **Palliser Expedition** traveled up the Bow River into the Rockies and split into three groups.

Captain Palliser took a group over **North Kananaskis Pass** in modern Kananaskis Country to the Palliser River, then recrossed eastward just south of the Crowsnest area through **North Kootenay Pass.** Lieutenant **Thomas Blakiston** led a group to the **Waterton area. Dr. James Hector,** a physician and geologist, led a third group up the Bow valley and west over **Vermilion Pass,** now crossed by Highway 93, to the Kootenay River.

Hector's crew did the most exploring in the Rockies. A series of misadventures with a confused Stoney guide took them up the Kootenay, down the Beaverfoot, up the Kicking Horse (where Hector was the one kicked) to **Kicking Horse Pass** (1643 m); then up the Bow, down the Mistaya, back west nearly to Howse Pass and finally east to Edmonton in late fall.

Hector was soon off again, this time journeying up the Athabasca in January of 1859 with **Tekarra,** an Iroquois guide. The group reached the Whirlpool River, named by Hector after he realized that it was not the upper Athabasca. In the spring Hector ventured up the Bow again, exploring the Pipestone and Siffleur Rivers; the following year he crossed Howse Pass to the Columbia.

Another member of Palliser's expedition was **Eugène Bourgeau,** a respected European botanist. Part of Hector's party but hopelessly incompetent on horseback, he remained in the Banff area to collect plants while Hector and the others continued their explorations, meeting later at Fort Edmonton.

## 1859

**James Carnegie, Earl of Southesk,** went hunting in the front ranges between the Athabasca and Bow rivers, crossing **Pipestone Pass** among others. An interesting and light-hearted account of his adventures was published, somewhat making up for the amount of killing he indulged in.

By this time commercial and native hunting was on the increase generally in western North America, and by the 1880s most of North America's elk and bison had been hunted nearly to extinction. The isolation of the Canadian Rockies offered some protection, but accounts of the time show that game in the main valleys was becoming scarce here, too. Southesk may have found more because he hunted the tributary valleys.

## 1862

**Gold** was discovered on the western slope of the Cariboo Mountains south of Prince George. Two hundred and thirty-eight would-be miners from eastern Canada were dubbed the **"Overlanders,"** because they took the continental route west instead of going by sea. Divided into several groups, and all men except for one woman, those who had not turned back crossed the Rockies by way of Yellowhead Pass. They suffered mightily. Several drowned in the Grand Canyon of the Fraser River upstream from Prince George, still called "Fort George" at that time. The trip was a bust—the gold strike was overrated—but many of the Overlanders stayed in the west to become pioneers.

## 1863

English travellers **William Fitzwilliam,** titled Viscount Milton, and his physician **Dr. Walter Cheadle** found Canadian Rockies accommodation, food and travel arrangements in 1863 to be rather more primitive than expected. Along with a wimpy, unwelcome companion named **Eugene F. O'Beirne** (sometimes spelled "O'Byrne"), Lord Milton and Dr. Cheadle barely survived to write a popular book about their adventures. By this time there was very little game left along their route.

## 1868

**John "Kootenai" Brown** was the first non-native settler in the Waterton area. Hearing of America's Yellowstone park, founded in 1872, he petitioned Ottawa for a national park in his area and became the first superintendent of **Waterton Lakes National Park** when it was created in 1895.

## 1871
**British Columbia** joined the Canadian confederation.

## 1872
**Walter Moberly** surveyed Yellowhead Pass, which was to be the Rockies crossing for the **Canadian Pacific Railway.** This easy grade was intended to be coupled with equally easy Albreda Pass through the Columbia Mountains to the west.

But the proposed route was not used. In 1881 Kicking Horse Pass was chosen for the CPR instead, to keep the tracks close to the international boundary and thus to prevent American railways from siphoning off business on lines leading into Canada from the south.

To mark the site for an important 1872 meeting with **Sir Sanford Fleming,** who was directing the survey, a Douglas-fir along the Athabasca just east of modern Jasper was stripped of all branches except those near the top. In the lingo of that era, the tree was a **lobstick.** At time of writing in 1995, the tree is long-dead but still standing.

Under Fleming's direction, botanist **John Macoun** crossed the Rockies via the Peace River in 1872 and 1875, cataloging hundreds of species—including Macoun's buttercup, page 321. Farther south, Macoun collected plants and animals for the Canadian government along the CPR route between 1879 and 1904. His daughter married A.O. Wheeler, page 702, in 1888.

Between 1871 and 1875, **Alfred Selwyn,** English director of the Geological Survey of Canada, mapped the rocks along the proposed CPR route. In Albreda Pass, west of Tête Jaune Cache, Selwyn's horse ate his field book.

## 1873
**Crowsnest Pass** (1396 m) had somehow escaped non-native attention until now, when **Michael Phillipps** and **John Collins** blundered through it looking for new trapping territory. An easy route over the Rockies, Crowsnest had been avoided by the aboriginals, perhaps because of legends surrounding Turtle Mountain. (See the Frank Slide, 1903 item.) But there was plenty of evidence to show that the pass had been used for a long time by migrating bison.

## 1875
**Henry McLeod,** a CPR surveyor, explored Maligne River as a possible rail shortcut southeast through the Rockies. He reached a big lake at the end of the valley, named it "Sore-foot Lake" in memory of the difficult trip up the rock-slide-strewn streamcourse and dismissed the idea. This was the first written reference to **Maligne Lake.**

### Also in 1875
**Peter Younge** and **Benjamin Pease** received directions from local Stoneys to hot springs on Sulphur Mountain in the Bow Valley. Although the Stoneys knew of these springs long before, the two American hunter/trappers were the first non-natives to record a visit to what would become **Banff Hot Springs.** Younge built a shack at the Cave and Basin, but lacked the money to register a claim and abandoned the springs the following year.

**Frank McCabe** and the brothers **William and Tom McCardell** rediscovered the Cave and Basin hot springs in 1883. The three young men applied unsuccessfully for a homestead permit (of all things) and were also denied a mineral lease.

Interlopers soon arrived at the springs, bringing on legal and not-so-legal maneuvering. When the steam finally cleared in 1885, the three lads had been bought out for a pittance, and the government had set aside a federal reserve around the springs, later expanded to become today's **Banff National Park.** Banff is the second-oldest national park in North America, following Yellowstone National Park, Wyoming, founded 1872.

## 1879
The **Dewdney Trail,** a wagon road built across southern British Columbia to the Rocky Mountain Trench in 1860, was extended to Crowsnest Pass. The 1.2-m-wide road connected B.C. with

established routes east to become the first improved route across the Canadian Rocky Mountains. Today's Highway 3 follows the Dewdney route; the first auto road over the pass dates to the early 1920s.

## 1881–1884

Geologist **George Dawson** and his assistant, **Richard McConnell,** mapped the topography and rocks of the southern and central Canadian Rockies for the Geological Survey of Canada. This despite Dawson's handicaps; he was hunch-backed and very small.

## 1882

Town of **Golden** founded.

## Also in 1882

**Tom Wilson,** who horse-packed supplies for the CPR construction crews, was taken up into a cirque fronting the Bow River to see the "Lake of Little Fishes" by a Stoney named **Edwin Hunter, the Gold Seeker.** Wilson named it "Emerald Lake," but it was renamed **Lake Louise** in 1884. The CPR construction camp in the valley was named "Laggan"; that community is now named for the famous lake up the hill.

In 1884 Wilson started an outfitting (horseback trip) business in Banff, attracting such notable trail guides as the colorful **Bill Peyto,** for whom **Peyto Lake** is named, and **Jimmy Simpson,** who built lovely **Num-ti-jah** ("Num-TIE-jaw") **Lodge,** given the Stoney name for the pine marten, at Bow Lake in 1923.

## 1883

The CPR reached **Banff.** Carelessness in camping and construction set fires that swept the Bow Valley. Railway-related fires burned a great deal of land along Canada's new transnational railway.

## 1884

The CPR crossed Kicking Horse Pass and headed down the steep, avalanche-prone western slope to the Rocky Mountain Trench. The last spike was driven at Craigellachie in the Columbia Mountains in 1885. In 1909, the **Spiral Tunnels** were drilled under the western lip of Kicking Horse Pass to lessen the grade from a dangerous 4.5 percent to a steep but manageable 2.2 percent.

## 1885

**Banff National Park** was founded as the "Banff Hot Springs Reserve," a 26-km$^2$ tract surrounding the springs on Sulphur Mountain above Banff. It was named "Rocky Mountains Park" in 1887 and expanded to 673 km$^2$. In 1902 the park was expanded again to include all the land between Kananaskis Lakes, now Peter Lougheed Provincial Park, and the Red Deer River east of Lake Louise. The park was reduced considerably in the teens and stabilized at its present size (6641 km$^2$) by the National Parks Act of 1930. The town of **Canmore** has been built on what was originally national-park land.

## 1886

**Banff townsite** was laid out. The name came from **Banffshire,** a district in Scotland in which George Stephen, a principal in the CPR, was born.

"Banff" is properly pronounced as spelled, but just try it. One usually hears something between "Baf" and "Bamph." The pronunciation to avoid is "Ban-iff."

## Also in 1886

**Steamboat service** began between Golden, British Columbia, and Libby, Montana along the lakes and rivers of the southern Rocky Mountain Trench. The boats ran until 1914, when the crews went off to war. In 1921 a railway line up the trench ended the business permanently.

### Further, in 1886

**Coal-mining** began in the Rockies at **Canmore** and **Anthracite,** east of Banff along the CPR. The federal government actually encouraged mining in Banff park because it brought royalty payments. In 1903 the CPR opened a mine near Banff, on the lower slopes of Cascade Mountain, and founded a company town there called **Bankhead** in 1905.

Over the next 20 years collieries opened in the **Crowsnest Pass** area, in the **Nordegg** foothills along the North Saskatchewan River, in the **Coal Branch** foothills south of Hinton, at **Pocahontas** in Jasper park and in the foothills along the Peace River. World War I created a coal-mining boom as the Allies bought all the Rockies coal they could get to fuel troop ships crossing the Atlantic. Reason: it was semi-anthracite and burned without making telltale smoke. After the war, a depressed market closed most of the mines, many of them permanently.

There was a resurgence in coal-mining in the 1960s, when Japan started to buy Rockies coal for use in making steel. **Open-pit mining,** despite its heavy environmental damage, was by now the usual mining method; it had been practiced sporadically in our area since the 1950s, but major new pits were opened in the Crowsnest area, where the new town of **Sparwood** was created, in the Coal Branch and at **Coal Valley,** near the Brazeau River. By this time, the National Parks Act of 1930 had banned coal-mining in the mountain parks. Still, some old leases remained, and mining continued at Anthracite until 1950.

In 1969 a large combination underground/open-pit mine started up in the foothills along the Smoky River. The Alberta government built a town here, not far from the old Metis community of **Grande Cache.** Like other coal towns, Grande Cache went through periods of boom and bust, leading the locals to give it the nickname "Grande Crash."

The most recent Rockies coal town is **Tumbler Ridge,** built in the foothills southeast of Pine Pass by the B.C. government in 1982. Critics warned that the development was uneconomic; by 1985 they had been proven correct, as the provincial government wrote off 300 million dollars in loans to the companies there.

### Yet one more event in 1886

**Yoho National Park** was established.

### 1887

**Richard McConnell,** of the Geological Survey, travelled the Liard River, mapping the strata of the remote north end of the Rockies. This was no mean feat, for the Liard runs in a deep, dangerous canyon.

### Also in 1887

Government topographic surveyor **James J. MacArthur** seems to have been the first non-native visitor to **Lake O'Hara.** With the camera he used for mapping, MacArthur climbed **Mt. Stephen** that year—the first ascent of a summit over 3000 m in the Canadian Rockies.

### 1888

The CPR opened the original, log-frame **Banff Springs Hotel. William Cornelius Van Horne,** head of the CPR, visited during construction and discovered that the hotel was being built facing the wrong way. The wonderful view to the east was going to be enjoyed by the kitchen staff rather than by the guests. He quickly designed a viewing pavilion on the kitchen side.

Between 1904 and 1928—helped along by a fire in 1927—the hotel was entirely rebuilt in its present form. It is much larger than the original, made of concrete instead of wood and covered with Spray River siltstone from nearby outcrops. And it faces the right way.

### Also in 1888

In Yoho park, the **Monarch** and **Kicking Horse mines** opened along the Kicking Horse River near Field, producing 826,000 t of lead/silver/zinc ore until closure in 1952, the last mining operation in the mountain-parks block. These were the only sizable metal-ore mines in the

Canadian Rockies. See also copper-mining in Glacier park, page 59, and Bill Peyto's talc claim, page 705.

At the time the mines opened there were many other prospecting sites in Yoho park, perhaps related to a nearby igneous intrusion called the Ice River Complex, page 119. Small deposits of low-grade malachite/azurite copper ore were found in the Castle Mountain/Copper Mountain area of Banff park; a trail up Protection Mountain leads past two cabins to some prospecting holes above treeline. Higher-grade lead/copper ore was found at **Silver City,** a short-lived prospectors' camp under Castle Mountain. But the mines at Field were the only ones developed. Today, the entrances to the Kicking Horse Mine are plainly visible from the TransCanada Highway at the turn-off for Takakkaw Falls. Look north, on the cliffs of Mt. Field. Those of the Monarch Mine are on the south side of the valley, in Mt. Stephen.

## More in 1888

**A.P. Coleman** and **Frank Stover** followed the Columbia River from Golden to Boat Encampment, intending to climb two peaks flanking Athabasca Pass: Mt. Brown and Mt. Hooker, which had been reported by David Douglas (see the 1826 item, page 692) as being about 5000 m high. But lacking a guide or outfitter, geology-professor Coleman and his friend got no farther than Kinbasket Lake, the original lake from which the modern reservoir takes its name. Illness and lack of food forced them back.

Thus began an interesting story, typical of its time.

In 1892 Coleman tried again, this time with his brother L.Q. and a stronger party. They followed the mountain front from the Bow River to the Brazeau River, then over **Poboktan Pass** to the Sunwapta, which they thought was the Athabasca. They came to the junction with the real Athabasca, which they assumed to be Whirlpool River, and followed it to a lake that they took to be the Committee's Punch Bowl in Athabasca Pass. But they noted that this lake was much too big to be the Committee's Punch Bowl and realized that they were not in Athabasca Pass at all. Instead, they were lost. They climbed the adjacent peaks, saw no sign of the giants they sought, and went home, having discovered **Fortress Lake.**

Undeterred, the Coleman brothers returned the following summer for one more try, this time following the North Saskatchewan and Cline rivers to Pinto Lake in the north end of Banff park and thence to the Sunwapta and the Athabasca. Yet again they missed Athabasca Pass, this time by overshooting it and mistakenly following the Miette River toward Yellowhead Pass. The group soon backtracked south and finally reached the pass, but where were the two great mountains? The Coleman party climbed what they thought was a minor peak buttressing the pass—it was actually the fabled Mt. Brown—and headed home terminally mystified.

Next up at the wicket: **Walter Wilcox,** in 1896. A climber from Washington, D.C., Wilcox made the first recorded trip from Banff to the Athabasca River along the route of today's Icefields Parkway (Highway 93). But like the others he could not find the huge peaks.

The saga continued. In 1898 British peak-hunters **Herman Woolley** and **Norman Collie** failed to reach Athabasca Pass, but along the way they climbed **Mt. Athabasca.** From the top they beheld the **Columbia Icefield,** the first recorded non-native view.

Our story ends back in England, when chemistry-professor Collie read David Douglas's journal carefully and discovered a discrepancy. How could Douglas have climbed a 5000-m peak from a 1700-m pass in only *five hours,* as he stated? A fit mountaineer would have taken at least 10 hours to climb the 3300 m—probably more, considering the altitude. Douglas must have been incorrect.

He was right. Mt. Brown's elevation was later determined to be 2799 m; that of Mt. Hooker, 3286 m. Neither is particularly high for a continental-divide peak.

A final note: David Douglas can't be held responsible for the error. David Thompson (see item for 1810) reported an elevation for Athabasca Pass of 3050 m, apparently based on the boiling temperature of water at the pass. This is an error-prone technique for estimating elevation. If Douglas had actually started at 3050 m, his climbing time of five hours would have been reasonable.

## 1889

Noting that as the Kootenay River entered the Rocky Mountain Trench it came within 2.5 km of Columbia Lake, which is the headwaters of the Columbia River, **William Baillie-Grohman** built a **canal** between the two, intending to divert Kootenay water down the Columbia and thereby end annual floods at the inlet of Kootenay Lake, farther west in B.C. He hoped to develop the lakehead as farmland.

This scheme was scuttled by the CPR, who feared flooding along the Columbia and convinced Ottawa to install a government-controlled lock in the canal.

Never put to its original purpose, the canal was used once to move a steamboat from Columbia Lake to the Kootenay River. An attempt to move a second boat through damaged the lock and the canal was permanently closed. Legacy of this fiasco was the town of **Canal Flats.**

### Also in 1889

**Montana,** in which the southern physiographic end of the Canadian Rockies falls, became a state.

## 1890

The CPR built a log chalet at Lake Louise, the forerunner of **Chateau Lake Louise,** which grew steadily larger as the years passed. In 1912–1913 the present concrete structure was built as a wing of 350 rooms. In 1924 the rest of the place, which was made of wood, burned. In the early 1990s the hotel was greatly expanded, along with most tourist accommodation in the Rockies, under a pro-development Tory government.

## 1893

**Lewis Swift,** an American who didn't talk much about his past, built a cabin under the **Palisade,** which is a big cliff just east of Jasper. He ranched, traded with the Metis **Cardinal** and **Moberly** families living in the valley, and mainly waited for the inevitable railway line that would buy him out and make him rich. But when the railway land agent finally showed up Swift received only a pittance for a small piece of his spread.

In 1910 a government representative arrived who wanted to clear settlers out of then-new Jasper National Park. The Metis accepted cash and deeds to land outside the park, mostly in the foothills around Hinton and Grande Cache. But Swift hung on, not selling out until the thirties, when a dude-ranch operator purchased Swift's ranch. The dude-rancher finally turned the property over to the government for a hefty price in 1962. This was the last privately held land in Jasper park. In Banff and Yoho, CPR and other private holdings remain to this day. There are none in Kootenay.

### Also in 1893

**Samuel E.S. Allen** and **Walter Wilcox** looked into the **Valley of the Ten Peaks,** near Lake Louise, seeing **Moraine Lake.** Wilcox explored the valley in 1899. Samuel Allen gave the ten peaks Stoney names for the numbers one to ten; these have since been replaced by English names, except for peaks nine and ten, which still bear the Stoney-language names **Neptuak** and **Wenkchemna.** What the Stoneys themselves called them, if anything, is unknown. Allen made an early, 1894 visit to **Lake O'Hara.**

### Yet more in 1893

The **Great Northern Railway** crossed Marias Pass. The pass had been explored as a railway route by engineer/surveyor **John Stevens** in December of 1889. Stevens achieved fame in 1905, when he became chief engineer of the American Panama Canal project.

## 1894–1913

This was the **golden age of mountaineering** in the Canadian Rockies, in which nearly all the major peaks were climbed, starting with Mt. Temple in 1894 and ending with Mt. Robson, the highest, in 1913. American and British climbers made most of the first ascents. They climbed with **Swiss guides** brought to Lake Louise by the CPR in 1899.

## 1896

Appalachian Mountain Club climber **Philip Abbot** fell from Mt. Lefroy, near Lake Louise, and thus became the first known mountaineering fatality in the mountain parks.

## 1897

A party of Mounties headed by Inspector **J.D. Moodie** crossed the Rockies north of the Peace River, bound for the Yukon goldfields to uphold law and order. Following a guide known only as "Dick," they traveled up the Halfway River and Cypress Creek, over **Laurier Pass** to the Ospika River, down the Ospika and west over **Herchmer Pass** to a Hudson's Bay Company post on the Finlay River known as **Fort Grahame,** a historical site now lost to posterity under Williston Lake. The following year the party continued up the northern Rocky Mountain Trench to **Lower Post** and on to Dawson City.

Most of the gold-rushers reached the Klondike from the west coast, an easier route, but some came from the east, up the Liard River.

### Also in 1897

**Fernie** was founded, named after **William Fernie,** a coal-mining developer.

## 1898

The CPR laid track across Crowsnest Pass, linking the main line at Medicine Hat with a line across southern British Columbia. Objective: to develop coal-mining in the area and to get the jump on American branch lines from Montana, Idaho and Washington. **Blairmore** was the first of ten communities to appear along a 20-km stretch through the pass at the turn of the century. See also the item on coal-mining, 1886.

## 1900

**Bill and Jim Brewster** started an outfitting service in Banff to compete with Tom Wilson's. Brothers **Fred and Jack** set up shop in Jasper soon thereafter, and by the twenties the family had come to dominate tourist transport throughout the mountain-park block—until 1965, when the Brewsters sold out to Greyhound.

## 1901

**James Outram,** a Scottish climber who settled in Canada, ascended **Mt. Assiniboine** on his first try. Walter Wilcox had failed on the peak several times and was annoyed, as was **Edward Whymper**, the conqueror of the Matterhorn, who ostensibly came to try Assiniboine but was now too old (62) and apparently too alcoholic to attempt it. Outram was an upstart companion of Whymper's.

## 1902

The first **oil well** in the Rockies was drilled at **Oil City** along Cameron Creek in Waterton park, near seeps known since 1886. Other wells were drilled in the Glacier park area along Swiftcurrent Creek and on the western slope at Kintla Lake. The oil had moved up through the thin Lewis Thrust Sheet, page 36, from oil-bearing Cretaceous rock below. Insufficient flow from these shallow wells caused abandonment a few years later.

But in 1913 oil in quantity was discovered in the foothills at **Turner Valley,** southwest of Calgary. Alberta has never been the same.

Deeper drilling in the years ahead showed that the Rocky Mountain foothills held a great deal of **natural gas.** The foothills were gradually crisscrossed by straight **seismic lines** cut out of the forest by exploration crews using dynamite shock waves to map the folds and faults below. Foothills gas was loaded with stinky, poisonous hydrogen sulphide, so processing plants popped up throughout the foothills to remove it from the gas headed for market. People living downwind of these plants discovered that Alberta was becoming industrial. Air-pollution battles in the Pincher Creek area and elsewhere are still unresolved at time of writing.

Meanwhile, **clear-cut logging** on the western slope had been turning the forests of the Rocky Mountain Trench into patchwork since the arrival of the CPR, and the atmosphere there had become smoky from the burning of slash (discarded limbs) and sawdust. The Alberta side saw little activity at first—the lumber industry considered eastern-slope timber too short and scrubby—until the late 1950s, when the paper-making industry built large **pulp mills** at Hinton and Grande Prairie. Loggers, coal miners and seismic crews found themselves in competition to get government permits and tax concessions for carving up a particularly exploitable part of the foothills: the section between Highway 16 and the North Saskatchewan River.

Today, the pulp mill at Hinton spreads rotten-egg odors up and down the Athabasca valley; Hintonites depend on the mill for jobs and accept the pollution. Occasionally the fumes reach Jasper, 70 km away, where the locals are forcibly reminded of what is happening to the Rockies outside the national parks.

## Also in 1902

An underground explosion in a coal mine near Fernie killed 128 miners. In 1914 another explosion killed 189 at **Hillcrest,** Canada's worst underground accident. This and other mining accidents have taken over 500 lives in the Crowsnest area.

## 1903

Photographer **Byron Harmon** arrived in Banff. His photos, films and postcards publicized the Canadian Rockies worldwide.

At about this time, **Bill Oliver** set up a photo and film business in Calgary. Ottawa was a steady client, and Oliver produced a string of educational films about the mountain parks.

## Also in 1903

The **Frank Slide** killed at least 76 people in the Crowsnest Pass area. In the slide, some 36.5 million cubic metres of rock fell from Turtle Mountain—a peak known to the Kootenays as "the mountain that moves"—and smashed part of the town of Frank, established just two years before. The CPR line through the pass was temporarily blocked.

## 1904

The first **automobile** entered Banff park, along the railway tracks. Thought to scare the animals, and certain to interfere with the Brewsters' livery service, cars were immediately banned. A road reached the park gates from Calgary in 1909, but visitors were not permitted to drive into the park until 1915, when the future was seen by both the park and the tour company, and the ban was lifted.

One-lane wagon tracks were widened in the teens for tough Brewster touring cars to follow from Banff to Lake Minnewanka and from Lake Louise to CPR "bungalow camps," which were groups of cabins—the first motels—at Moraine Lake and Wapta Lake. The government completed a road from Banff to Lake Louise in 1921. The section to Castle Junction had existed since 1914; it was extended to Field in 1926 and to Golden in 1928. Side roads led to bungalow camps at Lake O'Hara, Takakkaw Falls and Emerald Lake. In Yoho park, west of the divide in very British B.C., cars had been driven on the *left* side of the road for a few years.

In 1923 a road between Banff and Radium then known as the **Banff-Windermere Highway,** now part of today's Highway 93, opened as a link in the first public highway across the Canadian Rockies. It used Vermilion Pass, connecting with routes from the United States on the west and from Calgary on the east to form part of what the Americans called the "Grand Circle Tour," which included Yellowstone and the Grand Canyon. Motorized tourism had been invented.

Construction of the modern **TransCanada Highway** over Kicking Horse Pass began in 1956; the highway opened officially in 1962.

## Also in 1904

Sixty-year-old butterfly-collector **Mary de la Beach Nichol,** who was British in spite of the continental-sounding name, engaged outfitter Jimmy Simpson in a collecting expedition that saw the famous big-game hunter running about the meadows of Yoho park with a butterfly net. It was so much fun that Simpson worked for her again in 1907, this time in northern Banff park.

## 1905
**Alberta,** previously part of the North West Territories, became a province.

## 1906
**A.O. Wheeler,** Irish-born topographic surveyor, formed the **Alpine Club of Canada.** Annual ACC camps drew climbers from round the world, and a string of mountain huts was established. At the camps, A.O. lined up the climbers and shook their hands as they left to make official club ascents.

## 1907
**Jasper National Park** was founded.

## 1908
**Mary Schäffer,** a middle-aged Quaker widow from Philadelphia, followed the directions of Stoney **Samson Beaver** to a lake in Jasper park the young man called "Chaba Imne," meaning "Great Beaver Lake." There were no beaver at the lake, and probably never had been; the name may have come from the shape of the lake, or it may have been named for the Beaver band, or Samson Beaver may simply have named it for his own family. At any rate the name is now **Maligne Lake,** known the world over from travel posters.

Schäffer spent her summers exploring the Rockies with her friends **Mollie Adams** and **Mary Vaux** (pronounced "VOX," in the American manner, not the French "VOE"), guided by outfitters **Sidney Unwin, Billy Warren** and **Jack Otto.**

*Mollie Adams, Mary Schäffer, Billy Warren and Joe Barker at a back-country camp. Photo courtesy of the Whyte Museum of the Canadian Rockies (their negative V439/PS-1, photographer unknown).*

Schäffer painted wildflowers, took photos and kept a journal. In 1911 she published an illustrated book about her adventures called *Old Indian Trails of the Canadian Rockies.* It was a hit; she wrote humorously and well about roughing it in the remote Canadian mountains. Still available under the title *A Hunter of Peace,* the book captures the feeling of that age: ladies and gentlemen enjoying the Rockies area for its wildness and beauty. Schäffer's work helped to establish the value of the region as a place for wilderness journeys and scientific study—right in line with the objectives of the growing national park system.

Mary Schäffer moved to Banff in 1912 and married Billy Warren in 1915. She died in Banff in 1939.

The Vaux family included Mary's brothers **George and William Vaux,** who became enthusiastic amateur glaciologists in the Rockies and Selkirks. In 1914 Mary Vaux married Charles Walcott, the paleontologist famous for his work on the Burgess Shale fossils in Yoho National Park.

## 1909

**Curly Phillips,** an Ontario trapper and canoe guide, arrived in Jasper to start an outfitting business. In his first summer he met **Rev. George Kinney,** a Methodist minister who needed help in making the first ascent of Mt. Robson, highest peak in the Canadian Rockies (3954 m). Kinney was experienced, but Phillips had never climbed a mountain in his life. Still, the two very nearly reached the summit.

Kinney insisted that they actually *did* reach it. Doubtful of his story, A.O. Wheeler organized further attempts, leading to undisputed success in 1913 by Austrian guide **Conrad Kain** and two ACC members: **Albert MacCarthy,** who was an American rancher in southeastern B.C., and **William Foster,** who was British Columbia's deputy minister of public works.

Curly Phillips went on to become Jasper's premier back-country horse-group guide. He was killed in an avalanche in 1938. Kain settled near Invermere, B.C.

*Conrad Kain (at left), Albert MacCarthy and William Foster after the first ascent of Mt. Robson, July 31, 1913. Photo by Byron Harmon courtesy of the Whyte Museum of the Canadian Rockies (their neg. V263/NA-1046).*

## Also in 1909

**Charles Walcott,** a paleontologist who ran the Smithsonian Institution in Washington, D.C., located the **Burgess Shale** fossil beds of Yoho National Park, one of the more important geological sites in the world. See page 80.

## 1910

**Glacier National Park, U.S.A.** was established. In 1913, **Glacier Park Lodge** opened in East Glacier, Montana, and the tourist business began there.

## 1911

The **Grand Trunk Pacific Railway** reached the mountain front from the east. The remains of an old log structure near the mouth of the Snake Indian River were dismantled by railway surveyors needing a raft to cross the Athabasca—and thus did Jasper House meet its end. Tracks were laid all the way to Yellowhead Pass in that same year. "Fitzhugh" was established, renamed **Jasper** in 1913.

A second transcontinental railway was built through Yellowhead Pass in 1913: the **Canadian Northern,** headed for Vancouver (the GTP line went to Prince Rupert). One line would have done the job as far as Yellowhead Pass; the government assumed control during the World War I and sent some redundant track to France. Both lines went broke after the war, so in 1922 Ottawa picked up the pieces and created the **Canadian National Railways** system.

## 1912

The CPR installed a narrow-gauge railway from Lake Louise station to the chateau at the lake. It ran until 1930, replaced by an improved auto road. Lot-leasing by the government in the years ahead allowed more hotels, restaurants and other commercial operations to open at the lake, creating a textbook example of wilderness despoilment. See the item for 1971, page 706.

## 1913

**Mount Robson Provincial Park** was established.

## 1914–1920 (World War I and after)

Canadians of Ukrainian origin or background were imprisoned in concentration camps near Banff, Castle Junction, Field and Jasper. Most of them were put to work building roads. The Castle Junction camp held over 600 men. All were suspected of being sympathetic to the Germans in World War I because the Ukraine was part of the Austro-Hungarian empire, even though most Ukrainians resisted the empire. Without benefit of trial, 8500 Canadian citizens and residents were "interned" across Canada. After the war, many continued to be held during the post-Bolshevik "Red Scare." Their property and belongings were seized, and no compensation was paid. A monument at the site of the Castle Junction camp commemorates this exercise in national paranoia and state theft.

## 1916

In a burst of patriotic indignation, Canada named the great white peak south of Jasper **Mt. Edith Cavell,** after a British nursing instructor who stayed behind in fallen Brussels to treat wounded soldiers. She was executed by the Germans for helping Allied prisoners of war to escape.

## 1917

**Elk,** which had been hunted to extinction in the southern and central Rockies by the turn of the century, were reintroduced in Banff National Park (63 animals) and Waterton Lakes National Park (58 animals) from large herds in Yellowstone National Park, Wyoming. Jasper park received 88 elk from Yellowstone in 1920, and 194 more elk were translocated to Banff park in that year. The animals have prospered.

### Also in 1917
**Bill Peyto,** the famed outfitter and by this time Banff park warden, staked a mining claim at Talc Lake, just outside the Banff park boundary near Redearth Pass. Robert O'Hara, for whom Lake O'Hara is named, had found talc in the area in the mid-1890s. The talc was mined intermittently until 1944, but little was removed.

### 1920
**Kootenay National Park** was established.

### 1922
Having begun as "Tent City" in 1915, **Jasper Park Lodge** was opened by the Grand Trunk Pacific Railway. A set of cabins surrounded a central dining hall, ballroom and lounge housed in what was billed as the largest log structure in the world. The lodge burned in 1952, to be replaced by a fireproof building in a style resembling that of Frank Lloyd Wright, the great American architect.

### Also in 1922
The first **auto** to reach Jasper from Edmonton used abandoned railway grades. The trip took six days. An all-weather road—today's Highway 16—was not built until 1951. Much of it followed the railway route, which accounts for the wide curves and gentle grades.

Although motorists could drive through Yellowhead Pass to Valemount and McBride on a narrow dirt road built during World War II, there was no paved road west of Jasper until the **Yellowhead Highway** opened in 1970.

### 1925
**Mt. Alberta,** most difficult of the major Rockies peaks, was climbed by a Japanese party employing Swiss guides from Jasper Park Lodge. Rumor had it that the group left a silver ice axe on the summit, but an ice axe found on a later climb was of the ordinary sort.

### 1928
Sisters **Agnes and Mona Harragin** (later Agnes Truxler and Mona Matheson) of Jasper became the Rockies' first and second licenced female guides for horse trips.

### 1930
Parliament passed the **National Parks Act,** establishing the current park boundaries (minor adjustments since then) and names. The act has been amended several times, most recently in 1988, when it strengthened its park-protection provisions.

### 1931
As make-work during the Great Depression, construction began on Highway 93, the **Icefields Parkway,** then called the Banff-Jasper Road or more colloquially the "B-J." The sum heavy equipment used was one medium-sized farm tractor and two smaller ones. The road was completed in 1939; it opened in 1940 as a single-lane of gravel, upgraded in the 50s and 60s to the current all-weather standard.

### 1933
The **Going-to-the-Sun Road,** another depression-era project, was opened over **Logan Pass** in Glacier park. A road over Marias Pass, now Highway 2, had been completed in 1930.

### 1939–1945 (World War II)
As in World War I, **internment camps** were set up in Banff and Jasper parks, and in the Kananaskis area. This time the internees were Canadian civilians of Japanese ancestry. Work camps for **conscientious objectors to conscription,** dubbed "conchies," were also established. The men were assigned to park road-building projects. After the war some of the camp buildings were moved to locations along the Icefields Parkway to become **youth hostels;** see page 744 for more on these hostels.

## 1942
The **Alaska Highway** was completed. The northern tip of the Rockies was now accessible.

## 1949
The **Forestry Trunk Road**, now Highway 40, was surveyed across **Highwood Pass** in the Kananaskis region. At 2230 m above sea level, this was and still is the highest highway pass in Canada.

## 1952
The Trans Mountain Pipe Line was built through Yellowhead Pass, carrying oil from Alberta to Vancouver.

## Also in 1952
The **Hart Highway** (Highway 97) crossed Pine Pass. In 1958 the **Pacific Great Eastern Railway,** now part of the British Columbia Railway, used Pine Pass to link Prince George with Grande Prairie and the east. The line was completed to Fort Nelson in 1971.

## 1959
**Willmore Wilderness Park** was created as the largest provincial park in the Rockies. It was named in 1965 for Alberta minister of lands and forests Norman Willmore.

## 1962
The **TransCanada Highway** opened, making travel over Kicking Horse Pass much easier. But the new highway was hard on park animals, prompting park-warden poet Sid Marty to refer to it as "the Meatmaker." Much of the route through Banff park has since been fenced. This has practically ended the carnage, but it has also hindered wildlife movement.

## 1967
The **W.A.C. Bennett Dam** on the Peace River near Hudson's Hope backed up **Williston Lake,** as of 1995 still the largest reservoir in the world, submerging a 360-km stretch of the northern Rocky Mountain Trench and endangering the ecology of the Peace River delta downstream at Lake Athabasca, home of the whooping cranes. But there was now lots of electricity for northern British Columbia.

## 1971
Following an American lead, Parks Canada planned new roads and other developments for the mountain parks. However, reaction at public hearings was so negative that the plans were scrapped. This was an early skirmish in today's ongoing struggle between developers and environmentalists. The next fight was in 1972, over plans for a large development at Lake Louise. The preservationist faction appeared to win, but a toned-down development proceeded in the 1980s. On the positive side, some of the problems noted there were solved.

By 1976 Parks Canada no longer held public hearings on its plans, preferring instead to have something it called "open houses" for "public input." In this atmosphere two bitterly contested enlargements of Sunshine ski area went ahead, despite protest marches in Banff. Piecemeal commercial development continues to occur in the parks, despite supposedly protective policies and legislation.

## 1973
**Mica Dam,** along the Columbia River upstream from Revelstoke, backed up **Kinbasket Lake,** called "McNaughton Lake" for a few years, which flooded the Rocky Mountain Trench from Golden to Valemount.

## 1977

**Kananaskis Country** was formed in the foothills and front ranges between the TransCanada Highway and Highwood River. It became the largest provincial recreation area in Alberta, enclosing the older Kananaskis and Bow Valley provincial parks.

This new mountain playground pleased those who liked motorized recreation, with upgraded roads and more accommodation. In an attempt to control and concentrate previously uncontrolled and widespread land abuse by motorcyclists and snowmobilers, large blocks were set aside for these activities. Golfers got a 36-hole course and lodge; downhill skiers got a new ski area built on Mt. Allan for the 1988 winter Olympics, complete with lodge. Environmentalists got hopping mad: most of these projects were hard on the land, and all were paid for with public funds.

## Also in 1977

The Alberta government presented its landmark **Eastern Slopes Policy,** which protected much of the foothills and mountains outside the national parks from development. Several new provincial wilderness areas were also declared in the 1970s. But in 1984 the policy was revised to make it easier for development to occur.

## 1988

The National Parks Act was amended to increase fines for poaching, to set permanent boundaries around towns and ski areas, and to enshrine protection as the first priority in national-park planning and operations. In that same year, 20-year management plans were instituted for Banff, Jasper, Kootenay and Yoho parks. Whether these progressive actions will halt the ongoing commercialization of the parks or the growth of the in-park towns remains to be seen.

## 1990

After a local vote in favor of autonomy, Banff became a municipality incorporated under provincial laws, no longer governed by Parks Canada. The land itself stayed within Banff National Park, and park regulations continued to apply, but municipal development matters came under the control of a locally elected town council and mayor. Tourist-industry development increased. Jasper remained under direct control of the park superintendent, having voted against autonomy in 1986. At time of writing, though, Ottawa seems about to impose some form of autonomy on Jasper unilaterally.

## 1991

The Oldman River was dammed by the province of Alberta near Pincher Creek despite determined opposition. Originally planned in the 1960s, the dam had little apparent value except in a large-scale water-diversion scheme to send water southward along the front of the Rockies from the North Saskatchewan River to the Milk River, which feeds into the Missouri system of the United States. Interbasin transfer of water is still against federal and provincial policy at time of writing, but under the North American Free Trade Act, signed by Canada and the United States, water can be bought and sold as a commodity.

## 1994

Ottawa allowed the mountain national parks to raise money internally through user fees, something Parks Canada had wanted for many years. All such fees increased immediately, and for the first time ever, hikers were charged $5 per person per night to walk in the back country.

*For some thoughts about the accelerating pace of wilderness erosion and environmental damage in the Canadian Rockies, see the afterword, page 783.*

# Population of the Canadian Rockies
## Based on provincial estimates current in 1995

This is a short table that was long in preparation. The numbers may not be very accurate; they are a mix of recent head-counts and projections from older figures. Some of the Alberta census regions extend from the foothills east into more populated areas, in which case mountain and foothills populations have been estimated roughly. Getting accurate figures for some of the First Nations reserves was not possible.

### Alberta 1993

| | |
|---|---:|
| Banff | 7615 |
| Black Diamond | 1727 |
| Blood Reserve (incl. Stand Off) | 5292 |
| Bragg Creek and area (M.D. 44)* | 1500 |
| Brazeau (M.D. 77)* | 1300 |
| Calgary to Nanton (M.D. 31)* | 6000 |
| Canmore | 6621 |
| Cardston | 3480 |
| Cardston rural area (M.D. 6)* | 2000 |
| Crowsnest Pass and I.D. 9* | 6779 |
| First Nations small reserves | 200 |
| Glenwood | 301 |
| Grande Cache | 3842 |
| Grande Cache to Brazeau (I.D. 14)* | 550 |
| Hinton | 9108 |
| Jasper and east (I.D. 12) | 5414 |
| Kananaskis area (I.D. 5) | 420 |
| Lake Louise (I.D. 9) | 1311 |
| Longview | 304 |
| Morley and the Stoney Reserve | 3500 |
| Nanton to Ft. Macleod (M.D. 26)* | 1000 |
| Piegan Reserve (includes Brocket) | 1899 |
| Pincher Creek | 3660 |
| Pincher Creek rural area (M.D. 9)* | 1400 |
| Sundre | 2027 |
| Tsuut'ina Nation (Sarcee) Reserve* | 350 |
| Turner Valley | 1478 |
| Waterton Park townsite | 167 |

| ***Total Alberta*** | ***79,245*** |
|---|---:|

### British Columbia 1991

| | |
|---|---:|
| Alaska Highway settlements | 1338 |
| Columbia Valley small centres | 8940 |
| Cranbrook | 17353 |
| Elkford | 2779 |
| Fernie | 4987 |
| Golden area | 4510 |
| Invermere | 2451 |
| Kimberley | 6675 |
| Mackenzie area | 5737 |
| Penny to Upper Fraser | 210 |
| Peace River area | 4472 |
| Sparwood | 4083 |
| Tumbler Ridge | 4277 |
| Valemount to McBride area | 4100 |

| ***Total British Columbia*** | ***71,912*** |
|---|---:|

### Montana 1990–1993

| | |
|---|---:|
| Blackfeet Res. (excl. Browning)* | 5693 |
| Browning | 1186 |
| Columbia Falls | 3044 |
| East Glacier | 326 |
| Eureka | 1039 |
| Hungry Horse | 642 |
| Martin City | 322 |
| Rural areas | 1257 |
| West Glacier | 117 |
| Whitefish | 4551 |

| ***Total Montana*** | ***18,177*** |
|---|---:|

**Total population of the Canadian Rockies: 167,334±**
Population density: 0.94 persons/km$^2$

### Sources

*1993 Municipal and Regional District Population Estimates* (1994) BC Stats, British Columbia Ministry of Government Services, Victoria

*Official Population List, 1993* (1995) Alberta Municipal Affairs, Edmonton and calls to First Nations offices

*U.S. Bureau of the Census, 1992 figures* (obtained through Montana state government, Helena)

*Census region that extends east of the foothills. "M.D." stands for "Municipal District." "I.D." stands for "Improvement District."

## Further reading

There is a voluminous historical literature on the Canadian Rockies. For this list, I have chosen only those publications that bear mainly on the region and that are still either on sale or likely to be available in libraries in the area. A couple of local-history books are included; most small Rockies communities prepared these in the late 1970s and early 1980s, when government funding for such projects was readily available. They are full of family-by-family reminiscences and photos. Check locally. Some reprints of early journals have been included, along with a few spot references from the history outline. Publications that include references, bibliographies and indexes, so important to historians, are noted.

Akrigg, G. and H. (1986) *British Columbia Place Names*. Sono Nis Press, Victoria. Long-awaited update to the Akrigg's 1969 *1001 British Columbia Place Names*. 346 pages.

Anderson, F. and E. Turnbull (1984) *Tragedies of the Crowsnest Pass*. Frontier, Calgary. Accounts of the Frank slide and Hillcrest mine explosion; 96 pages.

Bella, L. (1987) *Parks for Profit*. Harvest House, Montreal. A scholarly study of the history of the mountain national parks and the role of commerce in their origin and development. Referenced, indexed, 216 pages.

Beers, D. (1991) *The World of Lake Louise: a Guide for Hikers*. Highline Publishing, Calgary. A unique combination of trail information and history, with excellent illustrations. Place-name information, index, bibliography; 240 pages.

— (1993) *Banff–Assiniboine: a Beautiful World*. Highline Publishing, Calgary. The second in this series of hiking/history guides, 216 pages.

— (1994) *The Wonder of Yoho: Scenes, Tales, Trails*. Rocky Mountain Books, Calgary. The third in this series of hiking/history guides, 192 pages.

Brewster, P. (1977) *Weathered Wood*. Altitude Publishing, Canmore. Memoirs of one of the famous Brewster brothers, well-known outfitters in Banff and Jasper who started the tour company that still bears their name. 64 pages.

— (1979) *They Came West*. Altitude Publishing, Canmore. More reminiscences as above, 63 pages.

— (1982) *Wild Cards*. F.O. Brewster, Banff. Yet more vintage Brewster, 64 pages.

Camp, F. (1993) *Roots in the Rockies*. Frank Camp Ventures, Ucluelet, B.C. Memoir of Frank Camp, a long-time warden in the mountain national parks. Photos, index, 167 pages.

Carnegie, J.; Earl of Southesk (1969) *Saskatchewan and the Rocky Mountains*. McClelland and Stewart, Toronto. Reprint of Carnegie's 1875 travelogue.

Cavell, E., ed. (1980) *A Delicate Wilderness: the Photography of Elliott Barnes, 1905–1913*. Altitude/Whyte Foundation, Banff. Scenes from early Banff park and east along the Bow Valley, with a biography; 32 pages.

— (1984) *Legacy in Ice: the Vaux Family in the Rockies*. Altitude, Canmore. Excellent photo collection, with biographies and amusing diary entries; 100 pages.

— and J. Whyte, eds. (1982) *Rocky Mountain Madness, a Bittersweet Romance*. Altitude, Canmore. Selection of whimsical historical photos and texts; 127 pages.

Cousins, J. (1981) *A History of the Crow's Nest Pass*. Historic Trails Society of Alberta, Lethbridge. Illustrated, referenced, 152 pages.

Dixon, A. (1985) *Silent Partners: Wives of National Park Wardens*. Dixon and Dixon, Box 1893, Pincher Creek, AB. Biographies of women in the mountain parks, with many anecdotes; 205 pages.

Dowling, P. (1979) *The Mountaineers: Famous Climbers of Canada*. McClelland and Stewart, Toronto. Covers many exploits in the Rockies; 258 pages, 15 photos, glossary of climber's terms.

Findlay, N. (1992) *Jasper, a Backward Glance*. Collection of weekly historical-interest newspaper columns by Nora Findlay that appeared in the Jasper *Booster* in 1990 and 1991. Illustrated, 133 pages.

Forster, M. (1987) *A Walk in the Past*. Friends of Jasper National Park, Jasper. Spiral-bound guide to historical buildings in the town of Jasper. Illustrated, map, 61 pages.

Fraser, E. (1969) *The Canadian Rockies: Early Travels and Explorations*. McClelland and Stewart, Toronto. Still the only historical summary on the region, but out of print and in need of updating; 252 pages.

Fryer, H. (1982) *Ghost Towns of Southern Alberta*. Heritage House, Surrey, BC. Short items on Bankhead, Anthracite, Silver City and other extinct Alberta communities south of the Bow River. Illustrated, 62 pages.

Gadd, B. (1989) *Bankhead: the Twenty-year Town*. Friends of Banff National Park, Banff. Account of national-park coal-mining at Bankhead, near Banff, 1903–1922. Illustrated, 74 pages.

Gest, L. (1979) *History of Mount Assiniboine*. Whyte Museum, Banff. A short account of early mountaineering and skiing in the Assiniboine area, written by one of those mountaineers, with info on the cabins and huts. Illustrated, short bibliography, 60 pages.

Guest, R. (1995) *Trail North: a Journey in Words and Pictures*. Lone Pine Publishing, Edmonton. Unique blend of art, folklore and history. The story of the Hinton Trail, set against 70 of Robert Guest's renowned paintings; 160 pages, with additional photos.

Hallworth, B. (1985) *Pioneer Naturalists of the Rocky Mountains and the Selkirks*. Calgary Field Naturalists' Society. Biographies of John Macoun, Arthur Wheeler, Eugene Bourgeau, James Hector, Norman Sanson, Mary Schäffer, the Vaux family and Mary de la Beach-Nichol; a few photos and maps, 39 pages.

Harmon, C., ed. (1978) *Great days in the Rockies*. Oxford University Press, Toronto. Selected photos of Byron Harmon, with a biography by Bart Robinson and afterword by Jon Whyte; 110 pages.

— and B. Robinson (1992) *Byron Harmon, Mountain Photographer*. Altitude Publishing, Banff. Biography and better work of the Canadian Rockies' best-known photographer; 112 pages.

Hart, E. (1979) *Diamond Hitch: the Early Outfitters and Guides of Banff and Jasper*. Summerthought, Banff. Detailed, interesting accounts of Tom Wilson, Bill Peyto and the like. References, index; 160 pages.

— (1981) *The Brewster Story*. EJH Enterprises, Banff. Detailed account of the major tourist-transport business in the mountain parks; 161 pages.

— (1983) *The Selling of Canada: the CPR and the Beginnings of Canadian Tourism*. Altitude, Banff. Exactly as stated; 180 pages.

— (1991) *Jimmy Simpson, Legend of the Rockies*. Altitude Publishing, Banff. Biography of the British remittance man who became Banff National Park's premier back-country guide and who later built Num-Ti-Jah Lodge at Bow Lake. Illustrations, index; 219 pages.

— (1995) *Ain't it Hell: Bill Peyto's "Mountain Journal."* EJH Literary Enterprises, Banff. Private writings of the famed Banff-park eccentric, edited and annotated by Ted Hart. A few illustrations, 224 pages.

Hart, H. (1980) *History of Hinton.* Hazel Hart, Hinton. Family-history collection for this foothills community, including material relevant to Jasper and Grande Cache; photos, index, 352 pages.

Houk, R.; P. O'Hara and D. On (1984) *Going-to-the-Sun: the Story of the Highway across Glacier National Park.* Woodlands Press, Del Mar, CA. Short, well-illustrated account—with an incongruous photo of the Weeping Wall in Banff National Park. 48 pages.

Jonker, P. (1988) *The Song and the Silence: the Life of Stoney Indian Chief Frank Kaquitts.* Well-written biography of a native elder who spent most of his life in and near the Rockies. Illustrations, 218 pages.

Kane, P. (1968) *Wanderings of an Artist.* McClelland and Stewart, Toronto. Reprint of Paul Kane's famous 1859 travelogue; 329 pages.

Karamitsanis, A. (1991) *Place Names of Alberta, Volume I: Mountains, Mountain Parks and Foothills.* University of Calgary Press. The official provincial government source for place-name information, alphabetized. Short bibliography, 292 pages.

Liddell, K. (1981) *Exploring Southern Alberta's Chinook Country.* Frontier Books, Calgary. Historical and other features from the TransCanada south to the international boundary; 62 pages.

Long Standing Bear Chief (1992) *Ni-Kso-Ko-Wa: Blackfoot Spirituality, Traditions, Values and Benefits.* Spirit Talk Press, Browning, Montana. Good introduction to Blackfoot culture. Illustrated, 68 pages.

Lothian, W. (1987) *A Brief History of Canada's National Parks.* Parks Canada, Ottawa. The official account, brought up to 1984. Illustrated, referenced, 156 pages.

Luciuk, L. (1988) *A Time for Atonement: Canada's First National Internment Operations and the Ukrainian Canadians, 1914–1920.* Limestone Press, Kingston, ON. Short account of little-known ethnic concentration camps during WWI, including those in the Rockies. Illustrated, referenced, 31 pages.

MacGregor, J. (1974) *Overland by the Yellowhead.* Douglas & McIntyre, Vancouver. History of the area traversed by Highway 16, from Edmonton to the Rocky Mountain Trench; good coverage of Jasper park. Indexed, 270 pages.

Marty, S. (1978) *Men for the Mountains.* McClelland & Stewart, Toronto. Reminiscences from Marty's years as a Parks Canada warden; 270 pages.

— (1984) *A Grand and Fabulous Notion: the First Century of Canada's Parks.* NC Press, Toronto. History of Banff National Park; 156 pages.

Oltmann, R. (1997) *My Valley the Kananaskis.* Rocky Mountain Books, Calgary. History of the Kananaskis River area, written by a long-time resident. Illustrations, references, 240 pages.

— (1995) *Lizzie Rummel, Baroness of the Canadian Rockies.* Rocky Mountain Books, Calgary. Biography of the Rockies' most famous lodge-keeper. Illustrated, 160 pages.

Parks Canada (1986) *In Trust for Tomorrow: a Management Framework for Four Mountain Parks.* Parks Canada, Ottawa. Policy statements for Banff, Jasper, Kootenay and Yoho parks; illustrated, 80 pages.

Patton, B., ed. (1993) *Tales from the Canadian Rockies.* McClelland & Stewart, Toronto. Selections from original journals and historical accounts. Biographical notes; 303 pages.

Pole, G. (1991) *The Canadian Rockies: a History in Photographs.* Altitude Publishing, Canmore. Centres mainly on Banff National Park. Profusely illustrated, with a very good text; 112 pages.

— (1995) *The Spiral Tunnels and the Big Hill: a Canadian Railway Adventure.* Altitude, Canmore. History of the Canadian Pacific Railway's struggle with Kicking Horse Pass. Well-illustrated, reading list, index; 80 pages.

Potter, M. (1997) *Central Rockies Placenames.* Luminous Compositions, Banff. Pocket-size guide to about 1000 geographic names in Banff, Yoho and Kootenay parks, plus Kananaskis Country; 134 pages.

Pollon, E. and S. Matheson (1989) *This Was Our Valley.* History of Hudson's Hope, the tiny Peace River community at the mountain front that found itself in a losing struggle with B.C. Hydro and the W.A.C. Bennett Dam. Illustrated, referenced, 401 pages.

Pringle, H. (1986) "Vision quest," *Equinox* 26, pages 73–85. Good summary of Rockies archaeology, with photos.

Putnam, W.; G. Boles and R. Laurilla (1990) *Place Names of the Canadian Alps.* Footprint Publishing, Revelstoke, B.C. Compiled by three mountaineers with extensive knowledge of the Rockies. Also covers the neighboring Columbia Mountains. Map, photos of peaks, index; 384 pages.

Raczka, P. (1979) *Winter Count: a History of the Blackfoot People.* Oldman River Cultural Centre, Brocket, AB. Interesting description and interpretation of hide-painting symbolic historical records (1764–1924) of the North Peigan tribe of the Blackfoot Confederacy. Illustrated, bibliography, 96 pages.

Robinson, B. (1973) *Banff Springs: the Story of a Hotel.* Summerthought, Banff.

Ross, T. (1974) *Oh! The Coal Branch, a Chronicle of the Alberta Coal Branch.* Shannon Ross, Edson, Alberta (contact the Edson *Leader*). Locally written history of coal-mining and settlement in the Rockies foothills southwest of Edson. Photos; 339 pages.

Sandford, R. (1991) *The Canadian Alps: the History of Mountaineering in Canada, Volume 1.* Altitude Publishing, Banff. Early climbs and climbers, from the untrained mountaineers of the fur-trade days to the formation of the Alpine Club of Canada in 1906. Illustrated, indexed, 296 pages.

— (1993) *Yoho: a History and Celebration of Yoho National Park.* Altitude Publishing, Banff. Historical treatment devoted to a single national park. Entertaining reading, with historical quotations. Illustrated, 144 pages.

— (1996) *A Mountain Life: the Stories and Photographs of Bruno Engler.* Rocky Mountain Books, Calgary (Alpine Club of Canada). Biography of Banff's well-loved mountain guide and photographer. Illustrated, 152 pages.

Scace, B. (1973) *Banff, Jasper, Kootenay and Yoho: an Initial Bibliography of the Contiguous Rocky Mountains National Parks.* Parks Canada, Ottawa. Not a public document, but can be seen in park libraries or at the western regional office in Calgary.

Schäffer, M. (1980) *A Hunter of Peace.* Whyte Foundation, Banff. Mary Schäffer's 1911 *Old Indian Trails of the Canadian Rockies.* Reprinted with color separations of her hand-tinted lantern slides, plus the previously unpublished account of her 1911 trip to Maligne Lake and a biography by Ted Hart; 153 pages.

Scott, Chic (1999) *Pushing the Limits: the Story of Canadian Mountaineering.* Rocky Mountain Books, Calgary. A carefully researched and well-written history by a renowned Rockies climber. Many illustrations; maps, references, index; 432 pages.

Smith, C. (1985) *Jasper Park Lodge, in the Heart of the Canadian Rockies.* Cyndi Smith, Jasper. History of the CNR hotel; referenced, 87 pages.

— (1989) *Off the Beaten Track: Women Adventurers and Mountaineers in Western Canada.* Carefully researched, readable biographies of Mary Vaux, Mary Schäffer, Lillian Gest and others active in the Rockies. Illustrated, indexed, referenced, 290 pages.

Smyth, D. (1984) "Tête Jaune," *Alberta History* 32/1. The life of Pierre Bostonais, also known as Pierre Hatsinaton.

Sokoloff, C. (1993) *Eternal Lake O'Hara.* Ekstasis Editions, Victoria. Mostly the author's poetry, with 16 pages of historical information at the front. Illustrated, short bibliography, 144 pages.

Spry, I. (1963) *The Palliser Expedition.* Macmillan, Toronto. Authoritative account of this early political/scientific endeavor.

Strom, E. (1977) *Pioneers on Skis.* Smith Clove, Central Valley, NY. Autobiographical account of early ski-touring in Banff, Jasper, Assiniboine and Glacier parks. Illustrations, index, 239 pages.

Taylor, W. (1973) *The Snows of Yesteryear: J. Norman Collie, Mountaineer.* Holt, Rinehart and Winston, New York. Biography emphasizes climbing in the Rockies; 186 pages.

— (1984) *Tracks across My Trail: Donald "Curly" Phillips, Guide and Outfitter.* Jasper-Yellowhead Historical Society, Jasper. Biography of Jasper's most famous outfitter; illustrated, references, index, 146 pages.

Tetarenko, L. and K. (1996) *Ken Jones, Mountain Man.* Rocky Mountain Books, Calgary. Humorous biography of the well-known Banff/Assiniboine climber, guide, ski racer and park warden. Illustrated, 192 pages.

Thompson, D.; B. Belyea, ed. (1994) *Columbia Journals.* McGill-Queen's University Press. Scholarly presentation and interpretation of David Thompson's records of his Rockies explorations, 1800–1811. Includes reproductions of his famous maps. Bibliography, index, 336 pages.

Touche, R. (1990) *Brown Cows, Sacred Cows: a True Story of Lake Louise.* Gorman Publishers, Hanna, AB. Entertaining history of what is now the big Lake Louise ski area, told by one of the owner-developers. A few illustrations, 205 pages.

Valemount Historic Society (1984) *Yellowhead Pass and Its People.* Valemount Historic Society, Valemount, BC. Family-by-family accounts of settlers in the British Columbia Rockies communities west of Jasper. Illustrated, detailed contents list, 617 pages.

Waiser, B. (1995) *Park Prisoners: the Untold Story of Western Canada's National Parks, 1915–1946.* Fifth House, Saskatoon. Well-documented history of the park internment camps. Illustrated, indexed, 294 pages.

Whyte, J. (1982) *Lake Louise: a Diamond in the Wilderness.* Altitude, Banff. Early history of the Lake Louise area, with much about climbing; 128 pages.

— (1983) *Tommy and Lawrence: the Ways and the Trails of Lake O'Hara.* Lake O'Hara Trails Club, Banff. History of the area, centring on George "Tommy" Link and Lawrence Grassi. Historical quotes, illustrations, 56 pages.

— (1992) *Mountain Chronicles.* Altitude Publishing, Banff. A collection of Jon Whyte's lively and informative weekly columns in the Banff *Crag and Canyon*, 1975–1991; 160 pages.

Wilson, T. (1972) *Trail Blazer of the Canadian Rockies.* Glenbow Alberta Institute, Calgary. Wilson's memoirs, as told to W. Round and edited by H. Dempsey; 54 pages.

*On the summit of Mt. Athabasca (3491 m), July 1, 1987.*

# Enjoying the Rockies
## From car window to crux pitch

Here is some information about **auto-touring, hiking, mountaineering, cross-country skiing, bicycling and boating** in the Canadian Rockies, condensed from many years of personal experience. I'm a perpetual novice at paddling, so the section on boating has been written by someone else. There are recreational guidebooks available that hold far more detail than these pages can. See page 756 for a list.

You will find little in this book of interest to devotees of fishing, hunting, off-road motorcycling or back-country dynamiting—activities in which I will probably never gain much expertise.

**Summer institutes** offer education as well as enjoyment. Highly qualified instructors, often university professors on summer leave, share their knowledge and enthusiasm with the general public during short field courses about birds, bears, wildflowers, geology, etc. At time of writing there are six institutes in and near the Canadian Rockies, all operated by non-profit associations.

- **Friends of Banff Summer Institute and Speakers Series,** Box 1695, Banff, AB T0L 0C0 (403-762-8918)
- **Friends of Yoho Summer Institute** Box 100, Field, BC V0A 1G0 (250-343-6393)
- **Glacier Institute,** Box 1457D, Kalispell, MT 59903 (406-752-5222)
- **Heritage Education Program,** Waterton Natural History Association, Box 145, Waterton Park, AB T0K 2M0 (403-859-2624)
- **Jasper Institute,** Friends of Jasper National Park, Box 992, Jasper, AB T0E 1E0 (780-852-4152 or 4767)
- **Friends of Wells Gray Park Summer Field Courses,** Box 1386, Kamloops, BC V2C 6L7 (250-372-1198)

*Class in alpine wildflowers held by the Jasper Institute in the Opal Hills above Maligne Lake, 1994. Photo by Jill Seaton.*

# *The must-see list*
## Auto-accessible highlights of the region

Each of the places listed below offers a whopping view right out the car window. In your glove compartment you should have a copy of Brian Patton's excellent *Parkways of the Canadian Rockies*. It covers all the scenic stuff in the four-mountain-parks block (Banff, Jasper, Kootenay and Yoho).

### Logan Pass and the Going-to-the-Sun Highway in Glacier National Park

The high point along the Going-to-the-Sun Highway is Logan Pass, 2031 m, with an interpretive centre and a short hike to nearby Hidden Lake Overlook (4.1 km return). See castle-like peaks cut in colorful Purcell Group rock. See marmots, ptarmigan and other high-country dwellers going about their business among hordes of people.

The road itself is narrow and winding, very slow in afternoon traffic—but a marvel, etched along the steep valley walls and lovingly built during the Great Depression, with stone guard-railings and many viewpoints. Closed in winter.

*Saint Mary Lake, near the start of the Going-to-the-Sun Highway in Glacier National Park. Photo courtesy Glacier National Park.*

### Highway 5 between Cardston and Waterton Lakes National Park

In the grassy foothills south of Crowsnest Pass, the rangeland carries on right to the mountain front—a unique situation, for the inner foothills are normally forested. There are interesting glacial features between the park gate and the townsite.

### Wilmer Marsh, Columbia National Wildlife Area

See flora and fauna typical of the southern Rocky Mountain Trench. Dry terraces, complete with juniper trees and the only cactus in the Canadian Rockies, page 329, slope down to the marshy valley floor, which is usually quacking with water birds. Hoodoos have formed at the terrace edges, and they display Quaternary sediments.

This delightful sanctuary is not widely known. To find it, turn off Highway 93/95 toward Invermere. After crossing the Columbia River, take the road to Panorama ski area, turning off shortly to the little community of Wilmer. Continue north from Wilmer (road unpaved at time of writing) for a kilometre or two until you come to an obvious but undeveloped parking area on the right. Stroll down toward the water on sandy trails.

## Southern Alberta foothills and front ranges scenic drive

Here is a one-day field trip that can easily be stretched into a week of puttering. Start along Highway 3 west of Pincher Creek, which follows the Oldman River across foothills hogbacks set with gnarled Douglas-firs and limber pines. Turn north on Highway 22 near Lundbreck Falls and continue between the craggy limestone of Livingstone Ridge and the soft contours of the Porcupine Hills to the Chain Lakes, where Highway 532 takes you up through the aspen-covered inner foothills and over the mountain front to Highway 940.

Following 940 north, it becomes Highway 40, running over Highwood Pass and among the cockscomb ridges of Kananaskis Country. Watch for the great fold on Mt. Kidd, which marks the northern end of the Lewis Thrust (photo on page 196). The route finishes across the Morley glacial-outwash flats, where Highway 40 meets the TransCanada Highway.

## The view west of Calgary from the TransCanada Highway

Just east of the Highway 22 junction, or from nearby Highway 1A atop the hill overlooking Cochrane, you can take in a grand perspective of the foothills and front ranges of the central Rockies. There is no official viewpoint pull-off here, but there ought to be; wooded ridges and meadowy dales roll up to the mountain wall in a scene that is beautiful enough to bring on the tears. These days you can weep for another reason: the Alberta government has let loggers clear-cut patches of it.

## The Ten Peaks above Moraine Lake, in Banff National Park

This may be the greatest of all cliffs in the Rockies, if you are figuring by height and length combined. It's over 1000 m tall from base to ridgeline, and 15 km long between hikable passes. Wow! Reach it from the road to Lake Louise. See also the Larch Valley trail, page 724.

*Moraine Lake and the Valley of the Ten Peaks, near Lake Louise in Banff National Park*

### Lake Louise

Lake Louise is the cliché capital of the Canadian Rockies, and the centrepiece of Banff National Park. Enjoy with the multitudes. Or leave them behind by walking to Lake Agnes or the Plain of Six Glaciers, page 723. The color of the water? Rock flour from the glaciers feeding the lake. See page 180.

### Takakkaw Falls in Yoho National Park

There it is at the end of the Yoho Valley Road: 380 m tall, one of the higher waterfalls in Canada. Icefield-fed, the falls are slim in the morning, swelling with gray meltwater in the afternoon. Stentorian. Every now and again you hear the crack of a water-flung boulder.

### The Icefields Parkway
### in Banff and Jasper parks

This is the most beautiful road in the world, I am told by well-travelled people who ought to know. Highlights: Crowfoot Glacier Viewpoint, the closest auto approach to an ice cliff in the region; Bow Lake, graceful in its subalpine bowl, with views of the Wapta Icefield to the west; Bow Summit, with its short interpretive trail and high-level view of Peyto Lake, turquoise-like in the valley below; the Weeping Wall, in which filmy waterfalls pour over a big cliff of Palliser limestone, forming wonderful ice drapery in winter; and Athabasca Glacier, the friendliest glacier in the Rockies (lets you walk right up and pet it). Farther north, the huge glacial-outwash gravel flats at Beauty Creek bloom pink in the latter half of July.

If all that scenery hasn't burned you out, stop at Athabasca Falls before reaching Jasper. That'll do it.

*Takakkaw Falls*

### The Maligne Valley near Jasper

Three wonders—Maligne Canyon, Medicine Lake and Maligne Lake—lie within an hour of one another on the same road.

At 50 m deep and so narrow in places that the squirrels jump across, Maligne Canyon is the most impressive of the easily accessible limestone gorges in the Rockies; there is a list of others on page 167. To see this one best, walk from Fifth Bridge up the canyon to the main parking area at the top, 2.7 km one way.

Medicine Lake is next, with its disappearing water and strange annual cycle, page 169. Interpretive signs at the north-end viewpoint explain. Peaks made of huge limestone slabs flank the highway.

At road's end, Maligne Lake spreads serenely down the rest of the valley. This is the longest natural lake in the Rockies, 22.3 km from end to end. Parks Canada has allowed only a day-use operation at the lakehead, instead of the tourism disaster at Lake Louise, so the place remains beautiful. A short walk along the left-side lakeshore trail leads past picnic tables to interpretive signs about Mary Schäffer, the explorer from Philadelphia (more on page 702) and a fine view of the lake.

*Maligne Lake at the end of the day. This lake is not, as one often hears, "the second-largest glacially fed lake in the world." There are many larger lakes in British Columbia and elsewhere that, like Maligne, receive meltwater from nearby glaciers.*

## Mt. Robson

See it, if the clouds aren't hiding it, 80 km west of Jasper on Highway 16. Mt. Robson is not the highest, but the *biggest* peak in the entire Rockies, Canadian and American.* With the summit at 3954 m above sea level and the base at 985 m (Kinney Lake), Robson presents 2969 m of mountain mass—618 m more than runner-up Pikes Peak, in Colorado. Stop in at the provincial park visitors' centre at the Robson viewpoint. Climbers: see page 735.

*Mt. Robson, 3954 m, highest point in the Canadian Rockies. The name should be pronounced with a short "o" (rhymes with "Hobson"), not long "o" ("Robe-son" is incorrect). The peak is probably named for Colin Robertson, an officer of the Hudson's Bay Company. The aboriginal name is* **Yuh-hai-has-kun,** *"the mountain of the spiral road to heaven," which seems much more appropriate.*

*Highest peak in the entire Rockies chain is Mt. Elbert in central Colorado, 4399 m.

### The chinook salmon run in the Fraser River drainage

At Rearguard Falls, between the Mt. Robson visitor centre and Tête Jaune Cache on Highway 16, a short trail leads to excellent viewpoints from which to watch the salmon trying to jump a step in the Fraser River. Few manage it. Season: late August to mid-September. A 20-minute drive away at Swift Creek on the northern outskirts of Valemount, there is a viewing bridge and interpretive display right beside Highway 5. The big red fish are practically close enough to touch in the clear water as they spawn and die. For more on the salmon run, see page 481.

### Pine Pass

This is the lowest road-or-rail pass in the Rocky Mountains: 933 m. Reach it along Highway 97, the Hart Highway, between McLeod Lake and Chetwynd. Even at such a low elevation the pass is in the subalpine zone. Stop at the Lake Azouzetta overlook for good views of the long whaleback ridges typical of the northern Rockies.

*Lake Azouzetta, along Highway 97 in Pine Pass. This pass is the most northerly rail pass in the Rockies, as well as the lowest (933 m).*

### Trutch Viewpoint, on the edge of the Interior Plains escarpment

Reach it on a side road from the Alaska Highway near Mile 200. View is west across the long valley that fronts the northern Rockies, toward the rolling foothills and the mountain backbone sticking up beyond.

### The northern foothills along the Tetsa River

Seen along the Alaska Highway west of Fort Nelson, the glacially gravelled valley floor winds between rounded ridges, with subalpine forest on the south side of the road and montane forest on the north side (see page 208 for the reason).

### Summit Lake, in Stone Mountain Provincial Park

Summit Lake lies astride a pass, as is typical of the major gaps in the Canadian Rockies. You may be able to drive higher. From just west of the restaurant, a rough road leads up to a microwave station above treeline. This road is not recommended for passenger cars, and it may be gated anyway. But it is a walk of only a few kilometres through high-subalpine woods and tundra with rewarding views of the lake, of Mt. St. Paul and the Stone Range to the north, MacDonald Creek to the west, with its colorful peaks of ancient rock (page 60) and the slopes of Mt. St. George near at hand.

### Liard Hot Springs Provincial Park

These are my favorite thermal springs in the Rockies. Well, not quite *in* the Rockies, for they are on the far side of the Liard River, which is the northern boundary. Extensive marshes between the parking lot and the springs are quite interesting, traversed via boardwalk. Schools of little warmth-tolerant lake chub swim under the walkway, while mew gulls screech in for mock attacks on half-dressed people coming and going from the pools. These are the most natural of the popular springs in the region—and the hottest.

# *Hiking*

## If you want to *really* see the Rockies, you have to leave the car

For most hikers, the season begins in early April and ends in late October. At low elevations in the southern and central sections, the snow is so thin in the winter that you can walk year-round on the more-popular trails. For hikes above treeline, expect to cross patches of snow until mid-July, and be prepared for snowfalls in August. These normally melt away in a day or two until mid-October, when the winter accumulation starts to pile up.

Between early May and mid-August, the days are so long in the Canadian Rockies that one can cover amazing distances between dawn and dusk. By about 5 a.m. or 6 a.m. there is enough light to see, and the evenings are bright enough for comfortable walking until about 10 p.m. or 11 p.m. Around the summer solstice, June 21 or 22, it never gets really dark from Jasper north, so you could walk around the clock if you wanted to.

**Wheelchair users:** try the Fenland Trail near Banff, the shoreline trail at Lake Louise, the upper interpretive trail at Peyto Lake, or the Clifford E. Lee wheelchair trail around Lake Annette, near Jasper. Parts of the Johnston Canyon and Maligne Canyon trails are also good for wheeling, as is the opening stretch of the Cavell Meadows Trail, pictured below.

*The Path of the Glacier Trail at Mt. Edith Cavell takes you through a rough and bouldery place, but there's strength in numbers. Photo courtesy Jasper National Park.*

## *Four things to do right while hiking in the mountains*

- If you're reading this book, you're probably already careful about littering. Why not carry out some of the trash you find on the trail? The Canadian Rockies are still pretty clean, but governments are doing less garbage-picking these days, which means that we responsible citizens will have to do more. A trashy trail attracts more trash, and we don't want to pass the point of no return. Every time I go out, I pick up the few dropped items I see, sticking them in my back pocket or in a plastic bag in my pack. On a dirty trail it's impractical to pick up everything, of course, and I don't pick up nose-wipe tissues by hand for health reasons.

- Carry apple cores, peach pits and so on back with you. They are not natural foods for Rockies critters, and the seeds of many grocery-store fruits are poisonous to the chipmunks that will eat them. Orange peels have dye in them and will be rejected by all scavengers, so carry these back lest they lie around for years.

- Resist the urge to cut switchbacks. Instead of taking that steep shortcut you'll often find just before a trail doubles back, stay on the main route. Switchback cutoffs erode quickly, producing gullies that wreck both the trail and the hillside. As much as possible, stay on the trail in muddy stretches, or the mudholes will just get wider. Write to Parks Canada about the outrageous damage to trails done by commercial horse parties in the national parks.

- If there is no toilet available, excrete at least 100 m away from water and carry your toilet paper away or bury it. Same for used menstrual pads and tampons. Even though feces breaks down faster on the surface than when buried in cold Canadian Rockies soil, and even though the vegetative cover is disturbed by digging, on balance it is better to bury your poop. This helps to prevent the spread of *Giardia lamblia* parasites (see page 773) and reduces the number of smelly piles in the woods. Bury feces in a small hole 15–20 cm deep. For more on this fascinating topic, read *How to Shit in the Woods* (see reading list on page 758).

## Recommmended clothing and equipment for day hikes

Light boots are fine, as long as hikers from drier climes realize that the trails here can be boggy and these boots will get wet. A coat of wax waterproofing—Sno-seal or some such—on both the leather and fabric parts helps in repelling the wet and hastens drying.

Short-pants hiking weather here runs only from early July to mid-August, which gives you an idea of typical daytime temperatures. I always have a jacket in my pack, plus a sweater, knit cap and light gloves if I'm going above treeline, where the wind is cold and the storms come suddenly. Recommended: long pants with zip-off lower legs.

There is usually water along trails in the Canadian Rockies, but it is often contaminated with *Giardia lamblia*, page 773. To avoid this pest, carry water from a safe source or pack a filter-pump. Except on the hotter days, a litre of water will do for most people. You'll want a non-leaking, unbreakable bottle to carry it in. And some lunch to go with it. And some snacks to go with the lunch.

Small items always with me on hikes: sunglasses, small pocketknife with scissors and tweezers, bug repellent, sunburn protectant, small first aid kit (see page 775 for contents), lighter or waterproof matches, handkerchief, small flashlight, small binoculars, equally small camera, maps (often one that covers a large area, so I can identify peaks in the distance, plus the appropriate detailed map), compass (seldom used, but useful for bushwhacking when no landmarks are in sight or for settling arguments about which mountain in the distance is which) and assorted nature guides (lucky you; all you need is this book). Yikes; almost forgot the toilet paper, and the zip-lock bag for packing out used.

# Representative day-hikes

The walks listed below are my favorites among the popular, easy-to-follow routes. I have chosen outings in the national parks, where the trails are kept up and unpleasant surprises are rare. In unprotected places last year's trail can become this year's road, the forest can be logged off and the destination can change from wilderness meadow to coal-mine pit or oil-company wellsite.

There are many fine off-trail routes in the Rockies, most of them semi-mountaineering routes up the easier peaks. See *Scrambles in the Canadian Rockies* in the list of guidebooks, page 757.

### Avalanche Lake in Glacier National Park *4.5 km one way, 3–4 hr return*

A moderate climb from the red-cedar groves along Lake McDonald to the lower subalpine ecology of Avalanche Lake, with its spectacular backdrop of cliffs and waterfalls. The first kilometre is along the Trail of the Cedars: a stroll through classic Columbian forest. A well-made boardwalk keeps you out of the mire, and a free interpretive pamphlet at the trailhead keys to signs along the way. This place contrasts wonderfully with the windy heights of nearby Logan Pass along the Going-to-the-Sun Highway.

### Siyeh Pass in Glacier National Park *13.8 km total, 6–8 hr*

A classic Glacier-park hike. Steep climb from the Going-to-the-Sun Highway takes you up to Preston Park, a hanging valley at treeline. Cross the rocky alpine pass at 2362 m, then trudge steeply down to Baring Creek, for a touristy finish at Sunrift Gorge. Note that this route starts at one place and ends at another.

### The Carthew Trail in Waterton Lakes National Park *20.1 km total, 7–9 hr*

From Cameron Lake up a well-graded woodsy trail to fields of beargrass and the alpine zone at Carthew Summit, 2410 m. Then down past three lakes (alpine, subalpine, upper montane) to Waterton townsite at Cameron Falls. A long day, but it hits every life zone in the region.

### Lake Agnes, above Lake Louise
*3.4 km one way, 2–3 hr total, or loop trip by way of Plain of Six Glaciers trail, 18 km, 6–7 hrs*

Hike up to a textbook tarn lake (glacially carved basin), with teahouse treats recalling the ladies-and-gentlemen days of the pre-war Rockies. From Chateau Lake Louise, follow the lakeshore trail northwest and branch off at the Lake Agnes sign. Fairly steep climb finishes up wooden stairs to the tarn. The teahouse is open July 1 to Labour Day. Enjoy freshly baked goodies and start back, or, fueled by teahouse caffeine, continue up the rougher trail over the Beehive (2268 m) and down to yet another teahouse in the next valley to the south, the Plain of Six Glaciers. Complete the loop downhill to Lake Louise, having seen some glacial geology and taken in the best views of Canada's postcard-image paradise.

Lake Agnes, a tarn reached in a walk of one or two hours from Lake Louise. There is still a little ice on the lake in July. The Lake Agnes Teahouse is visible in the centre of the photo, Lookout Point beyond. The Lake Louise area is famous for its concentration of spectacular day-hikes. And its crowds.

### Larch Valley and Paradise Valley via Sentinel Pass *16.9 km, 6–8 hr*

Another classic of the Lake Louise area. Begin at Moraine Lake. Occasional views across the lake to the great Ten Peaks wall (photo on page 717) enliven the steady 3-km climb to Larch Valley. Here the grade eases through high-subalpine larch woods and tundra ponds. Either return, 2–3 hrs total, or continue through the narrow gap of Sentinel Pass at 2611 m and down a steep, bouldery section into Paradise Valley, with Hungabee Mountain lurking at the end. A gentler trail leads past the waterfalls of the Giant Steps and back to the Moraine Lake Road. Hitch-hiking back to the car usually doesn't take too long.

### The Ink Pots in Banff National Park *5.8 km one way, 3–4 hr return*

Lots of variety. Start on the Johnston Canyon Trail, joining the throngs along the metal walkway, then leaving them behind as you take the stairs up and out of the canyon near the end. Steady climb through the woods ends with a steep but short descent to lower subalpine meadows and the Ink Pots, which are several interesting karst springs (for more on karst, see page 168). Impressive views there of Mt. Ishbel and other slabby front-range peaks.

### Opabin Plateau in Yoho National Park *5.1 km loop; 2–3 hr*

Take the bus to Lake O'Hara, which is the only way to get in unless you walk. Mountain bicycles are not allowed. Info and reservations from Parks Canada in Field, B.C., 250-343-6433. Opabin Plateau is a hanging valley at treeline, with larch trees among heathery meadows and reflecting ponds. All trails beginning at Lake O'Hara are wonderful; the place offers the best selection of day-hikes on the western slope of the Canadian Rockies. Get Don Beers's guidebook (see page 756).

### The Iceline in the Yoho Valley *18.4-km loop, 6–8 hr*

The name fits this trail perfectly; the route skirts the Emerald Glacier, taking you through 5 km of spectacular glacial forefield high on the western wall of the Yoho Valley. It's a long day, though, with lots of elevation gain. From the Yoho Valley trailhead at Whiskey Jack Hostel near Takakkaw Falls you can head up to the ice directly, via the trail toward Yoho Pass, or take the main Yoho Valley trail north to the Celeste Lake junction and a more gradual climb. Be prepared for rough weather up there in the moraines.

### Chephren Lake and Cirque Lake in Banff park *4.0 km one way to Chephren, 2–3 hr; add 5.8 km and another 2 hrs to include Cirque Lake*

Moderate climb through subalpine forest that opens suddenly on the lakes, set against immense cliffs. Pronunciation: "KEFF-ren" is correct, for the name is indeed Egyptian; Mt. Chephren was originally named Pyramid Mountain, then renamed for Chephren, builder of pyramids, to avoid confusion with the Pyramid Mountain located near Jasper.

### Parker Ridge in northern Banff park *2.4 km one way, 2–3 hr*

A popular alpine-zone hike. Steady grade through upper subalpine woods and tree islands to treeline, then over a broad ridge to views of Saskatchewan Glacier and the Columbia Icefield. Fossils en route—white corals in black Southesk limestone, page 108—and a good variety of alpine flowers from mid-July to early August.

### Cavell Meadows/Path of the Glacier in Jasper National Park *9 km total, 3–4 hr*

From the Mt. Edith Cavell parking lot, through Little Ice Age moraines into subalpine forest and alpine meadows above, famous for wildflowers. Smashing views of the north face of the mountain and Angel Glacier. On your way back, branch left shortly before reaching the paved part of the trail to take in the short Path of the Glacier interpretive loop, which finishes at the parking lot.

## The trail network surrounding the town of Jasper *Half-day hikes, mostly*

For those who like short walks in easy terrain, the Jasper trails are ideal. Montane meadows and Douglas-fir woods; feather-moss forests; low gritstone ridges; lots of lakes. Recommended: Valley of the Five Lakes, Old Fort Point, Wabasso Lake, Mina Lakes–Riley Lake Loop. Be prepared for a lot of horse crap and mud on most of these. The network is complex, but comprehensive directional signage installed and maintained by the Friends of Jasper National Park makes it easy to find your way around.

## Opal Hills in Jasper park *8.2 km return, 4–6 hr*

A steep but rewarding climb to the alpine zone. Keep left at the junction reached well up the hill; the righthand trail is steeper. The trail passes by hill-size piles of shaly rock-slide debris on the right. These heaps are not the Opal Hills; the name refers to the higher summits on the east side of the trail.

The other classic hike in the Maligne Lake area is the Bald Hills Trail, unfortunately taken over by a horse-ride concession in 1989 and thus rendered less pleasant for walking. The rolling alpine country beyond the horse-accessible section is quite lovely.

## Overlander Trail in Jasper park *15 km, 4–5 hr*

Takes the roadless side of the Athabasca River from the Sixth Bridge picnic site on the Maligne River to the Cold Sulphur Spring viewpoint on Highway 16. Easy walking, with good views and a variety of forest and meadow; good birding for hawks near the northeastern end. Passes by the photogenic ruins of John Moberly's ranch (see page 699).

# *Back-packing*

This is where the national-park block really distinguishes itself, with its enormous back country open to everyone for overnight and multi-day walks. (Open, that is, to those able to pay. In the summer of 1994, Parks Canada started charging overnight fees.) The deeper rivers are bridged, although you may have to wade the odd stream. Primitive campsites are provided. Warden patrols add to safety. Many people walk these mountains alone, knowing that they will probably meet others on the way should they get into trouble. Still, it is wise to have at least one companion on any hike in the wilds.

# *Suggested equipment, clothing and food*

In addition to the day-hiking items suggested on page 722, you might want to consider the following for longer walks. They have worked well for me.

**Internal-frame pack.** My nice old external-frame pack gathers dust these days, replaced by an internal-frame model that is light, comfortable, holds lots, and doesn't catch in the trees as I walk. Further, it goes small for day use from a back-country campsite and rides low for overnight ski trips. In the rain, a large plastic garbage bag covers it completely.

**Light self-supporting tent.** The kind you can pick up and move after you discover The Lump. Look for a tent that pops up in a trice, requires as few stakes as possible and weighs less than 3 kg. The more you pay, the better off you will be when the weather gets nasty.

Guyed, staked-out tents are harder to set up on stony ground—next to impossible on the hard-packed gravel tent pads that park officials often inflict on back-packers.

With a light tent, you can afford the small extra weight of a hiker's tarp. This provides head-high shelter for cooking and eating in bad weather, or for just waiting out a thunderstorm. Slung over a cord strung between trees, a tarp makes a rainy-day camp far more pleasant. Car-camping tarps are typically too heavy. Buy a lightweight back-packer's tarp (weight 1 kg), or make your own 2.5-m by 3-m rectangle from tent-fly material. Hem the edges, then add nylon-tape ties at each corner and halfway along each side.

Wading Poboktan Creek on the way to Jonas Shoulder in Jasper National Park

**Long sleeping pad.** The ground is always cold in the Canadian Rockies, and any part of you that touches it through your sleeping bag will be, too. A feather-light closed-cell foam pad is fine for summer; you will sleep warmer if it reaches from head to toe. Middle-aged types like me appreciate the extra comfort of an inflatable pad such as the Therm-a-Rest.

**Down or synthetic-fill sleeping bag.** My summer bag weighs only 1 kg and stuffs into a small sack that forms the bottom layer in my pack. If the weather is cool and rainy, though, the down gets damp overnight and I have to dry the bag every couple of days to keep it cozy. The synthetic-fill bags don't have this disadvantage, and they are half the price, but they weigh nearly twice as much for equivalent warmth and don't pack as small.

**Gasoline or butane cooker.** An evening fire is always pleasant, but it is seldom necessary and is always hard on the surrounding vegetation—especially if you are in an upper-subalpine area, where every stick of wood has a purpose, even the dead snags, and should be left alone. I use the lightest, hottest white-gas stove on the market and spare the forest. Implements: fuel bottle, pot with lid, edge-gripping lifter, insulated plastic cup and nylon spoon.

**Incidentals.** Light line for stringing up the food sack at night, more toilet paper than I carry on day hikes, more complete first-aid kit (see page 775 for suggested contents), spare glasses, extra flashlight batteries, plastic garbage bags for keeping your sleeping bag and clothing dry.

**Clothing.** In addition to the usual day-hike stuff, I always pack a pair of long pants, a change of socks and underwear, gloves and a tuque (the Canadian knit cap; rhymes with "Luke," and it's not spelled "toque"). A light down jacket takes the chill off in the morning and evening, and it could save your life if your only sweater gets wet in a four-day storm. For wading streams, a pair of light plastic sandals or moccasins will protect your feet from the stones; you can also wear them in camp while drying your boots out.

**Food.** Freeze-dried stuff for supper and breakfast on trips of three days or more. Minimal breakfast: instant porridge and dried fruit. My favorite breakfast: black-bean flakes and instant rice. Good at lunch: peanut butter and other spreads on crackers; dry salami, cheese, dried fruit, cookies, granola bars. Good anytime: GORP (acronym for Good Old Raisins and Peanuts). To bulk up supper, try Japanese instant noodles mixed with Swiss instant soup—made thick. Hot drinks: tea, cocoa (nice with a touch of peppermint schnapps), hot Jello (don't knock it 'til you've tried it). Cold drinks: plain water, usually, because drink mixes don't quench the thirst as well.

With four days of food, my pack comes to about 18–22 kg when I am going alone; a couple of kilos less when I'm with someone else and sharing the weight of tent and cooking stuff.

*"Such a great spot to pitch the tent, right beside this pond, but when we came back at the end of the day the place had kind of changed." Camp well above water; lake and stream levels can vary by the hour. Parks Canada photo by Brian Luckman.*

# Representative back-packing trips

As in the case of the day hikes listed earlier, the ones described here are all within national or provincial parks, and for the same reasons: reliable trail maintenance and ongoing land protection. They require back-country permits, and usually a fee must be paid.

### Gunsight Pass in Glacier National Park *35.3 km, overnight*

An east-west traverse through the heart of the park, from St. Mary Lake to Lake McDonald. En route are two high passes: Gunsight and Lincoln—Gunsight is one of the better places in the park to see mountain goats—and two high lakes. On the eastern approach to Gunsight Pass the trail has been blasted out of the cliff in classic Glacier-park style. There is a shelter (not for camping) in the pass. Usual campsites: at either Gunsight Lake or Ellen Wilson Lake, depending on whether you make it over the pass on the first day.

### North and South Kananaskis passes in Kananaskis Country *40 km, three days*

Perhaps the best K-Country loop trip, set among the great folds and flatirons of the front ranges. Routes in the region are becoming easier to follow as the province improves the trails, but this one has an unmaintained section on the B.C. side of the divide, so expect a few problems there, made easier if you have a copy of the *Kananaskis Country Trail Guide* along.

From the trailhead on the north side of Upper Kananaskis Lake, hike to Three Isle Lake, climbing into the meadows of South Kananaskis Pass and then crossing the divide for a night at Beatty Lake, with the impressive Royal Group to the west. Next day, drop precipitously down the Beatty Creek drainage until possible to head north across the slopes of the peak west of Mt. Beatty and bushwhack down into the valley of Leroy Creek, where a good trail on the north side heads toward North Kananaskis Pass. Once over, there is camping downstream from Maude Lake, near the amazing Turbine Canyon. Finish by way of Lawson Lake, along the high-line trail past Mt. Putnik and beside the Upper Kananaskis River to close the loop.

### Mt. Assiniboine in Banff National Park and Mount Assiniboine Provincial Park *54–70 km, three days*

Pilgrimage to the Matterhorn of the Canadian Rockies. If the weather is poor, go in via Bryant Creek (take the Smith-Dorrien Road from Canmore past Spray Lake to a marked turnoff and side road to the trailhead) and over Assiniboine Pass to Magog Lake under the peak, 27 km one way. This route stays in the valleys. If the weather report is optimistic, consider going from the opposite direction by way of the beautiful alpine Sunshine Meadows and the interesting Valley of the Rocks, 35.5 km one way, starting at the Healy Creek parking lot west of Banff. Gondola or shuttle service up to the Sunshine ski area saves 6.5 km of uphill hiking. Inquire 403-678-4099.

Going in one way and out the other is the best, of course, but hitch-hiking between the two trailheads can take all day. A popular plan is to go in from Sunshine and out over Wonder Pass, a variation of the Bryant Creek route that offers views of Assiniboine's enormous east face hulking over Marvel Lake.

*Backpacker near Assiniboine Pass on the trail to Mt. Assiniboine*

## Nigel Pass, Jonas Shoulder, Poboktan Creek in Jasper park *55 km, three days*

A straightforward and scenic hike through the front ranges east of the Columbia Icefield. Good trail all the way. From the southern trailhead along the Icefields Parkway near Parker Ridge, the first high point is Nigel Pass, with its interesting orange dolomite lumps. Then steeply down to the headwaters of the Brazeau River (picturesque ponds) and a campsite near the Four Point warden cabin. Up Four Point Creek to the high country next morning, with rusty-colored, glacier-spotted peaks of Gog quartzite, page 71, on the west side of the valley. Keep right for the high pass over the Jonas Shoulder, which forms the eastern wall of the valley, and down to Poboktan Creek on the other side. The last day is all downhill along Poboktan Creek to the Sunwapta Warden Station.

## Tonquin Valley loop in Jasper park *44 km, two or three days*

The grandest place in the park and perhaps in the entire Canadian Rockies. Most people do this hike with two cars, leaving one at the Portal Creek trailhead on the access road to Marmot Basin Ski Area south of Jasper on the Icefields Parkway and Highway 93A, and continuing in the other to Mt. Edith Cavell, farther south off 93A. The trailhead is near the end of the Cavell Road, opposite Cavell Hostel.

A wide trail contours the southern side of the Astoria River Valley, crossing the river and switchbacking up the northern side to reach lush high-subalpine country characteristic of the main ranges in Jasper park. (A nearby pass is named "Verdant.") Suddenly one sees the tops of mountains peeking up, then more and more of them: the sensational Ramparts, a mountain wall on the scale of the Ten Peaks ridge near Lake Louise. On a good day the Ramparts reflect in Amethyst Lakes. No wonder this scene is known worldwide.

So are the bugs, the mud, and the horse-dung here. The Tonquin Valley is mosquito-plagued all summer, and it's the fly capital of the park in August. There are two groups of horse-supplied commercial cabins at the lakes. Parks Canada's trail crews can't keep ahead of the wear and tear.

Camping at the lakes makes for a long day of 23 km; you may want to camp sooner and stretch the hike to three days. Continue the loop north, past the Moat Lake junction, and pick up the trail heading east to Maccarib Pass, where you may see the pass's namesake: caribou. Beyond the pass it is mostly downhill along Portal Creek.

## The Skyline Trail in Jasper park *44.1 km, two or three days*

The best hike in the Rockies, I think. It runs from Maligne Lake to Maligne Canyon, and over half of it is above treeline, which means that in bad weather it is the *worst* hike in the Rockies. There are three high passes. On one of these, the trail tops out and stays well above treeline for about 5 km, following the crest of the Maligne Range. Supreme views of the Maligne Lake peaks, the gray waves of the front ranges, the Athabasca River far below and the glacier-draped main ranges to the west. You can see everything from the Columbia Icefield to Mt. Robson.

Park at the second lot at Maligne Lake—the one past the bridge over the outlet stream—and choose the righthand of two trailheads there. For a two-day trip, a good campsite is the one below Curator Lake; three-day hikers often camp in the Snowbowl and at Tekarra Lake.

## Berg Lake in Mount Robson Provincial Park *17.4 km one way, two or three days*

The best view of the biggest mountain in the Rockies, if the weather allows you to see it at all. The trailhead is at the end of a short road leading to the Robson River from the Mt. Robson viewpoint and park information centre, 80 km west of Jasper along Highway 16. A busy trail follows the river 4.2 km uphill through a red-cedar forest to Kinney Lake, then up and down along the shore to the far end and a warden cabin beyond. After the Whitehorn Campground, the trail begins a steep ascent to the lip of the hanging valley on the north side of Mt. Robson. This is a tough pull with a heavy pack, so keep it light. Waterfalls along the way are distractions from the toil, especially Emperor Falls, the sight of which means that you are nearly up the hill. But not at your objective, yet, because the campground at Berg Lake lies 6 km farther.

# Long walks in the mountain parks

These are possibly unique in North America. I can't think of anyplace else on the continent where it is possible to go hiking for two weeks in the wilderness, never crossing a road, yet travelling on maintained trails with bridged rivers. (Well, *mostly* bridged rivers.) But that is what you can do in the Canadian Rockies. There isn't room here to describe these hikes in detail, so be sure to consult one of the trail guides listed on page 756. Maps on page 759.

### The North Boundary Trail in Jasper and Mt. Robson parks
*178 km, typically ten days*

Starts along the Snake Indian River in eastern Jasper park, curves through the northern part of the park along the Smoky River and comes out by way of Berg Lake to Highway 16 at Mt. Robson. A trip of this duration makes for a heavy pack until you have made a dent in your food supply, and much of the North Boundary Trail is in forested valley bottoms, but it's great for woodsy wildlife, alpine scenery over two passes—plus an unspectacular grind over the shoulder of Twintree Mountain—and the knowledge that you are a long way from the nearest used car lot. There are seldom-visited side valleys to explore en route. Recommended: Blue Creek.

### The South Boundary Trail in Jasper park *170 km, 10–14 days*

More serious than the North Boundary route, with longer high-country stretches, trickier route-finding and a couple of over-the-knees stream fords. Reward: better scenery, more sense of adventure. Starting from Medicine Lake (arbitrarily; these long trips go equally well from either direction), the route runs past Beaver Lake and Jacques Lake to the Rocky River; up the Rocky and the Medicine Tent to Southesk Pass, down the Cairn River to the Southesk, across a low height of land in the foothills to the Brazeau River, then up the Brazeau to Nigel Pass and down Nigel Creek to the Icefields Parkway near Sunwapta Pass.

### The Sawback Trail in Banff and Jasper parks *149 km, 10–14 days*

Lies entirely within the front ranges and mostly in Banff park. Very scenic, with five passes. Start at the lowest parking lot near the end of the Norquay Road near Banff. Route: Forty Mile Creek, Mystic Pass, Johnston Creek, Pulsatilla Pass, Baker Creek, Baker Lake, Red Deer Lakes (either via the upper Red Deer River, which is shorter, or via Deception Pass and Skoki, which are more scenic), Little Pipestone Creek, Pipestone River (over-the-knees ford), Pipestone Pass, Siffleur River (fords at Dolomite Creek and Porcupine Creek) to the North Saskatchewan River (bridged) and Highway 11.

This route is about as difficult as the South Boundary Trail, perhaps tougher beyond Red Deer Lakes because of the fords. Shortly after Dolomite Creek you cross out of the park and into the provincial Siffleur Wilderness, where trail maintenance is spotty and the route not as clearly indicated. If you want to stay in the park, double back at Dolomite Creek and follow it over Dolomite Pass to the Icefields Parkway at the Crowfoot Glacier Viewpoint. For a shorter trip of 8–10 days, take the trail west to Fish Lakes from the Pipestone River beyond Cataract Peak, continuing over North Molar Pass to Mosquito Creek and out to the Icefields Parkway at Mosquito Creek Campground.

# The longest hike in the Canadian Rockies

In the first edition of this book I pointed out that no one had yet walked the full length of the Canadian Rockies, from the international boundary to the Liard River, a distance of 1350 km as the raven flies. English long-haul hiker Chris Townsend accepted the challenge and did it— alone. The trip took him all summer and then some, from June 22nd to October 24th, 1988. Total distance walked: 2575 km. Difficulties: many, but he knew what he was doing, having already hiked the Rockies from Canada to Mexico (May 30th to November 27th, 1985). Read about Townsend's adventure in his book *High Summer,* Oxford Illustrated Press, 1989.

# Mountaineering
## Why did we climb it? Well, *somebody* had to

This information is for climbers with enough experience to take the lead on fairly difficult rock, snow and ice. If you are a beginner, or if you haven't climbed but would like to learn, then please hire a mountain guide and/or get some good instruction before attempting to do any of the routes listed here. To be blunt: without training in this sport you stand a good chance of getting killed. The organizations and guides' companies listed below teach climbing in the Rockies at the time of writing.

- **Alpine Club of Canada,** Box 2040, Canmore, AB  T0L 0M0 (403-678-3200)
- **Association of Canadian Mountain Guides,** Box 1537, Banff, AB  T0L 0C0 (403-678-2885)
- **Banff Alpine Guides,** Box 1025, Banff, AB  T0L 0C0 (403-678-6091)
- **Company of Canadian Mountain Guides,** Box 1149, Canmore, AB  T0L 0M0 (403-678-4662)
- **Canadian School of Mountaineering,** Box 723, Canmore, AB  T0L 0M0 (403-678-4134)
- **Guides Office,** Box 1913, Canmore, AB  T0L 0M0 (403-678-2642)
- **Glacier Mountaineering Society,** Box 291, Whitefish, MT 59937
- **Jasper Alpine Guides,** Box 2495, Jasper, AB  T0E 1E0 (780-852-4161)
- **Lac des Arcs Climbing School,** 1116 19th Avenue NW, Calgary  T2M 0Z9 (403-289-6795)
- **Mountain Adventure Canada,** Box 99, Canmore, AB  T0L 0M0 (403-678-4338)
- **Pacific Granite Mountaineering,** Box 1267, Banff, AB  T0L 0C0 (403-762-3484)
- **Peter Amann, Guide,** Box 1495, Jasper, AB  T0E 1E0 (780-852-3237)
- **Yamnuska Inc.,** Box 1920, Canmore, AB  T0L 0M0 (403-678-4164)

*Rappelling ice cliffs on the southwest face of Mt. Robson*

## Climbing season

Rock-climbing begins in late April here, when south-facing cliffs at low elevations become clear of snow and the rock warms up. After doing mostly rock climbs in the front ranges during spring, many Canadian Rockies climbers turn to the glacier-hung main ranges for mountaineering during July and August. Here they find classic alpine-style climbs of 1000–2000 m on snow and ice. The higher peaks are usually at their driest and warmest in the first week of August. Many one-day climbs can be done from the Icefields Parkway, although in the same area it is possible to walk in the wilderness for a couple of days to a back-country peak and do a climb in splendid isolation.

Winter snow (November to May) provides ski-mountaineering ascents. The peaks between Kicking Horse Pass and Bow Summit are the most popular for this, and there are mountain huts in the area. Contact the Alpine Club of Canada, 403-678-3222 in Canmore, for more information on huts. From November to April, frozen waterfalls also attract climbers.

The following sections include recommended routes on rock, snow and ice for competent climbers. These are not the hardest climbs; they show what the region has to offer, and they are all favorites of mine. The guidebooks on page 756 offer more detail.

## Rock-climbing

Rock-climbing in the Canadian Rockies is mostly on steep limestone of the Eldon and Palliser formations (see pages 79 and 113 for geology), with short crack systems and less-than-trustworthy rock. A typical route takes you up a series of short faces and inside corners on small, square-cut holds. Overhangs are common, and stemming is probably the most-used technique.

This is all rather different from jamming the long, solid cracks found in granite. Climbers not used to limestone often find that they must lower their standard for a few days until they catch on. Limestone offers one great advantage: it is less slippery when wet than other kinds of rock.

The usual granite gear-rack also works on limestone, but be aware that limestone is harder to protect than granite, for the rock is softer and splittier, while the cracks are less common and placements trickier. Limestone cracks often take keystone-shaped nuts better than they take hexagonal ones. Camming devices (Friends, etc.) are terrific in the shallow cracks and holes you often find in this rock; they are perhaps an even greater leap forward in protecting limestone than they are in protecting granite. Most climbers carry a few small pitons on routes they are unsure of, although driving and removing pitons in limestone quickly damages the rock and should be avoided wherever possible. Rather than packing a hammer, I use a nut hook with a small hammer head on one end.

There is also some very good climbing on quartzite in the main ranges of the Canadian Rockies, especially in the Jasper area, where quartzite faces of 1300 m are climbed on Mt. Edith Cavell, in the Ramparts and elsewhere. These routes are moderate in difficulty–many are graded 5.7 to 5.9–but the length and objective dangers make them serious climbs of alpine grade III–VI.

_Will Gadd making a first ascent in Maligne Canyon, March 1984_

Beginning in the early 1980s, many **sport-climbing routes** have been established in the Canadian Rockies. Some popular locations for these short, difficult, bolt-protected climbs include Heart Creek, Grotto Canyon and Cougar Canyon near Canmore; Back-of-the-Lake at the far end of Lake Louise; Dune Wall beside Mt. Edith Cavell; the Rock Gardens near Jasper, and Hidden Valley between Jasper and Hinton. Inquire locally.

The most popular cliff in the region is 300-m **Yamnuska,** the original Stoney name for what is marked on the map as "Mt. Laurie" at the mountain front west of Calgary. Approach via the TransCanada Highway. Turn north on Highway 1X, cross the valley to Highway 1A, and turn right on 1A. Follow for 2 km to the gravel access road on the left (there is no sign; take the first obvious left). There are many routes up the two-kilometre-long cliff face, with easy hiking descents on the back side.

Here are four popular multi-pitch climbs. Two are on Yamnuska and two are on other mountains. See page 756 for current guidebooks.

### Red Shirt on Yamnuska *8 pitches, II, 5.7*

Considered to be the best introduction to limestone climbing in the Canadian Rockies, Red Shirt is steep and sustained, but at a moderate grade and on excellent rock. However, it is easy to get off-route on the fourth and fifth pitches; follow the guidebook carefully or (better) go with someone who knows the climb.

### Direttissima on Yamnuska *10 pitches, III, 5.8*

Here is the classic Yamnuska climb, directly to the summit. Route-finding is fairly straightforward; beyond the second pitch the climbing is in a great inside corner leading to a crux overhang at the top.

### Reprobate on EEOR *13 pitches, III, 5.9*

A long climb offering the best limestone in the Bow Valley corridor. "EEOR" is short for "East End of Rundle," the cliff marking the southeast end of Mt. Rundle above Canmore. Approach is via the road to Spray Lakes, scrambling from the gap between EEOR and the next peak to the south, which is Ha Ling (formerly "Chinaman's") Peak, also with good climbs. Reprobate takes a fairly direct line between the big left buttress and two prominent cracks to the right. Three easy pitches up a rottenish pillar lead to excellent rock and a two-grade jump in difficulty. Getting into the huge inside corner above goes free at 5.9, then things ease somewhat from there to the top. Easy ridge-walking descent.

### Tower of Babel at Moraine Lake *10 pitches, II, 5.6*

Located in the Valley of the Ten Peaks near Lake Louise, this is a moderate quartzite climb in glorious terrain with a spectacular finish. The tower is the obvious buttress southeast of Moraine Lake. Starting near the centre of the base, work up and right for two pitches to the right edge, then more easily up and left into a big corner that ends at the huge ledge two-thirds of the way up: the Ski Jump. The excellent rock above goes most easily from just right of centre, straight up, then slightly left to a belay ledge below the last pitch. Off the right end of the ledge, angle right into a crack and follow it to the top. Descent is south along the crest of the buttress, then to the right down the steep gully along the tower's right (west) side.

## *Summer mountaineering on snow and ice*

We are speaking now of the big main-range peaks of the central Rockies. A word of warning: these peaks are for climbers experienced in glacier travel, use of crampons, ice axe, ice screws and so on.

Those used to climbing in the sunny Colorado Rockies or California Sierras will find greater objective danger here: crevasses, summer avalanches of wet snow and ice, more rockfall, poorer holds, colder and more frequent storms, loss of visibility on glaciers. But the altitude is lower—summit elevations are typically 3000–3500 m rather than the 4300-m elevations of the southern Rockies—and there is less lightning.

**Crevasses** claim a mountaineer every now and again in the Canadian Rockies. It is surprising how few climbers practice or even understand crevasse rescue. If this applies to you, get some training. You'll learn that a party of three is really the minimum for safety. This group size is also ideal for climbing ice faces quickly by using **simul-climbing:** the party moves together, the leader putting in an ice screw every 20–25 m until she/he runs out of screws, whereupon he/she waits for the tail end to transfer them.

Popular equipment for main-range mountaineering: 10-mm single rope, helmet, seat harness and chest sling for the glacier travel involved, fairly long ice axe for use in steep snow as well as on ice, ice hammer in holster, a dozen ice screws, two or three snow-belay plates if a knife-edged snow ridge or avalanche-prone slope is in the plan, a half-dozen carabiners and slings, a few nuts or pitons if it is a mixed climb (rock sections on ice peaks are inclined to be terribly rotten), rappel gadget if required, warm single boots or double plastic boots, waterproofed gloves, long underwear, Goretex or wool climbing pants, gaiters, pile jacket or thick sweater, Goretex jacket, tuque, sunglasses. Don't forget the map and compass in case you get into a white-out; for compass instructions see page 777.

The most dangerous part of a glacier in summer is the **firn line:** the first snow you come to as you walk up. Snow bridges over crevasses are thinnest here. Most accidents happen on the way down, when the snow is soft in the late afternoon, the footfalls heavier (one is going downhill) and the views limited by the stair-step character of most crevasse fields. Going down-glacier, you often can't see a crevasse until right on the lip.

Here are some popular mountaineering routes in the Canadian Rockies.

## Mt. Victoria, above Lake Louise

This is a two-day ascent, with an elegant ridge traverse. Take the trail from the lake to the Plain of Six Glaciers, passing the teahouse and getting onto the Lower Victoria Glacier at the point at which the trail begins to fade. Follow the glacier to Abbot Pass—some danger of avalanche from above on the narrow approach—and stay overnight in the Abbot Hut. Reservations: 403-678-3200. Bring sleeping bag, fuel and food; stove and foamies are in the hut. Start at dawn the next morning, scrambling up easy rock at the west side of the col to the south summit. Follow the narrow ridge north to the centre summit; 4–6 hr. Avoid straying out on the east face, which is avalanche-prone. Most parties return to the hut and descend the glacier to Lake Louise the same day.

## Mt. Athabasca, in the Columbia Icefield area

Mt. Athabasca is the most popular snow-and-ice peak in the Canadian Rockies. The approach to most routes is from the first major stream along the Athabasca glacier-ride road, a little beyond the first kilometre. The road is open only to shuttle buses most of the day, but climbers may drive up to the small parking spot beside the stream if they do so before 7 a.m. A trail along the right (west) moraine leads through a rubbly gully in the cliff and up to the glacier well right of centre. Gain the ice easily—a little steep at the start—then angle up and left toward the base of the ice-clad Silverhorn.

From there the regular route, called the **Saddle Route** (UIAA grade II), traverses right across fairly steep slopes to the long col—the Saddle—right of the horn. Head south across a flat section to the rocky west ridge of the peak and follow it east to the top of the Silverhorn. It is only a short way from there to the summit along a narrow and very beautiful snow/ice ridge. Descend the same way, or, if you are good at self-arrest with your ice axe, consider dropping down one of several long snow gullies from the saddle into the next cirque west—a quick descent in bad weather. Once down, keep to the east (right) side of the cirque, scrambling down ledges at the lip to the glacier-ride concession and the road.

**Silverhorn Route** *II–III:* from the base of the horn, climb left a hundred metres to the entrance of the north cirque, then to the right up the Silverhorn over mixed snow and ice to the summit ridge.

**North-face Route** *III–IV:* cross the north cirque and take to the face in about the middle, heading up 50° ice toward a somewhat steeper snow/ice gully through the rock band just below the summit. Climb a short, steep section of water ice or rotten rock to get into the gully. Ten rope-lengths in all.

## Mt. **Edith Cavell** near Jasper, east-ridge route *III, 5.5*

Cavell's east ridge is a moderate mixed climb on quartzite, usually in good condition after mid-July. Leave Jasper well before first light. Park at the end of the Cavell Road and follow the trail to Cavell Meadows for 20 minutes or so, until it switchbacks away from the mountain. A faint climber's trail leads southeast just inside the moraine to the snow/ice patch that takes you to the col at the foot of the east ridge. Scramble up the ledgy first buttress. The alternatives gradually diminish as the buttress narrows and you are forced over to a steep, narrow snow/ice gully on your left. Crossing it there avoids a longer ice patch higher up.

Beyond the flat spot in the ridge the grade goes up to lower fifth class in spots; most parties belay steadily from there to the summit. Bring a dozen nuts/cams up to 5 cm. Occasional patches of ice usually require crampons, but not screws.

Descent: back down the ridge, or continue over the summit and down the regular route on the west side. This is much longer, but it offers a scenic hike. To descend the regular, follow the summit ridge west, working north (right) onto the wide col between Cavell and Sorrow Peak. From the centre, head down over scree, talus and ledges, angling gradually right; cliffs near the bottom will force you into a through-going gully down to the meadows at Verdant Pass. Angle right to a stream, where you should pick up the trail at treeline; it stays on the east (right) side of the creek, well above it. Joining the Astoria River Trail, turn right and head east to the parking lot. In late summer most parties finish in the dark.

## Mt. **Robson,** Kain Route

At 3100 m to the top, this is a mini-expedition for experienced climbers. Plan to spend a week on the mountain. "Kain" refers to Conrad Kain, leader of the first-ascent party in 1913. See page 703 for photo. The best climbing conditions are often in the first half of August.

**Day one:** to Berg Lake from Highway 16. A hard grind, but get as close to Robson Pass, beyond the east end of the lake, as you can.

**Day two:** up the Robson Glacier, following a rough trail along the moraine on the east (left) side for the first kilometre or so and gaining the glacier where it peters out. At the icefall, move left off the glacier and up rock benches, passing in front of Extinguisher Tower and then easily back onto the glacier. Higher up, the glacier steepens toward the Robson-Resplendent Col, and big crevasses here will have you shuttling left and right around them. A flat pocket under the col is suitable for a camp. Or, if you are travelling fast and have six hours of climbing time left, do the next day's work.

**Day three:** if there is lots of snow, the icefall on the south side of the Dome may be an easier route than the Robson-Resplendent Ridge, which is very narrow and often double-corniced early in the summer. But if the icefall looks nasty and the snowmelt season is well on, then the ridge will probably be easier because the snow along it will have melted back on the south side, exposing a ledge for walking. There is still a 20-m pitch of rotten fourth-class rock on the ridge, nasty if iced-up. The Dome is flat on top, a safe and spectacular spot to camp.

*Climbing the Kain Route on Mt. Robson. Photo by Greg Spohr.*

**Day four:** take the Kain Face—angle 52°—on either side of the central ice bulge for 10–12 rope-lengths to the ridge. Left is shorter and steeper than right. Follow the ridge up the Roof, staying on the right side of the face but moving left if need be among the cauliflower-ice formations there, and thence along the short summit ridge. Descend the same way. Climbing time is quite variable, 12–20 hr, depending on weather, snow conditions and stamina. Be prepared to wait awhile atop the Kain Face if it has softened into avalanche soup.

**Retreat:** it is usually possible to go from the Dome to Berg Lake in one day, then out the next, for a total of five or six days on the mountain. But count on losing at least one day to the weather.

The key to this ascent is to go lightly and quickly. Too many parties labor up the peak under 30-kg loads, burning themselves out. Try for 20 kg. Gear considerations: you will need a strong tent, bags good to -15°C, two or three snow-deadmen for belaying the Robson-Resplendent Ridge and 10–15 ice screws for doing the Kain Face with running protection (see page 734). No rock gear required. Most parties carry a dozen-or-so wands to mark important points on the route beyond the Dome, for it often whites out and new snow can fill tracks.

## High peaks

Peaks in the Canadian Rockies 3500 m or higher in elevation

| | |
|---|---|
| Mt. Robson | 3954 |
| Mt. Columbia | 3747 |
| North Twin | 3718 |
| Mt. Clemenceau | 3657 |
| Twins Tower* | 3627 |
| Mt. Alberta | 3619 |
| Mt. Assiniboine | 3618 |
| Mt. Forbes | 3609 |
| South Twin | 3566 |
| Mt. Goodsir, S. | 3562 |
| Mt. Temple | 3544 |
| Mt. Goodsir, N. | 3524 |
| Edward Peak | 3514 |
| Ernest Peak | 3511 |
| Mt. Kitchener | 3511 |
| Rudolf Peak | 3507 |
| Mt. Bryce | 3507 |

*If counted separately from North Twin

Thanks to John Martin of Calgary for researching this table.

*The east face of Mt. Robson*

# *Ski-touring*
## Including ski-mountaineering

Many summer trails in the Canadian Rockies make terrific winter ski routes. The season is long—six months at subalpine and alpine elevations—and the variety is endless.

By mid-November there is usually enough snow on the ground to ski the easier trails, dodging the rocks. Around Christmas the skiing frequently improves dramatically: a major Pacific storm has often deepened the accumulation and in the subalpine zone the snowpack is becoming solid enough to support one's weight off the packed trails.

January is often quite cold. Daytime temperatures seldom rise above -15°C. But by mid-February the weather is warmer and the days are longer. Late February to early March is perhaps the prime period: plenty of snow-cover, good base, small accumulations at night and sunny days. Late March and April are frequently stormy, with poor visibility at high elevations. By mid-April the avalanche danger is high and for many people the skiing season is over.

In about one year out of four the skiing is generally poor in the Canadian Rockies, more often from the Columbia Icefield north. This is because the Rockies are drier and colder than other ranges in western Canada, climatic factors that tend to produce **depth hoar:** loose, sugary-textured snow created at the base of the snowpack by recrystallization of normal flakes. Aboriginal words for depth hoar include the Cree "muskowkoonawum" and Innuit "pukak," which sounds particularly apt. When there is a thick layer of depth hoar, the snow cannot support a skier's weight. One step off the packed trail and you're floundering.

In such conditions the avalanche hazard is usually extreme, too. See page 764 for more on avalanches and depth hoar.

Skiing on steep mountain trails is more difficult than skiing on groomed tracks in gentler terrain. Good instruction helps. See page 731 for a list of skiing/climbing schools and guides.

*Winter in the high country. If you're careful, you can take the kids. View is along the trail to Helen Lake, two hours from the Icefields Parkway north of Lake Louise.*

# Skiing equipment and clothing for the Canadian Rockies

Twenty-five years of ski-touring hereabouts have taught me a few things about the gear required to enjoy it best. The key words are *strong* and *warm*.

**Skis.** I use shorter skis than those preferred by most nordic skiers. Mine are just a little over head-high. Such skis turn more easily on steep, switchbacking trails than longer ones do, yet they still provide enough flotation for powder skiing. When the base is poor, though, and my pack is heavy, I tend to break through more easily than people wearing longer skis. The camber is soft, which gives good uphill grip, and the tips are floppy, which means that the skis turn easily in powder and tend to stay up on crusty snow rather than digging in.

A typical mountain trail runs steadily uphill from the valley floor to a treeline pass, lake or summit, followed by lunch and a long downhill run. There is little kick-and-glide on such trips; the idea is to get up with minimal back-slipping and get down with the fewest falls. A short, soft ski works best on such trails.

**Boots.** Single for day trips in reasonable temperatures, double for longer tours, icefield trips or very cold days. The higher the boot-tops, the better the control on downhill runs. The sole should resist twisting but should bend fairly easily at the toe. When buying single boots, I get them big enough to fit two pairs of heavy wool socks and an insulating insole, which greatly increases the warmth. Long and narrow is the ticket here, so that you have plenty of toe room and adequate width when the laces are loose, but foot-huggers when the laces are tightened up for better control on the hills. I wear my socks inside out, with the smooth side against the skin to delay the blisters.

**Bindings.** I still use three-pin bindings, choosing stout models with large pins that hold the boot firmly in place and thus prevent any motion, which causes wear to the pin sockets that eventually rips them out. Pin bindings with removable cables have two advantages: the binding will still work when the pins sockets wear out, and a cable binding allows you to lift the tail of the ski up when side-stepping in deep snow.

**Poles.** A lot of telemarkers use adjustable poles, which can be lengthened or shortened to suit conditions. Some people prefer one-piece poles for strength. Powder snow requires large baskets. Pole length: just reaching my armpit when I'm standing in socks. This is somewhat shorter than nordic skiers recommend, and admittedly a bit too short for elegant kick-and-glide skiing, but with short poles I don't reach as high on each step, which my arms appreciate after a long day, and short poles are not as awkward on the sideslope. They work fine for doing either unweighted turns or telemark turns, the two more-popular techniques these days.

**Clothing.** Layers work well in winter, for they can be donned and shed as the weather changes. A popular combination: turtleneck shirt, for a warmer neck on downhill runs and in icy winds; heavy shirt and a sweater or pile jacket.

When needed for wind or snowfall, slip on a *breathable* (i.e. not waterproof) shell parka or anorak. It should be long enough to reach over your rear and cut large enough to fit over a down jacket. The front should zip up to your nose, and there should be a deep hood that can

*The color-coordinated Compleat Skier finding that, alas, there are some places in the Rockies in which one cannot ski. Photo by Greg Horne taken along the Eight-pass Route in Jasper National Park.*

be closed with a drawstring. I use a single-layer uncoated ripstop anorak with those features; it is extremely lightweight and packs to a handful, yet has proved adequate in the worst winter conditions. All it has to do is stop the wind from penetrating the underlying insulating layers while letting the sweat out. For some reason this kind of shell is hard to find. Cheap shells of coated nylon with inferior hoods and flimsy zippers are plentiful, but a *proper* one is a prize; buy two.

On very cold days, a light down jacket over the sweater and under the shell has always sufficed for me. Heavy down jackets are good for only two things: climbing K2 or waiting for the bus in Edmonton in January.

Concerning **Goretex** clothing in winter: jackets that claim to be both waterproof and breathable tend to ice up inside at low temperatures. However, near the freezing mark Goretex breathes just fine. It also has the advantage of repelling wet snow, which tends to melt on your jacket. If that jacket is not waterproof …

For my hands, I like long-wearing leather gloves soaked with wax boot waterproofing and large enough to hold knit liners. These are warm enough for most days, but I also carry a pair of light down-filled mitts just in case.

**Headwear.** Anything that keeps your ears warm. A billed cap with earflaps will keep the sun out of your eyes. Some knit caps (tuques) also have bills on them.

**Pack.** A large fanny pack is great for day trips. Low centre of gravity and no shoulder straps to hinder poling—but a down jacket won't go in. However, I seldom carry my downie on day trips, and my sweater can be tied round my waist when not needed. When I must carry more, a slim day pack with a waistbelt, done up during downhill runs to stop balance-disturbing flopping, also keeps the weight low. For longer trips, an internal-frame back-pack offers plenty of room and, again, keeps the weight low.

**Items always in the pack.** Wax bag, spare tip (even though I haven't broken a ski in years—but if it ever happens it will occur 10 km from the highway), lunch, water bottle (tightly capped, wrapped up in clothing to delay freezing and carried upside down so the bottom freezes first rather than the lid), dark glasses, compass (necessary if you are going above treeline into white-out country; see page 777 for compass-using essentials), map and guidebook, matches, first aid kit (see page 775 for contents), toilet paper and extra plastic bag to pack out used; a headlamp (not a flashlight; you need both hands for skiing) and an avalanche beacon and shovel on trips with slide hazard.

Although rarely needed, a balaclava (knit head-sock with holes for eyes and mouth) prevents facial frostbite in extreme conditions. At the very least, pack a scarf.

**In the wax bag.** These days I seldom use anything but Swix Dry Snow, which is the colder wax in a two-wax all-purpose pair, and purple. Either the waxes are getting better or I'm getting less fussy. For long, steep climbs in untracked snow, such as you find on most icefield trips, **skins** made for skinny skis are just the thing. There are times when wax simply will not work, but skins will see you through. And you can use them on downhill runs through the woods in fast conditions or in the dark.

Also in the wax bag: a scraper and smoothing cork, roll of strapping tape for mending poles, an extra binding screw and a Leatherman all-purpose tool that fixes everything. If the bale from your binding (the plate or wire that tightens down on the boot) is of the type that can come loose and be lost, bring a spare. If you have plain cable bindings be sure to bring an extra cable.

**For trips requiring camping** you will need a winter sleeping bag, or an overbag for your three-season bag, or a slim summer-weight bag to slip inside a three-season bag, which is the combination I use. Pack a thick sleeping pad such as the Therm-a-Rest, a full-length one long enough to keep your whole sleeping bag off the tent floor. Long-enough foam pads are seldom available, but you can lengthen a shorter one by sticking on a piece from another pad. Duct tape works well for joining the two.

## *Places to ski*

The Canadian Rockies are most heavily skied in Banff, Jasper and Peter Lougheed parks. These are all eastern-slope areas offering excellent snow: dry and even for easy waxing. South of Kananaskis Country on the eastern slope, frequent chinooks and lighter snowfalls tend to cause uneven conditions, while north of Jasper the depth-hoar buildup in most winters produces breakable crust. The problem gets worse the farther north you go.

The entire western slope of the Canadian Rockies is generally warmer and wetter in winter than the eastern slope. There is more snow there, but it's harder to wax for. The valleys are deeper, with correspondingly bigger and more numerous avalanches. Outside the national parks, auto access is not as easy on the western slope and there are fewer trails. Popular places include Yoho park, Kootenay park between Vermilion Pass and Floe Lake, and western Glacier park.

This is not to say that you can't find good skiing in other parts of the western slope, or north of Jasper or south of Kananaskis Country on the eastern slope. Frequently you can. You just have to look a little harder.

### Prepared trails in Peter Lougheed Provincial Park west of Calgary

The trails strarting at Pocaterra Creek are mostly easy with intermediate sections. The Boulton Creek area offers intermediate trails with some difficult sections. A good loop for intermediate skiers takes in the Boulton Creek, Elk Pass, Tyrwhitt and Whiskey Jack trails, 16 km total. Pick up a map at the Barrier Lake information office.

### Boom Lake, near Vermilion Pass in Banff National Park *4 km one way*

Wide most of the way, and easy with intermediate sections. Skiable early in the season and quite popular; expect a lot of company in the afternoon. Trailhead is 7 km west of the Trans Canada Highway on Highway 93.

### Stanley Glacier, in Kootenay National Park *4.4 km one way*

Passes through the Vermilion Pass burn of 1968; see how the forest is regenerating. Intermediate skiing in the lower parts, with fairly steep grades and switchbacks; easier higher up, with some gentle powder slopes at treeline that are good for learning to do turns. Avalanche danger increases quickly if you go farther. Trailhead is on Highway 93.

## *Ratings used for Canadian Rockies ski trails*

**Easy:** suitable for skiers without much experience.

**Intermediate:** enjoyable for competent skiers, who can turn easily and can control their speed on hills.

**Difficult:** for experienced skiers only, who can handle tight turns, narrow, steep sections and powder snow.

**Insane:** see photo at right.

For figuring times, an average for reasonably fit intermediate skiers is about 5 km/hr, uphill and back. But times vary a great deal from group to group.

*Photo by Chris Harvey*

### The Ink Pots, in Banff National Park *6 km one way*

An intermediate trip, with one difficult section. Begins at Johnston Canyon, which is lovely in winter. You can start immediately north of the cabins, where the fire road begins, or see the canyon first by carrying your skis along the walkways, then climbing out of the canyon up the stairway and steep path at the end to join the main ski trail. The trail climbs steadily through the trees to its high point, then drops very steeply to the Ink Pots, which are springs situated in meadows surrounded by superb scenery.

### Plain of Six Glaciers, in Banff park *7 km one way*

Takes you around Lake Louise to the west end and on to treeline. Excellent scenery in good weather and a variety of skiing: easy around the lake, intermediate in the forest and difficult in the powder higher up. Do this one from February on, when there is usually enough snow to ski Louise Creek rather than the avalanche-prone route of the summer trail.

### Lake O'Hara Fire Road in Yoho National Park *13 km one way*

An easy trip with rewarding scenery at the end, although the round trip makes for a long day. The summer road from Wapta Lake, near Kicking Horse Pass, to Lake O'Hara is not plowed in winter; it is wide, with moderate grades—ideal for beginners with stamina, who will learn a lot in skiing it. Many skiers use the road to get to the Elizabeth Parker Hut near Lake O'Hara, a centre for many fine day trips in this famous area. Call the Alpine Club of Canada, 403-678-3200.

### Parker Ridge in northern Banff park

Many an intermediate skier has advanced to the high-country powder here. From the large Parker Ridge lot near Sunwapta Pass, ski the open glades in the forest and the alpine tundra above, keeping well left of the big, steep, open slope on the right, which can avalanche. The skiing above nearby Hilda Creek Hostel is also good. Inquire about avalanche conditions.

### Whistlers Creek in Jasper National Park *6.5 km one-way*

From the highest parking lot at Marmot Basin ski area, follow a trail north into the trees. It soon contours west along the valley wall of Whistlers Creek, then follows the creek (intermediate skiing; brushy until February) to spectacular alpine slopes higher up. Of these, the route to Marmot Pass is the most popular. Stay in the valley bottom until you reach the toe of a big rockslide, then turn left to follow a clear line upward between the edge of the slide and the trees until you swing right at treeline to gain the gentle pass.

## Overnight and multi-day trips with hut accommodation

Don't try these until you are able to handle intermediate trails while wearing a fairly heavy pack. More endurance is required than that needed for the average day trip. Leaders of these trips should be seasoned back-country skiers, who know what to do in case of white-out, avalanche, frostbite, etc. See the safety section, page 761. Back-country permits are required; contact Parks Canada, 403-762-1550. For hut reservations, call the Alpine Club of Canada, 403-678-3200.

### Healy Pass and Redearth Creek in Banff park *34 km total*

Varied skiing with good views throughout and a high pass to cross. Good introduction to back-country skiing.

Start at the Sunshine ski area parking lot, taking the ski-out trail at the southwest end of the lot for a few hundred metres then turning right onto the Healy Creek Trail. The trail climbs gradually at first, then quite steeply to the high-subalpine meadows below a long whaleback ridge called the rampart (not the Ramparts southwest of Jasper). Cross this long ridge at treeline on its northern end. On the other side is a north-angling intermediate run through scattered larch into heavier woods and the exquisite setting of the Egypt Lake Shelter.

This hut can be hard to find. It sits on the west side of Pharoah Creek, out of sight from the creek bed that most skiers descend to and follow when they have lost the regular trail in new snow. If you come to the warden cabin, you went by the hut. Backtrack south along the west side of the creek for about half a kilometre.

The following day, head north down Pharoah Creek to its junction with Redearth Creek and a long kick-and-glide run—one of the few like it in the Rockies—to the TransCanada Highway. Strong skiers often do this loop in a day, starting at dawn, lunching at the hut and finishing at dusk. You may want two cars for this one because the trip doesn't end where it began. Hitching back to the Sunshine lot can take a long time, especially after the ski area closes.

## Wapta and Waputik icefields in Banff and Yoho parks *35 km total*

Also called the "Bow-Lake-to-Wapta-Lake traverse," this is the classic icefield ski trip in the Canadian Rockies. The route goes from Bow Lake on the Icefields Parkway to the Bow Hut, visible from the highway below St. Nicholas Peak if you know where to look, then over the Wapta Icefield, through the Nicholas-Olive Col and down the Vulture Glacier to Balfour Pass and a hut there. Then along the eastern slopes of Mt. Balfour to a very high pass over the continental divide and across the Waputik Icefield on the other side to the col between Mt. Niles and Mt. Daly, where there is a third hut. On the last day, the run down to Sherbrooke Lake and the TransCanada Highway at Wapta Lake can be terrific. Or awful, depending on the snow.

If you are going to try this trip without someone who has done it before, I strongly recommend that you carry a copy of Murray Toft's excellent route map *Touring the Wapta Icefields*. For hut reservations, call the Alpine Club of Canada, 403-678-3200.

Most parties take three days to do this trip, although I have spent up to a week at it, enjoying ski ascents of the peaks along the way and waiting out bad weather. For many skiers an overnight visit to Bow Hut is a good introduction to icefield skiing.

*Icefield skiers on their turf, the Waputik Icefield of Yoho National Park. Mt. Daly at centre, peaks around Lake Louise to right.*

# *Bicycling*
## The hills aren't all that tough, really. But the weather ...

Main roads in the Canadian Rockies are good, often with shoulders wide enough for comfortable cycling. There are large national and provincial parks with plenty of campsites. Hostels—cheap overnight accommodations for people of all ages—are found along the major routes. Thus, the region is just *made* for bicycle tours.

Cycling is a fine way to see new country: slow enough to take in the passing scene in detail; fast enough to cover a lot of ground in a day. A few must-do tours are presented here. For many other good routes in the Rockies, pick up one of the guidebooks listed on page 757.

### *Season, weather*

Bicycling becomes practical at low elevations in the Canadian Rockies in late April, when daytime temperatures are above freezing—but cyclists here must watch for icy patches until mid-May, when it is more likely to rain than to snow. The higher passes are still chilly until July, and near-freezing temperatures are possible anywhere in the mountains throughout the summer, so bring long pants, a jacket, warm gloves and a knit cap to keep your ears warm on any multi-day ride in the Rockies.

After the usual early-September nasty spell, there is often lovely fall cycling until late October, when the roads are becoming icy and most cyclists pack it in for the season.

### *How tough are the Canadian Rockies?*

The Canadian Rockies are very rugged, but the highway grades are not as long or as steep as one might think. Glaciation has given cyclists some help, by carving deep passes through the mountains. But be prepared to bike many kilometres between towns and food stores. And keep your supplies hung up at campgrounds, for there are bears here. Cyclists have been killed by bears, although not in the Rockies. If you see a bear along the road, approach cautiously. If it pays you no attention, just cruise on by. My wife was once delayed along the Icefields Parkway by an aggressive moose that would not let her pass. She had to sneak through beside a slow-moving auto.

*July bicycling weather near Sunwapta Pass. Bring your woollies.*

## Accommodations for cyclists

Campgrounds abound in the southern and central Rockies. Provincial road maps and Parks Canada brochures show campground locations. However, many cyclists prefer to use the **Hostelling International** non-profit cabins and lodges in the region. Most of these are simple accommodation. You bring your own sleeping bag and food; the hostel provides bunks, kitchen, cooking and eating implements.

Here is a list of hostels in and near the Canadian Rockies. Except as noted, they are open seven days a week May–September. Some are closed one day a week October–April. Reservations are advised; call the numbers given for the individual hostels listed below, or 403-237-8282 in Calgary or 780-439-3139 in Edmonton. By mail for hostels without addresses: Hostelling International, 10926 88 Avenue, Edmonton, AB  T6G 0Z1 or #203, 1414 Kensington Road NW, Calgary, AB  T2N 3P9.

- **Fernie.** 892 Sixth Avenue. Box 580, Fernie, BC  V0B 1M0 (250-423-6811). 68 beds, family rooms, laundry, storage.
- **Blairmore.** Box 982, Blairmore, AB  T0K 0E0 (403-562-7314). 30 beds, family rooms, showers.
- **Calgary.** 520 7th Avenue SE, Calgary, AB  T2G 0J6 (403-269-8239). 114 beds, family rooms, showers, laundry, lockers, snack bar.
- **Ribbon Creek.** 24 km south of TransCanada on Highway 40 (403-591-7333). Reservations 403-762-4122 Banff. 44 beds, family rooms, showers, laundry.
- **Banff.** 3 km from Banff on Tunnel Mountain Road. Box 1358, Banff, AB  T0L 0C0 (403-762-4122). 154 beds, family rooms, showers, laundry, cafeteria, bike/ski workshop.
- **Castle Mountain.** 1.5 km south of Castle Junction on Highway 1A, the Bow Valley Parkway (403-762-2367). Reservations 403-762-4122 Banff. 36 beds, showers.
- **Lake Louise.** In the village. Box 115, Lake Louise, AB  T0L 1E0 (403-522-2200). 105 beds in various-sized rooms, family rooms, showers, sauna, laundry, cafe, bike/ski workshop. Operated in conjunction with Alpine Club of Canada.
- **Whiskey Jack.** Near Takakkaw Falls, 13 km north of Field in Yoho park. Reservations 403-762-4122 Banff. 27 beds, showers, lockers. Open mid-June to September.
- **Mosquito Creek.** 26 km north of Lake Louise on Icefields Parkway. Reservations 403-762-4122 Banff. 38 beds, family rooms, sauna, food store.
- **Shunda Creek.** Near Nordegg, 3 km north of Highway 11 on road to Shunda Creek Recreation Area (403-721-2140). 47 beds, family rooms, showers, hot-tub, laundry.
- **Rampart Creek.** 12 km north of Saskatchewan Crossing (34 km south of Columbia Icefield Centre) on Icefields Parkway. 30 beds, sauna. Reservations 403-762-4122 Banff.
- **Hilda Creek.** 8.5 km south of Columbia Icefield Centre on Icefields Parkway. 21 beds, sauna. Reservations 403-762-4122 Banff.
- **Beauty Creek.** 86.5 km south of Jasper on Icefields Parkway. 24 beds. Reservations 780-852-3215 Jasper. Open May to September; key system for groups in winter.
- **Athabasca Falls.** 32 km south of Jasper on Icefields Parkway (780-852-5959). 40 beds, bike shelter. Reservations 780-852-3215 Jasper.
- **Mt. Edith Cavell.** Near end of Cavell Road, 13 km from Highway 93A junction south of Jasper. 32 beds, sauna. Open mid-June to October. Reservations 780-852-3215 Jasper.
- **Jasper International Hostel.** Along road to Jasper Tramway off Icefields Parkway, 7 km from Jasper. Box 387, Jasper, AB  T0E 1E0 (780-852-3215). 70 beds, family rooms, showers, lockers, mountain-bike rentals.
- **Maligne Canyon.** 11 km east of Jasper on the Maligne Road (780-852-3584). 24 beds. Reservations 780-852-3215 Jasper.
- **Edmonton.** 10422 91 St., Edmonton, AB T5H 1S6 (780-429-0140). 50 beds, family rooms, showers, laundry, snack bar, mountain-bike rentals.

## *Bicycle tours*

If you'd like to bike the Rockies with a group, here are some contacts:

- **Adventure Cycling Association,** Box 8303, Missoula, MT 59807 (406-721-1776)
- **Cycle High,** 2221 Fourth Ave. NW, Calgary, AB T2N 0N8 (403-283-9167)
- **Foothills Adventure Cycle Tours,** 1515 110 Ave. SW, Calgary, AB T2W 0E2 (403-252-8548)
- **High Country Cycle Tours,** 617 Second Ave. NW, Calgary, AB T2N 0E2 (403-283-0527)
- **Canusa Cycle and Adventure Tours,** Box 45, Okotoks, AB T0L 1T0 (403-560-8959)
- **Castle River Mountain Biking,** Box 723, Pincher Creek, AB T0K 1W0 (403-627-5283)
- **Rocky Mountain Worldwide Cycle Tours,** Box 1978-T, Canmore, AB T0L 0M0 (403-678-6770)
- **Southern Alberta Hostelling Association,** #203, 1414 Kensington Rd. NW, Calgary, AB T2N 3P9 (403-283-5551)

*A young bicyclist enjoying Beauty Creek Flats along the Icefields Parkway. The kid should be wearing a helmet.*

# Cycling the Icefields Parkway

The ride between Jasper and Banff is generally considered to be the finest short bicycle tour in the world. I am not exaggerating; this route is internationally famous, attracting thousands of cyclists from all over the globe each summer. It follows the valleys of the Athabasca, North Saskatchewan, Mistaya and Bow rivers, paralleling the continental divide through the heart of the Canadian Rockies.

Total distance: 287 km. Most cyclists take four or five days for the trip, doing 60–70 km per day, but very strong riders can do it in a couple of days. Starting from Banff means easier grades on the two passes than starting from Jasper. But you are more likely to get headwinds if you start from Banff. Take your pick. I usually go from Jasper, getting the hills done in strenuous but short climbs and enjoying the long downhill grades beyond, often with a tail wind. So the tour is described here from Jasper to Banff.

**Day one (32 km):** Jasper to Athabasca Falls Hostel. A short day, but recommended if your behind hasn't put in many warm-up kilometres before starting the tour. The next hostel is at Beauty Creek, 54 km farther, if you feel like doing more distance the first day and taking a shorter ride on the second, which will provide time for a hike in the Columbia Icefield area before supper on the second day.

**Day two (80 km):** reach Hilda Creek Hostel, just over Sunwapta Pass and close to treeline, 80 km from Athabasca Falls or 26 km from Beauty Creek Hostel. From Athabasca Falls the day starts with a couple of moderate hills, then things get serious as you tackle Sunwapta Pass, the steepest, longest hill on the route. But for diversion there are often bighorn sheep along here, mingling with the tourists at the viewpoints. If you arrive at the hostel with a couple of hours of daylight left, and any energy, take the walk up to the alpine zone on Parker Ridge, well known for wildflowers and fossils (illegal to grab either in the national park) and views of the glaciers and peaks roundabout.

*What to do at the Athabasca Glacier, high point of the Icefields Parkway tour*

**Day three (94 km):** blast down the long grade south of Sunwapta Pass, stopping on the high bridge to admire Nigel Falls, missed by motorists because it is hidden under the bridge. There is another hostel at Rampart Creek, only 30 km from Hilda Creek and often used by cyclists going from the Beauty Creek Hostel through the Icefield area without stopping at Hilda. Copious carbohydrate-pigging at the Saskatchewan Crossing restaurant will stoke the fires for the long climb up the Mistaya River Valley, past Waterfowl Lakes and over Bow Summit, the only other pass on the route. Reach Mosquito Creek Hostel 16 km beyond.

**Day four (83 km):** Cruise the last of the Icefields Parkway, joining the TransCanada Highway near Lake Louise. It is a strenuous side trip up to the lake, but if you start early that morning you can see the Gem of the Rockies and the Valley of the Ten Peaks at Moraine Lake. This adds 34 km to the day's ride.

Banff-bound traffic on the TransCanada is usually heavy, but at Lake Louise you can take the **Bow Valley Parkway** (Highway 1A), a low-speed paved road with many pull-offs and interpretive displays–and a couple of hills you don't have to do if you stay on the TransCanada.

The parkway ends west of Banff, forcing you onto the TransCanada, but you need follow it for only a kilometre, watching on the right for an unlocked gate in the fence. Beyond, a short unpaved section connects with lovely Vermilion Lakes Drive, Banff's back door.

Continuation from Banff to Calgary is a ride of 122 km, usually done in one day. The grades are very easy and you often get a whopping tailwind through the foothills in the afternoon. In the morning, though, there are likely to be headwinds, especially out on the prairie.

## Going-to-the-Sun Highway in Glacier park (85 km)

Shorter than the Icefields Parkway, but offering scenery nearly as grand, the route over Logan Pass is steep and narrow, with so much traffic that cyclists are banned on the middle 24 km between 11 a.m. and 4 p.m., June 15 to Labor Day.

Check at the park gates for advice on cycling this road. It is possible to do it all in one day, by starting early and going partway in the morning, then taking a hike or a snooze during the hours of moto-madness, leaving the afternoon to finish up. The days are long in late June and July, so there is plenty of daylight. Accommodation: campgrounds along St. Mary Lake and at Avalanche Creek, east of Lake McDonald. No hostels. A paved trail runs between West Glacier and Apgar.

## Cycling in Kananaskis Country

Kananaskis Country is a large provincial recreation area in the mountains west of Calgary. The roads in it make very good cycling trips, and there are paved trails designed with bicycling (and ski-touring) in mind.

Riding from the TransCanada Highway to Kananaskis Lakes, 56 km one way along Highway 40, is a fine way to see the front ranges. There is hostel and hotel accommodation at Ribbon Creek (23 km), camping at Eau Claire (41 km) and at Kananaskis Lakes in Peter Lougheed Provincial Park. Groceries can be had at the hotel complex near Ribbon Creek, at the Fortress Mountain service centre (48 km) and at Boulton Campground in the park.

For a longer tour with a 2206-m pass, keep going past the park entrance for 17 km to reach Highwood Pass, 74 km from the TransCanada. The pavement continues over the pass to Highwood Junction, where the road east to Longview, Highway 541, is also paved. Food is available at a small store at the junction. For a terrific loop trip from Calgary, go south on highways 2, 7 and 22 through the foothills to Longview, then west on 541 to Kananaskis Country, north through the mountains to the TransCanada and back to Calgary. Total distance 300 km.

Hardy types on mountain bikes continue south of Highwood Junction, travelling the gravelled Forestry Trunk Road through the front ranges all the way to Crowsnest Pass (112 km). Another good trip for mountain bikers is the Smith-Dorrien Road between Kananaskis Lakes and Canmore, by way of Spray Lakes (75 km). This road may be paved by the time you read this, providing a two/three-day loop if you travel the TransCanada Highway between Canmore and the Kananaskis Country turnoff. The TransCanada is not particularly dangerous in this section; it is a four-lane divided highway.

**Paved trails** suitable for touring bicycles connect the visitor centre near the entrance to Peter Lougheed park with Upper Kananaskis Lake, passing the Elkwood and Boulton parking lots along the way. Total distance one way: 29 km. Another bike trail runs for 8 km between Ribbon Creek and Wedge Lake, north of the park within Kananaskis Country.

## Trail bicycling

With its fat tires and low gears, a mountain bike can carry you down the trail at two or three times the speed of hikers and back-packers—whose territory, already shared with trail-destroying, polluting horse parties, is now being invaded by people on wheels. Reaction is mixed. Trail wear and tear caused by bicycles is heavier than that caused by hikers, but lighter than that caused by horses. Safety problems include the inevitable crashes (I go over the bars once or twice each summer), breakdowns in the back country and high-speed encounters with other trail users, including bears. In 1993 a mountain-biker was hurt by a grizzly bear near Jasper.

On the plus side, trail bicycling is good exercise and a lot of fun. It's easier on the back, knees and feet than hiking. Bicycles are self-propelled and non-polluting, meeting two of the criteria normally applied in finding a particular sport acceptable in a national park.

All the national and provincial parks in the Canadian Rockies allow trail bicycling, although not on all trails. Jasper park is currently the most liberal. Waterton is the most restrictive. Regulations vary from park to park, and they are subject to change, so I am hesitant to recommend good trails for off-pavement cycling. Enquire locally.

---

## Mountain-biking etiquette

The following is from *River City Rides,* a biking guide to the Grand Junction, Colorado area by Toby Gadd and Alix Craig, reproduced with their permission.

**Be friendly**
Say, "Hi."

**Don't intimidate other trail users**
Hikers and horses aren't used to speeding, whooping, titanium-clad superhumans.

**Yield to other trail users**
If approaching from the front, pull over and let them pass you.
If approaching from behind, slow down and announce your presence before passing.
Downhill riders yield to uphill riders.
Dismount when meeting horses, and move your bike off the trail on the downhill side.

**Don't litter**
The weather gods aren't nice to litterbugs.

**Abuse your body, not the trail**
Abused bodies grow stronger; abused trails wash away.

**Don't ride in the mud**
Tire-ruts collect water, eventually becoming either bogs or streams. People and cyclists go around bogs, which widens the trail and kills vegetation. Streams wash away the tread, leaving only rocks. The trail crew—if there is one at all—will hate you.

**Stay on the trail**
Keep trails narrow—AIM!
Don't cut switchbacks.

**Don't skid**
Don't skid.

# Paddling in the Canadian Rockies
## Special section by Stuart Smith*

Travelling by water has some advantages. Paddling allows you to explore remote valleys, and it provides spectacular views from open areas on the river. On overnight trips the carrying capacity of canoes and the larger kayaks means river travellers can enjoy comforts that would severely burden most back-packers.

Most popular are lake trips, which do not demand the boating skill needed to negotiate swirling waters. However, the consequences of an upset on a lake can be just as serious as a spill on a river, for there is one thing that characterizes just about all the water in the Rockies, hot springs excluded: it is cold! With the exception of some shallow and sheltered bays on a few lakes, swimming and water play are out.

## Boating season

Rivers fed from snowmelt reach peak flow early in the year in a sudden rush, then seldom rise later in the summer except during extended rains. Many of the rivers on the eastern slopes of the Rockies fit this category. In the area west of Lethbridge rivers peak in May, and paddling on many of those rivers is typically over by June. Farther north, peak flow is delayed. Streams in the foothills west of Calgary tend to peak in early June; farther north they peak in late June.

On the western slope the lower-elevation rivers follow a similar pattern, with May peak flows in the south and June peaks in the north. A few rivers with high-elevation drainages peak in July rather than June. See page 178 for a table of river-discharge data.

Glacially fed rivers respond early in the year just like the snowmelt rivers, but they usually peak in July, and they can be counted on to provide reasonable flows when many of the snowmelt-fed rivers have all but dried up. Of course, it takes warm, sunny weather to feed that meltwater to the rivers; years with cool, cloudy summers produce less flow.

For an ideal paddling vacation in the Rockies, I would start in the south in mid-May and work my way north to catch all the good water.

## Water temperature

During spring runoff, most snowmelt-fed streams have water temperatures of 4–8°C, with some warming later in the season. Glacially fed streams rarely exceed 5–6°C and can be as cold as 2–3°C. The closer you get to the headwaters of the streams, the colder they get. Pooling and longer exposure to solar radiation raise the temperature of the water downstream. A river with a lake or reservoir at the headwaters or partway along can have surprisingly warm (for the Rockies!) water, particularly after long spells of sunny weather.

## Personal equipment

Required by law: a personal flotation device (PFD) for each person in the boat, something for bailing, and a whistle or other noisemaker. It may be tempting to use your PFD for a cushion, but putting the thing on after being tossed into frigid water may be impossible. Wear it!

Thermal protection for Rockies paddling is a problem. The water temperature and air temperature can differ by as much as 30°C. What is comfortable when you are rightside up may not be adequate when you are upside down. This is more of a concern for open canoeists or rafters, who seldom can flip themselves rightside up again. The same also applies to novice closed-boat (kayak or closed canoe) paddlers who have not mastered their rolls.

At the minimum, consider a wicking layer of polypropylene underwear next to the skin, an insulating layer consisting of a wool sweater or pile jacket, or more than one of each, and an

*Past President, Alberta Whitewater Association, and author of *Canadian Rockies Whitewater*, a series of river guides.

outer wind/waterproof shell such as a windbreaker or rain jacket. At the other extreme is the **dry suit,** a waterproof garment with latex rubber seals at the wrists, neck and ankles. **Wet suits** of 2–3 mm neoprene offer excellent warmth in the water, although with some movement restriction. The classic "farmer John" suit—full length legs in a one-piece combination with an upper vest—gives good freedom of movement. You'll want foot protection, too. The newer neoprene boots offer good warmth and reasonable soles. For extended trips or trips requiring a fair bit of walking, you'll want to wear or carry something with harder soles; a pair of light running shoes worn with neoprene socks provide an excellent combination of warmth and protection. Be sure that the laces are cut short and well secured so as not to catch on anything.

Every whitewater paddler should wear a sturdy helmet. This protects you not only from impacts with rocks, but also from paddles, boats … and sometimes from other paddlers. Hockey helmets offer all the right protection for a reasonable cost. Any helmet should have a secure chin strap that cannot come undone inadvertently.

## Group equipment

In addition to each person's gear, add an extra change of clothes, waterproof matches (not the kind with waterproof matches and a cardboard striker, which is useless when wet), some high-energy food and a lightweight stove. Dry clothing and a warm sweet drink such as hot chocolate help in recovering from a dunking in the river.

Carry a water filter or carry water. Rockies water may look clean, but *Giardia* parasites are usually present; see page 773 for more on giardiasis. Waterproof binoculars add little weight but a lot of enjoyment, and a camera can be protected in waterproof bags available at most sporting goods stores. Hard-shell waterproof cases are available as well.

## Safety considerations

Most emergency-response agencies are not equipped or trained for river rescues, so you must be well prepared for mishaps. Each boat should carry a rescue throw rope and a small rescue kit including 3 or 4 carabiners, 2 prusik loops, and a 3-m loop of nylon webbing. A couple of lightweight rescue pulleys can also be useful. More important than the equipment is the knowledge required to use it effectively. *River Rescue,* by Les Bechdel and Slim Ray, is an excellent river-safety reference.

A first aid kit is essential. The most common whitewater injuries are sunburn, bruises, abrasions, and cuts. Prepare your kit accordingly and place it in a good waterproof container.

Make sure all boats have lots of flotation and that all equipment in the boats is well secured, with no loose lines in which to become entangled. Painters or bow lines should be tied down, so they cannot come loose in an upset. Bring a spare paddle for each canoe or raft and a spare paddle per group of kayakers. As a minimum, travel in groups of three boats. Carry a map of the area, in case you need to walk out. When in the national parks, register your trip plan with Parks Canada. If you are outside the parks, leave word with a friend, so that someone knows when you are expected back. See page 762 for more on leaving word.

## Whitewater classification used

The classes below are used to describe particular rapids.

Class I     Passages wide open and easily seen from the river. Few obstacles, small waves.
Class II    Rapids with small obstacles that may require maneuvering, but not scouting.
Class III   Larger waves, bigger holes, more maneuvering. Scouting may be required.
Class IV    Highly irregular features and complicated passages. Scouting may be required.
Class V     Risky, violent, congested passages with vertical drops. Scouting advised.
Class VI    Very risky, extremely violent water with big drops. Advance planning required.

Grades: same as above, applied to the run generally. Higher-class rapids are noted.

*Kayaking the Bighorn River, in the Alberta foothills near Nordegg. Photo by Stuart Smith.*

## *Popular runs*

The descriptions in this section are necessarily brief, and much detail has been eliminated. Be sure to stop and scout downriver whenever you're not sure of what you're getting into, and don't hesitate to portage.

### Sheep River, from Bluerock Creek to Sandy McNabb, southern Alberta
*20 km, grade III–IV with class III–V+ rapids*

The upper part of this low-volume run is suitable for kayaks and expert canoeists, while the lower part is suitable for less experienced canoeists and kayakers. A marvelous tight and technical run through a small canyon with many bedrock ledges that produce interesting rapids. The valley is very picturesque, and as the name suggests, bighorn sheep are common in the area. There are three major waterfalls in the upper run and numerous tight spots in a narrow canyon. The lower part of the run is much easier, with class II–III rapids in a more open canyon.

From Turner Valley go west on Highway 546 to the take-out at Sandy McNabb Campground. Follow the picnic-area signs to a spot by the river. The mid-point take-out/put-in is at Gorge Creek. Bluerock Creek, upstream near the end of the road, is the put-in for the upper run.

### Wildhay River, from Collie Creek to Highway 40, northern Alberta
*26 km, grade II with class II–II+ rapids*

This low-volume run is suitable for canoes, kayaks and rafts, although water levels need to be high for rafts to negotiate the shallow river channels. An open, yet technically challenging run for novice and intermediate paddlers, with many small, well-defined eddies and waves. The first half of the run is the most challenging. The river flows through a remote valley with abundant wildlife in foothills terrain.

Just west of Hinton, turn north on Highway 40 and go approximately 30 km to the take-out bridge. To get to the put-in, continue north to the first big gravel road on the west side of the highway. Follow that road west for a couple of kilometres to a T-intersection. Turn left and go to the next junction, where you stay right; mid-point access is straight ahead down the hill. When you reach a fork in the road just past the base of a large hill, stay left onto a smaller road that leads to an old bridge site in a few hundred metres, which is the put-in. The mid-point access allows you to choose between the more-challenging upper section or the easier lower run to the bridge.

### White River, from Thunder Creek to the Kootenay River, southern B.C.
*42 km, 2–3 days, grade II+ – III with class III–III+ rapids.*

Suitable for rafts, canoes, and kayaks. A classic, scenic trip with an excellent class II+ – III+ technical whitewater section in the upper part, followed by an easier but more remote section down to the Kootenay. This medium-volume river flows over a boulder bed, with occasional constrictions and short canyon walls. At high flows, large irregular waves appear and holes develop behind the larger boulders, which are exposed at low water.

The upper section can be run unloaded to the White River bridge access point on the first day, where you can pick up your overnight gear, then head down to the Kootenay. The top section has some easy class II+ – III rapids that can be seen from the road on the way up beside a large avalanche chute on the south side of the river, as well as a class III – III+ rapid just downstream of Blackfoot Creek, which enters from the left on a sharp right turn. Here you should scout on the right below the creek confluence.

Below the White River bridge, rapids consist of sharp turns and small chutes with waves and a few holes. Paddlers attempting to do the whole run in two days should try to camp at or below Elk Creek, which is the first big tributary below the bridge. It enters from the right. Those with three days can camp at the White River bridge the first night and at Jack Creek, the second large tributary entering from the right (about 5 km below Elk Creek), on the second night.

Go south from Canal Flats on Highway 93/95. Turn east at the Whiteswan Lake Provincial Park sign and follow this road approximately 32 km past Alces and Whiteswan lakes until you reach the White River bridge. To reach the take-out, cross the bridge, turn left and follow the

White-Rock Forest Service Road downstream for 35 km, then turn left on the White-Clay Forest Service Road and go 2 km to the confluence of the White and Kootenay Rivers. To reach the put in, return to the White River bridge and continue upstream on the north side of the river for 9 km, at which point the river is close to the road.

### Highwood River, from Eyrie Gap to Ings Creek, southern Alberta
*34 km, two days, grade III–IV with class III–IV+ rapids*

Suitable for canoes, kayaks, and rafts. A powerful pool-and-drop foothills stream flowing through a scenic gorge, with rapids created by bedrock ledges. Run the upper section to the Eden Valley Bridge the first day, then do the rest the second. Below Ings Creek the canyon is much more difficult, with river-wide ledges that create serious holes.

To find the take-out, travel 10 km west on Highway 541 from Highway 22 at Longview. Watch for a pronounced bend to the left, followed by a kilometre-long straight, then a right turn. Just past the right turn is a short section of guardrail on the south side, where a narrow gully leads down to the river. Respect adjacent fences and avoid trespassing. To reach the put-in, continue upstream for about 30 km until you reach the Eyrie Gap picnic area. The mid-point take-out/put-in is the Eden Valley Indian Reserve bridge, 27 km from Longview.

### Red Deer River, from Highway 40 to Coal Camp, southern Alberta
*40 km, two days, grade II–III with class II–IV rapids*

Suitable for canoes, kayaks and rafts, and quite scenic; a great weekend trip for all levels of ability. Most of the rapids are created by bedrock ledges, many of which have well-developed holes downstream, so be prepared to stop and scout frequently.

To find the take-out, go west from Sundre on Highway 584 for approximately 8 km. Turn south at the Mountainaire Lodge sign and follow the road until it comes close to the river. Coal Camp Ledge, the first easily seen ledge on the river, is the take-out. Put in farther up the road at the Highway 940 bridge. There are many access points along the river, so shorter runs can be arranged.

*Stopping for lunch on the Athabasca River in eastern Jasper National Park. The main hazard on this trip, a three-day float from Jasper to Hinton, was going aground on a sandbar in the middle of Jasper Lake. Photo by Barbara Zimmer.*

### Athabasca River, from Athabasca Falls to the Whirlpool River, Jasper National Park
*9.5 km, grade II–II+ with class II–III rapids*

Suitable for canoes, kayaks and rafts, this stretch of the Athabasca is very popular with intermediate kayakers. The river is big on hot summer days that load it with glacial meltwater, and it runs through scenic bedrock canyons with ledges, boulders and sharp turns. The rapids are mostly in the upper canyon of the two; the lower is surprisingly calm–then it ends at Kerkeslin Ledge (class II–III), a roaring double drop. Near the end of the run lies the 200-m-long Rock Gardens, class II–II+.

The put-in is about 1 km from the south end of Highway 93A, just below Athabasca Falls. Park on the west side of the road, where the Geraldine Lakes Road branches off, and carry your boat across Highway 93 and downhill a short distance to the river. The take-out is 10.3 km south of the Athabasca River bridge on Highway 93A.

### Elk River, from pipeline crossing to Highway 93, southern B.C.
*13 km, grade II–III with class III–III+ rapids*

Suitable for rafts, canoes and kayaks, although the extremely steep carry to the put-in will discourage those with large or heavy boats. This large-volume river runs through a narrow and intimidating canyon with big waves, hydraulics and surfing. In the most-constricted section, small ledges provide plenty of excitement. Paddlers should be prepared to boat-scout the canyon, since the steep walls prevent river-level scouting from shore.

Directions to the take-out: from the junction of Highways 3 and Highway 93 west of Elko, head south on Highway 93 for 14km to the Elk River Bridge. Just past the south end of the bridge on the east side is a small gravel road that winds back around under the bridge.

To reach the put-in, go back toward Elko, looking for a gravel turnoff for Crestbrook Forest Industries Ltd. Turn right and go 1.4 km to the pipeline-access road, which angles right. Follow the pipeline road for 1.3 km up a steep hill to a small metal shack near a fence. Follow the fence left, to an opening in the trees where a short dirt road leads to a small meadow. The put-in trail drops off from the northwest corner; it's a steep cat-track that drops 150 m to the river. Watch your step here!

### Kicking Horse River, from Crozier Bridge to Glenogle Siding, southern B.C.
*16 km, grade II–III with class III–IV rapids*

Suitable for canoes, kayaks and rafts. A large-volume run with some big waves and holes when the river is high. The cold glacial water makes any dunking serious. There is lots of good surfing and playing on the river; the more-difficult rapids are fairly short and can be easily portaged. Be aware that below the take-out the river increases in difficulty to grade IV–IV+, before reaching a class V+ rapid under the Yoho Bridge. Mark the take-out to be sure.

Just outside the western boundary of Yoho National Park along the TransCanada Highway, the gravelled Beaverfoot Road leads south off Highway 1. The put-in bridge is about 1 km south on the road. The take-out is 2.4 km east of the Yoho Bridge, which is the first bridge over the river on the TransCanada east of Golden, or 16 km west of the Beaverfoot Road. A large gravel pullout on the north side has access to the river.

### Kicking Horse River, from Yoho Bridge to Golden, southern B.C.
*7 km, grade III–IV with class III+–IV+ rapids*

Suitable for canoes, kayaks and rafts. This is a popular big-volume, difficult and pushy section of whitewater. The railroad runs along the river in the canyon, so you can portage on the tracks if you need to. The most difficult rapids are just downstream of the Yoho Bridge; the lower part of the run has a long stretch of calmer water.

The put-in is at the Yoho Bridge, which is the first bridge east of Golden on the TransCanada Highway. A switchback road on the east side of the bridge allows steep access to the river. If you wish to avoid the section below the bridge, or if you are using rafts and would like better access, then go west of the bridge for 900 m to a steep gravel road on the south side of the highway that leads down to the river. Take out upstream of the Highway 95 bridge in Golden, which is south of the Highway 1/95 junction.

## Fraser River, from Moose Lake to Robson Ranch Bridge, northern B.C.
*20 km, grade III–IV, with class III–V rapids, plus a 13-m waterfall*

Suitable for experienced kayakers and expert rafters. A big-volume technical river with long continuous sections of constricted rapids. At high flow the river becomes much more difficult; rafters should go at lower flow. The most difficult section is below Overlander Falls, where the river flows through a narrow canyon and is for experts only. This is a spectacular, world-class whitewater run.

The run is located in Mount Robson Provincial Park, on Highway 16 west of Jasper. To find the take-out, go south on the paved road across from the gas station at Mt. Robson, past the campground to a small road on the right just before the narrow bridge. The put-in is located 17 km upstream off Highway 16, at the Red Pass railroad siding. Watch for a gravel road on the south side of the highway. Cross the tracks and put in near the railroad bridge.

## North Saskatchewan River, from Highway 940 to Rocky Mountain House
*115 km, 2–3 days, grade II with class II–III rapids*

Suitable for rafts, canoes and kayaks. A relaxed, big-volume river trip through the forested foothills of Alberta. Many rapids are created by low-angled sandstone ledges, which produce large waves and small reversals; you can avoid them by choosing one side of the river or the other. Most of the bigger rapids are in the lower third of the run. For the most part the river traveller is alone in a scenic valley.

If doing this run in two days, camp near the Ram River, the only large tributary river entering from the right. A campsite on the right just below the confluence is ideal. If you have three days, camp on the first night between Shunda Creek, which is the second major creek on the left below the Gap, and Jackfish Creek, the third major creek on the left below the Gap. The Gap is the short, steep sided valley where the river cuts through the Brazeau Range, with a powerline crossing the river just downstream. Jackfish Creek is approximately 20 km downstream of the gap.

Follow Highway 11 west of Rocky Mountain House to just past Nordegg. Turn south on Highway 940 and follow it 8 km to the bridge over the North Saskatchewan. The take-out is the Highway 11 bridge near Rocky Mountain House.

## Smoky River, from Grande Cache to below the Cutbank River, northern Alberta
*165 km, 4–6 days, grade II with class III–IV+ rapids*

Suitable for rafts, canoes, and kayaks. A large-volume glacially fed run through remote wilderness in the foothills. There are many rapids, and your party can expect no help if trouble occurs, so do not take this run lightly. Most of the whitewater consists of large standing waves on bends in the river. Low ledges create the more difficult rapids, and the portages are complicated by cliffs along the banks.

The put-in is at the Highway 40 bridge just west of Grande Cache. Take out at Smoky Flats Campground, which is located approximately 140 km north on Highway 40, then 20 km east on the gravel road leading to Highway 734. An alternative take-out that extends the trip a day or two on an easier section of river is the Highway 34 bridge east of Grande Prairie.

# Recreational guidebooks

Some of these publications can be hard to come by. If a title is in print, it will be at Mountain Equipment Co-op, 1009 4th Avenue SW, Calgary, AB  T2P 0K8 (403-269-2420), or the Banff Book and Art Den, Box 1420, Banff, AB  T0L 0C0 (403-762-3919), or at Woodruff & Blum Books, Box 118, Lake Louise, AB  T0L 1E0 (403-522-3842).

Ambrosi, Joey (1984) *Hiking Alberta's Southwest.* Douglas and McIntyre, Vancouver. Much-needed guide to the eastern slope south of Kananaskis Country. Photos, maps, trail profiles; 166 pages.

Beers, Don (1981) *The Magic of Lake O'Hara.* Rocky Mountain Books, Calgary. Trails in the Lake O'Hara area of Yoho park.

Blaxley, Bob (1997) *The Whaleback: a Walking Guide.* Rocky Mountain Books, Calgary. Trails in the Porcupine Hills area of the southern foothills. Illustrated, maps, 96 pages.

— (1991) *The World of Lake Louise: a Guide for Hikers.* Highline Publishing, Calgary. A unique combination of trail information and history, with excellent illustrations. Place-name information, index, bibliography; 240 pages.

— (1993) *Banff–Assiniboine: a Beautiful World.* Highline Publishing, Calgary. The second in this series of hiking/history guides, 216 pages.

— (1994) *The Wonder of Yoho: Scenes, Tales, Trails.* Rocky Mountain Books, Calgary. The third in this series of hiking/history guides, 192 pages.

Boles, Glen; Robert Kruszyna and William Putnam (1979) *The Rocky Mountains of Canada, South.* Standard climber's guide to the Rockies between Waterton and the North Saskatchewan River. The other volume in this set: see Putnam, 1974. Illustrations, maps; 473 pages.

Cameron, Aaron and Matt Gunn (1998) *Hikes Around Invermere and the Columbia River Valley.* Rocky Mountain Books, Calgary. Trails in Kootenay National Park, the western Mt. Assiniboine area and south. Maps, photos, index; 208 pages.

Daffern, Gillean (1992) *Kananaskis Country Ski Trails.* Rocky Mountain Books, Calgary. Covers every known ski route in K-Country, and the set-track trails at Canmore Nordic Centre. Amusing commentaries. Maps, photos, index; 296 pages.

— (1994) *Canmore and Kananaskis Country.* Rocky Mountain Books, Calgary. The first in an interpretive series dubbed "Short Walks for Inquiring Minds," written in Daffern's enjoyable style. Maps, photos, index; 296 pages.

— (1997) *Kananaskis Country Trail Guide.* Rocky Mountain Books, Calgary. Indispensable in K-Country; well-informed and entertaining writing. Photos, maps; two-volume set, 272 and 320 pages.

Dodd, John and Gail Helgason (1998) *The Canadian Rockies Access Guide.* Lone Pine, Edmonton. Compendium of places to see and easy things to do in all five of the mountain national parks and Kananaskis Country. Illustrated, indexed, 400 pages.

Donaldson-Yarmey, Joan (1992a) *Back Roads of Northern Alberta.* Auto-traveller's directory, including the interesting Coal Branch area south of Hinton and Edson. Illustrated, index, 144 pages.

— (1992b) *Back Roads of Southern Alberta.* Companion book to previous item, 144 pages.

Dougherty, Sean (1991) *Selected Alpine Climbs in the Canadian Rockies*. Rocky Mountain Books, Calgary. Two hundred classic mountaineering routes, written up by someone who's climbed a lot of them. Maps, annotated photos, index; 320 pages.

Eastcott, Doug and Gerhardt Lepp (1999) *Backcountry Biking in the Canadian Rockies*. Rocky Mountain Books, Calgary. Routes from Waterton to Grande Cache, including the western slope. Maps, photos, index; 408 pages.

Edwards, J. Gordon (1990) *A Climber's Guide to Glacier National Park*. Distributed by Glacier Natural History Association, West Glacier, MT. How to get up and down those wonderful crumbling glacial horns—alive. Maps, illustrations, 352 pages.

Haberl, Keith (in press for 1995) *The Alpine Club of Canada Backcountry Huts and Facilities Directory*. Alpine Club of Canada, Canmore, AB. Will have photos and descriptions of all the ACC huts and cabins in the Rockies. About 160 pages.

Hampton, Bruce (1986) *Soft Paths: How to Enjoy the Wilderness Without Harming It*. Stackpole Books, Harrisburg, PA. Must reading for any outdoorsperson, put together by the famous National Outdoor Leadership School. Illustrated, 173 pages.

Harmon, Will (1992) *The Hiker's Guide to Alberta*. Falcon Press, Helena and Billings, MT; distributed in Canada by Rocky Mountain Books, Calgary. Covers the whole province but concentrates on the mountains. Maps, photos, 186 pages.

Helgason, Gail and John Dodd (1986) *The Canadian Rockies Bicycling Guide*. Lone Pine Publishing, Edmonton. Careful descriptions of 60 tours in the Rockies and Columbia Mountains. Illustrated, indexed, maps; 256 pages.

Howatt, Bruce and Colin Zacharias (1987) *The Back of the Lake: a Rockclimber's Guide to Lake Louise*. OFC Enterprises. Sport-climbing routes on the superb quartzite at the west end of Lake Louise. Climber's topos, 32 pages.

Josephson, Joe (1994) *Waterfall Ice*. Rocky Mountain Books, Calgary. Illustrated guide to all the better-known ice climbs in the Canadian Rockies between Waterton and Grande Cache. Maps, photos, index; 272 pages.

—, Chris Perry and Andy Genereux (1997) *Ghost Rock: Front Range Rock Climbs Near Calgary*. Rocky Mountain Books, Calgary. Guide to the limestone cliffs along Ghost River and Waiparous River. Annotated photos, route diagrams, maps; 240 pages.

Kane, Alan (1999) *Scrambles in the Canadian Rockies*. Rocky Mountain Books, Calgary. Non-technical ascent routes on peaks between Waterton and Jasper. Maps, annotated photos, index; 336 pages.

Kariel, Patricia (1987) *Hiking Alberta's David Thompson Country*. Lone Pine Publishing, Edmonton. Trails in the foothills and front ranges between the Ghost River and Blackstone Creek. Good human-history section. Maps, photos, index; 158 pages.

Krause, Karl and Mike Vincent (1992) *The Climber's Guide to Lake Louise*. Available at Woodruff & Blum Books, Lake Louise. Guide to the sport-climbing routes at the west end of the lake. See also Howatt, 1987. Maps, climbing topos, 32 pages.

MacDonald, Janice (1985) *Canoeing Alberta*. Lone Pine, Edmonton. Covers the eastern slope between Waterton and Grande Cache; includes whitewater runs. Photos, maps, hydrographic charts; 240 pages.

Martin, John; Chris Perry and Jon Jones (1991) *Bow Valley Update: a Guide to New Climbs East of Banff.* Updates Perry et al.'s 1988 *Bow Valley Rock,* q.v. Photos, topos, index; 56 pages.

— David Dancer and Jon Jones (1992) *Kananaskis Rock.* From the Barrier Bluffs south to the huge, seldom-climbed Half-Dome-like wall of Gibraltar Mountain west of Turner Valley. Maps, annotated photos, climbing topos, index; 96 pages.

— and Jon Jones (1998) *Sport Climbs in the Canadian Rockies.* Rocky Mountain Books, Calgary. Compendium of short routes between Lake Louise, the Ghost River and Kananaskis Country. Climbing topos, illustrations, index; 288 pages.

McLean, Celia (1992) *Hiking the Rockies with Kids.* Orca Book Publishers, Victoria. Somebody had to do it: a guide to 65 walks, including some overnight trips, you can do with children. Lots of good advice, too. Maps, photos, index; 215 pages.

Meyer, Kathleen (1989) *How to Shit in the Woods.* Ten Speed Press, Berkeley, CA. Yes, instruction is needed. Illustrated, amusing, with glossary (glossary?); 77 pages.

Nelson, Bob (1982) *The Prince George and District Trail Guide.* Caledonia Ramblers. Popular hikes on the western slope between Valemount and Pine Pass. Maps, 56 pages.

Norheim, B. (1982) *Prince George and District Cross-Country Ski Trails.* Sons of Norway Skitouring Club, Prince George. Popular trails on the western slope between Valemount and Pine Pass. Maps, survival information, 25 pages.

Patton, Brian (1995) *Parkways of the Canadian Rockies: an Interpretive Guide to Roads in the Mountain Parks.* Summerthought, Banff. Descriptions of roadside features in Banff, Jasper, Yoho and Kootenay parks. Roadlogs, maps, photos, index; 160 pages.

— and Bart Robinson (1994) *The Canadian Rockies Trail Guide.* Summerthought, Banff. Covers Waterton, Banff, Jasper, Kootenay, Yoho, Mount Assiniboine and Mount Robson parks. The original; photos, maps, index; 363 pages.

Perry, Chris; John Martin and Sean Dougherty (1988, new edition due late 1999) *Bow Valley Rock.* Rocky Mountain Books, Calgary. Everything east of Banff, from EEOR to Yamnuska. Annotated photos, index, 224 pages.

Pole, Graeme (1992) *Walks and Easy Hikes in the Canadian Rockies.* Altitude Publishing, Banff. The shorter, less-strenuous outings. Beautifully illustrated, maps, index; 160 pages.

— (1994) *Classic Hikes in the Canadian Rockies.* Altitude Publishing, Banff. Exactly as purveyed, with special attention to trailside natural history. Beautifully illustrated. Maps, photos, index; 304 pages. Also available in a three-ring binding for carrying just the pages you need.

Potter, Mike (1992) *Backcountry Banff.* Luminous Compositions, Banff. Meticulous hiker's guide, with lots of natural-history info. Maps, photos, index; 212 pages.

— (1994) *Hiking Lake Louise.* Luminous Compositions, Banff. Another of Potter's carefully prepared books; *the* guide to the best day-hiking area in the Rockies. Maps, photos, index; 126 pages.

Putnam, William; Robert Kruszyna and Chris Jones (1974) *Climber's Guide to the Rocky Mountains of Canada—North.* American Alpine Club/Alpine Club of Canada. Covers the Rockies north of the North Saskatchewan River. Photos, maps; 259 pages.

Robinson, Dave (1999) *Jasper Rock.* Otto Press, Box 640, Jasper, AB T0E 1E0. The long-awaited guide to sport-climbing routes in Jasper National Park, with selected traditional climbs, too. Annotated photos, route diagrams, index; 117 pages.

Ross, Jane, and Daniel Kyba (1998) *David Thompson Highway: a Hiking Guide.* Rocky Mountain Books, Calgary. Trails heading along Alberta 11, between Nordegg and the eastern boundary of Banff National Park. Illustrations, maps, 256 pages.

Ruhle, George (1986) *Roads and Trails of Waterton-Glacier International Peace Park.* Distributed by Glacier Natural History Association, West Glacier, MT. Lots of detail for hikers and motorists. Photos, maps, peak-finder diagrams; 143 pages.

Russell, Charles, et al. (1984) *Waterton and Northern Glacier Trails for Hikers and Riders.* Waterton Natural History Association, Waterton Park, AB. Covers all major trails in Waterton and those in Glacier from Helen Lake North. Photos, maps, trail profiles, references; 110 pages.

Russell, Elizabeth, et al. (1987) *Short Hikes and Strolls in Waterton Lakes National Park.* Waterton Natural History Association, Waterton Park, AB. Similar to previous item, covering short day hikes only; 32 pages.

Savage, Brian and Margaret Barry (1985) *Ski Alberta.* Lone Pine, Edmonton. Includes some areas not covered in any other guide. Emphasis on short, easy tours. Illustrated, maps, 239 pages.

Schmidt, Esther and Dennis (1991) *Photographing Wildlife in the Canadian Rockies.* Lone Pine Press. Techniques, places to get photos, and lovely examples; 192 pages.

Scott, Chic (1998) *Ski Trails in the Canadian Rockies.* Rocky Mountain Books, Calgary. The definitive guide for skiing and ski-mountaineering in Waterton, Banff, Jasper, Kootenay and Yoho national parks, with good information in the front on equipment and safety. Illustrated, maps, index; 224 pages.

— (1994) *Summits & Icefields: Alpine Ski Tours in the Rockies and Columbia Mountains of Canada.* Rocky Mountain Books, Calgary. The best ski-mountaineering guide available. Includes details of some great long-haul trips. Maps, photos, index; 304 pages.

Smith, Stuart (1995, 1996) *Canadian Rockies Whitewater: the Southern Rockies* and *Canadian Rockies Whitewater: the Central Rockies.* Rocky Mountain Books, Calgary. Two essential books for kayakers making runs between the international boundary and the Fraser River drainage northwest of McBride. Illustrated, maps, indexes; 312 and 336 pages.

Spring, Vicky (1994) *Glacier National Park and Waterton Lakes National Park.* Rocky Mountain Books, Calgary, and the Mountaineers, Seattle. Hiking, cycling and skiing trails amid the colorful rock and the mountain goats. Photos, good route diagrams; 280 pages.

Strong, Janice (1998) *Mountain Footsteps: Hiking the East Kootenay.* Rocky Mountain Books, Calgary. One of the few guides to the southwestern part of the Canadian Rockies. Maps, photos, index; 280 pages.

Tobey, Kelly (1987) *Barrier Bluffs: the Guide.* Rocky Mountain Books, Calgary. Well-designed pocket guide to the popular climbing area in Kananaskis Country. Annotated photos, index, 91 pages.

## Maps

For a list of topographic maps of popular areas, see page 802.

*Is this person in trouble? No. Despite the situation and the weather, he knows exactly what he is doing. Photo taken on the north face of Mt. Athabasca during a storm.*

# Safety and emergencies
### Keeping yourself together in the mountains

We humans live by our wits. Physically unimpressive, we can still survive nearly anywhere by figuring out what to eat, what to wear, where to find shelter, what to do and—equally important— what *not* to do. Success in the Canadian Rockies is no different.

Suppose we wish to reach the top of a great big icy mountain. We give the problem some thought, find out what others who have climbed it recommend, prepare for the task and gather the necessary gear. Clever and cautious, we practice on small mountains first. Then, when we know what we're doing, we go for the big one. We tread carefully up, protecting ourselves with rope in places where a fall would break our fragile bodies. We insulate our nakedness with layers of feathers and animal hair and plastic as we climb higher, to the land where the wind sticks its cold fingers under our shirts. We stand on the summit and smile, magically saving the scene in our cameras, then tread carefully back down again, unscathed.

Mountainous terrain is risky terrain. It's easy to get into trouble. According to the Parks Canada mountain-rescue service, the situations they respond to most often stem from (a) not following the trail, (b) getting caught in an avalanche, (c) trying to go down the mountain a different way than the way the party went up, (d) slipping on snow patches, and (e) falling from climbing routes that are not particularly difficult.

A perennial fatal-accident site is at Athabasca Falls, where people climb over the railings to get pictures of the gorge and slip into it on the wet, water-polished rock. Another is the Athabasca Glacier, where people ignore the many posted warnings, walk onto the glacier and fall into a crevasse hidden under the snow.

Seldom is an accident caused by an act of nature. Usually accidents happen because of bad judgement.

## Avoiding trouble

The simplest, best advice is to **approach new places and new activities cautiously.** People who are new to the mountains and get carried away with the Rockies—"Wow! I'm going up there, Wilma!"—may literally get carried away later. If you are a novice at mountain travel, it is wise to limit yourself at first to well-traveled trails not far from civilization. These are the safer places. Later, when you understand the lay of the land, you will be competent enough to travel off the beaten track safely. Regardless of how experienced you become, the basics still apply:

### 1. Get competent leadership

When you are headed off on something potentially risky—a hike off established trails, for example—**go with other people,** not alone, and be sure that the organizer/leader is someone whom you *know* to be **able and experienced.** If the leader is going to be you, be sure you are competent before agreeing to lead.

If you don't know the group leader, then do some checking beforehand. Who is this person? Is he or she reliable? Or does the person have a reputation for generating fiascos? Most of the nasty experiences I have had in the mountains were the result of relying on poor judgement and bad advice. Trips put on by large clubs and schools are particularly subject to screw-ups of this sort, for the participants seldom know the people with whom they entrust their lives.

The best approach to learning your way around the mountains is to join a small, experienced group with a good reputation. Go with them on several outings. If you do well, you will soon become one of the gang. The next-best approach is to book trips with respected organizations or guides and pay for competent leadership. Outdoor-skills courses offered in the Rockies area are good training; there is a list on page 731.

## 2. Carry creature comforts

In my pack I carry the essentials required to protect myself from the weather, to take care of thirst and hunger, to keep from getting lost and to deal with minor injuries or equipment failures. This is second-nature to those of us experienced in the mountain environment.

But consider the many newcomers who are not. A couple from Ontario, enjoying their first visit to the Rockies, may intend to walk for an hour. They carry no jackets, no water, no lunch, no sunburn protection, no insect repellent, no map and no matches. Because they are having fun, they push on and on. Eventually they find themselves 10 km from the car, above treeline, drenched in a cold and frightening thunderstorm.

This is a common experience, unpleasant but seldom fatal. Lots of people who stride unprepared into these hills are quickly humbled, having discovered that the Canadian Rockies are tougher than they look. Next time, these folks come prepared, more knowledgeable and better-equipped—and they enjoy themselves, snug in their warm jackets, eating their lunches in comfort as they wait out the storm inside the trail shelter that was mentioned in the guidebook they were smart to bring.

Things get serious when the unpleasantness gets out of hand. The blisters become more painful and the steps slower, the body is running out of fuel, there is nothing to eat or drink, the rain turns to snow, the slope steepens, lightning hits close by, the mind panics, the body starts to run, the ankle twists … and they read about you in the papers.

## 3. Leave word

Tell someone back home where you are going and when you expect to be back. Leave thorough and accurate information about your trip. Write the following down and leave the note with a responsible person.

- Who is going? List names and phone numbers.
- Where, exactly, are you going? If it's a climb, what is the route?
- How difficult is the trip supposed to be? Have you done it before?
- Where is the car being left? Write down the make and the licence number.
- When do you expect to be back? When should people start to worry?
- What should be done if you don't show up?

These items of information will be of great help to the authorities if they have to look for you. In the national parks, you may also want to use the voluntary safety-registration system.

## If an accident occurs

**Keep cool, assess the situation before acting, reassure the victim, and above all don't endanger yourself.** Be glad you have taken a first-aid course recently. Readers who haven't should do so.

### If you have to go for help

Once the victim is safe, sheltered and prepared to wait for help:

- **Determine exactly where the person will be found.** Look around, identify the landmarks, and describe the place to yourself so you can describe it to rescuers. If possible, write down the location and carry the note with you. You may not be able to go back.

- **Stay long enough** to determine the nature of the injured person's condition. This will help in mounting the rescue. Again, write these things down.

- **Take your time if you have to cross difficult terrain to alert rescuers.** Hurrying can cause another mishap. You may be alone, and the victim will be depending on you to get help. Whenever possible, more than one person should go.

## Getting lost

To get lost, fall behind the group you're with. Tell them it's okay; you'll catch up later. And be sure you've never been in the area before.

That's the usual getting-lost situation. The main party takes the left branch of the trail, then the stragglers come along and take the right branch. Each group frantically spends the rest of the day looking for the other instead of enjoying the hike. This happens all too often with improperly led groups of school kids. So the rule for leaders is **keep the group together.** A well-led party proceeds no faster than the speed of the slowest member. Look back to see if gaps are developing in the line of hikers. If so, wait for everyone to catch up—especially at trail junctions. Explain the reason for this to your charges.

Another way to get lost is to assume that you know more than the person who built the trail. The trail jogs left when you think it should jog right, so you leave it and take to the bush. Hours later, far from home in the dark, you wish you had stayed on the trail. Avoid taking shortcuts when a trail seems to be going the wrong way. It may be bypassing impassable cliffs, or detouring around a gorge, or leading to a better, safer stream-crossing.

Few people become lost for long in the mountains. I'm speaking now of winding up in the wrong valley, quite confused. Landmarks are plentiful, and if you keep checking your location on a topographic map—the key to not getting disoriented—then you won't become lost.

If you do get lost, remember that in most valleys a trail of some sort can be found beside the stream running down the middle. Along the trail will be other human beings, most likely. If not, one valley joins another; as long as you're going downstream, you're probably going to come out on a road eventually.

Young children may become separated from the adults for only a moment. In that moment, though, kids are inclined to panic. They may run down the trail in the wrong direction, or take to the woods, or hide from rescuers because they think they've done something wrong and may be punished for it. Obviously, adults should keep an eye on youngsters at all times, even when they're just stepping off the trail to pee. And teach youngsters that if they should find themselves alone, they should **stay where they are until somebody comes for them.** Give each child a whistle to blow while waiting.

To a lost child, the voice of a parent may represent punishment and the voice of a stranger may be interpreted as dangerous, particularly to a child taught by his or her parents not to associate with people she or he doesn't know. My wife and I taught our kids that any adult will help you if you're lost. We reasoned that very few adults present a danger to a lost child, but a child afraid to seek help is in real trouble.

If you must scour the woods looking for someone, prepare a plan first. Divide the search area into natural sections, e.g. "We'll take this side of the creek. You take the other side." Search in pairs. Call the lost person's name often, each time stopping quietly to listen for a reply. Plan for all rescuers to meet at a certain place at a certain time. If a quick search doesn't turn up a lost child, send for help before returning to the hunt.

## Storms and lightning

A warm rain is unheard-of in the Canadian Rockies. The stuff comes down cold, quickly chilling unprepared people caught outdoors. So carry a waterproof rain jacket in the summer, even if the weather looks good, and a sweater if you are going above treeline. Alpine-zone squalls are windy, often carrying snow mixed with rain—a chilling combination that can sweep in quite suddenly, catching hikers off guard. For the results, read the section on hypothermia, page 769. In spring and fall, alpine-style weather reaches down to the valley bottoms.

The **thunderstorm** season is June to September, with August the prime month. Even though it may be clear overhead, keep an eye on the clouds farther away. Evidence of a general cloud buildup elsewhere means that there is probably something similar headed your way; you just can't see it yet over the crest of the ridge.

One sure way of telling whether the clouds starting to stream over are tugging in a thunderstorm is to carry a pocket radio and tune it between stations. Popping and crackling will be caused by you-know-what.

**Lightning** is so common in the mountains that you would think climbers and hikers would come to ignore it, but not so. Most of us have lived through several close calls, during which we have felt like flies about to be swatted, and thus we try to avoid future encounters.

We know that when wispy strands of rain are starting to hang down from the cumulus clouds, or when a blue-black wall of cloud is approaching, it is time to head back down to treeline. Caught in the open, get at least a hundred metres down from the crest of a ridge or the top of a mountain.

There are two kinds of relatively safe places in the high country: low spots or depressions without tall rocks or trees nearby, and the bases of cliffs. Squat in such places, keeping your contact with the ground small so as to get the minimal dose of ground currents, which spread out within a 30-m radius of a strike. Like a lightning rod, which shields a cone-shaped area under it, a cliff above you offers some protection. But you should move out a few metres from the cliff base to avoid currents traveling over the surface if the top is struck.

**Places to avoid:** high points such as summits and ridges, large open areas such as glaciers, where you are the only pointy thing, stands of trees in open, flat or gently sloping places—sheltering under a lone tree is statistically quite dangerous—and under overhangs or in shallow caves in cliffs, where current running through the rock can take a shortcut through your body.

Metal alone does not attract lightning, but touching your ice axe or other metallic climbing gear during a close strike can give you burns, as can coins and a knife in your pants pockets, or metal watches and jewelry. Caught in a risky spot during an electrical storm, I get metal items off my body.

Deep woods, with many trees, are statistically safe, unless you are standing under the tallest tree in the woods, as are deep rock shelters. Stay a metre away from the walls, and well back from the entrance. Climber's huts above timberline are protected from lightning by metal cables running over their roofs or by the metal skin of most such huts. You are safe inside, protected by the **Faraday-cage effect:** electricity will pass through the metal rather than the air within the structure. Same with a metal-roofed automobile.

Should someone in your party receive a jolt, be sure that this person is breathing properly afterward and has a steady heartbeat. If knocked unconscious, the victim will probably need mouth-to-mouth resuscitation, page 767. Check for burns.

# Avalanches

Avalanches are slides of snow. Some people refer to rock slides as "avalanches," but this isn't correct. In the Canadian Rockies a few people die each winter in avalanches, along with a fair bit of wildlife. Mountain goats are especially endangered by avalanches.

It is easy to avoid avalanches: don't go to the mountains. But for oromaniacs like me, life is inordinately dull elsewhere, so we have had to learn something about staying alive in avalanche country. Much wisdom is contained in Tony Daffern's excellent *Avalanche Safety for Skiers and Climbers* (see "Further reading," page 781). You might wish to attend a course or seminar on the subject.

**Avalanche tracks** are usually obvious: you break out of the woods into an open strip that reaches well up the mountain, often into a gully capped by a **cornice,** which is an overhanging mass of wind-driven snow built out on the leeward side of a ridge. There may be small, bent-over and stripped-looking trees in the track, and if an avalanche has come down already that winter the lumpy, over-deep snow remains as evidence. Despite these indications, I often see skiers stopped for lunch in sunny, scenic avalanche tracks.

**Only one person should cross an avalanche track at a time.** On wide ones, where solo crossings would use up too much time, the party should space themselves well apart. Consider the warning signs given next before crossing it at all.

The most dangerous time is the 24 hours following a snowfall of 20 cm or more. It takes a day or two for new snow to settle somewhat and stabilize. Early-winter snowfalls are quite dangerous when new, especially at high-subalpine levels—where the best skiing is, of course. November and December storms often dump copiously on grassy slopes that avalanche easily. **Beware of Parker Ridge and Bow Summit,** popular early-season skiing spots along the Icefields Parkway. There have been fatalities here on innocent-looking slopes.

Determining avalanche hazard is a tricky business, even for experts. Every skier should know and listen for the **settling sound:** a dull "whoomph" spreading from under your skis. This indicates that the snow is unstable and the hazard is high.

Another way to estimate stability is to poke your ski pole down, basket first. If you encounter increasing resistance all the way down, then probably the snow is stable. If the snow is uniformly soft throughout, or if there is reduced resistance at depth, then the snow is likely to slide. On a slope I'm unsure of, I test the snow with my pole every few metres. If indications are worsening, I pick another route or go home.

**Places to avoid in unstable conditions:** any slope over 30°, especially leeward slopes that are convex—avalanches frequently start from such bulges—and any spot threatened by a **cornice**: a drift of snow built out over space along a ridge.

Ridgecrests offer avalanche-free routes in poor conditions—the western sides of ridges in the Rockies are often blown clear of snow—but ridges present another danger: you may be walking on a cornice, treading over thin air. Cornices are seldom obvious from the upwind side; all you see is the edge of the snow and the sky beyond. That edge can overhang several metres, and it can break off anytime. Or you can simply fall through. A friend of mine was killed this way, by falling unroped through a cornice on the summit of Mt. Assiniboine, and another friend was badly injured in a similar accident. I make it a habit to keep at least 10 m back from ridgelines unless I can clearly see that neither side is corniced.

On one trip a cornice let go above us. It seemed a safe distance away, but the avalanche that resulted ended at our ski tips. On another trip, a helicopter passed low overhead while I was crossing a steep gully. The vibration knocked off a cornice at the top. The gully avalanched, but a flattening in it stopped the slide just above our crossing point. Whew.

**Depth-hoar buildups** often result in avalanches. Depth hoar is a layer of loose grains at the base of the snowpack. Other terms are more descriptive: "sugar snow," "rotten snow" and the wonderful northern aboriginal term "pukak," pronounced "POO-kack."

This is snow that has recrystallized from the ground up. The greater the temperature difference between the soil and the air, the faster it develops and the thicker the depth-hoar layer gets. A long stretch of cold, clear weather can rot most of the snowpack. This is bad news for skiers. There is no **base** (no firmness), so skiing off the trails or outside the ski areas means constantly breaking through to your knees. Snow underlain by a lot of depth hoar also slides quite easily, reducing the safe-slope angle from 30° to 20°.

In 1973, while skiing up the trail to Stanley Glacier near Vermilion Pass, a friend and I noted depth hoar over a metre deep, and

*These climbers on the summit ridge of Mt. Robson don't realize how little substance lies beneath their feet.*

settling all around us. But it lay deceptively under a solid layer that supported our weight. As we approached treeline, a long sighing sound indicated that a big depth-hoar avalanche had let go on the steep slope just ahead. Most avalanches crack or rumble; depth-hoar avalanches swish along almost silently. Hurrying over a knoll to get a better view, we saw the last movements of a slide a kilometre wide and a kilometre long. On that slope there had been a party of four inexperienced skiers. Unaware, they had skied into the middle of it and triggered that huge slide. Two of them died.

Large, plate-like crystals of **surface hoar** sometimes form overnight atop the snow. Surface hoar is fragile stuff, and buried under successive snowfalls it remains as a thin zone of weakness above which a thick slab may slide. You may not be able to detect these zones in the ski-pole test described earlier, but you can feel layers of crust caused by sun or wind. Such layers also form sliding surfaces.

With the beginning of April, skiers must be wary of **climax avalanches,** especially on the western slope, where the valleys are deep and the avalanche chutes are long. A climax avalanche is the main one of the year in any particular chute. It involves the whole thickness of the snow, right down to the ground, or to the ice on a steep glacier. Such slides can come earlier in the proper conditions, and they continue through June and into July on the

*In April the sun is strong and the avalanches are big. This one came down a west-facing slope on Paget Peak in Yoho National Park. It missed us by a day.*

higher peaks, presenting a danger to summer mountaineers.

Park wardens and ski patrollers seem obsessed with avalanches—as well they might, for they are the ones who have to recover the twisted, suffocated victims. Parks Canada wardens assess the avalanche hazard regularly through the winter by digging pits in the snow and doing various measurements and tests, the details of which are beyond the scope of this book. The experts know of what they speak; **before heading into the high country in winter, get the latest avalanche forecast and heed the warnings.**

If you regularly ski in avalanche-prone terrain, wear an **avalanche beacon,** which is a small radio-signal-emitting device used to locate avalanche victims. There isn't space here to describe how to track down the transmitting victim, so be sure to practice the technique. Wear that wonderful gadget **close to your body,** not slung over your clothes or left in your pack; an avalanche can easily rip these away, and searchers will find the beacon or the pack, not you.

Further, resist the false sense of security an avalanche beacon can give. You must still be cautious, still be aware of the condition of the snowpack, or the beacon will serve only to lead rescuers to your dead body.

Carry a lightweight **collapsible snow shovel** on or in your pack, in case you have to dig someone out. You can also use this shovel for digging test pits in the snow—the only way to actually see those weak layers I was talking about—and for digging snow-holes to give you some shelter while you're having lunch on a windy day above treeline.

If you are caught in an avalanche, try swimming uphill in the snow. This will help you to stay on the surface. As the motion stops, **bring your hands to your face** and hollow out a breathing space. Then try to get one arm up closer to the surface, where it may be seen.

If someone is buried, and the party on the surface is small—two or three—all should stay and search for a while, trying to try to find the victim in the first half-hour, after which the chance of survival diminishes quickly. Consider the possibility that another slide may come down while you are absorbed in the rescue. Keep an eye on what is above, and if the situation looks very dangerous, leave the area before you, too, become a victim.

If the group was carrying avalanche beacons, **be sure all members on the surface switch theirs to receive,** so someone isn't confusing the search by transmitting like the victim. Forgetting to switch over to receive is common during the tension of an emergency.

If a victim was not wearing a beacon, note where he or she was last seen and search below that point for the victim's hat, ski poles, skis, pack or any other clues. If you find something that is obviously not attached to a buried person, **don't touch it.** Placing your scent on it can confuse a rescue dog. Leave the item as it lies, and mark the location with a ski or a pole.

Check very carefully downhill from anything you find, probing suspected spots with ski poles—pull the baskets off—in hope of finding the buried person(s) quickly.

If a half-hour search turns up no sign, then it is time to send one person for help, two if the party is larger. Send out fast, strong skiers, so help arrives as quickly as possible.

Those remaining on the scene should continue the search. Thoroughly check the whole slide downhill from where the tracks entered it, then begin probing systematically. Stand shoulder to shoulder and probe uphill, one short step at a time, starting at the toe of the slide directly below the last-seen point and working uphill.

- Don't probe systematically going downhill. Your steps will be too long.
- Don't piss in the slide, or drop cigarette butts, food wrappers or anything else human into the snow nearby. These things also tend to confuse a rescue dog, just like touching an item belonging to a victim's.
- When the victim is found, uncover the person's head first. If she or he is unconscious, check for breathing. If there is no apparent breathing—chest does not rise and fall, pair of glasses held over mouth does not fog—begin mouth-to-mouth resuscitation immediately (see next section), while the others free the victim's chest. Check for injuries. Hypothermia is likely; see page 769.

## Mouth-to-mouth resuscitation

Tilt the head gently back to open the airway. Clear the mouth and upper throat of any obstructions, such as snow, or food if the person has been choking on a meal. Pinch the victim's nostrils closed and place your mouth over the victim's mouth. Make sure there is a good seal. The chance of serious disease transmission in doing this is quite small.

Breathe out into the victim's airway one time, filling the victim's lungs enough to see the chest rise. Remove your mouth and let the air expel naturally. If something is blocking the airflow, check the airway again and clear it.

Repeat about 12 times per minute. For children, the rate is 20 times per minute and the breaths should be shallower to prevent damage to a child's small lungs. For infants, breathe in small puffs. On a small face, cover both the nose and the mouth with your mouth.

While you are doing the resuscitation, get someone to check for heartbeat by taking the pulse in the neck or listening to the chest. As long as a heartbeat is detected, no matter how faint or slow, continue with resuscitation. It may be an hour or more before the victim can breathe on her/his own. To detect a faint heartbeat, open or pull up the victim's shirt and press your ear onto the bare chest, just left—victim's left—of centre.

If the heart has stopped, and someone in the group is practiced at CPR (cardio-pulmonary resuscitation), then try CPR. First-aid organizations used to recommend that untrained people not attempt CPR, but now they suggest that you try anyway, because a person without a heartbeat has nothing to lose. Just be *sure* that there is no heartbeat, because CPR is often damaging. The illustration on the next page shows the method.

## Cardio-pulmonary resuscitation

After making *sure* there is no heartbeat, kneel beside the victim as shown, locate the victim's breast bone, interlock your fingers and press down on the breast bone hard enough to depress it 4–5 cm. Do 80–100 chest compressions per minute, letting the chest come back up each time. Check once each minute for a pulse. If there is one, stop chest compressions but continue doing mouth-to-mouth resuscitation. If you must do both, give two breaths for each 15 chest compressions. Remember to check for a pulse.

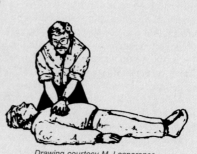

*Drawing courtesy M. Lesperance*

## Stopping heavy bleeding

This is caused by a broken artery or large vein. First, try putting pressure directly on the wound. Don't wait to dig a bandage out of the first-aid kit; use anything handy: a handkerchief or a glove will do. It helps to elevate the wound above the heart. Direct pressure will usually stop the bleeding in a few minutes, at which point you can apply a dressing to keep the pressure on the wound, to protect it and sop up any seepage. A sterile dressing is preferable, of course, but anything soft, such as a folded handkerchief or a teeshirt or clean sock, will do. Tape it or tie it over the wound, putting it on fairly tightly but not so tightly as to cut off the circulation.

If pressure doesn't stop the bleeding, then a major artery has been cut. The victim may die quickly from loss of blood. Apply strong pressure with the fingers, searching for the spot that stops the flow. When you find it, **keep the pressure on,** trading off with someone else when your hand tires. If there are just two of you, the victim may be able to help.

Heavy bleeding causes **shock:** the effect of blood loss, or otherwise lowered blood pressure, on the major organs. Shock produces paleness, cool skin, thirst and a weak, rapid pulse, followed if blood loss is great by confusion, stupor, coma and death. A person who has lost more than a litre of blood will probably show signs of shock, and many other injuries and conditions can cause shock, so **always treat a victim for shock,** as follows. The victim lies down with head slightly lower than hips, except if there is a head injury, in which case the head should be higher than the hips. Raise the legs 25–30 cm to allow the blood to reach the major organs more easily. Keep the victim warm, providing external heat as per hypothermia, facing page, if shock is severe. If the victim asks for a painkiller, non-aspirin types such as Tylenol are okay. Aspirin interferes with clotting. Give nothing alcoholic, and give no liquids to an unconscious person.

## Head injuries

A knock on the head hard enough to cause unconsciousness often creates **concussion,** which is a reaction to brain motion within the skull. Concussion is often made worse by the tearing of small blood vessels inside the skull or on the surface of the brain. A pool of blood forms between the brain and the skull, usually (but not always) at the point of impact, putting pressure on the brain and causing the following symptoms:

- Confusion. The victim asks the same questions over and over.
- Aggressive, out-of-character behavior.
- Upset stomach, often with vomiting.
- Pupils unequal in size.
- Return of unconsciousness, a sign that the victim's condition is worsening. Get to the hospital, fast.

There is no field treatment for concussion. Since it comes on gradually, watch anyone who has suffered a head injury for symptoms and head for the hospital at the first sign.

## Moving an injured person

Should the victim try to walk out? Should you try to carry a person out? Sometimes yes, sometimes no.

If the victim can walk without much difficulty, *and* the distance is not too far, *and* the victim is not likely to become incapacitated en route, then sure; the victim should walk out. Why burden society with an unnecessary helicopter rescue?

On the other hand, society will be a lot more burdened if a walking evacuation goes wrong. If the injury is serious, and/or the rest of the party is not strong, the victim should remain in a safe place and wait for rescue.

Much is made of carrying injured people out of the woods, using many ingenious rigs for doing so, but professional mountain-rescuers advise that **you should move a non-walking victim only to the nearest shelter, if at all,** then go for help. This is usually quicker; a helicopter can be summoned and will normally arrive a lot sooner than the time it takes to carry someone out. And it's a whole lot easier on the victim.

## *Hypothermia*

Definition: failure of the body to produce enough heat to keep the inner organs at the proper temperature.

This used to be known as "exposure," as in, "He died of exposure." The usual cause is fatigue and hunger coupled with inadequate insulation from wet clothing or not wearing enough clothing. Skinny people are more susceptible to hypothermia than fat people are. The condition often strikes near the end of a long, wet day at higher elevations, when everyone is tired and soaked and the temperature is near freezing. Surprisingly, it's just as common in summer as it is in winter, perhaps more so. In winter, people dress warmly; in summer they often dress lightly and don't carry enough extra clothing.

When you are very tired and/or hungry and thirsty, your metabolic furnace is not burning as hot as usual. In warm surroundings this is not a serious condition. You eat, drink, sleep and feel better. But when the surroundings are cold—and they needn't be very cold, for hypothermia can occur at temperatures well above freezing—and when there is no rest in sight and no food in the tummy, then the body cannot produce enough heat to overcome the steady loss and hypothermia results.

The body's first defense is to slow the circulation in the hands and feet. This decreases heat loss from body the core, where the essential organs lie. If you know you are tired, and your hands and feet are getting cold, then put on your jacket, pull up your hood, put on your gloves and do whatever else you can to avoid further chilling. Moving more quickly will generate more heat and get you back home sooner.

**Shivering** is a sign of incipient hypothermia. The result of millions of years of mammal evolution, this response gives the furnace a vigorous stoke; it is intended to get you through the episode before the fire flickers out.

Normal body-core temperature is 37°C. At 37–35°C shivering starts. At 35–34°C there is obvious uncoordination, a sluggish pace and apathy. At 34–32°C there is stumbling and inability to use the hands. At 32–30°C severe

*Typical hypothermia weather in the Canadian Rockies. A few hours after this photo was taken, one member of the party had to be treated for hypothermia.*

hypothermia sets in. Shivering stops. The victim can no longer walk. He or she is confused, irrational, helpless. At 30–28°C death is close. The victim is semiconscious, with dilated pupils, and is barely breathing. There is practically no heartbeat. At 28°C the heart stops.

Obviously, the idea is to keep the situation from going beyond the shivering stage.

If someone in your group is cold and tired, watch her or him for these symptoms: a fatigued look and irritability, followed by shivering, dullness and inattentiveness. Be alert for signs of hypothermia and do something about it *before* you note poor coordination (fumbling with pack straps, staggering). If the shivering stops but the victim doesn't brighten up, that person is in big trouble.

At the first sign of hypothermia in your group, consider how far it is to the car, the cabin or the tent. If it is only an hour or two at the most, call a short halt. Be sure that any victim is wearing the warmest, driest clothing available. A soaked sweater, for example, might be replaced by a dry one or by a warm jacket if there is an extra available. Cover the victim's head. Make the victim eat *and drink* something—dehydration is a contributor to hypothermia—and then **get him or her moving as quickly as possible toward home.** The victim may not be very cooperative, saying something like "I'm okay; leave me alone." But that person is *not* okay and needs help.

If the victim cannot walk any farther and you have no camping gear, find a sheltered spot and **build a fire for warmth.** Use the brown needles of evergreens as tinder; they burn explosively when dry and can even be coaxed into flaming when wet. Add small twigs at first, gradually building the fire up until it is large and throwing off plenty of heat. Get the victim to stand beside it, removing layers of clothing and thus allowing the heat to penetrate. Use the fire to dry out the clothing.

If you haven't brought matches, or your fire fails, make an all-out effort to reach civilization. The victim's life probably depends on it. If she or he comes to a halt and cannot be cajoled or shouted into continuing, and you are still in good condition, it might be best to go for help. Most people can take several hours of severe hypothermia before they die.

Suppose the worst: going for help is not possible, there just isn't enough clothing to keep warm and you can't build a fire. You still have a chance. Break off evergreen boughs—the driest ones are those near the ground—and quickly build a nest in a sheltered spot, perhaps under another evergreen. Put down a thick layer of boughs, for insulation against the cold ground, and another thick layer over you and victim. Open your clothing to get skin-to-skin contact. Cuddle and rest, eating any food you have.

If you are hiking or skiing in the back country and have camping gear with you, **get a tent up** when you notice an attack of hypothermia. This assumes that other measures have failed, such as changing into dry clothing, eating and moving faster. Get the victim inside, undressed if his or her clothing is wet, and into a sleeping bag. Prepare a warm, not hot, sugary non-alcoholic drink.

Give this to the person and note the response. If she or he brightens up, the emergency is over. Feed the grateful victim and allow enough rest before moving on. It is often wise to simply camp on the spot.

But if a cup of hot chocolate taken while in a dry sleeping bag doesn't do the trick, then the victim cannot generate enough heat on his own. Someone will have to **strip down and get in the sleeping bag with the victim,** warming him or her by skin-to-skin contact. This works very well; never mind the social taboos.

A word of warning: do not try to rewarm a victim of severe hypothermia *rapidly.* For example, a comatose person dragged into a mountain hut should not be stripped and laid out in front of the stove. Cold, acidic, poorly oxygenated blood in the extremities will move into the heart, possibly causing **fibrillation** (random twitching of the heart muscle) and death. For the same reason, do not rub the victim's arms and legs. Put the person into a sleeping bag, surrounded with more insulation. Then try to get her or him to drink warm liquids—be careful not to cause choking—so the body temperature rises internally. Be gentle in handling the victim; the heart rhythm is unstable, and roughness can bring on fibrillation. At the same time, someone should go for the helicopter. The victim will probably get no worse than he or she already is, and in hospital the rewarming can be done internally.

Apparently dead victims, with practically undetectable heartbeats, have recovered from severe hypothermia. To quote the old medical adage, "No one should be considered cold and dead until that person has been warm and dead."

In the Canadian Rockies we frequently have a rash of hypothermia cases during the week-long summer drizzles that are caused by upslope weather (see page 209). The sun doesn't shine and the air is very cool, often just above freezing for days on end. Hikers in the back country find themselves in trouble when all their clothing gets wet and they can't dry it. In really miserable conditions above treeline it is not even possible to start a fire to warm up and dry out. The same thing can happen during lengthy "cold-low" storms, page 210, that dump a lot of low-temperature rain.

**Prevention:** bring several plastic garbage bags to keep your sleeping bag and spare clothing out of the wet. A good, leak-proof tent and a stove that can be fired up inside it, ignoring in this case the reasons for not running a stove in a tent, can get you out of a jam. Make sure the tent door is partly open, for adequate ventilation.

## Frostbite

Frostbite is the killing of cells caused by freezing. You cannot become frostbitten at temperatures above freezing, and you can develop frostbite without showing signs of hypothermia. Noses, faces and ears are seldom badly damaged by frostbite, but fingers and toes often are.

Once frostbitten, always susceptible, for the circulation is permanently impaired. So the idea is to **avoid that first encounter.** Wear boots, gloves and clothing warm enough for the lowest temperatures you are likely to encounter. Don't wear metal earrings in very cold weather. Metal-framed glasses can cause frostbite where they touch the skin. The skin of light-colored people becomes quite pink when threatened by frostbite; skin of any color goes pale as it freezes. Amazingly, the face feels little pain when it is being frostbitten. Keep an eye on your companions' noses, ears and cheeks, looking for telltale white patches.

Feet and hands complain bitterly as they cool. The feet are the most difficult parts to keep warm—and the most awkward for someone else to have to warm for you out of doors—so choose your footwear carefully. For walking or working in the cold, I have found **bush boots,** also called "shoe pacs," to be the best. They have rubber bottoms, leather tops, and thick felt liners that surround the foot. Unlike fabric-topped snowmobile boots or military arctic boots, bush boots can get wet without wetting the insulation within. This is good to know if you have broken through the ice into the creek.

Mountaineering boots with removable inner boots are fairly good, and they are essential for climbing with crampons, but the insulation is not as thick as the average felt liner and the toes don't bend, so they won't keep you as warm as bush boots will. Single-layer mountaineering boots are cold, a factor in the high incidence of frostbite among climbers.

For cross-country skiing at low temperatures, double ski boots or loose-fitting single boots with insoles and overboots are usually adequate. Gaiters add warmth and keep the snow out of your boots. Double boots are best for multi-day trips; their outer surfaces are not warmed by body heat and thus these boots don't get wet from snow melting on them.

The toes of cross-country boots bend with every step; as long as you keep moving, your feet stay warm at surprisingly low temperatures, even in light, low-cut boots, which bend the most. But when you stop, light boots cool rapidly. I don't recommend them for anything other than short jaunts, not far from the car. See page 738 for more on selecting ski boots for mountain touring.

If your feet are getting cold, **loosen your boots and pick up the pace.** Put on your hat if it isn't on already. Some skiers carry a pair of extra-large wool socks to pull over their boots. These add more comfort than one might imagine.

On overnight trips in the winter I always carry a pair of lightweight insulated **booties.** They offer comfort in a tent or a mountain hut, they keep my feet warm in my sleeping bag, and they provide extra protection in an emergency.

Bring a very warm pair of mitts to put on if your hands get cold under the gloves or light mitts that most people wear. Don't take your mitts off and blow on your fingers; this will just make them colder as the moisture in your breath condenses on them. Flinging your arms round and round may warm the arm muscles and thus the hands. The best thing for cold hands is the same as for cold feet: ski or walk faster, causing the whole body to heat up.

Many people, especially kids and women, tend to get cold feet and hands at the beginning of a trip. Then their extremities warm up comfortably as they continue to exercise. If your feet or hands have gone numb within a few minutes of the trailhead, be patient. They will most likely warm up soon, although you can expect some pain as they do. If there is no further pain once feeling and warmth have returned, then you haven't been frostbitten.

But if your hands or feet just aren't warming up after an hour or so, **turn around and go home.** You will probably make it back before frostbite occurs.

If you can't do that—it is too far to go, say, or you have been injured—then **take off your gloves or boots and quickly stick your hands or feet under a companion's shirt,** warming your fingers or toes on his or her bare abdomen.

This feels awfully chilly for the person offering the abdomen, of course, but it works well and has a wonderfully positive effect on children. You simply take off a kid's mitts and stick his cold hands up under your sweater and onto a large, warm, grown-up tummy. There is some psychology at work, here: the snivelling youngster, whose hands are becoming more and more painful, realizes that the adults aren't going to let him or her die after all. Once the pain of warming stops, she or he feels much better and usually has warm hands for the rest of the day.

I have been on trips in which my feet were miserably cold for days, yet no frostbite resulted. As long as you can feel your toes wiggling, you are okay, no matter how uncomfortable you are—up to a point. Cold feet, especially cold *wet* feet, can be injured by constant blood-vessel constriction and accompanying oxygen deprivation, a condition known mainly in the military, where it is called **trench-foot.**

If sensation is lost for many hours, and the pain at rewarming is strong and continues, then you probably have frostbite. Frostbitten flesh is hard and white when frozen; it blisters the day after rewarming and often discolors. As the days go by, the skin peels. Badly frostbitten toes and fingers often become infected and even gangrenous if untreated. Frostbite can kill you.

The preferred treatment is to warm frostbitten limbs in a carefully controlled sequence in hospital, where medications can be used to improve circulation and prevent infection. In this way, fingers and toes are seldom lost.

So don't attempt to treat frostbite out of doors, or in a mountain hut. Get the victim to hospital. Warming the injured parts above body temperature will damage them further, as will rubbing them. Put the victim in a sleeping bag and keep the frostbitten hands or feet protected from heat.

It is quite possible to ski for days on frozen feet, but often impractical once they thaw; the pain is too severe. So if your toes are really frozen—the skin is hard and white, with no sensitivity, and you can't wiggle the toes—get to civilization before you are disabled. If your feet thaw en route and you are unable to continue, stay in a protected place, for example in a tent or cabin, inside your sleeping bag, while others go for help. You may be tough enough to walk or ski in spite of the pain, but you will damage the tissues further if you do. And you may get frostbitten all over again, worsening the injury considerably.

## Asthma: many people don't even know they have it

If a quick start in cold air makes it hard for you to breathe—especially on the exhale and after you have stopped for a moment—then you may suffer from mild exercise-induced asthma. Many skiers have this condition. Untreated, it takes the fun out of winter sports. See your doctor if you suspect that you may have this easily treated problem.

Trip leaders should be aware that in any group of ten or more people, at least one person is likely to have asthma. Whether in winter or summer, start slowly, work up to speed gradually and stop as little as possible.

# Mountain sickness

Symptoms: nausea, headache and weakness caused by an inadequate supply of oxygen to the brain.

Although the proportion of oxygen in the atmosphere (21 percent) is nearly the same from sea level to the height of the Himalayas, the low pressure of the atmosphere at high elevations makes it difficult for the body to extract enough oxygen from the air because there are fewer oxygen molecules per litre. The air really *is* thinner up there! Some people can function atop Mt. Everest without breathing bottled oxygen, while others may feel queasy at 2500 m. Mountain sickness symptoms often start at 3000–3500 m, elevations typical for summits in our area. So mountain sickness is a climber's problem here, not a hiker's.

General rule: as long as you are not feeling sick to your stomach you can go higher— cautiously. But once you are nauseous the only thing to do is to go back down, or probably you will soon be sitting in the snow throwing up. Keep moving down, even though you won't want to walk, until you feel better. Losing only a couple of hundred metres in elevation can bring a big improvement.

To avoid mountain sickness, **acclimate** yourself by working up to higher elevations gradually. This increases the concentration of red blood cells in your body and increases the efficiency of your heart and lungs. Spend the day at elevations just below those that make you sick, and return to lower elevations to sleep.

Research on Mt. Rainier has shown that drinking plenty of water helps. Drink several litres over the course of the day, enough for normal urine production. There is some evidence that taking antacid tablets helps, too. Drinking alcohol at altitude can bring on mountain sickness—save the summit bottle for back at camp—and drinking the night before a climb causes dehydration, which exacerbates the effects of altitude.

# Giardiasis (folk name: "beaver fever")

Any surface water in the Canadian Rockies is possibly contaminated by *Giardia lamblia,* a protozoan parasite that attaches inside the small intestine and sometimes the gall bladder. It affects most mammals, including humans. It enters streams and lakes as cysts in the feces of a carrier.

Studies in Montana have shown that beavers do indeed carry the parasite there, and the increase in Rocky Mountain beaver populations has been accompanied by an increase in giardiasis. But let us not blame the beaver only. Human population growth in the Canadian Rockies area and the boom in wilderness travel have sent a great number of people into the back country. They have also brought dogs and horses, known to carry and spread *Giardia lamblia.* Once established in a watershed, *Giardia* tends to remain there.

The organism is not killed by simple chlorination. It requires the heavy-duty chemical treatment used in big-city water systems. Giardiasis outbreaks in Banff and Jasper have prompted these high-profile tourist centres to change from surface water supplies to wells, for *Giardia* cysts are naturally filtered out of groundwater—most of the time. Shallow wells in gravel are not entirely safe.

If you have drunk water contaminated with *Giardia,* the symptoms begin in about 15 days. They include gas, diarrhoea, abdominal cramps, lack of appetite and weakness.

These cover a multitude of illnesses, but giardiasis often shows a couple of additional symptoms that are more diagnostic: soft, yellowish, greasy-looking and very foul feces caused by a reduced ability to process sugars and dairy products; ongoing flatulence and a bloated feeling in the belly; more-frequent but less-productive trips to the toilet. When a giardiasis attack is at its height there is often localized pain in the lower abdomen, sharp when stepping down stairs or walking down a steep trail.

It is this kind of abdominal pain that frequently sends a victim to the doctor for treatment of what feels rather like a bladder infection. A stool sample is necessary for firm diagnosis, but in many samples *Giardia* is not detected, even though the sufferer obviously has the disease.

Annoying but seldom incapacitating, giardiasis is so common in third-world countries that it is rarely treated there. Some people carry the parasite and hardly notice it. Others (like me) suffer miserably with it. Kids are hit harder than adults. In most untreated cases the victim kicks the parasite or develops a tolerance that keeps the symptoms at low levels for years, with occasional flare-ups. The anti-protozoan drug metronidazole (trade name: Flagyl) is used to treat giardiasis.

**Prevention of giardiasis:** bring to a boil (continuous boiling is unnecessary) all mountain water used for drinking and washing, or put it through a portable pump-action water-purifying filter with a pore size of 0.4 microns or smaller. These filters are small and light, sold at many outdoor equipment shops. Large-capacity, untended drip filters are available for cottages and lodges. Treating water with iodine tablets is an alternative, although it takes a lot of iodine to kill the cysts.

Keep your hands clean in the mountains, washing them with soap. Wash after handling pets. Carry your washwater away from the source, so the suds don't contaminate it. To slow the spread of the parasite, defecate at least 100 m from any stream or lake and bury your poop. See page 722 for further advice on excreting in the wilderness.

**Three other pathogenic illnesses** to watch out for in our area are two kinds of tick-borne diseases (see page 458) and the hantavirus pulmonary syndrome (page 600).

## Minor injuries

Prevention is just as important as treatment in dealing with minor injuries.

### Blisters

These are the most common injuries in the mountains, and they can spoil a four-day backpack on the first day. As soon as you feel a hot spot, **stop and put on a piece of moleskin,** a Bandaid "Compeed" blister pad or adhesive tape large enough to cover it. Too many people keep walking until the hot spot has become a blister, at which point there is little you can do to get relief.

However, further blistering can often be prevented by cutting the centre out of a bandaid or two and placing the hole around the blister. This makes a pressure-relieving ring around the blister. Apply a blister pad over the top. Taking your sock off when you are not walking will help to dry the loose skin and thus speed callus formation. It's better not to open a fluid-filled blister; the wound may infect.

*Treat that hot spot before it gets like this.*

### Scrapes and cuts

For minor ones, with little bleeding and nothing foreign stuck in the injury, just put on a bandaid. For deeper ones that have bled freely, pick out any bits of dirt or whatever, and clean the wound with water that has been boiled (and allowed to cool, of course). Cover the injury with a bandage. Antiseptics such as iodine and mercurochrome do more harm than good. **Tetanus** is possible with any open wound; update your immunization if need be.

### Burns

For a minor burn, quickly head to the creek, or the nearest cold water, and stick the burned place into it for several minutes. This will reduce the degree of injury. Burns infect rather easily, so keep a burn clean. Cover it lightly with a gauze dressing, to allow air circulation. Don't use creams or other ointments on a burn when it's new. Later on, when it scabs over and gets tight and flaky, you could apply some hypoallergenic lotion for comfort. For a serious burn, do not get it wet. Cover it loosely with a clean dressing and get medical help ASAP.

## Sunburn

Prevention is quite easy. Keep your shirt on, wear a hat, put on sunglasses and use sunblock with a rating of 15 or higher, reapplying it several times during the day. Make sure children are protected well.

This sounds elementary, but it is advice often ignored. Following a typical cloudy, rainy spring in the Rockies, the first few days of cloudless summer weather bring with them terrible cases of sunburn. Untanned hikers wander the high country in shorts and no shirt; untanned climbers get up on the glaciers and broil their faces in the first two hours of the day.

There is little you can do for a sunburn, although drinking lots of water will prevent the accompanying dehydration. Cool, wet cloths may make a burn feel somewhat better. A severe sunburn should be seen by a doctor. File away under "Lessons learned."

*Result of crossing a glacier in June without using enough sunblock.*

### Insect bites and stings

See page 444 for mosquito bites, page 451 for bee stings, page 459 for tick bites.

## *First-aid kit*

My always-in-the-pack kit is small, but it has everything I have ever needed in an emergency. When guiding for hire, I carry a more complete one. Note that many of the items are for repairing broken equipment, which seems to need first aid more often than people do.

- A pair of **latex gloves,** which take hardly any space, to prevent contact with someone else's blood (danger of AIDS).
- Several **triangular bandages,** the first-aider's do-everything cloth. If these take up too much space in your first-aid kit, carry some of them elsewhere. I keep a couple in the bottom of my binocular pouch. Good padding.
- **Moleskin pieces and Bandaid "Compeed" blister pads:** several of each, for putting on hot spots *before* they become blisters.
- **Bandaids:** three regular ones, three small ones, a couple of large ones for big scrapes and a butterfly type for a deep cut.
- **Large sterile bandage** or a clean pocket handkerchief. Either of these will work as a compress.
- **Adhesive tape,** supposedly for holding on bandages but used mostly for fixing broken equipment. Fibreglass strapping tape is the best repair tape.
- **Some twist ties,** for closing plastic bags or making repairs.
- **Tylenol,** or some other non-aspirin painkiller (aspirin inhibits clotting). I pack a half-dozen Tylenol 3 tablets. Don't give prescription medicine to someone else. Give over-the-counter medicine only if the person asks for it and is not allergic to it.
- **Ear plugs,** the kind that deaden noise, so I can sleep at night in a tent or hut when others are snoring. I sometimes take a mild, over-the-counter antihistamine sleeping pill before going to bed at higher elevations. This overcomes the sleeplessness that I, like most people, experience on my first couple of nights up there.
- **Can opener.** One of those little flat ones.
- **Butane lighter,** in case the one in my pocket quits working, or I lose it.
- **Pack of waterproof matches,** in case the lighter fails.

- A short **candle.**
- **Needle and thread.** A heavy needle and dental floss, which makes extra-strong thread. Dental floss can also be used for its intended purpose.
- A couple of **safety pins,** half a metre of **wire** and some **rubber bands,** all for fixing things.
- A piece of **stick-on nylon repair material,** to cover holes in down sleeping bags and jackets. Moleskin also works for this.
- **Coleman mantles,** for making a hut lamp work. All guests will praise you.
- A **pamphlet on first aid,** for looking up things one might not remember in the crunch. How can you tell whether a person is in a diabetic coma? What do you do for a person with a broken neck? Check the pocket guides listed in "Further reading," page 781.
- **Pencil and a couple of filing cards,** for leaving notes or keeping track of who's winning at cards in the hut. Also essential for writing down details of an accident to send out with whoever is going for help.
- **Money:** a twenty-dollar bill, and a couple of quarters for making phone calls.
- Not in the kit, but always with me: **pocket knife with scissors and tweezers** on it. My wife packs a tiny knife like this right in her first-aid kit. Some people carry little folding scissors and separate tweezers.

All these items fit into a small polyethylene freezer container 12 cm by 13 cm by 5 cm. On back-packing trips and when guiding for hire I bring an additional container with an **elastic bandage** (Tensor bandage) for holding a heavy compress or wrapping up a sprained ankle. Also in the container I have some of the larger-sized dressings and extra triangular bandages.

A **large plastic garbage bag,** kept folded until needed, can be used as an emergency raincoat or shelter. It can be used to carry water or to keep a dressing dry. It can also be used to pack out garbage.

Tim Auger, who leads Banff National Park's mountain-rescue team, suggests carrying a **cardboard splint.** This is a simple, flat item of folded cardboard (don't get the heavier plasticized ones) that can be refolded in various ways for splinting a broken arm or leg. Such a splint weighs next to nothing and slips down the inside of your pack, next to your back. You can use it to sit on, and Auger told me that he has slept on his more than once. To get one, contact any safety supply store.

Rick Kunelius, another long-time Banff park warden and mountain-rescuer, recommends carrying a couple of **menstrual pads** to use as dressings for large wounds, and **pantyhose** to use in holding a compress in place. You cut a section from the hose to slip over the bandaged arm, leg, tummy, head or whatever. Chic hikers and skiers could also wear the pantyhose at formal parties in mountain huts.

## Animal bites and attacks

Don't feed or touch any wild animal. It might bite you. Even a deer can bite, and coyotes bumming food in picnic grounds are well-known for it. Handling any small animal can result in a bite, and there is always the danger of infection and rabies.

*Serious* wild-animal attacks on humans are rare in the Rockies. They include, roughly in order of frequency, attacks by elk (page 649), coyotes (page 629), moose (page 650) and bears (page 637). Keep clear of all of these species, even if they seem friendly.

If you are bitten by any animal, wash the wound out well with soap and water. Go to the doctor.

# How to use a compass

Be sure to carry a compass on any ski trip that will take you above treeline, or on any mountaineering route that may put you out on a glacier in a white-out. The clouds can roll in, leaving you a choice of (a) relying on your sense of direction—in my case always a mistake— (b) waiting until the fog lifts, which is often a reasonable plan, for white-outs in the Canadian Rockies seldom last more than an hour, although the clouds can sock in for several days at a time on an icefield, (c) using a GPS unit, which some hikers and skiers carry, or (d) following a compass, which many hikers and skiers carry—and generally don't know how to use. Map-grid locations, magnetic declination and other navigational matters are just too intimidating.

Yet following a compass is quite easy. In most situations you don't even need a map. The method explained below can also be applied when bushwhacking through dense forest. It does require a compass with a rotating bezel; that is, the needle housing must turn. The compass models I recommend are the Silva "Ranger" and the Suunto "Leader." These also have a mirror, which helps for sighting, and a built-in declination adjustment, which helps a lot when doing more advanced compass work.

## The basic sequence

1. Get the compass out before the fog rolls in, or before you enter the woods, while you can still see the place you are headed for.

2. Point the compass at your objective, holding the instrument flat so that the needle is free to swivel, not jammed up against the glass.

3. Keeping the compass pointed in the direction you want to go, turn the bezel (the movable ring surrounding the needle) so that the red arrow on it lines up with the compass needle. If the compass has a mirror, angle the mirror so you can see the needle better.

4. Check your setting. When you point at your objective with the compass, the needle should line up with the red arrow, or it should lie between the two marks.

5. And away you go, keeping the needle aligned but following the compass, not the needle.

Nine times out of ten, that is all there is to using a compass. There is no need to deal with numbers or to get out the map. Just point, turn the bezel, check the setting and stride confidently into the fog. Keep an eye where you are walking, though; you don't want to stride confidently over a cliff or into a crevasse.

*By angling the mirror, you can see your objective and the compass bezel at the same time. Turn the bezel until it aligns with the compass needle.*

## Getting more accuracy

The method described above is okay for rough orienteering, but there are times when you need greater accuracy in following your course. People are inclined to drift off course when holding a compass and trying to go in a straight line. After a couple of kilometres, that drift adds up. So here is how to navigate through a white-out with very little error, sans GPS. One person acts as the **compass-reader,** while another person acts as the **leader.**

1. Send the leader forward in the direction of travel. When she or he reaches the limit of visibility, call out "Stop!"

2. Sight at the leader with the compass. Is he or she left or right of the true line? Ask the leader to step left or right to come back onto the true line. Sight again, just to be sure.

3. When the leader is on the true line, then the compass-reader and the rest of the party ski/walk up to the leader and the process repeats.

This procedure can be amazingly accurate. On one trip, we crossed a four-kilometre stretch of socked-in icefield by compass, aiming to hit the gap between two peaks. A couple of hours later we came up against a rocky slope in the fog. We figured that we must have erred to right or left. Suddenly the clouds broke and we found that we were on a small nipple of rock sticking up exactly in the centre of the gap!

## When to get out the map

If you cannot see your objective, you must use a topographic map, preferably a 1:50,000-series map, to set a compass course.

If you have a compass with adjustable declination, set the declination before you leave home. **Declination** is the difference between true north—meaning the direction to the north pole—and magnetic north, which is not the same. Maps are drawn in alignment with true north, while a compass needle aligns with magnetic north. So you need to correct the compass if you're using it with a map. The declination angle is shown on all Canadian government topo maps. In the central Rockies it is about 19° east at Banff and 20° east at Jasper. So work the adjustment, which is usually a tiny screw on the bezel ring, until the red arrow on the face of the bezel is pointing 19–20° to the east of true north, which is the 360° marking on the bezel's ring. This has nothing to do with the way the compass *needle* is pointing as you make the adjustment; what matters here is the alignment of the markings on the compass bezel.

If your compass has no built-in declination adjustment, the red arrow and the bezel ring are in one piece and can't be moved independently. But you can still compensate for declination, as shown further on in these instructions.

To get a bearing from a map:

1. You don't have to orient the map to north; just set it on a flat surface. Find your location and the point you are trying to reach, and imagine a straight line connecting the two. This will be your compass course. Lay the compass down with one of its straight sides on that line. Make sure the front end points **toward** the objective, not away from it, or you could set your compass incorrectly by 180° and take off in the wrong direction.

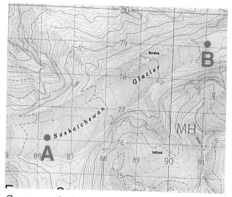

Suppose that you need to travel down this glacier, from point A to point B. It's foggy, and the glacier is featureless.

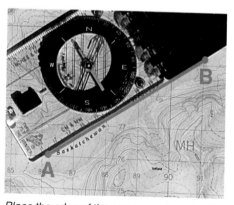

Place the edge of the compass along the line you wish to travel. Turn the bezel until the black lines in it match the alignment of the blue lines on the map—provided the blue lines are close to proper north/south alignment themselves. If not, adjust the angle of the black lines a little.

2. Keeping the compass aligned with your intended route, turn the bezel until the parallel lines in it are lined up with something on the map that is true north/south. The blue grid-lines on the Canadian government topo maps are close to true, but usually not *exactly* true. That is because they are based on **UTM zones** (the Universal Transverse Mercator worldwide grid), which align with true north only on maps that happen to cover the centre of a zone.

You can see how close the UTM grid is to perfect alignment by noting how the blue grid lines converge with the left and right map edges, which are true north/south lines. Turn the compass bezel a little (often just a tiny bit) so the lines in it mimic the convergence you see on the map. Or line up the bezel with something on the map that *is* properly oriented, such as a map edge, a township line, a line of latitude or a north/south boundary of some kind. In wilderness areas these lines are few.

3. If your compass has a declination adjustment, you're ready to go, no arithmetic required. Keeping the compass needle lined up with the red arrow will keep you pointed in the right direction.

If your compass has no declination adjustment, then you have to do some arithmetic. Read the compass setting in degrees; that is, read the number along the edge of the bezel that lines up with the mark inscribed on the plate. **Subtract** the 20° of magnetic declination from the bezel setting. For example, if the compass setting is initially 75°, or roughly northeast, then change it to 55°. If the initial reading is 212°, or roughly southwest, change it to 192°. If it is 12°, set it to 352°, having subtracted past the zero mark. And off you go.

### How to triangulate your position

You may not know exactly where you are, but if the weather is clear, if at least three good landmarks are present, if you have a 1:50,000-scale map and a compass that gives accurate sightings, then you can determine your position to within 100 m. I suggest you try this only with a compass that has a declination adjustment and a mirror.

Photos illustrating the sequence below are given on the next page.

1. Identify the first landmark. It must be obvious on the map, and the pointier the better. A sharp summit is ideal. You could also use a spot where two streams intersect, a point where two ridges come together, or where a stream enters a lake.

2. Sight on your first landmark with the compass. Keep the landmark squarely in the sight, hold the instrument flat and turn the bezel until the red arrow is lined up with the needle, as seen in the mirror. Once the bezel is set, don't disturb it.

3. Now lay the compass on the map. You don't have to orient the map by using the compass; just make sure that the compass is pointing roughly from you toward the point on the map identifying the landmark. Put one of the straight sides of the compass in contact with the landmark point. Keeping that side against the landmark, turn the compass—not the bezel, the whole compass—until the parallel lines in the bezel are lined up with a north/south line on the map, as described in the previous section. Check again to see that the side of the compass still contacts the landmark point, hold everything steady, and use that side to draw a straight line from the landmark in the direction from which you're viewing it. You can draw that line only two ways from the landmark point—toward you or away from you—so try to choose the right one.

4. Repeat for two more landmarks, setting the bezel each time. Ideally, these landmarks should be about 120° from one another. But you can get good results with landmarks not spaced so evenly.

If you have triangulated correctly, the three lines you have drawn on the map will come together at your position. If all three lines cross at exactly the same place, congratulations; your triangulation was quite accurate. If the three lines form a large triangle, something went wrong. Better sight again. That's why you need three landmarks instead of two. The third performs a check.

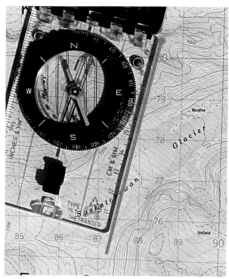

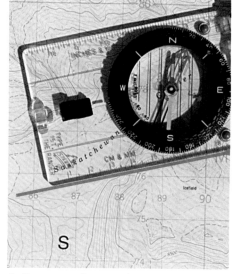

1. Compass edge crossing the first landmark and angled so the lines in the bezel match the blue UTM lines on the map.* Draw a line along the edge of the compass.

2. Compass edge crossing second landmark and correctly angled. Draw a  second line on the map.

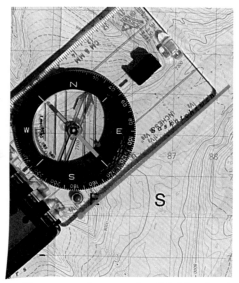

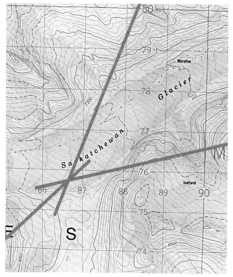

3. Compass edge crossing third landmark and correctly angled. Draw a third line.

4. The point where all three lines cross is your position.

*If the UTM grid does not line up accurately with true north/south on the map, angle the lines in the bezel a little to compensate.

## Further reading

Bezruchka, S. (1994) *Altitude Illness, Prevention and Treatment.* Douglas & McIntyre, Vancouver/The Mountaineers, Seattle. Compact guide to take on the mountain with you; indexed, 93 pages.

Daffern, T. (1992) *Avalanche Safety for Skiers and Climbers, Second Edition.* Rocky Mountain Books, Calgary. The definitive treatment on snow accumulation, metamorphosis of the snowpack and slides, with the latest advice on safety. Well-illustrated, glossary, bibliography, index; 192 pages.

Fredston, J. and D. Fesler (1994) *Snow Sense: a Guide to Evaluating Snow Avalanche Hazard.* Alaska Mountain Safety Center, Anchorage. Up-to-date, inexpensive book covering all the essentials. Illustrated, with reading list, 116 pages.

Graydon, D., ed. (1992) *Mountaineering, the Freedom of the Hills, Fifth Edition.* Douglas & McIntyre, Vancouver/The Mountaineers, Seattle. The classic work on climbing, with emphasis on safety. Illustrated, indexed, 474 pages.

Kochanski, M. and D. Driscoll (1991) *Basic Wilderness Survival in the Boreal Forest.* Mors Kochanski, RR1, Peers, AB T0E 1W0. Very small guide to the essentials: how to light a fire, build a shelter, signal for help and so on. Illustrated, 30 pages.

LaChapelle, E. (1985) *The ABC of Avalanche Safety.* Douglas & McIntyre, Vancouver/The Mountaineers, Seattle. Compact guide intended for field use. Indexed, short bibliography, 112 pages.

Lentz, M.; J. Carline and S. Macdonald (1990) *Mountaineering First Aid and Accident Response.* Douglas & McIntyre, Vancouver/The Mountaineers, Seattle. Compact first-aid manual. Illustrated, indexed, 112 pages. See also the pocket first-aid guide by The Mountaineers, below.

Letham, L. (1998) *GPS Made Easy.* Rocky Mountain Books, Calgary. How to get the most out of your Global Positioning Satellite receiver. Illustrations, maps, 208 pages.

McKown, D. (1992) *Canoeing Safety and Rescue.* Rocky Mountain Books, Calgary. Required reading for anybody taking to the water in the Canadian Rockies. Photos, index, 128 pages.

Merry, W. (1994) *St. John Ambulance Official Wilderness First-Aid Guide.* Ontario Council of the Order of St. John. Written by a mountaineer specifically for Canadian conditions, this excellent book is used in St. John Ambulance wilderness first-aid courses. Illustrated, glossary, index; 387 pages.

Mountaineers (1982) *First Aid.* Douglas & McIntyre, Vancouver/The Mountaineers, Seattle. The essentials in a pamphlet that will go into your first-aid kit. Illustrated, indexed, 34 pages.

St. John Ambulance (1988) *Pocket Guide to Emergency First Aid.* St. John Ambulance, Ottawa. The smallest guide available, 8 by 10 cm, but not specifically about wilderness first aid. Illustrated, 34 pages of English and 34 pages of French back-to-back.

Toft, M., ed. (1998) *Playing it Safe.* Rocky Mountain Books, Calgary (Alpine Club of Canada). Essays and reports on mountaineering safety. Sobering reading! Illustrated, 160 pages.

Wilkerson, J. (1995) *Medicine for Mountaineering.* Douglas & McIntyre, Vancouver/The Mountaineers, Seattle. The standard work on mountain first aid, written by a doctor. Recently updated. Index, glossary, 384 pages.

*In the Victoria Cross Ranges, Jasper National Park. If you're Canadian, you own this. Sort of.*

# Afterword
*Tell 'em what you've told 'em*

Three hundred thousand words after starting this book, I have learned something about the Canadian Rockies: this place is special, unlike any other place on earth. So we have to protect it, which means we have to keep it *wild.*

Have you heard the latest argument for protecting wildlands? It is wonderfully convincing: *wilderness pays.* In the age of the bottom line, studies have shown that mountain wilderness is worth far more to the economy as a place for nondestructive forms of recreation than it is as a place for tough-on-the-land activities such as logging, mining, drilling for oil and gas, building roads and so on.

We are speaking of dollars here; income and jobs. Add up the value of everything that can be dragged off or ripped out of a typical chunk of the Rockies, then compare that with what the public would spend over the years to enjoy that land in its original state. Surprise! Hands down, it is worth more as wilderness. People put an amazing amount of money into such things as bird books, binoculars, backpacks … and especially *vacations,* which are often taken in pretty parts of the outdoors.

Once the loggers and miners and oil companies are allowed in, these places are not very pretty anymore. Farmers and ranchers alter the landscape and its natural biota to their own ends. Resort developers take over prime pieces of wildland and make the rest of us pay to enjoy it, turning mountain meadows into golf courses and forested slopes into ski areas. The tourist industry, which has a stake in keeping beautiful places beautiful, nonetheless prefers that the scenery be viewed from hotel balconies and tramway gondolas. The friendly folks at the Chamber of Commerce haven't yet realized how easy it is to love the mountains to death.

The Canadian Rockies haven't much to interest the hard-rock miner (yet), but there are people who want the coal, the natural gas, the trees, the water and the big game. They want more roads, more towns, more motels, more dams—more of everything human and thus less of everything natural.

But these incredible mountains are *ours.* Most of the Rockies is public land, belonging to all Canadians. We shouldn't give it away to people who want bits and pieces for themselves. If we do, the Canadian Rockies will look like the American Rockies: full of mines and mills and fences and cows and ski areas and condominiums and roads and jeeps and reservoirs. Missing: much of the forest, most of the native animals and all of the views that stretch from horizon to horizon without anything manmade for the eye to trip over. Why do so many American visitors come to the Canadian Rockies each year? They are amazed at the wilderness we have saved, and they ache for what they have lost.

Despite their perennial problems, the *national parks* still have the best record of wildland protection in Canada. Outside the parks, wilderness-exploiters find a sympathetic ear at the provincial level, where that sneaky euphemism "multiple use" is accepted and practiced by the governments of Alberta and British Columbia. What those governments allow in wild parts of their jurisdictions—what they *promote*—is senseless, unconscionable, outrageous. They do not understand.

Parks Canada is not the owner, but rather the trustee,
of a national inheritance that must never be spent.
—*Message posted by Parks Canada in Jasper*

My conclusion: we Canadians need to get more of our Rockies under federal control, i.e. inside national-park boundaries.

Currently about 24,000 km² are federally protected, which is only 13 percent of the total. That 13 percent is mainly in the form of four large interlocking parks (Banff, Jasper, Kootenay and Yoho), which together just might hold enough wilderness to preserve the ecosystems typical of the central Rockies. The mountain parks block is internationally important; it has been declared a World Heritage Site.

However, the southern end of the range has only Waterton/Glacier, a popular and crowded pair of parks that have lost some of their naturally occurring animals and plants. And in the northern half of the Canadian Rockies there are no national parks at all. The Northern Rockies Wilderness, a provincially managed area of 4.3 million hectares, confers some protection, but it's too weak. Hunting, trapping, motorized access and resort-building will continue. Logging, oil and gas extraction and mining will be allowed in three-quarters of it.

Nearly 1500 km long, the Canadian Rockies have a characteristic style that is consistent from end to end (see page 13). Preserving only a bit here and a bit there, while letting the rest fall to human encroachment, will destroy that integrity. With it will go the marvelous ecosystems that depend on it. Our islands of wilderness must be *large;* large enough to give the big animals enough range; large enough to give the big fish unpolluted water and the big birds an uncluttered sky.

The islands must be linked. As the **Yellowstone to Yukon Conservation Initiative** proposes, wildlife-movement corridors should be established up and down the range, connecting each wildland to neighboring ones. Governments should cooperate in protecting species that cross boundaries. As things stand, a grizzly bear that is protected under the Endangered Species Act in Montana can step across the international boundary and be killed legally by hunters in Alberta.

The northern Rockies are especially vulnerable. We need a new national park there, running from the Liard River on the north to the Kwadacha River—ideally to the Peace—on the south. Let's give this park a name right now: **Tuchodi National Wilderness,** from the Tuchodi River, which would be central to it. Tuchodi wilderness park would cover everything from the foothills to the western side of the Rocky Mountain Trench. We need this park soon. We have perhaps ten years left before the tide of humanity will have washed its wildness away.

My parting message, then, dear Canadian reader, is this. The next time the opportunity presents itself, please take your Member of Parliament aside and whisper in his or her ear the magic phrase, "I will vote for you if you will get me a big national park in the northern Rockies." I'm sure that a whole lot of mountain goats and wolverines and wildflowers would appreciate it.

*Ben Gadd, Naturalist*

## *Further reading for appreciating the Canadian Rockies*

See page 831 for a list of literary works (essays, poetry, fiction).

# Atlas of the Canadian Rockies

Reproduced from the International Map of the World Series 1:1 000 000

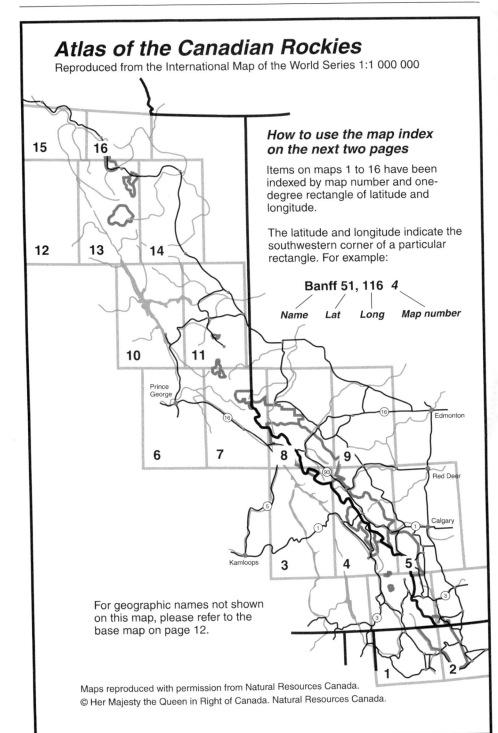

### How to use the map index on the next two pages

Items on maps 1 to 16 have been indexed by map number and one-degree rectangle of latitude and longitude.

The latitude and longitude indicate the southwestern corner of a particular rectangle. For example:

**Banff 51, 116  4**

*Name     Lat     Long     Map number*

For geographic names not shown on this map, please refer to the base map on page 12.

## Atlas index

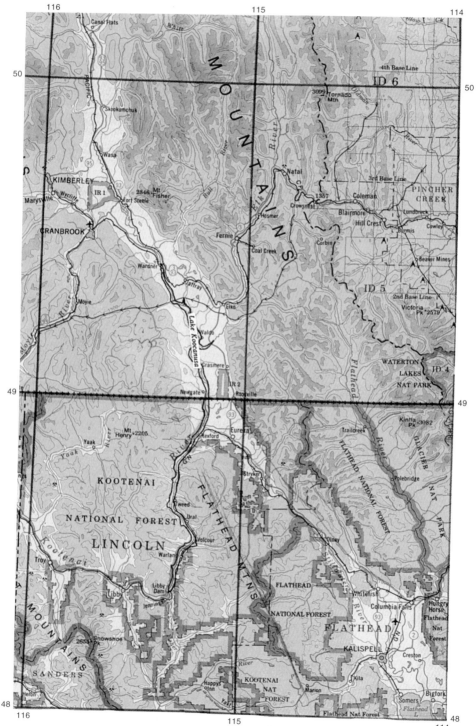

# Map 2

*Atlas*   789

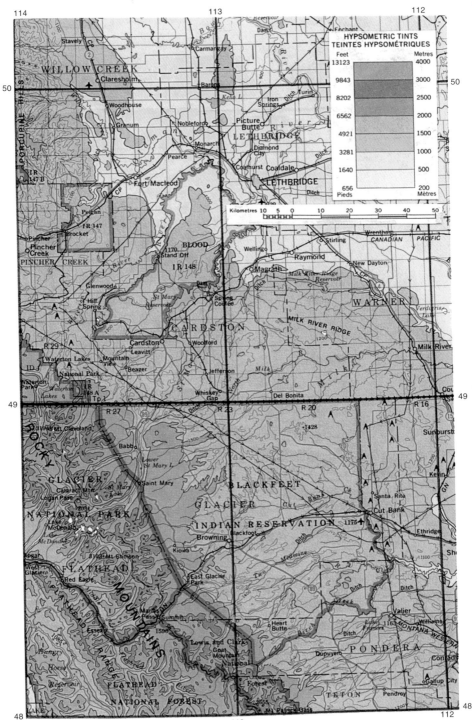

HYPSOMETRIC TINTS
TEINTES HYPSOMÉTRIQUES

| Feet | Metres |
|------|--------|
| 13123 | 4000 |
| 9843 | 3000 |
| 8202 | 2500 |
| 6562 | 2000 |
| 4921 | 1500 |
| 3281 | 1000 |
| 1640 | 500 |
| 656 | 200 |
| Pieds | Mètres |

Kilometres 10  5  0    10    20    30    40    50

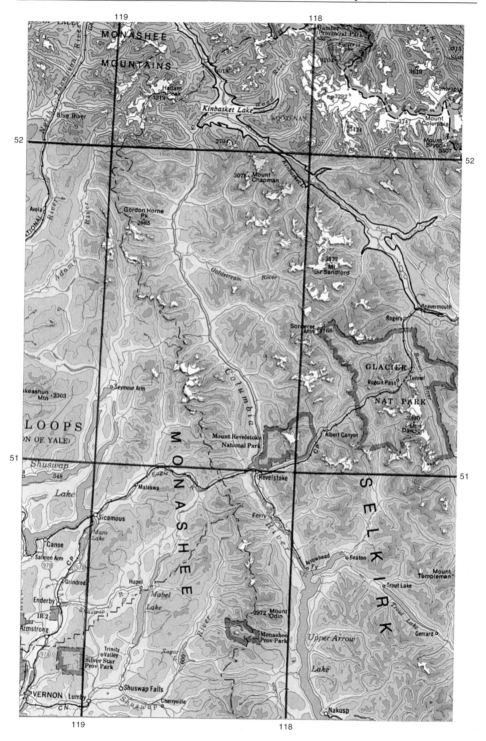

# Map 4

*Atlas* 791

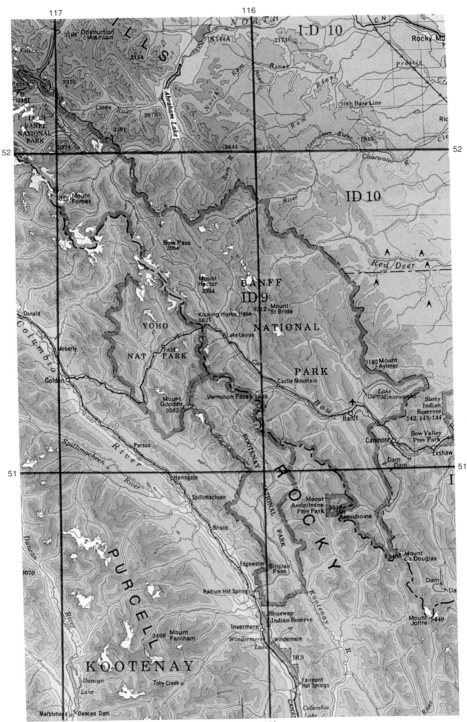

115    114

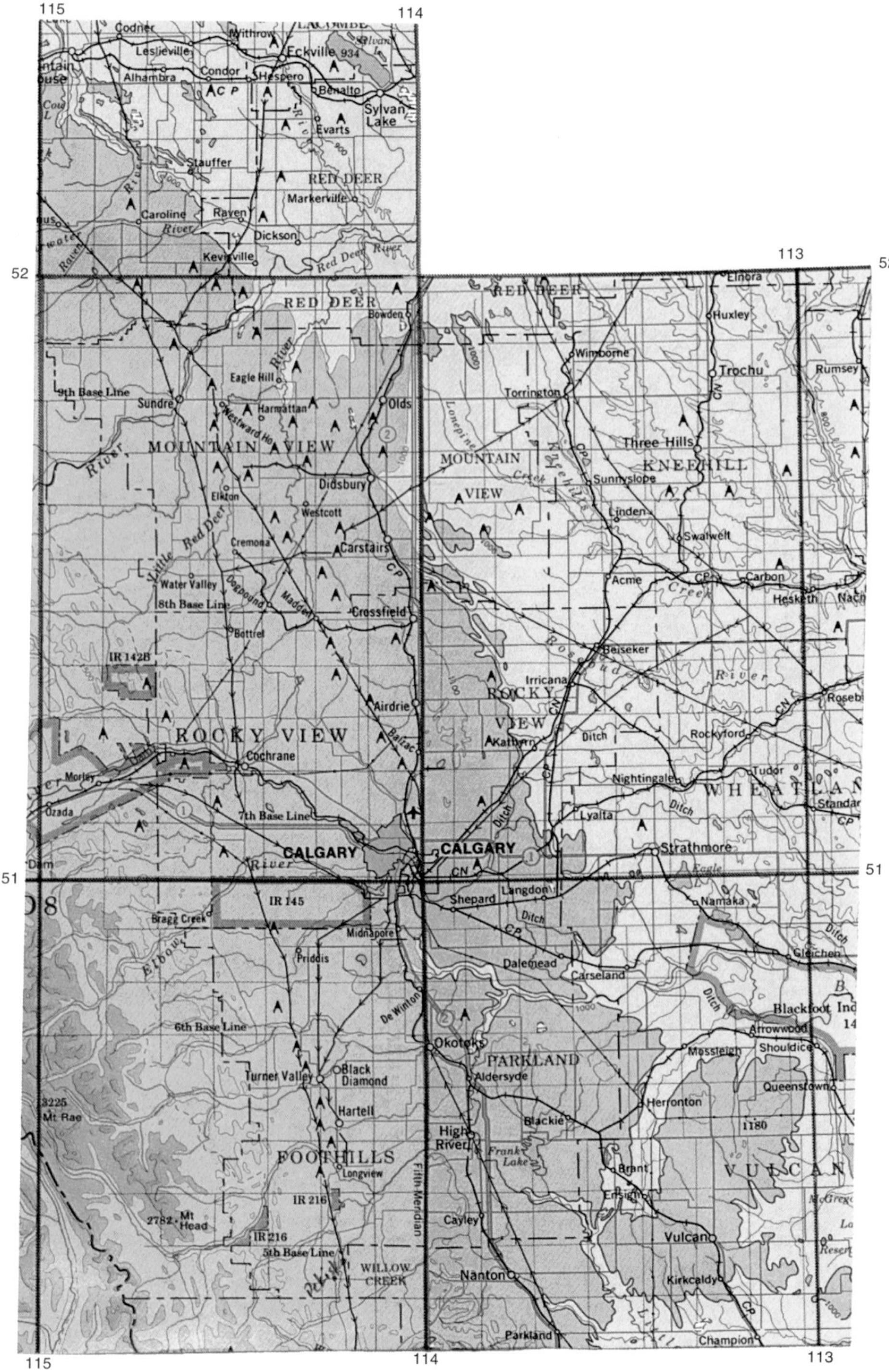

Codner
Leslieville    Withrow    LACOMBE
Alhambra    Condor    Eckville 934    Sylvan
House    Hespero    Benalto    Sylvan Lake
Stauffer    Evarts
Caroline    Raven    RED DEER
Markerville
Kevisville    Dickson
Red Deer River

52    113    52

RED DEER    Elnora
Bowden    Huxley
8th Base Line    Eagle Hill    Wimborne    Trochu    Rumsey
Sundre    Harmattan    Olds    Torrington    Three Hills    KNEEHILL
MOUNTAIN VIEW    MOUNTAIN    Sunnyslope
Elkton    Didsbury    VIEW    Linden    Swalwell
Westcott    Acme    Carbon
Cremona    Carstairs    Hesketh    Nach
Water Valley    CP    Beiseker
8th Base Line    Madden    Crossfield    Bosebud    River
Bottrel    Irricana    Roseb
IR 142B    Airdrie    ROCKY
ROCKY VIEW    VIEW    Rockyford
Morley    Cochrane    Kathry    Ditch    Tudor
Ozada    7th Base Line    Nightingale    WHEATLAN
Standard
Dam    CALGARY    CALGARY    Lyalta    Ditch    Strathmore
Eagle

51    51

IR 145    Shepard    Langdon    Namaka
Bragg Creek    Ditch    Gleichen
Midnapore    Dalemead
Priddis    Carseland    Blackfoot Ind
6th Base Line    Arrowwood    14
De Winton    Massleigh    Shouldice
Okotoks    Queenstown
Turner Valley    Black    PARKLAND    1180
3225    Diamond    Aldersyde    Herronton
Mt Rae    Hartell    Blackie
High    Brant    VULCAN
FOOTHILLS    River    Frank    Ensign
IR 216    Longview    Lake    Cayley    Vulcan
2782    Mt    Vulcan
Head    IR 216    Kirkcaldy
5th Base Line    WILLOW    Nanton
CREEK    Champion
Parkland

115    114    113

# Map 6

*Atlas* 793

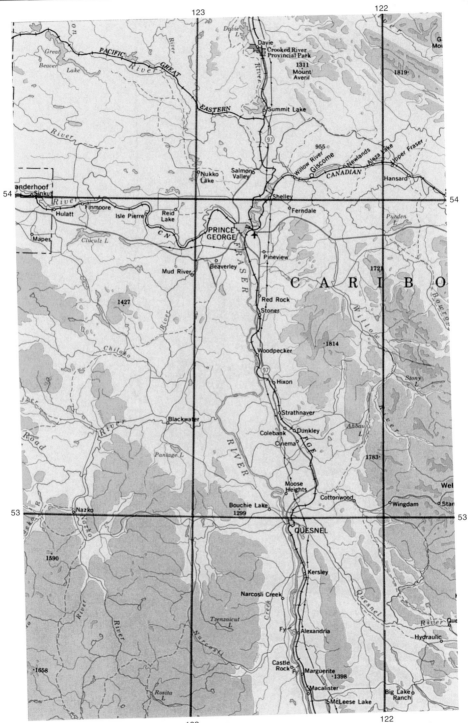

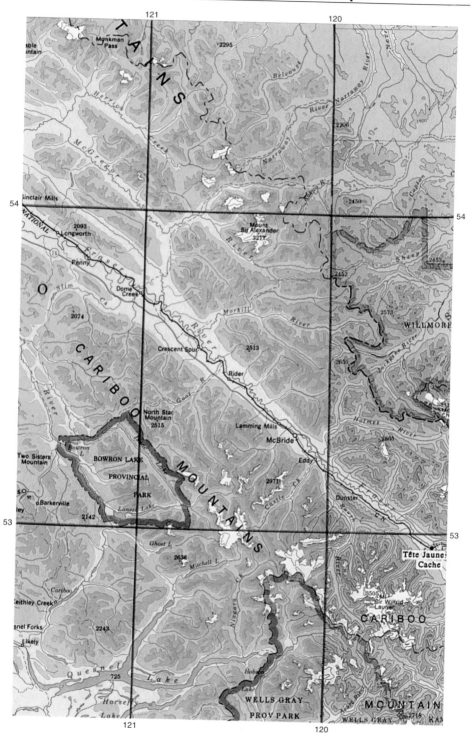

# Map 8

*Atlas* 795

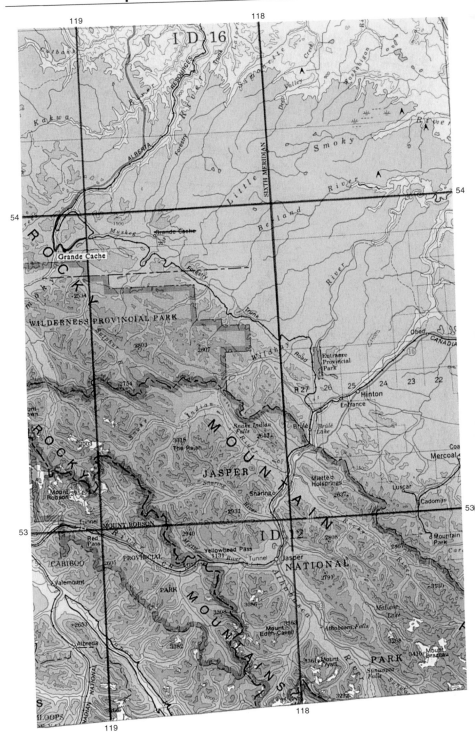

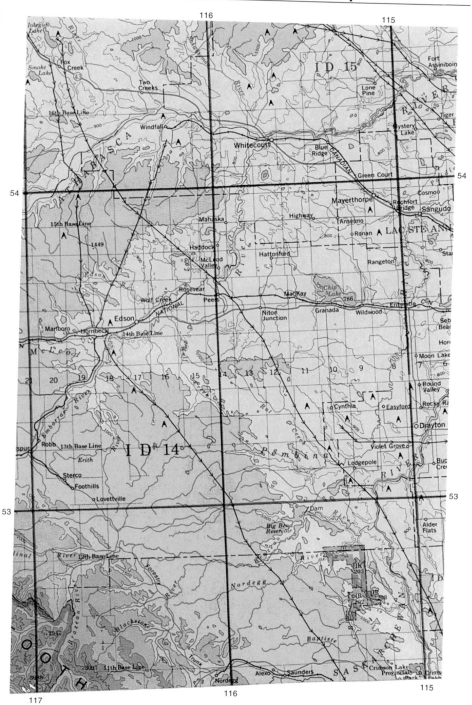

# Map 10

*Atlas* 797

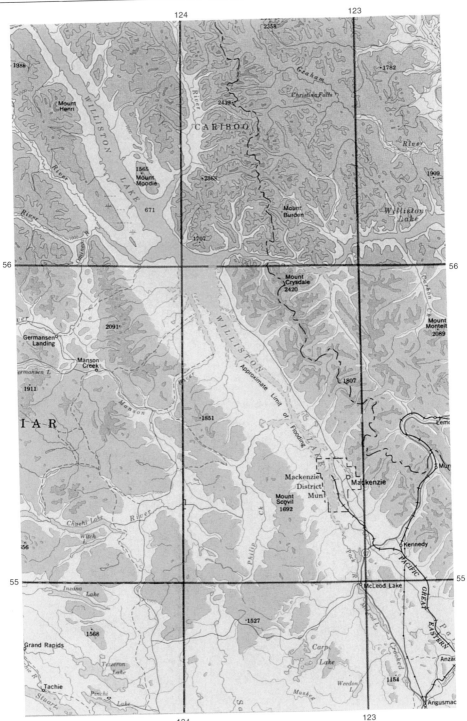

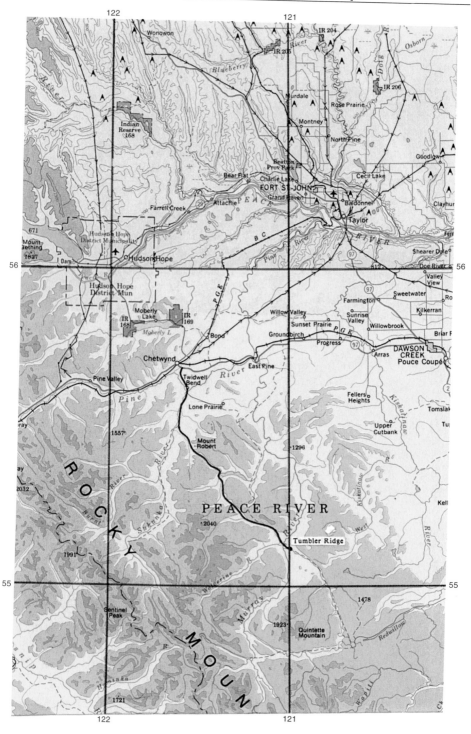

# Map 12

*Atlas* 799

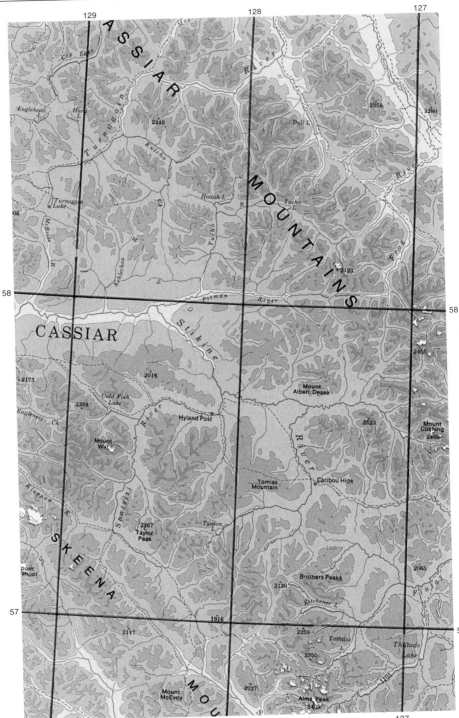

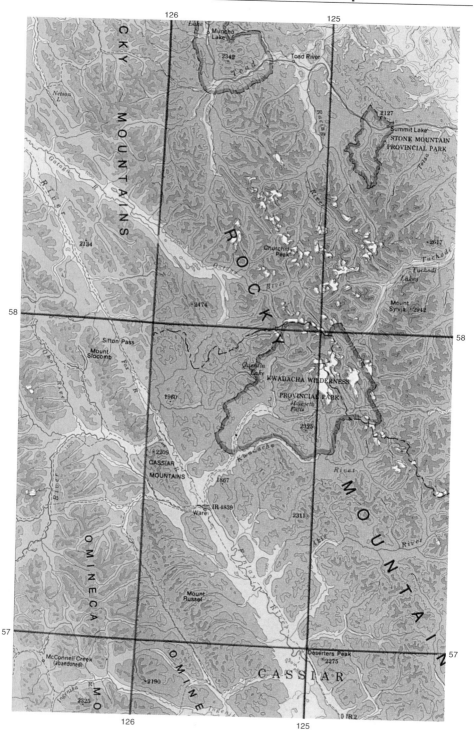

# Map 14

Atlas    801

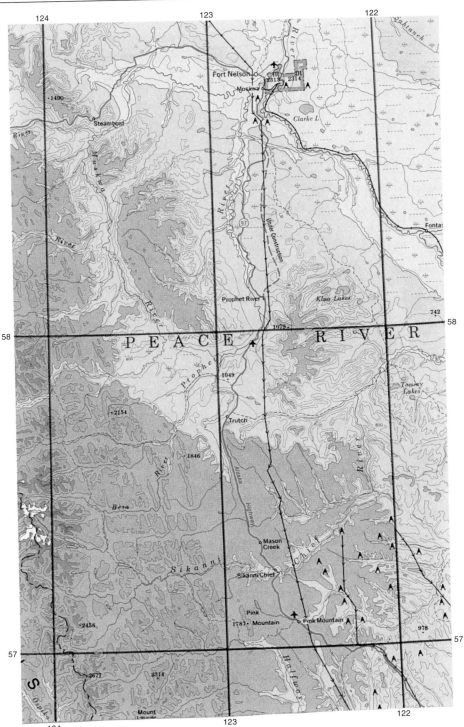

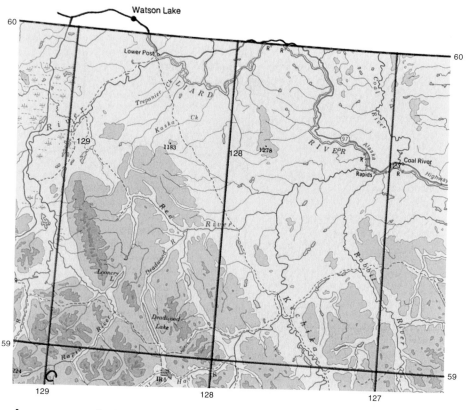

## Larger-scale topographic maps of popular areas

### Official Parks Canada maps, available at park information centres:

*Banff, Kootenay and Yoho National Parks* 1:200 000
*Columbia Icefield* 1:50 000
*Jasper National Park* 1:200 000
*Waterton Lakes National Park* 1:50 000

Federal maps of the National Topographic Series, 1:50 000 and 1:250 000, are available at many park information centres, Mountain Equipment Co-op stores, Map Town shops and some smaller retailers that cater to outdoor recreationists.

### The following excellent recreational maps are available from Gem Trek Publishing, Box 1618, Cochrane, AB T0L 0W0 (403-932-4208):

*Banff & Jasper* 1:400 000
*Banff & Mount Assiniboine* 1:100 000
*Banff Up-Close* 1:35 000
*Bow Lake & Saskatchewan Crossing* 1:70 000
*Bragg Creek and Elbow Falls, Kananaskis Country* 1:50 000
*Canmore & Kananaskis Village, Kananaskis Country* 1:50 000
*Columbia Icefield Guide and Map* 1:75 000

# Map 16

*Atlas* 803

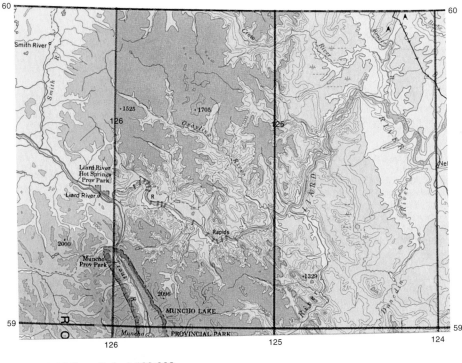

*Jasper & Maligne Lake* 1:100 000
*Jasper Up-Close* 1:35 000
*Kananaskis Lakes and Region, Kananaskis Country* 1:50 000
*Kootenay National Park* 1:100 000
*Lake Louise & Yoho National Park* 1:50 000
*Southwest Alberta and Southeast B.C.* 1:600 000

Altitude Publishing, Box 1410, Canmore, AB  T0L 0M0  (403-678-6888), has produced an oblique-view artist's rendering of the Banff-Yoho-Kootenay area: *Panorama Map of the Canadian Rockies,* painted by Murray Hay.

# Index

## *Further reading for appreciating the Canadian Rockies*

Some of these literary works (essays, poetry, fiction) are hard to find. But persevere; they're all worth the effort.

Allan, Mary (1992) *The Inward Trail,* Jannis Hare, Box 227, Banff, AB  T0L 0C0

Burles, Gordon (1984) *The Old Cabin, Crossing the Pass,* and other books of poems, Box 2245, Banff, AB  T0L 0C0

Christensen, Lisa (1996) *A Hiker's Guide to Art of the Canadian Rockies,* Glenbow Museum, Calgary

Deegan, Jim (1994) *Timberline Tales,* Coyote Books, Canmore

Gadd, Ben (2001) *Raven's End,* McClelland & Stewart, Toronto

Harrap, David (1994) *The Littlest Hiker in the Canadian Rockies,* Tekarra Books, Jasper, AB  T0E 1E0

Kerr, Michael (2000) *When Do You Let the Animals Out?* Fifth House, Calgary

McIntyre, David and Martha (1993, 1995) *Tales from the Alberta Woods,* vols. I and II, Sweetgrass Comunication, Crowsnest Pass, AB  T0K 0E0

McLay, John (2001) *On Mountaintop Rock,* Cobblestone Creek, Edmonton

Marty, Sid (1973) *Headwaters,* McClelland & Stewart, Toronto

— (1978) *Men for the Mountains,* McClelland & Stewart, Toronto

— (1995) *Leaning on the Wind,* Harper Collins, Toronto

— (1999) *Switchbacks,* McClelland & Stewart, Toronto

Patton, Brian, ed. (1984) *Tales from the Canadian Rockies,* McClelland & Stewart, Toronto

Pole, Graeme (1998) *Healy Park,* Rocky Mountain Books, Calgary

Russell, Andy (1975) *The Rockies,* McClelland & Stewart, Toronto

— (1987) *The Life of a River,* Voyageur Press, Stillwater, Minnesota

Wharton, Thomas (1995) *Icefields,* NeWest, Edmonton

Whyte, Jon (1981) *Gallimaufry,* Longspooned Press (Book & Art Den, Banff)

— (1983) *The Cells of Brightness,* Longspooned Press (Book & Art Den, Banff)

— edited by Brian Patton (1992) *Mountain Chronicles,* Altitude Publishing, Canmore

## *Five things that people have actually done to pass the time in a small tent on a rainy day*

- Sat at opposite ends of the tent and talked to each other as if they were using CB radios

- Grabbed the noses of mosquitoes when they stuck them through the netting and held onto them while they buzzed

- Played worms by crawling into their sleeping bags head-first and wiggling around

- Torn pages out of *Handbook of the Canadian Rockies* to make tiny paper airplanes to fly in the tent

- Enjoyed *Handbook* humor, pages 156, 185, 203, 340, 435, 448, 556, 594, 600, 647, 656, 659, 740